THE OXFORD HANDBOOK OF
EUROPEAN ROMANTICISM

THE OXFORD HANDBOOK OF

EUROPEAN ROMANTICISM

Edited by

PAUL HAMILTON

OXFORD UNIVERSITY PRESS

OXFORD
UNIVERSITY PRESS

Great Clarendon Street, Oxford, OX2 6DP,
United Kingdom

Oxford University Press is a department of the University of Oxford.
It furthers the University's objective of excellence in research, scholarship,
and education by publishing worldwide. Oxford is a registered trade mark of
Oxford University Press in the UK and in certain other countries

First published 2016
First published in paperback 2019

Published in the United States of America by Oxford University Press
198 Madison Avenue, New York, NY 10016, United States of America

British Library Cataloguing in Publication Data
Data available

Library of Congress Cataloging in Publication Data
Data available

ISBN 978–0–19–969638–3 (Hbk.)
ISBN 978–0–19–883114–3 (Pbk.)

Contents

German

Hungarian

Italian

Greek

PART II DISCOURSES

List of Figures

List of Contributors

Richard Aczel is Professor at the English Seminar of the University of Cologne. He is the author of *National Character and European Identity in Hungarian Literature 1772–1848* (1996) and has published widely on Central European cultural history, narrative theory, and Renaissance rhetoric. He has also translated Robert Musil's *The Confusions of Young Törless* and Dezso Kosztolányi's *Skylark*.

Roderick Beaton is Koraes Professor of Modern Greek and Byzantine History, Language and Literature at King's College London, a post he has held since 1988. He has published books and scholarly articles on many aspects of Greek literature and culture from the twelfth century to the present, including *An Introduction to Modern Greek Literature* (1994, revised 1999) and *George Seferis: Waiting for the Angel. A Biography* (2003). From 2009 to 2012 he held a Major Leverhulme Fellowship, to work on his most recent book, *Byron's War: Romantic Rebellion, Greek Revolution*, published in 2013.

Andrew Bowie is Professor of Philosophy and German at Royal Holloway, University of London. He has written extensively about music and literature as well as philosophy and is the author of, amongst other books, *Aesthetics and Subjectivity: From Kant to Nietzsche* (Manchester); *Schelling and Modern European Philosophy: An Introduction* (Routledge); *From Romanticism to Critical Theory* (Routledge); *The Philosophy of German Literary Theory; Music, Philosophy, and Modernity* (Cambridge); *Philosophical Variations: Music as Philosophical Language* (ISD). His latest book, *Adorno and the Ends of Philosophy*, has just been published by Polity Press.

Michael Caesar is Emeritus Serena Professor of Italian at the University of Birmingham (UK). His main interests are in nineteenth- to twenty-first-century literature, with studies ranging from the European reception of Dante (*Dante: The Critical Heritage*, Routledge, 1989) to the post-structuralist turn in Italy (*Umberto Eco: Philosophy, Semiotics and the Work of Fiction*, Polity, 1999). With Ann Hallamore Caesar he has co-authored *Modern Italian Literature* (Polity, 2007) and is co-editor, with Franco D'Intino, of the first complete English edition of Giacomo Leopardi's *Zibaldone* (New York: Farrar, Straus & Giroux; London: Penguin, 2013; 2nd, rev., paperback edn scheduled for 2015).

Leon Chai is Emeritus Professor of English and Comparative Literature at the University of Illinois at Urbana/Champaign. He is the author of four books, including *Romantic Theory* (Johns Hopkins University Press, 2006). More recent work can be found at <http://www.leonchai.net>.

Monika Coghen is Reader in English Literature at the Jagiellonian University in Cracow. She has worked on British Romanticism and Anglo-Polish cultural relations in the eighteenth and nineteenth centuries. She has published numerous articles, particularly on dramas by Coleridge, Wordsworth, and Byron, and the Polish reception of Coleridge and Shelley. Her other areas of interest include the British nineteenth-century novel and Polish Romanticism. She is currently working on the reception of Byron in Poland.

Roberto Dainotto is Professor of Italian and of Literature at Duke University. His publications include *Racconti Americani del '900* (Einaudi, 1999), *Place in Literature: Regions, Cultures, Communities* (Cornell University Press, 2000), and *Europe (in Theory)* (Duke University Press, 2007), winner of the Laura Shannon Prize in Contemporary European Studies in 2010.

Benjamin Dawson is Lecturer in Literary Theory, Queen Mary University of London.

Franco D'Intino is Professor of Modern Italian Literature at the University of Rome 'La Sapienza'. His main areas of research are: theory and history of autobiography (*L'autobiografia moderna: Storia forme problemi*, 2nd edn, 1998) and the work of Giacomo Leopardi. He has published the editions of Leopardi's *Scritti e frammenti autobiografici* (1995), *Poeti greci e latini* (1999), *Volgarizzamenti in prosa 1822–1827* (2012), and the monograph *L'immagine della voce: Leopardi, Platone e il libro morale* (2009). He is Director of the Leopardi Centre (University of Birmingham) and Director of the Laboratorio Leopardi (School for Advanced Studies at 'La Sapienza'). He has edited, with Michael Caesar, the complete English translation of the *Zibaldone*, Leopardi's notebooks (New York, Farrar Straus & Giroux; London, Penguin, 2013).

Angela Esterhammer is Principal of Victoria College and Professor of English and Comparative Literature at the University of Toronto. Her publications include *Creating States: Studies in the Performative Language of John Milton and William Blake* (1994), *The Romantic Performative: Language and Action in British and German Romanticism* (2000), *Romanticism and Improvisation, 1750–1850* (2008), and the edited volumes *Romantic Poetry* (2002) and *Spheres of Action: Speech and Performance in Romantic Culture* (2009). Her current research examines interrelations among improvisational performance, print culture, periodicals, and fiction in the early nineteenth century.

Jan Fellerer is Associate Professor in Slavonic languages at Oxford University. He studied at the universities of Vienna, Prague, Cracow, and Basel. His research focuses on the history of Polish, Czech, and Ukrainian, with special reference to the modern period from the late eighteenth century to the present day, and on topics in the modern grammar of Slavonic languages, especially the relation between lexical semantics and syntax.

Derek Flitter is Professor of Spanish at the University of Exeter. The main focus of his research has always lain with Spanish Romanticism and modern Spanish intellectual history, beginning with his monograph, *Spanish Romantic Literary Theory and Criticism* (1992) and continuing with *Spanish Romanticism and the Uses of History: Ideology and* *the Historical Imagination* (2006). He is currently completing a book on eschatological elements in Spanish romantic drama. Professor Flitter has published extensively also on modern Spanish poetry and on Galician literature. He is the editor of a number of collections of essays in the area of modern Spanish literature, and has been Hispanic Editor of *Modern Language Review* since 2006.

Biancamaria Fontana is Professor of the History of Political Ideas at the Institut d'Études Politiques et Internationales of the University of Lausanne. Her works focus on the history of classical liberalism and the shaping of representative government before and after the French Revolution. She is the author of many books including *Benjamin Constant and the Post-Revolutionary Mind* (1991), *The Invention of the Modern Republic* (1994), *Montaigne's Politics, Authority and Governance in the 'Essais'* (2008), and *Du Boudoir à la révolution: Choderlos de Laclos et les Liaisons dangereuses dans leur siècle* (2013).

Giuseppe Gazzola is Assistant Professor of European Literatures and Fellow of the Humanities Institute at Stony Brook University. He holds a Ph.D. from Yale University and an MA from the University of Notre Dame; his research focuses on European literature and cultural history of the nineteenth and twentieth centuries. He has published articles on Foscolo, Petrarch, and Italian Orientalism in various international journals. His most recent books include *Versi e Prose: Marinetti traduce Mallarmé* (forthcoming); *Futurismo: Impact and Legacy* (2011); *Ugo Foscolo: Essays über Petrarca* (with Olaf Muller, 2008). He is currently completing a book project on the analysis of landscape and autobiography in the poetry of Eugenio Montale.

Luba Golburt is Associate Professor in the department of Slavic Languages and Literatures at UC Berkeley where she teaches eighteenth- and nineteenth-century Russian literature and culture. Her publications include *The First Epoch: The Eighteenth Century and the Russian Cultural Imagination* (University of Wisconsin Press, 2014) and a number of articles on eighteenth-century Russian poetry, Romanticism, Pushkin, history of genre, and word and image criticism.

Rüdiger Görner is Professor of German with Comparative Literature and Founding Director of the Centre for Anglo-German Cultural Relations at Queen Mary, University of London. He is Fellow of the Japan Society for the Promotion of Science and Corresponding Fellow of the Deutsche Akademie für Sprache und Dichtung. His most recent monograph is *Georg Trakl: Dichter im Jahrzehnt der Extreme* (Vienna/Munich: Zsolnay/Hanser, 2014).

Katya Hokanson is Associate Professor of Russian and Comparative Literature at the University of Oregon. She is the author of *Writing at Russia's Border* (2008) as well as numerous articles including 'Russian Women Travelers in Central Asia and India', *Russian Review* (Jan. 2011), and 'Suwarrow, Souvaroff: Byron's Russia and Pushkin's Political Poems of 1831', in *Zapadnyi pushkinizm i rossiiskii baironizm: Problemy vzaimosviaze* (2009).

Andrew Kahn is Professor of Russian Literature at the University of Oxford. He is the author of *Pushkin's Lyric Intelligence* (2008) and amongst other Russian writing, he has edited N. M. Karamzin, *Letters of a Russian Traveller* (2003) and Mikhail Lermontov, *A Hero of Our Time*, with Alexander Pushkin, *Journey to Erzurum* (2013). He is also the editor of *The Cambridge Companion to Pushkin* (2007).

Katherine Lunn-Rockliffe is Faculty Lecturer in French at Oxford University and Fellow and Tutor at Hertford College. She is the author of *Tristan Corbière and the Poetics of Irony* (2007) and is currently working on a book on Victor Hugo.

Joseph Luzzi teaches at Bard and is the author of *My Two Italies* (Farrar, Straus & Giroux, 2014) and *A Cinema of Poetry: Aesthetics of the Italian Art Film* (Johns Hopkins University Press, 2014). His first book, *Romantic Europe and the Ghost of Italy* (Yale University Press, 2008), won the Scaglione Prize for Italian Studies from the Modern Language Association and was selected as an Outstanding Academic Title by *Choice*. An active critic, Luzzi's essays and reviews have appeared in the *New York Times*, the *Los Angeles Times*, *Bookforum*, and *The Times Literary Supplement*.

Dennis F. Mahoney is Professor of German in the Department of German and Russian at the University of Vermont. He is the author of numerous articles on Goethe, Novalis, Schiller, and others. He has written books on the *Roman der Goethezeit*, three books on the German romantic writer Novalis, two written in German and one in English. He recently edited *The Literature of German Romanticism* (2004), which is volume 8 in the Camden House History of German Literature series.

Francesco Manzini is Fellow of Oriel College, Oxford, and Stipendiary Lecturer in French at Oriel and University Colleges, Oxford. He is the author of *Stendhal's Parallel Lives* (2004) and *The Fevered Novel from Balzac to Bernanos* (2011), as well as of various articles on nineteenth-century French literature. He is currently co-editing (with Maria Scott) a Special Issue of *Dix-Neuf* on 'Stendhal in the Twenty-First Century'.

Tim Mehigan is Professor of German and Head of the School of Languages and Comparative Cultural Studies at the University of Queensland. He is the author of amongst other things *Heinrich von Kleist: Writing After Kant* (2011), 'Robert Musil: *Der Mann ohne Eigenschaften*', in *Literatur und Wissen: Ein interdisziplinäres Handbuch* (2013), and *Raumlektüren: Der Spatial Turn und die Literatur der Moderne* (2013). He has also published, with B. Empson, the first English translation of K. L. Reinhold's major work of philosophy *Versuch einer neuen Theorie des menschlichen Vorstellungsvermögens* (2011).

Douglas Moggach is Distinguished University Professor at the University of Ottawa, and Honorary Professor in the Department of Philosophy, School of Philosophical and Historical Inquiry, University of Sydney. He has published widely in the field of German philosophy, and has held visiting appointments in Beijing, Cambridge, London, Münster, Pisa, and Sydney.

Klaus Müller-Wille is Professor in the Deutches Seminar at the University of Zurich. He is the author of *Schrift, Schreiben und Wissen: Zu einer Theorie des Archivs in Texten von C. J. L. Almqvist* (2005) and is the editor of several critical collections on Scandinavian literature including, most recently, *Wechselkurse des Vertrauens: Zur Konzeptualisierung von Ökonomie und Vertrauen im Zeitalter des nordischen Idealismus 1800–1870* (2013).

Angus Nicholls is Senior Lecturer in German and Comparative Literature and Chair of the Department of Comparative Literature and Culture at Queen Mary University of London. He is the author of *Goethe's Concept of the Daemonic: After the Ancients* (2006), *Myth and the Human Sciences: Hans Blumenberg's Theory of Myth* (2014), and has co-edited Hans Blumenberg, *Präfiguration: Arbeit am politischen Mythos* (2014).

Wm. Arctander O'Brien is Professor of German and Comparative Literature at the University of California, San Diego. His publications on Romanticism include *Novalis: Signs of Revolution* (Durham, NC, and London: Duke University Press, 1995).

Maike Oergel is Associate Professor in German Studies, Director of the Centre for Translation and Comparative Cultural Studies, Faculty of Arts, University of Nottingham. She is the author of *The Return of King Arthur and the Nibelungen: National Myth in 19th Century English and German Literature* (1998), and *Culture and Identity: Historicity in German Literature and Thought 1770–1815* (2006). She has co-edited, amongst other collections, *Counter-Cultures in Germany and Central Europe: From Sturm und Drang to Baader-Meinhof* (2003), *Re-Writing the Radical: Enlightenment, Revolution and Cultural Transfer in 1790s Germany, Britain and France* (2012) and, most recently, *Aesthetics and Modernity: From Schiller to the Frankfurt School.*

Sotirios Paraschas is Lecturer in French Studies at the University of Reading. His research interests include nineteenth-century fiction, the theory and history of realism and the novel, law and literature, the history of intellectual property, and comparative literature. He is the author of *The Realist Author and Sympathetic Imagination* (London: Legenda, 2013).

Thomas Pfau is the Alice Mary Baldwin Professor of English, with secondary appointments in Germanic Languages and Literatures and in the Duke Divinity School. To date, he is the author of three monographs: *Wordsworth's Profession* (Stanford University Press, 1997) *Romantic Moods: Paranoia, Trauma, and Melancholy, 1794–1840* (Johns Hopkins University Press, 2005) and *Minding the Modern: Human Agency, Intellectual Traditions, and Responsible Knowledge* (Notre Dame University Press, 2013). He has published some thirty-five essays on a wide range of writers, including Rousseau, A. Smith, Kant, Wordsworth, Wollstonecraft, Coleridge, Shelley, Goethe, Beethoven, Eichendorff, Schleiermacher, Thomas Mann, Walter Benjamin.

Alexander Regier is Associate Professor of English at Rice University and editor of the scholarly journal *SEL: Studies in English Literature 1500–1900*. He is the author of *Fracture and Fragmentation in British Romanticism* (Cambridge University Press, 2010) and the co-editor of *Wordsworth's Poetic Theory* (Palgrave, 2010). His articles on rhetoric, Wordsworth, Walter Benjamin, ruins, utopianism, contemporary poetry, the aesthetics of sport, and other topics have appeared in *FMLS, European Romantic Review, Germanic Review, Sport in History*, and elsewhere. He is currently working on a comparative study of William Blake and Johann Georg Hamann's poetry of progress.

Jean-Marie Roulin is Professor at the University of Lyon (campus of Saint-Étienne) and a member of UMR CNRS IHRIM ('Institute of History of the Representations and Ideas in Modernity'). His research bears on French literature from the Enlightenment to Romanticism, especially on the relations between literature, society, politics, and history. His principal works include *Chateaubriand, l'exil et la gloire* (Champion, 1994), and *L'Épopée de Voltaire à Chateaubriand: Poésie histoire et politique* (Oxford: SVEC, 2005). He has edited Benjamin Constant's fictional works (GF, 2010) and several critical collections, including *Masculinités en Révolution, de Rousseau à Balzac* (Presses Universitaires de Saint-Étienne, 2013) and *Les Romans de la Révolution 1790–1912* (A. Colin 'Recherches', 2014).

Diego Saglia is Associate Professor of English Literature at the University of Parma (Italy). His research focuses on British romantic-period literature and culture, as well as their links and exchanges with other European traditions. He is the author of *Poetic Castles in Spain: British Romanticism and Figurations of Iberia* (2000), and co-editor of *British Romanticism and Italian Literature: Translating, Reviewing, Rewriting* (with Laura Bandiera, 2005). A contributor to *The Encyclopedia of Romantic Literature* (ed. Frederick Burwick, 2012), he has also recently completed the first critical edition of Robert Southey's *Roderick, the Last of the Goths* (2012), and *European Literatures in English: 1813–1832* (2018).

Bradley Stephens is Senior Lecturer in French at the University of Bristol and works on the reception and adaptation of French romantic writers, with a particular interest in Victor Hugo. He is the author of *Victor Hugo, Jean-Paul Sartre, and the Liability of Liberty* (Legenda, 2011), and the co-editor of both *Transmissions: Essays in French Literature, Thought and Cinema* (Peter Lang, 2007) and a special issue of *Dix-Neuf* (Maney, 2014) on adaptations of nineteenth-century French literature. He has also published various articles and book chapters in this field, including a new introduction to Hugo's novel *The Hunchback of Notre-Dame* (Signet Classics, 2010), and two co-edited books are forthcoming: *'Les Misérables' and its Afterlives: Between Page, Stage, and Screen*, with Kathryn M. Grossman (Ashgate), and *Approaches to Teaching Victor Hugo's 'Les Misérables'*, with Michal P. Ginsburg (Modern Language Association).

Paul Stock is Assistant Professor in Early Modern International History 1500–1850 at the London School of Economics and Political Science. His publications include *The Shelley-Byron Circle and the Idea of Europe* (Palgrave Macmillan, 2010) and *The Uses of Space in Early Modern History* (ed., 2015), as well as scholarly articles on Napoleon Bonaparte, Romanticism, eighteenth-century racial thought, and philhellenism.

Stefan H. Uhlig is Assistant Professor of Comparative Literature at the University of Davis California. He has written numerous articles, most recently, 'Ferguson's School for Literature', in *The Poetic Enlightenment: Poetry and Human Science, 1650–1820* (2013), and co-edited *Wordsworth's Poetic Theory: Knowledge, Language, Experience*, introduced and edited with Alexander Regier (2010) and *Aesthetics and the Work of Art: Adorno, Kafka, Richter*, introduced and edited with Peter de Bolla (2009).

Patrick Vincent is Professor of English and American literature at the University of Neuchâtel. His books include *The Romantic Poetess: European Culture, Politics and Gender 1820–1840* (2004), *La Suisse vue par les écrivains de langue anglaise* (2009), *Chillon: A Literary Guide* (2010). He also co-edited *American Poetry: Whitman to the Present* (2006), and Helen Maria Williams, *A Tour of Switzerland* (2011).

Caroline Warman is Associate Professor in French at the University of Oxford and a Fellow of Jesus College. She is the author of *Sade: From Materialism to Pornography* (SVEC, 2002) and has written widely on eighteenth- and nineteenth-century literary and intellectual history. She is currently preparing a book on Diderot's late text, the *Eléments de physiologie*. She and Kate Tunstall edited and translated a volume of Marian Hobson's essays, *Diderot and Rousseau: Networks of Enlightenment* (SVEC, 2011), and their translation of Diderot's tricksy dialogue *Le Neveu de Rameau* is published in a multimedia edition by Open Book Publishers (edited by Marian Hobson, music researched and directed by Pascal Duc, 2014). Caroline Warman is also the translator of Isabelle de Charrière's novellas, *The Nobleman and Other Romances* (Penguin, 2012).

Astrid Weigert is Assistant Visiting Professor at Georgetown University. She is the author of many articles including 'Gender-Art-Science: Elsa Bernstein's Critique of Naturalist Aesthetics' in Helga W. Kraft and Dagmar C. G. Lorenz (eds), *From Fin-de-Siecle to Theresienstadt: The Works and Life of the Writer Elsa Porges-Bernstein* (Peter Lang, 2007).

Jonathan White is Professor Emeritus in Literature, University of Essex. His two books on Italy are *Italy: The Enduring Culture* (Leicester University Press, 2000; Continuum, 2001) and *Italian Cultural Lineages* (University of Toronto Press, 2007). A portion of his Cambridge thesis on Shakespeare appeared earlier as a monograph in Italian: *Teatralità e politica nel 'Coriolano' di Shakespeare*, tr. and ed. Daniela Corona (Libreria Dante, 1979). He has edited *Recasting the World: Writing After Colonialism* (Johns Hopkins University Press, 1993) and co-edited *The City and the Ocean: Journeys, Memory, Imagination* (Cambridge Scholars Publishing, 2012). White is currently co-editing *Landscape, Seascape and the Eco-Spatial Imagination*, as well as completing a monograph titled *Conversing with the Dead: A Poetics of Cultural Memory*.

INTRODUCTION

PAUL HAMILTON

ROMANTICISM has always been a systematically contested subject in modern criticism. From the start, it presented itself as a patchwork of different manifestos. Poets, especially, from Wordsworth to Hugo, Hölderlin to Leopardi, published or recorded privately their reasons for writing in the ways they did in order to show that self-consciousness was a significant part of their endeavour and contributed to its content. What they thought of their writing was part of what it was about. These professional explanations often involved philosophical, political, ethical, as well as literary reformulations for which the time and place of Romanticism were deemed to offer exclusive opportunities. The major and learned dispute between Arthur Lovejoy and René Wellek in the 1940s about the very definability of Romanticism actually renewed a foundational controversy; Wellek and Lovejoy debated the usefulness of a term for a period of literary history whose main characteristic had always been contestation of its terms of reference. Their *querelle* anticipated the more recent new historicist project of resisting a major feature of Romanticism, its habit of cajoling its readers into defining it on its own terms. Objective, properly historical discussion, historicists alleged, tends to be assimilated to Romanticism's own version of itself. But, equally, to resist this self-portrait could confirm Lovejoy's scepticism about the viability of discriminating any single thing called Romanticism, and so to perpetuate another self-image of the Romantic age, its original self-questioning, if not its 'ideology'

Lovejoy and Wellek, though, wrote about Europe, while new historicists have tended to write almost exclusively about British Romanticism, incorporating some continental allies, such as the young Marx and Heine, when convenient, but usually contextualizing British Romantic poetry's claim to autonomy with the local archives it purported to transcend—political, educational, economical, medical—or, in other words, the disciplines in contrast to which a Romanticism led by poetry had, in Coleridge's terms, proposed 'pleasure' rather than 'knowledge' for its object. European Romanticism, however, is more plausibly viewed as the comparative subject of its earlier commentators. The local was often transcended in a spirit not of sublimation but of practical political necessity. The collaborations between different disciplines generated the idea of a general creativity, the *Poesie* of the age. This transferable skill or formative impulse in response to historical circumstance is what is explored through the diversity of subjects in the chapters of this book.

Viewed in most general terms, Romanticism was implicated in the creation of modern Europe, a process extending from the revolutionary throes of France in the 1790s to the reconstruction that took place after the Napoleonic era. Modern Europe did not of course leap fully formed from post-Napoleonic settlements such as the Congress of Vienna (1814), yet historians are still agreed that at least the groundwork out of which arose the continent's formative national antagonisms was laid at this time. This Europe was the culmination of a series of 'dry-runs': the *internationale* coming out of the French Revolution, and the subsequent Napoleonic imperialism, with its simultaneously emancipating and domineering 'code', clearly had European pretentions. Their universalizing rhetoric for a while belied their French origins and only gradually subsided into an exclusive and aggrandizing nationalism, although much to the chagrin of sympathizers as far apart as Wordsworth and Ugo Foscolo. The invasion of Switzerland did it for Wordsworth, 'Another year, another deadly blow', and the tyrannies emerging from collaboration with Napoleon for Ugo Foscolo's hero Jacopo Ortis, 'si servono della libertà come i Papi si servivano delle crociate' ('they make use of liberty as the Popes used to do of the Crusades'). But Romanticism re-established the precedent of justifying nationalism by reference to a (lost) universalism equated with Europe. When Burke talked of a vanished 'chivalry' he appeared reactionary; but, as Novalis recognized, the recovery of the idea of a united Europe implied by his polemic could be regenerated in the undeniably progressive ideologies supporting or anticipating Greek, Italian, and German unification. Napoleon had scented such revivals in Mme de Staël's *De l'Allemagne*, and pulped as many copies as he could. The entire 1816 Italian controversy, provoked by Staël's subsequent letter on translation, continued this debate over ways in which a national literature could be modern and show that its moment had come by being European.

Less sweepingly, one can claim as well that the naturally interdisciplinary quality of European Romanticism, the typical transitions writers of the time made between different discourses and periods, set up an internal comparative dynamic. Again, the manifesto beckons. Literatures ancient and modern, dramatic or prosaic, or traditionally belonging to distinct genres or kinds became regarded as different sorts of writing seeking their recognizable translation into each other. They did so, it was argued, on the understanding of a common ground, a shared denominator whose evocation is most easily figured as the Romantic project. We should accept that queries will always persist as to when the term 'Romantic' was first used, or became an accepted category of classification, or if it can ever escape the retrospective legislation of later pedagogical or cultural purposes. At the same time, though, we should perhaps recognize that it is in its European or comparative character that the post-neoclassical period behaves in what became known as a Romantic manner. A resistance to generic boundaries of all kinds, and a cultural investment in the transgression of inherited boundaries permitted a *choice* of the traditions with which one defined oneself. No longer an inalienable birthright, history became historicized, ideas became ideologized, and the possible relativity of everything became a determinate indication of the cultural needs and priorities of the present. The 'occasionalism' for which the Fascist Carl Schmitt consequently derided the German Romantics actually confirmed the Romantic period as the one which inaugurated that series of redefinitions or occasions of modernity, unconstrained by static traditions, extending into our own post-modern or post-post-modern times.

Schmitt's contempt was focused on the irony powering much romantic writing. In a scenario in which everything was provisional, offered as a temporary description, nothing, he argued, was for real or could be taken with unequivocal seriousness. Wilful obfuscation, a captious blindness to the realities of politics, or sheer escapism characterized the Romantic unwillingness to acknowledge certain fundamentals. How could a tradition be an optional rather than an inherited characteristic and still remain a tradition? How could an imagined polity retain any credibility without a real rather than a speculative basis in violent self-preservation? In Romantic reply one might claim that Schmitt is too narrow in his understanding of irony, himself blind to its defining links with a cultural expansiveness which actually supplanted its ironic beginnings. An aesthetic indecisiveness before choices obligatory in real life translates into a deliberate acceptance of varieties of social and anthropological realism, an urbanity made available, though, by that initial openness. This latitude was anticipated by Montesquieu to some extent, but it is forward-looking thinkers like Herder, interested in advancing a consciously modern literature, who are pre-Romantic in this sense.

But just as its irony exceeded a merely rhetorical role, becoming 'Romantic irony' proper, so Romanticism exploded an original literariness and proposed a much wider cultural repertoire. At one end of its agenda, there is Friedrich Schlegel's theory of the artwork, the novel or *der Roman*, whose hybrid generic form possessed for him the strict political correlate of a mixed republican constitution. At the other end, a byword for ultimate philosophical explanation, Hegelian phenomenology shuttles between a metaphysics of becoming and the stance of criticism and reflection which that metaphysics justifies. Everything, but everything, must be brought to reflection in this critical age; everything must be critiqued in the post-Kantian sense of an interrogation of its logical presuppositions, and in the further Hegelian sense of subordinating *that* logic to the movement of history and the cunning of *its* reason. Hegelian logic only corroborated the way the world goes, *der Weltlauf*, which prioritized a series of different perspectives and descriptions. Again, the crossovers are crucial: movements between different expressions of experience are undertaken with a view to questioning just what might be at stake in the possibility of this translation. Such unfolding supports my suggestion here that it is in its comparativism that Romanticism can be approached most profitably and least controversially. Hegel certainly had little time for Romanticism, which he thought too ironical and inward, but even in attack he replicates its drive beyond initially aesthetic boundaries into a wider discursive geography. The European view of Romanticism stresses its compulsive dissipation of its talents across various fields. The refusal of European Romanticism to restrict conclusions to any single language-game, and the consequent difficulty in defining it posed by this comparative dynamic, is what turns the academic question debated between Lovejoy and Wellek into something more practical and symptomatic. The question becomes a profounder one about the timeliness of those changes which Romanticism typically makes in its discursive investments in response to changes in historical circumstance. This comparative habit may trouble later desires for disciplinary tidiness but has to be represented in any adequate discussion of the period.

How does one handle an area full of discourses constantly seeking their own past and each other's company? Any scheme used must be competent to suggest, in effect, the transformation of the great encyclopedic project of the *philosophes* into something much more interactive. What sort of economy is it appropriate to try to impose here?

One chapter below shows the 'Frenetic Romanticism' that can grow out of the recurrent Romantic habit of self-reflection. The frenetic inflection of reflective judgement is fascinated by boundaries and limits of the human because of the temptation to cross them. No doubt the origins of this are in respectable, acculturated moments of sublimity, and a sense of dignity supervening on scenes of weakness or belittlement by nature's grandeur or our own inarticulacy. But the 'frenetic' reveals that, logically, the door is left open to a delight in perversity, the unnatural, or anything staging a refutation of the quotidian identity sublimity leaves behind. Whether, on such journeys, the individual remains intact, or suffers a fatal expansion, enjoyably dissolute or horrifically destructive, is the main curiosity.

The modern destination for Romantic versatility is often evident in this *Handbook* and its authors encourage us to see it. We are also, I trust, given the tools with which to preserve historical difference from the hindsight historicism encourages. In what follows, individual discussions do not cross-reference each other, but stand on their own, lodged within a commentary alive to its subject's characteristically comparative impulse. There are two main editorial decisions taken, geographical and disciplinary. There is an obvious problem of anachronism in any attempt to divide Romanticisms up between nations. Nevertheless, dominant nationalist aspirations are so much a subject of Romanticism that it won't do either to treat subjects as if they inhere within a neutral geography. The answer offered here is to observe divisions with relation to languages rather than places. This is in any case an age in which the explanatory force of the phenomenon of language is beginning to irradiate all fields in a way we too often think of as modern or contemporary. Most of the chapters, once one is alert to this, have language as a major actor.

The *Handbook*, then, is organized under the two headings of languages and discourses. Languages particularize nations or nations about to be. The discourses section fills out and develops the comparative logic which will have been noticeably present in the largely author-based language studies, but will not have been their main subject. The title of 'discourses' is also meant to raise the question of the extent to which subjects are produced by ways of writing about them. So, in a pragmatic and not exact fashion, I am in debt to the approach to the organization of knowledge associated with Michel Foucault, itself arguably the inheritor of a comparative approach which it transformed. The mutually reflective or symbiotic character of literature, science of all kinds, biography or life-writing, political economy, and so forth is part of a general economy of

Romanticism which, I have argued, Romanticism was itself eager to stress. When Shelley, defending the cultural relevance of 'poetry', tells us that we want 'the poetry of life' or that the poetry of Rome lay 'in its institutions' he is speaking in a continental idiom in which poetry inspires an acquaintance with the different 'knowledges' of his time. In its range, this poetic resource recalls a medieval fluency in Latin culture or the Renaissance ideal of rounded learning which followed it. An English word for this might be 'Coleridgean', suggesting the hazards as well as the fascination of such intellectual freedoms.

But of course it is not English definitions that we are interested in primarily here. The most interrelated European areas are French, German, and Italian Romanticism. Otherwise, this book is about the Romanticisms of countries who joined the Romantic conversation later and the idioms in which they characteristically did so. 'Europe' is then repeatedly generated as the background noise against which each linguistic or discursive intonation becomes audible. By that I mean that characteristically Romantic or of the time is just to claim as much right to represent Europe as one's competitors. There is, to greater and lesser degrees, a continental habit from Stäel onwards, to cast national success as the achievement of taking one's place in a European context—whether that be cultural or political. Disappointment in political aspiration, especially after the Congress of Vienna, puts greater responsibility on the cultural effort; but the resulting nationalist movements still aspire to a European franchise. Stäel envisages a 'Europe of nations', and Friedrich Schlegel argues that different countries at different times represented and continue to represent the definitive way of being European. At one time Spain, at another France or Italy, and more recently Germany were the leading ways of being European—a cultural rota and not a series of empires, one should emphasize. But the same goes for discourses, something more visible within a Romantic context, when the sense a discourse gives of being written knowledgeably against other pretenders to completeness or comprehensiveness of understanding does so by pushing its claims to resume the European spirit of history, drama, theology, language, sexual and racial egalitarianism, care of the body, mind, and so on.

The neoclassicism which Romanticism is popularly thought to succeed is itself a shape-shifter. On the one hand, it is associated with rigid adherence to the unities, an allegiance to traditional forms which, with Voltaire, found Shakespeare outrageous and, with Dr Johnson, found imagination to be a sort of madness. On the other hand, classical precedent was founded on a notion of propriety which undid such formal prescriptions. Propriety, in the writing of an adept like Ben Jonson, for example, is evidenced by a language equal to all occasions. The fit between usage and circumstance shows the judicious art of the poet, its pronouncement on rather than immersion in its subject, and exonerates the poet artist from contamination by the content of the poem. The most elevated and scabrous of subjects find themselves judged by the happiness of the diction in which they are addressed, rather than possessing any power to incriminate or degrade the language in which they are so felicitously described. But such poetry's authority over its content does not produce a dry formalism. Getting things right in a way that generates the pleasure of recognizing the fit of word and object, genre and occasion, feeling and situation, is an activity on which depend ideas of authenticity, experience, maturity, skill, sense—in fact a diet of techniques for living. And the instruction is convincing and palatable only in proportion as it also registers poetic success, mixing the *utile* with the *dulce*.

It is not a huge jump from here to the European Romantics' theory of the novel or *der Roman*: that literary portmanteau or *poème multiforme*, as Hugo called it, which, in approaching a subject from all sorts of directions, provides an adequate treatment through its mixture of genres and discourses. Just as European Romanticism saw itself as creating a grasp of modernity fit for its own time, so it thought of its stylistic expansiveness as setting new standards for realism, more usually described as what succeeded Romanticism. But chapters here, especially on French Romanticism, repeatedly remark on the romancing of realism common to the work of writers as different as Stendhal, Balzac, and Dumas *père*. Such interpretation raises the possibility that it is in its realistic ambitions or appetite for experience that Romanticism differs from the similar but different ambitions of neoclassicism to be stylistically adequate to experience.

Different aspects of experience demand of their writer different proprieties, and the divine tolerance of comedy with which to accommodate them. But the studies in this volume show that writing which is interdisciplinary and comparative does not necessarily create cosy agreements about synergies. Conflicts made to cohabit the same discursive space are real ones. In line with the integrity Staël imagined for Europe, what is fostered is a common *autonomy*, one contrasting definitively with subjection to Napoleon's imperium. Staël links things by seeing them as alternatives to each other. Indeed she is a creator of alternatives: travel and exile let her map another Europe; an alternative kind of edification therefore arises from her subversive enthusiasm for each country's potential future in contrast to the antiquarian pleasures of the previous century's Grand Tour; an alternative female character emerges from her narration of her flight into autonomy, her unofficial embassy on behalf of her liberal ideas; an alternative critical practice, a sociology of literature, evolves from the unprecedented number of cultural issues her literary histories keep in focus. Other female writers, especially German ones, refuse to be air-brushed out of cultural history in which they played an important role. They show that, even where a literary genre is shared with men, women can give it a startlingly innovative treatment, one in several ways different from the canonical radicalism of the male writers. After the Terror, when radicalism itself was being reconceived, this was to give the lead: their revisionism was not supplementary but avant-garde.

Roman and *Mischgedicht* provide in discursive miniature a general Romantic toleration of conflict or reconciliation of opposites. The largest display of the Romantic talent for negotiation comes when, along with Chateaubriand and, later, Leopardi, German writers mediate between Classicism and Romanticism. Again, though, this settling of differences is not a superficial elision of them. Exemplary in this regard is Goethe, and it takes two chapters to sketch the range of his achievement, as it does with Leopardi. Goethe's inclusiveness, as described across the two chapters devoted to him here, maintains the oppositions necessary to his overall project of remaining receptive to a world forever more various than our descriptions of it. This 'healthy' realism, though, is achieved through the Romantic habits of irony, generic cross-overs, and the catholic or Shakespearean range of sensibility culminating in *Faust*. Goethe shows that accommodations so sensitive to the differences in what they bring together lead back to what Hölderlin, another 'classicist', called *Urteil*: judgement originating in a primal severance from the Being judged. Hölderlin's own 'measure', 'tone' and 'caesura', it is shown here, then stage a reconciliation extremely knowing about its own aesthetic status. The knowingness is of the need either to champion that achievement in absolute terms, or to accept its provisional character through calculated nostalgia for an (invented) Hellenic era when aesthetic absolutism was possible. Kleist and Schelling, in their different ways, see the abyss opening up in the very moment of judgement, differentiation and definition. Unlike the crises which they plot, Hegelian logic works its way back to the unity with essence which knowledge or the creation of the concept originally forfeited. These varieties of Jena thinking, it is suggested, recall the alternatives of Reformation or the revitalized Catholicism driving a Counter-Reformation.

Another conspicuous mix of competing elements becomes visible when we consider the traditionally vexed problem of pre-Romanticism. The prehistory of European Romanticism suggests a long, mutating Enlightenment whose continuity is obscured by the epochal disruption of the French Revolution of 1789. For some, Enlightenment ends with revolution, and an equally epochal reaction sets in. The Restoration ensuing in Europe after the Congress of Vienna in 1814 then characterizes Romanticism. What gets forgotten in this simple story is the resistance to Napoleon, a Napoleon no longer understood as the 'child of the Revolution' beloved of English Jacobins like Hazlitt, but as an impediment to the rethinking of revolution altogether analogous to the Romantic rethinking of Enlightenment. ('Why should the Revolution remain French?', Novalis was to ask.) As the chapters here show, Diderot and Hamann, whether writing from within the *philosophes* or from the heart of *Sturm und Drang*, are already participants in Romanticism's strenuous self-fashioning.

Similarly, Europe's view of Britain, and its construction of a European identity for Britain in interaction with continental interests, also exhibits a dialectic of division and resolution. The European writing of Britain in the Romantic period describes it as a place of moderation. The idea of Britain encouraged the thinking of forms of mediation between Europe's polarities—ethical, political, and aesthetic. Advocates of highly partisan positions were perhaps bound to interpret British liberalism as prevarication, parliamentarianism as Old Corruption, and the famous English eccentricity as dissolute self-indulgence. But the notion of Britain as a challenge to determinate self-images of all kinds found an echo in Romantic hybridity, its mixed economies, constitutions and love of difference. While continental latitudes of this kind took a self-defining effort of imagination, though, British equanimity owed more to the laissez-faire economics of Adam Smith and the urbane scepticism of David Hume—the opposite, in other words, of the transformative alliances of the Romantic worldview. Yet these virtues, in turn, were influentially linked by Staël to a Northern sensibility whose greatest author was Shakespeare, stylistically generous and versatile to a fault, and so the wheel comes full circle again.

In individual countries, Spain for example, it is striking in the context of the *Handbook* that while Romantics of other nations (especially Germany) are praising the Shakespearean latitude of Calderón, Spanish Romantics themselves are returning to an earlier, more starkly agonistic paradigm. This allows extreme forms of gendered oppositions, which are Romantic or of their time, although created by preserving older conflicts between traditions (religious, social, literary) and individual desire. The modernization comes in the Romantic concentration on conflict, usually between male love and female tradition, here described as 'ferocious'. By contrast, in Russia, Romantic sensibility, competing with a classical heritage of form and genre, became a general aptitude which, like Rousseau's 'heart', increased the number of loci and topoi traditionally used to corroborate subjectivity. This writing largely distinguished itself from what had gone before without having to formulate Romantic manifestos or stage battles with a preceding classicism. Pushkin constantly negotiates positive results out of literary redeployments, grounding the extraordinary achievement of the Russian novel to come. And novels of the time are often founded on a common geography, even if, paradoxically, it primarily describes periphery and exile.

Geography and history, as the chapter in the Discourses section suggests, are Romantically intertwined, in theory and in practice. Kant's philosophy had appeared to show that the form of our most inner sense of ourselves is a temporality which can only be expressed spatially. So the age's philosophical crux is, arguably, played out in the interdisciplinary relations of history and geography. Herder makes history as plural as geography. We coerce free particulars, unrelated in themselves, into society with each other in order that we can be made coherent subjects by belonging to the same history of national places. Geography traces the consequences of political decisions in this age of political remapping; it thus fuels the most ordinary conversation about the status quo as well as raising larger questions of political metaphysics. What are borders for? What is a nation? What do we still have in common despite political difference? What is Europe's 'other'?

In Poland, history and geography constantly shift in response to each other, and the preservation of an individual voice in the face of Russian annexation draws on adjacent nationalisms, Lithuanian and Belarussian, without, though, sharing their languages. The complexity with which the self is represented by Polish writers grows with these acknowledgements; they help sketch an orientation within Europe very different from that of countries less oppressed by others. In Hungary, on the other hand, the deal struck after the Great War emancipated Austro-Hungarian subject peoples in the name of the nationalist credentials denied to Hungary's claims to retain her distinctive hegemony. Linguistic sustainability, for which poetry is the flagship, becomes the touchstone of national identity. The question then settles on the degree to which that revival of Hungarian carries with it allegiances to aesthetics transformative of Enlightenment universals and to cosmopolitanism of a Kantian kind. Scandinavian Romanticism is the most varied and in many ways the most fascinating developer of its individuality through a critical orientation towards mainstream European ideas. Oehlenschläger is capable of startling annexations and cooptings of different kinds. Andersen can simultaneously take up a critical stance towards German *Märchen, Romantik*, and contemporary Biedermeier culture to anticipate, as strikingly as Kierkegaard, a 'modernity' to come, a supposedly new realism free of Romanticism's self-generating ironies. And the uses of Greece as iconic support for nationalism set in motion a historicizing of antiquity essential to Romantic conceptions of modernity, from Hölderlin to Leopardi. Like architecture, the novel, epitome of Romantic emancipation, is rooted in classical precedent, in this case Greek romance. The differences of past and present can inspire the thinking of modernity as much as they can impose the enervating belatedness which Byron lamented. He could therefore recast the anachronism of a Greece in rebellion against Asia Minor as a scandal for a modernity which could not resuscitate it in modern aesthetic and political form.

Italy is the other iconic precedent for the cultural advancement of claims to belong to Staël's Europe. And yet its most outstanding Romantic literature emerged from Leopardi's disagreement with Staël's advice to Italian writers on how to be modern. Arguably, much of Italian literary expression in the Romantic period is energized and even structured by the shape of the polemic with Staël. This debate explicitly connects literary and political questions. Once that connection is established, the possibilities for a literary politics expand considerably. In the absence of a contemporary Italian society creatively and critically conversant with itself, Leopardi's range of writing, his imagined sociability of different discursive activities in his encyclopedic *Zibaldone di Pensieri*, acquires an exemplary political charge. But other avenues to modernity as well as this one are mooted here, most vividly in Manzoni's genuine interest in an underclass whose subjection revealed a myriad different purposes too complicated for a single ideological solution. Manzoni's piety in fact anticipates that immersion in horror of post-Holocaust narrating of the unmanageable task of redress and compensation.

The management of discourses, then, can be strikingly in tune with nationalist aspirations. Or investments in individual discourses can help characterize a European *leitmotif* momentarily in the possession of one nation rather than another. We have seen that an economical way of explaining this, taken up here, is to show that Geography is always historical and History always geographical. Both discourses reciprocally locate each other in spatial and temporal coordinates borrowed from the other, each lending their own national colouring to the abstract grid or chronology of the other. Within national geographies, too, the historical plot of writing and thinking can sometimes be best caught in spatial shifts—Heidelberg, Dresden, Berlin, and Vienna. Medical research shows France taking over from Germany, and demonstrating the way forward for the emergent life-sciences. German self-experimentation, though, relocated the logic of scientific research closer to speculation in ways that recruited the philosopher poets, like Goethe, Novalis and Ritter, and set up new analogies between artistic and scientific creativity—practically and not just existing in the wish-list of the Jena *Frühromantiker*. These affinities may have appeared subsequently to have gone underground for a while, but have been rediscovered in the narrative art of Darwin and others.

Other discourses, even those as apparently different as religion and celebrity, reach for the exception rather than the rule. They target a particularity in human experience or character which suspends the usual order of things, whether scientific, ethical, or even aesthetic. Both expand on an inherent instability in the Romantic conception of the self, in the case of celebrity doubling the individual through the growing development of mass media and improved communication which the study of celebrity simultaneously maps. Religion is shown to use older teleological arguments to describe the human project as a continual outgrowing of a succession of institutional accommodations. And hence we can be shown an intelligible line running through the affective expansiveness of Schleiermacher to its Hegelian rationalization. This conceptualization is certainly something initially necessary for religion to keep its identity, but, for Hegel, it tends to transform religion, like art, into its own philosophy.

The issue, then is whether religion can retain its specificity or characteristic power of deregulation, thus impacting on other discourses to describe 'a hyper-pluralist conception of moral and political community'. Of course, the varied political discourses of the time can themselves be seen to be engaged in the remedying of a modern 'diremption', or sundering of the ties of community and belonging on which politics had been thought to be founded. National myth and tradition tend to replace public opinion as the foundation of political legitimacy. Liberalism is only maintained by an open-endedness or 'post-Kantian perfectionism' which, in Benjamin Constant's case, converged on a religious interest. Philosophy, too, supports aesthetics because 'dissonances' between key constituents of Romantic modernity—between the warm 'life-world' and the cold world of a growing free-market capitalism, between ideas of a common culture and the specialized technological sophistication or esotericism increasingly expected of scientific explanation—cry out for new myths and narratives to connect these parts to a whole. The breadth of the conceptual front on which this took place is perhaps what is distinctive of the Romantic confrontation of the crisis.

Both religion and celebrity *dramatize* rather than describe; they set up performative opportunities for us, roles in excess of our conventional identity, place-holders for what we are capable of or what our human potential actually might be. Correlatively, the contemporary sense of theatre exceeded any discipline or tradition to produce a new, active culture, a formative praxis rather than a literary or philosophical reflection. Literally, drama spilled into the streets. The piazza then returned the compliment and filled the theatres with plays fuelled by its contemporary political debates. Both street and playhouse combined to translate current discontent or aspiration into articulate dramatic form.

Behind all discourses, however, lies the enabling idea of language as such. Romantic period writers and thinkers in almost every country were engaged in the study both of the plausibility of language as *the* human universal, and, locally, of the consequences of the alignment of linguistic specificity and nation. These could conflict. A linguistics could be constrained to serve particular political purposes, the emancipation of a group of native speakers of a language from the hegemony of non-native speakers. At the same time, for international emancipatory movements like pan-Slavism, linguistic boundaries had to be politically porous. A language was one source of identity, but language as such seemed an inalienable human character. But was our access to language always not nationally inflected, always the language of a particular interest? And, if so, was to establish the identity of a particular language-community also to establish an undeniable political interest, or, in the language of the time, a national interest—an interest which could either justify the forming of new nations, or fuel a kind of irredentism of older nations directed at pockets of those speaking their language in newly established nations?

As the chapter here on language concludes, questions of this kind take us far beyond Romantic period disputes, but highlight the influence of the way Romantics brought such questions to reflection. They also take us back to the principles organizing this *Handbook*. To group Romanticisms by language, but with this kind of knowingness, is precisely to avoid mapping Romanticism by country; but it is also to recognize that the themes of Romanticism are still primarily located in particular nations and their struggles for ascendancy. Fundamentally, though, the survey of cultural activity of the kind given by this book must imply that validation of success in this international competition is the achievement of a sense of European belonging which had many more versions than the remapping of Europe coming out of the Congress of Vienna. Romantics for the most part were engaged in writing another unofficial story, and their literatures, philosophies, and discourses, taken generally, build up an alternative picture which events of 1820, 1830 and 1848 tried to realize. At these moments Europe is virtually defined by the ubiquitous unrest and unease with itself generated from Romantic manifestos.

The unofficial story, so visible in political aspiration, is, I have been emphasizing, what is made detectable across many forms of Romantic endeavour by these chapters. Collaboration, hybridity, historical transformations cast by 'the magic wand of analogy' as Novalis called it, are the source of those transpositions of discourses characteristic of the period. These shape-shiftings are not intended to flout the discipline of individual discourses so as to produce mixed metaphors or pathetic fallacies. To 'Romanticize' the world, for minds like Novalis and Friedrich Schlegel, was to be 'progressive', and it is that Romantic notion of the progressive which is the burden of Romantic lateral transfiguration in contrast to the orthodox linear model more familiar to us. A dedicated European perspective is needed to present this ambition in all its strengths and weaknesses, and here it is.

PART I

LANGUAGES

French

CHAPTER 1

PRE-ROMANTIC FRENCH THOUGHT

CAROLINE WARMAN

Much of French Romanticism, in both its first and second waves, was pre-figured in eighteenth-century writing, if by first wave we understand the rejection of reason and the turn to a mystical inexplicable union (or communion) with nature, and by the second the development of an anti-classical aesthetic particularly in the domain of the theatre, broadly understood as pro-Shakespeare, anti-Racine, and as disseminated by Stendhal and Hugo. When we think of the pre-figuring in the first case we might think first of Rousseau and of his many statements about the alienation of individual from society, whether generally conceptualized (*Le Discours sur les sciences et les arts, Le Discours sur l'origine et les fondement de l'inégalité, Du Contrat social*) or personally expressed (*Les Confessions, Les Rêveries du promeneur solitaire*), and in the second case we might think again of Rousseau, this time for the part he played in the violent controversy about the respective merits of French and Italian musical styles, the Querelle des Bouffons, with his arguments in favour of 'natural' song and against the classical French style encapsulated by Rameau.[1] Or perhaps we might think of the way Diderot theorized the 'drame' as being more natural than the accepted comic or tragic forms. And all these cases are included in literary history in the 'precursor' format: Rousseau (for example) heralded Goethe's *Werther*, and Diderot heralded Lessing, although generally if we think of Diderot at all in this context, we don't consider him as a Romantic or isolated figure, as symbolically important, as embodying Romanticism, in the same way as we do when we think of the Rousseau of the *Confessions*.[2] However, even if

[1] Rousseau's views about music and his contribution to the Querelle des Bouffons are lucidly explained by Catherine Kintzler, 'Rousseau, Jean-Jacques', Grove Music Online, Oxford Music Online, <http://www.oxfordmusiconline.com/subscriber/article/grove/music/23968> (accessed Sept. 2012). See also Marian Hobson, 'Kant, Rousseau and Music', in her *Diderot and Rousseau: Networks of Enlightenment* (Oxford: Voltaire Foundation, 2011), *SVEC* 4 (2011): 261–80.

[2] Peter Gay writes about 'the vitalism of Diderot, the passion of Rousseau, or the skepticism of Hume, as foreign bodies, as harbingers of Romanticism', *The Enlightenment: An Interpretation* (New York: Knopf, 1973), i, pp. xii, 3, cited by Aidan Day, *Romanticism*, 2nd edn (London: Routledge, 2012), 59.

Diderot is the minor partner in this familiar account, he features, and the prehistory model therefore does its job, doing justice to the earlier links in the chain without disrupting the established sequence. But a series of connected questions force themselves on our notice: is the precursor argument *enough*? In what way is it *important* to situate the centre of gravity of the Romanticism movement later rather than earlier? And do these later properly Romantic texts/statements articulate their positions *more fully* or *better* than the earlier ones? Further, is it sufficient always to focus on Rousseau, leaving Diderot with a much smaller role? Does that not follow literary history as it was written and rewritten in the Revolution, and thereby follow not so much an *incorrect* version as a *polemical* one, without acknowledging or perhaps even realizing the fact?[3]

This chapter will consider all these questions, exploring what is at stake for these supposedly 'pre-Romantic' thinkers in France, and trying to understand what 'pre-Romanticism' is. It will try to argue that many of the most resonant themes associated with Romanticism had already been compellingly and unflinchingly explored by Diderot. As a corollary, it will require us to abandon the familiar models of straightforward transmission and influence which we can fruitfully use in the case of Rousseau, because with Diderot we simply don't have all the evidence about who said what to whom, or who read what when. Instead, we have sudden astonishing eruptions of presence and attention, such as Goethe's 1805 translation of the *Neveu de Rameau*, its first publication in any language. We shall also have to abandon the idea of a literary history in which classicism dominated then faded to make way for the Enlightenment, which dominated and then faded to make way for Romanticism. As a model it's simply too easy, too crass, although its very convenience explains its existence: it's a teaching tool, but it's a teaching tool that originated in a politically motivated whitewash with the likes of La Harpe in the newly founded Ecole normale, a whitewash which sought to discredit Diderot as belonging to the reviled atheist materialist camp, and which conveniently blamed what tend to be known as the 'excesses' of the Revolution on the 'excesses' of 'reason', 'reason' here being synonymous with something arid, abstract, lacking in humanity,

Guides to or histories of Romanticism, generally *English* Romanticism, whether this is acknowledged in the title or not, tend to mention Rousseau numerous times, and generally don't mention Diderot at all, as their indexes confirm. See J. Faflak and S. Chaplin (eds), *The Romanticism Handbook* (London: Continuum, 2011), and James Chandler (ed.), *The Cambridge History of English Romantic Literature* (Cambridge: Cambridge University Press, 2009). For a precise account of the extent of Diderot's influence on Lessing, see Francis Lamport, 'Lessing traducteur et critique de Diderot', in Nicholas Cronk (ed.), *Études sur* Le Fils naturel *et les* Entretiens sur le Fils naturel *de Diderot* (Oxford: Voltaire Foundation, 2000), 171–80.

[3] Jean-François La Harpe's *Lycée ou Cours de Littérature* (1799–1805), based on his 'Leçons de littérature' at the Ecole normale in 1795, is a key example here: having initially been a disciple of Voltaire's, and an eager revolutionary, his time in prison during the Terror turned him against it and anything he associated with it, and he spent the rest of his life redefining literature as eloquence broadly speaking, and turning back to antiquity as well as seventeenth-century tragedy. See Philippe Roger's 'Introduction aux Leçons de La Harpe', in *L'Ecole normale de l'an III: Leçons d'analyse de l'entendement, art de la parole, littérature, morale*, ed. G. Gingembre et al. (Paris: Editions ENS Rue d'Ulm, 2008), 523–33, esp. p. 531. See also R. Tarin, *Diderot et la Révolution française* (Paris: Honoré Champion, 2001), 60.

and thus being *atheist, materialist.*[4] Reason was cold, amoral, inhuman; religion was love, moral, human. Or so the argument went, as Robespierre in full Rousseauian flight had it, as Chateaubriand argued it in his *Génie du christianisme* (1802).[5] Jessica Riskin has looked at how this argument was initially erected in the 1790s, and also at how totally it rewrote the numerous attempts of eighteenth-century thinkers working in the wake of Locke to understand what a world which could only be apprehended through sensation actually looked and felt like, appropriating their own anxiety about over-rationalizing systems (the 'esprit de système' is a commonplace insult for systems wedded to their own self-enclosed perfection throughout the eighteenth century).[6] Pierre Daled has looked at how sensationist empiricism of the period was renamed 'sensualisme' by the first Napoleonic historian of French philosophy, Joseph-Marie Dégérando, and thereby discredited and dismissed.[7] Alain Viala has looked at why and how the term 'classicism' was adopted, and at why it should be replaced.[8] So we must accept that the sequence of movements and influences that we are most familiar with and which has been very generally accepted as the history of French literature and thought was first proposed by political opponents of materialist positions and writing, who have thereby hidden important strains of materialism in Romanticism, such as the ways in which nature is conceptualized as something dynamic and sublime, and how it is conceptualized in connection with mankind, that is to say, in terms of fraught opposition to society. How nature and society impose competing and terrible strains on individuals is repeatedly investigated in eighteenth-century writing. And it's simply not helpful to chop it all up into pre-Revolution Enlightenment reason, and post-Revolution Romantic reaction against reason. What we have instead is repeated iterations of various intersecting quarrels. Here for example is Stendhal's argument in *Racine et Shakespeare* (1823), broadly summarized: the constraints and conventions of seventeenth-century French theatre are out of date and unreal; they are pale imitations of Sophocles and Euripides;

[4] La Harpe described Diderot as 'un auteur immoral et subversif mais aussi sanguinaire' (quoted by Tarin, *Diderot*, 143).

[5] See Robespierre: 'Qui t'a donné la mission d'annoncer au peuple que la Divinité n'existe pas, ô toi qui te passionnes pour cette aride doctrine, et qui ne te passionnas jamais pour la patrie?' 'Sur les rapports des idées réligieuses et morales avec les principes républicains, et sur les fêtes nationales, 18 floréal an II (7 mai 1794)', in Robespierre, *Discours et rapports à la Convention* (Paris: Union générale d'éditions, collection 10/18, 1965), 262. See Chateaubriand: 'Un écrivain qui refuse de croire en un Dieu auteur de l'univers, et juge des hommes dont il a fait l'âme immortelle, bannit d'abord l'infini de ses ouvrages. Il renferma sa pensée dans un cercle de boue, dont il ne peut plus sortir', or 'Il est possible que la somme de talents départie aux auteurs du dix-huitième siècle, soit égale à celle qu'avaient reçue les écrivains du dix-septième. Pourquoi donc le second siècle est-il au-dessous du premier? Car il n'est plus temps de dissimuler, les écrivains de notre âge ont été en général placés trop haut.' In 'Que l'incrédulité est la principale cause de la décadence du goût et du génie', *Génie du christianisme*, ed. Pierre Reboul (Paris: Garnier-Flammarion, 1966), ii. 25–6 (part III, bk IV, ch. 5).

[6] Jessica Riskin, *Science in the Age of Sensibility: The Sentimental Empiricists of the French Enlightenment* (Chicago and London: University of Chicago Press, 2002).

[7] Pierre F. Daled, *Le Matérialisme occulté et la genèse du 'sensualisme': Ecrire l'histoire de la philosophie en France* (Paris: Vrin, 2005).

[8] Alain Viala, *La France galante* (Paris: Presses Universitaires de France, 2008).

their mannerisms suit bewigged and befrocked aristocrats, and bear their characteristics; now (the early nineteenth century) needs reality and prose and tasteless detail, not alexandrines and good taste; Shakespeare's representation of the human heart in a play such as *Macbeth* is more grandiose and more moving than anything Racine could offer, although more tasteless and grotesque. And here is Hugo, in the famous 'Préface de Cromwell': in the grown-up era of the Christian world, where the real is melancholy and complex, there is no room for powder and panier: the grotesque must dominate, and genres and tones must mix and clash. Yet Diderot's *Fils naturel, ou les épreuves de la vertu* (1757), that 'espèce de roman' (sort of novel) as he called it his *Discours sur la poésie dramatique* (1758), or play plus accompanying theoretical dialogues as it's generally considered today, demonstrates and argues for family drama as a new genre, neither comedy which ridicules its subject, nor tragedy, which limits too narrowly what can be called tragic and heroic.[9] It talks about being real and about being recognizable to its audiences, about stirring a chord in them, about setting aside questions of taste and convention, moving on from seventeenth-century models and 'returning' to antiquity, and it is triggered by a curious character called Dorval whose principal attribute is melancholy. Its main protagonist takes tea and was a self-conscious testing of the boundaries of taste, as the dialogues reveal;[10] it mixes genres (of play, of novelistic narrative character description and scene-setting, of dialogue), and some of the dilemmas it poses (principally why Dorval remains so melancholy and solitary despite the seemingly happy resolution) are not even discussed, even in all the hyper-articulate 'rational' exposition that follows the play. There is therefore a significant chunk which is placed beyond words, in untouchable mystery. So, although we could also look at the typical Romantic themes of solitude, alienation, misery, of being crossed in love because of social convention, and of the opposition between natural drives and social requirements through almost any of Rousseau's texts, especially *Julie ou la nouvelle Héloïse* (1761), it may jolt us out of our usual sense of Enlightenment-Romanticism chronology to look at the question through Diderot instead, with the subsidiary advantage of drawing attention to the extraordinary richness of his treatment.

Le Fils naturel ou les épreuves de la vertu (comédie) contains a five-act play framed within a narrative presenting the circumstances of Diderot first hearing of the 'true' story the play relates, and followed by three dialogues between the protagonist of the play, Dorval, and 'moi' (Diderot) about theatre which propose various far-reaching reforms to do with dramatic conventions of genre, taste, theme, and how a play relates to its audience. The way these four broadly distinguishable sections relate to each other is complex, and the multi-levelled views of its subjects provided by the narrator, identifiably Diderot himself as we know from being told in line 1 that he has just brought out the sixth volume of the *Encyclopédie*, and by a series of overlapping Dorvals—as

[9] Diderot, *De la poésie dramatique*, in *Œuvres*, ed. Laurent Versini (Paris: Bouquins, 1996), iv. 'Esthétique, Théâtre', 1303. All references to Diderot are to this volume unless otherwise specified, and for ease of reference will appear in the text as VER xxx.

[10] 'Moi' challenges Dorval about it in the *Entretiens*, VER 1135.

interlocutor, as intriguing 'sombre et mélancolique' figure (VER 1081, 1111), as actor in the play, and as the original for the character which he acts, switch dizzyingly between interiorizing and involved, and external and spectating. Further, the fact that the play is not for an audience (although 'Diderot' watches from a hidden corner unbeknownst to the actors apart from Dorval), is supposed to be based on a series of real events, and is not provided for entertainment (however defined), but is an annual re-enactment decreed by the now dead father, disturbs preconceptions about how a play might relate to recognizable unchanging types of comedy (the old man, the miser, etc.) or to the similarly recognizable fatally flawed but larger than life heroic characters of tragedy, and resituates drama as quasi-sacred rite. So, even in a summary as summary as this, we can see that whatever early Romantics such as Novalis and Chateaubriand, second-generation Romantics such as Stendhal and Hugo, or we as literary historians in the wake of Isaiah Berlin define as *preceding* Romanticism, presumably intellectually something to do with prioritizing reason, and in terms of literary convention determined by classicism, in no way accounts for what Diderot is doing with his *Fils naturel.* Such definitions so totally fail to account for what he is doing that they fall away completely. In fact, 'reason' does not have very much to do with *Le Fils naturel*, as much of it does not add up in any logical way, key features remaining unexplained and mysterious, and a blanket of melancholy, unassuaged yearning, and miserable solitude persisting throughout, affecting not only Dorval but 'moi' also, who, evoking his state in the closing narrative of the play, writes: 'Je suis seul, parmi la poussière des livres et dans l'ombre d'un cabinet ... Et j'écris des lignes faibles, tristes et froides.' ('I am alone, amidst the dust of books and in the darkness of a study ... writing these feeble, sad, and cold lines') (VER 1127[11]). Nostalgia and fear at time passing are strikingly present, and are an inextricable part of the melancholy mood that frames and disturbs the meanings of the whole. Being in nature—understood as the sublime outside—is the only possible comfort, as well as the appropriate arena for expressing distress. The protagonists' relationship with nature underscores and amplifies their attitude to circumstance, being at once as immense and therefore as grand as their sublime emotion, and the living unbearable contrast to social constraint. The opening section of the *Second Entretien* shows all these aspects at play:

> Le lendemain, je me rendis au pied de la colline. L'endroit était solitaire et sauvage. On avait en perspective quelques hameaux répandus dans la plaine; au-delà, une chaîne de montagnes inégales et déchirées qui terminaient en partie l'horizon. On était à l'ombre des chênes, et l'on entendait le bruit sourd d'une eau souterraine qui coulait aux environs. C'était la saison où la terre est couverte des biens qu'elle accorde au travail et à la sueur des hommes. Dorval était arrivé le premier. J'approchai de lui sans qu'il m'aperçût. Il s'était abandonné au spectacle de la nature. Il avait la poitrine élevée. Il respirait avec force. Ses yeux attentifs se portaient sur tous les objets. Je suivais sur son visage les impressions diverses qu'il en éprouvait; et je commençais

[11] This is my own translation, as Geoffrey Bremner (see n. 12) only translates the 'Entretiens' and not the 'play' itself.

à partager son transport, lorsque je m'écriai, presque sans le vouloir: 'il est sous le charme.'

Il m'entendit, et me répondit d'une voix altérée: 'Il est vrai. C'est ici qu'on voit la nature. Voici le séjour sacré de l'enthousiasme. Un homme a-t-il reçu du génie? Il quitte la ville et ses habitants. Il aime, selon l'attrait de son cœur, à mêler ses pleurs au cristal d'une fontaine; à porter des fleurs sur un tombeau; à fouler d'un pied léger l'herbe tendre de la prairie; à traverser, à pas lents, des campagnes fertiles; à contempler les travaux des hommes; à fuir au fond des forêts. Il aime leur horreur secrète. Il erre. Il cherche un antre qui l'inspire. Qui est-ce qui mêle sa voix au torrent qui tombe de la montagne? Qui est-ce qui sent le sublime d'un lieu désert? Qui est-ce qui s'écoute dans le silence de la solitude? C'est lui. Notre poète habite sur les bords d'un lac. Il promène sa vue sur les eaux, et son génie s'étend. C'est là qu'il est saisi de cet esprit, tantôt tranquille et tantôt violent, qui soulève son âme ou qui l'apaise à son gré ... Ô Nature, tout ce qui est bien est renfermé dans ton sein! Tu es la source féconde de toutes vérités! ... (VER 1141–2)

The next day, I went to the foot of the hill. It was a lonely, wild place. The view was of a few hamlets spread out over the plain; beyond, a range of irregular, jagged mountains which formed a part of the horizon. We were shaded by some oak trees, and the muted sound could be heard of an underground stream flowing nearby. It was that season when the earth is covered with the fruits it grants to the toil and sweat of men. Dorval had arrived first. I went up to him without him noticing me. He had abandoned himself to the spectacle of nature. His chest swelled out and he was breathing deeply. His eyes were fixed keenly on everything around him. I could see on his face the various impressions of what he saw and I was beginning to share in his rapture when I cried out, almost involuntarily: 'He is under the spell.'

He heard me and replied in a troubled voice: 'It is true. Here it is that nature can be seen. This is the sacred abode of enthusiasm. If a man has been granted the gift of genius he quits the town and its people. He takes pleasure, as his heart inclines him, in mingling his tears with the crystal waters of a spring, in bearing flowers to a grave, in walking lightly across the tender grass of a meadow, in wandering slowly through fertile fields, in contemplating the work of men, in fleeing to the depths of the forests. He loves their secret horror. He wanders on. He seeks a cavern to inspire him. Who is it that mingles his voice with the torrent falling from the mountainside? Who feels the sublime nature of a wilderness? Who listens to his heart in the silence of solitude? It is he. Our poet dwells on the shores of a lake. He casts his eyes over the waters and his genius takes flight. There he is gripped by that spirit, now tranquil, now violent, which lifts his soul or calms it as it will ... O Nature, all that is good has its place in your breast! You are the fertile source of every truth! ...[12]

The passage presented here is curtailed for practical reasons (but not internally abridged or cut: the ellipses are Diderot's own), but is coherent in itself, and with its own formal completeness. It starts with a description of the prospect and then describes a man

[12] Diderot, 'Conversations on *The Natural Son*, in *Selected Writings on Art and Literature*, tr. Geoffrey Bremner (London: Penguin Classics, 1994), 18.

(Dorval) contemplating that prospect, not with detachment but with observable emotion. Dorval having been the object of observation then takes over the narrative, and he replicates the movement from general to particular, initially describing the relationship of the genius to nature, then asking a series of open questions, and finally addressing 'Nature' as in the form of a prayer: the 'génie' is no longer generalized, but is himself. It starts with a visual description and ends with an emotional invocation, all focused on 'nature'. Not everything can be said (there are a series of ellipses), and not everything which is said is consciously controlled or presented as coming from the reasoning mind (the exclamation by 'moi' is 'almost involuntary'). Nature is sacred, enthusiasm or transport is contagious, and indeed the 'génie' seems to be defined by his ability to feel these emotions in a pure extreme form, as opposed to being designated by the possession of any exceptional abilities. Town-life (although not humble hamlets), and by extension society, are inimical to the genius, who seeks and understands the sublimity of solitude, who in his heart is unhappy and who has suffered loss, who seeks inspiration, whose voice is at one with the mountain torrent. His identification with nature and with the sublime is complete.

He sounds like a straight down-the-line Romantic, does he not? As a subsidiary point, he sounds like Rousseau, or rather, he sounds like the alienated figure that Rousseau will come to embody in his *Confessions* and *Rêveries*, both published posthumously. And indeed Rousseau himself drew attention to this, devoting a passage in his *Confessions* to his distress at what he felt was a remark directed at him (the aphorism 'il n'y a que le méchant qui soit seul' ('Only the wicked man is alone') VER 1111).[13] But it blurs the issues to assume that Diderot was describing Rousseau, or that the point of this argument is to displace Rousseau in favour of Diderot: the real point is that their thought and writings are entwined to a conceptually very deep extent, and remain so from their first collaboration to the end of their lives: we need look no further than the allusion to the 'cristal d'une fontaine' to recall the famous passage in Rousseau's *Essai sur l'origine des langues* (*c.*1755), in which he imagines love and language as song being born from the 'pur cristal des fontaines', to see that Diderot is here thinking with and through Rousseau, who will himself react to *Le Fils naturel* and embed it in his thinking. The famous split that was occurring at precisely this point in their lives, triggered by the argument over d'Alembert's entry on 'Genève' in volume vi of the *Encyclopédie* (which had just come out, as the first line of *Le Fils naturel* declares), is not a false split, but it is simply unhelpful to read their work as henceforth separate *as if* in opposition to one another. Further, if we assume an opposition of this sort, we fall automatically into the chronology literary history has bestowed on us and according to which reason and Enlightenment reigned, Diderot being in this first camp not least because of his editorship of the flagship *Encyclopédie*, and thereafter came Rousseau with the first intuitions of Romantic alienation and disturbance. We can see, if only from the passage just quoted, that this cannot be the case.

[13] Rousseau, *Confessions*, bk IX, in Rousseau, *Œuvres complètes*, ed. Bernard Gagnebin and Marcel Raymond (Paris: Gallimard Pléiade, 1959), i. 455.

So, returning to the earlier point about Diderot giving us what looks like a portrait of pure Romanticism here, and bearing in mind these larger questions of literary history and chronology, as well as the subsidiary but important points about Diderot's position with respect to Rousseau, we could make two different arguments. We might want to conclude that Diderot like Rousseau should be admitted to the pantheon of (very) early Romantics, without otherwise disturbing the sequence from Enlightenment to Romanticism. Or we might want to review whatever it is we think the Enlightenment actually is. Because if we move Diderot over into the Romantic camp without otherwise disturbing the landscape, and thereby lose the editor of the *Encyclopédie*, the Enlightenment loses its centre. We can't argue that the aim of the *Encyclopédie* was *not* to support progress, reason, explicability, the general availability of knowledge, and thereby the improvement of mankind. That *was* its aim. And we can't argue that Diderot as a writer independent of the *Encyclopédie* didn't believe in the advancement of knowledge and the ability of human reason to tease out the implications moral, logical, political, and other of any given stance, because any number of his works, from the *Lettre sur les aveugles* (Letter on the Blind, 1749) to the *Religieuse* (The Nun, 1780) do just that. What it means is that we have to amend our sense of what 'reason' was and meant, and accept that it was not merely dry, unemotional, abstract, and uninspired: some Romantics did argue this (Novalis, Schlegel, Chateaubriand) but they argued it for *polemical reasons*, in order to establish their own positions, draw attention to themselves, and to create distance from anything that looked too French (in the case of the Germans) or too atheist (in Chateaubriand's case).[14] I would argue on the contrary that there are deep continuities here, and that what is continuous is in part the polemic itself. We will come back to this aspect. Let me turn first to another more simply demonstrated area of continuity, the theme of incest.

Thus far I have lingered on the complexities of *Le Fils naturel ou les épreuves de la vertu (comédie)*: the story that the play recounts, irrespective of its framing and of the questions it raises, is relatively straightforward, and involves a group of intimate friends who are crossed in love. Dorval has fallen in love with Rosalie, the fiancée of his best friend, Clairville. Clairville's sister, Constance, has fallen in love with Dorval, and declares it. Clairville senses that Rosalie no longer loves him, and asks Dorval to probe Rosalie for her reasons. He does so, against his will, and it turns out she loves him: he allows her to see that he loves her too. They both feel that their duty is to Clairville. Rosalie leaves Dorval a letter confessing her dilemma and stating her passion. Dorval, overwhelmed, writes a few words in reply, and then leaves his letter half-written on learning that Clairville is being attacked. Constance finds his letter, and assumes it is written to her, and declares her joy to Clairville who now returns unscathed with Dorval, owing him his life. Dorval is speechless. Clairville then communicates his happiness at Constance

[14] Denis Thouard presents a lucid and scholarly account of the relationship between Enlightenment and Romantic writers as it has traditionally been perceived, and which the present chapter is attempting to problematize, in his 'Qu'est-ce que les Lumières pour le premier romantisme?', *SVEC* 12 (2006): 197–212.

and Dorval's union, in front of Dorval who is given no opportunity to explain the mistake. Rosalie faints, and then leaves. An unknown man then asks for an audience: it is André, Rosalie's father's servant, comes to announce that they have lost all their money and that Rosalie is therefore without dowry. Dorval immediately writes to his banker to transfer half his money to her, and after a conference with Constance where she stuns him with her virtuous perspective on life, decides to embrace the constraints from which he cannot extricate himself without causing great distress, and marry her, while doing what he can to forward Rosalie's marriage to Clairville. Dorval makes a long exalted speech to Rosalie urging her not to reject and destroy pre-existing ties, to embrace virtue, that is, legitimate social constraint, and renounce passion. At this point, Rosalie's father finally arrives, and Dorval, amazed, recognizes him as Lysimond, his own father. Rosalie and Dorval face each other as brother and sister. Lysimond expresses his desire that his children should know and love each other. He unites Rosalie and Clairville, and then Constance and Dorval, whose gift of his fortune to Rosalie becomes known, triggering what seems to be a general realization that he has sacrificed fortune, passion, and liberty. Dorval and Rosalie accept the situation. The final scene is missing because the actors (acting their own past parts) become overwhelmed with grief for reasons that are not completely clear, although one of them is that Lysimond has died in the year that has passed since this is supposed to have taken place. In brief, therefore, passion is sacrificed to virtue, it subsequently emerging that the passion had been incestuous. The tension of the play is between passion and virtue, inclination and duty, nature and society. Virtue, duty, and society prevail, but Dorval and Rosalie only just choose them, and only because they haven't really got any choice. To betray the best friend/fiancé is too obvious a crime against honour and loyalty, and the expectations made on them by the *other* brother and sister are too publicly stated for it to be possible without transgressive discourtesy to evade them. So they renounce passion in favour of public politeness. And they do that under great pressure, and at great personal cost, as all the marks of sensibility tell us (fainting, weeping, sinking down, covering their faces). And then it turns out that they have escaped a worse fate, that of transgressing a legal and religious taboo. The play thereby seems incontrovertibly to confirm the dominance of virtue and society over desire, the incest theme being brought in to underscore that the union of Dorval and Rosalie would have entailed the triumph of vice. And yet the framing narrative and dialogues show that their thwarted love appears to have left behind it lasting melancholy, as if the personal cost of complying with publicly recognized conventions and expectations has simply been too great. As James Fowler points out, the words point to a virtuous and happy resolution, but the actions and attitudes suggest the opposite, and this tension is left open, unresolved, untidy.[15] Reason, virtue, and the social good may well all be in alignment in the sort of way we would expect from an Enlightenment writer, but against it, more powerful because impossible to resolve or even articulate, are ranged nature, passion, and pain.

[15] J. E. Fowler, *Voicing Desire: Family and Sexuality in Diderot's Narrative* (Oxford: Voltaire Foundation–Vif, 2000), 45–6.

Incest is the tragic knot at the centre of this tension, and Diderot shows us that the intensity of desire is only equalled by the totality of the taboo. And Diderot is not the only one to use incest as an emotionally charged way of exploring the competing demands of nature and society. We meet it again and again. Voltaire uses it in his play *Sémiramis* (1749) and again exploits the ambiguities it casts on intimate relationships in *Zaïre* (1732) (sibling intimacy looks exactly the same to an outsider as lovers' intimacy), looking at the taboo in theoretical terms in his *Questions sur l'Encyclopédie* (1770–4). Diderot makes incest seem perfectly natural in his value-reversing experimental dialogue, the *Supplément au voyage de Bougainville*. Rousseau casts the prohibition of incest as the founding moment of society in the *Essai sur l'origine des langues* (written 1755). Bernardin de Saint Pierre gives us a Pierre and Virginie (1788) effectively brought up by their two virtuous mothers as brother and sister on the Ile de France (now Mauritius), and whose intimate relationship very naturally develops into sexual love as they grow up: social convention in the symbolic form of education and geographical separation leads to their misery and ultimately to Virginie's death. Sade in his usual unpalatable way uses incest as the first principle of following nature and desire, casting society as the deforming unnatural force, and none of his pornographic works is without numerous incestuous relationships, whether forced or freely chosen. It also features in his unpornographic short story collection, *Les Crimes de l'amour* (1800): 'Eugénie de Franval' is analysed in detail in Georges Benrekassa's study on incest in the *siècle des Lumières*.[16] Chateaubriand's *René* (1802) also uses it, of course, and the way in which desire and obedience to the dictates of social virtue are set in opposition to one another, the latter winning, but the former setting the prevailing tone of melancholy and despair, can be mapped almost identically onto the pattern we find in Diderot's *Fils naturel*. In the context of the phrase 'natural son', 'natural' clearly has two meanings, the commonplace idiom of 'natural' or illegitimate son, and what the words actually mean, that is, the son who is *natural*, who is close to nature. The combination of the two meanings gives us a compact poetic signal of how to interpret the play as a whole: the child who is close to nature is *for that reason* illegitimate, unlegalizable because unacceptable to society, not of it, in opposition to it.

If we look at these texts as a series which repeatedly come back to the same question of the contrasting needs of nature and of society, all of them using the motif of incest to cast those needs as irreconcilable, we can see how unhelpful, how artificial, it is to separate them into Enlightenment (pro-reason) and Romantic (anti-reason). Rational, articulatable, public, social morality remains deeply problematic before and after the Revolution. Optimistic resolutions based on some fiction of reason and improvability are not available. Alienation from oneself, melancholy, and solitude are the invariable consequences that this series of texts display, and when we talk about *René*, Constant's *Adolphe* (1816), Senancour's *Oberman* (1804), or Musset's *Confessions d'un enfant du siècle* (1836) as founding texts of 'le mal du siècle' we can see that in fact they are simply continuing

[16] Georges Benrekassa, 'Loi naturelle et loi civile: L'Idéologie des Lumières et la prohibition de l'inceste', *SVEC* 87 (1972): 115–44, 141–3.

a theme which remains of urgent importance to all these writers, throughout this extended period. What we generally call 'Romanticism' is a delimited period within that longer span, known to us by that name and accepted as a new movement in contrast to what went before not least because the 'Romantics' loudly trumpeted that contrast and that novelty. It is not my task here to explore the reasons motivating the claims they make beyond what was sketched out in the opening paragraphs of this chapter.[17] However, it will be the subject of the next section to show that the aesthetic claims made by Stendhal and Hugo are not disconnected from the themes of alienation and solitude we have already been discussing.

I outlined earlier Stendhal's argument about embracing modernity, reflecting reality, and rejecting the constraints of theatrical convention, all of which were characterized as being to do with outmoded taste, and likened to the ridiculous wigs and clothes of their long-dead admirers. In the *Second Entretien* of the *Fils naturel*, Dorval exclaims, 'Ah! Bienséances cruelles, que vous rendez les ouvrages décents et petits! …' ('Ah! cruel proprieties, how proper and how feeble you make our plays', VER IV 1154, ellipsis in text; Bremner, pp. 32–3). The earlier text claims these *bienséances* to be cruel, and therefore powerful, whilst the political changes that have occurred between its writing and that of Stendhal's *Racine et Shakespeare* mean that it is easy to deride the conventions where once they were feared, as well as pragmatic to reinforce the criticism of outmodedness by likening it to the aristocrats whose *régime* is now *ancien*. The point both Diderot and Stendhal are making is nonetheless the same one: convention and decorum detract from the quality of the plays written. They stifle the drama. They don't show life and death and people as they are. They don't show nature. Dorval exclaims 'Je ne me lasserai point de crier à nos Français: La Vérité! la Nature! les Anciens! Sophocle! Philoctète!' ('I shall never cease crying out to the French: Truth! Nature! the Ancients! Sophocles! Philoctetes!' VER IV 1155; Bremner, p. 34). So the aesthetic that rejects conventions of decorum is continuous with the theme which pits nature against society. Further, we see Dorval explicitly bringing in 'les Anciens', thereby aligning his aesthetic and philosophical arguments with the long-running quarrel of the Ancients and the Moderns which periodically convulsed European theoreticians and practitioners of all the arts.

Its initial expression seems to be when vulgar languages start to replace Latin (the medieval poet Dante was an important and eager participant in the debates with his *De volgari eloquentia*, *c.*1302–5), and became urgent again during the Renaissance, that period which we name in reference to the *rebirth* of classical, particularly Greek, learning. The forms of poetry and drama (to focus on what is most relevant to the current discussion), as categorized and defined by Aristotle and Horace, are the object of heated discussions: which are the best metres, the best forms, does 'best' mean 'closest to the original', which original is the optimum original, are all questions which preoccupy

[17] See my 'Caught between Neologism and the Unmentionable: The Politics of Naming and Non-Naming in 1790s France', in Kate E. Tunstall and Wilda Anderson (eds), 'Naming, Unnaming, and Renaming', *Romance Studies*, 31: 3/4 (Nov. 2013): 264–76, for an analysis of the issues around claims of innovation during and after the Revolution.

intellectuals across early modern Europe. It was generally the view that a novel, for example, was a non-form, it not having existed in antiquity, and not being mentioned by Aristotle or Horace. (Classical prose romances and narratives such as *Daphnis and Chloe* or *The Golden Ass* seem not to count.) A play (especially a tragedy) was a pure form; a novel was an unform. In this context, we can begin to assess how formally bizarre *Le Fils naturel* would look: Diderot himself called it an 'espèce de roman' as we have already seen, Voltaire clearly read it as a play with a series of discussions about plays rather than a whole, and many publications split the two.[18] Voltaire nonetheless took its formal proposals seriously, and argued against it and for formal purity in the preface to his play *Les Scythes* (1767).[19] He is therefore aligned in his dramatic theory with the Ancients, and Diderot with the Moderns. All parties in fact call on classical authorities for their proposals, they just use different ones, for different purposes, each person claiming to know their sources better than their rivals. So, when Stendhal calls on Sophocles and Euripides in his *Racine et Shakespeare*, he is not only following Diderot, he is also part of Quarrel of the Ancients and the Moderns, and therefore not only, or not even principally, a Romantic, unless we use Romanticism as the 'modern' label for the Moderns.

When we think about this entire early modern period in France and map the quarrel of the Ancients and the Moderns onto it, a slightly revised landscape comes into focus. John D. Lyons argues that the politeness and convention-driven nature of much of seventeenth-century French literature should be seen in the context of anxiety in the wake of the Wars of Religion: 'in this climate flourished a literature that promoted an idea of moderation, discretion, and even concealment'.[20] He sees it as fear of disagreement, fear of the big ideas about man and nature that came with the Renaissance and with humanism. In that context, it is suggestive to identify *two* humanisms: the first more familiar one, encapsulated by the ebullient experimentalism of writers such as Rabelais and Montaigne, which was repressed in favour of orthodox polite thinking and aesthetics, but whose recurrent concerns with the nature of man and the nature of nature persisted in the writings of figures such as Cyrano de Bergerac or Pierre Bayle, and then re-emerged into cultural dominance in the second humanism, better known as the Enlightenment, with writers like Diderot and Rousseau. Romanticism comes at the end of this second wave, and provides us thematically and aesthetically with the results of this centuries-long thinking, in the form of a rejection of politeness, an assessment of society as inimical to the nature of man, and of nature as the only real value.

Unsurprisingly, if we pursue this line of enquiry into areas which we would now (no doubt anachronistically) see as more directly linked to nature, that is to say, into areas we now group together as 'the life sciences', we find that the sorts of questions being researched, as well as their theoretical underpinnings, are absolutely consistent with

[18] See Russell Goulbourne, 'Essai bibliographique', in Cronk, *Études*, 182. Geoffrey Bremner includes only the *Entretiens* in his translation, *Selected Writings on Art and Literature*.

[19] See Nicholas Cronk's chapter 'Dorval et le dialogue à trois voix: La Présence de Rousseau et de Voltaire dans *Le Fils naturel* et les *Entretiens*', in Cronk, *Études*, 122–37.

[20] John D. Lyons, *French Literature: A Very Short Introduction* (Oxford: Oxford University Press, 2010), 34.

what we've identified so far. We can therefore map them onto the grand narrative which tells us that throughout the early modern period, natural philosophy was increasingly displacing theology as the primary object of knowledge. We sometimes call this the rise of science, and indeed it is symptomatic that a word which etymologically derives from the Latin *scio* 'I know', and means 'knowledge', over the course of the nineteenth century, particularly in English, comes to mean 'science', a designation which we now consider as meaning empirical provable research about nature (broadly defined), and as distinguished from such areas as 'the humanities' and 'the arts', which are not empirical in the same way, not provable. During the eighteenth and nineteenth centuries, the sorts of research questions are broadly humanistic ones, as already suggested, that is to say, what is man, what distinguishes him from the rest of creation, what is thought if it is a *natural* property, what is morality if it is defined by *natural* and not theological needs, is nature organized and how, what is the role of time with respect to nature, does nature change? All of these questions are propelled by an approach that can be broadly translated as materialist, that is to say, one which supposes that everything that exists is made of matter in different combinations, and which tries to understand the processes that make this possible as well as what their social and moral consequences might be. It is absolutely to falsify the situation to suppose that materialists deny the spirit and are only interested in *things*, mechanisms, etc. Their *major* question is how matter can think, and that obviously involves acknowledging that 'consciousness' is quite different from 'unconsciousness', that animate beings are quite different to inanimate ones, and these questions lead to a further set of investigations about how they all relate. Diderot's experimental dialogue, *Le Rêve de d'Alembert* (1769), explores these questions in a deliberately provocative and zany fashion, returning to them in more serious mode in his less well-known *Eléments de physiologie* (1769–82). His position can generally be labelled as vitalist: vitalism was defined against mechanism, and held that one cannot try to understand nature by assuming it is some sort of very complex machine that only needs to be taken apart to be understood. The great Dutch physician Herman Boerhaave who flourished in the early eighteenth century was an important exponent of the mechanistic approach, and it is encapsulated in his pre-eminence as an anatomist: he wanted to know how bodies worked, how they fitted together. Vitalism counters this approach with the objection that you cannot understand what a human being is from a dead body, given that the key aspect, life, is missing. By 1800, the *Dictionnaire des sciences médicales* will baldly state that 'il n'est guère permis à l'époque actuelle de n'être pas vitaliste' (it is barely conceivable these days to be anything other than a vitalist).[21] This is the precise period when the term 'sciences de la vie' or 'life sciences' comes into being, and of course it is exactly contemporaneous with Romanticism.[22]

[21] François Victor Mérat de Vaumartoise, 'Vitalistes', *Dictionaire* [sic] *des sciences médicales*, ed. Alard et al. (Paris and Liège: Panckoucke & Plomteux, 1812–22), lviii. 281.

[22] The two unsurpassed scholarly works in this area are Jacques Roger's *Les Sciences de la vie dans la pensée française du dix-huitième siècle* (Paris: A. Colin, 1962), tr. by Robert Ellrich under the title *The Life Sciences in Eighteenth-Century French Thought* (Stanford, Calif.: Stanford University Press, 1997), although interestingly without the chapter on Diderot, and Roselyne Rey's *Naissance et développement*

Much of the work which seems to reach out to medical and biological research underpinned conceptually by vitalism, and also to philosophical and aesthetic concerns associated with Romanticism, was done by a group working in the 1790s and 1800s, known by their self-coined term 'Idéologues' (or scientists of ideas), and especially by two of their most prominent members, the physician Cabanis and the philosopher Destutt de Tracy. Cabanis's *Rapports du physique et du moral de l'homme* (1802) took forward Diderot's work on the relationship between consciousness and thought (the Ideologues were known to be the intellectual legatees of Diderot) to conclude that 'Vivre, c'est sentir' ('to live is to feel').[23] His aphorism reaches back to sensibility, out to Romanticism, and defines medicine's object of research: sensation and consciousness, and their properties. His work inspired Bichat, whose innovative work on human tissue was cut short by an early death at the age of 1802. Cabanis's vitalist materialist views of the relation of 'le physique et le moral'—what we now call psychology—are a complex mix of determinism and unpredictability, that is to say, the physical determines the moral, although the sequence of chain reactions is not necessarily predictable, and may be transformed in unrecognizable ways.[24] Destutt de Tracy's *Mémoire sur la faculté de penser* (1798), *Traité de la volonté et de ses effets* (1815), and *De l'amour* (published in Italian in 1819) pursued these insights into different areas of psychology, and Stendhal's own *De l'amour* (1822) owed much to it, and directly to Destutt, claiming to be 'un livre d'idéologie'.[25] Another Ideologue was Maine de Biran (1766–1824), more famous now as a spiritualist and Romantic opponent of theirs, but whose early 1802 *Influence de l'habitude sur la faculté de penser* was deeply influenced by their work, and promoted by them. He subsequently developed in mystical directions, but what he is most celebrated for now is his *Journal intime*. Significantly, it was Chateaubriand who promoted its publication, which finally occurred in 1858, and it had immediate and widespread popularity and influence. It is remarkable for its introspection, its careful observation of thought, its self-conscious reflection on its own patterns of behaviour.

Given these multiple links and filiations, it is tempting to return to *Le Fils naturel* and exclaim with Dorval that 'dans l'art, ainsi que dans la nature, tout est enchaîné' ('But in art, as in nature, everything is connected.' VER 1155; Bremner, p. 34). Romanticism,

du vitalisme en France de la deuxième moitié du 18e siècle à la fin du premier empire (Oxford: Voltaire Foundation, 2000). A recent re-evaluation of the field can be found in the collection of essays edited by Pascal Nouvel, *Repenser le vitalisme: Histoire et philosophie du vitalisme* (Paris: Presses Universitaires de France, 2011).

[23] P.-J.-G. Cabanis, *Rapports du physique et du moral*, in *Œuvres philosophiques*, ed. C. Lehec andt J. Cazeneuve (Paris: Presses Universitaires de France, 1956), ii.

[24] For the background and history of the extremely influential and initially chemical concept of 'action and reaction' during this period, see Jean Starobinski's *Action et Réaction: Vie et aventures d'un couple* (Paris: Seuil, 1999), tr. Sophie Hawkes, *Action and Reaction: The Life and Adventures of a Couple* (New York: Zone, 2003).

[25] Stendhal, *De l'amour*, ed. Victor Del Litto (Paris: Folio, 1980), 35n. I explore the scientific bases for Stendhal's metaphor of love as a crystallized branch as well as his links with the Ideologues in '"La cristallisation à la mode" ou le vocabulaire de la matière amoureuse', *L'Année stendhalienne*, 8 (2009), special issue 'Stendhal et la femme', ed. Lucy Garnier: 35–50.

neatly delimited in literary history as *not* Enlightenment, and *not* post-Romanticism or Realism, is, it turns out, not so easily located. Diderot emerges at the nexus of materialist investigations into nature and aesthetics, its concerns seeming continuous with Romanticism as we normally understand it.[26] This chapter would argue that Romanticism is more accurately seen as playing out and amplifying those concerns, as participating in the ongoing Quarrel of the Ancients and Moderns, and as a moment of crisis at the end of a second wave of humanism. Its vaunted distance from Enlightenment materialism arises from a polemical stance made necessary or inevitable by the pressures of the French Revolution. This chapter would therefore encourage a rethink.

Further Reading

Readers keen to explore pre-Romantic eighteenth-century texts, either in French or in translation, will enjoy the works by Diderot and Rousseau mentioned here, and might also want to read Voltaire's *Treatise on Tolerance* (1763), La Mettrie's *Man Machine* (1748), Prévost's *Manon Lescaut* (1731), Laclos's *Dangerous Liaisons* (1782), Beaumarchais's trilogy of Figaro plays (1773–92), or any of Charrière's novellas, including *Letters from Mistress Henley* (1784), and *Saint Anne* (1799). Diderot and d'Alembert's *Encyclopédie* (1751–72) is an endlessly stimulating and polyphonic resource, now easily consultable in a wonderful digital edition <https://encyclopedie.uchicago.edu> that has also inspired an ongoing translation project: <http://quod.lib.umich.edu/d/did>. A free online database of quarrels in Europe and Britain in the Early Modern period can be consulted at: <www.agon.paris-sorbonne.fr/en>.

For English-language orientation in eighteenth-century French literature and thought, set sail from the following:

Burgwinkle, William, Hammond, Nicholas, and Wilson, Emma (eds), *The Cambridge History of French Literature* (Cambridge: Cambridge University Press, 2011).

Delon, Michel (ed.), *Encyclopedia of the Enlightenment*, tr. Gwen Wells, 2 vols (Chicago and London: Fitzroy Dearborn, 2001).

Douthwaite, Julia, *The Wild Girl, Natural Man and the Monster: Dangerous Experiments in the Age of Enlightenment* (Chicago and London: Chicago University Press, 2002).

Edelstein, Dan, *The Enlightenment: A Genealogy* (Chicago: Chicago University Press, 2010).

Haakonssen, Knud (ed.), *The Cambridge History of Eighteenth-Century Philosophy* (Cambridge: Cambridge University Press, 2006).

Holmes, Richard, *The Age of Wonder: How the Romantic Generation Discovered the Beauty and Terror of Science* (London: Harper, 2008).

Riskin, Jessica, *Science in the Age of Sensibility* (Chicago: Chicago University Press, 2002).

Starobinski, Jean, *The Emblems of Reason*, tr. Barbara Bray (Cambridge, Mass.: MIT Press, 1988).

[26] Michel Delon's *L'Idée d'énergie au tournant des lumières (1770–1820)* (Paris: Presses Universitaires françaises, 1988) shows in great detail how fruitful it is to see this period as continuous.

Starobinski, Jean, *Jean-Jacques Rousseau, Transparency and Obstruction*, tr. Arthur Goldhammer (Chicago: Chicago University Press, 1988).

Starobinski, Jean, *Action and Reaction: The Life and Adventures of a Couple*, tr. Sophie Hawkes (New York: Zone, 2003).

Thomson, Ann, *Bodies of Thought: Science, Religion, and the Soul in Early Enlightenment* (Oxford: Oxford University Press, 2008).

Warman, Caroline, 'Nature and Enlightenment', in John D. Lyons (ed.), *Cambridge Companion to French Literature* (Cambridge: Cambridge University Press, 2015).

CHAPTER 2

LITERARY HISTORY AND POLITICAL THEORY IN GERMAINE DE STAËL'S IDEA OF EUROPE

BIANCAMARIA FONTANA

THE key question that needs to be addressed when considering Germaine de Staël's contribution to what is conventionally called European Romanticism is: how did she get there? How can we trace the path that led from the shapeless intellectual ambitions of an exceptionally talented young woman, thoroughly educated in the tradition of the Enlightenment, to a set of novel intuitions about modern society, about the politics, morals, and aesthetics of a new age?

Taken as a whole, the production of Staël's oeuvre[1]—including her political, literary and historical writings—stretched over three decades: from 1788, when, at the age of 22, she published *Lettres sur les ouvrages et le caractère de Jean-Jacques Rousseau*[2] for a confidential audience of family and friends, to 1817, when she died, a celebrated authoress, leaving unfinished her major historical work, *Considérations sur la révolution française*.[3] In particular it was after 1800—when, following Napoleon's access to power, her exile from France became irrevocable—that Staël became an international celebrity,

[1] A first collected edn of Staël's works was published posthumously by her son Auguste de Staël: Mme de Staël, *Œuvres complètes*, 17 vols (Paris, 1820–1). A new edn of Staël's collected works is in the making, but some of the texts cited here have not yet appeared in it; only very few of her works are currently available in English translation.

[2] In *Lettres sur Jean-Jacques Rousseau, De l'influence des passions et autres essais moraux, Œuvres complètes*, series 1, *Œuvres critiques*, i, ed. Florence Lotterie (Paris: Honoré Champion; Geneva: Slatkine, 2008), 35–110.

[3] *Considérations sur la Révolution française*, ed. Jacques Godechot (Paris, Tallandier, 1983); English tr.: *Considerations on the Principal Events of the French Revolution*, ed. Aurelian Craiutu (Indianapolis: Liberty Fund, 2008).

producing her best known and most successful works: her novels *Delphine* (1802)[4] and *Corinne ou l'Italie* (1807),[5] and her pioneering contributions to the history of literature: *De la littérature considérée dans ses rapports avec les institutions sociales* (1800),[6] and *De l'Allemagne* (1810–13).[7]

Yet the sources of these influential literary achievements were contained and, as it were, compressed within a much shorter time-span, roughly the years 1789 to 1792, years that, as Staël herself repeatedly observed, counted as centuries in terms of the upheaval and changes they brought to the lives of those who experienced them. It was mainly during this earlier period that the established views she had absorbed from her precocious and extensive readings of ancient and modern classics, and from her privileged contacts within European intellectual circles, were tested and transformed into a novel, highly original perspective.

The Voice of Opinion

There is a particular sense in which the French Revolution of 1789 represented the founding episode in Staël's formation. Naturally her life—like the lives of all the people in her Parisian entourage—was profoundly marked by the impact of revolutionary events, though she was sheltered from their most disruptive consequences by her status as the daughter and wife of foreign dignitaries: her father, the Genevan banker Jacques Necker, was until 1790 a minister of the crown; her husband, Baron Erik-Magnus de Staël, was the Swedish ambassador to the Parisian court. Her family's large and solid fortune, a good part of which was placed outside France, offered an additional protection against uncertain times.[8]

However Staël was probably less affected by the evils that accompanied the Revolution, much as she deplored them, than by the gap they revealed between expectations and

[4] *Delphine*, in *Œuvres complètes*, series 2, *Œuvres littéraires*, ii, ed. Lucia Omacini and Simone Balayé (Paris: Honoré Champion; Geneva, Slatkine, 2004). English tr.: *Delphine, a novel*, 3 vols (London: G. and J. Robinson, 1803).

[5] *Corinne ou l'Italie*, in *Œuvres complètes*, series 2, *Œuvres littéraires*, iii, ed. Simone Balayé (Paris: Honoré Champion; Geneva, Slatkine, 2000). English tr., *Corinne or Italy*, 3 vols (London: S. Tippen, 1807).

[6] *De la littérature, considérée dans ses rapports avec les institutions sociales*, ed. G. Gengembre and J. Goldzink (Paris: Flammarion, 1991). English tr., *Politics, Literature and National Character*, ed. Morroe Berger (New Brunswick, NJ: Transaction Publishers, 2000).

[7] *De l'Allemagne*, ed. Simone Balayé, 2 vols (Paris: Flammarion, 1968). English translations: *Germany*, 3 vols (London: Murray, 1813); *Germany*, ed. O. W. Wight, 2 vols (New York: Derby & Jackson, 1859).

[8] For basic biographical information on Staël see: J. Christopher Herold, *Mistress to an Age* (London: Hamish Hamilton, 1959); Simone Balayé, *Mme de Staël, lumières et liberté* (Paris: Klincksieck, 1979); Ghislain de Diesbach, *Madame de Staël* (Paris: Perrin, 1983); Maria Fairweather, *Mme de Staël* (London: Constable & Robinson, 2005); also, on her family background: Jean Denis Bredin, *Une singulière famille: Jacques Necker, Suzanne Necker et Germaine de Staël* (Paris: Fayard, 1999).

reality. In 1789 she had seen, in the transformation of France into a modern constitutional monarchy, the triumph of the ideals of the Enlightenment: civil freedom, religious toleration, and the equality of all citizens before the law, set in the framework of a moderate constitution. She had also passionately identified with that elite of enlightened reformers who, by their writings and political action, had made that transformation possible. Staël's unusual personal circumstances had in fact placed her from the start at the very heart of political power: first as her father's self-appointed helpmate and adviser; then, thanks to her own relentless activity, as a rallying presence for the party of the constitutional monarchists (*constitutionnels*) in the Constituent Assembly; finally, as a backstage influence on the *feuillant* cabinet of 1791–2, when she obtained for her lover, Count Louis de Narbonne-Lara, the post of minister of war. For her the collapse of the moderate regime established by the constitution of 1791, the crippling partisan divisions within the royalist camp, and the emergence of the most radical groups as leading forces in the Revolution, were the steps leading to a tragic, all-engulfing failure.[9]

In the first place such developments sealed the defeat of the political cause she had served, a cause in which considerable hopes and ambitions had been placed by many; it was a shipwreck that led a whole generation of talented intellectuals and idealistic reformers to their death, to the betrayal of their political ideals, or to a protracted exile (Staël herself, heavily pregnant and terrified for the safety of her closest friends, managed to escape from Paris just in time as the infamous massacres of September 1792 began).[10] But for the 26-year-old ambassador's wife this disastrous political outcome was also a personal existential debacle. In the heat of political struggle and in the (however derivative) exercise of power, the young woman had found a degree of enthusiasm and gratification that she had never felt before, and would never experience again, neither in her sentimental and family life, nor in the many exceptional intellectual contacts she was able to develop, not even in her own literary success.

Until her death the memory of the Revolution dominated Staël's imagination like that of all the writers in her generation. Like them she recalled the sufferings, the fear, the loss of friends, the horrors she had witnessed; but above all she remembered what it was like to be in Paris, amongst her political friends, at the heart of great events, making history. Significantly, in her recollections of the Revolution she described some initial episodes—such as the colourful ceremony for the opening of the Estates General on the 5 May 1789—as unique moments of collective enthusiasm and expectation.[11]

> I think I can affirm that in my generation [she wrote many years later] the one that entered society with the French Revolution, there were very few young people, or

[9] The best insight on Staël's personal as well as political experience is offered by her own letters, admirably edited by Béatrice Jasinski in the 1960s: Germaine de Staël, *Correspondence générale*, ed. B. Jasinski, 6 vols (Reprinted Geneva: Editions Slatkine, 2009).

[10] For Staël's own narrative of this episode, see *Considérations*, part III, ch. X, pp. 280–6.

[11] For an often cited account of the opening of the Estates, see *Considérations*, part I, ch. XVI, pp. 139–42.

> young women, who were not filled with the hope that the Estates General represented for France. [12]

On a more personal register she referred to another of these occasions—the scenes of popular rejoicing in front of the Hôtel de Ville when her father, who had been dismissed by the King Louis XVI, was recalled to office after the insurrection of 14 July—as the last day of ease (*prospérité*) of the life that at the time was still in front of her.[13] Any future prospect of happiness and gratification would be set forever against these very exacting standards. In addition to its political and personal consequences, the rapid shift of the revolutionary movement from constitutional reform to terrorist dictatorship also had significant theoretical implications. The sudden collapse of the monarchy, the advent of a republican regime in a large nation such as France, the new republic's unexpected military triumphs and her equally surprising economic survival, were to some extent the empirical refutation of widely accepted beliefs about the functioning of societies and political regimes, that had dominated eighteenth-century thinking.

In Staël's analysis, one crucial issue that had to be seriously reconsidered in the light of the revolutionary experience was that of the nature and role of public opinion. Staël believed that the development of public opinion in France during the eighteenth century had been the main force behind the revolutionary movement. It was a view she repeatedly expressed in her writings, arguing that it was opinion, the novel ideas and principles set forth by writers and philosophers, that had made the Revolution and led to the collapse of the Ancien Régime.[14] It was the impulse behind these ideas, rather than any specific political design, that had triumphed in 1789.

To some extent this interpretation corresponded well enough to the expectations of Enlightenment theorists concerning the progress of societies. The dissemination of publications, the development of education and scientific knowledge, the circulation of ideas not just inside one country, but within the international arena, were the preconditions for political reform and social improvement. As Staël herself had written in 1788, on the eve of the summoning of the Estates General, France was about to gain by the progress of her lights what other nations had conquered at the cost of floods of blood.[15] This optimistic vision of the impact of ideas considered opinion as an essentially rational force: not the immediate expression of popular passions, or an impulse of the moment that pushed the crowds in this or that direction, but an established consensus within the nation; this consensus must be initially shaped by the views of an educated elite, then tested and clarified by open debate, and finally accepted by the public at large.[16]

[12] Mme de Staël, *Dix années d'exil*, ed. Simone Balayé and Mariella Vianello Bonifacio (Paris: Fayard, 1996), 45. The translation of all the quotations from Staël's works in this chapter are my own.

[13] *Considérations*, 168.

[14] See e.g. *Des Circonstances actuelles* … *Œuvres complètes*, Part 2, 'Des écrivains', 433 ff.

[15] *Lettres sur Jean-Jacques Rousseau* …, *Œuvres complètes*, letter IV, p. 83.

[16] On the vast subject of the notion of public opinion in the French 18th-century context, see, for an overview, Mona Ozouf, 'Le Concept d'opinion publique au XVIIIème siècle', in *L'Homme régénéré, essais sur la Révolution française* (Paris: Gallimard, 1989), 53; Keith Baker, *Au tribunal de l'opinion, essais sur l'imaginaire politique au XVIIIème siècle* (Paris: Payot, 1995). See also B. Fontana, 'Public Opinion in the

The problem was that in France this ideal scenario had soon gone off the rails. The pondered views of philosophers had been replaced by a flood of ephemeral publications—pamphlets, journals, satires—far more partisan and intemperate in their expression. The very notion—so prominent in earlier eighteenth-century thinking—that writers had the crucial task of enlightening and guiding the nation, had become a risible formula: writers could now choose between remaining silent or risking their head. New radical factions, such as the Girondins or the Jacobins, had deployed considerable talent in exciting and manipulating popular sentiments to their own advantage: set into a kind of rhetorical overdrive by their propaganda, political discourse had become corrupted and almost meaningless. Even formal debates within the Assembly had been disrupted by the shouts and invectives of the tribunes that cowed any opposition. The advent of the war that opposed France to the other European powers had cut off the country from the peaceful discussions of the Republic of Letters, abandoning her to the squabbling of her own domestic factions.

As a result of these developments, what should have been the well-considered opinion of the nation at large had been reduced to silence. In her first political article: 'A quels signes peut-on connaître quelle est l'opinion de la majorité de la nation'—published in 1791, just after the death of the leader of the constitutional monarchists Mirabeau—Staël deplored the difficulty of discerning the true sentiments of the public; the question of what was the opinion of the majority of the nation

> in quiet times would be easy enough to answer; but during an insurrection, that apparently shows the emergence of a dominant opinion, things need to be considered with particular attention. It is in fact necessary to distinguish between what belongs to the moment, and what will last through time; what is dictated by fear, and what is inspired by reason; finally between what stems from hatred of the old regime, and what comes from an attachment to the new one.[17]

The voice of public opinion, that leading force that had guided France in 1789, had now become a chorus of discordant claims, to the extent that it was impossible for a divided and disoriented political class to interpret the will of the people. This elusiveness of opinion, made more dramatic by the policies of the revolutionary regime that terrorized and silenced any opposition, became a recurrent theme in Staël's writings throughout the 1790s. In her accounts there was no shortage of retrospective explanations for this state of affairs. The condition of France before the Revolution had been too backward, the gap in experience and understanding between educated elites and the mass of the people too deep, to allow a smooth transition from the old to the new regime; overdue reforms had come too late and too abruptly; a complete freedom of the press had been permitted in

French Enlightenment', in M. Albertone (ed.), *Il repubblicanesimo moderno* (Naples: Bibliopolis, 2006), 305–19.

[17] 'A quels signes peut on connaître quelle est l'opinion de la majorité de la nation', in *Des circonstances actuelles et d'autres essais politiques sous la Révolution, Œuvres complètes*, series 3, *Œuvres historiques*, i, ed. Lucia Omacini (Paris: Honoré Champion; Geneva: Slatkine, 2009), 559.

a country used to centuries of censorship, leading to all sort of excesses; unlike England, France had no tradition of parliamentary debates or electoral campaigns, no established political parties that could discipline the disputes amongst factions.

In her work of 1796, *De l'influence des passions sur le bonheur des individus et des nations*, Staël described the difficulty for the French people in reaching the tranquillity of spirit necessary to address rationally any public issues.[18] In France popular demands and aspirations had been repressed for centuries by a rigid caste system, then suddenly liberated and driven by fanatical demagogues into a kind of spiritual frenzy.[19] The result, by the end of the Revolution, was a sort of emotional exhaustion, that kept most people from taking any interest and investing any more energy in public life. This retreat of opinion away from public concerns, though easy enough to understand, constituted a major political problem. After the collapse of the terrorist regime in 1794, the new government of the Directory had established a moderate republican constitution, to which Staël had pledged her support.[20] In order to survive, the new republic was doubly in need of the presence of a vigorous public opinion: first, because any sovereign nation ruled by representative institutions relied on an independent opinion to control the actions of its representatives; secondly, because in France the stability of the political system was constantly under threat from attempted insurrections and conspiracies organized by the ultra-royalists or by the die-hard Jacobins, and required a large popular consensus to keep them at bay. Thus the passive attitude of the majority was

> a fatal disposition in a republic; it is guilty in those who govern, and those who are governed must join all their efforts to overcome it, since their opinion, so quiet, so submissive in front of any act of authority, is at the same time the only invincible force; ... because it represents the true power of the nation, either such opinion will be on the side of the republic, or republican government will never be established.[21]

But how could the moderate majority sustain the government, when the mass of the people looked upon their rulers with suspicion and mistrust? Staël thought that in normal circumstances, when a political regime was well-established, it was perfectly acceptable for citizens to be more focused upon their own private concerns than upon public affairs. Indeed, one of the reasons that made representative government best suited to large modern societies was precisely the freedom that under it people enjoyed to pursue

[18] *De l'influence des passions*, in *Lettres sur Jean-Jacques Rousseau ..., Œuvres complètes*, 111–302. English translation: *A treatise on the influence of the passions upon the happiness of individuals and of nations* (London, 1798). On some of the political implications of this work, see B. Fontana, 'Mme de Staël, le gouvernement des passions et la Révolution française', in *Le Groupe de Coppet et la Révolution française: Actes du IV colloque de Coppet* (Lausanne and Paris: Jean Touzot, 1988), 175–81.

[19] *De l'influence des passions*, 226.

[20] On Staël's political position in this period, see B. Fontana, 'The Thermidorian Republic and its Principles', in B. Fontana (ed.), *The Invention of the Modern Republic* (Cambridge: Cambridge University Press, 1994), 118–38.

[21] *Des circonstances actuelles ..., Œuvres complètes*, 352.

their own private goals, instead of being pressed into some form of public service like the citizens of ancient republics.

Unfortunately in France, in the absence of a stable regime of long standing, the government was faced with an impossible choice: public debate was dominated by the most extreme political factions, while the mass of peaceful citizens was unable or unwilling to express their views, as their massive abstention at the elections showed. If, however, coercion was exercised by the government to silence extremists and to limit their electoral influence, constitutional guarantees were suspended, the freedom of opinion was violated, and the country fell back into some form of emergency rule, just as during the Revolution. There were simply no means available in the short term to a constitutional government for attracting the support of an indifferent population, for influencing their beliefs or their choices.

Staël discussed at length this problem in her draft *Des circonstances actuelles qui peuvent terminer la révolution et des principes qui doivent fonder la république en France* in 1798: it was her last political work, and she left it unpublished, turning instead to a new project, a history of European literature. There were, as far as we know, a number of circumstantial reasons that led her to abandon publication, the main one being that France was once again on the verge of a change of regime. But the fact remains that in *Des circonstances actuelles* the question of the autonomy of opinion, so central to the whole argument, remained unresolved.[22]

As Benjamin Constant was to argue in 1819 in his famous *Discours sur la liberté des anciens comparée à celle des modernes*, while free opinion was one of the cornerstones of modern representative government, it was also its most unpredictable element. Naturally, given enough time, a government could hope to make public institutions more popular by improving the education of the citizens or by promoting civic values. But no pedagogical or institutional measure could guarantee the emergence of the kind of opinion that was needed to preserve a free constitution.[23]

The difficulties and contradictions encountered by Staël when writing *Des circonstances actuelles* showed that the issue of opinion was far more complex than Enlightenment theorists had originally suggested. Opinion was not just an abstract form of public consensus, automatically produced by given mechanisms (such as the circulation of information or public debate). For one thing opinion was not wholly rational, but was subject to emotional tensions and swings; it was not just ignorant

[22] On the context and making of this work, see Bronislaw Baczko, introduction to *Des circonstances actuelles*, 'Opinions des vainqueurs, sentiments des vaincus', in *Des circonstances actuelles* . . ., *Œuvres complètes*, 184–275; see also Lucia Omacini's introduction to the first critical edn of the same work, *Des circonstances actuelles*, ed. Lucia Omacini (Paris and Geneva: Droz, 1979), pp. xvii–lxxxvii.

[23] Benjamin Constant, *Discours sur la liberté des anciens comparée à celle des modernes: Discours prononcé à l'Athénée royal de Paris en 1819*, in *Ecrits politiques*, ed. Marcel Gauchet (Paris: Gallimard, 1997), 589–619; English tr.: *Discourse on the Liberty of the Ancients and the Moderns*, in Benjamin Constant, *Political Writings*, ed. and tr. B. Fontana (Cambridge: Cambridge University Press, 1988), 307–28. On Constant's attitude to public opinion, see B. Fontana, *Benjamin Constant and the Post-Revolutionary Mind* (New Haven and London: Yale UP, 1991), ch 6, 'The Government of Opinion', 81–97.

crowds who succumbed to blind impulses: intelligent, educated individuals could react in the same way, when they were driven by party interests and fanaticism (Staël's favourite example of a personality dominated by a partisan temperament was the philosopher Condorcet).[24] Opinion had a history, since collective beliefs and attitudes evolved through time, though not always at the same speed, and not invariably in the sense of progress. While nations within the European continent shared some features, and to some extent influenced one another, in each country public discourse had peculiarities that depended on its traditions, customs, religion, and institutions. The analysis of public opinion, adapted to its different contexts, led directly to the consideration of a much wider field of inquiry represented by the ethos and cultural identity of nations.

The Literature of Nations

The reflection on literature in a European context that Staël developed since 1798 was to some extent the pursuit of the political questioning she had practised since the beginning of the Revolution. No doubt, it would be far too reductive to consider the work she published in 1800, *De la littérature considérée dans ses rapports avec les institutions sociales*, as a kind of sequel to *Des circonstances actuelles*. There is no evidence to support this interpretation, and the two works are very different in their choice of themes as in their style of address. In the same way it would be misleading to see *De l'Allemagne* simply as the pursuit of a political struggle, an exercise in anti-Bonapartist propaganda.[25]

All her life Staël had cultivated an interest in literature in parallel to her other intellectual concerns. The somewhat derivative literary works she wrote in the 1780s (and in some cases published later on) illustrated her interest in a wide variety of genres: the historical novel, historical drama, poetry, and the sentimental and moral narrative.[26] Even a political text such as her pamphlet in defence of Marie-Antoinette published in 1793—'Refléxions sur le procès de la Reine, par une femme'—contained motifs borrowed from historical romances and Gothic narratives.[27] Her essay of 1795, 'Essai sur les fictions'—much appreciated by Goethe, who translated it into German—attributed to literature a very distinctive role, that neither history nor philosophy could perform: that of representing the individual condition and exploring individual moral choices.[28] But

[24] *De l'influence des passions, Œuvres complètes*, ch. VII: 'De l'esprit de parti', pp. 221–33.

[25] John C. Isbell, *The Birth of European Romanticism: Truth and Propaganda in Staël's 'De l'Allemagne', 1810–13* (Cambridge: Cambridge University Press, 1994).

[26] See the texts collected in Mme de Staël, *Œuvres de jeunesse*, ed. Simone Balayé and John Isbell (Paris: Desjonquères, 1997).

[27] 'Refléxions sur le procès de la Reine', in *Des circonstances actuelles …, Œuvres complètes*, 29–66; see also the post-face by Monique Cottret to the 2006 edn of the same work, *Refléxions sur le procès de la Reine* (Paris: Editions de Paris); and B. Fontana, 'Mon triste écrit sur la Reine: Mme de Staël et le fantôme de la révolution', in *Cahiers Staëliens: Les Biographies Staëliennes*, 61 (2011), 197–208.

[28] In Mme de Staël, *Œuvres de jeunesse*, 131–56.

if Staël's interest in the subject was of long standing, *De la littérature* addressed it from a radically new perspective, that grew largely out of her need to come to terms with those questions that the failure of the republic established under the Directory had left unanswered.

In her text Staël adopted an unusually broad definition of literature, extending the term to include the writings of historians and philosophers, as well as the tradition of political rhetoric. Her work aimed at a systematic and comparative approach, in the style of Montesquieu's *Esprit des lois*,[29] something she had attempted before, unsuccessfully, with *De l'influence des passions*. Just as did the diversity of the laws in Montesquieu, literature was to offer a point of entry into the variety of past and present national histories and cultures, showing the relation between literary production and social and political institutions. (Benjamin Constant employed a very similar method in his vast, never completed *De la religion*, yet another attempt to reproduce the model of the *Esprit des lois*.[30])

The idea that literature should be examined in relation to particular historical contexts had been anticipated, during the mid-1790s, by the contributors to the journal *Décade philosophique*, who had set forth the claims of a new republican aesthetics, adapted to the post-revolutionary age.[31] However Staël's design was far bolder and more ambitious than anything the group of the *idéologues* had produced before. She did not confine herself to the traditional comparison between ancient and modern canons, or between pre- and post-revolutionary literature, but presented a broad and diversified picture of national literary traditions across Europe. In particular she abandoned the conventional approach that placed France at the centre of the picture as the uncontested leader of style and taste: her discovery and appreciative assessment of the literatures of the North, until then largely unknown or underestimated, led eventually to the production of what was possibly the most influential of her books and the main nineteenth-century reference work on German culture: *De l'Allemagne*.

Staël's approach to the history of literature was essentially dynamic. The vast tableau outlined by Montesquieu in the *Esprit des lois* presented a relatively static picture of past and present laws and customs, with long-term continuities and cyclical recurrences. Staël on the other hand was especially keen to prove that, in spite of setbacks and periods of stagnation, the slow but continuous march of human spirit in philosophy, and of its quick, but often interrupted achievements in the arts,[32] showed the tendency of

[29] Charles-Louis Secondat, baron de Montesquieu, *De l'Esprit des lois*, in *Œuvres complètes*, ed. Roger Caillois, 2 vols (Paris: Gallimard, Bibliothèque de la Pléïade, 1951), ii.

[30] Benjamin Constant, *De la religion considérée dans sa source, ses formes et ses développements*, ed. Tzvetan Todorv and Étienne Hofmann (Arles: Actes Sud, 1999).

[31] See Joanna Kitchin, *Le Journal 'philosophique' La Décade (1794–1807)*, Thèse de doctorat, Université de Paris, 1956 (Paris, 1966). On the ideologues, see Sergio Moravia, *Il tramonto dell'illuminismo, filosofia e politica nella società francese (1770–1810)* (Bari: Laterza, 1986); Xavier Martin, 'Mme de Staël, Napoléon et les iéologues, pour un réajustement des perspectives', *Bulletin de la société française d'histoire des idées*, 7 (1990), 11–30.

[32] *De la littérature*, 65.

human societies towards progress. Moreover, where Montesquieu's comparative analysis stressed the specificities and differences of human civilizations, she was more interested in their interaction, and in the stimulus they offered to each other's evolution.

At a time when many saw the years of the Revolution as a parenthesis of ideological folly and vulgar propaganda, Staël was anxious to prove that some positive elements of that experience could still be rescued. The mistake was to assume that, in subverting traditional order, the Revolution had also removed all the criteria by which public discourse and literary contributions may be judged. On the contrary, the establishment of a new republican government in France required high standards of style, rigour, and public morality. For a society based on equality, promoting excellence and merit was far more important than for a traditional society of ranks. Unless exacting standards were preserved in all fields, a democratic regime would see the triumph of banality and ignorance. In particular democratic leaders must excel for their moral and intellectual qualities: if mere popularity became the only criterion of distinction, then vulgarity would become the prevailing feature:

> In a democratic state there is always the risk that the desire for popularity might lead to the imitation of vulgar customs; ... the people would become used to selecting coarse and ignorant magistrates; such magistrates would stifle intellectual improvement, and by an inevitable circularity the loss of enlightenment could then lead to the enslavement of the people.[33]

Such considerations helped to explain the corruption of opinion during the Revolution. Public views should be promoted when they contribute to the moral and intellectual progress of the people. The mere dissemination of opinions and arguments, in the absence of any guiding principles, could only multiply worthless formulas and ephemeral commonplaces. One dimension of public discourse that, in Staël's view, required special attention, was political rhetoric. The Estates General as well as the Constituent and National Assemblies had failed to provide a space for real deliberation, in which opposite views could be exchanged and discussed: speeches delivered from the tribune were often inaudible, minority speakers were prevented from expressing themselves, debates, and even voting procedures, were disrupted by the rowdy interventions of the public. In the constituencies deputies—unlike their English counterparts—were not in habit of communicating with their electors and exchanging views with them.[34] Just like opinion, eloquence—political rhetoric—could be preserved from corruption and improve only if the conditions for free and open exchanges in the public domain were guaranteed. Together with eloquence, literature could also seriously contribute to

[33] *De la littérature*, 77.

[34] In the *Considérations* Staël quoted Étienne Dumont and Jeremy Bentham on the question of deliberative practices in the French revolutionary assemblies, *Considérations*, part III, ch. XXIII, pp. 248–50. Cf. Jeremy Bentham, *Tactique des assemblées législatives*, ed. Étienne Dumont (Paris, 1822; repr. Charleston: Nabu Press, 2010).

improving and stabilizing opinion, as the creations of imagination were very effective in promoting new ideals and in discrediting old prejudices. [35]

But how could one measure the progress of any nation, even in relation to a particular object, such as literature? Should literary production be considered in isolation from progress in other fields, like wealth, education, or civil liberties? Was it possible to set universal standards of judgement, and if so, could it be said that some nations progressed more than others? Here too the Revolution altered the nature of the problem: the disruption of the balance of powers in Europe showed that the position of France could no longer be understood in isolation from that of the countries she had suddenly undertaken to fight and to conquer.

A New Idea of Europe

Unsurprisingly, given the major upheavals the European continent underwent during her lifetime, Staël's attitude towards the issue of nationality as a political and cultural reality changed significantly through time. Born in France from Swiss parents, Staël felt a passionate attachment to the country in which she had been raised. Her attitude towards Switzerland (where she spent a considerable part of her time) can be described at best as ambivalent,[36] while she resented the fact that by marriage she had become the subject of a kingdom, Sweden, she had never even visited. [37] For years, she battled in vain against various hostile governments to obtain the French citizenship to which she thought she was naturally entitled.

Her strong attachment to France went together with an equally dedicated anglophilia—a trait she shared with her father and with many protagonists of the Constituent Assembly of 1789, the so-called *parti anglais*. She considered English political institutions and practices as a model to imitate; her interest in English history and politics—fed by extensive reading but also by personal contacts with some prominent public figures in the Whig camp—lasted all her life. A substantial part of her work *Considérations sur la révolution française* was in fact dedicated to a presentation of the English Constitution and of the functioning of the English political system.[38]

[35] *De littérature*, part 2, ch. VIII, 'De l'éloquence', pp. 393–406; see also *Considérations*, 540.

[36] Pierre Kohler, *Mme de Staël et la Suisse* (Lausanne and Paris: Payot, 1916). For a recent assessment of Staël's attitude towards Swiss culture see Roger Francillon, *De Rousseau à Starobinski: Littérature et identité en Suisse*, Le Savoir Suisse (Lausanne: Presses polytechinique et universitaires romandes, 2011), 40–6.

[37] One of the conditions set by Necker for his daughter's marriage was that Baron de Staël should be appointed to a post in Paris so that Germaine should not be obliged to live in Sweden; she only visited her husband's country several years after his death, in 1813. She did however learn Swedish and studied diligently her acquired country's history and institutions. She also corresponded regularly with the King of Sweden Gustavus III, in Mme de Staël, *Corréspondance générale*, i. *Lettres de jeunesse*, 1777–Dec. 1791, *passim*.

[38] *Considérations*, part VI.

Until the Revolution Staël's vision of Europe reflected the common attitude of most Enlightenment intellectuals: the European continent was merely the space in which the great powers deployed their natural rivalry, a rivalry kept in check by a system of mutual threats and alliances. In this perspective a closer integration of European nations could only come from two sources: from conquest, if some form of military government were to prevail in one of the great powers; or from commerce, as the growth of public debt and the extension of markets reduced the autonomy of individual states, making them increasingly dependent on extra-national factors.[39] Neither prospect was especially appealing. The affirmation of a military regime in one country might bring to an end free constitutional government in the whole continent. Unity by commerce seemed a more benign option to some observers; yet writers such as Rousseau were ready to denounce its deleterious consequences: the loss of national identities and traditions, the decline of civic values, the spreading of greed and corruption across the frontiers of a soul-less continent.[40]

To these uninspiring alternatives, the Revolution added a third, more appealing possibility: a closer unity of European states may be realized by the voluntary choice of nations who shared common values and compatible forms of free government. The notion of a federation of sister republics made a fleeting appearance after 1792, as the new French republic claimed a special relation with America, and encouraged the creation of democratic republics in the countries the French army proceeded to liberate in the course of the war waged against the European monarchies. Soon however it became clear that the sister republics of Italy, Holland, or Switzerland were treated by the French just as conquered territories subject to military occupation.[41]

In 1791, when a conflict between France and the other major European powers seemed inevitable, Staël exercised whatever influence she had within the government and in diplomatic circles to avoid this prospect. She was partly motivated by the (well-founded) belief that France was unprepared for war; she also thought that a war would not, as some hoped, put an end to the Revolution, but rather sustain and prolong it. This conviction was confirmed by events: the same patriotic sentiment that enabled the republic to resist her enemies represented the main obstacle to a return to normality; the war became the engine of the Revolution, by creating a condition of permanent alarm and mobilization that justified exceptional measures. In her pamphlet of 1795,

[39] On the economic dimension of European integration in Staël's and Constant's reflection see my articles: B. Fontana, 'The Napoleonic Empire and the Europe of Nations', in A. Pagden (ed.), *The Idea of Europe*, Woodrow Wilson Centre Series (Washington, DC, and Cambridge: Cambridge University Press, 2002), 116–28; and 'A New Kind of Federalism, Benjamin Constant and Modern Europe', in M. Albertone and A. De Francesco (eds), *Rethinking the Atlantic World* (London: Palgrave Macmillan, 2009), 161–79.

[40] Cf. Rousseau's comments in the opening pages of his work on the government of Poland, Jean-Jacques Rousseau, *Considérations sur le gouvernement de Pologne*, ed. Jean Fabre in *Œuvres complètes*, ed. B. Gagnebin and M. Raymond, 4 vols (1969), iii. 951–1041.

[41] Michel Vovelle, *Les Républiques sœurs sous le regard de la grande nation, 1795–1803* (Paris: L'Harmattan, 2000); M. Turchetti (ed.), *La France et les républiques sœurs en 1798: Invasion ou liberation?* (Geneva: Georg, 2005); Pierre Serna (ed.), *Républiques sœurs: Le Directoire et la Révolution atlantique*, Actes du colloque de Paris 2008 (Rennes: Presses universitaires de Rennes, 2009).

'Refléxions sur la paix intérieure', addressed to William Pitt, Staël pleaded for peace, urging the English minister to abandon a war that—she claimed—his Tory government pursued for purely partisan motives. She also denounced the danger of a protracted war between France and the rest of Europe, a conflict that would devastate the continent, reducing it to the condition of the deserts of Africa and of enslaved Asia.[42]

On the whole, given the duration of the war and the victories of the revolutionary army, Staël did not find it surprising that some form of military government should finally prevail in France—indeed she had anticipated this outcome long before the coup d'état of Brumaire that brought Bonaparte to power in 1800. The conquering republic, and later Napoleon's empire, turned into a reality the Enlightenment nightmare of military government, with all its dreaded consequences: endless war, disruption of trade relations, loss of freedom both in France and in the European states subject to French occupation. The aspirations to national unity and independence of those Italian, Hungarian, Polish, or Greek patriots who wished to free their countries from foreign domination, were cynically exploited and betrayed by the new conquerors. Even the positive features of imperial conquest—such as the reforms introduced in public administration, education, or penal law—were judged by Staël insufficient to compensate the suffering and disruption they had cost. As she observed in the *Considérations*:

> was the earth to be inundated by blood, so that Prince Jerome might take the place of the Elector of Hesse; and so that the Germans might be governed by French administrators, who appropriated for themselves fiefs of which they could scarcely pronounce the titles, though they carried them, promptly pocketing their revenues regardless of the language in which they came ...?[43]

In the end, by the time of Napoleon's final defeat in 1815, far from being transformed into a modern federation of free states, Europe appeared as an odd combination of the feudal empire of Charlemagne with some despotic Asian potentate.

Yet in spite of this generally disastrous outcome, the protracted imperial experiment had also some positive—if largely unintended—consequences. To begin with, the resistance to French expansionism and to the uniformity imposed by the conquerors, showed the resilience of European nations, a resilience that was enhanced, rather than diminished, by their diversity. It was not surprising that England, with her wealth and her strong traditions of political liberty, should become the leader of the opposition to Napoleon; and yet a remarkable capacity for resistance was displayed by backward countries—such as Spain and Russia—whose obstinate patriotism largely compensated for any deficiencies in their institutions and social organization. The threat of conquest brought out in the European peoples unexpected depth of heroism and virtue. Staël recalled that, when the French army threatened Switzerland in 1798, the representatives

[42] *Refléxions sur la paix intérieure, adressées à M. Pitt et aux français*, in *Des circonstances actuelles ...*, *Œuvres complètes*, 133–82, 108–9.

[43] *Considérations*, 401–2.

of the small cantons came to Berne to declare in their noble ignorance that they were ready to fight, as they had already mobilized four hundred men, and could double that number if necessary. If their response was touchingly pathetic, and if their desperate resistance failed to stop the invaders, in the end it was the French who had to bend to the national will of these small populations, who refused to be integrated into the new republic the victors had established. It was the people, not their rulers or generals, who won the long war against oppression.[44]

The qualities that enabled European nations to fight for their independence were the same qualities that conferred on their literature its distinctive character and vitality. Style, elegance, and rational reasoning were not all; imagination, passion, creativity had also an important role to play: it was their love of liberty for example that sustained the imagination of the barbarous people of the North, enabling them to build better institutions than their more sophisticated counterparts in the South of Europe:

> The poetry of the North is far better suited than that of the South to the spirit of a free people ... Independence was the first and unique source of happiness of northern people. A certain fierceness of the soul, a detachment from life born of a harsh land and melancholic sky, made servitude unbearable; long before England discovered the advantages of representative governments, the war-like spirit that Erse and Scandinavian poets sung with such enthusiasm gave to man an extraordinary sense of his own individual strength, and of the power of his will. [45]

While the Napoleonic experience had offered to European nations the occasion to display and defend their diversity, it created at the same time an interaction that left durable traces. Even if the unity imposed by the empire was ill-conceived, hopes were raised, new ideas circulated, reforms tested; people were given the opportunity to compare their circumstances and institutions as never before. Thus it would be unrealistic to expect that, with the defeat of Napoleon and the collapse of the Empire, things could simply go back to what they were before the Revolution. Frontiers may be re-established and monarchs reinstated; however those who imagined it was possible to revert to the Ancien Régime—like many of the supporters of the restored Bourbon monarchy, or the promoters of the new Holy Alliance—were clearly mistaken. The ideals the French conquerors had proclaimed and circulated, largely out of opportunism, had not lost their value because an instrumental use had been made of them. If the Revolution and the Empire had failed to give substance to the ideal of a federation of free states, in the concluding pages of the *Considérations* Staël could still assert with confidence that only limited monarchies and republics—that is to say, only free constitutional governments—had their place in modern Europe and could shape her future.

Once again there were parallels between the political order of Europe and the development of literature. The diversity of contributions, far from pointing to some inequality

[44] *Considérations*, part III, ch. XXVIII, 'Invasion de la Suisse', pp. 344–7.
[45] *De la littérature*, 206–7.

of achievement, must be regarded as a richness of resources. It was thanks to this diversity that national literary traditions could be preserved from the monotony and mediocrity that came from the repetition of conventional patterns. Staël discussed this issue provocatively in her essay 'De l'esprit des traductions', published in Milan, in the journal *Biblioteca italiana* in 1816. [46] The French, she argued, had always shown a tendency to modify the spirit of the foreign authors they translated, impressing on them their own national colour; this, however, was a mistake, since the translation of foreign works could, better than any other means, preserve the literature of one country from those banal expressions that are the certain indication of its decadence.[47]

It was significant that the imperial regime, that at home could tolerate only a servile, sycophantic literature, should consider the circulation and discussion of foreign works, even on non-political subjects, as a threat to its own authority—witness the fate of Staël's own book *De l'Allemagne*, the first edition of which was destroyed at the printer's, before it could be distributed, by order of the imperial police.

> For my part [she confessed in 1816] I have supplied continual refrains to the French journalists for fifteen years—the melancholy of the North, the perfectibility of the human species, the muses of romance, the muses of Germany ... The good instincts of despotism made the agents of the literary police feel that originality in the manner of writing may lead to independence of character; and that great care must be taken to prevent English and German books from being introduced into Paris, in order to stop those French writers, while they observe the rules of taste, from keeping pace with the progress of the human mind in countries where civil troubles have not retarded its advancement.[48]

The form of literary works could not be separated from their content. Originality in style and creativity could contribute to the promotion of new values, as much as the subject and the choice of themes. If the experience of the Revolution had largely discredited the works and doctrines of the Enlightenment, a new generation of writers across Europe, following different individual paths and experimenting with new aesthetic approaches, had already taken their place in the ongoing struggle for liberty.

A World of Exiles

It is difficult to imagine what Staël's profile as a writer would have looked like, had there been no Revolution and no Empire, leaving her free to spend all her life presiding

[46] On the background of the composition of this article, see Simone Balayé, *Les Carnets de voyage de Mme de Staël* (Geneva: Droz, 1971), 410–11.

[47] 'De l'esprit des traductions', in Mme de Staël, *Œuvres complètes*, ed. Auguste de Staël, 17 vols (Paris, 1820–1), xvii. 389.

[48] *Considérations*, 428.

undisturbed over her Parisian salon. As it is, first revolutionary terror, then the repeated interdictions, issued by governments of different political colours, to reside in the French capital, led her to undertake a series of foreign explorations: a period of residence in England (in a country house in Surrey quaintly named Juniper House) in the early months of 1793; the journeys to Germany in 1803–4 and to Italy in 1804–5 famously reflected in her literary production; and finally the adventurous escape from the surveillance of the French authorities that led her to Vienna, Moscow, St Petersburg, Stockholm, and London in 1812–13. The same prohibition to live in Paris transformed the Neckers' chateau of Coppet near Geneva (a place Staël disliked and had tried to avoid for the best part of her life) into a refuge for dissident intellectuals and the symbolic centre of post-revolutionary European liberalism.[49]

Towards the end of her life, while working on the *Considérations*, Staël began another draft, the unfinished version of which was published posthumously with the title *Dix années d'exile*.[50] In this text she retraced the progress of Bonaparte's career as she had witnessed it, and described the journey across Northern Europe she had undertaken in defiance of his injunctions in 1812–13. To some extent *Dix années* was written as a conventional travel journal: based on annotations taken during the journey, it duly described roads and landscapes, local folklore and monuments, receptions at the royal courts and encounters with famous personalities.[51] Being a journal, it had the form of an autobiographical narrative; this time it was not Delphine or Corinne, or some other literary alter ego, who sat between Napoleon and Sièyes at dinner, listened to the songs of Russian coachmen, and conversed with the Tsar, but the writer herself, whose life-story was revealed for what it was, a series of experiences outside any established pattern, far more adventurous than any fictional creation.

For this was no ordinary Grand Tour, undertaken to broaden one's horizons. It began as an escape, with moments of great suspense every time the travellers, equipped with passports of uncertain legitimacy, crossed the frontier from one state into another; it then became a flight from the phantom of tyranny, as Staël's party arrived in Moscow just ahead of Napoleon's invading army and hastened north towards the safety of the British fleet anchored in front of St Petersburg. Inevitably, given the circumstances, the journey was also a reviewing of the troops, as in her conversations with diplomats and monarchs Staël tried to ascertain the prospects of a victory of the anti-French coalition: would Austria stick to the alliance with France stipulated by the marriage of Napoleon to the Archduchess Marie-Louise? Could the Tsar Alexander I be trusted to continue the fight?[52] Was Bernadotte—the dissident Napoleonic general who had been adopted by

[49] On the international profile of the Coppet group, see: *Madame de Staël et l'Europe*, Colloque de Coppet 1966 (Paris: Klincksieck, 1970); Kurt Kloocke and Simone Balayé (eds), *Le Groupe de Coppet et l'Europe, 1789–1830*, 5ème Colloque de Coppet, 1993 (Lausanne: Institut Benjamin Constant; Paris: Touzot, 1994).

[50] Mme de Staël, *Dix années d'exil*, ed. Simone Balayé and Mariella Vianello Bonifacio (Paris: Fayard, 1996).

[51] Simone Balayé, *Les Carnets de voyage de Mme de Staël* (Geneva: Droz, 1971).

[52] On Alexander I's position, see Marie-Pierre Rey, 'Le Projet européen d'Alexandre Ier', in Thierry Lenz (ed.), *Napoléon et l'Empire: Regards sur une politique européenne* (Paris: Fayard, 2005), 288–317.

the King of Sweden as his heir—ready to confront his former master?[53] The narrative of *Dix années* stopped abruptly just as Staël was about to embark for Sweden. The picture of the European continent it conveyed was that of a vast no-man's land, crossed by rival armies and suspended on the brink of the abyss; but the same no-man's land was also the blank page on which the common future of European nations was about to be redesigned, the backdrop to a whole parade of new identities and imagined futures.

It is of course impossible to distinguish, in Staël's choice of years of compulsive travelling, the objective constraints of political persecution from her own existential disquiet and agitation. After all nothing prevented her from sitting out her banishment in Switzerland, or even in some French country residence, had she truly suffered (as she claimed) from the deprivation of familiar people and places. Indeed it is only too easy to attribute her frequent journeys not to necessity, but to an irresistible craving for new people and new settings—a reaction to the condition of latent depression by which she clearly felt constantly threatened. By her own admission, the anxiety to escape from boredom was one of the dominant motivations in her life, one that made her vulnerable to those powers that could restrict her access to society.[54]

Yet setting aside the question of the writer's own psychological make up, the fact remains that she was part of a generation that the revolution had forced into a condition, if not of exile, at least of displacement. This was true in the first instance of those young French aristocrats who had survived terror, but lost their fortune and their place in society. However dislocation had become the fate of many other people: revolutionary militants defeated in one or other of the political battles engaged since 1789; foreign intellectuals who had moved to France attracted by the Revolution and could not, or did not want to go back home; patriots in different European countries whose fate had become entangled with that of their French liberators; professional soldiers to whom the Revolution had offered undreamt of prospects of advancement, but at the price of presiding over some remote province of the conquered continent.

In a world in which a lowly officer from Pau could become King of Sweden, Rousseau's metaphor of exile as the exemplary condition of modern man, isolated and homeless in an alien world, took on new proportions and a new significance.[55] In one of the abandoned drafts of *Dix années*, Staël denounced exile as a subtly cruel form of persecution: from the outside it looked as a rather mild form of punishment, as the victim was not imprisoned or physically harmed, only sent away; and yet through exile people were deprived of all those familiar presences, places, and habits that gave meaning to

[53] Cf. Mme de Stael and August Wilhelm von Schlegel, *An Appeal to the Nations of Europe against the continental system published in Stockholm by authority of Bernadotte* (London: Richardson, 1813). On this particular moment in Bernadotte's career, see Frank Favier, *Bernadotte, un maréchal de l'Empire sur le trône de Suède*, preface by Jean Tulard (Paris: Ellipses, 2010), 225–47.

[54] 'All my life—she wrote—I have been pursued by the phantom of boredom'. *Dix années d'exil*, 85.

[55] On the meaning of exile for Rousseau and Staël, see Jean-Marie Roulin, 'Ontology and the politics of return in Germaine de Staël', in Karyna Szmurlo (ed.), *Germaine de Staël, Forging a Politics of Mediation* (Oxford: Voltaire Foundation, 2011), 137–49; see also Angelica Goodden, *Madame de Staël, the Dangerous Exile* (Oxford: Oxford University Press, 2008).

their life.[56] This description of the experience of exile might have been accurate when the victims had solid roots somewhere; it seemed more dubious as the new generation of exiles (Staël included) had gradually drifted away from their original attachments. They had got used to alien lifestyles, fell in love with and married foreigners, became involved—sometimes dangerously—with the political passions of other nations,[57] flirted with their taste and way of thinking, discovered and imitated their literature.

If they experienced an uneasy sense of non-belonging, this was not necessarily associated with sentiments of pain and loss; on the contrary, it could be seen as a condition of freedom from those limitations and constraints that came with the membership of traditional communities. The fluctuation between these two moods—frustrating isolation and liberating detachment—was apparent in Benjamin Constant's account of the liberty of the moderns: the anonymous citizen of the new, shapeless European continent could at least chose to live wherever and however he wished, without the burden of any specific bonds and obligations.[58] In contrast with Constant's careless indifference, Staël showed she was closer in sensibility to Rousseau's, when she associated exile with suffering, with the loss of an idealized condition of safety and happiness that she had in fact rarely (if ever) experienced.

The paradox, in her case, was that displacement, the collapse of the secure and privileged circumstances in which she had been raised, had allowed her to reshape her own personal destiny, to an extent that would normally be beyond the power of any individual, let alone a woman. Before the Revolution she had been a diplomat's wife with a literary salon and a penchant for politics. Had she died in childbirth on the occasion of her first pregnancy in 1787, she would be remembered as a minor personality on the fringe of the French salon tradition. Instead she had become a political activist, a leading figure (if not a leader) in her own party, the catalyst of a set of converging reflections on republicanism and representative government; a dissident writer and intellectual with an international reputation, the promoter of exchanges amongst cultures and of new aesthetic trends;[59] a historian whose narrative of the Revolution of 1789 would become an essential reference for posterity.

Of all the expectations raised by the Revolution the promise of happiness was the one that had been most cruelly betrayed, more so than any political or philosophical ideal. If Staël did not find fulfilment in the extraordinary life she had made for herself, her failure was at least immensely creative and fertile.

[56] *Dix annés d'exil*, 317.

[57] The expression is Staël's, see *Considérations*, 345.

[58] This ambivalence is especially apparent in Constant's novel *Adolphe* (1816); *Adolphe, Anecdote trouvée dans les papiers d'un inconnu*, ed. Jean-Marie Roulin (Paris: Flammarion, 2011); cf. B. Fontana, *Benjamin Constant and the Post-Revolutionary Mind*, 118–33.

[59] For a recent assessment of this 'collective' dimension of Staël's contribution, see Alain Vaillant (ed.), *Dictionnaire du romantisme* (Paris: Editions CNRS, 2012), 709–11.

Further Reading

Baker, Keith, *Au tribunal de l'opinion, essais sur l'imaginaire politique au XVIIIème siècle* (Paris: Payot, 1995).

Balayé, Simone, *Mme de Staël, lumières et liberté* (Paris: Klincksieck, 1979).

Bredin, Jean Denis, *Une singulière famille: Jacques Necker, Suzanne Necker et Germaine de Staël* (Paris: Fayard, 1999).

Diesbach, Ghislain de, *Madame de Staël* (Paris: Perrin, 1983).

Fairweather, Maria, *Mme de Staël* (London: Constable & Robinson, 2005).

Fontana, B., 'Mme de Staël, le gouvernement des passions et la Révolution française', in *Le Groupe de Coppet et la Révolution française, Actes du IV colloque de Coppet* (Lausanne and Paris: Jean Touzot, 1988), 175–81.

Fontana, B., *Benjamin Constant and the Post-Revolutionary Mind* (New Haven and London: Yale, 1991).

Fontana, B., 'The Thermidorian Republic and its Principles', in B. Fontana (ed.), *The Invention of the Modern Republic* (Cambridge, Cambridge University Press, 1994), 118–38.

Fontana, B., 'Public Opinion in the French Enlightenment', in M. Albertone (ed.), *Il repubblicanesimo moderno* (Naples: Bibliopolis, 2006), 305–19.

Fontana, B., 'Mon triste écrit sur la Reine: Mme de Staël et le fantôme de la révolution', *Cahiers Staëliens, Les biographies Staëliennes*, 61 (2011), 197–208.

Francillon, Roger, *De Rousseau à Starobinski, Littérature et identité en Suisse*, Le Savoir Suisse (Lausanne: Presses polytechinique et universitaires romandes, 2011), 40–6.

Goodden, Angelica, *Madame de Staël, the Dangerous Exile* (Oxford: Oxford University Press, 2008).

Herold, J. Christopher, *Mistress to an Age* (London: Hamish Hamilton, 1959).

Isbell, John C., *The Birth of European Romanticism, Truth and Propaganda in Staël's 'De l'Allemagne', 1810–13* (Cambridge, Cambridge University Press, 1994).

Kloocke, Kurt, and Balayé, Simone (eds), *Le Groupe de Coppet et l'Europe, 1789–1830*, 5ème Colloque de Coppet, 1993 (Lausanne, Institut Benjamin Constant and Paris, Touzot, 1994).

Kohler, Pierre, *Mme de Staël et la Suisse* (Lausanne and Paris: Payot, 1916).

Martin, Xavier, 'Mme de Staël, Napoléon et les iéologues, pour un réajustement des perspectives', *Bulletin de la société française d'histoire des idées*, 7 (1990), 11–30.

Moravia, Sergio, *Il tramonto dell'illuminismo, filosofia e politica nella società francese (1770–1810)* (Bari: Laterza, 1986).

Ozouf, Mona, 'Le Concept d'opinion publique au XVIIIème siècle', in *L'Homme régénéré, essais sur la Révolution française* (Paris: Gallimard, 1989).

Roulin, Jean-Marie, 'Ontology and the politics of return in Germaine de Staël', in Karyna Szmurlo (ed.), *Germaine de Staël, Forging a Politics of Mediation* (Oxford: Voltaire Foundation, 2011), 137–49.

Serna, Pierre (ed.), *Républiques sœurs: Le Directoire et la Révolution atlantique*, Actes du colloque de Paris 2008 (Rennes: Presses universitaires de Rennes, 2009).

Turchetti, M. (ed.), *La France et les républiques sœurs en 1798: Invasion ou liberation?* (Geneva, Georg, 2005).

Vovelle, Michel, *Les Républiques sœurs sous le regard de la grande nation, 1795–1803* (Paris: L'Harmattan, 2000).

CHAPTER 3

FRANÇOIS-RENÉ DE CHATEAUBRIAND

Migrations and Revolution

JEAN-MARIE ROULIN
(TRANSLATED BY TRISTA SELOUS)

FRANÇOIS-RENÉ de Chateaubriand (1768–1848) was born under Louis XV and died at the start of the Second Republic, living through French Romanticism from its emergence to its decline. His dates are closer to those of Wordsworth, Coleridge, Foscolo, and even Schiller and Goethe, than Victor Hugo and Alfred de Musset, putting him in the first generation of French Romantics. He belongs to the period between the two centuries, more aesthetically unstable than that of 1830s Romanticism. A contemporary of Germaine de Staël and Benjamin Constant, he was marked, like them, by the experience of the French Revolution. This sets him apart from the Romantics of the 'battle of *Hernani*' (1830), for whom the Revolution was a pre-existing narrative, an inherited source, as Hugo indicates when he speaks of the war in Vendée as one that 'my father fought in'. For Chateaubriand's generation the Revolution was crucial, posing ontological, political, and metaphysical questions—how could that 'river of blood' be crossed, to borrow one of his recurrent metaphors? How could they set sail from the bank of the Ancien Régime? What should the new literature be like, and for what type of society in revolutionized France? Chateaubriand's Romanticism was first of all an answer to these questions, an elegiac adieu to a past forever lost and an uneasy questioning of the future. For a man whose youth was rooted in the eighteenth century and intellectually shaped by the great Enlightenment texts, it was also a critical summation of its philosophical thought, including that of Jean-Jacques Rousseau, who was still the great model, in an ambivalent relationship of admiration combined with resistance. Chateaubriand's seminal debate with de Staël at the dawn of the nineteenth century around perceptions of literary history and the orientations of modern literature was largely focused on what aspects of this Enlightenment legacy should be retained or rejected.

In the early nineteenth century Chateaubriand distilled the essence of French Romanticism in the iconic character of the disillusioned René, who yearns for an elsewhere. Less widely translated and less well known outside France than writers such as Hugo, Chateaubriand was nevertheless at once the most profoundly inspired by modern European literature, from Dante to Ossian, via Torquato Tasso and Shakespeare, and also the least Parisian, even less so than Stendhal, who was involved in the Romantic circles of the 1820s. Before being called *le grand Sachem*, the 'big Chief of Romanticism', Chateaubriand, who rose instantly to prominence in 1802 as the great writer of his generation, was above all a decentred writer. Unbound in time due to his position between two worlds—on the one hand the Ancien Régime and the Enlightenment, on the other the era of democracy and literary modernity—he was also without roots in space, sometimes a Breton nomad with an 'instinct to travel', sometimes an internal émigré. Although he was at the centre of literary life in the Empire, and then of political life in Paris during the Bourbon Restoration, he was always being called away, to America or the East. This is reflected in his work, which is polymorphous and shifts between genres, from essays (*Essai sur les révolutions*) to political writings (*De Buonaparte et des Bourbons*), autobiography infused with history (*Mémoires d'outre-tombe*), novels (*René*, *Atala*), and travel writings (*Voyage en Italie*, *Itinéraire de Paris à Jérusalem*). Yet, paradoxically, although he often felt himself to be on the margins, his literary practice was always rooted in the contemporary world, while his press articles and pamphlets were concerned with current affairs. It was one of his particularities that he played a more important role in political life than any other European Romantic. His formulation of Romanticism and his poetic practice can be understood in terms of two responses to reality, two notions of capital importance to him: migration and revolution.

Migrations and Returns: The Spaces of Chateaubriand's Romanticism

One of the great characteristics of Romanticism was its discovery of new spaces, or new explorations of known spaces that it had invested with subjectivity and imagination. These places shaped the artists' view of the world and, in return, the artists endowed them with aesthetic representations: Goethe with Italy, Hölderlin with Greece, Byron with Switzerland and Greece. In France writers (Nerval, Lamartine) and painters (Delacroix) had a special relationship with Italy and the East. In this respect, Chateaubriand was a pioneer who opened up new perspectives and marks a transition from the encyclopedic travels of the *savant* seeking new forms of knowledge to those of the Romantic traveller who notices landscapes and the picturesque, seeking out the emotions and sensations aroused by exotic worlds through subjective experience of other places. The exploration of new lands and construction of a personal geography, placing the writer in a space where his imagination can unfold, is a profound, structural element of Chateaubriand's oeuvre, in which travel writing occupies pride of place. This is because his global travel relates to an investigation that is at once ontological (what is my position in space?), historical (what are the cultural and religious origins of modern Europe?), political (what social model and political regime should be adopted?), and even metaphysical (does nature bear traces of the divine?). In Chateaubriand's work, human beings are thrown at birth into a world in which they do not necessarily have a designated place, like the child described by Lucretius in a well-known phrase cited in *Mémoires d'outre-tombe* (III, 6): '*Tum porro puer ut saevis projectus ab undis / Navita.*' Travel, at once the ontological condition of the subject and an imposed destiny, offers the possibility of an answer. In the back and forth between exile and return, abandonment and reintegration (Roulin, 1994; Müller, 2013), Chateaubriand's spatial imagination is stretched between an unstable here and elsewheres given consistency by layers of time and symbolic values.

His relationship to space is first of all an experience of rootlessness. Describing his departure for America, aged only 25, in the first books of the *Mémoires d'outre-tombe*, Chateaubriand already identifies with the words from *Childe Harold*: 'Again to sea!'[1] The phrase stands as the motto of his life, with its perpetual travel, and his work, which looks always elsewhere. Symbolically, everything starts with an original rootlessness. Grounded in the ancestral soil of Brittany, the Château de Combourg is established in the *Mémoires d'outre-tombe* as a legendary place of origins. In fact Chateaubriand spent little time there, between 1777 and 1786. The château is a feudal edifice, barely adapted to the comforts of the late eighteenth century, and symbolizes the attachment to lineage and aristocratic pride of his father, descendant of an old Breton family. The château thus becomes the ambivalent symbol of a lineage and its provincial status, greatness and decline. As an outmoded building emptied of inhabitants,[2] Combourg already evokes ruins and Romantic chateaux of the kind described in *René*, or La Vivetière, portrayed by Balzac in *Les Chouans*. Where the occupation of space is concerned, young François-René has a room apart. As the youngest child, he is already decentred within the family home. Despite its obsolescence, the château still has roots in a territory elevated to the status of paradise at a time when the young François-René must leave it forever, borrowing a significant farewell from Milton's *Paradise Lost*, XII. 646: 'The world was all before him.' In the tradition of Dante—one of the poets he most readily cites—Chateaubriand faces the world as a man in an exile that is both geographic and historic, at once Adam and Wandering Jew, since Combourg is a place and also a time of childhood and the Ancien Régime.

Chateaubriand describes his world as characterized by wandering from his first breath, since, before he puts down roots in Breton soil, his birthplace is given as Saint-Malo, in a room with a window overlooking the ocean. Resistant to the enthusiasm for the

[1] Chateaubriand is thinking of Canto III, stanza 2, line 10: 'Once more upon the waters! Yes once more!'

[2] Francesco Orlando, 'La sala troppo vasta', in *Infanzia, memoria e storia da Rousseau ai Romantici* (Padua: Liviana editrice, 1966), 79–105.

Alps that emerged in early European Romanticism, Chateaubriand's spatial imagination was initially maritime—Atlantic, and then Mediterranean. So the young Breton set sail from Saint-Malo on his first great journey to America—one of the few, if not the only Romantic to travel there. His time in America provided him with some of the most original elements of his thought. It was the first major stage in the constitution of his Romantic anthropology. His declared objective was encyclopedic in nature: he intended to follow in the footsteps of the great explorers to discover the North-West Passage; but he also—and perhaps primarily—hoped to find Rousseau's 'good savage' in the inhabitants of the new land. However, on arriving in the United States, Chateaubriand realized that the state of nature was merely a hypothesis and that even the American wilderness was a fallen world. Abandoning Rousseau's vision, he turned towards a more Augustinian view of nature and human beings, marked by the Fall. The *Natchez* cycle, from which *Atala* and *René* were taken, with its superimposed layers of editing apparent in the successive prefaces and variants, illustrates the destruction of the dream of a state of nature, since the characters, both Indians and settlers, are inhabited by Evil. In this cycle René, the founding figure of French Romanticism, updates *Werther* in an American setting. Chateaubriand makes him the vehicle for the issues facing French youth at the dawn of the nineteenth century—an Augustinian unease and the feeling that, due to the historical break of the Revolution, a young nobleman no longer has a place in French society (Barbéris, 1976). René's exile is ontological (a deficit of being), historical (inability to integrate into the new social order), and metaphysical (worry and an inability to find peace in God). This first major anthropological exploration was supplemented by another. In America, Chateaubriand witnessed the dispersal, and indeed disappearance, of Native American tribes under pressure from the settlers. This was bound to resonate with his own feeling, as a product of the minor Breton aristocracy, of belonging to a society that was bound to disappear and being the last of his lineage. Before Fenimore Cooper and *The Last of the Mohicans*, he developed the theme of the death of civilizations and the last survivor. These themes are orchestrated in *Atala*, notably in the epilogue, and in *Les Natchez*. These two major investigations of the Romantic anthropology that developed in the fertile soil of religion and history in France crystallized in America. Emerging in Chateaubriand's American writings, they are a constant presence throughout his work and fuelled French Romanticism.

America was also an opportunity to explore expanses of wilderness, fulfilling aspirations to find new exotic landscapes. It was there that Chateaubriand found his palette and colours, from the 'magnificent picture' of the banks of the Mississippi in the prologue to *Atala*, to the sense of infinity provoked by the vast landscapes or nocturnal descriptions such as the moonlit scene of Atala's funeral. One reason for the immediate success of *Génie du christianisme* in 1802 is undoubtedly Chateaubriand's skilful use of these American scenes, which exerted a fascination over the public of the day through their combination of nostalgia for a lost world and the enchantment created by the exotic landscapes, fauna, and flora. The effect was confirmed some thirty years later by the grandchildren of Charles X, who still remembered the American snakes described in the *Génie*. So Chateaubriand's America was not confined to the epitaph of the good savage or an elegy for lost worlds but, through his use of landscapes to reflect states of the soul, gave impetus to a new relationship between human beings and the spaces they live in. An additional dimension appears in the notes taken by Chateaubriand on 'policed America'. Published later, in *Voyage en Amérique*, these offer an analysis of the emerging democracy and its customs, which can be seen as prolegomena to the systematic study provided some ten years later by Tocqueville in *De la démocratie en Amérique*.

Brought back to Paris by the news of the King's death, Chateaubriand soon set off again as an émigré, exchanging exploratory travels for political exile. He spent the years 1793–1800 in England, in London and Suffolk. These miserable years as a poor émigré also proved highly productive, since they brought him great familiarity with English literature. For a Frenchman in 1793, *Paradise Lost* in particular, which he translated, offered a poetic depiction of Hell that recalled scenes from the Revolution, a comparison made easier by the fact that Milton himself had lived in a period of political disturbance and witnessed another revolution. It was also an example of a Christian epic poem, in contrast to a classical French tradition wary of embracing the marvels of Christianity. From this point of view, the figures of Adam and Eve offered examples of the path to be taken in founding a new literature, as proposed by *Génie du christianisme*. *Paradise Lost* and *Gerusalemme liberata* illustrate the fact that, compared to antiquity, modernity is defined by a greater wealth and depth of feeling, which is the product of Christianity. Chateaubriand was an assiduous reader of not only Milton, but also Shakespeare, Macpherson, and contemporary English writers such as Thomas Gray, Byron, and Beattie. His reading gave rise to an essay published much later, *Essai sur la littérature anglaise*, some chapters of which were subsequently included in *Mémoires d'outre-tombe*. So his years in England enabled Chateaubriand to become familiar with a literature that had a crucial influence on the emergence of French Romanticism, just as Voltaire's time in London had proved fertile a little less than a century before.

It was in a later period, under the Empire, that Chateaubriand discovered the Mediterranean world. Not that he had been unaware of it until then—he knew it well through books by the Latin writers, Virgil foremost among them, with whom he had become familiar during his schooling. But he had not directly encountered the 'classical' landscape. In 1803 he was sent to Rome as *secrétaire de légation* by First Consul Bonaparte, providing him with the opportunity for his own Italian journey. Ideologically and aesthetically, Rome primarily embodied the encounter and synthesis of ancient paganism and Christianity. Chateaubriand's Romanticism was not defined in opposition to antiquity, but sought the reappropriation of the Greek and Latin past by the moderns. His quest for ideal beauty found its full expression in his encounter with the Italian landscape. He was an atypical traveller who also explored the fringes of the *Urbs* and revealed the evocative power of the Roman countryside (Berchet, 1969; Tucci, 2010). Rome, the eternal city, was also paradoxically the city of tombs. The death of his friend of the time Pauline de Beaumont, who died in his arms a few days after a visit to the Coliseum, gave particular resonance to all that the ruins evoked. Henceforth he would identify this city formed of layers of ruins as the place where his memories were rooted, in an autobiography itself grounded in tombs.

In a desire to go back to the Greek and Judaic sources of Western culture in order to reshape the modern world, Chateaubriand took French Romanticism to the East (Berchet, 2006; Guyot and Le Huenen, 2006). As Napoleon's regime grew ever more tyrannical, he devised a tour around the Mediterranean—*Itinéraire de Paris à Jérusalem et de Jérusalem à Paris*, to borrow the title of the resulting travel narrative published in 1811. For Chateaubriand this was as much a journey through time as through space, as the shores of the Mediterranean, charged with history, bore the traces of French travellers, for whom they were both memory and cultural homeland. It was a 'Journey to the self', both because the narrative Chateaubriand drew from it offers a slice of life and because he was exploring the cultural origins of an early nineteenth-century Frenchman (Berchet, 1983). The journey traced a line between Athens and Jerusalem and linked Greek antiquity and Christianity in a movement towards freedom. This was contrasted with Oriental despotism, embodied in the Ottoman Empire and reflected in Napoleon's despotism (Berchet, 1994). Armed with this experience, in the 1820s Chateaubriand became involved in the fight to liberate Greece, as did Byron and other Romantic writers.

While this journey to the sources of European culture and Christianity has political resonance, it would be wrong to see it as no more than a critique of the deviations of the imperial regime. For Chateaubriand is more concerned with the principle that underpins liberty, which for him was Christianity. With its personal tone and the place it gives to the Mediterranean landscape, for example in the meditation at Cap Sounion, *Itinéraire de Paris à Jérusalem* introduces a series of travels to the Orient described by nineteenth-century writers. It was also the source of two pieces of fiction. One was the epic *Les Martyrs* (1809), in which the heroes criss-cross the Mediterranean in a plot that takes them from Arcadia to Judea to the Coliseum in Rome. Their ultimate martyrdom enables them to regain a symbolic lost paradise, as it marks the moment when Christianity was established as the official religion of the Roman Empire. The narrative interweaves pages of Romanticly inclined, wild, rocky, and storm-battered landscapes with more neoclassical descriptions of idyllic places (Berchet, 1986). Written in 1810 but published in 1826, *Les Aventures du dernier Abencérage* describes the Granada of the Reconquista, contrasting the nostalgia of a young Moor exiled from Granada with the uncertainties of a young Catholic who has moved back to Andalusia.

Brittany, America, England, Rome, and the Orient are the spatial components of Chateaubriand's Romanticism; he modulates their significance throughout his work and weaves connections between them. On returning to Rome and London, he evokes his first visits to these cities, linking and comparing two periods of his life. Space is an analogical support in his work, as reflected in the visit of 1833 to Prague Castle (Hradschin), where the old French king, Charles X, was in exile. With its reverberations of time in space, this castle giving refuge to an ageing, deposed monarch has echoes of the Château de Combourg (Richard, 1967). Similarly, Venice, where Chateaubriand paused in 1833, becomes a crossroads and site of an imaginary encounter between Rousseau and Byron. In this forerunner to 'Death in Venice', the city is elevated to an allegory of fading desire, just as Venice itself is irremediably sinking into the waters of the lagoon.

In this interplay of exile and return, Paris gradually becomes the central point. While Chateaubriand spent more time there than in any other place, he was at first an intermittent resident, often away travelling, and on the fringes of the city's life and movements. For René, paraphrasing *La Nouvelle Héloïse*, Paris was 'a vast desert of men'. Chateaubriand was often on the periphery with the status of an internal émigré—both physically, since he chose to live some 15 kilometres to the south in la Vallée-aux-Loups from 1807 to the end of the Empire, and symbolically, as he kept apart from the inner circles of Romanticism formed at the end of the Restoration. He was involved in the political rather than the literary life of Paris, particularly at the time of the publication of *Génie du christianisme* (1802) and during his time as a minister under the Restoration. It could be said that, for Chateaubriand, Paris was primarily the centre of political life, and particularly the Revolution, an event that was central to his life and creativity. Indeed, while the city is largely absent from his fictional oeuvre, in *Mémoires d'outre-tombe* it is the subject of careful descriptions in the great revolutionary scenes, notably the two striking and contrasting tableaux of 1789 and 1792 and the burlesque account of the Revolution of 1830.

Revolution: Political Action and the Understanding of *Histoire*

The French Revolution is key to Chateaubriand's centrifugal life and decentred work, with effects discernible throughout his literary creation (Fumaroli, 2003; Berchet, 2012). As a Catholic nobleman, Chateaubriand found himself on the side of the victims and exiles. Yet, it was the consequences of the upheaval that enabled him to play a prominent political role during the Empire and particularly during the Restoration, when he even became Minister for Foreign Affairs (1822–4). In this way, he bridged the worlds of letters and political affairs in post-revolutionary France; he was one of the driving forces behind the transformation of the writer from *philosophe* and critical observer of social injustice, exemplified by Voltaire, into man of letters involved in the affairs of the day, who was by turns journalist, member of parliament, ambassador, and member of the government (Gracq, 1960). So Chateaubriand's Romanticism is inseparable from political life and history.

In the first place, the Revolution had a direct, decisive impact on his life, and hence on his oeuvre, into which it etches a fundamental tension between exile and return, destruction and new beginnings. In 1789 he was 21 years old, living in Paris, a direct witness to the eruption of the 'climacteric' event. Although he was curious, he was also immediately disturbed by the early manifestations of violence, symbolized, both for him and for other writers like Sénac de Meilhan in *L'Émigré* (1797), by the heads of Foullon and Berthier placed on pikes on 22 July 1789. The slide towards the Terror drove Chateaubriand first to Germany, where he joined French aristocrats preparing for war against the revolutionary government. But his scruples and lucidity in relation to this group are apparent in the depiction of the army of princes in *Mémoires d'outre-tombe*, which criticizes the blind arrogance of the high aristocracy in relation to the inevitable evolution of French society. Wounded and on the verge of death, Chateaubriand set off for London, where he suffered the trials of the impoverished petty aristocracy.

This first phase gave rise to what I shall call the ethos of émigré expression. Chateaubriand's first great prose work, *Essai historique, politique et moral sur les Révolutions*, opens with the question: 'Who am I, and what do I have to tell humanity that is new?' Returning in interrogative form to the introductory question of Rousseau's *Confessions*, Chateaubriand offers a historical answer: the subject speaking these words is defined by the public as a 'suffering actor' of history and 'an émigré'. This exiled speech is also that of the narrators of *René* and *Atala*, who are migrants, and the memorialist whose voice emerges from the final exile 'beyond the grave'. Similarly, Chateaubriand chose to be buried on the small island of Le Grand Bé, separated from Saint-Malo by a narrow stretch of sea—the autobiographical voice speaks from a place of isolation, away from the land, the city, and other human beings. These émigré narrators tell the stories of rootless characters, wandering in search of an impossible return. This sense of exile has its origins in a concrete historical situation, and extends more widely through Chateaubriand's fictions, which are haunted by the theme of emigration (Roulin, 2013). It has an ontological dimension—these exiled characters are seeking their lost identity—and also the metaphysical dimension of human beings who, in Christian anthropology, wander over the earth yearning for paradise. We can see this in René, Chactas, Eudore, and Aben-Hamet, but also, surprisingly, in St Augustine, whom Chateaubriand portrays in *Les Martyrs* as haunted by a desire for elsewhere. So the Revolution gave new resonance to a motif developed notably by Rousseau in *La Nouvelle Héloïse*, giving it a historical dimension and, crucially, new metaphysical depth in an indictment of the Enlightenment's vision of religion.

Chateaubriand's novels are fictions about the Revolution, insofar as they are elegies to a lost world and investigate the identity of human beings thrown into a new society. The French Revolution is never explicitly present in them, but it is there in their patterns of mismatches and decentring. The characters live in worlds turned upside-down, in a state of mutation, bearing the marks of the violence of history: in London René evokes the execution of Charles I, obviously echoing that of Louis XVI; the Granada of *Le Dernier Abencérage* is described during the transition from the Moorish occupation to the Reconquista by the Catholic kings; more clearly, *Les Natchez* depicts Native American tribes rising up against the settlers. Political struggles and internal conflicts are a transposition of the atmosphere of Paris in the revolutionary years. In particular, the descriptions of assemblies are marked by memories of the French Revolution (Principato, 2003; Roulin 2005, 2008), from the assemblies of Native Americans in *Les Natchez* and Roman senators in *Les Martyrs* to the gathering of demons led by Satan, for which the descriptions of hell in *Gerusalemme liberata* and, crucially, Milton's *Pandemonium* provided powerful inspiration.

In a world of violence and ruins it is necessary to start afresh, cross the river, leave the ancient parapets behind and set foot on a new shore—to cite this image again. So the response to migration is a return and new beginnings. *Essai sur les Révolutions*, published in London in 1797, sought to understand the French Revolution using the eighteenth-century historiographic method of parallels. On his return from emigration in 1800, Chateaubriand was arriving in 'France and the century' (*Mémoires d'outre-tombe*, XII, 6). So he saw his return as a new beginning, with an aesthetic and religious programme formulated in *Génie du christianisme*. Resolutely adopting the movement of history, this essay follows the religious reconciliation sought by Napoleon and realized in the Concordat, which restored relations between France and the Holy See. While it is not very original in terms of its apology, its ideological background is clear. In order to lay the foundations of post-revolutionary society, it is necessary to return to the Catholic tradition, which can provide a sound basis for the social and intellectual cohesion of the new France. For the purposes of this argument, Chateaubriand included in his manifesto diverse writings from his travels in America, notably *Atala* and *René*, which appear here as *exempla* of the greatness and benefits of Catholicism. Though they retain a tone of despair, these narratives were the founding texts of what Baudelaire called 'the great school of melancholy established by Chateaubriand'. This melancholy is a product of the human condition, which sees us yearning for the infinite in a finite world, longing for the ideal and bound to reality. In this manifesto of the first wave of Romanticism, Chateaubriand creates an unusual synthesis of nostalgia for a lost France and new possibilities for a different relationship to the world; his argument draws on his experiences as a traveller (the infinite American landscape and the exoticism of American nature) and the culture he acquired during his years as an émigré, identifying French writers—Racine, Fénelon, and Rousseau—and European poets—Tasso, Milton, and Ossian—as the pillars of modern Christian poetry.

Supported notably by his friend Louis de Fontanes, whom he met in London and who later occupied important posts for the First Consul, and following an effective publicity campaign, *Génie* was an instant success, propelling Chateaubriand to the rank of great writer of the day. The fact that his essay perfectly met the expectations of a public hungry for sentiment, who found in it an updated and, more precisely, Catholicized version of Rousseau's tone in *La Nouvelle Héloïse*, also largely explains the great success enjoyed by the book on publication. Offering an ideological understanding of society, art, and literature, *Génie* countered the thesis of perfectibility developed by de Staël's *De la littérature* with a vision of progress and modernity entirely rooted in Christianity, seen as the sole civilizing factor. The debate related to philosophical issues dividing the continuers of the Enlightenment, who were close to the 'Ideologues', from the advocates of a return to Christian fundamentals. It also related to political divisions between the 'liberals' of monarchist, even republican tendencies, and the royalist legitimists. The debate that opened the French literary nineteenth century was thus highly political. The divisions it represented remained present in French Romanticism, which was split between a liberal conception of the modern world espoused by writers such as Stendhal, and a royalist, Catholic vision adopted by the early Hugo (who wanted 'to be Chateaubriand or nothing') and Alfred de Vigny. In *Illusions perdues*, Balzac notes that under the Restoration the liberals were Classics and the royalists Romantics; this is a slightly schematic vision, but has some truth in it.

So the Revolution left deep traces in Chateaubriand's oeuvre and influenced the development of aesthetic conceptions at the dawn of the modern world. It also had another, unexpected and indirect consequence on the direction taken by Chateaubriand's oeuvre and career. For while the Revolution lasted and then gave way to military tyranny, the return of the Bourbons marked a new phase for the French monarchy within the framework of a new 'Charter'. So the Restoration saw the development of regular parliamentary activity, with debates in the chambers and a press that experienced moments of freedom. This crucible led to the involvement of writers in political life that became a characteristic of French culture. The Revolution drove writers to engage in public debate—we can think of, among others, de Staël and Constant—and to speak in the revolutionary assemblies, which were for a while hotbeds of eloquence. Throughout the nineteenth century and on to the illustrious example of Malraux, writers applied their skills to debates in the chambers, the press, and government ministries. Notable among the Romantics were Lamartine, a very active member of parliament during the July Monarchy and Second Republic, and Hugo, member of parliament during the Second Republic and Senator during the Third.

So, on his return to France, Chateaubriand responded to a need created by the Revolution and entered political life, notably through the press in *Mercure de France* (Berchet, 2004). It was primarily after his break with Napoleon in 1804 that his articles took on a political tone, opposing the hardening of the imperial regime. In 1807, in a review of a book by his friend Alexandre de Laborde, Chateaubriand included a sharp, visionary attack against the power of the Emperor: 'Nero prospers in vain; Tacitus was already born under the Empire'—the modern writer portrays himself as the critical historian of the aberrations of his time. But under the Empire the press was muzzled by censorship. So at the start of the Restoration Chateaubriand declared he was abandoning literature and embarked on a 'political career'. He began with pamphlets, such as *De Buonaparte et des Bourbons*, which he later described as worth an army to Louis XVI. Heir to the Enlightenment *philosophes*, who used their pens to criticize contemporary 'affairs', the Romantic Chateaubriand adapted to the new political context and used his eloquence in the service of the public debate, seeing it as a weapon and establishing an activist literature.

With the return of the Bourbons, Chateaubriand had an opportunity to integrate fully into political life. During the fifteen years of the Restoration he was a member of the Chamber of Peers and Minister for Foreign Affairs 1822–4, and also ambassador to Berlin (1821), London (1822), and Rome (1828–9). So he was very actively involved in political life, with some success, notably ensuring that France intervened against the liberals in Spain to restore the power of the Bourbon Ferdinand VII. He was always involved in the machinations of political life, with its makeshift alliances and betrayals. So, although a fairly moderate royalist, he found himself swept by alliances and rivalries into the camp of the Ultras. In these years literary works gave way to writings in response to events—speeches in the chamber and newspaper articles published in *Le Conservateur* (1818–20) and the *Journal des Débats*. Beyond the trivial debates of everyday politics, his constant fight for press freedom is worthy of note. In 1829, hearing that the ultra-royalist Polignac, who opposed press freedom, had been appointed to replace Martignac as President of the Council, Chateaubriand handed his resignation to Charles X, marking the end of his political career. He was very hostile to Louis-Philippe and the July Monarchy (1830–48) and remained outside public life after 1835.

In a context of profound change in France and across Europe during these years, alongside his political activity Chateaubriand engaged in more distanced thinking about the processes of history. The French Revolution had given him a sharp awareness of the weight of history. In the preface to *Études historiques* (1831), he notes: 'Everything today takes the form of history—polemic, theatre, novels, poetry'. This new awareness that individuals are caught up in a collective story much greater than themselves is one of the profound aspects of his work. Reflecting on the influence of this theme, Augustin Thierry declared in the preface to *Récits des Temps mérovingiens* that his vocation as a historian came to him on reading *Les Martyrs*, and particularly the page that describes the Franks going into battle and sounding their war chant—the 'bardit'. Chateaubriand's sensitivity to lost worlds and the passing of time, and his ability to resuscitate vanished peoples, as Jules Michelet put it, were very clearly perceived by young historians at this time when romantic French historiography was just emerging. Chateaubriand was one of the great artisans of a new kind of historicity, ensuring the transition between the *magister vitae* approach to history and a new vision that saw the present as a key for reading the past (Hartog, 2002). Yet, although history is everywhere in Chateaubriand's work, he never completed his great historical projects *Études historiques* and *Analyse raisonnée de l'Histoire de France*. Of the two, the preface to *Études historiques* is the most finished piece, offering a penetrating critical analysis of the French historical schools at the end of the Restoration (Rosi and Roulin, 2009).

Rather than in his historical writings, Chateaubriand's thinking on history is at its most profound in *Mémoires d'outre-tombe*. This autobiography occupied him for many years, as its conception developed towards the perfect integration of self and history. In an early, incomplete version, the book was entitled *Mémoires de ma vie*, linking a life story on the model provided by Rousseau in the *Confessions* to 'memoirs' in the aristocratic tradition of the high-ranking individual providing an account of the historic events of his day. With *Mémoires d'outre-tombe*, Chateaubriand distances himself from Rousseau more explicitly, by refusing to make the book a place for 'confessions', and by integrating himself into the history of his period. At the end of the Restoration, Michelet published an abridged translation of Vico's *Scienza nuova* with the title *Principes de la philosophie de l'histoire*, and Quinet translated Herder's *Idées sur la Philosophie de l'Histoire*, while Ballanche published *Essais de Palingénésie sociale*. Each of these in its way took a symbolic approach to history, influencing Chateaubriand's conception of his autobiography. *Mémoires d'outre-tombe* thus became an 'epic of my time' in a conception summed up in a phrase of the 'testamentary preface': 'In my person portrayed in my memoirs I shall represent principles, ideas, events and disasters, the epic of my time.' Quite unlike the myth of an egocentric Chateaubriand that Stendhal helped to spread, this history of a life is also that of a period; the 'self' is a metonymy for the history of France from the end of the Ancien Régime to the July Monarchy (Berchet, 2005; Cavallin, 2000). The most striking element in this new conception is the place occupied by Napoleon, a man who left an indelible footprint on the century, as Alessandro Manzoni observes in 'Il Cinque Maggio'. Relegating the story of his own life to a secondary level, Chateaubriand includes a remarkable narrative of Napoléon's life in books XIX–XXIV of his memoirs. Though a harsh judge of the despot and soldier greedy for conquest and careless of human lives, he is sensitive to Napoleon's legendary dimension and the greatness of actions that seemed to lift him above the destiny of common mortals. The escape from the island of Elba and Napoleon's return to Paris in 1814 are among the finest pages on the Napoleonic myth. This man who embodied his century and symbolized it in himself is described by the shadowy figure of the memorialist who nevertheless wields the power of the pen. From the encounter between the two emerge both the spirit of Empire and two figures of Romantic mythology—the Promethean genius and the prophetic writer. In *Génie du christianisme*, Chateaubriand suggested that, when it comes to history, the French have only memoirs. At the end of this career he was himself an eminent example of this, introducing a profound change in the relationship between the self and history in French autobiography.

A Poetics of Prose: Turbulent Times, Vain Desires

Chateaubriand's early works are contemporary with 'Weimar classicism'. Although he had very few contacts with German literary circles—apart from reading *Die Leiden des jungen Werthers* of course—he shares with the Goethe of that period the aspiration to an updated form of classicism, in an aesthetic approach marked by Winckelmann's thought. Influenced by Fontanes among others, Chateaubriand centres his aesthetics on the cult of ideal beauty and the search for noble simplicity. His great familiarity with the Latin authors, particularly Virgil, led him to seek out this ancient simplicity, finding concrete materials and images in the form of landscapes, monuments, and sculptures on his trip to Rome. In French painting David and his pupils drew on antiquity to glorify first the Revolution, then the Empire. Although Chateaubriand took this aesthetics down a different path, he can be said to manifest a literary neoclassicism (Saliceto, 2013), not in the sense of a return to the classicism of the seventeenth century, but insofar as founding a modern literature required the Ancients to be assimilated. His sense that history was tending towards tragedy and fragmentation led him to give art a custodial mission as the royal road to new beginnings. The ideological significance of Chateaubriand's neoclassicism thus sets it apart from references to antiquity and the persistence of classicism to be found in the work of later French Romantic writers, such as Théophile Gautier and

Baudelaire. As in the work of Goethe—and to draw on the presence of two great works associated with the figure of Werther—in Chateaubriand's work there is a Homer side and an Ossian side. This can be seen particularly in his epic *Les Martyrs*, part of which unfolds in the classical landscape of Arcadia, where Christians and pagans, the Bible and Homer, coexist in harmony, whereas the storm-battered landscape of Armorica is conversely embodied by Velléda, a priestess carried away by the torments of her desires. This thematic division between the Mediterranean and the Atlantic reflects the contrasting poetic options of ideal beauty and the energy of images, and is present throughout Chateaubriand's literary work.

Secondly, Chateaubriand is unusual within French and indeed European Romanticism for his choice of literary genres. As a young man he wrote a few poems and later a verse tragedy, *Moïse*, but, like Stendhal, he was primarily a prose writer. However, unlike Balzac, who identified with the novel, and more similar to de Staël, Chateaubriand explored several genres—the novel, travel writing (Antoine, 1997), and autobiography—reshaping them each time. This is most eloquently illustrated by his successive transformations of *Les Natchez* and *Les Martyrs*—novels in one version, epics in another, and even both, as with *Les Natchez*, which was published late, in 1826, the first part in epic form and the second part as a novel. Underpinning this shift between genres was his prose style. Following the great prose writers of the eighteenth century—Fénelon, whose *Les Aventures de Télémaque* remained exemplary, Rousseau, and even Bernardin de Saint-Pierre—Chateaubriand gave his prose a poetic dimension (Moore, 2009). It is characterized by a sharp sense of rhythm, no doubt inherited from his constant reading of the Latin authors, a very free use of syntax (Mourot, 1960), a rich and highly inventive lexical palette and a very powerful use of images, again showing traces of his reading of classics including Homer, Virgil, Racine, and Bossuet, and also Dante, Shakespeare, Tasso, and Milton. Chateaubriand's strength lies in his art of descriptive prose, whether for pamphlet or elegy. He is primarily an assembler of mosaics, as can be seen from his reuse of sequences. His description of the American night reappears several times in different genres, illustrating the porosity of genre boundaries.

With this prose Chateaubriand introduces a new relationship to the world, which underpins his poetics. Although he rejected a materialist vision, leaving the French Enlightenment behind, he did not reject the substance of the world along with it. He was trying instead to establish a different relationship, a new alliance, which would displace rational, scientific approaches in favour of a sensitive, emotional, and symbolic understanding of things. In short, he was seeking to restore the full power of the imagination (Porter, 1978). So, in *Génie du christianisme*, he criticizes Voltaire for failing to use the evocative power of landscapes and forests in *La Henriade*. Chateaubriand's imagery is dominated by two great underlying themes: time and desire. These are ontological themes, because they involve a definition of the individual and his relationship to the world.

Chateaubriand was above all a writer of time. First of course because the Revolution effected a sharp break in the continuity of time. Secondly because the Enlightenment had introduced the idea of progress and perfectibility, requiring writers of the new generation to adopt a position in relation to those ideas and to reformulate them. This raised the central issues to which French Romanticism constantly returned: the desire to resurrect the past and restore the lost heritage—we can think of Nerval's fascination with old French tunes—and to understand evolution as a tension between progress and backward steps, between *corsi* and *ricorsi*. Chateaubriand's poetics approach these issues directly and powerfully, first in the language itself. The textual fabric is a marquetry of quotations, a library of reassembled fragments; his lexicon is deliberately heterogeneous, boldly combining archaisms and neologisms; narration in the present brings both past and future into an unstable present. In this way the narrator becomes a figure of time, as a synthetic phrase indicates: 'I'm no longer anything but time' (*Vie de Rancé*). This is also why vanity, in the philosophical and pictorial sense, is central to Chateaubriand's work (Verlet, 2001), often expressed in references to the book of Job, from which he took the epigraph of *Mémoires d'outre-tombe*: '*Sicut nubes ... quasi naves ... uelut umbra*'. Similarly, his preferred season is autumn, the time of storms and falling leaves.

Proust took from Chateaubriand his ability to transform everyday life, both ordinary and historical, into something immortal, and his expression of involuntary memory. The song of a thrush that Chateaubriand hears in the grounds of the Château de Montboissier, suddenly recalling his childhood, has been read as an important precursor to the famous episode of the madeleine in *À la Recherche du temps perdu*. In its development of a poetics of memory—a palimpsest memory (Sheringham, 2000)—*Mémoires d'outre-tombe* is an elegiac resurrection of childhood time spent in a family and social context that are gone forever, and of the entire period through which Chateaubriand lived. This fresco of the past leads, in the final pages, to a prophetic vision of 'the future of the world'. The encounter with distant times is grounded in a shifting, unstable present. It is moreover one of the most remarkable, recurring traits of *Mémoires d'outre-tombe* that it associates different periods and combines them on the same page, in a manner reminiscent of Calder's mobiles, creating improbable temporal syntheses.

This world made ungraspable by the passing of time is nevertheless intensely *desired*: in a profound way Chateaubriand is a writer of desire. His characters combine two antithetical qualities—melancholic lifelessness and the force of desire. The melancholic René longs for an object, an 'Eve drawn from myself'; Amélie struggles with her passion for her brother by withdrawal; Atala escapes her powerfully carnal love for Chactas by suicide; Cymodocée and Eudore are drawn to each other, but place their longing for another life higher still (Bercegol, 2009). The initial erotic desire is not without sensuality and fantasy (Glaudes, 1994).

If passion and lifelessness are inseparable, it is because there is always a mismatch between the desire and its object: 'The imagination is rich, abundant and wonderful, life is poor, dry and disenchanted. With a full heart, we inhabit an empty world.' There is always an awareness that the world cannot fully respond to the individual's yearnings: 'Rise quickly, desired storms which will sweep René away to the spaces of another world!' exclaims René, in a cry that can be read as an appeal to God. Similarly, and at the risk of countering orthodoxy, Augustin in *Les Martyrs* and Rancé in *La Vie de Rancé* are Christians tormented by lack of satisfaction, filled with unease and longing for another world amid the disappointments of reality. Chateaubriand the traveller is also split between contemplation of the sensory world and disenchantment. In the *Itinéraire de Paris à Jérusalem*, the narrative of the visit to Sparta—a name invested with strong desire—tells of disillusion at the absence of any trace of the vanished city. His writing often adopts a poetics of the negative, in which things and beings are named to state their absence (Roulin, 1997). The sylphide, a mythical feminine spirit of the air borrowed from the Comte de Gabalis and Rousseau, returns several times in Chateaubriand's work. She embodies the power of desire and the fleeting nature of its object. When the sylphide is caught, she loses her wings. It is significant that this figure was the subject of the first Romantic ballet performed in Paris in 1832—she is the emblem of a Romantic vision of an ungraspable ideal (Roulin, 1987).

Yet, in this disappointing world of negativity, there are also moments of plenitude when time stops for a while, as Lamartine describes in 'Le Lac'. Significantly, for Chateaubriand such moments are nocturnal—night among the American Savages, the night that follows the death of Atala, a night at Cap Sounion and the moonlit landscapes of the Roman countryside. Chateaubriand was a master of the literary nocturne, the musical equivalent of which was developed during those years by John Field and then Chopin. Proust observes as much in a passage that hits the nail on the head despite its sarcasm. In *À l'ombre des jeunes filles en fleurs*, Mme de Villeparisis speaks of great writers she has known, telling the narrator that Chateaubriand always recited the same page on 'moonlight in the Roman countryside'.

More profoundly, in the mismatch between the fragmentation of time and memory, the calls of desire and the deceptive nature of reality, Chateaubriand develops a poetics of fragments and analogy. Memory and the imagination form the link that is missing from the world, establishing continuity in discontinuity. The structure of *Mémoires d'outre-tombe* in many fairly short chapters expresses the fragmentary, exploded nature of his life. As the text unfolds, characters, places, and circumstances call up other characters, places, and circumstances in a sometimes frantic process of analogy. The world is a universe of signs that refer to each other in perpetual motion, a theatre of shadows in search of embodiment. It is in the written expression of the analogical imagination that reality acquires consistency and depth. *Vie de Rancé*, written in Chateaubriand's old age and often read as his most 'modern' work, provides the supreme illustration of this poetics. What gives the text coherence is not the dismantled syntax of broken sentences, which Gracq describes as written 'in Morse code' (1960) and Barthes calls frantic anacolutha (1965)—but the very free associations of an unbridled imagination. This power of the imagination to make analogies and create metaphors is one of the most profound and original features of Chateaubriand's oeuvre.

Instantly acknowledged as a great writer in 1802, Chateaubriand was nevertheless absent from the circles and debates of 1820s Romanticism. He died in 1848, leaving as his last work *Mémoires d'outre-tombe*, which found little appreciation when published. So he was not part of the great period of French Romanticism, which developed later than elsewhere in Europe. He was nevertheless one of its most fertile sources of inspiration, whose traces can be seen in the work of many writers, including Balzac and Baudelaire. It was only at the very end of the nineteenth century, with Edmond Biré's new edition of the *Mémoires d'outre-tombe*, that Chateaubriand's work began to resonate fully, finding its best echoes in Proust. In Europe his work did not have the resonance that it deserved, unlike that of Goethe, Byron, and other great Romantics. This lack of echoes remains to be examined, particularly at a time of growing interest in Chateaubriand's writngs among translators. In our own period of revolutions and migrations, his particular Romanticism, in which literature, politics, and history entwine in a global vision of the world, is acquiring a new resonance.

Further Reading

Antoine, Philippe, *Les Récits de voyage de Chateaubriand: contribution à l'étude d'un genre* (Paris: Champion, 1997).

Barbéris, Pierre, *Chateaubriand une réaction au monde moderne* (Paris: Larousse, 1976).

Barthes, Roland, 'Chateaubriand: *Vie de Rancé*' (1965), in *Le Degré zéro de l'écriture* (Paris: Seuil 'Points', 1972), 106–20.

Bercegol, Fabienne, *Chateaubriand, une poétique de la tentation* (Paris: Classiques Garnier, 2009).

Bercegol, Fabienne, and Glaudes, Pierre (eds), *Chateaubriand et le récit de fiction* (Paris: Classiques Garnier, 2013).

Berchet, Jean-Claude, 'Chateaubriand et le paysage classique', in *Chateaubriand e l'Italia* (Rome: Academia nazionale dei Lincei, Quaderno, 133, 1969), 67–85.

Berchet, Jean-Claude, 'Chateaubriand poète de la nuit', in *Chateaubriand. Actes du congrès de Wisconsin* (Geneva: Droz, 1970), 45–62.

Berchet, Jean-Claude, 'De Paris à Jérusalem ou le voyage vers soi', *Poétique*, 53 (1983), 93–108.

Berchet, Jean-Claude, 'Et in Arcadia ego!', *Romantisme*, 51 (1986), 85–103.

Berchet, Jean-Claude, 'Chateaubriand et le despotisme oriental', *Dix-huitième siècle*, 26 (1994), 391–421.

Berchet, Jean-Claude, 'Le *Mercure de France* et la "Renaissance des Lettres"', in J.-C. Bonnet (ed.), *L'Empire des Muses* (Paris: Belin, 2004), 21–58.

Berchet, Jean-Claude, 'Les *Mémoires d'outre-tombe*: Une autobiographie symbolique', in D. Zanone (ed.), *Le Moi, l'histoire, 1789–1848* (Grenoble: ELLUG, 2005), 39–69.

Berchet, Jean-Claude (ed.), *Le Voyage en Orient de Chateaubriand* (Houilles: Manucius, 2006).

Berchet, Jean-Claude, *Chateaubriand* (Paris: Gallimard, 2012).

Cavallin, Jean-Christophe, *Chateaubriand mythographe: Autobiographie et allégorie dans les* Mémoires d'outre-tombe (Paris: Champion, 2000).

Fumaroli, Marc, *Chateaubriand: Poésie et terreur* (Paris: de Fallois, 2003).

Glaudes, Pierre, Atala, *le désir cannibale* (Paris: PUF, 1994).

Gracq, Julien, 'Le Grand Paon' (1960), in *Préférences, Œuvres complètes* (Paris: Gallimard Pléiade, 1989), i. 914–26.

Guyot, Alain, and Le Huenen, Roland, *L'*Itinéraire de Paris à Jérusalem *de Chateaubriand: L'invention du voyage romantique* (Paris: PUPS, 2006).

Hartog, François, 'Chateaubriand: Entre l'ancien et le nouveau régime d'historicité', in *Régimes d'historicité: Présentisme et expérience du temps* (Paris: Seuil, 2003), 77–107.

Moore, Fabienne, 'Chateaubriand's *Atala*', in *Prose Poems of the French Enlightenment* (Farnham: Ashgate, 2009), 223–37.

Mourot, Jean, *Le Génie d'un style: Chateaubriand. Rythme et sonorité dans les* Mémoires d'outre-tombe (Paris: A. Colin, 1960).

Müller, Olaf, 'Exil als Schreibort: Chateaubriand und das Porträt des Autors als Exilant', in *Literatur im Exil: Zur Konstitution romantischer Auorschaft in Frankreich und Italien* (Frankfurt am Main: V. Klostermann, 2012), 265–341.

Orlando, Francesco, 'La sala troppo vasta', in *Infanzia, memoria e storia da Rousseau ai Romantici* (Padua: Liviana editrice, 1966), 79–105.

Porter, Charles, *Chateaubriand: Composition, Imagination and Poetry* (Saratoga: Anma libri, 1978).

Principato, Aurelio, 'L'*Essai historique* et l'épopée de sauvages en vis-à-vis', *Bulletin de la société Chateaubriand*, 46 (2003), 33–45.

Richard, Jean-Pierre, *Paysage de Chateaubriand* (Paris: Seuil, 1967).

Rosi, Ivanna, and Roulin, Jean-Marie, *Chateaubriand, penser et écrire l'Histoire* (Saint-Étienne: PUSE, 2009).

Roulin, Jean-Marie, 'La Sylphide, rêve romantique', *Romantisme*, 58 (1987), 23–38.

Roulin, Jean-Marie, *Chateaubriand, l'exil et la gloire: Du roman familial à l'identité littéraire dans l'œuvre de Chateaubriand* (Paris: Champion, 1994).

Roulin, Jean-Marie, 'Le Travail de la négation: L'Ombre et le reflet', in *Chateaubriand e i* Mémoires d'Outre-Tombe (Pisa andGeneva, ETS/Slatkine, 1998), 129–45.

Roulin, Jean-Marie, 'Chateaubriand: Une "parole nouvelle de politique et de poésie"', in *L'Epopée de Voltaire à Chateaubriand: Poésie, histoire et politique*, Studies on Voltaire and the Eighteenth Century (Oxford: Voltaire Foundation, 2005), 181–207.

Roulin, Jean-Marie, 'Assemblées et discours dans *Les Natchez* et *Les Martyrs* de Chateaubriand: Fictions de la Révolution', *Dix-huitième siècle*, 40 (2008), 665–82.

Roulin, Jean-Marie, 'Chateaubriand: La Fiction émigrée', in F. Bercegol and P. Glaudes (eds), *Chateaubriand et le récit de fiction* (Paris: Garnier, 2013), 229–43.

Saliceto, Elodie, *Dans l'atelier néoclassique: Ecrire l'Italie de Chateaubriand à Stendhal* (Paris: Classiques Garnier, 2013).

Sheringham, Michael, 'La Mémoire-palimpseste dans les *Mémoires d'outre-tombe*', in J.-C. Berchet and P. Berthier (eds), *Chateaubriand mémorialiste* (Geneva: Droz, 2000), 119–31.

Tucci, Patrizio, 'Introduzione', in F.-R. de Chateaubriand, *Viaggio in Italia*, ed. P. Tucci (Rome: Carocci, 2010), 9–59.

Vasarri, Fabio, *Chateaubriand et la gravité du comique* (Paris: Classiques Garnier, 2012).

Verlet, Agnès, *Les Vanités de Chateaubriand* (Geneva: Droz, 2001).

CHAPTER 4

STENDHAL

FRANCESCO MANZINI

MARIE-HENRI Beyle (1783–1842) only properly became a writer once the collapse of the French Empire in 1814 had brought his career within its civil and military bureaucracy to an abrupt halt.[1] It is often forgotten just how successful this first career had been. In 1810, Beyle had been appointed as an *auditeur* within the Imperial Conseil d'État; in 1812, he had followed Napoleon to Moscow and then back again, serving—by all accounts, including of course his own[2]—with no little distinction during the horrific winter retreat; in 1813, he had been appointed as the *intendant* of Sagan (Żagań) in Silesia; thereafter he had returned to his native Grenoble to help organize an improvised defence of the city. But in 1815, during the Hundred Days that followed Napoleon's dramatic return from exile in Elba, Beyle stayed put in Milan, the city he was coming to think of as his spiritual home.[3] Unlike Fabrice Del Dongo, the quixotic young hero of *La Chartreuse de Parme* (1839), Beyle did not leave Lombardy in order to join Napoleon at Waterloo. Rather, he continued to devote his energies to literature. For the end of Beyle's administrative career had in fact been experienced as a release: 'Qui le croirait! quant à moi personnellement, la chute me fit plaisir' (Who would believe it! As for me personally, the fall gave me pleasure) (*OI* ii. 540).

At the end of January 1815, Beyle had brought out a first work, his partly plagiarized lives of Haydn, Mozart, and Metastasio, under the self-consciously absurd pseudonym

[1] In the *Vie de Henry Brulard* (1836), Stendhal observes that: 'Je tombai avec Nap[oléon] en avril 1814. Je vins en Italie vivre comme dans la rue d'Angivilliers.' (I fell along with Nap[oleon] in April 1814. I came to Italy to live as I had lived in the Rue d'Angivilliers.) In other words, he resumed the life he had led in Paris in the first years of the century, studying literary and other texts with a view to one day becoming a writer. See Stendhal, *Œuvres intimes*, ed. Victor Del Litto, 2 vols (Paris: Gallimard Pléiade, 1981–2), ii. 540 (hereafter *OI*).

[2] See Prosper Mérimée, *H.B.*, in *Carmen et treize autres nouvelles*, ed. Pierre Josserand (Paris: Gallimard Folio, 1965), 447–9 (hereafter *H.B.*) and *OI* ii. 979.

[3] Beyle first discovered the delights of Milan as a soldier in 1800. Thereafter, he returned to the city periodically until his definitive expulsion by the Austrian authorities in 1821. Stendhal's two projected epitaphs, dated by him to 1820 and 1821 respectively, sought to fix his identity in death as either 'Errico Beyle Milanese' (*OI* ii. 472) or 'Arrigo Beyle Milanese' (*OI* ii. 981).

of Louis-Alexandre-César Bombet.[4] It was almost as though this first publication were intended as a joke in which he himself served as a kind of punchline—*Armance* (1827), his first novel, can be read as another such joke, again very much on its author. Thereafter, Beyle continued to work on his *Histoire de la peinture en Italie*, first conceived of in 1811. This work finally appeared in 1817, attributed to M. B. A. A. [Monsieur Beyle Ancien Auditeur]: as we shall see, it is telling that Beyle should have sought to present himself as qualified to pronounce on the art of the Italian Renaissance by his administrative rank.[5] Later that same year, he published *Rome, Naples et Florence en 1817*. Now, for the first time, Beyle passed himself off as 'M. de Stendhal, officier de cavalerie' (M. de Stendhal, cavalry officer). Thereafter, insofar as Beyle came to be known in his own lifetime, it was as Stendhal.[6] And it is Stendhal, the elusive Beyle's artfully constructed authorial persona, that Stendhalians study and (like to think they) get to know.

The pseudonym is derived from the Prussian town of Stendal, and possibly also from Mme de Staël, the author of *De l'Allemagne* (1810), one of the most important French texts to theorize Romanticism. The pseudonym could, characteristically, be read in two quite different ways. M. de Stendhal might be a Prussian officer with (nearly) perfect French.[7] Or he might be a Napoleonic officer, rewarded for his valour in the field with a title alluding to the military conquest of German territory (the pseudonym occasionally appears as 'le baron de Stendhal'). If the former, the German name, made more obviously Germanic by its extra 'h', hinted at the author's possible Romanticism, for Romanticism was often construed in France, not least after Mme de Staël, as a German phenomenon. Stendhal's *Mina de Vanghel* (1831) represents just such an officer—the eponymous heroine's francophile father—as an enthusiastic devotee of Kant and Fichte, entirely given over to philosophy and the pleasures of the imagination. But Henri Beyle, as he set about constructing Stendhal, sought to lay claim to expertise not just in German but in European Romanticism more generally.

Stendhal spent much of his considerable free time between his expulsion from Milan in 1821 and the 1830 Revolution—after which he resumed his bureaucratic career at a much lower level, as the seemingly feckless French Consul General in Civitavecchia, an uninspiring port not quite near enough to Rome—posing as an expert on Romanticism, whether German, English, Scottish, or Italian. In 1816, he had met Byron in Milan: he went on to publish an opportunistic and inaccurate account of this meeting—*Lord*

[4] Stendhal enjoyed combining the grandiose with the absurd. The names of Louis XIV, Alexander the Great, and Julius Caesar are here combined to portentous effect, only to be rendered absurd by the bathetically bourgeois and bombastic Bombet.

[5] Elaine Williamson has argued that Stendhal's habit of borrowing from the work of others can be related to the training he received in the bureaucratic art of preparing reports synthesizing existing opinion. See *Stendhal et la Hollande*, ed. Elaine Williamson (London: IGRS, 1996).

[6] Stendhal is only one of more than 170 pseudonyms that Beyle is known to have used in the course of his life. See the often reprinted list compiled by Paul Léautaud. See also Jean Starobinski, 'Stendhal pseudonyme', in *L'Œil vivant* (Paris: Gallimard, 1961), for a classic account of Stendhal's obsession with pseudonyms, masks, and disguises.

[7] Balzac, Hugo Flaubert, and Proust all note that Stendhal wrote French incorrectly. See Georges Kliebenstein, *Figures du destin stendhalien* (Paris: Presses Sorbonne Nouvelle: 2004), 61.

Byron en Italie (1830)—contradicted, point by point, by Byron's friend John Hobhouse. In Milan, he also crossed paths with Alessandro Manzoni and Vincenzo Monti and became rather better acquainted with other luminaries of Italian Romanticism connected to the Milanese literary journal *Il Conciliatore*, most notably Silvio Pellico and the critic Ludovico di Breme. In 1816, Stendhal had also devoted time to reading more about Romanticism in the *Edinburgh Review*: inspired by this example, he wrote his own unpublished survey of the field: *Qu'est-ce que le romanticisme* [*sic*] (1818). Once back in Paris, he published two brief polemical tracts theorizing and defending Romanticism—*Racine et Shakspeare* [*sic*] (1823) and *Racine et Shakspeare* [*sic*] *II* (1825). He completed a further survey, dealing once again with several major figures of European Romanticism, in *Les Gens dont on parle* (1829). The latter text, unpublished in his lifetime, came at the end of what has often been regarded as Stendhal's Romantic phase, assuming, as many have done, that the publication of his second novel, *Le Rouge et le Noir* (1830), marked the start of some new realist phase. In the words of D. G. Charlton, Stendhal's 'maturer work ... is commonly felt to overflow, to transcend, the category of "Romantic prose fiction"'.[8] Yet in this chapter, I shall be arguing that *Le Rouge* is at least as Romantic as it is Realist and that this novel, as well as many of Stendhal's subsequent literary productions across a wide variety of genres, not only maintained his dialogue with various currents of European Romanticism, but also reflected his ongoing, highly critical engagement with the multiple strands of French Romanticism.

Stendhal was a very odd kind of Romantic and in some ways not a Romantic at all, just as he was a very odd kind of realist, and in some ways not a realist at all. Another way of putting this is that he was by turns, or even at one and the same time, a Romantic *and* a realist, for, in his fiction, he is forever treading a line between idealism and irony, ascribing value both to the Romantic illusions of an overheated imagination and to the cold truths produced by a calculating and logical apprehension of 'le réel' (the real). This doubling of authorial point of view is characteristic of Stendhal's approach in general: the preface to *Armance* turns in large part around a discussion of such a doubling of perspective, presumably as a way of preparing the reader for what remains to this day one of the most oddly and frustratingly indeterminate novels ever written.[9] More generally, Stendhal's works are forever setting up tensions between rival perspectives, whether those of men and women,[10] Parisians and provincials, the French and Italians (or Germans), the young and the old, aristocrats and commoners; or between perspectives

[8] D. G. Charlton (ed.), *The French Romantics* (Cambridge: Cambridge University Press, 1984), i. 13.

[9] As Stendhal puts it, 'la même chose, chacun la juge d'après sa position' (everybody judges the same thing from his or her standpoint). See Stendhal, *Œuvres romanesques complètes*, ed. Yves Ansel et al., 3 vols (Paris: Gallimard Pléiade, 2005–14), i. 85 ('Avant-propos', *Armance*; hereafter *ORC*). See also Jean-Jacques Hamm, *'Armance' ou la liberté de Stendhal* (Paris: Champion, 2009) for an account of *Armance* as a novel that deliberately sets out never to answer the many questions posed by its narrative.

[10] See Maria Scott, *Stendhal's Less-Loved Heroines: Fiction, Freedom, and the Female* (Oxford: Legenda, 2013) for a brilliant account of Stendhal's inscriptions of female perspectives. See also Richard Bolster, *Stendhal, Balzac et le féminisme romantique* (Paris: Minard, 1970) and Leslie W. Rabine, *Reading the Romantic Heroine: Text, History, Ideology* (Ann Arbor: University of Michigan Press, 1985).

informed by cynicism and innocence, boldness and timidity, hypocrisy and sincerity, irony and idealism, reason and feeling.[11] As Scott points out, for Stendhal, writing in *De l'Amour* (1822), 'il y a peut-être autant de façons de sentir parmi les hommes que de façons de voir' (where humans are concerned, there are perhaps as many different ways of feeling as there are ways of seeing).[12]

It is the tension between perspectives differentially informed by reason and feeling that should interest us most here, for it is this that helps explain the striking unromanticism of Stendhal's Romantic texts or, if one prefers, the striking Romanticism of his unromantic (Realist?) texts, depending, of course, on one's point of view. In *H.B.* (1850), a character sketch of his late friend, Prosper Mérimée observes that 'toute sa vie [Beyle] fut dominé par son imagination, et ne fit rien que brusquement et d'enthousiasme. Cependant il se piquait de n'agir jamais que conformément à la raison. "Il faut en tout se guider par la LO-GIQUE", disait-il en mettant un intervalle entre la première syllabe et le reste du mot' (all his life, [Beyle] was dominated by his imagination, and never did anything if not impulsively and out of enthusiasm. Nevertheless, he prided himself in never acting other than in accordance with the dictates of reason. 'One must always take LO-GIC as one's guide', he would say, pausing between the first syllable and the rest of the word).[13] On the one hand, Stendhal's love of logic and reason led him to decry what he refers to as 'l'emphase germanique et romantique' (German and Romantic bombast) (*ORC* i. 87, 'Avant-propos', *Armance*). On the other hand, Stendhal identified his own brand of Romanticism with the enthusiasm and idealism of the young, as well as with (Germanic) imagination, frequently contrasted with the relative 'a-imagination' (complete absence of imagination) of a prosaic and utilitarian nineteenth-century France.[14] Mérimée appears to find such inconsistency baffling; yet Stendhal's infuriating or very funny *inconséquence*—depending, of course, on one's point of view—can be seen as a highly conscious strategy. To understand this strategy, we must turn to the earliest origins of French Romanticism, not German, Italian, English, or even Scottish, but Genevan.

A-imagination tells the story of Robert Macaire, a stock character made famous by the satirical plays of Frédérick Lemaître and the caricatures of Honoré Daumier deriding the cynical values of the age. It opens as follows:

> L'âme passionnée, le jeune Jean-Jacques [Rousseau] s'attache aux prédictions de son imagination, Robert ne fait cas de ce qu'il voit.

[11] See Roger Pearson, *Stendhal's Violin* (Oxford: Clarendon Press, 1988) for perceptive discussions of many of these rival perspectives. See also Michel Crouzet, *Stendhal et l'italianité: Essai de mythologie romantique* (Paris: Corti, 1982) for a detailed account of Stendhal's construction of an Italian perspective.

[12] See Maria Scott, 'Stendhal, Mathilde et le regard oblique', in Johnnie Gratton and Derval Conroy (eds), *L'Œil écrit* (Geneva: Slatkine, 2005), 221.

[13] See *H.B.* 444–5.

[14] See, in addition to *Mina de Vanghel*, the short story *A-imagination* (1838).

> ... L'auteur voulait il y a dix ans faire un jeune homme tendre et honnête, il l'a fait ambitieux, mais encore rempli d'imagination et d'illusion dans Julien Sorel [the hero of *Le Rouge et le Noir*].
>
> Il prétend faire Robert absolument sans imagination, autre que celle qui sert à inventer des tours pour parvenir à la fortune.
>
> Passionate souls, such as the young Jean-Jacques [Rousseau], fix their attention on the predictions made by their imaginations. Robert only pays attention to what he can see before his eyes
>
> ... Ten years ago, this author tried to write the story of a tender and honest young man. He made this young man ambitious, but still full of illusion and imagination, in the shape of Julien Sorel.
>
> He now wishes to make Robert completely lacking in imagination except insofar as it helps him to come up with the confidence tricks by which he hopes to make his fortune. (*ORC* iii. 3)

As late as 1838, therefore, Stendhal was still associating the Romantic quality of imagination, as exhibited by his own Julien Sorel, with the example provided by Rousseau. However, Stendhal's view of Rousseau was as ambivalent as his view of Romanticism more generally.

As a very young man, Beyle appears to have been uncritically enthusiastic about the Citizen of Geneva; the slightly older Beyle found such enthusiasm worrying and potentially unhealthy. In 1804, Beyle first formulated the ambition to 'se *dérousseauiser*' (un-Rousseau himself): he decided to do so by throwing himself into a study of the French Idéologues, especially the work of Destutt de Tracy.[15] Beyle aimed thereby to acquire a hard-headed, scientific understanding of men and women in order to counteract what he felt to be the extravagant madness of Rousseauian idealism, misanthropy, and paranoia. But this is not to suggest that Beyle, and thereafter Stendhal, sought to reject Rousseau outright. The latter remained safely ensconced in Stendhal's personal pantheon, alongside Mme Roland (herself an ardent disciple of Rousseau), Napoleon, and Louis-Gabriel Gros (the young Beyle's republican mathematics teacher). To this list would eventually be added Adrien Lafargue (a murderer).[16]

Rousseau's continuing status as an exemplar for Stendhal's protagonists to emulate is significant for our purposes because the French Romantic emphasis on feeling derived in large part from his writings, and was used by Romanticism in the early years of the nineteenth century to challenge the uncompromising rationalism of the Idéologues

[15] Destutt's *Élements d'idéologie* (1801–15) built on the work of 18th-cent. sensationalists in order to found a new science of ideas. See Victor Del Litto, *La Vie intellectuelle de Stendhal: Genèse et évolution de ses idées (1802–1821)* (Paris: PUF, 1959) for a classic account of Stendhal's engagement with such ideas. See also Fernand Rude, *Stendhal et la pensée sociale*, 2nd edn (Brionne: Monfort, 1983) for an overview of Stendhal's interest in political economy. Stendhal eventually became friends with Destutt, frequenting his Parisian salon in the 1820s.

[16] Stendhal agreed with the Italian playwright Vittorio Alfieri that, in a debased 19th cent., violent criminals alone possessed 'âmes ardentes supérieures à toute crainte'. See Stendhal, *Voyages en Italie*, ed. Victor Del Litto (Paris: Gallimard Pléiade, 1973), 426 (hereafter *VI*).

to whose work Beyle was devoting his free time (Destutt de Tracy never quite made it onto the top table of Stendhalian exemplars). Just as Stendhal's interest in Ideology was intended to cure him of the worst excesses of Rousseauian idealism, so Rousseau's writings continued to serve as checks on the worst excesses of Stendhal's potentially reductive rationalism.

Stendhal's Romanticism, so often buried beneath multiple layers of irony, suddenly reveals itself when he represents uncontrollably irrupting feeling overturning all the careful analysis of reason. An authorial comment in the margins of the manuscript of *Lucien Leuwen*—detailing Lucien's unexpected overturning of his father's plans to embroil him in an affair in Paris and so keep his mind off Bathilde de Chasteller, the woman he (thinks he) loves—captures this Romantic process of devastation: 'tout le plan de M. Leuwen est barbarement renversé' (M. Leuwen's entire plan is barbarously overturned) (*ORC* ii. 934). For a secret finally disclosed by the text is that Lucien's father is too old to love properly, (political) ambition having become his 'dernière passion'; he is jealous of—because incapable of—the Romantic feeling intermittently exhibited by his son.

Stendhal's works stage many moments of inexpressible and finally inexplicable feeling, particularly at culminating points in their narrative. At these times, 'le sujet surpasse le disant' (the subject exceeds what can be said) (*OI* ii. 958, *Vie de Henry Brulard*): all analysis, and even irony, is suspended.[17] Such feeling often turns around love, as in the case of Lucien and Bathilde. But it is just as often provoked by the experience of reading: reading Rousseau; reading accounts of Napoleon's heroism and grandeur. Love, as analysed by Stendhal, is a largely illusory projection deriving from uncontrollable admiration for the love-object, typically amplified by feelings of relative unworthiness; it exists also in an asexual form, as the 'passions d'admiration' (passions of admiration) that Henry Brulard conceived for Gros, Destutt, and Giuditta Pasta (*OI* ii. 863). Such 'passions d'admiration' centre very frequently in Stendhal's fictions around the Romantic figure of Napoleon, even though Stendhal's own view of the Emperor appears to have been highly ambivalent (*H.B.* 446–7). Beyle had met his idol several times and conceived a passion for him: Mérimée reports him as claiming that 'j'ai eu le feu sacré' (I was touched by the sacred fire) (*H.B.* 446). Characteristically, however, he appears also to have made strenuous efforts to *se dénapoléoniser* (un-Napoleon himself) in order to counteract the potential unhealthiness of this fixation.

Julien Sorel, the hero of *Le Rouge et le Noir*, learns to love Napoleon immoderately through books: the *Bulletins de la Grande-Armée* and Las Cases's *Mémorial de Sainte-Hélène* form part of a 'coran' that informs Julien's unhealthy fanaticism throughout the novel; the other part of this 'coran' is made up of Rousseau's *Confessions*. These texts engender contradictory 'passions d'admiration' that prompt Julien to want to be just like both Rousseau and Napoleon: this idiosyncratic Romantic project takes the form of trying to prove himself their worthy peer by emulating their strikingly different

[17] Stendhal uses this phrase to break off the narrative describing his discovery of Italy and, more particularly, Milan.

examples. This fanaticism produces another form of pure feeling analogous to love: the madness that afflicts, or elevates—depending, of course, on one's point of view—so many of the heroes and heroines of Stendhal's fictions. Shoshana Felman has argued that such Stendhalian madness takes the form of 'la parole solitaire' (the solitary voice): the speaking of words that can no longer be understood except by the (Romantic?) self.[18] Certainly, the Romanticism of many of Stendhal's protagonists involves them becoming incomprehensible to the reader in precisely this way, yet the text holds out the lure that they might occasionally remain comprehensible to other characters whom they may, or may not, love and who may, or may not, love them back, depending, of course, on one's point of view. Perhaps Stendhal's ideal readers, the 'Happy Few' that he so insistently, idealistically, and ironically posits, will understand these characters also? Maybe they too will manage to decipher the wordless 'langage sacrée' (sacred language) that the Romantic Stendhal gives every impression of using to fill up the ellipses of his fictions.[19]

This 'langage sacrée' must remain unspoken and unwritten. Its only trace is the feeling engendered in the (ideal) reader.[20] This is because Stendhal, the incompetent stylist decried by Balzac, Hugo, Flaubert, and Proust, sought to write clearly and simply, rather than portentously or ecstatically. There is an irony, therefore, that his name should have come to be given to a 'sindromo di Stendhal' (Stendhal syndrome), the main symptom of which is the gushing verbiage produced by modern tourists as they become overwhelmed by their first encounters with Italian art and architecture. Stendhal's model was never Chateaubriand, Flaubert's great literary idol, for Stendhal objected not only to Chateaubriand's right-wing politics and narcissistic posturings, but above all to the 'emphase' (bombast) of his prose. From Stendhal's perspective, Chateaubriand sought to take the unspoken 'langage sacrée' of fine feeling and speak it, at length. (Rousseau can, at times, appear guilty of a similar crime.[21]) The result was to cheapen feeling. Instead, Stendhal famously set himself the task of writing, whether about feeling or its lack, in the concise and limpid style of the Code civil, the legal text produced at Napoleon's behest and first promulgated in 1804.[22] To this

[18] See Shoshana Felman, *La 'Folie' dans l'œuvre romanesque de Stendhal* (Paris: Corti, 1971), 162, and also Ann Jefferson, *Reading Realism in Stendhal* (Cambridge: Cambridge University Press, 1988), 128.

[19] In the *Promenades dans Rome* (1829), Stendhal lists his ideal readers in the following terms: 'Il est sans doute parmi nous quelques âmes nobles et tendres comme Mme Roland, Mlle de Lespinasse, Napoléon, le condamné Lafargue, etc. Que ne puis-je écrire dans un langage sacré compris d'elles seules!' (There are no doubt among us some noble and tender souls such as Mme Roland, Mlle de Lespinasse, Napoleon, the condemned man Lafargue, etc. Would that I could write in a sacred language intelligible only to them!) (*VI* 880).

[20] Hence Stendhal's observation, in the *Vie de Henry Brulard*, that 'un roman est comme un archet, la caisse du violon *qui rend les sons* c'est l'âme du lecteur' (a novel is like a bow, the soundbox of the violin *that resonates* is the soul of the reader) (*OI* ii. 699). See also Pearson and Jefferson for detailed analyses of this metaphor.

[21] See e.g. Stendhal's letter to Balzac of 10 Aug. 1840, in which he complains that Rousseau's style, as well as that of the overtly Romantic George Sand, contains 'beaucoup de faussetés' (much that is false). Stendhal, *Aux âmes sensibles: Lettres choisies (1800–1842)*, ed. Mariella Di Maio (Paris: Gallimard Folio, 2011), 469.

[22] 'En composant *la Chart[reuse]*, pour prendre le ton, je lisais de temps en temps quelques pages du Code civil.' (When dictating *The Chart[erhouse]*, in order to strike the right tone, I would from time to

extent, all of Stendhal's works, including even *De l'Amour*, might be ascribed to M. B[eyle] A[ncien] A[uditeur]. For even though, on the one hand, *De l'Amour* serves as an intensely personal, cryptically emotive account of Henri Beyle's unhappy passion for Matilde Dembowski (the ending of his hopes in her regard had led him to give his active consideration to suicide[23]), on the other hand, Stendhal insists, in the *Vie de Henry Brulard*, that 'je n'ai jamais dit un seul mot des femmes que j'aimais' (I have never said a single word about the women that I loved) (*OI* ii. 541). Thus *De l'Amour*, written in part as a cure for his melancholy, is laconically described in a footnote as 'un livre d'idéologie' (a book of Ideology), that is to say, a dispassionate analysis of the many stages and symptoms of love, finally posited as a form of madness.[24] The extreme delicacy and intricacy of this analysis owes something both to Rousseau's *Confessions* and to Destutt's *Éléments d'idéologie*, for both Rousseau and the Ideologues, in a manner of speaking, sought to render transparent the motivations of human beings. The difference in approach is pinpointed by Stendhal: 'si l'idéologie est une description détaillée des idées et de toutes les parties qui peuvent les composer, le présent livre est une description détaillée et minutieuse de tous les sentiments qui composent la passion nommée *amour*' (if Ideology consists of a detailed and minute description of ideas and all the parts which make them up, this book consists of a detailed and minute description of all the feelings that go to make up the passion we call *love*) (*DA* 35).[25]

It is against this background that we should reassess the relationship between Stendhal's idiosyncratic Romanticism and his alleged realism. In the second preface to *Lucien Leuwen*—a novel that represents its Romantic hero comically mired in the reality of Orleanist France, that least Romantic of worlds—Stendhal observes that 'l'auteur pense que, excepté pour la passion du héros, un roman doit être un miroir' (the author believes that, except for the passion of its hero, a novel should function as a mirror) (*ORC* ii. 722). On the face of it, Stendhal is recycling an analogy between novels and mirrors already famously set out in *Le Rouge et le Noir*. The force of this analogy seems quite clear: Stendhal, lacking our theoretical sophistication of the twenty-first century, thought that 'reality' could be represented unproblematically on the printed page in unmediated form. It does seem a shame that an author so apparently sophisticated in other ways should prove so obtuse in this regard, but there it is. Yet, as has already been noted, Stendhal also develops a completely different analogy in which the novel is a violin, producing sounds only when brought to life by the bow that is each individual reader's (Romantic) soul. To borrow the terms of M. H. Abrams, the Stendhalian novel can therefore be seen as either a mirror or a lamp, depending of course on one's point of view.[26] In any case, to return to Stendhal's mirror metaphors,

time read a few pages from the Civil Code.) Stendhal, *Aux âmes sensibles*, 473 (letter to Balzac of 17–28 Oct. 1840).

[23] See *OI* ii. 540 (*Vie de Henry Brulard*) and 979 (*Notices autobiographiques*, 1837) for assertions of this suicidal intent.

[24] See Stendhal, *De l'Amour*, ed. Victor Del Litto (Paris: Gallimard Folio, 1980), 35 (hereafter *DA*).

[25] See Jean Starobinski, *Jean-Jacques Rousseau: La transparence et l'obstacle* (Paris: Plon, 1957), for a classic account of Rousseau's attempts to render himself transparent to his readers.

[26] See M. H. Abrams, *The Mirror and the Lamp: Romantic Theory and the Critical Tradition* (New York: Oxford University Press, 1953).

our author turns out to be highly interested in the ways in which the angles of his tilting mirror cause arbitrary, incomplete, and misleading images to pass across it. Furthermore, to return to the second preface of *Lucien Leuwen*, the passion of the hero—along with the even more jealously guarded passion of the heroine(s)—is deliberately excluded from the novel's mimetic representation, even though this passion might be held to be the final object of Stendhal's fictional representations. This is quite some caveat, and can be interpreted in a number of possible ways, depending, of course, on one's point of view.

Perhaps this is another case of 'le sujet' surpassing 'le disant': the hero's passion (his love for a woman, or, more typically, two women; his various *passions d'admiration*; his abstract love of heroism; his idealism) simply exceeds the representational powers of language.[27] Put another way, the story of such passion is not one that can be told with propriety, for its Romantic expression would require a vulgar and gaudy display of reheated and hyperbolic feeling-as-language (as opposed to feeling-as-feeling) if it is not otherwise simply to fall flat. The Romantic text ought instead to use language in an effort to provoke Romantic feeling in its readers: to show, not tell. But there is also another way of looking at the problem posed by the second preface to *Lucien Leuwen*. Perhaps Stendhal is trying to tell us that such passion is no longer possible in the dismal reality of a nineteenth century defined by Stendhal, after Byron, as '*this age of cant*' (*ORC* ii. 1123, *Les Cenci*)? (As far as Stendhal is concerned, the nineteenth century begins only in 1815.[28]) For one of the most striking features of Stendhalian heroism is its anachronism: the protagonists of his fictions possess the heroism of earlier ages, whether the sixteenth and seventeenth centuries analysed in the *Chroniques italiennes* and held up as exemplary by Mathilde de La Mole and Fabrice Del Dongo in *Le Rouge et le Noir* and *La Chartreuse de Parme* respectively, or the historical parenthesis opened up by the French Revolution and closed by the fall of the Empire. This last golden age offers Stendhal's Romantic heroes and heroines further models to emulate: Lafayette, Mme Roland, Danton, and Napoleon, first in his guise as youthful republican general and then, more problematically, in his guise as Emperor.

Stendhal is often portrayed as an uncritical enthusiast, utterly besotted with Napoleon.[29] Yet Stendhal's autobiographical writings often ironize such a love for the Emperor. Indeed, another way of looking at the problem posed by the second preface to *Lucien Leuwen* is that the passion of the Romantic hero fails altogether to engage with reality, itself perhaps finally unknowable? Rather Stendhal's heroes endeavour to exhibit a heroism modelled on the fanciful constructs of literary and historical narratives, quixotically and delusionally imagined as somehow transposing a former lived reality. In this last sense, Stendhal's literary heroes and heroines are Romantic in yet another way: they are

[27] By contrast, Stendhal uses his short fiction very much to foreground the passion of two 19th-cent. heroines: Mina de Vanghel and Vanina Vanini. However, this passion reveals itself through actions rather than words.

[28] See *ORC* i. 86 ('Avant-propos', *Armance*).

[29] See Pieter Geyl, *Napoleon: For and Against*, tr. Olive Renier (London: Penguin, 1965), 32–3, for a classic articulation of this view.

self-constructed, the products of the narratives of self that they fashion from their identificatory reading, imagined as a kind of *cristallisation*.[30]

Stendhal's desire to construct the self appears to derive both from the concerns of Romanticism and Ideology. It is striking, however, that his representations of his most intimate self are never representations of Henri Beyle, but rather of endlessly proliferating pseudonymous projections of himself, such as Dominique (after Domenico Cimarosa, the composer of *Il matrimonio segreto*, Stendhal's favourite opera), Arrigo Beyle, or Henry Brulard. The Stendhalian self is organized around a screened off central space that is either stable or unstable, full or hollow, depending, of course, on one's point of view.

This last point hints at both Stendhal's optimism and his pessimism. Either the self can be fashioned, in which case it can be turned into something substantial—a Romantic self—and the hero and the heroine can find ways of emulating the exemplars, whether real or imagined, that they so admire.[31] Or all notions of a substantial constructed self are finally delusional, to be replaced by a realist account of the actions of the hero especially, but also perhaps the heroine(s), as no more than the random and barely understood epiphenomena of amorphous emotion. Stendhal's autobiographical texts (the *Souvenirs d'égotisme*, the *Vie de Henry Brulard*) turn around this question of the self and its stability.

In the *Souvenirs d'égotisme*, Stendhal asks:

> Quel homme suis-je? Ai-je du bon sens, ai-je du bon sens avec profondeur?
>
> Ai-je un esprit remarquable? En vérité, je n'en sais rien. Ému par ce qui m'arrive au jour le jour, je pense rarement à ces questions fondamentales, et alors mes jugements varient comme mon humeur. Mes jugements ne sont que des aperçus.
>
> Voyons si, en faisant mon examen de conscience la plume à la main, j'arriverai à quelque chose de *positif* et qui reste *longtemps vrai* pour moi.
>
> … Je ne me connais point moi-même et c'est ce qui quelquefois, la nuit, quand j'y pense, me désole. Suis-je bon, méchant, spirituel, bête? Ai-je su tirer un bon parti des hasards au milieu desquels m'a jeté et la toute-puissance de Napoléon (que toujours j'adorai) en 1810, et la chute que nous fîmes dans la boue en 1814, et notre effort pour en sortir en 1830?
>
> What kind of man am I? Do I possess good sense, do I possess good sense and also penetration?
>
> Do I have a remarkable mind? To tell the truth, I have no idea. Caught up in the emotion of day-to-day events, I rarely give any thought to these fundamental questions, and so my judgements vary in the same way as my moods. My judgements are no more than fleeting insights.
>
> Let us see if, by examining my conscience, my pen in my hand, I can arrive at some *positive* conclusions that might remain *enduringly true* as far as I am concerned.

30 See *DA* 30–40 for an account of the role played by *cristallisation* within the process of falling in love.

31 See Francesco Manzini, *Stendhal's Parallel Lives* (Berne: Peter Lang, 2004) for an extended development of this point.

… I do not know myself, and this is something that, at night, when I think about it, sometimes distresses me. Am I good or bad, clever or stupid? Have I known how to make the most of the chance events that befell me in 1810 thanks to the omnipotence of Napoleon (whom I still adored), or in 1814 when we all fell into the mire, or in 1830 when we tried to extricate ourselves from it. (*OI* ii. 429–31)

Certainly, Stendhal would like to imagine his own self as fairly substantial: 'je ne conçois pas un homme sans un peu de *mâle énergie*, de constance et de profondeur dans les idées, etc.' (my conception of a man necessarily involves a measure of *male energy*, thought that is constant over time and penetrating, etc.) (*OI* ii. 451). Yet his fictions seem to allow for the possibility than men are in fact condemned to hollowness or superficiality, in the sense that they appear, not least to themselves, to be unknowable and so unpredictable and unreliable. (Equally, Stendhal appears frequently to conceive of radical changeability as a virtue.) Put another way, Stendhal's male (anti)heroes are shown to be incapable of effective self-construction. Women, by contrast, tend to be represented as much more capable in this, as well as most other regards. It is this defect of hollowness or superficiality that Stendhal's (anti)heroes endeavour to remedy as they in turn try to find the answer to Stendhal's questions just cited, misleadingly reformulated by Lucien as the 'Ai-je bien ou mal agi?' (Have I acted well or badly?) that he asks of his (hollow, superficial) father (*ORC* ii. 589). Lucien is not in fact asking whether he has acted well or badly, but rather whether he has acted purposely or haphazardly: he is asking whether he in fact possesses a stable self and, if so, whether this self has any value.

As far as Stendhal is concerned, the answer to this question can only be found through action, or what Montaigne refers to as '*se colleter avec la nécessité*' (*coming to grips with necessity*) (*ORC* ii. 369). If *Armance* teaches its readers anything, it is that the answer to such a question can never come from the inaction and introspection that characterize the more hand-wringing variety of Romantic hero, including of course *Armance*'s own Octave de Malivert, a hero of unrealized potential. Octave's potential is in fact unrealizable precisely because he is unwilling to enter into contact with others and so never puts himself to the test (never comes to grips with necessity): rather than challenge either himself or others through action, he remains very largely passive and perpetually evasive. As Stendhal was to ask in *Lucien Leuwen*:

Qu'est-ce qu'un jeune homme qui ne connaît pas les hommes? qui n'a vécu qu'avec des gens polis, ou des subordonnés, ou des gens dont il ne choquait pas les intérêts? …] Il n'a point éprouvé l'effet des autres sur lui-même, il n'est sûr de rien ni sur les autres ni, à plus forte raison, sur soi-même. Ce n'est tout au plus qu'un brillant *peut-être*.

What is a young man who does not know his fellows, who has only lived in polite society, or in the company of subordinates, or people who do not go against his interests? … He has not felt the effect others have on him, he can be sure of nothing as regards others or, even more so, as regards himself. At best, he can be no more than a brilliant *perhaps*. (*ORC* ii. 369)

Ideally, the self, as it acts, would appear transparently to these others, hence Lucien's desire to show himself for what he is and his eagerness to obtain the judgements of others and in particular those characters who might reasonably be counted by Stendhal amongst the 'Happy Few'. But such self-exposure risks provoking the censure of the far from happy many and so action often requires dissimulation and the exercise of hypocrisy (this again is a problem posed by Rousseau in *Les Confessions*). In particular, the essentially narcissistic self (the Rousseauian and then the Romantic self) risks being traduced, that is to say, seen to be something s/he feels (or hopes) her/himself not to be. More generally, this narcissistic self may traumatically discover its own insubstantiality. Scott has argued persuasively that Lucien Leuwen's various encounters with mud serve to lay this process bare, for example when he is identified as an agent of the Orleanist government and pelted with mud by an angry mob. For mud figures in *Lucien Leuwen* not so much as a marker of moral squalor, as more commonly in realist fiction, but rather as an emblem of what cannot be symbolized by the hero. The mud with which Lucien is pelted, and which even enters his protesting mouth, cannot be decoded by Lucien or integrated within the narrative of his stable personality: it represents a 'malfunctioning of metaphor' that prompts Lucien to suffer a traumatic blow to his sense of self.[32] Hence his extreme anger and disarray at a phrase tossed out by an onlooker: 'vous avez mis son âme sur sa figure' (you have put his soul on his face) (*ORC* ii. 494).

Scott ties her analysis in part to a reinterpretation of Stendhal's famous mirror metaphor as deployed in *Le Rouge et le Noir*, which now deserves to be cited in full:

> Hé, monsieur, un roman est un miroir qui se promène sur une grande route. Tantôt il reflète à vos yeux l'azur des cieux, tantôt la fange des bourbiers de la route. Et l'homme qui porte le miroir dans sa hotte, sera par vous accusé d'être immoral! Son miroir montre la fange, et vous accusez le miroir! Accusez bien plutôt le grand chemin où est le bourbier, et plus encore l'inspecteur des routes qui laisse l'eau croupir et le bourbier se former.
>
> Yes, Sir, a novel is a mirror proceeding down a main road. At times it shows you reflections of azure skies, at times the mire of muddy puddles along the road. And the man who carries this mirror in his knapsack, you will accuse of immorality! His mirror shows mud, and you accuse the mirror! You should rather accuse the main road where the muddy puddles have formed, or better still the roads inspector who allows the water to collect and the mud to form. (*ORC* i. 671)

This passage relates specifically to the novel's representation of the character of Mathilde de La Mole, described (ironically) by the narrator as 'tout à fait d'imagination' (entirely of the imagination) (*ORC* i. 670) and 'impossible dans notre siècle, non moins prudent que vertueux' (impossible in our century, marked no less by its prudence than by its virtue) (*ORC* i. 671). Mathilde's representation therefore threatens the novel's verisimilitude: her passion must elude the reflecting surface of the novel-as-mirror, for example

32 See Maria Scott, 'Stendhal's Muddy Realism', *Dix-Neuf*, 16/1 (2012), 15.

because she contrives to be radically free in an '*age of cant*' that denies the individual all freedom (to this extent she is a Byronic heroine). Mathilde therefore cannot be contaminated by the mud that so destabilizes the hapless Lucien, even though the narrator appears, antiphrastically, to be claiming that it is her character that constitutes the mud so unfortunately represented in the novel. Indeed, there is a great deal of textual evidence to suggest that Mathilde, far from being 'la fange', is actually the blue sky. From a realist perspective, mathilde might be the mud that resists symbolization, a glitch; from a Romantic perspective, she offers instead the celestial transparency of freedom, only too rarely glimpsed in a text that concerns itself in large part with the squalor of nineteenth-century French civilization. As Scott puts it:

> If this reading were to be followed through to its logical conclusion, it would mean that Stendhal's famous description of his own textual practice actually gives priority to the transformative imagination over the reflected reality or, to take up M. H. Abrams' terms, to the expressive lamp over the mimetic mirror. More modestly, it would mean that the referent of the mud metaphor is unstable. In other words, the very image by which the text ostensibly anchors itself in the material world would itself be unstable.[33]

Stendhal's Romantic pessimism, which insists on mathilde's impossibility in the muddy world of the nineteenth-century, is therefore artfully balanced by his idealistic Romantic optimism: it may after all still be possible to extract oneself from the quagmire that is the nineteenth century and merge with the blue sky. But what does merging with the blue sky entail? As has already been noted, it appears to involve a radical performance of freedom. Yet many of Stendhal's male heroes fail spectacularly to attain the freedom of a Mathilde de La Mole (this may appear paradoxical given that realist literature has often been seen as denying the very possibility of female freedom).[34] Their failure may perhaps have something to do with politics.

Stendhal's theoretical writings on Romanticism insist largely (and unremarkably) on the need to renew the theatre by reflecting contemporary manners on the stage.[35] More generally, they suggest that Romantic writers should seek to emulate the great writers of the past rather than imitate them in the manner of the Classicists, that is to say that they should not be afraid to innovate as Racine himself had done in his own era. *Qu'est-ce que le romanticisme* also posits a new Romantic outlook, created by the experience of Revolution and Empire. This outlook is very different to that commonly associated with the reactionary Romantics of the early 1820s. Stendhal imagines a literature written by a new generation that has tested itself through action:

[33] See Scott, 'Stendhal's Muddy Realism', 19.

[34] See in particular the arguments put forward in this regard in Naomi Schor, *Breaking the Chain: Women, Theory, and French Realist Fiction* (New York: Columbia University Press, 1985).

[35] One of the few fixed chronological points in the narrative of *Le Rouge et le Noir* is the première of Hugo's *Hernani* on 25 Feb. 1830 (*ORC* i. 620), which Stendhal had managed to attend.

> Toujours les arts font de grands progrès dans le premier moment de repos *réel* qui suit les convulsions politiques. Les pédants peuvent nous retarder de dix ans; mais, dans dix ans, c'est nous, *ignorants en livres*, mais savants *en actions* et en émotions, c'est nous, qui n'avons pas lu Homère en grec, mais qui avons assiégé Tarragone et Girone, c'est nous qui serons à la tête de toutes choses.

> The arts always make great advances during the first *real* moment of calm following a period of political convulsions. The pedants may hold us back for ten years, but in ten years' time, we, the *ignorant in terms of our book-learning*, but the learned in terms of *actions* and emotions, we, who have not read Homer in the Greek, but who have besieged Tarragona and Girona, we shall be everywhere in the vanguard.[36]

Stendhal conceived of his Romantic heroes not as bewildered émigré aristocrats, wallowing in ever more bathetic self-pity, but rather as men of action and emotion; men who might deserve the admiration and even, at a push, the love of free women.

As a small child, Henri Beyle witnessed the 'journée des Tuiles' in Grenoble (7 June 1788), often viewed as a prequel to the Revolution proper. The *Vie de Henry Brulard* represents the impact of the Revolution on young Henry: its subject, in many ways, is his bid to free himself from the patriarchal authority of his father, just as France was freeing itself from the patriarchal authority of the monarch. Stendhal's fictional texts often stage fantasies of illegitimacy: the male hero must find a way of extracting himself from the control and dominance of the biological father. Patriarchal and, more ambiguously, matriarchal authority are represented by Stendhal as a form of tyranny that must be either evaded through the exercise of dissimulation and hypocrisy, or, better, challenged by means of radical self-assertion and self-invention made possible in large part by the examples set in this regard by the French Revolution and Napoleonic Empire. These were epochs, in Stendhal's analysis, that allowed for moments of quite radical freedom and, in particular, the exceeding of prescribed models of behaviour as (re)imposed in '*the age of cant*'. To this extent, the era of Revolution and Empire restored something of the originality of French manners, as exemplified by the spontaneity of sixteenth-century mores. Such spontaneity, Stendhal argues, had been stifled first by the centralized model of monarchy imposed by Louis XIV and more recently by the tyranny of public opinion that characterized the post-Napoleonic nineteenth century. The question of politics therefore turns around reactionary attempts to stifle freedom and spontaneity. It is against this background that we should read another of Stendhal's famous pronouncements about novels, first given in *Le Rouge et le Noir* and then repeated in *La Chartreuse de Parme*: talk of politics in a novel is like a pistol-shot at a concert. The harmony of the music is destroyed by the sound of the shot going off: a horrible, grating noise that irrupts, bringing with it all the excitement of sudden unpredicatability. Stendhal's problem with ordinary Romantic heroes is precisely

[36] Stendhal, *Œuvres complètes*, ed. Ernest Abravanel and Victor Del Litto, 50 vols (Geneva: Cercle du Bibliophile, [1967]–74), xxxv. 120. See also Pierre Barbéris, *Sur Stendhal* (Paris: Messidor, 1982), 27–39, and Christopher Prendergast, *The Order of Mimesis* (Cambridge: Cambridge University Press, 1986), 131–2, for an analysis of similar optimism in *Racine et Shakespeare*.

his problem with their predictability: they are always playing a role, conforming to dictates of good taste. His own Romantic heroes are unpredictable, to the point of appearing mad, unstable, contradictory, or even, finally, hollow.

It is Stendhal's faith in the lingering potential for spontaneity that informs his optimism with regard to political revolution, for it is this potential that explains, as far as Stendhal is concerned, how conformist slaves can suddenly become unpredictably free. It is this spontaneity that also allows his characters to appear anachronistic, in the manner of Mathilde in *Le Rouge et le Noir*. She is impossible, just as Julien is impossible in the France of 1830, for *Le Rouge et le Noir* (subtitled both a 'Chronique du XIXe siècle' and a 'Chronique de 1830') represents a nineteenth-century world of absolute conformity; at the same time, the novel represents (and yet deliberately chooses not to represent)[37] the uncontainable energy that produces the Revolution of 1830. It is this latent (Romantic) energy that explains how the apparently stable world of the Ancien Régime could so rapidly have been swept away by the first great Revolution; how the Restoration could be overturned in a mere three days in 1830: how the whole 'plan' of society can be 'barbarement renversé' (barbarously overturned) (*ORC* ii. 934). For Stendhal, revolutions represent an uncontrollable outpouring of emotion: *La Chartreuse de Parme* opens with a description of Milan being liberated by Napoleon's revolutionary army in 1796. In the *Vie de Henry Brulard*, Stendhal likewise represents young Henry as 'un esclave' (a slave), being educated to comply with his father's curious brand of unfreedom. Yet, at any moment, there is the potential for a revolution to take place, not in the old sense of a turn of the wheel of fortune, but in the new sense of a radical break with the past. This discontinuity is effected in Henry's life by the experience of being taught mathematics by the republican Gros: 'enfin le hasard voulut que je visse un grand homme et que je ne devinsse pas un coquin' (in the end, chance decreed that I see a great man and that I not become a scoundrel) (*OI* ii. 859). Brulard's first 'passion d'admiration' taught him to seek freedom at both a personal and a political level.

As far as Stendhal is concerned, most notably in *Le Rouge et le Noir*, evasion and challenge are both legitimate life strategies so long as they are employed in the pursuit of freedom (as opposed to the pursuit of mastery over others). Evasion, whether by means of flight or dissimulation, is the more practical of the two, permitting the self to screen off a private space that allows for the creation and preservation of a limited form of freedom, although prolonged dissimulation risks damaging the natural or constructed Rousseauian or Romantic self.[38] Challenge often leads to social censure and ridicule; sometimes it leads to prison and even death. However, such challenge also allows the self to assert itself radically in a kind of performance of freedom. Hence in part the paradox of the Romantic prison whereby freedom is attained in confinement;[39] a paradox

[37] By the chronology one can extrapolate from the fixed point given by the first representation of *Hernani*, the action of the novel spills over into the period that followed the July Revolution of 1830. Mme de Renâl is represented, however, seeking clemency for Julien from the already deposed Charles X.

[38] See David Place, 'Stendhal, *Le Rouge et le Noir* and the Untouchable Self', *Neophilologus*, 80 (1996), 377–84, for an excellent discussion of Romantic and social selves.

[39] See Victor Brombert, *La Prison Romantique* (Paris: Corti, 1975).

that can be extended to the freedom of being condemned to death—a freedom explored by Julien Sorel in *Le Rouge et le Noir*. Of all the exemplary characters represented in Stendhal's novels, only two—Mathilde de La Mole and Lucien Leuwen—survive; only they will be given the opportunity to continue exercising their Stendhalian freedoms in their unwritten futures.[40] To this extent, both *Le Rouge et le Noir* and *Lucien Leuwen* end the way that Édouard X. hopes his *Les Faux-Monnayeurs* will end in André Gide's *Les Faux-Monnayeurs*, which also ends this way:

> Je considère que la vie ne nous propose jamais rien qui, tout autant qu'un aboutissement, ne puisse être considéré comme un nouveau point de départ. 'Pourrait être continué …' c'est sur ces mots que je voudrais terminer mes *Faux-Monnayeurs*.
>
> I believe that life never presents us with anything which, just as much as an ending, cannot be viewed as a new beginning. 'Could be continued …' It's with these words that I should like to end my *Counterfeiters*.[41]

All the other major characters die, unless one counts Mosca as a major character, but his survival despite the otherwise ruthless cull at the end of *La Chartreuse de Parme* quite pointedly serves to exclude him from 'the Happy Few'. The question then might be whether death represents failure? From a Stendhalian perspective, revolutions are doomed to fail, for they always end up reconstituting the (patriarchal) power they had sought to eliminate. Similarly, sexual relationships (and resulting paternity) risk reconstituting the male/paternal tyranny from which the young hero had sought to free himself. From Stendhal's peculiar Romantic perspective, death frees the hero from the risk of himself becoming a tyrant. Death therefore, in Stendhal's fiction, represents failure as a type of success. The manner of death is, however, of crucial importance.

Stendhal's fictions set up a system of values that allows Stendhalians to (think they can) differentiate between good and bad ways of being. (Every now and again, it becomes apparent that they have got this system of values wrong.) From this system of values, it ought to be possible to deduce a right way of challenging society, and even a right way of evading the normative controls it is forever seeking to impose. More particularly, it ought to be possible to deduce a right and wrong way of being Romantic.

As has already been noted, Stendhal's first novel poses many problems of interpretation. Its hero, Octave de Malivert is a very serious young man. Perhaps his many qualities will one day turn him into somebody quite special. But does he possess any real worth? More to the point, what is wrong with him? It is possible that he is mad, as his concerned and controlling mother fears. But a letter written by Stendhal to Mérimée (what should the critic do with this paratext?) suggests that his problem may in fact be that he is impotent, a topical medical condition given that the restored monarch, Louis

40 Lamiel dies only in a draft sketch; it seems highly likely from what we have of this unfinished novel that she too would have been allowed to start again. In Stendhal's short fiction, Vanina Vanini finishes her story by starting a new plot for herself.

41 André Gide, *Les Faux-Monnayeurs* (Paris: Gallimard Folio, 1989), 322.

XVIII, was afflicted by it and given that this sexual impotence came to symbolize the political problems faced by the Restoration (Octave is himself the scion of an aristocratic Restoration family impotently wrestling with these political problems). Octave may in part have been modelled on the writer Astolphe de Custine who was not impotent, but rather gay (Mérimée tells us, in *H.B.*, that Stendhal believed all great men to have been gay; the examples he apparently liked to cite included Napoleon and Jesus). The novel appears to have been written as a spoof of *Olivier ou le secret*, an unpublished novel by Mme de Duras dealing with the delicate subject of sexual impotence; this novel had, confusingly, been spoofed already by ... Custine! So far, so confusing. By the time the novel appeared, Stendhal's few readers were unlikely to have been in a position to remember Mme de Duras's *Olivier*, much less understand his cryptic and sometimes rather silly allusions to the novel and its subject (Octave fantasizes at one point about being placed in charge of a perfectly functioning cannon). *Armance* must have seemed and might still seem a perverse way of embarking on a late career as a novelist.

Insofar as the novel has any point to make, Pearson has argued that this might be a point about Romanticism. He follows J. M. Sykes in reading *Armance* as a parody of Chateaubriand's *René*, and also shows how the novel's ending has the effect of ironizing his imitation of Byron.[42] As we have seen, however, the novel's point may well be to have no point, but rather to present a series of points of view as reflected and distorted by its mirrored surfaces. The question, then, returns to being one about Octave's personal value (his cousin and love interest, Armance de Zohiloff, is almost certainly of inestimable value, but the reader is shown too little of her, and from her perspective, to be able to develop a clear view of her worth). In particular, this question of Octave's value, either real or potential, turns around the vexed problem of his Romanticism.

Octave is not normally a man of action, except once when he takes offence at the words of a servant and throws him out of a window. Instead, he is prone to self-pity (as will be Lucien), extreme dissimulation (as will be Julien), and increasingly absurd fantasies of evasion. His problem, finally, is his Romanticism, the *mal du siècle* that prevents him from realizing his potential, even in death. Thus Octave finally kills himself, but this death in no way constitutes a Romantic challenge to reality, the endlessly disappointing order of things. Mina de Vanghel shoots herself in the heart when disappointed by the inadequacies of the man she has loved: the narrator observes that 'ce fut une âme trop ardente pour se contenter du réel de la vie' (she was too passionate a soul to content herself with the realities of life) (*OI* i. 329). Julien Sorel commits a kind of judicial suicide, challenging the authority of his bourgeois jurors to have him executed for the scandalous double shooting of his former lover, the aristocratic Mme de Rênal. Octave's suicide instead takes the form of more evasion and dissimulation: 'Le genre de sa mort ne fut soupçonné en France que de la seule Armance' (Back in France, Armance was alone in guessing at the manner of his passing) (*ORC* i. 243). He is on his way to Greece, to imitate Byron by fighting on behalf of Greek independence. 'Je te salue, se dit-il, ô terre des

[42] See Roger Pearson, *Stendhal's Violin*, 47, 58–9 and also J. M. Sykes, '*Armance*, roman romantique?', *Stendhal Club*, 16 (1973–4), 135.

héros!' ('Oh land of heroes, I salute you!' he exclaimed to himself) (*ORC* i. 243) Can he see the irony in repeating this line, taken from a poem written in honour of Byron, given that he has come not to fight but to pretend to die of natural causes?[43] He then takes a poison '[qui] délivra doucement Octave de cette vie qui avait été pour lui si agitée' (that gently delivered Octave from this life that, from his perspective, had been so agitated). Even in death, he manages to continue his Byronic pantomime, for, when he is found, his features are fixed in the same beautiful smile that allegedly played on Byron's dead face.[44] But there are important differences between Octave and Byron. The latter's life had indeed been agitated: from Stendhal's perspective, he had repeatedly challenged the tyranny of opinion characteristic of the '*age of cant*'. Octave's life had been agitated in quite a different way: he had fretted and wrung his hands, in the manner of a René. He had never performed freedom, nor even created freedom for himself by means of his evasions. Octave's brand of Romanticism leads him instead to ever greater constriction. For Stendhal, there was a right and a wrong way to be a Romantic.

Further Reading

Abrams, M. H., *The Mirror and the Lamp: Romantic Theory and the Critical Tradition* (New York: Oxford University Press, 1953).
Barbéris, Pierre, *Sur Stendhal* (Paris: Messidor, 1982).
Bolster, Richard, *Stendhal, Balzac et le féminisme romantique* (Paris: Minard, 1970).
Charlton, D. G. (ed.), *The French Romantics*, 2 vols (Cambridge: Cambridge University Press, 1984).
Crouzet, Michel, *Stendhal et l'italianité: Essai de mythologie romantique* (Paris: Corti, 1982).
Del Litto, Victor, *La Vie intellectuelle de Stendhal: Genèse et évolution de ses idées (1802–1821)* (Paris: PUF, 1959).
Felman, Shoshana, *La 'Folie' dans l'œuvre romanesque de Stendhal* (Paris: Corti, 1971).
Geyl, Pieter, *Napoleon: For and Against*, tr. Olive Renier (London: Penguin, 1965).
Hamm, Jean-Jacques, *'Armance' ou la liberté de Stendhal* (Paris: Champion, 2009).
Jefferson, Ann, *Reading Realism in Stendhal* (Cambridge: Cambridge University Press, 1988).
Kliebenstein, Georges, *Figures du destin stendhalien* (Paris: Presses Sorbonne Nouvelle: 2004).
Manzini, Francesco, *Stendhal's Parallel Lives* (Berne: Peter Lang, 2004).
Pearson, Roger, *Stendhal's Violin* (Oxford: Clarendon Press, 1988).
Place, David, 'Stendhal, *Le Rouge et le Noir* and the Untouchable Self', *Neophilologus*, 80 (1996), 377–84.
Prendergast, Christopher, *The Order of Mimesis* (Cambridge: Cambridge University Press, 1986).
Rabine, Leslie W., *Reading the Romantic Heroine: Text, History, Ideology* (Ann Arbor: University of Michigan Press, 1985).

[43] See *ORC* i. 924, and George M. Rosa, 'Sailing to Mount Kalos: The Poetical Denouement of *Armance*', *FMLS* 23 (1987), 31.

[44] See *ORC* i. 925, and Rosa, 'Sailing to Mount Kalos', 30–1.

Rosa, George M., 'Sailing to Mount Kalos: The Poetical Denouement of *Armance*', *FMLS* 23 (1987), 21–37.
Rude, Fernand, *Stendhal et la pensée sociale*, 2nd edn (Brionne: Monfort, 1983).
Schor, Naomi, *Breaking the Chain: Women, Theory, and French Realist Fiction* (New York: Columbia University Press, 1985).
Scott, Maria, 'Stendhal, Mathilde et le regard oblique', in Johnnie Gratton and Derval Conroy (eds), *L'Œil écrit* (Geneva: Slatkine, 2005), 221–36.
Scott, Maria, 'Stendhal's Muddy Realism', *Dix-Neuf*, 16/1 (2012), 15–27.
Scott, Maria, *Stendhal's Less-Loved Heroines: Fiction, Freedom, and the Female* (Oxford: Legenda, 2013).
Starobinski, Jean, *Jean-Jacques Rousseau: La transparence et l'obstacle* (Paris: Plon, 1957).
Starobinski, Jean, *L'Œil vivant* (Paris: Gallimard, 1961).
Sykes, J. M., '*Armance*, roman romantique?', *Stendhal Club*, 16 (1973–4), 127–35.

CHAPTER 5

THE NOVEL AND THE (IL)LEGIBILITY OF HISTORY

Victor Hugo, Honoré de Balzac, and Alexandre Dumas

BRADLEY STEPHENS

In the mid-1820s as the second wave of French Romanticism was surging, its soon-to-be figurehead, Victor Hugo, noted an unmistakable vortex in his generation's history: 'You will not find any bridge linking our century to the previous one, for in effect no such bridge exists. Between Frederick and Bonaparte, Voltaire and Byron, van Loo and Géricault, there lies the abyss of the Revolution.'[1] Simultaneously inviting fascination and obliterating durable meaning, 1789 is less a reference point than a natural phenomenon in Hugo's mind: a violent force that engulfed old ideas of the past as being linear and coherent, and one whose destructive power radically affected how he and his contemporaries related to their present. The downfall of Louis XVI had revealed the continuity of the French monarchy to be worldly rather than divine, and any subsequent social order would have to reckon with the ruinous reality that had now become apparent. In the decades following the Revolution, successive and often rapid change in the structure and status of France made it painfully clear to many of her citizens that the world they lived in was far from perpetual. A revolutionary dream could become the nightmare of civil war, and a conquering Emperor could become a defeated exile. Come *les Trois Glorieuses* of July 1830, a revolution could even hand the throne from one king to another rather than cast aside monarchy altogether, bringing novelty and nostalgia into a knotted bind. The symbolism of Pauline's kitten chasing the crumpled-up morning paper of political news round and round the garden in Balzac's *The Wild Ass's Skin* (1831)[2] would not have been lost on a country now familiar with the contortions and rotations of modern history.

[1] 'Littérature et philosophie mêlées' in *Œuvres complètes: Critique*, ed. Jean-Pierre Reynaud (Paris: Laffont, 1985), 166. All translations of French sources in this chapter are my own, unless reference is made to translated edns.

[2] *The Wild Ass's Skin*, tr. Helen Constantine (Oxford: Oxford University Press, 2012), 169.

The question of how to make sense of, or at the very least map, France's recent experience as a society was symptomatic of a culture that became progressively more interested in how to write and to think about history. The Enlightenment had promoted a rigorous and penetrating approach to knowledge, hence Voltaire's famous argument in Diderot's *Encyclopédie* (1751–72) that the modern historian should engage with the past as would the scientist with the disciplines of mathematics and physics. In turn, Condorcet's *Sketch for a Historical Picture of the Progress of the Human Mind* (1795) recognized that the scientific method of observation and deduction, which had transformed human knowledge of the physical world, should now be applied to develop an understanding of the social one as well. Amidst the fallout from the Revolution, this historical consciousness was being amplified by the allure of exotic pasts and unfamiliar lands as a stimulus for the European Romantic imagination, channelled in part by Napoleon's 1798–1801 expedition to Egypt. If history as a discipline had become an educational institution in France as it had in Germany,[3] then the writing of history also became a literary concern, both as it had happened and as it was happening at the time. It kindled a taste for modes that could accommodate this ever-changing social experience by reflecting the spirit of both the time and place in which events unfold, recalling Germaine de Staël's ideas from *De la littérature* (1799). Crucially, the abyss of the Revolution that Hugo spoke of could not be curbed by such a taste. How were writers to capture the vast interplay of different ideologies and discourses that had been energized by 1789, and how was meaning to be negotiated amidst the complex matrix of rival desires and reciprocal demands which it had generated in society?

These questions heightened interest in the novel as a vehicle for dealing with people and particulars rather than with the statistics and abstract situations common to more academic writing. The appeal lay in its ability to construct a narrative understanding of experience as both subjective and transient, breaking with the classical promotion of a universal morality which imagined men and women only as they could or ought to be. Through its powers of plotting, description, and dialogue, the novel allowed for a vivid, immersive and broad animation of history as an authentic rather than idealized experience. Exceeding the measured viewpoints of academic study, it was also free from both the physical and practical constraints of the theatre. More urgently still, the novel challenged classical rules through its focus on individual situations rather than on general instruction. For centuries, the novel had been denigrated as being incapable of providing any useful knowledge to readers. Undefined as a genre, it lacked the systematic poetics that Aristotle privileged for art, but that same embrace of particularity was recognized by the French Romantics as its key strength. In his influential examination of plot, Peter Brooks reinforces the connection between Romantic self-awareness and its development of a historical consciousness with 'the making and the interpretation of narrative plots'. The novel takes on new importance 'no doubt because of a

[3] By the 1820s, university chairs of history had become an established feature of the French educational system, and multi-volume studies such as Adolphe Thiers's *History of the French Revolution* (1823–7) and François Guizot's *History of Civilisation in France* (1829–32) were published to great acclaim.

large movement of human societies out from under the mantle of sacred myth into the modern world where men and institutions are more and more defined by their shape in time'.[4] At the same time, the novel's vivacity was proving essential in seducing readers. The novel had begun to catch the attention of the French Romantics during the early stages of the century, in which it had proven itself to be in tune with contemporary experiences of violence and self-reflection. The Gothic *roman noir*, exemplified in Matthew Lewis's *The Monk* (1796), and the *roman de l'âme*, typified by Chateaubriand's *René* (1802), had both proven themselves to be in sync with contemporary experiences of terror and self-reflection. But neither of these genres openly tackled the problem of how to seize and unpack the complexity of a post-Revolutionary social order so as to better plot the course of the country. The previous literary fascination with the supernatural and the sentimental was overtaken by a desire for the 'real' as readers and writers alike yearned for a greater understanding of their environment and its origins. In particular, it became clear that the *roman de l'individu* would not be vibrant or wide-ranging enough to respond to the pace and scale of change since the Napoleonic Wars, the Bourbon Restoration of 1814, and the rise of the bourgeoisie. The future *académicien* Désiré Nisard called for a more dramatic genre: 'The age we live in is too turbulent for a writer to indulge in the patient examination of his passions, or in the withdrawn study of those experienced by someone else.'[5]

This period's experimentation with the novel has of course been extensively documented: every French Romantic would test the genre, from Étienne Senancour with his epistolary novel *Obermann* (1804) to Théophile Gautier with the historical romance *Mademoiselle de Maupin* (1835), establishing a massive corpus of fiction. What is perhaps less clear, however, is the relationship in French literary history between the Romantic imagination which helped to broaden socio-historical consciousness in the nineteenth century, and the Realist aesthetic which would become synonymous with narrative fiction by that century's midpoint. The Realist interest in materiality, observation, and the everyday that is promoted by the redoubtable combination of Balzac and Stendhal from the 1830s onwards seems prima facie to be at odds with the Romantic emphasis on feeling, imagination, and the transcendent that is inherited from the late eighteenth century. Yet such a distinction can be unhelpful when factored into an account of the novel's development during this period. It wrongly suggests that a narrative focus on 'the real' is antagonistic towards any sense of the intangible, and conversely that an interest in human potential is somehow at odds with the desire to depict actual human nature. A less divisive and more measured scrutiny of this distinction is needed, both to understand the integral role played by Romantic thinking in the evolution of the Realist novel on the one hand, and to recognize literary Realism as more than the

[4] *Reading for the Plot: Design and Intention in Narrative* (Cambridge, Mass.: Harvard University Press, 1984), p. xii.

[5] Review of Hugo's *Notre-Dame de Paris*, *Journal des débats politiques et littéraires* (15 June 1831), 4. Mme de Staël's novels in particular had received noticeable criticism during this period for their more contemplative pace.

straightforward representation of material reality on the other. In the novel's development of an alert and expressive narrative that could effectively represent both the past and the present without glossing over their complexities, these two approaches reveal themselves to be indispensable to one another. Romanticism and Realism forged parallel and even intersecting contours for the novel from the 1820s onwards that marked out the genre's eminent position at the top of the literary hierarchy. Ian Watt's observation in his seminal account of the novel's ascendance remains as relevant now as it was over half a century ago: 'The novel is more intimately related to the general literary and intellectual situation than is always remembered, and the close connection of the first great French Realists with Romanticism is an example of this.'[6]

Indeed, the fortunes of the French novel under the Bourbon Restoration of 1814 and the July Monarchy of 1830 reveal a shared critical edge amongst key writers (including Stendhal) which cuts through the supposed divide between 'Realist' and 'Romantic' at this crucial stage in the modern novel's history. To illustrate how the relationship between Romanticism and Realism may be conceived, and by extension how important the novel became to expressing a Romantic worldview, this chapter will explore the stylistic and thematic affinities between three writers in particular. The choice of focus, although necessarily selective, is by no means arbitrary. If Hugo, Balzac, and Dumas *père* are rarely discussed together, such hesitation is arguably the result of factors surrounding their work rather than the actual substance of their writing. While the colourful biographies of these larger-than-life individuals can often prove distracting, the problems represented by the temptation towards biographical readings are secondary to the more practical difficulty of scale. The combined number of fictional works written by these three men approaches the 200 mark (9 for Hugo, approximately 100 for Balzac, and well over 60 for Dumas): the majority of these texts run to at least several hundred pages each, and amazingly form part of a yet larger artistic oeuvre in the cases of both Dumas and Hugo. Understandably, even the most conscientious of readers can therefore be prompted to approach their work in isolation and remotely through the clichés that distance affords, casting Hugo as the irrepressibly poetic dreamer, Balzac as the conservative secretary of bourgeois society, and Dumas as the shamelessly sensationalist entertainer. Notwithstanding these reputations, their individual traits need not narrow any focus at the expense of the broader structures and stylistics that

[6] *The Rise of the Novel: Studies in Defoe, Richardson and Fielding* (1957; reprint London: Chatto & Windus, 1960), 301. Following similar thinking, Maurice Z. Shroder emphasizes that Realism, along with Naturalism, 'seem more like extensions or developments of Romanticism than like outright alternatives to the school of the 1820s and 1830s'. 'Roman—Romanesque—Romantique—Romantisme', in Hans Eichner (ed.), *Romantic and its Cognates: The European History of a Word* (Toronto: University of Toronto Press, 1972), 264–92 (287). This argument continues to be aired, suggesting that clichés persist. Bruno Blanckemann notes that: 'Realism does not succeed Romanticism in the sense that it replaces it, rather it accompanies and emerges out from it.' *Le Roman depuis la révolution française* (Paris: Presses Universitaires de France, 2011), 54. Consequently, 'the realist novel is not a rival phenomenon of Romanticism, but one of its essential components', as Claude Millet argues, indicating that the history of French Romanticism is not strictly linear. See *Le Romantisme: Du bouleversement des lettres dans la France postrévolutionnaire* (Paris: Livre de Poche, 2010), 102 and 21.

each draws upon. All three figures found in narrative the potential to animate rather than fix the meaning of history in ways that corresponded to the cultural and political changes of their day. Yielding significant reflections on the world, the novel could also sweep the reader off their feet through the high drama of plot and the depth of its characters, allowing each writer to talk about fundamental concerns whilst speaking to the ever-widening audience of an increasingly literate and commercialized France. In the late 1820s, Hugo, who by now was the poet commander-in-chief of the Romantic Cénacle, had begun experimenting with narrative fiction that disclosed 'his own uneasy and continuous ideological grappling with the fundaments of time and history'.[7] At the same time, Balzac embarked on what would become the immense novelistic cycle of the *Comédie humaine*, becoming 'the experimental scientist who funnelled the phantasmagoria of Romanticism into the test-tube of the modern novel'.[8] As the next decade began, Dumas, the veteran of French Romantic drama, started to gather historical information for his own wildly successful novels, each marked by 'the exhilarating vitality of his characters and the dynamic narration of history'.[9]

Any fraternity between Hugo, Balzac, and Dumas is usually conceived in historical and cultural terms: born within three years of one another at the turn of the century, they all became part of Charles Nodier's celebrated soirées in the Arsenal Library in the late 1820s. Each man was a literary celebrity by the 1840s, achieving unprecedented commercial success for their novels, and their fiction has today become part of an international popular culture thanks to a wide range of multimedia adaptations. But these writers are not only brothers in terms of age, of their historical experience of both Napoleonic Empire and Restoration monarchies, and of their immense success. In spite of the 'Romantic' and 'Realist' labels which subsequent literary criticism has tried to pin on them, their shared artistic culture and mutual interest in the diverse character of history indicates that they may also be considered as brothers-in-arms, especially in the attempt to maximize the novel's capabilities in their generation's expression of fluid meaning. All three men indicated in their writing that no attempt to understand past events or present happenings could lay claim to knowledge unless it relied on a dramatic vision of human experience, itself revealing the cultural impact of the German *Sturm und Drang*. This vision finds a natural expression in their fictional works, and each took care to reflect on its demands in a series of non-fictional commentaries which underline the modern writer's obligation to probe both the surfaces and the depths of history.

In his famous *Préface de Cromwell* (1827), Hugo argues that the modern age could only be conceived as dramatic in nature, thereby providing the Romantics of the 1820s with a forthright manifesto for freedom from the neoclassical 'cage' of proportion and

[7] Isabel Roche, *Character and Meaning in the Novels of Victor Hugo* (Indiana, Ind.: Purdue University Press, 2007), 3.

[8] Graham Robb, *Balzac* (London: Picador, 1994), 421. Robb is paraphrasing Zola's argument in *Le Roman expérimental* (1880).

[9] Matthias Alaguillaume, 'Le Roman de cape et d'épée d'Alexandre Dumas: Une écriture cinégraphique', in Christian Chelebourg (ed.), *Alexandre Dumas, 'raconteur'* (Paris: Minard, 2005), 101–21 (119).

regularity. Hugo splits history into what he calls the primitive and antique eras: the times of the Bible and the *Iliad*, lyric and epic respectively. What he sees in the modern era is the excitement of both impulses caught together, with lyric poetry characterized as a 'tranquil lake' and epic writing as its 'rushing river' which both feed into the 'ocean of drama': 'like the lake, drama reflects the heavens above; like the river, it reveals its brinks on the ground; but drama alone has depth and turmoil'. Christianity's recognition of human existence as at once eternal in its divine origins and worldly in its mortal coil enables such a realization: '[Man is] double and made of two beings: one ephemeral and embodied; the other immortal and ethereal.'[10] Opposites must hence feed into one another in art so as to mobilize the relationship between what is transcendent and what is actual. Hugo stresses that: 'The real comes from an entirely natural combination of two types, the sublime and the grotesque.... Everything binds together and pulls apart as in reality, and so true poetry lies in the harmony of contrasts.'[11] For Hugo, such truth is embodied primarily by Shakespeare's works, whose 'double flame' is fanned by Dante and Milton as artists who demonstrated that ugliness could be beautiful, and vice versa. The 'interior and exterior human worlds' of ideas and facts—the subjective sphere of feelings and thoughts, and the objective realm of things and physical laws—necessarily cross into one another without aligning their individual natures into an integral or objective whole. Nothing is absolute or fully finished within a universe of endless creation where moods interchange and where night and day rely upon one another. Categorical thinking, whether it were the black and white of the moral or the aesthetic spectrums, would never understand such a dramatic world whose reality was more than a matter of either flesh and bone or heart and mind alone. Consequently, the modern artist had to envisage himself as part of an infinite divine energy which could be channelled but never fully controlled, and whose workings could be known without ever being entirely mastered. The poet had to represent the world not in terms of fixed descriptions and self-sufficient meanings, but as a transient and boundless space, 'changing shape and course with the wind'.[12] To connect with this flux, the artist's mind needed to be *un miroir de concentration*, or magnifying mirror, avoiding what Hugo believes to be the dull, flat images of a standard reflective surface so as to concentrate the depth and intensity of his poetic visions under the guise of what he came to call a *voyant*: 'thereby making a light out of a flicker, and a flame out of a light'.[13]

Less than five years after this preface appeared, Balzac would echo Hugo's endorsement of an imaginative and attentive artist seeking out fundamental meanings. In his preface to *The Wild Ass's Skin*, he declared: 'The writer must be familiar with all effects, all natures. He is obliged to have within him a sort of concentric mirror (*miroir concentrique*) in which, according to his imagination, the universe comes to be reflected.' In

[10] *Préface de Cromwell*, in *Œuvres complètes: Critique* ed. Jean-Pierre Reynaud (Paris: Robert Laffont, 1985), 16.

[11] *Préface de Cromwell*, 16–17.

[12] *Préface de Cromwell*, 5.

[13] *Préface de Cromwell*, 25.

addition to the faculties of observation and lively self-expression, the writer requires a further talent that reflects the poetic *voyance* which Hugo promotes: 'a sort of second sight which permits them to guess at truth in all possible situations' and which 'science can only grasp with difficulty'.[14] The key, for Balzac, is not to deduce a definitive solution to problems encountered amidst his observations, but to describe those problems and to suggest their meaning. Looking back over the twenty-five years since the fall of Napoleon, he noted that: 'Drama, colour and science have penetrated all genres, and the most important books are obliged to follow this movement that makes compositions so attractive.'[15] In his celebrated attempt to display his own commitment to this mobility in the foreword or *Avant-propos* to the *Comédie humaine* in 1842, Balzac affirmed the importance of Romantic self-determination: 'I believe in progress, in man's ability to develop, and so those who want to see in my work the intent to consider man as a finite creature are oddly mistaken.'[16] Believing this titanic corpus of fiction to be another of mankind's great voyages of discovery, akin to Columbus approaching the New World or Galileo looking to the stars, Balzac is emphatic about the need for careful study, which in Hugo's thinking had remained more implicit. In a society motivated by capital, Balzac's primary inspirations are not a dramatist like Shakespeare or a poet like Milton, but men of science such as the zoologists Étienne Geoffroy Saint-Hilaire and Georges Louis Leclerc, Comte de Buffon. Treating men and women as objects to be observed and interpreted in their natural habitats, Balzac asks: 'If Buffon has produced a magnificent work that tries to represent the whole of zoology in one book, is there not a book of this genre to be written for society?' His goal is 'to write the kind of human history that is forgotten by so many historians': a history of social mores for his own age, the likes of which were lacking from previous major civilizations such as those of Athens and Rome. But to unveil the potential significance of his findings, the inventive *voyance* that Hugo privileged remains paramount. Unnerved by the vice of modern living, Balzac holds both the monarchy and the church as key social functions to promote stability, and so the quest for unseen moral orders drives his approach. 'A writer can become a more or less faithful painter ...; but to merit the acclaim that every artist should aspire towards, must I not also catch the hidden meaning in this immense throng of people, passions and events?'[17] In this respect, the opening references in the *Avant-propos* to Corneille and Molière, the master wordsmiths of the French stage, have potentially deeper implications than to note the need for artistic modesty before an audience: a suggestion lingers from the start that the *Comédie humaine* must be read as much as a creative work of art in search of sublime meaning as it should a scientific study.

Dumas's oeuvre may lack prefaces as distinguished as those of *Cromwell* or the *Comédie humaine*, but there is ample evidence that he too had been deeply influenced

[14] *Wild Ass's Skin*, 227–8.

[15] Letter of 15 July 1840 to Mme la Comtesse E, *Revue Parisienne*, 1/1 (1840), 49.

[16] 'Avant-propos', in *La Comédie humaine*, 12 vols, ed. Pierre-Georges Castex (Paris: Gallimard, 1976–81), i. 16.

[17] 'Avant-propos', 8–11.

by this Romantic investment in the twin powers of invention and observation. Writing the preface to his weekly serial novel *The Countess of Salisbury* in one of the earliest editions of *La Presse* in 1836, Dumas expressed his dissatisfaction with previous representations of France's history. In his view, works by historians 'starved the life' out of the past, whereas literary accounts had turned that same past into an embellished and 'disfigured' performance. Where Balzac honed the need for a material awareness and Hugo detailed a poetic drive, Dumas here struck a more openly even tone between what he sees as the deficits and excesses of studious inspection and stunning imagination. If historians lent shape to the past and writers gave it emotional substance, then the successful artist needed to bring both qualities to bear on their work. 'We have hoped that there remains a stance to take between those men who simply do not see with their mind's eye enough and those who do so too often.' In response, 'the drama that is history' establishes a relationship between fact and meaning, whereby 'the truth of the past, with both a body and a soul, would be rigorously observed'.[18] The artist need only follow the line left by history and link its episodes accordingly, using the imagination to cut through any fog and allow a human portrait to emerge. This activity is less an indulgence than it is the duty of the Romantic writer, who as Hugo had so emphatically argued in the late 1820s must recognize the correlation between the artistic dexterity and social diversity that were necessary to a free-thinking democracy. Dumas's toast during a banquet in early May 1834 smacks of the same conviction in the power of writing to change the reader's perception of reality that is present in Hugo's manifesto and in Balzac's mission: 'To Art! May both the pen and the paintbrush be as effective as the rifle and the sword in the regeneration of society to which we have dedicated our lives!'[19] Dumas's inspiration is the concealed, essential nature to all life, which like Hugo and Balzac he believes can only be accessed by a creative imagination. Reflecting on his early career in his memoirs in the 1850s, he likened the cosmic essence of the universe to a natural force which comes to rest atop writers of great talent as clouds would on mountain peaks. There, this phenomenon is obliged to release downpours which nourish the artist's mind and quench their thirst for inspiration, revealing that 'the spirit of God is poetic'.[20] This qualification of the divine as a dynamic rather than dictatorial force, priming the powers of signification as opposed to yielding immediate meaning, recalls the independence of spirit that both Hugo and Balzac highlighted.

For each writer, this Romantic drive to align feeling with knowledge, to force subjective values into dialogue with objective facts, required a dynamic expression that they each had come to believe the novel could provide thanks to Sir Walter Scott. 'One of the fetishes of the romantic cult', as one reviewer put it in 1821,[21] *walterscottmanie* became a fashion in France, from plays and paintings to tartan dress at society balls. A collective admiration of these writers for Scott is clear. Hugo claimed that 'few historians are as

[18] 'Introduction à nos feuilletons historiques', *La Presse*, 15 July 1836, 1–2 (2).

[19] *Mes Mémoires*, ed. Pierre Josserand, 5 vols (Paris: Gallimard, 1954–68), iv. 332.

[20] *Mes Mémoires*, 365.

[21] *Le Miroir*, 203 (Sept. 1821), 2.

faithful to the truth as this novelist';[22] Balzac respected how Scott 'combined drama, dialogue, portraiture, landscape, and description all at once, bringing wonder and truth into the genre';[23] and Dumas believed that Scott 'bonded a knowledge acquired from studying the hearts of men with the science of national histories.'[24] Scott's mixture of colourful adventure and historical detail immersed the reader in times gone by, utilizing the past not as a decoration within the narrative but as one of its key motors in the development of its characters. Mikhail Bakhtin's theories of narrative offer a useful elucidation of the novel's appeal in this respect through his concept of the 'chronotope'. Literally defined as 'time-space', the chronotope expresses the inseparability of temporal and spatial relationships: 'Time, as it were, thickens, takes on flesh, becomes artistically visible; likewise, space becomes charged and responsive to the movements of time, plot and history.'[25] Meaning becomes loosened in its reliance on context over text, on subjective situations and perspectives as opposed to an objective or continuous sense of truth. Crucial to this release is the melange of genres that the novel in turn could initiate as a hybrid literary form. Much as Hugo had called for an embrace of contrast rather than neoclassical symmetry, Scott noticeably mixed tones in his writing. Stepping beyond the Gothic and sentimental genres, he offered at once populist spectacle through his work's comic and fantastic moments, and thought-provoking insight through its more melancholic attributes. In a France whose cultural tastes were still governed by the insistence on uniformity, Scott had revealed the diversity of historical experience as opposed to any universal principle. Whereas Nicolas Boileau's *Art poétique* (1674) had disdainfully dismissed the novel as a frivolous form that was incapable of any greater reaction than simple amusement, Scott's writing indicated that fiction was capable of great depth precisely because it articulated a chronotopic image of history. In a clear broadside at Boileau's students, Nodier observed that: 'under Scott's pen, the novel has shed its meaningless frivolity, becoming an abundant and untainted source of useful instruction and valued knowledge.'[26]

Although Hugo, Balzac, and Dumas each acknowledged an individual debt to Scott's historiography in their own fiction, they made a case for developing rather than simply imitating his style. Alfred de Vigny's *Cinq-Mars* (1826) was the first major attempt to turn the French novel in the directions which Scott had opened up, but Vigny did not necessarily offer anything that had not already been seen with Scott's accomplishments. In admiration of the novel, Hugo politely implied that Vigny may have relied more on memory than imagination: 'There's no doubt that if someone had presented you with this book as one of Walter Scott's new works, you would not be the only reader to have initially been taken in.'[27] Following Scott, the aim would be to introduce a more

[22] 'Sur Walter Scott, à propos de *Quentin Durward*', in *Œuvres complètes: Critique*, 146.

[23] 'Avant-propos', 10.

[24] 'Introduction à nos feuilletons historiques', 1.

[25] Mikhail Bakhtin, *The Dialogic Imagination*, tr. Caryl Emerson and Michael Holquist (Austin, Tex., and London: University of Texas Press, 1981), 84–5.

[26] Review of *Han d'Islande*, *La Quotidienne*, 21 Mar. 1823; cited in Marguerite Iknayan, *The Idea of the Novel in France: The Critical Reaction 1815–48* (Geneva: Droz, 1961), 36.

[27] *La Quotidienne*, 30 July 1826; cited in Victor E. François, 'Sir Walter Scott and Alfred de Vigny', *Modern Language Notes*, 21/5 (1906), 129–34 (133).

pronounced sense of Romantic verve into the novel so as to optimize its ability to represent indeterminate and ever-shifting meanings. In his review of *Quentin Durward* (1823), Hugo found the inspiration in Scott's novels to demand a lyric quality for fiction that would heighten and quicken the drama through the form itself. 'Following on from Walter Scott's picturesque but prosaic novel, another novel waits to be created, and one that I feel is yet finer and more complete. At once dramatic and grand, it is a novel that is picturesque but poetic; realistic yet idealistic; truthful, but also extraordinary.' The novelist, to be a true artist, must 'look for the depths in everything' to create a narrative that is as profound as it is broad.[28] This is the *roman dramatique* that Hugo pointed to in the *Préface de Cromwell*, acknowledging storytellers and prose writers like Cervantes and Rabelais as those who strengthen the transition from epic to dramatic art.[29] For Balzac, Scott may be developed on two fronts, not only to lend greater substance to a text's verisimilitude but also to impart a more distinct personal vision to a writer's work. First, he detected a Protestantism in Scott's depiction of female characters which reduces them all to symbols of virginal wholesomeness. Balzac stated that he would stomach a more morally dubious set of traits in the women of the *Comédie humaine*, paying close attention to contemporary reality. Secondly, he promised that each of his works would plug into an expansive network so as to represent a wide-ranging vision of society that leaves no stone unturned. In contrast to Scott, who 'had not thought of linking his works to one another so as to coordinate an overarching narrative, each chapter of which would have been an individual novel',[30] Balzac intended to evoke a broader, more ambitious chronicle, full of cross-references and recurring characters, that would testify to his own ingenuity. Only Dumas was implicit in his declarations to progress from 'the Scottish bard', possibly because he held greater personal affection for Scott's novels.[31] But his comment that his thematic focus would be 'the history of those passions which Satan thrust into our tranquil hearts before the Fall'[32] betrays a sympathy for Balzac's criticism of Scott's Protestant standpoint towards his characters, and a penchant for more salacious action.

If we read these arguments alongside and through one another, a mutual understanding emerges of reality as a constructed and mobile space rather than a predetermined and static object of enquiry. If Scott stoutly exercised the power of fiction to represent the world as defined by time and place, then Hugo, Balzac, and Dumas wanted to expose and explore that power as the basis for all human knowledge. Respectively bringing philosophical scope, narrative sweep, and dramatic stealth to the novel, their fiction is characterized by flexible narrative frames, indeterminate meanings, and the need for agile reading strategies. Each writer engaged with the prospects and problematics of trying to pattern a historicized, socialized reality whose truths are therefore relative rather than unvarying in nature.

[28] 'Sur Walter Scott', 149–51.

[29] *Préface de Cromwell*, 14.

[30] 'Avant-propos', 11.

[31] In his memoirs, Dumas recalls that Scott's descriptions of the Roman dining room in *Ivanhoe* (1820) electrified his imagination when he first read it in his late teens: ii. 279–80.

[32] 'Introduction à nos feuilletons historiques', 2.

In order to evoke the drama of human experience so as to entice their readers, all three writers make the act of assembling and interpreting narratives a thematic and formal concern in their fiction, whether casting their eyes back over past history or turning towards history in the making in contemporary society. In so doing, the legacy of Romantic individualism itself emerges as both a growing social reality and a moral dilemma about how to behave. Human reality is revealed as a construct, powered by subjective and individual inputs which, although not real in material terms and certainly not rock-steady in duration, acquire both weight and shape as the basis of truth. The tension between reality and its meaning is cultivated by these writers, so as to dramatize the human experience of history and indeed the reader's encounter with the texts themselves as a manifestation of that same experience. Such drama is reinforced by each writer's ability to draw upon the traits of populist literary genres, especially melodrama. The appeal of their thinking is thereby broadened through thrilling emotions, thwarted desires, and theatrical confrontations which have inserted characters like Quasimodo, Rastignac, and d'Artagnan into a popular consciousness.

Hugo's very first novels, *Hans of Iceland* (1823) and *Bug-Jargal* (1826), both incorporate elements of this dramatic approach, albeit in a tentative manner as the poet searched for both his narrative and political voice during a decade which would see him become increasingly liberal-minded. That voice—so distinctive in his later novels of the 1860s, such as *Les Misérables* (1862)—became considerably more audible with the publication of *The Last Day of a Condemned Man* (1829), an anonymous narrator's first-person reflection on his own impending execution, and *Notre-Dame de Paris* (1831), the hugely popular story that today is most associated with the hunchback Quasimodo. Each novel relies on a visual imagination to immerse the reader vigorously within a credibly physical space, from the purple faces and shivering bodies of the convicts in the Bicêtre prison to Notre-Dame's architectural face and her symbolically ocular *rosace* window that sees out across fifteenth-century Paris. At the same time, they espouse a plea for self-determination and human tolerance that is clear in the plight of both the condemned man and the hunchback of Notre-Dame cathedral, neither of whom possesses the contemptible character that their social status as murderer and monster would suggest. In turn, these texts oblige both their characters and their readers to look more closely and acknowledge a less objective, more diverse world in which meaning is not only inscribed but may also be effaced and rewritten. The condemned man frets over his decision to write down his thoughts as he awaits death, introducing a notion of writing as an anxious rather than self-certain foundation of meaning: 'But what to write? What can I have to say, I who have nothing left before me in this world?'[33] Similarly, his exploration of his prison cell one night throws into question his ability to make sense of what he finds. The walls reveal a 'strange book': they are covered with a continuous mix of scribbles, drawings, odd shapes and numerous names, all written using a variety of materials from chalk to blood, and none of which is fully discernible. The prisoner

[33] *Le Dernier Jour d'un condamné, in Œuvres complètes: Roman*, 3 vols, ed. Jacques Seebacher (Paris: Laffont, 1985), i. 437.

yearns 'to rediscover each man beneath these names, to give both meaning and life to these mutilated inscriptions', but deprived of a future, he realizes that such a narrative is beyond him.[34] With regard to his own history in chapter 47, there exists only a title (*Mon histoire*), with the implication that he was as unable to put such a narrative together under this heading as he has been throughout the novel to give anything other than a highly suggestive impression of his past. Condemned to death and haunted by terrifying visions, he feels that time now lacks regularity, deepening both the reader's sense of disorientation and their unease at the horrific plight of this dignified man. Not only does such an effect strengthen Hugo's ethical plea against the death penalty, but it also reiterates to the reader the close connection between narrative and truth. In *Notre-Dame de Paris*, Hugo again toyed with the power of narrative to establish and eradicate meaning. The narrator persists in reminding his reader that his representations of the novel's medieval setting and action are precisely that: attempts to depict scenes and determine meanings which are at once insistent and insufficient. The abundance of vivid images used to describe Quasimodo ('that tetrahedral nose, that horseshoe mouth, the tiny left eye') are still not enough to render the creature fully present, and so the reader is encouraged to imagine the sight for themselves.[35] The hunchback is described as an approximation of a human being, acting as a potent metaphor for the always unfinished nature of human reality that is enlarged by the cathedral he calls home. As a Gothic structure, Notre-Dame is a heterogeneous presence that bears testament to a transient reality through the assortment of changes in taste and tone across French history that can be read upon her walls. Offering sanctuary to the innocent gypsy girl Esmeralda, the cathedral, like her hunchbacked bell-ringer, is furthermore allied with a revolutionary spirit of freedom and creativity which stands in stark contrast to its archdeacon, whose self-consciousness proves to be his undoing. Claude Frollo yearns for an all-encompassing value system to lend meaning to his existence. He becomes 'more and more rigid as a priest, and more and more unhappy as a man',[36] through both the absolutist morality of his dogmatic Catholicism and the promise of godlike personal power over the natural world offered by his study of alchemy. His faith in the narratives of the Fall and of science respectively distorts rather than enhances his humanity, leading to the tragic downfall of all three central characters amidst the epic siege of the cathedral by the Parisian underclass. This denouement reminds the reader of a point stressed by the narrator in his numerous digressions: that objective and totalized systems of truth are ill-equipped to showcase the shifting reality of a multifaceted human experience.

With his eyes on bourgeois society and the trappings of wealth, Balzac is more explicitly anxious than Hugo with regard to how a freedom from dogmatic orders and the consciousness of individual desire may fashion a posture of egotism. His own narrative interventions in *La Cousine Bette* (1846) tend towards a more reactionary standpoint that is best represented by one of his many recurring characters, Dr Horace Bianchon. When asked

[34] *Le Dernier Jour*, 441.

[35] *Notre-Dame de Paris*, tr. John Sturrock (London: Penguin, 2004), 70.

[36] *Notre-Dame de Paris*, 172.

what the cause of their society's growing moral depravity can be, he replies: 'Lack of religion and the pervasion everywhere of finance which is nothing but the concrete manifestation of selfishness.'[37] But Balzac's famous narrative interjections of *voici comment* ('here is how it happened') and *voici pourquoi* ('here is why it happened') do not justify any reading of his novels as epistemologically assured or morally objective. The drive towards causality and a transparency of meaning is countered by not only the fluid reality of modern living, which the narrator catalogues with extensive detail, but also Balzac's inability to resist the excitement and intrigue that this flux generates. In a jungle-like, morally unregulated Paris, the climate of his novels is unsettled rather than cool. He relies on illustriously dense descriptions not to paint a static picture but to animate a mobile experience. Entering into the curiosity shop towards the beginning of *The Wild Ass's Skin*, Raphael and the reader work their way through the 'immense pasture' of its rooms, whose countless artefacts across page after page span all of human civilization: 'this sea of furniture, inventions, fashions, works of art, and wreckage made up an endless poem. Forms, colours, ideas, everything came alive once more in that place. But he could perceive nothing whole in it.'[38] At the level of plot, this brimming and eerie environment introduces the notion of excess which will be the fate of both the hero and the indulgent consumerist society he represents, typified in the mouth-watering delicacies and luxurious bodies served up at the banker's orgy. At the yet more fundamental level of narrative, the shop presents human history as an accident of happenings that create an infinite mystery whose meanings can be proposed but never made unconditional. The symbol of the arabesque from Laurence Sterne's *Tristram Shandy* (1759–67) which marks the start of the novel visualizes the twisting movements that Balzac evokes for human experience, and which the reader is made to undergo more readily still through a conspicuous reference to Goethe. Raphael sees each work of art come alive, as if in 'a weird Sabbath worthy of the fantastical scenes witnessed by Doctor Faust on the Brocken'. But before offering Raphael the titular supernatural talisman that will fulfil his every wish, the shop owner bears not just the 'sly mask of Mephistopheles' from Goethe, but also the 'clear serenity of an omniscient God', subsequently playing with expectations.[39] When the old man later reappears at the opera, it is only the demonic visage which remains, as if the narrator wishes to categorize the talisman as evil. Yet the earlier ambiguity, reinforced by the talisman's Sanksrit inscription which proclaims that 'God will grant your wish', leaves the reader less sure as to whether the human pursuit of desire and knowledge can be qualified in absolute moral terms. One year later in *Le Colonel Chabert* (1832), Balzac dwells yet more intently on the difficulties of cohering experience into an understandable form. Near the novel's start in the lawyer Derville's offices, his clerk Godeschal is dictating a legal motion to his colleagues on which he offers a simultaneous and highly self-conscious commentary. Godeschal insists on certain punctuation and adjectives with the express intent of charming the Courts, even

[37] *Cousin Bette*, tr. Sylvia Raphael (Oxford: Oxford University Press, 1992), 434.

[38] *Wild Ass's Skin*, 16.

[39] *Wild Ass's Skin*, 20–2.

though he mocks the King as a 'big joker'.[40] Language, as the essential tool for representing meaning, is exposed by Balzac as performative in nature, placing the reader on guard against its potential manipulations. That caution is amplified by both the office's layout, full of bundles of papers and indistinguishable boxes, and the deficient sunlight allowed into it by the dirty window-panes: such a scene paints the truth-seeking practice of law through which bourgeois society is regulated as being tangled and unclear rather than organized and obvious. Within this environment, and trying to inhabit a monarchical era that does not care to remember its Napoleonic past, a man with a straightforward set of values like Chabert fails to adapt, unlike his calculating wife. Chabert's faith in the apparent moral clarity and social order under his beloved Napoleon smacks of childlike naivety when framed in terms of a filial relationship: 'I had a father, the Emperor! Oh, if he were standing today, the dear man, and he could see *his Chabert*, as he called me, in the outcast state I find myself in now—why, he would be outraged!'[41] As echoed in the demise of the eponymous central character of *Le Père Goriot* (1835), the certainties of patriarchal systems are no more, either for the characters or the reader. The new, democratic social model of capital and self-interest offers no moral guarantees.

Complementing Balzac's impeccable social perceptions and Hugo's ardent philosophical visions, there is a relentlessly energetic pace to Dumas's writing which is as acutely aware of the variable nature of human history as that of his two peers. Much of this velocity is charged by his use of the *roman feuilleton* in France's booming newspaper business from the late 1830s onwards. The emerging popularity of serialization allowed Dumas to maintain a substantial narrative line over an episodic structure that relies on subplots and cliff-hanger endings. The relentless deadlines from editors also further encouraged his use of collaborators with whom to develop his novels, most famously Auguste Maquet, raising scandalous accusations in the 1840s about the authorship of his work which were dismissed even at the time by associates like Maquet himself.[42] As with Hugo and Balzac, the use of local colour and visual detail is evident in Dumas's narratives in order to ground his fiction in a historicized reality, for example in the meticulous descriptions of Marseille's streets and Albert's bourgeois Parisian lodgings in *The Count of Monte Cristo* (1844–6), and of the royal ballet of La Merlaison in *The Three Musketeers* (1844). Noticeably, Dumas does not experiment with the novel's capacity for digression or extended authorial intervention, unlike Hugo and Balzac. The swift tempo of his writing at times obliges his narrator to apologize for having forgotten key details, such as a proper introduction of Valentine de Villefort in *The Count of Monte Cristo*, and leaves little time for such direct narrative involvement as an author. Instead, his novels are driven more singularly by character, with Edmond Dantès's intricate

[40] *Le Colonel Chabert*, in *La Comédie humaine* (Paris: Gallimard, 1976), iii. 312.

[41] *Le Colonel Chabert*, 331.

[42] Eugène de Mirecourt's notorious written assault on the 'novel factory' of 'Dumas and co.' in 1845 was met with disavowal from collaborators like Maquet and Paul Meurice, who insisted that the central and driving creative force in these texts was Dumas himself. Mirecourt was in fact fined by the Parisian authorities and jailed for fifteen days.

plans for revenge as the Count and d'Artagnan's spirited love of adventure captivating the reader's attention. Despite these stylistic differences, Dumas's fiction holds the same interest and investment in the workings of narrative as the means of instituting and inverting truth. The narratives of both *The Count of Monte Cristo* and *The Three Musketeers* are loaded with instances of characters narrating stories about themselves. Each of these is revealed as a practice that is at best individual and at worst illusory so as to cue the reader's own interpretive caution, from Bertuccio's loaded recounting of the events behind his vendetta against Villefort to Milady de Winter's siren-like deceptions of Felton and Constance through her pretence of virtue. This exposure is perhaps best observed in how each novel refuses to give an unambiguous sanction for its heroes' own self-perceptions, further complicating the individualist heritage of 1789's *liberté, égalité*, and *fraternité*. Full of valour and youthful passion, d'Artagnan leads a hero's life of indiscriminate swashbuckling and carefree romance. However, his self-confidence is doubly rocked by the novel's climax. First, Milady's murder of Constance confounds his characteristic faith in Fate: his pleas to God unanswered, he throws himself 'like a madman' upon his mistress's body.[43] The subsequent offer of promotion to the rank of musketeer further confuses his moral compass, since this proposal does not come from a paternal or trustworthy figure like Tréville, but from the supposedly villainous Cardinal Richelieu, whose ulterior motives for greater power are well-established. Dantès especially exhibits a core belief in Providence which ostensibly serves to validate his identity, but which Dumas again displaces. Dantès thirsts for revenge on the men whose betrayal condemned him to fourteen years of imprisonment, the horrors and injustice of which demand the reader's sympathy. Given that his incarceration coincides with Napoleon's final defeat in 1815, and that each of his targets (Fernand, Danglars, and Villefort) represent three cornerstones of monarchical France (the military, the banking system, and the King's lawcourts), a clear moral indictment of the new, corrupt social order seems apparent. Believing himself appointed by God as his 'agent of Providence', he deals out 'my own justice, which suspends no sentences and hears no appeals'.[44] The tragic fate of Villefort's family, however, which is triggered by Dantès's plotting, confirms suspicions that the narrative has encouraged through his increasingly inhuman obsession: that his powers as the extraordinarily resourceful Count do not serve a perfect justice. What complicates the scenario further still is that his realization of having become 'vengeful, secretive, and cruel', and that man should have faith in God's own design by 'waiting and hoping',[45] does not automatically negate the moral value of his previous actions, especially as the future happiness of Maximilien and Valentine has depended on his stratagems of revenge. Dumas's fiction invokes both the well-oiled myths and the coarse-ridden reality of autonomous and patriarchal power embodied in both the Napoleonic and monarchist traditions.

[43] *The Three Musketeers*, tr. Richard Pevear (London: Penguin, 2006), 643.
[44] *The Count of Monte Cristo*, tr. Robin Buss (London: Penguin, 1996), 317.
[45] *Count of Monte Cristo*, 1192 and 1243.

Evidently, for Hugo, Balzac, and Dumas, only a fiction of this dramatic kind could effectively represent the disorderly march of social history and survey the subjective nature of its meanings. Moreover, the interplay between Romantic imagination and Realist scrutiny is both pronounced and lively, forcing systematic modes of understanding to collapse through the intuition of drama. This fluidity may ultimately be read as both a reflection of and a response to the ideological vertigo that France experiences as she reckons with the abyss of 1789. In this context, Sandy Petrey's shrewd analyses of Realism's expansion in the early 1830s put forward a structural model which may highlight the interchanges between Balzac's 'Realist' narrative and Hugo's and Dumas's 'Romantic' fiction. The interest in how truth is at once created and essentialized not only enables a socio-historical consciousness but also empowers a political awareness, given that the Orleanist monarchy at once harnessed and then denied the historical narrative of the Revolution in July 1830. 'Like the revolution that became a monarchy, realism has as its armature representation's power to make and unmake reality.... Realism's great accomplishment is not to represent reality but to represent representation as it configures reality, as it generates and destroys reality.'[46] The narrative engagement with both the desire for a meaning to human experience and the devices through which it comes into (and slips out of) existence is one shared by these three colossal figures of French Romanticism. As the journalist Beauchamp declares after another extraordinary episode in *The Count of Monte Cristo*: 'Let anyone now deny that drama is only in art and not in nature!'[47] But perhaps above all else, Hugo, Balzac, and Dumas possessed an instinctive feel for the novel in its ability both to engage and to entertain the swelling readerships of nineteenth-century society. Their ability to connect with audiences both in their own time and thereafter demands joint attention in any consideration of the novel's rise to prominence during *le siècle romantique*, even if such joint attention has not always been forthcoming. Helping to find ever-greater depth to the novel form and to lend it a sense of pensive sobriety, they also understood its aptitude for the fizz and froth of popular spectacle.

Further Reading

Primary Sources

Balzac, Honoré de, *Le Colonel Chabert*, in *La Comédie humaine*, iii (Paris: Gallimard, 1976).

Balzac, Honoré de, *Cousin Bette*, tr. Sylvia Raphael (Oxford: Oxford University Press, 1992).

Balzac, Honoré de, *The Wild Ass's Skin*, tr. Helen Constantine (Oxford: Oxford Classics/Oxford University Press, 2012).

Hugo, Victor, *Préface de Cromwell*, in *Œuvres complètes: Critique*, ed. Jean-Pierre Reynaud (Paris: Robert Laffont, 1985).

[46] *In the Court of the Pear King: French Culture and the Rise of Realism* (Ithaca, NY: Cornell University Press, 2005), 35 and 55. As Petrey notes, such a condition does not disenfranchise this reality or place it within the quotation marks adopted by poststructuralist criticism, since Balzac's novels demonstrate that it remains 'aggressively real' for all those who inhabit it (p. 145).

[47] *Count of Monte Cristo*, 1174.

Hugo, Victor, *Le Dernier Jour d'un condamné*, in *Œuvres complètes: Roman*, 3 vols, ed. Jacques Seebacher (Paris: Laffont, 1985).
Hugo, Victor, *Notre-Dame de Paris*, tr. John Sturrock (London: Penguin, 2004).
Dumas *père*, Alexandre, *Mes Mémoires*, ed. Pierre Josserand, 5 vols (Paris: Gallimard, 1954–68).
Dumas *père*, Alexandre, *The Count of Monte Cristo*, tr. Robin Buss (London: Penguin, 1996).
Dumas *père*, Alexandre, *The Three Musketeers*, tr. Richard Pevear (London: Penguin, 2006).

Secondary Sources

Bakhtin, Mikhail, *The Dialogic Imagination*, tr. Caryl Emerson and Michael Holquist (Austin, Tex., and London: University of Texas Press, 1981).
Blanckeman, Bruno, *Le Roman depuis la Révolution française* (Paris: Presses Universitaires de France, 2011).
Brooks, Peter, *Reading for the Plot: Design and Intention in Narrative* (Cambridge, Mass.: Harvard University Press, 1984).
Chelebourg, Christian (ed.), *Alexandre Dumas, 'raconteur'* (Paris: Minard, 2005).
Eichner, Hans (ed.), *Romantic and its Cognates: The European History of a Word* (Toronto: University of Toronto Press, 1972).
Iknayan, Marguerite, *The Idea of the Novel in France: The Critical Reaction 1815–48* (Geneva: Droz, 1961).
Millet, Claude, *Le Romantisme: Du bouleversement des lettres dans la France postrévolutionnaire* (Paris: Livre de Poche, 2010).
Robb, Graham, *Balzac* (London: Picador, 1994).
Petrey, Sandy, *In the Court of the Pear King: French Culture and the Rise of Realism* (Ithaca, NY: Cornell University Press, 2005).
Roche, Isabel, *Character and Meaning in the Novels of Victor Hugo* (Indiana, Ind.: Purdue University Press, 2007).
Watt, Ian, *The Rise of the Novel: Studies in Defoe, Richardson and Fielding* (1957; repr. London: Chatto & Windus, 1960).

CHAPTER 6

ROMANTIC DRAMA
The Mask of Genius

SOTIRIOS PARASCHAS

> CHATTERTON: 'j'ai résolu de ne me point masquer et d'être moi-même jusqu'à la fin' (I have decided to throw off my mask and be myself until the end).[1]

CHATTERTON's determination in Alfred de Vigny's eponymous play can be seen as summarizing the desire for authenticity voiced insistently and repeatedly by Romantic authors and fictional characters in the first half of the nineteenth century—a desire condemned as a 'romantic lie' by René Girard. In *Mensonge romantique et vérité romanesque*, he argues that the authenticity the Romantic subject lays claim to is an illusion; according to Girard, this claim is of a 'metaphysical' nature and obscures the fact that desire imitates and is mediated by the desires of others.[2] If the Romantic subject in general is substituted for the artist, Romantic texts offer a series of more down-to-earth reasons which demonstrate the impossibility of authenticity: the artist, if he is to survive, must face a utilitarian, Philistine society which values productivity over inspiration, views art as a kind of innocuous amusement and is envious of men of genius, taking any opportunity to cast them out. In such a context, the artist often has to define his place and his function in society in ways external to the essence of his work or to the aesthetic domain: he has to assume a mask. This conflict between the artist of genius or the exceptional individual and his time is explored in multifarious ways in Romantic texts.

This confrontation manifests itself more vividly in the theatre for a variety of reasons. Strategically, drama was of crucial importance for the Romantics, not least because it was the last stronghold of neoclassicism; the stage was the field in which the battle between the

[1] Alfred de Vigny, *Œuvres complètes*, ed. François Germain, André Jarry, and Alphonse Bouvet (Paris: Gallimard, 1986–93), i. 771. Further references are given after quotations in the text.

[2] René Girard, *Mensonge romantique et vérité romanesque* (Paris: Hachette, 1961).

'Classicists' and the 'Romantics' was fought at its fiercest. One of the most prominent models for the Romantics was Shakespeare; his disregard for the Aristotelian unities of time, place, and action as well as the combination of verse and prose, and tragedy and comedy in his plays were not merely proof of the right of genius to assert his own originality by breaking venerated rules but also represented the grievances of the Romantics against French neoclassical theatre, as Stendhal had discussed in his *Racine et Shakespeare* (1823–5).[3] In his preface to *Cromwell* (1827), which soon acquired the status of a manifesto of Romanticism, Victor Hugo, reviewing the history of literature from antiquity to his time, claimed that every age was characterized by the dominance of a particular genre whose main qualities pervaded all literary productions—drama being the one suited to the 'modern age'.[4]

In 1830, at the premiere of Hugo's *Hernani*, the Comédie Française became a literal battlefield from which the Romantics emerged victorious. The 'battle of *Hernani*' became a symbol of the emancipation of the Romantic artist from the shackles of the neo-classical tradition and its antiquated rules; this liberation, however, was far from signalling the absolute artistic freedom usually associated with Romanticism. The theatre, in particular, was a highly regulated cultural field. The freedom of the theatres established in 1791 had been severely restricted by Napoleon who, in 1807, had limited their number and distinguished between 'official' and 'secondary' theatres with specific repertoires in terms of genre—the domain of the secondary ones being the 'minor' genres of the vaudeville and the melodrama. Censorship was virtually omnipresent throughout the nineteenth century: even during the period 1830–5, when it was temporarily abolished, plays could be banned after their premiere, as was the case with Hugo's *Le Roi s'amuse*. Most importantly, the theatre was the most commercial form of literature, in which the Romantics could not pretend to be addressing themselves to the 'happy few': this immediate confrontation of the author with the public brought to the forefront the conflict between genius and society.

This conflict acquires even greater intensity if one takes into account the fact that 'Romantic drama' is not synonymous with 'drama in the age of Romanticism'. Histories of Romanticism and of French literature tend to reserve the term 'Romantic drama' for the works of only a handful of authors: Victor Hugo, Alfred de Vigny, Alexandre Dumas, Alfred de Musset, and, occasionally, Honoré de Balzac. With the exception of Dumas, who had a twin career as a novelist and as a dramatist, none of these authors was a professional playwright. The fact that they were poets and novelists who ventured on the stage is decisive in terms of their approach to drama, their authorial status, and of the reception of their plays. Unlike professional playwrights who would engage in an empirical approach to their art, the Romantics were intent on theorizing their practice. Professional playwrights would produce several plays per year and their publication would not be certain, if the performances were not successful. The Romantics (with the

[3] Stendhal, *Racine et Shakespeare*, in *Œuvres complètes* (Geneva: Cercle du bibliophile, 1968–74), xxxix.

[4] Victor Hugo, 'Préface de *Cromwell*', in *Théâtre complet*, ed. J.-J. Thierry and Josette Mélèze (Paris: Gallimard, 1963–4), i. 424.

exception of Dumas) not only had a relatively meagre dramatic output[5] but the plays would be intended for publication, independently of their performance: Hugo never intended *Cromwell* to be staged and he published *Le Roi s'amuse* before the premiere, while Musset, after the failure of his first play to be performed, *La Nuit vénitienne* (1830), abandoned the stage and started publishing his plays under the general title *Un Spectacle dans un fauteuil* or 'armchair theatre'. Their plays would also be accompanied by prefaces which would explain the aesthetic *credos* of their authors or defend them against contemporary critics. At the same time, professional playwrights were systematically engaged in collaborations which would often involve more than two authors: in the first half of the nineteenth century, collaboratively authored plays were never less than 50 per cent of the entire dramatic production, while the percentage in the late 1820s and the 1830s often rose up to 70 per cent.[6] By contrast, the Romantics subscribed to the idea of the solitary genius and, when they employed collaborators, they would often do so without acknowledging them. Dumas (who, unlike the rest of the Romantics, did not merely operate within the context of this authorial model of collaboration but had also transferred it to prose fiction) would usually acknowledge only his long-term collaborators, such as Auguste Maquet, and would often sign plays which were largely based on the work of others (as is the case with *Kean, ou Désordre et génie*). Finally, the works of the Romantics would habitually be perceived by critics as plays written by poets or novelists: Vigny's *Chatterton* was described as an elegy, 'une poésie mélancolique et triste plutôt qu'un drame' (a melancholy and sad poem, rather than a play);[7] Balzac's *Les Ressources de Quinola* as 'plutôt un roman qu'un drame' (a novel rather than a play);[8] Hugo's *Le Roi s'amuse* as a highly undramatic but 'admirable poésie qui n'a pas pu être entièrement exécutée sur la scène ... et ... elle sera mieux goûtée encore sur le papier' (admirable poem which could not have been performed properly on the stage ... and ... will be enjoyed better on the page).[9] In fact, their plays were often derived from their non-dramatic works or based on recurrent themes of their oeuvre: *Chatterton* is an adaptation of a section of Vigny's own *Stello*; Balzac's first play to be performed, *Vautrin*, resurrects a character from *La Comédie humaine* on the stage, while Dumas systematically adapted his own novels as soon as their serial publication was completed.

The Romantics' intention to revolutionize the stage cannot be seen independently of the material benefits of a dramatic career for a nineteenth-century author: despite the prestige of poetry and the slightly higher respectability of the novel in comparison to drama, a play could have the benefit of being instantly translated in immediate popularity

[5] Vigny produced three original plays; four of Balzac's plays were staged during his lifetime; between 1827 and 1843, Hugo staged nine plays and adapted *Notre Dame de Paris* into an opera; Musset's plays (with the exception of *La Nuit vénitienne*) began being staged from 1847 onwards.

[6] F. W. J. Hemmings, 'Co-Authorship in French Plays of the Nineteenth Century', *French Studies*, 41/1 (1987), 37–51 (41).

[7] Anonymous, 'Comédie Française. *Chatterton*', *L'Artiste*, 1st ser. 9 (1835), 33–6 (36).

[8] Gabriel-Désiré Laverdant, '*Les Ressources de Quinola*', *Phalange*, 3rd ser. 5/37 (27 Mar. 1842), cols 595–606 (col. 604).

[9] L.H., 'De Victor Hugo: A propos du *Roi s'amuse*', *L'Artiste*, 1st ser. 4 (1832), 198–200 (199).

and commercial success. This, however, clashed with one of the main authorial strategies employed by these authors, namely, their marketing themselves as geniuses—a quality which, as *Chatterton* demonstrates, is predicated on being unappreciated and impoverished. This contradiction generates tensions in several key Romantic dramas which thematize the clash between exceptional individuals and their time and society—problematizing thus the very status of Romanticism on the stage and that of the Romantics as authors venturing on a foreign and (more often than not) hostile territory. The underlying idea of the plays which will be discussed in what follows is the internal conflict between the 'authentic', 'pure', 'innocent' self of the artist (the genius) and the 'mask' he has to assume in order to survive in a materialistic society and in the literary marketplace.

The protagonist of Alfred de Vigny's *Chatterton* (1835) is the eighteenth-century English poet Thomas Chatterton, famous both for his suicide and for attributing his own poems to a fictional fifteenth-century monk by the name of Thomas Rowley. The play focuses on Chatterton's suicide and presents him as a young, penniless poet who, pursued by his creditors, hides his identity and lodges with the Bell family. His fellow lodger, referred to only as 'the Quaker', suspects his intention to commit suicide as well as the mutual feelings that begin to develop between Chatterton and his landlady, Kitty Bell. When Lord Beckford, on whose patronage Chatterton has placed his last hopes, offers him the humiliating position of a valet and when a credulous critic declares that his poems have indeed been written by Thomas Rowley and that Chatterton is a plagiarist, the poet poisons himself and is followed to the grave by Kitty Bell who dies from the shock.

As the first reviewers of the play noticed, Vigny had omitted any unsympathetic traits of Chatterton's character.[10] His portrayal of the young poet (whose story he had already recounted in *Stello*)[11] had been tailored to match the stereotypical image of a genius: brilliant and tortured, penniless and humiliated by society, driven to suicide as the only option—an ideal figure to dramatize what Vigny called, in his preface, 'le martyre perpétuel et la perpétuelle immolation du Poète' (the perpetual martyrdom and the perpetual sacrifice of the Poet) (750). Vigny specified that he wanted to 'montrer l'homme spiritualiste étouffé par une société matérialiste' (show the spiritual man stifled by a materialist society) (759) whose representatives in the play are Chatterton's landlord, John Bell, and Lord Beckford, both equally exaggerated characters. John Bell is the self-made capitalist who is shown mercilessly firing an injured worker from his factory, while Lord Beckford is presented as a condescending patron who dismisses poetry as a mere useless amusement (806) and believes that the young poet is well suited to be his valet.

At first sight, the play seems to support this distinction between poetry and materialism: Chatterton distinguishes between 'le travail du corps' and 'le labeur de la tête'

10 R., 'Théâtre français. Première représentation de *Chatterton*', *Journal des débats*, 14 Feb. 1835.

11 On the differences between the two versions, see Barbara T. Cooper, 'Exploitation of the Body in Vigny's *Chatterton*: The Economy of Drama and the Drama of Economics', *Theatre Journal*, 34/1 (1982), 20–6 (21–2).

(manual and mental labour) (772) and declares that he is, by nature, unfit for any profession (773), vehemently opposing the idea of productivity: 'qu'importe, si une heure de cette rêverie produit plus d'œuvres que vingt jours de l'action des autres? Qui peut juger entre eux et moi?' (what does it matter, if an hour of this reverie produces more works than twenty days of action others may undertake? Who can judge what is best, their way or mine?) (772). This belief in idleness as a condition of poetry (confirmed in the preface to the play, in which Vigny claims that the poet 'a besoin de *ne rien faire*, pour faire quelque chose en son art' (needs to *do nothing*, in order to create something in his art) (753)) is the characteristic trait of what Vigny calls 'le Poète' (753), one of the three distinct types of people who engage in the work of the intellect. 'L'homme de lettres' (the man of letters) is appreciated and at ease in society and, while he does not possess real emotions, he can express himself felicitously (750–1). 'L'écrivain' (the writer) is disciplined and of a philosophical disposition: his work springs from a deep conviction and consists in a fight for his principles (751–2). The Poet is a plaything of his own imagination, prone to involuntary reveries (752) and unable to function in everyday life (753). In the play, Chatterton himself hesitates, for a moment, between 'les deux poésies possibles' (the two kinds of poetry possible). According to the first option, the author has to 'saisir [s]on âme et l'emporter tour à tour dans le cadavre ressuscité des personnages qu' [il] évoque' (grasp his soul and drag it into one after another of the resuscitated corpses of the characters he is evoking). According to the second, 'il faut que, devant Chatterton malade, devant Chatterton qui a froid, qui a faim, [s]a volonté fasse poser avec prétention un autre Chatterton, gracieusement paré pour l'amusement du public, et que celui-là soit décrit par l'autre; le troubadour par le mendiant' (before a Chatterton who is sick, who hungers and thirsts, his will must place, pretentiously, another Chatterton, gracefully attired for the public's amusement, and the latter must be described by the former; the troubadour by the beggar). He has to 'faire jouer de misérables poupées, ou l'être soi-même et faire trafic de cette singerie' (animate miserable puppets or become one himself and trade on this mockery) (792). The rejection of this option summarizes the desire for authenticity and the idea that Chatterton is determined 'de ne [s]e point masquer et d'être [s]oi-même jusqu'à la fin' (to throw off his mask and be himself until the end) (771). In his preface, Vigny argues that, since any attempt on the part of the poet to assume a different role in society, or even to become a 'man of letters' would result in a part of himself dying, in a series of 'demi-suicides', the only 'authentic' option is to commit suicide (754–5)—a statement at which several reviewers took offence, seeing the play both as an immoral apology for suicide and as a false representation of the rather prosperous status of poets in the July Monarchy, many of whom were present at the premiere of the play.[12]

A closer look at the play, however, reveals that, despite what Vigny claims, the desire for authenticity is not the most accurate motive for Chatterton's suicide. In fact,

[12] H.B., 'Théâtres. Théâtre français. *Chatterton*', *L'Epoque*, 1st ser. 1 (1835), 557–8; anonymous, 'Théâtre français. *Chatterton*', *Le Figaro*, 15 Feb. 1835; anonymous, 'Théâtre français. *Chatterton*', *Gazette des théâtres*, 15 Feb. 1835; anonymous, 'Spectacles. Th. Français. *Chatterton*', *L'Indépendant*, 15 Feb. 1835.

Chatterton is far from having thrown off his mask. In terms of the plot, he is hiding his identity at the Bells: he has been renting a room for three months (764) under the familiar version of his first name, Tom, and he is terrified of being recognized by one of his former friends, Lord Talbot: 'il ne pouvait rien m'arriver de pis que de le voir. Mon asile était violé, ma paix était troublée, mon nom était connu ici' (nothing worse could happen to me than to see him. My sanctuary would be violated, my peace disturbed and my name would be known here) (777). More importantly, in terms of his work, he has assumed the mask of Thomas Rowley. Despite the fact that Vigny presents the Poet in his preface as only being appreciated by few, Chatterton's poems are successful, as long as they are attributed to a fifteenth-century monk. A significant component of the Romantic notion of genius is not merely the fact that genius is not appreciated in its own time, but also that it will be recognized as such by future generations of readers. Chatterton claims that his 'muse' would have been ignored if he had not transported her to the past: 'ils l'auraient brisée s'ils l'avaient crue faite de ma main: ils l'ont adorée comme l'œuvre d'un moine qui n'a jamais existé' (they would have crushed her if they believed her my creation: they have adored her as the work of a monk who never existed) (773). In pretending to be Rowley, Chatterton manages to present himself as a genius of the past who is only appreciated three centuries later.

The contradiction between Chatterton's statement that he wants to be himself and the fact that he masquerades as Rowley seems to be resolved, since the characters of the play are aware of who is the real author of the poems (773). However, the poet cannot throw his mask off easily—and it is precisely this fact that precipitates his suicide. A critic who has fallen prey to Chatterton's hoax denounces him as a plagiarist and, as Chatterton puts it in *Stello*, his mask turns into a shroud: 'j'espérais que l'illusion de ce nom supposé ne serait qu'un voile pour moi; je sens qu'elle m'est un linceul' (I was hoping that the illusion of this invented name would be nothing more than a veil for me; I feel that it has become my shroud) (533).

In addition to his inability to unmask himself, the very act of suicide can be seen as an instance of Chatterton's participation in the economy of productivity he despises, rather than as an authentic act which confirms his true self. Chatterton, during the course of the play, struggles with a work that he must finish on time, if he is to repay his debts: in calculating and quantifying his gift, '[il a] manqué de respect à [s]on âme immortelle, [il] l'[a] louée à l'heure et vendue' (he has disrespected his immortal soul, he has rent it by the hour and sold it away) (803). More importantly, according to his agreement with his creditor, Skirner, if he dies before he completes the work, his body will be sold to the College of Surgeons as a way of paying his debt (801): the poet is therefore complicit, body and soul, in the discourse of productivity; as John Bell puts it, 'tout doit rapporter, les choses animées et inanimées' (everything must yield a profit, both the living and the inanimate things) (768).[13]

[13] On the body as a commodity in *Chatterton*, see Cooper, 'Exploitation of the Body', 20–6; on *Chatterton* as 'une version économique du mal du siècle', see Nathalie Buchet Rogers, 'L'Or du poète et l'or du financier: Une lecture de *Chatterton* de Vigny, avec Mallarmé', *Nineteenth-Century French Studies*, 31/1–2 (2002–3), 84–103.

Chatterton can also be seen as participating in the other materialist discourse of the play, represented by Lord Beckford, the discourse of utility. In response to Beckford's opinion that writing verses is good for nothing and that every Englishman should be useful to his country, Chatterton retorts that England resembles a ship and every Englishman is part of the crew and therefore useful in his own way. He claims a higher order utility for poetry since the poet is the one who 'lit dans les astres la route que nous montre le doigt du Seigneur' (reads in the stars the path pointed by the Lord) (807). However, the metaphor of the poet as a navigator or a look-out points towards an instrumentalization of genius which is taken further in Honoré de Balzac's *Les Ressources de Quinola* (1842), in which the man of genius becomes literally a ship's engineer. A reviewer who compared the two plays claimed that 'il y a deux motifs qui font affronter les périls de la mer, le désir de s'enrichir et le désir de servir le pays; en un mot, il y a deux marines, la marine royale et la marine marchande' (there are two reasons to face the perils of the sea, the wish to be rich and the wish to serve one's country; in short, there two navies, the royal and the merchant one).[14] Alfonso Fontanarès, the fictional sixteenth-century inventor of the steam engine, seems to belong to the merchant navy.

Fontanarès, thanks to the machinations of his servant, the escaped convict Quinola, is given permission by Philip II of Spain to demonstrate his invention. Fontanarès wishes to acquire wealth and fame in order to be able to marry Marie Lothundiaz whose father has promised her to Sarpi, the viceroy's secretary. Faustina Brancadori, a Venetian courtesan, falls in love with the inventor and vows to destroy him because he has rejected her advances. The proliferation of enemies and debts force Fontanarès to collaborate with the ignorant don Ramon. Quinola, who has recourse to several tricks in order to help his master realize his project, enlists the help of another former convict, Monipodio, by means of the false promise that they will betray their master and steal his invention. Marie, who returns Fontanarès's feelings, helps them and eventually accepts to marry Sarpi in order to save the inventor. When, at the end of the play, the demonstration of the steam engine is about to begin, Fontanarès's enemies announce that the invention belongs to don Ramon; while the crowd cheers for the latter, the outraged Fontanarès is informed that Monipodio has sabotaged the engine and, knowing that the penalty for destroying a ship of the royal fleet is death, renounces his invention, asserting don Ramon's claim, and leaves Spain for Paris, accompanied by Quinola and Faustina.

Balzac's second play to be staged did not fare well with the critics. Their objections summarize its differences from *Chatterton* and the way in which it depicts the man of genius: reviewers criticized the inventor's lack of disinterestedness[15] and his association with a criminal.[16]

[14] Paul Gaschon de Molènes, 'Revue dramatique: *Les Ressources de Quinola*', *Revue des deux mondes*, 4th ser. 30 (1842), 136–51 (149).

[15] Ferdinand de La Boullaye, '*Les Ressources de Quinola*', *L'Indépendant*, 24 Mar. 1842; Gaschon de Molènes, 'Revue dramatique'.

[16] D—y, '*Les Ressources de Quinola*', *Le Constitutionnel*, 21 Mar. 1842; anonymous, '*Les Ressources de Quinola*', *Revue de Paris*, 4th ser. 3 (Mar. 1842), 301–3.

Fontanarès's primary motive is not his passion for science but his love for Marie: he admits that 'si je n'aimais pas Marie, je rendrais au hasard ce que le hasard m'a donné' (if I did not love Marie, I would return to chance that which chance has given me).[17] In this sense, he resembles less the disinterested geniuses of *La Comédie humaine* (such as Frenhofer and Gambara or Balthazar Claës, the scientist who neglects his own family and spends his fortune in his search for the absolute) and more the numerous representatives of the type of 'l'ambitieux', such as Rastignac in *Le Père Goriot*. Both Faustina and the Grand Inquisitor accuse him of viewing his invention as a means: 'Vous vous dites inventeur, et vous ne pensez qu'à la fortune! Vous êtes plus ambitieux qu'homme de génie' (You call yourself an inventor and you think of nothing but money! You are a man of ambition rather than one of genius) (466). Monipodio agrees: 'cet homme m'inquiète! il me paraît posséder mieux la mécanique de l'amour que l'amour de la mécanique' (this man worries me! He seems to have a firmer grasp of the mechanics of love than of the love of mechanics) (504).

According to a reviewer who compares *Les Ressources de Quinola* with *Chatterton*, Balzac

> aussi a voulu créer un homme de génie portant sous son front une pensée méconnue de tous; mais après des efforts dont nul n'a réussi …, au lieu de se résigner ou de mourir …, son héros tend une main à la femme perdue, une autre à l'homme flétri, et, fort de ces appuis indignes, se redresse pour défier la société.
>
> also wished to create a man of genius harbouring an idea no one appreciates; but after a series of failed efforts …, instead of resigning or dying …, his hero reaches out to a fallen woman and a branded man, and, with the support of these unworthy companions, rises to defy society).[18]

This association between genius and crime (a more benevolent version of the relation between Vautrin and Lucien in Balzac's *Splendeurs et misères des courtisanes*), however, serves an important function in the play. On the one hand, Fontanarès is presented as a pure genius who, like Chatterton, cannot survive in a materialist world: he is 'un savant qui ne sait pas compter' (a scientist who cannot count) (482), 'un sublime rêveur' (a sublime dreamer) (579), his 'délicieuse simplicité' (delightful simplicity) being 'le cachet du génie' (the mark of genius) (590). As Quinola claims, 'il ne suffit donc pas d'avoir du génie et d'en user …, il faut encore des circonstances' (possessing the faculty of genius and exploiting it is not enough …, one also needs favourable circumstances) (460), which are the domain of Fontanarès's servant. In order to ensure the survival of genius, Quinola has to engage in shady dealings, acting as the 'agent' of the man of genius without the latter being tainted by any of them. On the other hand, *Les Ressources de Quinola*, unlike *Chatterton*, is a comedy: the streetwise Quinola who is free to make jokes, use prison slang, and engage in unlikely disguises is meant to

[17] Honoré de Balzac, *Œuvres complètes*, ed. Jean-A. Ducourneau (Paris: Les Bibliophiles de l'Originale, 1965–76), xxii. 466.

[18] Gaschon de Molènes, 'Revue dramatique', 141.

assume the comic burden while keeping the unappreciated genius outside the scope of humour.

However, this distinction between genius and crime is gradually undermined. Quinola draws a parallel between his and his master's character when he states that 'vous êtes inventeur, moi je suis inventif' (you are an inventor, I am inventive) (580), but the play insists on deeper affinities between genius and criminal which have to do with their position in society. An exasperated Fontanarès, faced with persecution, exclaims: 'O mon Dieu! le talent et le crime seraient-ils donc une même chose à tes yeux?' (my God! Is talent and crime the same thing for you?) (551). It is the very gift of genius, originality, which is the cause of this persecution: 'Invente et tu mourras persécuté comme un criminel, copie et tu vivras heureux comme un sot' (invent and you will die persecuted like a criminal, copy and you will live happy like an idiot) (483). The genius in Balzac's play is forced to the margins of society, acquiring the status of a criminal and, in this sense, it is quite fitting that Fontanarès allies himself at the end of the play with a thief and a prostitute, two occupations which, in *Splendeurs et misères des courtisanes*, 'sont deux protestations vivantes, mâle et femelle, de *l'état naturel* contre l'état social' (are a living protest, male and female, of *nature* against the social condition).[19] Their leaving for Paris has something of the challenge mounted by Rastignac against Parisian society at the end of *Le Père Goriot*.

In the last act, Fontanarès finds himself in a position similar to Chatterton: if Chatterton cannot take off Rowley's mask because he is unable to convince his readers that the poems are his own works, Fontanarès, faced with a crowd celebrating don Ramon, admits that that he is a fraud and that the latter is the real inventor of the steam engine, assuming the mask his jealous enemies are forcing him to wear.

The impossibility of distinguishing between the mask and the man, as well as the challenge to society, are the central themes of Alexandre Dumas's *Kean, ou Désordre et génie* (1836) which dramatizes the life of Edmund Kean, the famous early nineteenth-century English actor. Dumas's Kean, a former acrobat of humble origins who has become one of the most acclaimed Shakespearean actors and has the reputation of 'un héros de débauche et de scandale' (a hero of debauchery and scandal)[20] has an affair with Elena de Koefeld, and becomes the protector of Anna Damby, a middle-class heiress who abandons her fiancé, Lord Mewill, after Kean's performances convince her to pursue a career in acting. Kean saves Anna from being kidnapped by Lord Mewill and, finding a rival for Elena's attentions in the Prince of Wales, asks him to stop pursuing her. When he refuses, Kean feigns madness during a performance and insults both Lord Mewill and the Prince of Wales in public. The well-meaning Prince saves Elena's honour by lying to her suspicious husband and, when a warrant is issued for Kean's arrest and imprisonment, manages to convert his sentence to a year of exile.

[19] Honoré de Balzac, *La Comédie humaine*, ed. Pierre-Georges Castex (Paris: Gallimard, 1976–81), vi. 830.

[20] Alexandre Dumas, *Théâtre complet* (Paris: Michel Lévy frères, 1874–83), v. 106. Further references are given after quotations in the text.

Kean, who realizes that Elena does not really love him, leaves with Anna for America, announcing their marriage.

Dumas's *Kean* portrays another aspect of genius: while Chatterton and Fontanarès are both unappreciated, Kean is not only a man of genius but a successful celebrity. Jules Janin, who disapproved of the play, described the real Kean, whose performances in Paris he had witnessed, as 'un homme gâté et corrompu par le succès' (a man spoiled and corrupted by success).[21] The novelty of Dumas's play, according to another reviewer, consisted in the fact that it focused on the depiction of 'l'artiste dramatique' (the dramatic artist) and not of 'le comédien de métier' (the professional actor).[22] The very subtitle of the work, *Désordre et génie*, implied 'une intention philosophique et sociale, un enseignement' (a philosophical and social purpose, a moral), which, according to the reviewer of the play in *La Phalange*, was not realized in a work which, while showing both genius and disorder, did not demonstrate the relation between the two.[23] The reviewer implies that Dumas wanted to demonstrate that disorder is the condition of genius, according to the widespread Romantic belief that alcohol (which Kean is shown to consume in generous quantities) would trigger the imagination and the creative potential of artists. The play, however, seems to depict, inversely, genius as the cause of disorder by emphasizing the continuity and the confusion between life and art, between the role and the self, both on the level of the plot and on that of the performance and the staging of the play.

Unlike the actor described in Diderot's *Paradoxe sur le comédien* (published for the first time in 1830) who is an 'insensible' being and does not feel but is only able to reproduce the emotions of others, Kean is described as a predominantly emotional and sensitive actor: 'il faut qu'un acteur connaisse toutes les passions pour les bien exprimer. Je les étudie sur moi-même, c'est le moyen de les savoir par cœur' (an actor should be familiar will all passions in order to express them. I study them on myself; this is the way to learn them by heart) (124). This continuity between life and the stage is not limited to Kean rehearsing in real life the emotions of the characters he is to impersonate; his chameleonic ability to represent them on stage also transmits these emotions to the audience. Anna relates that she had been suffering from spleen and from an inability to feel which was cured by watching Kean performing Othello's jealousy, Romeo's love, and Hamlet's despair (153–4).

Kean's genius is described as a kind of vampire (162–3) feeding off his life and he resents the fact that he is unable to feel his own emotions:

> métier maudit ... où aucune sensation ne nous appartient, où nous ne sommes maîtres ni de notre joie ni de notre douleur ... où le cœur brisé il faut jouer Falstaff, où le cœur joyeux, il faut jouer Hamlet! toujours un masque, jamais un visage.

[21] Jules Janin, 'Théâtre des Variétés. *Kean, ou Désordre et génie*', *Journal des débats*, 3 Sept. 1836.

[22] Anonymous, 'Théâtre des Variétés. Première représentation. *Kean, ou Désordre et génie*', *L'Indépendant*, 4 Sept. 1836.

[23] Anonymous, 'Feuilleton de la Phalange. *Kean, ou Désordre et génie*', *La Phalange*, 1st ser. 1/9 (1 Oct. 1836), cols 273–92 (cols 277, 292).

> accursed trade ... in which no feeling belongs to us, in which we are masters neither of our joy nor of our pain ... in which the broken heart must play Falstaff and the joyous one Hamlet! Always a mask, never a face. (179)

In this sense, he is wearing masks in his real life: 'Edmund Kean' is a pseudonym behind which hides 'le pauvre bateleur' (the poor street performer) David, and he is shown to visit pubs disguised as a sailor. But, more importantly, in the key scene of the play, he is shown to be unable to contain his real emotions on stage: he interrupts his performance and vents his jealousy of the Prince of Wales and his indignation for Lord Mewill who is persecuting his ex-fiancée. This confusion between life and the theatre was also reflected on the staging of the play: precisely in the scene in which Kean breaks the illusion of the stage to express his own feelings, the actors impersonating Lord Mewill, the Prince and Elena were sitting in the stalls and the boxes, thus creating an inverse confusion between stage and life which critics did not appreciate and which, according to Jules Janin, constituted a 'burlesque idée'.[24]

An aspect of the play which was not commented on by the reviewers is the thematization of the status of the artist in society—in this case, the successful artist. If Chatterton presents genius as the moral compass of the nation, Kean presents himself as a king (134). The idea that genius conferred the status of nobility or royalty to an artist was widely diffused in the Romantic age, with authors such as Gérard de Nerval and Honoré (de) Balzac adopting aristocratic names or pseudonyms. While Kean is tolerated by and occasionally invited in society 'comme on invite ces messieurs, en qualité de bouffon' (as one invites these gentlemen, in their capacity as jesters) (110), his relation with the Prince of Wales is depicted as one of equals, with the Prince admitting that Kean is 'un front couronné depuis longtemps, tandis que le mien attend encore sa couronne' (a head long since crowned, while mine still awaits its crown) (112). Despite his camaraderie with the Prince of Wales, Kean only dares attack him and Lord Mewill through the qualified immunity of the stage and he immediately chooses to cloak his outburst under the veil of madness; eventually, he fails to take his stand and he is expelled to America.

The theme of challenging society and royalty takes more sinister dimensions in Victor Hugo's *Le Roi s'amuse* (1832). If Kean is an actor who blurs the boundaries between classes, Triboulet, the main character of *Le Roi s'amuse*, has a very clearly circumscribed social position which forces him to wear a single mask. He is the king's fool and he is forced to be merry: 'Je suis bouffon de cour! | ne vouloir, ne pouvoir, ne devoir et ne faire | que rire!—Quel excès d'opprobre et de misère!' (I am a court jester! Being disposed, able, obliged to do nothing but laugh! There is no greater disgrace and misery).[25] In mocking the courtiers and in encouraging the king to seduce their wives, he makes enemies and he is cursed by Saint-Vallier, who accuses the king of corrupting

[24] Janin, 'Théâtre des Variétés'.

[25] Victor Hugo, *Théâtre complet*, ed. J.-J. Thierry and Josette Mélèze (Paris: Gallimard, 1963–4), i. 1380.

his daughter, Diane de Poitiers. Triboulet's enemies decide to punish him by abducting his daughter (whom they believe to be his mistress) and deliver her to the king, who also tries to seduce her, without knowing who she is. The courtiers kidnap Blanche and, after she is raped by the king, Triboulet hires an assassin, Saltabadil, to have the king murdered. Saltabadil lures his victims by having his sister seduce them but the latter, who is taken with the king, implores her brother to kill the first passer-by who knocks on their door; Blanche, who overhears their conversation, decides to save the king and Triboulet's triumph turns into a tragedy when he realizes that the dead body he is presented with is his own daughter's.

While Triboulet is not introduced as the most sympathetic character, Hugo's summary of the play in his preface presents him in an entirely unsympathetic light: according to Hugo, Triboulet's 'triple misère', the fact that he is deformed, sick, and a fool, makes him 'méchant' (mean) (1326). The 'real subject of the play' is Saint-Vallier's curse and its fulfilment, the rape of Blanche, which Hugo presents as Triboulet's just punishment for his corruption. In such a reading of the play, the only positive character is the inexplicably self-sacrificial Blanche whose altruism for her rapist puzzled the critics.[26]

Hugo's preface, however, was meant to be a defence of his work against the charges of immorality that prompted its prohibition the day after its premiere—a bias which explains its somewhat monolithic interpretation of the play. Triboulet is the kind of fool who would soon become the symbol of the idealist artist in the work of Baudelaire and the symbolists,[27] and he possesses the traits of the Romantic artist: like Chatterton, he is by nature incapable of any other profession than that of a fool; because of his physical deformity and his sharp wit, he is an outcast; it is thought impossible that he may have a semblance of a normal life, a mistress, much less a daughter; like Kean, he belongs to no class and in virtue of this social status he can challenge all classes. However, he represents a more rebellious side of the Romantic artist; in attempting to have the king assassinated, he challenges the established order. As Triboulet explains, his 'wickedness' is the result of the humiliation he has endured (1381) and, in this sense, he can be read as a Romantic martyr who rises against a society which despises him.

In this context, Triboulet activates the sinister aspects of the characters so far examined: Vigny, in his preface to *Chatterton*, likens the Poet to a scorpion which, trapped in a circle of fire by cruel children, is forced to turn its sting on itself (755–6). This image, while conveying the inevitability of suicide, also presents the artist as a potentially dangerous being. Even though this sinister potential is not realized in *Chatterton*, genius is associated with criminality: in killing himself, Chatterton becomes 'criminel devant Dieu et les hommes' (a criminal in the eyes of God and men), since 'le suicide est un crime religieux et social' (suicide is a crime against religion and society) (755); Fontanarès associates himself with a thief and a prostitute; and Kean rises

[26] See e.g. anonymous, 'Théâtre français. *Le Roi s'amuse*', *Le Constitutionnel*, 25 Nov. 1832; anonymous, 'Théâtre français. *Le Roi s'amuse*', *Le Figaro*, 24 Nov. 1832.

[27] See Jean Starobinski, *Portrait de l'artiste en saltimbanque* (Geneva: Albert Skira, 1970).

up against the royal family and the aristocracy. Triboulet explicitly compares himself to Saltabadil: 'Nous sommes tous les deux à la même hauteur, | une langue acérée, une lame pointue. | Je suis l'homme qui rit, il est l'homme qui tue' (We are equals, a sharp tongue and a pointed blade. I am the man who laughs, he is the man who kills) (1379). Instead of killing himself or eventually resigning and leaving, Triboulet decides to exact his revenge.

The most controversial scene of the play is the abduction of Blanche and Triboulet's unwitting complicity in the act: the courtiers who have vowed to punish Triboulet run into him while he is leaving his daughter's house and tell him that they intend to abduct Mme de Cossé, a woman who lives nearby and whom the king wants to seduce. They all wear masks and offer one to Triboulet but also cover his eyes with a blindfold and make him hold the ladder by which they enter the house. Triboulet does not realize he is wearing a blindfold until after the abduction. While the blatant lack of verisimilitude of this scene exasperated Hugo's reviewers,[28] it also reiterates the central motif of the play; the fact that the mask Triboulet is wearing has become a part of his being he is barely aware of: he is blindly complicit both in the court's corruption and in the kidnapping of his own daughter.

The impossibility of tearing off one's mask is a leitmotif in the plays examined here: whether the mask is the artist's own invention (as is the case with Chatterton's Rowley) or imposed to genius by society (in the case of Fontanarès and Triboulet), it takes on a life of its own and is attached to the exceptional individual like 'cette robe de Nessus qu'on ne peut arracher de dessus de ses épaules qu'en déchirant sa propre chair' (this shirt of Nessus which one cannot take off his back without tearing his own flesh off) (134), as Kean puts it when he describes what it is to be an actor. The metaphor of the poisoned robe which the centaur Nessus deceives Deianeira into believing will regain her Hercules's affection does not merely recur in Musset's *Lorenzaccio* (1834) but it becomes the main theme of the play.

Lorenzaccio ('bad Lorenzo'), the cousin of Alexandre, the duke of Florence, is at first presented as a cynical and malicious friend of the duke who chooses the women the latter seduces and spies on the republicans, and as an effeminate coward who faints at the sight of a sword. It is only in the third act of the play that Lorenzo reveals he plans to murder the duke in order to restore the republic. After he realizes his plan, Lorenzo flees to Venice and is assassinated in his turn and the play concludes with the failure of the republicans to take control of Florence.

Musset's play seems to be ill at ease in the company of the plays I have examined, since the main character is not an artist nor does he overtly lay claim to genius; at first sight, he can only be connected to Triboulet, since he aims—and, unlike the fool, succeeds—to commit a tyrannicide. Lorenzo, however, can be read as a would-be artist on account of the idealism of his youth which is the reason why he undertakes to kill the duke—an idealism whose description reveals an affinity between Lorenzo and Chatterton. The duke

28 See e.g. *Le Constitutionnel*, 25 Nov. 1832; anonymous, 'Théâtre français. *Le Roi s'amuse*', *Gazette des théâtres*, 25 Nov. 1832.

calls Lorenzo 'un méchant poète qui ne sait seulement pas faire un sonnet!' (a bad poet who cannot even write a sonnet)[29] and his mother remembers him as a bookish young man who had 'un saint amour pour la vérité' (a sacred love for truth) and who was passionate about Plutarch's biographies of great men (160). Lorenzo himself speaks of his youth as being 'pure comme l'or' (pure as gold) (198). His disillusionment, as critics have frequently noticed, can be connected not only to the general disillusionment that certain Romantic authors were feeling in the aftermath of the July 1830 revolution but also to the moral role of the Romantic author who, like Vigny's Chatterton, wanted to be a moral compass connecting the mundane with the ideal.[30] The staging of the duke's murder lends it a distinctly aesthetic character: Lorenzo carefully prepares, almost rehearses the murder,[31] he wants to use a blade which has not previously drawn anyone else's blood (189) and he lures the duke to his own bed, promising to deliver his aunt. Lorenzo resembles Balzac's Vautrin, the criminal who describes himself as a poet of actions: 'Je suis un grand poète. Mes poésies, je ne les écris pas: elles consistent en actions et en sentiments' (I am a great poet. I do not write my poems down: they are made of actions and feelings).[32]

On the other hand, he is also, like Fontanarès, an 'ambitieux'; it is not only his idealism that leads him to the determination to kill a tyrant. Modelling himself on Plutarch's great men, he decides that 'il faut que je sois un Brutus' (I have to be a Brutus), admitting that his motive is also pride: 'si la Providence m'a poussé à la résolution de tuer un tyran, quel qu'il fût, l'orgueil m'y a poussé aussi' (if Providence has led me to the decision to kill a tyrant, whoever he be, pride has also led me to it) (199). After choosing Alexandre as his victim, he realized that in order to achieve his aim, he had to become 'vicieux, lâche, un objet de honte et d'opprobre' (a man of vice, a coward, ashamed and disgraced) who would feel no shame, since 'les masques de plâtre n'ont point de rougeur au service de la honte' (plaster masks do not blush in the service of shame) (200). Lorenzo henceforth becomes an off-stage actor whose mask is impossible to remove, like Kean's: when Philippe Strozzi claims that, once Lorenzo has killed the duke, 'tu jetteras ce déguisement hideux qui te défigure, et tu redeviendras d'un métal aussi pur que les statues de bronze d'Harmodius et d'Aristogiton' (you will throw off this hideous disguise which disfigures you and you will turn back into a metal as pure as the bronze statues of Harmodius and Aristogeiton), Lorenzo replies that 'le vice a été pour moi un vêtement, maintenant il est collé à ma peau' (vice used to be a garment for me, now it is stuck to my skin) (203). In fact, he realizes that he has internalized his role to such an extent that he automatically tries to seduce his own aunt on the duke's behalf: 'le vice, comme la robe de Déjanire, s'est-il si profondément incorporé à mes fibres, que je ne puisse plus répondre de ma langue, et que l'air qui sort de mes lèvres se fasse ruffian malgré moi?' (is vice, like the shirt of Deianeira, so deeply intertwined in the fibres of my being that

[29] Alfred de Musset, *Théâtre complet*, ed. Simon Jeune (Paris: Gallimard, 1990), 152.

[30] See Paul Bénichou, *L'Ecole du désenchantement: Sainte-Beuve, Nodier, Musset, Nerval, Gautier* (Paris: Gallimard, 1992), esp. 144–8.

[31] See Alain Heyvaert, *L'Esthétique de Musset* (Paris: SEDES, 1996), 80–2.

[32] Balzac, *La Comédie humaine*, iii. 141.

I cannot even use my own tongue to speak and the air which comes out of my lips is corrupted, in spite of myself?) (225). According to his mother, even his physical appearance has changed and his corruption is legible on his face (160); in fact, he is significantly described as an incorporeal entity, as a shadow (204), a spectre (175), or a vapour (160, 175, 198)—the implication being that there is nothing left behind his mask.[33]

Starring in this 'hideuse comédie' (195), he loses faith in his cause: everyone believes he is harmless, laughable, and contemptible, like Triboulet. Despite the fact that he warns the republicans that he will kill the duke, no one believes him—not even the duke who hears of his threats (233–4). At the end of the play, it is not liberty which motivates him: as he confesses to Philippe Strozzi, he is painfully aware that the murder of the duke will change nothing. His motive is now to avenge his own lost innocence (204–5) and, in killing Alexandre, he stages an elaborate suicide. On the one hand, the duke can be read as Lorenzo's alter ego and, in choosing to commit the murder in his own room and bed, Lorenzo seems to be killing his own corrupt self. On the other, even though he flees Florence for Venice and, despite the fact that he knows that there is a price on his head, he fails to take any precautions and is killed by a random stranger who has recognized him.

The examples of Romantic drama discussed in this chapter trace a poetics of failure: the protagonists of the plays fail to convince the world of their genius (in the case of Chatterton and Fontanarès), to find their proper place in society (in the case of Kean), or to exact their revenge on it because it has forced them to assume a role they despise (in the case of Triboulet and Lorenzo). In all cases, the exceptional individual is not only forced to wear a mask but discovers that taking the mask off and 'being himself', as Chatterton wishes, is impossible.

The failure of the characters, however, extends its grasp to include the plays themselves: with the exception of Dumas who was judged as a playwright, Hugo, Vigny, Musset, and Balzac remained, at least in the opinion of their critics, strangers to the stage. Even when their works were appreciated for their literary qualities, they were still considered to be fundamentally unsuited for the theatre. Half a century after the battle of *Hernani*, Emile Zola (who was also haunted by his own failure to introduce naturalism on the stage) was unequivocal in his criticism of Romantic drama as a whole:

> Certes, je ne suis pas injuste envers le mouvement romantique. Il a eu une importance capitale et définitive, il nous a faits ce que nous sommes, c'est-à-dire des artistes libres. Il était, je le répète, une révolution nécessaire, une violente émeute qui s'est produite à son heure pour balayer le règne de la tragédie tombée en enfance. Seulement, il serait ridicule de vouloir borner au drame romantique l'évolution de l'art dramatique.... A une rhétorique lymphatique, le mouvement de 1830 a substitué une rhétorique nerveuse et sanguine, voilà tout.[34]

[33] See Barbara T. Cooper, 'Breaking Up/Down/Apart: "L'éclatement" as a Unifying Principle in Musset's *Lorenzaccio*', *Philological Quarterly*, 65 (1986), 103–12 (107).

[34] Emile Zola, *Œuvres complètes* (Paris: Nouveau monde, 2002–10), x. 25.

> I certainly do not wish to be unfair to the Romantic movement. It has played a major and definitive role; it has made us who we are, that is, free artists. It was, I repeat, a necessary revolution, a violent rebellion which occurred at the right moment in order to brush aside the reign of tragedy which had lapsed back into childhood. However, it would be ridiculous to restrict the evolution of dramatic art to Romantic drama.... The movement of 1830 replaced a lymphatic rhetoric with a nervous and sanguine one—that is all.

What was perceived by contemporary reviewers as the artistic failure of Romantic drama was often accompanied either by the actual failure of the performances or their prohibition for political or moral reasons: Balzac's *Vautrin* and Hugo's *Le Roi s'amuse* were banned immediately after their premieres; Hugo's plays often attracted the attention of the censors, while the failure of *La Nuit vénitienne* had a traumatic effect on Musset.

Failure, however, is not merely a theme of the plays, nor exclusively a matter of circumstances; it is also an integral component of the myth of genius. The Romantic artist is often described as a kind of Icarus who rises to the skies only to fall.[35] In this sense, genius is often prioritized over his works which are considered to be mere symptoms of genius and whose absence or incompleteness does not disprove his greatness—the cause for the latter often being the inability or unwillingness of genius to conform to the taste of his contemporaries, the requirements of the literary marketplace, or the dominant norms of behaviour in society. In his preface to *Chatterton*, Vigny claims that 'on dira que les symptômes du génie se montrent sans enfantement, ou ne produisent que des œuvres avortées; ... que des essais ne sont pas des preuves ... Je dis, moi, que quelques vers suffiraient à les faire reconnaître de leur vivant, si l'on savait y regarder' (people will say that the symptoms of genius manifest themselves unexpectedly or that they only produce abortive works; ... that drafts are not proof ... I say that a few lines are enough for a genius to achieve recognition while alive, if only they knew where to look) (756–7). Balzac goes a step further in his *Études philosophiques* and presents a series of geniuses whose inability to produce a work of art becomes a condition or even a proof of their genius: Frenhofer's attempts, in *Le Chef d'œuvre inconnu*, to perfect his painting result in its destruction; in *Gambara*, the protagonist's sublime music is perceived by listeners as hideous cacophony; in *La Recherche de l'absolu*, Balthazar Claës, the chemist in search of the 'absolute', spends his fortune, reduces his family to poverty, and makes his discovery shortly before he dies, taking it to the grave; the philosopher Louis Lambert, in the eponymous novel, becomes immersed in reflection and reaches an almost catatonic state which hinders him from communicating with others. In this context, the failures portrayed in or exemplified by the Romantic dramas I have discussed do not merely present their protagonists as geniuses but also confirm the genius of their own authors; in wearing the 'mask' of the playwright, the Romantics themselves

[35] See Maurice Z. Shroder, *Icarus: The Image of the Artist in French Romanticism* (Cambridge, Mass.: Harvard University Press, 1961).

engage in a performance which tests their authorial status and strategies both on and off the stage.

Further Reading

Bénichou, Paul, *Le Sacre de l'écrivain 1750–1830: Essai sur l'avènement d'un pouvoir spirituel laïque dans la France moderne* (Paris: José Corti, 1973).

Cahiers Textuel, 8 (1991), 'Lorenzaccio', ed. José-Luis Diaz.

Dimoff, Paul, *La Genèse de 'Lorenzaccio'* (Paris: Marcel Didier, 1964).

Guise, René, 'Un grand homme du roman à la scène ou les illusions reparaissantes de Balzac', *L'Année balzacienne* (1966), 171–216; (1967), 177–214; (1968), 337–68, and (1969), 247–80.

Halsall, Albert W., *Victor Hugo and the Romantic Drama* (Toronto: University of Toronto Press, 1998).

Hemmings, F. W. J., *The Theatre Industry in Nineteenth-Century France* (Cambridge: Cambridge University Press, 1993).

Hemmings, F. W. J., *Theatre and Stage in France, 1760–1905* (Cambridge: Cambridge University Press, 1994).

Krakovitch, Odile, *Hugo censuré: La Liberté au théâtre au XIXe siècle* (Paris: Calmann-Lévy, 1985).

McCormick, *Popular Theatres of Nineteenth-Century France* (London: Routledge, 1993).

McCready, Susan, *The Limits of Performance in the French Romantic Theatre* (Durham: Durham University Press, 2007).

Masson, Bernard, *Musset et le théâtre intérieur* (Paris: Armand Colin, 1974).

Sices, David, *Theater of Solitude: The Drama of Alfred de Musset* (Hanover, NH: University Press of New England, 1974).

Ubersfeld, Anne, *Le Roi et le bouffon: Étude sur le théâtre de Hugo de 1830 à 1839* (Paris: José Corti, 1974).

Wicks, Charles Beaumont, *The Parisian Stage: Alphabetical Indexes of Plays and Authors*, 5 vols (Tuscaloosa, Ala.: University of Alabama Press, 1950–79).

CHAPTER 7

FRENCH ROMANTIC POETRY

KATHERINE LUNN-ROCKLIFFE

FRENCH Romantic poetry marked a dramatic break with a national tradition of verse which had been inherited almost unaltered from the seventeenth century. During the eighteenth century, the neoclassical conception of poetry as a rule-governed and highly stylized art had continued to prevail; verse was characterized by a solemn tone and narrow lexis, and there was a rigid distinction between poetic genres. Whereas Romantic poetry in England and Germany seemed already to allow the imagination free rein, in France poets needed first to reject these neoclassical conventions. Victor Hugo declared in the preface to his *Odes et ballades* of 1822 that 'La poésie n'est pas dans la forme des idées, mais dans les idées elles-mêmes' (poetry lies not in the form of ideas but in the ideas themselves), and the French Romantic poets were all in different ways engaged in reshaping the forms of poetry to suit their individual purposes.[1]

Hugo concludes that preface by declaring that 'La poésie, c'est tout ce qu'il y a d'intime dans tout' (Poetry is what is intimate in everything), and in the years following the Restoration of 1815 poets began to treat an increasing number of subjects from the perspective of the individual, for example in the highly personal elegies of Marceline Desbordes-Valmore and Lamartine written around 1820. The emphasis on subjectivity was closely linked to the emergence of new ways of expressing religious belief. Poets were influenced by Rousseau's and Chateaubriand's suggestive evocations of the spiritual in nature, and intensified the effects of this style of writing by transposing it into verse. Moving away from classical abstractions and an ideal of clarity, they evoked mystery by creating novel metaphors which suggested new relationships between the material and the transcendent realms, and ventured far beyond the repertoire of conventional images.

In the 1820s, poets sought in increasingly daring ways to fashion a poetry suited to the modern world, and Hugo emerged as a leading voice in this polemic and the foremost poet of the 'Cénacle', a group including the poets Vigny, Sainte-Beuve, Lamartine,

[1] Preface to *Odes et Ballades*.

Musset, and Nerval. Breaking free of classical influences, the poets in Hugo's circle revived forms used before the classical model had come to dominate, and rediscovered Renaissance poets such as Ronsard.[2] They also looked to other European literatures, and were influenced by writers including Shakespeare, Scott, Byron, Goethe, and Schiller. Experimentation extended to the freeing of conventional verse rhythms, a tendency which had already been apparent in the eighteenth-century poet Chénier, whose work was only published in 1819. The classical line of French verse, the alexandrine, which consists of twelve syllables, traditionally fell into two halves, but was used with increasing liberty, especially by Hugo and Musset.[3] In a later poem, 'Réponse à un acte d'accusation' (Reply to a bill of indictment), Hugo boasted that he had overthrown the monarchy of traditional verse, stamped on good taste, banished clarity, and introduced darkness, breathed a revolutionary wind, put a red cap on the old dictionary, and banished the hierarchy between words of different social levels.[4]

In 'Réponse à un acte d'accusation', Hugo systematically deploys the rhetoric of political revolt to describe his poetic innovations, and this is more than just metaphorical verve, because in France the Romantic assault on poetic forms was closely bound up with the political turmoil in the decades which followed the Revolution. The directions taken by the leading poets were partly determined by their own allegiances. Lamartine, Vigny, and Hugo made their names as royalists during the Restoration, although they moved away from this position as that regime faltered and was overthrown in 1830, the year that is generally said to mark the triumph of Romanticism in France. Lamartine and Hugo moved towards liberal positions and eventually adopted roles on the political stage. Both poets came to view the poet as a kind of prophet in a secular age, and Hugo used his poetry to address political questions, declaring later on that, although art for art's sake is a fine thing, art for the sake of progress is even better.[5]

Discussion of French Romantic poetry has often concentrated on the public personae of these three poets and the associated myth of the poet as a genius, but there were other models of poetic creativity in the period—Marceline Desbordes-Valmore's exploration of new modes of subjectivity led to a more radical liberation of verse form and a more self-conscious reflection on the authority of the poetic voice. Critics have also tended to focus on the lyric, traditionally charting the triumphant emergence of the self-expressive subject and more recently drawing attention to ways in which these apparently unified voices are discontinuous, polyphonic, or decentred. As a consequence, the historical and political poems have been read more in relation to their extra-literary context than for their poetic qualities. However, the poets themselves invariably emphasized the continuities between these different projects, and the interest of much of their verse lies

[2] See Sainte-Beuve, *Tableau historique et critique de la poésie et du theatre français au seizième siècle* (1828).

[3] See Clive Scott, *French Verse-Art: A Study* (Cambridge: Cambridge University Press, 1980) on the conventions.

[4] *Les Contemplations.*

[5] Victor Hugo, *William Shakespeare* (1864), 2. 6. 1.

precisely in the ways in which it makes connections between intimate experience and a wide range of religious, political, social, and philosophical concerns. Poetry is a kind of thinking and, although this notion is more frequently associated with the German Romantics, the intimacy with which French Romantic poets engaged with their subjects was also a way of thinking about them.

Alphonse de Lamartine

Like many of the early French Romantic poets, Lamartine was of noble origin and began writing in a royalist Christian vein. His *Méditations poétiques* (1820) is conventionally said to mark a turning point because he adapted the themes and forms of neoclassical poetry to express the contemporary sensibility: a sense of profound melancholy and yearning to transcend material reality. His most famous poem, 'Le Lac' (The Lake), portrays nature as an enduring reality in contrast to the transience of human life. It is a meditation on memory and death uttered by a solitary speaker on the occasion of his return to a lake where he had previously been happy with a lover who is now departed. It follows the pattern of what Abrams has called the 'greater Romantic lyric', widespread in European Romantic poetry, in which a speaker's response to a changed landscape is intertwined with a reflection on transience closely bound up with the place.[6] Lamartine is particularly good at conveying a subjective perception of temporality, and opens 'Le Lac' by comparing the continual passing of time to the flow of water:

> Ainsi, toujours poussés vers de nouveaux rivages,
> Dans la nuit éternelle emportés sans retour,
> Ne pourrons-nous jamais sur l'océan des âges
>   Jeter l'ancre un seul jour?

> So, driven incessantly to new shores, swept forever into eternal darkness, will we never be able to anchor on the sea of time even for one day?

It is the intense musicality of these lines which turns the comparison into a harmonious pattern, the repeated echoes suggesting that experience has an underlying unity despite its apparent turbulence. In the stanzas that follow, the speaker apostrophizes the lake and implores it to remember his lost happiness, as though the landscape could hold his feeling. Although the lake is described in less concrete terms than the landscapes of Wordsworth and much of the vocabulary remains neoclassical, the personal

[6] M. H. Abrams, 'Structure and Style in the Greater Romantic Lyric', in Harold Bloom, *Romanticism and Consciousness* (New York and London: Norton, 1970), 201–27; Lloyd Bishop, '"Le Lac" as Exemplar of the Greater Romantic Lyric', *Romance Quarterly*, 34 (1987), 403–23.

note was strikingly new to French readers in 1820. In the 1849 preface to the *Méditations*, Lamartine declared that he had been the first poet whose muse had a lyre with strings made of the very fibres of man's heart.[7]

Lamartine often builds up long sequences of verse 'by using sets of images as a musician uses variations'.[8] 'Les Etoiles' (The stars) (*Nouvelles méditations poétiques*, 1823) combines a number of very conventional metaphors—the sky as sea, personification of the night—but the dense sound patterns blend them into a rich new unity:

> Alors ces globes d'or, ces îles de lumière,
> Que cherche par instinct la rêveuse paupière,
> Jaillissent par milliers de l'ombre qui s'enfuit
> Comme une poudre d'or sur les pas de la nuit;
> Et le souffle du soir qui vole sur sa trace,
> Les sème en tourbillons dans le brillant espace.

> Then these spheres of gold, these islands of light, which the dreaming eye instinctively seeks, spring in their thousands from the fleeing darkness, like a golden powder on the heels of night; and the breath of the evening, rushing after her, scatters them in whirls in the dazzling space.

Evoking a transitional moment between day and night, Lamartine does not highlight contrasts but instead suggests that light and dark blend softly into one another, hinting at the existence of a greater harmony. He was reflecting a modern understanding of the divine, closely bound up with nature and expressed by a profoundly human voice. At the same time he saw the poet as resuscitating a lost sacred poetry, and this conviction that poetry was an echo of a divine language became increasingly important to him. He thought that human language was inadequate to express the ineffable and the task of the poet was to bring it closer to the language of the Gods. In the *Méditations*, this divine language is spoken by the soul, burning with sighs, ardours, and transports ('Dieu' (God)), and by the time he wrote *Harmonies poétiques et religieuses* (1830), it had become an echo of the Old Testament prophets, a sign of genius which permitted the transformation of the material world ('Invocation'). Although Lamartine started out expressing a religious sensibility in conventional terms, he gradually moved away from orthodox Catholicism, influenced by the proliferation of new religions and occult spiritualisms in this period.[9] He became concerned with the spiritual life of humanity as a whole, in which he saw the poet as having a leading role.

Much of Lamartine's later poetry was written when he was pursuing a political career. In 1833 he was elected a deputy in the Chamber of Deputies, and in 1848 stood unsuccessfully as a presidential candidate. Like many of his contemporaries, he aspired

7 Lamartine, *Méditations*, ed. Letessier (Paris: Garnier, 1968), 303.

8 J. C. Ireson, *Imagination in French Romantic Poetry* (Hull: University of Hull, 1970), 18.

9 See D. G. Charlton, *Secular Religions in France 1815–1870* (Oxford: Oxford University Press, 1963).

to write a vast epic of the human spirit, but completed only two episodes, although these are very long.[10] The first, *Jocelyn* (1836), extended his celebration of man's spiritual communion with nature and explicitly criticized the church as an institution, in the story of a young priest who suppresses his intense feelings in order to conform to religious order. He flees from the fallout of the Revolution to live an idyllic life in an Alpine cave with a lover, but has to renounce this when he is recalled to the church. Where *Jocelyn* was widely read and appreciated for its novel focus on an unexceptional hero in modern times, the second episode, *La Chute d'un ange* (1838), was less popular. The eponymous angel becomes the human Cédar after falling in love with Daïdha, has twins with her, and they journey in search of a just God, whilst persecuted by enemies including a tyrant pagan deity. When Daïdha and the children die, Cédar is left deploring how distant he is from God. Although such works are uneven and now little read, the epic ambition was important to Lamartine, and indeed in French Romanticism as a whole.[11]

After *Recueillements poétiques* (1839), in the same vein as *Harmonies*, Lamartine abandoned poetry. His verse is expansive and eloquent, and he was criticized by his successors for lacking control—Flaubert's remark that he was like a tap was not untypical.[12] However, his *Méditations* had set the tone for a new kind of poetry. The volume was widely read and its recasting of neoclassical commonplaces in a subjective mode had a major influence on contemporary poets. Gautier described Lamartine's voice as seeming to come from the heavens,[13] and although his verse was still metrically conventional, it had harnessed the musicality of the alexandrine to convey a sense of modern spirituality, and thus opened up new ways of conveying moods and beliefs without proclaiming them directly.

Marceline Desbordes-Valmore

Although Lamartine has traditionally been considered the father of French Romantic poetry, an equally innovative poet was Marceline Desbordes-Valmore, an actress, who published her first volume, *Élégies, Marie et Romances*, in 1819. She took many more liberties with metrical structure than Lamartine and departed further from neoclassical rhetoric to convey a striking sense of a real speaking voice. Her early poems, collected in *Poésies* (1830), often deal with personal loss, for instance this elegy of 1820 expresses yearning for an elusive lover and alternates between obsessive repetition and stuttering when words fail:

[10] See Herbert J. Hunt, *The Epic in Nineteenth-Century France* (Oxford: Blackwell, 1941).

[11] Aurélie Loiseleur, *L'Harmonie selon Lamartine: Utopie d'un lieu commun* (Paris: Champion, 2005) considers his lyric and epic works as part of a unified project.

[12] Letter to Louise Colet, 16 Sept. 1853.

[13] Théophile Gautier, *Histoire du Romantisme* (1874), ed. A. Goetz (Paris: Gallimard, 2011), 477.

> Ma sœur, il est parti! Ma sœur, il m'abandonne!
> Je sais qu'il m'abandonne, et j'attends, et je meurs,
> Je meurs. Embrasse-moi, pleure pour moi ... pardonne ...
> Je n'ai pas une larme, et j'ai besoin de pleurs.

> My sister, he has gone! My sister, he is abandoning me! I know that he is abandoning me, and still I am waiting and I am dying, I am dying. Embrace me, cry for me ... forgive ... I have not a single tear, and I need to weep.

The repetitions create a sense of uncontrolled outburst and the third line tails off, imitating the rhythm of speech. The speaker of this poem is confiding in her sister, and Desbordes-Valmore dealt with the whole panoply of relationships, writing poems not only about lovers but also her friends, children, and mother.

Sensations of longing permeate her verse, but, in contrast to the metaphysical yearnings of Lamartine, they are often rooted in everyday situations like waiting for a lover or missing a child who is at school. Where Lamartine had his speakers step back from their pain to frame questions in universal terms, Desbordes-Valmore conveyed raw psychological states without either generalizing or resorting to abstract reflection. Instead, she would comment lucidly on the intense states she expressed, as in 'je sais fuir: en fuyant on cache sa douleur' (I know how to flee, by fleeing one hides one's pain) ('Elégie', *Poésies*, 1830). Where her early poems above all voice surprise at new feelings and evoke their immediate force, her three later collections increasingly reflected on the nature of transience and explored the psychic struggle involved in remembering and grappling with loss: *Les Pleurs* (1833), *Pauvres Fleurs* (1839), and *Bouquets et Prières* (1843). For example, 'Tristesse' (Sadness), evokes nostalgia for a childhood home and only records happy memories after a lengthy description of the difficulty of uncovering them. As in Lamartine's 'Lac', the description of remembering conflates space and time:

> Vous aussi, ma natale, on vous a bien changée!
> Oui! Quand mon cœur remonte à vos gothiques tours,
> Qu'il traverse, rêveur, notre absence affligée,
> Il ne reconnaît plus la grâce négligée
> Qui donne tant de charme au maternel séjour! (*Les Pleurs*)

> You, my birthplace, have changed greatly too! Yes! When my heart returns to your gothic towers, and, like a dreamer, crosses our suffering absence, it no longer recognizes the neglected grace which makes life with one's mother so precious

These lines convey simultaneously an impression of a physical return to the real place and a sense that it is being revisited only in the heart of the absent speaker, with words like 'remonte' and 'traverse' referring both to physical and mental movement. This kind of subtle intensity is typical of Desbordes-Valmore, who was greatly admired by Baudelaire for her freedom: 'Jamais aucun poète ne fut plus naturel;

aucun ne fut jamais moins artificiel.' (Never was any poet more natural, none was ever less artificial.)[14] Her preoccupations may appear to be sentimental, but she also wrote some powerful political poems about the repression of workers' rebellions in Lyon, reflected explicitly on the contradictions inherent in the position of a woman asserting herself as a poet, and constantly addressed ethical questions of autonomy, communication, and identity in her more personal verse. Her range and originality is only now being fully recognized, and she is beginning to be read alongside Lamartine as expressing the mood of longing which is so characteristic of her time, without needing to meditate on history or pronounce herself a prophet.[15] Instead she refuses the traditional role of poetic authority, using quotidian experience to articulate the broader concerns with subjectivity and temporality which preoccupied her generation.

Alfred de Vigny

Vigny was a noble who served in the army during the Restoration but was disillusioned by the lack of action and rich enough to retreat to his ivory tower to devote himself to his art. He wrote a small number of dense poems whose innovation was to use the medium of verse to chisel ideas rather than to express emotion. He expressed profound disillusionment and, unlike Lamartine, offered no religious consolation, but instead gazed upon the world with an undeluded eye, and reflected on human suffering.

In *Poèmes antiques et modernes* (1826), Vigny reinvented the 'poëme', a short narrative genre.[16] He recounted episodes which were often historical or mythical, and had epic grandeur, in short poems which explored their philosophical implications. In 'Moïse', the biblical leader produces a melancholy monologue, describing his forehead as too heavy to sleep on a woman's breast, his hands as horrifying to those he touches, and his voice as a storm which makes people tremble. He begs God to free him from this condition:

> Vos anges sont jaloux et m'admirent entre eux.—
> Et cependant, Seigneur, je ne suis pas heureux;
> Vous m'avez fait vieillir puissant et solitaire,
> Laissez-moi m'endormir du sommeil de la terre!

[14] 'Réflexions sur quelques-uns de mes contemporains: Marceline Desbordes-Valmore in Baudelaire, *Œuvres complètes*, ed. C. Pichois Pléiade (Paris: Gallimard Pléiade, 1975-6), ii. 146.

[15] Aimée Boutin, *Maternal Echoes: The Poetry of Marceline Desbordes-Valmore and Alphonse De Lamartine* (Newark, Del.: University of Delaware, 2001).

[16] See Laurence Porter, *The Renaissance of the Lyric in French Romanticism: Elegy, Poëme and Ode* (Lexington, Ky.: French Forum, 1978) on the reinvention of these genres.

> Your angels are jealous and admire me amongst themselves, and yet, Lord, I am not happy. You have made me grow old as a powerful and solitary man, let me sleep the sleep of the earth!

The biblical hero is thus transformed into a solitary Byronic man of genius. Being more pessimistic than Lamartine or Hugo, Vigny was more profoundly influenced by Byron, especially the earlier *Manfred*.

Many of Vigny's poems reworked familiar themes in this way. 'Éloa' takes up the fallen angel myth, to describe an angel born from one of the tears of Christ, who is so afflicted by melancholy that the usual consolations of celestial life cannot keep her from exploring the terrestrial realm. She is lured to earth by Satan, who has taken the form of a boy, and tempts Éloa to save him. In trying to do so, she falls to earth, only to be confronted with Satan who declares himself sadder than ever. Vigny remarked that this poem was very much his own creation because the female angel did not exist, and the language was made of new terms rather than drawn from existing discourses.[17] Even this most restrained of Romantics was engaged in a project of innovation, and he emphasized that the undertaking required a heroic effort.

Vigny's Moses has much in common with the myth of the poet as melancholy leader which proliferated in the 1820s, a myth to which Vigny's strange novel *Stello* (1832) contributed. It consists of a dialogue between a splenetic emotional poet pondering whether to write about an ideal form of government and a pragmatic Docteur Noir who treats him by recounting the stories of three poets who died as a result of not being understood by society: Gilbert, Chatterton, and Chénier (Vigny developed the Chatterton story into a successful play in 1835). These poets suffered under three different kinds of regime, and the doctor concludes his consultation by issuing the prescription that the poet should keep politics and art firmly separate. This was ultimately the route that Vigny chose, retreating to art as a refuge from politics. The novel also includes an early articulation of the myth of the poet as a prophet, anticipating Hugo's later pronouncements: Stello declares that he can feel in his heart a secret but indefinable power, like a premonition of the future and a revelation of the causes of the present.[18] For Vigny, the poet's task was to stand aside from his era and look beyond surface appearances in order to grasp more fundamental truths.

The stark nature of these truths was apparent in the poems published posthumously as *Les Destinées* (1864), originally entitled *Poèmes philosophiques*. This volume includes many of Vigny's most famous works, such as 'La Maison du berger' (The shepherd's house), a dense three-part meditation on the relationships between man's suffering, nature, and poetry. Where other poets qualified nature as responsive or impassive in accordance with the speaker's state of mind, Vigny charts a progression of thought from one of these positions to the other, using the stately seven-line stanza which he made

[17] *Le Journal d'un poète*, in Alfred de Vigny, *Œuvres complètes*, ed. A. de Baldensperger (Paris: Gallimard Pléiade, 1965), ii. 891.

[18] *Stello*, in *Œuvres Complètes* (Paris: Gallimard Pléiade, 1964), i. 586.

his own. The first part, addressed to an idealized 'Éva', celebrates nature as a refuge from the confinement of urban society. It evokes a shepherd's wagon in which the poet and Éva might travel to distant landscapes, and laments the increasing speed of transport in a world which seems to be rushing out of control, including a famous description of a railway:

> Sur le taureau de fer qui fume, souffle et beugle,
> L'homme a monté trop tôt. Nul ne connaît encore
> Quels orages en lui porte ce rude aveugle,
> Et le gai voyageur lui livre son trésor.

> Man has mounted too soon the iron bull which smokes, puffs, and lows. Nobody knows yet what storms this crude and blind beast will bring with it, and the carefree traveller entrusts his precious cargo to it.

Here Vigny personifies the steam train as both mechanized and animalistic, a force over which humanity has little control. He emphasizes its threat to more measured modes of existence and subsequently portrays it as an emblem of capitalism. The second part of 'La Maison du berger' celebrates poetry, a pearl of thought which is far more durable than political speeches which are lost in the wind, and the third celebrates the humanity of 'Éva' and views nature from a new perspective, describing it as an impassive theatre akin to a tomb and concluding that the dignity of human suffering is far more admirable than the vain splendours of nature. Having gradually developed this idea from the initial scene of nature as a refuge, the poem performs the aesthetic ideal which it has expounded, that of preserving profound thoughts in a condensed form.

Another poem which explicitly celebrates thought is 'Bouteille à la mer', a sober evocation of a shipwreck. Instead of using verbal pyrotechnics to lament the maritime disaster, the poem coolly notes how a sailor folds his arms as his ship goes down, how he and his fellows drink champagne, how he inserts into the empty bottle a map drawn in the storm to show future sailors the reef which has sunk them, and tosses it into the waves, from which it is eventually retrieved by a fisherman. The poem ends by underscoring its moral, that knowledge is precious and will outlive those who discover it, although the value of thought has already been indirectly evoked by the stark contrast between the catastrophe and the serene stillness of the poet's voice. Vigny described himself as 'un moraliste épique' and ideas in his verse invariably emerge from such carefully described concrete situations.[19]

Although Vigny stated that all the great problems of humanity could be discussed in the form of verse, he was by no means a heavy-handed didactic poet.[20] Even the lines which explicitly expound morals have great resonance—'La Mort du loup' describes the

[19] *Le Journal d'un poète*, 1018.
[20] *Le Journal d'un poète*, 1204.

stoical death of a wolf at the hands of man and interprets the animal's final stare as offering the following lesson to humanity:

Fais énergiquement ta longue et lourde tâche,
Dans la voie où le Sort a voulu t'appeler.
Puis après, comme moi, souffre et meurs sans parler.

> Undertake your long and arduous task energetically, in whatever realm Fate has called you to. Then afterwards, like me, suffer and die silently.

There is something intractable in the universe for Vigny, which is reflected in the austere tone and often strained texture of his language. His verse always has a carefully hewn quality, and he maintains a consistently elevated register and avoids heightened emotion. Where Lamartine produced long poems which create the illusion of an overflow of feeling, Vigny built mental struggle into the very form of his poems. This was his way of communicating an absolute, and represents a distinct contribution to French Romanticism.

Victor Hugo

Hugo was the greatest of all the French Romantic poets, first and best known for his verse. His mountainous oeuvre lives up to his ambition to encompass the whole of creation in art and to fashion new forms appropriate for new subject matter. In his Romantic manifesto *Préface de Cromwell* (1827), he recognized that creation included both the sublime and the grotesque, and called for this duality to be integrated into art. In his own poetry, this led to startling juxtapositions of the material and the spiritual within single lines of verse. He was constantly blurring boundaries, between the introspective and the political, religion and science, aristocracy and people, concrete and abstract, high and low registers.

Like Lamartine, Hugo started out as a royalist poet with *Odes* (1822), reinventing the traditional ode for modern times by introducing a subjective element. The book was republished as *Odes et ballades* in 1826, with the addition of ballads with mystical overtones, modelled on the English and German genre. His second volume, *Les Orientales* (1829), was radically different, describing itself as a useless book of pure poetry. Drawing on the fashion for the exotic, it created an intense atmosphere using vivid pictorial language, and experimented with local colour, striking images, and unusual rhythms. 'Les Djinns', a poem which describes evil spirits attacking a town, underlines the drama by opening with lines of two syllables, and gradually building up to decasyllables at the height of the onslaught. Such playfulness was typical of this flamboyant early work, but Hugo was taking more fundamental metrical liberties in his verse drama, and the scandal of *Hernani* (1830) had much to do with its startling use of enjambement in the opening lines. Looking back at this period in the later poem 'Réponse à un acte d'accusation', Hugo boasts of having liberated the traditional alexandrine, which he describes as a shuttlecock of twelve feathers being sent backwards and forwards by the two rackets of prosody and etiquette, to produce a freer modern version, which he compares to a divine lark released from the cage of the caesura and flying free. One way in which Hugo broke away from the binary structure was by writing ternary alexandrines which fell into three parts, like this reflection on the mysterious richness of the word: 'Créé, par qui? Forgé, par qui? Jailli de l'ombre.' (Created, by whom? Forged, by whom? Sprung from the shadows.)[21]

By 1830, Hugo was moving towards a liberal position, and settling into a mode of more introspective lyricism, combining reflections on the present historical moment with expressions of personal melancholy. *Feuilles d'automne* (Autumn leaves) (1831), deliberately seeks refuge from the social turmoil following the 1830 revolution, and includes an early intimation of his characteristic visionary style, 'La Pente de la rêverie' (The slope of reverie), about a spiral descent from reality towards an invisible sphere, where the poet can see all his friends living and dead, who then dissolve into the massed whole of humanity. By concentrating hard, the poet sees strange cities and ruins from the past, which then come alive and seem to be populated. He grasps the totality of the world, both past and present, conjuring a vision of a great edifice made of teetering piles of centuries, before the spectacle is gradually overwhelmed with darkness. Subsequent collections wove increasingly close connections between personal emotion and socio-political ideas. *Les Chants du crépuscule* (Songs of twilight) (1835) begins by pondering the 1830 revolution directly, asking whether the present tumult is the dawn or the sunset, and setting out the poet's task: to express hope as we wait to find out. The penultimate poem describes the corrosive effect of doubt, vividly presented as a short-sighted and deaf spectre made of dark and light. Both poems are expressions of the same state, the yearning and disillusionment of modern man. This play of contrasts was accentuated in *Les Voix intérieures* (1837) which both reflects on the violence of historical change and celebrates nature in an ecstatic Virgilian mode.

These volumes of the 1830s reflect Hugo's move away from the monarchic Christian model and betray the influence of the diverse range of illuminist and Saint-Simonian thought which was proliferating at the time. The preface to *Les Rayons et les Ombres* (Rays and shadows) (1840) asserts that a poet should contain the sum of the ideas of his time whilst remaining free from specific allegiances. Although Hugo never adhered to any identifiable doctrine, his verse, more than any of that period, absorbed contemporary thought and transformed it into metaphors. While he had always affirmed the strength of the poet's voice, at this point he adapted the religious notion of prophecy to the secular mission of envisaging the future of humanity, as expressed in 'Fonction du poète': 'Le poète en des jours impies | Vient préparer des jours meilleurs. | Il est l'homme

[21] 'Suite', *Les Contemplations.*

des utopies; | Les pieds ici, les yeux ailleurs.' (The poet in ungodly times anticipates better days. He is the man of utopias, with his feet on the ground but looking elsewhere.) Meanwhile, he intensified the introspective elegiac mode, for example in 'Tristesse d'Olympio' (Olympio's sadness), in which a melancholy speaker returns to a landscape where he had once been happy and finds the place overgrown. He reproaches nature for being indifferent to his sadness and beseeches it to respond to his pain, but is forced to rely on his own memory for consolation.[22]

Hugo published little poetry in the 1840s, when he was engaged in political activity, culminating in his exile to the Channel Islands after Napoléon III's coup d'état of 1852. The first volume he published in exile was the satirical *Châtiments* (1853), which combines invective against Napoléon III with affirmations of belief in progress. Thereafter he began to develop the visionary style for which he is now most renowned. *Les Contemplations* (1856) is generally acknowledged to be the richest volume of French Romantic poetry, despite coming long after the battle lines had originally been drawn up, and only a year before Baudelaire published *Les Fleurs du Mal*. It is presented as an autobiography following the structure of Hugo's life and centring on the death of his daughter Léopoldine. The first half, 'Autrefois', evokes the poet's youthful enthusiasms, and the second, 'Aujourd'hui', evokes his grief and reflects on death in a densely metaphorical style. The book includes poems written between 1834 and 1856, and Hugo wrote many new poems about his youth but dated them much earlier, to enhance the illusion that the verse was an unmediated expression of his life.

In the first half, poems of innocent love and family life are interspersed with ecstatic nature poetry affirming the centrality of both God and the poet. Hugo celebrates the dynamism and diversity of living nature, cramming his poems with lists of creatures and plants whilst showing how they are all connected. Tiny concrete phenomena constantly open onto the vast and ineffable. In the ten-line poem titled 'Unité', a humble daisy announces to the sun that she too has rays, and the analogy is echoed both in the description of the sun bending over like a flower at sunset and in the sequence of rhymes which each in turn bind an earthly reality to a divine attribute. So often in Hugo's verse, such dualities are both stated with grandiloquence and hinted at by a subtle network of patterns, and modern readers too often deride the grandiosity while neglecting the artistry.

For Hugo, unity was a reflection of the divine, and nature a dark network of branches criss-crossing to spell the word God (III, 8), but he also emphasizes the role of the poet in grasping and expressing this unity: 'Et j'étudie à fond le texte, et je me penche, | Cherchant à déchiffrer la corolle et la branche.' (And I study the book in depth and I learn, seeking to decipher the corolla and the branch.) (III, 8). Contemplating the world involves reciprocal relationships; flowers may bow down before the poet, but the poet also absorbs creation and allows it to flower within him. Furthermore, he is not

[22] Patricia Ward situates this poem in European Romanticism, viewing it as an example of the 'greater Romantic lyric', in '"Tristesse d'Olympio" and the Romantic Nature Experience', *Nineteenth-Century French Studies*, 7 (1978–9), 4–16.

just transmitting meanings guaranteed by God, but creating ingenious analogies and extending metaphors. Like Lamartine, Hugo transformed the religious language which he had inherited into a highly individual idiom.

The second half of *Les Contemplations* is much darker, mourning the lost daughter and ultimately transcending the personal with cosmic speculations about what lies beyond the grave. Hugo's mingling of lyric postures is often unsettling: in 'A Villequier' private grief is declaimed in an elegy which has an oddly public ring, whilst 'Demain dès l'aube' (Tomorrow at dawn) expresses lament for his daughter in the form of a love poem whose speaker only reveals at the end that the object of his longing is the girl's grave. What Hugo means by 'contemplation' becomes clearer in the second half of the book, in which he peers beyond the bright surfaces of nature, into the abysses of the unknown. A visionary shepherd looks at nature so hard that it disappears, blood runs through the veins of marble, and trees become a hydra ('Magnitudo Parvi', II). In 'Pasteurs et troupeaux' (Shepherds and flocks), a sheltered valley full of sheep is contrasted with the wild sea overlooked by an incongruously personified headland: 'Le pâtre promontoire au chapeau des nuées, | S'accoude et rêve au bruit de tous les infinis.' (The shepherd promontory with its hat of clouds leans on its elbows and dreams to the sound of all infinities.) The yoking of two nouns is an idiosyncratic feature of Hugo's later style, as is the use of an abstract noun in the plural. Elsewhere his style makes it hard for the reader to distinguish figure and ground, as in:

> Mon esprit, qui du doute a senti la piqûre,
> Habite, âpre songeur, la rêverie obscure
> Aux flots plombés et bleus,
> Lac hideux où l'horreur tord ses bras, pâle nymphe,
> Et qui fait boire une eau morte comme la lymphe
> Aux rochers scrofuleux. ('Pleurs dans la nuit')

My spirit, which has felt the stab of doubt, inhabits, harsh dreamer, a realm of obscure reverie with blue and leaden waves, a hideous lake where horror, a pale nymph, twists its arms, and makes the scrofulous rocks drink water as dead as lymph. (Tears in the night)

The poet's mind inhabits a landscape, which is compared to a state of reverie, itself in turn compared to an eerie lake, which becomes a concrete embodiment of the mental torment of doubt. Mind and matter seem to have become interchangeable in this accumulation of analogies, just as inanimate objects have agency and abstractions are given concrete form.

Such doubt is counterbalanced by celebrations of the visionary power of the poet-prophet who, with the wings of an eagle and the mane of a lion, ventures far into the cosmos and steals fire from God ('Ibo'). The secrets of the cosmos are unveiled in the long visionary poem 'Ce que dit la bouche d'ombre' (What the mouth of darkness says), influenced by the ideas of metempsychosis then in vogue and Hugo's own experiments with table-turning in 1853–5. This poem borrows the myth of the ladder of being, and evokes the mire at the bottom, rising up through plants and animals to man, and dissolving into the divine at the top, with humanity torn between the extremes. Its originality lies not in the idea itself, but in the striking images which Hugo forged from it, such as imprisoned souls struggling to escape from flowers, and reincarnated souls streaming from one planet to another like hair hanging behind the face of stars. The description of the bottom of the ladder is particularly rich in proto-surrealist images: 'Là sombre et s'engloutit, dans des flots de désastres, | L'hydre Univers tordant son corps écaillé d'astres' (There sinks and is engulfed, in the waves of disasters, the hydra Universe twisting its body covered in scales of stars). He who dares look to the very bottom will glimpse 'Un affreux soleil noir d'où rayonne la nuit!' (a terrible black sun from which the night shines). Where Lamartine softly modulated contrasts between dark and light, Hugo revelled in thunderous antitheses.

Poetic metaphors were no longer just ornaments standing for an identifiable idea, or even analogies in which concrete reality hinted at an invisible world beyond, but had instead become the structuring principle of the verse. The notion of the symbol was commonly discussed in France in the 1820s and Hugo was recognized as the prime exponent of a new kind of writing—in a famous article of 1829, Pierre Leroux defined the symbolic style as elaborating images without giving the abstract term to which they refer.[23] He remarks that in such poems the same idea may be expressed in twenty different forms, whereas in the seventeenth or eighteenth century it would have been impossible to have more than two comparisons for a single idea in a text of the same length.[24] By the time *Les Contemplations* was published, Hugo's early pictorial experiments had effloresced into disturbing visions, whose originality anticipated Baudelaire and the Symbolists, and much criticism of Hugo's verse explores his inventive use of figurative language.[25]

In the 1850s Hugo wrote an enormous quantity of visionary verse, including poems only published posthumously but now recognized as some of his greatest achievements: the epics *Dieu* (God) and *La Fin de Satan* (The end of Satan), as well as his epic *La Légende des Siècles*. He remained in exile until 1870 and continued to write in this manner on a wide range of themes until the 1880s, dominating French verse to the extent that all later poets were in different ways writing in his shadow. Hugo described himself as a sonorous echo of the voices of nature,[26] and his verse also echoed the cacophonous chorus of humanity, incorporating utopian, political, religious, and scientific ideas. Whereas Vigny viewed poetry as a vessel for pure thought, Hugo transformed contemporary ideas into imaginative images. He used the formal resources of verse to create

[23] Pierre Leroux, 'Du Style symbolique', *Le Globe*, 23 (8 Apr. 1829), 220–3 (221).

[24] Leroux, 'Du Style symbolique', 222.

[25] e.g. Michael Riffaterre, *Essais de stylistique structural*, tr. Daniel Delas (Paris: Flammarion, 1971); Suzanne Nash, *'Les Contemplations' of Victor Hugo: An Allegory of the Creative Process* (Princeton: Princeton University Press, 1976).

[26] The opening poem of *Les Feuilles d'automne*.

harmony out of multifarious ideas and clashing dualities, but also struggled with conflicts which could not be resolved by aesthetic means. Although often accused of bombastic optimism, he was haunted by the violence of revolutions and wrestled in verse with the question of whether suffering was necessary for good to emerge.[27] Recent criticism has increasingly emphasized both his resistance to conventional categories and the paradoxical aspects of his writing, questioning the traditional view of his voice as a unified force.[28]

Alfred de Musset

Younger poets would extend the scope of the aesthetic freedoms won in the 1820s, whilst challenging the notion of the poet as a seer. Amongst these was Musset, who began writing at the end of the 1820s but in many ways belongs to a new generation. Aware of his belatedness, he grew increasingly disenchanted with the social sphere, and uses verse above all to register the private torments and excesses of disappointed individuals. He launched himself with a flamboyant collection called *Contes d'Espagne et d'Italie* (Tales of Spain and Italy) (1830), reminiscent of Hugo's *Orientales*. In it Musset celebrates the intensity of emotions—he urges 'Frappe-toi le cœur, c'est là le génie!' (strike your heart, that is where genius lies)—but simultaneously derides excessive sentiment.[29] This first volume juxtaposes short theatrical pieces with long narrative poems and shorter lyric poems, including many sonnets, a form generally avoided by poets of the 1820s.

The narrative poems recount adventures of passion and revenge, in which intense pleasure constantly borders on intense pain. 'Portia' is the story of an affair between a married woman and the enigmatic stranger Dalti, who kills her husband in a duel. The pair flee and, while serenading her in a Venetian boat, Dalti reveals that he is not the rich noble she thought, but a fisherman who made a fortune gambling only to lose it again. This kind of sting in the tail is typical of Musset, who constantly mingles sorrow and frivolity, especially in the tone of the narrators. The worldly narrator of 'Mardoche' ironically maintains a lively running commentary on his hero, a young Parisian rake in love with a married woman, Rosine. This flippant voice mocks his hero's Romantic tendencies, saying he has attacks of spleen four times a week, and would happily have used skulls as lanterns and soup bowls. The verse is full of daring enjambments, often between stanzas, and the narrator intrudes to reflect on the process of writing, pointing out how much of his own fantasy enters into the description of Rosine, and calling on female readers to remember the ardour of their first lover as a way of

[27] Especially in *Verso de la page* (1857–8), *Œuvres complètes*, ed. G. Rosa and J. Seebacher, Poésie (Paris: Laffont, 1986), iv. 1085–1109.

[28] Ludmila Charles-Wurtz, *Poétique du sujet lyrique dans l'œuvre de Victor Hugo* (Paris: Champion, 1998) emphasizes the plurality of his voice.

[29] 'A mon ami Edouard B.'

justifying Mardoche's haste. Utterances are constantly interrupted, commented upon, or derailed by the narrator's digressions, often punctuated with dashes which add to the breathless pace.

Where the first generation of Romantics had been influenced by Byron's earlier works, especially the melancholy *Manfred*, but bemused by the more mordant *Don Juan* in 1820, Musset, like many later poets, preferred the sardonic later work, as is evident in 'Namouna' (1832), about a rake called Hassan. It begins by describing Hassan reclining naked on a bearskin sofa, and wittily reflects on what female readers might make of this. The narrator has to race through the story of Hassan's affair with Namouna very hastily at the end, because the bulk of the poem is taken up with digressions about how difficult it is to pin down his hero's character: 'Il était très joyeux, et pourtant très maussade, | Détestable voisin,—excellent camarade' (He was very joyful, and yet very gloomy, a terrible neighbour and an excellent friend). The narrator explains that this contradictory being is not a heartless libertine but an idealist who dissipates himself in desperate and vain adventures searching for an unattainable ideal in a world which is constantly unsatisfactory.

Musset's emphasis on the disproportion between desire and reality generated increasingly agonized verse. 'Rolla' (1833) reprises the familiar Byronic theme in more serious terms—a melancholy libertine spends three years spending his inheritance and living a life of debauchery, to commit suicide as the money runs out. The narrator underlines that his hero is a child of a corrupt century, calling on Voltaire to survey contemporary society, and reflecting on how poverty has driven innocent girls to prostitution. He further explored the theme of the melancholy libertine suffering from 'la maladie du siècle' in his novel *La Confession d'un enfant du siècle* (1836).

Musset is best remembered for 'La Nuit de Mai' (1835), a dialogue between a suffering poet and a muse who urges him to return to his abandoned art and use his pain as inspiration, saying that the most desperate songs are the most beautiful. Following the legend that the pelican feeds its young with its own flesh, she describes poets as sacrificing themselves to their audience, and the extended metaphor culminates in these lines describing their verse:

Leurs déclamations sont comme des épées:
Elles tracent dans l'air un cercle éblouissant,
Mais il y pend toujours quelque goutte de sang.

their declamations are like swords; they trace a dazzling circle in the air, but there hangs on them always some drop of blood.

Vigny and Musset both represent the poet as a misunderstood martyr, and this conception of the 'poète maudit' would be elaborated by later poets.

Musset describes what it feels like to have overwhelming desires which are frustrated, and develops the gulf between the ideal and reality which had already haunted Lamartine's *Méditations*, and which would reappear in Baudelaire's depiction of the ravages of spleen and the impossibility of the ideal. Musset developed the practice of poetry as self-expression, evoking the impulses and defence mechanisms of sensitive individuals grappling with a meaningless world, and yet also undercut sentiment by showing speakers constantly ironizing themselves and commenting on the artifice of their poems.

The self-consciousness typical of Musset also characterized the works of many lesser known poets, particularly from 1830 onwards. After the initial ferment of the 1820s, poets took increasingly individual paths. A group including Gautier, Nerval, Pétrus Borel, and Philothée O'Neddy broke away from the original circle to proclaim a more radical rebellion, styling themselves as the *Jeunes-France* and scorning the bourgeoisie; if poetry had been put back in touch with life, life itself was now to become a work of art. Ultimately Gautier forged an aesthetic of Art for Art's sake, which paved the way for Baudelaire, and Nerval took the experiments with mysterious metaphors to extremes in his hermetic sonnets *Les Chimères* (1854). The distinction between prose and poetry became blurred, partly because foreign verse was often read in prose translation and partly because of the new emphasis on experience shaping the very form of poetry, and a new hybrid genre of prose poetry emerged, notably in Aloysius Bertrand's *Gaspard de la nuit* (1842).

What poets in this period all shared was an ambition to adapt received forms to suit their new purposes, and what resulted was 'a poetry liberated from convention yet concerned with form'.[30] Whilst the novel was rising in stature, verse retained its appeal and prestige—although many of the later poets lament their isolation and martyrdom, the works of Lamartine and Hugo were in fact widely read. Lamartine, Vigny, and Hugo all made their names in the 1820s and their later verse refined the aesthetic born in that decade, elaborating a conception of the poet as a privileged spiritual voice. Paul Bénichou has surveyed the process by which poetry replaced religion as a source of value, showing how poets forged a myth of themselves as guides in a world where secular and religious values were in flux.[31] He emphasizes that the idea of the poet-prophet was not a manifestation of the individual authors' vanity but grew out of contemporary systems of thought, and was fed by utopian thinkers like Saint-Simon who themselves attributed considerable importance to poets in their projections of a new social order. However, this social and intellectual turmoil did not just provide subject matter for visionary poetry but led the poets to reinvent conventional modes, extend their imaginative scope, and rethink the poetic vocation itself. Above all, poetry about the most private experience invariably reflected broader concerns about a changing world, and the intimate ways in which poets engaged with their themes was also a way of reflecting on them. Marceline Desbordes-Valmore's refusal to declaim and insistence on immediacy was just as much a symptom of the age as was Hugo's styling himself as a prophet.

[30] Margaret Gilman, *The Idea of Poetry in France* (Cambridge, Mass.: Harvard University Press, 1958), 142.

[31] Paul Bénichou, *Le Sacre de l'écrivain* and *Les Mages romantiques*, in *Romantismes Français* (Paris: Quarto Gallimard, 2004).

In the hands of a range of very distinct creators, verse was being reinvented to suit a variety of modern needs, standing in for religion, registering the intensity of subjective moods, and attempting to define an absolute. In the process it became a much more versatile medium and the proliferation of highly individual poetic idioms forged the way for more extreme formal innovations later in the century, beginning with Baudelaire and culminating in Rimbaud's visionary revolt and Mallarmé's radical atheist aesthetics.

Further Reading

Bénichou, Paul, *Le Sacre de l'écrivain* and *Les Mages romantiques*, in *Romantismes Français*, 2 vols (Paris: Quarto Gallimard, 2004).

Bishop, Lloyd, *The Poetry of Alfred de Musset: Styles and Genres* (Frankfurt: Peter Lang, 1987).

Boutin, Aimée, *Maternal Echoes: The Poetry of Marceline Desbordes-Valmore and Alphonse De Lamartine* (Newark, Del.: University of Delaware Press, 2001)

Castex, Pierre-Georges, *Vigny* (Paris: Hatier, 1969).

Gaudon, Jean, *Victor Hugo: Le Temps de la contemplation* (Paris, 1969; repr. Paris: Champion, 2003).

Gilman, Margaret, *The Idea of Poetry in France* (Cambridge, Mass.: Harvard University Press, 1958).

Houston, J. P., *The Demonic Imagination: Style and Theme in French Romantic Poetry* (Baton Rouge, La.: Louisiana State University Press, 1969).

Ireson, J. C., *Victor Hugo: A Companion to his Poetry* (Oxford: Oxford University Press, 1997).

Loiseleur, Aurélie, *L'Harmonie selon Lamartine: Utopie d'un lieu commun* (Paris: Champion, 2005).

Nash, Suzanne, *'Les Contemplations' of Victor Hugo: An Allegory of the Creative Process* (Princeton: Princeton University Press, 1976).

CHAPTER 8

FRENETIC ROMANTICISM

FRANCESCO MANZINI

INTRODUCTION: FRENETICISM

FRENETICISM, in its broad sense, is a mode of writing with a long and ongoing tradition in European literature. The term derives from the notion of frenzy, an altered state typically induced either by madness or by fever. To this extent, frenzy is synonymous with delirium, unsurprisingly given that both frenzy and freneticism are derived from the Greek and late Latin *phrenesis*, itself synonymous with the Latin *delirium*. Frenetic literature is typically frenzied or delirious in its style, often resorting to the (black) comedy of the grotesque, to hyperbole and to hyperbolic punctuation, especially block capitals and the incontinent use of exclamation marks. It is also frenzied or delirious in its subject matter: frenetic heroes and heroines themselves frequently enter altered states induced by either madness or fever. These altered states typically allow them to access intuitive truths, inaccessible to reason, and, more generally, to explore the sexual and other impulses that would eventually come to be associated with the Freudian subconscious, and in particular the death drive.

Pierre-Georges Castex observes that

> comme l'extase mystique, le délire frénétique est une fièvre d'Absolu. Les deux états répondent à un même désir d'échapper aux servitudes de la condition humaine et d'atteindre en un instant privilégié à un bonheur incommensurable. Mais le mysticisme suppose une soumission, une ascèse, la frénésie implique une révolte et un défi.
>
> mystical ecstasy and frenetic delirium are both fevers of the Absolute. The two states fulfil the same desire to escape the bonds of the human condition and to attain boundless happiness in a privileged instant. But mysticism presupposes submission and asceticism, whereas freneticism implies revolt and defiance.[1]

[1] See Pierre-Georges Castex, *Horizons romantiques* (Paris: Corti, 1983), 15.

Indeed, nineteenth-century French freneticism descends from the mystical tradition of the early-modern period, with its *rêveries* (in their now archaic sense of ravings) and its *ravissements* (raptures). This tradition was exemplified by the scandalously erotic Quietism expounded by Mme Guyon (1648–1717) and Antoinette Bourignon (1610–80), as well as by the sexually immodest, masochistic spectacles provided by Jansenist Convulsionaries in the cemetery of the Parisian church of Saint-Médard until its closure by the authorities in early 1732. It then leads—via late-nineteenth-century theorizations and stagings of (female) hysteria[2]—finally to the self-professedly convulsionary and hysterical psychic automatism of Surrealism, as defined by André Breton in his *Manifeste du Surréalisme* of 1924:

> SURRÉALISME, n.m. Automatisme psychique pur par lequel on se propose d'exprimer, soit verbalement, soit par écrit, soit de toute autre manière, le fonctionnement réel de la pensée. Dictée de la pensée, en l'absence de tout contrôle exercé par la raison, en dehors de toute préoccupation esthétique ou morale.
>
> SURREALISM Pure psychic automatism, whereby one sets oneself the task of expressing, be it verbally, be it in writing, or be it in any other manner, the real workings of the mind. A dictation of the mind, in the absence of any control exercised by reason, and free from any aesthetic or moral preoccupations.[3]

It is on account of its evident psychic automatism that freneticism has tended also to be associated with Gothicism in its various forms and in particular with the latter's subgenres derived from the European folklore relating to vampires and werewolves. For to become a vampire or a werewolf is to enter an automatic and self-revealing state related in part to medieval and early-modern conceptualizations of demonic possession, in part to the nightmares that derived, in the early-modern imagination, from possession by incubi and succubi, in part to sleepwalking or oneirodynia (another recognizable

[2] On the construction of hysterical women in 19th-cent. France, see Janet Beizer, *Ventriloquized Bodies: Narratives of Hysteria in Nineteenth-Century France* (Ithaca, NY: Cornell University Press, 1994), Sander L. Gilman et al., *Hysteria beyond Freud* (Berkeley, Calif.: University of California Press, 1993), and Jann Matlock, *Scenes of Seduction: Prostitution, Hysteria, and Reading Difference in Nineteenth-Century France* (New York: Columbia University Press, 1994). Jean-Martin Charcot, the young Freud's mentor, notoriously stage-managed spectacles of hysteria at the Hospital of La Salpêtrière in the course of his *Leçons du mardi*, put on between 1872 and his death in 1893. See Jacqueline Carroy-Thirard, 'Hystérie, théâtre, littérature au XIXe siècle', *Psychanalyse à l'université*, 7 (1982), 299–317, and Stephen Heath, *The Sexual Fix* (London: Macmillan, 1982), 33–49.

[3] See André Breton, *Œuvres complètes*, ed. Marguerite Bonnet et al. (Paris: Gallimard Pléiade, 1988–2008), i. 328. Famously, as far as Breton was concerned, 'la beauté sera CONVULSIVE ou ne sera pas' (beauty will be CONVULSIVE or will not be at all) (i. 753, *Nadja* (1928)). See also Jeremy Stubbs, 'Les Épidémies de l'esprit: Convulsionnaires et hystériques dans l'imaginaire surréaliste', in Christopher Lloyd (ed.), *Epidemics and Sickness in French Literature and Culture* (Durham: University of Durham, 1995), 113–23, for an account of Breton's efforts to recuperate the Convulsionaries and hysterics within Surrealism, as well as Breton and Louis Aragon, 'Le Cinquantenaire de l'hystérie 1878–1928', in Breton, *Œuvres complètes*, i. 948–50.

trope of frenetic literature), and in part also to Freudian sexual anxiety and repression.[4] As Castex puts it,

> l'imagination frénétique, en effet, se plait non seulement dans la singularité, mais dans la surréalité. Non contente d'aller *jusqu'au bout* de l'expérience possible, elle tend à s'aventurer *au-delà*. Elle crée des êtres maudits, qu'habite une rage démoniaque: criminels qui subjuguent par l'éclat fascinant de leur regard et qui tuent avec une sombre exaltation; ogres qui boivent le sang de leurs victimes dans la coupe de leur crâne. Elle donne aussi la vie à des êtres surnaturels dont les pouvoirs terrifiants accomplissent les plus insensés ou les plus inavouables de nos rêves: vampires qui sortent de leurs tombes pour venir sucer le sang des vivants, stryges qui rongent le cœur des jeunes gens en proie au mal d'amour, sorcières qui éprouvent des philtres de mort. Ces créations hallucinantes ne sont pas des fantaisies gratuites. Nous y reconnaissons bien l'image des hantises qui traversent le cauchemar.
>
> indeed, the frenetic imagination takes delight not only in the singular but also in the surreal. Not content with testing *the very limits* of possible experience, it tends to venture *beyond* such experience. It creates accursed beings, possessed by demonic rage: criminals who subjugate by virtue of the sparkling fascination of their gaze and who kill in a state of solemn exaltation; ogres who drink the blood of their victims in cups made from their skulls. It also brings to life supernatural beings whose terrifying powers allow them to fulfil the maddest and most shameful of our fantasies and dreams: vampires who climb out of their graves to suck the blood of the living, striges who eat away at young lovelorn hearts, witches who try out death-dealing potions. These hallucinatory creatures are not gratuitous fantasies. We can well recognize in them the dreadful images that pass through our nightmares.[5]

Anthony Glinoer has shown that French freneticism additionally owes its origins to literary models, most notably the Italian *Novelle* of Matteo Bandello (1554), a collection of hideous and demoniacal tales which served to inspire the French 'histoires tragiques' (tragic tales) of the seventeenth century, produced by such authors as François de Rosset. The latter's *Histoires tragiques de notre temps où sont contenues les morts funestes et lamentables de plusieurs personnes arrivées par leurs ambitions, vols, rapines et autres accidens divers et mémorables* (1614) were read (and partly recycled) in the nineteenth century by Charles Nodier, Alexandre Dumas, Stendhal, and Jules Barbey d'Aurevilly among others.[6] The tradition exemplified by Rosset would go on variously to produce the *roman-charogne* of the 1820s and 1830s identified by Théophile Gautier,[7] the

[4] Ernest Jones explores this last relation in his *On the Nightmare* (1931). Jean Cocteau uses *La Machine infernale* (1932) to underline the connection between freneticism and sexual repression by introducing folk-tales of vampires in his play based on the Oedipus myth.

[5] See Castex, *Horizons romantiques*, 17–18.

[6] See Anthony Glinoer, *La Littérature frénétique* (Paris: PUF, 2009), 35–6.

[7] 'A côté du roman moyen âge verdissait le roman-charogne, genre de roman très agréable, et dont les petites-maîtresses nerveuses et les cuisinières blasées faisaient une très grande consommation.' See Théophile Gautier, *Mademoiselle de Maupin*, ed. Geneviève van den Bogaert (Paris: Flammarion

fin-de-siècle theatre of the *Grand-Guignol*, and a number of the horror genres of the twentieth century, including those that sought once again to disinter the vampires and werewolves of Mittel-European legend. The epithet 'frénétique' (frenetic) first came to be applied, however, to a disparate literary movement that emerged in France towards the end of the second decade of the nineteenth century.

Frenetic Romanticism

Frenetic Romanticism developed as a specifically French hybrid form, tracing its lineage back to Bandello and Rosset, via such eighteenth-century intermediaries as Jacques Cazotte—the author of *Le Diable amoureux* (1772), traditionally regarded as the first important example of the *conte fantastique*. However, it also derived from the more recent literary and historical models variously provided by Jean-Jacques Rousseau, Sade, German Romanticism in its many forms, the English, Scottish, and Irish Gothic novel, Byron, Polidori, the Shelleys, and the French revolutionaries, particularly the Jacobins, figured, after Joseph de Maistre, as 'héautontimorouménos' or psychically automatic self-torturers and self-executioners.[8]

The term 'frénétique' was coined by Charles Nodier to describe and deplore a new, late form of Romantic literature that was emerging in the France of the Second Restoration (1815–30). This epithet was initially applied to a cluster of literary texts, including some by Nodier himself, that were deemed at one and the same time to derive from a variety of foreign influences and to present a peculiarly Gallic solution to the problem of how to write in a Romantic idiom. From the outset, French frenetic Romanticism was portrayed by Nodier as a minor, immature, and degenerate subgenre, lacking in proper seriousness. This is a view that has persisted. As Lisa Downing puts it, 'waning Romanticism spawns the delirious Gothic hyperbole of the Frenetic Romantics'.[9]

The frenetic Romanticism of the 1820s is often ignored.[10] Instead the movement, insofar as any coherence is imputed to it, is assumed to revolve around a later group of writers, who first achieved a measure of notoriety not on account of their publications but rather their eye-catching leading roles in the 'battle of *Hernani*' staged on 25 February 1830 and then again two nights later. Indeed, even Gautier—by some margin the most successful (former) member of the group in his own lifetime, and along with Nerval, the most critically celebrated in the twentieth and twenty-first centuries—ruefully concluded towards the end of his life that he was probably still chiefly famous for the bright

GF, 1966), 37 ('Préface') and also, more generally, Mario Praz, *The Romantic Agony*, 2nd edn, tr. Angus Davidson, ed. Frank Kermode (London: Oxford University Press, 1970 [1931]).

8 See Pierre Lepère, *L'Âge du furieux 1532–1859: Une légende dorée de l'excès en littérature* (Paris: Hatier, 1994) for an analysis of 'les hommes frénétiques' (pp. 205–58).

9 See Lisa Downing, *Desiring the Dead: Necrophilia and Nineteenth-Century French Literature* (Oxford: Legenda, 2003), 11.

10 See Max Milner, *Le Diable dans la littérature française de Cazotte à Baudelaire (1772–1861)* (Paris: Corti, 1961), i. 314–43, for the first detailed analysis of the frenetic Romanticism of the 1820s as a phenomenon in its own right.

(cherry) red waistcoat he wore to the première of Hugo's emblematically Romantic play.[11]

This group was first known as 'le Petit Cénacle', to distinguish it from the more august earlier 'cénacles' (literary circles) that had clustered around Nodier, Hugo, and Sainte-Beuve. In 1831, it was given the new name of 'les Jeunes-France' by *Le Figaro*. Gautier went on to publish his semi-satirical *Les Jeunes-France, romans goguenards* (1833), which served both to fix this new name for 'le Petit Cénacle' and to distance Gautier himself from the group. 'Les Jeunes-France' spent much of the 1830s shocking bourgeois opinion, whether by hosting parties at which a guest (Alexandre Dumas) allegedly ate custard out of a skull,[12] or simply by living semi-communally—successively in the rue Rochechouart, the rue d'Enfer, and the impasse du Doyenné—whilst indulging in a great deal of inappropriate nudity. 'Les Jeunes-France' produced a steady dribble of commercially unsuccessful literary works in the course of that decade, but, as led by the flamboyant figure of Pétrus Borel, they constituted above all a literary avant-garde committed to the extreme pursuit of artistic freedom, as well as to the acceptance of abject poverty and the other privations of a Romantic lifestyle.

'Les Jeunes-France' came to be associated with another broader grouping, the Bousingots or Bousingos, who combined the radical literary ideas and attention-seeking of the former with the radical (republican) politics fanned by Orleanism's frustration of the hopes engendered by the July Revolution. 'Les Jeunes-France' cheerfully adopted this new epithet also and planned to mythologize themselves further by producing a collection of *Contes du bousingo, par une camaraderie*. Both 'les Jeunes-France' and the Bousingots belonged to what eventually came to be known as 'la Bohème', after Nodier's *Histoire du Roi de Bohème et de ses sept châteaux* (1830). This counter-culture would go on to be celebrated by Henry Murger in his *Scènes de la vie de bohème* (1851) and inspire like-minded movements in other countries, most notably the Italian 'Scapigliatura' of the 1860s and after.

'Les Jeunes-France' continue to figure in modern literary histories of France partly because they counted Gautier and Nerval in their ranks, as well as Aloysius Bertrand, the author of *Gaspard de la nuit* (1842), latterly celebrated as the first collection of modern prose poems in the French language (Alphonse Rabbe, another writer associated with the group, also produced an earlier species of prose poem); partly also because Gautier and Baudelaire both went on to write affectionate and (semi-)admiring retrospective accounts of the movement's leading figures.[13] Modern literary histories tend

[11] See Théophile Gautier, *Histoire du Romantisme*, followed by *Quarante portaits romantiques*, ed. Adrien Goetz and Itaï Kovács (Paris: Gallimard Folio, 2011), 127 and pp. 127–46 more generally for a discussion of the first production of *Hernani*.

[12] See Max Milner, 'Romantics on the Fringe', in D. G. Charlton (ed.), *The French Romantics* (Cambridge: Cambridge University Press, 1984), ii. 382–422 (388).

[13] See Gautier's *Histoire du Romantisme* and Charles Baudelaire, *Réflexions sur quelques-uns de mes contemporains*, in *Œuvres complètes*, ed. Claude Pichois (Paris: Gallimard Pléiade, 1975–6), ii. 129–81, esp. 153–6 dedicted to Borel. See also Philothée O'Neddy, *Lettre de Philothée O'Neddy, auteur de 'Feu et Flamme', sur le groupe littéraire romantique dit des Bousingos* (Paris: Rouquette, 1875).

to define the leading lights of 'les Jeunes-France'—Borel, Philothée O'Neddy, Rabbe—as minor Romantics, if for no other reason than convenience. As Jean-Luc Steinmetz observes in his anthology of their work, 'je ne m'en suis servi que faute de mieux, et avec toutes les restrictions qu'on imagine' (I have availed myself of this appellation in the absence of a better one, and with all the caveats that one might imagine).[14] Milner, who cites Steinmetz to outline the problem he himself had faced when writing his own survey of the movement, ends up referring to these authors as 'Romantics on the fringe' or 'les Romantiques marginaux'.[15] They might more properly be known as the unread Romantics: Gautier, Nerval, and, to a lesser extent Bertrand, are often held no longer to count as part of a movement they evidently spent quite some time identifying themselves with precisely because their works are now read. By contrast, the works of Borel, O'Neddy, and Rabbe, of Xavier Forneret, Alphonse Esquiros, and Charles Lassailly, have gone through long periods of remaining out of print and continue to this day to count as highly specialist taste. Perhaps the legend of these works depends on our never finding out quite how bad they might actually be? Put another way, they might best be read as an intriguing list of titles: *Album d'un pessimiste; Feu et Flamme; Les Roueries de Trialph, notre contemporain avant son suicide*. Writing from the fringe of the fringe that was frenetic Romanticism, Forneret is the undoubted master in this regard, producing such unimprovably titled works as *Rien ... Quelque chose—au profit des pauvres* (1836), *Sans Titre, par un homme noir blanc de visage* (1838), *Vapeurs, ni vers ni prose* (1838), *Encore un an de Sans Titre, par un homme noir blanc de visage* (1839), *Pièce de pièces, Temps perdu* (1840), and *A mon fils naturel* (1847).[16] There appears to have been no question of these publications, published very much at their author's expense, actually being read, at least until their partial revival by the Surrealists. As Forneret himself observed: 'Le plus grand voleur que je connaisse,—c'est moi, si vous me lisez' (The greatest thief I know,—that would be me, if you read my work (*LFF*, 515, *Encore un an de Sans Titre*).

There have, however, been two sustained attempts to secure a readership for this varied corpus of texts. The first of these was indeed made by the Surrealists, and in particular by André Breton, who sought to lend his own fame to their cause, eventually using his *Anthologie de l'humour noir* (1940) to republish a number of excerpts from the works of Borel and Forneret, as well as from the *Mémoires* (1836) of the murderer Pierre-François Lacenaire, sensationally tried and executed in the year of their publication (this last text has come, after Breton, sometimes to be associated with frenetic Romanticism, although it was perhaps too widely read properly to take its place alongside the works of 'les Jeunes-France'[17]). More recently, the indefatigable Steinmetz has conducted a one-man

[14] See Jean-Luc Steinmetz, *La France frénétique de 1830* (Paris: Phébus, 1978), 32 (hereafter *LFF*) and also the same author's more strident 'Pour en finir avec les "petits romantiques"', *Revue d'histoire littéraire de la France* (2005), 891–912.

[15] See Milner, 'Romantics on the Fringe', ii. 382–422.

[16] Forneret was atypical on account of his large private income, which he used to fund the staging and publication of his works, as well as to live the life of a frenetic dandy not in Paris, but in his native Burgundy. See Eldon Kaye, *Xavier Forneret dit 'l'homme noir' (1809–1884)* (Geneva: Droz, 1971).

[17] See Pierre François Lacenaire, *Mémoires*, ed. Jacques Simonelli (Paris: Corti, 1991). Simonelli discusses the many differences between Lacenaire's text and the works of frenetic Romanticism proper,

campaign to draw the attention both of specialists and a wider public to the works of the 'minor' Romantics. In addition to his influential anthology, already cited, he has produced new editions of Borel's two best works, *Champavert: Contes immoraux* (1833) and *Madame Putiphar* (1839), as well as a biography of Borel and several critical studies of the author.[18]

The story of French frenetic Romanticism appeared to end with the commercial failure of Borel's *Madame Putiphar*—subsequently hailed by Baudelaire as demonstrating flashes of 'un talent véritablement épique' (a truly epic talent), by Breton as 'un ouvrage traversé d'un des plus grands souffles révolutionnaires qui furent jamais' (a work crossed by one of the most revolutionary currents there has ever been) and by Steinmetz, on the back cover of his edition, as 'LE roman noir de la littérature française' (THE Gothic novel of French literature).[19] It is true that Borel gamely limped on, publishing occasional journalistic pieces, but by the end of the 1840s he was to be found incongruously pursuing a bureaucratic career as a colonial administrator in Algeria. The group that had once coalesced around him no longer existed. Yet frenetic Romanticism was to live on by forming an essential component of another hybrid literary movement: the frenetic Catholicism first adumbrated by Balzac—a freneticist, on and off, since the early 1820s[20]—then developed by Barbey d'Aurevilly, and finally taken up at the end of the nineteenth century by Léon Bloy.[21]

Frenetic Catholicism concerned itself with the intuitive delirium produced by the altered state of fever, not least as a means of attacking Enlightenment rationalism. Chateaubriand had used his version of Romanticism both to serve the ends of his Catholic apologetics and to hark back to the Counter-Enlightenment intuitivism of Rousseau; Balzac and Barbey looked instead to the radical and polemical Counter-Enlightenments of Louis de Bonald and Joseph de Maistre as they made their first attempts to fuse freneticism (in its Romantic form) with their versions of Catholicism. This Balzac was not so much a realist, but rather, in Baudelaire's famous formulation, a 'visionnaire' (visionary), just as, for Steinmetz, 'les Jeunes-France' were 'voyants' (seers).[22] In the 1830s, Balzac had produced his heterodox *Livre Mystique*

whilst also pointing out a parallel between the ironic prefaces of Lacenaire's *Mémoires* and Lassailly's *Les Roueries de Trialph* (pp. 9–11).

[18] See Pétrus Borel, *Madame Putiphar*, ed. Jean-Luc Steinmetz (Paris: Phébus, 1999); *Champavert: Contes immoraux*, ed. Jean-Luc Steinmetz (Paris: Phébus, 2002); and Jean-Luc Steinmetz, 'L'Ouïë du nom', in *Le Champ d'écoute* (Neuchâtel: La Baconnière, 1985), 79–103; *Pétrus Borel: Un auteur provisoire* (Lille: Presses Universitaires de Lille, 1986); *Pétrus Borel, vocation: Poète maudit* (Paris: Fayard, 2002).

[19] See Baudelaire, *Œuvres complètes*, ii. 153; and André Breton, *Anthologie de l'humour noir* (Paris: Le Livre de Poche, 2002), 105.

[20] Balzac produced a series of novels in a broadly frenetic manner in the course of the first half of the 1820s. See Honoré de Balzac, *Premiers romans*, ed. André Lorant (Paris: Laffont Bouquins, 1999). *Le Figaro* identified Balzac as its first example of a '*Jeune France*'. See the front page of its issue of 30 Aug. 1831. This is available for consultation at <http://gallica.bnf.fr/ark:/12148/bpt6k267083n>.

[21] See Francesco Manzini, *The Fevered Novel from Balzac to Bernanos: Frenetic Catholicism in Crisis, Delirium and Revolution* (London: IGRS, 2011) for an extended account of Frenetic Catholicism.

[22] See Baudelaire, *Œuvres complètes*, ii. 120; and Steinmetz, *LFF* 33.

(1835), which had served to collect *Les Proscrits* (1831), the partly autobiographical *Louis Lambert* (1832), and the Swedenborgian *Séraphîta* (1835). In the 1840s, he went on to produce the Mesmerist *Ursule Mirouët* (1841) and the Maistrean *L'Envers de l'histoire contemporaine* (1843–8). These texts explored what might broadly be referred to, after the Surrealists, as psychic automatism. Balzac—who continued also to produce frenetic texts uninflected by Catholicism, most notably the splendidly hyperbolic *La Fille aux yeux d'or* (1833–5)—drew on Gothicism, for example, in his *Melmoth réconcilié* (1835), but also on the examples provided by 'les Jeunes-France', with whom he remained in sporadic contact. Indeed, he collaborated extensively with Lassailly (one of his famous *nègres* (ghostwriters)), as well as with Philarète Chasles and Charles Rabou on *Les Contes bruns par...* (1832), a work associated directly with the movement (it was Chasles who first drew the distinction between Balzac the 'voyant' and Balzac the 'observateur' (observer)).[23] Barbey d'Aurevilly, by contrast, returned to the source of frenetic Romanticism as it had been defined by Nodier, for he used his major fictional works—especially *Un prêtre marié* (1865)—to fuse the freneticism of Byron and Polidori with the theosophy of Maistre. In 1832, the 24-year-old Barbey had written *Léa*, a short story that set the tone of his own frenetic Romantic manner.[24] He continued to write in a defiantly frenetic Romantic idiom until well into the 1880s.

Nodier and the Frenetic Romanticism of the 1820s

Charles Nodier was an influential figure in the Romantic circles of the French Restoration. From his position as the librarian of the Bibliothèque de l'Arsenal, to which he had been appointed in 1824, he emerged as the first leader of the Romantic 'cénacle' that formed itself in 1826 and counted Vigny, Lamartine, Hugo, and Sainte-Beuve amongst its more illustrious members. Nodier's claim to leadership rested in part on his own previous fictional output, which included a number of texts in the frenetic manner: the best known of these are the novel *Jean Sbogar* (1818) and the short-story *Smarra ou les démons de la nuit* (1821).[25] It also rested, however, on his status as a leading literary

[23] See Baudelaire, *Œuvres complètes*, ii. 1135–6 and Claude Pichois, *Philarète Chasles et la vie littéraire au temps du romantisme* (Paris: Corti, 1965), i. 431–2.

[24] See Thomas Löw, 'Vampires et suceurs de sang', *Revue des lettres modernes*, 965–70 (1990), 83–99, for a comparison of Polidori's *The Vampyre* and Barbey's *Léa*.

[25] Castex identifies *Smarra* and *Les Aventures de Thibaud de la Jaquière* (1822; probably by Nodier) as together forming a 'cycle frénétique'. See Charles Nodier, *Contes*, ed. Pierre-Georges Castex (Paris: Classiques Garnier, 1961), 25–31. In his preface to *Smarra*, Nodier suggests that Dalmatia, the scene of his story, is a land of 'délires' (deliria) and 'frénésies' (frenzies) (34). Steinmetz includes three *contes* by Nodier dating from the 1830s in his anthology of frenetic Romanticism (*LFF* 51–124). Glinoer notes that Steinmetz's anthology chooses to ignore the frenetic Romanticism of the 1820s (*La Littérature frénétique*, 27).

critic: as has already been noted, Nodier had himself introduced the epithet *frénétique* to describe the new form of Romanticism being produced by the France of the 1820s.[26] This Romanticism took its inspiration from Byron and from Charles Maturin: Byron's complete works appeared in a ten-volume French translation between 1819 and 1821 and Maturin's *Melmoth the Wanderer* (1820) appeared in two different translations in 1821. In particular, however, it took its inspiration from Polidori's *The Vampyre* (1819). Nodier reviewed Henri Faber's French translation of this work (also 1819).[27] However, he first used the word *frénétique* in his review of Christian Spieβ's *Das Petermännchen* (1791, translated into French by Henri de Latouche in 1820).[28] Spieβ's text proved an important point of reference for Nodier; however, *The Vampyre*, attributed first to Byron and only belatedly to Polidori, clearly functions as the founding text of the frenetic Romanticism of the 1820s. Nodier would go on to collaborate on *The Vampyre*'s adaptation as a melodrama in 1820 and to allow his name to be associated with the publication of Cyprien Bérard's spin-off novel, *Lord Ruthwen* [*sic*] *ou les vampires* (also 1820).

Nodier claimed to doubt the value of the frenetic Romanticism he had been the first to identify, for this was a literature 'qui promène l'athéisme, la rage et le désespoir à travers des tombeaux; qui exhume les morts pour épouvanter les vivants, et qui tourmente l'imagination de scènes horribles, dont il faut demander le modèle aux rêves effrayants des malades' (which parades atheism, rage and despair through graveyards; which exhumes the dead to frighten the living, and which torments our imagination with horrible scenes, modelled on the terrifying dreams produced by diseased minds').[29] Thus,

> il est de l'honneur national de faire tomber sous le poids de la réprobation publique ces malheureux essais d'une école extravagante, moyennant qu'on s'entende sur les mots; car ce n'est ni de l'école classique, ni de l'école romantique que j'ai l'intention de parler. C'est d'une école innommée … que j'appellerai cependant, si l'on veut, l'école frénétique.
>
> it is a matter of national honour for the full weight of the public's reprobation to fall on the unhappy literay productions of this extravagant school, although we should be clear about the use of this term, for I do not intend to speak either of the classical or the Romantic school. Rather I intend to speak of a school with no name … that I shall nevertheless call, if nobody objects, the frenetic school.

This extravagant form of literature served primarily to provide the titillation and excitement required to stimulate a jaded society, exhausted by the wars of the Revolution and Empire. As a result, it functioned both as a symptom and as a possible

[26] See Jean Larat, *La Tradition et l'exotisme dans l'œuvre de Charles Nodier* (Paris: Champion, 1923), 368–74; and Terry Hale, 'Frénétique School', in Marie Mulvey-Roberts (ed.), *The Handbook to Gothic Literature* (London: Macmillan, 1998), 58–63.

[27] See Charles Nodier, *Mélanges de littérature et de critique*, ed. Alexandre Barginet (Paris: Raymond, 1820), i. 409–17.

[28] Nodier's review appeared in *Annales de la littérature et des arts*, 3 (1821), 77–83. The review ends with a discussion of frenetic Romanticism (80–3).

[29] Charles Nodier, *Annales de la literature et des arts*, 3 (1821), 82–3.

cure for the *mal du siècle* already afflicting the Restoration.[30] In the preface to his adapted translation of Maturin's tragedy *Bertram*, Nodier argues that Chateaubriand (and Népomucène Lemercier) had missed the opportunity to create around them a true and valuable French Romanticism. Instead, the nation had been left with mere freneticism:

> Le genre souvent ridicule et quelquefois révoltant qu'on appelle en France romantique, et pour lequel nous croyons n'avoir pas trouvé trop malheureusement l'épithète de *frénétique*, ne sera jamais un genre, puisqu'il suffit de sortir de tous les genres pour être classé dans celui-là. Distraction innocente d'une étude plus sérieuse; ou essai d'une imagination fatiguée qui s'ennuie dans sa sphère; ou aberration d'un esprit malade, qui se dédommage dans le vague infini des malheurs imaginaires de la réalité de ses souffrances; ou ressource d'un talent méconnu qui consulte le goût de son temps pour conquérir le pain que d'utiles travaux ne lui auraient pas donné, on ne peut considérer ses tristes amplifications que comme les rêveries délirantes des fiévreux. Cependant l'état de notre société fait très-bien comprendre l'accueil qu'elle accorde aux folies sentimentales et aux exagérations passionnées. Les peuples vieillis ont besoin d'être stimulés par des nouveautés violentes. Il faut des commotions électriques à la paralysie, des horreurs poétiques à la sensibilité, et des exécutions à la populace.
>
> The often ridiculous and sometimes revolting genre that in France passes for Romanticism and to which I have applied, not too unhappily, the epithet *frenetic*, will never be a genre proper, for it is sufficient not to belong to any genre to fall into this one. An innocent distraction from more serious pursuits; or the product of a tired imagination tired of its limited sphere; or an aberration of a sick mind that compensates for the reality of its suffering by exploring the endless vagueness of imaginary misfortunes; or the resort of a misunderstood talent responding to the tastes of the age in order to earn a living that more useful work would not have provided? In any event, one can but view its sorry manifestations as the delirious reveries of the fevered. Nevertheless, the current state of our society explains well enough the enthusiastic reception it gives to sentimental follies and exaggerated passions. Aged peoples require stimulation by violent novelty: their paralysis needs electric shocks, their sensibility needs poetic horrors, and the mob needs executions.[31]

It is these 'commotions électriques' and 'horreurs poétiques' that were to become the mainstay of French frenetic Romanticism not just in the 1820s, but also in the 1830s.

Nodier's diagnosis would eventually be confirmed by Musset, himself a sometime member of the 'cénacle' towards the end of the 1820s, in his *La Confession d'un enfant du siècle* (1836). The second chapter of this novel presents the classic Romantic survey of the impact of Napoleon's extraordinary rise and fall on the generation that immediately

[30] See Nodier, *Mélanges*, i. 411; and Larat, *La Tradition*, 369.

[31] See Charles Maturin, *Bertram ou le château de Saint-Aldobrand*, tr. Charles Nodier and Justin Taylor (Paris: Gide fils; Ladvocat, 1821), pp. iii–vi; and Larat, *La Tradition*, 371–2.

followed him: 'alors il s'assit sur un monde en ruines une jeunesse soucieuse' (it was then that anxious youth took its seat amidst a world in ruins).[32] The impact of the Empire, along with the impact of the earlier Revolution, on the worried youth of the Restoration had already been analysed by Nodier. As he laconically observes, 'on sait où nous sommes en politique, et en poésie nous en sommes au cauchemar et au vampires' (we know where we've ended up politically, and in poetry we've ended up with nightmares and vampires).[33]

The young Hugo served as an exemplary illustration of Nodier's (and eventually Musset's) theory, for this prodigy of Romanticism was the son of a Napoleonic general who chose to emerge from the shadow cast by his father by producing two broadly frenetic novels—*Han d'Islande* (1823) and *Bug-Jargal* (1820, 1826)—dealing with various electric shocks and poetical horrors, including especially the executions required by the mob. He was to follow these two texts with his *Le Dernier Jour d'un condamné* (1829), which has been incongruously described as a work of 'réalisme noir' (Gothic realism), that is to say frenetic realism.[34]

Balzac's *Le Centenaire* (1822) is also often cited as an example of what Glinoer describes as 'le roman frénétique romantisant' (the romanticizing frenetic novel).[35] Inspired directly by Maturin's *Melmoth*, it opens a frenetico-Gothic Balzacian cycle that closes only in 1835 with the publication of *Melmoth réconcilié*. This thematic and stylistic continuity illustrates the arbitrariness of the literary historical convention that divides Balzac's juvenilia of the first half of the 1820s from the great 'realist' project of *La Comédie humaine*, launched only in 1842, but retrospectively made by Balzac to include texts that extend as far back as *Les Chouans* (1829), another novel heavily inflected by freneticism.

For Nodier, as for its other practitioners, frenetic Romanticism represented excess in art: to be frenetic was to be extreme and therefore to possess energy to an unusual degree. Glinoer is surely right to suggest, after Christine Marcandier-Colard, that this lesson was lost neither on Balzac nor on Stendhal:

> avec l'édification du mythe napoléonien et l'éclosion du romantisme, cette idée a été développée sur tous les modes et dans tous les arts, mais le roman, avec Stendhal et Balzac notamment, s'est révélé un habitacle ideal pour donner vie au déploiement de l'énergie, comme forme de beauté liée à la violence, comme force physique, corporelle que l'homme oppose aux obstacles de la destinée.
>
> with the construction of the Napoleonic myth and the flowering of Romanticism, this idea was developed in all sorts of ways across the arts, but the novel, especially as produced by Stendhal and Balzac, proved the ideal vehicle for representing the

[32] See Alfred de Musset, *La Confession d'un enfant du siècle*, ed. Claude Roy and Gérard Barrier (Paris: Gallimard Folio, 1973), 22.

[33] See Castex, *Horizons romantiques*, 17.

[34] See Glinoer, *La Littérature frénétique*, 112–14.

[35] See Glinoer, *La Littérature frénétique*, 84–91.

> deployment of energy as a form of beauty linked to violence—as a physical, bodily strength used by men to overcome the obstacles of fate.[36]

It is this energy, exemplarily embodied by Julien Sorel in Stendhal's *Le Rouge et le Noir* (1830), that Baudelaire detects in Balzac:

> Tous ses personnages sont doués de l'ardeur vitale dont il était animé lui-même. Toutes ses fictions sont aussi profondément colorées que les rêves. Depuis le sommet de l'aristocratie jusqu'aux bas-fonds de la plèbe, tous les acteurs de sa *Comédie* sont plus âpres à la vie, plus actifs et rusés dans la lutte, plus patients dans le malheur, plus goulus dans la jouissance, plus angéliques dans le dévouement, que la comédie du vrai monde ne nous les montre. Bref, chacun, chez Balzac, même les portières, a du genie. Toutes les âmes sont des armes chargés de volonté jusqu'à la gueule. C'est bien Balzac lui-même. Et comme tous les êtres du monde extérieur s'offraient à l'œil de son esprit avec un relief puissant et une grimace saisissante, il a fait se convulser ses figures; il a noirci leurs ombres et illuminé leurs lumières.
>
> All his characters are endowed with the same vital ardour by which he himself was animated. All his fictions are as highly coloured as dreams. From the heights of the aristocracy to the depths of the masses, all the actors in his *Comedy* prove fiercer in the way they live their lives, more active and more cunnning in their struggles, more accepting of their misfortunes, more greedy in their pleasures and more angelic in their devotion than they ever appear in the comedy of the real world. In short, everyone in Balzac possesses genius—even the door-keepers. Everyone is like a gun, loaded to the muzzle with will, just like Balzac himself. And, given that everyone in the external world appeared to his mind in powerful relief, grimacing memorably, he made their faces convulse, darkening their shadows and illuminating their light.[37]

Balzac's frenetically energetic fictions often tip into absurdity, but this absurdity appears quite knowing and qualitatively different to the grotesque grimaces deployed by Hugo. Balzac appears in control of the self-parodic elements that also feature in the frenetic Romanticism of the 1830s. These had already been foregrounded in Jules Janin's *L'Ane mort et la femme guillotinée* (1829), the last major frenetic Romantic text of the 1820s. This set out at once to provide its readers with electric shocks and poetic horrors—criminality, impalements, etc.—in the best frenetic Romantic manner, and to parody this manner in such a way as to make a mockery both of the reader and of the text itself. Janin went on to enjoy a long and illustrious career as a critic; Gautier would eventually follow this same path by using the self-parody of his *Les Jeunes-France, romans goguenards* to establish distance between himself and his dubious companions on the literary fringe, prior to embarking on his more orthodox literary career as a critic, poet, and novelist. But self-parody was in any case to become the stock-in-trade of the frenetic Romantics that clustered around Pétrus Borel.

[36] See Glinoer, *La Littérature frénétique*, 89–90; and Christine Marcandier-Colard, *Crimes de sang et scènes capitales: Essai sur l'esthétique romantique de la violence* (Paris: PUF, 1998), 94.

[37] See Baudelaire, *Œuvres complètes*, ii. 120.

Borel and the Frenetic Romanticism of the 1830s

Baudelaire argues that Borel was doomed to fail, the eternal victim of *le Guignon* (persistent bad luck). Everything about him offended, including even his handwriting, that sloped the wrong way, and his determination to use unfamiliar spellings (including *phrénétique* for *frénétique*). These idiosyncrasies appeared to Baudelaire as symbols of Borel's broader intransigence:

> Cet esprit à la fois littéraire et républicain, à l'inverse de la passion démocratique qui nous a plus tard si cruellement opprimés, était agité à la fois par une haine aristocratique sans limites, sans restrictions, sans pitié, contre les rois et contre la bourgeoisie, et d'une sympathie générale pour tout ce qui en art représentait l'excès dans la couleur et dans la forme, pour tout ce qui était à la fois intense, pessimiste et byronien.
>
> This mind at once literary and republican, at the other extreme of the passion for democracy that has since oppressed us so cruelly, was possessed at once by a boundless, unreserved, pitiless aristocratic hatred for kings and for the bourgeoisie, and by a general sympathy for everything that, in art, represented formal and chromatic excess—everything at once intense, pessimistic and Byronic.[38]

As Baudelaire suggests, this intransigence was both literary and political: it was the intransigence that led Borel to take Sade and Robespierre as his self-professed exemplars. Borel, in other words, was a Byronic rebel who sought to take such rebelliousness to new extremes.

Baudelaire's reference to Borel's alleged *Guignon* is knowing, for example when he poses the rhetorical question: 'Quel méchant esprit se pencha sur son berceau et lui dit: *Je te défends de plaire?*' (What evil spirit bent over his crib and said to him: *I forbid you from giving pleasure?*)[39] For Baudelaire is alluding to the central conceit of *Madame Putiphar*, namely that divine Providence often fails the very best of us (no doubt because God does not in fact exist):

> Je ne sais s'il y a un fatal destin, mais il y a certainement des destinées fatales; mais il est des hommes qui sont donnés au malheur; mais il est des hommes qui sont la proie des hommes, et qui leur sont jetés comme on jetait des esclaves aux tigres des arènes; pourquoi? … Je ne sais. Et pourquoi ceux-ci plutôt que ceux-là? Je ne sais non plus: ici la raison s'égare et l'esprit qui creuse se confond.
>
> I do not know whether there is such a thing as fateful destiny, but there are certainly some destinies that proved ill-fated; but some men are given over to misfortune; but

[38] See Baudelaire, *Œuvres complètes*, ii. 155. In his *Conseils aux jeunes littérateurs* (1846), Baudelaire reveals himself to be sceptical about 'le Guignon' as an excuse for commercial and critical failure: 'si vous avez du guignon, c'est qu'il vous manque quelque chose'. See Baudelaire, *Œuvres complètes*, ii. 13–20 (14).

[39] See Baudelaire, *Œuvres complètes*, ii. 153.

> some men are the prey of other men and are thrown to them as slaves were thrown to tigers in the arena; why? ... I don't know. And why these and not others? I don't know either: at this point, reason loses its way and the enquiring mind becomes confused.][40]

Or, as Forneret puts it:

> L'Homme commet une faute en naissant; celle de naître.—
> Man is born into sin; the sin of being born.—
> (*LFF* 511, *Sans Titre par un homme noir blanc de visage*)

Thus, for Borel, 'beaucoup d'entre nous ne ressemblent-ils point par leur existence à ces scarabées transpercés d'une épingle, et piqués vivants sur un mur; ou à ces chauves-souris clouées sur une porte servant de mire pour tirer à l'arbalète' (in the lives we lead, many of us ressemble, do we not, those beetles pierced through with a pin and mounted on a wall whilst still living; or those bats nailed to a door to serve as targets for crossbow practice) (*MP* 45). Certainly, Borel's fictions focus on man's unthinking or else consciously sadistic infliction of pain on other men and, a fortiori, on women: Borel is one of the great chroniclers of nineteenth-century and transhistorical misogyny. His stories and novels present the animal sufferings of their human victims. Thus Borel, when he presents himself as a lycanthrope (or werewolf), appears both as a (republican) hunter of the bourgeoisie and as its tortured prey; he is at once possessed of the bestial energy that had also marked out Hugo's Han d'Islande and the eternal victim of a bourgeois dynamic still more bestial in its cruel indifference to suffering. As Forneret puts it,

> On regarde un chat mort, et l'on passe le Pauvre.—
> We stop to look at a dead cat, and pass the Pauper by.—
> (*LFF* 511, *Sans Titre par un homme noir blanc de visage*)

Finally, however, Borel is fated to lose: he can only be 'la proie' (prey), as figured at the end of the long poem that serves as a prologue to *Madame Putiphar*:

> Quand finira la lutte, et qui m'aura pour proie,—
> Dieu le sait!—du Désert, du Monde ou du Néant?
> When will the struggle end, and who will have me as its prey,—
> God knows!—out of the Desert, Society or the Void?
> (*MP*42)

The end-point of many of Borel's narratives is a particularly horrible death. Thus, included among the stories that make up *Champavert: Contes immoraux*, we have the execution of a young woman, prosecuted for an unwitting infanticide by the man who had raped her ('Monsieur de l'Argentière'), two men hacking each other to

[40] See Borel, *Madame Putiphar*, 43 (hereafter *MP*).

pieces ('Jaquez Barraou'), and an impotent old man vivisecting his much younger wife to punish her for an infidelity, or rather for her sexual desire ('Don Andréa Vésalius, l'anatomiste'). Death alone is a release:

> Il n'est de bonheur vrai, de repos qu'en la fosse:
> Sur la terre on est mal, sous la terre on est bien;
> Là, nul plaisir rongeur; là, nulle amitié fausse;
> Là, point d'ambition, point d'espoir déçu ...—Rien! ...
> There is no true happiness, no rest outside the grave:
> Above ground all is bad, underground all is well;
> There, no gnawing pleasure; there, no false friends;
> There, no ambitions, no dashed hopes...—Nothing! ...
> (*MP* 41)

Or, as Forneret puts it:

> Cimetière veut dire: Allons nous reposer.—
> Graveyard means: let's take a nap.—

and

> Quand la mort frappe, le bonheur entre.—
> When death knocks, happiness walks in.—

and

> Dans le creux d'une fosse, il y a l'Espérance.—
> In the hollow of a grave, there is Hope.—
> (*LFF* 511–13, *Sans Titre par un homme noir blanc de visage*)

It is for this reason that fateful destiny (the malevolent Providence of a God who does not exist) decrees that death should come as horribly as possible, to spoil the otherwise happy event. (As Stendhal was apparently fond of observing, 'ce qui excuse Dieu, ... c'est qu'il n'existe pas' (God's only excuse ... is that he doesn't exist).[41]) Luckily,

> Le sapin, dont on fait des cercueils, est un arbre toujours vert.—
> The fir, from which coffins are made, is an evergreen tree.—
> *LFF* 515, *Encore un an de Sans Titre par un homme noir blanc de visage*)

The first text associated with the frenetic Romanticism represented by Borel's circle was Rabbe's *Album d'un pessimiste*, only published in 1835, but written before the

[41] See Prosper Mérimée, *Carmen et treize autres nouvelles*, ed. Pierre Josserand (Paris: Gallimard, 1965), 445.

latter's death in 1830. Much of this text is given over to an apologia for suicide, also celebrated in Lassailly's *Les Roueries de Trialphe, notre contemporain avant son suicide* (1833). Rabbe had contracted syphilis in his early twenties and become hideously disfigured by the disease, to the point where suicide appears to have struck him as an attractive proposition. When his death finally came—whether or not by his own hand is unclear—it appears not to have been an easy one.[42] As Forneret observes:

> L'homme qui songe au temps passé, sourit aux jours qu'il a de moins à vivre.—
> The man who reflects on the past smiles at the days he has less to live.—

and

> Celui qui sait Mourir, a su Vivre;—
> He who knows how to Die knew how to Live;—
> (*LFF* 512, *Sans Titre par un homme noir blanc de visage*)

After Rabbe, Borel and his circle developed a pervasive (Frenetic Stoic?) interest in suicide and the nothingness of death as counterpoints to hope and ambition. Baudelaire suggests Borel's ambition is an important part of his 'génie manqué' (unfulfilled genius).[43] Certainly those in Borel's circle assumed that this ambition would be fulfilled, at the very least negatively. As Gautier puts it,

> nous le trouvions *très fort*, et nous pensions qu'il serait le grand homme spécial de la bande. Les *Rhapsodies* s'élaboraient lentement et dans une ombre mystérieuse pour éclater en coup de foudre et aveugler ou tout au moins éblouir la bourgeoisie stupéfiée.
>
> we thought him *really talented*, and decided he would be the greatest of the great men in our group. The *Rhapsodies* were coming together slowly, in myserious shadow, only eventually to flash like a bolt of lightning and blind, or at least dazzle, the stupefied bourgeoisie.[44]

But the *Rhapsodies*, a collection of poems published in 1832, provoked a small measure of derision and were otherwise met with indifference. At this point, it appears to have become clear to all concerned that 'les Jeunes-France' would never succeed in integrating themselves within the literary establishment, not even as licensed jesters. It was around this time that Gautier decided to fend for himself; Lassailly, for his part, made a virtue of the inevitability of his own failure, responding to the ineluctable mockery of fate by means of the following epigraph to his novel:

[42] See *LFF* 125–6.

[43] See Baudelaire, *Œuvres complètes*, ii. 155.

[44] See Gautier, *Histoire du Romantisme*, 75.

Ah!
Eh! hé?
Hi! hi! hi!
Oh!
Hu! hu! hu! hu! hu!
Profession de foi par l'auteur
Ah!
Eh! hey?
Ha! ha! ha!
Oh!
Hu! hu! hu! hu! hu!
The author's profession of faith[45]

Lassailly goes on to explain that the name of his hero, Trialph, is derived from the Danish word for 'Gâchis' (waste), suggesting that his story, leading to the suicide announced in his title, will be one of confusion and wasted talent.[46] In 1832, Lassailly had in any case already signalled his aim to court failure by announcing his intention to publish a pair of novels, to be entitled *Robespierre* and *Jésus-Christ* respectively. This bridge-burning attitude would be ironized by Gautier in his preface to *Mademoiselle de Maupin* (1835), by which the latter further marked his detachment from 'les Jeunes-France'.[47]

However, Borel and his circle would also continue to fail because, as the generally sympathetic Baudelaire observes, their works were simply not good enough. This conclusion does not prevent Baudelaire from noting that Borel in particular played 'un rôle non sans importance.... Sans Pétrus Borel, il y aurait une lacune dans le Romantisme' (a role not without its importance.... Without Pétrus Borel, there would be something missing from Romanticism).[48] What Baudelaire means is that Borel performed his lycanthropic role, as he had himself defined it in the preface to his *Rhapsodies*: over the course of the 1830s, he committed himself fully to the freedom in art that had been contested over three days at the end of February 1830 during the 'battle of Hernani', as well as to an abstracted version of the political freedom that had been contested over three days at the start of July during the Revolution of 1830. It is thanks to this commitment that, again according to Baudelaire, Borel's name became proverbial:

> quand un petit journal veut, en 1859, exprimer tout le dégoût et le mépris que lui inspire une poésie ou un roman d'un caractère sombre et outré, il lance le mot: *Pétrus Borel!* Et tout est dit. Le jugement est prononcé, l'auteur est foudroyé.
>
> when, in 1859, some little review wants to expess all the disgust and contempt it might feel for a sombre and outré poem or novel, it hurls out the name *Pétrus Borel!*

[45] See Charles Lassailly, *Les Roueries de Trialphe, notre contemporain avant son suicide*, ed. Thierry Galibert (Arles: Sulliver, 2006), 34.

[46] See Lassailly, *Les Roueries de Trialphe*, 34.

[47] See Gautier, *Mademoiselle de Maupin*, 27. Gautier goes on to make a dismissive reference to Trialph's 'roueries' (32).

[48] See Baudelaire, *Œuvres complètes*, ii. 155.

> No more needs to be said. Judgement has been passed, and the author has been struck down.[49]

One of Forneret's most frequently anthologized pieces, 'Un pauvre honteux', continues in part where Borel had left off in his *Contes immoraux*. It ends in an extraordinary flourish of psychically automatic orality:

> Il l'a palpée
> D'une main décidée
> A la faire mourir.—
> —Oui, c'est une bouchée
> Dont on peut se nourrir.
> Il l'a pliée,
> Il l'a cassée,
> Il l'a placée,
> Il l'a coupée;
> Il l'a lavée,
> Il l'a portée,
> Il l'a grillée,
> Il l'a mangée.
> —Quand il n'était pas grand, on lui avait dit:
> Si tu as faim, mange une de tes mains.
>
> He felt her
> With a hand determined
> To make her die.—
> — Yes, she's a mouthful
> On whom one can feed.
> He folded her,
> He broke her,
> He positioned her,
> He cut her,
> He washed her,
> He carried her,
> He grilled her,
> He ate her.
> —When he wasn't big, he'd been told:
> If you're hungry, eat one of your hands.
> (*LFF* 532, *Vapeurs, ni vers ni prose*)

Stendhal was to explore similar territory in the brief account he gives of the fifteenth-century would-be alchemist and child-killer Gilles de Retz (more usually Rais) in his *Mémoires d'un Touriste* (1838), associated via Stendhal's peculiar conceptualization

[49] See Baudelaire, *Œuvres complètes*, ii. 153.

of the Don Juan, to the eminently frenetic figure of Francesco Cenci.[50] The latter had been murdered at the behest of his daughter Beatrice, whom he had previously repeatedly raped. This last story formed the subject of Stendhal's *Les Cenci* (1837), a short story in large part translated from an original Italian manuscript dating from shortly after Beatrice Cenci's execution in 1599 (the same subject had of course been treated by Shelley in his *The Cenci* of 1819).[51] Stendhal's various excursions to his imagined world of sixteenth-century Italy can be explained by his own quest for freedom in both art and politics: a quest that was Romantic in inspiration, but prefigures Bataille's post-Surrealist notion of sovereignty.

The anglophone Gothic novel had long identified Spain and Italy as sites of freneticism. Frenetic Romanticism followed suit, producing texts such as Borel's 'Don André Vésalius', Alphonse Royer's *Venezia la bella* (1834), and Jules Lefèvre-Deumier's *Les Martyrs d'Arezzo* (1839) that explored the possibilities presented by Spanish and Italian frenzy. Alphonse Esquiros's *Le Magicien* (1838) located freneticism instead in a parallel world of the occult—a world also explored by Nerval, for example in *L'Alchimiste* (1839), co-authored with Dumas, and *Les Illuminés ou les précurseurs du socialisme* (1852). The figures of Gilles de Rais and Francesco Cenci, the occult, and eighteenth-century illuminism (as also recast in the theosophy of Joseph de Maistre) would all continue to feed into the new form of frenetic Romanticism that was to take off in the 1850s and 1860s: the frenetic Catholicism developed by Barbey d'Aurevilly.

Conclusion: Frenetic Catholicism

The frenetic Romanticism of the 1830s can be seen to lead directly not only to the late works of Nerval but also to the post-Romanticism of Barbey's friend Baudelaire. Barbey, for his part, did not look back to Borel and his circle, but rather to the Byronic origins of the frenetic Romanticism of the 1820s. Stylistically, he participated in the Dutch auction of excess initiated in France by Nodier and Hugo. Around 1863, the latter wrote *Promontorium somnii*, a text that looked back at his younger self of 1834 and that sought to recuperate excess within his mature poetics:

> Poëtes, voici la loi mystérieuse: Allez au delà.
> Laissez les sots la traduire par *extravagare*. Allez au delà, extravaguez …

[50] Gilles de Rais would go on to attract the attention of Huysmans in *Là-bas* (1891) and Bataille. See Joris-Karl Huysmans, *Là-bas*, ed. Yves Hersant (Paris: Gallimard Folio, 1985); and Georges Bataille, *Le Procès de Gilles de Rais* (Paris: Pauvert, 1965).

[51] See Belinda Jack, *Beatrice's Spell* (London: Chatto & Windus, 2004) for an account of the many treatments of the Cenci story, e.g. by Melville, Hawthorne, and Artaud as well as by Shelley and Stendhal.

> Ce que les pédants nomment caprice, les imbéciles déraison, les ignorants hallucination, ce qui s'appelait jadis fureur sacrée, ce qui s'appelle aujourd'hui, selon que c'est l'un ou l'autre versant du rêve, mélancolie ou fantaisie, cet état singulier de l'esprit qui, persistant chez tous les poëtes, a maintenu, comme des réalités, des abstractions symboliques, la lyre, la muse, le trépied, sans cesse invoquées ou évoquées, cette ouverture étrange aux souffles inconnus, est nécessaire à la vie profonde de l'art. L'art respire volontiers l'air irrespirable. Supprimer cela, c'est fermer la communication avec l'infini. La pensée du poëte doit être de plain-pied avec l'horizon extra-humain.
>
> Poets, here is the mysterious law: Go beyond.
> Let fools name this law *extravagance*. Go beyond, be extravagant ...
>
> What pedants call capriciousness, what idiots call unreasonableness, what the ignorant call hallucinations, what was once called sacred fury, what is today called either melancholy or fantasy, depending on which side of dreams one looks at, this singular state of mind which, common to all poets, has preserved as realities, as symbolic abstractions, the endlessly invoked or evoked lyre, muse and oracle's tripod seat, this strange openness to the breaths of inspiration of the unknown is necessary to profound artistic life. Art likes to breathe unbreathable air. Get rid of all this and you interrupt communication with the infinite. The poet's thoughts must be on a level with an inhuman horizon.[52]

Frenetic Catholicism sought precisely to communicate with the infinite in this way, or rather the Infinite, figured as the Catholic God. It did so in increasingly lurid prose, culminating in Léon Bloy's two novels: *Le Désespérée* (1887) and *La Femme pauvre* (1897). As far as Bloy was concerned, the excesses produced by Barbey, Baudelaire, and Lautréamont had rendered Byron's 'frénésie décorative de Manfred' (Manfred's decorative frenzy) entirely obsolete.[53] Similarly, Byron, Chateaubriand, Lamartine, and Musset are all lumped together by Bloy as 'postiches lamentateurs' (false wailers). However, Bloy's hero and alter ego, Caïn Marchenoir, refers to himself as a 'lycanthrope' (40, 266): Bloy posits Marchenoir as a Catholic Pétrus Borel, writing to the dictations of his deliria in the certain knowledge that he was forever condemned to critical and commercial failure not by his own lack of talent but rather by a vast conspiracy mounted by the bourgeoisie. Bloy, a self-professed 'pèlerin de l'absolu' (pilgrim of the absolute), followed Barbey in pursuing the 'fièvre d'absolu' (fever of the absolute) identified by Castex as a symptom of both mystical ecstasy and frenetic delirium. The difference between the nihilistic black humour of the frenetic Romantics of the 1830s and the (only involuntarily humorous) despair obsessively treated by the frenetic Catholics is pinpointed by Milner:

[52] See Victor Hugo, *Le Promontoire du songe*, ed. Michel Crouzet (Paris: Les Belles Lettres, 1993), 41–3.

[53] See Léon Bloy, *Le Désespéré*, ed. Marie-Claire Bancquart (Paris: La Table Ronde, 1997), 50.

> In the most virulent of the fringe Romantics two tendencies are detectable: on the one hand a reactivation of the polar concepts of belief/blasphemy, for the purpose not of giving new life to belief (as was to happen in the case of Barbey d'Aurevilly), but of lending greater force to blasphemy; on the other, a radical rejection of all the values that man might claim in order to take the place of a dethroned God.[54]

Frenetic Catholicism explored blasphemy, whether in Barbey's *Les Diaboliques* (1874), Huysmans's *Là-bas*, or Bernanos's *Sous le soleil de Satan* (1926). Breton deliberately excludes po-faced Catholic literature from his *Anthologie de l'humour noir*, for example including only excerpts from Huysmans's work prior to the publication of his conversion novel *En route* 'en 1892, date à laquelle nous le perdons' (in 1892, the year in which we lose him).[55] However, Breton and other figures associated with Surrealism went on to associate themselves with the mystico-frenetic tradition exemplified by the convulsionaries of Saint-Médard—most notably Artaud, who wrote, directed and acted in *Les Cenci* (1935), having already produced a 'translation' of Matthew Lewis's Gothic novel *The Monk* that simply took Léon de Wailly's 1840 translation and exaggerated its already marked freneticism.[56] Artaud similarly identified with Bernanos, his contemporary, and the last of the frenetic Catholics, despite obvious differences in outlook.[57] In the preface to his version of *Le Moine*, Artaud writes:

> nous ne saurions trop insister sur le fait que le *Moine* doit être lu justement hors de son romantisme qui fait date,—ou que son romantisme doit être entendu hors de ce qui le rend d'actualité et le remet présentement à la mode,—dans son sens profond et libérateur.
>
> we cannot stress enough the fact that *The Monk* must precisely be read separately from its dated Romanticism,—or that its Romanticism must be understood separately from what makes the novel relevant today and has brought it back into fashion,—in its profound and liberating sense.[58]

Artaud here puts his finger on the contribution made by frenetic Romanticism in all its various forms: it produces what he goes on to refer to as a psychic phosphorescence that serves to break down psychic barriers. It is this phosphorescence that made (and continues to make) frenetic Romanticism appear profound and liberating to some, even as it made (and continues to make) it appear extravagant and ephemeral to others.

54 See Milner, 'Romantics on the Fringe', ii. 396.

55 See Breton, *Anthologie de l'humour noir*, 189.

56 Wailly was himself associated with Borel's circle. *The Monk* had been extolled by Breton in the *Manifeste du Surréalisme* of 1824. See Breton, *Œuvres complètes*, i. 320.

57 See Manzini, *Fevered Novel*, 216–18, 227–31, on the identification and also Simon Kemp, 'Representing the Mind in the French Catholic Novel', *Modern Language Review*, 107 (2012), 408–21, on the differences in outlook that separated Bernanos and his fellow Catholic novelists from their Surrealist, Existentialist, and other inter-war contemporaries.

58 Matthew Lewis, *Le Moine, raconté par Antonin Artaud*, in Antonin Artaud, *Œuvres complètes* (Paris: Gallimard, 1976–94), vi. 13–14.

Further Reading

Bataille, Georges, *Le Procès de Gilles de Rais* (Paris: Pauvert, 1965).

Beizer, Janet, *Ventriloquized Bodies: Narratives of Hysteria in Nineteenth-Century France* (Ithaca, NY: Cornell University Press, 1994).

Bloy, Léon, *Le Désespéré*, ed. Marie-Claire Bancquart (Paris: La Table Ronde, 1997).

Breton, André, *Anthologie de l'humour noir* (Paris: Le Livre de Poche, 2002).

Carroy-Thirard, Jacqueline, 'Hystérie, théâtre, littérature au XIXe siècle', *Psychanalyse à l'université*, 7 (1982), 299–317.

Castex, Pierre-Georges, *Horizons romantiques* (Paris: Corti, 1983).

Downing, Lisa, *Desiring the Dead: Necrophilia and Nineteenth-Century French Literature* (Oxford: Legenda, 2003).

Gautier, Théophile, *Histoire du Romantisme*, followed by *Quarante portaits romantiques*, ed. Adrien Goetz and Itaï Kovács (Paris: Gallimard Folio, 2011).

Gilman, Sander L., et al., *Hysteria beyond Freud* (Berkeley, Calif.: University of California Press, 1993).

Glinoer, Anthony, *La Littérature frénétique* (Paris: PUF, 2009).

Hale, Terry, 'Frénétique School', in Marie Mulvey-Roberts (ed.), *The Handbook to Gothic Literature* (London: Macmillan, 1998).

Heath, Stephen, *The Sexual Fix* (London: Macmillan, 1982).

Jack, Belinda, *Beatrice's Spell* (London: Chatto & Windus, 2004).

Kaye, Eldon, *Xavier Forneret dit 'l'homme noir' (1809–1884)* (Geneva: Droz, 1971).

Kemp, Simon, 'Representing the Mind in the French Catholic Novel', *Modern Language Review*, 107 (2012), 408–21.

Larat, Jean, *La Tradition et l'exotisme dans l'œuvre de Charles Nodier* (Paris: Champion, 1923).

Lepère, Pierre, *L'Age du furieux 1532–1859: Une légende dorée de l'excès en littérature* (Paris: Hatier, 1994).

Löw, Thomas, 'Vampires et suceurs de sang', *Revue des lettres modernes*, 965–70 (1990), 83–99.

Manzini, Francesco, *The Fevered Novel from Balzac to Bernanos: Frenetic Catholicism in Crisis, Delirium and Revolution* (London: IGRS, 2011).

Marcandier-Colard, Christine, *Crimes de sang et scènes capitales: Essai sur l'esthétique romantique de la violence* (Paris: PUF, 1998).

Matlock, Jann, *Scenes of Seduction: Prostitution, Hysteria, and Reading Difference in Nineteenth-Century France* (New York: Columbia University Press, 1994).

Milner, Max, *Le Diable dans la littérature française de Cazotte à Baudelaire (1772–1861)*, 2 vols (Paris: Corti, 1961).

Milner, Max, 'Romantics on the Fringe', in D. G. Charlton (ed.), *The French Romantics*, 2 vols (Cambridge: Cambridge University Press, 1984), ii. 382–422.

Pichois, Claude, *Philarète Chasles et la vie littéraire au temps du romantisme* (Paris: Corti, 1965).

Praz, Mario, *The Romantic Agony*, 2nd edn, tr. Angus Davidson, ed. Frank Kermode (London: Oxford University Press, 1970 [1931]).

Steinmetz, Jean-Luc, *La France frénétique de 1830* (Paris: Phébus, 1978).

Steinmetz, Jean-Luc, 'L'Ouïe du nom', in *Le Champ d'écoute* (Neuchâtel: La Baconnière, 1985), 79–103.

Steinmetz, Jean-Luc, *Pétrus Borel: Un auteur provisoire* (Lille: Presses Universitaires de Lille, 1986).

Steinmetz, Jean-Luc, *Pétrus Borel, vocation: Poète maudit* (Paris: Fayard, 2002).

Steinmetz, Jean-Luc, 'Pour en finir avec les "petits romantiques"', *Revue d'histoire littéraire de la France* (2005), 891–912.

Stubbs, Jeremy, 'Les Épidémies de l'esprit: Convulsionnaires et hystériques dans l'imaginaire surréaliste', in Christopher Lloyd (ed.), *Epidemics and Sickness in French Literature and Culture* (Durham: University of Durham, 1995), 113–23.

German

CHAPTER 9

JOHANN GEORG HAMANN

Metacritique and Poesis in Counter-Enlightenment

ALEXANDER REGIER

Johann Georg Hamann is one of the most enigmatic yet central figures of the eighteenth century and for Romanticism. His work, especially his views on language, is amongst the most unusual, important, and yet understudied of this period. The theory of language we encounter in Hamann's publications and letters disrupts many of the most fundamental philosophical assumptions of the age, as well as our subsequent construction of it. Throughout Hamann's oeuvre, the relation between thinking and language remains the central subject of his complex thought. In a letter to his one-time pupil Johann Gottfried Herder, Hamann provides a succinct and elliptical introduction to his position: 'Without word, no reason, no world' (Ohne Wort, keine Vernunft, keine Welt).[1] As this short remark suggests, Hamann's insights into the privileged and fundamental interconnection between language and reason make him not only one of the most innovative thinkers of the era but also one of its most intriguing stylists.

There are many areas of theology, philosophy, and cultural transmission in which Hamann's role as a radical innovator is considerable. His work on the status of reason, linguistic theory, and the materiality of language is groundbreaking, and his eloquent voice on matters of style, systematicity, and cosmopolitanism, amongst other topics, of considerable importance. Given that Hamann's work is not very familiar to many readers, I focus here on one of the most relevant and central parts of his thinking, namely his work on the interconnection of language, thought, metacritique, and poetry, especially since this connection is tremendously important for European Romanticism and its reception.[2] A further reason to concentrate on this area of Hamann's work is that the

[1] Johann Georg Hamann, *Briefwechsel*, ed. Walther Ziesemer and Arthur Henkel (from vol. iv on, ed. Henkel alone), 8 vols (Wiesbaden/Frankfurt am Main: Insel, 1955–75), v. 95. Hereafter ZH. All translations, unless indicated otherwise, are my own.

[2] In the case of Hamann, his influence on contemporary thinkers we can also call Romantic, such as Walter Benjamin, Martin Heidegger, or Paul Celan, gives ample—if understudied—evidence of that. More on this later.

radicality of his project becomes clear very quickly. His account of thinking and language (poetical language, specifically) interferes equally productively with the Kantian epistemological project and the building Cartesian legacy of a philosophy of the subject, both central to European Romanticism. For Hamann, language negates and side-steps the stark division between empiricism and idealism that troubles much of the Enlightenment and Romantic thought.

As readers of the works of Novalis, Friedrich Schlegel, William Wordsworth, or Percy B. Shelley, to pick a selected band, we should prick up our ears if a crucial figure in mid-eighteenth-century Germany pronounces that thinking is the 'uterus of language' (Gebärmutter der Sprache),[3] that philosophy is mostly a 'play with words' (Wortspiel) (ZH vi. 534), and that reason is the centre of its 'misunderstanding with itself' (Missverstandes der Vernunft mit ihr selbst) (N iii. 286). Consider in this light Novalis's statement made in 1798 that 'proper conversation is merely a word game' (das rechte Gespräch ist ein bloßes Wortspiel).[4] Novalis's formulation clearly represents a Romantic continuation of Hamann's thinking. By poeticizing the world, these 'word games' lead us to Novalis's blue flower, the image at the very heart of the *Frühromantik*. We can also think here of Schlegel's suggestion that 'words often understand themselves better than those by whom they are used' (die Worte sich selbst oft besser verstehen, als diejenigen von denen sie gebraucht werden).[5] While this statement is more optimistic than Hamann's account of reason and language as a 'misunderstanding with itself', it does insist on the primacy of language over the human and certainly our ability to give a coherent account of it. The fact that Schlegel published some of Hamann's writings further illustrates that these examples are not atypical, but that Hamann is an important reference point for the Jena circle and beyond.[6]

Given these clear lines of influence, it is not surprising that, in German scholarship, Hamann has counted for some time as an important thinker who is relevant to the formation of European Romanticism. His work is understood to be central to eighteenth-century intellectual life, and especially relevant for literature of the *Sturm und Drang* (and thus Romanticism).[7] He is a constitutive part of the most important German intellectual circles along with Immanuel Kant, Friedrich Heinrich Jacobi, Herder, Moses Mendelssohn, Christoph Friedrich Nicolai, Ephraim Lessing, and Johann Kaspar Lavater. As this *Handbook* evidences, all of these figures were deeply influential for the

[3] Johann Georg Hamann, *Sämtliche Werke*, ed. Josef Nadler, 6 vols (Vienna: Thomas Morus Presse im Verlag Herder, 1949–57), iii. 239. Hereafter N.

[4] Novalis, *Philosophical Writings*, tr. and ed. Margaret Mahony Stoljar (Albany, NY: State University of New York Press, 1997), 83. Novalis, *Werke*, ed. Gerhard Schulz (Munich: Beck, 1981), 426. On Novalis and Hamann, see Katie Terezakis, *The Immanent Word: The Turn to Language in German Philosophy, 1759–1801* (New York: Routledge, 2007).

[5] Friedrich von Schlegel, *Kritische Friedrich-Schlegel-Ausgabe*, ed. Ernst Behler and others, 35 vols (Paderborn: Schönigh, 1958–), i/1. 364.

[6] On Schlegel's publication of Hamann, see John R. Betz, *After Enlightenment: The Post-Secular Vision of J. G. Hamann* (Chichester: Wiley-Blackwell, 2009), 13–14.

[7] As an example, see Larry Vaughan, *The Historical Constellation of the Sturm und Drang* (New York: Peter Lang, 1985).

self-definition of European Romanticism. Alongside Wilhelm von Humboldt, Hamann is considered the most important figure in relation to theories of language of his time. Even G. W. Hegel's highly critical 1828 review of Hamann's works in *Jahrbücher für wissenschaftliche Kritik* allows for his stature as an eminent thinker on matters linguistic.[8] Moreover, as we shall see in more detail later, Hamann is a truly European and cosmopolitan figure. He translates and reads across Anglo-German contexts in particular (something he was known for in his own day) and contributes to creating a backdrop for a European Romanticism whose strength lies in its heterogeneity.

Within the distinguished circle of thinkers and writers just mentioned, Hamann is the loudest and most idiosyncratic voice against the Enlightenment (or at least a common account of it). After a conversion experience (Schlüsselerlebnis) during a London visit in 1755–8 he turns his initial sympathy for the Enlightenment project into fierce criticism, especially of his fellow Königsberg citizen and philosopher, Kant (although the two remained respectful and even helpful towards each other throughout their lives). For all the recognition his work receives (Goethe calls him the 'brightest head of his time' (den hellsten Kopf seiner Zeit)), Oswald Bayer aptly describes Hamann as a 'contemporary in dissent' (Zeitgenosse im Widerspruch).[9] Crucially, *Widerspruch* can here mean 'dissent' (as in 'disagreement', not as a term in specifically Anglo-religious debates) as well as '(self-)contradiction', dissent with oneself. Hamann's complex disagreement with versions of the Kantian Enlightenment have been the subject of much sophisticated and insightful commentary.[10] One emblematic example that scholarship regularly returns to is the discussion surrounding Kant's and Christoph Berens's attempt to rekindle Hamann's initial enthusiasm for the Enlightenment[11] after his return from London. Hamann's resistance ultimately leads to his 1759 work, *Socratic Memorabilia* (Sokratische Denkwürdigkeiten), and its dedication, 'To the Two' (An die Zween) (N ii. 57), the two being Kant and Berens.[12] In those works, Hamann articulates his opposition

[8] On Hamann and Hegel, see G. W. F. Hegel, *Hegel on Hamann*, ed. and tr. Lisa Marie Anderson (Evanston, IL: Northwestern University Press, 2008).

[9] Oswald Bayer, A *Contemporary in Dissent: Johann Georg Hamann as a Radical Enlightener* (Grand Rapids, MI: Eerdmans, 2011). Oswald Bayer, *Zeitgenosse im Widerspruch: Johann Georg Hamann als Radikaler Aufklärer* (Munich: Piper, 1988).

[10] A good starting point is Oswald Bayer, *Vernunft ist Sprache: Hamanns Metakritik Kants* (Stuttgart: frommann, 2002). Another invaluable source is vol. i (*Die Hamann Forschung*) of *Johann Georg Hamanns Hauptschriften Erklärt*, ed. Fritz Blanke and Lothar Schreiner, 7 vols [only six are completed] (Gütersloh: Bertelsmann; Mohn, 1956–).

[11] After these initial conversations do not yield the desired results, Kant tries to persuade Hamann to co-author an introduction to physics for children. Hamann, probably suspecting Kant wants to use this as a further platform to convince him of a particular worldview (including natural science and pedagogy), declines. The most accessible introduction to the *Memorabilia* is Sven Aage Jørgensen's introduction to Johann Georg Hamann, *Sokratische Denkwürdigkeiten, Aesthetica in Nuce* (Stuttgart: Reclam, 1968).

[12] Kant and Berens are not the only objects of this attack, though. The *Memorabilia* also feature Hamann's resistance to 18th-cent. French subjectivism championed by people like Charles Batteux. Batteux's account of successful art as an 'imitation of beautiful nature' that is based on clear aesthetic principles is precisely the kind of project that Hamann already fiercely objects to in *Aesthetica in Nuce*, namely a *mordlügnerische Philosophie hat die Natur aus dem Wege geräumt.* (N 2, 206.) ('*lying,*

to what he believes to be the coercive nature of any systematic philosophy (for which a certain version of the Enlightenment becomes the most obvious representative example). Whatever our assessment of his intellectual project in these wide-ranging conversations, it is beyond doubt that he is pivotal for the way the Enlightenment and Romanticism formulate their self-understanding.

Hamann's position in the anglophone reception is considerably different, for a number of reasons. Until recently, translations of Hamann's works into English were not in wide circulation and limited to some three or four texts, namely, the *Socratic Memorabilia* (1759), the *Aesthetica in Nuce* (1762), and the *Metacritique of the Purism of Reason* (1784). Between 1950 and 1967, Walter Lowrie, Ronald Gregor Smith, W. M. Alexander, and James O'Flaherty initiated a first phase of modern transmission into English, but there was little echo outside of a small theological community.[13] Without considering Hamann's wider oeuvre, it was difficult for anglophone readers to confirm whether the early introductions that were on offer were accurate and faithful. The authors of many of these, not surprisingly, had strong agendas. For instance, Isaiah Berlin, whose 1993 essay on Hamann subsequently formed part of his popular *Three Critics of Enlightenment* (2000), remains one of the most commonly cited sources in relation to Hamann. Berlin's characterization of Hamann as an antirationalist—a label Hamann still struggles to shed—is highly problematic once we take into consideration the wider context from which Berlin chooses to present his selection (and that he articulates his dislike against Hamann from a position of extreme allergy to irrationalism, which he sees as one of the major sources of totalitarianism). Nevertheless, since Berlin's account was standard for many years, many of even the most sophisticated accounts of the period, such as Jonathan Israel's *Radical Enlightenment* (2001), fail to mention Hamann[14] or treat him as a negligible figure.

The few scholars in the fields of British eighteenth-century studies and Romanticism who do include Hamann in their discussions in more than a passing way, such as M. H. Abrams in *Natural Supernaturalism* (1971) and Elizabeth Harries in *The Unfinished Manner* (1994), rely on their own translations to bring their very specific arguments across. More recently, Gwen Griffith-Dickson's more extensive translations of Hamann's works in 1995 and Kenneth Haynes's selected translations (2007) have begun to change the field somewhat.[15] Dickson's splendid work is one of the most singularly impressive

murderous philosophy has cleared Nature out of the way'); see Gwen Griffith Dickson, *Johann Georg Hamann's Relational Metacriticism* (Berlin and New York: de Gruyter, 1995), 420. Hereafter D.

[13] See Walter Lowrie, *Johann Georg Hamann: An Existentialist* (Princeton: Princeton Theological Seminary Press, 1950); Ronald Gregor Smith, *Johann Georg Hamann: A Study in Christian Existence, with Selections from His Writings* (London: Collins, 1960); W. M. Alexander, *Johann Georg Hamann: Philosophy and Faith* (The Hague: Martinus Nijhof, 1966); James O'Flaherty, *Hamann's Socratic Memorabilia: A Translation and Commentary* (Baltimore: Johns Hopkins University Press, 1967).

[14] I mention Israel here precisely because his work is so encompassing, thorough, and comprehensive, making the omission all the more noteworthy, especially since Hamann could be seen as a relevant figure for the story of a Radical Enlightenment that Israel wants to tell. While certainly no Spinozist, Hamann represents a very important influence on a group of people who are central to Israel's account (especially Mendelssohn and Lessing).

[15] Johann Georg Hamann, *Writings on Philosophy and Language*, tr. and ed. Kenneth Haynes (Cambridge: Cambridge University Press, 2007).

(and underrated) achievements in eighteenth-century studies. Its thorough translations and commentary are responsible for the fact that anglophone Hamann scholarship is beginning to flourish, albeit relatively quietly. Interventions like Carol Jacobs's *Skirting the Ethical* (2008); John R. Betz's *After Enlightenment: The Post-Secular Vision of J. G. Hamann* (2009), which also contains some new translations; and edited collections such as *Hamann and the Tradition* (2012) have opened up new avenues within and outside Romanticism. All of this, together with the 2012 translation of Oswald Bayer's 1988 standard monograph that I mentioned above ought to rectify the one-sided picture that emerged from Berlin's book and has served as the standard introduction, paradoxically ensuring Hamann's marginalization in the anglophone world.

Hamann's oeuvre, we should realize, is substantial. The current standard editions of his work in German encompass fourteen volumes of writings, seven of which are works, the others correspondence.[16] The early selective anglophone reception of these texts is a fascinating way to track what *kinds* of arguments Hamann allows us to make in the scholarly realm of European Romanticism, especially since his establishment as a central figure in the period was mostly monolingual. And while the current surge of scholarship is encouraging in this respect, too, it is also worth gesturing towards a connection with seemingly unrelated work which generates some of the most fruitful and serious work on poetry and thought, such as the studies of Paul Fry, Geoffrey Hartman, Marjorie Levinson, and Simon Jarvis. All of these investigate the status of poetic thinking in ways that are immediately related to Hamann's work, since they, for all their substantial differences, make the connection of poesis and thinking the central piece of their account both of Wordsworth (in the specific cases mentioned) and of Romanticism.

My discussion here of Hamann's views of language, metacritique, and poetry is an attempt to contribute to these growing possibilities for connections. It is part of a recovery project, to be sure, but with a twist, since it also attempts to test what it means to follow Hamann in his thinking on language and thought (rather than present him as an archival oddity). So, this chapter illustrates what attending closely to Hamann's work *does* in a context of the study of the Enlightenment and Romanticism in a European context. More specifically, I want to show how Hamann, throughout his work, thinks through the consequences of the link between thinking and language within philosophy as well as phenomenological experience. The second major dimension, more implicit than the exposition of Hamann's thought, is my suggestion that Hamann holds a particularly important position in relation to our construction of European Romanticism. His work has often been pigeonholed as either one of anti-Enlightenment or Counter-Enlightenment. The latter of these is a label that has been most useful in understanding Hamann's position vis-à-vis Kant and Herder. When it comes to Hamann's relation to Romanticism, however, many of the accounts relegate him to a secondary influence, since by the time Romanticism rolls around, Hamann had already been superseded by

[16] For an editorial history of Hamann's works, see the first volume (*Die Hamann Forschung*) of the excellent Hamann, *Johann Georg Hamanns Hauptschriften Erklärt*, vol. 1.

the Enlightenment, the bulwark against which Romanticism supposedly defines itself (remember that Hamann died before the French Revolution). In the more complete variations of this lineage, Hamann is accounted for as an early representative of the *Sturm und Drang*. While this is not unreasonable, it ultimately often ends up trying to provide a clear genealogy that separates the Enlightenment (and its countercurrent) and the isolated precursor to Romanticism (*Sturm und Drang*), in order to retain the more general periodization of Enlightenment versus Romanticism. This move does none of these three distinct yet related movements any favours. There are, of course, exceptions to this version of European and German literary history (the works of Andreas Huyssen or David Wellbery come to mind), but it remains a tacit assumption in much scholarship. Following Hamann's thinking, I suggest, is one way to address these shortcomings and offer an alternative account.

We all know that deeply idiosyncratic work can illustrate particularly well why periodization is both necessary and highly problematic. Hamann's case is no different, and his work challenges us to consider the way even very recent accounts, which are often committed to rethinking periodization and literary chronologies, fall into familiar patterns. My version of Hamann here implicitly suggests that we can use his work to disrupt these patterns in a serious and thoughtful way. It seems to me that Hamann offers a new way of looking not just at language and its importance to Enlightenment discourse and Romanticism. He also suggests, and opens up, a highly relevant connection between the early Enlightenment and early Romanticism. It bypasses the idea that there is the small 'test run' of sensibility and rejection of reason (or rationality) in the *Sturm und Drang* that then leads to Romanticism. Hamann not only becomes a forerunner of Romanticism in its most radical form, namely, philosophical and metacritical, but he thereby also opens up a set of possibilities of reading the Enlightenment and Romanticism in a new way. Here is a figure whose recovery marks an opportunity to imagine a version of the Enlightenment that is more attentive to the connection of language, thought, and poesis, more metacritical in its use of our most powerful intellectual tools, and thus an early Enlightenment that is more radical in its imagination about what the status of representation could be. It is a version of early Romanticism that connected with the Enlightenment through a critique of reason, its links to poesis, and an unorthodox and visionary understanding of central categories of the period, such as the origin of language, the status of representation, or the role of the human body (especially the sexual body) in aesthetic production.

Hamann's Method: Metacritique

The idea and term of 'metacritique' are at the centre of Hamann's work and writing. He first uses the terminology in a letter to Herder on 7 July 1782: 'Because of Hume & Kant everything in my head turns sour; must live to see the *Prolegomena* of metaphysics, which is still to be written, if it is God's will, before I come out with my *Metacritique*'

(Ueber Hume u. Kant versauert alles in meinem Kopf; muß erst die *Prolegomena* der Metaphysik, die noch geschrieben werden soll, erleben, wenn es Gottes Wille ist, ehe ich mit meiner *Metakritik* herauskomme) (ZH iv. 400). This small moment from a much more thorough engagement with Kant's work and method can serve as a good way into the discussion of his *Metacritique on the Purism of Reason*. The work, despite its four-page brevity, one of Hamann's most important, was completed though not published during his lifetime. What leads Hamann, the thinker on language, to speak about the first Kantian *Critique* in such a way? Simply put, he believes that Kant's approach of thinking through the conditions of the possibility of thought neglects to acknowledge the medium in which this thinking is performed and uttered, namely language. Kant's attempt in the *Critique* to 'purify' thought of its assumptions ignores language's status as the medium in which this process takes place.

Hamann reads Kant's 'purification' in three stages. First, there is the attempt 'partly misconceived, partly unsuccessful' 'to make reason independent of all custom' (D 520) (dem theils misverstandenen, theils mislungenen Versuch, die Vernunft von aller Ueberlieferung ... unabhängig zu machen) (N iii. 284). The second step, according to Hamann, 'is still more transcendental and aims at nothing less than an independence of experience and its everyday induction' (D 520) (ist noch transcendenter und läuft auf nichts weniger als seine Unabhängigkeit von der Erfahrung und ihrer alltäglichen Induction hinaus) (N iii. 284). Both of these lead, ultimately, to an apotheosis of reason, an apotheosis that is blind to its original inaccuracies. As Hamann puts it, Kant 'turns God into the ideal without knowing that his pure reason is precisely the same' (Kant macht Gott zum *Ideal* ohne zu wißen, daß seine reine Vernunft eben daßelbe ist) (ZH vi. 163). Kant's pure reason ends up as the theologically inflected glue that holds the supposedly non-theological critical project together.

But it is the third purism that is the 'most sublime and as it were *empirical*': it 'concerns *language*, the single, first and last *organon* and criterion of reason' (D 520); ('höchste und gleichsam *empirische* Purismus betrift also noch die *Sprache*, das einzige erste und letzte Organon und Kriterion der Vernunft') (N iii. 284). For Hamann, language is the 'organon' of reason. An organon connects the physical and the mental; it is a 'bodily organ, esp.... an instrument of the soul or the mind' (*OED*). Kant's first mistake, according to Hamann, is to ignore that language is precisely such an instrument, that it generates thought. As a result, Kant also neglects how the process of that production shapes the outcome in a significant way. Hamann suggests that reason and language are not to be separated, since we need them in unison to identify, qualify, and judge their results. Language is both the productive and declamatory 'organon' but also the 'criterion' by which language judges itself and the thoughts it produces with reason. Hamann's elliptical reference towards Kant's transcendental method suggests that he views language as the ultimate illustration of why the Kantian procedure is doomed to fail. The bridge between empirical experience and conceptual representation cannot be bridged by 'purifying' both of them.

For Hamann, language links the physical and the mental sphere: 'Words ... have an *aesthetic* and *logical* capacity' (D 524) (Wörter haben ... ein *ästhetisches* und *logisches*

Vermögen) (N iii. 288). Importantly, they do this in a generative way. Given the central role language plays for thought, it thereby also stands at the very centre of knowledge and experience. The 'organon' of language is a constitutive part of the production of knowledge and cannot be 'purified'; it is also both physical and mental. Hamann's comments on 'aesthetic capacity' point towards his wider criticism of the idealization of reason. They also refer to an account of thought itself that is central to how (and why) critique is often understood. Any substantial critique of thought, he intimates, must also include the critique of the form, the medium, in which this thought is generated. Metacritique asks us to think about the forms in which analysing the conditions of the possibility of critique take place. And, while that way of thinking about metacritique is applicable across a wide spectrum, Hamann posits its linguistic incarnation as the most crucial dimension (I will return to this privileging of language in the next section).

For Hamann, Kant's neglect of the generative dimension of language is a symptom that is connected to his assumptions of the supposed neutrality of thought. Two of these assumptions stand out: first, that Kant's attempt to 'purify' is particularly resistant to the idea of the physicality of language. Hamann links this to what he sees as an overall resistance to aesthesis in Kant's projected outcome. Secondly, that Kant's project unwittingly betrays his desire to achieve a clear and coherent outcome at the price of ignoring a piece that is in fact central to its construction (though it threatens to introduce interference). If language and thought are so intrinsically connected, Hamann insists, we need to include linguistics in our philosophical field of vision, not simply as an external object of study (such as in the work of John Locke) but rather as a constitutive part of any method that philosophy develops.[17] This method is, in turn, subject to a form of critique, namely, metacritique.

A very short historical contextualization is useful here. As I mentioned before, Hamann's criticism and his whole enterprise should not be understood as a crass anti-Kantianism, an irrationalist intervention, or even an appeal against reason as such. Bayer's direct, lucid remarks and his quotation from Hamann are helpful on this specific aspect of the *Metacritique*: 'As contemporary in contradiction he neither flatly dismisses the Enlightenment nor does he argue for an uncritical conservatism—just as "*healthy reason* and *orthodoxy* in the root of the matter, and even in their etymology, are synonymous words"' (Als Zeitgenosse im Widerspruch lehnt er weder die Aufklärung pauschal ab noch vertritt er einen unkritischen Konservatismus—wie denn '*gesunde Vernunft* und *Orthodoxie*, im Grunde der Sache und selbst in der Etymologie,

[17] It is important to note that Locke does not always relegate language this way. In what has become known as Draft B of the *Essay Concerning Human Understanding* (1689) he does seem to present a variation of his more widely known view on language and its relation to the formation of ideas. This does not affect the overall argument here, but should serve as a reminder that his (and, more widely, 18th-cent.) linguistic theory is more complicated than it is often presented to be. See John Locke, *Drafts for the 'Essay Concerning Human Understanding', and Other Philosophical Writings*, ed. Peter Nidditch and G. A. J. Rodgers (Oxford: Clarendon Press, 1990), i. 167–203. For an introductory overview, see Nicholas Hudson, 'Theories of Language', in H. B. Nisbet and Claude Rawson (eds), *The Cambridge History of Literary Criticism* (Cambridge: Cambridge University Press, 2005), iv. 35–48.

ganz gleichbedeutende Wörter sind').[18] We can qualify Hamann's attitude towards the Enlightenment and Kant in many ways, but the most comprehensive scholarship consistently shows that it is certainly a misunderstanding to think of his distanced (and humorous) engagement with that movement and its pivotal figure as a simple rejection of the project of reason, critique, or even rationality.

Hamann's thesis of the inextricability of language and thinking puts the analysis of language squarely at the centre of philosophy. It cannot divide intellectual or conceptual inquiry from linguistic form. Philosophy has to account for language, not just as a supposedly controlled object of study. Two years after his letter to Herder in which he first mentions metacritique, Hamann articulates the consequences of this view again when he suspects that 'our philosophy consists more of language than reason' (unsere Philosophie mehr aus Sprache als Vernunft besteht) (ZH v. 272). This is not just a swipe at verbose philosophers; it is also an insistence that we had better put language centre stage in our philosophical analysis. To Hamann's mind, his contemporaries show a lack of engagement with the question of how language shapes thinking and how the structures of language are a meaningful and important aspect of this shaping process. And though Enlightenment philosophy, at least in some quarters, is concerned with language, 'we still lack a *grammar* of reason' (Es fehlt uns ... noch immer an einer *Grammatik* der Vernunft) (ZH v. 272). The '*grammar*' is a grammar of reason which takes seriously the inextricability (or analogy, as we will see) between language and thinking and understands that the structure—the grammar—of thought reveals its linguistic aspect and meaning.

We can understand Hamann's drive behind his linguistic diagnosis (that 'we still lack a *grammar* of reason') in various ways. Initially, it seems to encourage an account that clarifies and clears up the relation between thought and language. Once we have established that, so the argument would go, we can map language and thought onto one another as clearly as possible, and not risk any interference (the grammar would be clear, unambiguous). The clearer that relation, the better the philosophy (much like later attempts by positivism and certain strands of analytical philosophy). However, this way of approaching the issue runs directly counter to the spirit and meaning of Hamann's remark. Most crucially, it ignores that the relationship of language and thought, for all its importance, is precisely *not* transparent. Philosophy's great error is to maintain that the relation is (or needs to be) clear and unambiguous. This is deeply misguided. To address the lack of our structural understanding of language, our grammar, does not translate into a claim that we can elucidate (or even manipulate) the entirety of that structure. Just because we identify that the structure is important does not mean that we are able clearly to discern how the structure works.

For Hamann, then, language is not a neutral medium. It is linked to thinking. That link needs to be part of any philosophy, albeit with an understanding that it will not be elucidated completely. In other words, language is the source of our epistemological, ethical,

[18] Bayer, *Vernunft ist Sprache*, 73; also see D 19–20.

and aesthetic frameworks. It allows us to articulate our experiences within these frameworks and the thinking that shapes them. However, its link to the faculty of thought is not straightforward or transparent, and we have to resist attempts, in philosophy and elsewhere, to make it appear as if it were. For Hamann, the assumption that rational thinking is neutral and somehow 'outside' of language is, thus, deeply mistaken. While there is an interconnection between the two, the link is not open to easy inspection and, certainly, is in need of philosophical scrutiny. In an important sense, philosophy is precisely the continuous investigation of that relation. As Hamann states in August 1784 in a letter to Herder: 'Reason is language, Λογος; I gnaw on this marrowbone, and will gnaw myself to death over it' (Vernunft ist Sprache, Λογος; an diesem Markknochen nag' ich und werde mich zu Tod drüber nagen) (ZH v. 177). The remarkable image of the 'marrowbone' turns Hamann into a dog whose repetitious and visceral engagement is, by definition, both profoundly pleasurable and lacking an ultimate solution. Language and thought provide the backbone of philosophy; they are what lies behind the outer appearance of much thought, but they themselves are irreducible and cannot be further broken down, however much they entice us to try. The engagement with language cannot be teleological or linear; the complexity and resistance of its object of study (the marrowbone) necessitates a return to it over and over again. Hamann positions himself against philosophers who qualify the inescapable obliqueness of that relation as a stultifying frustration. Implicitly, he does not conceive of this oblique relation as something that is necessarily negative. That we gnaw on a bone without having a tangible result does not mean that we should stop gnawing, or that the activity itself is not pleasurable. We do not just gnaw the bone to sharpen our teeth, but we find some delight in this repetition. In fact, it makes our mouths water.

'Without praxi, all theory is a numbskull'

For Hamann, language is the medium through which we think and construct the world, the 'organon of thought'. For him, we engage with the world in a linguistic way. Consider again that 'Language' here is not limited to natural language alone. All of our communication, our being, is linguistic in nature. Natural language is a particular instantiation of it (it is akin to what Walter Benjamin, in his early work, will call 'The Language of Man'). Even though it is particularly important, we also evidently use vastly different systems of communication beyond natural language that are relevant here. Our ability to move from one system to another is, for Hamann, related to the ability to translate:

> *Speaking* is *translation*—from a *tongue of angels* into a *human tongue*, that is, *thoughts* in *words*—*things* in *names*—*images* in *signs*; that can be *poetic* or

> kyriological, *historical*, or symbolic or hieroglyphic—and *philosophical* or characteristic. (D 413)
>
> *Reden* ist *übersetzen*—aus einer *Engelssprache* in eine *Menschensprache*, das heist, *Gedanken* in *Worte*,—*Sachen* in *Namen*,—*Bilder* in *Zeichen*; die *poetisch* oder kyriologisch, *historisch* oder symbolisch oder hieroglypisch—und *philosophisch* oder charakteristisch seyn können. (N ii. 199)

When we speak, or think, we translate from one register that we encounter to the next, in a linguistic process. The carrying-over (meta-phero) is a linguistic operation. Importantly, however, translation is not a simple one-to-one transposition that is either transparent or perfect. The difficulties with how to render the quotation here in more than one natural language is only one example. Crucially, any translation from one register to another is itself not a 'neutral' event. When we translate from one sphere to another (angels to humans, 'thoughts in words', etc.), the linguistic event—we have learned from the *Metacritique*—is not itself void of character and meaning. Thus, such a translation can be 'poetic or kyriological, historical, or symbolic or hieroglyphic—and philosophical or characteristic'. We will look at some of the terms in this list in due course, but what I want to foreground first is that all of these characterisations point towards the complexity and ultimate impossibility of translating 'accurately'. Again, this need not be a source of despair. Translations that are 'poetic or kyriological, historical, or symbolic or hieroglyphic—and philosophical or characteristic' are productive and allow us to communicate, but they will not be immediately transparent or easily accessible. According to Hamann, this tense process describes the way we speak and think; it does not describe an event that needs to be purged of its complicated (or, say, poetic) character.

Language and thinking, in their multiple translations, are not transparent or clear. Translation is possible and allows communication from one sphere to the other, but it also contains misunderstandings or difficulties. The complexities of translation are mirrored in each linguistic act. We can locate them in natural language itself, by attending to the fact that it creates misunderstandings not as an aberration from its norm but, rather, as one of its defining features: 'Language is also the centre point of the misunderstanding of reason with itself'[19] (Sprache ist auch der Mittelpunct des Missverstandes der Vernunft mit ihr selbst) (N iii. 286). Reason's misunderstandings about and with itself are self-generated through the modes of its thinking and its articulation. Since the misunderstanding is at the centre of production, it means that reason cannot be non-linguistic or transparent. This suggests that we need to re-evaluate, analyse, and interpret how we claim dominion over texts, including their interpretation. There are no clear, distinct, or self-evident statements that do not, at their centre and in their translations, also carry the potential of being a 'misunderstanding of reason with itself'.

[19] For the Wittgensteinean echoes of this claim, see Jonathan Gray's chapter 'Hamann, Nietzsche and Wittgenstein on the Language of Philosophers', in Lisa Marie Anderson, *Hamann and the Tradition* (Evanston, IL: Northwestern University Press, 2012), 104–21.

Hamann's metacritical stance and his self-deprecating humour are two ways in which he reflects this dynamic in his own writing.

For Hamann, the translations (and misunderstandings) that language and reason produce have immediate conceptual and empirical consequences. Remember that language is crucial in the construction of the world, and that this is not 'simply' a metaphor. Translations are not an abstractly remote business. They are a condition under which we produce thinking and shape our experiences, as well as our accounts of these experiences. Such an ambitious and comprehensive account needs to position itself within the philosophical landscape. How does it see these translations between different spheres in relation to now standard philosophical categories? Not surprisingly, Hamann rejects most of these conventional categories (or categories that have since become conventional) and explains why language cuts through many of them. For instance, the perceived conflict between empiricism and idealism, or rationalism, and the assumption that one of the two will dominate, he argues, relies on a misunderstanding about the nature of their contrast.[20] For him, any convincing philosophical conceptualization of theory and praxis, and therefore of experience, must account for their interdependence. Theoretical insight has to be (imaginatively or actually) 'filled' with the experience it relates to, even if it concerns abstract categories that shape our empirical accounts. This comes to be one of Hamann's main philosophical tenets, and he turns, once again, to language in order to illustrate how central it is to all our thinking and experience.

According to Hamann, to imagine an experience that is not empirical at all is philosophically non-sensical (quite literally). Conversely, any empirical account always relates to the theoretical sphere that makes it possible as the experience of a particular kind. In effect, the problem lies with our attachment to a model that divides experience in such a manner to begin with. To split our experience between an empirical part and one of understanding is to commit a major mistake. It reveals an attachment to a philosophical impetus and system that will present this division as either central, intuitive, or both. In contrast, Hamann questions the first assumptions of such a philosophical account, including, and this is key, attempts to supposedly bridge the areas of understanding and perception (such as the Kantian epistemological project):

> but if *sensibility* and *understanding* spring as two stems of human knowledge from *One* common root, so that through one objects are *given* and through the other *thought*;

[20] The negotiation of this contrast for Hamann comes directly out of reading David Hume on natural belief (or 'faith' as Hamann terms it). Kant's attempted solution to the problem of seemingly incommensurate areas of empiricism and idealism is, according to Hamann, faulty because it does not (contrary to self-proclamation) connect 'Realismo and Idealismo', giving the latter ultimately primary status. One can see why, for this critique, Hume is a highly important figure for Hamann. See Bernhard Gajek (ed.), *Johan Georg Hamann und England: Hamann und die englischsprachige Aufklärung: Acta des siebten internationalen Hamann-Kolloquium zu Marbur/Lahn 1996* (Frankfurt am Main: Lang, 1999); Thomas Brose, *Johann Georg Hamann und David Hume: Metaphysikkritik und Glaube im Spannungsfeld der Aufklärung* (Frankfurt am Main: Lang, 2006).

> to what end such violent, unwarranted, obstinate divorce of what nature has joined together! (D 522)

> Entspringen aber *Sinnlichkeit* und *Verstand* als zwey Stämme der menschlichen Erkenntnis aus *Einer* gemeinschaftlichen Wurzel, so daß sie durch jene Gegenstände *gegeben* und durch diesen *gedacht* werden; zu welchem Behuf nun eine so gewaltthätige, unbefugte, eigensinnige Scheidung desjenigen, was die Natur zusammengefügt hat! (N iii. 286)

Kant's dichotomy, presented by him as a given that has to be overcome, is in fact the opposite. It presents an artificial division that is deeply inattentive to human experience (so quite the opposite of intuitively evident). If we pay close attention to the nature of experience, we notice that it does not follow the division that Kant presents as a given. In fact, the continuous interaction of sensibility and understanding in language precedes any 'obstinate divorce' of them in a Kantian thought-experiment.[21] Language is the one 'common root', Hamann maintains, which needs not to be divided but rather understood as containing all aspects of human existence.

It is a mistake, then, to focus on solely one aspect of human experience or thought in the belief it could provide an adequate and truly insightful philosophical account. As Hamann puts it succinctly: 'Without *praxi*, all theory is a numbskull, and to crack that open I like my rotten teeth too much' (Ohne *praxi* ist alle Theorie eine taube Nuß, und die aufzubeißen, habe ich meine morschen Zähne zu lieb) (ZH vi. 534). Knowledge is always complex because it *relates* to something. A 'taube Nuß' (literally, an 'emptynut') is not only bereft of sense, but also empty and hollow. It does not contain what it promises and therefore cannot be productive. It is relevant here that in eighteenth-century German the expression was also used to describe an infertile woman: pure theory is barren.[22] In many ways, this is not simply an appeal to theoretical endeavours to exemplify their practical application, but rather it is a statement rejecting the usefulness of thinking about them as separate in the first place.

For Hamann, the split between a theoretical account and an empirical experience is empty and false. Crucially, language illustrates and performs the truth that there is a necessary connection between the two spheres, since there cannot be reason without language, and language implies a particular experience of the world. The interaction between the two supposedly different spheres of 'realism' and 'idealism' occurs through the word, which becomes the bridge, or sticky lubricant, between empirical experience and thought. Brian Jacobs succinctly points out that 'Nothing remains of reason, Hamann claims, if it is purified of all experience: for language is always bound up

[21] On this point also, see Bayer, *Vernunft ist Sprache*, 338–41.

[22] There is an important and complicated pattern of images of sexuality and fertility in Hamann's work. The references range from not being able to imagine a God without genitalia to language being repeatedly, almost obsessively, figured as the '*pudenda* of our nature' (*Pudenda* unserer Natur) (ZH v. 167), to, as I already mentioned, describing thought as the 'uterus of language' (Gebärmutter der Sprache) (N iii. 239).

with that experience; indeed, it *is* experience.'[23] We can see how Hamann's deep-seated assumption cuts through linguistics as well as through the classical opposition between empiricism and idealism in various ways. In a much-quoted passage from his correspondence with Jacobi some years before, Hamann states,

> I am neither speaking about physics nor about theology—but *language*, the *mother* of reason and revelation, its A and Ω. It is the two-edged sword for all truths and lies. So do not laugh if I have to attack the thing from this side. I keep harping on about it, but through it all things are made.
>
> Bey mir ist weder von Physik noch Theologie die Rede—sondern *Sprache*, die *Mutter* der Vernunft und Offenbarung, ihr A und Ω. Sie ist das zweyschneidige Schwert für alle Wahrheiten und Lügen. Lachen sie also nicht wenn ich das Ding von dieser Seite angreifen muß. Es ist meine alte Leyer—aber durch sie sind alle Dinge gemacht.[24] (ZH vi. 108)

Language is, like the *organon*, the mother of the faculty of thought as well as the articulation of its insights (for Hamann, revelation). These two poles are both the beginning and the end of our conceptual universe, adequately represented by two letters. 'A and Ω' indicate that language spans the totality of the world.

Hamann's writings make it clear that for him language reaches across aspects of the world that are commonly (and often mistakenly) thought to be divided or separate; this includes 'physics' and 'theology'. And, crucially, language is not reducible to either one or the other. For him, it is two-sided and cuts both ways. Language is a Hydra-like mother that is the fundamental medium through which we know as well as err. He is aware that this is a position that can be easily attacked; thus he asks Jacobi not to ridicule him ('do not laugh') but rather consider that his position comes from a different vantage point altogether (he attacks 'the thing from this side'). It is a topic he has been 'harping on about' for a while. Since Hamann maintains that language is not transparent, there is much variety and difference between the A and the Ω. It is not a coherent plane, nor is its linguistic description one-sided: as he intimates, language cuts both ways. It is a sword that is double-edged, and whose power allows both 'truths and lies'.[25] That does

[23] Brian Jacobs, 'Self-Incurrence, Incapacity, and Guilt: Kant and Hamann on Enlightenment Guardianship' with an Annotated Translation of Hamann's Letter to C. J. Kraus, *Lessing Yearbook/ Jahrbuch*, 28 (1996), 147–61 (150).

[24] Hamann mentions the imagery of Alpha/Omega again in a later letter to his friend and admirer Amalie of Gallitzin: 'Herewith consists the Alpha and Omega of my whole philosophy, on which I need to daily suck and gnaw for my comfort and pastime. More I do not know, and do not demand to know more. Despite my insatiable wantonness and curiosity I do not find the truly divine all and whole for everbody, without consideration of person and of sex, anywhere else but in this single One.' (Hierinn besteht das *Alpha* und *Omega* meiner ganzen Philosophie, an der ich täglich zu meinem Troste und Zeitbertreibe saugen und kauen muß. Mehr weiß ich nicht, und verlange auch nichts mehr zu wißen. Trotz meiner unersättl. Lüsternheit und Neugierde finde ich nirgends—als in diesem Einzigen das wahre göttliche *All* und *Ganze* für Jedermann, ohne Ansehn der Person und des Geschlechts) (ZH vii. 377).

[25] The formulation of these 'truths and lies' is only one of a number of phrases that find a surprisingly exact echo in Friedrich Nietzsche's work (another is the idea of a 'grammar of thought').

not mean we discard it, just as we do not give up on reason. We are simply more cautious about our ability to manipulate it and about its potential dangers.

Hamann is very invested in the double-edged character of language, not only in its power to deliver verdicts. The Hamannian double edge does not fall into the trap of reductive or static dualism. Similarly to the rest of his theoretical outlook, Hamann insists that the multiple structures in language undermine and complement each other continuously. He elaborates on the ones he considers most important, especially the physicality and materiality of the word. As I pointed out earlier, Hamann insists multiple times that language contains, within itself, the physical, the sensuous, on the one hand, and the metaphysical, the spiritual revelation, on the other. The inextricability of sensuality and intellect, or experience and appearance, is mirrored in Hamann's description of language as containing both of these aspects:

> Words ... have an *aesthetic* and *logical* capacity.... As visible and audible objects they belong with their elements to *sensibility* and *intuition*, but according to the spirit of their *employment* and *meaning*, belong to *understanding* and *concepts*. Consequently words are as much pure and empirical *intuitions*, as they are pure and empirical *concepts*. (D 524)
>
> Wörter haben ... ein *ästhetisches* und *logisches* Vermögen. Als sichtliche und lautbare Gegenstände gehören sie mit ihren Elementen zur *Sinnlichkeit* und *Anschauung*, aber nach dem Geist ihrer Einsetzung und Bedeutung, zum *Verstand* und *Begriffen*. Folglich sind Wörter sowohl reine und empirische *Anschauungen*, als auch reine und empirische *Begriffe*. (N iii. 288)

The fact that words cut across these spheres goes for the experience of these words (and what they produce), too. Language, in both its 'logical' and 'aesthetic' aspects, is integral to an account of thinking and its preconditions, because thought and language are intertwined. This offers us an account that completely side-steps the widely accepted view of language as a system that conceives of words as clothing for ideas, or arbitrary signs that should be, in Locke's representative formulation, 'subservient to Instruction and Knowledge'.[26] In its unfamiliarity and in his willingness to embrace the obliqueness of the relation between language and thought, Hamann's is more radical than most philosophical accounts of language either then or now. Importantly in this context, his views have a recognizably Romantic commitment to poesis at its core.

Language cannot be a purely cognitive ability that is neutral and transparent. But neither is it 'simply' experienced noise or sound. The sensual quality of language is an integral part of the way it generates understanding and knowledge. And this character of language points towards a larger principle:

> It is pure idealism to separate *belief* and *feeling* from *thinking*. *Fellowship* is the true *principium* of reason and language.

[26] John Locke, *An Essay concerning Human Understanding*, ed. Peter H. Nidditch (Oxford: Clarendon Press, 1975), 404.

> Es ist reiner Idealismus *Glauben* und *Empfinden* vom *Denken* abzusondern. *Geselligkeit* ist das wahre *Principium* der Vernunft und Sprache. (ZH vii. 174)

Hamann inists that the sharp separation of feeling from thinking is 'pure idealism', a purity that he deems to be negative. (It is a similar desire for purity that ultimately turns reason into an idol.) If we want to understand the relation between feeling and thinking, we need to turn to the simultaneity of reason and language. What makes their connections possible, according to Hamann, is the 'true *principium*'—both their logic and the beginning of their relationship—of '*fellowship*'. The social fellowship is not solitary and 'pure'. Neither is it predetermined to be all-harmonious. Sociability, with both its difficulties and possibilities, is ultimately the principle that produces language and reason and, thereby, our understanding of the world.

The attempt to reduce such a complex relationship to a single, clear, and pure principle leads to a distorted view that Hamann laments ironically in his letters:

> Just such a pity that the deepest experience depends on an appearance, and the highest reason amounts to a play of words.
>
> Nur Jammerschade, daß die tiefste Erfahrung von einer Erscheinung abhängt und die höchste Vernunft auf ein Wortspiel hinausläuft. (ZH vi. 534)

Hamann offers a critical corrective to the way in which many of his philosophical colleagues describe the mediation and understanding of the world. Deep experiences rely on the seemingly unrelated appearance without which no experience at all is possible. The supposedly controlled and pure 'high reason' is a 'play of words' in both senses. First, the phrase 'pure reason' is a confused rhetorical image. Second, reason itself, since it is always connected to language, is determined to function according to the rules it has established with language.

Though the similarities are striking, Hamann's 'word play' goes beyond a socially constructed Wittgensteinean language game. He follows his statement on the 'play of words' with an explanation that returns us to the importance of the intertwined nature of reason and empiricism:

> Reason and experience is fundamentally all the same: as reason and practice are all the same. Where does the difference of this opposition come from. Does not the whole secret of our reason, its antitheses and analogies, rest in nothing but a *licentia poetica* to part what nature has joined together and to match what she wanted to part, to mutilate and to mend again.... All our babble and imitation is non-sense.
>
> Verstand und Erfahrung ist im Grunde einerley: wie Verstand und Anwendung einerley sind. Woher komt die Verschiedenheit des Gegensatzes. Beruht das ganze Geheimnis unserer Vernunft, ihrer Antithesen und Analogien in nichts als einer *licentia poetica* zu scheiden, was die Natur zusammengefügt und zu paaren, was sie hat scheiden wollen, zu verstümmeln und wider zu flicken.... All unser Lallen und Nachahmen ist *Non-sense*. (ZH vi. 534)

Hamann posits language as one of the main ways to understand and illustrate the complexity of components to knowledge. It poses the problem and the solution. In a self-reflexive and self-deprecating moment, he acknowledges that the way that we have been instituting the supposedly intuitive division between 'reason and practice' is itself a product of language. 'Antitheses and analogies' are not 'natural' or a neutral faculty. They are produced by language, too. Funnily, though, even in such destructive and simplistic divisions we can find a characteristic of language that is irreducible, namely, its poetic character. The divisions are produced by a language that takes poetic licence. In this case, the *licentia poetica* comes up with fictions that are deeply misguiding, since they 'part what nature has joined together and . . . match what she wanted to part'. This is an example of Hamann's return to his 'marrowbone' and its partly inconclusive outcome since the *licentia poetica* creates the divisions through which we understand, but also misunderstand, the world. Language contains the 'secret of our reason, its antitheses, and analogies', yet it is also liable to produce inadequate or imprecise categories, even uncontrolled utterances, such as our 'babble' or 'slurring' (lallen).[27]

We produce a lot of '*Non-sense*', yet we return to our marrowbone. Reason is at the centre of its own self-misunderstanding, yet we continue to value thought. The relationship of word and idea is oblique and difficult, yet it remains centrally important, necessary, and, crucially, pleasurable to realize it as such and continue to analyse it. Hamann is under no illusions: language and thought, for all their connection, do not a simple pair make. However, it is imperative to understand that he does not conceive of this oblique relation as something that is terrifying or needs to be purged of all complexity. He reacts positively to the fact that human language is illuminating as well as confusing. His style is an intense indication that he addresses this characteristic of language head-on. Language can reveal unknown qualities through its complexities, and we should not shy away from it but rather embrace it. To put it in anachronistic terms: it is almost as if Hamann intuits a linguistic negative capability. Hamann opens a world to us that is strange and idiosyncratic. It takes risk and patience to work ourselves into it. It rewards us with a completely new view, with an unorthodox and powerful critique of our patterns of thinking. However, it also produces confusion and, with it, the insight that our common assumptions might be far more difficult to sustain than we think. And yet, just as negative capability, this can be seen as a productive dynamic.

There remains a lot to be said about Hamann's thinking, as well as how his work relates to other sources relevant to European Romanticism. Much of this work needs translation, some needs excavation, and some of it needs our ability to listen to a voice

[27] There is a biographical dimension to this since Hamann suffered from a stutter. This was, some conjecture, the reason for his inability to become an academic. The 'babble' is not quite a stutter, but both make us intensely aware of the bodily dimension of the spoken word and how its physical representation through the linguistic sign remains an inadequate witness to this complexity. For a particularly sophisticated, and funny, discussion of this aspect, see Hamann's most intriguing texts *The New Apology of the Letter h by itself H*. Also see Marc Shell, *Stutter* (Cambridge, MA: Harvard University Press, 2005), 72. For a delightful short commentary on the history of 'h' and the *Apology* see Daniel Heller-Roazen, *Echolalias: On the Forgetting of Language* (New York: Zone Books, 2008), 33–44.

that sounds very unfamiliar. This ability to listen also includes the willingness to be attuned to the historical and conceptual echoes of a version of the eighteenth century (a Hamannian century, for instance), together with its thinkers, that is powerful but hardly ever scrutinized. It is to take seriously the idea that Hamann represents a moment of thinking about poesis and language that is central to European Romanticism and its legacy. For a study of the period, that means to be open to make connections between Hamann and other figures of historical Romanticism, such as Wordsworth or William Blake.[28] But it also includes perceiving that Hamann stands at the beginning of a Romantic genealogy that continues to think through the philosophical and poetical questions that the connection of poesis, logos, and language produces.

My last formulation invokes a genealogy of Romanticism that goes beyond its chronological limitation of an eighteenth- and nineteenth-century literary or cultural movement. It includes many thinkers who have been understood to be part of the wider Romantic project, such as Søren Kierkegaard, Walter Benjamin, Martin Heidegger, or Paul Celan. I mention these four very different writers in particular since for all of them Hamann was a pivotal figure in their reading and an important reference point for their thinking and writing. Kierkegaard cites Hamann regularly, including in his opening to *Fear and Trembling* (1843), and adopts his strategy of openly masked authorship as a philosophically significant move.[29] Hamann is the single most relevant figure to Benjamin's thinking on language, especially in his early work (he cites him twice, both times approvingly, in the seminal 'On Language as Such and on the Language of Man' (1916)).[30] Heidegger refers to Hamann as one of the 'three Hs' (die drei H) that are the central reference points in Enlightenment language philosophy (the others are Herder and Humboldt).[31] And Paul Celan's utterly neglected annotations to Hamann's works are extensive (Celan owned several volume of Hamann's writings) and include a particular focus on many of the passages discussed in this chapter.[32] All these figures

[28] The relation between the works of Blake and Hamann is particularly relevant. While Hamann's work has meaningful connections to other British authors of the 18th cent. (Hume, Bishop Berkeley, and Laurence Sterne, to name a few), his intellectual, rhetorical, and spiritual affinity to Blake has a special status. Currently, I am preparing a book that contains a comparative study of Hamann and Blake in which I hope to illuminate their relation in some detail.

[29] A good starting point for the relation between Hamann and Kierkegaard is provided in John R. Betz, 'Hamann before Kierkegaard: A Systematic Theological Oversight', *Pro Ecclesia*, 16/3 (2007), 299–333. Also see Joachim Ringleben, 'Søren Kierkegaard als Hamann-Leser', in Bernhard Gajek (ed.), *Die Gegenwärtigkeit Johann Georg Hamanns; Acta des achten Internationalen Hamann-Kolloquiums an der Martin-Luther Universität Halle-Wittenberg 2002* (Frankfurt am Main: Lang, 2005).

[30] See Walter Benjamin, 'On Language as Such and on the Language of Man', in *Selected Writings*, ed. Michael Jennings et al. (Cambridge, MA, and London: Harvard University Press, 1996–2003), i. 62–74. On Benjamin and Hamann see the still standard Winfried Menninghaus, *Walter Benjamins Theorie der Sprachmagie* (Frankfurt am Main: Suhrkamp, 1987).

[31] Martin Heidegger, *Vom Wesen der Sprache: Zu Herders Abhandlung 'Über den Ursprung der Sprache'*, Gesamtausgabe, lxxxv (Frankfurt am Main: Klostermann, 1999), 38. Heidegger's remark is particularly apt, since Hamann wrote a whole treatise on the letter *H* (and is himself, of course, the H-mann). It stands to reason that Heidegger would like to think of himself as H number four.

[32] Paul Celan, *La bibliothèque philosophique: Die philosophische Bibliothek* (Paris: Rue d'Ulm, 2004), 108–15. Especially with regard to Heidegger's interest, Celan's continuous study of Hamann is

find in Hamann a problem that, in its many different forms, becomes the problem of a Romanticism that goes beyond a Kantian framing of philosophy, namely, the problem of poetical thinking that encompasses the world or, to put it in Schlegelian terms, conceiving of the world *as poesy*.

It seems worthwhile to take up their invitation to reconsider this fundamental problem and engage with a way of thinking through it. One of the ways through which we, as scholars, can approach this issue, both in its eighteenth- and nineteenth-century articulation, as well as in its legacy, is to listen to some of the more unorthodox primary sources, including Hamann. In his case, we discover a figure who offers original and unusual ways of thinking about issues that we consider central to our understanding of the Enlightenment, Romanticism, and modernity. One example for this is the connection of thought and language, which I have been pursuing here, though there are many more (such as his stance on ethics or institutionalized religion, for instance). Such enquiries can uncover historically specific, and important, material as well as go beyond this recovery. They suggest that Hamann's unorthodox way of framing the problem of poesis, thinking, and language, constitutes a real invitation to radically reconsider many assumptions that we recognize as central to both us and the period.

Further Reading

Bayer, Oswald, *A Contemporary in Dissent: Johann Georg Hamann as a Radical Enlightener* (Grand Rapids, MI: Eerdmans, 2011).

Bayer, Oswald, *Vernunft ist Sprache: Hamanns Metakritik Kants* (Stuttgart: frommann, 2002).

Betz, John R., *After Enlightenment: The Post-Secular Vision of J. G. Hamann* (Oxford: Wiley-Blackwell, 2009).

Blanke, Fritz, and Schreiner, Lothar (eds), *Johann Georg Hamanns Hauptschriften Erklärt*, 7 vols [only 6 are completed] (Gütersloh: Bertelsmann; Mohn, 1956–).

Böhme, Hartmut, *Natur und Subjekt* (Frankfurt am Main: Suhrkamp, 1988).

Dickson, Gwen Griffith, *Johann Georg Hamann's Relational Metacriticism* (Berlin and New York: de Gruyter, 1995).

Gajek, Bernhard (ed.), *Johan Georg Hamann und England, Hamann und die englischsprachige Aufklärung: Acta des siebten internationalen Hamann-Kolloquium zu Marbur/Lahn 1996* (Frankfurt/Main: Lang, 1999).

Hegel, G. W. F., *Hegel on Hamann*, ed. and tr. Lisa Marie Anderson (Evanston, IL: Northwestern University Press, 2008).

Jacobs, Carol, *Skirting the Ethical* (Stanford, CA: Stanford University Press, 2008).

Jørgensen, Sven-Aage, *Querdenker der Aufklärung: Studien zu Johann Georg Hamann* (Göttingen: Wallstein, 2013).

O'Flaherty, James, *Johann Georg Hamann* (Boston: Twayne, 1979).

significant. To imagine that *The Meridian* was composed while Celan was reading the *Socratic Memorabilia* opens up this text of contemporary Romanticism completely anew. Celan was also interested in Hamann's intellectual formation in England. See Celan, *La bibliothèque philosophique*, 476.

CHAPTER 10

FREEDOM, REASON, AND ART IN IDEALIST AND ROMANTIC PHILOSOPHY

ANDREW BOWIE

EVEN though its authorship is still widely disputed, only part of it survived, and it only surfaced in 1913, the text, probably from 1796 or 1797, to which Franz Rosenzweig gave the title 'The Oldest System-Programme of German Idealism' (OSP) (see Appendix) has been remarkably influential in debates over the aims and significance of German Idealism. The text was written in Hegel's hand, but is often taken to be either by Hölderlin or Schelling, the three being friends at the time at the theological seminary in Tubingen. I do not propose to give a detailed interpretation of the text here, or speculate on who was the author, but instead want to take key motifs from it and show how they adumbrate tensions that are decisive for European Romanticism's significance in modern philosophy.[1]

The most obvious fact about the OSP in this respect is that it revolves around the divisions in Kant's philosophy which Habermas has seen as reflecting the core aspects of modernity, namely the divisions between the cognitive, the ethical, and the aesthetic, which he argues are concretely manifest in the differing spheres of modern science, modern law and the state, and modern art. It is notoriously difficult to characterize Romanticism in any unified sense, but it undoubtedly does have to do with tensions and contradictions between the way the modern world is understood in the terms of these notional spheres, an idea later suggested by Edmund Husserl's contrast between scientific and 'life-world' forms of understanding, and Wilfrid Sellars's contrast between the 'scientific' and the 'manifest' image of the world. The aim of German Idealism, broadly

[1] See Christoph Jamme and Hans Schneider (eds), *Mythologie der Vernunft: Hegels ältestes Systemprogramm des deutschen Idealismus* (Frankfurt am Main: Suhrkamp, 1988), and Frank-Peter Hansen, *Das älteste Systemprogramm des deutschen Idealismus. Rezeptionsgeschichte und Interpretation* (Berlin: de Gruyter, 1989).

understood, is to reconcile the conflicting demands of the modern world, so that the divisions between what we can know, what we should do, and forms of expression that cannot be reduced to the cognitive and the ethical, can be negotiated. The way in which Idealist thinkers can be said to differ from the thinkers of 'early German Romanticism', such as Novalis and Friedrich Schlegel, will be in the image of philosophy which results from engaging with these divisions.[2]

The sense of division in question here is in part a result of precisely what the modern period often sees as essentially differentiating it from the pre-modern world. The OSP makes freedom, initially in the sense of the capacity for self-determination in defiance of dogmatic traditional authority, the centre of its contentions. Once freedom is no longer subordinated to theological and other traditional demands, the problem is how it is to be understood, how it is to be exercised, and how its results can be legitimated. At this point new contradictions become apparent, between seeing the world in terms of necessity and seeing it in terms of freedom. Kant famously separates the account of someone acting in the world into two aspects: as an empirical, observable phenomenon what is done is wholly subject to the laws of nature, whereas in the world 'in itself', the 'intelligible' world, the action can be free, because the subject can take their own stance on the norm which governs their action. They act in terms of a conception of a rule, rather than just in terms of a rule. This means that nature in what Kant calls the 'formal' sense is just a system of deterministic laws, and it becomes unclear how it relates to freedom. How are we to understand the way in which freedom affects the world of appearance, if the world as seen in terms of freedom and as seen in terms of natural laws are in some sense not the same? Kant essentially wants to make freedom subject to the necessity generated by the categorical imperative, such that one makes the maxim of one's action into what one would freely decide should be universally applicable like a law of nature. A reconciliation of the normative and the natural of the kind Kant seeks with this idea is also the aim of German Idealism, but the Idealists, Fichte, Schelling, and Hegel, question Kant's version of the reconciliation.

It is important to remember here that the location and understanding of freedom in relation to the world seen in scientific terms is not just an abstract philosophical problem, of the kind familiar from the metaphysical debate over 'freedom of the will', because it concerns how the new sciences and their applications affect human culture and everyday human practices. This question is the essential theme of the OSP, and it is then played out both in the history of Idealist and Romantic philosophy, and in crucial aspects of modern history.

The key phrase in the OSP, which also occurs in Schelling's *System of Transcendental Idealism* (1800), is 'mythology of reason'. The Enlightenment is supposed to free people from dogmatic beliefs which have not been subject to rational criticism, of the kind that inform mythology, so the phrase would appear to involve a contradiction. The author of the text, and Schelling, whether or not he wrote the OSP, evidently do not think the

[2] Andrew Bowie, *Aesthetics and Subjectivity: From Kant to Nietzsche*, 2nd edn (Manchester: Manchester University Press, 2003).

phrase entails a contradiction, and maintain that an Enlightenment conception of reason needs to be rethought. The suggestion is that this has to happen via art and aesthetics, and this idea even today generates controversy both within and beyond philosophy. The notional division between much of analytical philosophy, for which art has at best marginal philosophical significance, and much of European philosophy, for which art is central to philosophical understanding, clearly has to do with differing construals of the relationship between aesthetics and rationality.

One reason why the idea of art as a means of responding to philosophical dilemmas is so controversial is that, while many forms of art remain central to sense-making in modernity, the importance of philosophy as a discipline declines during the period between the OSP and the present, mainly as a result of the growing reach of scientific explanations and the technological application of such explanations. The overheated expectations of a renewal of society via a new philosophy of freedom in the OSP have been replaced by the sometimes abstruse and specialized concerns of much contemporary philosophy, concerns which can seem to have little relevance for the orientation of people's lives. The call for a mythology of reason may in this respect be understood as involving an awareness of what Max Weber called the 'disenchantment' of the modern world. The concern in the OSP is with the consequences of not developing rational means to respond to a world in which more and more becomes explicable in terms of necessary causal laws, while human existence itself can come to seem more and more arbitrary and contingent.

In the *Critique of Pure Reason* Kant makes a distinction between 'understanding', which produces particular knowledge of natural laws, and 'reason', which gives the principles according to which the particular laws can be seen as cohering into a systematic whole in terms of 'ideas', such as the idea of the universal lawfulness of nature. The problem lies in the status of 'ideas', and this is what gives rise to the move towards aesthetics, both in Kant, in the 1790 *Critique of Judgement*, and in the OSP. The dissonance between the results of analysing the law-bound functioning of the world in ever greater detail, which leads to ever greater specialization and a disintegration of unified conceptions of the world, and the need to make sense of one's place within things as a whole, generates the orientation towards modes of sense-making which are neither straightforwardly cognitive nor straightforwardly ethical. The reason for the link to mythology is evident here: mythology provides a way of making sense of things by embodying general understandings of the world in particular images and stories. The problem is how to make general sense when mythology is discredited by the results of the sciences. Art is regarded as taking over this role precisely because it manifests general sense in a particular form, making ideas 'sensuous'.

This account of the way in which aesthetic issues change their significance might seem rather abstract, but one particular manifestation of the change can help make the account more concrete. Towards the end of the eighteenth century music, in its least representational, wordless, purely instrumental form, moves from being a subsidiary form of art to being seen by many Romantic thinkers as the highest form of art.[3] At

[3] See Bowie, *Aesthetics and Subjectivity*, and Andrew Bowie, *Music, Philosophy, and Modernity* (Cambridge: Cambridge University Press, 2007).

the historical moment when rational explanation in the terms of the understanding is becoming the dominant form of responding to the world, the form of art which connects people to the world and themselves in a non-conceptual, affective, and somatic way (particularly through rhythm) takes on a cultural significance in the work of Mozart, Beethoven, Schubert, and others, which it had previously not possessed. The change in question involves a deep-rooted questioning of the capacity of rational explanation to make complete sense of human existence. The simultaneous revaluation of the beauty of wild nature, which had previously been regarded as ugly or threatening, further underlines such questioning by finding a new kind of sense in the objective world which replaces mythological or theological forms of sense.

The OSP may not offer plausible answers to the question of how the new form of reason can be realized, but it is striking for the way in which it points to dilemmas which will play a role in subsequent philosophy and politics. The basic course of the 'argument' of the OSP, exposition of which fails to capture its aesthetic and performative force, is as follows. The idea that the whole of metaphysics should come within ethics, which the OSP links to Kant's 'postulates' of God, the freedom of the will, and the immortality of the soul, results from Fichte's prioritization of the practical, where the essential core of reality is the 'deed-action' (*Tathandlung*) of the I in 'positing' the not-I, the objective world. Without the self-determining activity of spirit, the world would, for Fichte, not be a world in any meaningful sense, because it would be opaque. As such, the subjective gains a priority over the objective, which gives it 'absolute freedom'. The subject's ability to take a stance on its own nature in reflection upon itself elevates it above the rest of nature. The reflection is absolute because it is not caused by something natural, which would render it relative, like all parts of nature which are the effects of preceding causes. In the hyperbolic interpretation of what Kant terms 'spontaneity'—that which is 'cause of itself' both in theoretical and practical reason—characteristic of early Idealism, attributes of God from theology often become transferred onto the subject. If dogmatic beliefs about nature as, in Hilary Putnam's phrase, 'ready-made', fall prey to the 'Copernican turn' towards the subject, the very constitution of nature itself as something intelligible becomes a product of freedom, and this is what lies behind the call for a new physics.

If ideas, as that which makes sense of the totality, are the product of freedom, then what matters in science is not just the particular explanations produced by the understanding, but how what we know in this way can be used to make sense of a world governed only by human self-determination—in Kant's terms, we give the law to nature in cognition and to ourselves in practical action—so that it is fit for a 'moral being'. Implicit in such an approach is the idea that relying on a rigid 'fact/value distinction' misconstrues how we should conceive of our understanding of the world. The significance of facts, though not necessarily the facts themselves, depends on contexts of evaluation constituted in the practices of human societies. Mechanical accumulation of facts and theories—which may be true in themselves—does not suffice to make sense of the world we inhabit as practical beings, because that sense is holistic, generated by interactions within society and with nature that cannot be grasped in piecemeal fashion.

The startling anarchist attack on the state that immediately follows the reflection on physics in the OSP results from a related prioritization of the idea of the organic coherence of the totality over the law-bound particulars of which it consists. In the same way as nature seen in terms of the understanding can appear as just a system of laws, like a machine, the state, as that which imposes laws on its subjects, rather than allowing them to be self-determining, is merely mechanical. It should be remembered that the Germany in which the text is written consists mainly of small states whose laws are often the result of arbitrary imposition of authority by their rulers. The utopian idea here is that if people are truly free the need for the imposition of law will be obviated, because the law would be the result of people's own self-determination, of, in Kant's terms, autonomy rather than heteronomy. The strikingly different construals of the relation of freedom to the law on the part of Kant (and the mature Hegel), for whom duty to the state is an essential part of self-determination, and of the OSP, for which the state is precisely the obstacle to real self-determination, should not obscure the fact that they begin from the same premise, namely of reconciling freedom and necessity. The differences between the ideas of how such reconciliation is to be achieved are paradigmatic for essential conflicts in modernity. Reconciliation can be seen in political and ethical terms, whereby the individual comes to acknowledge the need to follow the collectively constituted law of the state. Doubts about what this entails are, however, precisely what leads the OSP to the issues we shall now consider, which will turn out to have often deeply problematic consequences.

The fact that the abrupt move in the OSP towards consideration of art and beauty is a response to the issue just considered is indicative of fundamental contradictions in modernity. One of the decisive factors in disenchantment is that, as warranted knowledge of natural laws increases, such knowledge can become more and more divorced from how the world is experienced in everyday terms. The sense we make of important life events tends to have a teleological element, connecting things in such a way that they cohere as part of a perceived meaningful pattern of development towards something that makes more sense at the end than at the beginning. Modern science is largely directed against teleological explanation and so can add to the nihilistic sense that all that really exist are arbitrary causal chains in a notional system. When dogmatic theological belief in the inherent meaningfulness of nature can no longer be defended, not least because it had been linked to the justification of feudal hierarchies as part of a natural order of things, aesthetic forms of production and reception take on new significance.

There is, though, a crucial ambiguity with respect to aesthetic issues. On the one hand, aesthetic production comes to be seen as linked to human freedom to create without the restrictions of tradition and received authority; on the other, without what is aesthetically apprehended or articulated transcending the individual and subjective, it can be or can seem to be merely arbitrary. The association of artists and madness that is present in Romantic literature, like that of E. T. A. Hoffmann, testifies to this dilemma. Kant famously says in the *Critique of Judgement* that nature gives the law to art in the production of the genius, who is compelled by something beyond their capacity for creating according to intersubjectively acknowledged rules, and so can establish new aesthetic norms. This idea is another attempt to square the circle between freedom and necessity, but the history of modern art suggests that the kind of reconciliation Kant intends actually often results in something more conflictual than the at least apparent reconciliation of subjective and objective, mind and nature, which Kant associates with the idea of the genius.[4]

In the OSP the idea that the 'highest act of reason' is an 'aesthetic act' is explained by the contrast of the aesthetic form of reason with the reason of the 'pedantic philosophers', who do not think in terms of 'ideas'. In the 'Platonic' sense the idea of 'beauty' has to do with Kant's link between the organism—whose parts just involve the series of mechanical laws which govern each part, the whole of which, in contrast, coheres in a way explanation of the particular laws cannot account for—and the work of art, where there is an analogous transcendence of the whole over the parts. The hyperbolic future role attributed to 'poetry', which generally at this time has the sense of 'creative production', may seem naive in the light of the way in which the sciences have come to dominate how the world is understood since the time of the OSP. The significance of the claims becomes clearer in relation to the idea of a 'new ... mythology of reason', which fulfils the need for a 'sensuous religion'.

What is at issue is an aspect of disenchantment which has vital ramifications that play a role both in Romantic philosophy and modern politics. The dissonances between the way in which the life-world is experienced, how the world is rationally explained, and how modern forms of exchange and technology impact on people's lives create key aspects of the space in which modern politics takes place. If people can see no continuity between these three ways of relating to the world, the result is forms of disorientation which create the need for narratives which restore a sense of orientation of the kind provided previously by traditional and theological forms of myth. The idea of a new mythology, which would restore the link between the products of what will later be termed 'instrumental reason', and the kind of sense people make of their everyday existence, is therefore both a necessity and a source of great political danger. The OSP's insistence that this be a mythology of reason, which counters both the philosophical temptation of abstract rationalism, and the popular tendency to irrationality based on a failure critically to interrogate prejudices, of the kind that will later emerge, for example, in nationalist and racist beliefs, is in many respects based on a pious hope. Looking at responses to the essential tension here is, though, a good way of charting the course of some key aspects of modern philosophy in relation to decisive developments in modern history.

What lies behind the hyperbolic desire for 'general freedom and equality of spirits' in the OSP is a sense of dissonance between subject and object, mind and nature—the indeterminacy of the terms can be seen as part of the issue—that demands a resolution.

[4] See Andrew Bowie, *Adorno and the Ends of Philosophy* (Cambridge: Polity, 2013), and later in this chapter.

The problem is that the freedom which separates us from a dogmatic, supposedly natural order that does not involve a division between self and world is also precisely what is supposed to enable us to establish a new kind of harmony. The difference between broadly construed German Idealist, and early German Romantic philosophy is that the former seeks a philosophical account of how unity can be articulated through division, whereas the latter sees such unity as only accessible at all in our sense of failure when we strive to achieve definitive unity.[5] The role of art in the respective philosophies reflects this difference, in that the former, paradigmatically in the mature Hegel, sees art as being transcended by philosophy in modernity, whereas the latter sees art as the key to understanding why the attempt at a systematically complete philosophy fails. At the same time it is notable that Hegel kept returning to aesthetics in his lectures and that the issues he raises pose questions for his philosophical project which are far from resolved.[6] If philosophy cannot exhaustively comprehend what art reveals by converting the kind of sense made by art into a conceptual account, this changes the very nature of what philosophy is understood to be, as later thinkers such as Adorno, Heidegger, and Wittgenstein will also suggest.[7]

It is important to see both how different levels of the issues here are connected, and how there are significant divergences between these levels. This is most obvious with respect to the relationship between the political and the philosophical levels. Germany is in this respect paradigmatic for the extremes of modernity, both producing many of the most insightful philosophical understandings of modern freedom, and the most catastrophic manifestations of what happens when the contradictions between objective developments and subjective responses (albeit ones fundamentally influenced by objective factors) become what determines politics.[8] The prescience of the OSP's call for a new mythology lies in the realization that a world determined more and more by the effects of science's new insights into laws of nature and by the rationalized social forms of modern capitalism can become alien to those inhabiting it, because the kind of narratives via which they make sense are not commensurable with what is happening around them and to them. Germany's notorious failure to modernize politically as it modernizes in scientific, economic, and industrial terms—what Ernst Bloch would later see in terms of 'non-simultaneity'—clearly has to do with a falling apart of differing forms of understanding of the world to which people respond in ultimately self-destructive ways based on mythical thinking that can also, of course, issue in appalling violence against others.

[5] See Andrew Bowie, *From Romanticism to Critical Theory: The Philosophy of German Literary Theory* (London: Routledge, 1997); Bowie, *Aesthetics and Subjectivity*; Manfred Frank, *'Unendliche Annäherung': Die Anfänge der philosophischen Frühromantik* (Frankfurt: Suhrkamp, 1997).

[6] Robert Pippin, *Kunst als Philosophie* (Frankfurt: Suhrkamp, 2013).

[7] See Bowie, *Adorno*; Lee Braver, *Groundless Grounds* (Cambridge, MA: MIT Press, 2012); M. Wrathall, *Heidegger and Unconcealment* (Cambridge: Cambridge University Press, 2011).

[8] Andrew Bowie, *Introduction to German Philosophy from Kant to Habermas* (Cambridge: Polity, 2003); A. Bowie, *German Philosophy: A Very Short Introduction* (Oxford: Oxford University Press, 2010).

One of the most well-known critical responses to the extreme manifestation of the problems here, fascism, is Walter Benjamin's critique of the 'aestheticization of politics', to which he, in the wake of Brecht, opposes the 'politicization of aesthetics'. However, it is arguable that Benjamin does not fully articulate the problem he confronts, which is evident in the OSP's awareness that if reason does not take a form which makes sense to people they will not respond to it. Schiller, an obvious influence on the OSP, was aware of part of what this meant in his ideas about 'aesthetic education' as the means of creating moral cohesion that rational moral arguments may not achieve. It is now clear that the most such ideas can achieve in political terms may be to enable us to grasp the sources of their failure to be realized. Bloch would point out that the successes of the Nazis depended in part on what the OSP sees as the making sensuous of ideas, and that the Left failed to see how the failure to do this weakened its political effectiveness, even as it also meant it sometimes avoided the kind of irrationalism that fuelled aspects of the Nazi terror. The specifically philosophical insights that emerge in relation to the OSP point in other directions which can help relocate aesthetic issues at the heart of modern philosophy, rather than making them peripheral, as they still are for many kinds of contemporary philosophy.

It has been quite plausibly argued that Hölderlin is in fact the author of the OSP, but even if he isn't, some of his theoretical work offers ways of elaborating core issues from the OSP. In two texts, 'Being and Judgement' of 1794/5 (the title is often given as 'Judgement and Being', but the logic of the text suggests that being should come first), and 'On the Workings of the Poetic Spirit', probably of 1800, he explores issues arising out of the sense of division between subject and world. In much modern philosophy, especially in the anglophone traditions, this division is seen in terms of epistemological scepticism. The vital fact is that Hölderlin does not couch the issues in these terms, for the following instructive reason.

If anything is most characteristic of modernity it is probably the growth of warranted scientific knowledge, without which much that is characteristic of the modern human world would not exist. In the light of this fact the obsession with scepticism in philosophy since Descartes, which continues to this day in the analytical tradition, must appear strange. A. C. Grayling makes a characteristic statement in this respect when he says: 'The problems facing the justification of knowledge-claims can best and most powerfully be described by framing them as sceptical challenges, meeting which—if possible—will certify that we are at least sometimes indeed entitled to make claims to knowledge.'[9] The fact that such a remark may well appear very odd to anyone but a philosopher should be taken seriously. How can it make sense, in the light of the success of scientific prediction and the resulting technological developments, seriously to doubt whether we are entitled to claim we know anything? There are many ways in philosophy of suggesting problems with what is suggested here, but my response to these will not be arguments against the objections to the centrality of epistemological scepticism

[9] <http://www.acgrayling.com/scepticism-and-justification>.

in modern philosophy. Instead I want to suggest why the Romantic approach to issues that also give rise to modern scepticism-obsessed epistemology is philosophically more important than has usually been realized.

The point here is not to claim that concern with scepticism is merely a mistake, but to see that it is part of an expression of something broader, in which a sense of division that is not just concerned with knowledge of the world is constitutive of the modern condition. The sense of division can be manifest in the difficulty of actually giving a warranted philosophical account of what it is that justifies warranted scientific knowledge, but it can also be manifest in other forms which are central to the experience of subjects in modernity in ways that epistemological, as opposed, say, to existential doubt, often is not, and this is where Hölderlin's texts are significant. The broader issue here can be seen in terms of 'alienation'. Talk of alienation has often been regarded as too vague to do much critical work, not least because it is sometimes unclear whether what is at issue is ontological, defining the very nature of human being in the world, or whether it is a specific phenomenon characteristic of modernity, of the kind that Marx sees as resulting from the new phenomenon of widespread social mobility, where the awareness of possibilities of self-realization grows at the same time as systemic economic and political obstructions to such self-realization. The second notion relates to the fact that in the wake of Kant the fear arises that the subject is alienated from itself, in ways which will later be explored by Freud, Lacan, and others, and this fear takes us to the heart of Romantic philosophy.

The basic contradiction in self-knowledge, namely that what does the knowing must be identical with what is known for it to be self-knowledge, but different from it for there to be any meaningful sense in which what results is knowledge at all, becomes acute if, as it is for Fichte, the I is supposed to be the generative principle of the world's intelligibility. How does what makes things intelligible make its own activity intelligible to itself, and what would enable us to be sure of the point and legitimacy of such activity? In the *Vocation of Man* (1800) Fichte himself asks: 'And do I really think or do I just think a thinking of thinking? What can stop speculation acting like this and continuing asking to infinity?'[10] The problem of self-knowledge can therefore lead to doubts about the very nature of our relationship to the world, an issue which Schelling, Heidegger, Adorno, and others will see, not in terms of epistemological scepticism, but in terms of the danger of such contact merely becoming an narcissistic imposition of its own nature on the world by the subject. As such, the desire for understanding self-consciousness's relationship to being is an expression of a real contradiction, of the kind that now informs concern with the modern destruction of the natural environment, in ways which were already suggested by Schelling in his Hölderlin-influenced critiques in the late 1790s and early 1800s of Fichte's failure to see nature as anything more than a resource to be used by the subject.[11]

[10] Johann Gottlieb Fichte, *Werke*, ii (Berlin: de Gruyter 1971), 252.

[11] Andrew Bowie, *Schelling and Modern European Philosophy* (London: Routledge, 1993).

Hölderlin's first text revolves around a notion that plays a role in Kant's reflections on the limits of knowledge, 'intellectual intuition', which Kant sees as the manner in which a deity actually produces the object of its thought, unlike human thought which can only produce representations based on what is given in receptivity. The idea in 'Being and Judgement' is that if the subject's essential nature is spontaneity, its reflective awareness of itself could, as Fichte thinks it is, be a production of the object of its thought, making it absolute, not dependent on something else. Hölderlin, however, contests the idea that the self-relation of the subject can be absolute, in a way which maps out a path for philosophy which questions the reliance in certain parts of German Idealism on the idea of the philosophically articulable identity of subject and object. The notion of 'judgement', 'Urteil', is seen as inherently involving a division (following a possible etymology of the word as meaning 'original separation', 'Ur-Teil'). Even the statement of identity 'I = I' must involve a difference between the I in the subject- and the I in the predicate-position. Anything entailing a relationship cannot be absolute, so identity must be grounded in something which carries the two related poles, which Hölderlin calls 'being', the 'whole of which subject and object are parts'.[12]

The problem is then that a sense of alienation seems constitutive of how we understand ourselves and the world. The subject that seeks to understand itself splits itself in the process, and nothing it can know could ultimately overcome the split, because knowledge entails a relation, and thus a difference. This situation points to the core difference that determines subsequent thinking in German Idealism and Romanticism and subtends other important aspects of modern philosophy.

Hegel famously attacks Schelling's version of 'intellectual intuition', which relies (admittedly in a rather questionable manner) on something like what Hölderlin claims, as the 'night in which all cows are black', because Hegel thinks that for Schelling the unity of being is arrived at just by suppressing all differences. Hegel contends in the *Phenomenology of Spirit* (1807) that the unity presupposed in intellectual intuition has in fact to be a result, not a prior foundation. For Hegel, by seeing that knowledge inherently involves division and contradiction, progressing by 'determinate negation'—each particular piece of knowledge resulting from the refutation of a preceding claim, so no Copernicus without Ptolemy to prove wrong—we realize that the absolute must be understood as the articulation of all differences in a comprehensive system, rather than as a presupposition which renders relative all the differences that follow from it. The 'reflexive' Hegelian relationship between subject and object obviates the need for any kind of foundational ground, because all determination results from the process of negation where what 'stands against' the subject (the German for 'object' often used here is *Gegenstand*) enables the subject to articulate new knowledge. At the end, having gone through and incorporated all the negations, the divisions between subject and object, including those present in self-consciousness's reflection upon itself, are dissolved in the realization that unity is made manifest by rationally articulating differences, not by any

[12] Friedrich Hölderlin, *Werke Briefe Dokumente* (Munich: Winkler, 1963), 490–1.

founding principle. As an approach to epistemology this is a plausible stance, answering the sceptic by turning the sceptical position against itself: the very fact that things turn out to be false in the process of inquiry is what enables us to understand the real nature of knowledge as generated by determinate negation, and so to articulate that nature philosophically. But here we encounter the decisive point.

As we saw, it seems hard to explain why so much modern philosophy, especially in the analytical tradition, has focused on the difficulty of providing a philosophical account of warranted knowledge. In the Hegelian response the sense of the division of subject and object that inspires sceptical thoughts is incorporated into a new, dynamic conception of how to think about knowledge. What Hegel fails to do, however, is adequately to address the wider modern sense of dislocation between mind and world, which cannot be overcome by showing a better way of understanding the new ability to know and manipulate the world that defines one view of modernity. It is here that Hölderlin's further reflections point in a crucial, often neglected direction. The need he sees is to find a way of understanding self-consciousness which gets over the problem that reflection on the unity it must in some way entail if it is not to disintegrate into unintelligibility is, as 'Being and Judgement' suggests, precisely what destroys that unity. How does the subject gain a sense of the totality of subject and object that does not either involve a mystical dissolution of the self into the whole, or a sense of ineliminable alienation between self and world, or an objectification of the subject that results from the claim to comprehensive self-knowledge on the basis of a general theory? The last of these is what lies behind contemporary reductive naturalist accounts of subjectivity, and this suggests why the perspective Hölderlin seeks to develop is still significant. The key point is that what Hölderlin seeks cannot take the form of a theoretical claim that would explain the relationship between self and world in conceptual terms. 'Knowing the answer' could be seen as actually increasing the subject's alienation, because the meaning of its existence would take a form which objectified it, so taking away precisely the dynamic, individual, potentially creative aspect of the self which gives rise to new meaning and so resists being fixed in conceptual terms.

'On the Workings of the Poetic Spirit', a text of considerable conceptual complexity and stylistic density, owes its literary form to the nature of what it seeks to reveal, namely a way of the subject understanding its relationship to the world and itself which takes account of both unity and division in manner that does not issue in a claim to a definitive philosophical theory. The basic idea[13] is that without divisions there would be no self-consciousness, merely an undifferentiated state akin to that of a contented baby, but that the self would disintegrate into 'isolated moments' if the division were not also grounded in some kind of unity. Without change the point of self-consciousness is absent, but change lacks any meaning if it does not involve connections between what precedes and what comes after each moment of change. In Kant the continuity demanded here is seen in terms of the 'transcendental unity of apperception', the 'I think

[13] For a detailed analysis see Bowie, *Aesthetics and Subjectivity*, ch. 3.

that must be able to accompany all my representations',[14] thus in epistemological terms. Hölderlin's concern, in contrast, is that such an identity, which Kant infers as a necessity for knowledge to be possible at all, because without it experience would disintegrate into unconnected moments, fails to offer resources for responding both to the divisions in the self that result from self-reflection and to the related alienation of the self from the world: 'It is a matter of the I not simply remaining in interaction with its subjective nature, from which it cannot abstract [by reflecting on itself] without negating itself.'[15] Only by responding to the divisions within the I in relation to something in the world beyond the I can the I realize itself in a manner that creates unity out of division. At the same time the relationship to the aspect of the world is not cognitive, because that does not give any motivating force to the relationship: what is the point of the I knowing the world, if the I merely adds to its alienation by a further objectification?

Here the significance of aesthetics for modern philosophy is adumbrated in ways which even today have often not been adequately appreciated. Hölderlin sees the subject's way out of the dilemmas just outlined in its 'free choice' of an object of 'poetic' representation. The free choice is not some kind of arbitrary subjective preference, but rather the result of engaging with the world and finding fundamental sense in aspects of the world via that engagement. The idea is not to lose oneself in the object, nor to subject it wholly to oneself, but rather to come to an awareness of oneself via the manner in which the object both resists one and yet enables one to make individual and supra-individual sense through the way one responds to that resistance. Hölderlin talks in this context of that which is 'harmoniously opposed'[16] both in the subject and in the object. Rather than the idea of some kind of inherent epistemological division between mind and world that we need a philosophical theory to overcome, which, as we saw, failed to address the more significant divisions that haunt modernity, Hölderlin takes on board the divisions that modern self-reflection necessarily entails and tries to use them to arrive at a mode of being which incorporates contradiction.

Unlike the child that is 'identical with the world',[17] the free subject realizes itself via what can result from the object's difference from itself, which enables it to make individual sense via the object. Hölderlin is referring to any aspect of our world which we seek to make sense of by giving it a meaningful form. One instructive way to understand what Hölderlin means is to think of language in these terms, as something which both resists us by being the 'discourse of the other', and enables us to realize our individuality when we master it as an individual means of expression, whose highest form is 'poetry', which includes all forms of creative literature. Along with the use of the idea of harmony as the unification of difference, Hölderlin talks elsewhere of finding the *Ton*, meaning something between 'note' and 'tone', that embodies 'inner and outer life', and of *Stimmung*, 'mood',[18] with the sense of 'attunement' that will later recur in aspects of

[14] Immanuel Kant, *Kritik der reinen Vernunft* (Frankfurt: Suhrkamp, 1968), B 131.

[15] Hölderlin, *Werke Briefe Dokumente*, 518.

[16] *Werke Briefe Dokumente*, 512.

[17] *Werke Briefe Dokumente*, 521.

[18] *Werke Briefe Dokumente*, 528–9.

Heidegger's reflections on moods as fundamental ways of being in the world that are not willed by the subject.

The link to music suggests the philosophical implications that I want to bring out here. Instead of being concerned with crossing an epistemological gap, Hölderlin is seeking to understand ways of being in the world which overcome the kind of alienation that results from the loss of traditional connections to the world. In this view involvement in music is one way in which I can gain sense from connecting to a world which objectifying forms of knowledge may render alien to me. The idea of freedom he associates with these ideas is not Kantian self-determination via norms, nor is it the licence which Rousseau saw as making one the slave of one's passions, but instead, as Schelling would later see it, a liberation which 'directs or determines itself according to the reality of that from which it liberates itself'.[19] This can be understood by the way that great art in modernity, from Hölderlin's own poetry to Beethoven and Bruckner's symphonies, gains its greatness from responding to the negative aspects of life and transforming them. The resistance of the objective material, be it of language, or music, or the material of the plastic arts, is precisely what generates the impetus to overcome that resistance and so make sense of it in ways which can connect us to the world and potentially transform both the world and ourselves.

The philosophical point about this kind of understanding of the nature of the modern relationships between subject and object is that it can only be grasped via concrete investigation of and engagement with the historical forms in which they are manifest, and not solely in philosophical terms abstracted from those forms. What is suggested here involves in one respect a version of what Hegel will do in the *Phenomenology of Spirit* in relation to the philosophical situation following Kant. In the *Phenomenology* the sceptical attitude is undermined by showing how it arises out of the changing historical forms in which the mind–world relationship manifests itself, there being no way of meaningfully separating mind from the world it articulates. However, the crucial difference is that the related aesthetic perspective suggested in Hölderlin, which is not predicated on an essentially cognitive relationship to the world—the *Phenomenology* does concern itself extensively with more than cognitive relations, but 'absolute knowing' is its ultimate scepticism-dissolving goal—may be more able to register and respond to the ways in which what Axel Honneth has referred to as modernity's 'pathologies of reason' arise.

What this means is that if philosophy seriously wishes to comprehend the ways in which, while enabling so many advances in human well-being, modernity has also led and can lead again to disaster, it cannot just rely on many of the dominant concerns of academic philosophy, of the kind epitomized by the focus on scepticism, realism, and the like. Instead philosophy needs to widen its focus, in the manner characteristic of the best thinkers in the European tradition, to consider the other ways in which relations to the world are constituted and in which they can become problematic: Adorno's interpretations of the effects of commodity form on modern culture are an obvious example

[19] F. W. J. Schelling, *Sammtliche Werke*, ed. K. F. A. Schelling, i/1–10, ii/1–4 (Stuttgart: Cotta, 1856–61), ii/4. 20.

here. It can be argued in this context that art in modernity offers in many respects the most illuminating manifestations of the tensions between subject and world. The OSP's connection of art and freedom is decisive here.

If the 'highest act of reason' is an 'aesthetic act', the kind of relationship to the object cited by Hölderlin offers a post-theological model of how the subject can make more than merely individual sense by engaging with and forming aspects of the world, and this model helps to understand the development of art in modernity as offering new semantic and affective resources. The history of the arts in modernity is, though, as Adorno will insist, also characterized by the increasingly problematic relationship between the desire to make sense by aesthetic production and the fact that so much of what happens in modernity may really make little or no sense, as events like the Holocaust, the growing systemic pressures produced by capitalist forms of exchange, and what Adorno calls the 'fall of metaphysics' as a means of creating universal sense, can suggest. Even Beethoven, whose music embodies the ideals of a new self-determining humanity, comes in his late works to question the hope for harmony which is expressed by his most heroic 'middle period' works, by fragmenting forms and undermining the vocabulary of Viennese classicism. The subsequent emergence of modernism and the avant-garde both reflects the way in which freedom in relation to the object of art opens up radical new constructive possibilities that allow the escape from pre-given forms, and at the same time threatens the making of sense of the kind that the OSP associates with a mythology of reason, by no longer seeking to reconcile whole and part in a wider, shared context of meaning. Such a reconciliation can be regarded merely as an illusion in relation to a world where the ever expanding human ability to manipulate reality too rarely results in a humane existence for the majority of people.

In the light of the growing commodification of modern culture, the nature of the subject's relations to the objective world becomes more problematic because the ways in which consciousness is formed by diverse symbolic pressures from aesthetic norms and practices, advertising, the media, etc., cannot be easily be separated into those which result in merely ideological effects and those which truly enable the subject to make sense. The same piece, say, of commercial pop music can be both a crucial emotional support for its individual listener and yet also part of a wider industry-driven emotional manipulation that ultimately can contribute to the coarsening of affective life. Significantly, the common failure to reflect on the political and economic factors which produce this situation aligns with some influential reductionist tendencies in Anglo-American philosophy, when all such issues are consigned to the status of being 'merely subjective' preference, much as that philosophy regards the phenomenology of human experience as mere 'folk psychology', or regards ethical issues as mere subjective emotional projection. The value of the Idealist and Romantic traditions lies not least in their refusal to accept the picture of the world behind such attitudes.

Rather than regarding the fact that aesthetic responses are constitutively contested as a reason to exclude them from the domain of rational argument,[20] this tradition

[20] See Stanley Cavell, 'Aesthetic Problems of Modern Philosophy', in *Must we Mean What we Say?* (Cambridge: Cambridge University Press, 1976), 73–96, for a brilliant account of this issue.

precisely takes the fact that they are not justifiable in the same way as empirical truth claims as an indication of their importance in disclosing crucial aspects of meaning in modernity which would otherwise remain hidden by the dominant forms of understanding and justification.

By taking seriously the need for shared forms of sense of the kind established by art, and the ways in which art in modernity both creates and destroys those forms, the scope of our understanding can be widened. Art can critically question the objectification which grounds the success of the natural sciences by reminding us both that objectification is only one way in which we understand things and that it cannot account for the content of many forms of relation to the world. Honneth talks of the 'ruling idea, according to which an epistemic subject stands opposite the world in a neutral manner',[21] which is questioned by thinkers influenced by German Idealism and Romanticism, like Heidegger, Adorno, and Merleau-Ponty.[22] The neutral stance is, for them, a derivative stance, depending on what Heidegger refers to as the 'care structure' of *Dasein*, the fact that our primary investment in the world is motivated by things we care about, which are not necessarily things we rationally choose. That these can be often better brought under our control by the neutral objectifying stance is in many respects the underlying principle of modernity, but this can give rise to a repression of the kind of relations to things we saw Hölderlin making central to the subject's self-understanding.

The contemporary resurgence of interest in Hegel and German Idealism in philosophers like John McDowell is expressly directed against a reductionist naturalism that tries to reduce everything in the world to the 'space of causes', and thereby fails to give an adequate account of the 'space of reasons'. The importance of the way the aesthetic dimension is invoked by the OSP and explicated by Hölderlin and by parts of Romantic philosophy lies, though, not least in the fact that what is disclosed by art cannot be fully understood in terms of reason-giving and normativity. This is because the aesthetic has to do with connections to things which involve responses that, even as they can generate reasons and norms, cannot themselves be adequately understood in terms of reasons and norms. That such connections cannot be grounded in philosophical terms, if these are thought of as inferential forms of justification, suggests the dangers they involve: they involve dimensions of sense that must be directly felt and experienced, and so cannot be legitimated in terms of publicly agreed criteria.

At the same time, though, this connects these dimensions to questions about freedom. The contingency involved in aesthetic connections to the world is not just an indication of meaninglessness, but can also be what opens up the space of new meanings. The notion of the subject developed in Hölderlin and Romantic philosophy depends precisely on the mobility and openness to the world of the subject, not on a conceptual

[21] Axel Honneth, *Verdinglichung: Eine anerkennungstheoretische Studie* (Frankfurt: Suhrkamp, 2005), 31.

[22] Honneth, 31.

fixing of its nature. However much the history of modern Western music, for example, can be rationally reconstructed in terms of a progression which comes to incorporate more and more sonic material by finding harmonic, rhythmic, and melodic forms which make sense of it, the ability of such music to express aspects of modern human existence that are otherwise inaccessible relies on an ungroundable openness to the contingency of the new which is a perennial, if always threatened, possibility of human life. The philosophical tension suggested here between the desire for rational, conceptual control of the world, and the realization that such control can make us blind to some of the most crucial forms of sense has, in much academic philosophy, often been neglected in favour of the first option.

The recent interest in the European Romantic philosophical tradition, a tradition which, it is vital to remember, does not abjure the need for rational understanding, is based on a new attention to the fact that the freedom to make sense goes beyond what reason-based understanding can offer. This move beyond an agenda defined by epistemological concerns towards aspects of human existence which can often only be understood by direct participation in cultural practices opens up productive ways of connecting philosophy to the humanities at a time when the legitimation of the humanities in relation to the natural sciences has once again become a pressing issue. The sense made by real participation in art is not something whose truth is revealed by its being objectified in a philosophical or scientific theory. It is rather something which gives us ways of grasping how dominant ways of making sense, which in contemporary culture are generally and in many ways justifiably seen as defined by what the sciences can legitimate on the basis of observation and experiment, can hide the kind of participatory sense which both motivates human lives and offers critical perspectives on the effects of presupposing a complete priority of objective knowledge over other relationships to the world.

APPENDIX: THE SO-CALLED 'OLDEST SYSTEM PROGRAMME OF GERMAN IDEALISM' (1796?)

RECTO

An Ethics. As the whole of metaphysics will in future come under *Morality*—of which Kant only gave an *example* with his two practical postulates and *exhausted* nothing, this ethics will be nothing but a complete system of all Ideas, or, which is the same, of all practical postulates. The first Idea is naturally the notion *of my self* as an absolutely free being. With the free self-conscious being (*Wesen*) a whole *world* emerges at the same time—out of nothing—the only true and thinkable *creation from nothing*—Here I will descend to the fields of physics; the question is this: how must a world be for a moral being? I should like to give wings again to our physics which is progressing slowly and laboriously via experiments.

Thus—if philosophy gives the Ideas and experience the data we can finally achieve the grand physics which I expect from later epochs. It does not appear that our present physics could satisfy a creative spirit which is like ours, or like ours should be.

From nature I come to *human activity* (*Menschenwerk*). Putting the Idea of humanity first—I want to show that there is no Idea of the *State* because the state is something *mechanical*, just as little as there is an Idea of a *machine*.

Only that which is an object of *freedom* is called an *Idea*. We must, then, also go beyond the state!—For every state must treat free people as a piece of machinery; and it should not do this; thus it must *come to an end*.

You can see yourselves that here all the Ideas, of eternal peace etc. are only *subordinate* Ideas of a higher Idea. At the same time I want here to establish the principles for a *History of Mankind* and to completely expose the whole miserable human creation of state, constitution, government, legislature. Finally come the Ideas of a moral world, divinity, immortality—the upturning of all superstition, the pursuit of the priesthood, which has recently been feigning reason, by reason itself.—Absolute freedom of all spirits who bear the intelligible (*intellektuelle*) world in themselves, and may not seek either God or immortality *outside themselves*.

Finally the Idea which unites all, the Idea of *beauty*, the word taken in the higher platonic sense. I am now convinced that the highest act of reason, which embraces all Ideas, is an aesthetic act, and that *truth and goodness* are brothers *only in beauty*—The philosopher must possess just as much aesthetic power

VERSO

as the poet (*Dichter*). People without aesthetic sense are our pedantic philosophers (*BuchstabenPhilosophen*). The philosophy of spirit is an aesthetic philosophy. One cannot be spiritual (*geistreich*) in anything, one cannot even reason spiritually about history—without aesthetic sense. It should here become apparent what it is that people lack who understand no Ideas—and admit faithfully enough that everything is a mystery to them as soon as it goes beyond charts and registers.

Poetry thereby gains a higher dignity, at the end it again becomes what it was at the beginning—*teacher of (History) Mankind*; for there is no philosophy, no history any more, poetry alone will survive all the remaining sciences and arts.

At the same time we hear so often that the masses should have a *sensuous religion*. Not only the masses but also the philosopher needs monotheism of reason of the heart, polytheism of imagination (*Einbildungskraft*) and of art, this is what we need!

First of all I shall speak here of an Idea which, as far as I know, has never occurred to anyone—we must have a new mythology, but this mythology must be in the service of the Ideas, it must become a mythology of *reason*.

Before we make the Ideas aesthetic i.e. mythological, they are of no interest to the *people* and on the other hand before mythology is reasonable the philosopher must be ashamed of it. Thus enlightened and unenlightened must finally shake hands, mythology must become philosophical and the people reasonable, and philosophy must become mythological in order to make the philosophers sensuous. Then eternal unity will reign among us. Never the despising gaze, never the blind trembling of the people before its wise men and priests. Only then can we expect the *same* development of *all* powers, of the individual as well as all individuals. No power will be suppressed any more, then general freedom and equality of spirits will reign!—A higher spirit sent from heaven must found this new religion among us, it will be the last, greatest work of mankind.

(Translated by Andrew Bowie)

Further Reading

Bowie, Andrew, *Schelling and Modern European Philosophy* (London: Routledge, 1993).

Bowie, Andrew, *From Romanticism to Critical Theory: The Philosophy of German Literary Theory* (London: Routledge, 1997).

Bowie, Andrew, *Aesthetics and Subjectivity: From Kant to Nietzsche*, 2nd edn (Manchester: Manchester University Press, 2003).

Bowie, Andrew, *Introduction to German Philosophy from Kant to Habermas* (Cambridge: Polity, 2003).

Bowie, Andrew, *Music, Philosophy, and Modernity* (Cambridge: Cambridge University Press, 2007).

Frank, Manfred, *Der kommende Gott. Vorlesung über die neue Mythologie I* (Frankfurt: Suhrkamp, 1982).

Frank, Manfred, *'Unendliche Annäherung': Die Anfänge der philosophischen Frühromantik* (Frankfurt: Suhrkamp, 1997).

Henrich, Dieter, *Selbstverhältnisse* (Stuttgart: Reclam, 1982).

Henrich, Dieter, *Der Grund im Bewußtsein: Untersuchungen zu Hölderlins Denken (1794–5)* (Stuttgart: Klett-Cotta, 1992).

Jamme, Christoph, and Schneider, Hans (eds), *Mythologie der Vernunft. Hegels ältestes Systemprogramm des deutschen Idealismus* (Frankfurt am Main: Suhrkamp, 1988).

Lypp, Bernhard, *Ästhetischer Absolutismus und politische Vernunft: Zum Widerstreit von Reflexion und Sittlichkeit im deutschen Idealismus* (Frankfurt: Suhrkamp, 1972).

Pinkard, Terry, *Hegel's Phenomenology. The Sociality of Reason* (Cambridge: Cambridge University Press, 1996).

Pippin, Robert, *The Persistence of Subjectivity* (Cambridge: Cambridge University Press, 2005).

Pippin, Robert, *Kunst als Philosophie* (Frankfurt: Suhrkamp, 2013).

CHAPTER 11

FRIEDRICH VON HARDENBERG (PSEUDONYM NOVALIS)

WM. ARCTANDER O'BRIEN

for Darius

On 2 May 1772 at the family manor of Schloß Oberwiederstedt, Georg Friedrich Philipp, Freiherr (Baron) von Hardenberg was born the eldest son in an aristocratic family with unbroken lineage from the twelfth century. Hardenberg's father had left the military and diplomatic careers most often associated with the Hardenbergs, especially during this turbulent period, and dedicated himself and his family to a pious life in the countryside. The family manor was a secularized thirteenth-century monastery, given to Hardenberg's great-great-grandfather a hundred years before. The boy grew up in this house until he was 13, when his father's promotion to Director of Salt Works (a significant position, given the importance of salt to the state) occasioned their moving to a large, more urban house in the city of Weißenfels. Hardenberg thus grew up in surroundings both religious and secular, medieval and modern, rural and urban, aristocratic and professional, at the very moment these pairs were about to collide in the French Revolution. When the Bastille was stormed in 1789, Hardenberg was 17, and he had just spent the year with his uncle at the latter's Schloß Lucklum, where life was enjoyed in the style of the Ancien Régime.

When he returned home, Hardenberg, along with his entire generation of the 1770s—the first generation of Romantics—excitedly awaited all news of the cataclysmic event which was said to promise a new, young world of *liberté, egalité, et fraternité*. For Hardenberg, as for his contemporaries, the French Revolution would prove to be the central event of his life—and peculiarly so, since his world so starkly embodied the contradictions of the Revolution, and he would not live to see, much less foster, the Reaction.

(To take the example closest to Hardenberg, Friedrich Schlegel converted to Catholicism in 1808; accompanied the Duke of Teschen to war against Napoleon in 1809; began service to Metternich in 1809 lasting through the Congress of Vienna; received for his service a patent of nobility that made him 'von Schlegel' (and thus ushered him into the pantheon with Goethe and Schiller, the high and low bourgeois whose *von* certified their stardom and service); became a Knight of the Papal Order of Christ through Pius VII in 1816, etc.)

In 1790 Hardenberg matriculated at the University of Jena, ostensibly to study law, but increasingly to attend lectures on Kant and medieval history. The latter were taught by the young Schiller, whom Hardenberg, a member of his circle, helped nurse through illness. In Jena Hardenberg met the now legendary Herder, and had a juvenile poem published by Wieland. Eventually Hardenberg's father wrote Schiller to request help getting his son back on track. The professor obliged the baron.

The young Hardenberg followed his teacher's advice and his father's prodding, and transferred to the University of Leipzig in 1791. He soon began a lifelong friendship with Schlegel, who wrote his brother August describing Hardenberg:

> Fate has placed in my hands a young man from whom all is possible.... Still quite a young person—of slender good build, very fine face with black eyes that take incredible fire when he speaks of something beautiful—indescribable how much fire—he speaks three times more and three times more quickly than the rest of us—the quickest understanding and sensibility. Philosophical studies have given him a fully developed ease in forming beautiful philosophical thoughts—he tends to the beautiful rather than the true ... I have never seen such youthful cheer. His sensibility has a certain chastity based in the soul and not in inexperience. For he has been much in society (he gets acquainted with everyone right away) ... He is very happy, very soft, and right now taking every shape impressed on him. (IV 571–2)[1]

Schlegel's letter as a whole betrays a slightly wicked delight in Hardenberg's naiveté and provincialism (judgements Schlegel never entirely abandoned), but his words help answer the obvious question: How was Hardenberg able to pen so much in so short a time—while advancing a practical career? While Hardenberg published scarcely eighty pages in his lifetime, he was drawing upon thousands, and he even once wrote to a friend:

> Literary scribbling is a mere sideline for me. You judge me clearly by the main thing—practical life.... I treat my writing as a means of education—I learn to think and to work things through carefully—that is all I ask of it. (IV 266)

According to Schlegel, Hardenberg is a young man on fire, speaking three times more quickly and saying three times more than 'the rest of us'. Schlegel's observation may

[1] Arabic and roman numerals in parentheses refer to the *Novalis Schriften* (1960–). All translations are by the author, informed by those already in print.

seem exaggerated, but it is corroborated by other witnesses, such as Hardenberg's eventual supervisor and biographer, Coelestin Just:

> He did nothing by halves; what he set his mind to do, he did completely. Nothing was done superficially; he was thorough in everything.... He read a new book in a quarter of the time we ordinary mortals need. When done, he set the book aside as if he had never touched it. Weeks or months later, if it entered a conversation, he was able to muster its entire contents ... (IV 540)

Hardenberg could also sleep as little as five hours a night. It all adds up. Cheerful and social, Hardenberg talked, read, and thought four times more quickly than anyone in his distinguished company, and he could do it almost around the clock. It makes sense that his mature writing, produced in only six years, appears the product of many more.

At the university Hardenberg played understudy to Schlegel, two years older and more savvy. His education proceeded rapidly. Together, the two neglected their formal studies, as Schlegel led Hardenberg to contemporary philosophy, introduced him to aesthetic and literary theory, and, perhaps most importantly, awakened him to the delight in wit and paradox that would henceforth enliven his work. Hardenberg also followed Schlegel's lead in romance and chose the sister of Schlegel's own sweetheart—but it was here the party ended. For Schlegel to dally with a charming bourgeois girl was expected, but for Hardenberg, the eldest son in an aristocratic family, to fall in love with one was out of the question. His father made this furiously clear.

Hardenberg transferred to the University of Wittenberg in 1793 and applied himself exclusively to legal studies, passing his final examinations in June 1794 with the highest grade. Yet he continued to follow the news. When he was matriculating at Wittenberg, Robespierre was beginning the Reign of Terror. A month after he left university, Robespierre was beheaded and the Terror replaced by the Directory. Things were moving quickly.

The logical next step for Hardenberg was to find a position with the diplomatic side of the family, but negotiations through the Prussian Minister Karl August von Hardenberg went nowhere. Greatly relieved, Hardenberg's father decided to bring his eldest son closer to home, and helped set him up as legal assistant to the local district director of nearby Tennstedt. Less than a month after starting work, Hardenberg accompanied him on a winter business trip to nearby Schloß Grüningen, where he instantly fell in love with Sophie von Kühn, one of five children in a respected family of the newer nobility. The 22-year-old Hardenberg was initially led to believe Sophie was 14 (she was actually 12-and-half, just proper for the times), and the two got secretly engaged the following spring. Of this union the father would eventually approve. Throughout the year Hardenberg and his brothers playfully courted all three sisters in the more relaxed atmosphere of Sophie's house. Soon, however, in November 1795, Sophie fell gravely ill. After a series of painful operations (performed by Schiller's own surgeon) she died on 17 March 1797. One month later she was followed by Hardenberg's favourite brother, Erasmus. Hardenberg was so overcome that he could attend neither funeral. The two deaths plunged him into a period of mourning and melancholia.

Yet the years in Tennstedt had been fruitful. In addition to his professional work and love of Sophie, Hardenberg had immersed himself in studies of Fichte's philosophy, a crucial spur to the invention of early Romanticism. Hardenberg had met and studied with Fichte in Jena, and his notebooks contain roughly 700 entries, running from a few lines to a few pages. The notebooks show exactly how Hardenberg, in writing, would 'think and work something through'. As do all of Hardenberg's fragments—a privileged genre in early Romanticism, whether published or not—the notes capture Hardenberg's thought in mid-flight, and it is a rare pleasure to read the handwritten manuscripts, where pages can explode visually with corrections and original thoughts spilling into the margins.

In the *Fichte Studies* Hardenberg first of all works to understand Fichte's philosophy. At the same time, he pushes, criticizes, and extends certain of Fichte's thoughts. Finally, he uses Fichte as a springboard for his own thoughts. In his early philosophy—all of which Hardenberg had read—Fichte presents himself less as an innovator than as an explicator of Kant, someone drawing out certain implications of Kant's philosophy that Kant himself had not seen. In this sense, Fichte's most famous statements—'I = I' and 'I ≠ -I'—respond to Kant's crucial distinction between our perception of things and their unknowability, the way they exist at an unbridgeable distance from our knowing of them. Despite all the qualities humans perceive in objects, the objects themselves remain simply blank 'things-in-themselves'. Kant claimed, however, that the distance between our perceptions and things-in-themselves is nevertheless reconciled by what he calls the 'schemata' of our minds—which, as part of the same world, operate with the same logic as things-in-themselves. Our perception of things may take place at an unbridgeable remove from things-in-themselves, but there is nevertheless an inherent agreement and harmony between the two. Fichte uses the shorthand of 'I = I' to show that even in Kant our perceptions are *projections* onto things, so that while we initially experience the world as outside us and different from us—in Fichte's shorthand 'I ≠ -I'—we can realize that all we perceive is really projected by us, and in that sense is simply an extension of the I. Our relation to the world is really one of confronting the I again, of understanding that in the end, the formula 'I = I' clearly expresses the relation of self to the world, and of the self to itself. For all German Romanticism, this ability of the self to project itself onto things, in a sense to make them, became fundamental for elaborations of the self as both 'creative' and 'artistic' in its activity.

The *Fichte Studies* show Hardenberg hard at work understanding all of Fichte's painstaking elaborations of this philosophy, and he eventually makes the remarkable claim: 'Spinoza climbed as far as Nature—Fichte as far as the I, or the person. I [climb] as far as the thesis, God' (150).[2] Hardenberg does not mention Kant here—for he accepts Fichte's philosophy as the logical extension of Kant's—and he instead evokes Spinoza, the philosopher most closely associated in this period with pantheism, the view of nature as itself divine. The combination of precisely these two philosophers is explosive, and Hardenberg's logic is less conventionally religious than it might at first appear. (One does well to remember that suspicions of heresy followed anyone sympathetic to

[2] Roman numerals alone in parentheses refer to the standard numbering of the passage under discussion, in both German eds. and English tr. (where available).

the Jew, Spinoza; and that charges of atheism would soon drive Fichte from his post in Jena.) Hardenberg's logic runs thus: Spinoza discovered the divinity of nature. Fichte discovered that nature is a projection of the self, identical with the self. Thus, the divinity Spinoza found in nature is identical with that of the self. This divinity is ours too: we too partake of divinity, and in a sense, we are divine, we are as gods, we are God.

Hardenberg's formulation is a germ of Romanticism, which later Romanticism would often trivialize and falsify. For the *Fichte Studies* expand Hardenberg's discovery very precisely. His coupling of Fichte and Spinoza extends the revaluation of *creation* that had been ongoing since the mid-century, when creation was reserved for the deity alone: *creatio ex nihilo*. By the end of the eighteenth century, creation and creativity were beginning to become human endeavours, and Hardenberg is pivotal in this regard. Kant and Fichte's *projection* of human qualities upon the world became a *creation* of this world, and in this sense everyone is creative, most especially artists. It also extends the reformulation of the idea of *genius*, which changed from the mid-eighteenth century—when the genius was understood as a spirit, a kind of genie and muse, that inspired the artist—to the nineteenth century, when the artist himself was seen as a *creative genius*. Fichte spurred the Romantic cults of the 'creative artist' and 'genius', both alive to this day (their theological implications largely forgotten). Hardenberg, however, saw that the issue was not as simple as it would later become. For the divine, creative self does not experience itself as the whole, but as part of the whole, a part of nature, and—as Rousseau had made clear—always already distant from it, always strangely 'separate' from it. Hardenberg is acutely aware of this alienation, and for this reason the Whole, the Real, the True, or—in Romantic terms—the Absolute, *can never simply appear as such, nor be adequately described or designated as such*. For in the very gesture of supposedly describing it, we stand *outside* it, and thus break it, falsify it. As Hardenberg first comes upon this realization in the *Fichte Studies*, he stops to note: 'Grasp then, a handful of darkness' (3). No problematic in the difficult theory of early Romanticism would be more vulgarized in later Romanticism.

Hardenberg's stance towards all supposed representations of the Absolute—which can be neither properly thought nor not-thought—has radical implications for all representation, especially language. Strictly taken, *representation* means the *re*-presentation of the real, of that which is, of that which has *already presented itself*. For Hardenberg, drawing out the implications of both Kant and Fichte, such a representation is simply impossible, because the Real, the Absolute, indeed *all that is* lies beyond re-presentation, simply because it never *presents itself as such*. The mind *projects* all qualities: 'The I has a hieroglyphic power' (6).

Hardenberg's first fragment already assumes this by calling Fichte's proposition, 'A = A', an 'apparent or illusory proposition' (*Scheinsatz*). In other words: 'We abandon the Identical in order to present it' (1). The gesture is radical. Hardenberg is not approaching representation as a philosophical problem among others. Instead he is approaching philosophy as a problematic instance of language. Hardenberg dismisses the pre-eminent claims of philosophy to truth, to the *re-presentation of what is*. In a long, worked-out passage, Hardenberg gives the dearest claims of philosophy short shrift: 'Truth—fiction or illusion'; 'Illusion is mind (*Geist*)'; 'All thought is thus an art of illusion'; 'Illusion alone is the ground of form and matter'. In short: 'Illusion is thus everywhere' (234). For Hardenberg, this is a power to celebrate, for while philosophy fails to recognize the inherent problem of language and thought as illusion (*Täuschung* and *Schein*), Hardenberg sees our ability, not to re-present, but simply to present (*darstellen*), as part of the wondrous, fantastic, creative principle of nature. In thought and language we make illusion, but we do it naturally; and at best, one can learn to do it in harmony with nature.

In Tennstedt, after the death of Sophie, Hardenberg began his short but remarkable *Journal*, a painfully frank diary of his activities and thoughts while in mourning. None of his writings better displays the strange mixture—a hallmark of Hardenberg's writing—of passionate feeling stated in precise, almost emotionally detached language. Like everything Hardenberg penned after the *Fichte Studies*, his *Journal* is also, unavoidably, a self-conscious work of fiction. In a sense it is Hardenberg's first fiction, a precise record of his gradual apotheosis of Sophie, his projection of her to a sacred 'beyond' where she both joins and reveals, as mediatrix, the divinity. A few days before the *Journal's* end, Hardenberg concludes a long entry with the words, centred on the page: 'Xtus and *Sophie*'. The terse jotting posits Sophie, traditionally, as reunited with Christ in death, but in the context of the *Journal* it remains ambiguous, suggesting Sophie as the bride of Christ (and thus never really Hardenberg's fiancée), or more radically, as an equal or equivalent of Christ. Hardenberg will elaborate, and reconcile, these possibilities later.

Hardenberg spent the rest of the year recovering by reading German mystics, visiting old friends, and travelling with his father. In December Hardenberg arrived at the Mining Academy in Freiberg to begin a year and a half of scientific studies. Hardenberg plunged headlong into studies of geology, chemistry, and mathematics, excelling at all three; and he quickly became engaged to a retired Academy teacher's daughter, Julie von Charpentier—making both families happy.

The Mining Academy—one of the earliest such professional schools—had been founded by Frederick the Great in 1765 to apply fast-growing scientific knowledge to strategic enterprises of the state, such as coal, salt, and mineral extraction. The Mining Academy attracted celebrated scientists to its faculty, and catered to a demographic in transition: aristocrats in positions of state oversight, who now needed to be trained technically and scientifically. In pursuing a professional career—as in his aristocratic lineage—Hardenberg differed from everyone else in the Jena Circle. Although they would later portray Hardenberg as the dreamiest of them all, he was actually the only one who held a steady job. Tieck, the Schlegels, and Schleiermacher were all pioneers in the new intellectual and literary careers open to the bourgeoisie. Professional writers and critics, they pasted together an income—eventually quite lucrative—from patronage, book sales, and the university, where the new bourgeois reading public eagerly attended lectures about world literature (itself a Romantic invention). Although he was the only aristocrat among them, Hardenberg was also the only early Romantic who got his hands dirty—at least, with anything but ink. When he wrote of his 'literary scribbling', he was not only continuing the aristocratic tradition in which *belles lettres* remain a strictly personal amusement. Hardenberg also took his work seriously: he went out to the salt works, down into the mines, and if need be, into the miners' homes to help them. Unlike his fellow Romantics, Hardenberg had no need at all of literary success, and he cared very little about it when writing or publishing—as his friends soon learned.

Only a month after his arrival at the Academy, Hardenberg sent his first major manuscript to August Schlegel with a small request. Were the Schlegels' new journal, the *Athenaeum*, to publish it, Hardenberg asked that it appear under the pseudonym 'Novalis', which, he explained, 'is an old family name of mine, and not quite inappropriate' (IV, 251). Prone to understatement only when he had the most up his sleeve, the 25-year-old Hardenberg had chosen a pseudonym not only 'not quite inappropriate', as he rather disingenuously claimed, but cleverly filled with revelations and concealments. As the young baron implied, a form of 'Novalis' had indeed been used by his twelfth-century ancestors at their Hannover estate of Großenrode bei Nörten. This branch of the family had referred to itself as *de novali* or *von der Rode*, 'from the cleared land'. In this familial sense 'Novalis' was no pseudonym at all, and Hardenberg was surreptitiously writing under his proper, aristocratic family name in reviving it. It was, however, a proper name with a difference. Hardenberg cleverly played with his aristocracy by unobtrusively replacing the German *von* of *von der Rode* and, more urgently, the *de* of *de novali* (the Latin now suggesting French) with the German possessive *s*. The name 'Novalis' retained a trace of Hardenberg's aristocratic lineage, while at the same time announcing—for the French Revolution too had 'cleared the land'—a change in the order. So while it was fashionable for both aristocratic and bourgeois writers of the period to adopt pseudonyms, Hardenberg's choice also reflected a politic discretion on his part. Prussia had an effective censor in the 1790s, and in the wake of the Terror not everyone was enthusiastic about having *their* land 'cleared'.

Romanticism announced itself in 1798, when its three foundational and self-consciously programmatic texts appeared—all within six months of the other, none bearing the author's name. In this brief year of peace in Europe, Wordsworth and Coleridge published the *Lyrical Ballads* anonymously in the fall; the previous June Friedrich Schlegel printed his annunciatory *Fragments* (*Fragmente*) anonymously in his new journal, the *Athenaeum*, openly edited by him and his brother; and a month still earlier the *Athenaeum*'s inaugural issue published *Pollen* (*Blüthenstaub*) by 'Novalis'. Though it appeared first, *Pollen*'s privileged place in the history of Romanticism has remained unrecognized for obvious reasons: Hardenberg's text was not republished as such until the twentieth century, and it remained untranslated into English until 1996. *Pollen* thus missed the boat for comparative (and even German) histories of Romanticism. Today, *Pollen*'s importance is as clear as it first was to Friedrich Schlegel, who delayed publishing his own *Fragments* to print *Pollen* first. For Hardenberg's text, like those of Schlegel, Wordsworth, and Coleridge, openly announces the programme of the first Romantics. Schlegel first put the word 'Romantic' into print to describe the new movement (a word he and Hardenberg had been using all year), and his 116th *Fragment* famously claims: 'Romantic poetry is a progressive universal poetry.... The Romantic kind of poetry is the only one that is more than a kind and, as it were, the poetic art itself: for, in a certain sense, all poetry is or should be Romantic.' Wordsworth's brief 'Advertisement' to the first edition of the *Lyrical Ballads*, though less famous than his 'Preface' to the second (1800), expects its poetical 'experiments', which use 'the language and conversation of the middle and lower classes', to provoke, as he delicately puts it, 'feelings of strangeness' in his readers. All anonymous for good reason, the three texts of 1798 announce a programme that seeks to expand poetry's reach, and by doing so, to revolutionize it.

With *Pollen* from 'Novalis'—pollen from the cleared land—both the title and pseudonym situate the text as *post-revolutionary*—not reactionary, but simply in the wake of the Revolution. The text also presents itself as *revolutionary*, for it self-consciously continues the work begun by the Revolution in form and content: a mobile aphorism collection very freely assessing the new changes in politics and society. *Pollen* explicitly states the scope of change envisioned by the first Romantics: 'We are on a mission: we are called to the education of the earth' (32). This early Romantic mission differs from that of the Enlightenment because it is not more, but less mystical and colonialist. First, it makes no claim to understand or even encounter the Absolute or Infinite. This is amusingly implied in *Pollen's* first aphorism: 'Everywhere we *seek* the infinite, and always we *find* just finite things' (1). Romanticism does not differ from the Enlightenment by leaving the empirical for the mystical, the Absolute; on the contrary, it insists from the start that the Absolute cannot be grasped. It rejects all Enlightenment claims to absolute or all-encompassing truths, such as a discovery of the universally 'human'. (Earlier in the year Hardenberg had casually jotted down: 'The Human—a metaphor' (II 561).)

Pollen is concerned not with how we can attain the Infinite or the Absolute, but what we can do in the realm of 'things'. Its second aphorism observes:

> Signifying with sounds and marks is an amazing abstraction. Three letters signify God to me—a few strokes a million things. How easy it is to handle the universe this way! ... A single word of command moves armies—the word liberty—nations. (2)

On this side of the Absolute—and there is no other—there are only things, and the thing called 'signifying' or language moves other things: it can suggest God, it can compute the otherwise unthinkable (exactly 'a million things'), and it can command armies (tellingly here, with the word 'liberty'). Romanticism may be self-reflective about language, but it is not self-absorbed: it knows the power of language in the world.

Pollen applies Hardenberg's insights about 'signifying' pressingly to politics: 'In the state, everything is theatricality; the life of the people is a play' (76). Hardenberg is not introducing the idea of an aesthetic society—Schiller had already done that—but he is extending it by pointing out the role of fiction within all society. Still further, he asserts that the power of fiction organizes the state, just as the Revolution had restaged a state and commanded its people to war. These are dangerous words in 1798, and *Pollen* goes still further by delegitimizing Europe's rulers, deposing them by denying them the title: 'By the way, it is an undeniable fact that most rulers are not rulers' (76). Impudently, as a mere aside, the sentence topples most of Europe's (crowned) rulers—an audacious gesture in the German states of 1798. Hardenberg goes so far in his manuscript as to claim, 'Democracy, in the usual sense, is at bottom no different from monarchy, except that here the monarch is a mass of heads' (122). This is beyond the pale of acceptability and Schlegel, in reworking Hardenberg's manuscript, withheld it from *Pollen*. The German public, and the Prussian censor, never read it.

Pollen is equally inflammatory about religion. Decades before Marx, Hardenberg says of conventional religion: 'Their so-called religion simply works as an opiate: stimulating, dulling' (177). *Pollen* attacks what it calls religious 'philistines' relentlessly, calling their Sunday services 'a poetic seventh-day fever', and mocking their idea of heaven as a product of class: 'The coarse philistine imagines the joys of heaven in the guise of a church festival, a wedding, a voyage, or a grand ball; the more refined make heaven into a splendid church with beautiful music, much pomp, chairs for the common people on the ground, and chapels and balconies for the more distinguished' (77).

Hardenberg also examines Christian theological dogma at length:

> Nothing is more indispensable for true religious feeling than an intermediary—which connects us to the divinity. A human being is utterly incapable of an unmediated relation to it. In choosing this intermediary the person must be wholly free.... Fetishes, stars, animals, heroes, idols, gods, *one* god-man. One soon sees how relative such choices are ...
>
> It is idolatry, in the broader sense, when I accept this mediator as in fact God himself. It is *irreligion*, when I accept no mediator at all; and to this extent superstition or idolatry—and unbelief—or theism, as one can call older Judaism—are both *irreligion*. At the other extreme, atheism is merely negation of religion altogether and thus has nothing to do with religion. True religion is that which accepts the mediator as mediator—takes him for an instrument of the divinity—for its sensual appearance.... (74)

Hardenberg approaches religion as what one would later call an anthropologist of religion. He flatly states the need for mediators of the divine, since the Absolute cannot appear to us simply as such. He then matter-of-factly lists off their developing forms, right up to the God-man (or god-man, *Gottmensch*) of Christianity. The implied point here is that, since Christianity understands the mediator (Jesus or Christ) as identical to God, as God Himself, Christianity is idolatry. Hardenberg's further twist—which combines his notion of pantheism with his personal apotheosis of Sophie—is to define truly religious people (those who follow what he elsewhere calls 'Romantic religion') as those who understand themselves as free to choose whatever or whomever they wish for their mediators. Here, as throughout *Pollen*, Hardenberg can get away with such a radically subversive idea by eschewing overt rhetoric and by sounding so coldly factual—and by moving very, very quickly.

Hardenberg pushed his luck still further with his next publication, the fragment collection *Faith and Love, or, The King and Queen*. A concise political tract of exceptional tropological complexity and mobility—and radical experimentation—*Faith and Love* ostensibly presents an over-the-top panegyric to the recently crowned Prussian

King and Queen, Friedrich Wilhelm III and Louise. As such, nothing seemed strange about Hardenberg's insistence that Schlegel place it with the *Yearbook of the Prussian Monarchy*, the state monthly devoted to official news, travelogues, and reports about the royal couple. Schlegel generously obliged his friend, and the *Yearbook* even planned to follow *Faith and Love* with Hardenberg's 'Political Aphorisms' in its next issue. After *Faith and Love* appeared, Schlegel mischievously described to Hardenberg how it had been read by the King himself, who, perplexed, had given it to his ministers to read, who agreed among themselves that it was probably another incomprehensible scheme of the Schlegel brothers. Schlegel was delighted: a little scandal is good publicity, especially when you are launching a fledgling journal. He and the publisher agreed: 'The essay has provoked general amazement. Everyone is satisfied with it' (IV 497–8).

Their smirks did not last long, and the following week Schlegel writes again, this time nervous and upset: 'The slight exasperation of the king ... has so frightened the censor that he has forbidden publication of the political aphorisms—I do not know where the general rumor arose that a nephew of Minister v. Hardenberg was the author.' Clearly annoyed as well as worried—the little scandal had gotten a little too big—Schlegel now tells his friend, 'It would also be good if you were to change your assumed name', and he conveys the exasperated publisher's assessment: 'Nothing can now be printed under the name Novalis' (IV 499).

Most strange in all of this was Hardenberg's reaction: he doesn't seem to care at all. He neither shares Schlegel's initial glee, nor expresses any contrition, nor voices any fear of the court. No surprise, no delight, no worries—nothing.

Hardenberg's insouciance is revealing about him and his relation to publishing. Hardenberg never bothered to develop connections in the publishing business—he always left that to Schlegel—but he was no fool about the topicality of his work. By insisting that *Faith and Love* appear in the *Yearbook*, he was enjoying a very private joke, one that could turn dangerous for Schlegel and his publisher—but not for him. By all accounts, Hardenberg never pulled rank or stood on ceremony as an aristocrat with his bourgeois acquaintances; but it is a great error—one successfully begun by his first biographers—to infer that Hardenberg himself was oblivious to his standing. His reaction to the court scandal shows this plainly. No one without a title and a well-placed relative in government would ever have risked such a stunt with the *Yearbook* and its royal sponsors. 1798 was a year of declared peace, but the political mood throughout Europe was still tense (and would remain so until Waterloo). *Faith and Love* contained passages that could easily (and rightly) be construed—and prosecuted—as politically subversive: 'The king is a man raised to the fate of the earth. This poetic fiction necessarily forces itself upon man.... All men should become worthy of the throne' (18); 'A time will come, and soon, when there will be a general conviction that no king can exist without a republic, and no republic without a king' (22); 'There is no monarchy where the king and the intelligence of the state are no longer identical. Hence the King of France had been dethroned long before the Revolution, and so most of the rulers in Europe' (28). The essay borders on sedition, and though it opens by pointing out, eloquently and precisely, how its 'language will be strange or foreign ... a language of tropes and riddles'

(1), written in such a way 'that only he would understand, who should understand' (2), such hermeneutical niceties do not tend to hold up well with angry kings. Hardenberg published *Faith and Love* with the *Yearbook* because he knew his title and family connections afforded him protection—and he was right: as soon as 'Novalis' was thought to be Minister von Hardenberg's nephew, the flurry appears to have dissipated.

The scandal of *Faith and Love* reveals a secret in plain sight about Hardenberg. A great deal of what makes him such a unique critic of his times is his complicated class status. Bourgeois criticism has historically avoided discussing class, since bourgeois institutions have supposedly abolished class. Yet the bourgeoisie has never forgotten its old enemy, and it has a tendency to brand all aristocrats in the revolutionary period as reactionary (until proven innocent). This bourgeois prejudice became amplified when it passed into leftist, Marxist, and Communist criticism. The problem with Hardenberg is that he was *both* an aristocrat *and* a child of the Revolution. He accepted the Revolution as fait accompli, never doubted its epochal significance, and made little effort to conceal his republican sympathies. Even after the Terror, when the older generation, and much of the younger, had turned away from the Revolution in disgust, he and Sophie celebrated his twenty-third birthday (rather frivolously in wartime) around a cake topped with the enemy's revolutionary tricolour and cockade. Yet he greeted the Revolution, with its promises of freedom, equality, and democracy, with more scepticism than most admirers. Not a bourgeois, Hardenberg did not have the same kind of stake in the Revolution that his bourgeois friends shared.

At the same time, Hardenberg was a professionally trained technocrat and bureaucrat, employed in precisely the kind of field that soon became peopled with bourgeois administrators. For this reason, his thinking about the Revolution also differed from that of his fellow aristocrats. For a moment, the old regime and the new were still facing each other: the one was passing away and the other had yet to be fully institutionalized—or indeed, fully conceptualized. Because Hardenberg was in a sense *both* aristocratic and bourgeois, yet at the same time *at a remove* from both, he was able to observe and analyse contemporary developments from a most peculiar position. His aristocratic standing did not make him more reactionary than the other members of the Jena Circle. On the contrary, it permitted him to be more, not less, daring in his assessments of both the old and the new regimes. More grounded by daily work and less afraid of scandal, he repeatedly scandalized his fellow Romantics.

Hardenberg was also a mystic. Mystical reflections run throughout his notebooks, and while at the Mining Academy he wrote his first mystical text—the third 'work' of his spare hours there. *The Novices of Sais* proceeds directly out of Hardenberg's scientific studies, documented in his technical notebooks and his largest notebook, the *General Studies* (*Allgemeine Brouillon*). Hardenberg conceived the latter as a Romantic encyclopedia of the sciences and all other branches of knowledge. More exactly, Hardenberg referred to his project as 'encyclopedistics', an attempt to develop the theory of such a project, and to show the analogical harmony of all studies. So alongside notes about current science are others on 'the physics of politics', 'mathematical philosophy', 'poetic physiology', 'literary politics', 'the poetics of maladies', and so forth.

Hardenberg's thinking here is by no means anti-Enlightenment or anti-reason. As in his social theory, he builds upon the knowledge and sciences of the Enlightenment. (There is much of the French *philosophe* in Hardenberg.) The *General Notebook* approaches sciences as 'sign-systems', extending Hardenberg's notes on linguistics and semiotics in the *Fichte Studies*. In the earlier notebook, Hardenberg also had given an important mystical turn to his analyses of Fichte, where he argues the split between self and world—I and not-I—is more properly and productively seen as a relation between self and other—I and You. The *General Notebook* pulls all these strains of investigation together by stating that the universe speaks to us: 'Not only does man speak—the universe also speaks—everything speaks—infinite languages' (143). Nature addresses us as interlocutors in conversation, and we *translate* some of what it says into the various languages of science: biology, physics, mathematics, botany, etc. Because they are all translations of nature's speech, the various scientific languages correlate analogically or 'grammatically' with one other: the structures of nature, of the sciences, and of the mind are identical. 'What is nature?' asked Hardenberg the previous year, answering, 'An encyclopedic systematic index or plan of our mind' (II 582). Yet no encyclopedia can exhaustively describe the whole of nature or the law of its 'infinite languages'. Nature, a Romantic Absolute, only appears in the finite—but the finite too suggests the Absolute.

The *Novices of Sais* traces this move from science to mysticism in its opening words:

> Men go various paths. Whoever follows and compares them, will see wondrous figures arise; figures that seem to belong to the great cipher script that one glimpses everywhere, on wings and eggshells, in clouds and snow, in crystals and stone formations, on freezing water, on the inside and outside of mountains, plants, and men, in the lights of the heavens, on swept and striated sheets of pitch and glass, in iron splinters around a magnet, and in remarkable conjunctions of chance. In them, one feels a sense of the key to this wondrous script, of its very grammar; only this feeling will not adopt any fixed set form, and does not want to become any more elevated key. (I 79)

Nature surrenders neither the key nor grammar of its language. No other language can fully express or translate this language—it appears to us as signs we do not fully understand. This primeval, as it were 'natural', language, will not surrender itself to any master translation or narrative. Nothing can comprehend it, and it does not even comprehend itself:

> One does not understand this language, because it does not understand itself, it does not want to understand itself; authentic Sanskrit only speaks in order to speak, because speaking is its delight and essence. (I 79)

Incomprehensible even to itself, impossible to think (much less understand), Hardenberg's nature is both present (always here now) and absent (never fully revealed). It is constant and ever changing, understandable but incomprehensible, reassuring and mysterious. Romantic nature is natural and supernatural. The famous yearning

(*Sehn-sucht*, literally: yearning-seeking) of the Romantics, which Hardenberg decisively develops, is our *feeling* towards nature (and other forms of the Absolute). Romantic yearning is the *feeling* of nature's wholeness and the *seeking* of its key—but neither can ever appear. The whole remains beyond reach, even as we are part of it; and its over-arching system remains formless, even as our knowledge conforms to it. We yearn for what is present, but cannot be grasped; we yearn for what we already have, but cannot 'have'. (Hardenberg illustrates this prettily in the fairy-tale of *Hyacinth and Roseblossom*, in *Sais*'s second part; and his one-page *Monologue*, written just before it, expounds the ironies of speaking a language that doesn't understand itself.)

Hardenberg left the Mining Academy in May 1799 and returned to Weißenfels to work with his father. Alongside his professional duties and constant notebooks, Hardenberg produced three works in the coming year that are generally considered religious and mystical: seven short hymns for a projected church *Songbook*; an essay titled *Europa* about the lost Christian unity of the Middle Ages; and his *Hymns to the Night*. *Pollen* had already made it clear that Hardenberg had few pieties, and while all three writings *work in the genre* of the religious text, they turn it sharply towards Hardenberg's own agendas. At the time, Hardenberg noted, 'The artist is thoroughly irreligious—he can therefore work in religion as in bronze', adding too that religion's importance for the spiritual life was as an 'hors d'oeuvre' (III 488). Such convictions do not lead to the writing of religious texts in the conventional sense of the word.

The *Songbook* and *Europa* recall Hardenberg's perverse sense of humour in publishing *Faith and Love* under the King's nose. The *Songs* and *Europa* attempt similar projects. The *Songs* are ready-to-use church hymns that aim to put Romantic religion on the lips of unsuspecting church-goers. *Europa* praises the Catholic Middle Ages and hopes for their 'return' in order to mock both reactionaries and what we would term progressives. Like *Faith and Love*, however, each also presents a serious programme while playing a hoax on its audience.

The *Songs*, while posing as traditionally Christian, serve Hardenberg as a vehicle for the dissemination of Romantic religion. They seamlessly weave together stock Christian imagery (the Crucifixion, Resurrection, Eucharist, etc.) with Hardenberg's own experience and understanding of divine mediation (through Sophie). Christian tropology is invoked and undermined, for the use of Sophie as divine mediatrix contradicts (or more exactly: tries to move beyond) Christianity's doctrine of a unique mediator and incarnation. The *Songs* cannot, of course, mention Sophie by name, and they repeatedly use ambiguities, double entendres, suggestive images, and deeply personal references to invoke her as the equivalent of Christ (Himself hardly named). In short, they aim to get Romantic religion into the church by sneaking it in. Although Hardenberg did not live to see it, they were surprisingly successful. Hymnals began to include some *Songs* as early as 1803, and they were quite popular.

Europa is as extravagant as the *Songs* discreet. It is Hardenberg's most outrageous work, provoked by dramatic political changes and by intellectual disagreement within the Jena Circle. Politically, like all his generation, Hardenberg came of age in wartime. While Prussia sided against France from 1792 to 1797, Hardenberg grew from 20 to 25.

When the Second War of Coalition broke out in March 1799, it ended what now suddenly seemed like fifteen months of mere respite, and it opened the prospect of more wars to come (as they did). Partly in response to this change, the following summer Schleiermacher published his speeches *On Religion*, which argued that progress could only come through more enlightenment of the public and of religion. Hardenberg immediately penned a response.

In *Pollen* Hardenberg made it clear that the clock of history could not be moved back to before the Revolution—which was exactly what the Coalition sought to do. Hardenberg also insisted that, while the Revolution opened a new era, politics and religion still nevertheless depended upon manipulations of the masses. *Europa* was Hardenberg's response to the reactionaries of contemporary politics (supporters of the war) and to believers in progress through more Enlightenment (Schleiermacher). To mock those who would cling to the vanishing Holy Roman Empire, *Europa* waxes ridiculously effusive in praise of the Catholic Middle Ages (along with the Inquisition, the Papacy, etc.) and calls for their return. To mock Schleiermacher, it rages against the Reformation, Luther, Protestantism, and the Enlightenment itself.

Europa's diatribes were utterly alien to the rest of Hardenberg's thinking, but no one in the Jena Circle seems to have caught the joke. Hardenberg even read *Europa* and the *Songs* aloud to it the week after Napoleon's coup d'état of the Eighteenth Brumaire. Squabbles soon broke out about publishing the essay: Friedrich Schlegel wanted to publish it, August disagreed, and everyone had an opinion. Eventually the Schlegels asked Goethe to decide the issue for them, and the manuscript was shelved. The little controversy suggests early rifts in the Circle (which dissolved soon after Hardenberg's death), and its growing distance from Hardenberg (who remained completely detached from its deliberations).

More boisterous than *Faith and Love* in political parody, *Europa* is quieter in voicing its programme. The essay maintains a thread of argument tracing Europe's progressive loss of what it calls 'the holy sense'—sense for the sacred. Hardenberg's serious criticism of the Enlightenment is that it ossified into 'a religion' of unbelief. Of course for Hardenberg, this 'loss' of 'the holy sense' is not primarily a historical issue (the essay opens like a fairy-tale: 'Once there were beautiful, glorious times') but a personal one. After the disappointing relapse into war, Hardenberg urges his readers not to historical action, but to a study of history 'with the magic wand of analogy'(III 518). The real fight in Europe is one for peace and sanity: 'Blood will stream over Europe until nations become aware of their terrible insanity'. Cloaked in outlandish calls for a return to Christianity—when the essay repeatedly states that Christianity is long dead—*Europa* urges its readers to abandon political strife for the peace of 'a new, higher religious life'(II 518–19).

This turn inwards, here given new weight by Hardenberg, was nothing new in his writing. *Pollen* famously states, 'Inside goes the mysterious path. Within us, or nowhere, is Eternity with its worlds—the Past and Future' (16). In late 1799, when Hardenberg advises his readers to turn inward and away from the war against with France, his gesture is not that of an escapist reactionary. On the contrary: it expresses Hardenberg's disgust with incipient Reaction.

At year's end Hardenberg produced the *Hymns to the Night*. A centrepiece of European Romanticism, it is generally taken as Hardenberg's masterpiece (along with *Heinrich von Afterdingen*, which remains fragmentary). Whereas the *Songs* seek to infiltrate churches with Romantic religion, the *Hymns* clearly lay out its programme, heavily camouflaged by the Christian imagery dominating its closing sections. The *Hymns* are a *tour de force* in the interweaving of poetry, prose, philosophy, mysticism, and religion. The *Hymns* bring all of Hardenberg's resources to bear on the project: his writings about Sophie, his facility in philosophy, his readings in mysticism, his theory of religious mediation, his skill in prose and verse, and now, his awareness of his impending death.

The formal invention of the *Hymns* strikes, as usual with Hardenberg, at first glance. The opening words of *Hymns to the Night* are prose to the day:

> What living, sensual creature does not love, above all the wondrous appearances in the spread-out space around him, the all-gladdening light—with its colors, its beams and rays, its mild omnipresence as waking day? As life's innermost soul it is breathed by the restless, gigantic world of the celestial bodies, swimming and dancing in its blue tide—breathed by the glittering, ever-motionless rock, the sensing, sucking plant, and the wild, burning, multiform animal—and above all, by the splendid stranger with eyes full of sense, a hovering gait, and tenderly closed lips, rich in tones.

The prominent prose in the *Hymns*, changed from free verse just before printing, make it an early, extended experiment in prose poetry, prose that even strikes a claim to be hymnic. The ever-rhyming verse in the *Hymns* is unconventional as well, for Hardenberg uses relatively short lines for the hymnic genre (especially in the German tradition), with only two, three, and (once) four stresses per line. Counting pages, a reader must get almost to the mid-point of the text to encounter any verse at all, and the *Hymns* as a whole, with its pages breaking evenly between prose and verse, is thus written mostly in prose.

The six *Hymns* logically develop a meditation on the Night, on death, and the Absolute. The first four are dominated by the first person, an 'I' both lyrical and philosophical. This 'I' progressively to come to grips with death and the Absolute, both figured as Night. The fifth *Hymn* expounds a history of religion from classical antiquity through Christianity, the latter understood as a revelation of personal resurrection back into a mundane life filled with a sense for the Absolute. It also presents Jesus as the first in a series of henceforth (chosen) human mediators. The sixth *Hymn*, 'Yearning for Death', celebrates death not only (and conventionally) as a promised rest from the travails of life, but as a reunion with the Absolute. The *Hymns* push back against their Christian tropes by repeatedly alluding to the Night as impossible to represent, unspeakable and unsayable (*unaussprechlich* and *unsagbar*). The *Hymns* 'represent' the Absolute by systematically elaborating, in phrase and image, its unpresentability.

Hardenberg's last work is the unfinished novel, *Heinrich von Afterdingen*. This name (perhaps serendipitously a near-anagram of his own) was invariably used by Hardenberg, who had taken it from among his readings about the old masters (*Meister*) of the medieval poetic form, *Minnesang*. Hardenberg devoted the last year and a half of his productive life to the novel, from spring 1799 to early 1801, just months before his death on 25 March.

Set in the late Middle Ages, the novel follows the experiences of its eponymous 20-year-old protagonist, who is destined to become a poet. Hardenberg conceived the novel as a reply to Goethe's *Wilhelm Meister's Apprenticeship*, which Hardenberg, like his fellow Romantics, initially revered and studied. Later, Hardenberg became disenchanted with it, calling it 'pretentious and precious', a '*Candide* against Poesy', and (more *ad-hominem*) Goethe's 'pilgrimage to the patent of nobility' (III 646). Hardenberg saw Goethe's work as that of a bourgeois social-climber accommodating himself to a reactionary old regime. Hardenberg claimed that he would write 'The apprenticeship of a *nation*' (IV 281) and, most significantly, what he called 'my *political novel*' (III 652). His would be a different, decidedly Romantic kind of *Bildungsroman*. No tale of accommodation, *Heinrich von Afterdingen* is a novel of poetic and political education—not reactionary, but *post-revolutionary* with a vengeance.

The education of Heinrich proceeds, as it were, through detours—mostly stories told to him by the characters he meets. There is barely any plot: in the ten chapters of Part I, *Expectation*, the only external developments are Heinrich's carriage ride with his mother to Augsburg and their reception there; in the fragmentary Part 2, *Fulfilment*, Heinrich briefly appears as a pilgrim in mourning. The real action is in the stories and conversations: the first chapter describes a dream within a dream, where Heinrich glimpses the 'blue flower' (later used as a synecdoche for all of German Romanticism); the second and third chapters relate two stories told by merchants; in the fourth Heinrich hears drunken, brutish crusaders sing of their wars, and he listens to the sad story of Zulima, their sweet captive; in the fifth chapter Heinrich stumbles upon a book about what appears to be his own life, as if Heinrich von Afterdingen were reading the novel, *Heinrich von Afterdingen*; the seventh and eighth chapters relate discussions about poetry; and the final chapter narrates an extended allegorical fairy-tale of universal renewal.

The heart of Hardenberg's 'political novel' are the stories of the travelling merchants, especially their fairy-tale about Atlantis. The plot is simple: the only daughter of the widowed king gets lost in the woods, meets and secretly weds the naturalist's son, and two eventually return to the king with their new baby. After the boy sings three songs to the king and crowd, everyone hails the child as heir. Within this frame, Hardenberg extends his thinking about the state as theatre, taking aim at the fundamental issue of legitimacy and relating it to mass psychology. Through the elaborate allegory woven around a fairy-tale plot (as in chapter 9, 'Klingsohr's Fairy Tale'), Hardenberg strikes at the heart of political theory since Plato (for whom Atlantis was the arch-enemy of the *Republic*). He presents the legitimacy of the state as a fiction spun by poets and foisted upon the mass (and unwitting king). For Hardenberg, the poets are surely 'unacknowledged legislators of the world', as Shelley would have it; and still more, they are the makers of the legitimacy that grounds legislation, that grounds the very existence of the state. In *Heinrich von Afterdingen*, legitimacy is a product of the poets' manipulation of spectacle, convention, sign. It is a fiction that becomes a working fiction, a fiction actualized and institutionalized in the reality of the state. Hardenberg's tale is no escape from political realities, as some claim of the Romantics, but a lesson in how political reality is made. Fiction makes the real, or, as Hardenberg noted at the time, *not* sentimentally: 'The more poetic, the more true' (III 647). In politics, as in all else, this is the final word in Hardenberg's Romanticism.

Further Reading

Novalis, *The Novices of Sais*, tr. Ralph Manheim (New York: Curt Valentin, 1947).

Novalis, *Henry von Ofterdingen*, tr. Palmer Hilty (New York: Frederick Unger, 1964).

Novalis, *Novalis Schriften*, 3rd edn, ed Paul Kluckhohn, Richard Samuel, and Hans-Joachim Mähl (Stuttgart: Kohlhammer, 1964–).

Novalis, *Hymns to the Night*, 2nd edn, tr. Dick Higgins (New Paltz, NY: McPherson & Co., 1984).

Novalis, *Philosophical Writings*, tr. and ed. Margaret Mahony Stoljar (Albany, NY: State University of New York Press, 1997); includes *Pollen* (manuscript version), *Faith and Love, Europa*, etc.

Novalis, *Fichte Studies*, tr. Jane Kneller (Cambridge: Cambridge University Press, 2003).

Novalis, *The Birth of Novalis. Friedrich von Hardenberg's Journal of 1797, with Selected Letters and Documents*, tr. and ed. Bruce Donehower (Albany, NY: State University of New York Press, 2007).

Novalis, *Notes for a Romantic Encyclopaedia: Das Allgemeine Brouillon*, tr. David W. Wood (Albany, NY: State University of New York Press, 2007).

CHAPTER 12

JENA 1789–1819

Ideas, Poetry, and Politics

MAIKE OERGEL

THOSE familiar with German Romanticism, will be familiar with Jena. Literary criticism has named a whole branch of the multifarious Romantic movement after this town in Thuringia—the *Jenaer Romantik*. According to this narrative, which favours geographical markers, Jena Romanticism was followed by the *Heidelberger Romantik*, although many of Jena's key players decamped to Berlin after—or even during—'Jena', so a case could be made for a Berlin phase, too. For those who prefer organic-historicist terminology, the Jena phase is otherwise known as *Frühromantik*, followed by *Hoch*- and then *Spätromantik*. Later nineteenth- and early twentieth-century criticism set Jena up as the counterpart to neighbouring Weimar, the home of German classicism, for which there is also a choice of programmatic names: initially called *Deutsche Klassik*, it is now generally referred to as *Weimarer Klassik*, or Weimar Classicism.[1] According to this—bipolar—narrative, *Romantik* was born in Jena, whereas *Klassik* happened in Weimar, at the same time. This astonishing simultaneity was considered singular in modern (West) European intellectual history: in both France and Britain, those models of early twentieth-century developmental normality, Romanticism neatly *follows* classicism. This simultaneity was proof to those critics imbued with the spirit of modern intellectual nation-building that the *German Geist* was special, strong, and destined for greatness.[2] The double-edged nature of the *Sonderweg* trajectory, i.e. exhibiting signs of singularity

[1] Cf. e.g. Fritz Strich, *Deutsche Klassik und Romantik oder Vollendung und Unendlichkeit* (1922) and Dieter Borchmeyer, *Weimarer Klassik: Portrait einer Epoche* (1994).

[2] This is evident in the almost talismanic invocation of the notion of 'deutscher Geist', and the 'deutsche Bewegung', that dominate the accounts of *Geistesgeschichte* (intellectual history), this speciality of German historiography. Cf. Rudolf Haym's *Romantische Schule* (1870), which he subtitled 'contribution ... to the history of the German spirit', a point he reiterates in his introduction (*Die romantische Schule: Ein Beitrag zur Geschiche des deutschen Geistes*, facsimile repr. (Hildesheim: Ohlms, 1961)); or, two generations later, Paul Kluckhohn's *Ideengut der deutschen Romantik* (1941), who identifies his subject as 'Teil der deutschen Bewegung', 4th edn (Tübingen: Niemeyer, 1961), 7). 'German movement' was the title given to Herman Nohl's posthumously published collection of essays and

and greatness (which Peter Watson's *The German Genius*[3] has recently reiterated), but actually heading for doom, *Untergang*, as the Germans tended to refer to the events leading up to 1945 and by implication the Nazi dictatorship, is evident and well known.[4] After the 'German catastrophe' of the 1940s, as the long-lived German historian Friedrich Meinecke called it,[5] who began his academic career in Wilhelmine Germany and still saw the creation of the two post-war German states, the split nature of the Jena-Weimar complex offered different ways of dealing with the past. One could prioritize the classical heritage, because classicism was considered to have strong links to Enlightenment thinking, with its priority of rationality and reason. This approach was frequently taken in the 1950s and early 1960s, when Enlightenment thinking, once the natural property of Britain and France, was reclaimed for German thought.[6] Or, one could focus on the politically revolutionary rather than the mystically folkish Romantic heritage as a trajectory for the socialist state of workers and peasants, which GDR criticism tended to do, celebrating as political heroes anti-feudal nationalists such as Ernst Moritz

lectures on this topic, *Die deutsche Bewegung: Vorlesungen und Aufsätze zur Geistesgeschichte von 1770–1830*, ed. Otto Friedrich Bollnow and Frithjof Rodi (Göttingen: Vandenhoeck & Ruprecht, 1970). Nohl had trained with the (intellectual) historian Wilhelm Dilthey, whose monumental 'Studien zur Geschichte des deutschen Geistes' was never fully realized; its completed parts appeared as *Von deutscher Dichtung und Musik: Aus den Studien zur Geschichte des deutschen Geistes* in 1933 (cf. Dilthey, *Schiller* (Göttingen: Vandenhoeck & Ruprecht, n.d.), 4). For these scholars the 'German spirit' was as evident in literary achievements as in intellectual ones: for the historian Friedrich Meinecke the concept of historicism is the application of the new existential principles that the 'große deutsche Bewegung' produced and in which 'deutscher Geist' revealed its singular brilliance; cf. Meinecke, *Die Entstehung des Historismus*, 1st publ. 1936, ed. Carl Hinrichs (Munich: Oldenburg Verlag, 1959 = *Werke*, iii. 2).

[3] Peter Watson, *The German Genius: Europe's Third Renaissance, the Second Scientific Revolution and the Twentieth Century* (London: Simon & Schuster, 2010).

[4] The origins of the negative interpretation of the German *Sonderweg* tend to be related to the Fischer-controversy in the 1960s, when Fritz Fischer in *Griff nach der Weltmacht: Die Kriegszielpolitik des kaiserlichen Deutschlands 1914–1918* (1961) put forward the thesis that many of Hitler's policies originated in pre-1914 German power-political thinking and that the Third Reich was a likely conclusion to developments beginning during the Second Reich. The idea that there is a continuity in German thinking from early modern German history to the NS dictatorship, i.e. a direct descent from Luther to Hitler, or at least from Herder to Hitler, had already been put forward by American historians from Peter Viereck in 1941 (cf. his *Metapolitics: The Roots of the Nazi Mind)* onwards and persists to Daniel Goldhagen's *Hitler's Willing Executioners* (1995).

[5] Meinecke, *Die deutsche Katastrophe: Betrachtungen und Erinnerungen* (Zurich: Aero-Verlag, 1946).

[6] Although this is by no means a new approach: the lively *Romantik*-debate of the first half of the twentieth century had a strong *Klassik* party, which tended to denigrate, even demonize *Romantik*. Cf. Ernst Behler, *German Romantic Literary Theory* (Cambridge: Cambridge University Press, 1993), 32–3; or earlier, Kluckhohn, *Ideengut der deutschen Romantik*, 7–8. An interesting example of 1950s criticism is the 'all-German' volume *Schiller. Reden im Gedenkjahr 1955*, a collection of lectures and essays occasioned by the 150th anniversary of Schiller's death, whose table of contents boasts a roll call of eminent Goethezeit experts from *both* fledgling German states and which styles the 'deutscher Klassiker' as a 'Nothelfer' (p. 8), then as now, who showed his 'Zeitgenossen ein Idealbild künftiger Wirklichkeit ..., in der sich einst der geistesmächtige, vernunftsstarke, sinnenfrohe Mensch in seiner Freiheit und Schönheit darleben wird, in der die Menschheit endlich vermenschlicht, der Mensch wahrhaft Mensch geworden sein wird—ein Bild in dem wir das Vermächtnis Schillers wie der deutschen Klassik erblicken dürfen.' Joachim Müller, 'Bürgerfreiheit, Nationalbewuβtsein und Menschenwürde im Werk Friedrich Schillers', in *Schiller. Reden im Gedenkjahr 1955*, ed. by Deutsche Schillergesellschaft (Stuttgart: Klett, 1955), 235–6.

Arndt,[7] who in early West German criticism tended to be seen as a rather suspect nationalist.[8] On the whole GDR criticism, however, focused on Klassik as the 'good' legacy of German *Geist*.[9] Or, in a more recent trend, one could view the intensity of intellectual and artistic activity focused on Jena and Weimar between the late 1780s and the years following the Congress of Vienna as a more integrated phenomenon, that is to say, integrated not just in mutually complementary terms.[10] This approach eventually culminated in the programmatically named and publicly funded research cluster *Event Weimar-Jena*, which concluded in 2010.[11] It has now also become common in literary and intellectual criticism, especially that issuing from the *Ereignis Weimar-Jena* research group, to refer to Jena and Weimar as a *Doppelstadt*.[12] In many respects, Jena always remained the junior partner in this union: Weimar was the residence, not so much of Grand Duke Karl August, but of Goethe, and eventually also of Schiller. These two together outshone everything else, and together they have been taken to represent Weimar Classicism, as the 1857 *Goethe und Schiller-Denkmal*, the monumental double statue of the two friends on the Theaterplatz in Weimar clearly suggests. While this is all reception history, which tells us little about Jena around 1800, it is indispensible to approach what one might find there

[7] Cf. the catalogue of the exhibition to mark the bicentenary of Arndt's birth in 1969 put on by the Ernst-Mortiz-Arndt-University at Greifswald. Manfred Herling and Horst-Dieter Schröder (eds), *Ernst Moritz Arndt 1769–1969: Ausstellungskatalog der Ernst-Moritz-Arndt Universität Greifswald zum 200. Geburtstag von Ernst Moritz Arndt* (Greifswald: Ernst-Moritz-Arndt-Universität, 1969). This closely associates Arndt with the developments that prepare, from the wars of liberation via the *Vormärz*, the Labour movement and the GDR, 'our socialist state of German nation', p. 4. Cf. also later in this chapter the GDR research into the early Burschenschaften movement.

[8] Cf. Walter Erhard and Arne Koch (eds), *Ernst Moritz Arndt (1769–1860): Deutscher Nationalismus, Europa, Transnationale Perspectiven* (Tübingen: Niemeyer, 2007), 1–14.

[9] Cf. Karl Robert Mandelkow, 'Deutsche Literatur zwischen Klassik und Romantik aus rezeptionsgeschichtlicher Sicht', *Europäische Romantik I = Neues Handbuch der Literaturwissenschaft*, xiv (Wiesbaden: Athenaion, 1982), 1–26.

[10] Already Strich looked at *Klassik* and *Romantik* in conjunction, as did Hans August Korff in his 4-vol. *Geist der Goethezeit* (1923–57), which explicitly set itself the task to make visible the interrelatedness of the different 'phases'. But both studies see the two 'movements' as essentially distinct entities, a tradition that still informs Gert Ueding's 'social history' of *Klassik und Romantik: Deutsche Literatur im Zeitalter der Französischen Revolution 1789–1815* (Munich and Vienna: Hanser, 1987), cf. 65–135. Mandelkow, on the other hand, provides, by producing a reception history of appropriations of *Klassik* and *Romantik*, a platform from which the *Goethezeit* might be viewed as marked by common features and concerns, to which its contemporaries may have reacted differently, a circumstance that in turn made the dichotomy possible and ready to be utilized, cf. Mandelkow, 'Deutsche Literatur zwischen Klassik und Romantik'.

[11] The Deutsche Forschungsgemeinschaft (German Research Foundation/DFG), the main public funder of academic research in Germany, funded *Ereignis Weimar-Jena: Kultur um 1800* (SFB 482) as one of its *DFG-Sonderforschungsbereiche*, <http://www2.uni-jena.de/ereignis/index.html>, accessed May 2014.

[12] The term features prominently on the homepage of SFB 482 and is frequently used in the publications associated with the research cluster (vicariously cf. Gerhard Müller, Klaus Ries, and Paul Ziche (eds), *Die Universität Jena: Tradition und Innovation um 1800* (Stuttgart: Steiner, 2001), Einleitung, p. 12). But it predates this project: already in 1995 a volume on Jena's history (Jürgen John and Volker Wahl (eds), *Zwischen Konvention und Avantgarde: Bausteine zu Jenas Stadtgeschichte* (Cologne: Böhlau, 1995)) uses this term in its subtitle, albeit reversed: *Doppelstadt Jena-Weimar*. It clearly has considerable kudos: it features on the homepage of the Weimar Jena Akademie, an association (*Zusammenschluss*) of local education providers founded in 2004, cf. <www.weimar-jena-akademie.de>, accessed May 2014.

through the lens of posterity in order to get a sense of the ideological battleground these two places represent, and of the shifting lines between them.

None of the thinkers and poets who made Jena one of the key centres of European Romanticism hailed from this town, or even the region. What was this place like, to which they came? Today's Jena is a town in the Freistaat Thüringen, one of the smaller states in the Federal Republic, whose territory was, from the late Middle Ages to the nineteenth century, part of the German principality of Saxony. The name Thuringia, or Thüringen, recalls Dark Age central European history; it refers to the tribal fifth-century Thüringerreich, whose territory later and relatively briefly formed a medieval feudal fief, before the name came to designate a region within Saxony. The name was picked up again for a more independent entity after the First World War when the fairly federal German Reich was restructured into the federal Weimar Republic. Thuringia continues its federal independence today, a history it shares with most other German *Bundesländer*. In its Saxon days Jena belonged to the Eastern, or Ernestine,[13] duchies of a principality that was gradually becoming more and more subdivided due to complex inheritance rights. This potentially overdetailed, and possibly even tedious, account of historical geography serves to illustrate the typicalness of Jena's history within the German lands, and of its position within German history. Imperial frameworks and borders change, but the town, and its geo-cultural region, do not necessarily change correspondingly. Jena has its own distinct history that is again rather typical, exemplifying key European socio-historical and cultural developments: the twin rise of the middle classes and formal secular education. Jena blossomed as a late-medieval town, with a rich, confident, corporately oriented cast of burghers, many of them wine merchants selling the fermented produce of the Thuringian slopes. From the early modern period the town came to be defined by the presence of its large and influential university. Jena University was founded in 1558 by the Saxon Prince-Elector Johann Friedrich the Magnanimous. Although it remained at least nominally in the hands of the aristocracy—its *Nutritoren* were four independent Saxon courts—the very fact that its overlords were so split up reduced their power to interfere in university matters and allowed a fairly independent running of the institution. The University of Jena lies 'geo-academically' in the heartland of late medieval–early modern *Wissenschaft*, a sort of 'golden academic square' in central Germany, not to say central Europe. Within roughly 50 square miles we find the universities of Erfurt (founded 1389/92), Leipzig (1409), and Wittenberg (1502), which were joined by Halle in 1694. Both Erfurt and Leipzig are part of the rush into secularized science and academic enquiry towards the end of the fourteenth century north of the Alps, which also saw the foundations of Cologne, Prag, Heidelberg, and many of the older colleges in Oxford and Cambridge (although in England, as in Paris, the university foundations date back to the thirteenth century). The foundations of Wittenberg and Jena fall in the sixteenth century, when the Reformation accelerates the disappearance of the medieval world and modern paradigms and conditions arise. Both Erfurt and Leipzig had excellent reputations in central Europe during the early modern period, and Wittenberg is of course one of the iconic places of the German Reformation,

[13] Named after the founding ancestor of the Eastern line of the ruling house of Wettin, Ernst.

where Martin Luther—while being a professor at the newly established academic institution in this town—nailed his theses to the local church door.

Protestantism was crucial to the development of intellectual life in Jena and for the outlook its university developed. In this respect Jena's affiliation with Saxony was critically important: Saxony is one of the cradles of European Protestantism. Its early sixteenth-century Prince-Elector was sympathetic to church reform and wary of (Catholic) imperial dominance, so he supported his subject Martin Luther in his reformatory efforts, rescued and sheltered him from the imperial ban, effectively a death sentence, on the Wartburg, which is situated a stone's throw from Jena, where Luther famously produced the first authoritative Bible in German. Saxony remained a stronghold of central European Lutheran Protestantism for centuries. Modern intellectual historians have, from the inception of the discipline in the eighteenth century, shown how Protestantism has driven European thought towards scientification, secularization, and individualism; and the special role the Reformation's intellectual trajectory played in the German contribution to modern European thought through the works of Herder, Kant, Goethe and Schiller, Fichte, Hegel, and Marx has been much rehearsed. Protestantism, in its reformatory and radical forms, lies at the heart of Jena intellectual life. The university at Jena was not only a Protestant foundation, but also the site of much intra-Protestant dispute. Intellectual ground-breaking, radicalism even, was a local tradition. By the early eighteenth century it had grown, in terms of student numbers, into the largest university in the German territories.[14]

However, at first sight, little of the above seems to be related to Romanticism, of German or Jena description. And indeed at the time the crucial people, from Schiller and Fichte to the Schlegel brothers, begin to arrive in Jena, at the university, the latter had been in serious decline for well over a generation. Contemporary observers, if they were versed in local history, might have predicted a fate similar to that of the neighbouring institution at Erfurt, which after dominating higher learning far beyond the region of central Germany from the fifteenth to the seventeenth century, had—in modern terms—entirely lost its global ranking. But exactly the opposite occurred: Jena University became the birthplace of post-Kantian German philosophy, German Idealism, and gave its name to *that* first phase of German Romanticism which is often considered the most exciting. So Jena, largely through the personnel who gathered at the university and who brought their friends and partners with them, came to host a closely interacting, densely concentrated social and intellectual milieu of exceptional dynamism; an intensity, dynamism, and concentration, one might add, that is more typical of large capital cities. In hindsight the cast is truly stellar: between 1789 and 1807, the years between Schiller's arrival and Hegel's departure, Fichte, Friedrich and August Wilhelm Schlegel, Schelling, Novalis, Hölderlin, Schleiermacher, Wilhelm von Humboldt, Brentano, and Tieck were all spending time in Jena, and nearly half of these held chairs at the university. In terms of fame, the stellar nature of this list may not have been quite so evident in the early 1790s: although none of them lacked a sense of their own brilliance, only Schiller was a household name, Fichte was just 'breaking' and August Wilhelm

[14] Cf. Ulrich Rasche, 'Umbrüche—Zur Frequenz der Universität Jena im ausgehenden 18. und frühen 19. Jahrhundert', in Müller et al., *Die Universität Jena*, 79–134 (97).

Schlegel an exciting newcomer, while his younger brother Friedrich was to achieve fame and notoriety overnight in 1796.[15] The others, with the only exception of Schelling, achieved renown mainly *after* the heyday that will be described here. However, all of them *remained* famous, i.e. they are still household names now, which is testimony to the significance of what they came up with. The heyday is brief, only slightly more than a decade. Hegel was the last to leave by a long shot, most of the aforementioned had gone by the time Novalis died in 1801. Only Hegel actually experienced in situ the collapse of Prussia, the capitulation of 'Germany'—still only a construct in people's heads—to Napoleon after the nearby Battle of Jena (and Auerstedt) in 1806. Fichte (was made to) depart in 1799; Schiller made the move to Weimar in the same year; the Schlegels and Brentano were gone by the end of 1801, while Tieck had already moved on in 1800; Schelling left in 1803.

With its twin focus on philosophy and literary culture, this gathering indeed appears to be some kind of apogee of the modern German *Geist*, which Hans August Korff defined in early twentieth-century tradition along hero-worshipping lines as *Geist der Goethezeit*, which Herman Nohl called, along national lines, *Deutsche Bewegung*, and which had throughout the later nineteenth and the early twentieth century been taken as the basis for the definition of modern German identity. To this link between aesthetic and philosophical enquiries one needs to add a new methodology: practised by all is the newly dominant historical perspective, which Meinecke, a contemporary of Korff's and Nohl's, defined as the *Entstehung des Historismus*.[16] The historically oriented aspects of Hegel's and Schelling's philosophies, along with Schiller's and the Schlegels' aesthetic and intellectual histories, represent one of the fonts of German historicism and the historical school from Leopold von Ranke to Meinecke himself (although Meinecke preferred to define a descent from Herder and Goethe, both residents of Weimar). Those three, German philosophy, historicism, and literature energized nineteenth-century European intellectual life far beyond German-speaking lands.

Energized intellectual life in what way? Through what? Their key concerns were time and meaning. These issues were being grappled with across Europe, are quintessentially *Romantic*, but they seemed to come into particularly sharp focus in the minds of the people just listed. This occurred against the familiar background of the acute crisis that precipitated the paradigm shifts of what Reinhard Koselleck has defined as the *Sattelzeit* of epochal change around 1800.[17] Contemporaries were keenly aware of the interlinking web of different crises. Intellectually reason was in crisis: the founding principle of Enlightenment was increasingly being seen as itself unfounded. Fichte's *Wissenschaftslehre* (1st edition 1794), in many respects the foundational text of the transcendental philosophy of post-Kantian

[15] With his essay on the 'Studium der griechischen Poesie' (On the Study of Greek Poetry), which was published in preliminary excerpts in 1796 in J. H. Reichardt's journal *Deutschland*. The journal was closed down the following year due to its Revolution-friendly tendencies, only to be replaced by Reichardt's new effort *Lyceum der schönen Künste*. Friedrich Schlegel featured prominently in both. It was publications in *Deutschland* that sparked the Schlegels' famous spat with Schiller (and Goethe), who proceeded to retaliate with their *Xenien*. Cf. Behler, *German Romantic Literary Theory*, 38–40.

[16] Cf. n. 2.

[17] Reinhart Koselleck: *Einleitung*, in Otto Brunner, Werner Conze, and Reinhart Koselleck (eds), *Geschichtliche Grundbegriffe*, i (Stuttgart: Klett Cotta, 1979), p. xv.

German Idealism, aims at bridging the gap that had opened up in Kant's split epistemology of the world as the human mind sees it and the world as it is.[18] Kant's *Critique of Pure Reason*, a text that concludes and explodes the omnipotent primacy of reason, sums up the growing contemporary uncertainty: how can we know that reason is infallible, and hence the font of knowledge and truth, i.e. meaning, and how can we prove that reason exists in the way we define it? Fichte's answer to the separation of the human understanding of the world and the world in itself was to propose that the two would gradually come to overlap in the thinking individual's consciousness: meaning would reveal itself over time as cognition. Fichte's process is not historical in any primary sense, but his description of a consequential development over time is a form of historical narrative. Fichte was primarily interested in the workings of the mind and consciousness of the thinking individual: the ego, or I, will gradually come to understand the world (the not-I) more and more fully and advance toward the absolute ego, the full overlapping. While Kant's own answer in his *Critique of Judgement* (*Urteilskraft*) was already triadic, only in Fichte does this process become dialectical: the I encounters the world as antithesis in order to engage with it in productive synthesis. The dialectical process will be the basis for much historical, political, and critical theory to come.

Politically order was in crisis: the Revolution in France was demonstrating that social and religious order could be reconfigured, even if it did not show conclusively how to do this or what the reconfiguration should look like. Politics was always present in Jena, and not unexpectedly so: it was impossible *not* to deal with the Revolution, which changed the late eighteenth-century world irrevocably, rather like 9/11 changed ours. Fichte was an extremely politically minded person. A staunch supporter of the early phase of the Revolution, he never lost his belief that philosophy must inform politics and that working towards the establishment of reason in freedom within the political framework of a state was not just the obligation of the scholar and philosopher, but achievable. It was in Berlin, where he went after losing his job in Jena due to his radicalism (the famous *Atheismusstreit*), that he formulated his more historically based political theories, which envisaged general education as the basis for ensuring that citizens were politically and morally mature enough to cope with the liberties and responsibilities that political revolution would bring. Fichte's nationalist stance against Napoleon has, especially after 1945, seen him cast as a figure whose ideas have supported the far right. In his own time, however, he can only be considered as politically left-wing. Rather like Friedrich Schiller, who when he arrived in Jena in May 1789 was mainly known as the radical author of *The Robbers* and whose views were, in the eyes of social conservatives, nothing short of seditious: the man who as a poet felt he 'war keines Fürsten Untertan', was subject to no feudal prince. Like Fichte, Schiller felt part of a vanguard of modern citizens of a new political order. However, both, like many intellectuals who had initially welcomed the Revolution, had to deal with the escalating internal violence of the revolutionary republic: the bloodbath of the Terror prompted revisions of their earlier positions. Schiller's *Aesthetic Education*, which he wrote in Jena while Fichte was putting

[18] For a summary of the protracted genesis of the *Wissenschaftslehre*, of which the 1794 version is only a first stage, cf. Walter E. Wright's introduction in *The Science of Knowing: J. G. Fichte's 1804 Lectures on the Wissenschaftslehre*, tr. Walter E. Wright (Ithaca, NY: State University of New York, 2005).

together the first *Wissenschaftslehre*, diagnoses that the Revolution in France had had to fail because the people had not been ready, a view to which Fichte, and later Hegel, would subscribe to great effect. The philosophical dialectic of mind and world returns on the political level as the dialectic between freedom and necessity, between spiritual, intellectual, and moral aspirations on the one hand and physical needs and moral and power-political coercion on the other. Fichte would present a similar picture when he discussed the failure of the French Revolution, at great personal risk, in occupied Berlin in his *Reden an die deutsche Nation*, the latter still an imagined community. But Fichte's and Schiller's paths towards the educational goals are different: while Fichte advocates more thinking, Schiller argues for more art and beauty, aesthetics. The disinterested—'un-needy'—experience of beauty will afford the learning human the training for full humanity and citizenship. It is important to note that neither Schiller nor Fichte ever repudiated the aims of the Revolution; they did forcefully criticize their not being reached, and the subversion of the revolutionary process by terror and tyranny. The Jena answer to the problem of how to achieve a successful revolution was, according to Schiller and Fichte, education, to equip the human being with the skills necessary to make a modern society work, where political responsibility could be shared by the citizens. This notion informs Wilhelm von Humboldt's concept of higher education which was—more or less—implemented in the foundation of the new (model) university at Berlin, whose first *Rektor* was Fichte, later followed by Hegel. Humboldt too had made his home in Jena between 1794 and 1797.

But if Schiller believed in the educational, not to say redemptive power of beauty, aesthetics was in crisis, too. The classical rule book, on which the different neoclassical concepts of beauty were based and which had informed (high) Enlightenment aesthetics, was gradually being torn up by a preference for the unbound, the irregular, the intense, and the homegrown: the rise of the Gothic (both architectural and literary), the ballad, the bardic, and Shakespeare. In the area of aesthetics the challenge to the rule of classical and rational order (they are slightly different things) goes back to the middle of the eighteenth century. It is the basis for all types of pre-Romanticism, whether in Britain (Richard Hurd, Thomas Percy, Thomas Gray, or Horace Walpole), France (Jean-Jacques Rousseau) or the German-language-based *Sturm und Drang*, of which Herder and the young Goethe, inspired by Johann Georg Hamann and the British pre-Romantics, were the first and the young Schiller the last exponent. In Jena it was August Wilhelm and Friedrich Schlegel who established Romantic aesthetics in the narrower sense, in the guise of a new literary theory, and a new concept of criticism, both triggered by a fresh look at literary and cultural *history*. The literary ideas of *Frühromantik* are highly theoretical and cerebral, in many respects a far cry from the unbound emotionalism and the glorification of the dark Other of reason that dominated the different aspects of the Gothic and the 'Ossianic'. This, however, cannot be surprising, permeated as they were with the ideas of Fichte's 1790s thinking. Their most significant *actual* output from this period is the journal *Athenäum* (1798–1800). The *Athenäum* experimented with form just as much as with content. Mixing (hundreds of) fragments with imagined discussions and essays, the journal sought to find ways of expressing the fragmentary, incomplete nature of knowledge and understanding, their dependence on perspective and context, and inherent diversity. With the *Athenäum* the Schlegels took up position against an established organ of literary criticism, the *Allgemeine Literatur-Zeitung*, also a Jena undertaking. The *ALZ*'s famous offices Am Engelsplatz, with its growing *Präsenzbibliothek* (they required reviewers to return all review copies to them!), were the gathering place of writers, critics, and academics. Here the idea of modern German literary and cultural criticism was taking shape.[19] Initially the Schlegels were frequent reviewers, as was Fichte.

For the Schlegels, knowledge, and the art which expressed it, was a process governed by time, subject not just to augmentation (*more* being known), but more importantly to qualitative change (things being known *differently*), which is why both Schlegels were so interested in history. To express this new understanding of knowledge adequately a new poetry was required: *their* Romantic art and poetry. It is important to note that this Romanticism represents no rejection of reason as such, but a revision of the capabilities of reason with the aim to transcend its limitations, a kind of qualitative augmentation of reason. Critique, criticism, and critical reflexion, all based on analytical reason, play a key part in the make-up of the 'progressive universal poetry'.

> Die romantische Poesie ist eine progressive Universalpoesie. Ihre Bestimmung ist nicht bloß, alle getrennte Gattungen der Poesie wieder zu vereinigen, und die Poesie mit Philosophie und Rhetorik in Berührung zu setzen. Sie will, und soll auch Poesie und Prosa, Genialität und Kritik, Kunstpoesie und Naturpoesie bald mischen, bald verschmelzen ..., und die Formen der Kunst mit gediegenem Bildungsstoff aller Art anfüllen und sättigen, und durch die Schwingungen des Humor beseelen.... Nur sie kann gleich dem Epos ein Spiegel der ganzen umgebenden Welt, ein Bild des Zeitalters werden. Und doch kann auch sie am meisten zwischen dem Dargestellten und dem Darstellenden, frei von allem realen und idealen Interesse auf den Flügeln der poetischen Reflexion in der Mitte schweben, diese Reflexion immer wieder potenzieren und wie in einer endlosen Reihe von Spiegeln vervielfachen. Sie ist der höchsten und allseitigsten Bildung fähig ... Die romantische Dichtart ist noch im Werden; ja das ist ihr eigentliches Wesen, daß sie ewig nur werden, nie vollendet sein kann.[20]

> Romantic poetry is a progressive, universal poetry, Its aim isn't merely to reunite all the separate species of poetry and put poetry in touch with philosophy and rhetoric. It tries to and should mix and fuse poetry and prose, inspiration and criticism, the poetry of art and the poetry of nature, ... and fill and saturate the forms of art with every kind of good, solid matter for instruction, and animate them vibrantly with humour ... Like the epic, it alone can become a mirror of the whole surrounding world, an image of the age. Best of all it can hover in the middle between the represented and what represents, free from all real and ideal interest on the wings of poetic

[19] Cf. Stefan Matuschek (ed.), *Die Organisation der Kritik: Die Allgemeine Literatur-Zeitung in Jena 1785–1803* (Heidelberg: Winter, 2004).

[20] Athenäum Fragment 116, *Kritische Friedrich Schlegel Ausgabe*, ii. *Charakteristiken und Kritiken I (1796–1801)*, ed. Hans Eichner (Munich: Schönigh, 1967), 182–3.

> reflection. It can raise that reflection again and again to a higher power and multiply it in an endless series of mirrors. It is capable of the highest and most rounded formation ... The Romantic kind of poetry is still in a state of becoming; indeed its real essence is eternally to be becoming, never perfectible.

This kind of art links reality and the ideal, as well as the aesthetic creation and its critique. The inherent heterogeneity of their concepts also finds expression in Friedrich Schlegel's twin focus on mythology and irony, each representing different approaches to knowledge, to knowing, and to the representation of knowledge in artistic form. (Romantic) irony opens up the gap between the known, or the representation, and its context, it is critical and questioning.[21] Mythology attempts to close the gap without denying heterogeneity: it is complex and simple at the same time.

Transcending the fragmentary and the momentary, without denying one's awareness of the potential impossibility of doing this, was a key aim of the Schlegels' inner circle, which included two other precocious and brilliant young men, the poet Novalis (Friedrich von Hardenberg) and the philosopher Friedrich Wilhelm Josef Schelling. The latter shared a house with both brothers and their partners for a few months, which resulted in August Wilhelm's wife Caroline falling in love with the young Schelling and her divorce from August Wilhelm. Novalis had actually been the first to arrive in Jena after Schiller, in 1790, to study law at the university. A keen admirer of Schiller's, he attended his lectures on history and struck up a friendship with his hero that lasted throughout the decade.[22] Novalis shares the preoccupation with the human telos, the historical vision of its eventual fulfilment in history. He also engages in both writing (mystical) poetry *and* an attempt at a comprehensive reordering of knowledge, which is his unfinished 'Allgemeine Brouillon'.[23] His life, and works, retain their fragmentary character due to his early death, but were doubtlessly also intended to be so (only to what extent we do not know) because he was in close discussions with the Schlegels about the progressive universal poetry in the late 1790s. Novalis shared the Romantic vision of poetry as the medium in which the present as well as the history and the aim of human striving could be expressed. His concept of poetry was enthusiastically redemptive and at the same time existential. The Schlegels published his fragments *Blütenstaub*

[21] Cf. M. Oergel, entries 'Romantic Irony' and 'Mythology' in Matthias Konzett (ed.), *Fitzroy Dearborn Encyclopaedia of German Literature* (Chicago: Fitzroy Dearborn, 2000).

[22] The student Novalis, aged 19, kept watch at Schiller's sickbed in Jan. 1791, when Schiller was first struck down with the illness that would eventually kill him; despite the break between Novalis's close friends, the Schlegels, and Schiller in 1797, Novalis retained his admiration for his hero. Cf. Rüdiger Safranski, *Schiller oder die Erfindung des deutschen Idealismus*, 1st publ. 2004 (Munich: Deutscher Taschenbuchverlag, 2007), 343 and 426.

[23] Novalis, *Notes for a Romantic Encyclopaedia: Das Allgemeine Brouillon*, tr. and ed. David W. Wood (Albany, NY: State University of New York, 2007). For a discussion of its epistemological importance, cf. Peter Krilles, 'Detours of Knowledge: Aspects of Novalis' Aesthetic Epistemology', in M. Oergel (ed.), *(Re-)Writing the Radical: Enlightenment, Revolution, and Cultural Transfer in 1790s Germany, Britain and France* (Berlin and New York: de Gruyter, 2012), 204–18.

and his mystically idealistic *Hymnen an die Nacht* in the *Athenäum*, as examples of the new poetry and the new way of grasping human reality.

Schelling visited Jena in 1796, to see Schiller, while he was engaged in his second programme of study at Leipzig, where he studied mathematics, natural sciences, and medicine, after already having completed a degree in theology at the Tübinger Stift in 1792, as had his friends Hölderlin and Hegel. His *Ideen zu einer Philosophie der Natur* of 1797, published while he was in Leipzig, brought Schelling to the attention of Goethe—who was at the time keenly interested in the natural sciences—and through Goethe a chair in philosophy at Jena in 1798. Schelling's initial *Naturphilosophie* here developed into the *System des Transzendentalen Idealismus*, which he published in 1800, aged 25, and which provides another answer to the Kantian problem. Schelling puts forward his identity philosophy, which is another history of consciousness and also the story of reason. But by including nature in his developmental system Schelling goes beyond the scope of Fichte before him or Hegel after him. Consciousness emerges from unconscious nature in order to finally return to it on a higher level. Schelling assumes an identity between nature and history, history being the conscious part of nature. This identity, however, is only postulated and remains obscure. It can only be glimpsed in art. This links his thinking to that of the Schlegels, and their theory of poetry, and will eventually earn him the intellectual disdain of his friend Hegel, who disliked this intellectually impenetrable notion of identity. Schelling would move on to elaborating the link between knowledge and art in his *Philosophie der Kunst* of 1802 before leaving Jena for a position at Würzburg in 1803.

Complexity had to be faced, embraced, and acknowledged. There were no easy answers, only the hope that the (historical) process could give. Not surprisingly all of them, the Schlegels, Novalis, and Schelling, engaged intensively with Fichte's *Wissenschaftslehre*, which set out a cognitive process that promised enlightenment and empowerment and provided a basis for independent and synthetic thinking as well as independent and responsible activity. During the time between Schelling's arrival in 1798 and Fichte's dismissal in 1799, Fichte was a frequent visitor in the Schlegel-Schelling residence, and after Fichte's departure Schelling stayed in touch with him until 1802. Friedrich Schlegel's intense relationship with Fichte the man is well known; his intellectual encounter with Fichte, and eventual critique of his work, resulted in lengthy discussions in his notebooks,[24] which he shared with Novalis.[25]

All of the 'Tübingen Three' (Schelling, Hegel, and Hölderlin) came to Jena. Hölderlin, the poet, was actually the first of the three friends to set foot in the town in 1794, to visit Schiller, but unlike the others he did not stay. In 1801 Schelling brought Hegel to the university where the latter stayed until 1807. They collaborated on the *Kritisches Journal*

[24] Cf. *Kritische Friedrich Schlegel Ausgabe*, xviii. *Philosophische Lehrjahre*, ed. Ernst Behler (Munich: Schönigh, 1963), 31–9.

[25] Behler, *German Romantic Literary Theory*, 189. Regarding Friedrich Schlegel's critique of Fichte's ideas, cf. Behler, pp. 189–91, and M. Oergel, *Culture and Identity* (Berlin and New York: de Gruyter, 2006), 85 n. 143.

der Philosophie (1802–3) until Schelling left for Würzburg University. Fichte, Schelling, and Hegel all started from their engagement with Kant and all shared a sense of the need for urgent work on the 'fate of reason' in a post-Kantian, and post-revolutionary world. But eventually they ended up agreeing on very little. This did not preclude them from each—one after the other—holding the same chair of philosophy at the University of Berlin.

Hegel wrote his first major work, *Die Phänomenologie des Geistes* (*The Phenomenology of Mind* or *Spirit*, depending on the translation) in Jena, after almost everybody else had gone; the work would—finally, compared to Schelling's swift rise—make him famous. Again grappling with closing the gap that Kant had ripped open between world and mind, unlike Fichte who had focused on the individual mind, and different from Schelling who had focused on the relationship between mind and nature, Hegel focused on the species as a whole, on how humanity, or human communities, develop their consciousness(es) throughout history. General consciousness, here as Reason itself, will actuate itself in the process of history, i.e. acquire increasing self-consciousness of itself. Unlike Kant, Hegel was convinced that world and mind were compatible, and that the latter *can* know the former by gradually acquiring a more accurate and inclusive understanding of it. This actuation is dynamic and productive, a perpetual becoming, a feature it shares with the progressive universal poetry, except that Hegel had no need for irony: the self-reflexivity of mind was realized over time, not in the moment of ironic double entendre.

All approaches discussed here focus on the role of reason, which demands freedom, but is faced with the conditions of necessity. This constellation, which is identified as the constellation of modernity, is discussed in aesthetical as well as political terms, and approached historically: development over time will reconfigure and eventually resolve the dialectic of this constellation.

The Schlegels took the term *romantisch* as their emblem, took it to denote *their* specific interpretation of modernity and the issues of their time, as well as their equally contingent answers to them. August Wilhelm Schlegel would soon after leaving Jena provide the historical justification and definition for the 'Romantic' as the modern identity in his Berlin and then Vienna lectures; Friedrich grapples with this already in his *Griechische Poesie*. Behind *Romantic* stands a whole interpretation of cultural history that will only surface in the years after 1800. It defines a particular European modern identity, which can be, and frequently *was* narrowed down to a German(ic) one. Their deliberate choosing of this term, with its non-classical connotation evident to any educated contemporary, has been seen as a programmatic declaration of war against (classical) Weimar, against Goethe and Schiller.[26] Here lies the root of the interpretation of German Classicism and Romanticism as opposites, which, although questioned, still underlies many approaches to the *Goethezeit*, simply because of the deep resonance of

[26] For an elucidation of the programmatic, and combative, aspect of the German term 'romantisch', cf. Eudo Mason, *Deutsche und Englische Romantik: Eine Gegenüberstellung* (Göttingen: Vandenhoeck & Ruprecht, 1959), 3–8.

the two terms as fundamental oppositions. But especially in physically concrete terms, the dividing line between the two centres is not very neat: Schiller was equally connected to both places. Even when the first issue of the *Athenäum* appeared he was still living in Jena, although he would probably not have given the time of day to either Schlegel at that point; as people they had finally fallen out in 1797. Yet his *Naïve und Sentimentalische Dichtung*, written in Jena and published in 1795, grapples with the very issue of defining appropriate concepts for contemporary art. *Naïve und Sentimentalische Dichtung* is also an intellectual history of human culture, a rewrite of the *Querelle*, and hence a position paper on modernity; it is this pan-European identity that will make German thinking so influential, and so astonishing to contemporaries. Schiller's *Aesthetic Education* treats the same problem as the progressive universal poetry: based on the notion that art is the way to overcome the contemporary maze of moral, political, and existential uncertainty, it outlines how this might be done. The difference between Schiller and Schlegel here is the position of the 'ideal'. Although firmly out of reach, it is for Schiller clearly within sight on the horizon. Schlegel shares this aim-oriented outlook—the ideal exists and the task is to work towards it—but his focus is not so much on, but *within* the process: the dialectical dynamic between poem and critique, between imaginative synthesis and rational analysis, mythology and irony, almost comes to obscure the aim.[27] While the question is the same, the answers differ in focus. But to what extent these are opposing worldviews is perhaps less clear.

Schiller's essays and the Schlegels' *Athenäum* share two key approaches. The first is the primacy and priority of thinking, but thinking needs to be mediated through the aesthetic, through art and beauty. Reason (mind and thinking) and experience (the world) need to relate to each other in art and poetry. This would refine and mature the human being in such a way that s/he would be equipped to overcome the human condition through knowledge and beauty, and political oppression through justice and in freedom. The second is their preoccupation with the historical process, with the historicity of existence, knowledge, and experience, and its relation to reason and freedom. Time was experienced as critical because things were changing fast; and meaning was up for reconfiguration because the changes in political, intellectual, and aesthetic terms were so significant. Crisis was seen as opportunity: the underlying driver of all these changes was the desire for (more) freedom; crisis could create a platform for the realization of freedom in political, intellectual, and artistic terms. Friedrich Schlegel's much quoted *Athenäum* fragment 216 sums this up: 'Die Französische Revolution, Fichtes *Wissenschaftslehre* und Goethes *Meister* sind die größten Tendenzen des Zeitalters.' ('The French Revolution, Fichte's *Wissenschaftslehre*, and Goethe's *Wilhelm Meister* are the greatest tendencies of the age.')[28]

The preoccupation with (actual) history, so absent in Fichte's work of the 1790s, leads us back to Schiller, the Jena professor of *history*. Like Fichte's, his thinking connected in many significant ways with the circle of the Jena Romanticists around the Schlegels and Schelling. Schiller inspired Novalis before the latter had even met the Schlegels. Schiller had brought the older Schlegel to Jena: before he settled with Caroline in the

[27] Cf. Oergel, *Culture and Identity*, 90.
[28] *Kritische Friedrich Schlegel Ausgabe*, ii. 198.

town in 1796 August Wilhelm began, in 1794, to contribute to Schiller's *Horen* and *Musen-Almanach*, after much courting from Schiller.[29] And yet, literary history tends to group Schiller with Goethe, and Weimar, in the other half of the *Doppelstadt*. His friendship with Goethe is of course the key link. When he started out, Schiller had been rather antagonistically disposed towards the already much more established Goethe, and even during Schiller's early years in Jena the two were rather wary of each other. Against this background it cannot be surprising that in the minds of posterity the moment in which this changed, on that hot July evening in 1794, is conceived as both highly significant and highly dramatic. On 20 July both Goethe and Schiller had attended a paper on botany at the Naturforschende Gesellschaft (Society for Research into Nature) in Jena. Walking out of the room they, quite coincidentally, engaged for the first time in serious conversation with each other, so seriously that Schiller asked Goethe in to continue their debate when they reached his house. Sparked by what they felt was the paper's misapprehension of nature, Goethe outlined his notion of the metamorphosis of plants. According to Goethe, based on his testimony twenty years later, they promptly could not agree on whether Goethe's thoughts were based on 'experience' or 'ideas'.[30] According to Schiller, writing a few weeks afterwards, they were not mainly talking about nature, but about art. But Schiller, too, acknowledged that the exciting aspect of their discussion rested in their very different views and approaches to issues.[31]

Frequently the inception of their friendship, not least because it is so well documented, has been styled, mythologized, as one of the most—if not *the* most—significant moment in modern German literary and intellectual history.[32] The intensity of their mutual appreciation lines them up side by side against all others. This view is reinforced by the well-documented growing animosity between Schiller and the Schlegels. But how justified is this enduring division between the halves of the *Doppelstadt*?[33] To be sure, Goethe

[29] Schiller had been headhunting Schlegel since 1792, but August Wilhelm's close relationship with his mentor Gottfried Bürger at Göttingen made him unwilling to accept the invitation at the time, following the latter's critical slating by Schiller.

[30] Safranski, *Schiller oder die Erfindung*, 402.

[31] Letter to Körner of 1 Sept. 1794, *Schillers Briefe: Schillers Werke*, Nationalausgabe, xxvii, ed. G. Schulz (Weimar: Böhlau Nachfolger, 1958), 34.

[32] Wilhelm Dilthey in the introduction to his Schiller essay in the mid-1890s wrote (5) 'Es war in der Geschichte unserer Literatur der größte Moment, als in jenem Gespräch in Jena 1794 Goethe und Schiller sich zusammenfanden und ihre Freundschaft anhob.' Emil Staiger, in his epilogue to the paperback Fischer edn of the letters between Goethe and Schiller, published in 1961, calls their friendship 'eines der größten Wunder der europäischen Geistesgeschichte' (566), which represents, through the works and deeds it helped create and the love that nourished it, 'das vollkommenste Beispiel von Humanität, von reiner Menschlichkeit' (570). *Goethe-Schiller Briefwechsel* (Frankfurt am Main: Fischer, 1961), 566–70.

[33] It is maintained by both German and British scholars. Cf. T. J. Reed, *The Classical Centre: Goethe and Weimar 1775–1832*, 1st publ. 1980 (Oxford: Oxford University Press, 1985), esp. the chapter 'Divergences', pp. 186–9. Dieter Borchmeyer, in *Weimarer Klassik*, although steadfast in his complementary differentiation between the two, argues for an annexation of Jena to Weimar: the Jena 'achievements are part of "Weimar", there is a Weimarer Klassik and a Weimarer Romantik, which has its centre in Jena, each complementary to one another' (33–4).

kept his distance, he was the oldest of them and the least enamoured of the Revolution, so he had least in common with the 'Romantic' Jena circle.[34] But, unlike Schiller, Goethe remained on speaking terms with even Friedrich Schlegel in 1797, and the Schlegels' veneration for Goethe remains evident in the *Athenäum*. He, too, is in creative and artistic terms, not very far from 'Jena' concerns: the *Bildungsroman* is a genre imbued with Romantic notions of individuation (consciousness!) through education and increasing knowledge and empathy, and as a *Roman*, a novel, it embodies what Friedrich Schlegel considers the new, all-encompassing type of literature of the Romantic literary future. The *Faust* poem—which Goethe revisited during the period of Jena's heyday and published the year after Hegel left Jena—remains, in both form and content, one of the undisputed highlights of European Romanticism.[35] And, although it is an incidental detail, an accident of history, the fact is that Goethe's and Schiller's famous meeting of minds took place in Jena, not Weimar.

My discussion suggests that there are a number of aspects that indicate Schiller is far more rooted in the intellectual milieu of Jena than is sometimes assumed. His substantial theoretical output—his famous will to theorize, to define ideals theoretically—is as akin to the Schlegels' approach to literary theory as it is alien to Goethe. His philosophical tendencies, so clearly expressed in his essays of the 1790s, are similar to those of the Idealist thinkers. His aesthetic essays are, rather like Schelling's *System* and especially Hegel's *Phenomenology*, histories, of cultural and intellectual development, presenting trajectories, teleologies, meaning embodied in time. In the 1790s, out of the thinkers I have discussed here, Schiller is probably the *one* Jena writer most keenly interested in history: in Jena he researches and writes his *History of the Thirty Years War*.[36] Perhaps this subject matter was forced on him by his position at the University—his letters make clear that he saw doing the work of an historian as a viable economic (and spiritually economical) option—but his engagement with history was genuine. 'Ich sehe nicht ein, warum ich nicht, wenn ich ernstlich will, der erste Geschichtsschreiber Deutschlands werden kann', he writes to Körner in 1790.[37] In 1788, the year his first historical venture, the *Geschichte des Abfalls der vereinigten Niederlande von der spanischen Regierung*[38] appeared, he had told his friend: 'Geschichte ist ein Feld, wo alle meine

[34] As Reed argues (*Classical Centre*, 184–5).

[35] Mason, half a century ago, argued that considering Faust Romantic is based on a misunderstanding by anglophone readers, including educated and scholarly ones. Cf. Mason, *Deutsche und Englische Romantik*, 3–8. This was echoed a generation later by Dieter Borchmeyer (cf. *Weimarer Klassik*, 40), and this approach is still common among Germanists today, even if the persistent use of the epithet 'classical' for key German writers around 1800 identifies German literature as peripheral, out of step, in anglophone understanding.

[36] Schiller's *Geschichte des dreißigjährigen Krieges* appeared in English translation in 1799, only eight years after its original publication. *The History of the Thirty Years War in Germany*, tr. Captain Blaquiere (London: W Miller, 1799).

[37] 'I don't see why I shouldn't become, if I seriously try, the foremost historian in Germany.' Letter to Körner, 26 Nov. 1790. *Schillers Briefe: Schillers Werke*. Nationalausgabe, xxvi, ed. E. and H. Nahler (Weimar: Böhlau Nachfolger, 1992), 58.

[38] This account was translated by E. B. Bastwick as *The History of the Defection of the United Netherlands from the Spanish Empire* (1844).

Kräfte ins Spiel kommen.'[39] When the first two books of the *Thirty Years War* appeared in the autumn of 1790, they sold out within weeks and required a new print-run. The historicist school, and not least Meinecke himself, tended to deny Schiller a place in the genesis of the new historicist outlook. Meinecke disliked Schiller's priority of ideas and a priori parameters, which to him obscured the independent and organic vitality of historical developments, although the organic force of fanaticism is one of the key themes in Schiller's *Thirty Years War*. But the development of German historicist thinking around 1800 is equally evident in Idealist thought, to which Schiller's thinking was clearly close, and their contribution to the historicist turn of German thinking has been established.

Schiller wrote his Jena works against the background of events unfolding in France. Politics was always close to the surface in Jena, how close becomes even more evident once the stellar cast have left, after the events of 1806/7. The intoxicating emotions of patriotism and Germanness that carried the *Befreiungskriege* and the victory over Napoleon in the much mythologized *Völkerschlacht* near Leipzig in 1813 effected a 'political turn' in the students, and some of their teachers, at Jena (and elsewhere). Despite the absence of a posthumously famous professoriate, the university was still booming.[40] Jena students had had a reputation for a love of egalitarian freedom for some time (which may initially have been no more than a lack of restraint and a penchant for riots), but when Schiller visited Jena for the first time in 1787, he noted with satisfaction the republican atmosphere, which seemed free from feudal yokes.[41] This was to give him some uncomfortable pause in 1792, when the young Jena 'Jacobins' chanted slogans and songs from the *Robbers* in Jena's streets, which led to calls from Weimar for Schiller to distance himself. (Intriguingly, he considered travelling to Paris to lead the Revolution onto the right path.)

From 1815 matriculations saw a steep rise, peaking in 1818 at almost early eighteenth-century levels. In 1813 Jena had been a productive area for recruiting volunteers. Large numbers of Jena students had joined the—later much mythologized—free corps of the *Lützower Jäger*.[42] It would appear that after the war many came, or returned,

[39] 'History is a field in which all my powers come into play.' Letter to Körner, 17 Mar. 1788, *Schillers Briefe: Schillers Werke*, Nationalausgabe, xxv, ed. H. Haufe (Weimar: Böhlau Nachfolger, 1979), 29–30. See these two letters for Schiller's notion of the profitability of history and, from the writer's point of view, its less demanding nature.

[40] Cf. Rasche, *Umbrüche*, 101.

[41] In a letter to Körner dated 29 Aug. 1787, he noted 'dass Studenten hier etwas gelten, zeigt einem der erste Anblick ... sie wandeln mit Schritten eines Nichtbesiegten.... Die unter vier sächsische Herzoge [sic] vertheilte Gewalt über die academie macht sie zu einer freien und sicheren Republik, in welcher nicht leicht Unterdrückung stattfindet.... Die Professoren sind in Jena fast unabhängige Leute und dürfen sich nicht um eine Fürstlichkeit bekümmern.' The latter was to prove significant during and after the *Befreiungskriege*, see later in this chapter. *Schillers Briefe: Schillers Werke*, Nationalausgabe, xxiv, ed. K. J. Skrodzki (Weimar: Böhlau Nachfolger, 1989), 146 and 148 respectively.

[42] Cf. G. Steiger, *Aufbruch: Burschenschaft und Wartburgfest* (Leipzig: Urania Verlag, 1967), 42–3. This book is in itself a (historical) document of its own era: researched and published in the German Democratic Republic in the 1960s, it aims to show, using the tone and terms of the Marxist class struggle, how the GDR is the true culmination of the 19th-cent. democratic traditions in Germany. But before

here to press for what they had been led to believe they were fighting for: liberal constitutions, constitutional monarchies, freedom of the press, and a broadening of the franchise. Jena students organized themselves in a new Burschenschaft movement, which was vigorously supported by Jena's 'political professoriate'.[43] Prepared by careful planning and political agitation in the run-up to the victory in 1813, the so-called Ur-Burschenschaft was founded in Jena in 1815.[44] Students had been politicized by the events of the wars and the propaganda that had surrounded these events, propaganda both from the reformers in princely governments and the liberal intellectuals outside them. The political fervour that mobilized the volunteers who fought at Leipzig was based on the hope for constitutional government and increased civil rights within a united German nation. To many political reformers national unity was inseparable from political reform. Although nationalism is a well-established feature in the process of political modernization, here a perhaps unexpected mixture of progressive political radicalism and intense interest in ancient German traditions (so-called *Deutschtümelei*) emerged. One reason for this connection between forward- and backward-looking approaches lies in the widespread acknowledgement that any future political reform, and indeed revolution, must not repeat the mistakes of the French Revolution. It must in fact proceed from different conditions. Mindful of the assessments of why the French Revolution had failed, and had nearly led to the annihilation of the independence of German states—assessments such as Schiller's and Fichte's—the student reformers sought to connect their revolutionary tendencies to German traditions, especially German Protestantism, to Luther's Reformation. This was to produce the qualitative distinction from French Jacobinism and to lay the moral basis for a successful revolution. Jena lies in Luther-country, and it was only a few years before that Fichte had styled the Reformation as the 'Welttat des deutschen Volkes' (world deed of the German people),[45] endowing it with world-historical significance.

Progressive political approaches were at the heart of the foundation of the Jena Burschenschaft: in its ceremonial act of formation in June 1815, the regional Landsmannschaften, the traditional student organizations that replicated German federalism, symbolically disbanded, and all present joined the new undivided Burschenschaft. Their constitution focused on the social and political equality of its members and was based on democratic structures: their leaders were democratically

'Western' readers consign this book to the dustbin of Cold War history, they would do well to recognize the wealth of material relating to this democratic tradition that Steiger has brought together here.

43 Klaus Ries, 'Die Universität Jena als frühes Zentrum des politischen Professorentums', in *Die Universität Jena*, 175–90.

44 For a summary of these developments and the complex political, intellectual, and cultural intentions behind them, cf. Oergel, 'Revolutionaries, Traditionalists, Terrorists? The Burschenschaften and the German Counter-Cultural Tradition', in Steve Giles and Maike Oergel (eds), *Counter-Cultures in Germany and Central Europe 1770–1980: From Sturm und Drang to Baader-Meinhof* (Berne: Peter Lang, 2003), 61–86, but also cf. Steiger, *Aufbruch*.

45 Johann G. Fichte, *Reden an die deutsche Nation*, 'Sechste Rede', in *Johann Gottlieb Fichtes Sämmtliche Werke*, vii, ed. Immanuel Fichte (Berlin: de Gruyter, 1846), 344.

elected.[46] Their activities were part of the democratic opposition to the increasingly evident conservatism emanating from the courts and the ongoing congress at Vienna, where the post-war reorganization of Europe was being agreed. Although Sachsen-Weimar received a comparatively liberal constitution in 1816, which guaranteed freedom of the press, and elevated the duchy to being a model of (moderate) reform, many students and other political reformers felt the promises made before 1813 were not being kept. In 1817, to commemorate the 300th anniversary of the Reformation and the fourth anniversary of the Battle of Leipzig, the Jena Burschenschaft organized a student congress, the Wartburgfest, which was also attended by a number of Jena professors sympathetic to the students' demands and aims, such as Jakob Friedrich Fries and Lorenz Oken. The impassioned speeches revolving around the concepts of 'Freiheit' and 'Nation' and, most of all, the excesses, such as the book burning, put conservatives all over Germany on alert and led to a curtailment of press freedom in Sachsen-Weimar, before it was finally rescinded altogether in the general clampdown following the assassination of the writer August von Kotzebue in 1819. It is perhaps not entirely surprising that Kotzebue's assassin, Karl Sand, was a former Jena Burschenschaftler, who had gone through a process of political radicalization. In conservative circles, Jena, or more precisely its university, had been identified as a hotbed of Jacobinism. The students' anti-French stance (which was at least partly linked to their intention not to imitate the French revolutionaries' mistakes) was clearly lost on political conservatives, for whom all nationalism was Jacobinism.

While the Jena Burschenschaft in its progressive democratic form did not survive the measures of the Carlsbad Decrees, it is worth pointing out that the Jena Burschenschaft of 1815 was one of the first German organizations to resemble a modern political party and that at the Wartburgfest it quite deliberately sought out the public sphere for a kind of public party conference. This was not lost on the bourgeois-liberal democratic opposition of the mid-nineteenth century: the black, red, and gold of the students' tricolour, taken from the colours of the Lützow uniforms, was adopted by the Frankfurt Parliament and later the Weimar Republic.[47] They continue to represent modern German states, featuring on the flags of both the Federal Republic and the GDR.

What went on in Jena in the three decades between 1789 and 1819 is ultimately 'bigger' than the *Jenaer Romantik*. Philosophy, literature, and history inform each other to create a powerful new intellectual impetus. But politics, which looms so unavoidably large over everything that occurs after 1789, is never far from their thoughts and often prompts their ideas. The spark of intellectual radicalism of the Jena professoriate seems to ignite the political radicalism of the students. The link in their minds is no doubt a developing sense of a modern German identity that was finding expression in a new philosophy, literary theory, and understanding of history, as well as new political

[46] Cf. Oergel, 'Burschenschaften', 66–7.

[47] The tricolour of black, red, and gold was a key feature of the Hambacher Fest in 1832. The actual combination of colours originates in the flag of the Urburschenschaft, which sported a red-black-red tricolour with golden tresses. Cf. Steiger, *Aufbruch*, 19–32.

structures. One is almost given to wonder, bearing in mind the intellectual and political pedigree of this place, whether the first German republic would not have done better to call itself the Jena Republic.

Someone is missing in this essay, a poet and writer who engaged intensely with Kant, who experimented with poetics and topics as innovatively as Novalis or Friedrich Schlegel, and who engaged with the political and 'national' situation every bit as committedly as the *Lützower Jäger* or the Jena Burschenschaft: Heinrich von Kleist. But Kleist only came to Weimar. This may serve to illustrate the arbitrariness of such geo-physical demarcations and add a critical self-reflexivity appropriate to the subject matter of this chapter. While there is room, and reason, for the myth of Jena I have described here in German, or Romantic, or European intellectual history, there must equally be the slightly ironic critical awareness that it is just that, a myth, a construction to order and understand complex facts, and make visible how meaning, and identity, arise.

Further Reading

Behler, Ernst, *German Romantic Literary Theory* (Cambridge: Cambridge University Press, 1993).

Beiser, Frederick, *The Romantic Imperative. The Concept of Early German Romanticism* (Cambridge, Mass.: Harvard University Press, 2003).

Borchmeyer, Dieter, *Weimarer Klassik: Portrait einer Epoche* (Weinheim: Beltz Athenäum, 1998; 1st publ. 1994).

Deutsche Forschungsgemeinschaft (German Research Foundation), *Sonderforschungsbereich*, 'Ereignis Weimar-Jena. Kultur um 1800' (SFB 482) 2001–2010. <http://www2.uni-jena.de/ereignis/index.html>.

Dilthey, Wilhelm, *Von deutscher Dichtung und Musik: Aus den Studien zur Geschichte des deutschen Geistes* (Leipzig: Teubner, 1933; 2nd unchanged edn, Stuttgart: Teubner, 1957).

Fichte, Johann Gottfried, *Grundlage der gesammten Wissenschaftslehre*, 1st edn (Leipzig: Gabler, 1794).

Fichte, Johann Gottfried, *Reden an die deutsche Nation*, 'Sechste Rede', in *Johann Gottlieb Fichtes Sämmtliche Werke*, vii, ed. Immanuel Fichte (Berlin: de Gruyter, 1846), 344.

Fichte, Johann Gottfried, *The Science of Knowing: J. G. Fichte's 1804 Lectures on the Wissenschaftslehre*, tr. Walter E. Wright (Ithaca, NY: State University of New York, 2005).

Haym, Rudolf, *Die romantische Schule: Ein Beitrag zur Geschiche des deutschen Geistes*, facsimile repr. (Hildesheim: Ohlms, 1961).

Hegel, Georg Wilhelm Friedrich, *Phänomenologie des Geistes*, 1st publ. 1807, ed. Eva Moldenhauer and Karl Markus Michel on the basis of the *Werke* (1832–45) (Frankfurt am Main: Suhrkamp, 1970; = *Hegels Werke*, iii).

Hegel, G. W. F., *The Phenomenology of Mind*, tr. J. B. Baillie, 1st edn 1910 (Mineola, NY: Dover, 2004).

Kluckhohn, Paul, *Ideengut der deutschen Romantik*, 4th edn (Tübingen: Niemeyer, 1961).

Korff, Hans August, *Geist der Goethezeit*, 4 vols (Leipzig: i and ii by J. J. Weber, 1923; iii by S. Hirzel, 1949; iv by Koehler & Amerlang, 1953).

Mandelkow, Karl Robert, *Europäische Romantik I = Neues Handbuch der Literaturwissenschaft*, xiv (Wiesbaden: Athenaion, 1982).

Mason, Eudo, *Deutsche und Englische Romantik: Eine Gegenüberstellung* (Göttingen: Vandenhoeck & Ruprecht, 1959).

Meinecke, Friedrich, *Die deutsche Katastrophe: Betrachtungen und Erinnerungen* (Zurich: Aero-Verlag, 1946).

Meinecke, Friedrich, *Die Entstehung des Historismus*, 1st publ. 1936, ed. Carl Hinrichs (Munich: Oldenburg Verlag, 1959; = *Werke*, iii. 2).

Müller, Gerhard, Ries, Klaus, and Ziche, Paul (eds), *Die Universität Jena: Tradition und Innovation um 1800* (Stuttgart: Steiner, 2001).

Nohl, Herman, *Die deutsche Bewegung: Vorlesungen und Aufsätze zur Geistesgeschichte von 1770–1830*, ed. Otto Friedrich Bollnow and Frithjof Rodi (Göttingen: Vandenhoeck & Ruprecht, 1970).

Novalis, *Werke in einem Band* (Munich and Vienna: Hanser, 1981).

Novalis, *Notes for a Romantic Encyclopaedia: Das Allgemeine Brouillon*, tr. and ed. David W. Wood (Albany, NY: State University of New York, 2007).

Oergel, Maike, 'Revolutionaries, Traditionalists, Terrorists? The Burschenschaften and the German Counter-Cultural Tradition', in Steve Giles and Maike Oergel (eds), *Counter-Cultures in Germany and Central Europe 1770–1980: From Sturm und Drang to Baader-Meinhof* (Berne: Peter Lang, 2003), 61–86.

Oergel, Maike, *Culture and Identity: Historicity in German Literature and Thought 1770–1815* (Berlin and New York: de Gruyter, 2006).

Reed, T. J., *The Classical Centre: Goethe and Weimar 1775–1832*, 1st publ. 1980 (Oxford: Oxford University Press, 1985).

Ries, Klaus (ed.), *Romantik und Revolution: Zum politischen Reformpotential einer unpolitischen Bewegung* (Heidelberg: Winter, 2012).

Safranski, Rüdiger, *Romantik: Eine deutsche Affäre* (Munich: Hanser, 2007).

Safranski, Rüdiger, *Schiller oder die Erfindung des deutschen Idealismus*, 1st publ. 2004 (Munich: Deutscher Taschenbuchverlag, 2007).

Schelling, Friedrich, *System des Transzendentalen Idealismus*, 1st publ. 1800, *Historisch-Kritische Ausgabe: Friedrich Wilhelm Joseph Schelling*, in Auftrag der Schelling-Kommission der Bayerischen Akademie der Wissenschaften, ed. H. M. Baumgartner, W. G. Jacobs, H. Krings, and H. Zeltner, 1st ser. 9 (Stuttgart: frommann-holzboog, 1976–).

Schiller, Friedrich, *Naïve und Sentimentalische Dichtung*. ed. with introduction and annotations by William F. Mainland (Oxford: Blackwell, 1951).

Schiller, *Reden im Gedenkjahr 1955*, ed. Deutsche Schillergesellschaft (Stuttgart: Klett, 1955).

Schiller, Friedrich, *Über die ästhetische Erziehung des Menschen in einer Reihe von Briefen: Schillers Werke*. Nationalausgabe, xx, ed. Benno von Wiese and H. Koopmann (Weimar: Böhlau Nachfolger, 1962), 308–412.

Schiller, Friedrich, *On the Aesthetic Education of Man in a Series of Letters*, ed. and tr. with an Introduction, Commentary, and Glossary of Terms by Elizabeth M. Wilkinson and L. A. Willoughby (Oxford: Clarendon Press, 1967).

Schiller, Friedrich, *Geschichte des Abfalls der Niederlande von der spanischen Regierung: Schillers Werke*. Nationalausgabe, xvii, ed. K.-H. Hahn (Weimar: Böhlau Nachfolger, 1970), 7–356.

Schiller, Friedrich, *Geschichte des dreißigjährigen Krieges: Schillers Werke*, Nationalausgabe, xviii, ed. K.-H. Hahn (Weimar: Böhlau Nachfolger, 1976).

Schiller, Friedrich, *On the Naive and Sentimental in Literature*, tr. with an introduction by Helen Watanabe-O'Kelly (Manchester: Carcanet, 1981).

Schlegel, Friedrich, *Kritische Friedrich Schlegel Ausgabe*, xviii. *Philosophische Lehrjahre*, ed. Ernst Behler (Munich: Schönigh, 1963).

Schlegel, Friedrich, *Kritische Friedrich Schlegel Ausgabe*, i–ii, ed. Ernst Behler (vol. i contains *Über das Studium der griechischen Poesie*) and Hans Eichner (vol. ii contains *Athenäum*) (Munich: Schönigh, 1967 (ii) and 1979 (i)).

Schlegel, August Wilhelm. *Kritische Ausgabe der Vorlesungen*, 3 vols, ed. Ernst Behler (i), Georg Braungart (ii), Frank Jolles and Edith Höltenschmidt (iii) (Paderborn: Schönigh, 1989–2007).

Schlegel, Friedrich, *On the Study of Greek Poetry*, tr., ed., and with a critical introduction by Stuart Barnett (Albany, NY: State University of New York, 2001).

Schulz, Gerhard, *Die deutsche Literatur zwischen Französischer Revolution und Restauration*, 2 vols (Munich: Beck, 1983–9).

Steiger, G., *Aufbruch: Burschenschaft und Wartburgfest* (Leipzig: Urania Verlag, 1967).

Strich, Fritz, *Deutsche Klassik und Romantik oder Vollendung und Unendlichkeit: Ein Vergleich*, 1st publ. 1922, 2nd augmented edn (Munich: Meyer & Jessen, 1924).

Ueding, Gert, *Klassik und Romantik: Deutsche Literatur im Zeitalter der Französischen Revolution 1789–1815* (Munich and Vienna: Hanser, 1987).

Watson, Peter, *The German Genius: Europe's Third Renaissance, the Second Scientific Revolution and the Twentieth Century* (London: Simon & Schuster, 2010).

CHAPTER 13

GENDER AND GENRE IN THE WORKS OF GERMAN ROMANTIC WOMEN WRITERS

ASTRID WEIGERT

WHAT's in a name, or, more specifically, what's in the name of a female German Romantic author? Far from being an idle question, a closer look at the specifics of women's names in general and German Romantic women writers, in particular, provides important clues about class, ethnicity, religious affiliation, level of education, and unconventional lifestyle choices, to name only those most obvious. Additionally, such a consideration of names will also offer clues about both the singularities and the commonalities among the group of female authors discussed in this chapter.

Consider, then, the names of today's best-known German female Romantic writers: Dorothea (Brendel) Mendelssohn-Veit-Schlegel (1763–1839), Caroline Michaelis-Böhmer-Schlegel-Schelling (1763–1809), Sophie Schubart-Mereau-Brentano (1770–1806), Rahel Levin-Varnhagen (1771–1833), Karoline von Günderrode (1780–1806). What immediately catches the reader's attention is the number of hyphenated last names. A look at the initial family name in each listing provides information on the author's family background, class, and an indication of her level of education: in the case of Mendelssohn-Veit-Schlegel, the name 'Mendelssohn' identifies her as the daughter of the German-Jewish Enlightenment philosopher Moses Mendelssohn, a learned pedigree indeed. Similarly, Michaelis-Böhmer-Schlegel-Schelling was the daughter of the Göttingen University Professor Johann David Michaelis, who saw to it that his daughter received an exceptional education. Schubart-Mereau-Brentano whose father was a ducal secretary, is known to have attended Fichte's lectures. The other women in this group were also from families of lower nobility or administrators in various principalities who valued female education. Taken together, with regard to education level, German Romantic women authors were an unusually learned group of women for their time.

In some cases, the sequence of last names points to tragic or unconventional personal lives. The hyphenated names indicate a sequence of marriage, widowhood, even divorce, and remarriage, or, in the case of von Günderrode, an equally unconventional unmarried status. As such then, this group of authors includes a number of women whose lives did not fit the circumscribed traditional model of the time.

What is also noteworthy is the Jewish first and last names: Brendel, Rahel, Mendelssohn, Veit, Levin—a fact that highlights the contribution of female authors of Jewish descent to German Romanticism.

The attentive reader has no doubt noticed that two of the authors listed share the last name 'Schlegel'—and indeed, the two Schlegel couples (Dorothea and Friedrich; Caroline and August Wilhelm) were the most prominent 'Romantic couples', not only because of the formidable number of works produced between the respective couples, but also because of the intensive collaboration among the four of them during their time in Jena when they lived together under one roof (1799–1801). As such, the two Schlegel couples are representative of the close and productive learned sociability which marked what is known as the 'Jena Circle' of the early Romantics. It was indeed at the salon-like gatherings at the Schlegels' where Sophie Mereau and Clemens Brentano, another 'Romantic couple' got to know each other and began their personal and literary relationship.[1] Literary history traditionally assigned these women the roles of helpmate and muse. Over the last thirty years, though, significant feminist archival and interpretive scholarship has established that these female authors were highly productive and creative in their own right, and continues to articulate their specific contributions to (and interventions in) early German Romanticism.

Feminist scholarship on women Romantic authors in Germany has established that their creative and theoretical contributions span a wide variety of genres: from novels to dramas and from poetry to literary criticism. Mereau-Brentano even founded and edited a literary journal of her own (*Kalathiskos*). Many were exceptionally gifted letter-writers with an extensive corpus of correspondence. In addition, several Romantic authors were talented translators of source texts in a variety of genres (drama, novel, poetry) and from a range of periods (from the Italian Renaissance to Shakespeare to contemporary French literature).

This breadth of genres represented in the works of the relatively small group of Romantic women authors suggests that, like their male counterparts in the Romantic movement, they, too, saw the aesthetic category of 'genre' as key to both the literary and theoretical concerns of their endeavours. An analysis that links the author's gender with the genres of her oeuvre affords the reader the opportunity to look at the contributions, changes, and aesthetic decisions that female Romantic authors made to a variety of genres in their literary output. As such, then, this chapter is not so much concerned with the fact that Romantic women authors wrote novels, poetry, literary criticism, etc per se;

[1] See chs 4 (on Friedrich and Dorothea Schlegel) and 6 (on Sophie Mereau and Clemens Brentano) in Adrian Daub, *Uncivil Unions: The Metaphysics of Marriage in German Idealism and Romanticism* (Chicago: University of Chicago Press, 2012).

rather, it highlights how their generic contributions participated in and contributed to the circulation of Romantic thought in Germany. For the genres of the novel and literary criticism, Dorothea Schlegel's novel *Florentin* (1801) and her essay of literary criticism 'Gespräch über die neuesten Romane der Französinnen' (1803, 'Dialogue on the latest novels of French women writers') will serve as the basis for a brief case study. For other genres such as letters, plays, and poetry, those female authors whose oeuvre centres around these textual forms will be highlighted in less extensive ways.

As an aesthetic category, 'genre' (Gattung) played a major role in the Romantic reconceptualization of literature. Friedrich Schlegel, the leading theorist among the German Romantics, provided numerous aesthetic-programmatic statements on genre issues. In conjunction with the centrality of the concept of 'synthesis' in male Romantic thought, it is not surprising that those genres that allowed for the dissolution of boundaries in terms of form and/or content were favoured. Two such genres stand out: the then relatively new and undefined genre of the novel and the printed, multi-voiced 'Gespräch'. It is precisely these two genres that Dorothea Schlegel also engages with in her oeuvre and that, when viewed against the foil of F. Schlegel's novel and Gespräch, demonstrate her independent aesthetic contribution to German Romantic thought.

Friedrich Schlegel saw the genre of the novel as the ideal 'Romantic' genre: its flexible form allowed for a synthesis of various genres from fragments and poems to songs, literary criticism, and aesthetic/programmatic statements, while at the same time allowing for the inclusion of traditional narrative forms. His novel *Lucinde* (1799) is generally regarded as *the* German-language Romantic novel and as such as the literary exemplification of his theoretical thoughts on the very genre. He had claimed in the 'Brief über den Roman' ('Letter about the Novel') which forms part of the 'Gespräch über die Poesie ('Dialogue on Poetry')' that 'the theory of the novel must itself be a novel'. Indeed, Friedrich Schlegel's novel is an experimental, eclectic, and self-aware arrangement of genres with a centrally placed traditional narrative, 'Lehrjahre der Männlichkeit' ('Apprenticeship for Manhood') that is preceded and followed by six shorter genres (titled 'Allegory', 'Characteristic', 'Arabesque', 'Two Letters', etc.) that offer aesthetic reflections. The 'Lehrjahre' narrative recounts the development of a young artist whose sexual escapades culminate in the ideal figure of Lucinde, who becomes his muse and wife. In terms of its contemporary reception, it was the novel's content that provoked the strongest reaction, not its form. *Lucinde* was seen as a scandalous text due to its, for the time, pornographic details, and further due to the fact that Schlegel's contemporaries read the novel as a roman-a-clef about Friedrich and Dorothea's love relationship (a claim that F. Schlegel did not contest but indeed was refuted vigorously by D. Schlegel).

At first glance, D. Schlegel's *Florentin* may seem a much more traditionally structured novel than *Lucinde*. Lacking F. Schlegel's clearly labelled sections, D. Schlegel synthesizes the various genres in her novel more subtly. The novel incorporates poems and songs, a 'Ghost Story' labelled as such, and an unlabelled fairy-tale like section that recounts the protagonist's background.

If one reads the 'Lehrjahre der Männlichkeit' in *Lucinde* as a form of *Bildungsroman*, then a reading of *Florentin* quickly reveals that D. Schlegel playfully engages, parodies, or/and rejects the conventions of the novel of self-discovery and development.[2] This aesthetic approach is evident from the novel's very first page, where D. Schlegel's narrator ambiguously refers to the protagonist Florentin's life as both a 'Lebensreise' (life's journey) and 'Reiseleben' (a life of travels). On the plot level, all potential elements of 'discovery' are subverted: while presumably searching for his family roots, the protagonist does not progress through a series of various locales but remains in one place, the estate of the Schwarzenberg family, throughout the novel. He neither undertakes any activities to further his supposed goal of discovery, nor does he find his purpose in life, nor the love of his life or even a place to settle down. The novel's very last sentence epitomizes this 'Ziellosigkeit' (lack of a goal): 'Florentin was nowhere to be found.'

The novel's non-closure is a key concern in several of D. Schlegel's aesthetic statements. In the unpublished dedication to her novel's fictive editor, she explicates her decision for an open ending:[3] a satisfactory ending is one with the potential for longing and speculation ('Sehnsucht und Ahndung') that in turn allows the imagination to play with a limitless number of potential endings. She stresses her preference for this approach when she employs the metaphor of young girls playing with dolls: she compares herself to girls who favour playing with naked dolls that they can dress differently every hour to playing with a perfectly dressed up doll whose clothes have been sewn on tightly and cannot be taken off or changed. The radical non-closure that D. Schlegel conceives for her novel stands in stark contrast to the rather conventional ending in F. Schlegel's *Lucinde*, where the protagonist finds his purpose in life and settles down with his lover and muse. D. Schlegel's aesthetic reflections make clear that this is a purposeful and independent conception of a key aspect of the Romantic novel, one that is indeed much more radical than F. Schlegel's.

In another set of aesthetic statements, D. Schlegel again demonstrates significant independence of thought, this time with regard to her novel's lack of self-referentiality. In marked contrast to F. Schlegel's proclaimed Romantic synthesis and reflection of self in art, exemplified by the autobiographical references to himself (and Dorothea, for that matter) in *Lucinde*, D. Schlegel explicitly refuses to write herself into her novel—which may also explain her unusual choice of a male protagonist—and vehemently criticizes those who try to read autobiographical elements into or out of her text.[4] Indeed, D. Schlegel develops an independent aesthetic vocabulary for her novelistic endeavour: she terms her approach 'Bildergalerie' (picture gallery) and explicitly contrasts it with the 'male' notion of 'Spiegelsaal' (hall of mirrors). In the unpublished foreword to the unpublished sequel to the novel, she first describes her approach *ex negativo*, explaining that reading her novel is 'not like being in a hall of mirrors where one is alone among

[2] See Martha B. Helfer, 'Dorothea Veit-Schlegel's Florentin: Constructing a Feminist Romantic Aesthetic', *German Quarterly*, 69/2 (1996), 144–60.

[3] Dorothea Schlegel, 'Zueignung an den Herausgeber', in *Florentin: Roman, Fragmente, Varianten*, ed. Liliane Weissberg (Frankfurt am Main: Ullstein, 1987), 157–9.

[4] Dorothea Schlegel, *Briefe von Dorothea Schlegel an Friedrich Schleiermacher*, ed. Heinrich Meisner and Erich Schmidt (Berlin: Litteraturarchiv-Gesellschaft, 1913), 106.

the oft-repeated images', but rather corresponds to 'taking a pleasurable walk in a picture gallery in which the various portraits and figures ... surround us with memories'.[5] The key distinction between the two concepts is that 'Bildergalerie' refers to an associative approach that allows for a creative and enjoyable encounter with a variety of mental pictures and memories, as is typical when looking at pictures in a gallery, whereas 'Spiegelsaal' refers to repeated lonely encounters of the self only with itself. D. Schlegel's emphasis on the non-identification of author and work plays out in her novel as well. At one point in the narrative, Florentin recounts his childhood and youthful experiences to his friends. His female friend Juliane innocently asks for clarification about names, relationships, and persons mentioned in Florentin's memories. With an unexpectedly sharp rebuke, Florentin chastises her and refuses to provide more information that might identify him, saying that there is no point in recounting such 'coincidences that have nothing to do with him'.[6] Florentin's language not only obviates any need for precise identification or 'mirroring' of self, but also signals through the use of 'coincidences' a certain arbitrariness in terms of the associations and relationships the reader may conjure up in his/her mind. Read in conjunction, the aesthetic statement in the foreword and the passage cited above reiterate D. Schlegel's independent conception of another key aspect of the Romantic novel: a preference for speculative association over self-referentiality.

A third central aesthetic aspect of D. Schlegel's writings concerns the Romantic artist's creative process, and in particular the linkage of gender and creativity. Again, she uses both non-literary and literary texts to express her viewpoint. Her novel includes a section entitled 'Geistergeschichte' (Ghost Story) told by a female character, in which a devout noblewoman whose marriage has remained childless for years, claims to see a ghost child after a fainting spell in church. This vision of a child accompanies her every activity, day and night, for the duration of the next nine months. Her family and friends, unable to see the ghost child, consider her slightly deranged and leave her mostly alone. The vision ends at the end of nine months, when the noblewoman is delivered of a real child. While metaphors of pregnancy and birth have been employed by (mostly male) artists to represent the creative process for centuries, certain gender components in this particular version merit a closer look. First, the noblewoman becomes pregnant without any male involvement (her husband being out of the country)—an immaculate conception, so to speak; second, the woman becomes aware of her pregnancy only after a considerable time, and third, the story emphasizes the pregnancy itself and neither the act of giving birth, nor the newborn child per se. These three aspects can be read as D. Schlegel's comments on female creative originality that is independent of male

[5] Dorothea Schlegel, 'Vorrede', in *Florentin*, ed. Weissberg (ed.), 162. German original: 'nicht in einem Spiegelsaal in dem man sich mitten unter den oft wiederholten Gestalten allein befindet'; in einer Bildergalerie zu lustwandeln wo die verschiedenen Porträte und Figuren uns ... mit Erinnerungen umgeben.' My translation.

[6] German original: 'Fragen Sie mich nicht um dergleichen Zufälligkeiten, liebe Juliane, sie gehören nicht auf die entfernteste Weise zu mir .... In Dorothea Schlegel, *Florentin*, ed. Weissberg, 82. My translation.

influences (autopoiesis), on frequent female unawareness or excessive modesty to acknowledge that creative potential, and, finally, on the emphasis on the creative process as against the final product—the point at which women authors traditionally lost control of their 'product' in terms of acknowledgement of authorship or publishing. Parallel to the 'Geistergeschichte' in the novel, D. Schlegel explicitly reflects on her own gendered creative process. In several statements to Schleiermacher, she proudly announces herself as the creator of the poems in her novel (as opposed to Schleiermacher's assumption that F. Schlegel authored them) and explicitly states that F. Schlegel and Schelling imitated her style (and not, as traditionally expected, vice versa) in their own stanzas. In addition, not only does D. Schlegel demonstrate authorial pride and a good dose of self-confidence, she likewise is not shy about laying claim to high literary ambitions. In correspondence with Schleiermacher, she chastises him for expressing surprise at her poetic progress and reminds him that she always said, indeed insisted, that she would amount to something. Similarly, she comments to him, while working on *Florentin*, that this work might very well acquire a 'brilliante Stelle' (brilliant position) once finished. As such, then, D. Schlegel's reflections on female creativity and originality, as well as on the creative process and creative ambitions, add an important dimension to our understanding of Romantic authorship.

In addition to novels, D. Schlegel was also well versed in other genres characteristic of German Romanticism, such as fragments, reviews of theatre performances, descriptions of paintings, and literary criticism, all of which appeared in literary journals edited and published by F. Schlegel (*Athenaeum, Europa)*. As journal editor, F. Schlegel tended not to identify contributors of shorter pieces, or to only add initials. For this reason, there may still be contributions, especially of women, that have not been acknowledged as of yet: scholarly work in this area is ongoing.[7]

One lengthier piece of literary criticism acknowledged as authored by D. Schlegel is the 'Gespräch über die neuesten Romane der Französinnen' ('Dialogue on the latest novels of French women writers').[8] While the title clearly echoes F. Schlegel's 'Gespräch über die Poesie' ('Dialogue on Poetry'), it also points to gender-specific distinctions. The reader of D. Schlegel's essay expects a rather narrow discussion of contemporary French novels, further limited to works by women authors only, implicitly targeted towards a female readership. Given these indications, one could expect the piece to be of little import. A closer look at D. Schlegel's complex and multi-voiced text, however, reveals that she expertly makes use of this opportunity for publication in order to give voice to her aesthetic ideas on the novel. In her 'Dialogue', then, such contemporary novels as *Delphine* (1802) by Mme de Staël are simply used as an entry point into a more in-depth critique of key aspects of the novel as D. Schlegel saw them. One such key aspect for D. Schlegel is the conception of the protagonist ('Held'). Through the all-female

[7] A recent accomplishment in this area is the study by May Mergenthaler, *Zwischen Eros und Mitteilung: Die Frühromantik im Symposion der 'Athenaeums-Fragmente'* (Paderborn: Schöningh, 2012).

[8] Dorothea Schlegel, 'Gespräch über die neuesten Romane der Französinnen', *Europa: Eine Zeitschrift*, ed. Friedrich Schlegel, i/2 (1803), 88–106.

participants in the conversation, D. Schlegel lays out her view on the differences between protagonists in 'old' novels and those in 'modern' novels. The key distinction for her lies in the competing influence of exterior and interior factors on the main character. In the 'modern' novels, she claims, the protagonist's life (for whom she uses the German masculine pronoun 'he' throughout) is only minimally influenced by the vagaries of exterior events and, in turn, much more affected by ('determiniert') the tensions within himself, between his desires, principles, prejudices, and those of society.[9] Indeed, D. Schlegel's 'hero' Florentin can be read as an extreme representation of this 'modern' protagonist, as his character is portrayed as full of contradictions and inconsistencies, lacking any explicit desires, principles, or goals. Or to be more precise, desires and plans are stated, but neither mentioned again, pursued, nor executed. One example suffices to illustrate: At the beginning of the novel, Florentin declines Count Schwarzenberg's invitation to his estate because he is supposedly on his way to the coast from where he is going to take a ship to America. Despite announcing these plans, Florentin does accept the invitation and stays at the estate for several months. In the course of the novel, he never mentions his plans to go overseas again, nor does he undertake any steps towards this presumed goal. For a female author of her time, D. Schlegel's choice of a male protagonist, and one in the mould of the 'modern' hero she describes, is an unusual decision that can be seen as an explicit participatory gesture towards the dominant aesthetic discourse. At the same time, this gesture stands well apart from the prevailing decision of female novelists of the era with regard to the fictional lives of their female protagonists. Indeed, D. Schlegel expressly laments in her 'Gespräch' the circumscribed options available to female protagonists in novels of her time, in which the heroine's life is determined by external events and in which she shines through steady female virtue and quiet domesticity. She contrasts this 'modern' heroine with earlier times where, she claims, the models for female protagonists were women who possessed extraordinary gifts of power, courage, strength, and greatness. As D. Schlegel articulates her thinking on the conception of the protagonist, it becomes evident that her decision to create a male protagonist in her own novel was a conscious aesthetic choice for which her 'Gespräch' offered a platform for justification.

A last important aspect of D. Schlegel's oeuvre are her translations, an area of literary activity through which she again proved herself as a talented and active participant in the Romantic project in Germany. In many ways, the Romantic period was *the* era of translation in German literary history, with A. W. Schlegel's Shakespeare translation generally viewed as the crowning accomplishment.[10] In addition to the practice of translation, male Romantic authors were also invested in theoretical reflections on translation. Broadly speaking, they considered translation an integral part of the Romantic project, favoured adaptation over literalness, and viewed translating as a creative

9 J. M. Raich (ed.), *Dorothea von Schlegel, geb. Mendelssohn und deren Söhne Johannes und Philipp Veit*, i (Mainz: Kirchheim, 1881), 121.

10 See later in this chapter on the contribution of Caroline Schlegel-Schelling to A. W. Schlegel's Shakespeare translation.

process equal to crafting an original work.[11] This appreciation for translation as an aesthetic and intellectual endeavor did, however, not translate into appreciation for the actual work of women translators, as D. Schlegel's experience in this regard shows. D. Schlegel's translations include: the novel *Corinna oder Italien* by Mme de Staël (1803/4), *Geschichte der Jungfrau von Orleans: Aus altfranzösischen Quellen* (1803), *Geschichte der Margarete von Valois: Gemahlin Heinrichs des Vierten. Von ihr selbst beschrieben* (1803), *Geschichte des Zauberers Merlin* (1804), and *Lother und Maller: Eine Rittergeschichte* (1805). However, as with her novel, none of these translations were published under her own name but under that of F. Schlegel. As this list demonstrates, D. Schlegel translated these works within a very short timespan and was able to deal with source texts in contemporary French, medieval French, and old English.

Some of the details surrounding her translation of Mme de Staël's novel *Corinne ou l'Italie* (translated as 'Corinna oder Italien') shed further light on her translation practices. The offer to translate this particular novel came to F. Schlegel via his brother A. W. Schlegel, mentor and travel companion of Mme de Staël and her children, whose works were very popular with German audiences. The goal was to quickly produce the first translation of her new novel in order to secure some income for F. Schlegel (and by extension D. Schlegel) whose financial situation was constantly strained. F. Schlegel then turned the task over to D. Schlegel, who produced the translation under less than ideal conditions and in record time: instead of having access to the entire work to be translated, she received the manuscript in sections directly from Mme de Staël who was still in the process of finishing the novel. The time pressure was such that D. Schlegel complained about 'the factory-like conditions' under which she had to produce the translation. Despite these adverse circumstances, she achieved a highly readable and successful translation which received praise from the critics (who, of course, assumed that the translation was by F. Schlegel).

Her translation of the Merlin legend, undertaken while living in Paris, was initiated by F. Schlegel who discovered the French sources in the Bibliothèque National de Paris. Helmine von Chezy, D. Schlegel's friend in Paris, notes in her autobiography that she and D. Schlegel translated *Merlin* jointly[12] which means that not one, but two female translators remained unacknowledged upon publication. The combination of a lack of visibility or public acknowledgement of German female translators in the Romantic period, lack of agency in selecting the source texts, time pressures, and financial motivations point to a discrepancy between the theoretical sublimation of translation in Romanticism and its practice on the ground, so to speak.[13] On the other hand, leaving

[11] See e.g. Friedrich Schleiermacher, *'Ueber die verschiedenen Methoden des Uebersetzens. (1813)'*, ed. Hans-Joachim Störig, *Das Problem des Übersetzens* (Stuttgart: Goverts, 1963), 38–69. And *Novalis Schriften*, ed. Paul Kluckhohn (Stuttgart, Kohlhammer, 1975), iv. 237.

[12] See Lorely French, 'The Magic of Translation: Dorothea Schlegel's "Geschichte des Zauberers Merlin" ', *Pacific Coast Philology*, 40/1 (2005), 36–56, 51 n. 5. Interestingly, today's edn of the Merlin translation by Ullstein publishers lists both Dorothea and Friedrich as authors: Dorothea und Friedrich Schlegel, *Geschichte des Zauberers Merlin* (Frankfurt am Main: Ullstein, 1984).

[13] This Romantic practice is decidedly different from the independent manner with which Enlightenment author and translator Luise Gottsched chose her source texts. See 'Introduction', in Hilary Brown, *Luise Gottsched the Translator* (Rochester, NY: Camden House, 2013), 1–8.

aside the issue of source text selection, some scholars convincingly argue that female translators of the period often 'rescued' forgotten female characters or authors from oblivion and in the process of a quite liberal translation/adaptation practice were able to bend or subvert the source texts towards their own views on gender relations, religion, or politics. D. Schlegel's Merlin translation has been shown to do just that.[14]

Translation was also a very important part of Sophie Mereau-Brentano's oeuvre, considered one of the first professional women authors in Germany. Her source texts in Italian and French included Bocaccio's fourteenth-century novel *Fiammetta* (1806), the seventeenth-century novel *Die Prinzessin von Cleves* (1799) by Mme de La Fayette, and the letters of the seventeenth-century French feminist, *saloniére*, and courtesan Ninon Lenclos (1797, 1802, and 1805).[15] Due to her focus on source texts with female characters, Mereau-Brentano's translations have received attention from feminist scholars, in particular her choice to translate the extensive correspondence of Ninon Lenclos, whose life would have traditionally been considered anything but virtuous and domestic.[16] Even before she tackled the first set of translations from Lenclos's source text, Mereau-Brentano thought it important to introduce the author to the German reading public. She did so in an astoundingly provocative autobiographical essay on Lenclos in her own journal *Kalathiskos* (1801–2), in which she holds up Lenclos's life as a model of women's sexual equality. In her later translation, she interweaves her own poetic voice with that of Lenclos's original to such a degree that Mereau-Brentano masquerades as Lenclos in order to be able to voice her views on gender relations, sexuality, and equality.[17]

In her two novels, *Das Blüthenalter der Empfindung* (*The Blossoming of Sensibility*, 1794), published anonymously but identified as written by a female author in the preface ('Die Verfasserinn') and *Amanda und Eduard* (1803), Mereau-Brentano features young couples with emancipatory yearnings for political and individual freedom, inspired by the French Revolution, with the female characters particularly eager to achieve the latter. Unusually well educated, Mereau-Brentano participated in the heady intellectual life of 1790s Jena, was familiar with the writing of Kant, Humboldt, and in particular Fichte. Indeed, she was the only female member of Fichte's private seminar in Jena and well-versed in his philosophical views on autonomy and marriage. Scholars have read *Blüthenalter* as a first testing of Fichte's metaphysics of marriage in the realm of fiction, with a decidedly emancipatory bent in the context of political and gender emancipation[18] that predates F. Schlegel's *Lucinde* by five years. With its insistence on the distinction between love and marriage, *Blütenalther* features two plot strands that highlight

[14] This is the conclusion drawn by Lorely French in 'Magic of Translation'.

[15] An in-depth study of Mereau-Brentano's translations mentions also a possible translation from the Spanish: Britta Hannemann, *Weltliteratur für Bürgertöchter: Die Übersetzerin Sophie Mereau-Brentano* (Göttingen: Wallstein, 2005).

[16] See Daniel Purdy, 'Sophie Mereau's Authorial Masquerades and the Subversion of Romantic Poesie', *Women in German Yearbook*, 13 (1997), 29–48.

[17] This is essentially Purdy's argument.

[18] See Daub, *Uncivil Unions*, 208.

restrictions on women's choice of marriage partners on the one hand, and their potential personal fulfilment in a union marked by love on the other.

Told from the perspective of a highly sentimental and sensitive male character, the protagonists in *Blüthenalther* make their way, both separately and together, through revolutionary Europe in search of such freedom and, frustrated at every turn, decide to escape to the New World which they expect to be an utopian haven for personal freedom and gender equality. Similar concerns of female autonomy and emancipation feature in the later *Amanda and Eduard*. In 1797, Schiller published eight of the letters that would later constitute part of that epistolary novel in his journal *Die Horen*. In the 1803 publication of the completed novel, Mereau-Brentano subverts the genre of the epistolary novel, traditionally used by female authors for 'virtue-in-distress' plots,[19] to explore and lament marriages of convenience, loveless marital unions, and societal restrictions on happiness, especially female happiness, in the love story between Amanda and Eduard that spans several decades. Similar themes occupy Mereau-Brentano in her narrative 'Die Flucht nach der Haupstadt' (The Flight to the City', 1806), a story of love and elopement whose plea for love without societal restrictions could not be clearer. In this case, though, parodic and ironic elements—the couple are actors who play lovers and become lovers because they play those roles—provide a particular metanarrative twist to the story.[20] In addition to prose texts, Mereau-Brentano also published two volumes of poetry in 1801 and 1802. Among them, 'An einen Baum am Spalier' ('To a Trellised Tree', 1800) resonates again with the themes of personal freedom. The lyrical 'I' of the poem addresses a trellised tree and likens it to human life coerced into a rigidly determined societal structure.[21] Of note is that Beethoven set her earlier poem 'Feuerfarb' to music (Opus 52, 1805), after it had appeared years earlier in the *Journal des Luxus und der Moden* in 1792.

Poetry is the main genre that Karoline von Günderrode (1780–1806) chose for her creative endeavours and for which she is best known today. Scholars have read her poetic oeuvre more expressly along biographical lines than in the case of other Romantic women authors. This may be due in part to the easier identification of the autobiographical with the lyrical 'I' in poetry, yet also because there is a continued fascination with her short and unconventional life which included a series of unrequited love relationships (including with Clemens Brentano who later married Sophie Mereau), her taking up residence in the Frankfurter *Damenstift* (Lutheran convent for unmarried and widowed upper-class women), and, finally, her carefully planned dramatic suicide by dagger. The biographical approach to Günderrode's oeuvre is certainly also the result of Bettina von Arnim's account of her friend's life, *Die Günderrode* (1840), which consists of collected letters between the two and some of Günderrode's poems. In it,

[19] Consider in the German context Sophie von La Roche's epistolary novel 'Die Geschichte des Fräuleins von Sternheim' of 1771.

[20] The text is translated in Jeannine Blackwell and Susanne Zantop (eds), *Bitter Healing: German Women Writers 1700–1830. An Anthology* (Lincoln, Neb.: University of Nebraska Press, 1990), 380–99.

[21] Blackwell and Zantop, *Bitter Healing*, 378–9.

B. von Arnim's painful personal report on Günderrode's suicide has received particular attention. In the twentieth century, East German author Christa Wolf published two highly influential works on Günderrode: one, *Karoline von Günderrode: Im Schatten eines Traumes* (1979, *In the Shadow of a Dream*), presents selected poems and letters and uses events in Günderrode's life as reference points for reflections on the position of the female author in the early nineteenth century; the second novel, *Kein Ort. Nirgends. (No Place on Earth)*, imagines a fictional encounter between Günderrode and Heinrich von Kleist.

The interest in Günderrode's biography may also stem from a number of her remarks on gender and gender identity that are unusually radical and honest. Nearly every reference to Günderrode's life quotes the following passage

> I had often had the unfeminine wish to throw myself into the midst of a raging battle, to die. Why wasn't I born a man! I have no mind for feminine virtues, for feminine happiness. The wild, the great, the brilliant things are what I love. There is an ill-fated incongruity in my soul; and it will and must remain that way, for I am a woman and have desires like a man, without the strength of a man. For this reason I am so changing and so at odds with myself.[22]

Clemens Brentano identified this alienation from her own gender and the disunity with herself in Günderrode's poetry when he criticized her first collection of poems as being located 'between the masculine and the feminine'.[23] Günderrode explicitly takes on a male role, when, in parts of her correspondence with her married lover Friedrich Creuzer, she writes about her feelings towards him from the perspective of a fictive 'male friend'.

While Günderrode's biography is certainly intriguing, her oeuvre itself is just as fascinating. Two volumes of writing were published under the pseudonym 'Tian' in 1804 and 1805. Highly educated, including in mythology, history, and philosophy, her often dark and brooding poems approach the pain of unfulfilled desire, a yearning to live in a different world and time ('Einstens lebt ich süßes Leben'— 'Once a dulcet life was mine'),[24] and, quite often, for death ('Hochroth'—'Bright Red)'. The reader may find resonances with Novalis's poetry, especially the death wish in his 'Hymnen an die Nacht' and with the disenchantment of the world through reason (Novalis, 'Wenn nicht mehr Zahlen und Figuren'; Günderrode, 'Vorzeit und neue Zeit'). Indeed, Günderrode composed a poem titled 'Novalis' in which she addresses the poet, praises him for his prophetic vision, and sees the world's spirit revealed through him.

A particularly intriguing number of her poems reflect her fascination with ancient and oriental cultures, reflecting the nascent Orientalism and philological studies in

22 Letter to Gunda Brentano, 29 Aug. 1801. In Lorely French, *German Women as Letter Writers, 1750–1850* (Madison, NJ: Fairleigh Dickinson University Press, 1996), 145–6.

23 French, *German Women*, 146.

24 Tr. in Blackwell and Zantop, *Bitter Healing*, 428–39.

German Romanticism. Several poems treat Egyptian themes ('Egypten', 'Buonaparte in Egypten', 'Der Nil'), others appropriate Hindu religious practices and philosophy for her reflections on love, death, and afterlife. In the poem 'Die Malabarischen Witwen', she presents the Hindu custom of the widow's sacrifice on the pyre as a metaphysical reunion with the beloved and, by extension, suicide as a triumph of union over separation. Even in death, she chooses a Sanskrit poem, translated by Herder, as her epitaph or 'suicide note'.[25] Oriental themes occupy the author not only in poetry but also in prose and drama. In her narrative 'Geschichte eines Braminen', the search for fulfilment, virtue, and inner peace is presented as one of exile from the world, solitude, and death. With her play *Mahomed, der Prophet von Mekka*,[26] she confidently inserts herself into the contemporary discussion on the representation of Islam led by two of the great male thinkers of the time, Voltaire (*Le fanatisme ou Mahomet le prophète*) and Goethe's translation thereof entitled simply *Mahomet*. Contrary to Voltaire's and Goethe's depiction of the prophet, Günderrode aims to present a sympathetic and humanizing picture by reducing the prophet's essential 'otherness' evoked in Voltaire and Goethe. Her choice of the subgenre *Lesedrama*, i.e. a drama meant to be read not performed, similar to Lessing's *Nathan der Weise*, provides her with the opportunity to include some lengthy philosophical musings while providing her 'generic' cover to deflect contemporary critics who might have chafed at her daring to write a drama in the vein of Goethe and Voltaire.

Letters and correspondence have played a considerable role in the oeuvre of each of the women authors discussed so far. None, however, comes close to the volume and literariness of Romantic letter-writer par excellence, Rahel Levin Varnhagen (1771–1833), who is said to have written thousands of letters over the course of her life. Born in Berlin into a wealthy Jewish merchant family, this intelligent young woman hosted one of the city's most famous salons frequented by an unconventional mixture of members of the nobility and bourgeoisie, of Jews and Christians, men and women. Among the Romantic authors who participated were Ludwig Tieck, Clemens Brentano, Friedrich Schlegel, and Adalbert von Chamisso. She remained unmarried until her early forties when she became the wife of the much younger Karl August Varnhagen.

Gender has been a key factor in the aesthetics of letter-writing, with eighteenth-century male authors encouraging women to hew to letter-writing due their 'natural' affinity for this supposedly pre-literary form with its purported emphasis on the trivialities of life and sentiment. This encouragement was often coupled with a discouragement to write in forms traditionally associated with male authors such as the novel or the drama. Over the last two decades, feminist scholars have not

[25] See Dorothy M. Figueira, 'Karoline von Günderrode's Sanskrit Epitaph'. *Comparative Literature Studies*, 26/4 (1989), 291–303. Figueira is critical of *Günderrode*'s misinterpretation of the Sanskrit poem as one of despair.

[26] For the analysis of Günderrode's drama, I draw heavily on Stephanie M. Hilger, *Women Write Back: Strategies of Response and the Dynamics of European Literary Culture, 1790–1805* (Amsterdam: Rodopi, 2009).

only undertaken painstaking archival work to unearth letters by women authors but also developed an aesthetic of letter-writing as a multi-faceted and conscious means of female self-fashioning.[27] In their correspondence, women writers navigate deftly between public and private spheres, history and literature, and fiction and reality. In Rahel Varnhagen's case, letter-writing is a search for authenticity and truth that is at its most intense in her exchanges with intimate female friends such as Pauline Wiesel. In these exchanges, the two writers reflect on their outsider status—Varnhagen due to her Jewish ethnicity; Wiesel's as the mistress of Prince Louis Ferdinand of Prussia—and society's restrictions and lies, and vow to strive for truth in their personal relationship which, as Varnhagen states, is life-sustaining: 'Dear heart! Unique Pauline! Who must stay living! otherwise I will be in my grave, so lonely! There is only one person who knows who I am. You, you, you! Nobody will believe it: I know it.'[28] In another letter, Rahel Varnhagen imagines the friendship the two women could have had, had they known each other before Pauline's marriage and imagines the complementarity of their characters: 'This friend would have been I. What a life! ... Such people like you should have had my musings, my circumspection, my rationality! Such people as I your courage and your beauty.'[29] Today's readers may be struck by the intensity of feelings expressed between the two women that suggests homoerotic elements.

Rahel Varnhagen is the female Romantic author who most explicitly reflected on her persona as a letter-writer and who was most intent on actively shaping her legacy as a woman of letters. In characterizing herself in the above letter to P. Wiesel as one full of 'musings', 'circumspection', and 'rationality', she emphasizes intellectual qualities traditionally ascribed to men. Unlike many other women writers of her time, Rahel Varnhagen was not shy to claim her place among male intellectuals, philosophers, and writers, and even touts her own uniqueness. Tellingly, in a letter to the physician David Veit, she writes with astounding clarity and self-esteem: 'I am as unique as the greatest phenomenon on this earth. The greatest artist, philosopher, or poet is not above me. We are of the same element. Of the same order, and belong together.'[30] This confident sense of her place in the intellectual world of her time also comes through in her plans to publish her correspondence. Long before her later husband conceived of organizing and publishing her letters, Rahel Varnhagen, at age 29, expressed a sense that her correspondence would be an original poetic form: 'And if I die—try to acquire all my letters—through some ruse—from all my friends and acquaintances ... and put them in order with Brinckmann. It will be an original = story and poetic.'[31] Some years later, when Karl Varnhagen suggests that he organize her written exchanges for posthumous publication, she forcefully demands that she be the one to select and edit the letters for publication:

[27] See studies by Barbara Hahn, Lorely French, Margaretmary Daley, and Barbara Becker-Cantarino.

[28] French, *German Women*, 177.

[29] French, *German Women*, 178. One letter to Pauline Wiesel is tr. in Blackwell and Zantop, *Bitter Healing*, 411–14.

[30] Blackwell and Zantop, *Bitter Healing*, 409.

[31] Letter to Frau von Boye in 1800, in French, *German Women*, 163.

'But I myself want to examine my letters and discard; and not in forty, fifty years, as you wrote …, but much sooner. I want to live when it is read.'[32] Despite her insistence, none of her correspondence was published during her lifetime. Rather, her husband published a selection in the year after her death, titled *Rahel: Buch des Andenkens* (1834) (*Rahel: Book of Rememberance*). Despite its massive length of 1,800 pages, hundreds of her letters are omitted, as are all replies. This strategy gives the *Buch des Andenken* a unique monologic character. Scholars have criticized Karl Varnhagen's editorial interventions and recent decades have seen substantial archival and philological efforts to close these lacunae.[33]

While Rahel Varnhagen understood her correspondence very much as a vehicle for shaping her authorial persona and legacy, Caroline Schlegel-Schelling (1763–1809), also a prolific woman of letters, seems to have understood her epistolary work more as a way of 'preserving the self in progress'[34] and was not inclined to have her letters published. Her reluctance to see herself as a public artist stands in a somewhat paradoxical opposition to the artistry evident in her letters. A concern for truthful representation of her life as a woman in her time runs through her epistolary oeuvre. Indeed, Schlegel-Schelling's life was one of multiple tragedies, personal and political, but also of strength and resilience, all of which is reflected in her letters. Born into an intellectual family—her father was a professor of theology and oriental studies at Göttingen University—Schlegel-Schelling benefited from exposure to intellectual luminaries and their works during her youth. She found herself a widow with one young daughter at the age of 26 when she made her way to Mainz just as the city came under French occupation. Labelled a traitor, Schlegel-Schelling became a political prisoner while pregnant by a French officer and spent several months under extremely dire circumstances at a fortress near Königstein. Upon her eventual release, the newborn infant died prematurely, as had several previous newborns. Schlegel-Schelling's most productive years took place in Jena while she was married to August Wilhelm Schlegel. From 1796 to 1800, the couple lived in Jena and for part of that time shared a house with A. W. Schlegel's brother Friedrich and his partner Dorothea Veit, an arrangement that was often characterized by tension, particularly between the two women. Her marriage to A. W. Schlegel ended in divorce and, most tragically, her one living daughter Auguste Böhmer died at age 15. Her third marriage to philosopher Friedrich Schelling brought her to Munich where she died in her mid-forties in 1809. Given this biography, one would expect Schlegel-Schelling's letters to be full of emotion and passion, yet more than anything they reveal a restrained personality who is attempting to 'express and reconcile the various identities that she adopts in the course of her life'.[35] The editorial history of her letters is complex, with seven different

[32] French, *German Women*, 165.

[33] See studies by Heidi Tewarson, and by Barbara Hahn and Ursula Isselstein.

[34] This expression is the title for the chapter on Schlegel-Schelling in Margaretmary Daley, *Women of Letters: A Study of Self and Genre in the Personal Writing of Caroline Schlegel-Schelling, Rahel Levin Varnhagen, and Bettina von Arnim* (Columbia, SC: Camden House, 1998).

[35] Daley, *Women of Letters*, 21.

editors so far (the most recent being Sigrid Damm in 1997), each of whom has made individual choices on selecting from the voluminous correspondence based on personal agendas, ideological preferences, or customs of the time.[36]

In addition to being an accomplished letter-writer, Schlegel-Schelling was intimately and actively involved in the Jena Romantic project as an unacknowledged translator and contributor of literary reviews to such journals as Friedrich and August Wilhelm Schlegel's *Athenaeum*, Friedrich Schiller's *Die Horen*, and A. W. Schlegel's *Allgemeine Literatur-Zeitung*, although specific attribution is in many cases difficult.[37] Friedrich Schlegel, in particular, attests to Schlegel-Schelling's talent and intellect and encourages her to contribute to his journal. Interestingly, he provides conflicting suggestions in terms of the genre of her contributions. On the one hand, he states in a letter that she should stick with letters and reviews as genres that she is fully capable of producing. On the other hand, however, he asks her to contribute to his *Fragmente*, i.e. a genre that was traditionally considered beyond a woman's ability. Even more paradoxically, he urges her to create fragments out of her letters, a suggestion that she ignores.[38] Looking closely at the exchanges between Friedrich Schlegel and Schlegel-Schelling, it is evident that she was a truly important sounding board and interlocutor for specific texts in his Romantic project. For instance, F. Schlegel's critique of Ludwig Tieck's novel *Sternbald* in *Athenaeums-Fragment* 418 was preceded by several exchanges of letters in which F. Schlegel specifically solicited her opinion on Tieck's text.[39] With regard to her work and achievements as a translator, while her contributions to the ambitious translation project of Shakespeare's dramas *Shakespeares Dramatische Werke* (vols i–viii, 1797–1801; vol. ix, 1810) are today generally acknowledged, specific attributions have again proven difficult. However, for *Romeo and Juliet*, attribution has been clearer, in part because of a co-authored essay published in Schiller's *Horen* titled 'On Shakespeare's Romeo and Juliet'.[40] A. W. Schlegel's Shakespeare translation received uniform and universal praise at its publication and is still considered a milestone in translation practice today—an achievement that is as much Schlegel-Schelling's as her husband's.

The female Romantic authors discussed in this chapter—Dorothea Veit-Schlegel, Sophie Mereau-Brentano, Karoline von Günderrode, Rahel Varnhagen, and Caroline Schlegel-Schelling—constitute a vital part of German Romanticism. Their contributions span all genres characteristic of the period: the novel, literary criticism, poetry, drama, and letters. In each of these areas, they expand our traditional notions of German Romanticism and thus make this crucial period in German and European literary history even more fertile ground for scholars.

[36] Daley details editorial history of Schlegel-Schelling's letters, 27–31.

[37] See the excellent new website on Caroline Schlegel-Schelling's oeuvre, all translated into English: <www.carolineschelling.com>. This website lists Schlegel-Schelling's confirmed and also probable contributions.

[38] Mergenthaler, *Zwischen Eros und Mitteilung*, 218.

[39] See the meticulous research on this by Mergenthaler, *Zwischen Eros und Mitteilung*, 225–33, who views the exchange as an intellectual dialogue along the lines of Socrates and Diotima.

[40] *Die Horen*, 10/6 (1797), 18–48.

Further Reading

Berman, Antoine, *The Experience of the Foreign: Culture and Translation in Romantic Germany* (Albany, NY: State University of New York Press, 1992).

Blackwell, Jeannine, and Zantop, Susanne (eds), *Bitter Healing: German Women Writers from 1700 to 1830: An Anthology* (Lincoln, Neb.: University of Nebraska Press, 1990).

Brandstädter, Heike, and Jeorgakopulos, Katharina, *Dorothea Schlegel, Florentin: Lektüre eines Vergessenen Textes* (Hamburg: Argument Verlag, 2001).

Daley, Margaretmary, *Women of Letters: A Study of Self and Genre in the Personal Writing of Caroline Schlegel-Schelling, Rahel Levin Varnhagen, and Bettina von Arnim* (Columbia, SC: Camden House, 1998).

Daub, Adrian, *Uncivil Unions: The Metaphysics of Marriage in German Idealism and Romanticism* (Chicago: University of Chicago Press, 2012).

French, Lorely, *German Women as Letter Writers, 1750–1850* (Madison, NJ: Fairleigh Dickinson University Press, 1996).

Hahn, Barbara, and Ursula Isselstein, *Rahel Levin Varnhagen: Die Wiederentdeckung einer Schriftstellerin* (Göttingen: Vandenhoeck & Ruprecht, 1987).

Hannemann, Britta, *Weltliteratur für Bürgertöchter: Die Übersetzerin Sophie Mereau-Brentano* (Göttingen: Wallstein, 2005).

Helfer, Martha B., 'Dorothea Veit-Schlegel's *Florentin*: Constructing a Feminist Romantic Aesthetic', *German Quarterly*, 69/2 (1996), 144–60.

Hilger, Stephanie M., *Women Write Back: Strategies of Response and the Dynamics of European Literary Culture, 1790–1805* (Amsterdam: Rodopi, 2009).

Hopp, Doris, *Karoline von Günderrode* (Frankfurt am Main: Freies Deutsches Hochstift, 2006).

Purdy, Daniel, 'Sophie Mereau's Authorial Masquerades and the Subversion of Romantic *Poesie*', *Women in German Yearbook*, 13 (1997), 29–48.

Reulecke, Martin, *Caroline Schlegel-Schelling: Virtuosin der Freiheit. Eine kommentierte Bibliographie* (Würzburg: Königshausen & Neumann, 2010).

Rossbeck, Brigitte, *Zum Trotz Glücklich: Caroline Schlegel-Schelling und die Romantische Lebenskunst* (Munich: Siedler, 2008).

Schlegel, Dorothea Mendelssohn Veit, *Florentin: A Novel*, ed. and tr. Edwina G. Lawler and Ruth Richardson (Lewiston, NY: Edwin Mellen Press, 1988).

Stern, Carola, *'Ich Möchte Mir Flügel Wünschen': Das Leben der Dorothea Schlegel* (Reinbek bei Hamburg: Rowohlt, 1990).

Tewarson, Heidi Thomann, *Rahel Levin Varnhagen: The Life and Work of a German Jewish Intellectual* (Lincoln, Neb.: Nebraska University Press, 1998).

Von Gersdorff, Dagmar. *'Die Erde Ist Mir Heimat Nicht Geworden': Das Leben der Karoline von Günderrode* (Frankfurt am Main: Insel, 2006).

Von Hammerstein, Katharina, *Sophie Mereau-Brentano: Freiheit, Liebe, Weiblichkeit. Trikolore Sozialer und Individueller Selbstbestimmung um 1800* (Heidelberg: Winter, 1994).

CHAPTER 14

THE SCEPTICISM OF HEINRICH VON KLEIST

TIM MEHIGAN

In what follows I present a philosophical reading of the writer Heinrich von Kleist (1788–1811) and his oeuvre. Kleist's connections with the movement of Romanticism only become properly evident when measured against the weight of philosophical problems Kleist felt to be pressing even before his career as a writer began. The most considerable of these was the problem of philosophical scepticism, a by-product of his early encounter with the philosophy of Immanuel Kant. The picture of Kleist I present here is one of an earnest mind in search of an answer to a problem that emerged in the philosophical discussion after Kant and, in one sense at least, has never left us.

Kleist and his Time

Heinrich von Kleist never recoiled from the power of images and image-making. His early thinking is completely steeped in visual language. His first drama, *Die Familie Schroffenstein* (1803), for example, pivots on the power of a single image—the child's severed finger—to speak of the ruinous circumstances that characterize the feuding Warwand and Rossitz dynasties. It is Kleist's general attachment as a writer to the visual that makes the dramatic medium appear, as it had been for Goethe, a natural medium in which to ply his craft. This remains the case even when Kleist's subject matter ostensibly commits him in the manner of the conventional Romantic to something like the reverse: to adumbrating the limits of the visual and the power of the unseen to entrance the soul. In the story 'Die heilige Cäcilie oder die Gewalt der Musik' (1810), for example, the forensic interest in disclosing the source of entrancement that prevented an act of iconoclasm in the Aachen cathedral brings about a denouement in which the four iconoclastic brothers are said to bay like wolves whenever the captivating passages of the musical score are intoned. Yet Kleist's point is not to celebrate the triumph of an older sensibility so much as to unsettle any reliable sense of it. The ostensible message of 'Die heilige Cäcilie'—that an old-style auditory community, bound by and to a culture of music, has more 'combining power' than a new community of the visual (where iconoclasm as a pursuit is a consequence of the belief in the power of what is seen)—falls literally on deaf ears. Kleist allows no easy endorsement of a project seeking to forestall the emergence of a new image-based culture.

In 'Die heilige Cäcilie oder die Gewalt der Musik', then, Kleist appears decidedly out of step with his time. This is a time, at least in Germany, poised between the never fully actuated promise of Enlightenment and the sudden widening of the spirit that accompanied the movement of Romanticism. The rationale for the new poetic programme of Romanticism had been laid out by Friedrich von Hardenberg (Novalis) and the brothers Friedrich and August Wilhelm Schlegel on the suspicion that the old logic of reason-led, bloodless illumination of the mind, as promoted in Germany by late eighteenth-century 'enlighteners' such as Lessing and Moses Mendelssohn, would never truly capture the heart and the soul. But at this moment around 1800 in which a new type of writing was beginning to emerge, it was sooner a new philosophy, already dubbed 'the Kantian philosophy' (and not, say, 'Kant's philosophy') on account of its proliferating forms and complicated reception, that most promised to reset spiritual co-ordinates. In the turn towards this new philosophy, the chance to install a meaningful exchange in the German lands between the northern moral mind, with its Pietistic leanings, and the sensate body, with roots in southern Catholicism, seemed, at least for a time, clearly within reach. That a deeper union of mind and matter, Protestantism and Catholicism, might soon be realized animated every committed spirit in Germany around 1800.

That Kleist—just as much as Novalis and the Schlegel brothers—was driven by this urge to forge a union of spiritual and material opposites makes him seem from our present perspective in some ways at one with them. In truth, however, Kleist drew quite different conclusions from those of the early Romantics about the meaning and significance of the Kantian philosophy. These conclusions were initially laid out in letters he wrote to his fiancée Wilhelmine von Zenge in 1800 and 1801. The letters themselves document in a powerful way the impact of a new philosophy on a young mind. Nietzsche, who was later to pass through his own reckoning with the Kantian philosophy, read them as such and admired them. They reveal Kleist—an 'Augenmensch' of a special kind, as already intimated—rifling through his visual toolkit in an attempt to come to terms with the significance of Kantian precepts. In this reliance on a visual language Kleist was bound to draw out certain lessons from reading Kant, but to pass over others. In its poignant quality and far-reaching significance, the crisis can be seen as a mental and emotional point of rupture that had a major impact on Kleist's intellectual development and the literary career upon which he was later to embark.[1]

[1] The commentary to the first volume of the Deutsche Klassiker-Verlag's edn of Kleist's *Sämtliche Werke und Briefe* declares that 'der biographische Drehpunkt des Kleist-Verständnisses ... die Kant-Lektüre ist'. See Heinrich von Kleist,: *Sämtliche Werke und Briefe*, ed. Ilse-Marie Barth, Klaus Müller-Salget, Stefan Ormanns, and Hinrich C. Seeba (Frankfurt am Main: Deutscher Klassiker Verlag, 1991), i. 466, 470.

The 'Kant Crisis'

The philosophy Kleist digested, whether directly through a reading of Kant's philosophy or via the means of one or more of Kant's many interpreters, remains both significant and controversial even today. The promise inherent in Kant's philosophy in its own day was that it appeared to suggest a way beyond philosophical positions whose opposed nature had seemed intractable for more than half a century: positions which on one side dogmatically held to a rationally purposive nature, usually underwritten by some kind of rational theology (or, as Leibniz called it, 'theodicy'), and, on the other side, an empirically focused viewpoint that limited the material admitted to philosophical understanding to the data of experience—however such 'experience' itself was finally to be understood (Hume had introduced significant restrictions to the definition of experience in his *Treatise of Human Nature*). That Kant had successfully developed a middle path connecting a rationalism (or 'reason') of 'a priori' concepts antedating the facts of experience to an empiricism of sense data logically derivable from experience was the initial seed that led to the flowering of early German Romanticism.

Among those who held that Kant had offered a philosophically compelling account of the way forward beyond the stalemate between rationalism and empiricism was Kant's first great expositor in Germany, Karl Leonhard Reinhold. In expounding his own 'theory of the capacity for representation' in 1789[2] Reinhold saw himself working in fidelity with Kantian precepts: immediate knowledge of the outside world was rejected in favour of a complex account of the workings of the mind that representation as a fundamental activity of human consciousness brought forth. In Reinhold's view, representation occurred not by way of direct apprehension of objects so much as through reports, variously to intuition and the understanding, about an object's properties. Cognition of properties occurred under two linked but separate aspects: an aspect rendered on the side of the subject ('the representing'), and an aspect attesting to the material reality of the object on the side of the object ('the represented'). The triangulation of the representing entity or subject and the represented thing or object in the process of representation (*Vorstellung*) gave up in its union of these two aspects a stable—and to this extent arguably 'Kantian'—picture of receptively given, yet also productively engaged, human consciousness.

Even if this account of Kant's philosophy was never explicitly endorsed by Kant, it was taken as a coherent statement of Kantian positions well into the 1790s.[3] It also seemed to be a more readily intelligible version of Kant's philosophy than Kant himself had accomplished. Reinhold rose to prominence both because of the overall clarity of his exegesis

[2] Karl Leonhard Reinhold, *Versuch einer neuen Theorie des Vorstellungsvermögens* (Prague and Jena: Widtmann & Mauke, 1789). English: *Essay on a New Theory of the Human Capacity for Representation*, tr. Tim Mehigan and Barry Empson (Berlin and New York: Walter de Gruyter, 2011)—hereafter cited with the abbreviation *NT* and page number.

[3] See Tim Mehigan and Barry Empson, 'Introduction', in *NT*, pp. xviii–xxiii.

(although the *New Theory* is certainly quite turgid over long stretches) and because his earlier discussion of Kant's outlook in the *Briefe über die Kantische Philosophie* (1786–7) had been explicitly endorsed by Kant. Even if Kant remained tight-lipped about the *New Theory*, it appeared to others in the late 1780s and early 1790s that he was nevertheless largely in agreement with it. It was not until Johann Gottlieb Fichte's major work *Die Wissenschaftslehre*, promulgated in several versions from 1794, that a philosophy came into being which laid claim to being a more robust and authoritative expression of Kantian thought than the Reinholdian Kant then in vogue.

By the mid-1790s, then, a complicated picture of what was glossed under the heading of 'the Kantian philosophy' had emerged. Alongside ongoing debate about the meaning of Kant's critical philosophy was a new debate about the status of allegedly new forms of Kantianism as well as restated hostility to Kant and Kantianism from religious thinkers such as Friedrich Jacobi, who now openly held that Kantianism was atheistic. A tumult over the alleged atheism of Kantian thought was to engulf Fichte himself in 1798. Fichte and his colleague Forberg, who had attempted to mark out new positions in metaphysical thought on the basis of Kantian assumptions, were held in one anonymous polemic to be in contempt of the religious disposition of the day. The 'atheism dispute' which reverberated through German letters for nearly two years afterwards was only settled when Fichte, the more prominent of the two, was removed from his Chair of Philosophy at the University of Jena in an edict issued by Karl August, Grand Duke of Saxe-Weimar-Eisenach, in 1800.[4]

By 1800, then, the year in which the young Kleist first became aware of Kantian philosophy, this philosophy had already become much more than a theory or set of theories: it was by now an explosive new type of thinking that contained more than a suggestion of scandal. The taint of scandal, of course, can only have made it appear even more worthy of Kleist's attention than it might otherwise have been. Whatever the direct pretext for Kleist's attention to it, it is clear by early 1801 that he had already meditated at some length on it. This meditation, as I will discuss, took him through three distinct stages of comprehension. The crisis itself was to appear at the third stage. Later responses to Kant are also registered, but these must be inferred from the dramas and stories after Kleist commenced a career as a writer. Of these responses, at least one further stage in Kleist's reception of Kant can be considered significant. This final stage reveals not only that Kleist maintained an intellectual development beyond the initial encounter with Kant in the early letters. It also reveals that Kant and Kantianism remained a constant point of orientation, regardless of whether he continued to make explicit mention of Kantian philosophy in his writings.

As I have argued elsewhere, Kleist was scarcely a proper Kantian (of whatever persuasion) when he first described the nature of his encounter with Kantian thought around 1800. But Kleist was arguably to become a Kantian as a result of crisis, although by no

[4] For a complete documentation of the atheism dispute and Fichte's role in it, see Johann Gottlieb Fichte, *Appellation an das Publikum: Dokumente zum Atheismusstreit um Fichte, Forberg, Niethammer. Jena 1798/99*, ed. Werner Röhr (Leipzig: Reclam, 1987).

means an orthodox one.[5] The story of his intellectual development from 1801 to 1811, therefore, is a story of an increasing appreciation of new thinking that initially, and not without a touch of melodrama, had plunged him into despair. This development was also to witness distinct moments of clarity and accommodation to the new philosophy, even if it might not finally have brought about the settled mind and sense of self he glimpses, however fleetingly, through the hard-won victories of certain of his characters. In meeting a challenge he knew philosophically not to underestimate, Kleist's journey has representative dimensions for all those writers and thinkers, beginning with Nietzsche, who, with increasing levels of awareness, have journeyed precociously from the habits of thought and feeling of a lapsed age into a new era—an era already perceived, perhaps, in broad outline, though far from fully comprehended.

The Sceptical Turn

Among Kleist's juvenilia—indeed his first serious piece of writing—is an essay from 1799 now known under its abbreviated title 'Essay on the Secure Path to Happiness' ('Aufsatz, den sichern Weg des Glücks zu finden'). Its chief interest lies in the conceptual programme it unfolds: a Panglossian account of happiness predicated on rationalistic assumptions in the vein of Leibniz. Kleist, at this point, cannot have known of Voltaire's parody of such naïve optimism in his play *Candide* (1759), though he was later to journey to Paris and to acquire fluency in the French language (and even later spent several months in a French prison during the Napoleonic Wars). Untrammelled by such Voltairean wit and foreknowledge Kleist reads from the script of the late seventeenth-century rationalist in the essay with, indeed, unsuspecting candour. It is these instinctively embraced positions that were to become the first casualty of crisis a little more than a year later.

The first shift we discern in the young Kleist's thinking as a result of impending crisis, therefore, is an abandonment of naïvely held, rationalistically premised optimism: Kleist loses the sense that education (*Bildung*) will necessarily illuminate the path to moral virtue. Whilst Kleist's moral compass thereafter tilts in a new direction, it does so in what might be called, with reference to Kant, a 'pre-critical' way: more attention to the discernment of moral ends in life will need to be applied; the moral path, furthermore, must become a *philosophical* endeavour. The result of the first interruption of unsuspecting rationalism, then, is that Kleist sees the need to direct attention to philosophy. It is for this reason that philosophy becomes his focus in 1800, and, for the same reason, that a work of philosophy can become the source of the second—and far more

[5] In my *Heinrich von Kleist: Writing After Kant* (Rochester, NY: Camden House, 2011), pp. ix–x, 1–12, I discuss in detail the question of Kleist's Kantianism. Hereafter cited as *WAK* with accompanying page reference.

profound—disturbance by the beginning 1801. It is this second disturbance that ushers in crisis.[6]

The crisis as outlined in Kleist's letters is notable for its vivid use of visual imagery. The passage, from a letter written to Wilhelmine on 25 March 1801, which has been much quoted in Kleist scholarship, bears quotation again:

> Wenn alle Menschen statt der Augen grüne Gläser hätten, so würden sie urteilen müssen, die Gegenstände, welche sie dadurch erblicken, *sind* grün, und nie würden sie entscheiden können, ob ihr Auge ihnen die Dinge zeigt, wie sie sind, oder ob es nicht etwas zu ihnen hinzutut, was nicht ihnen, sondern dem Auge gehört. So ist es mit dem Verstande. Wir können nicht entscheiden, ob das, was wir Wahrheit nennen, wahrhaft Wahrheit ist, oder ob es uns nur so scheint. Ist das letzte, so ist die Wahrheit, die wir hier sammeln, nach dem Tode nicht mehr—und alles Bestreben, ein Eigentum sich zu erwerben, das uns auch in das Grab folgt, ist vergeblich—[7]

This passage marks a sceptical turn in Kleist's thinking. This sceptical turn clearly resulted from Kleist's reading of Kant, or a second-hand account of Kant's philosophy, for Kleist intends the passage as a gloss of Kantian philosophy for his bride-to-be. Of course the passage does not and cannot begin to do justice to the complicated project that Kant had issued in the three great Critiques from 1781 to 1790. It is doubtful that Kleist had more than limited awareness of the complexity of this philosophical project. It would be proper, therefore, to speak of Kleist's 'pseudo-Kantianism', as James Conant does in relation to Nietzsche's Kant reception in an important recent essay.[8] The use of this term, following Conant, should not be taken to suggest that Kleist gives a 'fake' account of Kant's philosophy in the letters or subsequently (even if this remains a conclusion that some commentators have readily drawn[9]). Rather, as I shall make clear, the term indicates a particular reading of Kant that lies at variance with what Kant himself intended but which nevertheless formed part of the complicated reception of Kant's philosophy in the two decades which followed the first Critique.

Whatever the limitations of Kleist's early reception of Kant, it is clear from this key passage in the letter of 25 March 1801 that Kleist has already moved two large steps away

[6] I have discussed these two stages in Kleist's path to Kant in *WAK* 33–51.

[7] References are to the following edn: Heinrich von Kleist, *Sämtliche Werke und Briefe*, ed. Helmut Sembdner (Darmstadt: Wissenschaftliche Buchgesellschaft, 1983), ii. 634. Hereafter cited with volume number and page number.

[8] James Conant, 'The Dialectic of Perspectivism', 2 parts, *SATS* (autumn 2005 and spring 2006). Hereafter cited as DP with part number and page reference.

[9] James Phillips (*The Equivocation of Reason: Kleist Reading Kant* (Stanford, Calif.: Stanford UP, 2007)) has argued that we cannot simply assume that Kleist interpreted Kant's philosophy 'correctly'. Phillips suggests that Kleist misunderstood Kant because he did not grasp 'that Kant has changed the rules of the game: the burden of the *Critique of Pure Reason* is an account of the transcendental structures of cognition, rather than a quest for things as they truly are' (p. x). He continues, however: 'Kleist's despair [at the loss of truth] is not without a resonance in Kant', and, '[i]nsofar as Kleist's reading of Kant fastens on the unassimilability of things in themselves, it can be argued that it is critical rather than obscurantist' (pp. xi–xii).

from rationalistic doctrine. A single step away would involve an intermediate position where Kleist might have retained a sceptically informed rationalism: one that overcomes the limitations of the naïve perspectivism that characterizes the 'Aufsatz, den sichern Weg des Glücks zu finden' but does not yet abandon the assumption of realism. There are signs, indeed, that this intermediate step is precisely the position Kleist takes up in 1800—the period after (what I argue to be) his first encounter with Kant's thinking but predating the actual crisis of early 1801. In this period, Kleist maintains scepticism about objects—objects appear distorted to proper vision and such vision is patently in need of correction—but the admission of distortion entails no final loss of objects themselves. Nevertheless, Kleist quickly moves beyond this point to a new position whose consequence is nothing less than the abandonment of the rationalistic endeavour itself.

This shift is accomplished not by applying 'ordinary' scepticism to the problem of knowledge, but scepticism of the severest kind—the kind Descartes invokes, but also attempts to quell, in his argument against the 'evil demon' of the Pyrrhonists in his *Meditations*. In invoking such scepticism and supplying no antidote for it, Kleist does more than Kant aims to achieve with his 'Copernican revolution'—a revolution which moves in the direction of the shaping disposition of the human mind. Where Kant applies scepticism about the outside world in order to defeat dogmatic rationalism and simple-minded empiricism, *but no more than this*, Kleist follows the Copernican turn towards the shaping disposition of the mind but draws far deeper and more extravagant conclusions. In a radical move, Kleist effectively dispenses both with the 'primary' qualities of objects, the formal aspects of their 'objective' appearance such as proportion, quality, relation, etc., as well as the 'secondary' (subjectively super-added) qualities by which they are known through the sensory apparatus to the mind of human beings (taste, colour, beauty, and so on). In collapsing the primary into the secondary qualities of objects on suspicion that they are mere 'appearances' (one might say in German: 'nur scheinbar *Erscheinungen*'), and not just apparent forms of the objects themselves ('dem Auge [so] scheinende *Erscheinungen*') which may or may not be the same as these objects, Kleist joins a complicated discussion about Kant's philosophy that began in the mid to late 1780s in a period Robert Pippin has called the 'Kantian aftermath'.[10] It is in this context that it becomes a legitimate enterprise to view Kleist's crisis and his subsequent literary production as part of such an aftermath. To convict Kleist's pseudo-Kantianism of being a gross misunderstanding of Kant, which scholarship has been wont to do, distracts from Kleist's intellectual contribution to such an aftermath, which in my opinion does indeed deserve our attention.

If we now review the conceptual changes outlined in Kleist's early thinking, we can see that he passes from a naïve perspectivism, premised on an arguably seventeenth-century account of Leibnizian rationalism, to a brief period of attenuated realism where a distorting perspective is identified but the possibility of a higher order perspectivism still left open, through to a third stage in which radical scepticism is applied to discount the

[10] See his *The Persistence of Subjectivity: On the Kantian Aftermath* (Cambridge: Cambridge University Press, 2005).

possibility that any kind of independent knowledge of the world is possible. Kleist's crisis appears at this last stage. Kleist now declares that we cannot know if what we call knowledge truly is knowledge at all or only appears as such. According to Kleist's visually informed way of understanding, human beings do not just wear 'green spectacles'[11] that can be dispensed with and where some form of limited rationalism might still be conscionable. As the passage from the letter makes clear, human beings are now encumbered with *non-dispensable* 'green glass eyes' as a condition of our perceptual humanity. The cognitive perturbation that the green glass eyes introduce must therefore be regarded as irreparable; the impairment is unalterable and lasts a lifetime. This impairment also invalidates the rationalist project of knowledge, since no corrective to the distortions of perspective can possibly result. According to this new stage in the order of cognition, all our thinking has become irreparably distorted.

In reaching this third stage, Kleist has also made problematic the 'appearances', which Kant had established in the still productively philosophical meaning of 'phenomena': the technically unreachable aspect of things-in-themselves whose effects on human beings can nevertheless be regulated through a properly tutored understanding based on a full account of the enterprise of knowledge. Phenomena are now the appearances of unreachable 'noumena', which can never be known by human beings and whose essence, therefore, is never subject to correction. A world of ubiquitous, yet potentially governable, 'Erscheinungen' has been turned into a world of 'Schein' which can never be philosophically appeased. As Kleist, on this view, correctly observes, anticipating a radical strain in modern thinking known to us in many versions of the postmodern, 'all striving to secure a stock [of ideas and values] which pursues us to the grave is in vain'. In a temper, then, that is decidedly of a much later age, the epistemological turn towards what we can know of objects themselves, what we are now obliged to take 'objective knowledge' to be, has, under the operation of Kleist's visually led understanding, now acquired a fateful ontological dimension: the perturbations of spirit, being radically subjective and unconducive to correction, bring about a tragic view of the human being. This view on its own makes Kleist's subsequent engagement with dramatic form seem entirely logical. As classical drama in the Greek mould revealed only too clearly, human actors must be assumed to be predisposed to error. In Kleist's worldview, they are not only given to error, but bound by the absence of any Archimedean point of orientation for thought forever to repeat it.

'No Way Out'?

At first glance, the trenchantly sceptical position expressed in the letter of 25 March 1801 seems characteristic of Kleist's later epistemological commitments as a whole. A study

[11] This translation of the phrase 'grüne Gläser' in the 1801 letter, though commonly favoured, is erroneous.

of Kleist's works, with the early letters in mind, would seem broadly to support a position according to which there can be 'no [epistemological] way out'. According to this view, recently restated by Luanne Frank,[12] Kleist's imaginative scenarios in the plays and the stories end badly almost without exception and indeed are bound to end badly, for the attempt to construe positive outcomes from a starting point premised on deep epistemological scepticism must, by definition, undo the designs of even the most sober and knowing among Kleist's cast of characters (and, it must be said, there are precious few of these). There are signs that such a conclusion—whether it is overtly connected to Kleist's thinking in the crisis letters or not—is in fact warranted, since remarkably few of the plots Kleist constructs end with any kind of endorsement of the aims of the characters, and most of them appear to end outright with their demise. The would-be Good Samaritan Piachi in the story 'Der Findling' (1811), for example, is so unhinged by the errant behaviour of the foundling he takes into his family as a replacement for his dead son that he resolves at the end of the story not only to kill the foundling but also to pursue him to the hell to which he believes he has successfully consigned him. Even the innately clever and wisely affectionate Alkmene in the play *Amphitryon* (1807) is compromised by the very quality of a monogamous love she herself considers to be unimpeachable. When the god Jupiter, into whose arms she has sunk and to whom she has pledged her allegiance, unmasks himself at the end as a god and not as her husband Amphitryon, whose form he has assumed, Almene's only response is a poignant, but also deeply lamenting, 'Ach!' While Kleist spares his audience in this instance the spectacular resolution he organizes for readers of 'Der Findling', his conclusion nevertheless seems to be broadly of the same kind: we are bound to be misled by the constructions of our mentally and emotionally impaired perceptual apparatus; unimpeachable knowledge is not of a sort that can be directly or even indirectly accessed by human beings. Since no correction to this perceptual apparatus can be hoped for, a 'no way out' situation must logically result.

Even if such epistemological scepticism is allowed its due, it by no means appears exceptional in the context of the Kantian aftermath. Arthur Schopenhauer, in the midst of the blossoming of German Romanticism, brings a somewhat similar type of scepticism into play in his major work *Die Welt als Wille und Vorstellung* (1818). Much earlier, but perhaps no less significantly, Gottlob Ernst Schulze, known through his pseudonym Aenesidemus, undertook a full airing of equally profound scepticism in his critical discussion of Reinhold's *Beiträge zur Berichtigung bisheriger Missverständnisse der Philosophen* (1790).[13] Schulze's point is to highlight the fact that no kind of philosophy premised on Kantian assumptions can resist falling victim to the sceptical genie Kant

[12] Luanne Frank, 'No Way Out: Heinrich von Kleist's Erdbeben in Chile [sic]', in Theodore E. D. Braun and John B. Radner (eds), *The Lisbon Earthquake of 1755: Representations and Reactions* (Oxford: Voltaire Foundation, 2005), 265–81.

[13] *Aenesidemus oder über die Fundamente der von dem Herrn Professor Reinhold in Jena gelieferten Elementar-Philosophie: Nebst einer Vertheidigung des Skepticismus gegen die Anmassungen der Vernunftkritik* (no place of publication, 1792).

had already let out of the bottle. Schulze's account of Reinhold can therefore be taken not merely as criticism of Reinhold, but also as criticism of the epistemological standpoint developed by Kant in response to the challenge of Hume's scepticism.

In his influential review of Schulze's critique of Reinhold, Fichte also falls in behind the potency of the sceptical viewpoint in large measure.[14] Fichte's own discovery that the ego, as a product of 'intellectual intuition', is no more verifiable than the thing in itself, commits his system, in turn, to a liberal serving of scepticism, for the discrepancy between what the ego intimates (Fichte: 'posits') about the world and the way that world appears to the mind becomes technically and actually unbridgeable. Though this pulling apart of the 'ego' (*Ich*) and 'non-ego' (*Nicht-Ich*) was, for Fichte, nothing more than an invitation to expand the brief of 'practical' thinking about the world and thereby to increase philosophy's claim to constitute a science, the early Kleist, based on the testimony of the crisis letters, cannot allow even this limited kind of rationalistic enterprise to flourish.

The question therefore is: was Kleist to know no other type of perspectivism than the trenchantly sceptical, and must we assume a fateful continuity between the sentiment of the crisis letters and the creative work which followed, such that the letters and the creative work are, as has been most recently maintained, really of a piece?[15]

'Über das Marionettentheater'

The answer to this question is far from straightforward. A first response might be sought in a much later work, the essay 'Über das Marionettentheater' (1810), one of the last pieces of Kleist's writing that gives evidence of a clear philosophical standpoint. The essay is set out in distinct stages, with the question of the mismatch between the pictures of the world presented to cognition and the capacity of cognition to issue reliable copies or reports of them appearing at the first stage of argumentation. The late essay, then, begins with a basic proposition that had first been set out in the crisis letters of 1801. This proposition is rendered in the essay in the following way: a beautiful youth, engaged upon extracting a thorn from his foot next to a pond, finds he cannot repeat the gesture and thereby 'copy' the image he had first caught sight of in the pond. A separation accordingly results at the level of subjective imagination between image and gesture, self and world. The sceptical position, that human consciousness cannot, through its own processes, deliver an exact representation of (the beauty of) the world, is accordingly registered. One might extend from this insight and conclude that the hope of the

[14] Johann Gottlieb Fichte, 'Recension des Aenesidemus oder über die Fundamente der vom Herrn Prof. Reinhold in Jena gelieferten Elementarphilosophie', *Jena Allgemeine Literaturzeitung*, 47–9 (1794): *Fichtes Werke*, ed. Hermann Fichte, i (Berlin: Walter de Gruyter, 1971), 1–25.

[15] As suggested most recently in Gisela Dischner, *'Der ganze Schmutz zugleich und Glanz meiner Seele': Die Briefe Heinrich von Kleists als Teil seines Werks* (Bielefeld: Aisthesis, 2012).

early Romantics that an authentic report of the world might come about as a result of a 'Copernican' turn to the shaping disposition of subjective consciousness, or, failing this, a representation providing, if not exact correspondence, then at least the world in a form that somehow approximates its true state, must be dashed. To dismiss such a hope, as Kleist appears to do from the outset, is thus also to express a level of doubt about a Romanticism predicated on some authorizing form of human consciousness—a form promoted, for example, by Reinhold in his *Versuch*, conceding to 'the capacity for human representation' a philosophically reliable connection between the represented world and the representing aspect of the mind triangulated in consciousness at the level of representation itself. To the extent that early German Romanticism grew from this 'Reinholdian' version of Kantian philosophy—Reinhold tutored Schiller in Kantian principles and, as Manfred Frank has demonstrated, was also important for Novalis and Friedrich Schlegel[16]—it may be seen that Kleist's indubitable scepticism separates him from Romantic assumptions at the end of his career as a writer, just as it had done at the beginning of it.

Yet if Kleist, in the episode of the 'thorn-extracter' at the beginning of the 'Marionettentheater' essay, remains true to his default scepticism in the vivid image of the limitations of image-making, he appears to progress beyond it over the course of the essay. It is the type of progression the essay describes that becomes important in assessing Kleist's intellectual development towards the end of his life.

The pretext for the reflection on themes that address core concerns in the representationalist tradition is established by the report of a theatre practitioner who has allegedly witnessed the innate perfection of a performing puppet. Both puppet and, it is assumed, puppeteer have mastered mechanism at the level of form so as to execute perfect movement. This contention, if true, would offer the prospect of nullifying the perturbations of consciousness that otherwise separate form from content, mind from matter, nature from culture. Kleist, no less than the Romantics, had been heavily invested in such a prospect in the period before the Kant crisis, as we have seen. Yet, as the essay progresses, this prospect becomes increasingly distant. The dialogic form of the essay already establishes a type of Socratic distance from opinions of the theatre practitioner couched as statements of fact. The episode of the thorn-extracter then introduces a counter-discourse constructed on the basis of methodological scepticism. Subsequent episodes interpolated into the dialogue throw the assumptions advocated by the theatre practitioner into sharp relief: the episode of the fencing bear—itself, perhaps, no more likely than a perfectly 'instinctual' wooden puppet—suggests that the divide between the consciousness of 'nature' and human consciousness, which for the purposes of comparison is considered not as nature itself but as a form of culture and thereby artificial, cannot be bridged. The effect of such counter-examples is to establish not only a contrast with the initial contention about the alleged perfection of the puppet theatre, but also to reduce its conceptual reach. The capacity to bridge two ostensibly incommensurate

16 See his discussion in *Unendliche Annäherung: Die Anfänge der philosophischen Frühromantik* (Frankfurt: Suhrkamp, 1997).

realms therefore cannot be conceded to any 'thing' found in the world without profound reservations. At most this capacity is made over to the task of literary endeavour itself, which is to say, to cumulative acts of story-telling that might in the end constitute 'the last chapter in the history of the world' (where 'history' takes on the additional meaning of 'story' through the allusiveness of the word *Geschichte*).

At the end of the essay Kleist outlines a position that appears close to the platform of the early Romantics, namely that it falls to writing as a collective literary-philosophical endeavour to conjure circumstances in which the work of an 'infinite consciousness', the consciousness of God, might somehow be apprehended. At the same time, Kleist undercuts confidence in the viability of such a project, since nothing in the essay, and certainly not the essay's dialogic form, can be taken in support of it. A measure of distance from the Romantic programme of 'infinite approximation' (Manfred Frank) to infinite consciousness is thus implied.

A voice more recognizable in the essay as that of Kleist attaches not to this kind of sentiment, but to the assessment, altogether more cautious and ambiguous, that 'a journey around the world' would need to be undertaken in order that infinite consciousness, or something amounting to it, be accessed 'through the back door'. Significantly, it is the metaphor of travel with a destination however unlikely that suggests a deeper dimension to human striving. While vigilant scepticism still claims its due, the 'Marionettentheater' essay nevertheless opens the door to reconsideration of a position that would earlier have seemed anathema to Kleist. This position entails something like the 'hidden world realism' discussed by James Conant in his taxonomy of perspectivisms in relation to Nietzsche. The destination of Kleist's imagined journey is now quite literally hidden 'around the back'. Kleist *moves forward* to consideration of such a position after earlier rushing past it in a flight to thoroughgoing external world scepticism. If such a level of realism is allowed, it suggests a transformation in Kleist's thinking by 1810, and, more specifically, a narrowing of—nevertheless still readily discernible—differences between Kleist and the Romantics.

Is there evidence for such an intellectual development in other writings of the author? As I make clear in the final sections of this essay, I believe there is.

Kleist's 'Hidden Realism'

The early Kleist had started from a platform of rationalistically premised naïve perspectivism and moved through a brief period of non-naïve perspectivism still entailing a certain realism about the world, to a position at a third stage of logic involving the abandonment of rationalism. Such a position also implied condemnation of the Kantian attempt to revolve the epistemological project in convincing ways away from objects towards subjects, which is to say, from the externally (transcendentally) real to the internally and 'idealistically' real. The mature Kleist, however, might be seen to move back one step in this path leading to dogmatic scepticism and allow some kind of attenuated realism about the world to stand. This, at least, is a hypothesis to be drawn from the 'Marionettentheater' essay. Validating the hypothesis in relation to Kleist's works would appear to require the defeat of dogmatic scepticism. Under the countervailing hypothesis, which would witness the triumph of such scepticism, the outside world, held completely within the illusory projections and constructions of the mind, would completely collapse in on itself.

There are thus two possible routes to be traversed in the context of Kleist's later writing. One path involving the attempt to establish a case of anti-realism would forge connections at the end of Kleist's middle period between Penthesilea's fateful 'slip of the tongue' and the Prince von Homburg's similarly wayward somatic disposition in Kleist's last play *Prinz Friedrich von Homburg* (1811). This would constitute a movement from Penthesilea's inability to surmount the accidental phonological alignment of words linking 'kisses' (*Küsse*) with 'bites' (*Bisse*), where no homology, however constructive, is sustainable, but where some reality is still notionally entertained, to a strong reading of *Prinz Friedrich von Homburg* in which the Prince finally recognizes the full consequences of his act of insubordination against the Prussian Elector. On this strong reading, the inner world of the Prince collapses at the moment when the outer world secures its victory over all that which would oppose it (including the 'automatic' responses of the Prince). This victory of the outer world of Prussia over the inner world of the protagonist, according to this reading, would be recorded in the war cry at the end of the play 'In den Staub mit allen Feinden Brandenburgs!' (l. 1858) At the same time, and immediately preceding it, the Prince's alternative reality would be rejected and relegated to the status of a dream (in the words of the soldier Kottwitz: 'A dream, what else?'). This strong reading of one of Kleist's last works would retroactively impose a consistency over all works preceding it and also link back to the crisis letters, which would inevitably reclaim them. From this angle, all Kleist's works would be made to appear of a piece.

The second route would provide an alternative way of understanding Kleist's middle and later writings and argue for a trajectory of attenuated realism. The middle period, beginning with the early dramas *Der zerbrochne Krug* (1808) and *Amphitryon* (1807), would see Kleist moving backwards and forwards through differing shades of realism, all the while holding to the scepticism which would appear to be his constant companion. In *Der zerbrochne Krug*, for example, the need for scepticism in all affairs of life is emphatically linked to the duplicitous judge Walter, who both administers the justice of a fragile world and who is precisely the cause of its fragility. In *Amphitryon*, even a naturally vigilant (and not yet properly philosophical) scepticism is turned back by circumstances where the divine, commanding by instinctive belief the fealty and affection of all, is at once also the narcissistically parasitic divine—even worse, perhaps, than the ancient Greeks had held their humanly flawed 'pantheon of gods' to be. Jupiter, from this angle, would appear something like a devil, because he is an angel, and an angel, because he is a devil, in short, the same evocation of duplicitous humanity that Kleist constructs in the companion piece, the story 'Die Marquise von O ...' (1808).

According to this reading of Kleist, an outer world—no matter that it is inscrutable and its values unreliable—would still be held to exist. What prevents the slide into a thoroughgoing scepticism (where it is just as easy to maintain that an independent world cannot possibly exist) is the feeling—and it may be no more than a feeling—that a positive alignment of forces may just as easily be imagined as a disastrous misalignment of such forces.

Such is surely the case in the 'Marquise von O ...' where the protagonist moves steadily through a series of stages in which the reality of the world is denied—her saviour can under no circumstances be allowed to be her demonic betrayer—but finally upheld—the saviour is accepted as being a demon and an angel at the same time. Significantly, the Marquise is shown in a state of limited acceptance of a flawed reality at the beginning of the story: her decision to announce her pregnancy in a local newspaper in order that the father of the child might come forward already reveals that she has not succumbed to demonic unreality. The final triumph of outer reality over inner unreality, over the fantastic imaginary that the Marquise constructs in rejection of her tumescent condition, only comes about at the end of the story when the true defiler of her virtue, the Russian Count, to all other appearances impeccably credentialled and heroic, finally announces himself. At this point the Marquise has yet another fainting fit, but this time there is something that catches her and prevents the clouding of her consciousness. It is a vague stirring of something below her wakeful self that finally releases her into knowledge—a positive and fully certain knowledge of something perhaps long suspected but never admitted. It is not this positive knowledge, which of course remains unreliable, but its *possibility* among the general conditions that obtain for humanity that supports the subdued happy end of the story's coda. The Marquise's release into knowledge is also the author's concession, perhaps equally long denied, that the world is a real world after all and not some fantastic construction, however seemingly plausible, of an evil genius.

The Two Versions of 'Michael Kohlhaas'

While, on this evidence, a limited, 'hidden world' realism might readily be conceded, the question of whether Kleist continued to maintain such realism in the last phase of his life in the face of the temptation to succumb to a fantasy world—and thereby to the temptations of the evil genius—still has to be answered. That such attenuated realism did indeed predominate in the last years of Kleist's life is evident in 'Michael Kohlhaas', a story first published as a fragment in Kleist's journal *Phöbus* in 1808, then substantially revised and republished two years later. The changes Kleist made to the story, moreover, are not to be considered of a cosmetic kind, nor are they merely illustrative of a token alignment with those Romantics with whom Kleist maintained contact. Rather they signal a new level of philosophical commitment in his thinking. The adjustments Kleist undertook to his story brought about both a different conclusion to the narrative as well as a different energy to the realization of this conclusion.

Admittedly, there have been certain readers of the two versions of the story who have charged Kleist with a stylistic rupture, or else accused him of providing a final outcome that is scarcely credible in view of the patiently prepared build-up of the story—a build-up attuned to the historical chronicle Kleist was following. These charges may well be justified, but whether they have credence is a separate question from the matter of Kleist's epistemological commitments. The effect of Kleist's changes to 'Michael Kohlhaas', as I have discussed elsewhere (see esp. *WAK* 78–80, 202–5), is to prolong the protagonist's legal dispute with his adversary, the junker Wenzel von Tronka, at the precise moment when it had appeared certain to fail. In the 1808 version of the story, as far as can be gleaned from its fragmentary nature, Kohlhaas's journey through the legal courts of Saxony and Brandenburg to achieve redress for the crime perpetrated against him—the illegal use and abuse of the two horses offered to the junker as surety when passing across the junker's land—runs aground amid a network of aristocratic patronage arranged against him. In the later 1810 edition of the story, not only is the legal dispute itself revived, but a just outcome eventually, and somewhat improbably, achieved. That the protagonist's case is finally heard before the courts and that the courts find in favour of him seems improbable above all from a historical perspective, since a citizen of a lower social class (Kohlhaas is an 'ordinary' trader) is shown to triumph against a citizen of a higher social class (a member of the landed gentry) at a time when this caste-based order remained intact and unquestioned. But if the historical setting of the story is set aside and the story allowed to migrate into Kleist's present age where a challenge to caste-based assumptions had already been successfully mounted in France during the Revolution, then the decision to allow a present reality to be debated at a meta-level would appear entirely legitimate.

Among those who viewed Kleist's additions to the story in a critical light was Franz Kafka, who otherwise read the story with passionate enthusiasm in late 1912 or early 1913.[17] Kafka chides Kleist for stylistic imperfections in this part of the story—the conclusion, he opines, is in part 'roughly drafted'.[18] Yet equally obvious is the extent to which this new ending runs counter to the anti-realistic tenor of Kafka's own writing; the first version of 'Michael Kohlhaas', in any event, would appear more in keeping with the endings reserved for Kafka's protagonists, which are almost uniformly abysmal. Kafka's desire for a reality that cannot be endorsed as rational, not even in an attenuated or 'hidden' sense, can be read into his own 'rewriting' of 'Michael Kohlhaas' in his story *Der Prozeß*. In this story, the arduous attempts of the protagonist to gain an audience before the courts and have the lawsuit against him overturned prove fruitless, and the result is that an uncomprehended death sentence is carried out against an uncomprehending

[17] For a discussion of Kafka's response to 'Michael Kohlhaas', see John M. Grandin, *Kafka's Prussian Advocate: A Study of the Influence of Heinrich von Kleist on Franz Kafka* (Columbia, SC: Camden House, 1987), 14ff.

[18] 'der schwächere, teilweise grob hinuntergeschriebene Schluß …' See Kafka's letter to Felice Bauer, 10 Feb. 1913, quoted in *Heinrich von Kleists Nachruhm: Eine Wirkungsgeschichte in Dokumenten*, ed. Helmut Sembdner, ii (Frankfurt: Insel-Verlag, 1984), 335.

defendant. A world of putative rationality collapses thus into sheer unreality. No level of reality in the story can be endorsed.

By contrast, in the 1810 version of Kleist's story, justice is dispensed, the protagonist's good name is restored, the disputed horses are returned, fattened to their original condition if not beyond it, and Kohlhaas is put to death only on account of prior crimes committed against the state and its citizens—crimes perpetrated outside the strict confines of his legal dispute with the junker. This is arguably a just outcome, albeit a bitter-sweet one. Nevertheless, in a 'fragile' world,[19] a measure of logic and rationality, however inconsistent, is ultimately allowed to subsist. In the 1810 version of 'Michael Kohlhaas' we recognize a certain level of realism, but nothing we could yet construe as Kafkaesque. The distinction, I think, has instructive weight.

Conclusion

Heinrich von Kleist, in the end, must be allowed to remain something different from that which he was later made out to be by some of his more influential readers. The young would-be writer who had sunk into crisis as a result of an early encounter with Kantian thought, learnt to exercise a profound scepticism in relation to the world around him. But the initial effect of the encounter was rather more to end something (a rationalistically premised, naïve perspectivism) than to entrench something new (a thoroughgoing external world scepticism). So while posterity has noted the dramatic effects of Kant's philosophy on Kleist, in whatever form it came down to him, one must be cautious in extrapolating from these immediate effects to Kleist's works as a whole. The conclusion that Kleist was to remain within the orbit of crisis throughout his life[20] seems less justified than the view that he was to remain within the logic of conceptual positions that arose and were discussed at length in the Kantian aftermath. And it is in such a context that we recognize Kleist's connections—such as they were—with the German Romantics.

A distinction between the moment of early intellectual crisis and later moments appearing broadly within the context of the Kantian aftermath would appear justified in view of what can be discerned about Kleist's intellectual development once he embarked on a career as a writer. While there is persistent evidence in the plays and stories of scepticism attaching both to the world and what can be known through the process of representing it, there is also evidence that the mature Kleist pulled back as a matter of principle and conviction from the temper of searing scepticism evident in the crisis letters. To some extent this pull-back brought him closer to the Romantics, for not only

[19] References to 'the fragility of the world' and 'the fragile arrangement of the world' abound in Kleist's stories and may be considered of programmatic importance in his thinking.

[20] As recently maintained e.g. by Gerhard Schulz. See his biography: *Kleist: Eine Biographie* (Munich: Beck, 2007), 209.

does Kleist begin to favour motifs from the stock-in-trade of the Romantic writer (the soothsayer in Michael Kohlhaas is one example, Kleist's discussion of animal magnetism in his play *Das Käthchen von Heilbronn* another[21]), he also discusses in the late essay 'Über das Marionettentheater' global aspects of what might be considered a Romantic cosmology. Kleist, however, was to remain at arm's length from such a cosmology, even if it retained a certain appeal for him. It was Kleist's independence as a writer and thinker that set limits to the appeal of Romanticism, and equally brought him to the attention of later writers like Nietzsche and Kafka whose originality vied with that of Kleist's own. Kleist's originality consisted in a temperament that could not finally abandon the sense of a material reality he otherwise felt so much provocation to deny. This undenied reality remains palpable, I would argue, even where Kleist in his last play *Prinz Friedrich von Homburg* has his protagonist pass before an open grave—one that he assumes is being prepared for him—and thereby undergo some sort of spiritual death. Kleist's early crisis is remembered in this image, but equally it is transcended. It is transcended through the power of an image to speak of spiritual matters, which is to say, it is transcended at the level of the imagination. It was this singular capacity to imagine and represent through images an inner world—images firmly rooted in an outer 'real' world, however otherwise hidden and inaccessible—that is one of the hallmarks of Kleist's genius and, among many other things, a source of our continued fascination with his writing today.

Further Reading

Ameriks, Karl, *Kant and the Fate of Autonomy: Problems in the Appropriation of the Critical Philosophy* (Cambridge: Cambridge University Press, 2000).

Cassirer, Ernst, *Heinrich von Kleist und die Kantische Philosophie* (Berlin: Reuther & Reichard, 1919).

Conant, James, 'The Dialectic of Perspectivism', 2 parts, *SATS* (autumn 2005 and spring 2006).

Dischner, Gisela, *'Der ganze Schmutz zugleich und Glanz meiner Seele': Die Briefe Heinrich von Kleists als Teil seines Werks* (Bielefeld: Aisthesis, 2012).

Frank, Luanne, 'No Way Out: Heinrich von Kleist's *Erdbeben in Chile* [sic]', in Theodore E. D. Braun and John B. Radner (eds), *The Lisbon Earthquake of 1755: Representations and Reactions* (Oxford: Voltaire Foundation, 2005), 265–81.

Frank, Manfred, *'Unendliche Annäherung': Die Anfänge der deutschen Frühromantik* (Frankfurt am Main: Suhrkamp, 1997).

Grandin, John M., *Kafka's Prussian Advocate: A Study of the Influence of Heinrich von Kleist on Franz Kafka* (Columbia, SC: Camden House, 1987).

Kleist, *Heinrich von, Sämtliche Werke und Briefe*, ed. Ilse-Marie Barth, Klaus Müller-Salget, Stefan Ormanns, and Hinrich C. Seeba (eds) (Frankfurt am Main: Deutscher Klassiker Verlag, 1991).

Mehigan, Tim, *Heinrich von Kleist: Writing After Kant* (Rochester, NY: Camden House, 2011).

[21] For a discussion of Kleist's treatment of animal magnetism, see Jürgen Barkhoff, *Magnetische Fiktionen: Literarisierungen des Mesmerismus in der Literatur* (Stuttgart and Weimar: Metzler, 1995).

Phillips, James, *The Equivocation of Reason: Kleist Reading Kant* (Stanford, Calif.: Stanford University Press, 2007).

Pippin, Robert, *The Persistence of Subjectivity: On the Kantian Aftermath* (Cambridge: Cambridge University Press, 2005).

Reinhold, Karl Leonhard, *Versuch einer neuen Theorie des Vorstellungsvermögens* (Prague and Jena: Widtmann & Mauke, 1789). English: *Essay on a New Theory of the Human Capacity for Representation*, tr. Tim Mehigan and Barry Empson (Berlin and New York: Walter de Gruyter, 2011).

Schmidt, Jochen, *Heinrich von Kleist: Die Dramen und Erzählungen in ihrer Epoche* (Darmstadt: Wissenschaftliche Buchgesellschaft, 2003).

Sembdner, Helmut (ed.), *Heinrich von Kleist: Sämtliche Werke und Briefe*, 2 vols (Darmstadt: Wissenschaftliche Buchgesellschaft, 1983).

CHAPTER 15

FRIEDRICH HÖLDERLIN'S ROMANTIC CLASSICISM

RÜDIGER GÖRNER

POETRY operates with the literal and non-literal meaning of words. Some of their 'meaning', in Romantic contexts in particular, derives from the musical quality of poetic language as well as its sensual and intellectual appeal. Few poets around 1800 examined their language material as thoroughly as Friedrich Hölderlin (1770–1843). He studied the tonalities of language, so to speak, as well as the possibilities of contrasting sounds and rhythms in poems, and the dynamics generated by juxtaposing grammatical tenses. No other poet of his time was able to combine poetic vision and analytical thought, linguistic experiment and awareness of poetic universality, to such effect. Small wonder that critics like H. A. Korff referred to Hölderlin's 'lyrical symphonies' in words.[1] It was also Korff who, in his monumental and still unsurpassed study *Geist der Goethezeit*, argued that Hölderlin had attempted to reconcile in poetry 'Naturidealismus' (idealism of nature) with 'Vernunftidealismus' (idealism of reason) and with it Hellenism and Kantianism.[2] Korff suggested, quite rightly, that Hölderlin be discussed under the heading of 'romantische Klassik'.

Generating beauty in poetry was, arguably, one of Hölderlin's main concerns. Likewise, he engaged in what can be called the poetics of thought or, with Jean Paul, 'Denk-Kunst', the art of thinking.[3] Both ambitions seem ideally expressed by what Hölderlin's protagonist, Hyperion, discovers as the guiding principle of determining beauty, namely Heraclitus's expression ἑν διαφέρων ἑαυτου (the One differentiated in itself).[4] Differentiation and unification of related elements became a central feature of

[1] Hermann August Korff, *Geist der Goethezeit*, iii, 3rd edn (Leipzig: Koehler & Amelang, 1959), 438.

[2] Korff, *Geist der Goethezeit*, 353.

[3] In Jean Paul, *Vorschule der Ästhetik*, ed. Wolfhart Henckmann (Hamburg: Felix Meiner Verlag, 1990), 101.

[4] Cf. Andrzej Warminski, *Readings in Interpretation: Hölderlin, Hegel, Heidegger* (Minneapolis: University of Minnesota Press 1987), 55.

Hölderlin's poetics. This direction in his intellectual development was mainly influenced by the works of his friend Wilhelm Heinse and, perhaps to lesser extent than hitherto assumed, the Jena circle around the philosopher Fichte. Heinse's celebration of beauty and thinking as an intellectual *and* sensual experience, most notably in his novel *Ardinghello*,[5] left deep traces in Hölderlin's poetry and thought. It was therefore only natural that he should have dedicated one of his finest elegies, *Brod und Wein*, to Heinse. Published in 1787, Heinse's novel established the conception of the interrelation of all arts,[6] almost a decade before this thought became commonplace among the early Romantics from Heinrich Wackenroder and Ludwig Tieck to Friedrich Schlegel, and indeed Novalis.

Heinse's protagonist inhabits 'borders'—between epochs and forms of art, antiquity and modernity, aesthetic conventions and artistic innovation.[7] Blasphemy was part of this agenda, given that he refers to Christ's resurrection as an invention with a great sensual appeal.[8] Against social and religious convention, Ardinghello defends the freedom of the individual to begin something new, 'to be or not to be the cause of an effect, and to adopt a certain form or refuse it'.[9] This was exactly in line with Hölderlin's appeal in *Brod und Wein*: 'So komm! Daß wir das Offene schauen, | Daß ein Eigenes wir suchen, so weit es auch ist.'[10]

In the company of Heinse, Hölderlin eloped with his lover in the summer of 1796. She was the mother of his tutee and wife of a Frankfurt banker, Susette Gontard, the Diotima of his poetry. This was when Hölderlin was working on the final version of the first part of his novel *Hyperion*, published on Schiller's recommendation by Cotta in April 1797. Heinse's musical novel in three volumes, *Hildegard von Hohenthal*, seems to have been discussed in detail in this short-lived *ménage à trois* in Kassel and Bad Driburg. The cover of the first edition displays an oversized ear, leaving the reader in no doubt as to the purpose of this large-scale piece of epistolary fiction, which amounted to a narrated musical aesthetics.[11] This is of significance as the second half of part 1 of Hölderlin's own novel *Hyperion*, on which he was working at the time, includes explicit references to music, albeit in symbolic terms. They need to be considered together with Hölderlin's

5 Wilhelm Heinse, *Ardinghello und die glücklichen Inseln*, Kritische Studienausgabe, ed. Max L. Baeumer (Lemgo: Verlag der Meyerschen Buchhandlung, 1787; Stuttgart: Reclam Verlag, 1998).

6 Heinse, *Ardinghello*, 22. For an early discussion of this productive friendship see: Theodor Reuss, *Heinse und Hölderlin* (Stuttgart: J. F. Steinkopf, 1906); for a more recent discussion see: Bernhard Böschenstein, 'Heine in Hölderlins Dichtung: "Was nennst du Glück, was Unglück … mein Vater!"', *Bad Homburger Hölderlin-Vorträge*, 2 (1988/89), 49–64.

7 Heinse, *Ardinghello*, 136.

8 Heinse, *Ardinghello*, 216.

9 Heinse, *Ardinghello*, 306–7.

10 In Friedrich Hölderlin, *Selected Poems and Fragments: Bilingual Edition*, tr. Michael Hamburger, ed. Jeremy Adler (London: Penguin, 1998), 152/153: 'Let us go, then! Off to see open spaces, | Where we may seek what is ours, distant, remote though it be!'). (If not stated otherwise all quotations of Hölderlin's essays and letters in the text follow this edn = *PF*.)

11 Wilhelm Heinse, *Hildegard von Hohenthal*, part 1 (Berlin: Verlag der Vossischen Buchhandlung, 1795); parts 2 and 3 in 1796.

earlier fundamental statement on identity in his fragment *Urtheil und Seyn* (Judgement and Being) of 1795, which represents an intriguing attempt to bring together Kant's conception of judgement with Fichte and Pre-Socratic thought.[12] It centres around the significance of 'intellectuale Anschauung' (intellectual perception) as opposed to sensual perception. The latter presupposes the separation between subject and object, whilst the former suggests—in line with Kant and Fichte—the undivided unity of subject and object. Hölderlin's other friend from his student days in Tübingen, Schelling, argued that any form of perception was subjective, identifying it with self-perception. Hölderlin described his philosophical ambition in two letters at that time, first to Friedrich Schiller on 4 September 1795, and then to Friedrich Immanuel Niethammer on 24 February 1796. To Schiller he writes in a mode that brings together philosophical abstraction and geometrical imagery, which was to become one main characteristic of philosophical reflection in early Romanticism, as exemplified by Novalis. Hölderlin announces:

> I am attempting to work out for myself the idea of an infinite progress in philosophy by showing that the unremitting demand that must be made of any system, the union of subject and object in an absolute ... *I* or whatever one wants to call it, though possible aesthetically, in an act of intellectual intuition, is theoretically possible only through endless approximation, like the approximation of a square to a circle; and that in order to arrive at a system of thought immortality is just as necessary as it is for a system of action.[13]

Interestingly, in his letter to Schiller, who authored the recently published *Letters on the Aesthetic Education of Man* (1795), Hölderlin merely alludes to the possibility of such a 'union' being accomplished aesthetically. It is only in his next letter to Niethammer that it becomes clear why Hölderlin was not more elaborate in this connection: he evidently felt that Schiller's approach to this problem was not sufficient. Therefore, Hölderlin wanted to undertake the task of writing a 'new' set of letters with the purpose of finding 'the principle that will explain to my satisfaction the divisions in which we think and exist'. This very principle should also be 'capable of making the conflict disappear, the conflict between the subject and the object, between our selves and the world, and between reason and revelation—theoretically, through intellectual intuition, without our practical reason having to intervene'; hence the need for a new 'aesthetic sense' (*EL* 68).

This approach is consistent with the emphasis on aesthetics and the Beautiful in the 'Oldest System Programme of German Idealism' (1795/6), which called for the 'highest act of reason' to be regarded as an aesthetic one.[14] It claims that truth and generosity

[12] The most comprehensive reading of this fragment and its context is offered by Dieter Henrich, *Der Grund im Bewußtsein: Untersuchungen zu Hölderlins Denken, 1794–1795* (Stuttgart: Klett-Cotta, 1992).

[13] Friedrich Hölderlin, *Essays and Letters*, ed. and tr. with an introduction by Jeremy Adler and Charlie Louth (London: Penguin Classics, 2009), 62. (If not stated otherwise all quotations of Hölderlin's essays and letters in the text follow this edn = *EL*.)

[14] For further discussion of the 'system programme', see Ch. 10 of this volume.

of the heart are only related in Beauty. In this 'system' of thought the philosopher was attributed as much aesthetic energy as the poet. This line of argument culminated in what was to be become most significant for Hegel, namely the categorical statement that the philosophy of the mind (only) expressed itself as Neoplatonic aesthetic philosophy.

It now appears that this 'programme of German Idealism', which is just as 'Romantic' as it touched upon the classic concerns of Idealism with its emphasis on sensuality, a new mythology and regard for the 'people', was finalized by Schelling and Hegel after a concluding meeting on this subject with Hölderlin in April 1796. It was the third such meeting within one year between Schelling and Hölderlin, which suggests the urgency and intensity of their deliberations. Some of these thoughts are echoed in the published version of *Hyperion* since this novel demonstrates that even political concerns—in this case the real state of modern Greece (around 1800) as opposed to having once been the cradle of beauty and perfection—should be discussed in aesthetic terms, too. The assumption was that any intellectual or social formation radiates in a way that can best be judged through aesthetic arguments.

Hölderlin's protagonist Hyperion illustrates that human character manifests itself through contradictions. This thought was prefigured at the end of *Urtheil und Seyn* when Hölderlin argued that self-awareness is only possible if the individual separates itself from itself and, in so doing, posits or pitches itself against itself, thereby recognizing itself in the other part of itself. This argument exposes, and illustrates, a main problem of identity. Hölderlin's valid point on this subject is that personal identity cannot simply be achieved by claiming that object and subject are but one thing; instead, the individual needs to acknowledge that identity is the result of a process and cannot be a given quality.

If identity is not an unquestionable presupposition, but rather a quality that requires analytical premeditation, then the place to discuss those matters in a novel about a particular character is the preface, or foreword. This is indeed what Hölderlin does in *Hyperion*, more elaborately in the penultimate version of the novel and more succinctly, if not aphoristically, in the final version. The former explains that we are all following an 'eccentric curve' in our development ('exzentrische Bahn'). We tear ourselves away from the original state of being, the peaceful *Έν και Παν*, in order to recreate it in, and through, ourselves, but in a process of infinite approximation to this primordial state of ontological unity. Only when we experience Beauty, the preface to the penultimate version of Hölderlin's novel suggests, will we realize, or better, divine what this original state of Being entailed.

The narrator of the published version introduces his novel by calling the protagonist an 'elegiac character' but reduces the previous argument to the following sentence: 'The resolution of the dissonances in a particular character is neither for mere reflection nor for empty desire.' This sentence represents a significant shift from the ontological statement in *Judgement and Being*, together with the aforementioned letters, to a musically, and therefore primarily aesthetically, conditioned argument. As indicated earlier, this 'musicalization' of a quasi-existential discourse, or musical shift in Hölderlin's argument during and after 1796, seems to have owed a great deal to Heinse and his *Hildegard* novel, the story of an extraordinary singing voice that opens up emancipatory possibilities to Hildegard.

But the specificity of Hölderlin's 'musical shift' is the exposition of the dissonance, which goes beyond what Heinse had developed in the key passages on musical aesthetics in *Hildegard*. That said, there was a tendency in the musical culture since 1785, the year of Mozart's String Quartet No. 19 in C Major (KV. 465), his so-called 'Dissonance Quartet', to privilege reflections on how to use dissonances in musical compositions and how to judge them in music criticism.[15] At the beginning of the second part of volume I of his letters to his friend Bellarmin, Hölderlin's Hyperion compares the memories of his past with music for strings in which the composer 'runs through all tones mixing up discord and concord with a hidden structure'. Then, at times, he would listen to the 'astounding infinite consonance' within him always knowing, though, that his life had once resembled more of a 'torn playing of strings' with the only sounds emerging from within being a swansong. This dazzling array of musical metaphors in *Hyperion* includes reference to the quiet thoughts of the protagonist's beloved, Diotima, that 'governed above the rubble' (of modern-day Greece) like 'the playing of strings of the heavenly muses over the antagonising elements'. It extends to the realization that nature in the shape of the wind, 'the brother of coincidence', only played the Aeolian harp because real artists have deserted us and died. But the utopian vision which is, again, Romantic and Classical at the same time, implies that the 'one and only Beauty' will reunite mankind and nature, thus creating a new conception of an all-embracing divinity. As seen before, the very principle, or rather structural, feature of this Beauty is the Heraclitean ἐν διαφέρων ἑαυτῳ. The One that is differentiated in itself contains (resolved) dissonances, contradictions, and juxtapositions. It therefore resembles a contrapuntal structure of identity.

It has been observed that Hölderlin's accomplished musicianship made him favour 'the chord as an image of diverse but harmonious life: the tonic or key-note of a chord resonates more fully, more richly, when part of that chord than when played on its own; in a way its true (composite) character emerges'.[16] This remained indeed the basis for Hölderlin's further explorations into the nature of (poetic) language and substantiated in his belief that 'every genre is a modulation of the others'.[17] Attention to the sound quality of vowels and consonants, its implication for rhythmic structures, the consideration given to grammatical inversion, make Hölderlin probably the most language-conscious poet of his time. This consciousness was fully developed when he embarked on composing his odes, elegies, and hymns. While his odes and elegies followed more established patterns, chiefly

[15] In a literal and non-literal meaning this concept remained essential for the next 200 years of musical theory, with the 'emancipation of the dissonance' as one main feature of music modernism. Cf. Theodor W. Adorno, *Dissonanzen: Musik in der verwalteten Welt* (Göttingen: Vandenhoeck & Ruprecht, 1956).

[16] Adler and Louth, introduction to Friedrich Hölderlin, *EL*, p. xl.

[17] Adler and Louth, introduction to Friedrich Hölderlin, *EL*, p. xl.

influenced by Klopstock[18] and Schiller, the hymns were to exceed anything written before in German.

Hölderlin's emphasis on the interrelatedness of genres and forms of artistic expression brings him close to early Romantic aesthetics as developed by Friedrich Schlegel, Ludwig Tieck, and Novalis. At the same time, Hölderlin engaged in a particular quest for 'purity' of expression modelled on what had been perceived, since Johann Joachim Winckelmann's *History of Ancient Art* (1764), as the Greek principles of artistic production. This engagement in attaining, in Winckelmann's proverbial phrase, 'noble simplicity and quiet grandeur' brought Hölderlin closer to the ambition of Weimar Classicism. Tragically, though, what Hölderlin regarded as his major contribution to a new understanding of Greek culture, his translations of Sophocles, were at the time ridiculed by the Weimar classicists as the work of a deranged mind.

If one were to single out one particular theme in Hölderlin's works that features as a leitmotif, as it were, it would be experiencing and dealing with emotional, and existential, extremes and, eventually, attaining ἀταραξία, that is, tranquillity of the mind and soul. Hölderlin's poetry and thought were conditioned by this very ambition to discover, or re*create* a sense of measure or *Maß*, even-centredness, or *Mitte*.[19] This involved the balancing of extreme emotions, such as love and hate, anger and grace. In his hymn *The Rhine*, he captures this ambition in the following verse: 'Yet each of us has his measure. | For hard to bear | Is misfortune, but good fortune harder.' ('Nur hat ein jeder sein Maas. | Denn schwer ist zu tragen | Das Unglük, aber schwerer das Glük') (*PF* 206/7). It is often ignored that this very phrase ('Yet each of us has his measure') was prefigured by Johann Gottfried Herder, a thinker and poet who can claim to have been an inspiration to the German Romantics and Classicists alike; it reads as follows: 'Jeder Mensch hat sein eigenes Maß, gleichsam eine eigne Stimmung aller seiner sinnlichen Gefühle zu einander.'[20] The difference between both definitions of 'Maß' is Herder's emphasis on 'Stimmung', or mode, in this connection. Moreover, he associates 'measure' predominantly with 'sensual feelings' and the way they relate to each other but also, given the various meanings of 'Stimmung', the way in which they are tuned in order to resonate with each other.

But what conditions this process of identifying, and attaining, one's own measure and that of an entire culture? It appears from his *Notes on Oedipus* and those on *Antigone*, which accompanied his translations of both tragedies (1804), that, according to Hölderlin, this process included the individual's attempt to deal with the

[18] For further reference, see in particular Katrin Kohl, *Friedrich Gottlieb Klopstock* (Stuttgart and Weimar: Verlag J. B. Metzler, 2000), 88–90, 149–51.

[19] Cf. Rüdiger Görner, *Hölderlins Mitte: Zur Ästhetik eines Ideals* (Munich: Iudicium Verlag, 1993); Rüdiger Görner, 'Wanderung zwischen den Extremen. Hölderlins Sinngebung des Exzentrischen', in *Friedrich Hölderlin, Text + Kritik*, Sonderband 7 (Munich: Text + Kritik, 1996), 62–74.

[20] In Johann Gottfried Herder, Ideen. 7. Buch, 1. In: *Sämtliche Werke*, ed. Bernhard Suphan (Hildesheim: Olms Verlag 1967), xiii. 291. (Every human has his own measure, a mode of his own, as it were, in relation of all his sensual feelings.) For Herder's influence on Hölderlin, see Ulrich Gaier, *Hölderlin: Eine Einführung* (Tübingen and Basel: Francke Verlag, 1993), 312–13.

rhythmic, and counter-rhythmic, succession or collision of ideas. Hölderlin even speaks of 'counter-rhythmical interruption' which, in his terminology, defines a caesura in metric terms. The point is, however, that what looks like, and often is, a genuine exploration into the nature of metrics and the structure of the 'μηχανή of the ancients' (*EL* 317) always turns into a non-literal characterization of cultural, and indeed psychological, phenomena. The 'collision of ideas', interruptions in seemingly rhythmical developments, amounted to what psychology nowadays refers to as 'cognitive dissonances'; that is to say, various conflicting thoughts, feelings, and ambitions that *coexist* in an individual. By implication, Hölderlin described the psychopathography not only of Sophoclean tragedy but also of his own time and state of mind.[21] The intriguing, if not revealing, concept that underpins Hölderlin's highly idiosyncratic but poetically productive conception of rhythmical antinomies is 'calculable law' (*EL* 317). In order to fully appreciate the implication of this concept we need to remind ourselves of the debate in the late 1970s surrounding the question prompted by Pierre Bertaux in his biography of the poet: whether Hölderlin had faked his own insanity in order to escape political prosecution as a sympathizer with Jacobin revolutionary thought.[22] The point is not to reopen this discussion but, rather, draw attention to this fundamental principle ('the calculable law'), which was, by and large, overlooked during this debate on Hölderlin's supposedly psychopolitical manœuvrings. For what appears to be a solely aesthetic principle can suggest something else: that *any* kind of 'caesura', or 'counter-rhythmical interruption', let alone collision of (political) intentions, *can* be calculable, too. Hölderlin's stance as a poet and thinker was undeniably political, too. Again, this positions him between the Jena/Heidelberg Romantics and the Weimar/Berlin classicists. How else could it be with a poet whose main attempt at writing a drama, *Empedokles* (1797–9), which exists in three fragmentary versions, was essentially a political tragedy? 'Calculable' in this instance is the interplay of Empedokles's presence and absence. His power, or charisma, lies in his ability to use his presence and absence on the political stage of Agrigento to maximum effect.[23] In all three of Hölderlin's versions, Empedokles's self-deification and his self-sacrifice (taking his life into his own hands by throwing himself into Etna) happen off-stage. His union with the Gods, or rather ultimate hubris, leads him to being alienated from his people, whilst his decision to commit suicide amounts to a 'political testament'.[24] Through 'calculating' his own end to that extent, he not only remains in

[21] It is telling that the famous neurologist, Detlef B. Linke, summarized, at the end of his life, his insights into the neurological dispositions with a study on what brain research can learn from Hölderlin. In so doing he took the work of Karl Jaspers on Hölderlin's psychopathology to a different level, continuing P. Lacoue-Labarthe's studies on Hölderlin, too. Detlef B. Linke, *Hölderlin als Hirnforscher* (Frankfurt am Main: Suhrkamp Verlag, 2005).

[22] Pierre Bertraux, *Friedrich Hölderlin: Eine Biographie* (Frankfurt am Main and Leipzig: Insel Verlag, 2000).

[23] Cf. Rüdiger Campe, 'Erscheinen und Verschwinden: Metaphysik der Bühne in Hölderlins "Empedokles"', in Bettine Menke and Christoph Menke (eds), *Tragödie—Trauerspiel—Spektakel* (Berlin: Theater der Zeit. Recherche, 2007), 53–71.

[24] Cf. Anja Lemke, 'Die Tragödie der Repräsentation: Theater und Politik in Hölderlins "Empedokles"-Projekt', *Hölderlin-Jahrbuch*, 37 (2010–11), 68–87, quote 86.

charge of himself, but can also administer whatever it takes to appoint his heir, and thus secure his succession.

The people of Agrigento, or so we are told, react with ecstatic jubilation to the self-deification of their leader Empedokles. Ancient rites of worship are revolutionized by this 'heroic act' on Empedokles's part. But this Dionysian ecstasy is short-lived, for Empedokles realizes his hubris and retreats. In Hölderlin's fragmentary tragedy, the priest Hermokrates, as opposed to the politician Kritias, demands, however, that Empedokles should return for the people to see him being banned for his breaking sacred law. It is in this situation that Empedokles regains his initiative that is to lead him to his self-sacrifice. It has been pointed out that Empedocles, shortly before his suicide, asks his disciple Pausanias to bring him a last supper, strongly reminiscent of the 'communitas Christi' and the Eucharist.[25]

Hölderlin presents Empedokles's suicide as a moment of genuine self-elevation, as opposed to his initial ill-conceived self-deification. Therefore, and in line with classicist conceptions of the extraordinary, Empedokles can finally be associated with 'heroism' and 'idealism',[26] whereby his 'death drive' evokes Romantic connotations. Peter-André Alt argues that Empedokles's jump into the volcano represented a moment of ultimate beauty and, at the same time, horrific shock.[27]

In Schiller's poem 'Das Ideal und das Leben', which Hölderlin read in the poet's own journal *Die Horen* under the title 'In the Realm of Shadows', the future author of *Empedokles* discovered references to those who want to be like the Gods and move towards their dissociation from earthly ambitions. In a letter written in October 1795 to his friend Neuffer, Hölderlin spoke of the intoxication this poem had caused in him but invites him to comment on this philosophical poem by Schiller, whom Hölderlin regarded at that time as his mentor. Matters of taste, Hölderlin argues in this letter, are always decided with hindsight. Proper judgement can only emerge from the re-examination of one's initial enthusiasm for an object. The revisiting, or revision, of a particular opinion or stance generates value, Hölderlin implies, just in the way his own Empedokles was to scrutinize his self-deification once 'life' had shown him that his initial 'ideal' was fraud and detrimental to the common good.

Hölderlin's poetic productivity increased once he had completed his epistolary novel *Hyperion* in autumn 1797. This was then when he began to plan his tragedy *Empedokles* in more detail. What developed from there was an unprecedented intensification of his poetic work, poetological reflection, and creation of odes, elegies,

25 Cf. Mark Ogden, *The Problem of Christ in the Work of Friedrich Hölderlin*, Bithell Series of Dissertations, 16 (London and Leeds: Maney & Son, 1991), 89–129. Ogden makes a convincing case for a theological reading of 'Empedokles' at the expense of considering theatrical issues, such as the interplay of Empedokles's presence and absence. This is, however, an equally valid aspect of Christ's spiritual power.

26 Cf. Peter-André Alt, 'Subjektivierung, Ritual, implizite Theatralität: Hölderlins "Empedokles"-Projekt und die Diskussion des antiken Opferbegriffs im 18. Jahrhundert', *Hölderlin Jahrbuch*, 37 (2010–11), 30–67, here 62.

27 Alt, 'Subjektivierung', 66.

and hymns. That is to say, Hölderlin did *not* subscribe to the aesthetic principles of early Romanticism that saw in the novel the pinnacle of literary work, but he *did* follow Romantic principles in the way he treated reflection as an integral part of the poetic process. This becomes evident in, and through, his essay *The Ground of the Empedocles*, written in autumn 1799, which triggered work on the third and final fragmentary version of the play. Likewise, the fragmentary essay *On the Procedure of the Poetic Spirit* (1799/1800) may have inspired work on some of his hymns and elegies—and vice versa. One of the key-concepts in the latter essay, the 'harmonious opposition' (*EL* 281) does not only carry forward the conception of the 'One differentiated in itself' but also reflects the principle of contrasting actual lyrical composition with poetological reflection. This preoccupation with contrast was mirrored by Hölderlin's increasing use of the adversative conjunction 'aber' (but), which gained its own poetic validity.[28]

The highly complex syntax of these essays matches the complexity of thought or, more precisely, its layers. Furthermore, it resembles, if not prefigures, the extended periods and cadences found mainly in the hymns and some of the elegies. At the same time, these reflections, which only seem to meander in a Romantic fashion, strive for concision and classic simplicity. In Hölderlin's poetry this was to be achieved in some of the shorter hymn-like language compositions, such as 'Hälfte des Lebens' (Half of Life). Recent scholarship has shown that these two strophes, arguably Hölderlin's most known, not only celebrate the conception of *sobria ebrietas* (sacred sobriety)[29] but contain an entire poetology.[30]

The essay *Grund zum Empedokles* deals with ambiguities. They begin already with the very title. Hölderlin left it without an article, be it definite or indefinite, and uses the word 'Grund' in terms of 'ground', 'reason', or 'basis'. This therefore suggests that what is meant is the 'reason for Empedocles', 'the basis—in the sense of foundation—of Empdocles', or the motivation that led to writing this tragedy. Interestingly, Hölderlin refers to his drama as a 'tragic ode', thus emphasizing the lyrical and song-like quality of his tragedy. In addition, this connects his drama with one of the poetic forms which Hölderlin privileged at the time, the ode, with Klopstock, Schiller, and Pindar as his main models. It also marks the transition from the shorter to the more epic, or narrative, odes[31] which occurred around 1798/9. In the context of this discussion Hölderlin's ode 'Empedokles' is of particular significance:

[28] Cf. Rüdiger Görner, 'Hölderlins Aber oder: Die Kunst des Gegensatzes', *Sprachkunst* (1994), 293–307.

[29] Jochen Schmidt, 'Sobria ebrietas: Hölderlins "Hälfte des Lebens"', *Hölderlin-Jahrbuch*, 23 (1982–3), 182–90.

[30] Winfried Menninghaus, *Hälfte des Lebens: Versuch über Hölderlins Poetik* (Frankfurt am Main: Suhrkamp Verlag, 2005). Menninghaus's intriguing, and entirely convincing, starting point is to consider this poem as an expression of an early 'midlife crisis'.

[31] Cf. Jochen Schmidt, *Hölderlins später Widerruf in den Oden 'Chiron', 'Blödigkeit' und 'Ganymed'* (Tübingen: Niemeyer Verlag, 1978). This ground-breaking study also offers a comprehensive discussion of this particular genre in Hölderlin's work.

You look for life, you look and from deeps of Earth
A fire, divinely gleaming wells up for you,
And quick, aquiver with desire, you
Hurl yourself down into Etna's furnace.
So did the Queen's exuberance once dissolve
Rare pearls in wine; and why should she not? But you,
If only you, O poet, had not
Offered your wealth to the seething chalice!
Yet you are holy to me as is the power
Of earth that took you from us, the boldly killed!
And gladly, did not love restrain me,
Deep as the hero plunged down I'd follow. (*PF* 5)

Both Hölderlin's tragedy and his reflections on the 'Ground of the Empedocles' see this protagonist mainly as a 'religious reformer' and 'political being' (*EL* 269) but the poem not so. The ode celebrates him as a poet who set an example for the modern poet, too, which he would follow if 'love did not restrain' and prevent him from sacrificing himself. This ode does not immediately begin 'in the highest fire', rather with reference to an existential quest—the searching for the essence of life. But this very essence—and here is the fundamental dichotomy—represents life and destruction. This fire is aesthetically attractive ('gleaming') and, as the medium of sacrifice, seemingly connects Life with the Sacred.

The idea of sacrifice remained present in Hölderlin's thought, gaining particular prominence during the last phase of his creative life, mainly in connection with his Sophocles translations and his so-called 'Night Poems', or *Nachtgesänge*. To his new publisher, Friedrich Wilmans, he wrote in December 1803: 'It is a joy to sacrifice oneself to the reader and to enter with him into the narrow limits of our still child-like culture' (*EL* 217). This identification with the position of the reader and his limitations represents a significant shift in Hölderlin's attitude towards his social and cultural context. In his prefaces to *Hyperion* and the large-scale poem *Friedensfeier*, which came to light in London for the first time as late as 1954, his attitude was rather uncompromisingly Lutheran: If 'some should think such a language too unconventional, I must confess to them: I cannot help it. On a fine day—they should consider—almost every mode of song makes itself heard; and Nature, whence it originates, also receives it again' (*PF* 209). Now, though, Hölderlin saw himself on the way to a new 'naturalness' and 'originality' in his (use of) language, which was inspired by his renewed interest in translating from the ancient Greek. But this very 'originality' was not appreciated by his contemporaries; for it included an attempt to approximate ancient Greek and modern German. It is only in more recent times that this poetic experiment was fully appreciated, not least by Bertolt Brecht, who regarded Hölderlin's rendering of *Antigone* as an outstanding achievement.[32]

[32] Cf. Hellmut Flashar, 'Hölderlins Sophokles-Übersetzungen auf der Bühne', *Hölderlin-Jahrbuch*, 37 (2010–11), 9–29.

One concept is especially noteworthy in this connection: *Sangart* (mode of song). Once again, it confirms the musical foundations of Hölderlin's poetic projects and visions. In his much-quoted letter to Casimir Ulrich Böhlendorff of November 1802, Hölderlin speaks of the necessity to 'sing' with 'actual originality' (*EL* 214). Moreover, he asks his friend to write to him 'soon. I need your pure tones. Psyche among friends, the formation of thoughts in conversations and letters, is vital for artists' (*EL* 214).

Strangely or not, this notion of thoughts as the result of conversation is as close to Heinrich von Kleist's epistolary essay *On the Gradual Production of Thoughts Whilst Speaking* (1807/8) as it is to Goethe's interest in the string quartet as a conversation in tones from which further thoughts can develop.[33] What informs this 'mode of song' ranges from the melodic to the dissonant; it includes thunder and the fine-tuning of the psyche, expressions of anger and, in the elegies, the rustling of the 'leaves of mourning'.[34] One such mode of song is what Hölderlin refers to in his announcement to publisher Wilmans as 'the high and pure rejoicing of poems on our time' (*EL* 217). Hölderlin speaks quite explicitly of 'vaterländische Gesänge', which implies some patriotic meaning. 'Heimat' and 'Vaterland' become another leitmotif in Hölderlin's letters and poems after 1801, and especially during his stay in France in 1802. But this does not suggest a patriotic turn in Hölderlin's development, but rather the realization on his part that 'what is our own has to be learnt just as much as what is foreign', as he put it in a letter written in Stuttgart to Böhlendorff in December 1801 (*EL* 208). This amounts to another 'contrast', or potential dichotomy, in Hölderlin's work: the growing awareness of what constitutes one's 'own' culture and the expansion of his own horizon in terms of study and imagination.[35] Perhaps it is ironic and consequential that some of the most fertile discourses on Hölderlin, which contributed to his recognition as a representative of world literature, were generated by French intellectuals.[36]

Hölderlin's poetry, his hymns in particular, offer lyrical condensations of the human existence, often written 'at the edge of expression'.[37] One key to the understanding of the hymns is their triadic structure[38] as derived from the Pindaric ode, often termed

[33] Cf. Barbara Naumann, 'Stimmen vernünftiger Leute: Streichquartett und Gespräch', in Barbara Naumann and Margit Wyder (eds), *'Ein Unendliches in Bewegung': Künste und Wissenschaften im medialen Wechselspiel bei Goethe* (Bielefeld: Aisthesis Verlag, 2012), 205–20.

[34] Cf. Anselm Haverkamp, *Leaves of Mourning: Hölderlin's Late Work. With an Essay on Keats and Melancholy*, tr. Vernon Chadwick (Albany, NY: State University of New York Press, 1996).

[35] For further reference, see Eva Kocziszky, *Hölderlins Orient* (Würzburg: Königshausen & Neumann, 2009) and Rüdiger Görner, 'Hölderlins poetischer Kulturraum', in Maria K. Lasatowicz, Andrea Rudolph, and Norbert Richard Wolf (eds), *Deutsch im Kontakt der Kulturen: Schlesien und andere Vergleichsregionen* (Berlin: Trafo Verlag, 2006), 383–92.

[36] Cf. Geert Lernout, *The Poet as Thinker: Hölderlin in France* (Columbia, SC: Camden House, 1994); see also Manfred Koch, '"Hölderlin, ou le poète": Französische Lektüren des heiligen Worts', *Neue Zürcher Zeitung* (28/29 Apr. 2001), 53. Koch regards Maurice Blanchot as the main catalyst in this process and sees his essay on Hölderlin also in connection with a more radical reading of Heidegger and his interpretations of the poet. Blanchot argued that the space in which the work of the poet 'remains' was an abyss.

[37] Ian Cooper, *The Near and Distant God: Poetry, Idealism and Religious Thought from Hölderlin to Eliot* (Leeds: Legenda 2008), 44.

[38] Cf. *Hymns and Fragments by Friedrich Hölderlin*, tr. and introduced by Richard Sieburth (Princeton: Princeton University Press 1984), 26.

'hymnus' by Hölderlin.[39] The triadic structure is based on poetic progression from strophe to antistrophe to epode, but it is not appropriate to see in this Pindaric adaptation a form that 'perfectly suited the dialectical cast of Hölderlin's vision'.[40] Rather, one ought to appreciate the more comprehensive meaning of the triadic structure with all its theological, even musical, and political implications to get a proper sense of why the triad was of such interest to Hölderlin. There is an obvious thematic link between the poetic structure of the triad and the conception of a 'Holy Trinity'; likewise, whole sections of the New Testament follow the triadic structure, for instance the Letter of Paul to the Philippians, which has been interpreted in terms of a triadic hymn to Christ.[41] The triad in music as a three-note chord has dominated the basics of functional harmony since the Renaissance. The most important secular, and distinctly political, triad in Hölderlin's time, though, was the revolutionary three-value chord: *liberté—égalité—fraternité*. Decidedly more sinister was Carl Schmitt's use of this concept in his interpretation of the political situation in 1933, which he described in terms of a 'triadic structure of the political unity' as a 'three-part summation of State, Movement and People'.[42] The reference to Schmitt is significant in this connection, given his early analysis of 'political Romanticism' (in 1919), which he characterized as a combination of three main factors: revolutionary traditionalism, the formation of national consciousness, and a pronouncedly Christian system of values.[43] Again, the thematic scope of Hölderlin's hymns contains, at times in cryptic ways, the entirety of the above discourses. Even though they were prevalent then, the novelty lay in their poetic combination, mutual penetration, and cross-referencing to Greek antiquity—both in terms of motifs and poetic form. But it was the sheer character of Hölderlin's poetic language that turned these hymns and hymn-like fragments into something literally unheard-of in German. None of the poetry written by the German Romantics, or Weimar Classicists, engaged to such an extent in linguistic experiment as Hölderlin's did. Rather, they either attempted to attain a distinctly folk-oriented poetic speech or strove towards 'noble simplicity' in poetic expression. With Hölderlin, however, poetic language gained unprecedented intensity. His poetry seems to have developed on a different plane, and yet demonstrates an immediacy that directly engages with the ear and mind (in that order!). Hölderlin's words, even when they speak of ethereal calm and equanimity, self-possession and tranquillity, are on high alert, as it were. Rest and restlessness is but one experience in these poems, as the opening lines of some of his elegies and hymns suggest: 'Are the cranes returning

[39] Cf. the two masterly studies by Jochen Schmidt, *Hölderlins letzte Hymnen 'Andenken' und 'Mnemosyne'* (Tübingen: Niemeyer Verlag 1970); *Hölderlins geschichtsphilosophische Hymnen 'Friedensfeier', 'Der Einzige', 'Patmos'* (Darmstadt: Wissenschaftliche Buchgesellschaft, 1990).

[40] Schmidt, *Hölderlins geschichtsphilosophische Hymnen*.

[41] Ralph P. Martin, 'A Hymn of Christ: Philippians 2:5–11', in *Recent Interpretation and in the Setting of Early Christian Worship* (Cambridge: Cambridge University Press, 1967; new edn 1997).

[42] In Carl Schmitt, *State, Movement, People: The Triadic Structure of the Political Unity* (1933)/*The Question of Legality* (1950), ed., tr., and with a Preface by Simona Draghici (Corvallis, Oreg.: Plutarch Press, 2001), 11.

[43] Carl Schmitt, *Politische Romantik* (Berlin: Duncker & Humblot, 1919).

to you, and the mercantile vessels | Making again for your shores?' ('The Archipelago', *PF* 111); 'Daily I search, now here, now there my wandering takes me | Countless times I have probed every highway and path' ('Menon's Lament for Diotima', *PF* 127); 'Lonely I stood and looked out into African desert, unbroken | Plains; and, standing there, saw fire from Olympus rain down' ('The Traveller', *PF* 137); 'Round us the town is at rest; the street, in pale lamplight, falls quiet | And, their torches ablaze, coaches rush through and away' ('Bread and Wine', *PF* 151); 'For as when high from the gloriously voiced, the organ | Within a holy hall | Untainted welling from inexhaustible pipes, | The prelude, awakening men, rings out in the morning ...' ('At the Source of the Danube', *PF* 177); 'What is it that | To the ancient, the happy shores | Binds me, so that I love them | Still more than my own homeland?' ('The Only One', First Version, *PF* 219); 'Near is | And difficult to grasp, the God' ('Patmos', *PF* 231); and finally: 'Ripe are, dipped in fire, cooked | The fruits and tried on the earth, and it its law, | Prophetic, that all must enter in | Like serpents, dreaming on | The mounds of heaven' ('Mnemosyne', Third Version, *PF* 259).

Questions of orientation are raised by these openings and, interestingly, to a far lesser extent, issues of (personal) identity. The latter comes more into play when one asks who was meant by 'the Only One' ('der Einzige'), or 'the prince of the feast-day' in 'Celebration of Peace' (in reference to the peace treaty of Lunéville in 1801 between France and Austria, which ended the Second Coalition War). Plausible suggestions range from Christ to Napoleon. But could it also be 'the poet'?

As much as Hölderlin's (late) poems have tested the hermeneutical skills of their readers, it remains important to listen to their sound and, ultimately, respect that some of them follow what is said in 'The Rhine': 'A mystery are those of pure origin. | Even song may hardly unveil it' (*PF* 199). The original gives an ambiguous hint for a possible interpretation in the shape of the unusual compositum for 'pure origin': *Reinentsprungenes*. The assonance of the title of the hymn is striking: any origin, and that of a river in particular, represents a 'mystery' or rather 'riddle' (the German is 'Räthsel', a word that must have been particularly close to Hölderlin at the time of writing this hymn, given his preoccupation with translating *Oedipus*, with its reference to the riddle of the sphinx).

Hölderlin's hymns have the tendency to move the mind *ad fontes*, back to the origins, or sources, be it of rivers or human conditions. 'At the Source of the Danube' the poet celebrates the union of music and consciousness, the course of a river and the cultural developments that have occurred alongside through the centuries, from the archaic to the modern. Through the 'community's choir' the 'word came down to us from the East'. By the 'rocks of Parnassus and by Cithaeron' the poet even hears the echo of Asia. Then this very word, or so the hymn suggests, breaks—like the light in a prism—at the Capitol (in Rome), the Christian world in other words, and comes to us, freshly imbued with nature, 'from the Alps'. This hymn presents the word as a transmitter of culture and, at the same time, a 'weapon' (*PF* 181). What matters, however, is the 'voice that moulds and makes human' (*PF* 179). This one voice seems a distillation of all 'voices' of the 'inexhaustible pipes' of the organ near the source of the Danube and the choral voices, which blended the various cultural influences. This one voice, though, is initially perceived as a 'stranger'; something our ears have to get accustomed to in order to care for the word properly.

The 'ripe fruits' of the opening of 'Mnemosyne' can arguably be words, but they are, essentially, instruments of 'conversation' and 'expression of the heart', as the hymn 'Remembrance' states (*PF* 251/253). In another hymn, Hölderlin revisited the River Danube and gave it its ancient name 'Ister'. It displays a particular geographical imagination in the sense that it considers the possibility of the river flowing from East to West rather than the other way round. The point of this poetic speculation is that 'nobody knows ... what the river does' (*PF* 257). It is part of the 'mystery' that surrounds the life- and culture-giving streams. This repeated focus on rivers in Hölderlin's poetry further distinguishes it from that of his contemporaries. It underlines his interest in the Pre-Socratic notion of *παντα ρει*, the ever-flowing nature of life, with the human being floating mid-stream, or in the words of third stanza of the ode 'Dichtermuth' ('The Poet's Courage'): 'For, as quite near shores, or in the silvery | Flood resounding afar, or over silent deep | Water travels the flimsy | Swimmer, likewise we love to be' (*PF* 101).

In a famous discussion of this ode and another, 'Blödigkeit' ('Timidness'), Walter Benjamin singled out the poem's ambition to establish and praise the courage of the poet to seek death. 'This death', Benjamin writes, 'is the centre from which the entire world of poetic dying was to take its origin.'[44] Benjamin refers to the following strophe: 'Glad he died there, and still lonely his groves lament | Him whom most they had loved, lost, though with joy he drowned, | Often a virgin will hear his | Kindly song in the distant boughs' (*PF* 101).

Is such death 'Romantic'? Or does it rather have the hallmarks of classic 'heroism'? Or is it neither? This poet's death is clearly different from Empedocles's end in the sense that power did not matter in the poet's case. He was seen as the voice of people and his death amounts to a withdrawal from the public, but one that is not final. His 'song' continues and is performed by a 'virgin', suggesting an equivalent to the 'purity' of his poetry. A 'love death' it was not, for the poet dies alone. The task attributed to the 'poets of the people' in this ode is peculiar enough: they are to sing 'for each of them his god'. The obligation of the poet remains a sacred one. This connects the odes with the elegies and hymns in Hölderlin's late work. Thus poetry retains remnants of the sacred, but seems to absorb the poet's identity.

In Hölderlin's case this process had consequences, which, arguably, contributed more to his legacy than many of his works. The assumed loss of his identity became part of his mental pathology. The poems he wrote in his state of insanity from 1806 until his death in 1843—which time he spent in the care and open confinement of the iconic tower-house in Tübingen on the banks of the Neckar and in closest proximity to the Stift of his student days—show a complete absence of the first person singular but an overwhelming presence of nature in the form of the Four Seasons. Likewise, most of these poems—it is assumed Hölderlin wrote infinitely more of them, but only these survived—indulge in excessive repetition and formulaic language. The latter is particularly prominent in

[44] In Walter Benjamin, *Gesammelte Schriften*, ii/1. *Aufsätze, Essays, Vortrage*, ed. Rolf Tiedemann and Hermann Schweppenhäuser (Frankfurt am Main: Suhrkamp Verlag, 1991), 109.

the letters to his mother. Notably, the dates he gives for these poems are fictive and the author calls his own name in question. In doing so, he fictionalizes himself. The young poet Wilhelm Waiblinger, who visited Hölderlin on several occasions after July 1822, reports that he called himself Killalusimeno, and later Buonarroti and, most famously, Scardanelli. Waiblinger wrote this very first essay on Hölderlin from memory in Rome. It was published after Waiblinger's premature death in 1831 and was included in the first of Hölderlin's 'Collected Works' in 1839–46. Its main merit was Waiblinger's interest in Hölderlin's psychological disposition, his continuing interest in music and habit of speaking 'half in French', as well as the curious fact that he had a portrait of Frederick the Great on his wall.[45]

Other young Romantic admirers of Hölderlin, like the poets Ludwig Uhland and Gustav Schwab, visited him, left fragmentary accounts of his disturbed mind, and worked towards drawing attention to the extraordinariness of his works. Uhland and Schwab produced the first 'Collected Poems' in 1826, but public awareness remained limited and after his death in 1843 and, in particular, after the attempted revolution in 1848/9, Hölderlin seemed forgotten.

It is noteworthy, though, that none of Hölderlin's young 'friends', who belonged to the second generation of German Romantics (Waiblinger, Uhland, Schwab, and, most importantly, Eduard Mörike), felt inclined in any way to 'imitate' this poetry, or to (re) capture the Hölderlinian 'tone'. Perhaps only Mörike, whose art of translating from ancient Greek matched—to some extent—Hölderlin's mastery, felt challenged and able enough to continue Hölderlin's legacy in German late Romanticism, most notably in his poem 'To an Aeolian Harp'. One revealing aspect of the poetic reception of Hölderlin, or rather the rediscovery of this poet enabled by the ground-breaking edition of Norbert von Hellingrath,[46] was that the reverse occurred: it inspired poets of the time like Stefan George, Karl Wolfskehl, Georg Trakl, and, most notably, Rainer Maria Rilke, to write in a Hölderlinian mode. The lyrical 'key' of this reception was, however, distinctly non-Romantic and more interested in the classicist part of Hölderlin's legacy.

This edition soon turned into a literary monument of national proportions and significance, with the 'heroic' death of its editor supplying its own quasi-mythical aura. It was the very edition, the fourth volume in particular, which Walter Benjamin used when considering 'Zwei Gedichte von Friedrich Hölderlin'; Martin Heidegger, too, familiarized himself with Hölderlin, which led to his idiosyncratic and consequently controversial interpretations of the poet some ten years later under completely changed political

[45] In Wilhelm Waiblinger, 'Mein flüchtiges Glück', *Tagebücher, Briefe, Prosa*, ed. Wolfgang Hartwig (Berlin: Aufbau Verlag 1991), 285–338 ('Friedrich Hölderlins Leben, Dichtung und Wahnsinn').

[46] Hellingrath published the first of altogether 6 vols of this first 'critical edition' in 1913 (early poems), followed by Hölderlin's Sophocles and Pindar translations (vol. v), and one month before the outbreak of the First World War, what Hellingrath described in his introduction as the 'heart, essence and pinnacle of Hölderlin's works, its actual legacy': the odes, hymns, elegies, and some of the fragments. After Hellingrath's death in the Verdun in 1916 the edn was completed in 1923 in his memory. Hölderlin, *Sämtliche Werke: Historisch-kritische Ausgabe*, ed. Norbert von Hellingrath, with Friedrich Sebass and Ludwig V. Pigenot, 2nd edn (Berlin: Propyläen-Verlag, 1923). The Hellingrath quote is at vol. iv, p. xi.

circumstances.[47] There was no 'anxiety of influence' (Harold Bloom) among those poets and thinkers: quite the contrary, they *desired to be influenced* by Hölderlin's poetry. Stefan George led the chorus of Hölderlin admirers at that time suggesting this poet's uniqueness. He was at pains to dissociate Hölderlin from the Romantic movement, pointing at the Pindaric foundations of his poetry.[48] (This case can indeed be made if one compares, say, Novalis's *Hymns to the Night* with any of Hölderlin's hymns: while the former disregards Pindaric patterns, the latter celebrates them in German.) George saw in Hölderlin a precursor of Nietzsche, suggesting that this poet had already discovered the 'Dionysian' foundations of culture. Nietzsche himself had sensed just that, and he was in fact the first major thinker at the threshold of Modernism who perceived an elective affinity between Hölderlin, his novel *Hyperion* in particular, and his own ambitions. The poetic and intellectual dynamics that emerged from the reception of Hölderlin during the first two decades of twentieth century were so extraordinarily powerful because they merged with the Nietzschean cult of that time. In effect, what happened was the quasi-deification of the poet-philosopher Hölderlin and the philosopher-poet Nietzsche after the promulgation of the 'death of God'.

The young Walter Benjamin did not follow this cult. In his case, studying Hölderlin made him reflect on the meaning of happiness in Greek antiquity, on Socrates, and the odd paradox that Plato put him, the decidedly non-artistic 'ugly'-looking thinker, in the 'erotic centre of intellectual relationships', on the medieval origins of Romanticism, and, for the first time, on the meaning of tragedy (all in 1915/1916).[49] Heidegger's reading of Hölderlin was a different case altogether. After 1935, Heidegger who, as Vice Chancellor of Freiburg University, had compromised himself politically by publicly advocating a union between universities and National Socialism as early as 1933, 'used' Hölderlin and the 'purity' of his language to discreetly distance himself from his disastrous *faux-pas*. Heidegger detected an ontological quality in Hölderlin's language and, most importantly, a poetic turn in philosophy which he, Heidegger himself, attempted to emulate. This probably best-researched aspect of the philosophical reception of Hölderlin in the twentieth century does not require much additional comment[50] except, perhaps, a reference to Paul de Man, who rejected Heidegger's interpretation of Hölderlin on the followings grounds. The philosopher had not acknowledged the 'temporality' Hölderlin's poetry contained and had made him an 'apocalyptic poet and eschatological figure' and precursor of his, Heidegger's, own conception of 'temporary alienation from being'

[47] Martin Heidegger, *Erläuterungen zu Hölderlins Dichtung* (Frankfurt am Main: Klostermann, 1951). In English: *Elucidations of Hölderlin's Poetry*, tr. Keith Hoeller (Amherst, Va.: Prometheus Books, 2000); also Martin Heidegger, *Hölderlin's Hymn 'The Ister'*, tr. William McNeill and Julia Davies (Bloomington, Ind.: Indiana Press, 1996).

[48] Cf. Hans-Georg Gadamer, 'Hölderlin und George', in H.-G. Gadamer, *Poetica: Ausgewählte Essays* (Frankfurt am Main: Insel Verlag, 1977), 39–67, here 43.

[49] Benjamin, *Gesammelte Schriften*, ii.1. 126–40, quote 129.

[50] For a comprehensive discussion of the philosophical implications of his reception, see among others: Jennifer Anna Gosetti-Ferencei, *Heidegger, Hölderlin and the Subject of Poetic Language: Towards a New Poetic of Dasein* (New York: Fordham University Press, 2004).

('Seinsvergessenheit'), announcing 'the end of this barren time' and preparing the language for 'a renewal' of culture.[51] This is significant because this criticism reflects de Man's interest in Hölderlin as a master of rhetoric, which he considered more closely connected with the Romantic usage of language than with its existential dimension.[52] Furthermore, it highlights de Man's concern that the legacy of a poet like Hölderlin rested on close reading.

In conclusion, one example of a philosophical close reading of Hölderlin's late works should be considered in more detail, for it offers a synthesizing discussion of the main questions this chapter has attempted to address: Hölderlin's position between German Classicism and Romanticism, the philosophical essence of his poetry, and the specificity of his poetic style. The case in mind is Theodor W. Adorno's essay 'Parataxis' (1963), which was mainly devoted to exploring features of Hölderlin's late poetry. Adorno's starting point was a fundamental critique of Heidegger's interpretations of Hölderlin, based on the philosopher's supposed failure to take sufficient account of the poetic form of the late elegies, odes, and hymns. Adorno accuses Heidegger of having used inappropriate language in order to reflect the making and essence of Hölderlin's poetry and poetic stance in philosophy.[53]

Instead, Adorno elaborates on Hölderlin's stringing together of concepts ('Reihung') and his ability to create correspondences between hitherto unrelated concepts and emotions. He points out the use of parataxis, which generates the impression of poetic serialism and equality of arguments. Through applying a concept that is quintessential in musical Modernism, *Reihung* or serialism, to Hölderlin's poetry, Adorno alludes to its avant-garde-like quality. His occasional references to Beethoven's late works and their similarity with Hölderlin's ambition in poetry further testify to Adorno's interest in connecting Hölderlin with Modernism.[54] This is also confirmed when Adorno compares the tendency in Hölderlin's late work towards association and finding, or inventing, correspondences between abstract conceptions and tangible realities with Baudelaire's approach to writing poetry.

Adorno correctly attributes this poetic interest in 'real objects' to the Classicism in Hölderlin, whilst he identifies Hölderlin's ability to make language speak for itself in poetry as quintessentially Romantic.[55] For Hölderlin, though, working with abstractions possessed a sensual quality, too. It was as 'real' as any *res*, or object. Likewise, a 'real object' could turn, in his poetry, into an abstract entity. Somewhat surprisingly, given Adorno's own accomplishment in achieving just that in his philosophy, he did not detect this in Hölderlin. He emphasized instead Hölderlin's unease with ready-made syntheses and therefore with any plain, or mechanistic, understanding of dialectics. In this

[51] In Paul de Man, *Romanticism and Contemporary Criticism*, ed. E. S. Burt, Kevin Newmark, and Andrzej Warminski (Baltimore: Johns Hopkins University Press, 1993), 65.

[52] Paul de Man, *The Rhetoric of Romanticism* (New York: Columbia University Press, 1984).

[53] In Theodor W. Adorno, *Noten zur Literatur, Gesammelte Schriften*, xi, ed. Rolf Tiedemann et al. (Frankfurt am Main: Suhrkamp Verlag, 2003), 447–91, here 452–3.

[54] Adorno, *Noten zur Literatur*, 473.

[55] Adorno, *Noten zur Literatur*, 468 and 478.

connection, Adorno was right in recognizing that Hölderlin preferred symbiosis (for instance between ancient Greek and Christian values) to idealist synthesis.

At one point in his critique, Adorno observes that in Hölderlin, particularly in his elegy 'Brod und Wein', 'history' or historical events are 'cutting through the bond between idea and perception' that still existed according to classicist aesthetics.[56] This suggests, by association, a link between historical circumstances and Hölderlin's conception of 'caesura'. It also makes Adorno's argument anticipate Lacoue-Labarthe's interpretation of Hölderlin. For in *La Fiction du politique*, he applied Hölderlin's conception of tragedy to suggest an alternative to Heidegger's interpretation of what happened to Germany from 1933 to 1945. Lacoue-Labarthe maintains that Auschwitz represents what Hölderlin had called a *caesura*, a fundamental break in history that can occur when God and humanity become radically separated. 'In fact,' we are told, 'God died at Auschwitz, in any case the God of the Greco-Christian West.'[57] For Hölderlin, a caesura of such magnitude, given the radical withdrawing of God, constitutes the basic law of the tragic character of finite existence. Adorno, however, maintained that the overriding principle in Hölderlin's (late) work was 'the threshold of reflection', which guarded him against undue mysticism and (Romantic) emotionalism.[58]

Ultimately, though, Hölderlin's epigram 'προς εαυτόν' (to oneself), with which Hellingrath opened the fourth volume of his edition, reconciles, at least symbolically, the very tragedy of *caesura* in culture with the grace of Being; and he does so by virtue of its classic measure, Stoic effect, and yet latently Romantic appeal:

> Learn art in life, and in art learn about life,
> Can you rightly perceive the one, will you do so with the other, too.[59]

Further Reading

Cooper, Ian, *The Near and Distant God: Poetry, Idealism and Religious Thought from Hölderlin to Eliot* (Leeds: Legenda 2008).

Gaier, Ulrich, *Hölderlin: Eine Einführung* (Tübingen and Basel: Francke Verlag 1993).

Görner, Rüdiger, *Hölderlins Mitte: Zur Ästhetik eines Ideals* (Munich: Iudicium Verlag, 1993).

Gosetti-Ferencei, Jennifer Anna, *Heidegger, Hölderlin and the Subject of Poetic Language: Towards a New Poetic of Dasein* (New York: Fordham University Press, 2004).

Haverkamp, Anselm, *Leaves of Mourning: Hölderlin's Late Work. With an Essay on Keats and Melancholy*, tr. Vernon Chadwick (Albany, NY: State University of New York Press, 1996).

Hölderlin, Friedrich, *Selected Poems and Fragments: Bilingual Edition*, tr. Michael Hamburger, ed. Jeremy Adler (London: Penguin, 1998).

[56] Adorno, *Noten zur Literatur*, 465.

[57] Philippe Lacoue-Labarthe, *La Fiction du politique* (Paris: Christian Bourgeois, 1987), 62.

[58] Adorno, *Noten zur Literatur*, 488.

[59] Hölderlin, *Sämtliche Werke*, iv. 3: 'Lern im Leben die Kunst, im Kunstwerk lerne das Leben, | Siehst du das Eine recht, siehst du das andere auch' (my tr.).

Hölderlin, Friedrich, *Essays and Letters*, ed. and tr. with an introduction by Jeremy Adler and Charlie Louth (London: Penguin Classics, 2009).
Kocziszky, Eva, *Hölderlins Orient* (Würzburg: Königshausen & Neumann, 2009).
Menninghaus, Winfried, *Hälfte des Lebens: Versuch über Hölderlins Poetik* (Frankfurt am Main: Suhrkamp Verlag, 2005).
Ogden, Mark, *The Problem of Christ in the Work of Friedrich Hölderlin*, Bithell Series of Dissertations, 16 (London and Leeds: Maney & Son, 1991).
Warminski, Andrzej, *Readings in Interpretation: Hölderlin, Hegel, Heidegger* (Minneapolis: University of Minnesota Press, 1987).

CHAPTER 16

GOETHE THE WRITER

ANGUS NICHOLLS

Das Klassische nenne ich das Gesunde, und das Romantische das Kranke.

I call the Classical the healthy, and the Romantic the sick.

From Sickness to Health?

Of all Goethe's various statements on the relation between Classicism and Romanticism, this remark, apparently made to Johann Peter Eckermann on 2 April 1829,[1] has probably exerted the most influence upon his place in literary history. It was uttered by a 79-year-old man engaged in shoring up his legacy, which involved undertaking comparisons between his own works and those of a younger generation of authors that had, at least in Germany around 1800, initially taken Goethe to be their model.[2] The late Goethe's apparent total condemnations of what he called *das Romantische*—another claims that 'what is Romantic has already lost its way in its own abyss; one can hardly imagine anything more horrible than its quite disgusting recent productions'[3]—have often been used to argue that, although Goethe lived through and influenced the period known as German Romanticism, broadly defined in a recent account as spanning from

[1] Johann Peter Eckermann, *Gespräche mit Goethe in den letzten Jahren seines Lebens*, in Johann Wolfgang Goethe, *Sämtliche Werke, Briefe, Tagebücher und Gespräche*, ed. Hendrik Birus, Dieter Borchmeyer, Karl Eibl, and Wilhelm Voßkamp et al. (Frankfurt am Main: Deutscher Klassiker Verlag, 1985–2003), 2/12. 324. Hereafter cited as FA (= Frankfurter Ausgabe) followed by part, volume and page numbers. All translations of German passages in this chapter are my own unless otherwise noted.

[2] Here it should be noted that while Goethe's comment is couched in general terms, its specific context is a discussion of recent French literature.

[3] Goethe, *Maximen und Reflexionen*, in *Sämtliche Werke nach Epochen seines Schaffens*, ed. Karl Richter, Herbert G. Göpfert, Norbert Miller, and Gerhard Sauder (Munich: Carl Hanser, 1985–98), xvii. 893. Hereafter cited as MA (= Münchner Ausgabe) followed by volume and page numbers. Tr. Elizabeth Stopp in Goethe, *Maxims and Reflections* (Harmondsworth: Penguin, 1998), 132.

1789–1830,[4] he at the same time did not belong to it. Apparently existing in a parallel world of his own making, a world that his friend Friedrich Schiller is also said to have co-created before his untimely death in 1805, the middle phase of Goethe's life (roughly 1786–1805) came to be defined by the category of Weimar Classicism,[5] a reassertion of Classical aesthetic models that rejected all things redolent of mysticism and the Middle Ages, which in the early nineteenth century meant all things Romantic. But with even a cursory investigation of Goethe's famous remark on aesthetic health and sickness this narrative begins to unravel: only a few lines later he claims that the *Nibelungenlied*, that paragon of the mystical German Middle Ages, is *klassisch* and therefore healthy, suggesting that the surface opposition between the Classical and the Romantic is more complicated than one might have first thought.

Goethe's expressed opinions on Romanticism and his historical relation to Romanticism have often been conflated in unhelpful ways. The extent to which Goethe's pronouncements on his own works were afforded an almost unquestioned authority from the very beginnings of Goethe philology meant that their reception was dominated by Goethe's 'strategies of self-projection' until at least well into the twentieth century.[6] Wilhelm Scherer—writing in 1877, some eight years before the opening of Goethe's archive at Weimar—accordingly saw Goethe as a 'researcher of himself' who had, in his autobiography *Dichtung und Wahrheit* (Poetry and Truth, 1811–33), shown the way for future generations of scholars.[7] Similarly, for the purposes of Heinrich Heine's important 1833 study of German Romanticism, Goethe's own self-disaffiliation from German Romanticism was sufficient grounds upon which to see his works as being influential upon, yet also fundamentally different from, those of the so-called 'Romantic school', which Heine sees as having undertaken a reactionary revival of the Catholic Middle Ages. 'The Romantic School,' writes Heine with not a little irony

> suffered... a crushing protest from within its own temple, and indeed from the mouth of one of the gods whom they themselves had placed there. It was, namely, Wolfgang Goethe who stepped down from his pedestal and spoke this damning judgement concerning the Schlegels, the very same high priests who had surrounded him with frankincense.[8]

The importance of Heine's early account of German Romanticism, which focused mainly on local religious and political issues as opposed to broader philosophical

[4] Gerhard Schulz, 'From Romantick to Romantic', in Denis F. Mahoney (ed.), *The Literature of German Romanticism*, Camden House History of German Literature, 8 (Rochester, NY: Camden House, 2004), 28.

[5] This periodization is offered by Simon Richter in his introduction to *The Literature of Weimar Classicism*, Camden House History of German Literature, 7 (Rochester, NY: Camden House, 2005), 3–44.

[6] See Katrin Kohl, 'No Escape? Goethe's Strategies of Self-Projection and their Role in German Literary Historiography', *Goethe Yearbook*, 16 (2008), 173–91.

[7] Wilhelm Scherer, 'Goethe Philologie' (1877), in Erich Schmidt (ed.), *Aufsätze über Goethe* (Berlin: Weidmann, 1886), 12, 14.

[8] Heinrich Heine, *Die romantische Schule*, in *Werke*, ed. Helmut Schanze, iv. *Schriften über Deutschland* (Frankfurt am Main: Insel, 1968), 192.

content, goes a long way to explaining why, in German literary historiography, Goethe is often still seen to have somehow evaded Romanticism, whereas in many anglophone accounts he stands at the very centre of the European Romantic movement.[9] Indeed, Goethe's own reflections upon his literary development suggested that any subjectivist or Romantic tendencies that he might have had were quickly worked through and overcome. The narrative presented in *Poetry and Truth* involves a young man who divested himself of his own pre-Romantic excesses by writing *Die Leiden des jungen Werthers* (The Sorrows of Young Werther, 1774), the tale of an emotional protagonist who commits suicide on account of his unrequited love for a woman betrothed to another. Goethe describes his composition of the novel in therapeutic terms as a 'general confession' (*Generalbeichte*) that enabled him to surmount a youthful and stormy element in his personality.[10] In a much later novel—*Die Wahlverwandtschaften* (The Elective Affinities, 1809)—Goethe did revisit the theme of how natural passions may threaten the institution of marriage, and this novel was appreciated by some of his Romantic contemporaries for doing so.[11] But here Goethe's treatment of this seemingly high Romantic material was rather more controlled. Whereas the majority of *Werther* is narrated in the first person, from the perspective of Werther's own letters,[12] the dominant third-person narration of *Die Wahlverwandtschaften* did not necessarily encourage identification with the transgressors and was even seen by some contemporary interpreters as defending the institution of marriage against the uncontrolled forces of nature.[13]

Even with respect to *Die Wahlverwandtschaften*, therefore, the idea that Goethe had turned from youthful 'sickness' to mature 'health' could be maintained, and this biographical narrative would find its expression in the two dominant phases associated with Goethe's artistic development: the wayward subjectivism of the *Sturm and Drang* (Storm and Stress, spanning approximately from the late 1760s until the end of the

[9] See e.g. the account of Nicholas Boyle, who writes: 'Goethe was not just *a* poet—for the whole Romantic generation in England, Germany and even France, he was *the* poet, and through his influence on that generation he affected all subsequent notions of what poets are and what poetry does.' *Goethe: The Poet and the Age* (Oxford: Oxford University Press, 1991–2000), i, p. ix. For broader historical context on the anglophone categorization of Goethe as a Romantic poet, see also Robert C. Holub, 'The Romanticizing of Goethe: A Study in the Acquisition of a Label', in James Pipkin (ed.), *English and German Romanticism: Cross-Currents and Controversies* (Heidelberg: Winter, 1985), 349–61.

[10] Goethe, *Dichtung und Wahrheit*, FA 1/14. 369.

[11] See Friedrich Schlegel, 'Über Liebe und Ehe in Beziehung auf Goethes *Wahlverwandtschaften* (1810)', in Heinz Härtl (ed.), *Die Wahlverwandtschaften: Eine Dokumentation der Wirkung von Goethes Roman, 1808–1832* (Berlin: Akademie Verlag, 1983), 156–7.

[12] In response to allegations that the novel encouraged suicide, Goethe published a 2nd edn of *Werther* in 1787, which tended to discourage readers from identifying with its main character. See my discussion of these changes in *Goethe's Concept of the Daemonic: After the Ancients* (Rochester, NY: Camden House, 2006), 159–62. Both editions can be compared in FA 1/8.

[13] In particular, Johann Peter Eckermann, for whom the plot of this novel emerges from the conflict between the institution of marriage and the violence of nature (*Naturgewalt*). Goethe, according to Eckermann, sides with marriage when he has the character of Mittler exclaim 'You should have reverence for the bond of marriage.' Johann Peter Eckermann, 'Bemerkungen über Goethes *Wahlverwandtschaften* (1823)', in Härtl (ed.), *Die Wahlverwandtschaften: Eine Dokumentation*, 296, 293.

1770s),[14] which is later seen to be 'corrected' by the sober Kantian influence of Schiller and the balanced and formal qualities of Weimar Classicism—a 'movement' which, according to one of the pre-eminent anglophone proponents of German Classicism, was 'the doing of just two writers'.[15] Can two people a literary movement make? Perhaps not, since even in standard histories of German literature, other authors have been associated with this tendency in German literature—particularly Christoph Martin Wieland, who is seen to have conjoined late-baroque or rococo literature on the one hand with German Classicism on the other.[16] And was the Weimar Classicism of Goethe and Schiller really a separate phenomenon from Romanticism? Again, maybe not: since over the last forty years critical voices have instructed us that Weimar Classicism was in fact a 'legend' or 'pseudo-epoch' that was merely the retrospective ideological construction of a recently unified Germany in search of a national literature,[17] which meant that it was really only European Romanticism with a special German label.[18]

The question as to whether Goethe was a Romantic author tends to be an unfruitful one for precisely this reason: that aesthetic periods and categories such as Classicism and Romanticism always involve the retrospective projection of different criteria and values onto the diffuse realities of literary history. If this question must nevertheless be asked, then the mundane answer to it would be to say that, from a German perspective Goethe is probably still not quite Romantic, whereas from the broader vantage point of European literary history he undoubtedly is.[19] But this ambivalent answer says more about the function of the term 'Romanticism' in various national contexts than it does about Goethe's works, and decisively to adjudicate between these rival views would inevitably require one

[14] See David Hill's 'Introduction', to *The Literature of the Sturm und Drang*, Camden House History of German Literature, 6 (Rochester, NY: Camden House, 2003), 1–46.

[15] T. J. Reed, 'Weimar Classicism: Goethe's Alliance with Schiller', in Lesley Sharpe (ed.), *The Cambridge Companion to Goethe* (Cambridge: Cambridge University Press, 2002), 101.

[16] An example is Fritz Martini's *Deutsche Literaturgeschichte von den Anfängen bis zur Gegenwart*, 10th edn (Stuttgart: Kröner, 1960), 196–9.

[17] See Karl Robert Mandelkow, 'Deutsche Literatur zwischen Klassik und Romantik', in Karl Robert Mandelkow (ed.), *Europäische Romantik I*, Neues Handbuch der Literaturwissenschaft, 14 (Wiesbaden: Athenaion, 1982), 5–10.

[18] See e.g. Reinhold Grimm and Jost Hermand (eds), *Die Klassik-Legende: Second Wisconsin Workshop* (Frankfurt am Main: Athenäum, 1971); Hans Robert Jauss, 'Deutsche Klassik—eine Pseudo-Epoche?', in Reinhart Herzog and Reinhart Koselleck (eds), *Epochenschwelle und Epochenbewußtsein*, Poetik und Hermeneutik, 12 (Munich: Fink, 1987), 581–5; Klaus L. Berghahn, 'Das Andere der Klassik: Von der "Klassik-Legende" zur jüngsten Klassik-Diskussion', *Goethe Yearbook*, 6 (1992), 1–27; Dieter Borchmeyer, 'What is Classicism?' in Richter, *Literature of Weimar Classicism*, 45–62. It is also noteworthy, in this connection, that Weimar Classicism is included under the category of European Romanticism in *Neues Handbuch der Literaturwissenschaft*, 14, cited in n. 17.

[19] The broader European perspective on Goethe's relation to Romanticism is most clearly to be found in René Wellek's *Concepts of Criticism*, where he observes that 'it is impossible to accept the common German view that romanticism is the creation the Schlegels, Tieck, Novalis and Wackenroder. If one looks at the history of German literature between Klopstock's *Messiah* (1748) and the death of Goethe, one can hardly deny the unity and coherence of the whole movement which, in European terms, would have to be called "romantic".' See Wellek, 'The Concept of Romanticism in Literary History', in Stephen G. Nichols (ed.), *Concepts of Criticism* (New Haven: Yale University Press, 1963), 161.

to define European Romanticism across separate national literatures, a task that will not be attempted here.[20] What follows will be a rather more modest exploration not of Goethe's purported Romanticism or lack thereof, but of his indisputable relation to the philosophical discourses of Romanticism. What were the central poetic features of the Storm and Stress and of Weimar Classicism and what, if anything, do they have to do with German Romanticism proper? How was Goethe seen by self-consciously Romantic authors within Germany and how, in turn, did he view them? And finally, did the late Goethe attempt to overcome or undermine the perceived opposition between Romanticism and Classicism?

Back to the Poetry

When considering Goethe's relation to German Romanticism one might, as Heine had done, focus upon local literary schisms and claim that Goethe rejected the Catholic mysticism and medieval Germanic revivalism of his Romantic contemporaries. One could recall, in this connection, the unfortunate dinner gathering in Goethe's home on New Year's Eve in 1808, when the Romantic poet and dramatist Zacharias Werner recited a sonnet in which he likened a full moon to a consecrated wafer, upon which, according to a report from Heinrich Steffens, the outraged Goethe exclaimed to his hapless guest: 'I hate this skewed religiosity, do not imagine that I will somehow support it ... you have ruined my meal.'[21] One could also point out that Heinrich von Kleist, who was perhaps too delicately poised between Classicism and Romanticism for Goethe's taste, is likened by Goethe to a 'body that nature intended to be beautiful', but which seems to have been 'taken hold of by an incurable sickness.'[22] One might remember, too, that the Schlegel brothers are said by Goethe to have been 'unhappy people for their entire lives' because they 'wanted to represent more than what nature allowed them to'. Friedrich Schlegel, in particular—the leading and most self-conscious proponent of Romanticism in Germany—is said to have 'suffocated from masticating on moral and religious absurdities', which is why he eventually 'took flight into Catholicism' before 'moving in the direction of things Indian' as a desperate last resort.[23] Or one might, finally, call to mind Goethe's sweeping judgement concerning 'a half-dozen young talents' that included not only Werner, but also Achim von Arnim and Clemens Brentano: 'it is all moving thoroughly towards formlessness and characterlessness. None of them want to comprehend that the highest and only operation of nature and of art is that of form-giving' (*Gestaltung*).[24]

[20] A similarly pragmatic renunciation to my own has recently been taken up by Arndt Bohm. See his 'Goethe and the Romantics', in Mahoney (ed.), *Literature of German Romanticism*, 35.

[21] See Goethe, *Begegnungen und Gespräche*, ed. Ernst Grumach and Renate Grumach et al. (Berlin: De Gruyter, 1965–2011), vi. 619–20.

[22] Goethe, 'Ludwig Tiecks Dramaturgische Blätter', in *Werke: Weimarer Ausgabe*, ed. Gustav von Loeper, Erich Schmidt, et al. (Weimar: Herman Böhlau, 1887–1919), 1/40. 178.

[23] Goethe to Carl Friedrich Zelter, 20 Oct. 1831, in FA 2/11. 478.

[24] Goethe to Carl Friedrich Zelter, 30 Oct. 1808, in FA 2/6. 398.

Recounting these and similar anecdotes in order to make claims about Goethe's position in literary history is a commonplace of Goethe scholarship, and it is made possible by a plethora of critical editions, handbooks, and lexicons that allow one quickly to establish what Goethe said about whom and when.[25] Such statements—and, as we shall see, especially that concerning form and formlessness—*do* suggest important differences between Goethe's aesthetics and those of his younger contemporaries, and their rhetorical force has helped to draw an apparently clear dividing line between German Romanticism and Weimar Classicism. Yet it is also possible, as Heine and more recently Ernst Behler have suggested, that they might say more about an older author who felt threatened by younger talents than they do about purely aesthetic differences.[26] Goethe probably knew that even the damning judgements from his private correspondence would be published, and they can be seen as highly successful attempts to secure his central place in German literary history. But while this kind of chatter can provide a rich context for reading Goethe's literary works, it can also obscure them. The tendency of positivist Goethe scholarship to hang importance upon the poet's every anecdote and self-stylization can allow one to forget about the works as *texts* that operated in a particular historical and philosophical context. Thus, the approach taken here to 'Goethe the Writer'—to the author of the poetic works instead of the sometimes gossipy letters and reviews—does not polemically claim that the author is 'dead', or that his opinions are irrelevant, but simply emphasizes that not everything that Goethe says about his works and those of his contemporaries is incontrovertibly true.

Perhaps the most convincing reassertion of this sense of textuality in Goethe's works is that offered by David Wellbery in *The Specular Moment* (1996). Criticizing the biographical approach to Goethe that characterized the scholarly editions of the mid-twentieth century, Wellbery focuses upon Goethe's early poetry, arguing that it did nothing less than inaugurate 'a type of literary discourse that, from a European perspective, can be called the Romantic lyric'.[27] We note here Wellbery's emphasis upon a 'European perspective', since his implicit claim is that the period which German literary historians have called the Storm and Stress actually represents the early phases of European Romanticism. As Ernst Behler's more recent article on 'Romantik' in the *Goethe Handbuch* demonstrates, this position is now hardly disputed in German scholarship. Behler situates Storm and Stress within a broader category of early European Romanticism that includes Shaftesbury's and Edward Young's ideas about genius, Rousseau's reflections upon nature, and the discourses on poetic inspiration found in the works of Johann Georg Hamann and Johann Gottfried Herder. These tendencies continue into Weimar Classicism and into what Behler terms *Hochromantik* (High

[25] For further detail on Goethe's attitudes to individual authors associated with German Romanticism, see Hartmut Fröschle, *Goethes Verhältnis zur Romantik* (Würzburg: Königshausen & Neumann, 2002). Some of these episodes are related in Ernst Behler's article on 'Romantik', in Bernd Witte et al. (eds), *Goethe Handbuch* (Stuttgart: J. B. Metzler, 1996–9), 4/2. 918–25.

[26] Behler, 'Romantik', 923.

[27] David E. Wellbery, *The Specular Moment: Goethe's Early Lyric and the Beginnings of Romanticism* (Stanford, Calif.: Stanford University Press, 1996), 7.

Romanticism), by which he means the writings of the Schlegel brothers and Friedrich von Hardenberg (Novalis) around 1800, which were infused not only by Hamann and Herder but also, and to a far greater extent, by Kant's critical philosophy and its subsequent interpretations by Fichte and Schelling.[28] It can be argued, as Jane Brown has done, that Weimar Classicism and early (Jena) German Romanticism are both attempts to deal with precisely this collection of philosophical ideas in poetic terms,[29] with perhaps the central issue being the role played by art in mediating between human subjectivity and nature. When seen, then, within this broader philosophical context, it becomes clear that German Romanticism and Weimar Classicism represent 'not so much a polarity', but rather a 'family quarrel' within the broader context of post-Kantian European Romanticism.[30]

While Wellbery's focus is by and large upon Goethe's Storm and Stress poetry of the 1770s, our task here is to track, albeit schematically and in miniature, Goethe's literary and philosophical development from the Storm and Stress into the very late stages of Weimar Classicism, and to see what this development might have to do with the core issue expressed in what Wellbery calls the Romantic lyric: the relation between subjectivity and its world. This will be done through a consideration of two poems: the first, 'Mahomets Gesang' (Song of Mohammed), was written in 1773; while the second, 'Mächtiges Überraschen' (Unexpected Overwhelming) was composed during late 1807 and early 1808. A comparison between them will allow us to see how very differently Goethe treated the same metaphor for subjectivity, that of a rushing stream of water, at two separate stages of his development.[31] Goethe's choice of this metaphor was hardly coincidental, since it had been a topos for poetic inspiration since classical antiquity, and gained a renewed prominence during the eighteenth century. Horace, for example, compares Pindar's style to a river that 'bursts its banks and rushes down a | Mountain with uncontrollable momentum',[32] while Gotthold Ephraim Lessing, writing in 1765, observes that 'the true genius works its own way through the greatest of obstacles like a torrential stream', citing Shakespeare as his prime example.[33]

Although 'Mahomets Gesang' ostensibly takes the life of the Prophet Mohammed as its subject, it is not a poem that deals with the religious content of Islam. Its subject is much more the ability of a poet or prophet to found a national culture through the sheer force of his own subjectivity. Such a question was very much on Goethe's agenda during

[28] Behler, 'Romantik', 918.

[29] Jane K. Brown, 'Romanticism and Classicism', in Nicholas Saul (ed.), *The Cambridge Companion to German Romanticism* (Cambridge: Cambridge University Press, 2009), 124.

[30] Jauss, 'Deutsche Klassik—eine Pseudo-Epoche?', 583.

[31] This subject matter has been investigated at length by Richard M. Müller in *Die deutsche Klassik: Wesen und Geschichte im Spiegel des Strommotivs* (Bonn: Bouvier, 1959), and in chs 3 and 6 of Nicholls, *Goethe's Concept of the Daemonic*.

[32] Horace, Ode 5.2 in *The Odes and the Centennial Hymn*, tr. James Michie (Indianapolis, Ind.: Bobbs-Merrill, 1963), 187.

[33] Gotthold Ephraim Lessing, *Briefe, die neueste Literatur betreffend* (letter 332), in *Gesammelte Werke*, ed. Paul Rilla, 2nd edn (Berlin: Aufbau, 1968), iv. 434.

the early 1770s, since he and Herder had been considering, in their respective writings on Shakespeare, how they might throw off the shackles of French neoclassicism in order to found a national literature in which the natural German landscape and language would find their expression.[34] In his collection of fragments titled *Über die neuere deutsche Literatur* (On Recent German Literature, 1765–7), Herder again invoked Horace's use of the water metaphor in order to argue that such a poet would be akin to 'a great, violent stream', which, 'rolling itself with one hundred hands, roaring down from a cliff', would finally settle into a valley and become 'the name of its region'.[35] It is precisely this image of water streaming from rocks or cliffs (a *Felsenquell*) that we find in Goethe's poem:

Seht den Felsenquell
Freudehell
Wie ein Sternenblick!
Über Wolken
Nährten seine Jugend
Gute Geister
Zwischen Klippen im Gebüsch.

Jünglingfrisch
Tanzt er aus der Wolke
Auf die Marmorfelsen nieder
Jauchzet wieder
Nach dem Himmel
See the spring in the cliff
Bright with joy
Like the radiance of stars!
Over clouds
Its youth was nurtured
By good spirits
In the cliffs and scrub.

Youthful freshly
It dances from the cloud
Down to marble cliffs below
Jubilating
To the heavens

As the stream proceeds on its course, other *Bruderquellen* or 'brother-streams' join it, and their collective rush fertilizes the landscape, breathing life into the meadows below. Yet the joyous trajectory of this stream, now a literal band of brothers, is later threatened by exposure to the sandy desert and the sun, and by obstructive hills in the landscape.

[34] Johann Gottfried Herder, 'Shakespear', in *Werke*, ed. Günter Arnold and Martin Bollacher et al. (Frankfurt am Main: Deutscher Klassiker Verlag, 1985–2000), ii. 498–521; Goethe, 'Zum Shakespeares Tag', in FA 1/18. 9–12.

[35] Johann Gottfried Herder, *Über die neuere deutsche Literatur*, in *Werke*, i. 341.

The solution to this threat is to draw even more companions to the cause and finally to seek refuge in the arms of the father, the ocean:

Bruder nimm die Brüder mit!
Mit zu deinem Alten Vater
Zu dem ewgen Ozean
Der mit weitverbreiten Armen
Unsrer wartet
Die sich ach vergebens öffnen
Seine Sehnenden zu fassen
Denn uns frißt in öder Wüste
Gier'ger Sand
Die Sonne droben
Saugt an unserm Blut
Ein Hügel
Hemmet uns zum Teiche!
Bruder!
Nimm die Brüder von der Ebne
Nimm die Brüder von Gebürgen
Mit zu deinem Vater mit.

Brother, take your brothers with you,
To your age-old father,
To the eternal ocean
Where with outspread arms
Us it waits for;
Arms, alas, which open vainly
For the ones who're yearning for him;
For we're devoured in the barren desert
By greedy sand,
The sun up there
Sucks our blood,
A hillside
Hems us in as a pond.
Brother,
Take your brothers from the plains,
Take your brothers from the mountains
With you, with you to your father!

This survival strategy proves to be a success insofar as the stream swells further still in a manner that is suggestive of sexual arousal, and it is this potency that enables it to name lands and found cities as it passes:

Und nun schwillt er
Herrlicher, ein ganz Geschlechte
Trägt den Fürsten hoch empor
Und im rollenden Triumphe

Gibt er Ländern Namen, Städte
Werden unter seinem Fuß.

And he swells up
More resplendent, all a tribe
Carries a prince aloft,
And rolling in triumph,
He gives name to countries, cities
Spring up from his footsteps.

In this way, 'Mahomets Gesang' displays many characteristic features of the Storm and Stress that might also, from a European perspective, be seen as Romantic: the tendency to use foreign cultural models by way of analogy in order to found a national German literature in opposition to French neoclassicism; the emphasis on the disruptive but also vivifying powers of poetic genius, seen from a rather adolescent and masculine perspective; and the longing for consummation either with nature, with a love-object, or with an all-embracing and pantheistic conception of the divine, regardless of any obstacles that may stand in the way. The problem that Goethe eventually associated with this model of gushing subjectivity was that it proceeds only in the direction of formlessness. The poem shows how individual identities are subsumed under the auspices of a greater cause, and it ends with the brothers uniting themselves with the father, the eternal ocean:

Und so trägt er seine Brüder
Seine Schätze seine Kinder
Dem erwartenden Erzeuger
Freudebrausend an das Herz.

Thus he carries all his brothers,
All his treasures and his children,
Foaming joyfully to the waiting
Heart of their progenitor.[36]

The subject's unlimited desire for consummation with the object (whether that be nature, a lover, or God) leads to a regression and to a loss of identity—to the individual's sinking back into the infinite. It represents, in short, a failure to achieve individuation.

Some thirty-five years later, at the close of the period known as Weimar Classicism, Goethe revisits this topos in the sonnet 'Mächtiges Überraschen':

Ein Strom entrauscht umwölktem Felsensaale
Dem Ozean sich eilig zu verbinden;
Was auch sich spiegeln mag von Grund zu Gründen,
Er wandelt unaufhaltsam fort zu Tale.

Dämonisch aber stürzt mit einem Male –

[36] Goethe, 'Mahomets Gesang', FA 1/1. 193–5. Tr. John Whaley as 'Mohammed's Song', in *Selected Poems*, tr. John Whaley, introd. Matthew Bell (Evanston, Ill.: Northwestern University Press, 1998), 6–9.

Ihr folgen Berg und Wald in Wirbelwinden –
Sich Oreas, Behagen dort zu finden,
Und hemmt den Lauf, begrenzt die weite Schale.

Die Welle sprüht, und staunt zurück und weichet,
Und schwillt bergan, sich immer selbst zu trinken;
Gehemmt ist nun zum Vater hin das Streben.

Sie schwankt und ruht, zum See zurückgedeichet;
Gestirne, spiegelnd sich, beschaun das Blinken
Des Wellenschlags am Fels, ein neues Leben.

From clouded rocky vaults a river gushes,
To join the distant ocean downward racing:
Its course unchecked though mirrored valleys tracing,
Into the valley on and on it pushes.

But Oreas, daimonic, sudden rushes—
With cliff and forest too in whirlwinds chasing—
To seek contentment in that flow's embracing,
And halts it, forms a vessel ringed with bushes.

The wave spurts foam and then retreats, astounded,
And drinks itself in swirl of backwards streaming;
The striving to the Father is abated.

It sways and rests, and as a lake is bounded;
The constellations, mirrored, watch the gleaming
As wave laps rock, as new life is created.[37]

In this new version of the narrative, which has often been read as a direct response to the earlier poem,[38] limitation of subjectivity is no longer something to be avoided; rather it is actively to be embraced. In the second stanza, the protagonist-stream is blocked by a daimonic (in the sense of inexplicable and disruptive) mountain nymph, Oreas.[39] This leads, in the third stanza, to the protagonist undergoing a balancing switch in genders: what was once a masculine stream (in German *der Strom*) becomes a wave (the feminine *die Welle*). In the final stanza the protagonist, now referred to by the feminine *sie*, has been dammed into a lake that is able to reflect the constellations. It is precisely this dashing of the wave against a rock, this moment of limitation by external forces, which makes a new life possible, and the final stanza expresses the tension between movement (*schwanken* or swaying) and stasis (*ruhen*, to rest or repose) to which it gives rise. Here limitation means precisely form-giving power or *Gestaltung*, since only *Gestaltung* can render a mimesis of the infinite possible. And of course Goethe's strict reorganization of this thematic material into a sonnet—stylistically a world away from

[37] Goethe, 'Mächtiges Überraschen', FA 1/2. 250; tr. John Whaley as 'Unexpected Overwhelming', in *Selected Poems*, 89.

[38] See Müller, *Die deutsche Klassik*, 55–60, 69–78.

[39] See Nicholls, *Goethe's Concept of the Daemonic*.

the rushing, non-rhyming freedom of 'Mahomets Gesang'—also registers this preference for *Gestaltung* on a formal level.

There are numerous ways of reading 'Mächtiges Überraschen'. One trivializing approach is to suggest that it was merely a biographical reflection on Goethe's relationships with either Bettine von Arnim or Minchen Herzlieb, both of whom are said to be represented by the mountain nymph Oreas;[40] another is to argue that it depicts nothing less than Goethe's reckoning with the central question of post-Kantian idealism, and with what David Wellbery sees as the core content of the Romantic lyric: that of the relationship between subjectivity and its world. The latter approach is to be taken here. This is because the problem of subjectivity and its limits was an issue with which Goethe struggled already in the Storm and Stress, and which he later worked through during the period known as Weimar Classicism.

Self, World, and the Absolute in Post-Kantian Thought around 1800

The Storm and Stress model of subjectivity was one that Herder had adapted from Gottfried Wilhelm Leibniz's *Monadology*, according to which each individual soul is endowed with a divine potentiality, entelechy, or *Kraft*.[41] Leibniz's solution to the problem of how these separate *Kräfte* interact with one another was that of pre-established harmony: each monad has its preordained place within the divine scheme of things.[42] But the Storm and Stress theory of genius retained the sense of divine *Kraft* or force while dispensing with the limitations of a pre-established harmony underpinned by God: the monad-as-genius is the individual with literally limitless energies and wishes, who requires unobstructed self-development at all costs. It is the artist-as-upstart depicted in Goethe's poem 'Prometheus', who declares to his god Zeus: 'Ich dich ehren? Wofür? … Hier sitz' ich, forme Menschen | Nach meinem Bilde' (I honour you? For what? … Here I sit, fashion humans | In my own image).[43] Radical originality and total self-legislation, and not subjection to God or any other prior law, is the central feature of this notion of genius. Thus 'the genius', writes Herder in a typically hyperbolic passage from *Über die neuere deutsche Literatur*, 'rages, tears everything down, and terrifies the educated and uneducated'.[44]

This problem relating to subjectivity was also addressed by the critical philosophy of Kant. Pre-established harmony in the manner of Leibniz was for Kant a form of

[40] See Hans-Jürgen Schlütter's commentary on the poem's reception history in *Goethes Sonette: Anregung, Entstehung, Intention* (Bad Homburg: Gehlen, 1969), 111–15.

[41] See Herder, *Werke*, viii. 452; Robert T. Clarke, 'Herder's Conception of Kraft', *PMLA* 57 (1942), 737–52.

[42] See Leibniz, *Monadology*, §§1, 3, 7, 9, 17, 56, 78.

[43] Goethe, 'Prometheus', in FA 1/1. 204; tr. John Whaley in *Selected Poems*, 18–21.

[44] Herder, *Werke*, i. 411.

uncritical dogmatism: any sense of harmony that we might perceive in the world could only be a necessary idea of our reason rather than an objective aspect of reality. Yet Kant himself had quite a lot to say about the subject on the one hand, but on the other hand not quite enough. We know that the world which we perceive is synthetically assembled for us by our intuitions of space and time and by the categories of the understanding such as causality, and these aspects of our subjectivity are successful in creating for us a representation of the world that seems to accord with external reality, even if we cannot know the 'things in themselves'. But what the *self* actually is, *in itself*, was a question that Kant was only able to answer by way of inference. In the second or B version of the first *Critique*, the *Kritik der reinen Vernunft* (Critique of Pure Reason, 1787), it was called the transcendental unity of apperception, the 'I think' that must, logically, accompany all of my representations even if it cannot be a direct object of my perception.[45] But here many questions were left unanswered. If the self assembles its representations of the object-world, is it the primary and unconditioned force behind all perception, or is it in turn conditioned by something more primordial: by nature, by Being, or by God? This was one of the key debates of post-Kantian idealism, and Goethe followed it with interest after his initial encounter with the first *Critique* in 1789, and his immediate engagement with the third *Critique*, the *Kritik der Urteilskraft* (Critique of Judgement, 1790) in the year of its publication.[46] He was, moreover, directly involved in the academic careers of the two chief interlocutors in this post-Kantian debate: Fichte and Schelling. Goethe played a key role in the dismissal of Fichte from his post at the University of Jena in 1799, and he had helped to appoint Schelling to the same university in 1798.[47]

The respective answers offered by Fichte and Schelling to the problem of the self and its relation to the world were both eventually rejected by Goethe. In his *Grundlage der gesammten Wissenschaftslehre* (Foundations of the Entire Theory of Knowledge, 1794–5), Fichte decided the matter on the side of the subject: through a primary *Tathandlung* or deed-action, the transcendental ego initially posits itself as the absolute subject, and the object-world is then subsequently experienced as that which stands over against, or opposes, the ego.[48] The primary actor, is however, always the self-positing subject and not the object-world or nature. Writing to Goethe on 28 October 1794, Schiller causticly observed that, for Fichte, 'the world ... is merely a ball, which the I has thrown and which it once again catches through reflection!!'[49] Goethe probably agreed with this judgement,

[45] Immanuel Kant, *Critique of Pure Reason*, ed. and tr. Paul Guyer and Allen W. Wood (Cambridge: Cambridge University Press, 1998), 246–68.

[46] See Géza von Molnár, *Goethes Kantstudien* (Weimar: Hermann Böhlhaus Nachfolger, 1994); Robert J. Richards, *The Romantic Conception of Life: Science and Philosophy in the Age of Goethe* (Chicago: University of Chicago Press, 2002), 427–30.

[47] On Fichte, see Boyle, *Goethe*, ii. 625–30, and W. Daniel Wilson, *Das Goethe-Tabu. Protest und Menschenrechte im klassischen Weimar* (Munich: Deutscher Taschenbuch Verlag, 1999), 243–9; on Schelling, see Boyle, *Goethe*, ii. 593.

[48] See Johann Gottlieb Fichte, *Grundlage der gesammten Wissenschaftslehre*, in *Sämmtliche Werke*, ed. J. H. Fichte, i (1845; Berlin: Walter de Gruyter, 1965), §1, 91–101.

[49] Schiller to Goethe, 28 Oct. 1794, in MA 8/1. 36.

since he had already referred to Fichte's *Grundlage der gesammten Wissenschaftslehre* as a 'strange production' in a letter to Friedrich Heinrich Jacobi in September of that year.[50] The other option was presented by Schelling who, like Fichte, found Kant's transcendental unity of apperception to be a non-solution to the problem of the self. If, Schelling argued, this self is transcendental, then it can neither be an individual thing or object, nor can it be an individual subject; rather, it could only lie in what Schelling called the absolute.[51] In contrast to Fichte, Schelling then came to see this absolute as residing in Nature, explicitly opposing what he termed his own 'Idealism of Nature' to Fichte's 'Idealism of the I'.[52] The individual human subject, Schelling argued, is always conditioned by nature, which he also referred to as the *Weltseele* or world-soul. This move also presented an apparent solution to the Kantian question as to why our representations of the world seem to coincide with external reality: they do so, thought Schelling in his *Ideen zu einer Philosophie der Natur* (Ideas toward a Philosophy of Nature, 1797), because both are manifestations of the *Weltseele*: human thinking about nature is in these terms simply to be seen as nature, manifested in human subjectivity, engaged in the process of thinking about itself.[53]

In Goethe's opinion this solution was far too easy and elided the fundamental discontinuity between human representations of nature and what Kant called objects 'in themselves'. This position was worked out by Goethe during the 1790s, mainly in his writings on the philosophy of science. In one key essay from 1792 on the theory of experiments, he points out that it is precisely the 'disproportion of our understanding to the nature of things' which means that experiments are conducted according to ideal models that are later contradicted and corrected by the particulars of nature.[54] And in a similar piece written in 1798, he also claims that the use of such models in science is always accompanied by a tendency to pass over empirical realities that do not fit with the ideal type being proposed.[55] This is why, in a letter to Schiller written on 6 January 1798, Goethe argues that our knowledge of nature is not simply characterized by a transcendental unity between the mind and nature, but much more by our representations of nature being disrupted by sharp intrusions from external reality. 'While the idealist likes to be on guard against the things in themselves,' writes Goethe, referring to Schelling's critique of Kant, 'he still, without expecting it, runs into (*anstoßen*) things outside of himself.'[56] The subject who, like Schelling, imagines that complete consummation between the mind and nature is possible is deluded, and he or she will sooner or later be corrected by experience.

[50] Goethe to Friedrich Heinrich Jacobi, 8 Sept. 1794, FA 2/4. 24–5.

[51] Friedrich Wilhelm Joseph Schelling, *Vom Ich als Princip der Philosophie*, in *Werke*, ed. Wilhelm G. Jacobs, Jörg Jantzen, Walter Schieche et al. (Stuttgart: Fromann Holzboog, 1976–), ii. 90.

[52] Schelling, 'Über den wahren Begriff der Naturphilosophie und die richtige Art ihre Probleme zu lösen', in *Schellings Werke*, ed. Manfred Schröter, 4th edn, ii (Munich: Beck, 1992), 718.

[53] Schelling, *Ideen zu einer Philosophie der Natur*, in *Werke*, v. 98–9.

[54] Goethe, 'Der Versuch als Vermittler von Objekt und Subjekt', in FA 1/25. 34.

[55] Goethe, 'Das reine Phänomen', in FA 1/25. 125–7.

[56] Goethe to Schiller, 6 Jan. 1798, FA 2/4. 476.

'Mächtiges Überraschen' presents this critique of post-Kantian idealism in poetic terms. The subject, rushing headlong towards its unity with nature, is confronted by an incomprehensible obstruction that prevents it from achieving its goal. Total epistemological consummation—which means unity between subject and object, or between the self and the *Weltseele*—is thwarted, and in its place something more valuable and lasting is achieved. Stanza three depicts an astonished subject that has been forced into self-awareness (*sich immer selbst zu trinken*), and that is compelled to come to terms with its self-limitation. But it is precisely this newly established boundary between self and other that allows a great work of art to come into being: the stillness of the lake is only made possible by the new borders that surround it, and this very sense of containment allows it to mirror the heavens. In Goethe's simultaneously aesthetic and psychological language, then, Classical 'health' means the capacity to distinguish between one's ideas about nature on the one hand and nature 'in itself' on the other, and it is maintained by staying in touch with empirical reality, whereas Romantic 'sickness' refers to a situation in which one simply projects one's fantasies onto the external world. Seen in these terms, Weimar Classicism undertakes a dialogue with Romanticism, and might even be characterized as Romanticism's critique of itself.

Romantic Irony, or Ironic Romanticism?

The critical epistemology that underlies 'Mächtiges Überraschen' was already in place by the late 1790s, and its emphasis on borders, boundaries, and containment is suggestive precisely of the *Gestaltung* associated with Weimar Classicism. Yet here we must ask why the vanguard of German Romanticism, represented by Friedrich and August Wilhelm Schlegel, and also by Novalis, initially took Goethe to be such a central figure in their enterprise. 'The French Revolution, Fichte's *Wissenschaftslehre* and Goethe's *Meister* are the greatest tendencies of the age', according to Fragment 216 of the *Athenäums-Fragmente* (1797–8).[57] How could Goethe be fitted into this progressive triad when he so openly represented the old feudal order through his administrative role in the court of Duke Carl August Saxe-Weimar-Eisenach, and when he was so clearly opposed to the subjectivism of Fichte's *Wissenschaftslehre*? One answer to this complicated question lies in Friedrich Schlegel's interpretation of Goethe's novel *Wilhelm Meisters Lehrjahre* (Wilhelm Meister's Years of Apprenticeship, 1795–6), which he saw not as revolutionary in the political sense, but rather as announcing an *aesthetic*

[57] Friedrich Schlegel, Fragment 216 from the *Athenäum*, in *Kritische Friedrich Schlegel Ausgabe*, ii. *Charakteristiken und Kritiken I (1796–1801)*, ed. Hans Eichner (Munich: Ferdinand Schöningh, 1967), 198. See also Ernst Behler's discussion of the importance of Goethe's novel *Wilhelm Meisters Lehrjahre* for Friedrich and August Wilhelm Schlegel, for Novalis, and for Ludwig Tieck, in *German Romantic Literary Theory* (Cambridge: Cambridge University Press, 1993), 165–80.

revolution through its capacity to combine disparate literary genres and imbue them with irony.[58]

Now seen as the prototypical *Bildungsroman, Wilhelm Meisters Lehrjahre* concerns the eponymous protagonist's efforts to achieve full self-development through his life in the theatre. A central question that hangs over the narrative is thus precisely the problem that is already to be found in Goethe's early lyric poetry—the relation between self and world. To what extent is Wilhelm's life akin to a play that unfolds according to a preordained plot, and to what degree is it shaped by seemingly arbitrary external influences? Although Goethe began planning the novel as early as 1777, work on it continued up until 1796, which meant that the final stages of its composition came under the influence of Kant's three *Critiques*, especially as they were mediated by Schiller in his correspondence with Goethe. This meant that the ultimate answer to this question, at least from Schiller's perspective, turned out to be a Kantian one.

In a letter to Goethe dated 9–11 July 1796, for example, Schiller outlines in explicitly Kantian terms how the reader might respond to the narrative of *Wilhelm Meister*. The trajectory of Wilhelm's life, although apparently shaped by a series of disparate and conflicting influences, must appear to the reader to have an overall direction or teleology. Yet this meaning cannot simply be dictated by the author; rather, it must be the 'free and non-arbitrary production' of the reader.[59] Wilhelm, too, is described by Schiller as being sentimental in the sense that he had outlined a year earlier in his essay 'Über naïve und sentimentalische Dichtung' (On Naïve and Sentimental Poetry, 1795). While the purportedly 'naïve' poets of ancient Greece had lived in the pure immanence of nature, a world in which the gods and therefore meaning were always sensuously at hand, to be modern means to lack this unity with nature, which must be won back teleologically, via the path of reflection.[60] Wilhelm must in precisely this way have recourse to what Schiller calls the assisting means (*Hilfsmittel*) of philosophical speculation: always projecting what the possible purpose and meaning of his life may be.[61] Goethe incorporated these Kantian reflections into the final draft of the novel's eighth book (completed in October 1796), referring in particular to the human being's 'inborn drive to experience the origin and the end of things'.[62]

It was this idealist aspect of Goethe's novel that so excited Friedrich Schlegel, who refers in his essay 'Über Goethes *Meister*' (On Goethe's *Meister*, 1798), to the novel's playful contrasts between 'imagination and reality', which give rise to a sense of irony that 'hovers over the entire work'.[63] But it was not only this philosophical aspect of the novel

[58] On the relation between political and aesthetic revolutions, see Ernst Behler, 'Die Auffassung der Revolution in der deutschen Frühromantik', in *Studien zur Romantik und zur idealistischen Philosophie* (Paderborn: Schöningh, 1988), 66–85.

[59] See Schiller to Goethe, 9–11 July 1796, in MA 8/1. 211.

[60] Friedrich Schiller, *Über naive und sentimentalische Dichtung*, in *Werke und Briefe*, ed. Otto Dann et al. (Frankfurt am Main: Deutscher Klassiker Verlag, 1992–2004), viii. 724–7.

[61] See Schiller to Goethe, 9–11 July 1796, 213–14.

[62] See Goethe, *Wilhelm Meisters Lehrjahre* in FA 1/9. 882. See also the commentary in FA 1/9. 1247–73.

[63] Friedrich Schlegel, 'Über Goethes *Meister*', in *Kritische Friedrich Schlegel Ausgabe*, ii. 137.

that appealed to the Romantics. Wilhelm's idealistic decision to pursue the aesthetic life of the theatre instead of that of a bourgeois salesman also captured their imagination, as did the novel's tendency to combine prose fiction with other genres. These included drama (in the form of Shakespeare's *Hamlet*, which is staged in the novel); literary criticism, seen in the novel's own tendency to reflect upon and interpret Shakespeare's play; and lyric poetry—through the insertion of poetic interludes given to the characters of Mignon and the Harper, who, in the words of Friedrich Schlegel formed part of the 'holy family of natural poetry' that endowed the entire novel with 'Romantic magic and music'.[64] All of this accorded with one of the central features of Romantic poetry as outlined in fragment 116 of the *Athenäum*: the merging of literary genres to the extent that they become indistinguishable from one another.[65]

The question remains, however, as to whether Goethe's sense of irony was precisely the same as that of the Jena Romantics. In a much later essay, written in 1817, Goethe explicitly takes up the theme of irony and attributes it to Kant, whose critical philosophy is 'roguishly ironic' in asking us to remain within the limits of empirical experience while at the same time gesturing beyond them.[66] Kant of course maintained that any sense of teleology that we might find in the world is the necessary construction of our reason, which we should deploy only heuristically in order to gain an orienting sense of the whole. Fichte, however, went beyond this limitation by suggesting that the imagination is not merely a heuristic *Hilfsmittel*, rather it may actively shape the world that we perceive. Or this, at least, was the poetic sense in which Friedrich Schlegel and Novalis interpreted the *Wissenschaftslehre*, replacing the verb 'to philosophize' with their neologism 'to *Fichtecise*'.[67]

'Only when one begins to Fichtecise artistically', wrote Novalis in early 1798, 'can *wonderful artworks* come into being.'[68] And what it might mean to *Fichtecise* is expressed in fragment 116 of the *Athenäum*, where Romantic poetry is described as a 'progressive universal poetry' precisely because it hovers 'on the wings of poetic reflection' between that which is represented (*dem Dargestellten*) and the medium of its representation (*dem Darstellenden*), allowing this reflection to be 'intensified' and 'multiplied' as in 'an endless row of mirrors'. Romantic poetry is thus an 'infinite' (*unendlich*) poetry of becoming that can never be completed, because imaginative reflection is itself unlimited in its capacities. The genre of the fragment accordingly became the favoured mode of representing this situation. And while the fragment must be 'totally separated from the surrounding world like a small artwork, complete in itself like a hedgehog',[69] thereby

64 Friedrich Schlegel, 'Über Goethes Meister', 146.

65 Friedrich Schlegel, Fragment 116 of the *Athenäums-Fragmente*, in *Kritische Friedrich Schlegel Ausgabe*, ii. 182–3.

66 Goethe, 'Anschauende Urteilskraft', in FA 1/24. 447–8.

67 See Behler, *German Romantic Literary Theory*, 186–94.

68 Novalis, *Schriften*, ed. Richard Samuel, Hans-Joachim Mähl, and Gerhard Schulz, ii. *Das philosophische Werk I* (Stuttgart: Kohlhammer, 1960), 524.

69 Friedrich Schlegel, Fragments 116 and 206 of the *Athenäums-Fragmente*, in *Kritische Friedrich Schlegel Ausgabe*, ii. 182–3, 197.

suggesting a clear outline that might have pleased the 'Classical' Goethe, its very purpose *as a fragment* is to suggest the boundless expanses that lie beyond its fragile borders.

It is here that Goethe and the Jena Romanticism of the Schlegels and Novalis parted ways. At the conclusion of 'Mächtiges Überraschen', for example, we are certainly presented with a situation in which subjectivity engages in a mirroring of the stars, but the very point of the poem is the institution of the boundaries that were so lacking in 'Mahomets Gesang', not the gesturing beyond them. If, therefore, there is any sense of irony here, it merely arises from a purely Kantian disjunction between the protagonist's ideas about nature and empirical nature 'in itself'. It certainly does not correspond with the imagination's capacity to posit an infinite succession of representations, and thus to favour the ironic mode as that which is always provisional and pointing beyond itself. This, admittedly, is a matter of nuance within the common context of post-Kantian idealism, yet in Goethe's relation to the early German Romantics nuance is everything: while Goethe wants to preserve the limit for the sake of what might be called aesthetic health, which arises from a respect for the empirical forms of nature, the Jena Romantics wish to transgress it under the banner of the imagination.

In Goethe's *Winckelmann und sein Jahrhundert* (Winckelmann and his Century, 1805) this opposition becomes explicit, when he associates 'the healthy nature of the human being' with the Classical preference for sensuous forms, which is opposed to the modern desire to always approach the infinite (*das Unendliche*).[70] (Friedrich Schlegel took this to be a direct criticism of religiously informed Romantic art, writing to his brother August Wilhelm of Goethe's Winckelmann book: 'The old rascal has therein professed his paganism in a completely public way.'[71]) As Dieter Borchmeyer has shown, this opposition between 'finite' Classicism and 'infinite' Romanticism later becomes a typological distinction in nineteenth-century German aesthetics.[72] It can be found, for example, in August Wilhelm Schlegel's *Über dramatische Kunst und Literatur* (On Dramatic Art and Literature, 1809–11), where the Classical is 'simpler, clearer and closer to nature in the independent completion of its individual works', while the Romantic is despite (or perhaps because) of its 'fragmentary appearance, closer to the secret of the universe'.[73] Similarly, in Georg Wilhelm Friedrich Hegel's *Vorlesungen über die Ästhetik* (Lectures on Aesthetics, 1835–8), Romantic art, by virtue of its 'absolute inwardness' and its tendency toward subjective reflection, wants to

[70] Goethe, *Winckelmann und sein Jahrhundert*, in MA 6/2. 350–1.

[71] Friedrich Schlegel to August Wilhelm Schlegel, 15 July 1805, in *Krisenjahre der Frühromantik: Briefe aus dem Schlegelkreis*, ed. Josef Körner, 2nd edn, i (Bern: Francke, 1969), 214. For further context, see Volker Riedel, 'Zwischen Klassizismus und Geschichtlichkeit. Goethes Buch *Winckelmann und sein Jahrhundert*', *International Journal of the Classical Tradition*, 13/2 (2006), 217–42.

[72] Dieter Borchmeyer, 'Zur Typologie des Klassischen und Romantischen', in *Goethe und das Zeitalter der Romantik*, ed. Walter Hinderer (Würzburg: Königshausen & Neumann, 2002), 19–30; in this connection an important book that reinforced this typology in the 20th cent. was Fritz Strich's *Deutsche Klassik und Romantik, oder Vollendung und Unendlichkeit* (Munich: Meyer & Jessen, 1922).

[73] August Wilhelm Schlegel, *Sämmtliche Werke*, ed. Eduard Böcking (Leipzig: Weidmann, 1846–8), vi. 161, quoted in Borchmeyer, 'Zur Typologie', 26–7.

exceed sensuous representation, while Classical art concerns itself only with external and objective forms.[74]

The so-called 'late' period of Goethe's works—normally seen as falling between 1806 and 1832—both reinforces and plays with this typological distinction. Goethe's polemical relation to what he regards as the 'sickness' of later German Romanticism can be found in his essay 'Neu-deutsche religios-patriotische Kunst' (New-German Religious-Patriotic Art, 1817). There he accuses Wilhelm Heinrich Wackenroder and Ludwig Tieck of demanding, in their collection of essays titled *Herzensergießungen eines kunstliebenden Klosterbruders* (Outpourings of an Art-Loving Friar, 1797), that the artist should be subject to 'devotional inspiration and religious feelings, as though these were indispensable prerequisites for an artistic capacity', and they were soon accompanied in this, observes Goethe, by Friedrich Schlegel's new preference, outlined in the journal *Europa* that first appeared in 1803, for 'religion, mysticism and religious objects'. In the visual arts this enthusiastic-visionary (*schwärmerisch*) tendency, this regression to patriotic 'old-Germanness' (*alte Deutschheit*), is found by Goethe in Caspar David Friedrich's depictions of castles and ruins, which Goethe sees as alluding to 'mystical religious concepts'. All of this Goethe finds deeply distasteful, leading to an increase in subjective mannerism (*Manier*) and to a concomitant decrease in the simple imitation (*Nachahmung*) of nature found in the ancient Greeks. 'May ... all false religiosity (*Frömmeley*) disappear from poetry, prose and life as soon as possible,' he declares at the conclusion of this essay.[75]

But already in 1820, in the essay 'Klassiker und Romantiker in Italien, sich heftig bekämpfend' (Classicists and Romanticists in Italy, Fiercely Battling One Another) the opposition between Classicism and Romanticism has somehow become lighter and more tinged with irony. This may well be because Goethe, now over 70 years old, can wryly observe that in Germany the battle has already been won by the Romantics, who have captured the contemporary mood and are 'lacking neither readers nor publishers'. Thus, the fact that 'the fire that we [i.e. the Germans] lit is now starting to flare up on the other side of the Alps' is a source of some amusement. And here something like a dialectical relation between these two aesthetic tendencies also comes into play: an exclusive preoccupation with the past and with prior forms, according to Goethe, carries with it the danger of desiccating and mummifying the artistic sensibility, and in this way it calls forth a new revolutionary movement that wants to ignore the merits of the ancients.[76]

[74] Georg Wilhelm Friedrich Hegel, *Werke*, ed. Eva Moldenhauer and Karl Markus Michel (Frankfurt am Main: Suhrkamp, 1969–71), xiii. 89–92, 111–14.

[75] Goethe, 'Neu-deutsche religios-patriotische Kunst', in FA 1/20. 112, 115–18, 123, 125, 129. Here Goethe seems to be paraphrasing his earlier essay 'Einfache Nachahmung, Manier, Stil' (Simple Imitation, Manner, Style, 1798; see FA 1/15/2. 872–7) in which manner is presented as the subjective element in art which, if left unchecked, distorts the objects of nature. Only when manner has a secure empirical basis in simple imitation can there be style, in which imitation and manner are combined. It is also the perceived excess of mannerism in Romantic art that leads to Goethe's view, expressed in a conversation with Riemer on 28 Aug. 1808, that Romantic art is all 'coating' (*Anstrich*) without any foundation (*Unterlage*). See Goethe, *Begegnungen und Gespräche*, vi. 520.

[76] Goethe, 'Klassiker und Romantiker in Italien, sich heftig bekämpfend', in FA 1/20. 417–18.

In this way Goethe also tends, at times, to release the Classical and the Romantic from their historical frames of reference, allowing him to claim, as in the conversation with Eckermann on 2 April 1829, that medieval works such as the *Niebelungenlied* can also be seen as Classical insofar as they come to serve as formal aesthetic models.[77]

This new apparent lightness of touch with respect to the Classic–Romantic relation is then confirmed in *Faust Part Two* (mostly written between 1825 and 1831) in which the protagonist sets out on an absurd quest for Helen of Troy within the medieval setting of the Walpurgis Night. Writing to C. J. L. Iken about his depiction of Helen, Goethe observes: 'It is time that the passionate schism between Classicists and Romanticists finally be reconciled', before adding the following remark, which reveals that the old battle lines still existed under the surface: 'It is, though, a broader and clearer circumspection with respect to Greek and Roman literature to which we owe our liberation from monkish barbarity between the fifteenth and sixteenth centuries.'[78] In *Faust Part Two*, says Goethe to Eckermann on 16 December 1829, 'the Classical and the Romantic resonate and are brought to expression so that, as on a rising terrain, it can ascend to Helena, where both poetic forms come forth decisively and find a kind of equalization (*Ausgleichung*)'.[79] Even in Part One of *Faust* (first published in 1808) Goethe takes on what can only be regarded as Romantic themes, albeit from a position of ironic distance. In 'Wald und Höhle' (Forest and Cave), Faust invokes the key motif of 'Mahomets Gesang' and 'Mächtiges Überraschen' when he likens himself to a 'Wassersturz' or waterfall that has 'stormed in greedy fury from rock to rock towards the abyss below'.[80] And in 'Studierzimmer I' (Faust's Study I, probably written after April 1801),[81] Faust's rewriting of the Book of John, in which 'in the beginning was the Word' becomes 'in the beginning was the deed!' (*im Anfang war die Tat!*), has the ring of self-positing subjectivity found in Fichte's conception of *Tathandlung*.[82] Perhaps more than any other text from his oeuvre, it is *Faust* that—by dint of its emphasis on limitless subjective striving and through its revival of a story from older German folklore—has been responsible for Goethe being placed at the centre of European Romanticism.

Does one have to *believe* in Romanticism in order to be part of the European Romantic movement? The very question assumes that literary texts are always the representations of an author's beliefs, which of course they are not. And asking the wrong questions can also lead to one-sided answers. It is no coincidence that Percy Bysshe Shelley, writing in 1822, exclaimed that 'we admirers of *Faust* are on the way to Paradise', since the

[77] Eckermann, *Gespräche mit Goethe*, in FA 2/12. 324.

[78] Goethe to C. J. L. Iken, 27 Sept. 1827, in FA 2/10. 547.

[79] Eckermann, *Gespräche mit Goethe*, in FA 2/12. 366. See also Thomas Zabka, *Faust II: Das Klassische und das Romantische. Goethes 'Eingriff in die neueste Literatur'* (Tübingen: Niemeyer, 1993).

[80] Goethe, *Faust I*, in FA 1/7/1. 144. Tr. Stuart Atkins in Goethe, *Faust I and II* (Boston: Suhrkamp/Insel, 1984), 86.

[81] See the commentary in FA 1/7/1. 782.

[82] Goethe, *Faust I*, in FA 1/7/1. 61.

play arouses 'sensations which no other composition excites'.[83] And nor was Goethe's decision to base the character of Euphorion—the Apollo-like poetic spirit of *Faust Part Two*—on Lord Byron an arbitrary choice.[84] For the elderly Goethe, speaking to Eckermann on 5 July 1827, this English poet transcended all aesthetic dualisms: 'Byron is not antique, and not Romantic, rather he is like the present day itself. Such a one I had to have.'[85] In this his perceived status was something akin to what Goethe's had been around 1800, when the road between Jena and Weimar must have seemed to be the axis upon which German literature and thought turned. Along this road, according to Heine in *The Romantic School*, grow plums 'which taste very good when one is thirsty from the summer heat', and the Schlegels, he writes, took this route very often in order to pay homage to Goethe.[86] Yet Heine fails to mention that this road was by no means a one-way street, and that Goethe often travelled along it in the opposite direction. The perennial question as to whether Goethe himself was a Romantic writer cannot be answered in any satisfactory way, but many of his contexts, not to mention his works and their protagonists, undoubtedly were.[87]

Further Reading

Behler, Ernst, 'Romantik', in *Goethe Handbuch*, ed. Bernd Witte et al., 4 vols. in 6 (Stuttgart: J. B. Metzler, 1996–9), iv/2. 918–25.

Berghahn, Klaus L., 'Das Andere der Klassik: Von der "Klassik-Legende" zur jüngsten Klassik-Diskussion', *Goethe Yearbook*, 6 (1992), 1–27.

Bohm, Arndt, 'Goethe and the Romantics', in Denis F. Mahoney (ed.), *The Literature of German Romanticism*, Camden House History of German Literature, 8 (Rochester, NY: Camden House, 2004), 35–60.

Borchmeyer, Dieter, 'Zur Typologie des Klassischen und Romantischen', in Walter Hinderer (ed.), *Goethe und das Zeitalter der Romantik*(Würzburg: Königshausen & Neumann, 2002), 19–30.

Brown, Jane K., 'Romanticism and Classicism', in Nicholas Saul (ed.), *The Cambridge Companion to German Romanticism* (Cambridge: Cambridge University Press, 2009), 119–31.

Fröschle, Hartmut, *Goethes Verhältnis zur Romantik* (Würzburg: Königshausen & Neumann, 2002).

Holub, Robert C., 'The Romanticizing of Goethe: A Study in the Acquisition of a Label', in James Pipkin (ed.), *English and German Romanticism: Cross-Currents and Controversies* (Heidelberg: Winter, 1985), 349–61.

[83] Percy Bysshe Shelley to John Gisborne, 10 Apr. 1822, in *Letters from Abroad, Translations and Fragments*, ed. Mary Wollstonecraft Shelley (London: Edward Moxon, 1852), ii. 336–7.

[84] See the commentary in FA 1/7/2. 621.

[85] Eckermann, *Gespräche mit Goethe*, in FA 2/12. 251.

[86] Heine, *Die romantische Schule*, 193.

[87] My thanks to W. Daniel Wilson for his helpful comments on an earlier draft of this chapter.

Jauss, Hans Robert, 'Deutsche Klassik—eine Pseudo-Epoche?', in Reinhart Herzog and Reinhart Koselleck (eds), *Epochenschwelle und Epochenbewußtsein*, Poetik und Hermeneutik, 12 (Munich: Fink, 1987), 581–5.

Kohl, Katrin, 'No Escape? Goethe's Strategies of Self-Projection and their Role in German Literary Historiography', *Goethe Yearbook*, 16 (2008), 173–91.

Reed, T. J., 'Weimar Classicism: Goethe's Alliance with Schiller', in Lesley Sharpe (ed.), *The Cambridge Companion to Goethe* (Cambridge: Cambridge University Press, 2002), 101–15.

Wellbery, David E., *The Specular Moment: Goethe's Early Lyric and the Beginnings of Romanticism* (Stanford, Calif.: Stanford University Press, 1996).

CHAPTER 17

GOETHE'S FIGURATIVE METHOD

STEFAN H. UHLIG

The dimensions of the author's multiple careers as poet, natural philosopher, or even government official are in some ways bound to render Goethe an elusive figure for the patterns traced by literary or intellectual historiography. Conventional period concepts, or indeed the disciplines that map our sense of politics, the sciences, or arts, must struggle with a life and legacy that posed an early challenge to the protocols which shaped some of our favoured intellectual shorthands. Goethe's thought, his practical activities, writing, and poetry were obviously engaged with the historic transformations that marked his long working life: struggles for independence, wars, a revolution in philosophy and several more in politics, the coalescence of a German nation after the Vienna Congress, the Romanticisms of the European languages and arts alongside the enduring Classicism with which Goethe came to be identified. Equally, his recovery of a near-universal cultural range to which the poet could lay claim—much as the ancients had viewed Homer—broached decisive aspects of modernity which Goethe at the same time often sidestepped, or opposed outright. The dominance of Newton's legacy or the persistent resonance of literary Romanticism mark just two sites of this paradoxical relationship between the poet's epoch-making role and his profound misgivings about tradewinds of historical development.[1]

Even alongside these contemporary and, at the same time, retrospective forces of untimeliness, there is no denying Goethe's radiant presence to the period covered by his long and inexhaustibly productive life. Aside from the deep trail of evidence left by his writings, Goethe's personal encounters with the leading characters of his

[1] See Reinhart Koselleck, *Goethes Unzeitgemässe Geschichte* (Heidelberg: Manutius, 1997). Nicholas Boyle has challenged the assumption of an age defined by Goethe's authorship. See *Goethe: The Poet and the Age*, i. *The Poetry of Desire (1749–1790)* (Oxford: Oxford University Press, 1991), 5. On Goethe's contradictory perception as a Classicizing and Romantic writer, see Gerhart Hoffmeister, 'Reception in Germany and Abroad', in Lesley Sharpe (ed.), *The Cambridge Companion to Goethe* (Cambridge: Cambridge University Press, 2002), 233–4.

contemporary world afford a measure of his prominence: from the unfolding of his early interests under Johann Gottfried Herder's tutelage in Strasbourg to late engagements with Thomas Carlyle, or the transnational phenomena of Lord Byron and Sir Walter Scott. Goethe hosted Hegel, whose enthusiasm for the philosophical significance of history he could rarely bring himself to share.[2] At his first meeting with Goethe, Napoleon obliged the writer by critiquing aspects of his *Werther*. More importantly, he gratified the author's sense of his historic stature by assenting with a frequent 'oui!', or 'c'est bien'—and especially by ending his pronouncements with the coda, 'Qu'en dit Mr. Göt?', as Goethe proudly registered.[3]

Of course the author's copious works provide their own, enduring answers to Napoleon's question. Goethe supervised a number of large-scale editions of his works. These later culminated in the vast Sophien-edition, which helped to establish Weimar—once the author's haven from contemporary turmoil—as a shrine of European cultural history.[4] The primary corpus was in turn matched by the scholarship which trailed its literary and intellectual impact practically from the beginning. The sheer amplitude of Goethe's authorship would be remarkable enough (here is a writer, too, as Nicholas Boyle remarks, who had no need to repeat himself).[5] The qualitative breadth of his endeavours is, if anything, more startling, whether viewed from intellectual, artistic, disciplinary, or professional perspectives. Perhaps, to modern eyes, the most uncommon feature of the writer's open-ended boundary crossing is its exploration of variety and differences which, to the poet's mind, failed to uncover much resistant heterogeneity. Instead, his holistic confidence in a continuum—and hence compatibility between all different elements—informed the writer's sense of self and world no less than, by extension, the intimate relatedness of different cultural and intellectual activities.

Off the page, Goethe pursued a host of different roles and projects—by turns, a privy councillor, actor, theatre director, landscape architect, or university reformer. He devoted himself to a range of different arts, and spent a lifetime drawing, painting, and collecting. The focus of this chapter is, more narrowly, how Goethe's writing thought about, and to a point negotiated, the discontinuities it tracked between the visual arts, poetic writing, and the natural sciences. Even a modest set of Goethe's works offers art history and criticism alongside his novels, drama, lyric, epic, autobiographical, and aphoristic writings. What is more, his literary and critical achievements find some of their most expressive, corresponding interfaces in the scientific work to which the poet gave a large part of his life—as if he had undertaken to triangulate a map of creativity and method which late seventeenth- and eighteenth-century thinkers had worked hard to differentiate.

[2] See Koselleck, *Goethes Unzeitgemässe Geschichte*, 7–19.

[3] Entry for 2 Oct. 1808, 'Unterredung mit Napoleon', in *Werke: Hamburger Ausgabe* (Munich: Deutscher Taschenbuch Verlag, 2000), x. 547. Compare John R. Williams, *The Life of Goethe* (Oxford: Blackwell, 1998), 38–9. All translations from the *Hamburger Ausgabe* will be mine.

[4] Koselleck, *Goethes Unzeitgemässe Geschichte*, 9.

[5] Boyle, *Poetry of Desire*, 6.

The thirteen scientific Weimar volumes gather studies in geology, botany, or comparative anatomy, and they include Goethe's concerted challenge to Newtonian paradigms in his assiduously defended theory of colour. Nature claimed equal status alongside both artworks and the theory of art in Goethe's writings. It is hence not surprising that the poet would be led, in parallel, to question both the workings of mimesis and our less intentionally mediated, or intrinsically expressive, access to the natural world through science. A pervasive interest in analogy, in mediating figures, or, perhaps most forcefully, the figure of a mediating language ran through several of Goethe's efforts to stand back from his creative, active motivations. In reflecting on his own translations between subjects and their objects, or between the work of poetry, the visual arts, and science, Goethe frequently invoked the makings of a language, and its nesting of expressive forms. Yet this insistence on the powers of mediation was repeatedly shot through with silences, or failures of articulation. Goethe's effort to reflect on his encyclopedic writings critically evoked a kind of theory that would be nearly universal, and yet stay integral to distinctive kinds of understanding, practice, or analysis. The cognate idiom which bridged the labours of creation or discovery was torn, we might say, between naming archetypes in an intrinsically elusive labour and, coterminously, the desire to communicate. Goethe's rewriting of discontinuity accordingly foregrounded muteness even while promoting figurative consonance.

The peculiar constitution of his ample literary criticism has impeded efforts to position Goethe as a theorist in a way that would match his singular creative, or more broadly intellectual, stature. René Wellek's consternation at not having come by any 'systematic' treatment of a figure whom both Matthew Arnold and Sainte-Beuve already called a peerless critic has been often echoed.[6] Scholars have found good reasons for this lack of definition in the overwhelmingly occasional nature, and sheer mass, of critical perspectives which comprise his numerous brief essays, conversational exchanges, and reviews. They have pointed, also, to the poet's wariness of the enormous cultural leverage of abstraction—a hostility which certainly went well beyond his opposition to the mathematization of the natural sciences.[7] Yet if his own procedure seems elusively particular at times, its generalities have seemed just as evasive to historians of literary criticism. All too often, Goethe's harmonizing frame of mind refused to carve out a domain-specific argument that would pertain to one, and explicitly not another, discipline or cultural practice.[8]

[6] René Wellek, 'Goethe', in *A History of Modern Criticism: 1750–1950*, i. *The Later Eighteenth Century* (London: Cape, 1955), 201.

[7] Goethe described himself as 'someone who could lay no claim to mathematical or quantitative competence' (*einer, der keine Ansprüche an Meßkunst machte*). See 'Materialien zur Geschichte der Farbenlehre' (1810), in *Hamburger Ausgabe*, xiv. 264.

[8] See Wellek, 'Goethe', 201; Helmut Koopmann, 'Zur Entwicklung der literaturtheoretischen Position in der Klassik', in Karl Otto Conrady (ed.), *Deutsche Literatur zur Zeit der Klassik* (Stuttgart: Reclam, 1977), 30; and Frederick Amrine, 'Goethe, Johann Wolfgang von', in Michael Groden, Martin Kreiswirth, and Imre Szeman (eds), *The Johns Hopkins Guide to Literary Theory and Criticism*, 2nd edn (Baltimore: Johns Hopkins University Press, 2004), 465.

The early stages of this integrative strand of Goethe's criticism are conventionally identified with Herder's Storm and Stress, and with the all-important affect of a form 'most felt' in artworks which accordingly defied aesthetics.[9] Conversely, the trip to Italy with its exposure to the visual arts (as framed by Johann Joachim Winckelmann's art history) heralded a reworked Classicism which, as Wellek noted, referred literary theory to a unitary 'philosophy of nature'—though one which entailed a 'theory of symbolism' with attendant powers of mediation.[10] These holistic emphases have made it difficult, Wellek concluded, to derive a 'strictly literary' perspective from the 'speculations on the plastic arts', indeed on 'art and nature' as a whole, that form the primary mode of Goethe's self-reflection as a writer.[11] In a cogent further step, Ernst Robert Curtius identified the author's standing as a theorist emphatically with his encyclopedic studies. Unlike his literary essays, Curtius found the scientific writings to be laced throughout with the 'gold-bearing veins' of critical reflection.[12] Curtius read, moreover, Goethe's repositioning of his career within his late conception of an imminent 'world literature' as a reworking of late-humanist encyclopedism, or what had once been known as 'polyhistory'. For Curtius, the retrospective outlook of the author's final years resolved, or at least calmed, his lifelong quest for a 'comparative' perspective or, in the present terms, for some expressive mediation between discrete cultural and intellectual projects.[13]

Hermeneutic Science

I have noted Goethe's qualms about abstraction as a salient risk entailed by the controlling paradigms of modern natural philosophy. Established scientific protocols for him combined a fervour for technology with an immoderate faith in computation. Both seemed to disassociate the fullness of a subject's cognitive experience by means of specialized, and artificially constructed, series of experiments and measurements. The theory of colour was his most persistent effort to reverse these central tendencies of science, and perhaps the single long-term project he worked hardest to bring to fruition, and to vindicate. Writing to the composer Carl Friedrich Zelter, while preparing his contrarian account for publication, Goethe invoked the pitfalls of dissecting our experience of sound. He juxtaposed the technically objective methods, and experimental tools, of modern physics with the constant plenitude of interaction which a self has with the world that is present to its senses:

9 Wellek, 'Goethe', 203; and Amrine, 'Goethe, Johann Wolfgang von', 466.

10 Wellek, 'Goethe', 207.

11 Wellek, 'Goethe', 201.

12 Ernst Robert Curtius, 'Goethe als Kritiker', in *Kritische Essays zur Europäischen Literatur*, 2nd edn (Bern: Francke, 1954), 35 (tr. mine).

13 Curtius, 'Goethe als Kritiker', 47–8 (tr. mine). On Goethe's notion of world literature, see my 'Changing Fields: The Directions of Goethe's *Weltliteratur*', in Christopher Prendergast (ed.), *Negotiating World Literature* (London: Verso, 2004), 26–53.

> Der Mensch an sich selbst, insofern er sich seiner gesunden Sinne bedient, ist der größte und genaueste physikalische Apparat den es geben kann. Und das ist eben das größte Unheil der neuern Physik daß man die Experimente gleichsam vom Menschen abgesondert hat, und bloß in dem was künstliche Instrumente zeigen die Natur erkennen, ja was sie leisten kann dadurch beschränken und beweisen will. Ebenso ist es mit dem Berechnen. Es ist vieles wahr was sich nicht berechnen läßt, sowie sehr vieles, was sich nicht bis zum entschiedenen Experiment bringen läßt.
>
> The human being, as long as he makes use of his healthy senses, is himself the greatest and most precise physical apparatus there can be. And just that is the greatest bane of modern physics, that experiments have as it were been segregated from human beings, that we seek a knowledge of nature only in what artificial instruments will show, indeed that we seek thereby to confine and prove what she can do. It is the same with calculation. Much that cannot be calculated is true, as is a great deal that cannot be rendered susceptible to any decisive experiment.[14]

Goethe's aversion to the well-constructed measurement that overrides continuous experience, and thereby bars its further evolution, was brought into focus by his chief antagonist's *experimentum crucis* in the *Opticks*, first disclosed in 1704. Newton had famously deployed a prism to refract light into coloured 'rays', and then restored these differentiated colours to a single beam of white.[15] With his *Zur Farbenlehre* (or *On Colour*) which appeared in 1810, Goethe declared his resolution to 'disarm' that dominant 'abstraction, which we fear', in the Newtonian orthodoxy. He sought to sidestep these false guidelines with an 'experiential result' (*Erfahrungsresultat*) for which, as he declared, 'we hope' in a concerted effort.[16] This transformative result was to derive from sense experience without disrupting, like a law of concepts, its relationship with the particulars from which it grew. Goethe supplied a set of coloured tables with his text that were designed to let the reader replicate, perhaps even advance, his cumulative insights. In a typically analogizing fashion, he compared these compound offerings to the scripts for a 'good play', and stressed that he was counting on an actively perceptive audience.[17]

Newton's method had disaggregated light into the colours of the spectrum: a phenomenon one might explain as the absorption by an object, say, of certain wavelengths or, alternatively, particles. By contrast, Goethe's *Farbenlehre* categorically insisted that light was a unitary phenomenon. Colours must not be thought of as a part of light, or as its separable aspects. They were, rather, to be studied as the sensory, and partly physiological, result of viewing light or darkness through a 'turbid medium'—that is a mediation by an interface that would itself be luminous to varying degrees. Goethe derived the

[14] Letter to Zelter, 22 June 1808, in *Goethes Briefe*, ed. Karl Robert Mandelkow, 3rd edn (Munich: Beck, 1988), iii. 76 (tr. mine).

[15] See, for instance, Peter Dear, *Revolutionizing the Sciences: European Knowledge and its Ambitions, 1500–1700* (Houndmills: Palgrave, 2001), 143–4.

[16] 'Zur Farbenlehre' (1810), in *Hamburger Ausgabe*, xiii. 317. For a selection of Goethe's writings on science in translation, see Douglas Miller (ed.), *Scientific Studies* (Princeton: Princeton University Press, 1995).

[17] 'Zur Farbenlehre', 321.

full array of colours from this interplay of light and non-light, and their subtle mediations offered a prime instance of polarity, or the 'intensification' (*Steigerung*), which he thought fundamental to our experiential knowledge of the world.[18] Light in its highest 'energetic' form as, for instance, sun- or starlight, or the glare of burning phosphorus, was posited as 'colourless'. Where this intensity was mediated by its opposite, or darkness, it would take on an array of colours as experienced by the human eye. And the same process must hold in reverse, as brighter media colour absent light:

> Dieses Licht ... durch ein auch nur wenig trübes Mittel gesehen, erscheint uns gelb. Nimmt die Trübe eines solchen Mittels zu oder wird seine Tiefe vermehrt, so sehen wir das Licht nach und nach eine gelbrote Farbe annehmen, die sich endlich bis zum Rubinroten steigert .... Wird hingegen durch ein trübes, von einem darauffallenden Licht erleuchtetes Mittel die Finsternis gesehen, so erscheint uns eine blaue Farbe, welche immer heller und blässer wird, je mehr sich die Trübe des Mittels vermehrt, hingegen immer dunkler und satter sich zeigt, je durchsichtiger das Trübe werden kann, ja bei dem mindesten Grad der reinsten Trübe als das schönste Violett dem Auge fühlbar wird.
>
> When viewed through a medium which is the least bit turbid ... this light appears yellow. If the medium becomes more turbid or its depth increases, we will see the light gradually assume a yellow-red colour, which will ultimately intensify to ruby red .... If darkness is, by contrast, viewed through a turbid medium illuminated by light, we will see a blue colour growing ever lighter and paler as the medium becomes more turbid, but darker and more saturated as it becomes more transparent. With the minimal degree of the most rarefied turbidity, the eye will feel this colour as the most beautiful violet.[19]

Goethe inferred from this polarity of light and darkness, and the colours to which they gave rise, the undivided nature of the fact of light. Light both subtended infinitely variable phenomena, and marked a limit for what could be known about their presence in the world. In this resensitized conception of a scientific method, all discovery began from somebody's experience of the relevant phenomena. Whether the subject was an expert or, like readers working with their coloured plates, still new to the successful play to which Goethe had likened the experience, the process of investigation was explicitly in dialogue with the perceiving self. After initial observations, students would ascend through various 'rubrics' leading from the more 'empirical' impressions of a pattern to robustly 'scientific' categories. The observer thus became 'increasingly familiar' with what Goethe called the 'indispensable conditions for what manifests itself'. Yet these laws of nature must continue to be apprehended 'through phenomena', and hence remain accessible to the comparatively uninitiated.[20]

[18] See, for instance, Williams, *Life of Goethe*, 259.

[19] 'Zur Farbenlehre', 362.

[20] 'Zur Farbenlehre', 367–8.

In its analysis of colour, this account involved more than one, and literally turbid, medium. Goethe invoked a whole tropology of mediation to explain how colours must 'evolve' (*sich entwickeln*), like light or darkness, from their 'opposites'—while also 'pointing' (*deuten*) the cognizing subject through their 'reciprocity' back to 'a common unity': one that was both intuitive and scientifically compelling. The sheer range of Goethe's invocation of the *Mittel*—at once mid-point, median, or instrumental means—helped to account for the phenomena of colour and, more broadly, for his interactive method. His ascending figures stretched towards the limits of the understanding while attending, at the same time, to the intimacy of quotidian selves. This hybrid knowledge bred capacious metaphors for Goethe's rendering of the 'higher rules and laws' of nature.[21] He reabsorbed their clarity and mathematical detachment into his figure of a chain, or ladder, of subjectively attested science:

> Wir nennen sie Urphänomene, weil nichts in der Erscheinung über ihnen liegt, sie aber dagegen völlig geeignet sind, daß man stufenweise, wie wir vorhin hinaufgestiegen, von ihnen herab bis zu dem gemeinsten Falle der täglichen Erfahrung niedersteigen kann.
>
> We call these archetypal phenomena, because nothing that lies above them manifests itself in the world, whereas they make it quite possible for us to descend step by step, just as we previously ascended, from the archetypal phenomena down to the most common occurrence of daily experience.[22]

The polarities of colour, light, and darkness constituted one such archetype. For Goethe, their coherence both defined the scope of scientific understanding and evinced one of the basic mediations that helped constitute the natural world. His account of our correlative ascent to knowledge was explicit about the interpretative work this must involve for the perceiving subject. Hence 'turbidity' provided the material or physiological determinant of colour, while its function as a medium also glossed the category as metaphorical. Goethe expressly credited his explanation of the physical phenomenon to tools that were both intellectual and, in their public role, semantic. Where his colours emerged from the overlays of light and darkness, they required the explicit 'help of intellectual mediation' (*mit Hülfe gedachter Vermittlung*).[23] Within this experiential set of tropes, percept and thought appeared to paraphrase each other.

It will help clarify this interplay between analysis and figuration to note that the methodological reflections which suffused *On Colour* not only foregrounded metaphor, but also set themselves against more literal-minded parentheses, or linguistic interference, between subjects and phenomena. If the ascent to archetypes promised a more engaged cognition of the natural world than computation, or the trial by experiment, Goethe's project was no less resistant to the phraseology of scientific argument

[21] 'Zur Farbenlehre', 368.

[22] 'Zur Farbenlehre', 368.

[23] 'Zur Farbenlehre', 368.

or theory-formation. By insisting that discovery be channelled 'through phenomena', he equally defied its modelling 'through words', and the accretion of 'hypotheses', in standard forms of explanation.[24] In their place, a formulation like the 'medium of turbidity' could translate between thought, materiality, and language. By advancing this capacity of figuration, Goethe reworked a conception of the role of language within natural philosophy that was intrinsic to its mainstream protocols.

It is a well-known feature of empiricist and quantitative sciences that their first advocates all disavowed linguistic excess or presupposition. Bacon and Descartes explored alternatives to text-based learning partly by discrediting the flourishes of rhetoric. More importantly, they challenged classicizing scholarship in which discovery not only prompted texts and commentaries, but was itself conceived as a discursive construct. The Newtonian Royal Society advanced under the banner of 'nullius in verba', and its members rarely tired of opposing the 'mechanical', 'experimental', or, plainly, 'the *real*' Philosophy to studies of mere 'discourse' and perpetual 'disputation'. Robert Hooke charged that book-learning had done little more than endlessly refine the 'subtilty of its Deductions and Conclusions'. Instead, he urged that the foundations of enquiry 'ought', in future, 'to be well laid on the Sense and Memory'.[25] This would allow results to be communicated clearly, and without the philological entanglements which, for the champions of realia, had long blighted scholarship and intellectual debate.

Abraham Cowley's ode to the Society poetically reflected on the distance which this method must keep from the lure of eloquence. Whereas philosophy had relished the 'Desserts of Poetry' while they had jointly wandered through the 'Labyrinths of ever-fresh Discourse', the new agenda would need 'solid meats' to feed its quest for things behind the guise of words.[26] More than a century later, Goethe's effort to retrace these steps renewed the promise of companionship across the disciplines. He noted ruefully in *On Morphology* that modern readers had already lost all memory of how linguistic creativity had first been divorced from *Wissenschaft*. Despite this ignorance, and the resulting public scepticism about his unorthodox proposals, Goethe forecast that science and poetry could, with a single 'revolution of the times', again disclose their 'mutual benefit' on some accordingly 'more elevated' ground of knowledge.[27] He feared, in the meantime, that the pragmatism of hypotheses and their deliberate abstractions were eroding the experiential promise of his scientific project.

Goethe's meta-criticism sought to restore discourse to the full range of his intellectual curiosity—though as extended metaphor more than a literal means to abstract ends or,

[24] 'Zur Farbenlehre', 367–8.

[25] Robert Hooke, *Micrographia: Or some physiological descriptions of minute bodies made by magnifying glasses* (London, J. Martyn & J. Allestry, 1665), sig. a1[r]. On attitudes towards hypothesis in the early Royal Society, see Dear, *Revolutionizing the Sciences*, 139–42.

[26] Abraham Cowley, 'To the *Royal Society*', in Leonard C. Martin (ed.), *Poetry and Prose* (Oxford: Clarendon, 1949), 55 (ll. 21–4); first publ. in Thomas Sprat's *The History of the Royal-Society of London, for the Improving of Natural Knowledge* (London, J. Martyn & J. Allestry, 1667), sig. B[r].

[27] 'Zur Morphologie' (1817), in *Hamburger Ausgabe*, xiii. 107.

equally, the all-pervasive textualism of pre-modern thought.[28] He therefore prefaced his *On Colour* by envisaging a figurative idiom through which phenomena might nourish a capacious cognitive and cultural dialogue. In this perspective, nature's first address was to the senses, and yet this primordial appeal would find its analogue in our attempts to speak to the variety of patterns or, specifically, polarities which it presented to the self. Moreover, such engagement between discourse and phenomena looked set to resonate, by figurative extension, between idioms which otherwise described divergent fields and practices: be they poetic or mimetic, cognitive, or meta-critical.

Goethe began his effort to remediate these fault lines with the sobering premise that the 'nature of a thing', in this case the phenomenon of light, must necessarily deny our efforts to 'express' its full reality. This failure of description marked a robust cognitive constraint for his desire to reintegrate the paths of poetry and *Wissenschaft*. For his approach, no less than the hypotheses of mainstream physics, things in themselves defined a boundary of silence. Goethe broached the mysteries of light, therefore, by pointing to its palpable 'effects', and by suggesting that only a 'complete history' of what he called the 'deeds of light' could help elucidate their muted agency. The metaphors were, once again, performative. Just as, he argued, someone's character was hard to understand outside their agency, the colourations of these 'deeds and sufferings' would counteract the hubris of Newtonian definitions.[29]

If natural philosophy involved a kind of dramaturgy, Goethe trusted light to script 'the whole of nature' in a way that would compel the spectatorial and intellectual 'eye'. Though sight had long been thought of as the most capacious sense, Goethe's language-creating metaphor also recruited the remaining senses as effective proxies, or interpreters, of nature.[30] To this effect, the play of light transformed into a single voice of nature, and its cognate words and things came to join selves and objects in a new-found dialogue. In this proposal for a figurative method, nature vindicated the desire to know by drawing all our senses into conversation:

> Man schließe das Auge, man öffne, man schärfe das Ohr, und vom leisesten Hauch bis zum wildesten Geräusch, vom einfachsten Klang bis zur höchsten Zusammenstimmung, von dem heftigsten leidenschaftlichen Schrei bis zum sanftesten Worte der Vernunft ist es nur die Natur, die spricht, ihr Dasein, ihre Kraft, ihr Leben und ihre Verhältnisse offenbart, so daß ein Blinder, dem das unendlich Sichtbare versagt ist, im Hörbaren ein unendlich Lebendiges fassen kann.
>
> Let us shut our eye, let us open our ears, and sharpen our sense of hearing; and from the softest breath to the most savage noise, from the simplest sound to the most

[28] See Anthony Grafton, *Defenders of the Text: The Traditions of Scholarship in an Age of Science, 1450–1800* (Cambridge, Mass.: Harvard University Press, 1991).

[29] 'Zur Farbenlehre', 315.

[30] 'Zur Farbenlehre', 315. Plato famously discussed knowledge as a kind of vision in book 7 of *Republic*. In the *Metaphysics*, Aristotle postulated that sight, 'most of all the senses, makes us know and brings to light many differences between things'. See *Complete Works*, ed. Jonathan Barnes (Princeton: Princeton University Press, 1985), ii. 1552.

> elevated harmony, from the most intense cry of passion to the gentlest word of reason it is nature alone that speaks, that reveals its being, energy, life, and relations—so that a blind man who is denied the endlessly visible may grasp, in what he can hear, an infinite realm of life.[31]

Although things must within themselves stay silent, Goethe pledged that his attentive readers would find nature nowhere 'dead nor mute' in this pursuit of a discursive synaesthesia. And beyond the range of eyes and ears, the revelatory address which he envisaged even talked 'down' (*spricht die Natur hinabwärts*) to those 'other senses' which were otherwise 'misjudged' (*verkannt*), or virtually 'unknown'—perhaps because these lower senses still had to evolve their dialogic skills. If properly attended to, the voice of nature could speak copiously both 'with itself and to us' through 'a thousand' of its protean 'appearances'.[32] It was as if the natural world amounted to a complex lyric object that had long been waiting for its sensitive and, within Goethe's method, its interpretive community.

This faith in eloquent phenomena was clearly marked by a persistent risk of silence, or the muting of enquiry. Goethe granted that their paradoxically pre-cultural idiom had to strike the curious as 'manifold, entangled', or straightforwardly 'incomprehensible'. Still, this obscurity would simply prompt his cognitive interpreter to translate 'elements' into a series of expressive patterns. The 'movements and determinations' which might otherwise define the laws of chemistry or physics seemed, in Goethe's view, pre-linguistic. Mere 'appearances' within 'space and in time' would, in due course, suggest a grammar of, say, 'weight and counterweight', 'hither and thither', 'here and there', before or after. Soon, this exit from incomprehension joined the history of scientific metaphors. Goethe conjectured that where previous observers had perceived a set of tensions, or polarities, they had 'tried equally to name' this sense of a 'relationship'. Thus they had formed the corresponding idioms of, say, 'plus and minus, aggressive, resistant; acting, suffering; proactive, moderating', 'male' or 'female'.[33] Before long, these contrasts induced further paraphrase, or figuration, so that scientists were not just competent in nature's idiom but could, through their own growing eloquence, assuage the risks of dialogic failure. Though archetypes were inexpressible, Goethe recentred natural philosophy around these hermeneutic tools:

> so entsteht ein Sprache, eine Symbolik, die man auf ähnliche Fälle als Gleichnis, als nahverwandten Ausdruck, als unmittelbar passendes Wort anwenden und benutzen mag.
>
> in this way forms a language, a set of symbols, which can be used and applied to comparable (*ähnliche*) cases as a simile, as a closely related expression, or as an immediately (*unmittelbar*) fitting term.[34]

[31] 'Zur Farbenlehre', 315.
[32] 'Zur Farbenlehre', 315.
[33] 'Zur Farbenlehre', 316.
[34] 'Zur Farbenlehre', 316.

It is worth noting that, within this nested language of enquiry, the literally 'fitting' term could be derived from 'symbols' rather than the other way around. Goethe's rendition of his figurative process sidestepped questions about how to translate quantitative models, or the protocols for an experiment, into his terms. Instead, he championed discursive mediation as a trope for the most concrete interests of his experiential science. These included, for example, the phenomena of colour which he classed as 'physiological', since their enabling media formed part of the human eye.[35]

On Colour based its methodology on the conception of a speaking voice that allegorically addressed the self in para-human terms—terms which would need to be decoded and interpreted. Of course, this reinsertion of linguistic structures into natural philosophy stood in marked contrast to mainstream empiricist enquiry, where the experts looked for knowledge that was literally or, therefore, mathematically precise. The curiosity which Goethe urged on his participatory readers hinged so strongly on the notion of interpreting an unmade code that the resulting metaphors were hard to test against their cognitive results. Where we might ask what separates these figures from phenomena, the logic of *On Colour* urged that they act as each other's vehicle and tenor. Goethe's 'chief aim' for his favoured project was accordingly to amplify sensate experience through innate language skills. The researcher must listen to, learn to decode, elaborate, and, in its most capacious form, advance the idiom of phenomena—in other words,

> diese universellen Bezeichnungen, diese Natursprache auch auf die Farbenlehre ..., diese Sprache durch die Farbenlehre, durch die Mannigfaltigkeit ihrer Erscheinungen zu bereichern, zu erweitern und so die Mitteilung höherer Anschauungen unter den Freunden der Natur zu erleichtern.
>
> to apply these universal terms, this natural language, to the theory of color; to expand and enrich this language through the theory of color and the multiplicity of its phenomena; and thereby to facilitate the communication of higher insights amongst the friends of nature.[36]

The purpose of this 'universal' idiom was emphatically not to simplify a range of scientific insights for a wider audience. Instead, its figurative claim aimed to surpass all expert calculation and experiment, and in that sense democratize the work of natural philosophy. If it were possible to understand, while safeguarding, phenomena in all their sensory 'multiplicity', nature might speak about itself without hypotheses—in forms of words, that is, whose accuracy had been won through prior mediation.

[35] 'Zur Farbenlehre', 329.
[36] 'Zur Farbenlehre', 316.

Expressive Mimesis

Alongside his scientific work, Goethe's art criticism worked with its own notion of discursive mediation as a way to reconcile experience and concepts, thereby further testing the potential for conciliatory dialogue between the sciences, the visual arts, and poetry. An early essay which combined philosophy of science and the arts challenged the premium Newton placed on the definitive experiment by recontextualizing its experiential role as an effective 'mediator' between subjects and their objects of enquiry. The risk of dogma which arose from overreading a specific set-up was, in Goethe's view, best mitigated by a fellowship of different investigators, all engaging with a common object of cognition and, accordingly, debate. To lend added focus to this argument, Goethe contrasted the pragmatics of discursive consultation in the sciences with the creative process in the arts. While scientists did well to share, and 'publicly, each individual experience, even conjecture' by articulating them, the artist's work appeared almost defined by its reflective loneliness. Once they were finished, artworks rightfully became the target of 'reproach or praise'. Yet until then, the artist would 'do well' to realize that voices other than his own would never 'easily be able to advise or offer help' during his labours of production.[37] The interaction seemed, in this respect, to operate 'just in reverse' for the creative artist when compared to its substantial promise for the working scientist.

By contrast, in a longer essay of the late 1780s, Goethe argued that a meta-language of mimesis was precisely what allowed lone artists to develop their pictorial understanding. On returning from his formative Italian journeys in that decade through the landscape of exemplary art and architecture, Goethe sketched this figurative idiom in an effort to refine the central category of neoclassical art theory.[38] His separation of mimesis into 'simple' or straightforward 'imitation', 'manner', and then full-blown 'style' had precedents within the scholarly tradition.[39] Goethe, however, joined these various descriptors to a narrative whereby the artist rose through an increasingly sophisticated interaction between objects of mimesis and pictorial skills. Each mode might capture certain genres, from a basic still-life to more forcefully selective and, in that sense, mannered landscapes. Yet their chief interest was, more truly, to articulate a clear progression from naïve, or largely studious, attention to the fully conscious practice which defined a kind of wisdom in the artist's understanding of the world. And Goethe's scheme again

[37] 'Der Versuch als Vermittler von Objekt und Subject' (1793), in *Hamburger Ausgabe*, xiii. 13.

[38] Stephen Halliwell has used Goethe's thinking to define the vantage point for his study of mimesis as a leading classical and early modern category. He has rightly pointed to a progress from 'illusionism' towards some 'kind of entrancing idealism' as a feature of the poet's negotation between ancient and contemporary ideas. See *The Aesthetics of Mimesis: Ancient Texts and Modern Problems* (Princeton: Princeton University Press, 2002), 3, 1.

[39] 'Einfache Nachahmung der Natur, Manier, Stil' (1789), in *Hamburger Ausgabe*, xii. 30–4, 585–6. For selections of Goethe's writings on art in translation, see *Essays on Art and Literature*, ed. John Gearey (Princeton: Princeton University Press, 1994), and *Goethe on Art*, ed. John Gage (London: Scolar, 1980).

drew on a figurative idiom—a language through which artists learned to see, and draw or paint.

Goethe dealt briskly with the common-sense assumption that mimesis was a matter of descriptive competence: a faithful tracing of objective forms. No doubt much 'talent' and 'fidelity' went into even the most basic 'patterns' of, for instance, flower painting. The refusal to 'depart' from objects, to begin each time 'within their presence', no doubt helped representations to 'come true'. Yet Goethe also stressed that this rapport with things must, before long, give way to more expressive practices. It might well be that 'dead, or resting', objects matched the interests of a simple 'nature' (which referred both to the artist's temperament and to a narrow taste).[40] Soon further evolution must, however, complicate this object-oriented immanence. Once Goethe's manner superseded imitation, his explanatory tale used a semantic rendering of mimesis to explain how artists had advanced by thinking in a visually more expressive way. His argument for style as the supreme pictorial mode then once again reframed the process. In its highest form, the artist's idiom seemed to reliteralize itself, and to converge with science in the effort to grasp the deep structuration of phenomena.

Manner began as an attempt to amplify description. Once skilled artists strove to represent a larger whole than fruits or flowers—say a landscape with its numerous 'subordinate' parts—the copying of stable objects must be 'sacrificed'. Instead the artist would, now more self-consciously, leave small-scale referencing behind to seek the 'general expression' of a 'worthy object' (*des großen Gegenstandes*).[41] Goethe described this process characteristically as translating nature's unmade lexicon into a more capacious set of tropes. In art's search for the bigger picture, nature's horn book gives way to more meta-language when the artist, faced with too much detail, is forced to give up on 'seeing' literally. As Goethe put it,

> es verdrießt ihn, der Natur ihre Buchstaben im Zeichnen nur gleichsam nachzubuchstabieren; er erfindet sich selbst eine Weise, macht sich selbst eine Sprache, um das, was er mit der Seele ergriffen, wieder nach seiner Art auszudrücken, einem Gegenstande, den er öfters wiederholt hat, eine eigne bezeichnende Form zu geben, ohne, wenn er ihn wiederholt, die Natur selbst vor sich zu haben, noch auch sich geradezu ihrer ganz lebhaft zu erinnern.
>
> it displeases him merely to draw letter by letter, as it were, what nature spells out for him; he invents a manner for himself, creates a language for himself, to re-express in his own way what he has grasped with his soul; to lend its own significant form to an object he has repeated several times without seeing it before him, without even recalling quite what it looked like in nature.[42]

This more forcefully imaginative idiom launched the artist's rise from literal-minded imitation to the highest forms of 'characteristic' painting, which Goethe identified with

[40] 'Einfache Nachahmung', 30–1.
[41] 'Einfache Nachahmung', 31.
[42] 'Einfache Nachahmung', 31.

style. To an extent, his comments on this final, and artistically most valuable, stage of art curtailed the status of the artist's self-created 'medium' (*Mittel*) of visual tropes.[43] Yet their surpassing by more cognitive forms of mimesis also paralleled Goethe's forthcoming hopes for a discursive science in *On Colour*.

Goethe marked 'style' as the fulfilment of the artist's quest to understand the world through cognitive engagement. In its highest forms, mimesis became so aware of its distinctive resources that it showed no more need for the assistance of a method. Beyond copying or, equally, the help of a mimetic idiom, the artist rose to equal standing with the scientist:

> Gelangt die Kunst durch die Nachahmung der Natur, durch Bemühung, sich eine allgemeine Sprache zu machen, durch genaues und tiefes Studium der Gegenstände selbst endlich dahin, daß sie die Eigenschaften der Dinge und die Art, wie sie bestehen, genau und immer genauer kennen lernt, ... dann wird der *Stil* der höchste Grad, wohin sie gelangen kann; der Grad, wo sie sich den höchsten menschlichen Bemühungen gleichstellen darf.
>
> If art finally, through imitation of nature, through the effort of devising a general language for itself, through the rigorous and profound study of subject matter, comes to a point where it knows the characteristics of things, and their way of being, more and more precisely, ... then *style* becomes the highest level it can reach; the level, where it can equate itself to the highest human endeavours.[44]

Representation hence gained access, alongside analysis, to 'deepest cognitive foundations'—at least insofar as these were apprehensible to artists through the 'visible' or 'tangible forms' of the natural world. This rendered plausible an otherwise surprising twist: namely that some of Goethe's favourite artists had been able altogether to omit the stage of mannered art. Outside the language of mimesis, their experience in the sciences had raised them far beyond their humble origins as copyists. In this way, some Dutch painters (Goethe noted Rachel Ruysch and Jan van Huysum) managed to achieve their style through work in botany, thereby exchanging one domain of natural figuration for another. Although Goethe circumscribed the work of an imaginary language in the arts, his meta-critical manoeuvre coincided, in representation as much as in natural philosophy, with a commitment to rejoin these separate fields.

The narrow role for figuration in this genealogy of art points, at the same time, to a basic tension in how Goethe thought about concerted cultural or intellectual activity in its engagement with the natural world. His urge to use interpretation as a trope to bridge the gap between our agency and natural presences was frequently accompanied by a stark sense of difficulty, even failure. By extension, his support for mediations between disciplines appeared by turns enthusiastic and peculiarly reserved. Our discussion of the preface to *On Colour* found that, even in his strongest hopes for the formation of an hermeneutic idiom, Goethe stressed the boundaries around what could be said about

[43] 'Einfache Nachahmung', 34.
[44] 'Einfache Nachahmung', 32.

the natural world. The muteness of the archetype, or thing within itself, spoke only through the 'deeds' of its phenomena; and it was hence the voice of nature which observers parsed by gradually refiguring their terms. The limitations of this method were, if anything, more sharply phrased in his essays on art. Even the copia of 'manner' risked becoming 'ever emptier and insignificant' in cases where successful artists placed their own, characteristic idioms ahead of a more truthful style.[45]

Elsewhere, Goethe defined art quite generally as an intermediary between the world of objects and our selves. In these emphatic claims, the artwork functioned inescapably as mediation. And the critic's task was to elaborate on work that was already thought of as profoundly hermeneutic. Goethe introduced his journal *Propyläen* by expounding that the artist's duty was, invariably, to 'stick to nature, study it', and thereby to 'remake it'. This negotiation must prove deeply challenging, since 'nature' was 'from art', to start with, 'separated by an immense chasm' (*durch eine ungeheure Kluft getrennt*). Even 'genius' had to seek 'outward aids' or means (*äußere Hilfsmittel*)—such as the progression, say, from basic skills in imitation, via manner, to accomplished style. The promise, and the trial, of artistic work was to 'transcend' (*überschreiten*) this stark dichotomy.[46] In *Maxims and Reflections*, Goethe praised the intellect as an 'effective go-between' (*der tätige Kuppler*) designed to 'mediate' (*vermitteln*) the otherwise quite fearful self-disclosure of the archetypes. He argued likewise that artistic work served as 'the true', or most compelling, 'mediatrix' of the natural world. Hence 'to discourse on art' like critics was, in essence, 'to remediate the medium' (*die Vermittlerin vermitteln*). Goethe cautiously remarked that this elusive task had thus far offered much that was 'delightful' (*ist uns daher viel Köstliches erfolgt*).[47]

Quiet Cultivation

Read in the light of these endorsements, Goethe's own unsystematic literary criticism looks surprisingly resistant to the promise of a figurative method. Of course, verbal creativity inhabits those same symbols, similes, and so on, which he advocated as integral to descriptive knowing in the sciences or, likewise, to pictorial insight in the arts. However, some of his most forceful lines of argument overtly questioned the potential of exchange between poetic making and adjacent languages, whether in different fields or as instantiated in a work's reception by an audience. Goethe at times phrased the relationship between, say, word and image in a way that seemed to link poetics with his faith in the pictorial or cognitive effect of meta-languages. Another of his maxims and reflections thus defined all the 'tropes and similes' as an attempted dialogue between the eye and ear. Although these senses stayed 'perpetually in search of one another', they

45 'Einfache Nachahmung', 34.

46 'Einleitung in die Propyläen' (1798), in *Hamburger Ausgabe*, xii. 42.

47 'Maximen und Reflexionen', nos. 17 and 18, in *Hamburger Ausgabe*, xii. 367.

had helped to author discourse since the scriptures or, more personally, the child's first spelling book (*Bibel und Fibel*).[48] There is ample evidence that Goethe could not muster the same confidence in figuration from all angles of reflection. Hence John Neubauer has argued that his thought failed, overall, to reach 'a balanced symbiosis' between poetry and images. Perhaps surprisingly for this holistic thinker, a linguistic 'inability', as Neubauer describes it, to 'display what was intrinsically contained in images' instead gave rise to Goethe's famous contrast between allegory and symbol.[49]

This uneven trust in figuration as way to translate between fields was certainly borne out by Goethe's tribute, which he published in 1805, to the example set in this respect by Winckelmann. The art historian's writings now helped stress the odds against the kind of adaptation Goethe frequently pursued, and which Winckelmann had overcome in search of a new understanding of the ancient world. He had first studied ancient art and architecture in a largely textual tradition. That he had met with their distinctive 'beauty', therefore, in the 'writings of the ancients' and not 'personally', or in the flesh, moved Goethe all the more to praise his interdisciplinary success.[50] He now also underlined a sharp discontinuity between the visual and verbal arts, and their contrasting media:

> Von allem Literarischen, ja selbst von dem Höchsten, was sich mit Wort und Sprache beschäftigt, von Poesie und Rhetorik, zu den bildenden Künsten überzugehen, ist schwer, ja fast unmöglich; denn es liegt eine ungeheure Kluft dazwischen, über welche uns nur ein besonders geeignetes Naturell hinüberhebt.
>
> It is difficult, indeed almost impossible, to make the transition from literary concerns of any kind, yes even from the highest treatments of words and language, poetry and rhetoric, to the visual or plastic arts; this is because the two are separated by an enormous chasm, which only an especially well suited temperament may help us bridge.[51]

This separation of linguistic and concrete perception mirrored the deep 'chasm' Goethe placed, in *Propyläen*, at the heart of the mimetic enterprise. The obstacles the art historian had faced in parlaying his textual scholarship into outstanding visual observation showed the inverse of the figurative optimism propagated by *On Colour*. Though designed to praise him, Goethe's scepticism about Winckelmann's formation stressed the near-impossibility of mediation. His success in writing critically about the visual arts proved the exception from a rule that would, more commonly, split images from texts.

Goethe's account of his precursor's triumph drew a firm line around the significance of verbal creativity for other fields. This strangely literal detachment of the medium of tropes and figures was borne out by his, no more than loosely integrated, literary criticism. Goethe's scant efforts in poetic theory show, if anything, less interest in referring

[48] 'Maximen und Reflexionen', no. 907, in *Hamburger Ausgabe*, xii. 493.

[49] John Neubauer, 'Morphological Poetics?', *Style*, 22 (1988), 268. On Goethe's discussion of the symbol, see Nicholas Halmi, *The Genealogy of the Romantic Symbol* (Oxford: Oxford University Press, 2007), 1–2.

[50] 'Winckelmann' (1805), in *Hamburger Ausgabe*, xii. 103.

[51] 'Winckelmann' (1805), 106.

localized perceptions to some higher-order mediation than his writings on the visual arts or, certainly, the natural world. And, as we noted at the outset, scholars have long noted that the poet's broader contribution to the history of literary criticism is surprisingly oblique and variable in its focus. The recurrent themes include the theory of genre (or the 'natural forms' of poetic work), and Goethe's disambiguation between allegory and symbol.[52] It has, overall, proved hard to trace a structure in the poet's thinking about language that would match his eloquence about pictorial or sculptural mimesis, or the forms of nature.

At the rare points where they touch on meta-critical perspectives, Goethe's literary reflections must seem muted alongside his hermeneutic models for non-verbal disciplines. Curtius pointedly observed that Goethe's profile as a critic was 'the least' to be found in his writings about literature.[53] And more recent surveys find the same evasion of poetic theory that Wellek already mapped out. In this trajectory, Goethe's early, Sturm und Drang inspired commitment to expressive affect directly opposed aesthetic theorizing.[54] While the mature poet engaged in criticism from a range of different perspectives, his essays also sidestepped explicit poetics, though for different reasons, as a theory of expression. For one thing, Wellek pointed out that Goethe's literary criticism often raised its sights towards the arts in general, and then the visual and plastic arts ahead of poetry or fiction. Just as frequently, his observations simply skipped the theory of mimesis, and praised artworks as a virtual fact of nature—and not the intentional constructions of a subject whose designs might be articulated, or at least called into question. Wellek missed, in all this, 'a specifically *literary* theory'.[55] He blamed its absence largely on Goethe's reductive or, it seemed to him, quite plainly 'inconceivable' analogies between the natural world and works of art.[56]

The picture that emerges from this scholarly convergence shows a poet whose reflective stance remained implicit, even muted, in his native medium of figuration—a conclusion that is all the more remarkable in light of Goethe's figurative *copia* when reflecting on the non-discursive, and primarily perceptual, domains. In fact, his fullest rendering of a figurative method coincided, in the volumes of *On Colour*, with a commentary on

52 See, for instance, Wellek, 'Goethe', 210–15; and Amrine, 'Goethe, Johann Wolfgang von', 466–7.

53 Curtius, 'Goethe als Kritiker', 34 (tr. mine).

54 Wellek, 'Goethe', 203, notes that 'aesthetics mean little to the young Goethe', and quotes his jibe that the aesthetician Johann Georg Sulzer had, 'through all his theory (*durch alle Theorie*), blocked the path to true enjoyment'. See 'Die schönen Künste' (1772), in *Hamburger Ausgabe*, xii. 16.

55 Wellek, 'Goethe', 212. Compare Amrine, 'Goethe, Johann Wolfgang von', 466–7. Wellek concluded that 'the difficulty of isolating his strictly literary criticism from his speculations on the plastic arts and on art and nature in general, ... the constant shifts and changes in his views, are obstacles which could be overcome only by long study and meditation.' (201)

56 Wellek, 'Goethe', 226. Goethe suggested during his Italian travels that the greatest works of art were best conceived as if they were, in their formation, governed by the laws of nature: 'Diese hohen Kunstwerke sind zugleich als die höchsten Naturwerke von Menschen nach wahren und natürlichen Gesetzen hervorgebracht worden. Alles Willkürliche, Eingebildete fällt zusammen: da ist Notwendigkeit, da ist Gott.' See entry for 6 Sept. 1787, in 'Zweiter Römischer Aufenthalt' (1829), in *Hamburger Ausgabe*, xi. 395.

just this paradoxical relationship between poetic work and the extraneous motivations for the poet's turn to meta-criticism. Goethe followed his anti-Newtonian analysis with a corrective history of thinking about colour since the Greeks.[57] To this effect, Goethe included a 'confession of the author' in his role as an encyclopedic theorist, which traced the path from his beginnings as a poet, through art criticism, and towards his new brand of interpretative science.[58]

Within the telling of this retrospective, poetry, as his originary 'talent', marked the starting point of a trajectory that led the wider-ranging critic to add layers of reflection and description to his understanding of mimesis and, most forcefully, to his revision of Newtonian science. At the same time, the poetic sphere stood as an antonym of muted practice to the more expressive forms of critical reflection, which aspired to reintegrate adjacent fields (including, ultimately, poetry and science). Goethe began by looking back on how his first success as a creative writer had been characterized, in his own mind, by 'a strange relationship towards the art of poetry'—strange, as it must seem to the writer of *On Colour*, in presenting itself as 'no more than practical' (*bloß praktisch*). What he recalled was an experience of creativity which thrived on silence, be it self-directed or extended towards others. The materials he worked with had 'for years been cultivated quietly', before the poet 'fixed' what he had made of them 'at once', and 'as it were instinctively', on paper.[59]

Though it clearly served him well, Goethe reported that his gift to cope without sustained reflection led his writing down a number of dead ends. He found no profit in what he could learn about 'conception', 'style', or 'composition' from poetic manuals and rhetoric or, indeed, the 'lecterns' of the university. It was this deficit which first induced the writer to resituate himself 'outside of poetry', and to look elsewhere for an adequate 'position' by which to 'attain', at last, 'a comparison of some kind, and from where I might survey and judge at a certain distance what confused me from close up'. He had found 'nowhere better', for these purposes, to turn to than the realm of painting and the visual arts.[60] This was in part, as Goethe pointed out, because the ancient dictum of the sister arts suggested plausible connections between poetry and painting. Yet more importantly, his lack of a commensurate talent in this new sphere of activity left Goethe free to theorize the visual arts—in an exact reversal of his native gifts, which he had practised without any such reflective resonance. It was, in other words, the writer's mute poetics that had prompted these extensive critical, and meta-critical, investments in the first place:

> Je weniger also mir eine natürliche Anlage zur bildenden Kunst geworden war, desto mehr sah ich mich nach Gesetzen und Regeln um; ja ich achtete weit mehr auf das Technische der Malerei als auf das Technische der Dichtkunst: wie man denn durch

57 See the preface to 'Zur Farbenlehre' (1810), 319–20.

58 'Materialien zur Geschichte der Farbenlehre' (1810), in *Hamburger Ausgabe*, xiv. 251.

59 'Materialien zur Geschichte der Farbenlehre', 252.

60 'Materialien zur Geschichte der Farbenlehre', 252.

> Verstand und Einsicht dasjenige auszufüllen sucht, was die Natur Lückenhaftes an uns gelassen hat.
>
> The less I had accordingly been born with a gift for the visual arts, the more I looked around for laws and rules. Indeed I paid far more attention to the technical aspects of painting than to those of poetry: just as one tries to fill through understanding and insight what nature has left incomplete in us.[61]

This need for completion could explain the author's quest for intellectual mobility. His first exercise in mediating between native gifts and an explicit theory of painting could assuage the deficits of creativity. In a development which echoed Winckelmann's early formation, Goethe's 'confession' led him, via art, from poetry to science. In the end, neither the theorists nor travel writers, who had viewed artworks *in situ*, could relieve the early 'groundlessness (*das Bodenlose*) of my knowledge'—a persistent deficit which, after years of 'hesitation', led the poet south across the Alps.[62] There, his Italian travels finally allowed for the 'perpetual', and interchangeably art-critical and scientific, 'contemplation of nature and art'.

The finer points of colouring (*das Kolorit*) emerged in Italy as the cross-disciplinary 'unique point' for which Goethe realized he could not 'in the least' account within existing resources.[63] The poet's evolution as a theorist hence led him, in the end, to 'gain on art' (*etwas über sie gewinnen*) by casting questions of aesthetics first and foremost 'from the side of nature' (*erst von der Seite der Natur*).[64] It was not far from there to the elaborate method called for in *On Colour*. Yet its origins lay in the poet's self-confessed predicament in trying to reflect on his original gifts. In an exchange with Eckermann, Goethe continued to dismiss the notion that aesthetic experts might come to a 'clear result' about the poet's art. He had, after all, moved far outside the field to gain an adequate perspective. 'What is there really to define?', he pre-empted the discussion, and referred Eckermann back to his 'lively feeling' as the poet's primary, if unreflected, impetus.[65]

It is a paradox of Goethe's literary essays that they found poetic figuration less susceptible to hermeneutic dialogue than work in fields without an obvious discursive base. Their figuration of an audience for poetry likewise foregrounds the muted pragmatism which, by his account, helped shape the author's journey as a critic. In rebuking Johann Georg Sulzer's worthy theory, Goethe had aimed much of his scorn at the enlightened pundit's effort to explain the cultural effects of art. What did it matter, Goethe asked, whether a 'gawking public' could, or could not—once it 'finished gawking' (*wenn's ausgegafft hat*)—render an account of its experience of the work?[66] The early Goethe typically urged that, for his part,

[61] 'Materialien zur Geschichte der Farbenlehre', 253.
[62] 'Materialien zur Geschichte der Farbenlehre', 253.
[63] 'Materialien zur Geschichte der Farbenlehre', 254.
[64] 'Materialien zur Geschichte der Farbenlehre', 256.
[65] Conversation with Eckermann, 11 June 1825, in Johann Peter Eckermann, *Gespräche mit Goethe in den letzten Jahren seines Lebens*, ed. Christoph Michel (Berlin: Deutscher Klassiker Verlag, 2011), 160 (my tr.).
[66] 'Die schönen Künste', 20.

> um den Künstler allein ist's zu tun, daß der keine Seligkeit des Lebens fühlt als in seiner Kunst, daß, in sein Instrument versunken, er mit allen seinen Empfindungen und Kräften da lebt.
>
> it's exclusively about the artist, that he feels no blessedness of life but in his art, that, absorbed within his instrument, he lives there amidst all his powers and sensations.[67]

Likewise a draft advertisement for *Propyläen* pledged that essays published in the journal would defend the 'working artist' against audiences bound to subvert his purposes—a clash that Goethe bluntly termed a 'conflict between practice' and, as a receptive function, 'theory' (*ein Widerstreit des Praktischen und Theoretischen*).[68]

Goethe's most pointed characterization of the self-containment of poetic work came in a late essay which aimed to solve the crux, to his mind, of catharsis as a feature of Aristotelian criticism. Goethe blamed this aspect of the theory of tragedy for 'much embarrassment' (*viel Not*) among both exegetes and ordinary readers. It seemed, after all, as if the genre relied for its eminence on a capacity to draw its audiences, or even readers, into an affective ploy.[69] Goethe had no doubt that good tragic plots, with their conflicting agency or voices, were designed to mobilize the affects spanned by Aristotle's reference to pity and fear. What he could not accept was that the famed arousal, and then resolution, of these passions had to implicate a public in the form of audience members, readers, or, in consequence, interpreters. The poet sought to lay this claim to rest by retranslating the decisive section from *Poetics*. In his rendering, the only subjects Aristotle had in mind were those imagined by the poet to be speaking, acting, and responding on the stage. The shorter reach of their engagement, as internal to the tragic play, figured the inward-looking nature of poetics as a theory of verbal form. Goethe considered this an obvious inference to draw, not least because he found the ancient argument so clearly focused on the structure of the work:

> Wie konnte Aristoteles in seiner jederzeit auf den Gegenstand hinweisenden Art, indem er ganz eigentlich von der Konstruktion des Trauerspiels redet, an die Wirkung und, was mehr ist, an die entfernte Wirkung denken, welche eine Tragödie auf den Zuschauer vielleicht machen würde? Keineswegs! Er spricht ganz klar und richtig aus: wenn sie durch den Verlauf von Mitleid und Furcht erregenden

[67] 'Die schönen Künste', 20.

[68] 'Anzeige der Propyläen. Über strenge Urteile' (1798/99), in *Goethes Werke (Weimarer Ausgabe). Erste Abtheilung*, xlvii (Weimar: Böhlau, 1896): 51 (tr. mine).

[69] 'Nachlese zu Aristoteles' Poetik' (1827), in *Hamburger Ausgabe*, xii. 342. Though these did not loom large in neoclassical discussions, several passages in the *Poetics* are severely sceptical about theatrical performance and the role of 'spectacle' in tragedy (including music or 'excessive gestures'). Aristotle even argued that good tragedy must be as powerfully affecting when it is read as when it is performed in public. See *Poetics*, tr. Stephen Halliwell (London: Duckworth, 1987), 38–9, 64 (1450b16–20, 1462a5–13). Andrew Ford has argued that catharsis is itself extrinsic to the structural intent of the *Poetics* as the earliest analysis of works of poetry in their domain-specific forms and powers. See '*Katharsis*: The Ancient Problem', in Andrew Parker and Eve Kosofsky Sedgwick (eds), *Performativity and Performance* (London: Routledge, 1995), 109–32.

> Mitteln durchgegangen, so müsse sie mit Ausgleichung, mit Versöhnung solcher Leidenschaften zuletzt auf dem Theater ihre Arbeit abschließen.
>
> How could Aristotle possibly have thought of the effect and, what is more, the remote effect a tragedy might have on a spectator; when in his thoroughly demonstrative procedure he was properly discussing the construction of a tragic drama? By no means! He states quite clearly and correctly: once it has gone through means of arousing pity and fear, tragedy must conclude on the stage by balancing, by reconciling such emotions.[70]

Goethe took Aristotle to 'demand' this reconciliation, as a formal 'rounding off' (*Abrundung*), not only from a well-made tragedy, or drama in its various forms, but equally 'from all poetic works'.[71] Of course these works of poetry would still need to be read or viewed by somebody, and Goethe's stress on immanence had to involve its own subject-position for the audience. Yet his account of the post facto contemplation of catharsis clearly neutralized reception, and confined both agency and its effects to the poetic work.

For lay audiences, and we must likewise assume critics, the experience of a catharsis sealed within the work appeared, in equal measure, transient and disempowering. By refusing the suggestion of a cleansing, and hence morally instructive, process for spectators, Goethe blocked the expectation that the poet's work had consequences to be felt and, and perhaps clarified, elsewhere. By extension, his revisionist account left little room for the idea that central terms would form the subject of some open-endedly interpretative work, which had provided a key strand of his analysis in other fields. In the poetic realm, the work of figuration seemed directed inwards, to entangle and resolve itself within the work, rather than propagate through some additional linguistic mediation. If catharsis bound attention strictly to the work itself, the force of poetry was evidently that it left its public, and likewise its broader intellectual environment, much as it found them:

> Hat nun der Dichter an seiner Stelle seine Pflicht erfüllt, einen Knoten bedeutend geknüpft und würdig gelöst, so wird dann dasselbe in dem Geiste des Zuschauers vorgehen; die Verwicklung wird ihn verwirren, die Auflösung aufklären, er aber um nichts gebessert nach Hause gehen; er würde vielmehr, wenn er asketisch-aufmerksam genug wäre, sich über sich selbst verwundern, daß er ebenso leichtsinning als hartnäckig, ebenso heftig als schwach, ebenso liebevoll als lieblos sich wieder in seiner Wohnung findet, wie er hinausgegangen.
>
> If, then, the poet has for his part done his duty, has meaningfully tied a knot and then unravelled it with dignity, the same will happen in the mind of the spectator; the entanglement will confuse him, the resolution set him right, but he will in no way be improved when he goes home; if he were ascetically observant to the right degree, he would rather be surprised at himself for returning just as careless and obstinate,

[70] 'Nachlese zu Aristoteles' Poetik', 343.
[71] 'Nachlese zu Aristoteles' Poetik', 343.

> just as forceful and meek, and just as loving and unfeeling as he was when he left his quarters.[72]

For the method of *On Colour*, the dramatic presentation of the agency of characters provided an analogy for Goethe's vivid understanding of the 'deeds and sufferings' of light. In his recasting of a central element of the *Poetics*, tragic drama helped by contrast to delineate a markedly detached and, in its ideal type, effectively abstemious or ascetic mode of observation. It was as if spectators turned into men without qualities, with every affect 'just as' neutralized as every other, when the poet cast catharsis as absorptive form, and thereby barred the active mediation of the work.

The argument could even fit the one work in the poet's oeuvre which revolved most openly around motifs of metaphor and mediation. *Elective Affinities* included the elusive Mittler, who served as the figure of a marriage mediator, among its protagonists.[73] Its self-declared 'experiment' of disengaging and regrouping two Romantic couples resonated with the layers of figuration played on by its title.[74] Goethe's final novel thereby intertwined his lifelong polymathic interests with a textual narrative which, as its author promised, has proved daunting to interpreters.[75] Eduard's vignette of man as 'true Narcissus', converting his self-regard into a 'foil for the entire world', foretold how metaphorical relatedness and interaction, or conversely separation and divorce, would resonate throughout with amorous, scientific, or indeed meta-poetic implications. The novel's famous commentary on its title echoed Goethe's thinking about how 'peculiar terms of art' (*Kunstwörter*) must, in the sciences, also be 'reconciled' through 'sensory perception'.[76] And the Captain's explanation of the chemistry involved previewed the novel's basic plot. In doing so, it also recalled the array of media, means, and language systems which we have seen traverse Goethe's encyclopedic work:

> 'Wenn Sie glauben, daß es nicht pedantisch aussieht', versetzte der Hauptmann, 'so kann ich wohl in der Zeichensprache mich kürzlich zusammenfassen. Denken Sie sich ein A, das mit einem B innig verbunden ist, durch viele Mittel und durch manche Gewalt nicht von ihm zu trennen; denken Sie sich ein C, das sich ebenso zu einem D verhält; bringen Sie nun die beiden Paare in Berührung: A wird sich zu D, C

[72] 'Nachlese zu Aristoteles' Poetik', 345.

[73] Talking to Eckermann about the novel, Goethe commented on having met a stranger who had recognized himself in 'the person of *Mittler*'. He concluded that, 'the character must therefore have some truth to it, and exist more than once in the world'. See conversation with Eckermann, 9 Feb. 1829, in Eckermann, *Gespräche mit Goethe in den letzten Jahren seines Lebens*, 303 (my tr.).

[74] 'Die Wahlverwandtschaften' (1809), in *Hamburger Ausgabe*, vi. 252, 256.

[75] In his exchange with Eckermann, Goethe put it mildly when he noted that his text held 'more than anybody would be able to absorb within a single reading' (see n. 73). David Wellbery has offered an extraordinary account of its symbolic orders, and their dislocations. Yet he is also not the only critic to have flagged a lasting sense of feeling hermeneutically 'inferior' to Goethe's novel, 'unlike any other' in the German literary tradition. See David E. Wellbery, 'Die Wahlverwandtschaften', in Paul Michael Lützeler and James E. McLeod (eds), *Goethes Erzählwerk* (Stuttgart: Reclam, 1985), 291 (tr. mine).

[76] 'Die Wahlverwandtschaften', 276.

> zu B werfen, ohne daß man sagen kann, wer das andere zuerst verlassen, wer sich mit dem andern zuerst wieder verbunden habe.'
>
> 'If you do not think that it looks pedantic', said the Captain, 'I should be able to be brief by expressing myself in notational language. Think of an A, that is intimately linked with a B, and inseparable from it through many means and some considerable power; think of a C, that equally relates to a D; now bring both pairs into contact: A will throw itself to D, C to B, without our being able to say who left the other first, who first reconnected with another one.'[77]

Writing to Zelter in the last years of his life, Goethe chose this fictional conspectus of his stake in figurative methods to confirm, by contrast, the enclosure of poetic work. He identified *Elective Affinities* as the text in which he had sought, 'to complete (*abzuschließen*) the intimately true catharsis as purely and fully as possible'. As in his recasting of the *Poetics*, this claim served to detach the novel's formal qualities from real-world analogues or, by extension, from interpretative analysis in other fields. Goethe stressed that no degree of formal closure (and accordingly success) could, by poetic means, 'cleanse even one attractive man'—as if catharsis faced beyond the work—'from the desire to make eyes at someone else's wife'.[78] The more its figures challenged them, the more the work of poetry must leave its audiences effectively unchanged.

Where Goethe's literary criticism homed in on poetic making, it did so at the expense of its engagement with a wider public, the non-verbal arts, or other disciplines. His late readings of catharsis stressed the immanence of form in opposition to the kinds of interaction that elsewhere made Goethe's interests so susceptible to hermeneutics by merging their cognitive, sensory, or discursive strands. In this respect, the most overtly figurative domain of Goethe's interests presents a paradox. *Elective Affinities* famously reworked his polymathy within the microcosmic analogues and figures of its plot. What Goethe praised it for was then precisely its ability to fold in on itself. Like all good tragedies, it was to start and end on its specifically poetic stage. What was curtailed was its potential for cathartic transformation, and thereby its mediating force. The dialogic method for which Goethe made room in *On Colour* and explored, although more tentatively, in his genealogy of art, played no substantial part in his conception of poetic work. The poet's native gift of form remained sealed off from Goethe's figures of encyclopedic thought.

Further Reading

Amrine, Frederick, 'Goethe, Johann Wolfgang von', in Michael Groden, Martin Kreiswirth, and Imre Szeman (eds), *The Johns Hopkins Guide to Literary Theory and Criticism*, 2nd edn (Baltimore: Johns Hopkins University Press, 2004), 465–68.

Aristotle, *Complete Works*, ed. Jonathan Barnes (Princeton: Princeton University Press, 1985).

77 'Die Wahlverwandtschaften', 276.

78 Letter to Zelter, 29 Jan. 1830, in *Goethes Briefe*, ed. Karl Robert Mandelkow, 3rd edn (Munich: Beck, 1988), iv. 369 (tr. mine).

Aristotle, *Poetics*, tr. Stephen Halliwell (London: Duckworth, 1987).

Boyle, Nicholas, *Goethe: The Poet and the Age*, i. *The Poetry of Desire (1749–1790)* (Oxford: Oxford University Press, 1991).

Cassirer, Ernst, 'Goethe und die Kantische Philosophie' (1944), in Rainer A. Bast (ed.), *Rousseau, Kant, Goethe* (Hamburg: Meiner, 1991), 63–99.

Cowley, Abraham, *Poetry and Prose*, ed. Leonard C. Martin (Oxford: Clarendon, 1949).

Curtius, Ernst Robert, 'Goethe als Kritiker', in *Kritische Essays zur Europäischen Literatur*, 2nd edn (Bern: Francke, 1954), 31–56.

Dear, Peter, *Revolutionizing the Sciences: European Knowledge and its Ambitions, 1500–1700* (Houndmills: Palgrave, 2001).

Eckermann, Johann Peter, *Gespräche mit Goethe in den letzten Jahren seines Lebens*, ed. Christoph Michel (Berlin: Deutscher Klassiker Verlag, 2011).

Ford, Andrew, '*Katharsis*: The Ancient Problem', in *Performativity and Performance*, ed. Andrew Parker and Eve Kosofsky Sedgwick (London: Routledge, 1995), 109–32.

Gadamer, Hans Georg, 'Goethe und die Philosophie' (1947), in *Ästhetik und Poetik II: Hermeneutik im Vollzug* (Tübingen: Mohr, 1993), 56–71.

Goethe, Johann Wolfgang von, *Werke (Weimarer Ausgabe): Erste Abtheilung*, xlvii (Weimar: Böhlau, 1896).

Goethe, Johann Wolfgang von, *Goethe on Art*, ed. John Gage (London: Scolar, 1980).

Goethe, Johann Wolfgang von, *Briefe*, ed. Karl Robert Mandelkow, 3rd edn, 4 vols (Munich: Beck, 1988).

Goethe, Johann Wolfgang von, *Essays on Art and Literature*, ed. John Gearey (Princeton: Princeton University Press, 1994).

Goethe, Johann Wolfgang von, *Scientific Studies*, ed. Douglas Miller (Princeton: Princeton University Press, 1995).

Goethe, Johann Wolfgang von, *Werke: Hamburger Ausgabe*, 14 vols (Munich: Deutscher Taschenbuch Verlag, 2000).

Grafton, Anthony, *Defenders of the Text: The Traditions of Scholarship in an Age of Science, 1450–1800* (Cambridge, Mass.: Harvard University Press, 1991).

Halliwell, Stephen, *The Aesthetics of Mimesis: Ancient Texts and Modern Problems* (Princeton: Princeton University Press, 2002).

Halmi, Nicholas, *The Genealogy of the Romantic Symbol* (Oxford: Oxford University Press, 2007).

Hoesel-Uhlig, Stefan, 'Changing Fields: The Directions of Goethe's *Weltliteratur*', in Christopher Prendergast (ed.), *Negotiating World Literature* (London: Verso, 2004), 26–53.

Hoffmeister, Gerhart, 'Reception in Germany and Abroad', in Lesley Sharpe (ed.), *The Cambridge Companion to Goethe* (Cambridge: Cambridge University Press, 2002), 232–55.

Hooke, Robert, *Micrographia: or some physiological descriptions of minute bodies made by magnifying glasses* (London: J. Martyn & J. Allestry, 1665).

Koopmann, Helmut, 'Zur Entwicklung der literaturtheoretischen Position in der Klassik', in Karl Otto Conrady (ed.), *Deutsche Literatur zur Zeit der Klassik* (Stuttgart: Reclam, 1977), 30–43.

Koselleck, Reinhart, *Goethes Unzeitgemässe Geschichte* (Heidelberg: Manutius, 1997).

Molnár, Géza von, 'Goethe's Reading of Kant's *Critique of Esthetic Judgment*: A Referential Guide for Wilhelm Meister's Esthetic Education', *Eighteenth-Century Studies*, 15 (1982), 402–20.

Neubauer, John, 'Morphological Poetics?', *Style*, 22 (1988), 263–74.

Sprat, Thomas, *The History of the Royal-Society of London, for the Improving of Natural Knowledge* (London: J. Martyn & J. Allestry, 1667).
Steuer, Daniel, 'In Defence of Experience: Goethe's Natural Investigations and Scientific Culture', in Lesley Sharpe (ed.), *The Cambridge Companion to Goethe* (Cambridge: Cambridge University Press, 2002), 160–78.
Wellbery, David E., 'Die Wahlverwandtschaften', in Paul Michael Lützeler and James E. McLeod (eds), *Goethes Erzählwerk* (Stuttgart: Reclam, 1985), 291–318.
Wellek, René, 'Goethe', in *A History of Modern Criticism: 1750–1950*, i. *The Later Eighteenth Century* (London: Cape, 1955), 201–26.
Williams, John R., *The Life of Goethe* (Oxford: Blackwell, 1998).

CHAPTER 18

HEIDELBERG, DRESDEN, BERLIN, VIENNA

DENNIS F. MAHONEY

In the various permutations of German Romanticism from its beginnings in the 1790s, two factors remain constant: a penchant for collaborative, transdisciplinary work, and the formation of small circles—often in university towns—whose particular character often depended upon and contributed to the prevailing intellectual discourse of that locale. Jena Romanticism, for example, received impulses from the reworking of Kantian and post-Kantian thinking already undertaken by the philosophers Fichte and Schelling, but then applied to poetic theory and practice by the young Friedrich Schlegel, August Wilhelm Schlegel, and Novalis.[1]

For the four cities highlighted in the chapter heading, one further factor needs to be considered: the impact of the Napoleonic reorganization of central Europe. The breakup and dispersal of the Jena Romantics coincided with the collapse of the moribund Holy Roman Empire, which officially ended in 1806 but whose final dissolution began with the Treaty of Lunéville in 1801, which ceded territories west of the Rhine river to France, followed in 1803 by the amalgamation of ecclesiastical territories and many former free imperial cities into states such as Baden, Württemberg, and Bavaria as recompense.[2] After these three southern German territories allied themselves with Napoleon against Austria in 1805, they in turn were elevated to the status of archduchy, in the case of Baden, and even kingdom—as also happened with Saxony in the aftermath of the Prussian defeat at the battles of Jena-Auerstädt in October 1806. As a result, Heidelberg in Baden and Dresden in Saxony enjoyed a protected status that attracted students and scholars from across German territories. This, paradoxically, helped contribute to the growth of a sense of German cultural identity that found military and political expression in the so-called 'Befreiungskriege' (Wars of Liberation) of 1813. Berlin, by 1810, partook of the

[1] See Ch. 12 in this *Handbook*.

[2] See Michael Rowe, 'Napoleon and State Formation in Central Europe', in Philip G. Dwyer (ed.), *Napoleon and Europe* (Harlow: Longman, 2001), 204–24, esp. 204–7.

intellectual and cultural ferment of the Prussian Reform Movement that had a genuine Romantic component. Vienna, finally, was the capital of the only other major German state that was not a part of the Napoleonic Confederation of the Rhine. Here Friedrich Schlegel, who had converted to Catholicism in the Cathedral of Cologne in 1808 before moving to Vienna, argued that it was the Austrian emperor who represented the true heir to the Holy Roman Empire, as opposed to the usurper Napoleon. Schlegel's 1812 public lectures on literature had a profound effect on the young Joseph von Eichendorff, who completed his law degree in Vienna after earlier studies in Halle (Prussia) and then Heidelberg, but also finished here his first novel *Ahnung und Gegenwart* (Presentiment and Present, 1815) with the advice and encouragement of Friedrich Schlegel and his wife Dorothea, daughter of Moses Mendelssohn and herself a convert to Catholicism.

In the year of his death, Eichendorff wrote the autobiographical fragment *Halle und Heidelberg* (1857) that contributed not only to the image of Heidelberg as a 'Romantic' locale, but also to that of a Heidelberg Romanticism shaped by the presence of Joseph Görres, prophetic lecturer at the university, and his putative disciples Achim von Arnim and Clemens Brentano. As has been said about Goethe's autobiography *Dichtung und Wahrheit* (Poetry and Truth), Eichendorff's account contains more 'poetry' than 'truth'. Brentano, for example, only returned to Heidelberg in April 1808 after a one-year absence that coincided with the two semesters in which Eichendorff studied at Heidelberg and was in a position to write about what he had personally experienced; Arnim, for his part, had spent the year 1807 at the court in Königsberg, East Prussia, in a vain attempt to take part in the beginnings of the Prussian Reform Movement, and only recommenced writing and editing work in Heidelberg as of January 1808. True, Arnim's and Brentano's *Des Knaben Wunderhorn* (The Youth's Magic Horn, 1805, 1808), a three-volume collection of German folk songs, was published in Heidelberg as the initial offering of the young publishers Jacob Benjamin Christian Mohr and Johann Georg Zimmer, but the gathering of these songs took place prior to Arnim and Brentano's residence there and hence had little to do with Heidelberg as a locale. A commercial failure—copies of the first edition still remained unsold at the beginning of the twentieth century—the *Wunderhorn* did have an impact on the poetic style of Romantics such as Eichendorff, who was already reading the first volume in the summer of 1807, and later served as inspiration for the song settings of composers like Robert Schumann and Gustav Mahler. It also influenced, albeit more as a negative example, the theoretical premises of the Grimm brothers in Kassel (the residence of Napoleon's brother Jérôme as King of Westphalia), who objected to Brentano's and especially Arnim's modifications of their printed sources in the interests of revivifying folk tradition. In practice, however, the Grimms, particularly Wilhelm, 'managed to create a coherent narrative mode in which fairy tales originating from different traditions could be told to a contemporary public'.[3] It is no coincidence that the Grimms dedicated their collection of *Kinder- und*

[3] Fabian Lampart, 'The Turn to History and the *Volk*: Brentano, Arnim, and the Grimm Brothers', in Dennis F. Mahoney (ed.), *The Literature of German Romanticism* (Rochester, NY: Camden House, 2004), 186.

Hausmärchen (Children's and Household Tales, 1st edition 1812 and 1815) to Bettina von Arnim, Brentano's sister, whose engagement and marriage to Arnim had taken place during their 1810–11 residence in Berlin.

Another friend of Brentano and a true contributor to the intellectual ferment in Heidelberg was Joseph Görres, who had been his classmate at the former Jesuit Gymnasium in Coblenz. Görres, in his youth a zealous advocate of the French Revolution, returned from a stay in Paris from November 1799 to February 1800 deeply disillusioned by the lack of attention paid to his delegation's protests against corruption and injustice in the occupied Rhineland, as well as by the disparity between rich and poor in the French capital, which seemed anything but a realization of the principles of the Revolution.[4] Becoming a self-taught professor of physics in Coblenz whose essays in the spirit of Schelling's philosophy of nature won the respectful attention of Goethe, Görres came to the University of Heidelberg in the fall of 1806 as a private lecturer and remained there for four semesters. During this time, he collaborated with Brentano on a satire of philistine complacency and mistrust of music titled *Wunderliche Geschichte von BOGS dem Uhrmacher* (Wondrous History of BOGS the Watchmaker, 1807), whose name bears the opening and closing letters of the two friends' last names. Görres made use of Brentano's extensive private library while composing *Die teutschen Volksbücher* (German Folk Books, 1807), published in Heidelberg by Mohr & Zimmer, which includes a listing and retelling of forty-eight chapbooks such as Siegfried, Eulenspiegel, and Doctor Faust—to name a few of the more famous and extensively discussed tales. Integrating these works within a cultural development that began in ancient India and moved westward over the millennia, Görres took care to emphasize connections between medieval German literature and the romances of England, Spain, and Italy, as well as the importance of Nordic myths and interactions with Muslim traditions during the Crusades. Well aware that he was not a scholar by profession, Görres nonetheless hoped that the reading of his book would have the same animating impulse on others that the chapbooks had had upon him and rescue many a work from ill-deserved oblivion. One of these readers was Friedrich Creuzer, a rising star in classical philology at the University of Heidelberg who shared with Görres an interest in myth and symbolism in the religious and literary writings of ancient peoples. As Theodore Ziolkowski has observed, if one is looking for the roots of Heidelberg Romanticism, one should be sure to pay attention less to the residences of the poets than to the seminars at the university.[5]

Reacting to proponents of classical Greek and Latin at the expense of newer developments in literature, Görres agreed that it would be lamentable if the love for Greek art ever were to die among Germans, particularly when both nations were now so alike in

[4] For further information, see Jon Vanden Heuvel, *A German Life in the Age of Revolution: Joseph Görres, 1776–1848* (Washington, DC: Catholic University of America Press, 2001).

[5] Theodore Ziolkowski, *Heidelberger Romantik: Mythos und Symbol* (Heidelberg: Winter, 2009), 58. For further investigations of the philological, poetological, historiographic, and political dimensions of Heidelberg Romanticism, see the essays in Friedrich Strack (ed.), *200 Jahre Heidelberger Romantik* (Berlin and Heidelberg: Springer, 2008).

misfortune (i.e. as victims of imperialism); but neither should the Middle Ages' widening spiritual dimensions be neglected:

> Lassen wir so jeder Zeit ihr Recht, die Zukunft wird uns auch das Unsrige lassen; jede schnöde Herabwürdigung, jede einseitige Aufgeblasenheit ist verwerflich in sich selbst, und muß endlich am eignen Selbstmord sterben.
>
> If we give every age its due, the future will allow the same for us; each disdainful disparagement, each biased self-importance is reprehensible in itself and must finally die of its own self-eradication.[6]

These remarks near the conclusion of *Die teutschen Volksbücher* had a particular bearing on a growing controversy in Heidelberg, where Johann Heinrich Voß had been invited as honorary professor in 1805 as recognition for his translations of Homer in dactylic hexameter, a verse form he also employed in his *Luise* (1795), an idyllic representation of small-town German life. Soon Voß and his allies began attacking contemporary writers with the charge that they were 'Romantics' not only in content but also in their frequent employment of the sonnet—Voß would have been chagrined had he known that his friend Goethe himself had written a significant series of sonnets in 1807–8! Görres and Brentano responded with witty parodies in Arnim's bi-weekly *Zeitung für Einsiedler* (Tidings for Hermits, 1808) where they smote their opponents with their own weapons. Brentano's 'Der Einsiedler und das Klingding, nach der Schlacht bei Eichstädt' (The Hermit and the Clinging Thing, after the Battle of Eichstädt) employs a genuine Petrarchan sonnet written in classical Greek by the Heidelberg philologist August Böckh that is first quoted in the original, then amusingly misunderstood by the hermit, who does not understand Greek, and finally correctly translated as part of a dialogue of sonnets that reveals the female stranger to be the hermit's lover, who in her linguistic disguise has thereby survived the fearsome Battle of Eichstädt—a place in Thuringia but also the name of the editor of the *Jenaische Allgemeine Literatur-Zeitung* (Jena General Literature-News) who in June of 1808 had published in four instalments Voss's attack on the sonnet form and its practitioners.[7] Arnim's *Zeitung* ceased publication at the end of August, to the malicious satisfaction of his opponents. On 16 November 1808, Arnim left for Berlin, where he was later joined by Brentano in a new phase of their career concerned more with the present and future of Germany than its cultural past. Görres, meanwhile, had returned to Coblenz, where he was later to win fame as the editor of the newspaper *Rheinischer Merkur* (Rhenish Mercury, 1814–16) as a resolute opponent of Napoleon, Metternich, and the ever more conservative Prussian monarchy.

Ironically, neither Brentano nor Arnim had been making use of the sonnet form with any regularity before this so-called sonnet strife commenced. A more apt object

[6] Joseph Görres, *Die teutschen Volksbücher* (Repr. of the 1807 edn, Hildesheim and New York: Olms, 1982), 302.

[7] See Ziolkowski, 'August Böckh und die "Sonnettenschlacht bei Eichstädt"', in Strack, *200 Jahre*, 207–23.

for attack would have been the poeticizing efforts of Otto Heinrich Graf von Loeben, alias 'Isidorus Orientalis', whose novel *Guido* (1808) begins with two fulsome dedicatory sonnets and whose practically non-existent plot is overladen with a similar profusion of technically accomplished but virtually meaningless poems. Written during Loeben's stay in Heidelberg, where he was the centre of a cult of disciples that included the young Eichendorff, *Guido* was intended to be the continuation and completion of the unfinished novel *Heinrich von Ofterdingen* by Novalis; in the opinion of Gerhard Schulz it more accurately can be described as *Ofterdingen*'s parasitic reversal.[8] Set in a nebulous Middle Ages where the title figure encounters the Hohenstaufen emperor Frederick II, but also visits the tomb of Hans Sachs (who was born almost 250 years after Frederick's death in 1250), *Guido* documents that by 1808 the term 'Romantic' was being employed in inflationary terms by adherents and opponents alike. At one point in part II, the young minstrel Heinrich Frauenlob remarks to the hero:

> Ich weiß nicht—wenn ich oft keinen Namen für mein Verlangen habe, und weinen möchte vor schmerzlichen Vergnügen, und hinaus, hinaus in's Kühne und Grüne, in's Blaue und Graue—da ruf' ich: romantisch, nun wird die Brust mir frei und treu, als ob ich es besäße, als ob ich's in der Gestalt eines Mädchens mit beiden Armen auf ewig umschließen könnte. Ach! Es sieht aus wie grüne Luft und goldene Erde, wenn ich das Wort nenne.

> I don't know—when I often have no name for my desire, and would like to weep for painful pleasure, and [go] out, out, into the keen and green, the blue way and the gray—then I call out: Romantic, now my breast becomes free and faithful, as if I now possessed it, as if I could hold it forever with both arms in the form of a maiden. Oh! It looks like green air and golden earth, when I say the word.[9]

A more creative and congenial appropriation of the thoughts and works of Novalis and the early Romantics took place around this same time in Dresden. Unlike Heidelberg, Dresden did not possess a university, but as was true for Berlin's cultural life in the first decade of the nineteenth century, it made up for this lack by the staging of public lectures attended by the nobility as well as the educated middle class, male and female alike.[10] Pathbreaking in this regard were August Wilhelm Schlegel's 1802 Berlin lectures on literature, art, and the spirit of the age, which presented the aesthetic theories of Jena Romanticism in a more publicly accessible and less esoteric format than in the *Athenaeum*, the journal edited by the Schlegel brothers from 1798 to 1800. Adam Müller achieved a similar success with a series of twelve *Vorlesungen über die deutsche Wissenschaft und Literatur* (Lectures on German Knowledge and Literature, 1807) that he delivered in Dresden during the winter and spring of 1806 and that made him an

[8] Gerhard Schulz, Introduction to Isidorus Orientalis (Otto Heinrich Graf von Loeben), *Guido* (Bern: Lang, 1979), 23*.

[9] Isidorus Orientalis, *Guido*, 200–1.

[10] See Sean Franzel, *Connected by the Ear: The Media, Pedagogy, and Politics of the Romantic Lecture* (Evanston, Ill.: Northwestern University Press, 2013).

instant sensation upon their publication. Müller, the son of a Prussian fiscal bureaucrat and student of politics and diplomacy at the University of Göttingen, had already spent time in Dresden in 1803 with his mentor, the political publicist Friedrich Gentz, developing ideas that found their formulation the following year in his *Lehre vom Gegensatz* (Treatise on Contradiction, 1804), an early example of the Romantic fascination with opposites and their reconciliation. Already in his opening lecture on 28 January 1806, Müller stated that Germany was in an ideal geographical and cultural position to play the role of mediator in Europe between north and south, classical antiquity and medieval spirituality. He further developed this ideal of dynamic synthesis in his fifth lecture on the nature of German literature, praising Goethe's novel *Wilhelm Meisters Lehrjahre* for its reconciliation of poetry and economy; Goethe's only weak point, Müller contended, was the absence of an appreciation for the spirit of Christianity permeating history, poetry, and philosophy. Müller therefore called for a synthesis of the spirit of the medieval Christian world depicted in Novalis's *Heinrich von Ofterdingen* with the sphere of contemporary life depicted in *Wilhelm Meister*. As for Novalis, Müller elevated him to the status of a prophet of future times whose works are destined to find fulfilment in German art and life alike.[11] Literature, in other words, no longer required accreditation of its cultural legitimacy through recourse to Kantian aesthetics, as was still true for Schiller's letters on Aesthetic Education (1795) in his journal *Die Horen* (The Graces, 1795–7). Instead, Romantic literature accredited Müller's theory.

In his concluding lecture on 15 April 1806, Müller regarded the theatre as the place where national life most completely receives its expression and communication—an idea that received further development in his ten lectures *Über die dramatische Kunst* (On Dramatic Art) in the winter of 1806–7. No wonder, then, that Müller found his hopes for the future of German literature realized when he read in manuscript the reworking of Molière's *Amphitryon* by Heinrich von Kleist, still in French captivity as a suspected Prussian spy in the winter and spring of 1807.[12] For Müller, Kleist's treatment of the conception of Hercules—which Müller interpreted as an analogue to the Immaculate Conception—exemplified the union of antiquity and modernity, ideal and reality. Printed in Dresden in May 1807 by the same publisher as the *Vorlesungen* and with an enthusiastic foreword by Müller himself, *Amphitryon* made the hitherto unknown author a much sought-after guest upon his arrival in Dresden in late August of that same year. Kleist's appearance in Dresden took place six weeks after Napoleon's reception in that city following the peace treaty of Tilsit on 7 July 1807, which marked the height of Napoleon's power in Europe; Prussia, meanwhile, had lost all its territories west of the Elbe River and the bulk of its acquisitions in Poland, which now stood under the regime of the Saxon King Friedrich August I. Kleist and Müller made plans to establish a publishing house and bookstore in Dresden whose projected agenda itself

[11] Adam Müller, *Vorlesungen über die deutsche Wissenschaft und Literatur*, in Müller, *Kritische, ästhetische und philosophische Schriften*, ed. Walter Schroeder and Werner Siebert (Neuwied and Berlin: Luchterhand, 1967), i. 58.

[12] For further information on Kleist, see Ch. 14 in the *Handbook*.

seems a synthesis of pragmatism and idealism—on the one hand a German translation of the *Code Napoleon*, on the other a deluxe edition of the works of Novalis that would be more complete than the Schlegel-Tieck editions of 1802 and 1805—but the opposition of already existing Dresden booksellers led to a denial of royal permission for this venture.

Müller and Kleist were able to launch another ambitious project intended to accomplish what Schiller's *Horen* had attempted, namely a monthly journal containing the work of the intellectual elite of Germany, Goethe included, while also providing a forum for new developments in Romantic art and literature in a way similar to the *Athenaeum* of the Schlegel brothers. The first issue of *Phöbus: Ein Journal für die Kunst* (Phoebus: A Journal of Art), which appeared in January 1808, in fact included an essay on the significance of the dance by Schiller's friend Christian Gottfried Körner as well as the hitherto unpublished poem 'An Dorothee' by Novalis dedicated to Körner's sister-in-law, the artist Dora Stock. A further union of the classic and Romantic appeared in two drawings by Ferdinand Hartmann—not only an illustration of Phoebus Apollo in his chariot over Dresden, flanked by the Horen, but also a depiction of the angel appearing to the three Marys at the tomb of Jesus—for which Kleist alternately supplied poems in elegiac distich and Shakespearean blank verse, designed to stimulate a reconsideration of the question of the limits of painting and poetry in a future issue of the journal. For his part, Müller's essay on the character of the writings of Mme de Staël-Holstein demonstrated the editors' desire to develop a pan-European perspective on the arts, which was followed in the second issue of *Phöbus* by Müller's discussion of Mme de Staël's *Corinne ou l'Italie* (Corinna or Italy, 1807) and in issue 6 by 'La fête de la victoire où le retour des Grecs' (The Feast of Victory or the Return of the Greeks), de Staël's translation of Schiller's poem 'Das Siegesfest'. During her visit to Dresden from 30 May to 6 June 1808 in the company of August Wilhelm, Friedrich, and Dorothea Schlegel—the latter of whom had translated *Corinne* into German—Mme de Staël met at least with Müller, if not with Kleist, following her rendez-vous in nearby Teplitz with Friedrich Gentz, a fellow opponent of Napoleon. Both in the first and in future issues of *Phöbus*, Müller featured excerpts from his Dresden lectures on drama, which by the time of the twelfth and final issue included topics such as the religious dimensions of the ancient Greek stage, the character of Spanish poetry, Italian theatre, and an extensive section on Shakespeare. Such pan-European perspectives and interest in cross-cultural translation on the part of Kleist, Müller, de Staël, and the Schlegels anticipate aspects of what Goethe later was to call 'Weltliteratur', despite the marked reserve that he showed to all of them at this stage in his career.[13]

If Kleist had been hoping with this first issue of *Phöbus* to win the good graces of Goethe, who in the meantime had agreed to stage another of Kleist's dramas *Der zerbrochne Krug* (The Broken Pitcher, 1808) in Weimar, he was sorely mistaken in his choice

[13] For a discussion of the personal, political, and aesthetic reasons behind Goethe's refusal to meet with Mme de Staël and her entourage in Dresden, see Gabriele Bersier, 'Kulturbruch und transkulturelles Einvernehmen: Goethes deutscher Brief an Madame de Staël in Dresden', *Goethe-Jahrbuch*, 128 (2011), 217–27.

for the opening piece, namely the organic fragment of his drama *Penthesilea*. In his letter to Kleist from 1 February 1808 in response to the receipt of this first issue, Goethe freely confessed his difficulties in coming to terms with Kleist's protagonist, which is not at all surprising once one calls to mind Kleist's highly idiosyncratic modifications to Greek mythology. Whereas post-Homeric epics and novels had depicted the death of the Amazonian queen Penthesilea at the hands of Achilles, Kleist's fragment ends with a scene in which the high priestess of the goddess Diana likens Penthesilea not only to a Maenad, but also to a mad dog, after the Amazonian queen has rushed off, foaming at the mouth, with a pack of actual hunting dogs in search of what she describes as the most beautiful prey that ever walked the earth, i.e. Achilles.[14] In fact, Goethe's diplomatically expressed reservations were mild in comparison with the first reviews of the play in its complete form, which maintained that Kleist's tragedy does not induce pity and fear in its readers, but rather revulsion and disgust. In the scholarly literature dealing with *Penthesilea*, it has become a commonplace to see in this drama a repudiation of the measured self-control and belief in the transformative powers of humane behaviour epitomized in Goethe's *Iphigenie auf Tauris* (Iphigenia at Tauris, 1787).[15] When one considers, however, that Kleist sent the first issue of *Phöbus* to Goethe along with a letter in which he speaks of appearing before his revered contemporary upon the 'Knieen meines Herzens' (knees of my heart), an openly antagonistic approach to *Iphigenie auf Tauris* seems unlikely. The echoes of passages from Goethe's drama within the full version of *Penthesilea* suggest rather that Kleist made use of *Iphigenie* as a type of palimpsest which he then rewrote with the same kind of artistic freedom that Goethe did in his reworking of Euripides' *Iphigenia among the Taurians*—this time with the aim of constructing a 'Tragödie' (tragedy) rather than a 'Schauspiel' (play), as had been the case with Goethe's drama. Tragedy, for Kleist, seemed the appropriate form for the confluence of love and violence in his reworking of this saga from the Trojan War, where 'Küsse' (kisses), by the end of the completed play, rhyme with 'Bisse' (bites) and where Penthesilea loves Achilles so much that she literally eats him.[16] Kleist's fears that with *Penthesilea* he had written a play whose staging would have to wait for the future proved all too true, but its increasing fascination among critics and stage directors alike suggest that he, not Goethe, had judged this play correctly.[17]

[14] Heinrich von Kleist and Adam H. Müller (eds), *Phöbus* (Repr. of the 1808–9 original, with an afterword and commentary by Helmut Sembdner, Stuttgart: Cotta, 1961), 32–3 [34–5]. See also Heinrich von Kleist, *Sämtliche Werke und Briefe*, ed. Ilse-Marie Barth, Klaus Müller-Salget, Walter Müller-Seidel, and Hinrich C. Seeba (Frankfurt/Main: Deutscher Klassiker Verlag, 1987), ii. 140–1.

[15] Cf. Walter Müller-Seidel, '*Penthesilea* im Kontext der deutschen Klassik', in Walter Hinderer (ed.), *Kleists Dramen: Neue Interpretationen* (Stuttgart: Reclam, 1981), 144–71, here 163, and Helga Gallas, 'Antikerezeption bei Goethe und Kleist: Penthesilea—eine Anti-Iphigenie?', in Linda Dietrick and David G. John (eds), *Momentum dramaticum: Festschrift für Eckehard Catholy* (Waterloo, Ont.: University of Waterloo Press, 1990), 209–20.

[16] Kleist, *Sämtliche Werke*, ii. 254.

[17] For Hinrich Seeba's extensive survey of the reception of Kleist's drama on the page and the stage, see 'Wirkung' and 'Aufführungen' in *Sämtliche Werke*, ii. 693–749.

Nowadays, *Phöbus* has as its chief claim to enduring fame the first complete publication of *Die Marquise von O …* as well the partial publication of other works by Kleist such as *Penthesilea, Der zerbrochne Krug, Robert Guiskard, Michael Kohlhaas*, and *Das Käthchen von Heilbronn*. The fact, however, that so many works by Kleist and Adam Müller appeared in their journal betrays the fact that they had been unsuccessful in securing the collaboration of writers like Goethe, Wieland, Jean Paul, Friedrich Schlegel, and Ludwig Tieck, as they had been hoping. In part this was due to Goethe's break with Kleist after the unsuccessful staging of *Der zerbrochne Krug* in Weimar and Kleist's less than flattering reference to Goethe's optical studies in the epigram entitled 'Herr von Göthe' from the combined April/May issue of 1808: 'Siehe, das nenn' ich doch würdig, fürwahr, sich im Alter beschäftigen! | Er zerlegt jetzt den Strahl, den seine Jugend sonst warf' (See, I call that worthy, for sure, to occupy oneself in old age! | He now dissects the beam that his youth once cast).[18] But another factor leading to the speedy demise of both *Phöbus* and also Arnim's *Zeitung für Einsiedler* was the proliferation of other periodicals likewise seeking the work of famous authors at a time when the publishing industry was barely recovering from the after effects of the Napoleonic campaigns against Austria and Prussia. Still, the April/May 1808 issue of *Phöbus* contained an excerpt from Gotthilf Heinrich Schubert's immensely successful Dresden lectures soon to be published under the title *Ansichten von der Nachtseite der Naturwissenschaft* (Views of the Night Side of Natural Science, 1808), namely Schubert's account of the body of a Swedish miner preserved underground in its youthful beauty that E. T. A. Hoffmann and later Hugo von Hofmannsthal were to make use of for their retelling of *Die Bergwerke zu Falun* (The Mines of Falun).[19] And in the final double issue of *Phöbus*, which appeared in February 1809, the artist Ferdinand Hartmann published an essay that defended 'Das Kreuz im Gebirge' (The Cross in the Mountains, 1808), the oil painting of his friend Caspar David Friedrich, and its use of nature iconography to express Christian religiosity against the objections of the neoclassic art critic Friedrich Wilhelm Basilius von Ramdohr.[20] It is the presence of such themes in *Phöbus* and the underlying network of writers, artists, and scholars that has led Theodore Ziolkowski to argue persuasively that between 1805 and 1809 one can speak of a genuine Dresden Romanticism, and not just 'Romanticism in Dresden', as with the early Romantics' stay there in the summer of 1798 or E. T. A. Hoffmann's Dresden sojourn in 1813.[21]

When war broke out again between France and Austria in April 1809, Kleist left Dresden for Vienna, visiting the battlefield at Aspern, where Archduke Karl's forces had won a victory over Napoleon's army, and offering his services as a propagandist. The

[18] Kleist, *Phöbus*, 4/5, 69 [241].

[19] Gotthilf Heinrich Schubert, 'Fragmente aus einer Vorlesung', *Phöbus*, 4/5 (1808), 67–8 [239–40].

[20] Ferdinand Hartmann, 'Über Kunstausstellungen und Kunstkritik' (On Art Exhibitions and Art Criticism), in *Phöbus*, 11/12 (1809), 57–71 [573–87]. For a discussion of Friedrich's painting, Ramdohr's criticism, and also of Philipp Otto Runge's four engravings on 'Die Tageszeiten' (Times of Day, 1805) that were the subject of lectures by Görres in Heidelberg in 1807, see Beate Allert, 'Romanticism and the Visual Arts', in Mahoney, *Literature*, 273–306, especially 284–90.

[21] Theodore Ziolkowski, *Dresdner Romantik: Politik und Harmonie* (Heidelberg: Winter, 2010).

ensuing Austrian defeat at Wagram, however, eliminated the possibility for the publication of works like his *Hermannschlacht* (Arminius' Battle), completed in Dresden in the latter part of 1808, whose recounting of the crushing defeat inflicted upon the Romans and their German allies in 9 CE at the Battle of the Teutoburger Forest was a thinly disguised polemic calling for a united German rebellion against Napoleon and the Confederation of the Rhine. Kleist returned to Berlin in November 1809, now hoping to play a role in the Prussian Reform Movement, which received renewed impetus following the royal family's own return to the capital later that December.[22] Here he encountered not only Brentano and Arnim, but also Joseph von Eichendorff, who had accepted an invitation from Loeben to join him in Berlin, where Eichendorff remained until March 1810 before travelling to Vienna via his native Silesia. The satirical depiction of an 'ästhetische Teegesellschaft' (aesthetic tea gathering) in book 2, chapter 12, of *Ahnung und Gegenwart*, where a would-be poet reads 'einen Haufen Sonette mit einer Art von priesterlicher Feyerlichkeit' (a load of sonnets with a type of priestly solemnity) illustrates Eichendorff's growing scepticism with regards to Loeben's aestheticism, but also a good dose of self-criticism; when Graf (Count) Friedrich, the hero of the novel, says plainly 'Ihre Gedichte gefallen mir ganz und ganz nicht' (your poems do not please me in the slightest), Eichendorff's own Novalicizing is meant as well.[23] By way of contrast, Friedrich's words of praise at this same gathering for Achim von Arnim's novel *Armut, Reichtum, Schuld und Buße der Gräfin Dolores* (Poverty, Riches, Guilt and Penance of Countess Dolores, 1810), on which Arnim was working when Eichendorff first came into closer contact with him, testify to the importance of a poetry that deals with real contemporary problems and that wants to make a concrete contribution to the moral betterment of society.[24] In that regard, Arnim and Brentano both wrote texts to cantatas giving voice to popular sorrow at the untimely death of Queen Luise of Prussia in July 1810. Similarly, they wrote poems commemorating the opening of the University of Berlin in October 1810—in whose creation figures like Schleiermacher and Fichte played important roles and who like Wilhelm von Humboldt, its founder, used their experiences with the University of Jena and/or Jena Romanticism in promoting the concept of a university whose guiding principle would be academic freedom rather than narrowly defined state interests. Arnim and Brentano also contributed poems and articles to the *Berliner Abendblätter* (Berlin Evening Pages), the daily newspaper founded by Kleist and Adam Müller in October 1810, including the discussion of Caspar David

[22] For a discussion of the significance of Kleist's dramas *Die Hermannschlacht* and *Prinz Friedrich von Homburg*—both first publ. in 1821, ten years after Kleist's death—in the context of their intended contemporary effect and subsequent reception, see the 'Introduction', to Mahoney, *Literature*, 12–18.

[23] Joseph von Eichendorff, *Ahnung und Gegenwart*, ed. Gerhart Hoffmeister (Stuttgart: Reclam, 1984), 142 and 153.

[24] For a discussion of Arnim's defence of marriage as an institution and advocacy of a moral renewal of society, which represents a continuation of the German Enlightenment's use of morality as social criticism, see Klaus Peter, *'Gräfin Dolores'*, in Paul Michael Lützeler (ed.), *Romane der deutschen Romantik: Neue Interpretationen* (Stuttgart: Reclam, 1981), 240–63.

Friedrich's landscape painting 'Der Mönch am Meer'.[25] Although initially enjoying tremendous popularity, the *Abendblätter* proved to be another failure, owing to restrictions imposed by censors and the Prussian government, and ceased publication in March 1811.[26]

In one further attempt to combine commercial success with an impact on public opinion, in 1810 and 1811 Kleist also published two collections of his stories, including his longest and arguably greatest tale *Michael Kohlhaas*. In *Phöbus*, Kleist had interrupted his account of a sixteenth-century horse dealer seeking the return of unjustly confiscated horses at the point where Kohlhaas decides to take justice into his own hands when his quest is repeatedly frustrated by bureaucratic corruption and influence peddling in both Saxony and Prussia. As the story progressed in its 1810 publication, Kohlhaas first assails a castle, then a city, next the state of Saxony, until finally both Prussia and the Holy Roman Empire are drawn into legal battles. As in *Die Hermannschlacht*, Kleist provided plot details susceptible to contemporary political application.[27] Like his counterpart in Saxony, the Prince Elector of Brandenburg is surrounded by corrupt servants, but instead of making them his friends and confidants, he dismisses them and appoints more honest officials in their stead; and by laying charges against Kohlhaas's opponent, the Junker of Tronka, at the Imperial Court, he brings to a head the question of whether there is such a thing as a just society. Both electors bring charges before the Emperor in Vienna, and in a way both are successful, for the Emperor orders full reparation accorded to Kohlhaas for the crimes committed against him at the Tronkenburg, but at the same time condemns him to death because of his violation of the Imperial Peace. In the conclusion to his tale Kleist made use of new principles of contractualism and legal recognition derived in part from his discussions with Adam Müller in 1808 and 1809: 'This is communicated in the final scene of "Michael Kohlhaas", where the dispensing of justice to Kohlhaas is not just medieval spectacle, a scene of cautionary violence in the manner of the Roman or Spanish Inquisition, but also a scene where the right to justice—in this case the victorious outcome of Kohlhaas's dispute with the

[25] As with his books on Heidelberg and Dresden, Theodore Ziolkowski provides an informative and engagingly written cultural history of a city and its writers in *Berlin: Aufstieg einer Kulturmetropole um 1810* (Stuttgart: Klett-Cotta, 1802). For a discussion of the interaction between politics and literature in Prussia between 1807 to 1813 that also includes figures such as Ernst Moritz Arndt, Theodor Körner, and Friedrich Ludwig Jahn, see Otto W. Johnston, *The Myth of a Nation: Literature and Politics in Prussia under Napoleon* (Columbia, SC: Camden House, 1989).

[26] For an extensive discussion of satirical passages in the *Abendblätter* directed against friend and foe alike, see Wolfgang Wittkowski, 'Ein neuer Fund zu Kleists ironischer Fehde mit Iffland, Hardenberg und Müller in den *Berliner Abendblättern*', in Wolfgang Wittkowski, *Kleist: Wert-Ethik, Wahrheit, Widerstand und Wieder-Auf-Er-Stehung* (Frankfurt/Main: Peter Lang, 2013), 259–98.

[27] For a discussion of Kleist's *Michael Kohlhaas* as a critique of the Prussia of his own day see Wolfgang Wittkowski, 'Is Kleist's Michael Kohlhaas a Terrorist? Luther, Prusian Law Reforms, and the Accountability of Government', *Historical Reflections/Réflexions Historiques*, 26 (2000), 471–86. For an intriguing reading of Kleist's tale in light of Hannah Arendt's late work *On Violence*, see Jeff Champlin, 'Reading Terrorism in Kleist: The Violence and Mandates of *Michael Kohlhaas*', *German Quarterly*, 85 (2012), 439–54.

Junker—can be celebrated.'[28] Unlike his literary figure, Kleist enjoyed no such triumphant exit from this world; impoverished and discouraged, and feeling ever more isolated as one friend after another left Berlin, he committed suicide on 21 November 1811. It was left for future generations to see in Kleist a genius scarcely equalled by his older contemporaries Goethe and Schiller.

After his own unsuccessful attempt to secure a position at the newly founded University of Berlin and then the failure of the *Berliner Abendblätter* Adam Müller left for Vienna in May 1811, where this convert to Catholicism soon found government employment and re-established contact with the principal figure of later German Romanticism, namely Friedrich Schlegel. During the course of his Cologne researches into the medieval empire, Schlegel had become convinced that its heritage had been kept alive in the Austria of his own day; by way of contrast, he deemed both Prussia and the Napoleonic state that he had encountered during his various stays in Berlin and Paris between 1796 and 1804 as too modern in their break with tradition.[29] With great expectations he set out for Vienna in the summer of 1808, where earlier that year his brother August Wilhelm had delivered his lectures on the *Geschichte der dramatischen Kunst und Literatur* (History of Dramatic Literature and Art) with great success. Through his brother's help and that of Mme de Staël, the younger Schlegel soon made the acquaintance of the Emperor, Metternich, and other members of the Austrian high nobility. Not only was his status as archivist assured; in the spring of 1809 he was allotted a post on the field staff of the Archduke Karl in his campaign against the French. During this time Schlegel established and edited an army paper, the *Österreichische Zeitung*, which after the cessation of hostilities became in 1810 the *Österreichischer Beobachter* (Austrian Reporter), the official organ of the Austrian government until Metternich's deposition in 1848. Until 1810 there had existed no daily newspaper of any importance in Austria, the highly unimaginative Emperor Franz I regarding any so 'popular' a medium with deep suspicion. Metternich, however, his newly appointed Foreign Minister, had observed during his years of diplomatic apprenticeship in Paris the effective use made of the press by Napoleon, and determined to sway public opinion towards his own purposes with the help of the *Österreichischer Beobachter*. It was at this point that Schlegel, as editor of the paper during its first year of existence, began a long period of personal and professional association with Metternich marked at least as much by differences as by similarities.

In their polemics against Napoleon, Romantics like Kleist, Müller, and Friedrich Schlegel regarded his reorganization of German territory via the Confederation of the Rhine as an assault on the integrity of the nation's character. Such an attitude can be discerned in Kleist's *Hermannschlacht*, for example, and in Eichendorff's depiction of the Tyrolean revolts of 1809 in book 3 of *Ahnung und Gegenwart*, a novel written during

[28] See Tim Mehigan, 'Heinrich von Kleist's Concept of Law, with Special Reference to "Michael Kohlhaas"', in *Heinrich von Kleist: Writing after Kant* (Rochester, NY: Camden House, 2011), 78–9.

[29] Cf. Klaus Behrens, *Friedrich Schlegels Geschichtsphilosophie (1794–1808): Ein Beitrag zur politischen Romantik* (Tübingen: Niemeyer, 1984), 217–28.

a period of close association with Friedrich and Dorothea Schlegel, but only published after the end of the Napoleonic Wars, when a truly national outbreak against French rule had evinced itself during the so-called 'Befreiungskriege' of 1813 and 1814. This, however, was not the perspective of Metternich, the principal architect of the Quadruple Alliance of Austria, Prussia, Russia, and England against Napoleon. Observing that popular enthusiasm alone had not been enough to defeat the French in 1809, he had patiently and soberly forged an alliance of states, not nations, designed to restore a conservative social order to war-ravaged Europe. Regarding the trend towards the unification of states along linguistic lines and under constitutional rule as a grave threat to the subtle but fraying fabric of the Austrian Empire, Metternich resolved to define not only the conduct of the war but also the terms of the peace to conform with Austria's own internal interests.

During the years of the Congress of Vienna, Friedrich Schlegel, acting in the service of Metternich, drew up drafts of the constitution for the 'Deutscher Bund' (German Confederation) and also published articles in the leading North German newspapers propagating the Austrian perspective. Metternich demonstrated his satisfaction with Schlegel's service by awarding him a post within the Austrian delegation to the Bundestag (Diet) in Frankfurt, where he served from 1815 to 1818. Doubtless Schlegel saw in this institution a renewal of the supranational association of states that had existed during the Middle Ages and early modern period under the aegis of the Habsburgs. As George S. Williamson observes: 'there remained something "ideal" about Schlegel's conception of Germany. Moreover, insofar as the Reich was envisioned as having been part of a broader federation of states, this was a vision of Germany *in* Europe.'[30] Metternich's motives were neither so lofty nor grandiose: he aimed simply for a position of Austrian predominance in central Europe by means of the fragmentation of the German principalities and the frustration of national unity. Similar principles lay behind his reaction to Tsar Alexander's proposal of a Holy Alliance in 1815: 'But however Metternich might ridicule this effort and even if he ascribed it to the fact that the Tsar's mind was affected, it represented to the careful calculator of Vienna not a religious but a political document of the first magnitude.'[31] Under his guidance the Holy Alliance became an instrument not of renewal and fundamental reform but of stability and repression. Religious institutions themselves had significance for Metternich only in so far as they accustomed the common people to obey authority and keep their minds distracted from affairs of state.

Not so Friedrich Schlegel. Following dismissal from his post in September of 1818, in large part due to his zealous advocacy of ultramontane Catholicism, Schlegel pursued plans for the publication of a new periodical, the *Concordia*, intending it as an instrument of spiritual reconciliation in Germany. In the meantime, the March 1819

[30] George S. Williamson, 'Varieties of Conservatism in the Restoration Era: Friedrich Schlegel and August von Kotzebue', in Klaus Ries (ed.), *Romantik und Revolution: Zum politischen Reformpotential einer unpolitischen Bewegung* (Heidelberg: Winter, 2012), 199–200.

[31] Henry Kissinger, *A World Restored: Metternich, Castleragh, and the Problems of Peace 1812–22* (Cambridge: Cambridge University Press, 1957), 188.

assassination of August von Kotzebue, the German writer and correspondent for the Tsar, had led to the initiation of the so-called Karlsbad Decrees—co-authored by Adam Müller and Friedrich Gentz—that imposed strict censorship on the press and close supervision of the universities. Like Joseph Görres, whose condemnation of censorship and repression in *Kotzebue und was ihn gemordet* (Kotzebue and What Killed Him, 1819) and *Teutschland und die Revolution* (Germany and the Revolution, 1819) resulted in his flight to Strasbourg in order to escape arrest by Prussian authorities, Schlegel was convinced that such measures would fan the flames of rebellion rather than quell them. Indeed, he saw a potential for revolution existing not only in Germany, but also in France, Italy, Spain, and throughout the length and breadth of Europe. And so he devoted the entire first issue of *Concordia* to an instalment of his three-part treatise *Signatur des Zeitalters* (Sign of the Times, 1820–3), in which he attempted not only to analyse the fundamental illnesses of his age but also to propose a remedy at hand against them. As a counterbalance to the deep-laid inorganic spirit of absolutism affecting not only advocates of liberalism but also the more rabid monarchists, Schlegel praised what he termed 'das lebendig Positive' (the living Positive), which not surprisingly bore a striking resemblance to his conception of Austria: it is based on historical institutions and not on the spun-out theories and empty abstractions of individuals, and it respects the natural building blocks of society such as the family, the church, cities, principalities, and the various estates and trades.[32]

If Schlegel had intended the *Concordia* as a whole and his essay in particular to act as a balm for troubled Germany, his efforts fell far short of their goal. The list of Schlegel's detractors now included his brother August Wilhelm, who looked with deep disapproval upon Friedrich's rejection of the liberal religious and political ideals of their youth. More crushing, though, than his brother's opposition was the verdict pronounced on the *Concordia* by Metternich, who had no use at all for Schlegel's treatise on the virtues of a Christian state nor for Adam Müller's call for the restitution of lands to the Catholic Church in the latter's contribution to Schlegel's journal, namely 'Die innere Staatshaushaltung; systematisch dargestellt auf theologischer Grundlage' (The Inner Economy of State; Systematically Represented upon a Theological Foundation, 1820). Not only that: Metternich feared that a passage in Müller's essay condemning private property as being usurpation and robbery could even serve to fan the flames of rebellion.[33] Müller's own later career ran a course much similar to Schlegel's. Installed after 1815 as a diplomat and publicist in the city of Leipzig, he so antagonized the Prussian and North German governments by his aggressive Catholicism and insistent advocacy of his own theories on trade and duty payments that in 1827 Metternich finally was obliged to recall him from Austrian service. Müller and Schlegel died within one week of each

[32] Friedrich Schlegel, *Signatur des Zeitalters*, in *Kritische Friedrich-Schlegel Ausgabe*, ed. Ernst Behler (Paderborn: Schöningh, 1958ff.), vii. 522–5.

[33] Cf. the excerpts of the letter of 8 Oct. 1820 from Gentz to Müller that Ernst Behler provides in the afterword to his reprint edn of *Concordia* (Darmstadt: Wissenschaftliche Buchgesellschaft, 1967), 42*; for the passage in question from Müller's essay, see the boldface passage on p. 110 of *Concordia*.

other in January 1829; by the time of their deaths they had laid so much weight on organized religion as the Archimedean point for social reform that they had lifted themselves out of touch with the political and social realities around them. As Klaus Peter has observed with regard not only to Müller and Schlegel, but also Joseph Görres and Franz von Baader, 'one might say that political Romanticism stood in the way of its own goals. It was tragic that morality, in whose name Romanticism had fought, was not defined in connection with politics, but rather in opposition to it.'[34]

From its outset, German Romanticism had offered alternative visions for a Europe shaken by revolutionary developments and radical restructurings in politics, science, philosophy, economics, and organized religion. By the years after 1815, it was becoming evident that such visions had become less a solution than an expression of individual and social crises. Late Romantic writers like E. T. A. Hoffmann and Adelbert von Chamisso achieved popular success in cities like Berlin, to be sure, but also experienced the stress of producing for a marketplace where literature had become an article for consumption, not an instrument for changing the world, as it still had been for Kleist only a few years earlier. It would be intriguing to follow the efforts of these writers, as well as Romantics like Arnim, Brentano, and Eichendorff, to adapt their literary production to such changing developments. But this must be the topic for another chapter.

Further Reading

Johnston, Otto W., *The Myth of a Nation: Literature and Politics in Prussia under Napoleon* (Columbia, SC: Camden House, 1989).

Mahoney, Dennis F. (ed.), *The Literature of German Romanticism* (Rochester, NY: Camden House, 2004).

Strack, Friedrich (ed.), *200 Jahre Heidelberger Romantik* (Berlin and Heidelberg: Springer, 2008).

Vanden Heuvel, Jon, *A German Life in the Age of Revolution: Joseph Görres, 1776–1848* (Washington, DC: Catholic University of America Press, 2001).

Ziolkowski, Theodore, *Berlin: Aufstieg einer Kulturmetropole um 1810* (Stuttgart: Klett-Cotta, 1802).

Ziolkowski, Theodore, *Heidelberger Romantik: Mythos und Symbol* (Heidelberg: Winter, 2009).

Ziolkowski, Theodore, *Dresdner Romantik: Politik und Harmonie* (Heidelberg: Winter, 2010).

[34] Klaus Peter, 'Historical and Moral Imperatives: The Contradictions of Political Romanticism', in Mahoney, *Literature*, 204.

Hungarian

CHAPTER 19

HUNGARIAN ROMANTICISM

Reimagining (Literary) History

RICHARD ACZEL

> The great national poet of Hungarian romanticism differs from the conventional type of the patriotic poet, relatively uniform among all peoples, and this very difference makes him a great European poet. The Hungarian poet, Mihály Vörösmarty, lives out his patriotism in the name of humanity in general, infusing with feverish passion his consciousness of the tragic situation of the nation in the 'home of peoples', to which he cries out, which doesn't hear him and which, even at his graveside, looks on in indifference. This sense of tragic fate, in this special extreme instance, leads the Hungarian poet to face problems of European nationalism that are still pressing, if not even more pressing, today. The poet doesn't cease to be a poet of the East, even though his goals are thoroughly western.[1]

There is something tortured about the very urgency of these words by the twentieth-century Hungarian poet Mihály Babits, writing in the journal *Nyugat* (West) in 1927. The title of the journal is itself symptomatic of the historical debate—still raging in Hungary today—in which Babits attempts to situate Hungarian Romanticism. *Nyugat* was founded in 1908 to explore and promote the interconnectedness of Hungarian and West European culture. The journal and the project for which it stood was attacked by its critics from the start as 'un-Hungarian'. In fact, *Nyugat*, which ran for thirty-three years (until Babits's death in 1941), occupied a middle position in a polemic running from the eighteenth century to the present day between—only marginally to caricature the extremes—a cosmopolitanism dismissive of local provincialism and a nationalism that, at its most xenophobic, rejects this cosmopolitanism through the blinkers of anti-Semitism. At the time Babits wrote these words about Hungarian Romanticism, the political climate was

[1] Mihály Babits, 'Tanulmány a magyar irodalomról' (An Essay on Hungarian Literature), in Mihály Babits, *Esszék, Tanulmányok II* (Budapest: Szépirodalmi Könyvkiadó, 1978), 191. All trs. are my own, unless otherwise indicated.

particularly volatile. After the First World War, with the Treaty of Trianon (1920), Hungary had lost two-thirds of her 'historical' territory to the successor states. Post-Trianon revisionism affected not only Hungarian foreign policy, but also national historiography. In perhaps the most influential attempt to reformulate Hungarian cultural history in the light of the perceived national tragedy of Trianon, *Három nemzedék* (Three Generations, 1920), Gyula Szekfű opposed the liberal reading of the nineteenth-century 'Age of Reform' with a conservative, 'Christian-national' characterization of Hungarian Romanticism. Szekfű singles out Ferenc Kölcsey's poem 'Himnusz' (Hymn)—which, set to music by Ferenc Erkel in 1844, became and remains the Hungarian national anthem—as the 'most Hungarian product' of this Romanticism. According to Szekfű:

> In this poem there is no trace of classical reminiscence and foreign romanticism; these two supports have entirely disappeared, like the scaffolding when the proud edifice is complete. Because in 'Himnusz' for the first time, and at the highest level of perfection, the new imagination shows itself: a *Hungarian* romantic conception of history and nation, which … is Christian and national, that is to say, here, in our homeland, on Hungarian soil: Christian and Hungarian.[2]

The first book-length study of Hungarian Romanticism to appear in the twentieth century, *A magyar romantika* (1930), was written by Szekfű's disciple, Gyula Farkas, who states in the opening pages:

> [The] period of literary and national synthesis is what we term 'Hungarian romanticism'. The concept of romanticism is riddled with foreign elements. Hungarian romanticism, however, has very little to do with German or French romanticism. Here romanticism is understood as a process issuing from the depths of the national essence, which led to the wholesale renewal of national life and in so doing made use of the only means available to the national spirit for self-expression: literature. Literary romanticism expired at the moment when the national role of literature was taken over by politics.[3]

[2] Gyula Szekfű, *Három Nemzedék és ami utána következik* (Budapest: ÁVK-Maecenas, 1989), 60. Like many others, Szekfű saw Trianon as punishment for the short-lived communist Republic of Councils lead by Béla Kun, making a direct link between the 'catastrophe of the [1919] revolution' and the internationalism of 'its Jewish bolshevik leaders' (434)—a link which would be made again in connection with the communist dictatorship after the Second World War. In an expanded edn of *Three Generations* published in 1934, Szekfű went so far as to suggest that Jewish influence in urban culture could be radically diminished if only the latest wave of Jewish immigrants from the East would 'follow the logical consequences' of their own (Zionistic) national solidarity and leave the country. 'Therewith,' he added, 'the relationship between the sincerely Hungarianized, Hungarian-cultured Jewry and the Hungarians would be burden-free and could come closer to the final settlement expected in a Christian state' (444).

[3] Cited from the German tr., *Die ungarische Romantik* (Berlin: Walter de Gruyter & Co., 1931), 8. Farkas was also the author of a book on Jewish assimilation and integration, the German tr. of which—*Der Freiheitskampf des ungarischen Geistes, 1867–1914* (The Hungarian Spirit's Struggle for Freedom, 1867–1914)—was undoubtedly exploited by the Nazi propaganda machine. It should be added that the positions of both Farkas and Szekfű are considerably more complex than selective quotation might suggest.

The basic tenets of Farkas's book—that Hungarian Romanticism was a project of national renewal grounded in the celebration (or reinvention) of the national past and the rediscovery of folk poetry—have proved remarkably influential and durable in Hungarian literary historiography, even if the rhetoric has not always been so belligerent. I begin this chapter with the charged rhetoric of the interwar period to highlight from the outset the political vicissitudes involved in the definition of literary terms and movements within a national polemic that continues to frame Hungary's political life and highly politicized literary culture. Claims of the kind that 'Romanticism in its first phase meant the birth or revival of a national consciousness'[4] or 'the special relationship with folk poetry can be regarded as the most significant mark of Romanticism',[5] have different political resonances when made in the context of Percy's *Reliques*, the brother Grimm's *Märchen*, and the emergence of the popular-national tradition in Hungarian literature in the second decade of the nineteenth century.

To understand these resonances and their relationship to the concept of Hungarian Romanticism, it will be useful briefly to rehearse the traditional national narrative of the birth of modern Hungarian literature at the end of the eighteenth century. In the middle of the nineteenth century, the literary historian Ferenc Toldy traced the origins of Hungarian literary modernity back to the year 1772, which saw the publication of four important works by György Bessenyei, a member of Maria Theresa's Noble Hungarian Bodyguard set up in 1760, and this date has been broadly accepted ever since as a working point of departure. Linked to this periodization is a conventional perception of modern Hungarian literature as a belated child of the Enlightenment. As Bessenyei and his fellow Hungarian guardsmen in Vienna came into contact with the ideas of the *philosophes* and tried to translate them into Hungarian, they were forced to realize that the national language was in dire need of reform. The attempt to create a unified and modern Hungarian literary idiom became a key preoccupation of Bessenyei's generation and the generation that followed, led by the language reformer, translator, and 'literary dictator', Ferenc Kazinczy. The essentially enlightened (insofar as rationalistic) decision of Maria Theresa's successor, Joseph II, to make German the sole language of the Habsburg Empire (1784), inevitably came as a blow to the new Hungarian literati, qualifying their enthusiasm for enlightened universalism and making them more nationally defensive. Finding support for their project in the growing cultural relativism of Rousseau and the equivocal inspiration of Herder—who not only promoted ideas of national character, but also prophesied the eventual disappearance of the Hungarians from the map of Europe[6]—the newly born Hungarian literature began to look to its national past and popular traditions for the foundations of its identity. The result was the birth of the

[4] Tibor Klaniczay (ed.), *A History of Hungarian Literature* (Budapest: Akadémiai Kiadó, 1984), 213.

[5] István Sőtér, *The Dilemma of Literary Science* (Budapest: Akadémiai Kiadó, 1973), 179.

[6] In vol. 4 of the *Ideen zu einer Philosophie der Geschichte der Menschheit*, Herder had written: 'die Ungarn oder Madscharen ... sind ... jetzt unter Slawen, Deutschen, Wlachen und andern Völkern der geringere Teil der Landeseinwohner und nach Jahrhunderten wird man vielleicht ihre Sprache kaum finden'. Johann Gottfried Herder, *Werke*, ed. B. Suphan, xiv (Berlin: Weidmann, 1909), 269.

national historical epic, championed by the likes of Mihály Vörösmarty and a new lyric poetry based on the language of folksong which was to reach its heights in the poetry of Sándor Petőfi and, later, János Arany. These, so the story went, were the major representatives of Hungarian Romanticism, and their central theorist was Ferenc Kölcsey, the author of 'Himnusz', whose most influential prose work, *Nemzeti Hagyományok* (National Traditions, 1826), was predominantly drawn from the writings of Herder. Hungarian Romanticism, national, patriotic, and *völkisch*, was the direct product of the critical reaction to the Enlightenment which gave modern Hungarian literature its birth.

From the perspective of an attempt to understand Hungarian Romanticism, there are two ways in which this narrative seems to oversimplify. First, a notion of Romanticism that altogether bypasses questions of the imagination, the approach to nature, the irrational, and the post-Kantian dilemma of the experiencing subject, seems to run the risk of emptying the term of any fruitful comparative basis. I shall return to these problems of definition later in this chapter. Secondly, the cultural moment identified by Toldy and his followers to mark the birth of Hungarian literature is, in its relation to Hungarian Romanticism in its emergent forms, considerably richer than the notion of a belated enlightenment might suggest.

The case of Bessenyei is revealing here. Far from being the rather ponderous spokesperson for enlightened values he is often taken to be, much of his work reflects the crisis of these values rather than their inadequate articulation. One of the texts Bessenyei published in 1772 was *Az embernek próbája* (The Trial of Man), an ideologically charged misreading of Alexander Pope's classic compendium of enlightened aphorisms, *An Essay on Man*. The essential discontinuity between the two works is already anticipated by Bessenyei's title: for, in sharp contrast to the pragmatic optimism of Pope, Bessenyei will go on to describe human existence as an ultimately hopeless 'trial' *(próba)*, and closes with the distinctly Counter-Enlightenment claim that: 'only ignorance buzzes in the heads of men'.[7] Indeed Bessenyei's whole career seems to characterize in microcosm the Hungarian encounter with, and relatively rapid retreat from, the cosmopolitanism and rationalism of the West European Enlightenment. Initially attracted by the ratio-empiricism of Voltaire, Bessenyei becomes increasingly preoccupied with questions of national language, identity, and specificity, and ends his days, as the 'hermit of Bihar', deeply suspicious of the value of enlightened thought. As Kirakedes, Bessenyei's 'noble savage' in his last major literary work, *Tarimenes utazása* (The Travels of Tarimenes, 1804), says to Trezeni (with obvious echoes of Maria Theresa), the ruler of an 'enlightened' state: 'It is so true that the more educated and wise a man is the less cheerful his life; and the less reason he possesses, the more pleasures he will live amongst.'[8]

It is not surprising that literary works produced in the period 1772–95 should look beyond the Enlightement and reflect the crisis of its assumptions. By the end of the eighteenth century most of the important work of the Enlightenment had already been

[7] György Bessenyei, *Az embernek próbája*, ed. István Harsányi (Budapest: Franklin Társulat, 1912), 100.

[8] Bessenyei, *Prózai munkák* (Budapest: Akadémiai Kiadó, 1986), 541.

completed, and Kant's famous phrasing of the question 'Was ist Aufklärung?' in 1784 is already at least partly retrospective. The Rousseau of *Emile* and *Les Confessions* is no longer the confident *philosophe* of the first and second Discourses, and the classical ideals of Pope and Voltaire were being displaced as literary models by 'sentimental' works like Richardson's *Pamela*, Young's *Night Thoughts*, and Goethe's *Die Leiden des jungen Werthers*. The shift of focus from the head to the heart, from reason to feeling—reflected in Rousseau's famous statement from the *Lettres morales*: 'Exister pour nous c'est sentir; et notre sensibilité est incontestablement antérieure à notre raison meme'[9]—is echoed in Bessenyei's appendix to the 1772 edition of *The Trial of Man*: 'It seems as if the heart is nature's first born.'[10]

In addition to this, the last third of the eighteenth century witnessed a growing recognition of the importance of national character and traditions, which also finds expression in Rousseau's later writings, such as his *Considérations sur le gouvernement de Pologne* (1770–1). Thus it is the crisis of the Enlightenment, rather than the Age of Reason itself, which forms the cultural-historical context in which Hungarian literature comes of age as a modern, self-conscious discourse. Indeed, far from seeking belatedly to rehearse the old arguments of the Enlightenment, the aspirations of the Hungarian *literati* prove to be remarkably in tune with the preoccupations of the new moment.

The character of a group of more well-known works of art to come out of Hungary in 1772 will help us further to articulate the relationship between this new moment and the aspirations of Romanticism. Haydn's 45th Symphony, the 'Farewell' in the then still surprising key of F sharp minor, was composed, as anecdote has it, to prompt Prince Esterhazy to return with his musicians from Esterháza to Eisentadt. Representing the apogee of the composer's 'Sturm und Drang' period, Haydn's Farewell Symphony, like the String Quartets op. 20 and the Piano Sonata in C Minor Hob. 20 composed in the same year, are characteristic of the cultural context in which modern Hungarian literature comes to consciousness. In the personality of their expression, in the depth of their melancholy, and in their propensity to outbursts of intense passion, they share much in common with contemporary literary works like Rousseau's *Confessions* (1771) Mackenzie's *The Man of Feeling* (1772), the last canto of Klopstock's *Messias* (1772), or, perhaps most influentially of all, Goethe's *Werther* (1774).

'Sturm und Drang', 'Preromanticism', the 'Age of Sensibility' are all terms which have been employed to describe this cultural moment. In characterizing the ways in which it was experienced and articulated in Hungary at the turn of the eighteenth and nineteenth centuries, and in exploring the relationship between this experience and articulation and the idea of Romanticism, Schiller's definition in *Über naive und sentimentalische Dichtung* (1795) of his own age as *sentimental* in contrast to the essential *naivety* of the ancients may prove to be more productive. First, Schiller's notion of the sentimental embodies important continuities—both conceptual and historical—with Jena Romanticism. Friedrich Schlegel's initial enthusiasm for Schiller's 1795 essay has

[9] Jean-Jacques Rousseau, *Œuvres complètes* (Paris: Pléiade, 1969), iv. 1109.

[10] Bessenyei, appendix to *Az embernek próbája* (Vienna, 1772), 158.

been well documented, and his later rejection of the terminology does not detract from its influence on Schlegel's own oppositions between ancient and modern, objective and subjective poetry. Secondly, Schiller's essay, in addition to being equally influential in late eighteenth- and early nineteenth-century Hungary, provides a conceptual framework for understanding the continuities and negotiations between radically differing types of Romantic project (including Romantic theory) in Hungarian letters. That these continuities and negotiations are in part of a directly historical and political kind does not reduce the conceptual framework to the lowly status of *Geistesgeschichte*.

For Schiller, the dilemma of sentimentality is an essentially *modern* dilemma, naming a modern, post-Kantian moment of alienation. The sentimental poet is alienated from nature, society, and the objects of his own discourse. His 'feeling for nature is like that of a sick man for health'; he is unhappy in his experience of humanity, and 'has no more urgent interest than to flee out of it'.[11] Sentimental poetry marks not only 'the birth of isolation', but also of reflexive dislocation: the mind of the sentimental poet 'can suffer no impression without at the same time observing its own operation and what it contains, without placing it opposite and outside of itself by means of reflection'.[12]

Schiller's immediate, practical influence in Hungary is particularly evident in the translation projects of the young Kazinczy. Kazinczy begins with Gessner's *Idyllen*, which Schiller, in *Über naive und sentimentalische Dichtung*, had cited as an example of sentimental idyll. He then turns to J. M. Miller's *Siegwart*, again given special mention by Schiller as an example of sentimental elegy, and also translates various texts by Wieland, whom Schiller cites in the context of sentimental satire, praising him for his 'seriousness of feeling' in contrast to the excess of 'intellect' Schiller finds in Voltaire. Kazinczy had also intended to translate Goethe's *Werther*, considered by Schiller to be the one text in which 'everything which gives nourishment to the sentimental character is concentrated',[13] and, as Kazinczy himself states in his preface to his translation of Kayser's *Adolph's Gesammelte Briefe*, it was only circumstance that forced him to translate this 'Roman in dem Geschmack der Leiden Werthers' instead.

The significance of Schiller's concept of the sentimental for late eighteenth-century Hungarian literature is not, however, above all a matter of literary influence. For Schiller describes a cultural moment of which Hungarian literature is already an active part. The literary topoi which Schiller's notion of alienated 'sentimentality' seeks to understand are all widely represented in Hungarian literature in the last quarter of the eighteenth century. The sentimental projection of the alienated self onto the natural world is a major characteristic of the poetry of not only 'sentimental' poets like Pál Ányos and Gábor Dayka, but also of the more 'classical' Miklós Révai. The sentimental alienation of subject from object, of the poetic self from the world it can never approximate, is significantly refracted in the preoccupation of Kazinczy and his followers with style as a virtue in itself, over and above the objects of literary representation. Alienated from

[11] Friedrich Schiller, *Werke (Nationalausgabe)*, xx (Weimar, Bölhaus, 1962), 431.

[12] Schiller, *Werke*, xx. 452.

[13] Schiller, *Werke*, xx. 459.

the natural and social world, the sentimental writer's experience of reality is mediated primarily through the world of signs. Just as Werther's love for Lotte is negotiated textually rather than sexually through the ecstasy the couple share in reading Klopstock, Gessner, and Ossian, the most critical moment in the relationship between Fanni and Józsi T. in József Kármán's epistolary novel of 1794 *Fanni hagyományai* (The Memoirs of Fanny) is mediated through Józsi's reading of Gessner. Finally, the cult of solitude, born of the sentimental subject's sense of isolation, and promoted by the popularity of works like Young's *Night Thoughts* and Rousseau's *Les Reveries d'un promeneur solitaire* finds ubiquitous expression in the period, from the hermetic attitude of the mature Bessenyei, through the poetry of Ányos and Dajka, to the sentimental novel, represented at its best by Kármán's *Fanni hagyományai* and Ignác Mészáros's earlier *Kártigám* (1772).

It is in the poetry of Mihály Vitéz Csokonai (1773–1805) that the sentimental cult of solitude begins to take on more unequivocally Romantic dimensions. Csokonai, who experimented in a wide range of styles from the classical and rococo to the *völkisch*, certainly has, in the words of Antal Szerb, the author of what remains the most impressive single-author history of Hungarian literature written to date, a 'preromantic layer'[14] best expressed in his odes 'A magánnossaghoz' (To Solitude) and 'A Tihanyi Echóhoz' (To the Echo at Tihany). In the latter poem he compares himself to 'Rousseau in Ermenoville', a 'man and citizen' of solitude, while in the former he describes the poet as one who 'like lightning in dark night | creates new things | and out of nothing new worlds'. This essentially Romantic view of the poetic imagination is supported by Csokonai's distinction in an essay on 'Hungarian Prosody' (A maygar prozodiáról, 1799) between 'versification' and 'poesis', the latter being characterized by 'thought, imagination, and fire' and constituting 'a life-giving spirit'.[15]

It is likely, considering Csokonai's enormous breadth of reading, that his notion of imagination draws on the most important Hungarian study of the concept in the period, Ádám Horváth's treatise on psychology, *Psychologia* (1792)—one of the most fascinating Hungarian philosophical works of the eighteenth century. Horváth is the first Hungarian writer to develop a coherent theory of the imagination as something more than the 'power of visualization'[16] it had represented for most of the eighteenth century. Horváth devotes two chapters of his treatise to a finely differentiated examination of increasingly abstract forms of perception, cognition, and imagination, based on a series of terms sharing the same Hungarian stem, *kép* (image, 'Bild'). The first three stages of the examination are fairly conventional, consisting of: the *kép* (image or idea) presented to consciousness, the *képzés* ('cognitio') that the soul makes for itself of this image, and *képzelés* ('imaginatio'), 'the work of the soul through which a distant, but already cognized, object is imagined anew'.[17] If *kép, képzés*, and *képzelés* are still based in the neoclassical imitation of nature, Horváth's fourth and highest term, *képzelődés* ('phantasia'),

[14] Antal Szerb, *Magyar irodalomtörténet* (Budapest: Magvető, 1986), 285, first publ. 1934.

[15] Mihály Vitéz Csokonai, *Szépprózai művek* (Budapest: Szépirodalmi könyvkiadó, 1981), 279–80.

[16] See René Wellek, *A History of Modern Criticism*, i (London: Lowe & Brydon, 1955), 96.

[17] Ádám Horváth, *Psychologia* (Pest, 1792), 40.

which he directly associates with 'poetic talent' (40), involves the creation of a new order of images which has hitherto never existed in such a form or combination in the real world. In this sense, Horváth's *képzelődés* is analogous to Wordsworth's characterization of the Romantic imagination in the 1815 Preface to the *Lyrical Ballads*:

> Imagination ... has no reference to images that are merely a faithful copy, existing in the mind, of distant objects; but is a word of higher import, denoting operations of the mind upon those objects, and processes of creation or of composition ...[18]

Horváth's *Psychologia* has been almost completely ignored by historians of Hungarian literature, and Horváth's reputation rests instead on his historical epic, *Hunnias*, and an extensive collection of folksongs, *Ó és új mintegy ötödfélszáz énenkek* (Some 550 Old and New Songs), completed in 1813, but not published until 1953.

By the beginning of the nineteenth century such active concepts of the imagination were increasingly displacing the more passive alienation of the sentimental moment. József Teleki's important, if largely derivative, compendium of Romantic ideas in his essay of 1818, *A régi és az új költészet külömbségeiről* (On the Differences Between the Ancient and Modern Poetry) is a good index of this change, registering both the continuities and discontinuities of Schiller's 'sentimental' and the more active notion of Romanticism with which it is displaced. For while the project of sentimental writing is undoubtedly part of the 'great endeavor to overcome the split between subject and object, the self and the world, the conscious and the unconscious' which René Wellek sees as the central hallmark of Romanticism,[19] it does not yet possess the imaginative means to forge the illusion of a new poetic fusion between inner and outer worlds. As Antal Szerb argued in 1946:

> Sentimentalism passively waits for wonders. In exactly this it differs from the mood of Romanticism, which is also a complex of desire, sadness, and hopelessness. But the Romantic's inner setting of aims is active; Romantic desire strives for the infinite.[20]

Teleki's *A régi és az új költészet külömbségeiről* reproduces many of Schiller's central positions, but rejects the term 'sentimentalisch', which by then had already come to signify predominantly false or maudlin sentiment, and replaces it with the term *romántos* (Romantic).[21] Whereas the ancients, Teleki argues, described in their poetry 'what they thought, experienced, and felt', we modern, Romantic poets 'first form in our imagination a new *poetic world* that is completely different from that of the present reality, and then describe what we think, experience, and feel therein.'[22]

[18] William Wordsworth, *Poetical Works* (Oxford: Oxford University Press, 1978), 753.

[19] René Wellek, *Concepts of Criticism* (New Haven: Yale University Press, 1963), 161. Wellek concedes that this endeavour was 'doomed to failure' (221).

[20] Antal Szerb, *Gondolatok a könyvtárban* (Budapest: Magvető, 1981), 41.

[21] József Teleki, *A régi és az új költészet külömbségeiről*, repr. in Sőtér (ed.), *A Magyar kritika évszazadai* (Budapest: Szépirodalmi könyvkiadó, 1981), i. 12–13.

[22] Teleki, *A régi és az új költészet külömbségeiről*, 13.

These ideas are reflected upon and articulated with considerably more originality in the poetry and theoretical prose of Dániel Berzsenyi (1776–1836). In a treatise titled *Poétai harmonistika* (Poetic Harmony, 1832), Berzsenyi starts out, like Horváth, from an essentially gradatory concept of the imagination. Distinguishing between *képzelő erő* (the power or faculty of imagination) and *képzőszellem* (the spirit of imagination), he sees the latter as 'nothing other than the continuation of the eternal work of [God's] creation dressed in the mantle of beauty'.[23] Poetry involves both aspects, being, as it was for Wordsworth, a combination of what we see and half create. For Berzsenyi, 'Poetry is that free operation of the soul which strives to rise above the images of the outside world and of the imagination and ... to shape them into new forms.'[24]

The notion of poetic harmony in Berzsenyi's treatise is also informed by a fundamentally Romantic preoccupation with ideas of fusion, integration, and unification. The quest for unity and wholeness already underlies Berzsenyi's precarious morphological reading of the Hungarian word for beautiful, 'szép', in which the poet hears the morpheme 'ép' (whole). His subsequent definition of the beautiful has much in common with the pursuit of 'unity in diversity' so crucial to the likes of Schlegel, Novalis, Wordsworth, Coleridge, and Shelley: 'beauty is harmonious diversity—harmonious diverse wholeness'.[25] The same interest in harmony makes Berzsenyi critical of Schiller's naïve–sentimental opposition. Poetry should aspire to be neither 'purely nature nor purely ideal, but a harmonious medium between the two'; the task, for Berzsenyi, is 'to dissolve naïve and sentimental *poesis* into each other'.[26]

These aspirations are reflected in Berzsenyi's own poetry, most of which was completed long before he wrote *Poétai harmonistika*. Berzsenyi's finest poetry remains classical in form and metre, but proto-Romantic in its projected harmonies. His formal 'Classicism' has often diverted Hungarian criticism from his emergent Romanticism, although, like the Classicism of Hölderlin, it is closer to the visionary Hellenism of Byron, Shelley, and Keats than to the more measured and imitative neoclassicism of the eighteenth century.[27] What Berzsenyi most admires in Horace—that 'the thought is everywhere painted rather than spoken'—is no less characteristic of his own best poems. 'Lefestem szüretem estvéli óráit' (I paint the evening hours of my harvest) opens the second stanza of 'Levéltöredék barátnémhoz' (Epistolary Fragment to my Lady Friend)—and the object of the painting is less the mimetic reproduction of an evening scene than the metaphorical evocation of an inner state. The central images of the poem—an ancient oak, the fire the poet attempts to kindle, the flickering flame of the candle he observes—lead a double, yet indivisible life. We do not question the 'objectivity' of the scene they depict, but nor can we fail to

[23] Dániel Berzsenyi, *Összes művei* (Budapest: Szépirodalmi könyvkiadó, 1968), 297.

[24] Berzsenyi, *Összes művei*, 309.

[25] Berzsenyi, *Összes művei*, 299.

[26] Berzsenyi, *Összes művei*, 302.

[27] In his 900-page history of world literature, Antal Szerb has this to say on the relationship between Classicism and Romanticism: 'The great works of French Romanticism strike us as Classical, while in France and England, German Classicism inspired Romanticism. In the eyes of the French, *Faust* is a Romantic masterpiece ...' *A világirodalom torténete* (Budapest: Magvető, 1992; first publ. 1941), 400–1.

recognize that they are also the embodiment of a highly personal and spiritual reflection. Rather than employing figures of simile to name the contiguity of inner and outer worlds, Berzsenyi offers a series of images in which the dichotomy is already in solution and between which the relationship is not the neoclassical one of pictura to sententia, for the image is already the thought and the thought already the image.

This type of harmony is still more effectively achieved in 'A közelitő tél' (The Approaching Winter), where the whole poem reads as an unstated metaphor for the poet's inner struggle with mutability. The first three stanzas set the scene with a mixture of classical ease and rhythmic freedom that is impossible to reproduce in translation:

> Withered our grove, fallen its ornaments;
> yellow leaves rustle among the bare shrubs;
> no labyrinth of roses, and among balmy perfumes
> Zephyr no longer resides.
>
> No symphony sounds; between the green bowers
> no turtle-dove coos; under the willows
> the stream's violet valley is scentless, its surface
> covered with coppice run wild.
>
> In the vaults of the mountains twilight looms silent,
> no grape clusters smile on the scarlet vines.
> where late the sweet songs of joy resounded
> now all is fallow and still.

In the fifth stanza, Berzsenyi slides from the description of outer nature to the inner life without any interruption to the metaphorical intensity of the poem:

> Slowly the buds on my garland are paling,
> and sweet spring forsakes me with hardly a trace
> on my lips of its nectars, hardly a breath
> of one or two tender flowers ...[28]

Berzsenyi originally entitled the poem 'Ősz' (Autumn)—it was Kazinczy who suggested the title by which the poem has been known ever since—and autumn figures throughout the poem as a metaphor in which the worlds of subject and object, the life of man and the cycle of nature, remain in a tension of interdependence. Berzsenyi's imagery is well served by Paul de Man's characterization of 'the romantic image' as 'always a tension (not a mere analogy or imitation) between a consciousness and a natural object',[29] and 'A közelitő tél' certainly looks forward to the Romantic autumn poetry of Lamartine's 'L'Automne', Eichendorf's 'Herbstweh', or Keats's 'Ode to Autumn'.

[28] Berzsenyi, *Összes művei*, 81.

[29] Paul de Man, *Romanticism and Contemporary Criticism: The Gauss Seminar and Other Papers* (Baltimore and London: Johns Hopkins University Press, 1993), 130.

'A közelitő tél' and 'Levéltöredék barátnémhoz' were both written between 1804 and 1808. By the end of the next decade, the poet Berzsenyi had all but fallen silent. The reason for this—and also the reason for the composition of his theoretical reflections on Romanticism—was a devastating review of his poetry published by Ferenc Kölcsey in 1817. Kölcsey's review marked the end of the developmental process from sensibility to Romanticism we have been tracing, and the beginning of the hegemony of a very different response to Schiller's late eighteenth-century sentimental dilemma and a very different concept of Romanticism.

Poets 'will either *be* nature, or they will *look for* lost nature' (Schiller).[30] In the first case their poetry will be 'naïve', in the second 'sentimental'. The modern poet may try to overcome his sense of alienation by attempting to restore the 'lost' and naïve harmony enjoyed by the ancients with their 'simple' and 'natural' world, but this itself is an inherently sentimental impulse. The sentimental dilemma and the quest for its naïve resolution are, as Schiller so persuasively argues, two sides of the same 'modern' (or Romantic) coin. Concomitant with the sentimental cults of solitude and subjectivity in late eighteenth-century Hungarian literature we can identify the inception of a search for a more 'naïve' and 'native' sense of community and authenticity which was to prove particularly formative for the subsequent development of the national literature in general and for the dominant national view of Romanticism in particular. The literary object of this search is probably best described by Herder's concept of *Naturpoesie*, although it must be remembered that Herder's influence in late eighteenth-century Hungary was highly mediated. For Herder, *Naturpoesie* embodies an organic unity with the poet's immediate community and national traditions, lost to the modern *Kunstpoet*, who is the product not of an organic, but an imitative culture, devoid of its own coherent and collective identity.[31] In Hungary, especially after the centralizing and Germanizing reforms of Joseph II, the pursuit of such an identity would become one of the key cultural and political preoccupations of the late eighteenth and early nineteenth centuries. In Hungarian literature, it finds expression above all in three forms of 'naïve' recovery. First, there is an increasingly programmatic attempt to retrieve the lost or forgotten glories of the national past in order to foster a sense of collective historical purpose. Such efforts range from Bessenyei's historical tragedies, through Ádám Horváth's *Hunnias*, the epic fragments of Csokonai, Gedeon Ráday, and Benedek Virág, and the popular historical novel *Etelka* (1788) by Andás Dugonics—all dealing with the Hungarian Conquest of the Carpathian Basin at the end of the ninth century—to the cult of poetry lamenting the defeat of the Hungarian Kingdom by the Ottomans at Mohács in 1526. By the third decade of the nineteenth century, Mohács had become a symbol of both national tragedy and a byword for the tragic take on national identity.

A second form of naïve recovery can be identified in the pursuit of national identity through the cultivation of national traditions and customs as a source of shared,

[30] Schiller, *Werke*, xx. 432.

[31] See e.g. Herder's *Briefwechsel über Ossian und die Lieder alter Völker* in E. Purdie (ed.), *Von deutscher Art und Kunst* (Oxford: Clarendon Press, 1924).

common values. The most influential literary works in the early part of this process were Lőrincz Orczy's *A bugaczi csárdának tiszteletére* (In Praise of an Inn on the Bugac Plain, 1772) and József Gvadányi's *Falusi nótárius* (The Village Notary, 1796). It is often forgotten that Orczy's poetry of the previous decade is characterized by a distinctly Voltairean 'apologie de luxe' totally incompatible with the Spartan, *völkisch* values of *A bugaci csárda*. In addition to his dialogic reworkings of Voltaire's *Mondain* poems ('Le mondain', 'Defense du Mondain') in 'Barátságos beszédje egy úrnak káplánjával' (The friendly conversation of a Lord with his chaplain), the most pertinent example of his 'mondain' defence of luxury is the ode 'A magyar szépekhez' (To the Hungarian Beauties, 1760) in which he proposes an economic justification for (a)moral epicureanism. Orczy's rejection of his Voltairean position after 1772 is based in his response to the profoundly disturbing consequences of the first Partition of Poland in that year. Not only did Voltaire's open support for this intervention leave Orczy somewhat suspicious of the latter's enlightened values (just as Rousseau's condemnation of the Partition considerably consolidated his reputation in Hungary), it also led him to reconsider his earlier ideas on the proper extent of personal and political liberty. Thus the main section (fifty-five stanzas) of his longest poetic work, 'Futó gondolatok a szabadságról' (Fleeting thoughts about freedom), carrying the subtitle 'Lengyelek' (Poles) attributes Poland's downfall to the excessive vanity, luxury, and liberty enjoyed by the Polish nobility in their relations with both the monarch and the peasantry. The considerably shorter section on Hungary, on the other hand, pays tribute to the Hungarian nobility for its moral temperance and prudent acceptance of the limitations to its own political freedoms.

A third form of naïve recovery can be discerned in the attempt of late eighteenth-century Hungarian letters to restore a lost language of naturalness, simplicity, and immediacy as opposed to the imitative, modern language of refined or elevated style (*fentebb stíl*) championed by the likes of Kazinczy. This language is increasingly modelled on the living example of Hungarian folk poetry, as an equation of the 'authentically' national with the *völkisch* ('népi') becomes one of the key constituents of the national-cultural self-definition. From Révai's call for the collection of ancient and folk poetry in 1782 to Kölcsey's famous association of the national and the popular in *Nemzeti hagyományok* (1826), the naïve identification with the idiom and values of folk culture would lay the major foundations of a cultural populism that is still very much alive today.

Evidence of a renewed interest in ancient and folk poetry can be found throughout Europe in the second half of the eighteenth century, from Thomas Percy's *Reliques of Ancient English Poetry* to Herder's *Stimmen der Völker* and the widespread cult of Ossian. Wordsworth's *Lyrical Ballads* of 1798 are perhaps the supreme artistic achievement of a 'naïve' (in Schiller's sense) preoccupation with 'rustic life' and the 'language really spoken by men'. Where the literary populism (*irodalmi népiesség*) of the Hungarian late eighteenth century and Age of Reform differs from the Wordsworthian project is in the extent of its conflation of the concepts of 'naïve' and 'native'. When Wordsworth, in his Preface to the *Lyrical Ballads*, relates his interest in 'humble and rustic life' to a desire to reveal 'the primary laws of our nature', his use of the first-person plural evokes not a national, but a *universal* human community. For Wordsworth, the poet is not a bard addressing his nation, but 'a man speaking to men': for all their local specificity, Wordsworth's ballads aspire to the status of a Schlegelian 'Universalpoesie'. The Hungarian interest in folk culture—especially in the first four decades of the nineteenth century—is more exclusively related to the cultivation of distinctively *national* values and identity. As Kölcsey would claim in 1826: 'the original spark of an authentic national poetry has to be sought in the songs of the ordinary people'.[32]

Kölcsey's own literary development provides an instructive illustration of the close interaction of naïve and sentimental initiatives in Hungarian literature during this formative period in its history. While Kölcsey's earliest odes show the unmistakable influence of Csokonai, between 1808 and 1818 he would fall under the markedly sentimental influence of Kazinczy. Kölcsey himself stated in retrospect that 'in 1808 and 1809 I was sentimental-lyrical'[33] and much of his best poetry of the 1810s continues to draw upon the lexis of Young and the tone and disposition of Ányos and Dayka. Kazinczy's values also inform many of Kölcsey's critical evaluations during this period, such as his dismissal in 1815 of János Földi's claim that 'The true Hungarianness is that of the common people, a Hungarianness incompatible with foreign influences.'[34] The remarkable shift in Kölcsey's position after 1818 is largely the product of changing political considerations and the poet's crucial identification with the political aspirations of the Age of Reform: the transformation of the feudal *natio Hungarica* into a modern nation state capable of representing the interests of all its citizens. In this context the ideals of literary populism represented a potential cultural basis for a common national identity extending beyond the boundaries of private property and social class. The task of the true Hungarian patriot, Kölcsey will argue, is to ensure that 'the great mass of the tax-paying people should finally enter the bourgeois constitution'.[35] This liberal projection of national unity finds its most articulate and influential cultural expression in Kölcsey's most significant contribution to the discursive prose of the Age of Reform, *Nemzeti hagyományok* (National Traditions, 1826). Here the influence is no longer that of the 'sentimental' Kazinczy, but almost entirely of the (sentimentally) 'naïve' Herder. In one important sense *Nemzeti hagyományok* actually goes a good way beyond Herder—for whom there had been no 'Favoritenvolk'—in its insistence on the detrimental effect of foreign influences on the formation of the national character. Even the 'heroic' age of the fifteenth century is criticized on this basis: 'Painful to say, even in those days we gave place to foreign influences'.[36]

In his 1817 review of Berzsenyi's poetry, Kölcsey is still able to praise the poet for refining Hungarian poetic diction through classical example, but he finds that Berzsenyi's diction is often vacuous and his images 'bombastic' (*dagályos*). In his belated response

[32] Ferenc Kölcsey, *Összes művei* (Budapest, 1943), 369.
[33] Kölcsey, *Összes művei*, 1495.
[34] Kölcsey, *Összes művei*, 457.
[35] Kölcsey, *Összes művei*, 1240.
[36] Kölcsey, *Összes művei*, 637.

to Kölcsey, *Észrevételek Kölcsey recensiójára* (Observations on Kölcsey's Review, 1825), Berzsenyi defends his poetic language as 'the exalted images of exalted imagination' that belong to a 'the whole Romantic style' born of 'a new and individual spirit'.[37]

The charge of bombast or pompousness (*dagályosság*) would be used time and again against 'the exalted images of exalted imagination' that characterized Romantic writing in the Berzsenyi vein. The key spokesmen for the national-populist ideal in the 1840s, János Erdélyi, employs the same term in an essay on Berzsenyi, but, while holding the poet's 'painterly' style to be the product of regrettable foreign influences, he still finds enough of value in the poet's diction to claim that: 'Berzsenyi was foreign in his thought, but ours in his language'.[38]

By the 1840s, the 'naïve-native' critique of 'sentimental' Romanticism as bombastic and alien had emerged fully triumphant, paving the way for the characterization of national Romanticism which has survived to this day: 'Romanticism requires patriotism and populism as its primary basis and material.'[39] This is Erdélyi writing in 1847, the year of his Berzsenyi essay, in an article titled 'Valami a romanticzizmusról' (A Few Words about Romanticism). In opposition to the essential constituents of 'authentic' Romanticism ('homeland and national characteristics'), he sets the 'inauthentic Romanticism' or 'word-romanticism' of the likes of Victor Hugo and Lamartine and insists: 'This word-romanticism we despise and we desire for our literature ... the speediest possible liberation from French and all foreign influences.'[40]

According to the national-populist position, the two key representatives of Hungarian Romanticism are Mihály Vörösmarty, valued for his national poetic epics and appeals to the nation, and Sándor Petőfi, who embodied the ideal of the nationally engaged poet speaking the language of the common people. Even the most recent history of Hungarian literature, *Geschichte der ungarischen Literatur: Eine historisch-poetologische Darstellung*—written by Hungarian scholars but published only in German—can claim: 'Was die Romantik in der ungarischen Literatur ausmacht, formte sich durch das Auftreten von Sándor Petőfi in endgültiger Weise neu; Volkstumsdichtung und Tendenzliteratur kulminierten in seiner Dichtkunst.' ('It was the arrival on the scene of Sándor Petőfi that led to the ultimate transformation of what was Romantic in Hungarian literature; popular poetry and partisan literature culminated in his poetic art.')[41] Such claims equate Hungarian Romanticism unequivocally (and problematically) with the values of the process of 'naïve recovery' I have been outlining here.

Petőfi represents the epitome in Hungarian literature of Schiller's naïve genius. He speaks the language of a community in which he appears entirely at home, and

[37] Berzsenyi, *Összes művei*, 191.

[38] János Erdélyi, *Pályák és pálmák* (Budapest: Franklin Társulat, 1886), 68.

[39] János Erdélyi, *Tanulmányok* (Budapest: Franklin Társulat, 1890), 502.

[40] Erdélyi, *Tanulmányok*, 503.

[41] Ernő Kulcsár Szabó (ed.), *Geschichte der ungarischen Literatur: Eine historisch-poetologische Darstellung* (Berlin: de Gruyter, 2013), 183.

his diction is effortless and natural. In Schiller's phrase, he 'is the Creation, and the Creation is He';[42] all boundaries between poetry and biography, art and life, are blurred. For Petőfi, personal experience is inherently poetic, and poetry little more than the form and medium of that experience. Unlike Schiller's sentimental (and proto-Romantic) poet whose work involves 'the elevation of reality to the ideal', the naïve poet is concerned with 'the most complete imitation of the real'.[43] This imitation could be hardly more complete than in Petőfi's poetic descriptions of natural scenes, which are devoid of Romantic pantheism and have little in common with either the sentimental subjectivization of nature characteristic of Ányos and Dayka, nor the visionary and metaphorical transformation of nature we find in Vörösmarty. Both of these latter gestures are products of the alienation of subject from object, man from nature, which finds little expression in Petőfi's verse. In contrast to the cult of the folksong in the 1830s, there is nothing 'folkloristic' about Petőfi's identification with the common people and their culture. Petőfi does not collect folksongs as an outsider, but 'inhabits' and extends their idiom from within. The work of Petőfi, together with the early poetry of János Arany, represented the realization of the aspirations of Kölcsey and Erdélyi towards a new species of national poetry, which would both incorporate and further develop existing folk traditions.

The case of Vörösmarty is more complex. The more 'patriotic' poetry on which his reputation as a national Romantic is based presents a largely tragic vision of the national fate. Even in the celebrated 'Szózat' of 1836, which would become Hungary's 'second national anthem', Vörösmarty's darker vision repeatedly worries the confident grandiloquence of its stirring opening ('Unto thy homeland ever more be faithful, oh Magyar!') and the prospect of the death-of-the-nation (*nemzethalál*)—the Hungarian post-Herderian nightmare of the 1820s and 1830s—is never far away ('For it will come, if come it must, the all pervasive death').[44] In Vörösmarty's key epic on the national conquest, *Zalán futása* (The Flight of Zalán, 1825), the emphasis is, as the very title suggests, on the tragedy of the defeated Zalán rather than on the glory of the victorious Árpád.

Pál Gyulai, Erdély's chief successor as spokesman for the national-popular ideal, without questioning Vörösmarty's status as Hungary's central national Romantic poet, was none the less critical of the epic because:

> Vörösmarty didn't treat the legendary basis naively, but created out of his mythological imagination; he didn't pluck the strings of the folk-spirit, and instead of folksongs used Greek hexameters, which, while displaying the beauty of our language, still remain foreign to our point of view.[45]

[42] Schiller, *Werke*, xx. 433.

[43] Schiller, *Werke*, xx. 437.

[44] Mihály Vörösmarty, *Összes művei* (Budapest: Akadémiai kiadó, 1981), ii. 210–11.

[45] Pál Gyulai, *Kritikai dolgozatok (1854–1861)* (Budapest: Franklin Társulat, 1908), 93.

Concerning Vörösmarty's lyric poetry, Gyulai repeatedly raises the charge of *dagályosság*, and unsurprisingly so, as Vörösmarty is Berzsenyi's true (Romantic) successor.[46] While, unlike the earlier poet, he makes little claim on our attention as a Romantic theorist, the foundations of a Romantic concept of the imagination appear early in his work, as, for example, in the opening lines of the epic *Tündérvölgy* (Fairy Vale, 1825): 'What do you know, you short-lived mortals | If you've not been touched by the flame of imagination? ... I sing a song for the ears of the world which has never been heard in heaven or on earth'.[47]

Tündérvölgy, along with another early (unfinished) epic, *Délsziget*, anticipates the essentially tragic vision of the ungratifiable nature of human desire in the poet's most profound mature verse. In the extraordinary verse drama, *Csongor és Tünde* (Csongor and Tünde, 1831), unquenchable desire is reduced to meaninglessness as man, no more than the son of flies, disappears from a universe left alone to 'bleak, seclusive, all-forsaken night'; in 'Gontolatok a könyvtárban' (Thoughts in a Library, 1844), it is only the experience of tragedy, not all the wisdom of books, that can teach us to pursue meaning, nobility, and grace through struggle; in 'A vén czigány' (The Old Gypsy, 1850) it is only the figure of the storm that can ease our 'eternal promethean suffering', even if it cannot free us from the circularity and directionlessness of human existence. The natural world and its cycles become symbols of both inner suffering and cosmic doubt. A further aspect of de Man's description of the 'Romantic image' is pertinent here, as 'a longing of the language toward nature' which 'contains a constitutive element of tragic failure, because it is born from a conflict between two irreconcilable ways of being'.[48] Thus, in the late fragment, 'Előszó' (Preface, 1850), a temporal progression (spring, winter, spring) is presented as a deterioration in value, where the closing image of spring reinterprets the already metaphorical significance of the opening image. The remembered clear skies of the poem's opening give way, after a moment of stasis in which the whole universe briefly stops turning, to a characteristically Vörösmartyian storm whose 'blood-freezing hand throws human heads like balls into the air'. Then the poem reaches the present:

> Now all is winter, and quiet, and snow, and death.
> The earth turned white:
> Not hair by hair, like the fortunate,
> But at one stroke, like God,
> Who having created the world and man,
> This demi-God, half beast,
> In horror of his own grim work
> Turned grey at once and old.

[46] Vörösmarty wrote a paean to Berzsenyi in 1837, 'Berzsenyi emlékezete' (To the Memory of Berzsenyi).

[47] Vörösmarty, *Összes művei*, v. 29.

[48] De Man, *Romanticism and Contemporary Criticism*, 130.

After this, the prospect of spring's return is treated with characteristic Romantic irony:

> That old coiffeuse will come again, the Spring,
> To dress the grey earth in a periwig,
> And trim the flowers in silk and velvet suits.
> In her glass eye the ice will thaw,
> And on her perfumed, paint-smeared cheeks
> She'll fake fresh youth and cheer;
> But ask the ancient vixen then:
> Where has she buried her unhappy sons?[49]

Vörösmarty enjoyed a high reputation in his own lifetime, but himself complained that his verse was more widely praised than read. Celebrated as the author of the relatively early 'Zalán futása' and 'Szózat', he had already fallen into poverty by the 1840s, unable to find a wide readership for his work. 'The public treat my poems like water,' he complained in 1845; 'they praise it, then drink wine instead'.[50] It was the *Nyugat* generation that first reinterpreted the previously perceived weaknesses of his lyric poetry as its major strengths. Aladár Schöpflin, for example, directly takes issue with Gyulai's accusation of *dagályosság* in connection with 'A vén czigány': 'one cannot speak of bombast where true feeling speaks so directly'.[51] Today, the reputation of a poem like 'Előszó' as a Romantic classic is assured. It is quoted in full in the recent *Geschichte der ungarischen Literatur*, and, in the most recent history of Hungarian literature to be published in Hungary (*A magyar iradalom történtei*, 2007) a whole chapter is devoted to the history of its reception ('The belated canonization of a major Romantic work'). The editor of *A magyar iradalom történtei* ('Histoires of Hungarian Literature'—with an emphasis on the plural), Mihály Szegedy-Maszák, is an internationally renowned comparative literature scholar as well as a historian of Hungarian literature. Like Babits, who wrote a history of European literature, or Antal Szerb, another contributor to *Nyugat*, who, in addition to his fine history of Hungarian literature wrote an even more extensive *History of World Literature* (1941), Szegedy-Maszák manages successfully to negotiate the two-way boundary between national specificity and European identity, and has probably done more than any other post-war Hungarian scholar to promote the project of *Nyugat* to understand Hungarian culture within a broader European context. In an essay on 'A magyar romantika sajátosságai' (The Specificities of Hungarian Romanticism, 1987) he cautioned:

> One may argue that our national Romanticism possesses predominantly characteristics which differentiate it from other Romanticisms—but this is ultimately to make the use of the term superfluous.[52]

49 Vörösmarty, *Összes művei*, iii. 180.

50 Vörösmarty, *Összes művei*, iii. 364.

51 Cited in Vörösmarty, *Összes művei*, iii. 582.

52 Mihály Szegedy-Maszák, 'A magyar romantika sajátosságai', *Ars Hungarica* (1987), 21–9.

To figure Romanticism as 'a process issuing from the depths of the national essence',[53] whose most significant characteristics are 'the special relationship with folk poetry'[54] and 'the preoccupation with the nation's origins and glorious (if invented) past',[55] is not only to disregard the richness and complexity of Romantic initiatives in Hungarian literature at the turn of the eighteenth and nineteenth centuries, but to impoverish the notion of Romanticism as such. Romanticism, as Schlegel realized from the outset, is a bigger idea than can be comprised in any concept of locality or indeed period. If, as de Man suggests, even Yeats was 'premature in referring to himself as the *last* romantic' because 'there is little in the poetry of our century that cannot be included within [the] broadly considered framework of the romantic tradition',[56] Romanticism's beginnings may profitably be reread by its ends. Literary history, like any other history, is always still to be reimagined; and, as the great modern Romantic poet Wallace Stevens reminds us: 'It is one of the peculiarities of the imagination that it is always at the end of an era'.[57]

FURTHER READING

Aczel, Richard, *National Character and European Identity in Hungarian Literature 1772–1848* (Budapest: Nemzetközi Hungarológiai Központ, 1996).

Babits, Mihály, *Geschichte der europäischen Literatur* (Vienna: Europa Verlag, 1949).

Czigány, Lóránt, *The Oxford History of Hungarian Literature (From the Earliest Times to the Present)* (Oxford: Clarendon Press, 1984).

Farkas, Julius von (Gyula), *Die ungarische Romantik* (Berlin: Walter de Gruyter & Co, 1931).

Kósa, László, *A Cultural History of Hungary in the Nineteenth and Twentieth Centuries* (Budapest: Corvina/Osiris, 2000).

Szabó, Ernő Kulcsár, ed, *Geschichte der ungarischen Literatur: Eine historisch-poetologische Darstellung* (Berlin: de Gruyter, 2013).

Szegedy-Maszak, Mihály, 'Romanticism in Hungary', in Roy Porter and Mikulas Teich, *Romanticism in National Context* (Cambridge: Cambridge University Press, 1988).

Szegedy-Maszak, Mihály, 'Romanticism, Biedermeyer, and Realism', in Mihály Szegedy-Maszak, *Literary Canons: National and International* (Budapest: Akadémiai kiadó, 2001).

Szerb, Antal, *Magyar irodalomtörténet* (Budapest: Magvető, 1986).

[53] Julius von Farkas (Gyula), *Die ungarische Romantik* (Berlin: Walter de Gruyter & Co, 1931), 8.

[54] Sőtér, *Dilemma of Literary Science*, 179.

[55] George Bisztray, 'Awakening Peripheries: The Romantic Redefinition of Myth and Folklore', in Angela Esterhammer (ed.), *Romantic Poetry* (Amsterdam and Philadelphia: John Benjamins Publishing Co., 2002), 243.

[56] De Man, *Romanticism and Contemporary Criticism*, 131.

[57] Wallace Stevens, *The Necessary Angel: Essays on Reality and the Imagination* (London: Faber, 1960), 22.

Italian

CHAPTER 20

THE TASK OF ITALIAN ROMANTICISM

Literary Form and Polemical Response

JOSEPH LUZZI

ALTHOUGH it was written over a hundred years after the Italian Romantic debates, Walter Benjamin's description of translation as a 'mode' is eerily applicable to this contentious movement.[1] The essay that sparked the Romantic controversy in Italy, Mme de Staël's 'De l'esprit des traductions' ('The Spirit of Translation', 1816), anticipates Benjamin's theories by directing Italians to those works that call for translation. Italians, she argued, should avoid the obsolete neoclassical rhetoric and mythological references that rendered much of their literature unsuitable—figuratively speaking, untranslatable—for foreign readers, Instead, she urged Italians to merge with currents of Northern European thought that would rescue them from their backward-looking isolation. The most important event in Italian Romantic criticism, Staël's essay established a relation between literary form and polemical response that would drive the embattled movement.[2]

[1] Translations are my own unless otherwise indicated. Translations of foreign titles are given in capitalized italics when there is an English tr. (e.g. *The Betrothed*); and in sentence-style roman script when there is not (e.g. Italian Romanticism does not exist). See Walter Benjamin, 'The Task of the Translator: An Introduction to the Translation of Baudelaire's *Tableaux parisiens*', in Hannah Arendt (ed.), *Illuminations*, tr. Harry Zohn (New York: Schocken, 1968), 70: 'Translation is a mode. To comprehend it as mode one must go back to the original, for that contains the law governing the translation: its translatability. The question of whether a work is translatable has a dual meaning. Either: Will an adequate translator ever be found among the totality of its readers? Or, more pertinently: Does its nature lend itself to translation and, therefore, in view of the significance of the mode, call for it?'

[2] Stuart Curran discusses the contrasting dates of the European Romantic movements, *Poetic Form and British Romanticism* (Oxford: Oxford University Press, 1986), 209–10.

The student of Italian Romanticism faces a series of paradoxes. The 'movement', if we dare use this term, was one of the most self-conscious and publicly debated in all of Europe; yet some sceptics doubted its validity, none more so than Gina Martegiani in her influential and ominously titled study *Il romanticismo italiano non esiste* (Italian Romanticism does not exist, 1908). And the most famous Italian writers of the age—the *tre corone* (three crowns) of Italian Romanticism, Ugo Foscolo, Giacomo Leopardi, and Alessandro Manzoni—either disdained the advent of Romanticism in Italy (Foscolo), expressed outright hostility towards it (Leopardi), or conceived of it as a Christian phenomenon (Manzoni). Finally and most confusingly of all, the enormous presence of Italian Romanticism in its nation's cultural history—especially because of its links with the unification movement that it helped spawn, the Risorgimento—is countered by a near absence of interest in the movement abroad.[3]

In retrospect, we see that the virtues of Italian Romanticism were bound up with its vices. Though their names are now largely forgotten, the writers who publicized the movement in Italy succeeded in raising public debate about the relation between literary and national identity, which in turn did much to make authors aware of their political responsibilities towards the yet-to-be-born Italian nation. Meanwhile, since the triumvirate Foscolo, Leopardi, and Manzoni avoided direct alignment with mainstream Romantic thought, they enjoyed a greater literary and artistic freedom than their more doctrinaire (and less talented) contemporaries who actually aligned themselves with Italian Romanticism. Italy's isolation from much of European intellectual life gave the nation's controversies over Romanticism a dramatic, almost desperate air, as the subtext over whether Italy would become 'Romantic' was equal to asking whether it could become 'modern'.[4]

I will revisit the heated controversies over Italian Romanticism to show that they were no mere literary-historical phenomena; they actually represent a vital literary *mode*. In short, the debates over Romanticism in Italy led to the creation of literary masterpieces that carry within themselves the signs of the age's literary polemics.

[3] See my *Romantic Europe and the Ghost of Italy* (New Haven: Yale University Press, 2008), 27. The only study in English on the Romantic controversy in Italy is apparently Grazia Avitabile, *The Controversy on Romanticism in Italy: First Phase, 1816–1823* (New York: Vanni, 1959); the movement is not examined by Roy Porter and Mikulás Teich in their edited anthology on the different national versions of Romanticism: *Romanticism in National Context* (Cambridge: Cambridge University Press, 1988). Carlo Calcaterra anthologizes the major texts in the debates over Italian Romanticism: *I manifesti romantici* (Turin: UTET, 1951). Puppo and Raimondi consider the often-overlooked relation between Italian and European Romanticism: Mario Puppo, *Romanticismo italiano e romanticismo europeo* (Milan: Istituto Propaganda Libraria, 1985); Enzo Raimondi, *Romanticismo italiano e romanticismo europeo* (Milan: Mondadori, 1997).

[4] See René Wellek, *A History of Modern Criticism, 1750–1950* (New Haven: Yale University Press, 1955–72), ii, 260.

The Power of Cliché: Staël's Antiromantic Italians

On 1 January 1816, the journal *Biblioteca italiana* (Italian library) published Madame de Staël's essay on translation, and with it the Italian Romantic movement came violently to life. Even before the essay's publication, the journal had altered the literary life of the Italian peninsula. The editorship was first offered to Foscolo, the mercurial poet-patriot who had established his European fame with such masterpieces as the *Werther*-inspired *Ultime lettere di Jacopo Ortis* (*Last Letters of Jacopo Ortis*, 1798) and 'Dei sepolcri' ('On Sepulchers', 1807), a meditation on the relations between the living and the dead that transformed the Florentine Basilica of Santa Croce into the Italian pantheon. To the horror of his circle, Foscolo accepted the position at the Austrian-sponsored journal, then he realized the full implications of this acquiescence when he and fellow soldiers were asked to swear an oath of loyalty to the occupying Austrian government. He refused and decided to flee Italy, first to Switzerland then England, where he spent a difficult, impoverished decade writing what would turn out to be fundamental critical works that explained Italy's cultural riches to the anglophone world.[5]

In the meantime, the Austrians convinced Vincenzo Monti and his co-editor Pietro Giordani to take over the reins of *Biblioteca italiana*. Staël's essay appeared in the first issue and was translated from the French by the classically minded Giordani himself. A literary wildfire broke out. Immediately, leading Italian intellectuals including Pietro Borsieri, Ludovico di Breme, Silvio Pellico, and Ermes Visconti issued pro-Staël and pro-Romantic pieces; while Monti, Giordani, and an adolescent from the provincial town of Recanati—Giacomo Leopardi—retaliated with defences of Italian neoclassicism and mythology as well as attacks on Staël, a woman Foscolo called a 'donna di bellissimo ingegno' ('woman of great genius') before satirizing her 'metaphysical' understanding of Italian culture.[6]

In truth, the polemics about Italian literature had begun years earlier—once again in Staël's writing, albeit in the fictional universe of her bestselling novel *Corinne, ou Italie* (*Corinne, or Italy*, 1807), arguably the most influential statement about Italian culture ever produced by a foreigner. Staël's heroine, the half-English and half-Italian poetess Corinne, announces in book 7:

> La mélodie brillante de l'italien convient mieux à l'éclat des objets extérieurs qu'à la méditation. Notre langue seroit plus propre à peindre la fureur que la tristesse, parce

[5] See E. R. Vincent, *Ugo Foscolo: An Italian in Regency England* (Cambridge: Cambridge University Press, 1953), for a book-length study of Foscolo's English sojourn.

[6] See Ugo Foscolo, *Lettere scritte dall'Inghilterra*, ed. Elena Lombardi, in *Opere*, ed. Franco Gavezzeni (Turin: Einaudi-Gallimard, 1994–5), ii. 461.

> que les sentiments réfléchis exigent des expressions plus métaphysiques, tandis que le désir de la vengeance anime l'imagination, et tourne la douleur en dehors. (7.1; 114)
>
> The sparkling melody of Italian is more suited to the brilliance of external objects than to reflection. Our language is better suited to rage than sadness, because thoughtful feelings require more metaphysical language, while the desire for vengeance stirs the imagination and turns grief outwards. (109)

In a few words, Corinne outlines why Italians would be so ill-equipped for the birth of European Romanticism. Their musical language made them more attached to the surface charms of baroque and neoclassical rhetoric than to the sparse, transparent, and pared-down diction promoted by such exemplars of Romantic aesthetics as William Wordsworth in his 'Preface to *Lyrical Ballads*' (1800).[7] Moreover, their emotions tended towards the operatic and demonstrative instead of the gloomy and introspective, and their nation lacked a viable metaphysical tradition. This idea fills Staël's reflections in a pioneering work of European comparative literature, *De la littérature considérée dans ses rapports avec les institutions sociales* (*Literature Considered in Its Relation to Social Institutions*, 1800):

> Italians, except for a certain class of enlightened men, are in religion as in love and liberty: they like exaggeration in everything and can feel the true measure of nothing. They are vindictive yet servile. They are slaves to women yet strangers to profound and lasting feelings of the heart ... Such is the effect that must be produced upon a people by fanatical prejudices, by various governments that do not combine defense and love of the same fatherland, and by a burning sun that stirs up all the sensations and must induce voluptuousness if this consequence is not combated, as among the [ancient] Romans, by the force of political passions. (188)

The reductive nature of Staël's portrait of Italy and the Italians and her reliance on stereotypes are obvious. But we must ask ourselves why her two-dimensional view has had such lasting appeal. These words of hers would form the theoretical basis for her attack on contemporary Italian culture in 'The Spirit of Translation':

> Italian literature is now divided between the learned who sift and re-sift the ashes of the past to find some specks of gold in there, and the writers who trust in the harmony of their language to produce agreement without ideas and to put together exclamations, declarations, and invocations in which there is not a single word that issues from the heart or arrives there. (283)

Her indictment of Italian poetics becomes a critique of the nation's morality, as *Corinne* reveals the Italians as a people given to song and erudition, but incapable of genuine

[7] See Wordsworth on his desire to write in the 'language really used by men': 'Preface to *Lyrical Ballads*', in Willam Wordsworth and Samuel Taylor Coleridge, *Lyrical Ballads, 1798 and 1802*, ed. Fiona Stafford (Oxford: Oxford University Press, 2013), 97.

emotions. This emphasis on Italian superficiality, with all its connotations, also permeates *Corinne*, whose title character embodies the Italian nation's propensity for beautiful but highly decorative lyrical expression.

Early in the novel, Corinne appears on Rome's Capitoline Hill to accept the crown of poet-laureate, in the same spot where Petrarch had been crowned nearly five centuries earlier. The setting shows how she and Italian poetry are synonymous:

> Enfin, les quatres chevaux blancs qui traînoient le char de Corinne, se firent place au milieu de la foule. Corinne étoit assise sur ce char construit à l'antique; et de jeunes filles, vêtues de blanc, marchoient à côté d'elle. Partout où elle passoit, l'on jetoit un abondance des parfums dans les airs ... tout le monde crioit: *Vive Corinne! vive le génie! vive la beauté!* (2.1; 22)

> At last the four horses drawing Corinne's chariot made their way into the midst of the crowd. Corinne was sitting on the chariot, built in the style of ancient Rome, and white-robed girls walked alongside her. Everywhere she went people lavishly threw perfumes into the air ... everyone shouted, *Long live Corinne! Long live genius! Long live beauty!* (22–3)

I have noted elsewhere that readers of this passage feel as though they are about to encounter not just a person but a *people*, and that Staël uses the name 'Corinne', beautiful and brilliant but bereft of all honour not related to the arts, as a code for 'Italy'.[8] Corinne's poetic spell over the Italian people will eventually end with her own untimely death over heartbreak: she will be abandoned by her Scottish paramour Oswald in favour of her more traditional, more demure, and more 'English' half-sister, Lucile Edgermond. By extension, the delights and charms that Corinne represents as a poetic figure par excellence stand a world apart from the genre that Staël labelled the 'executive power' of literature in 'The Spirit of Translation': theatre (283). Lacking a viable socio-political ballast to create the genuinely national tragic stage, Italians must be content with Corinne's solitary lyrical effusions.[9] No wonder, then, that her musings on Italian cultural history seem always to occur, in the manner of all elegies, in the shadow of death. And so the novel ends where it begins: with Corinne once more at the Capitoline, but this time in death's throes and for her swan song, as she acts out

[8] See also my discussion of this scene in *Romantic Europe*, 215. See also Staël, *Corinne*, 2.1: 'Dans l'état actuel des Italiens, la gloire des beaux-arts est l'unique qui leur soit permise: et ils sentent le génie en ce genre avec une vivacité qui devroit faire naître beaucoup de grands hommes, s'il suffisoit de l'applaudisement pour les produire, s'il ne falloit pas une vie forte, de grands intérêts et une existence indépendante, pour alimenter la pensée' (New York: Leavitt, 1849), 20–1. 'In their present state, the only glory permitted to the Italians is that of the arts. They appreciate this kind of genius with a keenness which would give birth to many great men if acclaim would produce them, if strength of purpose, great interests, and an independent existence were not essential food for thought.' *Corinne, or Italy*, tr. Sylvia Raphael (Oxford: Oxford University Press, 1998), 21. Staël expresses a similar sentiment on Italy's melancholic artistic glory in 'The Spirit of Translation', tr. Joseph Luzzi, *Romanic Review*, 97 (2006), 284.

[9] The relation between Italy's socio-political fragmentation and its weak traditions in tragic theatre is the subject of my 'Tragedy without Society: Alfieri's Tragic Theater and the Discourse of Value', *European Romantic Review*, 20/5 (2009), 581–92.

her private drama in a land whose social and political fragmentation deny tragedy on a public scale.

A Woman of Genius: Foscolo and Leopardi contra Staël

The polemical responses to Staël's essay on translation have been well documented. Ranging from di Breme's *Intorno all'ingiustizia di alcuni giudizi letterari italiani* (On the injustice of some Italian literary judgements, 1816) to the now celebrated (yet then unpublished) reply of Leopardi, *Discorso di un italiano intorno alla poesia romantica* (*Discourse of an Italian on Romantic Poetry*, 1816), this outpouring of critical reaction to Staël's essay led to a hypertheorizing of Italian Romanticism. While it is impossible to reduce these responses to a single formula, they essentially sought to protect native Italian cultural idioms—principally, the propensity for allegory and mythology—from the imposition of foreign, Northern European norms. Thus, the struggle to define Italian Romantic poetics often became synonymous with the drive to define *italianità* (Italian identity), a link that would entwine the words *romanticismo* and *Risorgimento*.

Even an emphatically pro-Staël reply and the unofficial manifesto of Italian Romanticism, Giovanni Berchet's *Lettera semiseria di Grisostomo al suo figliuolo* (Semiserious letter from Chrysostom to his son, 1816), shared an essential quality with the negative rejoinders: his definition of Italian Romanticism was a defensive one, created as a rearguard act of cultural preservation against an outsider's view (Staël's) that exhorted Italy to imitate foreign cultures. Thus, Italian Romantic 'theory'—that branch of literary thought occupied with self-definition and self-reflection—lacked the optimism and energy of other Romantic movements that were unencumbered by the constant need to compare themselves to other countries and cultures. Even arguably the most powerful expression of Italian Romantic theory, Manzoni's dazzling recapitulation of the movement's growing pains and its implicit links to spiritual concerns, 'Lettera sul ' ('Letter on Romanticism', 1823), sought to explain Italian exceptionalism in the context of other Romantic movements. Hence his desire to divide his argument into 'negative' and 'positive' halves, the former saying what Romanticism in Italy *was not*, and the latter (and much shorter section of his essay) saying what it *was*.

Certain Italian literary works from the early nineteenth century reflect on Romantic theory in ways that implicate Staël. The case of Foscolo is instructive in this regard. In terms of the polemics over Romanticism, he said precious little that can be construed as an active contribution to the debates. Even his most explicit statement, on Italian Romantic tragedy in the *Edinburgh Review* in 1826, was more a self-promotion of his work as a tragedian than a meditation on the Romantic poetics that his essay maligns—especially in Manzoni.[10] For

[10] In 'Della nuova scuola drammatica in Italia' (On the new dramatic school in Italy, 1826), Foscolo critiques Manzoni's preoccupation with the 'historical' over the 'poetic' (quoted in Giorgio Pullini (ed.), *Le poetiche dell'Ottocento* (Padua: Liviana Editrice, 1959), 50, 56).

all the vagueness in Foscolo's attacks on *i romantici italiani*, the venom in his pen against Staël was rather explicit. In the first (and last) creative work of his British exile, *Lettere scritte dall'Inghilterra* (Letters written from England, 1817), he accused the author of *Corinne* of confusing the graves of Pietro Aretino and Leonardo Bruni, mistakenly listing Santa Croce as Boccaccio's burial site, and most egregiously of all offering seductive and superficial observations on the Italians that seemed issued by a woman gazing at Italians from a speeding carriage.[11]

Foscolo's 'On Sepulchers' takes on Staël in a different way: by implicitly exposing the weakness of her views on the problematic nature of Italian literary expression. Although the text was written about a decade before the Romantic debates of 1816, 'On Sepulchers' shows how neoclassical and mythological expression were indeed native Italian modes of feeling and thought that had little to do with the empty, rarefied erudition Staël accused them of. When Foscolo has Cassandra prophesy the future slavery of the Trojans in 'On Sepulchers', the allegorical link between ancient and modern Italian servitude is quite clear. That Foscolo has this political prophecy uttered by a well-known mythological figure shows just how connected the classical past and Italian present were to him. Such a link underwrites his belief in 'On Sepulchers' that the cities of the dead should never be separated from those of the living.

Leopardi also infused his feelings on Staël into creative forms that point to the uniqueness of Italian cultural expression and its ambivalent relation to European Romantic thought. Beyond his youthful polemic against Staël in *Discorso di un italiano intorno alla poesia romantica*, he was actually a very astute reader of the French author—much more so than Foscolo. But his views on *Corinne*, the subject of many insightful comments in Leopardi's massive philosophical notebook the *Zibaldone*, could also be inaccurate. In *Zibaldone*, 73, Leopardi quotes from book 5 of *Corinne* to show how Staël offers 'una solennissima condanna degli orrori e dell'eccessivo terribile tanto caro ai romantici' (very solemn condemnation of the horrors and terrible excesses that are so beloved of the Romantics) (104; 76).[12] But elsewhere in Staël's melodramatic *Corinne* we find many examples of that 'terrible' Romantic excess that Leopardi abhorred, and her novel eschews the classical forms that Leopardi spent his life defending (and defining as eminently Italian).

Leopardi's reading of Staël against the grain continues in *Zibaldone*, 86–7, when he cites Staël's description of the statue of Niobe from book 18, chapter 4, of *Corinne*: 'sans doute dans une semblable situation, la figure d'une véritable mère serait entièrement

[11] See Foscolo, *Lettere scritte dall'Inghilterra*, ii. 461.

[12] See *Corinne*, 5.2: 'mais l'ame est si mal à l'aise dans ce lieu, qu'il n'en peut résulter aucun bien pour elle. L'homme est une partie de la creation: il faut qu'il trouve son harmonie morale dans l'ensemble de l'univers, dans l'ordre habituel de la destinée; et de certaines exceptions violentes et redoutables peuvent étonner la pensée, mais effraient tellement l'imagination, que la disposition habituelle de l'ame ne sauroit y gagner' (84); 'but one's soul is so uncomfortable in this spot that no benefit can be obtained from it. Man is a part of creation; he must find his moral well-being in the universe as a whole, in the usual order of destiny. Certain fearful, violent expressions may astonish the mind, but they terrify the imagination so much that the usual state of the soul can derive no benefit from them' (80).

bouleversée; mais l'idéal des arts conserve la beauté dans le désespoir; et ce qui touche profondément dans les ouvrages du génie, ce n'est pas le malheur même, c'est la puissance que l'âme conserve sur ce malheur' (113); 'in a similar situation, no doubt, a real mother's facial expression would be utterly distraught; but in the arts, the ideal retains its beauty even in despair; and what touches us so deeply in works of genius is not misfortune itself but the power over misfortune that the soul retains' (83). Leopardi goes on to say that this reflects (once again) Staël's 'bellissima condanna del sistema romantico' (fine condemnation of the Romantic system):

> per conservare la semplicità e la naturalezza e fuggire l'affettazione che dai moderni è stata pur troppo sostituita alla dignità (facile agli antichi ad unire colla semplicità che ad essi era sí presente e nota e propria e viva), rinunzia ad ogni nobiltà, così che le loro opere di genio non hanno punto questa gran nota della loro origine, ed essendo una pura imitazione del vero, come una statua di cenci con parrucca e viso di cera ec. colpisce molto meno di quella che insieme colla semplicità e naturalezza conserva l'ideale del bello, e rende straordinario quello ch'è comune, cioè mostra ne' suoi eroi un'anima grande e un'attitudine dignitosa, il che muove la maraviglia e il sentimento profondo colla forza del contrasto, mentre nel romantico non potete esser commosso se non come dagli avvenimenti ordinari della vita ... (113–14)

> In order to preserve simplicity and naturalness, and to avoid affectation, which the moderns substituted, unfortunately, for dignity (which the ancients identified easily with simplicity, to them so present and familiar and right and living), the Romantic system eschews all nobility. As a result, their works of the mind bear no trace of this great feature of their origin, and, as a pure imitation of truth, like a rag statue with a wig and a wax face, etc., have much less effect than an imitation that, with simplicity and naturalness, preserves the ideal of beauty, and transforms the common into the extraordinary, that is, shows in its heroes a great soul and a dignified attitude, arousing admiration and deep feeling through the power of contrast. In the Romantic system, on the other hand, you cannot be moved except in the way you are moved by the everyday events of life. (83)

Leopardi's use of Staël in this manner is problematic on a number of fronts. First and most glaringly, he cites Staël out of context in claiming that her work rejects the 'Romantic system' because of her supposed refusal to let 'misfortune' triumph over the power of 'the soul' in her art. In truth, *Corinne* is very much a novel about excessive despair and pervasive melodrama, culminating in Corinne's swan song at the book's end, when she announces her impending death to an adoring public. That death is of course caused by the most sentimental of reasons—a broken heart over her failed relationship with Oswald and his marriage to Lucile. Second, the Romantic aesthetic that defines Staël's novel *Corinne* and many other works from her era was indeed concerned with the 'everyday', as the unusual and extraordinary became bywords of Romantic aesthetics. Corinne herself is a fantastic creature with little that is common about her. We can forgive Leopardi for such reductive dichotomies as Classical/Romantic and noble/common, as Staël among many others was guilty of the same vis-à-vis the Italians. But it is crucial to note that a great deal of Leopardi's—and Foscolo's—thinking on Romanticism grew out of his reflections on Staël, the foreign writer who had made the polemical mode a defining characteristic of early nineteenth-century Italian aesthetics.

From Polemics to Poetics: The Case of Manzoni

Manzoni's 'Letter on Romanticism' is an unusual document. Although it was initially drafted in 1823, it was first published without Manzoni's consent in 1846 and only appeared in an authorized edition in 1870, so it had no impact on the actual Romantic debates incited by Staël's essay on translation in 1816. Moreover, Manzoni's essay defended Romanticism in the most eccentric way imaginable: from a position of doctrinal Catholicism that few other writers would have promoted with such vigour. Manzoni writes:

> Era questa tendenza nelle intenzioni di quelli, che l'hanno proposto, e di quelli, che l'hanno approvato? Sarebbe leggerezza l'affermarlo di tutti, poiché in molti scritti di teorie romantiche, anzi nella maggior parte, le idee letterarie non sono espressamente subordinate al cristianesimo; sarebbe temerità il negarlo, anche d'uno solo, perché in nessuno di quegli scritti, almeno dei letti da me, il cristianesimo è escluso. Non abbiamo, né i dati, né il diritto, né il bisogno di fare un tale giudizio: quella intenzione, certo desiderabile, certo non indifferente, non è però necessaria per farci dare la preferenza a quel sistema. Basta che quella tendenza ci sia. ('Lettera', 452–3)

> Did those who first proposed and approved Romantic theory ever intend this Christian inclination? It would be frivolous to assert that this was everyone's intention, since in many Romantic theoretical writings, indeed in the greater part of them, literary ideas are not subordinated expressly to Christianity. It would be cowardly, however, to deny this Christian component, even in a single writer, for in none of these Romantic writings, at least in those I have read, is Christianity excluded. We have neither the facts, the right, nor the need to make such a judgment. Such a possible Christian intent, while certainly desirable and no small matter to us, is not, however, necessary to make us voice our preference for Romantic theory. It is enough for us that this Romantic tendency is present in Romantic thought. ('Letter', 313)

Those familiar with Manzoni's work will not be surprised to read his impassioned defence of what one might term 'Romantic Christianity'. Less obviously, Manzoni goes to great lengths to incorporate his vision of Christianity into his fictional writing. As we will see, his masterpiece *I promessi sposi* (*The Betrothed*, 1827; rev. edn 1840) gives life to his theoretical statements on the Romantic aesthetics in the 'Letter on Romanticism', especially his passage on the function of Romantic poetry:

> Dove poi l'opinioni de' Romantici erano unanimi, m'è parso, e mi pare, che fosse in questo: che la poesia deva proporsi per oggetto il vero, come l'unica sorgente d'un diletto nobile e durevole; giacché il falso può bensì trastullar la mente, ma non arricchirla, né elevarla; e questo trastullo medesimo è, di sua natura, instabile e temperario, potendo essere, come è desiderabile che sia, distrutto, anzi cambiato in fastidio, o da una cognizione sopravvegnente del vero, o da un amore cresciuto del vero medesimo. ('Lettera', 451)
>
> The area, then, in which the opinions of the Romantics were unanimous, it seemed and seems to me, was this: that poetry should make truth its objective, as the unique source of a noble and enduring delight. Although the false cannot fascinate the mind, it can neither enrich nor elevate it. This pseudofascination is, by its nature, unstable and temporary, since it is capable, as should be the case, of being destroyed or even changed into something tedious. Such a change may be brought about by a transcendent sense of truth or by an ever-increasing love of truth. ('Letter', 312)

Manzoni's term *true* is difficult to define in any context, especially in a domain as open to interpretation as the literary imagination. Yet Manzoni has something specific in mind for the word. He does not mean 'logical' or 'verifiable' in the scientific sense; rather, *il vero* functions here as an indicator of a moral ideal. Manzoni believed that literature must always serve a higher function—the glorification of God, the cultivation of national identity, the instruction of the public—and that the 'true' literary form was the one that best achieved such goals. As for his mighty predecessor Dante (who places Francesca and Paolo in hell for an adultery caused by reading *per diletto*, 'for pleasure' divorced from ethics), for Manzoni the aesthetic cannot exist independent of moral concerns. It is beholden to the laws governing human behaviour and the feelings motivating human faith. As such, there are times when aesthetic interests must give way to extraliterary claims.

We see this notion of truth at work in one of the final chapters of *I promessi sposi*, when Renzo, long separated from his fiancée Lucia, has a reunion both with the man who has helped him escape his persecutors (the priest Fra Cristoforo) and the evil nobleman whose lustful pursuit of Lucia led to Renzo's exile (Don Rodrigo). Renzo finds Fra Cristoforo at the *lazzaretto*, the quarantine compound where victims were sequestered during the bubonic plague of 1630, a pivotal event in the narrative that wipes out thousand of lives and many of the novel's characters. When the subject of Don Rodrigo comes up, Renzo speaks of his wish for vengeance, inspiring Fra Cristoforo to launch into a tirade:

> 'Guarda, sciagurato!' E mentre con una mano stringeva e scoteva forte il braccio di Renzo, girava l'altra davanti a sè, accennando quanto più poteva della dolorosa scena all'intorno. 'Guarda chi è Colui che gastiga! Colui che giudica, e non è giudicato! Colui che flagella e che perdona! Ma tu, verme della terra, tu vuoi far giustizia! Tu

> lo sai, tu, quale sia la giustizia! Va, sciagurato, vattene! Io, speravo … sì, ho sperato che, prima della mia morte, Dio m'avrebbe data questa consolazione di sentir che la mia povera Lucia fosse viva; forse di vederla, e di sentirmi prometter da lei che rivolgerebbe una preghiera là verso quella fossa dov'io sarò. Va, tu m'hai levata la mia speranza. Dio non l'ha lasciata in terra per te; e tu, certo, non hai l'ardire di crederti degno che Dio pensi a consolarti. Avrà pensato a lei, perchè lei è una di quell'anime a cui son riservate le consolazioni eterne. Va! non ho più tempo di darti retta.' (*Promessi*, 683–4)

> 'Look around you!' [Fra Cristoforo] went on. He held Renzo fast, and shook his arm with one hand, while he swept the other round in front of him to take in as much as possible of that terrible scene [in the *lazzaretto*]. 'Look and see who it is that chastiseth mankind, who it is that judgeth and is not judged, who layeth on sore strokes and who granteth men his pardon! And you, worm that you are, crawling on the face of the earth, *you* want to administer justice! *You* know what justice is! Go, wretched sinner, leave my sight! And I hoped—yes, I had hoped that before I died, God would have granted me the happiness of knowing that my poor Lucia was still alive, perhaps even of seeing her again, and of hearing her promise to offer up a prayer over my grave! Go! for you have robbed me of that hope. I know now that God has not left her in this world for you. And you for your part cannot dare to hope, to think yourself worthy that he should have any care for your happiness. He will have taken thought for her, because she is one of those souls that are destined to eternal felicity. Go! I have no more time to waste on listening to you!' (*Betrothed*, 660)

Following this scene, Fra Cristoforo leads Renzo inside a room of the *lazzaretto*, where none other than Don Rodrigo is lying ill—and under the care of his former mortal enemy, Fra Cristoforo himself (whom Don Rodrigo had actively opposed and insulted earlier in the text). Fra Cristoforo's speech shifts the narrative into a deeply didactic and biblical rhetoric through the repeated use of the pronoun introducing God ('Colui') and stock phrases like 'verme della terra' (worm of the earth).[13] The Christian themes are clearly delineated (the separation of human and divine justice, the promise of a better life to come, and Fra Cristoforo's righteous indignation over Renzo's inability to forgive Don Rodrigo). And the lexical choices point beyond the secular and into the sacred ('sciagurato', 'miserable sinner'; 'Colui che flagella e che perdona', 'who layeth on sore strokes and who granteth … pardon'; 'consolazioni eterne', 'eternal felicity'). Of course, the scene has a literal, diegetic function in the narrative as the expression of Fra Cristoforo's mix of piety and rage in confronting the hot-tempered Renzo's desire for vengeance. But the larger message of the episode, suffused as it is with such overtly Christian rhetoric, cannot help but recall Manzoni's insistence in the 'Letter on Romanticism' that only an art that seeks the 'true'—which in his view was synonymous with the godly and Christian—was worthy of the name 'Romantic'. Moreover, the passage reveals yet again the willingness of an Italian author to embrace that allegorical mode so often criticized as artistically insufficient in European Romantic thought.[14] By grafting a biblical subtext

[13] I describe a similar rhetorical tendency in Manzoni's verse play *Adelchi* (*Adelchis*, 1822), 2.167–93: Luzzi, *Romantic Europe*, 32–4.

[14] Hazard Adams summarizes the symbol–allegory debate in the Romantic period: *Philosophy of the Literary Symbolic* (Tallahassee, Fla.: University Presses of Florida, 1983), 46–98.

onto Fra Cristoforo's words, Manzoni reveals both his ardent faith and his willingness to use his fictional narrative to stake a theoretical claim central to what he called *il sistema romantico*, Romantic theory.

Conclusion

I have attempted to show how the polemical strain of Italian Romanticism, which often centred on reactions to either Staël's essay on translation or her novel *Corinne*, led to the creation of literary forms that gave aesthetic life to the theoretical debates over Romanticism in nineteenth-century Italy. It may seem ironic that the *tre corone* on whom this chapter has focused were not among the voices in the 1816 debates that developed in reply to Staël's essay (Leopardi did weigh in but his contribution was not published until long after the controversy). Yet it is plausible that the lack of investment in the actual polemics of Italian Romanticism by Foscolo, Leopardi, and Manzoni freed them to create works of the imagination that, indirectly and directly, pronounced on the issues central to the creation of a uniquely Italian version of Romanticism. The partisan and ideological nature of the Italian Romantic movement is well known. So it is fitting that the most towering works of art produced during the strange career of Italian Romanticism should be adversarial and argumentative. After all, such masterpieces were the aesthetic embodiments of a polemical mode that questioned whether Romanticism belonged in Italy, and whether Italians belonged in Romantic aesthetics.

Further Reading

Adams, Hazard, *Philosophy of the Literary Symbolic* (Tallahassee, Fla.: University Presses of Florida, 1983).

Avitabile, Grazia, *The Controversy on Romanticism in Italy: First Phase, 1816–1823* (New York: Vanni, 1959).

Benjamin, Walter, 'The Task of the Translator: An Introduction to the Translation of Baudelaire's *Tableaux parisiens*', in Hannah Arendt (ed.), *Illuminations*, tr. Harry Zohn (New York: Schocken, 1968), 69–82.

Calcaterra, Carlo (ed.), *I manifesti romantici* (Turin: UTET, 1951).

Curran, Stuart, *Poetic Form and British Romanticism* (Oxford: Oxford University Press, 1986).

Foscolo, Ugo, *Lettere scritte dall'Inghilterra*, ed. Elena Lombardi, in *Opere*, 2 vols, ed. Franco Gavezzeni (Turin: Einaudi-Gallimard, 1994–5), iii. 447–94.

Leopardi, Giacomo, *Zibaldone dei pensieri*, ii. *Tutte le opere di Giacomo Leopardi*, ed. Francesco Flora, 3rd edn (Milan: Mondadori, 1949); English tr., *Zibaldone*, ed. Michael Caesar and Franco D'Intino, tr. Kathleen Baldwin et al. (New York: Farrar, Straus & Giroux, 2013).

Luzzi, Joseph, *Romantic Europe and the Ghost of Italy* (New Haven: Yale University Press, 2008).

Luzzi, Joseph, 'Tragedy without Society: Alfieri's Tragic Theater and the Discourse of Value', *European Romantic Review*, 20/5 (2009), 581–92.

Manzoni, Alessandro, *I promessi sposi* [1840 edn], ii. *I romanzi*, ed. Salvatore Nigro, 2 vols (Milan: Mondadori, 2002). English tr., *The Betrothed*, tr. Bruce Penman (Harmondsworth: Penguin, 1972).

Manzoni, Alessandro, 'Sul romanticismo: Lettera al marchese Cesare d'Azeglio', in *Opere*, ed. Guido Bezzola, 3 vols (Milan: Rizzoli, 1961), iii. 425–57. English tr., 'A Gentle Prophecy: Alessandro Manzoni's "Letter on Romanticism"', tr. Joseph Luzzi, *PMLA* 119/2 (2004), 399–416.

Porter, Roy, and Mikulás Teich (eds), *Romanticism in National Context* (Cambridge: Cambridge University Press, 1988).

Pullini, Giorgio (ed.), *Le poetiche dell'Ottocento* (Padua: Liviana Editrice, 1959).

Puppo, Mario, *Romanticismo italiano e romanticismo europeo* (Milan: Istituto Propaganda Libraria, 1985).

Raimondi, Enzo, *Romanticismo italiano e romanticismo europeo* (Milan: Mondadori, 1997).

Staël, Mme la Baronne de, *Corinne, ou l'Italie* (New York: Leavitt, 1849); English tr., *Corinne, or Italy*, tr. Sylvia Raphael (Oxford: Oxford University Press, 1998).

Staël, Mme la Baronne de, *Literature Considered in its Relation to Social Institutions: Politics, Literature, and National Character*, tr. and ed. Morroe Berger (New Brunswick, NJ: Transaction, 2000), 139–256.

Staël, Mme la Baronne de, 'The Spirit of Translation', tr. Joseph Luzzi, *Romanic Review*, 97 (2006), 275–84.

Vincent, E. R., *Ugo Foscolo: An Italian in Regency England* (Cambridge: Cambridge University Press, 1953).

Wellek, René, *A History of Modern Criticism, 1750–1950*, 8 vols (New Haven: Yale University Press, 1955–72).

Wordsworth, William, 'Preface to *Lyrical Ballads*', in Willam Wordsworth and Samuel Taylor Coleridge, *Lyrical Ballads, 1798 and 1802*, ed. Fiona Stafford (Oxford: Oxford University Press, 2013), 95–115.

CHAPTER 21

VOICE, SPEAKING, SILENCE IN LEOPARDI'S VERSE

MICHAEL CAESAR

THE present contribution is concerned with what is often taken for granted in the Romantic lyric and in Leopardi's poetry in particular: that is, the act of speech in a poetic context, and its realization in the figure of voice. I shall be concerned with the liminal moment of enunciation, the poet's speaking, that speech which presents itself immediately, before any reference, and that, for the reader or listener, always re-presents itself, looping, so that even when we are absorbed in the reading of what the poem says, we never entirely succeed in forgetting its saying. On the contrary, this is one of the capital differences between lyric poetry—at least, in the affective, strongly personalized, version that it assumes in the eyes of Leopardi, 'where the poet and his own feelings are always to the fore' (*Z* 4417, 3 November 1828)[1]—and narrative forms, for while the reading of a novel allows us to enter into another, entirely imagined and imaginable reality, which leaves its sources and its departure points behind it, the poem continually reminds us that there is a someone or a something that is saying it.

For the Romantics this difference is constituted in terms of exteriority (of narrative) and interiority (of the subject speaking the lyric). The personalization of poetry conceived as extreme intimacy reaches its apex in Hegel's *Aesthetics*, where '[w]hat is most completely lyrical from this point of view' (that of the lyric poet's 'self-bounded subjective entirety') 'is a mood of the heart concentrated on a concrete situation, because the sensitive heart is what is inmost in the subjective life' ('das Innerste und Eigenste der Subjektivität').[2] The relationship between poetry and reading is seen as an interpersonal relationship, between poet and reader, to which is added, almost inevitably, a further

[1] It is customary to refer to Leopardi's notebooks, the *Zibaldone di pensieri*, by the author's own page numbers (here preceded by the abbreviation *Z*). The edn used (the first complete tr. into English) is Giacomo Leopardi, *Zibaldone*, ed. Michael Caesar and Franco D'Intino (New York: Farrar, Straus & Giroux; London: Penguin, 2013).

[2] G. W. F. Hegel, *Aesthetics*, tr. T. M. Knox (Oxford: Oxford University Press, 1975), ii. 1133.

element, that of sound, or of voice. Voice is a particularly privileged figure in Romantic poetics and criticism, and also in Romantic reading, because of the guarantees that it gives of presence, immediacy, and plenitude, whether of the speaker or the act of communication or the listener. Indeed, the poet speaks and the reader listens. But the kind of listening is particular. From the Romantic perspective, the poet does not speak to the listener directly, he does not attempt to explain himself or enter into a dialogue; on the contrary, he speaks as though the other were not there. It is for the reader to grasp the import of the words that are directed elsewhere, or that turn back upon themselves.

This is the point that is stressed by John Stuart Mill's celebrated synthesis of 1833, which illustrates the relation between the interiority that Hegel insists upon and the exteriority that is represented by the demands of a public: 'Eloquence is *heard*, poetry is *overheard*. Eloquence supposes an audience, the peculiarity of poetry appears to us to lie in the poet's utter unconsciousness of a listener. Poetry is feeling confessing itself to itself in moments of solitude.'[3] The enormously suggestive formula of speaking with oneself, alone, potentially with others but not in direct communication with them, a virtual colloquy in the form of soliloquy—readers of Leopardi's *Canti* will instantly recognize the emblematic situation of Brutus or Sappho in the poems that bear their name—spreads through the history of Romantic criticism at least as far as M. H. Abrams's fundamental essay on 'Structure and Style in the Greater Romantic Lyric' (1965). Under this rubric, the poems that Abrams proposes to discuss, for which, collectively, '[t]here is no accepted name', 'present a determinate speaker in a particularized, and usually localized, outdoor setting, whom we overhear as he carries on, in a fluent vernacular which rises easily to a more formal speech, a sustained colloquy, sometimes with himself or with the outer scene, but more frequently with a silent human auditor, present or absent'.[4] But if it is natural, Romanticly speaking, to think of the voice of poetry as the voice of a person, this does not necessarily mean that it is the person, that is, the content of the voice, that the reader is interested in. Hardly less strong than the tradition of the personal voice is that of the impersonality of the lyric, a doctrine formulated in an anti-Romantic key, but that has its origins in Romanticism itself and that takes on very different forms: from the multiple existence of 'the camelion Poet' to which Keats alludes in a letter ('A Poet is the most unpoetical of any thing in existence; because he has no Identity—he is continually in for—and filling some other Body')[5] to the transition from 'enthusiasm' to 'inspiration' as the motive force of poetic speech, to Leopardi's image of the poet traversed by the voice of Nature and an 'imitator' only of himself, in a way that tends to diminish the personality of the poet ('The poet does not imitate nature: rather is it true that nature speaks within him and through his mouth ... Thus the poet is not an imitator except of himself.... When through imitation he truly takes leave of himself, that really is no longer

[3] John Stuart Mill, 'What is Poetry?', now in *Essays on Poetry*, ed. F. Parvin Sharpless (Columbia, SC: University of South Carolina Press, 1976), 12.

[4] Now in Harold Bloom (ed.), *Romanticism and Consciousness* (New York: W. W. Norton, 1970), 201.

[5] John Keats, letter to Richard Woodhouse dated 27 Oct. 1818, in *Letters of John Keats*, ed. Robert Gittings (Oxford: Oxford University Press, 1970), 157; Gittings surmises 'informing' for 'in for' as written by Keats.

poetry, a divine faculty; that is a human art, it is prose, despite the verse and the language': *Z* 4372–3, 10 September 1828).

Impersonality, however, should not be seen as the simple reversal of personality, a mask, a person in disguise. It entails also the recognition of another dimension of the experience of the reader who is not interested, or not immediately interested, in the idea of someone who speaks, and whom one might wish or feel the obligation to know, or who, alternatively, is concealed and pursued through a scenario of disguises and recognitions. This other dimension focuses not on the speaker, but on the speaking, and more often than not a speaking that, rather than signalling a presence, points rather to an absence. What is read is precisely a trace, a sound which fills a void which could also not be there, which indeed is not there except in the moment of listening. The poet who says 'I' also says the opposite at the same time, saying 'I am not here', '*I* am not here', 'there is no I'. Word and silence break in upon each other. We may add that the voice the reader hears, materially, in the reading of the poem, is necessarily her own.

Further: for the reader, it is not only what the poem says that counts, but—even in advance of the reception of any specific message, and perhaps over and beyond it—the fact of its saying, in itself. The transmutation of signs on the page into an inner sense, the unravelling of sound from silence, these acts that occur on every occasion that the text is read are in themselves an involvement and a commitment that are not trivial. The opening of a dialogue between a reader who in the act of reading makes the inert text speak and the poem that speaks in the silence of the reader marks a privileged moment, suspended as it is in the entirety of the complex relations that pass between a reader and a text. A silence is broken, a relationship is instituted, a meaning will be produced, a transformation occurs from a pre-existing situation to another that would not necessarily have taken place. The announcement of the poem, its becoming present through its reading, is an event that ordinarily takes on the figure of voice, and corresponds to pure enunciation.

With the foregoing observations on enunciation in mind, I shall focus on moments in Leopardi's verse that pay particular attention to the figure of voice, which will be examined from three directions. First, I refer to those moments in which the rhetorical disposition of the text leads to a particular awareness of voice on the part of the reader, where there is a kind of actualization of voice. A particular instance of such actualization lies in the rhetorical figure of apostrophe. Secondly, I shall discuss a sample of given moments in the *Canti*, with particular reference to some of the *canzoni* (odes) written between 1818 and 1822, which Leopardi arranged to form the opening sequence of the editions that he oversaw in his lifetime and authorized for subsequent editions.[6] In these poems,

[6] Leopardi's earliest published poems (*All'Italia*, *Sopra il monumento di Dante*, and *Ad Angelo Mai*), written between 1818 and 1820, appeared in very limited edns (see also nn. 8 and 9). Between 1824 and 1826, Leopardi oversaw the publication, first of his *Canzoni*, including the three already published (Bologna: Nobili, 1824), and then of his shorter poems, including *L'infinito* (written in 1819), in Bolognese and Milanese literary journals (1825–6), subsequently gathered, with other compositions, in *Versi* (Bologna: Stamperia delle Muse, 1826). The Florentine edn of 1831 (Piatti), the first to appear with the title *Canti*, dropped various poems and translations from the Bologna 1826 edn, maintained the *canzoni* as the opening section of the collection, followed by the shorter *idilli*, and including the new poems written

voice is highlighted, dramatized, and to some degree problematized. The problematization of voice, finally, assumes more acute forms in several of Leopardi's very late poems, and these will be addressed in the final section of this chapter.

Apostrophe is a trope, as Jonathan Culler observed in a ground-breaking essay first published in 1977, that creates a good deal of embarrassment among critics, especially, we might add, among those who are inclined to regard lyric poetry as the expression of the interiority of one person that is destined to be internalized by another.[7] Repeatedly, in fact, the apostrophe upon which so much Romantic (and pre-Romantic) poetry is based, the voice of the poet there, on the scene, who invokes or evokes, who calls or animates or concretizes or makes present nature or the inanimate or the abstract or the absent or in general the other, is traduced and reduced, in critical discourse, to an instance of pure descriptiveness. Thus, anything and everything that might be strange, that might in some way arrest the reader of an *incipit* like 'O wild West Wind, thou breath of Autumn's being, | Thou, from whose unseen presence' etc. (note the 'unseen presence') is typically converted into an almost conventional description of an autumn scene with dead leaves and wind. From this premise, Culler develops an argument that is useful also for approaching Leopardi.

For Culler, the embarrassment felt in the presence of apostrophe derives from the fact that it is a trope that, unlike other tropes, does not concern the meaning of a word, but the very situation and circuit of communication. He analyses its role at four successive levels. First, apostrophe undoubtedly serves as a sign of intensification, as an image of passionate feeling, as an expression produced by the spontaneous impulse of a powerfully moved soul (61). This is not sufficient, however, because, at a second level, when poems 'address natural objects they formally will that these particular objects function as subjects'. What is formally at stake is 'the power of poetry to make something happen': 'The vocative posits a relationship between two subjects even if the sentence containing it denies the animicity of what is addressed' (62). This simple relation between an 'I' and a 'you' does not take account of possible listeners. Culler thus supposes a third level, 'where the vocative of apostrophe is a device which the poetic voice uses to establish with an object a relationship that helps to constitute him. The object is treated as a subject, an *I* which implies a certain type of *you* in its turn. One who successfully invokes nature is one to whom nature might, in its turn, speak. He makes himself poet, visionary. Thus, invocation is a figure of vocation' (63). But, in a final, more sceptical turn, Culler reaches his fourth level of reading, 'at which one must question the status so far granted to the *thou* of the apostrophic structure and reflect on the crucial though paradoxical fact that this figure which seems to establish relations between the self and the other can

in Pisa and Recanati between 1828 and 1830. The subsequent edn of *Canti* (Naples: Starita, 1835) included several new poems, two of which were strategically placed earlier in the volume, as will be mentioned later. The first posthumous edn (Florence: Le Monnier, 1845) included for the first time *Il tramonto della luna* and *La ginestra*.

[7] Jonathan Culler, 'Apostrophe', *Diacritics*, 7/4 (Winter 1977), 59–69; specific page references to passages from this article are given in the text.

in fact be read as an act of radical interiorization and solipsism, which either parcels out the self to fill the world, peopling the world with fragments of the self, or else internalizes what might have been thought external' (65–6).

No less interesting than this structuring of the argument is what Culler has to say about the relationship between apostrophe and temporality. The interiorization mentioned at the fourth level is important because it works against narrative, sequentiality, causality, time, and teleological meaning. Objects put together in a poem seem to require narrative linking. But if they are apostrophized, vocalized—ye hills, thou shepherd boy, or, in Leopardi, *voi collinette e piagge, garzoncello scherzoso*—they are associated with 'what might be called a timeless present but is better seen as a temporality of writing'. Apostrophized, the objects are located in the time of the apostrophe, 'a special temporality which is the set of all moments at which writing can say "now"'. This is discourse-time rather than story-time. Localized by apostrophe, the constituent parts are 'inserted in the poem as elements of the event' rather than being 'organized into events that can be narrated' (66).

In light of this theorization of apostrophe, one consequence of which is to shift attention from the enunciated to the enunciation, we might read certain poems by Leopardi, such as *Ad Angelo Mai* ('To Angelo Mai') and *Inno ai Patriarchi, o de' principii del genere umano* ('Hymn to the Patriarchs, or On the Origins of the Human Race'),[8] those in which apostrophe is more insisted upon and in which it is statistically more frequent, in an anti-narrative vein, not as the story of a decline so much as the attempt to remedy it. In these cases, apostrophe would have the function of underlining the (fictive) capacity of the poetic voice to actualize the absent at the moment of enunciation (that is, with each separate reading). It would follow then that the Romantic position is overturned. No longer can the integrity of the I act as guarantee of the product (the poem), for the guarantee is based on that trope, apostrophe, which lends itself least to a 'realistic' reading. Thus, when voice becomes an issue in Leopardi's poetic discourse, it is almost always to underline its precariousness. My intention in the pages that follow is to illustrate this assertion by attending to the figuration of voice, and its dramatization, in the early *canzoni*, initially through the speaker-protagonists Simonides, Brutus, and Sappho, and then through the 'ancient myths' of *Alla Primavera* (To Spring). The cumulative effect is that of an attenuation of the word, of its reduction to a thread in a hostile environment, of its destiny as a victim that is also in some measure a survivor (in a manner not dissimilar from the fate of 'the flower of the desert' in *La ginestra*), of the difficulty of enunciation (in this case, that of the protagonist-speaker, *within* the poem.)

In the first of the poems taken into consideration, *All'Italia* (To Italy), the voices that we hear discoursing, declaiming, that of the I speaking in the present and, subsequently, that of the historical personage Simonides, are both strangely dissociated from the reality into which they seek to insert themselves.[9] The poem opens with the speaker who,

[8] Also included among the early *canzoni*, written in Jan. 1820 and July 1822 respectively. The English titles, and all quotations in English from the *Canti*, are taken from: Giacomo Leopardi, *Canti*, tr. and annotated by Jonathan Galassi (New York: Farrar, Straus & Giroux; London: Penguin Classics, 2010).

[9] Written in Sept. 1818, originally with the title *Sull'Italia* (On Italy); along with its companion piece *Sopra il monumento di Dante che si preparava in Firenze* (On the Monument to Dante Being Erected

in tune with his fellow citizens ('noi', 'nostri', we, our), turns towards and apostrophizes an object ('Italia') that not only ought to come alive through this procedure but indeed should react—in the fiction of the poem—and respond to the poet's insistent demands, and see, speak in her turn. But instead, Italy, throughout the whole poem, does not respond at all, and after the first six lines the Italians too are left aside, and removed from the poem. The poem itself becomes a space that resembles a stage, occupied exclusively by a voice in the first person that addresses an object that does not respond, for the benefit of an audience that is silent. The voice penetrates and denudes the object (ll. 12, 14–17), amplifies and projects it beyond the limits of the stage (ll. 10–12, 25–7), generates rhetorical questions, hyperbolic demands, grandiose gestures, and affirmations and commands (ll. 10ff., 21–3, 37–8). Little by little the reader understands that this taciturn Italia is right not to be comforted by the sound of 'l'itala gioventude' (young Italians) fighting in battle, and her refusal to respond (ll. 49–52) exposes in turn the false rhetoric and the false vision of her bard. At this point, the *canzone* seems almost to portray the naivety of the sorcerer's apprentice trying at all costs to animate what cannot be in any way animated, as if to tell him that he is talking aimlessly, that the magic of apostrophe does not obtain in his case. To overcome the threat of blockage, from the fourth stanza on, the initial 'I' of the poem gives way to another, at first sight more authoritative, voice than the poet's own, more authoritative by virtue of its antiquity and its proximity to the fallen of Thermopylae celebrated in a sixth-fifth century lyrical fragment attributed to Simonides. But while for Leopardi, writing as humble author to the prestigious dedicatee of the two *canzoni patriottiche*, Vincenzo Monti, no greater or more suitable subject for a lyric poet could be imagined, before or since, than that which inspired Simonides and still inspires whoever reads or hears the story twenty-three centuries later, his own audacious bid, clad in appropriate modesty, to put himself 'in the shoes of Simonides' ('nei panni di Simonide') and to 'reconstruct' ('rifare') the latter's poem does not resolve the vexed relation between the figure of the bard and the addressees of the discourse (Italy and the young Italians), or, by extension, the author of the poem and his readers in the here and now.[10] There is something that does not square up in the performance of Simonides, a reversal of what we might expect to be the position of the visionary poet. Leopardi underlines the radical subordination of his position. In the words with which Simonides concludes his evocation of the heroes—'Così la vereconda || Fama del vostro vate appo i futuri | Possa, volendo i numi, | Tanto durar quanto la vostra duri' ('still may the modest glory of your bard, | if the gods will it, | endure as long as yours | in times to come': *All'Italia*, 137–40)—we understand that it is not the bard who will perpetuate the events in song, but the events that will perpetuate him. In reality, the memory of the

in Florence), written in Sept.—Oct. 1818, it was published in Rome at the beginning of 1819 (though dated '1818'), under the genre heading of *Canzoni*; the two poems together are referred to as the *canzoni patriottiche* (patriotic odes).

[10] The passages quoted or translated from Leopardi's dedication to Vincenzo Monti are taken from Giacomo Leopardi, *Poesie e Prose*, i, ed. Mario Andrea Rigoni (Milan: Arnoldo Mondadori Editore, 1987), 156.

battle, of the bravery, of the deaths, is already inscribed in the place; and already, before Simonides appears on the scene, the speaking I has told us: 'Io credo che le piante e i sassi e l'onda | E le montagne vostre al passeggere | Con indistinta voce | Narrin siccome tutta quella sponda | Coprìr le invitte schiere | De' corpi ch'alla Grecia eran devoti' ('It seems to me your trees and rocks, | your sea and mountains | murmur to the passing traveller | how the undefeated ranks | covered the entire shore | with undefeated bodies sworn to Greece': *All'Italia*, 68–73). Inspired in the manner of Ossian by a land that speaks, Simonides becomes its echo; and subsequently (in a time, to be clear, of Leopardi and us as readers), while the story of the heroes continues crystalline and imperishable, the song of the bard is lost, and must be reconstituted. In the two parts of the *canzone*, that which is Leopardi's and that which is Simonides', the human, in this case commemorative, voice is felt as something added. The poetic voice is displaced from the central position that it occupies at the beginning of each part and shifts towards the margins, leaving the space to a reality and a physicality that are far more eloquent.

The creation of figures or personages on the part of Leopardi, who speak for the whole or a large part of a poem written in the name of their author, poses interesting problems of identification. Limiting ourselves to the two most significant cases, those of Brutus and Sappho, it is unlikely that the reader will not ask herself, and that the question will not stimulate the reading, whether the historical figure should not be read in some way as the spokesperson of the author, or as a front or double. The difficulty with this kind of question is that it shifts attention from the text to the author and demands that it be deep in the folds of the author's psychology that the reader must probe in order to extract the reasons for such a delegation of meaning. Why, indeed, should the author have entrusted his meaning to another, to a messenger? The creation of a figure like Brutus or Sappho becomes, from this point of view, an extreme case of the poetic 'persona' or 'mask' offered as a vehicle for interpreting lyrical subjectivity, according to which the poetic I is not identical to the I of the poet's private self, but is a poetic version or projection of the same. But even if this way of looking at things helps us avoid the worst excesses of psychologism, it still refers back, ineluctably, to the interiority of the author as the origin and principle of interpretation: the poet adopts the role of a director or a ventriloquist, and it is legitimate to ask what is at the root of so strange an attitude. It would be preferable to be able to resist the temptation to enter back into the poet's mind, or to read the poems as copies or reflections or echoes of an antecedent, and prior, reality existing within their author.

That said, it should be added that the psychological dimension of *Bruto minore* (Brutus) and *Ultimo canto di Saffo* (Sappho's Last Song) is extremely powerful, given that, if what we are dealing with in these poems is dramatization, the stage on which these dramas are played out is human consciousness itself. In the first, the use of the opening stanza to set the scene creates a theatrical and existential space that is threatening and tragic. Everything that will pass in the remainder of the poem through the voice of Brutus is localized from the outset in silence, in the culmination of the opening scene: 'E di feroci note | Invan la sonnolenta aura percote' ('and [Brutus] assails the sleeping air in vain | with savage cries': ll. 14–15). The 'savage cries' that follow make themselves heard in an absolute present, next to which the past is consumed and the future, that of 'our corrupt descendants' (l. 116), is denied. This present is a time that is unusual for Leopardi, the poet par excellence of desire (ever denied), of memory, of the conditional mood, and the references to everything other than himself—to the gods, to the animals, to the moon, to the ignorant, to the descendants—as an attempt to defer the present, a last bathing in the familiar and comforting waters of possibilities, alternatives. But the attempt, or more precisely the temptation, is in vain, the present returns inexorably, the voice of the protagonist, unlike the song of the birds, echoes in an existential landscape in which every sound that has to do with the destiny of humankind is already an empty sound, like the word that stands for valour at the very beginning of Brutus's speech: 'Stolta virtù, le cave nebbie' ('Foolish valor, empty mists': 16): the echoing of that lonely place under the barbarian's heel ('Sotto barbaro piede | Rintronerà quella solinga sede': 89–90), the 'ululati spechi' (the 'caves resounding with our cries') of l. 103, undisturbed by our calamity.

In *Ultimo canto di Saffo*, on the contrary, everything is internalized, both in the purely material sense that there is no introductory stanza as in *Bruto minore* and we enter directly into the protagonist's speech—and this has the effect that the silence that surrounds her and awaits her is internalized as well, and so in a certain way is accommodated or adapted to herself by the speaker—and in the sense that Sappho, unlike Brutus, is endowed with a story and a past. In a poem that plays on two divisions, one within nature that is not, or is no longer, the 'spettacol molle' ('gentle scene': 6) of appearances, the other that which is proper to the human subject, Sappho pursues her lost innocence, the illusion of an originary unity within the self, even 'anzi il natale' ('before my birth': 38), without its existence or genuineness ever being confirmed. Sappho's self, furthermore, is a divided one, a self that is multiplied and fragmented, slipping from singular to plural and back, following tracks whose sense can be reconstructed a posteriori, but whose changes of direction, when they appear in the poem, signal radical and disconcerting swerves. Her recourse to the second person singular at a moment that is particularly dangerous for the identity of the speaker is also noteworthy: 'Incaute voci | Spande il tuo labbro' ('Your lips spill foolish words': 44–5). While in Brutus we had a voice that was as if disembodied and that echoes like a void, in Sappho interiorization does not lead to voice as a unifying agent but, quite the opposite, to voice as an instrument of discordance, discrepancy, and dismemberment.

In the three speaker-protagonists described, Simonides, Brutus, and Sappho, we can track the isolation of the voice. It is an exasperation of the condition identified by Mill, the poet who speaks with himself, 'overheard' and quite possibly not to be heard at all. They are poems that highlight—at an early stage in Leopardi's career—the constraints surrounding the poetic voice and its inner instability. The insecurity of the poetic voice is more than ever made apparent in the last two stanzas of *Alla Primavera, o delle favole antiche* (To Spring, or On the Ancient Myths), a *canzone* written immediately after *Bruto minore* in January 1822, in which the use in combination of the myths of Echo and Philomela leads to a generalization of the theme. The essential point to note, as far as Philomela is concerned, is that while nature in the present, from which all human meaning has fled, carries the voice of the 'musico augel' ('musical bird': 71; Philomela, the nightingale), its opposite, the humanized nature of another time, the nature of myth, tells the story of a voice that is cut or mutilated, Philomela's tongue ripped out, the sign of outrage and grief, the time of denunciation and lament. Paradoxically, humanized nature, the nature whose loss is mourned, is understood as itself being the scene of loss and privation; the originary voice of humankind, as Geoffrey Hartman put it in his study of the myth of Philomela, 'is intrinsically elegiac'.[11]

Alongside the figure of Philomela the poem introduces that of Echo (the two are often paired also in Renaissance poetry), an Echo who in the past has been the means of transmission of the 'luttuosi accenti' of 'umano affanno' ('the mournful sound of human suffering': 59, 58) to an only apparently insensible nature (harsh cliffs, fearful caves, grottoes, bare rocks, and lonely places). Clearly, this is a role that can no longer be performed in the demythicized world of modern times, but if the echo can no longer repeat the laments of humans, this function remains and is adopted, however dubitatively, by the first-person speaker at the end of the poem when he turns to nature: 'Tu le cure infelici e i fati indegni | Tu de' mortali ascolta, | Vaga natura, e la favilla antica | Rendi allo spirito mio' ('Hear the troubles | and unworthy fates of mortals, | lovely Nature, and imbue my spirit | with the old spark': 88–91). To be sure, there is no obligation on the poet to make nature aware of all human ills, but by addressing her, he disposes her to listen (perhaps). In a demythicized world, the mutilated voice is inherited by the contemporary poet.

One final observation on the themes explored so far, which imply a parallel research on the poetics of sound in Leopardi's verse, and on issues to do with 'person' and 'subjectivity' throughout Leopardi's work. Concerning the first aspect, there is an observable tendency, in at least part of his poetry, towards associating the human with an order of sounds that is broken, subject to the law of intermittency, while associating nature with an order that is relatively stable (see for example the contrast in *Il passero solitario* (The Solitary Thrush) between the bleating of the flocks and the lowing of the herds on the one hand and the bell-ringing and rifle-fire reports on the other, where the broken rhythm of human noise—peels and blasts—is linked to the non-linear rhythm of human time represented in the speaker's 'mistaken times' of youth and old age, in his putting off 'every pleasure and enjoyment | to another time' ('Ogni diletto e gioco | Indugio in altro tempo: e intanto ...': 37–8).[12] But when, as in *Bruto minore*, we find ourselves in the presence of a speaking which in its enunciation no longer makes sense to the enunciator and is at the mercy of the winds, this is no longer about the precariousness of time, it is not the sound or voice that, as in the concluding lines of *La sera del dì di festa* (The Evening of the Holiday), melts on the night air and disappears into silence. This precariousness is that of communication itself: it is the drama of the emptying of the subject.

[11] Geoffrey Hartman, 'Evening Star and Evening Land', in his *The Fate of Reading* (Chicago: University of Chicago Press, 1975), 163.

[12] The poem first appeared in the 1835 Naples edn of the *Canti*. But it is placed by the poet at the very beginning of the *idilli* of his youth, before *L'infinito* (no. 11 in the definitive ordering of the *Canti*). Sketched in 1819, finalized in 1834 or 1835, or at some point between these two extremes.

The scenario of communication takes on new dimensions in Leopardi's late poems, those written in Florence and Naples during his residence in those cities in the 1830s. What is it that changes? Change in the sense of a radicalization or an attenuation of the tragic scene that is inhabited in the early *canzoni*, or of a shifting of point of view, or of affective or philosophical priorities? From the answer to these questions we shall be able to judge whether the value that Leopardi assigns to vocal enunciation—staged in the first instance and continually through the medium of third persons, that is, characters who make their appearance in the poem, but fundamentally referring back to the poet's own vocal enunciation as a lyric poet Romanticly understood—is always one and the same, or evolves in time, and, in the latter case, how we should interpret this evolution. To tackle this question, we turn to selected passages drawn from three of Leopardi's last poems (last in order of composition): *Consalvo* (probably written in Florence in the spring of 1833), *Palinodia al marchese Gino Capponi* (Recantation for Marchese Gino Capponi, written in Naples in late 1834 or early 1835, the concluding poem of the 1835 edition of the *Canti*), and *Il tramonto della luna* (*The Setting of the Moon*, written in Torre del Greco, outside Naples, in the spring of 1836).

Consalvo is dying and will finally be granted the kiss so long desired from 'Elvira, famous for her godly beauty' ('Per divina beltà famosa Elvira': 13).[13] He is subject to a twofold submission, rendered speechless by his 'sovrano timor' ('great timidity': 22) and suffering a kind of physical and sexual mutilation: 'Così l'avea | Fatto schiavo e fanciullo il troppo amore' ('And so excessive love | had made him into a slave and a child': 22–3). The charged transition from the first to the second stanza emphasizes that it is only the approach of death, indeed, the acceleration of its arrival that finally loosens 'il nodo antico | Alla sua lingua' ('the age-old | knot in his tongue': 24–5). In a poem that is made up of silences, signs, and veritable floods of words, it is not really the long desired and dreamt-of kiss, even with all its melodramatic power, that is the focal point of the poem, but the mouth. Mouth, tongue, and more precisely, or more obsessively, the lips, mentioned no less than four times, with differing valences, in the extremely dense and agitated second and third stanzas (24–74). The lips are the strategic site of the yearned-for kiss, or rather of 'Più baci e più' ('many kisses': 72); of the still timid and hesitant beginning of what will become the torrent of Consalvo's words (see 29–33), the site of speaking and the counter-speaking that the beloved Elvira would wish in her turn to proffer, but from which she is prevented by the now unstoppable Consalvo (39–41), the site of his sighs (56–8, 69) and finally those of the still living Elvira (148), all of which—sighs, kisses, words—are expressed, we should remember, with the permission of death. If the approach of death unchains Consalvo's voice, and the voice sounds the word of life (his speech will lead to her kiss), it also marks its limit: the kiss will never be repeated. This is a juxtaposition that will also be confronted—on a completely different scale, with different but not totally unrelated means and points of reference—in one of the greatest

[13] This poem, like *Il passero solitario*, is chronologically 'displaced' in the order of the *Canti*, no. 17 in the 1835 edn, between *La vita solitaria* (1821) and the last of the ten *canzoni*, *Alla sua donna* (1823), itself already in 1831 separated by some distance from the other nine.

of Leopardi's late poems, *La ginestra, o il fiore del deserto* (Broom, or The Flower of the Desert, written in Torre del Greco, 1836), in which the dream of 'franca lingua' ('honest words': 114), of 'nom[are] ... apertamente' ('say[ing] ... openly': 95–6), and of 'l'onesto e il retto | Conversar cittadino' ('an honest, | just society of citizens': 151–2) has to measure itself against a reality that is literally under our feet, and which is also registered aurally: the 'impietrata lava, | Che sotto i passi al peregrin risona' (the 'hardened lava | that echoes to a wanderer's steps': 19–20), or again, in the here and now, the 'flutto rovente | Che crepitando giunge, e inesorato | Durabilmente sovra quei si spiega' ('the burning flood, | which advances hissing and unstoppable, | to pour over them unendingly': 266–8): the full richness of the conversation of citizens set against the empty sound of the footfall echoing across the hardened lava.

From one point of view, precisely that of impending death, Consalvo's situation might recall those of Brutus or Sappho, other orators awaiting death. But what seems to differentiate Consalvo's voice from those that are heard in the early *canzoni* (however different one from the other) is, in Consalvo's case, the relative absence of a subjective dimension. Although it starts from a highly 'personalized' position (Consalvo's extreme shyness, his virtually total abandonment, etc.), his words do not refer back to the protagonist's self or, which is even more important in the early *canzoni*, to the disintegration of that self. Rather, it is addressed to what relates the voice to its existential limits. The conversation of citizens will always be a conversation, if it occurs at all, but there is also, and perhaps more pressingly, the echoing of steps on the lava. Consalvo's words and sighs are real, but they depend strictly on death. And here we might turn to another case of voice at its limits: that of the infant that is twice invoked, and to effect, in a satirical, not to say a sarcastic key, in Leopardi's 'recantation' poem, *Palinodia al marchese Gino Capponi*.

The language of infants that is not yet language is mobilized in the *Palinodia* first and foremost as a comparison with the extravagant proposal of a 'former colleague' of the addressee (probably Niccolò Tommaseo), according to which the poet should give up exploring his 'propri affetti' and his 'proprio petto' ('your own affections', 'your [own] heart': 232, 235) and, turning from private questions to public ones, should think of what is useful for the community: 'Materia al canto | Non cercar dentro te. Canta i bisogni | Del secolo nostro, e la matura speme' ('Don't go looking | for a source of song inside yourself. | Sing our country's needs and its ripe hope': 236–8). The cry for public usefulness is the siren's song, the justification of an activity that is otherwise 'useless'. For the Leopardi before his palinode, the only possible response is laughter: either his antagonist is joking, or, without realizing it, he is talking a kind of nonsense, the nonsense uttered by the speech-less, infants, those who do not have command of language:

> Memorande sentenze! ond'io solenni
> Le risa alzai quando sonava il nome
> Della speranza al mio profano orecchio
> Quasi comica voce, o come un suono
> Di lingua che dal latte si scompagni.

> Memorable advice! To which I answered | with solemn laughter, the word 'hope' | sounding like a joke to my profane ears, | or a baby's tongue | that's sucking air (239–43)

This position of complete rejection is sarcastically reversed by a Leopardi who sees the error of his ways in the lines that follow. But this is the same 'pargoleggiar' (babble) that we will find in *La ginestra* (59) and the 'solemn laughter' is closely related to the 'suon giocondo | Che di secolo in secolo alle grotte | Più remote pervenne insino al fondo' ('mirthful sound | that from century to century carried to the depths | of the remotest caves') which greets the timid request of Count Leccafondi who has made it down to the underworld of his fellow mice in the eighth canto of the *Paralipomeni della Batracomiomachia* (8.25.2–4): a mirthful sound, not laughter, since 'Non è l'estinto un animal risivo' (which might approximately be translated 'The departed are not the laughing kind': 8.24.1).[14] In all these cases, the relationship between laughter, or its mousey underworld equivalent, and infancy is one of judgement and superiority, that of the mature person for whom infancy is by definition an exclusion from language, and consequently from reasoning and thought. But it should be added that the laughter of the mature echoes in some way the inarticulate sounds of the infant, not only in the sense that it is presented as the most adequate answer to such nonsense (there is no point in arguing with someone who does not reason), but also because laughter itself is part of the equipment of the child making its first sounds and is hard-wired into the adult-to-be (indeed, Leopardi continues, in octave 24 of *Paralipomeni*, 8: 'La virtù per la quale è dato al vivo | Che una sciocchezza insolita discerna, | Sfogar con un sonoro e convulsivo | Atto un prurito della parte interna' ('The power that is given to the living | who discern some unaccustomed folly, | to let out with a sonorous and convulsive | act an itching of the inner part': 3–6).

It is notable however that the *Palinodia al marchese Gino Capponi* closes, some forty lines after those already cited, on the image of an infant laughing. The infant joins with the child in the celebrated comparison in ll. 154–60, the child or boy whom nature resembles, who makes and unmakes, who builds, demolishes, and recycles her materials. The child, like nature, does not speak, he is intent on his work, completely absorbed in the task he has in hand; he is essentially busy, energetic, whether boy or man now it is difficult to say. The infant, by contrast, is at the threshold of the world of the grown-ups, and he does not know, nor can he know, whether that world is deception or self-deception, a lie invented also by men. The grown-ups may laugh at him, or with him, and can recognize in his laugh the unarticulated universe of sound from which they as adults have departed for good, from something that is in turn now only something ridiculous, or

[14] The *Paralipomeni della Batracomiomachia*, an unfinished satirical poem in ottava rima, was written in Naples between 1833 and 1837 and published for the first time in Paris (Baudry) in 1842. Drawing on the pseudo-Homeric poem of the war of the frogs and the mice that he had loved and translated and retranslated over the years, Leopardi recast it as a contemporary critique of Italian thought, politics, and society. In the war between the mice (Italian liberals) and the crabs (Austrians and reactionaries), the visit to the underworld quoted here is one of its most surreal moments.

they may recognize a part of themselves in that same universe, a reality to which they still in part belong.

E tu comincia a salutar col riso
Gl'ispidi genitori, o prole infante,
Eletta agli aurei dì: né ti spauri
L'innocuo nereggiar de' cari aspetti.
Ridi, o tenera prole: a te serbato
È di cotanto favellare il frutto;
Veder gioia regnar, cittadi e ville,
Vecchiezza e gioventù del par contente,
E le barbe ondeggiar lunghe due spanne.

And start smiling for your bearded fathers, | infant offspring, meant for golden days; | don't let the harmless darkening | of those beloved faces frighten you. | Smile, sweet offspring; the results | of all this chattering are meant for you: | to see joy reign in city and in country, | old age and youth both happy equally, | and beards flowing, two spans long. (271–9)

With this image the poem perhaps does not finish quite as Leopardi might have wanted it to. The heavy irony on the subject of beards, and the slightly weary listing of promises that will never be fulfilled do not close the argument decisively, but leave space for another point of view, that of the infant. This cheerful offspring cannot be interested in the 'results' which mean nothing to it; the treasure which it seeks is different: 'all this chattering', the discourse of adults, hairy or otherwise, which for now it cannot know as null and empty, only as fullness itself, as Consalvo does the lips of Elvira.

Death and infancy, and with infancy in particular the human voice at the limits of the inarticulate, or the inarticulable, a voice that, borrowing the adjective from Giorgio Agamben, we could define as 'bare voice',[15] whether it take the form of infantile babbling, of pure desire, of constricted laughter, a voice beyond, before or after, the discourse of mature people, outside the reach of 'civil conversation'. But this latter, with respect to that other voice, may also seem diminished, inconclusive, inadequate; sought-for but not secure.

Lines 15–19 of *Il tramonto della luna*, the last poem that Leopardi wrote, make many of his readers start. They are the lines that introduce the carter who sings at the end of the first stanza:

Orba la notte resta,
E cantando, con mesta melodia,
L'estremo albor della fuggente luce,

[15] The allusion is to the distinction, in Agamben's *Homo sacer* (Turin: Einaudi, 1995), between 'bare' and 'qualified' life and its relation to sovereign power.

Che dianzi gli fu duce,
Saluta il carrettier dalla sua via

Night is blind, | and singing with a mournful melody, | the carter on his way salutes | the last ray of the fleeting light | that led him on before.

These lines cannot but recall the final lines of *La sera del dì di festa* (The Evening of the Holiday, written at least fifteen years before):

Nella mia prima età, quando s'aspetta
Bramosamente il dì festivo, or poscia
Ch'egli era spento, io doloroso, in veglia,
Premea le piume; ed alla tarda notte
Un canto che s'udia per li sentieri
Lontanando morire a poco a poco,
Già similmente mi stringeva il core.

In my young years, in the time of life | when we wait impatiently for Sunday, | afterward I'd lie awake unhappy, | and late at night a song heard on the road | dying note by note as it passed by | would pierce my heart | the same way even then. (40–6)

The two passages, having in common the night scene, the song, and a certain idea of fading (of the song or of the light), are very different in reality. While the earlier poem is laden with symbolic allusions and specific references, held together by a strongly present poetic I, the *Tramonto* is more problematic. Is the carter's salute the poem itself (and vice versa), or are they different? (The syntax is not clear on this point.) Why does he sing? To prolong the light? To accompany it? To protect himself against the encroaching night? We know nothing of this. We know only that there is a countryside now almost entirely dark ('Spariscon l'ombre . . . ' shadows disappear: 13) and a carter passing—the 'passer-by' who is an emblematic figure in late Leopardi—and about to leave the stage definitively. The sense of the carter's song cannot be fixed, it does not refer to any other element in the poem. And yet, it is not simply decorative. What voice is this?

Further Reading

Camilletti, Fabio A., *Leopardi's Nymphs: Grace, Melancholy, and the Uncanny* (London: Modern Humanities Research Association and Maney Publishing, 2013).

Damiani, Rolando, *All'apparir del vero: Vita di Giacomo Leopardi* (Milan: Arnoldo Mondadori, 1998).

D'Intino, Franco, *L'immagine della voce: Leopardi, Platone e il libro morale* (Venice: Marsilio, 2009).

Gardini, Nicola, 'History and Pastoral in the Structure of Leopardi's *Canti*', *Modern Language Review*, 103/1 (Jan. 2008), 76–92.

Leopardi, Giacomo, *Poesie e prose*, ed. Rolando Damiani and Mario Andrea Rigoni, 5 vols (Milan: Arnoldo Mondadori, 1987).

Leopardi, Giacomo, *Canti*, ed. Lucio Felici (Rome: Newton Compton, 3rd edn, 2005).

Leopardi, Giacomo, *Canti*, tr. and annotated by Jonathan Galassi (New York: Farrar Straus & Giroux; London: Penguin Classics, 2010).

Leopardi, Giacomo, *Zibaldone*, ed. Michael Caesar and Franco D'Intino, tr. Kathleen Baldwin, Richard Dixon, David Gibbons, Ann Goldstein, Gerard Slowey, Martin Thom, and Pamela Williams (New York: Farrar, Straus & Giroux; London: Penguin Classics, 2013).

Prete, Antonio, *Il pensiero poetante: Saggio su Leopardi*, expanded edn (Milan: Feltrinelli, [1980] 2006).

Veronese, Cosetta, *The Reception of Giacomo Leopardi in the Nineteenth Century* (Lewiston, NY: Edwin Mellen Press, 2008).

Whitfield, John Humphreys, *Giacomo Leopardi* (Oxford: Basil Blackwell, 1954).

Williams, Pamela, *An Introduction to Leopardi's Canti* (Market Harborough: Troubador, 1997).

CHAPTER 22

LEOPARDI AS A WRITER OF PROSE

FRANCO D'INTINO

The Scholar, the Poet, the Prose Writer

Giacomo Leopardi (1798–1837) is famous above all as a poet. Yet he wrote only a small number of verses (forty-one compositions), collected in a single slender little volume (the *Canti*). His production as a prose writer in contrast is massive and comprises a large quantity of essays and scholarly works (1811–18), a book of moral dialogues and prose works (the *Operette morali*), largely written in 1824 and published in 1827, a number of translations of moral prose writing from the Greek (1822–7), around a thousand letters—arguably the finest in Italian literature—and an enormous intellectual diary of 4526 pages, which accompanied him in secret throughout almost the whole period of his life from 1817 until 1832, though three-quarters of it was written between 1821 and 1823. One of the merits of criticism in the last few decades has been that of re-evaluating Leopardi as a prose writer and philosopher, aspects which suffered from Benedetto Croce's negative criticism.[1]

In fact, viewed overall, the quality of Leopardi's prose is such that, while perhaps not agreeing entirely with Nietzsche's claim that he was the greatest prose writer of his century,[2] we may certainly recognise him as one of the greatest. It is to Leopardi that we owe

[1] Benedetto Croce, 'Giacomo Leopardi', in B. Croce, *La letteratura italiana per saggi storicamente disposti*, iii. *L'Ottocento* (Bari: Laterza, 1963), 74–8. The interest taken in Leopardi as prose writer and philosopher by Giovanni Gentile is worthy of note, though his Hegelian interpretation is tendentious and misleading. See *Opere*, xxiv (Florence: Sansoni, 1960).

[2] All statements by Nietzsche on Leopardi (in this case from the *Geschichte der Griechischen Beredsamkeit*) are usefully collected in Friedrich Nietzsche, *Intorno a Leopardi*, ed. Cesare Galimberti (Genoa: il melangolo, 1992), 60.

the creation of modern Italian prose outside the world of novel writing. This distinction is important, because it presents us with a problem. Among the different genres of prose writing practised by Leopardi, novel writing, the genre par excellence of his century, is absent, nor is it an absence which can be easily passed over. Let us not forget—and most critics do forget—that Leopardi is almost exactly contemporary with Balzac and only slightly younger than Stendhal, and he is no less capable of observing and describing social phenomena and the psychology of individuals. One may well ask then: what are the implications of the fact that, in contrast to what happens in every other European country, the greatest prose writer of the century in Italy does not write novels?

It would be as well here to give a description, albeit brief, of the daily life of this author, belonging to an impoverished aristocratic family in Recanati, a small town in the Marche, a somewhat isolated region of the Papal States. The first-born child of Conte Monaldo, an intellectual who managed to combine his Catholic faith with Enlightenment rationalism, Giacomo Leopardi lived through the years of his adolescence and youth cut off among the thousands of precious books in his father's library, the largest private library in Italy, a kind of treasure chest which acted as his only distraction, as he himself says, in a life bare of worldly attractions. Leopardi, who had mastered Latin perfectly as a child, read every day, with regularity and method, especially ancient texts, and texts by men of learning, scholars, and commentators, and perused dictionaries, encyclopedias, collections, miscellanies. While the Romantic revolution was exploding in the rest of Europe (the long wave of a political revolution resolutely opposed by his father), the young Leopardi lived a life typical of a monk or a scholar of the seventeenth century. He thus became the first philologist in Italy and possibly in Europe as well. This, then, was his life of seclusion until 1815. But, in the year which saw the Congress of Vienna, while the old order desired by his father and his uncle Carlo Antici (who advised him to read Bonald and de Maistre) was making a return, Leopardi discovered Greek poetry. Even as a child, he had worked on the composition and translation of poetry extracts, especially Horace, as was the custom in the eighteenth century. But when he taught himself Greek (for him the free language par excellence), he came into direct contact with the 'unveiled' body of Greek poetry (that is, something not cleaned up or expurgated), and especially with the erotic poetry of Anacreon and Sappho (whom he already knew through Longinus's *On the Sublime*), and, later, Homer.[3] This contact changed his life by making the most archaic classical poets a constant point of reference.[4] This opening towards antiquity was accompanied by an interest in politics which properly had its origin in Leopardi's observation of Greek and Roman society, but which also targeted the actual historical situation of a nation (Italy) which was still at this time only an 'imaginary community'.[5]

[3] On Leopardi and the sublime cf. Raffaele Gaetano, *Giacomo Leopardi e il sublime: Archeologia e percorsi di un'idea estetica* (Soveria Mannelli: Rubbettino, 2002); Margaret Brose, 'Leopardi's *L'Infinito* and the Language of the Romantic Sublime', *Poetics Today*, 4/1 (1983), 47–71.

[4] D'Intino, 'Introduzione', in Leopardi, *Poeti greci e latini* (Rome: Salerno, 1999), pp. vii–lix.

[5] Paul Hamilton, 'Leopardi and the Proper Conversation of a Citizen', in *Realpoetik: European Romanticism and Literary Politics* (Oxford: Oxford University Press, 2013), 189–220.

In this first phase poetry assumes a decidedly privileged position, and it will quickly become the only true object of Leopardi's aesthetic reflection. But this precise hierarchy, far from excluding, actually implies awareness of it as an outmoded genre, incompatible with the modern era which is an era of conspicuous rationality, in which poetry is quite out of place. From this moment on it shines with the brightness of distance, all the stronger the more it is rejected, and it is perceived as the projection of a body, a desire, an eroticism, all carefully repressed by the adolescent monk. Poetry, therefore, becomes the verbal condensation of the unconscious (and of political rebellion in the civic poems), contrasting with a prose which remains within the confines of a rational and scientific approach, controlled and methodical.

It was in this state that Leopardi was about to live through a crucial year, 1819, which shortly after he described in the following way in a famous page of his diary:

> The *total transformation* that took place in me, my passing from ancient to modern, happened, you might say, in the space of a single year, that is, in 1819, when, deprived of my sight and the constant distraction of reading, I began to feel my unhappiness in a much bleaker way, I began to abandon hope, *to reflect deeply on things ... to become a professional philosopher (instead of the poet I was before)*, to feel the incontrovertible unhappiness of the world, rather than knowing about it, in part also because of a state of bodily languor, which removed me even further from the ancients and brought me closer to the moderns. At that point, imagination in me was greatly enfeebled, and although the faculty of invention grew in me enormously, indeed that was almost its beginning, it was mainly directed *either to works in prose or to sentimental poems*.[6]

The 'total transformation' was the awareness of a modern condition which for Leopardi was static, immobile, melancholic, and which coincided with the hyper-development of the reflective faculty, of reason. In Restoration Europe, such an anthropological approach, which has much in common with that of Vico, naturally has political implications (as also in the case of Stendhal). This condition, from the expressive point of view, is the domain of prose or of reflective poetry of a sentimental nature. The modern poet cannot *not be* a philosopher. Here Leopardi, by routes which are entirely his own, and as a consequence of his existential experience, encounters the problems which had been the subject of debate for some time in Europe, especially in the German context, at the time of the first Romantic generation, whose progressive optimism, however, Leopardi does not share. Later (*Zibaldone*, 1742, 19 September 1821), Leopardi will attribute his growing maturity to a figure whom he considers decisive in his intellectual journey, Mme de Staël, whose *Corinne* he read in 1819 and her *De l'Allemagne* in 1821, which was his main source of information on Kant and the culture of Romanticism. Any discussion of Leopardi on a Europe-wide basis must take account of his isolation, of the scarcity

[6] Giacomo Leopardi, *Zibaldone di Pensieri*, ed. Giuseppe Pacella (Milan: Garzanti, 1991); tr. *Zibaldone*, ed. Michael Caesar and Franco D'Intino (New York: Farrar Straus & Giroux, 2013), 144.

of modern texts available to him in his library, and of what we might call the dilettante nature of his sharp philosophical reflection.

The Fragmentary Novel

It is in that same crucial year of his *transformation*, 1819, that Leopardi becomes a prose writer, or rather, that he begins to try out, in various different ways, the expressive path of prose. I have mentioned that Leopardi never wrote a novel. But in that terrible year, carried along on the emotional wave of depression, he tried to do so, without any success. A first narrative attempt had been completed in December 1817: a kind of diary in which he tells of his first experience of being in love (with observations which foreshadow Stendhal's *De l'amour*). The attempt was cut short, to be followed a year and a half later (spring/summer 1819) by a projected novel which began to take shape after he had read the fundamental text of *Sturm und Drang*, Goethe's *Werther* (followed by Foscolo's *Ultime lettere di Jacopo Ortis* and immediately afterwards, in the autumn, by Mme de Staël's *Corinne*).[7] It is a choice directed very precisely. The two texts which inspired him are autobiographical novels, intimate, reflective, and sentimental, and in addition they are epistolary, that is to say, fragmentary. In both, the protagonist is at the mercy of a whirlwind erotic passion (and in the case of *Ortis*, of revolutionary politics), while remaining the victim of history and society and, above all, of the rationality which surrounds him and tortures him without fully understanding his *sensibility* and his (self-)destructive impulses.

There are three essential elements which characterize this attempt at the novel. In the first place, it remained incomplete, that is, it is split into a series of jottings which were never brought to a conclusion; secondly, we know that the plot would have ended with a death caused by illness, or by weakness, through inability to bring to fruition a vital energy which has the potential to be beyond the ordinary (the plot as proposed corresponds deep down, therefore, with the failure of the project itself); thirdly the main character's life is a purely interior life, directed towards an absolute (nature, or even the 'beginning of the world') which cannot be expressed in words, but can only manifest itself in a musical dimension which borders on the divine. From all three points of view, which are naturally linked together, Leopardi's sketch, which is radical in a way far beyond anything by Foscolo, appears like a flower which is alien to the Italian cultural landscape of the time. In many aspects it recalls not only Goethe, the most important explicit model (of which it accentuates the metaphysical side), but also more radical Romantics such as Novalis, Schlegel, and Wackenroder (of a younger generation). It

[7] See Franco D'Intino, 'Fragmentariness and Performance: Leopardi's Autobiographical Sketches', in James Vigus (ed.), *Informal Romanticism* (Trier: Wissentschaftlicher Verlag, 2012), 115–30, and at greater length the 'Introduzione', to Leopardi, *Scritti e frammenti autobiografici* (Rome: Salerno, 1995), pp. xi–xcvii.

also shows notable consonance with Karl Philipp Moritz's *Anton Reiser*, a crucial representative of that pietistic *Stimmung* which, according to Isaiah Berlin, gave rise, through Hamann, to Romanticism.[8] This is a disposition with which the youthful Leopardi, although aristocratic, has much in common: poverty, timidity, melancholy, sense of isolation, of frustration and humiliation, intellectual ambitions which never found their voice, compensatory daydreams.

In a later letter, written in French, Leopardi recalls that fateful year, in which he tried in vain to flee, explaining how an excessive sensibility had led him to the terrifying consideration of the 'nothingness of things' and 'losing his reason' (*Epistolario*, 722–3, 23 June 1823). In the isolation of the library, with a sedentary life of reading and writing, his vital energy had transformed itself into the 'habit of reflection', in a thought process which, disconnected from the setting of everyday life as it was and rooted in the impossibility of acting or even of moving, had caused him to lose any perception of the reality of things. In this self-analysis, the ascetic readings of his early Christian upbringing, which warned him against the excesses of thought and the weaknesses of intellectual activity, merge with his personal myth of an antiquity which is nothing but realized energy, in which thought led to action. Long before Nietzsche, the result is a self-portrait of a young *homo theoreticus* of Platonic disposition ('Ultra-Platoniker' according to Nietzsche's definition),[9] whose capacity for abstraction prevents him from living:

> It is true that the habit of *reflecting*, which is always characteristic of sensitive spirits, often takes away the capacity to act and even to enjoy. The superabundance of the inner life always pushes the individual outwards, but at the same time has the effect that he does not know how to engage with what is outside himself. He embraces everything, he would like always to be filled; *yet all objects elude him*, precisely because they are smaller than his capacity. He demands even *of his slightest actions, his words, his gestures, his movements*, more grace and *perfection* than it is possible for a man to attain. Thus, never being able to be satisfied with himself, *or to cease examining himself*, and always mistrustful of his own powers, he cannot do what other people do.[10]

It is obvious that this mental state creates an impediment to the narration of a novel, which, as the Stendhal of the unfinished *Henri Brulard* will discover soon enough, must necessarily exteriorize by using those *objects* and those imperfect human actions—*words, gestures, movements*—which the Platonic rejects as not adequate to the ideal, nor to the image which precedes them. In the same months in which his novel sinks in a musical *reverie*, the confrontation with an unrepresentable absolute produces another

[8] Isaiah Berlin, *The Roots of Romanticism* (London: Chatto & Windus, 1999), ch. 6.

[9] Friedrich Nietzsche, *Nachgelassene Fragmente: Frühjahr-Herbst 1884*, in *Werke: Kritische Gesamtausgabe*, ed. Giorgio Colli and Mazzino Montinari (Berlin: de Gruyter, 1974), vii/2. 255 (Nietzsche, *Intorno a Leopardi*, 98).

[10] *Epistolario*, ed. Franco Brioschi and Patrizia Landi (Turin: Boringhieri, 1998), 723–4; tr. Prue Shaw, in *The Letters of Giacomo Leopardi 1817–1837* (Leeds: Northern Universities Press, 1998), 142, my italics. The letter is in French.

shipwreck in the idyll *L'infinito*, the verses with which Leopardi, breaking away from his experiments in civic poetry which precede the 1819 crisis, pioneers modern Italian poetry. For the time being, the text of the *Infinito* remains secret (it will only see the light of day in 1825). Reflexive and sentimental, it absorbs that narrative dimension which he had not been able to display in his prose, to the extent to which the 'I' narrates itself, but it is certainly not the story of outside events. More accurately, in fact, it is the story of how his thought ends by foundering sweetly in a 'sea' without boundaries and distinctions, ends, that is, by melting in a *sublime* dimension, beyond the *visible*: 'So my mind sinks in this immensity: | and foundering is sweet in such a sea' (tr. Galassi). In the *Infinito*, the general structure of a process of self-representation of thought is laid bare, the only representation possible for a subject which has become 'philosophical' and therefore cannot escape taking as its object its own analysis of its own thought, as Descartes had done in the myth which ushers in modernity, the *Discours de la méthode*. What is new about Leopardi's poem is the fact that it brings all of human experience to the point of view of an absolute subjectivity which has lost any external point of reference. Although the shipwreck is perceived as *pleasurable*, it is the sign of the possible risk of this new condition, which elsewhere in fact is represented as annihilation, loss of life force and tendency to suicide. This crisis is at the same time personal (that of a young man who is prevented from achieving self-realization in the world, from developing his energy) and historical, since it reflects the uncertainties of an epoch which has lost both its traditional political and religious co-ordinates (the *ancien régime*, of which his father Monaldo and his uncle Carlo Antici were typical exponents) and has also lost the revolutionary faith in progress and in the palingenesis of humanity. From this point of view, Leopardi is in tune with Chateaubriand, of whom he had read as a youngster the chapter of the *Génie du Christianisme*—'Du vague des passions'—where there is the description of the confused and uncertain state in which the faculties and energies of modern man ferment and turn against themselves. The same is true with Goethe, who portrays in *Faust*, the second part of which was published in 1832, the risks of demonic aspiration to action in a world without God.[11]

The Body of Thought: the *Zibaldone*

In this condition Leopardi finds another path along which to channel his energy, and it is for this purpose that he begins to forge a flexible new instrument: a prose composition which, while not being a novel, will encompass within it, as the material of thought reflecting upon itself, not only the wide sweep of human experiences (language, mind, body, emotions, behaviour), but also their metaphysical foundations. It is a *comédie*

[11] Franco D'Intino, 'Il monaco indiavolato: Lo Zibaldone e la tentazione faustiana di Leopardi', in *Lo Zibaldone cento anni dopo: Composizione, edizione, temi. Atti del X convegno internazionale di studi leopardiani* (Florence: Olschki, 2001), 467–512.

humaine which, in contrast to that of Balzac, is historical in so far as it constantly sets up the contrast between the ancient and the modern, but never forgets its metaphysical antecedents, its 'prologue in heaven'.

To be fair, however, we are not dealing with here with a proper *opera*, except in the Romantic sense of infinite *productivity*. In 1817 Leopardi had begun to jot down the odd note or two. In his year of crisis, 1819, this practice took on a more solid aspect, and was the beginning of the birth of what would later be called *Zibaldone di pensieri*, 4526 manuscript pages which accompanied the author secretly for fifteen years of his life (until 1832), written 'with the flow of the pen', that is, in a simple informal style of extraordinary efficacy and beauty.[12] Leopardi is very soon aware that his practice of writing is taking on a new, unforeseen physiognomy when in January 1820 (on p. 100), he begins with regularity to date every single thought. On p. 144 he writes the entry which I have already quoted on 'total transformation', which identifies, at the origin of the impulse to write, the perception of that internal breakdown which turns the subject into a thinking 'I' who observes himself, and Leopardi sets himself the task of reconstructing how this 'I' has travelled from his ancient condition (ingenuous, energetic, active, happy, child-like, spoken-word-based, animal) to a modern reflective condition, static, writing-based, and tending towards a continuous melancholic self-analysis. Naturally he is not dealing only with himself. The *Zibaldone* develops as an *anthropological autobiography*, in that, as Leopardi emphasizes on a number of occasions, the story of each single man epitomizes that of the whole human race (*Zibaldone*, 3029–30). And now that we are 'in the century of reason', he writes in one of the first notes, even those who incline to action, those who in antiquity would have been heroes, are brought to rational analysis (*Zibaldone*, 14). Thought, therefore, goes in search of its own foundations, and it follows, it spies closely upon the movements, the slightest oscillations, the different ways in which it reacts to experiences. Only 'few of the most learned', emphasizes Leopardi, are capable 'of retracing in detail, and holding accurately in their minds the origins, progress, mode of development, in short, *the history of their own notions and thoughts, their knowledge and their intellect*' (*Zibaldone*, 1376–7). If, on the one hand, the *Zibaldone* then has a diary structure, it is, on the other, a 'story' of the mind of an ancient 'hero' who has become a modern 'thinker'.[13] This means that there are two operations going on within him, that of the writer who writes every day, reflecting on his own experiences as a man and a reader, and that of the reader of his own text, who in retrospect observes, in a different way every day, the movement in time of himself as he writes, which in its turn is altered with respect to his ancient child self. This double and triple register, which in the novel corresponds to the changing relationships between character, narrator, and

[12] Leopardi, *Zibaldone*, 95 and 2541. See Luigi Blasucci, 'I registri della prosa', in *Lo stormire del vento tra le piante: Testi e percorsi leopardiani* (Venice: Marsilio, 2003), 106–8.

[13] On the structure of the *Zibaldone*, see Anna Dolfi, 'Le strutture cognitive dello *Zibaldone*' (1987), in *Ragione e passione: Fondamenti e forme del pensare leopardiano* (Rome: Bulzoni, 2000), 99–122; Joanna Ugniewska, 'Strutture saggistiche e strutture diaristiche nello *Zibaldone*', *La rassegna della letteratura italiana*, 91 (1987), 325–38.

author, materializes in corrections, internal cross-references, comments, additions, and cancellations. In short it is seen in all the innumerable manuscript traces of a continuous self-reflective activity, traces which are beginning to constitute a real proper textual body which will take the place of the biological body: a body of thought.

Thus the *Zibaldone* grows not so much as a planned work, but rather as a textual organism criss-crossed by innumerable tensions, so much so that it is difficult to find parallels in other literatures, let alone describe it. It is the product of an isolation and a historical paralysis (felt especially in the Papal States, where the climate of the Restoration is particularly intense), and at the same time of an incredibly powerful and inexhaustible activity of production, which remains, however, secret and interiorized (the text was not published until 1898). This diary-style of writing, as we have seen, emerges as compensation for an impossible flight (in obedience, therefore, to a repressive injunction at the same time erotic, political, and religious), and yet represents the energy of desire, the flight of thought beyond any limit on what can be seen and thought. From this point of view, allowing for its specific Italian connotations, it is clearly a Romantic piece of writing, tending to the infinite. Not, however, in the sense in which Schmitt means it, that is of a subjective productivity which in order to escape from reality seizes any opportunity to create an 'infinite novel'.[14] Leopardi's purpose is not to romanticize what exists but to understand it. This piece of writing, begun in the year of Leopardi's physical blindness, is the product of a great strengthening of his interior intellectual vision. The Romantic or Faustian aspiration towards the infinite takes the form of a rational inquiry of Enlightenment origin, the other important component of the explosive mix which was Leopardi's education and upbringing. Apart from classical texts, learned studies of the humanist tradition, manuals of asceticism, and the Bible, Leopardi also had access to a number of texts of Enlightenment philosophical literature, above all to the *Encyclopédie*, and this accustomed him to a scientific process of recognition which systematically passes through all fields of knowledge. The fragmentary structure and the zigzag progression of the *Zibaldone* do not trace the figure of the *arabesque*, so dear to Schlegel, but that of the *web*, which produces a methodical exploration 'of the *relationships* that exist between the most disparate things' (*Zibaldone*, 1922), with a view to a general *system* which embraces them all: 'any genuine thinker, absolutely cannot manage without forming for himself, or following, or generally having a system' (*Zibaldone*, 945). However, the search for the system cannot help but shine a light on the differences, the details, the contradictions which the thinker has the duty to record *against* his own system, which ends by becoming an anti-system, or in other words 'a Skepticism which is … reasoned and proven' since reason 'distances itself from truth whenever it judges with certainty' and 'not only does doubt serve to uncover the truth' but 'truth essentially consists in doubt, and whoever doubts knows, and knows as much as one can know' (*Zibaldone*, 1655).

[14] Carl Schmitt, *Politische Romantik* (1919); tr. *Political Romanticism* (Somerset, NJ: Transaction, 2011).

Even if here, as elsewhere, Leopardi keeps alive the image of 'truth', his radical doubt does not, as in Descartes, open the way to the possibility of knowing. In spite of his Enlightenment starting point, which is certainly important in his development, Leopardi suspects that every method and every system, no matter how rational and accurate they are, are no more than an imaginary construction superimposed on the real world, a speculative and fantastical hypothesis (*Zibaldone*, 3978), and in this sense reason and imagination (and therefore poetry, too) are the same thing. Although he is fascinated by the cognitive power of modern experimental science, Leopardi finally admits that while it has the capacity to dismantle ancient myths, it cannot arrive at positive truths. It can be destructive, but not constructive (*Zibaldone*, 4192). There is a temptation twisting and turning through the whole diary, becoming stronger the further on it goes, which is that of adhering to the gnoseological scepticism of Sextus Empiricus, that is, to the idea 'that there is no absolute truth' (*Zibaldone*, 661), 'except that *All is relative*' (*Zibaldone*, 452).

This idea, which Leopardi defines as 'the basis for all metaphysics' (*Zibaldone*, 452), is, however, contradicted in fact by the stubborn researches which with great effort gradually evolve every day in the pages of the *Zibaldone*, as if on a battleground. So in the diary two points of view in constant dialogue with each other begin to take shape: an 'I' which insists on searching out the conditions for a secularization of the absolute in terms of scientific-rational truths; and an 'I' which denies any such possibility, surrendering to the unknowable mystery of the 'nature of things'. This second option, which will in the end win out, presupposes a criticism of the Enlightenment not only as an 'idealistic' choice, but also self-destructive of the body which has sacrificed itself in a useless quest. Instead of burdening oneself with the toil and sweat of reflection, a point to which man has arrived after a long evolutionary process, it would have been much wiser to eschew excessive development of the faculty of reason, thus avoiding the possibility of erring: '*he who does not reason, does not err*. Therefore he who does not reason, or as the French would say, does not think, is supremely wise. Therefore men were supremely wise before the birth of wisdom, and of reasoning about things: *and the child is supremely wise, and the savage of California, who does not know* thinking' (*Zibaldone*, 2711–12; my emphasis; 'thinking' underlined by Leopardi; cf. also 4190). The Italian word 'errare' ('to err') used by Leopardi here means 'to make a mistake', 'to journey', 'to be on the move' (as English 'errant' in 'knight errant'). The failure of the Enlightenment method coincides with a warning to Leopardi from the other side of his upbringing, the religious, which comes to him from the fathers of the church. He tells us about this in an extremely important quotation transcribed in the *Zibaldone* during one of the most crucial moments of his life, when, for the first time, he was leaving home to explore the 'vast world', beyond the limits of the known. A journey to Rome was the most Faustian thing which a poor aristocrat of the papal domains could allow himself. So, in the carriage which takes him to Rome in November 1822, Leopardi writes: 'If man *breaks out* of his natural purity, then he sins. Keeping therefore our condition and virtue, let the natural ornament be sufficient to you, o man, and *do not change the work of your Creator, since wanting to change it is to corrupt it*' (*Zibaldone*, 2645,

Leopardi's emphasis). Leopardi uses here the same verb (*mutare*) which he had chosen to describe his 'total transformation' (*mutazione*), that is the abandoning of one's ancient ingenuous condition in favour of one which is reflexive and modern. However, here it is reinterpreted (in the voice of St Anthony) as sin, illness, corruption. Here there is evidently at work a theological model: the audacious interpretation of Genesis, not as the abandonment of divine reason for a weaker and more fallible human reason (as was the case in the early days of the Enlightenment, for example in Thomas Browne), but rather as the story of the transition from a total absence of awareness (which for Leopardi coincides with the animal condition) to the development of a reason which is enormously powerful and therefore also dangerous. It is significant that for Leopardi such a *transition* or *mutation* is depicted in the biblical text by the action of *opening one's eyes* to one's own natural *nakedness*: '*When they opened their eyes*, as it says in *Genesis*, then *they perceived* that they were naked, and they were ashamed of their nature ... and they fell from their natural state, or were corrupted. So *opening their eyes*, and therefore *perceiving*, was the same thing as falling or being corrupted; and thus this fall was a fall of their nature, not of their reason or knowledge' (*Zibaldone*, 399–400).

By opening one's eyes, thus illuminating the scene of nature, one cannot avoid understanding its *nakedness*, that is, the contradictions, monstrosities, sufferings, which Leopardi, turning to an ancient materialism of Lucretian stamp which sometimes produces visions worthy of the Marquis de Sade, describes as 'a perpetual circle of production and destruction'.[15] After having fought throughout the *Zibaldone* to hold firm to the myth of a perfect and harmonious nature (on to which, once he had lost his faith, he had projected his own aspiration to the absolute), at the end of the journey, Leopardi arrives at the vision of an inhuman nature; that is, of a nature which is literally not observed by a human gaze, as he himself had already described in one of the very early thoughts, which goes back to the year of crisis, 1819: 'Quiet life of animals in forests, deserted and uninhabited places etc., where the course of their lives is no less complete, with their doings, events, deaths, passing of generations etc., *just because no man is observing and disturbing them*, and they know nothing of events in the world, because *what we believe about the world concerns only human beings*' (*Zibaldone*, 55, my emphasis).

KRAPP'S LAST TAPE: THE *OPERETTE MORALI*

This encounter between the reflexive man, gifted with reason, and a nature which is absolutely indifferent to him, and therefore, from the human point of view, cruel and monstrous, is portrayed by Leopardi in one of the *Operette morali*, the 'Dialogue between Nature and an Icelander'. In fact, it was precisely the composition of this work, in May 1824, which signalled a change of direction in the writing of the secret diary and brought about its slow,

[15] Leopardi, 'Dialogo della Natura e di un Islandese', in *Prose*, ed. Rolando Damiani (Milan: Mondadori, 1988; 6th edn, 1997), 82. See also *Zibaldone*, 4130.

progressive abandonment.[16] From the point of view of the internal balance of the writing, this means that a prose which is diary in structure, questing, secret, private, free, open, restless, potentially infinite, as is that of the *Zibaldone*, gives way to a prose project which is completely different, and which in the space of scarcely a year (1824, but published in 1827) immediately takes on the form of a *book* of great stylization, difficult and disturbing, which has remained ever since marginal to the canon of Italian writing,[17] and very little known abroad. The *Zibaldone* was a seedbed of possible novel-style situations and narrative plots which have as protagonist the human race, the slow formation of its customary behaviour (or 'habituations'), and its numerous practices. From this point of view, by relegating metaphysics to second place, it dissolves into a fragmentary anthropology, in which, following the path opened by Vico, Leopardi attempts to reconstruct the history of men through their languages. On the contrary, the book of the *Operette* has nothing to do with human temporality. Notwithstanding the adjective *morali*, the point of view which the author of these prose compositions adopts (most of them in dialogue form) is fundamentally metaphysical; it is that of a disenchanted *post-human* thinker who looks at man as one of the many living species who for a short period have populated the universe, until they change form or are destroyed. From the point of view of this radical dehumanizing, human reason is a fantasy like any other, and there is no sense in making a distinction between the state of wakefulness and that of sleep, between the logic of man and that of gnomes and sprites; just as there is no sense in making a distinction between past and present, history and myth, reality and invention. For this reason on an ideal cosmic stage it is possible to find alternating and intermingling historical, mythological, and invented characters, real and fantastic animals, allegories, planets, stars, machines, mummies. The exchanges of dialogue which represent human emotions and feelings, hopes and yearnings for happiness are like the voices recorded on Krapp's last tape, commented on by a modern *Democritus ridens*. This is the landscape, devastated like the post-deluge landscape described in 'The Wager of Prometheus', which is spread out before the gaze of animal-man, who, in the course of a long evolution dictated by chance, has painfully won the capacity to think, to abstract, but who at the same time has ceased to believe in a transcendent being.

How are we to position this work in the context of Romantic thought? A quarter of a century earlier, in a crucial text, *Die Christenheit oder Europa*, Novalis had identified the problem of modernity in the inverted relationship between faith (or belief) and knowledge, condemning the 'audacious developments of the human faculties at the expense of sacred sense', that is, in other words, that disenchantment with the world which had been the object of the favoured enquiries of the Zibaldonian journey; that inability to believe which had reduced 'the infinite creative music of the universe to the

[16] The *operetta* is quoted in a crucial thought of 2 June 1824 in *Zibaldone*, 4099. After this, Leopardi only wrote another 400 pages in eight years. On the relationship between the *Zibaldone* and the *Dialogo* see Claudio Colaiacomo, 'Zibaldone di pensieri', in Alberto Asor Rosa (ed.), *Dall'Ottocento al Novecento, Letteratura italiana: Le Opere*, iii. (Turin: Einaudi, 1995), 246–50.

[17] See Liana Cellerino, 'Operette morali', in Alberto Asor Rosa (ed.), *Dall'Ottocento al Novecento, Letteratura italiana: Le Opere*, iii. (Turin: Einaudi, 1995), bibliographical note, 349–54.

monotonous clatter of a monstrous mill, driven by the stream of chance ..., a mill that milled of itself'.[18] This could be a very precise descriptive summary of the universe of the *Operette morali* (as it is described, for example, in the 'Apocryphal fragment by Strato of Lampsacus'), the comic *mise-en-scène* of a failed attempt at secularization, and also, perhaps, the most adventurous and integral nihilistic vision of the world before Nietzsche and Beckett, both admirers of Leopardi.

Novalis's solution is a return to faith; to a 'new visible Church' which will welcome 'all souls athirst for the supernatural'.[19] Leopardi certainly did not know Novalis, but, instead, in the phase of his search for the Romantic absolute, he had read and admired Chateaubriand's *Génie du Christianisme*, which, published in the self-same year (1802), said something quite similar:

> Morality is the basis of society; but if man is a mere mass of matter, there is in reality neither vice nor virtue, and of course morality is a mere sham. Our laws, which are ever relative and variable, cannot serve as the support of morals, which are always absolute and unalterable; they must, therefore, rest on something more permanent than the present life, and have better guarantees than uncertain rewards or transient punishments.[20]

In this one can understand the meaning of the adjective attached to the *Operette*. If the metaphysical foundations collapse, if, by accepting the hypothesis of an integral materialism, one loses one's faith in a 'world which is more stable' than the human, what is left of morality? And furthermore: is it really true, as Chateaubriand maintained, that morality, in order to be valid, must be 'absolute and inalterable'? These are the questions posed by the *Operette morali*, which in this sense permit a glimpse, beyond the metaphysical scenario, of an interest in problems which are not only ethical but also political, something always at the centre of Leopardi's reflections.[21]

Politics and Morality

Right from his adolescence Leopardi had been directed towards such interests by his uncle, Marchese Carlo Antici, who had been educated in Germany and who had a much

[18] Novalis, *Schriften*, iii/2. *Das philosophische Werk*, ed. Richard Samuel, with the collaboration of Hans-Joachim Mähl and Gerhard Schulz (Stuttgart, Kohlhammer, 1968), 508 and 515, my tr.

[19] Novalis, *Schriften*, iii/2. 524.

[20] François-René Chateaubriand, *Génie du Christianisme*, 1st part, bk 6, ch. 3, tr. Charles I. White: *The Genius of Christianity, or the Spirit and Beauty of the Christian Religion* (Baltimore: Murphy, 1856), 190.

[21] The first critic to underline Leopardi's moral interests was Francesco De Sanctis, *Studio su Giacomo Leopardi* (1876–83, publ. 1885), in *Opere*, xiii, ed. Carlo Muscetta (Turin: Einaudi, 1960), 261–77. In more recent times, two important essays which start a new phase in criticism (1947) focus on this aspect: Cesare Luporini, *Leopardi progressivo* (Rome: Editori Riuniti, 2006 [1st edn 1947]); and Walter Binni, *La nuova poetica leopardiana* (Florence: Sansoni, 1947).

deeper influence on his nephew than the critics have been prepared to admit.[22] In his frequent conversations with this able politician perhaps the first seed was sown of that 'total transformation', which, in 1819, as we have seen, brought Leopardi to deep reflection about 'matters of prose', and ethical problems, which did not of course exclude active participation in politics. From a psychological point of view, timidity, melancholy, and depression were the hidden side of a temperament which encouraged him to action and ambition, and which when he was a child manifested itself in a wish to become a saint,[23] and later in his energetic and bold youthful attempts to make contact with major Italian literary figures and editors in order to publish his own works and become famous. Because of his position, upbringing, and temperament, Leopardi could, like Novalis or Chateaubriand, have become a restorer of Christian morality or a politician of the Restoration, as Marchese Antici hoped. However, the latter made the mistake of encouraging Leopardi to read not only de Maistre, but also the Greek orators and moralists, which Antici interpreted in the key of Christian moralism. So in Leopardi was born a love for ancient oratory, and afterwards, more generally, for Greek culture, but as we have seen, in a very different sense. In his secluded condition, what attracted his energetic temperament was above all the call of liberty, of corporeality, of the light and pluralistic transcendence of luminous pagan mythologies, of beauty, youth, pleasure.[24] His love for Demosthenes and Homer shredded his faith in the absolute, and his boyhood desire for glory was turned in a secular national direction. This meeting ground—the idea of country and hatred for despotism—is the scene of the ambiguous encounter between Leopardi and the revolutionary and reforming disturbances in Italy, which never resolved itself, however, into any active participation. In fact, in the 1830s it will culminate in a savage satire on liberals in the *Paralipomeni della Batracomiomachia*.

Leopardi's initial patriotism, as expressed in the first civic poems (1818–20), is purely literary, and takes its inspiration from the cult of classicality and nature. In Romanticism, however, Leopardi saw a modern, European movement, substantially progressive, imbued with philosophy and directed by social interests. For this reason his first statements of position were anti-Romantic. These were a letter to the *Biblioteca Italiana*, a pro-Austrian publication, in response to a letter from Mme de Staël on translations (1816), and a lengthy *Discorso* against the Romantics (1818), not published in his lifetime, in which, however, without Leopardi being aware of it, there are numerous elements of Romantic poetics.[25] Leopardi's adherence to the Classicist or Romantic front line is, not by coincidence, one of the complex knots which criticism, frequently with ideological concerns, attempts without success to cut through, since it does not take into

22 D'Intino, *L'immagine della voce: Leopardi, Platone e il libro morale* (Venice: Marsilio, 2009), 85–131.

23 See Leopardi, *Scritti e frammenti autobiografici*, 123.

24 Franco D'Intino, 'Il rifugio dell'apparenza: Il paganesimo post-metafisico di Leopardi', in Paolo Tortonese (ed.), *Il paganesimo nella letteratura dell'Ottocento* (Rome: Bulzoni, 1999), 115–66.

25 See the English tr. (by Gabrielle Sims and Fabio A. Camilletti) in Fabio A. Camilletti, *Classicism and Romanticism in Italian Literature: Leopardi's Discourse on Romantic Poetry* (London: Pickering & Chatto, 2013), 113–73.

account the fact that Leopardi's thought is made up of tensions between different and sometimes opposite points of view.[26]

In later times, Leopardi's attention to politics never lessens, but continues as part of a general philosophical reflection of the ways of human behaviour, at the intersection of ethics, metaphysics, anthropology, and psychology, as for example in his recognition of self-love as the driving force behind human actions. It has been rightly said that Leopardi never abandons the concept of 'virtue',[27] in spite of the fact that he does not believe in the possibility that it can ever establish itself, and still less, like Nietzsche, that it can progress with the advancement of knowledge.[28] But in question is a virtue that arises from a tragic awareness, cut off from any transcendent consolatory vision, whether religious or secular, rooted in the movable and uncertain ground of habituations, needs, and illusions. From this point of view too Leopardi calls up the lesson of the ancients, carrying on a dialogue with Socratic philosophies, and in particular with Stoicism, one of whose key texts, the *Manual* by Epictetus, he translated in 1825.[29]

The Shadow of Plato and 'Half Philosophy'

The fundamental problem is the relationship between a morality which is compatible with the world (Leopardi calls it 'practical') and a morality which is in contrast with the world ('speculative' or 'theoretical'): between a thought which will be in solidarity with human action and interests, subject to time and transience, and one which is purely abstract, which aims towards non-temporal and absolute values. In short, between a philosophy close to the model of ancient wisdom and rooted in the art of persuasive and eloquent speech, and a purely speculative philosophy, which finds its own basis in a disembodied and disenchanted reason. The watershed between these two directions is marked by Plato, as Leopardi, following in the footsteps of Montesquieu and Locke, openly declares several times in the *Zibaldone*: 'once Plato's ideas have been taken away, the absolute is lost' (*Zibaldone*, 1463, 7 August 1821). In that same year perhaps,

[26] On Leopardi the classicist see Sebastiano Timpanaro, *Classicismo e illuminismo nell'Ottocento italiano* (Pisa: Nistri-Lischi, 1969 [1965]). An opening towards other philosophical perspectives comes from works by Antonio Prete, *Il pensiero poetante: Saggio su Leopardi*, 3rd rev. edn (Milan: Feltrinelli, 2006 [1980]), Mario Andrea Rigoni (*Saggi sul pensiero leopardiano*, Padua: Cleup, 1982, augmented as *Il pensiero di Leopardi*, 4th edn, Turin: Aragno, 2010), and Carlo Ferrucci (ed.), *Leopardi e il pensiero moderno* (Milan: Feltrinelli, 1989).

[27] Cesare Luporini, 'Introduzione al pensiero politico di G. Leopardi', in *Il pensiero storico e politico di G. Leopardi: Atti del VI convegno internazionale di studi leopardiani* (Florence, Olschki, 1989), 15–25.

[28] Friedrich Nietzsche, *Menschliches, Allzumenschliches*, §517, *Werke*, iv/2. 335.

[29] See Dolfi, 'Lo stoicismo greco-romano e la filosofia pratica di Leopardi', in *Ragione e passione*, 43–77; D'Intino, 'Introduzione', in Leopardi, *Volgarizzamenti in prosa 1822–1827*, ed. Franco D'Intino (Venice: Marsilio, 2012), 141–76.

Montesquieu is the inspiration of a project for a 'political book', in which politics is something which pertains to the natural and corporeal sphere of the senses and emotions. Without realizing it, Leopardi is here in step with the Schiller of the letters *On the Aesthetic Education of Man*: the goal of the ancients was not the 'true' but the 'beautiful' (that is, the aesthetic sphere of the senses), and from this the 'necessity to render interest in the state an individual thing, which was the reason for the greatness of ancient peoples'.[30]

A purely speculative philosophy is incompatible therefore with individual wishes, tastes, and interests, on which action depends. But how can the *modern*, Platonized, *homo theoreticus* still hope to be able to act in the world? Leopardi's answer is that he must, at least partly, turn back. This thesis is expounded in January 1821 in a note in which is coined the concept of 'half philosophy'.

While '[f]ull philosophy is totally inactive', and 'has never caused and could not have caused any revolution or movement or undertaking etc., public or private', on the contrary 'half-philosophy is compatible with action, indeed may cause it'. And this is because '[i]t is not pure truth or reason, which could not produce a movement', but is instead 'the mother of errors, and is itself an error' (*Zibaldone*, 520). 'Half philosophy' does not come *before* 'full philosophy'; instead it is *a step backwards* with respect to the openly displayed reason of modernity, a partial going back into the shadows to find protection from the blinding lights of an 'excess of civilization' which has also contaminated Christianity, so that, after the first century, as Leopardi specifies, it quickly became a rational religion. More than half a century later, Nietzsche will declare in an analogous formulation: 'Half-knowledge is more successful than complete knowledge: it conceives things as simpler than they are, and *therefore forms its opinion in the most comprehensible and convincing way*.'[31]

'Full philosophy' is not only ineffective but also dangerous, since, by following a cyclical route, it can lead to a new state of barbarism.[32] From this point of view, Leopardi, as critic of the revolutionary cult of reason (*Zibaldone*, 160–1), is in agreement with the anti-rationalist liberalism of Burke, for whom 'pleasing illusions' which only serve to harmonize 'the different shades of life' 'are to be dissolved by this new conquering empire of light and reason'.[33] One must, however, remain in the half-light,[34] that half-light (something half-way between seeing and not seeing) which is explicitly identified in a note on 27 November 1820 with *rhetoric* as an instrument of *mediation* and *action*: 'Eloquence, especially the judicial variety, but other kinds as well, consists largely

[30] Leopardi, *Prose*, 1212.

[31] Nietzsche, *Menschliches, Allzumenschliches*, §578, *Werke*, iv/2. 347 (my tr. and emphasis).

[32] On the complexity (and ambiguities) of Leopardi's reflections on history, see María de las Nieves Muñiz Muñiz, 'Sul concetto di decadenza storica in Leopardi', in *Il pensiero storico e politico*, 375–90.

[33] Edmund Burke, *Reflections on the Revolution in France*, ed. Leslie G. Mitchell (Oxford: Oxford University Press, 1993), 77. In other ways Leopardi considers the Revolution as a return (a positive one) to ancient natural illusions.

[34] On the relationship between light and shade, see Alberto Folin, 'Lo sguardo nell'ombra', in *Leopardi e la notte chiara* (Venice: Marsilio, 1993), 15–40.

of smoothing out the bumps, filling in the holes and gaps, levelling the surface and straightening out the kinks in things.'[35] Man, who lives amidst change and contradiction, 'needs to have beliefs' (*Zibaldone*, 437), and can only be brought back to believing by the power of an eloquent reviving word, which makes him 'see and not see, remember and forget at the same time' (*Zibaldone*, 359–60).

It is in this grey area of 'disillusioned illusions'[36] (to which poetry also belongs) that three years later the project of the *Operette morali* takes shape, born in the shadow of his full reading of Plato, which happened in Rome in 1823. It is a rational lucidity which, as so often in Plato, draws on a mythological and fabled imagination; written in a very elaborate way, but which, again as in Plato, imitates a dialogue structure, the motions of the living voice. It is a metaphysical and nihilistic satire which at the same time, as Francesco De Sanctis writes in a famous passage from his essay on *Schopenhauer and Leopardi*, attempts to stimulate action and virtue.[37] These are tensions which create the paradox of a poetic book written in prose: 'I swear to you that my intention was to write poetry in prose, as is the custom today' (*Epistolario*, 1740, 8 July 1830). This prose which is *poetic*, yet modern (in the sense that it *passes through* the rationality of a man who is by now *transformed* for ever), for Leopardi is *moral* in the sense that it is intended to 'stir the imagination': 'If any *moral book* could serve a useful purpose, I think it would mainly be *poetic books*; that is books intended to *stir the imagination*; and I am speaking here as much of books in prose as of those in verse.'[38] 'Poetry' (in the broadest sense, so that it applies also to prose) is a non-rational word which tries to transform men, to move them to action by playing on the imagination and on *feeling*: 'everything that is poetic *is felt* rather than being known or understood, or perhaps we should say, *is known or understood in being felt*' (*Zibaldone*, 3242, 22 August 1823, my emphasis).

The *Discorso sui costumi* and Modern Society

It has been said that between 1750 and 1850 the novel of *sensibility* is the attempt to reconstruct, through *feeling*, a community of readers, whose values are founded on the sacrifice of the protagonist.[39] After the failure of his *Werther*-style epistolary novel, Leopardi

[35] *Zibaldone*, 360. Leopardi, in common with the English and German Romantics, naturalizes the old rhetoric, transforming it, as other Romantic writers, 'from a highly coded art into a human representational capacity': David E. Wellbury, 'The transformation of Rhetoric', in Marshall Brown (ed.), *The Cambridge History of Literary Criticism*, v. *Romanticism* (Cambridge: Cambridge University Press, 2000), 189.

[36] Hamilton, 'Leopardi and the Proper Conversation of a Citizen', in *Realpoetik*, 213.

[37] 'He calls love, glory and virtue illusions, and he ignites in your breast an unexhausted desire for them': De Sanctis, *Opere*, xiii. 465, my tr.

[38] Leopardi, 'Dialogo di Timandro ed Eleandro', §9 (*Prose*, 173, my tr.).

[39] April Alliston and Margaret Cohen, 'Empatia e sensibility nell'evoluzione del romanzo', in Franco Moretti (ed.), *Il romanzo* (Turin: Einaudi, 2002), iii. 237.

with the *Operette morali* then turns to the same profound structure in a non-novel piece of prose which takes on the original fragmentary and dialogue form of a poetic philosophy. In 1819 the young protagonist succumbs to an excess of reflexivity which corrodes from the inside his morbid sensibility and produces a fragmentation of the subject. In 1824 the same author, who has lost the capacity for *feeling* and *imagining* on account of the 'total transformation' described in the youthful fragments, attempts to reconstitute it in a world which has become a desert by appealing to a modern reader who finds himself in the same position. The dialogue form guaranteed the character's presence, the sound of that living voice which, according to Diderot, succeeds, in Richardson's novels, in persuading the reader, something that abstract and general principles cannot achieve. Leopardi, who never quotes Diderot's *Eloge de Richardson*, did however share fully the theory of empathy developed in this manifesto of *sensibility*. In fact, before beginning to write the *Operette morali*, he entrusts to the *Zibaldone* a long reflection on theatrical dramas which moves in the same direction: dramas with a happy ending are to be preferred less than those in whose plot the protagonist dies and the evil-doer triumphs on the stage, so that the drama leaves in the spectator the desire to punish him (*Zibaldone*, 3448–60, September 1823). In the *Operette* there is no human plot, and one single evil-doer; it is the whole of nature which is evil, or incomprehensibly inhuman. And yet, as we have seen, this moral book has the task of leaving a trace, a living sign in the reader, of modifying his moral constitution and modes of behaviour.

The writing of this moral as well as metaphysical book responds therefore to the requirement to reproduce, in modernity, the mechanism of *mimesis* condemned by Plato. On the same foundations Leopardi bases an essay, the *Discorso sopra lo stato presente dei costumi degl'italiani*, written in 1824 at the same time as the *Operette morali*. In the initial description there is the portrayal of an open world, in movement, based exclusively on the dynamic of money and the frantic consumption of commodities (including literary ones). Against this background is placed at the forefront the destruction by the 'progress of Enlightenment concepts' of 'ancient national prejudices', or in other words of local opinions and traditions which remain in place until they are passed through the sieve 'of the spirit of philosophy and reason'. The dissolution of 'beliefs' brings with it the impossibility of 'establishing moral principles' since they are based precisely on those 'opinions outside of which it is impossible for the just and the honest to appear reasonable, and the exercise of virtue worthy of a wise man is also impossible'.[40] As a consequence, the hypothesis of the refoundation of advanced modern society in the *Discorso* demonstrates that the only possible grounds for the project are *illusion, opinion, authority*, and *example*. On the one hand, in fact, the rule of reason does not allow a 'good opinion' of anyone to be held; on the other, however, an instinct deriving from the force itself of social cohabitation drives man to imitate the ideas and modes of behaviour of

[40] Leopardi, 'Discorso sopra lo stato presente dei costumi degl'italiani', in *Prose*, 447. From this point of view, the *Discorso* is a retraction of his youthful *Saggio sopra gli errori popolari degli antichi* (1815), the work with which, in the wake of 17th–18th-cent. rationalism (Thomas Browne, Pierre Bayle, d'Holbach), Leopardi had accepted, though with grave reservations, the Platonic-Enlightenment line.

others, to follow the example of those nearest to him. From this perspective we should interpret Leopardi's interest in ancient moral prose writing, and especially in Isocrates, whose speeches, of which Leopardi translated four in 1824–5, propose exemplary models of behaviour, amplified by the orator's voice, which is reproduced in the writing.[41]

The orator-writer Isocrates, whose weak voice prevented him from delivering his speeches, anticipates what will be the modern condition, where greater social complexity does not allow the voice to spread rapidly (*Zibaldone*, 1203). The function of writing is precisely that of spreading and bringing together models of behaviour which can be imitated: 'Having read or in reading a book, no matter how stupid it is or thought to be by the one reading, … it is not possible for anyone who reads it or has read it … not to think, *at least for half an hour, even in spite of himself*, in a manner, one way or another, which is in agreement with the book's writer, not to take in something of his spirit, not to be affected by his authority, not to give it some weight.'[42] However, the reservation (*at least for half an hour*) is important because it clarifies the point that modernity does not reproduce the ancient system in its entirety. Once the concept of *tradition* has been demolished, and therefore that of *classicality*, authority is of very short duration. Born in 1798, Leopardi has assimilated thoroughly the historical trauma of the Revolution, and when he observes that the influence 'of the last book read' always prevails over 'that of books read further in the past',[43] he is already looking at the mechanism of the modern industry of culture, which foresees 'the shift from repeated readings in a few, mostly religious texts, to one-time readings of indefinitely many texts'.[44] It is not a coincidence that Benjamin quotes the *operetta morale* on Fashion and Death in his essay on Baudelaire and Paris.

Such clarity of vision, however, is like a condemnation: the writer who wished to acquire everlasting glory and become a 'classic' realizes that it has all been useless. In the world which is beginning to develop, from which Italy is for the moment excluded, the book can exercise an important function, but only for the briefest season. And perhaps it is only that genre of book, the novel, which can guarantee an almost complete illusion. We come back thus to our starting problem. In the *Discorso*, Leopardi maintains that modern society can only be established through the reiteration of ethical information which leads to the establishment of a habit of behaviour, of an *accustomed way of behaving*. The concept of *habit*, of familiarity, is not by chance at the heart of Leopardi's reflection on man in the *Zibaldone*, which in this sense lays down the theoretical premises for a novel-writing system, the centre of which is precisely the interplay of *accustomed ways of behaving* (as for instance with Jane Austen in England and Balzac in France). But the fragmentation and the civic backwardness of the Italian states, according to Leopardi, do not guarantee the formation of that *close-knit society*,

[41] See D'Intino, 'Introduzione', in Leopardi, *Volgarizzamenti in prosa*, 107–39.

[42] Leopardi, 'Discorso sopra lo stato presente dei costumi degl'italiani', in *Prose*, 457 (my emphasis).

[43] Leopardi, 'Discorso sopra lo stato presente dei costumi degl'italiani', 459.

[44] Wellbury, 'Transformation of Rhetoric', 188.

that is alive, active, rich in relationships and interchanges, which is at the same time the presupposition and the consequence of the development of the European novel. Hence the difficulty on Leopardi's part to measure himself against the plots and characters of the novel. This was something which Manzoni managed to achieve, but he of course lived in Milan, in a society much more similar to that *close-knit* society which Leopardi identifies in Northern Europe. In the *Discorso*, therefore, Leopardi could have explained to himself why an intellectual born in the Papal States could not write a novel. Leopardi does not say so explicitly, but he certainly reacted resentfully to the success of the most famous Italian novel of the nineteenth century, Alessandro Manzoni's *I promessi sposi*, published in the same year as his *Operette morali*, whose poetic nihilism was well nigh ignored by the wider public. In that same year (1827), he commented bitterly, transforming the anthropological observation into a metaphysical vision:

> The destiny of books today is like that of those insects called ephemerals (*éphémères*): certain species live a few hours, some one night, others 3 or 4 days; but it is always only a matter of days. In truth, we of today are travelers and pilgrims on the earth: our time is truly short: we are here for one day: the morning in flower, the evening faded, or dried up: destined also to outlive our own fame, and living longer than we are remembered.... This is because immortality has become impossible, not only for men of letters but now for all pursuits, among such an endless multitude of facts and human endeavors, ever since civilization, the life of civilized man, and the record of history has embraced the whole world.[45]

In under ten years, almost without moving from home, Leopardi has gone from a Romantic *reverie* nurtured on ancient memories to a lucid and disenchanted vision of future society: celebrity which lasts half an hour, the accumulation of *memory* which, according to Plato's prophecy in *Phaedrus*, wipes clean the memory of a globalized planet. A few years later (1840), Alexis de Tocqueville will write that American readers 'prefer books which may be easily procured, quickly read, and which require no learned researches to be understood'. Authors, for their part, 'will aim at rapidity of execution, more than at perfection of detail'.[46] Balzac described this world in a novel, *Illusions perdues* (1836–43), the first part of which was published the year before Leopardi died in Naples (1837). It would have been an excellent title for Leopardi's *Bildungsroman*, if he had written one. After the lack of success of the *Operette morali* (published 1827), he preferred instead to turn to the Homeric question and to poetry. Though he continued

[45] *Zibaldone*, 4270. On the concept of the 'ephemeral', see Dolfi, 'Della memoria, i libri e degli effimeri', in *Ragione e passione*, 79–96; D'Intino, 'Il libro effimero', in *L'immagine della voce*, 209–54; Fabio A. Camilletti, *Leopardi's Nymphs. Grace, Melancholy and the Uncanny* (Oxford: Legenda, 2013).

[46] Alexis de Tocqueville, *De la démocratie en Amérique*, ed. Harold J. Laski (Paris: Gallimard, 1961), ii. 64 (my tr.).

to write the odd page of the *Zibaldone*, to all intents and purposes he had finished with prose for ever.

Further Reading

Editions Used

Leopardi, Giacomo, *Scritti e frammenti autobiografici*, ed. Franco D'Intino (Rome: Salerno, 1995).

Leopardi, Giacomo, *Prose*, ed. Rolando Damiani (Milan: Mondadori, 1988; 6th edn, 1997).

Leopardi, Giacomo, *Epistolario*, ed. Franco Brioschi and Patrizia Landi (Turin: Boringhieri, 1998); partial tr. *The Letters of Giacomo Leopardi 1817–1837*, selected and tr. Prue Shaw (Leeds: Northern Universities Press, 1998).

Leopardi, Giacomo, *Poeti greci e latini*, ed. Franco D'Intino (Rome: Salerno, 1999).

Leopardi, Giacomo, *Volgarizzamenti in prosa 1822–1827*, ed. Franco D'Intino (Venice: Marsilio, 2012).

Leopardi, Giacomo, *Zibaldone di Pensieri*, ed. Giuseppe Pacella (Milan: Garzanti, 1991); tr. *Zibaldone*, ed. Michael Caesar and Franco D'Intino (New York: Farrar Straus & Giroux, 2013).

Secondary Sources

Binni, Walter, *La nuova poetica leopardiana* (Florence: Sansoni, 1947).

Blasucci, Luigi, 'I registri della prosa', in *Lo stormire del vento tra le piante: Testi e percorsi leopardiani* (Venice: Marsilio, 2003), 103–23.

Camilletti, Fabio A., *Leopardi's Nymphs: Grace, Melancholy and the Uncanny* (Oxford: Legenda, 2013).

Cellerino, Liana, 'Operette morali', in Alberto Asor Rosa (ed.), *Dall'Ottocento al Novecento, Letteratura italiana: Le Opere*, iii. (Turin: Einaudi, 1995), 303–54.

Colaiacomo, Claudio, 'Zibaldone di pensieri', in Alberto Asor Rosa (ed.), *Dall'Ottocento al Novecento, Letteratura italiana: Le Opere*, iii. (Turin: Einaudi, 1995), 217–301.

Croce, Benedetto, 'Giacomo Leopardi', in B. Croce, *La letteratura italiana per saggi storicamente disposti*, iii. *L'Ottocento* (Bari: Laterza, 1963), 68–90.

De Sanctis, Francesco, *Leopardi*, in *Opere*, xiii, ed. Carlo Muscetta (Turin: Einaudi, 1960, includes various essays).

D'Intino, Franco, *L'immagine della voce: Leopardi, Platone e il libro morale* (Venice: Marsilio, 2009).

Dolfi, Anna, *Ragione e passione: Fondamenti e forme del pensare leopardiano* (Rome: Bulzoni, 2000).

Ferrucci, Carlo (ed.), *Leopardi e il pensiero moderno* (Milan: Feltrinelli, 1989).

Folin, Alberto, *Leopardi e la notte chiara* (Venice: Marsilio, 1993).

Hamilton, Paul, *Realpoetik: European Romanticism and Literary Politics* (Oxford: Oxford University Press, 2013).

Il pensiero storico e politico di G. Leopardi: Atti del VI convegno internazionale di studi leopardiani (Florence, Olschki, 1989).

Lo Zibaldone cento anni dopo: Composizione, edizione, temi. Atti del X convegno internazionale di studi leopardiani (Florence: Olschki, 2001).
Luporini, Cesare, *Leopardi progressivo* (Rome: Editori Riuniti, 2006 [1st edn 1947]).
Prete, Antonio, *Il pensiero poetante: Saggio su Leopardi*, 3rd rev. edn (Milan: Feltrinelli, 2006 [1st edn 1980]).
Rigoni, Mario Andrea, *Il pensiero di Leopardi*, 4th augmented edn (Turin: Aragno, 2010, 1st edn, *Saggi sul pensiero leopardiano*, Padua: Cleup, 1982).
Timpanaro, Sebastiano, *Classicismo e illuminismo nell'Ottocento italiano* (Pisa: Nistri-Lischi, 1969; 1st edn 1965).

CHAPTER 23

'EUROPEAN MAN AND WRITER'

Romanticism, the Classics, and Political Action in the Exemplary Life of Ugo Foscolo

GIUSEPPE GAZZOLA

ACCORDING to the famous definition by Benedetto Croce, 'Ugo Foscolo was a European man and writer; even if ... the European literary world ignored him in the complexity of his personality and his major works.'[1] Almost a century later, Croce's assertion is still useful: Foscolo was an intellectual of European significance, and locating him in a transnational context offers an enriched perspective on his life and works. While he remained famous in Italy, his particular biographical and poetic trajectories made it easy for him to be overlooked in other national literary contexts.

Foscolo was a European intellectual, first of all, for biographical reasons. Born on a Greek island, moving as an adolescent to Venice, and then to Milan, Bologna, and Florence, when each of those cities was the capital of a different state, Foscolo identified himself as an Italian, even though Italy did not yet exist as a nation. He spent two years in France as a volunteer in Napoleon's army, and later travelled across Europe, ultimately taking refuge in England from the persecution of the Austrian government, which once again controlled Northern Italy after the Restoration following the Congress of Vienna (1815).

Beyond the biographical, returning Foscolo to a European context is also necessary for cultural reasons. He wrote in Latin, in Italian, in French, and in London, at the end of his life, he made an effort to write in English. He translated excerpts of the *Iliad* and Sterne's *A Sentimental Journey through France and Italy* into Italian. Above all, Foscolo was European because he knew, as a writer and as a scholar, by nature and culture, how

[1] Benedetto Croce, *Poesia e non poesia: Note sulla letteratura europea del secolo decimonono* (Bari: Laterza, 1923), 129. All translations are mine.

to escape the provincialism that permeated the academies of the Italian cities; far ahead of his time, he understood how to combine a classical education with encyclopedic culture and a critical sensibility in a way previously unknown in Italian letters. Foscolo appears in literary histories as a Romantic poet, even if his first attempts in the Italian language were Arcadian odes, and his debut as a writer happened with *Tieste*, a tragedy with a classical plot, respectful of the Aristotelian unities of place, time, and action.

Though Foscolo appears in literary histories in the section dedicated to Italian Romanticism, the patently Romantic works are a minority in his corpus. In addition to the epistolary novel, *Ultime lettere di Jacopo Ortis* (*Last Letters of Jacopo Ortis*, 1802), twelve *Sonnets* (1803), and the long poem in blank endecasyllables titled *On Sepulchres* (*Dei Sepolcri*, 1807), works that by consensus exhaust his participation in Romantic literature, Foscolo also wrote two tragedies of classical plot, *Tieste* (1797) and *Ajace* (1811); a collection of classical hymns dedicated to Antonio Canova titled *Hymns to the Graces* (*Le Grazie*, 1813); a political treatise in Latin titled *Hypercalypseos* (*Didymi Clerici Prophetae minimi Hypercalypseos liber singularis*, 1816), and several critical articles permeated with classical erudition.

To understand why Foscolo is deemed a Romantic writer, despite Romantic works being a minor part of his literary production, the cultural and biographical components of his literary persona must be examined together; he is considered a Romantic writer because his Romantic works appealed more to the *Weltanschauung* of the period and because of the way he lived his life. His restless and adventurous life came to be regarded, by the following generation of intellectuals and patriots, as the prototype of every Romantic life: driven by idealized notions of love, war, nationalism, and liberty, but in the end disappointed and scorned. Foscolo reinvented himself several times: as a cavalry officer on the battlefield, as a poet-ideologue on the podium, a polemicist in newspapers and magazines, a public intellectual, a professor in the university, and a *cicisbeo* in the salons. In his lifetime, he was known and occasionally feared in the centres of culture and power in Europe. In Vienna he was considered unreliable and seditious, but in London he was an indispensable, chic interpretive instrument for the culture of the southernmost peninsula that the British had started to consider as Europe's internal other. His epistolary novel, *Le ultime lettere di Jacopo Ortis*, earned him a serious literary reputation before age of 25. His essays, though long-winded (since he was paid by the page, excluding quotations), frequently display a visionary insight: the division of literary history into epochs, the elaboration of a criticism in control of its literary heritage, the opportunity to elect Dante, instead of Petrarch, as foundational father of both literature and the nation, are all intuitions still critically accepted today.

Ugo Foscolo was born in 1778 in Zante, the ancient Zakynthos, one of the Ionian Islands under the military and commercial dominion of the Venetian Republic. The tiny Mediterranean island, rich in vegetation and sunlight, immersed in a sea teeming with classical memories, made a considerable impression on him; he would later transfigure Zante into a mythical world of privileged beauty to which he would return in imagination during especially painful moments of his difficult life. Spending his formative years on a Greek island rooted Foscolo in a cultural tradition that enjoyed prestige and heightened consideration over the course of the century, both in Italy and in the rest of Europe. It was on Zante that the bonds of a lifelong affiliation with the art, language, and literature of Hellas, the affection for Homer, and the formal and insistent Classicism of his own verse were born.

After the death of his father, Foscolo's mother moved the family to Venice; thus, at the end of 1792, the 14-year-old Foscolo left his island forever, and made his entry into the sophisticated and worldly city, which, despite grave economic decline, was still illuminated by the academic and cultural pursuits of its inhabitants. In Venice Foscolo found a city glittering with life provided by salons and letters, academies and libraries, publishers and bookstores, and theatres and cafés. Between 1793 and 1797 Foscolo lived with great intensity, reading and studying the classics, as well as the works of Italian and foreign writers, poets, and thinkers. At the same time, he loved furiously and composed lyrics in various metres for his numerous Romantic interests, and exalted the ideals of liberty that the French Revolution had disseminated across Europe.

Italian intellectuals born in the last thirty years of the Settecento found themselves living through an epochal transformation, passing, in a brief period of time, from the Ancien Régime to the Restoration, while encountering the upheaval of the French Revolution and the Napoleonic Empire along the way. Judging the career of a preceptor to be unworthy of his aspirations, Foscolo became a *bourgeois* perennially short of money, divided between a military career and a love for literature, books, and teaching. He was introduced to Isabella Teotochi Albrizzi, and began to frequent her prestigious salon, where he had the opportunity to become acquainted with Ippolito Pindemonte, and to know Saverio Bettinelli, Aurelio de' Giorgi Bertola, and Antonio Canova. Foscolo was immediately infatuated with the older Isabella, and, over time, these sentiments were transformed into a bond of affectionate confidence that can be traced through his papers to the end of his exile in England.

Foscolo's political enthusiasm quickly turned to disillusionment when Napoleon ceded Northern Italy to Austria with the treaty of Campoformio.[2] In an imaginary letter, that is, the first in the novel *Last Letters of Jacopo Ortis*, fictionally dated 'Da' colli Euganei, 11 Ottobre 1797', he writes:

> Il sacrificio della nostra patria è consumato: tutto è perduto; e la vita, se pure ne verrà concessa, non ci resterà che per piangere le nostre sciagure, e le nostre infamie. Il mio nome è nella lista di proscrizione, lo so: ma vuoi tu ch'io per salvarmi da chi m'opprime mi commetta a chi mi ha tradito? Consola mia madre: vinto dalle sue lagrime l'ho ubbidita, e ho lasciato Venezia per evitare le prime persecuzioni, e le più feroci.... E noi, pur troppo, noi stessi italiani ci laviamo le mani nel sangue degl'italiani. Per me segua che può. Poiché ho disperato e della mia patria e di me, aspetto tranquillamente la prigione e la morte.[3]

[2] Campoformio is a town in Friuli, near Udine. In the treaty signed there between Napoleon and the Austrian Empire on 17 Oct. 1797, it was stipulated that Austria would abandon the Netherlands and the lands with the Rhine as a border; in exchange, France would cede the territories bordering the Adriatic Sea: Venice, Istria, and Dalmatia.

[3] I cite from the edn of 1802; see *Edizione Nazionale delle Opere di Ugo Foscolo* (Florence: F. Le Monnier, 1933), henceforth *EN*, iv. 137.

> The sacrifice of our country is completed; everything is lost. And our life, or what little remains of it, will be to cry after our misfortunes, and our infamy. My name is on the blacklist, I know; but do you want that I, to save myself from my oppressors, confide in those who betrayed me? Comfort my mother: overwhelmed by her tears I obeyed her, and I left Venice to avert the early persecutions, the most dangerous ones.... And we, alas, we Italians are washing our hands in the blood of other Italians. I am indifferent to what will happen next. Since I gave up hope for my homeland and for myself, I quietly await incarceration and death.

This letter, even in the fictional context of a novel, is intensely autobiographical. The difference between the author and his hero lies in the fact that Foscolo did not remain to quietly await 'la prigione e la morte' but, on 9 November 1797, left for Milan in voluntary exile. In Milan, then capital of the Cisalpine Republic, Foscolo found a vibrant cultural ambience and an atmosphere more receptive to his ideas than that of Venice. Here he met Parini, and established a friendship with Vincenzo Monti and his wife, Teresa Pikler, who would serve as the inspiration for the name of the female protagonist of the *Ortis*. He also began work as an editor of the *Monitore Italiano* with Melchiorre Gioia.

In the summer of 1798, Foscolo worked on the *Ortis*, the novel in which his unhappy political and amorous experiences converge. He concentrated intensely on this work and had already sent the first part to the publisher when he voluntarily enrolled in the Guardia Nazionale di Bologna in April 1799, as the city anticipated an Austrian attack. The publisher Marsigli confided the task of completing the novel to an obscure novelist, Angelo Sassoli, without the author's knowledge; an edition titled *Vera storia di due amanti infelici* (The True Story of Two Unhappy Lovers) was published, with numerous cuts and omissions owing to the Austrian censors, who had, in the meantime, seized control of the Bolognese media.

Upon his return to Milan, Foscolo was occupied with various missions in Northern Italy, particularly in Tuscany: between 1800 and 1801 in Florence, he met and fell in love with the young Isabella Roncioni, already betrothed to a wealthy marquis. This unrequited passion became the cause of acute lamentation for the poet, who drew on it as a source of melancholy for the sonnets composed at the time: 'Non son chi fui' (I'm Not Who I Used to Be); 'E tu ne' carmi avrai perenne vita' (You Will Live Forever in the Poems); 'Che stai?' (Why Do You Hesitate). The figure of Isabella, apart from merging into Foscolian verse, represented a model for the revised characterization of the female protagonist of the *Ortis*.

After completing the work of revision, Foscolo publicly complained about the edition of Sassoli[4] and authorized the printing of *Last Letters of Jacopo Ortis* in Milan in 1802. The novel is inspired by Goethe's *Die Leiden des jungen Werthers* (1774), but to the amorous chagrins of the joung Werther Foscolo's eponymous hero adds the political drama consequential to the Treaty of Campoformio. The letters that Jacopo addresses to his friend

[4] On the topic cf. Ugo Foscolo, 'Foscolo to the Editors of the *Gazzetta Universale*', Florence, 2 Jan. 1801, *EN, Epistolario*, i. 92–4.

Lorenzo Alderani, beginning from the one already quoted, express the disillusionment of their author at a demoralizing historical conjuncture. The plot is simple: Jacopo, a political exile from Venice, finds refuge in the nearby hills; but his reasons for suffering double when he falls in love with Teresa, who is already bethroted to Odoardo, a wealthy bourgeois unperturbed by the political vicissitudes of the Italian nation. After an idyllic scene in which Teresa and Jacopo visit Petrarch's last abode, a scene modelled precisely on Petrarchan motifs, Jacopo, trying to escape the sources of his suffering, starts wandering around Italy. In Florence he receives a strong impression from a visit to the tombs of the illustrious Italians in Santa Croce; in Milan he visits Giuseppe Parini; in Rimini he receives the news of Teresa's wedding. After visiting Dante's tomb and meeting his mother one last time, he commits suicide. Jacopo embodies the salient features of the Romantic hero: his feelings are intense, his soul magnanimous, his hopes unrequited. The final suicide is not an act of self-effacement, rather the bold affirmation of a character left without hope by an adverse destiny.

Foscolo had sent Goethe a copy of the first incomplete edition, with this accompanying note:

> Riceverete dal Signor Grassi il primo volumetto di una mia operetta a cui forse dié origine il Vostro *Werther*.... Ho dipinto me stesso, le mie passioni, e i miei tempi sotto il nome di un mio amico ammazzatosi a Padova. Non ho nissun merito nell'invenzione avendo tratto tutto dal *vero*.[5]
>
> You will receive from Signor Grassi the first part of a little work of mine, originated perhaps[6] from your *Werther*.... In it I have described myself, my ideals and my times under the name of a friend who has committed suicide in Padua. I do not take any credit for the argument, since I've copied everything from *reality*.

Goethe read and annotated the book but never acknowledged its reception, and there is no evidence that Foscolo attempted to send him a copy of the novel in its entirety. However, he did send a copy to his mentor, Vittorio Alfieri, accompanied by a letter dated October 1802:

> Al primo Italiano.
>
> In questo libercolo da me scritto in tre anni di sventure e di esilio, ed ora stampato, senza lusinga di gloria, a consolazione de' giovani sfortunati ed oscuri, ho ardito parlare di Vittorio Alfieri. Dipingendo sotto il nome di un mio amico infelice tutto me stesso, doveva a forza parlare di voi, perché la vostra gloria essendomi incitamento perpetuo a nobili imprese ed a liberi scritti, gran parte de' miei pensieri e delle mie passioni fu sempre l'esempio vostro. [7]

[5] Foscolo to 'Signor Goethe, illustrious German writer', Milan, 16 Jan. 1802, *EN, Epistolario*, i. 129–31.

[6] For an analysis of this adverb, and of the entire Foscolo–Goethe relationship, cf. F. Zschech, *Ugo Foscolos Brief an Goethe* (Hamburg: Realschule am Eilbeckerwege zu Hamburg, 1894).

[7] Foscolo to Vittorio Alfieri, Milan, Oct. 1802, *EN, Epistolario*, i. 129–31.

> To the First of the Italians.
>
> In this little book, written in three years of misfortune and exile, printed now, without ambition for glory, as a consolation for many humble and unfortunate youth, I dared to mention Vittorio Alfieri. Having described myself under the name of an unfortunate friend, I had to speak of you, since your glory incessantly incites me to noble actions and independent writing, and your example informs a great amount of my ideals and my thoughts.

The *adnominatio* of this letter is anything but casual: Alfieri, in writing and in conversations, had transmitted to his pupil a concept of *Patria* closer to that of the *Carboneria* of the following century than to that of the Milanese Jacobins. Thanks to Alfieri's teaching, Foscolo, barely 20 years old, was, in political terms, twenty years ahead of his contemporaries. His objective was not the reinforcement of the Repubblica Cispadana, but the constitution of Italy as a nation. In fact, with the essay *Su la Italia*, printed in Genoa in 1800, he asked the French general Championnet to promote an *Italian* republic; in the Meetings of Lyons in 1802, in which he participated as a representative for the Comitato di Governo giacobino, he provoked the assembly by reciting an *Orazione a Bonaparte*, which condemned the French malgovernance in the Cisalpine Republic and called on Napoleon to deserve his title of 'savior of the people'.

Vittorio Alfieri was also Foscolo's teacher in literary matters. From him, Foscolo learned that the critic ideally should also be a poet—or at least a potential poet. Reading Alfieri's treatise, *Del principe e delle lettere* (The Prince and Letters) he acquired several ideas on which he based, first, his oration, *Dell'origine e dell'ufficio della letteratura* (On the Origin and Function of Literature) and then, his entire critical apparatus. Central among these ideas was the understanding of literature as civic mission, and its corollary, that literature written for monetary gain was to be condemned—for the desire for wealth frequently constrained writers to support politicians and public opinion often prevented them from speaking truth and oberying the call of their particular genius.

While in the eighteenth century, the canon of Italian literature hinged around Petrarch and Tasso, Alfieri concentrated his attention on Dante and Machiavelli. Driven by his preference for the epic genre, Alfieri was convinced that the culmination of Italian poetry was not to be found in the love poets of the sixteenth century, as his contemporaries claimed, but in the fourteenth century, especially in Dante. The latter's merit, Alfieri argued, was to have understood literature as a sacred mission, to have affirmed the superiority of the poet over all other human beings, and to have provided an example of integrity as a man, artist, and citizen.

In April 1803 Foscolo published a volume of *Poesie*, composed of eleven sonnets and the two odes 'Luigia Pallavicini caduta da cavallo' (To Luigia Pallavicini, Who Fell from a Horse) and 'All'amica risanata' (To a Healed Friend). The definitive edition, which appeared a few months later, added just one sonnet, 'In morte del fratello Giovanni' (For the Death of My Brother Giovanni), who had recently committed suicide in Venice because of his gambling debts. The sonnets represents an interesting synthesis of Italian Romanticism, combining, as it does, Romantic images (the grief for an expired life, the emotional harshness of exile) with a vocabulary of classical derivation. The whole chapbook, in fact, presents a tension between a Romantic and a Classical pole: the sonnets, with their insistence on autobiography and the poetic persona epitomize and prove the existence of an Italian Romanticism; the two odes instead take inspiration from poems by Giuseppe Parini and tend towards a measured ideal of neoclassical beauty.

The following year Foscolo, now 26, requested, and was permitted by the Jacobin authorities, to be sent to France in the ranks of the army being prepared for the Napoleonic expedition against England. During the years he spent in Normandy, Foscolo went on with his studies and his literary experiments. He translated Laurence Sterne's *A Sentimental Journey* into Italian, under the pseudonym Didimo Chierico, and accompanied it with a *Notizia intorno a Didimo Chierico* (Notice on Didimo Chierico) which signalled the birth of a new autobiographical figure, as lucid and ironic as Jacopo Ortis had been Romantic and dramatic. Also while in France, between 1804 and 1805, in Valenciennes, Foscolo developed a relationship with Sophia Hamilton, a young Englishwoman. A child, Mary, born in this period, would later enter Foscolo's life; he would memorialize her with the name of Floriana and kept her close to him until his death.

When Napoleon had renounced the enterprise against England, Foscolo returned to Milan. Passing through Paris, in March 1806, he visited Alessandro Manzoni. The encounter between two pillars of Italian Romanticism was not particularly cordial, but this did not prevent either of them from writing, later, appreciative pages on each other's works. From Milan, he briefly went to Venice to meet his mother and the always affectionate Isabella Teotochi Albrizzi. During the return journey, he stopped in Verona to visit Ippolito Pindemonte. With Pindemonte, who was working on a poem titled *Cimiteri*, Foscolo discussed the so-called Edict of Saint-Cloud, with which Napoleon mandated that all burials were to be anonymous and should take place outside of the urban boundaries. The Edict, already enforced in France, was about to be extended to the Italian provinces. From the conversation with Pindemonte emerged the idea for the *Sepolcri*, composed and published in a matter of a few months.

The poem, in blank endecasyllables, has a colloquial and oratorical tone, as if it wanted to recreate the dialogue of the two friends in Verona. It is addressed to Pindemonte, and it begins with a question:

> All'ombra de' cipressi e dentro l'urne
> confortate di pianto, è forse il sonno
> della morte men duro? (ll. 1–3)
>
> In the shade of the cypresses and inside the urns
> comforted by tears, is the sleep
> of death more tolerable?

With this opening Foscolo captures in full the Enlightenment derivation of the Edict of Saint-Cloud. Yet, after having denied the rational function of the grave, the poem contradicts rational thought to confer on the sepulchre a universal significance. Graves connect the living and the dead, the past with the present; they are an incitement to virtue, since virtue allows the human being to survive in the memory of posterity. The sepulchre represents, first, a gathering of familiar remembrance, but also a religious function and a civil institution; it is the place where the memories of a nation are preserved and, hence, a supreme poetic inspiration. Taking as an example the graves of the illustrious Italians buried in the Franciscan church of Santa Croce in Florence (already visited, in the narrative fiction, by Jacopo Ortis) Foscolo explains how funerary monuments preserve the historical memory of a people and incite to great deeds:

> A egregie cose il forte animo accendono
> l'urne de' forti, o Pindemonte; e bella
> e santa fanno al peregrin la terra
> che le ricetta. (ll. 152–5)
>
> The urns of great men incite
> great souls to great deeds, Pindemonte;
> they transform the place where they are
> in a holy land for the pilgrim.

The poem, together with the *Esperimento di traduzione dell'Iliade*, was published in Brescia in 1807.

Thanks to the good offices of Vincenzo Monti, Foscolo was nominated the following year as professor of Italian and Latin eloquence at the University of Pavia. With this post, he thought he could finally enjoy that synthesis of public service, steadiness of income, and literary vocation which he had always desired and which had always eluded him. At the beginning of the term he pronounced a memorable prolusion, *Dell'origine e dell'ufficio della letteratura* (On the origins and the function of literature) his first attempt to express critical ideas in an organic manner. Receptive to the ideas expressed by Giambattista Vico in the *Scienza nuova* that related the origins and development of a civilization to the literary realm, Foscolo in his prolusionb outlined a new function for the academic intellectual. He was familiar with Vico's works through two of the latter's students—the Neopolitan patriots Vincenzo Cuoco and Francesco Lomonaco, who lived in exile in Milan after the Bourbons destroyed the short-lived Parthenopean Republic. Lomonaco, a historian and political thinker, was for several years Foscolo's doctor and friend, and encouraged him to study Vico's work. Soon, Foscolo adopted Viconian ideas on the origin and purpose of literature. Vico showed him the nature and value of language, the connection between the origin of words and concepts, and how literature itself, the most noble manifestation of the human spirit, grew out of intertwined words and concepts; indeed, in primitive populations, this vision of literature conincided, in the Viconian view, with poetry. Thus, in Vico's pages, Foscolo found a definition of poetry at once human and divine, which he found especially congenial. Already from Alfieri, he had learned to exalt poetry with great passion, but the Viconian system conferred an additional historical dignity to the poetic enterprise, converting poetry into the highest and most solemn manifestation of the will and culture of a people. It is not surprising, therefore, that Foscolo found in Vico's work an exhortation to the study of Homer and Dante, because they were, from the beginnings of their respective civilizations, the prophet-poets of their people and the creator of their language and literatures.

In sum, Vico was the stimulus that pushed Foscolo towards a methodological elaboration—if not a systematic unfolding—of his aesthetic thought. Through the Viconian system, Foscolo elevated literary historical study from the accumulation of facts to a critical and aesthetic system. Vico taught him to consider literature as an eternal moment of the human soul and, at the same time, an unmistakable manifestation of each civilization. For instance, the Viconian sources haunt all the pages in which Foscolo describes and theorizes the ancient ages of history from which emerges ancient poetry, or (as he would assert in his *Essays on Petrarch*, 1824), the only truly great poetry. By applying Viconian thought, Foscolo succeeded in transcending the neoclassical and Enlightenment strains in literary criticism and discovering a new vision, based on history, that profoundly influenced Italy's Romantic criticism.

In the *Prolusione* Foscolo specifically criticized the attitude of Italian intellectuals prone to celebrate the French government, which guaranteed their employment. Instead he proposed the task of educating the nascent national bourgeoisie, and exhorting Italians to a greater knowledge of history, so that they might better define the idea of a national identity.

Unfortunately for him, all chairs of eloquence were suppressed the following year by governmental decree; the newly minted professor was forced to return to Milan and give up pursuing his dreams of liberty and economic independence through academia. In his third Milanese period, from 1809 until 1811, Foscolo frequented various notable governmental officials, exciting envy and gossip in the circles of letters; the friendship with Monti, which had become strained and distant, transformed into one of open hostility. Foscolo's second tragedy, *Ajace*, performed at the Teatro alla Scala on 9 December 1811, did not garner public support. Worse still, the French censors claimed that the work had anti-Napoleonic allusions, perceiving the Emperor in the character of Agamennone, General Moreau in Ajace, and Fouché in Ulisse. The tragedy's lack of success, and the open hostility of some Milanese reviewers, induced Ugo to look elsewhere. During the spring of 1812 he decided to leave for Florence, now another province of the Empire.

Soon after his arrival in Florence, Foscolo met Quirina Mocenni Magiotti, the newly wed bride of a noble family who had been forced into a marriage with a wealthy man of feeble mind, and whom the critics have nicknamed 'Donna gentile' even though Foscolo did not reserve the term only for her. Quirina would dedicate passionate affection to Foscolo for the rest of her life, protecting him and helping him even during his exile in England.

The few years spent in Florence proved fecund for Foscolo's literary production: here he defined the project of *Le Grazie (Hymn to the Graces)*, a poem of classical inspiration and subject, dedicated to the daughters of Venus, but never completed. The Graces brought civilization and refinement to humanity and represent ideal beauty, perfect and radiant. Linked to the earlier *Odes*, the poem did not appeal to the Romantic admirers of Foscolo: it has only come to be appreciated in the twentieth century, when its fragments have been re-evaluated and its incompleteness taken as a virtue, since it fits the modernist idea that classical harmony can only be understood in fragments.

Also in Florence, Foscolo concluded and published his translation of Sterne's *A Sentimental Journey through France and Italy*, which attracted considerable attention, given the growing Italian interest in English narrative. The task of translation allowed Foscolo to experiment with a mode of writing and presentation profoundly different from the *Ortis*. From the influence of Sterne's detached, ironic style emerged Foscolo's second alter ego, Didimo Chierico, who made his debut in the preface of the Pisan edition of *Viaggio Sentimentale* in 1813. During his time in Florence he also wrote his third tragedy, the *Ricciarda*, which was performed in Bologna to little success in September 1813.

But the unstable political situation in Milan recalled Foscolo there one last time. In 1813, the forces of the Restoration organized an anti-Napoleonic offensive, and in August of that year the Austrian army repelled the resistance of the Cisalpine Republic. Foscolo had genuinely believed in the possibility of Italian independence and had fought and risked his life for it. The Austrians' return to Milan left him dejected.

Nevertheless the emissaries of the new government, attracted by his fame as a literary figure, approached him in early 1815 asking him to manage a pro-Austrian gazette, *La Biblioteca Italiana*.[8] The intellectuals hostile to Foscolo quickly became aware of the proposal and would accuse him of betraying his own principles on more than one occasion. The count Federico Confalonieri, a patriot and an active participant in the revolt of 20 April, was as a consequence challenged to a duel by the irritable poet:

> Signor mio—da più giorni mi viene ridetto che Ella parli poco discretamente di me. S'altri abusa del nome di Lei per avvalorare la propria malignità, è bene ch'Ella ne sia avvertita; ma se, come mi vien riferito, Ella mi attribuisce il progetto di rinnegare i miei principj e di prostituire la mia penna, Ella signor mio, ha il torto.... Spetta a Lei, signor mio, di far disdire la persona che le appone sì bassa calunnia ... Diversamente io mi vedrò costretto a parlare a Lei, caro signore, in guisa che Ella, o si ricreda, o mi faccia tacere per sempre.[9]

> Dear Sir—for a few days I have been told repeatedy that you are spreading untruths about me. If others abused your name to prove their own lies, it would be good if you were to know about it; but if, as it has been reported to me, you attribute to me the betrayal of my principles and the prostitution of my pen, you, dear sir, are wrong.... It remains for you, dear sir, to make the person who is spreading base calumnies

[8] Foscolo's reflections on the Austrian offer can be found in *Parere sulla istruzione di un giornale letterario*, *EN* viii. 315–20. The direction of the *Biblioteca Italiana*, after Foscolo's refusal, was offered to Vincenzo Monti, who accepted. In its opening issue, the journal published Mme de Staël's article *Sulla maniera e l'utilità delle traduzioni*. The article inaugurated the Romantic season in Italy, and sparked a momentous debate among Italian intellectuals, who divided into 'Classicists' (Pietro Giordani, Vincenzo Monti, Giacomo Leopardi) and 'Romantics' (Ludovico di Breme, Giovanni Berchet).

[9] Foscolo to Federico Confalonieri, Milan, 4 Mar. 1815, *EN*, *Epistolario*, v. 366–7. The following letters attest to the composition of the quarrel according to 19th-cent. custom in matters of honour.

> retract his claims ... Otherwise, I will be constrained to speak to you, my dear sir, in a form that either forces to you change your mind, or make me silent forever.

The duel was never carried out, but this letter indicates the increasing distance between Foscolo and the Milanese intellectuals, who would never forgive him for the gesture of taking control of a journal financed by the Austrian government. The emissaries of the new government, for their part, were interested in Foscolo because they assumed him to be disillusioned by the Napoleonic experience, but also because they saw in him the possibility of an example of political reconciliation.

Enlisting Foscolo to the imperial cause would have been a masterstroke of Austrian diplomacy. This was clear even in Vienna, as evinced by Baron von Hager's letter addressed to the Field-Marshal Count Bellegarde, commissioner of the government in Milan:

> Il fatto che il redattore proposto, come risulta dal secondo allegato, sia sospetto per le sue precedenti opinioni politiche, non dovrebbe impedire di prescegliersi ugualmente, dacché, avendo egli avuto di che lamentarsi del precedente regime, l'attuale Governo può fare buon uso di così eccellente ingegno com'è il Foscolo, ed è sempre meglio guadagnare al servizio dello Stato, pur con le debite cautele, questo scrittore stimato da' suoi concittadini procurandogli una conveniente occupazione, mostrandogli fiducia ed appoggiandolo, piuttosto che abbandonarlo, respingendolo da noi, in balia delle fazioni.[10]
>
> The fact that the editor proposed, as it results from the second attachment, is suspected for his former political positions should not impede us from choosing him anyway. Since he had much to complain about under the previous regime, the current Government would do well to use an excellent mind such as that of Foscolo. And it would be better to take into the service of the State, with all due prudence, this writer esteemed by his fellow citizens by finding him a convenient occupation, demonstrating our faith and support, rather than abandoning him, pushing him into the arms of the opposition.

Despite the pressure from the Austrians, Foscolo never directed the *Biblioteca Italiana*. When the new government imposed an oath of allegiance to Austria on all the officials of the Regno Italico, Foscolo chose to exile himself instead of taking it. He was meant to take the oath on 31 March 1815, but on the night before Foscolo chose to flee Italy by pretending to go on vacation. He was without means, without a passport, and without the support of his friends: the Countess of Albany, for instance, did not understand the gesture or the necessity of abandoning Milan and accused him of egotism. From Switzerland, Foscolo would later try to pacify her by describing, in his distinctive manner, his condition:

[10] Baron von Hagel to Count Bellegarde; Vienna, 3 Apr. 1815. Tr. from an Italian copy, as the German original has been lost. Cf. Giovanni Gambarin, 'Il Foscolo e la polizia austriaca: Con nuovi documenti', *Giornale Storico della Letteratura Italiana*, 140 (2° trimestre 1963), 428.

> ho pagato tutto quello che m'era stato dato molti anni innanzi meritatamente; ho rifiutato quel molto di più che mi sarebbe stato dato se avessi accettato di fare, o almeno *dire* a modo d'altri ... Ho perduto insieme le affettuose consuetudini della vita, preparate fin dalla gioventù, e che all'età mia non si possono rifare, e molto meno in terra straniera: ho perduto la Toscana ch'era per me ed ospizio, e teatro, e scuola, e giardino: ho perduto di rivedere quasi tutti gli anni, per le feste e il nuovo anno, la mia famigliuola, e la madre mia che già sudò tanto, ed ora piange tanto per me: ho fin anche perduto la compagnia de' miei libri, e non ho potuto condurre meco se non un Tacito, un Virgilio, e un Omero ...[11]
>
> I've paid for everything that had been given to me, deservedly, many years ago; I've refused the much more that would have been given to me if I had accepted to do, or at least to speak, as I was told ... I've lost the affectionate ties of life I cultivated since my youth, which, at my age, are so difficult to rebuild, especially on foreign soil; I've lost Tuscany, that was for me hospice, theatre, school, and garden; I've lost the ability to visit, almost every year, in the holiday season, my family and my mother, who has suffered so much, and now cries, for me; I've even lost the company of my books, and I couldn't take with me more than Tacitus, Vergil, and Homer ...

The restrictions and the difficulties of Foscolo's Swiss period are well-documented: without the economic support of his younger brother and of the Donna gentile, Foscolo would not have survived, particularly during the winter when his health deteriorated and he had to convalesce in a sanatorium several times. With the financial and social hardships of exile came political hardships; Foscolo's flight did not escape the attention of the Austrian regent, and with a slight delay a series of bureaucratic messages were dispatched with the intention of making his life as difficult as possible. Count Graf Strassoldo wrote from Milan:

> Als die reformirten Officiere der aufgelösten italienischen Armee von S. Exzellenz dem Herrn Feldmarschall zur Eidesablegung angewiesen wurden, so flüchtete er sich ... Er hat ausgezeichnete Talente, eine schöne Schreibart, eine lebhafte Einbildungskraft und vorzügliches Gedächtnis, aber wenig Verstand und wird unter jeder Regierung ein gefährlicher Mensch ohne Religion, ohne Moralität und ohne Karakter bleiben.[12]
>
> When the reformed officers of the disbanded Italian army were instructed by His Excellency the Field Marshal to take an oath [of fidelity to the Austrian government], Ugo Foscolo fled.... [Foscolo] has extraordinary talents, excellent writing style, a lively imagination and excellent memory, but little sense; he will remain under any government a dangerous man, without religion, without morality, and without character.

[11] Foscolo to the Countess d'Albany, Hottingen, 21 Dec. 1815. *EN*, *Epistolario*, vi. 157.

[12] Count Strassoldo to Baron von Schiller, vice-president of the Ausrian police. Milan, 3 May 1815. Cf. Gambarin, 'Il Foscolo e la polizia austriaca', 432–3.

Beginning with this report, the portrait of Foscolo as a dangerous subversive spread far, reaching Francis II Emperor of Austria, who mentioned him to the Minister of the Exterior, Fürst Metternich; Metternich, in turn, wrote to von Schraut, the plenipotentiary minister in Switzerland:

> Monsieur!
> D'après les derniers rapports d'Italie il se confirme, que les révolutionnaires qui s'enfuient de l'Italie trouvent en Suisse un asile. Parmi eux on nomme entr'eux [sic] un certain Hugo Foscolo, connu par ses mauvaises principes … La Suisse, en accédant à l'alliance générale, a dans ce moment un intérêt égal au nôtre à prendre des mesures rigoureuses contre le danger, qui résultrait nécessairement d'une condescendance déplacée envers des émissaires d'un gouvernement ennemi et révolutionnaire.[13]
>
> Monsieur!
> The recent dispatches from Italy confirm that the revolutionaries escaping from there are finding refuge in Switzerland. Among them is a certain Hugo Foscolo, known for his dangerous principles … Switzerland, being part of the general alliance, has at this moment an interest equal to ours in enforcing strict measures against the danger that would inevitably result from a misplaced act of condescention towards the emissaries of an enemy and revolutionary government.

The Austrian government, which had begun to magnify Foscolo's talents when they hoped to have him on their side, considered him a grave danger after the realization that it could not control him. Foscolo was frequently compelled to change his residence, to travel under a false name, and to be prudent in his relations with friends near and far.

Even in the unfavourable conditions of his exile, Foscolo did not abandon his vocation as an author, thanks to the friendship he developed with the Zurich bookseller Johann Heinrich Füssli. The third edition of the *Ortis* appeared under his auspices in 1816 (but bearing a false provenance of London, 1814), and it is in this edition that we find the famous letter, dated 17 March, against Napoleon. Again with Füssli, Foscolo under the pseudonym of Didimo Chrierico published the work known as *Hypercalypseos*, a satire in Latin prose directed against his political and literary adversaries—Napoleon, Eugenio Beauharnais, Vincenzo Monti, and others less famous, but mocked with equal vigour. Finally, the Zurich publisher arranged for the publication—at his own expense and in only three copies—of *Vestigi della storia del sonetto* (Vestiges of the History of the Sonnet), a florilegium of twenty-six sonnets extracted from the Italian literary tradition, with the final position reserved for Foscolo himself.

The cantons of Helvetia Felix did not offer him a safe sojourn nor that dimension of life or the possibility of earning a living that Sir Stewart Rose, a friend from his days in Florence, had led him to believe he could find in London. Accompanied by Andrea Calbo, a young man from Zante, who had already served him in the capacity of secretary

[13] Minister of the Exterior Metternich to the Plenipotentiary Minister of the Empire in Switzerland, von Schraut, Vienna, 31 May 1815.

and copyist in Florence, and who had now been hired by Quirina Mocenni Magiotti so that he could be a 'son and brother' to him, Foscolo set off once again.[14] He visited Basel and Frankfurt, and then set sail from Ostend to London, where he arrived on 12 September 1816.

Foscolo's first encounter with English society was a happy one, exactly as Sir Stewart had predicted. Considered the best living Italian poet, a celebrated patriot, well-versed in all the languages and literatures now appreciated in England, and famous for daring to criticize Napoleon in the period of his greatest power, Foscolo was immediately introduced into the best salons in London. He was a guest much in demand both in the city's best drawing-rooms and country estates.

> Qui per la prima volta mi sono avveduto ch'io non sono affatto ignoto a' mortali; e mi vedo accolto come un uomo che godesse già da un secolo di bella fama e illibata. Né starebbe se non in me di avanzarmi denaro alla prima; ma innanzi a questo s'ha da pensare alla dignità, tanto più che dove è più decoro, ivi corre spontaneo, col tempo, e più abbondante il danaro. Però mi sto sulle mie; e a questi signori che mi vanno offrendo aiuti e servigi rispondo signorilmente, con viso né superbo né modesto, e bado a studiare la carta per trovarmi sentiero alla fortuna, sicuro insieme e spedito e onoratissimo.[15]
>
> Here for the first time I realized how I am not completely unknown to mortals; and I am received as someone who has enjoyed untarnished fame for over a century. I would not have any difficulty in raising money quickly: but before that I need to take care of my dignity, even more so because where there is decorum, wealth flows more abundantly. Hence, I am reserved; to the gentlemen offering me help and services I respond in a gentlemanlike way, with a face neither proud nor modest, and I study the map to find my way to fortune, secure, and at the same time, expeditious and honorable.

But, other than creating a buzz in the elegant environs of the capital, the presence of Foscolo in London put the Austrian intelligence in turmoil. The governor of Milan,

[14] Quirina Mocenni Magiotti to Andrea Calbo, Florence, 14 May 1816: 'Quello di cui la prego con calore è il tenermi settimanalmente informata con lettere e della salute, bisogni, studi; e ogni altro che ad esso appartenga. Siategli figlio e fratello, sollevatelo, aiutatelo, sostenetelo nei differenti casi della vita, e non aspettate mai nella necessità a farmi sapere che li sarebbe necessario qualche denaro. Egli non importa che sappia che voi me ne informate, ed io farò in maniera che senza saperlo Egli si trovi non vuota affatto la borsa. Vi auguro un prospero e sollecito viaggio; salutate Ugo—e parlate qualche volta insieme di me.—Io sarò felice nella vostra memoria.' (I dearly pray that you keep me informed weekly, through the mail, about his health, his needs, his studies, and anything that concerns him. Be a son and a brother for him, help and sustain him in the adversities of life, and do not hesitate to let me know if he is in economic need. It is not necessary that he knows you are in contact with me, and I will make sure, without his knowledge, that he does not find the wallet empty. I wish for you a prosperous and solicitous journey. Bring my regards to Ugo, and mention me to him from time to time. I will be happy in your memory.) *EN, Epistolario*, vi, appendice III, 651.

[15] Foscolo to Quirina Mocenni Magiotti, London, 19 Sept. 1816, *EN, Epistolario*, vii. 11–12.

Count Saurau sent a note to Vienna concerning the notorious Foscolo, warning about his bad temper and his ready pen:

> Hochgeboren Graf!
> Der berüchtigte Ugo Foscolo, der Eurer Exzellenz aus vielen Vorachten ohnediess hinlänglich bekannt seyn wird, hat sich meinen erhaltenen Nachrichten zu Folge nach England begeben, wo er—wie die hiesige Oppositionspartei wenigstens auszuposaunen bemüht ist—mit vieler Auszeichnung empfangen wurde. Da Foscolo ein wahres Genie, in Gespräche hinreissend und mit der Alten litteratur sehr vertraut ist, so dürfte es ihm allerdings vielleicht gelingen, durch die englische Oppositionspartei—deren Mächtigwerden die Lordmayor's Wahl in London neuerdings bestättiget—einige Bedeutenheit zu erlangen. Den Englischen Journalen wird es in jedem Falle gewiss nicht an beleidigenden Artikeln gegen unsere Regierung in Italien fehlen, die aus seiner Feder fliessen dürfen, da es uns bis jetzt nur durch die sorgsamste Aufsicht gelungen ist, den Druck mehrerer Brochuren in diesem Sinne, deren Verfasser er war, in den Schweiz zu verhindern.[16]
>
> Noble Count!
> The notorious Ugo Foscolo, whom your Excellency will know from many episodes has, according to the information I have received, betaken himself to England where, as the local opposition party is trumpeting about everywhere, he was received with many honors. Since Foscolo is a veritable genius, captivating in conversation and very familiar with classical literature, it may well be possible for him to gain a certain importance through the English opposition party, whose increased power was recently confirmed by the Major's election in London. Insulting articles against our government in Italy, which will likely flow from his pen, will certainly not be lacking in the English newspapers, since we have up to now only through the most careful vigilance been able to prevent the printing in Switzerland of several brochures along this line, of which he was the author.

Climbing through the hierarchies of governmental officials, the report finally arrived on the desk of Metternich, who expressed his desire to alert the Embassy of the Empire in London:

> Il quadro che V.E. mi ha fatto dello scrittore Ugo Foscolo, col suo pregiato foglio del 1° corrente, non lascia in me sussistere alcun dubbio che egli impiegherà a Londra la sua penna contro di noi. La libertà di stampa inglese gli garantirà all'uopo il campo d'azione illimitato che gli aveva precluso in Italia e in Svizzera la saggia sorveglianza del signor conte di Saurau. L'I.R. Ambasciatore non ha a sua disposizione alcun mezzo per impedire l'inserzione sui fogli pubblici in Inghilterra di articoli sovversivi, e persino per la semplice sorveglianza di una persona si va incontro in quel paese a insuperabili difficoltà, che hanno il loro fondamento nella Costituzione.

[16] The Governor of Milan, Count Saurau, to the vice-president in charge of police and censorship in Vienna, Count Josef Graf Sedlnitzky, Milan, 22 Oct. 1816. Cf. Gambarin, 'Il Foscolo e la polizia austriaca', 440.

> Ciononostante, non mancherò di comunicare queste notizie al principe Esterhazy, e d'incaricarlo di far sorvegliare Ugo Foscolo con la maggior possibile cura.[17]

> The description of the writer Ugo Foscolo provided by Your excellency in the esteemed message dated November 1st makes me certain that he will use his pen against us from London. The English freedom of the press will ensure him the unlimited scope that the careful surveillance of Count Saurau precluded him in Italy and Switzerland. The Imperial Ambassador [to England] does not have any means to prevent the publication of subversive articles in the English newspapers, and even to simply monitor a person in that country there are insuperable difficulties, which have their basis in the constitution. Nevertheless, I will forward your dispatch to Prince Esterhazy, and request him to organize Ugo Foscolo's surveillance with the utmost possible care.

Leaving aside the involuntary praise of both the English political system and its freedom of the press we find in these letters, it is clear that Metternich was ultimately uselessly preoccupied: Foscolo's immediate worries were economic, not political. Already while in Switzerland Foscolo had decided not to publish the inflamatory *Discorsi sulla servitù d'Italia* (Discourses on the Servitude of Italy), nor did he ever actually finish the work. The highly praised Count Saurau did not have to exert much effort in order to contain Foscolo's pen in Switzerland, nor did he make the effort to read what Foscolo had effectively published. Never mind the *Hypercalypseos*, which, true to its title, must have appeared to be a rather obscure work to his contemporaries; had Count Saurau at least read the Swiss edition of the *Ortis* containing the oration against Napoleon (1816), he would have been aware that it was the French, not the Austrians, who should have been preoccupied by Foscolo's writings. Foscolo himself even refused to enter into contact with other exiles and expatriate politicians. A few years later, he would explain to Quirina Mocenni Magiotti:

> Fors'io m'inganno, ma questi Italiani che rifuggirono in Inghilterra, ed ora vanno e vengono dalla Spagna, mi hanno tutti chi più, chi meno, del pazzo. Sono fanatici senza ardire, e metafisici senza scienza, e deliranti per ottenere cose impossibili.... E qui da prima mi venivano intorno perch'io scrivessi contro imperatori ed eserciti, e contro parlamenti e senati, perché gli uni congiurano ad opprimere, e gli altri non si sbracciano a liberare l'Italia ... Ora, da che ho sempre risposto, che uno può, anzi deve, nella sua terra scrivere e predicare, se sa, e fare, se può, quanto gli pare utile a' suoi concittadini; ma che in paese d'altri s'ha da tacere come in casa d'altri, e portarsi da ospiti discreti e pacifici; da che io ho dato e ripetuto questa risposta, m'hanno bandito la croce addosso qui, come quei della setta contraria facevano contro di me in Italia.—Pur ci guadagno, dacché non mi vengono tanto dattorno, e mi lasciano riavere quello ch'io prima della loro venuta aveva ottenuto, di dimenticarmi ed essere dimenticato dagli Italiani.
>
> Io né scrissi mai né pensai di scrivere né per né contro la rivoluzione;—ch'io la lodo per l'intento, ma ne rido per l'evento in che riuscì, e per l'imbecillità di quelli che vi

[17] Fürst Metternich to Count Sedlnitzky, Vienna, 11 Nov. 1816. Cf. Gambarin, 'Il Foscolo e la polizia austriaca', 441.

> si ingerirono;—ch'io non ho cangiato mai, dacché ho potuto pensare, uno solo de' miei principj politici, né, spero, li cangerò mai;—però mi sono volontariamente eletto l'esilio, e le fatiche e la vecchiaja e la sepoltura in terra straniera: ma che contentandomi oggimai di serbare le mie dottrine per me, mi crederei forsennatissimo se ambissi di applicarle all'Italia ch'io credo cadavere, e dove le mie opinioni, se fossero instillate in cervelli vulcanici, riescirebbero perniciose ad essi ed a molte famiglie, senza la minima pubblica utilità. E d'altra parte mi vergogno a crescere il numero dei tanti Italiani da Dante in qua, che non han saputo se non che gridare, gridare, gridare.[18]

> I may be wrong, but all those Italians who took exile in England, and now come and go from Spain, seem to me more or less insane. They are fanatics without courage, metaphysicians without knowledge, and delirious to achieve impossible things.... Initially they courted me to make me write against emperors and armies, and against parlaments and senates, because the former come together to oppress Italy, and the latter do not hurry to set it free.... I've always answered that one can, or rather must, write and exhort, and be helpful to his compatriots in his own land: but in a foreign land one should behave like a guest, and discreetly and pacifically keep quiet. Since I've given and repeated this answer, they started treating me like the [pro-Austrian government] treated me in Italy.—Yet I still have an advantage from the situation, since they now do not crowd so much around me, and return to me what I had before they came, to forget the Italians and be forgotten by them.
>
> I never wrote, nor thought of writing, for or against the revolution [of 1821]; I praise it for the intentions, but laugh at the consequences, and at the stupidity of those who took part in it.—I've never renounced a single one of my political principles, nor I hope to ever change them—and I've willingly chosen the exile, and the infirmities of old age and the burial in a foreign land; today I am content with keeping my ideals for myself, and I would be an imbecile if I expected to apply them to the cadaver of Italy, where my opinions, instilled in incendiary spirits, would result in danger for them and their families, without the minimum public advantage. And on the other hand I would be ashamed in joining the many Italians who, since Dante, were only able to yell, yell, yell.

Foscolo, even if intimately he may not have abandoned his ideals of a free and Republican Italian nation, refused to participate actively in the political life of Italy after his arrival in London. In the essay 'On Parga', published in the *Edinburgh Review* in October 1819, he hoped for a Greek war for independence against the Ottoman Empire, but categorically refused to intervene in the debate about Italy's political destiny.

More than politics, Foscolo felt constrained to focus on making ends meet. Even if the letters written to Italian friends and family—particularly in this early period—did not let on about the writer's actual condition, they reflect the degree to which monetary concerns, in the absence of a stable income, were an unceasing preoccupation. Considering it unbecoming for a gentleman to abase himself by giving language lessons, and being used to the life of high society which continued to think of him as a favourite, Foscolo was busy living beyond his means.

[18] Foscolo to Quirina Mocenni Magiotti, South Bank, London, 6 Aug. 1823, *EN, Epistolario*, ix. 261–2. See also *Lettera apologetica: EN* xiii/2. 130.

He believed he could obtain independence and even economic prosperity as a critic and scholar of Italian literature through the publication of books and collaborations in literary journals. This idea was not entirely his own: it had been enthusiastically suggested to him by Sir Stewart, Lord Holland, Lord Wilbraham, Lady Dacre, and other friends, none of whom actually needed to work to earn income. However, the enterprise proved extremely difficult from the very beginning as he was not comfortable writing in English, and depended heavily on copyists and translators. Andrea Calbo's abandonment of Foscolo at the end of October 1816 compounded his difficulties.

Foscolo's personality, difficult to begin with, was tested by his struggles. With age, his health deteriorated, and in May 1817, his brother Giulio sent news of the death of their mother, which pushed him into a severe depression. He managed these intense months through loans, the generosity and companionship of his friends, reflection on his accomplishments, and an enthusiasm for that which he still had left to accomplish. During this time he conceived the *Lettere dall'Inghilterra*, a new epistolary novel, destined to remain incomplete; he wrote his first article on *Dante*, which was published in the *Edinburgh Review* and earned him glowing reviews.

Foscolo's relationship with the family of another political figure, Lord Russell, came to the forefront in December 1818. The lessons on the poetry of Petrarch that Foscolo gave to Lord Russell's two oldest daughters became the basis for the *Essays on Petrarch*. In the same period, Foscolo continued his translation of the *Iliad* (the third book, which he sent to his friend Gino Capponi, was published in the *Antologia Vieusseux* in Florence), and worked on the *Grazie* (of which two fragments, *Il velo delle Grazie* and *Di un antico inno alle Grazie* were published in a volume composed privately for the Duke of Bedford in 1822).[19]

The correspondence with his Italian friends dwindled, and his connections with English high society had ceased completely. It was only to his cousin Dionisio, who had remained in Zante, that Foscolo recounted his condition, hoping to be helped to find an occupation in the island of his youth.

> Se verso la fine di luglio passato, io non avessi finalmente pigliato il partito di vendere anche i migliori e più voluminosi de' libri miei, voi forse un giorno alzandomi un busto d'onore, avreste dovuto scrivermi anche nell'inscrizione, che mi moriva d'inedia.... Tanto a me, mio caro Dionisio, è giovata la *fama somma* ch'io godo in letteratura![20]
>
> If, at the end of July, I hadn't decided to sell even the best and most voluminous of my books, you perhaps one day, erecting a bust in my honour, would have had to write in the plaque that I had died of starvation.... How useful was to me, my dear Dionisius, the supreme fame that literature warranted me!

[19] Ugo Foscolo, *Outline Engravings and Descriptions of the Woburn Abbey Marbles* (Privately publ., 1822). Cf. *EN* i. 1077–94.

[20] Foscolo to Dionisio Bulzo, London, 25 Sept. 1826. In Orlandini and Mayer, *Opere edite e postume di Ugo Foscolo, Epistolario*, iii. 220–1.

And yet, Foscolo continued to write articles and to publish in London reviews, ranging across such a variety of subjects (*Ancient Encaustic Painting of Cleopatra; History of the Democratical Constitution of Venice;* an essay on Tasso's *Gerusalemme liberata*, another on the poetry of Michelangelo, one on 'erudite women', and on the *Mémoires* of Casanova) that we might doubt whether all these works, which appeared anonymously following the custom of the era, were entirely penned by Foscolo.[21] Even if not all the articles were to be attributed to Foscolo, it is clear that for a decade he had played the role of ambassador of Italian culture in London, in a way not dissimilar to that which Heinrich Heine would play in Paris.

He died on 10 September 1827, surrounded by his daughter and a few friends. From that moment, pro-independence Italian writers, guided by Giuseppe Mazzini, who took it upon himself to republish the texts of Foscolo, whose writings remained on the index of the Austrian censors in Italy, transformed his persona into a monument for the Italy to come, making him into the poet who inspired a generation of combatants. The Italian patriots ended up building a (literary) myth around Foscolo's figure: in the eyes of the following generation, Foscolo remained the author of the *Ortis* and the *Sepolcri*. The revolutionaries adored Foscolo, even when he himself, disillusioned in his own ideals by political defeats, weakened by illness and facing a difficult life, considered them a nuisance at best, and madmen, at worst. For these madmen, Foscolo was now an untarnishable myth, a warrior poet, the first incarnation in the contemporary era of the ideal union of thought and action: he had fought for the Venetian Republic against the Austrians, in the army of the French Republic for the ideals of liberty and equality, had challenged Napoleon for becoming a tyrant.

Twelve years after Foscolo's death, Mazzini retrieved and published the short text of the *Lettera apologetica* (1839), a political and literary testament in which Foscolo mirrored his own exile with Dante's, creating a genealogy that the idealistic revolutionaries rushed to imitate. Carlo Cattaneo with a much-celebrated epigraphic phrase summarized the importance of Foscolo's expatriation for the entire Risorgimento: 'Ugo Foscolo gifted the new Italy with a new institution: *exile!*'[22]

Eventually De Sanctis, the most successful critic of the epoch, would canonize Foscolo as the inspiration for national unity:

> Ugo Foscolo non rappresenta per noi alcun sistema politico, alcun ordine regolato d'idee. Egli è stato un'espressione poetica dei nostri più intimi sentimenti, il cuore italiano nella sua ultima potenza. Noi ci sentiamo in lui idealizzati ... Noi volevamo una patria e la patria fu per noi tutto.[23]

[21] See the prefaces by Cesare Foligno, *EN* x, p. xvi; and by Uberto Limentani, *EN* xii, p. xv.

[22] Cf. 'U. Foscolo e l'Italia', in Carlo Cattaneo, *Scritti letterari*, ed. Piero Treves (Florence: Le Monnier, 1981), i. 536.

[23] Francesco de Sanctis, *Giudizio del Gervinus sopra Alfieri e Foscolo*, in *Saggi critici*, ed. Luigi Russo (Bari: Laterza 1952), i. 192 and 197.

> Ugo Foscolo does not represent for us a political system, nor a systematic belief. He was a poetic expression of our most intimate sentiments, an Italian heart elevated to the highest power. We are idealized in him ... We wanted a homeland, and the homeland represented everything for us.

It was the beginning of the myth of Foscolo as a Father of the Nation, which culminated in the transferring of his remains to a sepulchre in the church of Santa Croce, next to the other great Italians he had exalted in his verses. But Foscolo, in the last part of his life, did not want to be associated with the patriots who adored him; and he would hardly have considered himself a Romantic writer. When the debate on Italian Romanticism exploded following Mme de Stäel's article published in the *Biblioteca Italiana* in 1816, he had already left Italy.

Further Reading

Allegri, Mario, '"Di Grecia in Italia:" Il Foscolo veneziano', in Alberto Asor Rosa (ed.), *Letteratura italiana*, vii. *L'età moderna* (Turin: Einaudi, 1989), 359–65.

Audeh, Aida, and Havely, Nick (eds), *Dante in the Long Nineteenth Century* (Oxford: Oxford University Press, 2009).

Binni, Walter, *Foscolo e la critica: Storia e antologia della critica* (Florence: La Nuova Italia, 1957).

Cambon, Glauco, *Ugo Foscolo, Poet of Exile* (Princeton: Princeton University Press, 1980).

Croce, Benedetto, *European Literature in the Nineteenth Century* (London: Chapman & Hall, 1924).

Foscolo, Ugo, *Edizione Nazionale delle opere di Ugo Foscolo*, 21 vols (Florence: F. Le Monnier, 1933).

Foscolo, Ugo, *Last Letters of Jacopo Ortis, and, Of Tombs*, tr. J. G. Nichols (London: Hesperus, 2002).

Isabella, Maurizio, *Risorgimento in Exile: Italian Émigrés and the Liberal International in the Post-Napoleonic Era* (Oxford: Oxford University Press, 2009).

Lindon, John, *Studi sul Foscolo 'inglese'* (Pisa: Giardini, 1987).

Luzzi, Joseph, *Romantic Europe and the Ghost of Italy* (New Haven: Yale University Press, 2008).

Nicoletti, Giuseppe. *Foscolo* (Rome: Salerno, 2006).

O'Neill, Tom, *Of Virgin Muses and of Love: A Study of Foscolo's Dei Sepolcri* (Dublin: Irish Academic Press, 1981).

Parmegiani, Sandra, *Ugo Foscolo and English Culture* (Oxford: Legenda, 2011).

Terzoli, Maria Antonietta, *Foscolo* (Rome: GLF editori Laterza, 2000).

Turchi, Roberta, *Ugo Foscolo e la patria infelice* (Padua: Liviana, 1981).

CHAPTER 24

MANZONI'S PERSISTENCE

JONATHAN WHITE

If as Alessandro Manzoni asserted in his *Letter to Monsieur Chauvet* the finest art ('la perfection de l'art') is 'like wealth that belongs to all, like a heritage available to every intelligence capable of appreciating it',[1] then on what terms are we in the twenty-first century best able to share in and appreciate what Manzoni himself bequeathed? Manzoni's effect upon Italian culture in his own lifetime and on into the early twentieth century has been well studied in the past.[2] He was visited by authors, artists, and statesmen, from Italy and other nations: Scott, Balzac, Longfellow, Gladstone, the Brazilian Emperor Pedro II, and Verdi are just a few of the prominent figures who paid their respects to Manzoni, sometimes on preplanned pilgrimages to his house in Via Morone, Milan. Balzac seems to have talked too much about himself to be able to measure his host's sensibility: Verdi may have been too overcome by Manzoni's greatness.[3] The young English

[1] '... comme la richesse de tous, comme un patrimoine acquis à toute intelligence capable de l'apprécier'. *Lettre à M. C*** sur l'unité de temps et de lieu dans la tragédie*, in *Opere varie di Alessandro Manzoni*, ed. M. Barbi and F. Ghisalberti (Milan: Casa del Manzoni, 1943), 370. The *Lettre* was composed in French in 1820 and publ. in 1823.

[2] For 19th-cent. approaches to Manzoni see in particular Alfredo Cottignoli, *Manzoni fra i critici dell'ottocento* (Bologna: Masimiliano Boni Editore, 1978). A helpful anthology of both 19th- and 20th-cent. critical responses is Lanfranco Caretti (ed.), *Manzoni e la critica* (Bari: Editori Laterza, 1971). David Forgacs in his Introduction to Manzoni's *Betrothed* writes succinctly about landmarks in reception of Manzoni. See also Luciano Parisi, *Come abbiamo letto Manzoni: Interpreti novecenteschi* (Alessandria: Edizioni dell'Orso, 2008).

[3] The fullest inspection of the surviving evidence of Balzac's meeting with Manzoni is offered by Raffaele de Cesare, 'Balzac e Manzoni: Cronaca di un incontro' (1975), included in his *Balzac e Manzoni, e altri studi su Balzac e l'Italia* (Milan: Vita e Pensiero, 1993), 189–290. Verdi and Manzoni met only once, in 1868, introduced to one another by Clarina Maffei, a friend of both, at Manzoni's home in Milan where she had previously taken Verdi's wife Giuseppina. Awestruck, Verdi wrote to Maffei afterwards: 'What can I say to you about Manzoni? How explain to you the sweet, new, indefinable sensation the presence of that Saint, as you call him, produced in me? I would have knelt before him if one could adore human beings. They say that we must not do that, and so be it, although at altars we worship many saints who have neither Manzoni's gifts nor his virtues ... When you see him, kiss his hand for me and convey to him all my veneration' (quoted in Franco Abbiati, *Giuseppe Verdi* (Milan: Ricordi & C., 1959), iii. 215). Internationally, Verdi was more famous than Manzoni at the time of writing those words.

painter Mary Clarke, on the other hand, gave an account of a stay in the Manzoni household in 1834 that might stand as representative of the author's effect upon others. Writing to Claude Fauriel, her sometime lover and Manzoni's close friend, Clarke tells of the cordial and responsive sensibility of the author: 'He has the same candour as ever, takes an interest in everything, seemed very delighted with all that I related about Paris, judges and knows people there as if he had just passed six months in their midst, does me so much good and so makes me believe anew in disinterested intelligence that I wish to return to Milan in a year or two to re-temper my soul and faith ...'[4]

The older tradition of generous tribute[5] was followed by accounts of Manzoni's writing that were well 'this side idolatry', in the criticism of Benedetto Croce as well as in a brief but suggestive comment by Antonio Gramsci.[6] While all such earlier tributes and criticism still provide us with guidelines for enquiry, we need to take further soundings, tracking forward in cultural consciousness from the Second World War into our own times. To mention just one interim point: the Italian novelist, art critic, and feminist Anna Banti (1895–1985) attested in 1956 that upon serious young writers of her generation Manzoni's novel *I promessi sposi*—in particular what she specifies as its 'historical memory' (*memoria storica*)—had a transformative impact. Banti confessed that her own appreciation of what she calls this 'foundational novel in our literature'[7] had progressively deepened during her formative years:

> When doubts and discontent overcame me, I had recourse to *I promessi sposi*, matchless restorative of the mind and of the pen. A random re-reading of three or four pages relaxed and reassured me: not in the sense of leading me into any kind of aping mimicry, but by means of infinite hints and possibilities revealed and offered, of style as well as of human content, as if Manzoni on every page endowed, so to speak, appropriate means for elucidating each human situation.[8]

Banti formulated this testimony more than half a century ago. What is Manzoni's present and potential future standing, not merely in Italian culture, but as a 'world' author?

[4] Quoted in Natalia Ginsburg, *La famiglia Manzoni* (Turin: Einaudi editore, 1983), 144–5.

[5] Not all 19th-cent. reaction to Manzoni was positive. In particular some critics took strong exception to his counsel of patient submission to providence in *I promessi sposi*. As early as 1832 Pietro Giannone was forthright: 'In the circumstances and in times as they are, the virtue of resignation is not the one necessary for our poor country.' In 1877 Luigi Settembrini was unsparing in his attack on what he interpreted as Manzoni's counsel of 'servile submission' to divine providence. See Mark Davie, 'Manzoni After 1848: An "Irresolute Utopian"?', *Modern Language Review*, 87 (1992), 847. There is a fuller discussion of Manzoni's handling of providence later in the present chapter.

[6] Croce's various pieces on Manzoni were gathered in *Alessandro Manzoni: Saggi e discussioni* (Bari: Editori Laterza, 1st edn 1930; 5th edn 1957). Gramsci's sharply critical remark is dealt with later.

[7] 'il romanzo principe della nostra letteratura': Anna Banti, *Opinioni* (Milan: Il Saggiatore, 1961), 54.

[8] 'Quando i dubbi e la scontentezza prevalevano, ricorrevo ai *Promessi*, insostituibile corroborante dello spirito e della penna. Una rilettura ad apertura di libro, per tre o quattro pagine, mi distendeva, mi rassicurava: e non nel senso di condurmi ad una specie di *singerie*, ma di infinite indicazioni e possibilità rivelate e offerte, così di stile, come di umano contento, quasi il Manzoni, in ogni sua pagina, accordasse, per così dire, gli strumenti buoni a commentare ogni umana vicenda.' Banti, *Opinioni*, 57–8.

This chapter, while not answering this important question head-on, will argue that in his novel and certain other works Manzoni has left much that is still of compelling relevance to troubled times such as our own.

Manzoni's dedication to history was a paramount preoccupation. His passion to understand long and complex lineages of the present anticipates much similar investigation of the *longue durée* of cultural change and development that more recent historians have pursued. Manzoni's focus was upon critical times of change in Italy or on the wider stage; not exactly '"hot years" in the calendars of European historiography', as James Chandler has named points in time such as 1642, 1789, or 1848,[9] but rather entire periods (lasting a generation or more) of development in society, politics, dominant discourse, or worldview. In parallel with his second tragedy, *Adelchi* (1822), treating of Charlemagne's defeat of the last Lombard kings, Manzoni produced a lengthy study of the centuries of Longobardian rule in Italy (568 to 774),[10] a period that in revealing ways anticipated later instances of foreign domination. As Stelio Cro has shown, Manzoni did not believe the Lombards had become Italians by reason of their two centuries of occupation, despite opinions to the contrary in histories from Machiavelli onwards.[11] Manzoni's historical novel *I promessi sposi* (first edition 1827, revised and definitive version 1840), set during seventeenth-century Spanish rule, focuses in particular upon Manzoni's own region of Milan at a crucial phase in the Thirty Years War. In 1842 he published an appendage to the novel titled *La Colonna Infame* (*The Column of Infamy*), a work of genuine historiography that investigates the victimization and torture of innocent commoners, falsely accused of spreading plague by smearing infected unguents upon walls in the Milan of the novel's setting. Its investigative narrative (*racconto inchiesta*) has possibly had more influence upon writers of the late twentieth and early twenty-first century than any other work by Manzoni. Leonardo Sciascia in particular paid tribute to 'this small great book'.[12] Sciascia's own writings and those of others adopt narrative strategies of investigation pioneered by Manzoni in *The Column of Infamy*. The work's relevance to instances of torture and victimization of the weak by the powerful in the twentieth century was pointed out in a landmark study by A. P. d'Entrèves.[13] I shall have more to say about why it retains equivalently searing messages for our own age.

Manzoni's fascination with history extended to a pursuit throughout his adult life of studies in the Italian language. He was preoccupied with problems of how best to achieve a 'standardized' language, based around phrasal and word usages in Italy's earlier literary masterpieces. As was widely acknowledged, the greatest of such literature

[9] James Chandler, *England in 1819: The Politics of Literary Culture and the Case of Romantic Historicism* (Chicago and London: University of Chicago Press, 1998), 77.

[10] *Discorso sopra alcuni punti della storia longobardica in Italia* (1822).

[11] Stelio Cro, 'Manzoni and the Lombard Question', in Sante Matteo and Larry H. Peer (eds), *The Reasonable Romantic* (New York: Peter Lang, 1986), 168.

[12] 'questo piccolo grande libro ... tra i meno conosciuti della letteratura italiana': Leonardo Sciascia, *Cruciverba* (Turin: Einaudi editore, 1983), 101.

[13] Introduction to Alessandro Manzoni, *The Column of Infamy*, prefaced by Cesare Beccaria's *Of Crimes and Punishments*, tr. Kenelm Foster and Jane Grigson (London: Oxford University Press, 1964).

had mainly emanated from the Tuscan region. Manzoni was fastidious about language, most notably in his extensive revisions of *I promessi sposi* for the revised 1840 edition. He even wrote to his mother explaining his having gone in 1827 to live for a period near Florence as a desire 'to wash his clothes in the Arno'; that is, to convert his novel into the Florentine idiom, which was generally perceived to be a more literary language. The phrase (*sciacquare i panni in Arno*) has became a well-remembered term not just for Manzoni's changes to his novel, but for an evolution towards standardization in language practices that he and others hoped for in Italy's coming together as a nation. For someone of a retiring temperament, Manzoni's concern about matters of language was highly public: one of his last publications was a report for the new Italian government, *Dell'unità della lingua e dei mezzi per diffonderla* (On Unity in Language Usage and the Means of Diffusing it, 1868). Late in life Manzoni also attempted *Saggio comparativo su la rivoluzione francese del 1789 e la rivoluzione italiana del 1859* (A Comparative Study of the French Revolution of 1789 and the Italian Revolution of 1859). This text remained uncompleted at his death in 1873, but is testimony to his undiminished immersion in historiography; in this instance, a desire to fathom what could be learned from the differing revolutionary pasts of France and of Italy.[14]

Manzoni first had cause in 1819 to challenge a significant historical reading produced by someone else. One of the important historical narratives of the European Romantic age was by the Swiss Protestant of Tuscan lineage, J.-C.-L Simonde de Sismondi. The first two volumes (of an eventual sixteen) of Sismondi's *History of the Italian Republics during the Middle Ages* had appeared in 1807, the last in 1818.[15] For many educated Italians of the early nineteenth century, so comprehensive an account of the earlier period of Italian greatness, followed by centuries of decline into domination by foreign powers, made for challenging reading. Francesco De Sanctis, the leading Romantic critic of his day in Italy, hailed the importance of Sismondi's *History* thus: 'more than novels or any other book it hastened the advent of our Risorgimento. It should still for a number of reasons stand as our legal code and gospel.'[16] Above all, Sismondi laid out a clear thesis regarding the cultural origins of Italy's present weaknesses. His points have resonance in our own times, given the long-running economic, social, and political crisis of Italy since well before its entry into the Eurozone of the European Union. Sismondi furnishes a comparative historical framework for thinking about the Italian people and nation; comparative in the sense that he is placing them not alongside other nations so much as in

[14] Mark Davie has pointed out that the Introduction to Manzoni's comparative study of France and Italy 'seeks to show how the Italian "revolution" was legitimate precisely because it had avoided the usurpation of power which had taken place in France'. Davie, 'Manzoni After 1848', 851. See the rest of Davie's article for the best single study of Manzoni's 'conflict of loyalties between his Catholicism and his patriotism' (856), both before and after 1859.

[15] J.-C.-L. Simonde de Sismondi, *Histoire des républiques italiennes du moyen age* (Paris: H. Nicolle and Treuttel & Würtz, 1809–18).

[16] 'vi raccomando quella storia che, più dei romanzi e d'altri libri, affrettò il nostro risorgimento. Essa dev'essere ancora per alcuni rispetti il nostro codice ed il nostro vangelo.' Francesco De Sanctis, *Manzoni: Studi e lezioni*, ed. Giovanni Gentile (Bari: Laterza & figli, 1922), 214.

relation to their own medieval and Renaissance forebears. Sismondi's text thereby operates in its final chapter as a kind of 'mirror' for Italian peoples, not unlike the function A. W. Schlegel had called upon Romantic nationalist drama to perform for Germans ('In this mirror let the poet enable us to see, while we take deep shame to ourselves for what we are, what the Germans were in former times, and what they must be again'[17]). When Sismondi completed his long text, his ascription in the final chapter of so many of Italy's contemporary faults to the dominating influence of the Catholic Church profoundly upset the devout Manzoni, and led to the latter's riposte of the following year (1819), titled *Observations on Catholic Morality*.[18]

Reviewing Sismondi's major arguments helps us to understand why Manzoni resolved to refute them. Sismondi's analyses of Italian decline were presented in the last chapter of his *History* (chapter 127), itself titled in the form of a question: 'What are the causes that have changed the character of Italians, since the enslavement of their republics?'[19] Italy's religion, education system, legislation, and morality of honour are all closely inspected, and the grounds of her decline found in them. Sismondi was unsparing in his account of how, after the Council of Trent (1545–63), rather than progress there had been regression on the part of the Catholic Church in Italy, with disastrous and ongoing consequences. Beginning under the pontificate of Paul IV (1555–9) a succession of popes, according to Sismondi, took the side of rulers of the various states in Italy, rather than of the people. Instead of concentrating on a true morality of individual conscience, as Protestantism in parts of Northern Europe had done, the Catholic Church had substituted the study of casuists. It went on trafficking in indulgences, in spite of attempts by the Council of Trent to put an end to such practices. Regularity of church devotion rather than genuine virtue was prioritized. In sum, Catholicism as practised taught Italians to ruse with their consciences rather than obey them. Educational practices were scarcely better by Sismondi's reckoning, intimately linked as they were with the bad influences of the church as an institution. He saw education as having been wrested during the sixteenth century from the hands of independent philosopher figures and handed over to the clergy. The great works of the ancients were still taught, but as a collection of facts and authorities rather than as a stimulus to original thought. Rote learning and ritualized prayer made for spiritual inertia, and became the breeding ground of something still worse, namely wide-scale hypocrisy. Sismondi's accounts of the Italian morality of

[17] *A Course of Lectures on Dramatic Art and Literature*, ed. John Black (London: Henry G. Bohn, 1846), 528–9. On works enabling contrast with a past historical standard, and conceptualization of a possible future, see Nathaniel Leach, 'The Shame of a Nation: Performing History in Schiller, Manzoni and Byron', *European Romantic Review*, 22 (2011), 155–72.

[18] An English tr., *A Vindication of Catholic morality: or a Refutation of the Charges Brought Against it by Sismondi in his 'History of the Italian republics during the Middle Ages'* (London: Keating & Brown, 1836), was made from a French tr. of 1834. Manzoni's work was titled in Italian *Osservazioni sulla morale cattolica* (1819).

[19] 'Quelles sont les causes qui ont changé le charactère des Italiens, depuis l'asservissement de leur républiques?', *Histoire*, xvi. 407–60.

honour and legislative practices are better dealt with later in relation to other works by Manzoni, principally *I promessi sposi* and *The Column of Infamy*.

Manzoni recognized the greatness of Sismondi's history, with the exception of what it had to say about the church:

> Without concurring in all the opinions of our author, we cannot but perceive how many questions of politics, jurisprudence, and literature he has considered frequently in a new and interesting and, what is more important, in a noble and generous point of view: how many truths he has re-established, which had fallen into a species of oblivion .... I state, however, distinctly, that I differ from the author in every case in which he dissents from the faith, and from catholic morality, for I hold these to be an infallible rule.[20]

Manzoni had reconverted to Catholicism in 1810, along with his mother Giulia and wife Enrichetta, whom he had originally wed in a Protestant ceremony on account of her faith of upbringing. By the time he was reading Sismondi's final chapter of 1818, Catholic morality was for Manzoni a truth not open to doubt or negotiation. Giovanni Carsaniga has asserted, unjustly, that all Manzoni's historical treatises and essays 'are notable mainly as evidence of his prejudiced ideas'.[21] The generosity of Manzoni's opening tribute to Sismondi shows that this is not true. Manzoni's dedicated pursuit of historical truth through thickets of error and contradiction is something that not only a Leonardo Sciascia but all readers can learn from, both in terms of practice and commitment. However, Carsaniga goes on rightly and acutely to define the one realm (an important one) in which Manzoni failed initially to distinguish adequately between the ideal and the real:

> For Manzoni 'it is unnecessary to use any evidence to justify the Church: its doctrines are enough': in other words, the test of Catholic doctrine is theological and a priori, not historical. To support this proposition, however, he had to keep stressing the distinction between Religion, as a perfectly moral system, and the Church, as an institution admittedly including fallible men; which was, of course, implicitly conceding Sismondi's point.[22]

[20] *A Vindication of Catholic Morality* (1836), 5–6. Manzoni's original reads: 'Senza ricevere tutte le opinioni dell'illustre autore, e rifiutando espressamente quelle che dissentono dalla fede e dalla morale cattolica, non si può non riconoscere quante parti della politica, della giurisprudenza, dell'economia e della letteratura siano state da lui osservate da un lato spesso novo e interressante, e, ciò che più importa, nobile e generoso: quante verità siano state da lui, per dir così, rimesse in possesso, ch'erano cadute sotto una specie di prescrizione ...' *Osservazioni sulla morale cattolica* (1819), in *Opere varie*, ed. Barbi and Ghisalberti, 35.

[21] 'Manzoni and the Novel', in Peter Brand and Lino Pertile (eds), *The Cambridge History of Italian Literature* (Cambridge: Cambridge University Press, 1996), 433.

[22] 'Manzoni and the Novel', 433. The Manzoni scholar Verina R. Jones makes a similar point in a somewhat different way, in reference to treatment of figures of the clergy in *I promessi sposi*. She shows how, in Manzoni's selective portrayal of aspects of the Counter-Reformation church, 'truth at the factual level did matter. But truth at the moral and ideological level counted even more.' 'Counter-Reformation

As a refutation of Sismondi, the hundreds of pages of Manzoni's treatise on Catholic morality were largely a wasted exercise, likely only to gain agreement from those already of similar faith. Even in later works Manzoni showed flexibility in historical thinking allied to rigidity over matters of religion. The changeover could occur in the space of a single sentence, such as the following from his treatise *On the Historical Novel*: 'What differentiates us from people of those [former] times is the possession of an historical criticism that seeks the real truth in past facts and, what is so much more important, the possession of a religion which, being the truth, cannot conveniently be adapted to arbitrary changes and fanciful elaboration.'[23] A much more finely nuanced and therefore intelligent reply to Sismondi than he produced in 1819, because one that engaged throughout in knowing as well as ironical ways with how the real differs from the ideal, came in the form of Manzoni's novel. Indeed from its early reception, in particular by the already mentioned De Sanctis, *I promessi sposi* was accounted to be a better response to Sismondi than had been furnished in *Observations on Catholic Morality*. The novel was a *practical* handling of Catholic morality. As De Sanctis explained to his students, 'the *Observations on Catholic Morality* form the basis for conceptions and situations in the novel, with the difference that in the treatise you see in the form of reasoned argument that which in the novel is represented in the form of action and feeling.' De Sanctis thought Manzoni far more effective in indirect reply to Sismondi, than in his earlier direct riposte, in which the 'artist had turned critic.'[24]

Shortly after his treatise refuting Sismondi, Manzoni turned towards poetic drama of a historical cast. The influence of Shakespeare's histories and tragedies is detectable throughout his own two tragedies, *The Count of Carmagnola* (1820) and *Adelchi* (1822). For Manzoni, Shakespeare was pre-eminent in having written plays that, rather than observing a rule-bound neoclassicism, created the very grounds by which they should be judged. In having combined 'the serious and the burlesque, the touching and the low', Shakespeare had taught writers of Manzoni's age that a work 'must be judged by its own rules.'[25] Such an aesthetic, important to German Romanticism (Manzoni admits that

and Popular Culture in *I promessi sposi*: A Case of Historical Censorship', *Renaissance and Modern Studies*, 36 (1993), 51.

[23] *On the Historical Novel*, tr. Sandra Bermann (Lincoln, Neb., and London: University of Nebraska Press, 1984), 125. 'Ciò che ci fa differenti ... dagli uomini di quelle età, è l'aver noi una critica storica che, ne' fatti passati, cerca la verità di fatto, e, ciò che importa troppo più, l'avere una religione che, essendo verità, non può convenientemente adattarsi a variazioni arbitrarie, e ad aggiunte fantastiche.' *Del romanzo storico e, in genere, de' componimenti misti di storia e d'invenzione*, in *Opere varie*, 673.

[24] De Sanctis, *Manzoni: Studi e lezioni*, 210–11. Alfredo Cottignoli showed how this idea of the novel being a more practical representation of the positions reasoned through in the earlier treatise predated De Sanctis's lessons. Domenico Ponisio in particular had first identified that *I promessi sposi* furnished Catholic morality 'with a force of examples adapted to the intelligence of a wide readership, making them love the beauty and benefits' imparted by their Catholic faith. Cottignoli, *Manzoni fra i critici dell'Ottocento*, 20–1.

[25] Much of his *Lettre à M. C *** [Chauvet]* is devoted to laying out a Romantic aesthetic of organic form, as opposed to a classical and rule-bound template for drama. The idea is repeated succinctly in a letter to Diodata Saluzzo di Roero, 16 Nov. 1827: 'I am profoundly persuaded of the truth of that principle expressed for the first time by A. W. Schlegel, that the form of compositions should be organic and not mechanical, resulting from the nature of the subject, from its interior development, from the

he had learned his sense of organic form from A. W. von Schlegel), would eventually achieve dominance in Italian culture as elsewhere, not least in contemporary assessment of Manzoni's own plays.[26] The elderly Goethe was quick to praise Manzoni for his first tragedy and to defend it against the kind of negative criticism that it had received in the British *Quarterly Review*.[27] Goethe detected in *The Count of Carmognola* an onward development of the historical drama that he and Schiller had successfully initiated on the German stage, they in turn having been so influenced by Shakespearean precedent. In spite of Goethe's early praise, any present judgement of Manzoni's two tragedies must acknowledge that they are less than ideally stageworthy. Their speeches are long, with the consequence that there is little to-fro dialogue in either work. Manzoni's division between 'historical characters' on the one hand and 'ideal characters' on the other in the cast list of *The Count of Carmagnola* is an early sign of something that would become more pronounced as his career developed, namely a dedication to the historically verifiable.[28]

If we concede that neither of Manzoni's plays is ideal for the stage, we must in the same breath assert how powerfully and movingly two different moments of Italian history are captured in their finest poetry. *Adelchi* in particular rings with memorable statement, especially when the protagonist's worldview is at its most tragic. Even in English translation, we detect the extent to which Manzoni has been influenced positively by Shakespeare's histories and tragedies, whether or not modified by his reading in intermediary drama by Schiller and Goethe. In the following passage, Adelchi pays homage to his opponent Charlemagne. The latter is figured in a way not unlike Caesar as presented in *Anthony and Cleopatra* ('Let determined things to destiny hold unbewail'd their way'), or Bolingbroke from *Richard II*, who manages to achieve dominance over a nation that under Richard had been become fractured and fragmented:

> My foe departs unpunished,
> Ready to accomplish more and more conquests.
> He has won here; he will stalk victory

relations of its parts and their natural arrangement, so to speak, rather than from the application of an exterior and extraneous template.' Marvin Carlson raises attention to this letter in his chapter 'The Italian Romantic Drama in its European Context', in Gerald Ernest Paul Gillespie (ed.), *Romantic Drama* (Amsterdam: John Benjamins Publishing Co., 1993), 244.

26 We must not suppose from the growing admiration for Shakespeare in Italy that fidelity to his plots or texts quickly won the day. Carlo Rusconi's 1839 Italian prose translations of Shakespeare are more accurate than Leoni's earlier versions, but even so *Hamlet* is given a happy ending.

27 The writer of the article titled 'Italian Tragedy: Manzoni, Foscolo, Pellico' has been identified as Henry Hart Milman. Milman was an Anglican clergyman and prominent intellectual who had by this point written an Italian tragedy of his own (*Fazio*, 1815). Treating in his article recent Italian dramatists beginning with Alfieri, Milman accounted Manzoni's *Count of Carmagnola* a 'feeble tragedy'. He acknowledged, however, that it included an affecting scene of parting by the Count from his family before execution, and also that one of its choruses, quoted in full in an English tr., was 'the most noble piece of Italian lyric poetry which the present day has produced.' *Quarterly Review*, 24/47 (1820), 87.

28 See on this point Sandra Bermann's Introduction to her translation of *On the Historical Novel* (Lincoln, Neb., and London: University of Nebraska Press, 1984), 25.

Elsewhere. And so he can because he reigns
Over a nation whose will is as firm
As the iron the king's sword is made of,
Cast solidly in one piece. As he handles
His sword nimbly in his hands, so does he
Handle, too, his own people.[29]

Not the least interesting feature of Adelchi's quoted lines is their adumbration of an important theme for the emergent Risorgimento movement. Charlemagne's Frankish realm is seen as a strong and powerful state, unified in ways unachieved by the fragmented Longobardian forces under Adelchi; not to say by the Italy of Manzoni's times, still a patchwork of smallish states, with large portions of its sub-Alpine plain and peninsula under Austrian rule.

In other respects what we see in finest detail in Adelchi's closing speeches is his abhorrence at oppression of the weak by the powerful. Manzoni's handling of that theme throughout his oeuvre constitutes one of his finest distinctions as a writer of the Romantic age. That Adelchi puts this oppression in such tragic terms makes it all the more powerful. The strong triumphing over the weak is figured in Adelchi's finest speech as unchanging throughout history.

There is no room
For guiltless action, 'tis only given
To either inflict wrongs or suffer them.
A fierce and dire force governs the world;
Men call it law! With blood-stained hands our
Forefathers cast the seeds of injustice;
Our fathers manured it with blood
And the land does not yield other harvest.
It is not sweet to rule ...[30]

Oppression of the weak comes from 'a fierce and dire force' that 'governs the world' ('Una feroce | forza il mondo possiede'). Adelchi has resented throughout the play the warmongering policies of Desiderio, his co-equal Longobardian king, to whom he has reluctantly deferred because he is his father. Adelchi has had to fulfil the role of a warrior king of his people, leading forces into battle and by his own admission killing many of Charlemagne's followers though personal feats on the battlefield. In council situations, however, and here again in speeches as he is dying, Adelchi proves himself an early and radical form of pacifist. Any adequate history of the lineages of pacifism would do well to take on board this tragic protagonist of Manzonian drama.

[29] *Alessandro Manzoni's The Count of Carmagnola and Adelchis*, tr. Federica Brunori Deigan (Baltimore and London: Johns Hopkins University Press, 2004), 248.

[30] *Manzoni's The Count of Carmagnola*, 306.

In the same year as he published *Adelchi*, 1822, Manzoni had already begun writing *I promessi sposi*. Manzoni had earlier displayed in correspondence his gratitude to Goethe for the notice given to his *Count of Carmagnola*. However, in the German author's next main responses to a work by Manzoni, Goethe was less pleased the further he read. The text was that of the 1827 version of *I promessi sposi*. After warm praise of the early portions of the novel, Goethe proclaimed in conversation with his friend Johann Peter Eckermann after reading the final volume:

> Manzoni takes off his clothing as a poet and presents himself for too long to us as a naked historian. That happens in the descriptions of the war, the famine, and the plague; things already repugnant in themselves, and which in the minute particularisation of arid representation by a chronicler become insupportable. The German translator must seek to avoid this weakness through abbreviations ...[31]

It took later criticism to address with subtlety the scale of Manzoni's achievement in the one historical novel he was to write. Recent responses widely differ from Goethe's, predominantly admiring the intense historical portrayals of, precisely, war, famine, and plague; sometimes even preferring them to many of the novel's more 'invented' materials and character portrayals. There is no need to cover old ground by tracing Walter Scott's influence upon Manzoni. Georg Lukács in *The Historical Novel* declares how, 'as a result of [his] superb and historically profound conception Manzoni creates a novel in which the human comes out even more powerfully than in his master'. In saying this, Lukács was explicating Scott's own admiration for Manzoni, which he goes on to relate: 'Scott himself recognized Manzoni's greatness. When in Milan Manzoni told him that he was his pupil, Scott replied that in that case Manzoni's was his best work.'[32] Lukács's positions have been critiqued by others, and are not the main line of enquiry here. My hope is rather that by addressing ways in which Manzoni dealt with history—in particular its forms of injustice, and the relative positioning of the powerful in relation to those weaker than themselves whom they oppress—comparative light may be shed on so important a topic.

For all his deceptive modesty and multiple disclaimers of authority, Manzoni had high ambitions in the realm of historical thinking. In the novel he treats figures of oppression (official or otherwise) and their support system of judges and administrators—including the *bravi* or bullyboys of tyrannical local seigneurs—as instances of enduring injustice in Italian culture. As Agnese, the mother of the peasant heroine Lucia puts it, 'They've made the Laws as they wanted them, and poor folk like us can't understand them all. Like so many other things' (80).[33] In such matters Manzoni is not at loggerheads

[31] Caretti (ed.), *Manzoni e la critica*, 244. For a different (19th-cent.) English tr. of Goethe's opinion, see Johann Peter Eckermann, *Conversations with Goethe*, tr. John Oxenford (London: Dent, 1971), 218.

[32] Georg Lukács, *The Historical Novel*, tr. Hannah and Stanley Mitchell (London: Merlin Press, 1962), 69–70.

[33] 'La legge l'hanno fatta loro, come gli è piaciuto; e noi poverelli non possiamo capir tutto. E poi quante cose ...' Manzoni, *I promessi sposi*, ed. Attilio Momigliano (Florence: Sansoni editore, 1951), 122.

with Sismondi's accounts of a debased and corrupted Italy, but closely in accord with the Swiss historian's generalizations. Sismondi had pointed out in the final chapter of his *Histoire* that the justice system practised in Italian states was another fallen pillar of Italy's greatness. The rise of absolutism had led to a crushing of legality, and to the primacy of mere privilege. Obedience was enforced from a largely downtrodden people. Legal process, potentially the very groundwork and foundation of public morality, being so often cloaked now in secrecy had given justice a bad name. More and more frequently an accused was not even informed of a charge and so could not mount an adequate self-defence. Bad justice itself had led, accordingly, to habits of dissimulation and of flattery. As if that were not enough, the frequent spectacles of state-sanctioned torture fostered further violence. Finally, with the exponential growth of legal cases, chicanery among lawyers thrived.

Almost every one of the points made by Sismondi about the decline in justice available to the peoples of Italy receives exemplification in Manzoni's novel, or in his follow-up work *The Column of Infamy*. The persons who represent civil authority in Spanish-dominated Milan by and large misrule the state. Those whom they protect, such as Don Rodrigo, the wicked abductor and would-be ravisher of Lucia the female protagonist, are eventually laid low not by human law but by the plague. Don Rodrigo's aider and abettor, the terrible Unnamed One, is only deflected from years of evildoing by his conversion to the Catholic faith, under the combined influence of the Franciscan monk Fra Cristoforo and the great prince of the church, Federico Borromeo (a real historical figure). The Unnamed One is the chief figure in a highly imaginative melodrama. His followers—the *bravi* who do his nefarious bidding—are hyperbolical elaborations on themes of injustice. When the Unnamed One converts to a life of goodness some of his *bravi* do so as well. Others leave him to continue a life of evil under different, still unconverted masters. None is shown by Manzoni as thinking for himself in a way that counts. If anything, they are rather comic Gothic creations. Their wickedness is not unlike that of Dante's band of devils taken straight from popular folklore, who guard and torment the barrators in their particular circle of Malebolge in the *Inferno* (Cantos 19–22).

One of Manzoni's other characters, nicknamed Dr Azzecca-garbugli (Quibbleweaver in the Colquhoun translation), is a comic exaggeration of the kind of chicanery pointed out by Sismondi. When the hero of the novel, Renzo, resorts to him for advice on how to re-establish and bring to fulfilment his interrupted wedding, Azzecca-garbugli at first believes that Renzo himself is a *bravo* who has prevented an honest marriage. He is perfectly willing to extricate him from the difficulties as he supposes them to be, but crossly reprimands Renzo for what he perceives as his stupid peasant honesty: 'You see, son, the man who tells lies to his lawyer is a kind of fool who'll end up telling the truth to the judge.'[34] By such a reckoning truth in tribunals must at all cost be subverted by 'quibbleweaving' lawyers. As Azzecca-garbugli reassures Renzo, 'As long, let it be understood,

[34] 'Chi dice le bugie al dottore, vedete figliuolo, è uno sciocco che dirà la verità al giudice.' *I promessi sposi*, ed. Momigliano, 61.

as you haven't offended anyone of consequence, I pledge myself to get you out of your fix; with a bit of outlay, of course' (41).[35] At this point in their conversation Azzecca-garbugli still has not grasped that Renzo is victim and not perpetrator of an act of oppression. The lawyer has consequently revealed forms of chicanery and hypocrisy that Sismondi had represented as strangling the Italian legal system. Plainly, lawyers of the type portrayed here by Manzoni were willing to lay right and wrong aside, arguing for whoever made an 'outlay' for their services, provided always that the offence had not been to 'anyone of consequence'. No sooner does Renzo mention Don Rodrigo as his opponent in the matter of the suppressed marriage (which Azzecca-garbugli has finally realized is Renzo's own) than the lawyer 'suddenly, frowning, wrinkling his red nose, and screwing up his mouth' (42)[36] orders the young man to be gone. There could be no more serio-comic portrayal than this of the law's collusion in tyrannical forms of oppression. As Attilio Momigliano wrote of Dr Azzecca-garbugli in notes to his excellent post-war edition of the novel, 'we have seen him so many times in the musty air of some provincial pettifogger's office, fossilised in his use of formulae that are a balance of the legalistic and the fraudulent'.[37]

One of Manzoni's treatments of a very different kind of injustice is his story within the larger story, of the nun Gertrude, trapped and tricked into a life of monastic devotion by her parents. These latter are leading nobility of the city of Monza, a lineage of Spanish grandees who wish to prioritize the male line of their family and are willing to sacrifice the happiness of their daughter in consequence. Manzoni's overall judgement is that such forcing of family members into a life of monastic service is deeply unjust to those upon whom it is perpetrated and that, worse still, it may lead to a more awful evil. Gertrude becomes implicated in the murder of a young novice who has discovered her secret liaison with a debauched young man in the environs of the monastery. Profound and committed Catholic that he was, Manzoni here makes the strong point via the story of Gertrude that the individual happiness of persons in their secular existences must never be sacrificed by forcing them into service to the church against their will. Her family sacrifices Gertrude in order to maintain and enhance their social standing. The case aligns closely with what Sismondi had had to say about the debased morality of honour in Italy. For Sismondi, punctilios of honour had become the equivalent of national institutions. To his mind the Spanish and the Arabs had been influential for the worse in such matters. Very importantly there had developed, according to him, an exaggerated delicacy over female chastity, which had led to women losing the honourable free will of action that they had possessed in the great former age of Italian republics, and to their coming under greater control of their families during the succeeding centuries. Many of

[35] 'Purchè non abbiate offeso persona di riguardo, intendiamoci, m'impegno a togliervi d'impiccio: con un po' di spesa, intendiamoci.' *I promessi sposi*, ed. Momigliano, 61.

[36] 'aggrottando le ciglia, aggrinzando il naso rosso, e storcendo la bocca': *I promessi sposi*, ed. Momigliano, 63.

[37] 'lo abbiamo veduto noi tante volte nell'aria ammuffita dello studio di qualche leguleio di provincia fossilizzato nelle sue formule tra legali e truffaldine': *I promessi sposi*, ed. Momigliano, 56n.

these increased constraints and restrictions apply to the case of Gertrude and are what makes hers such a tragic story within the larger narrative. Verina R. Jones rightly sums up Gertrude's personality as 'arrogant, haughty, sexually aware'. In her challenging study of Manzoni's two very different 'dark ladies' of the novel (Lucia and Gertrude), Jones shows, inter alia, how Manzoni's handling of the semi-historical figure of a cloistral nun from Ripamonti's *Historiae patriae* has interpellations of 'the stereotype of the contaminated beauty' from Gothic literature, as transmuted in particular through Italian translation from Manzoni's own period of Ann Radcliffe's *The Italian*.[38] Gertrude wishes for a life of self-fulfilment in the secular world, not the chastity of a nunnery. It is acutely painful as readers to witness how, step by step, she cedes free will of action under pressure from her wily and tyrannical parents, until there is no going back and she is trapped in the monastic life that they have unjustly chosen for her. Anna Banti ended her aforementioned tribute to Manzoni in terms of this particular narrative and character portrayal: 'If we modern narrators in Italy are inclined to consider ourselves "created" by Manzoni, I myself can profess this recognition as regards the episode of Gertrude with a humility and admiration that I might call religious.'[39]

I take up the specific matter of the novel's methodology at an interesting crux of Manzoni's own consideration of what went on in the mind of a minor historical character, Milan's Commissioner of Supply for the city, during the bread riots of 1628. The Commissioner is taking his own meal in peace when the starving rioters suggest going to his house and holding him to account for shortages of bread. After showing the Commissioner flee from his meal through private rooms of his residence and into the loft above, Manzoni writes:

> Crouching down in it, he listened to hear if the ghastly sounds were getting weaker or the tumult was abating a little; but instead he heard the bellowing getting louder and fiercer and the bangs on the door redoubling, so that his heart turned another somersault, and he hurriedly plugged up his ears. Then, completely losing control of himself, he clenched his teeth and twisted up his face, braced his arms and fists, as if he hoped they would hold the doors firm, then ... But what else he did we cannot tell, as he was alone; and history can only guess. Luckily, it is quite used to doing so. (184)[40]

Manzoni is equally critiquing here a characteristic practice of history as he is the strategies of his novel. History relies—because it has to—on too much guesswork. The historical novel, being an offshoot of history, is even more vitiated by this tack. As we have seen, Goethe had wanted more of Manzoni's novel to concentrate on its characters, not on long accounts of what actually happened in Milan and its region in the couple of years in which the work is set. Manzoni had by contrast sought to combine within a seamless piece what in other writers, such as Scott, consisted of a fictional text and accompanying

[38] Verina R. Jones, 'Manzoni's Dark Ladies', *Romance Studies*, 19 (Winter 1991), 37–52.

[39] Banti, *Opinioni*, 65.

[40] Manzoni, *I promessi sposi*, ed. Momigliano, 282.

paratext of historical notes. To judge from the words just quoted in relation to the Commissioner's hiding from the mob within his loft, Manzoni was perfectly able to imagine the man's inner plight and terrified thinking. This accords with concepts of Romantic sympathy and sensibility, here extended to a morally reprehensible character. The problem, however, lay in Manzoni's own sense of his role as a historical writer. He was not satisfied, either with his inferring what went through the Commissioner's mind or—and this is far more important—with history's own frequent resort, for lack of material evidence, to speculative guesswork. In Manzoni's opinion there had been far too much cultural forgetting of injustices in the Italian past. What was primarily of importance for him as a thinker was not to write further fictions about such injustice, much as his single novel proved that he had great powers to do so. Rather, he was concerned to bring forth by means of close study what was actually able to be discovered from historical records but had so far been neglected. This task he held to be more important than guesswork, even where the archival records left him short of sufficient detail. Manzoni is saying, let us look far more than we have done into what *can* be recuperated from historical records of the war and famine and plague, and the consequent human events and sufferings. This he does for chapters on end in his novel; all that constitutes its preponderance of history by Goethe's reckoning.

As Olga Ragusa has suggested, historical novels such as Manzoni's involve 'a fictional story set in a documented or documentable context which may also include actual persons who lived at the time'. This genre, Ragusa states, 'has one foot in fact and the other in fiction, one in a kind of scholarship or erudition and the other in a kind of entertainment'.[41] Manzoni was quick to see an irreconcilable gap between facts of the past and inventive elaboration in the present *about that past*, the two main components of a work such as *I promessi sposi*. He would not write another historical novel. As he explains in a theoretical disquisition on the subject, the full title of which hints at his thesis—*On the Historical Novel and, in General, on Works Mixing History with Invention*—the only faithful way to represent a state of past humanity or series of events (what can and cannot be known about them) is by means of rigorous historical methodology, without resort to invention. Believing as he did that historical novels were undermined by the contradiction upon which they were based—'The historical novel does not have a logical purpose of its own: it counterfeits two'[42]—Manzoni predicted an early demise of the very genre that he was foremost in Italy in having deployed. Antonio Illiano has noted 'Manzoni's disenchantment with literature as a vehicle of truth and his consequent turning to historiography as to the ultimate route of a moral inquiry into the perversity of a human and historical system based on oppression and victimization of the innocent'. This was, according to Illiano, 'a long and involved process of detachment and disillusionment which starts with the historical tragedies, and, through the lengthy

[41] Olga Ragusa, 'Alessandro Manzoni and Developments in the Historical Novel', in Peter Bondanella and Andrea Ciccarelli (eds), *The Cambridge Companion to the Italian Novel* (Cambridge: Cambridge University Press, 2003), 42.

[42] *On the Historical Novel*, 76. 'Non ha il romanzo storico un intento suo proprio e insieme logico: ne contraffà due.' *Del romanzo storico*, 635.

composition of the novel, motivates the work and commitment of the historiographer.'[43] Manzoni's own advice to any writer who wishes to illuminate a particular period and who is willing to undertake the tasks involved is, 'Search every document from that period that you can find. Even treat as documents writings whose authors never, in their wildest imaginations, dreamt they were writing in support of history. Select, discard, connect, contrast, deduce, and infer. If you do, rest assured that you will arrive at a far more precise, more definitive, more comprehensive, more accurate understanding of that historical moment than there was before.'[44] This constitutes an intense description of Manzoni's own investigative principles behind *The Column of Infamy*, the work that, so unlike the novel to which it was eventually appended, strictly eschews authorial invention and is even chary of straying overmuch into realms of historical conjecture. The sentence 'Select, discard, connect, contrast, deduce, and infer' could stand as cardinal advice today, not just for anyone engaged in ongoing historical studies but for work in the humanities more generally, as indeed in the sciences.

Manzoni writes that his aim in the chapters dealing with the plague that followed hard upon the heels of war is not so much to follow the lives of his characters but to address 'a page of our country's history which is more celebrated than it is known'. He reports in the thirty-first chapter that, although there were contemporary accounts of the plague, 'there is not one that gives a clear and connected idea of it', although also 'not one which cannot help us form one' (429).[45] Manzoni saw his task as that of drawing contemporary seventeenth-century chronicle history together into a nineteenth-century *summa* of the earlier events: 'No writer of a later period has tried to examine and collate these memoirs with a view to extracting from them a connected series of events' (430).[46] In the chapters following, Manzoni attempted to be the synthesizing writer who sifts through contemporary records in order to provide the joined-up history of the plague and its aftermath that had so far been lacking. What he provides is even more than he promised. For as well as condensing events into a comprehensible narrative, he extracts from them something that we should not flinch from calling moral understanding:

> In public calamities and prolonged disturbances of any normal order, one always sees an increase, a sublimation of virtue. But, unhappily, with it always and without fail

[43] Antonio Illiano, 'On Manzoni's Disillusionment with Literature', *Forum Italicum*, 24 (1990), 111.

[44] *On the Historical Novel*, tr. Bermann, 77: '[F]rughi ne' documenti di qualunque genere, che ne rimangono, e che possa trovare; faccia, voglio dire, diventar documenti anche certi scritti, gli autori de' quali erano lontani le mille miglia dall'immaginarsi che mettevano in carta de' documenti per i posteri; scelga, scarti, accozzi, confronti, deduca e induca; e gli si può star mallevadore, che arriverà a formarsi, di quel momento storico, concetti molto più speciali, più decisi, più interi, più sinceri di quelli che se ne avesse fino allora.' *Del romanzo storico e, in genere, de' componimenti misti di storia e d'invenzione*, in *Opere varie*, 636.

[45] '... un tratto di storia patria più famoso che conosciuto. Dalle molte relazioni contemporanee, non ce n'è alcuna che basti da sè a darne un'idea un po' distinta e ordinata; come non ce n'è alcuna che non possa aiutare a formarla.' Manzoni, *I promessi sposi*, ed. Momigliano, 653.

[46] '... confrontare quelle memorie, per ritrarne una serie concatenata degli avvenimenti': Manzoni, *I promessi sposi*, ed. Momigliano, 654.

> goes an increase, far more general in most cases, of crime. And this happened now, too. Rogues whom the plague spared and did not frighten now found new chances of activity, together with new certainty of impunity, in the common confusion following the relaxation of every public authority; in fact the very exercise of public authority came to be very largely in the hands of the worst of them ... They entered houses as masters, as enemies, and (not to mention their thieving or treatment of the wretched creatures reduced by plague to passing through their hands) they would lay those foul and infected hands on healthy people, on children, parents, wives, or husbands, threatening to drag them off to the lazaretto unless they ransomed themselves or got others to ransom them with money. (454)[47]

Manzoni writes with discursive calm, in a prose redolent of the Enlightenment because won from his long study of seventeenth- and eighteenth-century chroniclers. If asked to identify what his judgement on humanity at its foulest most resembles, we might choose writings since 1940 that have addressed without flinching the worst realities of ghettos and death camps. Manzoni like the later Italian author Primo Levi reminds us of human values that go missing in the extremes of behaviour that are unleashed by a terrible event. Both authors enable us to understand how shocking the world becomes when not governed by such values. Quite simply, Manzoni anticipated the finest of Holocaust literature.

An account of cartfuls of dead bodies seen by Renzo in Milan during the worst of the plague will have to serve as representative of a hundred pages or more of harrowing scenes. Only Dante had to this point in the genealogy of Italian literature known how to shape detail with this intensity, such that we might suppose we were 'reading' a painting. Manzoni shows how much he had learned to positive effect from the author of the *Inferno*.

> He heard the noise drawing nearer and nearer, then round the corner by the church saw a man appearing, ringing a bell. It was an *apparitore*. Behind him came two horses pulling ahead with difficulty, their necks straining and their hoofs pawing; drawn by these came a cartful of corpses, and after it another, and then another, and another, with *monatti* walking at the horses' flanks on either side, urging them on with lashes, prods, and curses. The corpses were mostly naked, a few roughly wrapped in rags; they were heaped up and entwined with each other, like a nest of snakes slowly uncoiling to the warmth of spring; for at every jolt and jar those ghastly heaps could be seen quivering and slithering revoltingly over each other, and heads dangling, and maidenly tresses unwinding, and arms sliding out and bumping against the wheels ... (482)[48]

We have seen such entwined dead bodies again in surviving photographs of the worst horrors of the Nazi era.

[47] For original Italian text, see Manzoni, *I promessi sposi*, ed. Momigliano, 684–5.
[48] Manzoni, *I promessi sposi*, ed. Momigliano, 728–9.

Alongside *I promessi sposi*'s taking up of the cause of justice there is another, in certain respects contrary, set of representations. The novel's providential Catholicism, as represented by the figure of its Franciscan monk Fra Cristoforo in his catechizing of the protagonist Renzo for wanting to take matters of justice into his own hands, holds that 'we must trust in God ... [W]on't you allow God one day, two days, as long as He needs, to make justice triumph?' Fra Cristoforo has just admitted, 'if men of power wanting to commit acts of injustice always had to give their reasons, things wouldn't be as they are' (86).[49] Manzoni's seeming trust throughout much of the novel in a divine providence for the working out of justice, in particular on behalf of the sufferings of the poor that have been caused directly or indirectly by the powerful and unjust, is what puts off a lot of Italian youngsters of today in their reading of the novel; that and having to read extracts of it at the hands of traditionalist educators. Franco Triolo offers a more sophisticated defence of Manzoni's representations of providence. Triolo first summarizes the many critics, including Croce and his followers, whom he wishes to refute: essentially, those who, in Croce's terms, 'observed that the novel was not a true work of art, but rather a work of "rhetoric," a very beautiful "poem of religious morality," an edifying sermon'.[50] According to Triolo a common and fundamental error of those who fault Manzoni for his providential reading of humanity is that of 'transferring to Manzoni his characters' more or less naïve, one-sided and often malicious ideas'.[51] Triolo reminds us that it was Manzoni who, in reflecting on history, described it as 'a state so natural to man, so violent and full of grief, which promotes so many designs whose fulfillment is impossible, which—rather than stopping for an instant—embraces at once all ailments and their remedies, ... a state which is a mystery of contradictions and in which the mind is lost unless it regards it as a state of trial and preparation for another existence'.[52] The ending of that quotation from Manzoni signals the direction Triolo is taking in defence of the author; one that provides a more complex but still religious and otherworldly spin to Manzoni's providentialism. Reminding us that Manzoni's tragedies also 'are based on the idea that sorrow, sadness, ill-fortune which strike the good can be for the spectator a stimulus to elevate the mind to higher thoughts and more transcendent realities', Triolo goes on to say of Manzoni's art that 'it is only within the framework and perspective of the other life that all things and sorrows of this world can find explanation and correction'.[53] For many, including schoolchildren who first meet *I promessi sposi* in the classroom, such a message still enshrines elements of what Triolo was determined to avoid or surpass, namely an edifying sermon. Instead of easily accepting Triolo's perspective, many first readers of the novel may concur more with Antonio Gramsci's very different and outrightly negative judgement: 'Manzoni's attitude towards the common people in

49 'Nondimeno, confidenza in Dio! ... [N]on vorrai tu concedere a Dio un giorno, due giorni, il tempo che vorrà prendere, per far trionfare la giustizia?' Manzoni, *I promessi sposi*, ed. Momigliano, 130.

50 Franco Triolo, 'Manzoni and Providence', in Matteo and Peer, *Reasonable Romantic*, 247.

51 Triolo, 'Manzoni and Providence', 254.

52 Triolo, 'Manzoni and Providence', 250, quoting Manzoni, *Discorso sulla storia longobardica*.

53 Triolo, 'Manzoni and Providence', 249, 251.

his novel is the attitude of the Catholic Church toward the people: an attitude of benevolent condescension, as opposed to the notion of human identity.' Gramsci had gone on to say that Manzoni 'finds "magnanimity", "elevated thought" and "lofty feelings" only in some members of the upper class but never among the people, who as a whole are inferior, like animals'.[54]

If Gramsci's judgement has relevance for certain aspects of the novel, it does not hold true for *The Column of Infamy* where Manzoni's devotion to archival evidence was at its most intense. That work breaks new ground in representing the way subaltern classes were mistreated by the strong. Sometimes in this far smaller text Manzoni recuperates from legal archives the very words of vulnerable citizens, extracted from them under the terrible duresses of torture—hardly a case of feeling that they are 'inferior, like animals'; rather a representation that underlines their humanity. Fiction had not permitted Manzoni to be as expansive and at the same time precise an historian as he wished. He made a promise to his readers that he would put further historical study into a separate work. The text that we know as *The Column of Infamy* had been substantially completed years earlier, but was only published along with the 1842 edition of the novel. When Goethe had said of Manzoni's writings about the war, famine, and plague that as a historian he was filled with too great a respect for reality, he had paid him the highest of unintentional tributes. *The Column of Infamy* is indeed a work sometimes overlooked, as Leonardo Sciascia had noted, when Manzoni's place in Italian or indeed European literature is being reviewed. In it Manzoni unravels each musty archival detail of the seventeenth-century case he studies, analysing to the full what it can be made to reveal. For Sciascia, Manzoni's study clearly established a methodology; a pressing to the limits of what could be known from old and mostly neglected archives about remarkable instances of 'ordinary people' standing up to those in power, and paying eventually with their lives rather than abandon their principles. Manzoni asks in *The Column of Infamy* whether we should look at injustice with different eyes when it is firmly in and of the past; in this case a specific cultural moment in the seventeenth-century region of Milan. His answer is broadly that we should not, because the perpetrators of injustice in that earlier time (even up to levels of advocates and judges) understood that their uses of torture were wrong, however long and deep the precedents for them in Roman and later constitutional law.

Manzoni's narrative in *The Column of Infamy* rests on a topic still not then regarded as—in his words—'a proper subject for history'; namely 'the sentences of criminal courts' and 'the fate of the poor (taken a few at a time)' (643).[55] Here we have on the part of a Romantic period writer the clearest statement possible that what he is attempting is focus upon subaltern classes that have previously been left out of historical reckoning. The Italian critic who has done most to fathom Manzoni's turn away from fiction

[54] Antonio Gramsci, *Prison Notebooks*, iii, ed. and tr. Joseph Buttigieg (New York: Columbia University Press, 2007), 196–7.

[55] 'I giudizi criminali, e la povera gente, quand'è poca, non si riguardano come materia propriamente della storia ...' *Opere*, ed. Barbi and Ghisalberti, i. 580.

into history, Giorgio Bárberi Squarotti, has finely explicated how, as early as the Author's Introduction to *The Betrothed*, Manzoni had jettisoned what he calls (in the words of the old and faded manuscript he purports to be retelling and modernizing[56]) the 'enterprises of Princes, Potentates, and mightie Personnages', to concentrate instead on 'persons of small import and low degree' (*gente meccaniche e di piccol affare* in the antiquated language of the so-called anonymous writer 'l'Anonimo').[57] Squarotti writes:

> By Manzoni's conception, as the Author's Introduction with its affirmations of the poetics of the 'Anonimo' testifies, the novel is a genre which allows for a voice to be given to figures who are outside of history when the latter is understood as the record of the powerful. Humble people would otherwise not be given space, since there is no trace of them in the annals and celebrations of princes and condottieri compiled by historians. The novel consents to dignify what happened to 'persons of small import' of a subaltern social condition. More fundamentally, it rereads the same history of the high and mighty in a perspective that overturns significances and values, showing their limits, errors, and crimes.[58]

Manzoni's feeling for the poor and making of them a new concern for history is comparable with Scott in *The Heart of Midlothian* and other works, or with the slightly later Dickens. Instead of writing accounts of the poor of his own age, however, as Dickens was frequently to do in succeeding decades, Manzoni attempts in *The Column of Infamy* to fathom weird and (partly from the lapse in time since their occurrence) well-nigh inscrutable instances from an earlier history of great injustice. This search to understand better the treatment of the weak by the powerful is undertaken not merely in homage to the victims of past oppression, but so as to shed light on injustice as a general phenomenon, not least within his own nineteenth-century Italy. It is also the reason, incidentally, why A. P. d'Entrèves was keen to promulgate the work in an English translation soon after the Second World War. In his introduction to that translation d'Entrèves commented upon Manzoni's relevance to an understanding of injustice in relation to the only recently defeated Nazism. In Italy, Sciascia would later point to Manzoni's relevance in the fight against enduring forms of fascism.[59]

56 This conceit of editing and retelling an older story that only exists in faded and anonymous manuscript form was becoming commonplace. It had been used by Scott, as well as by certain of his and Manzoni's forebears. What is at stake is the recovery of history from damaged, fragmentary, or obscure sources. Although use of the convention originally sought to engage readers' trust in the historical authenticity of the narrative, Manzoni's adoption of it is more ironic than that of most. He seems unwilling to hoodwink readers into believing that 'invented' aspects of the fiction were founded in some real document, presumably because already troubled that the historical novel is vitiated as a form by asking, precisely, for too much of such credence.

57 Squarotti's best essays on Manzoni's turn from fiction to history are 'L'altra faccia della storia', in his *Il romanzo contro la storia: Studi sui 'promessi sposi'* (Milan: Vita e Pensiero, 1980), 82–129, and both 'Manzoni e l'impotenza della letteratura' and 'La storia come dolore' in *Manzoni: Le delusioni della letteratura* (Rovito: Marra editore, 1988), 157–87.

58 *Il romanzo contro la storia*, 127–8.

59 Sciascia, *Cruciverba*, 108.

The investigative non-fiction genre as developed by Manzoni in *The Column of Infamy* was an attempt on his part to comment upon exact moves in a legal enquiry of 1630 into who and what had caused the plague to spread. Manzoni was, as it were, playing the role of a review tribunal at a later point in history, following how legal minds had arbitrated the original case two centuries previously. Manzoni frequently has to gloss for his readers certain legal procedures of the earlier age, and only then, as a separate analytical stage, note whether the judges had followed the letter of the law in their prosecution of the case. His overall position is that not only were the tortures of common people of Milan that they resorted to for extracting confessions abhorrent to the mind of his early nineteenth-century age: the judges did not even apply them according to strict legal constraints of their own times of the early 1630s.

Manzoni notes that the frequency and duration of any tortures used were prescribed in law in the seventeenth century, and that there were also limitations on the status to be accorded the confessions extracted by means of them. Even by these criteria (however dubious as a measure of justice they may appear to a later age) the judges were clearly at fault. Manzoni's argument embodies a sophisticated cultural relativism. He is saying that it is one thing to *judge these judges* of an earlier age by our standards. But it is another thing entirely to judge them by standards of their own times. Manzoni finds that *even* by the cruel allowance of specified usages of torture in their age, the seventeenth-century judges grossly erred in their prosecution of those whom they were demonizing as persons (*untori*) who deliberately went about Milan smearing unguents infected with plague.

It was one of Manzoni's fundamental cases that profound change is rare, because people do not have the audacity or brilliance to effectuate it. The last words of his text *The Column of Infamy* make this point. 'It happens quite often; good reasons come to the aid of bad ones, and then the combined effect of both is that a truth which has taken a long while to come to birth has still to remain concealed a while longer' (650).[60] This dictum seems like a repetition—certainly more than an echo—from Cesare Beccaria, Manzoni's maternal grandfather. Beccaria's famous Enlightenment text, *Of Crimes and Punishments*, had stated pessimistically that it was 'the fate of all great truths' to endure 'no longer than a flash, compared with that long dark night in which mankind is enveloped'.[61] *I promessi sposi* and the follow-up non-fictional investigative narrative *The Column of Infamy* are largely about one such long dark night in the years 1628, 1629, and 1630 in Milan and its surrounding region, during which famine was accompanied by unnecessary wars and followed by a devastating plague.

[60] 'Così è avvenuto più volte, che anche le buone ragioni abbian dato aiuto alle cattive, e che, per la forza dell'une e dell'altre, una verità dopo aver tardato un bel pezzo a nascere, abbia dovuto rimanere per un altro pezzo nascosta.' *Opere*, ed. Barbi and Ghisalberti, i. 585.

[61] Cesare Beccaria, in Manzoni, *The Column of Infamy*, prefaced by Cesare Beccaria's *Of Crimes and Punishments*, 51. '... la fortuna delle grandi verità, la durata delle quali non è che un lampo, in paragone della lunga e tenebrosa notte che involge gli uomini.' *Dei delitti e delle pene*, ed. Franco Venturi, 3rd edn (Turin: Einaudi editore, 1973), 69.

What transpires from Manzoni's research in the Milanese archives for the writing of *The Column of Infamy* is that there can be no final documenting of what were the deepest thoughts and the bedrock beliefs of subaltern persons engaged in an earlier century in great struggles against the injustice of the strong. The author cannot, as it were, speak for the subaltern, especially not during those moments when individuals went through extreme torture or were on the point of death from the suffering it caused. He can only present in evidence the subaltern's own words or screams, as recorded in the scribal testimony of those earlier trials and tortures. This he does painstakingly. Manzoni cannot add to such scribal testimony because, the novel once finished, he was adamant in not inventing thoughts and imputing them to any actual victim of past oppression: to do so would be to go back on his dedication only henceforth to deal with the historically 'real', no longer with fictional elaborations on it, however much verisimilitude they might enshrine. For Manzoni at this 'post-fictional' stage of his career there can only be speculation from the point of view of the present. He is left in puzzled admiration, unable finally to penetrate the minds of those who were tortured centuries earlier, during their ultimate acts of defiance. Having already faced almost unbearable pains, the victims go through the further torments of death sentences imposed on them, pathetically struggling but in an important sense morally undefeated.

Some of Manzoni's greatest writing is that which paid tribute to such instances of heroism on the part of the oppressed, as here in *The Column of Infamy*. 'The fate of the poor (taken a few at a time)' is very clearly made into 'a proper subject for history'. Manzoni thereby lays claims to being an important pioneer of 'history from below', not the more standard forms of history as seen from the point of view of the upper classes and those ensconced in power. Banti and Sciascia saw this greatness, whereas the somewhat earlier Gramsci wrongly characterized Manzoni as constitutionally locked into empathizing with the powerful and with the church. Manzoni's ability to represent the lives of the humble in *The Column of Infamy*, along with his searing treatments of famine, plague, and war in *The Betrothed*, or of oppressed beings like Gertrude who had been forced into unsuited service to the church, are in the final analysis his enduring legacy and a fundamental reason for his persistence.

Note

All quotation from *I promessi sposi* and from *La colonna infame* is given in English from Alessandro Manzoni, *The Betrothed and History of the Column of Infamy*, ed. David Forgacs and Matthew Reynolds (London: Dent, 1997), with page numbers in brackets in the main text. This version of the novel is the earlier Archibald Colquhoun translation, substantially revised and annotated by Reynolds. The translation in this same volume of *La colonna infame* is by Kenelm Foster, originally published by Oxford University Press (1964). Other quotations from Italian texts are in the author's own translation, except in the case of works for which a published translation already exists.

Further Reading

Abbiati, Franco, *Giuseppe Verdi*, 4 vols (Milan: Ricordi & C., 1959).

Banti, Anna, *Opinioni* (Milan: Il Saggiatore, 1961).

Beccaria, Cesare, *Of Crimes and Punishments*, in Manzoni, *The Column of Infamy*, ed. Kenelm Foster and Jane Grigson (London: Oxford University Press, 1964).

Beccaria, Cesare, *Dei delitti e delle pene*, ed. Franco Venturi, 3rd edn (Turin: Einaudi editore, 1973).

Bermann, Sandra, 'Introduction', to Manzoni, *On the Historical Novel*, tr. Bermann (Lincoln, Neb., and London: University of Nebraska Press, 1984).

Caretti, Lanfranco (ed.), *Manzoni e la critica* (Bari: Editori Laterza, 1971).

Carlson, Marvin, 'The Italian Romantic Drama in its European Context', in Gerald Ernest Paul Gillespie (ed.), *Romantic Drama* (Amsterdam: John Benjamins Publishing Co., 1993), 233–48.

Carsaniga, Giovanni, 'Manzoni and the Novel', in Peter Brand and Lino Pertile (eds), *The Cambridge History of Italian Literature* (Cambridge: Cambridge University Press, 1996), 427–40.

Cesare, Raffaele de, *Balzac e Manzoni, e altri studi su Balzac e l'Italia* (Milan: Vita e Pensiero, 1993).

Chandler, James, *England in 1819: The Politics of Literary Culture and the Case of Romantic Historicism* (Chicago and London: University of Chicago Press, 1998).

Cottignoli, Alfredo, *Manzoni fra i critici del Ottocento* (Bologna: Masimiliano Boni Editore, 1978).

Cro, Stelio, 'Manzoni and the Lombard Question', in Sante Matteo and Larry H. Peer (eds), *The Reasonable Romantic: Essays on Alessandro Manzoni* (New York: Peter Lang, 1986), 161–77.

Croce, Benedetto, *Alessandro Manzoni: Saggi e discussioni*, 5th edn (Bari: Editori Laterza, 1957; 1st edn 1930).

Davie, Mark, 'Manzoni After 1848: An "Irresolute Utopian"?', *Modern Language Review*, 87 (1992), 847–57.

De Sanctis, Francesco, *Manzoni: Studi e lezioni*, ed. Giovanni Gentile (Bari: Laterza & figli, 1922).

Eckermann, Johann Peter, *Conversations with Goethe*, tr. John Oxenford (London: Dent, 1971).

Entrèves, A. P. d', 'Introduction', to Manzoni, *The Column of Infamy*, ed. Kenelm Foster and Jane Grigson (London: Oxford University Press, 1964).

Ginsburg, Natalia, *La famiglia Manzoni* (Turin: Einaudi editore, 1983).

Gramsci, Antonio, *Prison Notebooks*, iii, ed. and tr. Joseph Buttigieg (New York: Columbia University Press, 2007).

Illiano, Antonio, 'On Manzoni's Disillusionment with Literature', *Forum Italicum*, 24/1 (1990), 111–15.

Jones, Verina R., 'Manzoni's Dark Ladies', *Romance Studies*, 19 (Winter 1991), 37–52.

Jones, Verina R., 'Counter-Reformation and Popular Culture in *I promessi sposi*: A Case of Historical Censorship', *Renaissance and Modern Studies*, 36 (1993), 36–51.

Leach, Nathaniel, 'The Shame of a Nation: Performing History in Schiller, Manzoni and Byron', *European Romantic Review*, 22 (2011), 155–72.

Lukács, Georg, *The Historical Novel*, tr. Hannah and Stanley Mitchell (London: Merlin Press, 1962).

Manzoni, Alessandro (1819), *Osservazioni sulla morale cattolica*, in *Opere varie*, ed. M. Barbi and F. Ghisalberti.

Manzoni, Alessandro (1822), *Discorso sopra alcuni punti della storia longobardica in Italia*, in *Opere varie*, ed. M. Barbi and F. Ghisalberti.

Manzoni, Alessandro (1823, composed 1820), *Lettre à M. C*** sur l'unité de temps et de lieu dans la tragédie*, in *Opere varie*, ed. M. Barbi and F. Ghisalberti.

Manzoni, Alessandro (1828), *Del romanzo storico e, in genere, de' componimenti misti di storia e d'invenzione*, in *Opere varie*, ed. M. Barbi and F. Ghisalberti.

Manzoni, Alessandro, *A Vindication of Catholic morality: or a Refutation of the Charges Brought Against it by Sismondi in his 'History of the Italian republics during the Middle Ages'* (tr. from an 1834 French translation of *Osservazioni sulla morale cattolica*) (London: Keating & Brown, 1836).

Manzoni, Alessandro, *Opere*, 3 vols, ed. M. Barbi and F. Ghisalberti (Milan: Casa del Manzoni, 1942–50).

Manzoni, Alessandro, *I promessi sposi*, in *Opere*, ed. M. Barbi and F. Ghisalberti (Milan: Casa del Manzoni, 1942), i.

Manzoni, Alessandro, *Opere varie*, ed. M. Barbi and F. Ghisalberti (Milan: Casa del Manzoni, 1943), ii.

Manzoni, Alessandro, *I promessi sposi*, ed. Attilio Momigliano (Florence: Sansoni editore, 1951).

Manzoni, Alessandro, *The Column of Infamy*. Prefaced by Cesare Beccaria's *Of Crimes and Punishments*, tr. and ed. Kenelm Foster and Jane Grigson, intro. A. P. d'Entrèves (London: Oxford University Press, 1964).

Manzoni, Alessandro, *On the Historical Novel*, tr. Sandra Bermann (Lincoln, Neb., and London: University of Nebraska Press, 1984).

Manzoni, Alessandro, *The Betrothed and History of the Column of Infamy*, ed. David Forgacs and Matthew Reynolds (London: Dent, 1997).

Manzoni, Alessandro, *Alessandro Manzoni's The Count of Carmagnola and Adelchis*, tr. Federica Brunori Deigan (Baltimore and London: Johns Hopkins University Press, 2004).

Matteo, Sante, and Peer, Larry H. (eds), *The Reasonable Romantic: Essays on Alessandro Manzoni* (New York: Peter Lang, 1986).

Milman, Henry Hart, 'Italian Tragedy', *Quarterly Review*, 24/47 (1820), 72–102.

Parisi, Luciano, *Come abbiamo letto Manzoni: Interpreti novecenteschi* (Alessandria: Edizioni dell'Orso, 2008).

Ragusa, Olga, 'Alessandro Manzoni and Developments in the Historical Novel', in Peter Bondanella and Andrea Ciccarelli (eds), *The Cambridge Companion to the Italian Novel* (Cambridge: Cambridge University Press, 2003), 42–60.

Schlegel, A. W., *A Course of Lectures on Dramatic Art and Literature*, ed. John Black (London: Henry G. Bohn, 1846).

Sciascia, Leonardo, *Cruciverba* (Turin: Einaudi editore, 1983).

Sismondi, J.-C.-L. Simonde de, *Histoire des républiques italiennes du moyen age*, 16 vols (Paris: H. Nicolle (i–viii) and Treuttel & Würtz (ix–xvi), 1809–18).

Squarotti, Giorgio Bárberi, *Il romanzo contro la storia: studi sui 'Promessi sposi'* (Milan: Vita e Pensiero, 1980).

Squarotti, Giorgio Bárberi, *Manzoni: Le delusioni della letteratura* (Rovito: Marra editore, 1988).

Triolo, Franco, 'Manzoni and Providence', in Sante Matteo and Larry H. Peer (eds), *The Reasonable Romantic: Essays on Alessandro Manzoni* (New York: Peter Lang, 1986), 245–57.

Spanish

CHAPTER 25

PERSONAL DEMONS AND THE SPECTRE OF TRADITION IN SPANISH ROMANTIC DRAMA

DEREK FLITTER

ONE thing which emerges as a consistent feature of Spanish Romantic drama, from Larra to Rivas, from Hartzenbusch to Zorrilla, is the contestatory exposition, normally by the male lead, of a radical and challenging prescription for a new understanding of love, life, and the world which is then either defeated by external forces or, more commonly, is mitigated by the mediating figure of the heroine.[1] Larra's Macías preaches natural love à la Rousseau while Elvira, at the same time as she makes a humanitarian rereading of a rigid honour code, remains with traditional religious principles as watchwords of her personal integrity. Rivas's Don Álvaro falls prey to religious scepticism and pays the price, while Leonor seeks old-fashioned atonement and penance for what she comes to regard as her transgressive love. At the heart of García Gutiérrez's *El trovador* is a pivotal dialogue in which the troubadour Manrique insists upon his erotic entitlement in the face of Leonor's profession of religious vows and her consequent moral conflict, and, subsequently, her consciousness that she has placed herself outside the reach of Grace. Hartzenbusch has the male half of the lovers of Teruel seek bloody vengeance while his female other half looks for redemption, not retribution, in Christian Stoicism. Zorrilla's Don Juan is inspired to embrace religion and the spiritual life in place of an existence of unbridled hedonism by the self-sacrificing love of a virtuous woman who speaks from beyond the grave. The emotionally explicit and sentimentally charged world configured on the Spanish Romantic stage, together with the unabashed high rhetoric of much of the plays' textual strategy, means that the internal commotions of their protagonists are enunciated metaphorically but customarily reflected in settings which appear to have been chosen principally for their symbolic resonance. Apart from

[1] For a full contextual introduction to the Spanish stage in the Romantic period, see David T. Gies, *The Theatre in Nineteenth-Century Spain* (Cambridge: Cambridge University Press, 1994), esp. 96–174.

the extravagant paraphernalia employed by Zorrilla, the demons and spectres that represent these commotions are textual ones, part and parcel of the plays' rhetorical fabric that remain within the mind, lexical choices which reveal with considerable intimacy the Romantic psychology of the various characters. At the same time, the demons that plague all of the male protagonists especially may be construed as those of nineteenth-century humanity acutely conscious of its loss of vital certainties, and the metaphorical spectres which can be perceived in the plays are shadows of the past: past orthodoxies, past views of the world, past literary traditions.

Relevant here, it seems to me, are trends prevalent in the narratives of Spanish historiography roughly contemporaneous with the various plays' performance, trends which I have examined in considerable detail elsewhere.[2] The choice of historical setting in Spanish Romantic drama, although sometimes anachronistic, is rarely neutral; modern concerns are dramatized within much earlier historical periods, principally within the Middle Ages. In this sense, playwrights and historians of the Romantic period in Spain employ comparable approaches: historians frequently read past events consciously transposing onto those events issues which have intellectual currency for their own generation, while Romantic dramatists superimpose on a deliberately chosen and often remote past the anxieties and uncertainties of their own day. In the most general terms, we shall see something of a common denominator here: a tension between contemporary questioning and Spanish Catholic tradition. Outside of the theatre, Espronceda's student of Salamanca, who suffers his ghastly demise at the hands of the spectre of the past (his past abandoned love, a past Calderónian play in the form of *El mágico prodigioso*, and uncompromising theocentric history) is a good example. We might regard Zorrilla's *Don Juan Tenorio*, the grand culminating phenomenon within Spanish Romantic theatre, as a play founded on a particularly famous centuries-old legend but emphatically conditioned by its own age, particularly by the prior development of Romantic drama in Spain in the most recent decade. Zorrilla attempts to square the circle of conflicts emerging from the previous plays in a bravura *deus ex machina* ending that seals the triumph of Romanticism over Enlightenment rationalism while sublimating and revising history, literary or otherwise.[3]

It might seem paradoxical that in Spain Romanticism, while stressing its own modernity, rarely uses contemporary settings: none of the canonical plays is set in their writer's own age, while narrative poetry was almost exclusively medieval in its elected backdrop and the dominant preference in prose fiction was for the historical novel. It is not difficult to account for this: the Schlegelian Romanticism which had come, over the twenty years prior to the appearance of the first original Romantic plays on the Spanish stage, to be very widely understood, virtually unanimously understood, as an effective template

[2] See my *Spanish Romanticism and the Uses of History: Ideology and the Historical Imagination* (London: MHRA Legenda, 2006).

[3] For an overall view, see Juan Luis Alborg, *Historia de la literatura española*, iv. *El romanticismo* (Madrid: Gredos, 1980); Leonardo Romero Tobar, *Panorama crítico del romanticismo español* (Madrid: Castalia, 1994).

for the new style of writing, was based on a fundamental *binomio* between Ancient and Modern in which the modern age was considered to have begun in, and quintessentially to belong to, the Middle Ages.[4] The closest thing to a model for Spanish prose writing of the Romantic kind was Walter Scott: not the Scott of the majority of his fiction located around the time of the 1745 rebellion but the Scott of *Ivanhoe* and, ironically, the narrative verse. In historical study the reclaiming of the Middle Ages in the face of perceived Enlightenment prejudice comes to be a keynote element, abundantly clear in all of the five general histories of Spain appearing in the decade of the 1840s.

Although Martínez de la Rosa's designated 'drama histórico' *La conjuración de Venecia, año de 1310*, premiered in Madrid in April 1834,[5] is more often seen as a 'transitional' play that points the way forward to later full-blooded Romanticism, it comes close to creating, on a number of levels, a paradigm for the plays which were to follow. It is set squarely in the Middle Ages, its hero Rugiero is an outsider of mysterious origins whose marginality is a barrier to the desired public consummation by marriage of his love (though here as elsewhere he is eventually discovered to be of noble birth, and, in Martínez de la Rosa's drama, married in secret) in conflict with an overweening traditional form of authority by which he is vanquished and, in this case, executed. What is missing from this play, when we come to compare it with its successors, are the rhetorical emphases that are more commonly found in later Romantic drama: the hero plagued by obsessive demons and the note of metaphysical protest that informs his defiance of authority (the direct cause of his arrest and execution is his involvement in a political conspiracy). One might argue that the spectre of tradition indeed looms large, as Rugiero is unwittingly condemned to death by his own father, who discovers his parentage too late to retract, just as Nuño, in *El trovador*, does not realize until too late that he is responsible for the death by decapitation of his own long-lost brother.

Larra's *Macías*, which came to the stage in October 1834, will be seen to foreground much more clearly the issues which I have outlined in my introduction. Again some preliminary considerations are relevant. First, Larra's education in Enlightenment principles made the choice of medieval setting for his play less of a natural choice: his dramatization of the personal history of the troubadour 'Macías el enamorado' is usually seen as the reflection of his own situation and an obsessive determining factor in his election of subject.[6] In addition, Larra famously declared, in the 'Dos palabras' prefacing the published edition, that his play could by no means be considered 'un drama romántico';[7] the specific indication on the page of the cast list is that the action is encompassed by events of a single January day in 1406, and located entirely within the palace of Don Enrique de Villena in Andújar, making its adherence to the Aristotelian prescriptions of

[4] See my study *Spanish Romantic Literary Theory and Criticism* (Cambridge: Cambridge University Press, 1992).

[5] The play had originally been published in Paris in 1830, which at least in part accounts for its transitional nature.

[6] See the section 'El drama personal de Larra' in Luis Lorenzo-Rivero and George P. Mansour's edn of the play (Madrid: Espasa-Calpe, 1990), 11–20.

[7] Larra, *Macías*, ed. Lorenzo-Rivero and Mansour, 70.

time and place complete. Thirdly, Larra's hero is not of noble birth, not even unexpectedly so; in the author's words, 'Macías es un hombre que ama, y nada más'.[8] Not only does Macías have no social standing but we see nothing of his artistic status either, as his troubadour pedigree is never evidenced textually. What we begin to see in Larra's play, notwithstanding, is a ferocious articulation of the centrality of love against all other social and religious factors, the transposition to a different age of modern issues and motifs, and the eventual defeat and death of the protagonist at the hands of an overshadowing tradition.

From the very start, Macías is regarded as an unsuitable potential husband, and the heroine Elvira's father Nuño Hernández is seen to favour the rival pretensions of the villainous Fernán Pérez, wealthy and of higher rank. Elvira, meanwhile, is presented from her first appearance as what will be the archetypal Romantic heroine, passionate and unconditionally committed. In Scene 2 of Act 1, the extremity of her language, communicated by the exclamation marks that accompany all of her initial words—'¡Suerte fiera!', '¿No he de llorar, ¡desdichada!',[9] and '¡Ah! ¿Cómo oculto el afán que el corazón me devora?' ('Oh, brutal fortune!', 'And shall I not weep in my wretchedness?', 'Oh, how can I conceal this yearning that is eating away my heart?')—and Larra's stage directions—(*Con dolor*), (*Contristada*), (*Violentándose*) (painfully, sorrowfully, doing violence to herself)[10]—leave us in no doubt.[11] Elvira is torn apart by the anxiety that Macías will not return as promised, and that she will therefore have no option but to marry his rival: 'si ya no vuelve Macías, | y dentro de pocos días | por mi palabra empeñada | vendrá Fernán Pérez' (if Macías should not return, | then in a few short days | and according to my given word | Fernán Pérez must come).[12] Here, then, is what comes to be a recurring feature in Spanish Romantic drama: the heroine agonizingly torn between a parental authority and a social obligation that are at war with personal feeling. The same pattern will be found in *Don Álvaro* and *Los amantes de Teruel*, and its variations in *El trovador* and *Don Juan Tenorio* will merely possess the complicating factor of bringing God into the equation.

Elvira's demons, then, are unleashed by Larra in Act 1. The intensity of her emotional persona needs to be convincing, as audience or reader will be required to accept that she immediately marries Fernán Pérez on the same day, erroneously believing in Macías's treachery; she has in fact been deliberately duped. Again we are confronted with a stock feature of Romanticism, found in Scott's *The Bride of Lammermoor* and Donizetti's grand opera on the same subject, for example. The predicament of the lovers is most forcefully shown, perhaps, by the unmistakable Romantic *coup de théâtre*: the returning

[8] *Macías*, ed. Lorenzo-Rivero and Mansour, 70.

[9] *Macías*, ed. Lorenzo-Rivero and Mansour, 87–8.

[10] *Macías*, ed. Lorenzo-Rivero and Mansour, 90–1.

[11] See Susan Kirkpatrick, 'Liberal Romanticism and the Female Protagonist in *Macías*', *Romance Quarterly*, 35 (1988), 51–8.

[12] *Macías*, ed. Lorenzo-Rivero and Mansour, 88.

Macías arrives just too late to prevent Elvira's marriage and, having forced his way into the palace, he raises the visor of his helmet to disclose his face as she passes him on her way out of the wedding ceremony at the end of Act 2. García Gutiérrez would use precisely the same theatrical device in *El trovador*, with the difference that Leonor has just become the bride of Christ by taking the veil.

The middle of Act 3 of Larra's play, meanwhile, sees the acting out of a pattern that will be repeated, with the aforementioned variant in *El trovador* but rather more closely in *Los amantes de Teruel*: the uncomprehending hero rebuking the heroine for her perceived perfidy (the word is especially appropriate) and emphasizing the primacy of love above all other considerations, and the latter placed in the traditional casuistic dilemma of the woman married to one man while loving another. In Romantic drama the hero's position is as blindingly clear as it is uncompromising, and the heroine's adherence to inherited sacramental values tested against the 'religion' of love. In Larra's drama, Macías's words seem to brook no contradiction:

> Rompe, aniquila
> esos, que contrajiste, horribles lazos.
> Los amantes son solos los esposos.
> Su lazo es el amor: ¿cuál hay más santo?[13]
>
> Break, destroy | the fearful contract you have made. | Lovers alone are groom and bride. | Their contract is that of love: what more sacred can there be?

Elvira's reply, on the other hand, reveals the ultimate subjugation of love to a more far-reaching moral authority:

> Juré ser de otro dueño, y al recato,
> y a mi nombre también y a Dios le debo
> sufrir mi suerte con valor, y en llanto
> el tálamo regar; si no dichosa,
> honrada moriré.[14]
>
> I swore myself to another, and to modesty, | to my reputation and to God I owe it | valiantly to bear my fate, and in tears | to water the marriage bed; if not happy | then honourable shall I die.

The respective views are as resounding as they are, in the light of later plays, paradigmatic: for Macías love for Elvira, independent of all other obligations, is what is most sacred, and her marriage vows constrain and pinion her instinctive feeling in ways that are unnatural; Macías's speech in its entirety reveals the clear imprint of Rousseau here, and

[13] *Macías*, ed. Lorenzo-Rivero and Mansour, 163.
[14] *Macías*, ed. Lorenzo-Rivero and Mansour, 164.

makes unnerving reading as voiced by an early fifteenth-century troubadour.[15] Elvira's reply is predicated on a much more traditional order of things: she has acquired a master in the form of her husband, and has sworn herself to him in terms that cannot be gainsaid; the imperative is to live the rest of her life in honour if in sorrow, and her obligation to God is to suffer that sorrow with fortitude and resilience. It is, in short, the Christian Stoic solution. If we move briefly ahead, we note insistent parallels in the plays by García Gutiérrez and Hartzenbusch. In Act 3, Scene 5, of *El trovador*, the pivotal dialogue acquires almost identical terms: Manrique tells Leonor that although she has taken religious vows she is irrevocably his, exclaiming: 'Vengo a salvarte, a quebrantar osado | los grillos que te oprimen, a estrecharte | en mi seno, de amor enajenado' ('I come to save you, audaciously to break | the shackles that bind you, to hold you close | to my breast, in love's delirium').[16] Her reply stands equally close comparison with the response of Elvira:

> Ya no puede
> ser tuya esta infeliz; nunca ... mi vida,
> aunque llena de horror y de amargura,
> ya consagrada está, y eternamente,
> en las aras de un Dios omnipotente.[17]

> This unhappy woman | can never now be yours ... my life, | though filled with bitter horror, | is already pledged, eternally, | at the altar of an almighty God.

Act 5, Scene 3, of Hartzenbusch's play, the only scene shared by Marsilla and Isabel, again strikes the same insistent note. Marsilla gives ultimate primacy to love, declaring: 'nada respeta quien bien ama. | Todo el amante fiel lo sacrifica | en el altar del numen que idolatra' ('He who loves well respects nothing. | The faithful lover sacrifices all | at the altar of his worshipped deity');[18] like Macías he loads traditionally religious words onto a love that stands outside of the sacramental by being, with her now married, adulterous and transgressive. Isabel's reply is once more steadfast in adversity, meanwhile, as she tells him:

> Ya lo ves, no soy mía, soy de un hombre
> que me hace de su amor depositaria.
> Deslindar sus derechos es en vano:
> yo debo serle fiel, Dios me lo manda.[19]

[15] See Javier Herrero, 'Romantic Theology: Love, Death and the Beyond', in John R. Rosenberg (ed.), *Resonancias románticas: Evocaciones del romanticismo hispánico en el sesquicentenario de la muerte de Mariano José de Larra* (Madrid: José Porrúa, 1988), 1–20.

[16] Antonio García Gutiérrez, *El trovador*, ed. Carlos Ruiz Silva (Madrid: Cátedra, 1997), 152.

[17] *El trovador*, ed. Ruiz Silva, 153.

[18] Juan Eugenio Hartzenbusch, *Los amantes de Teruel*, ed. Salvador García Castañeda (Madrid: Castalia, 1971), 147.

[19] Hartzenbusch, *Los amantes de Teruel*, ed. García Castañeda, 148–9.

> You must see it, I am not my own, but owned by a man | who has deposited his love in me. | Vainly can I trespass on his claims: | I must be faithful to him, as God commands me.

Just like Elvira, Isabel explicitly states that with marriage her husband has acquired over her rights that cannot be circumvented, as they are God-given. Her obligation (she uses the verb 'deber') is to keep that faith.

The three plays contain variants and nuances, of course, in dialogues that are much more substantial than the quotations suggest, but the essential tension is the same. The all-encompassing, obsessive degree of the hero's love is so absolute that in his mind it overrides all other obligations, which each of them refuses to countenance. The heroine will not compromise her traditional integrity, on the other hand, and her ultimate reliance resides with the authority of inherited tradition.

Each of the female figures, however, herself acts in ways that provide the plays with an extra dimension. In *Macías*, Elvira will not elope adulterously with the eponymous hero, but she does internally revise the honour code so as to take due account of instinctive humanity and natural justice: she employs the material signs of her more elevated status, her jewels, as bribes to attempt to secure Macías's escape from confinement, and thus places limits on her obligations to Fernán Pérez. In this way, Larra is effectively reworking what ought to be, in fifteenth-century terms, a rigid and unyielding moral code that exerts primacy even in the face of what seems to be morally just.

The full significance of the triumph of an overshadowing traditional order in *Macías*, though, only emerges when we make sense of the ending of the play. When Macías and Elvira are surprised by Fernán as she attempts to aid the former's escape, and after Macías has been fatally stabbed, Elvira commits suicide, placing herself in a deliberate act, by this final choice, outside of Grace. Her husband's words, with which the play concludes, are an apparently successful move to restore his own honour and to claim the justification of an intransigent honour code. Fernán, thinking adroitly at the imminent arrival on stage of others, says simply: 'Me vendían. | Ya se lavó en su sangre mi deshonra' ('They were betraying me. I have washed away the stain on my honour with their blood').[20] The words immediately recall, to Spanish audience and reader, the male entitlement that accompanies the traditional honour code, an entitlement which extends to the punishment by death of the adulterous wife; Calderón's wife-murder play *El medico de su honra* springs to mind both instinctively and textually. Fernán, in claiming to have murdered Elvira as well as Macías, is acting to shore up his personal social esteem when that esteem is threatened by what would amount to apocalyptic disaster: the widespread knowledge that his wife had committed suicide for love of another man.

As we move on from Larra's play to those less equivocally belonging to the Romantic canon, it is worth noting first that a pattern has begun to emerge, and, secondly, the component parts of what will be the characteristic Romantic set of antagonistic circumstances.

[20] *Macías*, ed. Lorenzo-Rivero and Mansour, 217.

Rivas's play, designated on the advertising playbills distributed before its first performance in 1835 as 'románticamente romántco', was the theatrical work apparently best placed to enshrine what Romanticism meant in the theatre. It moves on the largest possible level, moreover, its metanarrative coming to be predicated on final human destiny, with signposted religious dimensions: we go from Don Álvaro's initial words on his arrival to elope with Leonor, '¿Van ya los santos cielos | a dar corona eterna a mis desvelos?' ('Are finally the sacred heavens | to reward my tribulations with an eternal crown?') in Act 1, Scene 7,[21] in which a provident God is evoked in words that recall the vision experienced by John the Divine in chapter 2 of Revelation, to the apocalyptic ending redolent with the imagery and phrasing of Armageddon in the 'Escena última'.

Within the context I have been establishing here, several things seem significant. First, Rivas's drama is located, elusively but very specifically, in the 1740s, the decade in which the *Encyclopédie* edited by Diderot and D'Alembert began to be published. Don Álvaro's fall into religious scepticism can therefore be read as the potential disintegration of traditional Spanish society itself under the weight of widespread rationalism. The old order is wavering, as might be suggested of the impoverished traditional aristocracy represented by the Marqués de Calatrava, whose country estate reveals '*los adornos que se estilaban en el siglo XVIII, pero todo deteriorado*' ('those adornments in typical eighteenth-century vogue, but all in disrepair'), the stage direction to Act 1, Scene 5, indicates.[22] Secondly, Don Álvaro himself is the outsider whose view of the world is seemingly founded on his own sense of marginalization: 'el indiano' who has no acceptable pedigree has reminiscences of Martínez de la Rosa's mysterious orphan Rugiero, who like Rivas's protagonist is really of noble parentage, and of Larra's *doncel*, who is not. In Rivas's play, the role of Don Álvaro as an outsider doomed to suffering is bastioned textually by Preciosilla's reading of his catastrophic destiny in the lines of his hand and by his own self-conscious reference from an early point in time to 'mi adversa estrella' ('this adverse star of mine').[23] Thirdly, Rivas presents us with two divergent responses to the tragedy of the Marqués's death, one of which is acutely radical and the other profoundly traditional.

Don Álvaro's prioritization of love over religious reliance—his view of his own ultimate salvation or damnation is attributable to the constancy or otherwise of Leonor, as '¿Te complaces | en levantarme al trono del Eterno | para después hundirme en el infierno?' ('Would it please you | to raise me to the throne of Heaven | to bury me afterwards in Hell?') makes clear[24]—is what leads inexorably to his abandonment of faith and to the ferocity of the celebrated soliloquy in Act 3, Scene 3. What Don Álvaro signally fails to do is to accept moral accountability in line with religious teaching, so that he regards

[21] Duque de Rivas, *Don Álvaro o la fuerza del sino*, ed. Alberto Sánchez (Madrid, Cátedra, 1980), 67.

[22] *Don Álvaro o la fuerza del sino*, ed. Sánchez, 59.

[23] *Don Álvaro o la fuerza del sino*, ed. Sánchez, 67.

[24] *Don Álvaro o la fuerza del sino*, ed. Sánchez, 70. See my '*Don Álvaro*: Notes pour une lecture eschatologique', in Derek Fliiter, Luis F. Díaz Larios, and Georges Zaragoza (eds), *Don Álvaro* et le drame romantique espagnol (Dijon: Les éditions du Murmure, 2003), 41–60.

destiny, not his actions, as having caused the death of the Marqués, referring even in Act 4, Scene 1, to 'la desgracia inevitable | de que no fui yo culpable' ('the inevitable tragedy | for which I bear no blame').[25] This contrasts sharply with the response of Leonor, over whom looms much more entirely the weight of tradition. This is evidenced with considerable clarity in Act 2, Scene 3, where Leonor expresses her determination: 'el furor expiaré de mis pasiones' ('I shall atone for the fury of my passion') intimating that she believes her love for Don Álvaro to have been a sinful love and her need to seek atonement a moral imperative,[26] and informs the totality of her dialogue with Padre Guardián in Act 2, Scene 7. Leonor's deeply conservative solution is irresistibly founded, textually, on the paradigm of Job, while Don Álvaro is shown not to possess the fortitude to suffer stoically the reversals of personal fortune. The spectre of past tradition, however, also makes itself felt in less ostensible ways. After failing to achieve a recognized place in the aristocracy, Don Álvaro essays first the officer corps of the army and then the church, in neither of which does he find lasting integration. More elusively, one might say that the most significant thing of all in Rivas's play, nonetheless, is that Don Álvaro is never moved to atheism. When he rationalizes with increasing mental instability the reverses which life has thrown in his way, it is either to rail against God (rather than to read his catastrophic experience as proof of God's non-existence), or else to express his apocalyptic suicidal gesture in words that relate very directly to the destruction of the world contained in Revelation. Don Álvaro is always conscious of the repercussions of his struggle with his personal demons, their ultimate consequences indelibly marked by religious rhetoric, whether that rhetoric be providential or apocalyptic.

There is, it seems to me, manifest justification for this. As I have argued elsewhere, it is just as conscionable to read *Don Álvaro o la fuerza del sino* as a drama cautioning against religious scepticism and the erosion of faith as it is to view it as a protest play: who is to say that the eponymous hero functions as the playwright's spokesman, especially when the stance adopted by Leonor is given first and is unequivocally framed as the response expected of the traditional believer? Where Rivas's play takes us in the present context enables significant parallels to be drawn with Larra's *Macías*: a situation in which the protagonist explicitly shows love to be his most fundamental guiding principle and yardstick, the necessary questioning and turmoil resulting from that primacy, his ultimate defeat, and the counterbalancing prescriptions adduced by the dramatic heroine. The solution to personal woe, in the case of Elvira as much as in that of Leonor, and whether or not that solution will be workable or definitive, lies in religious observance and commitment.

The same patterning is seen to dominate the most popular Spanish Romantic drama, in terms of performances: that is, Antonio García Gutiérrez's *El trovador*, premiered in March 1836. Here at last was an original Romantic drama written by a young man who seemed more closely to resemble the paradigmatic 'romántico' depicted by Eugenio de Ochoa in the pages of *El Artista* than had been Larra, educated largely in

[25] *Don Álvaro o la fuerza del sino*, ed. Sánchez, 129.

[26] *Don Álvaro o la fuerza del sino*, ed. Sánchez, 86.

France and a child of the Enlightenment, or Rivas, who was close to 50 at the time of the first performance of his best-known drama and who had made a reputation as a neoclassical playwright.[27] The acclaim given to García Gutiérrez at the end of the first performance simply confirms Romantic drama as an exciting and sentimental new phenomenon which enabled unschooled and untried young men of genius to be lionized by a theatre-going public captivated by emotional experience. Leonor's words expressing the quasi-mystical effect of Manrique's song, 'una celeste ilusión | me abrasó de amor el alma' ('a heavenly vision | inflamed my soul with love'),[28] intimate textually the effect of Romanticism upon sensitive and self-consciously sentimental readers and audiences desiring transcendent experience through a sublime new literature. Galdós would render the point transparently clear in the recounting by his fictional character Pilar de Loaysa, of the sensational emotional effects of the first performance of García Gutiérrez's play in *De Oñate a La Granja*.

Nonetheless, *El trovador* is quickly seen to have much in common with its predecessors. Guillén's scathing words to Leonor in Act 1, Scene 2, 'Poco estimáis, Leonor, | el brillo de vuestra cuna | menospreciando al de Luna | por un simple trovador' ('You think little, Leonor, | of the brilliance of your birth | when you despise the Count of Luna | in favour of a mere troubadour'),[29] stand comparison with Nuño's words to his daughter Elvira in *Macías*: 'Mas, ¿qué bienes | son los suyos, Elvira? ¿Caballero | y no más? Hombre de armas, o soldado? | ¿Mal trovador, o simple aventurero?' ('But what assets | are his, Elvira? A knight | and no more? A warrior, or soldier? | A wretched troubadour, or mere adventurer?').[30] Not just this; Manrique, like Macías, is struggling within his own mind against the moral injustice of competing with a social superior while believing himself of equal worth. García Gutiérrez's presentation of Manrique as the son of a gypsy makes the social disparity appear more violent and extreme, one of many ways in which the young playwright seems bent on outdoing his predecessors; this is one of the anachronisms of the play, gypsies not having arrived in Aragón until after the date in which the drama is set. Another factor relevant here is the nature of the sacramental obstacle which Manrique must seek to circumvent: in Larra's play, it is marriage to a rival; in *El trovador*, Leonor, when Manrique confronts her as Macías had Elvira, is the bride of Christ. García Gutiérrez, at every juncture, underlines the enormity of the barriers which love has to confront, and the momentous nature of the consequential choices. He does not go so far as to have Leonor consciously and willingly leave her convent with the troubadour, who carries her off in a swoon, but her displacement from the spiritual world to that of the sacrilegiously erotic has, as she makes utterly clear in Act 4, Scene 5, placed her irrevocably outside of the reach of divine grace, and definitively damned:

[27] Eugenio de Ochoa, 'Un romántico', *El Artista* (1835); reproduced in *El romanticismo español: Documentos*, ed. Ricardo Navas-Ruiz (Salamanca: Anaya, 1971), 128–31.

[28] *El trovador*, ed. Ruiz Silva, 122.

[29] *El trovador*, ed. Ruiz Silva, 117.

[30] *Macías*, ed. Lorenzo-Rivero and Mansour, 101.

¿Esposa yo de Dios? No puedo serlo;
jamás, nunca lo fui ... Tengo un amante
que me adora sin fin, y yo le adoro,
que no puedo olvidar sólo un instante.
Ya con eternos vínculos el crimen
a su suerte me unió ... nudo funesto,
nudo de maldición que allá en su trono
enojado maldice un Dios terrible.[31]

A bride of God? I cannot be that; | I never was nor am ... I have a lover | who adores me forever, as I adore him. | cannot forget him for a moment. | Vice has, with bonds that are eternal, | linked my destiny to his ... fateful bonds. | an accursed bond that far off upon his throne | a terrible God has cursed in anger.

García Gutiérrez pulls no punches here in a display of rhetorical tour de force: the sworn vow of an 'esposa de Dios' has been rejected for the sake of 'un amante'; the lover attracts words drawn from a religious lexicon, as here 'adorar' (this has been systematically placed on display from the time of Leonor's important soliloquy in Act 3, Scene 4); Leonor is prey to the unremitting consciousness not just of having sinned, like her namesake of Rivas's drama who can still seek atonement, but of ineluctably having condemned herself to hell and attracted, by the perpetration of a morally criminal act, the curse of a vengeful God that may never be gainsaid. The spectre of traditional orthodoxy must now haunt her every step.

García Gutiérrez's heroine is unquestionably the most radical of the whole of Spanish Romantic drama. In a state not just of adulterous but openly sacrilegious love with her beloved, she takes the premeditated step of poisoning herself in order to free him from Nuño's clutches, an attempt that must, it goes without saying, be doomed to fail; the premeditation of the act, what is more, goes beyond even the suicide, *in extremis*, of Larra's Elvira. In fact, *El trovador* reaches its most daring when, after Leonor has died, Manrique dedicates to her a secular *trova* in lines that have manifest iconographical overtones. He will sing, he says, of Leonor's virtue, while, he declares: 'Una corona de flores | dadme también; en su frente | será aureola luciente, | sera diadema de amores' ('A crown of flowers | give me too; upon her brow | it shall be a shining ring of light, | it shall be a diadem of love').[32] The image of the Blessed Virgin, clothed in gold and crowned with stars, underlies the figure of the dead Leonor, her head framed by a gleaming halo and wearing a crown of human love.[33]

What we have seen up to this point, however, is little sign of redemption of any kind. Spanish Romantic drama has exalted human love and defied traditional authority,

[31] *El trovador*, ed. Ruiz Silva, 167.

[32] *El trovador*, ed. Ruiz Silva, 195.

[33] See Derek Flitter, 'Spanish Romanticism', in Michael Ferber (ed.), *A Companion to European Romanticism* (Oxford: Blackwell, 2005), 276–92.

but no meaningful attempt has been made to reconcile the two. What Hartzenbusch's *Los amantes de Teruel* sets out to do, and what Zorrilla's *Don Juan Tenorio* definitively accomplishes in its textual fabric, is to posit a vital solution.

At the start of Hartzenbusch's play, Isabel finds herself comparably placed to Larra's Elvira: awaiting the return of the man she loves while coming under increasing pressure, initially patriarchal pressure, to marry elsewhere. Act 2, Scene 6, her crucial long dialogue with her mother Margarita, crystallizes many of the most salient issues. We might detail the imperatives of the thirteenth-century world in Margarita's simple logic: 'Prendarse de quien le cuadre | no es lícito a una doncella, | pues entonces atropella | los derechos de su padre' ('To form an attachment to the man of your choice | is illicit in a well-born maiden, | for she thus tramples upon | her father's rights'), and the telling use of the active verb in 'Hoy día, Isabel, así | se conciertan nuestras bodas; | así nos casan a todas, | y así me han casado a mí' ('Today, Isabel, it is thus | our marriages are contracted; | it is thus that they marry us all, | and thus they have married me').[34] This is a dialogue between conservatism and rebellion, between an older woman entirely observant of conventional obligations and a younger woman inflamed by a passion that brooks no contradiction. Isabel's demons are metaphorically present in her response, where obedience to parental authority is subordinate to the dictates of a love which represents true faith: '¿Y podréis sin inquietud | sacrificarme a un abuso, | lazo pérfido que puso | el infierno a la virtud? ('And can you, without a care | sacrifice me to this abuse, | a perfidious bond placed | by hell itself on virtue?').[35] Isabel effects the by now customary dislocation of religious discourse from the world of conformity into that of the amorous imperative.

Los amantes de Teruel reflects the patterning established here in numerous other ways. When Marsilla returns to Teruel too late to prevent Isabel's marriage, he finds himself in the same position faced by Macías and one analogous also to that of Manrique after his failure to prevent Leonor taking the veil. Marsilla attributes his unhappiness to divine malevolence, and more or less precisely recreates the furious protest of Rivas's Don Álvaro: his line from Scene 4 of the second part of Act 4, 'No hay un amor, no hay Isabel, no hay nada' ('There is no love, no Isabel, there is nothing'),[36] is memorable for the definitive clarity of its unadorned sentimental logic. More striking is the rhetorical intensity of

> Potestades
> del mal, a quienes Dios para juguete
> me quiso dar, reid, ya conseguisteis
> llevar hasta su fin mi desventura.
> Solemnizad, espíritus dañados,
> mi desesperación. Tus calabozos
> ábreme, infierno[37]

[34] Hartzenbusch, *Los amantes de Teruel*, ed. García Castañeda, 78–9.
[35] Hartzenbusch, *Los amantes de Teruel*, ed. García Castañeda, 79.
[36] Hartzenbusch, *Los amantes de Teruel*, ed. García Castañeda, 135.
[37] Hartzenbusch, *Los amantes de Teruel*, ed. García Castañeda, 135.

> Powers | of evil, to whom God as a plaything | has chosen to give me, laugh out loud, you have now succeeded | in bringing my misfortune to its close. | Put your stamp, foul spirits, | on my despair. Your dungeons | open to me, o hell

which would seem consciously to rival the declamatory lines of Don Álvaro at the end of Rivas's play. Both dramas evoke their respective heroes' demons in concentrated graphic form.

While Marsilla, though, continues to enunciate a powerful sense of entitlement that, in his mind, overrides conventional sacramental obligations, as we have already seen, Isabel enters into a compassionate inner dialogue with a merciful God articulated in Act 5, Scene 2, her rhetoric belonging unquestionably to the discourse of Christian Stoicism:

> ¿No es cierto, Dios mío,
> que ya satisfecha
> con tantos afanes
> tu justicia queda?
> ¿Que, ya fenecido
> el tiempo de prueba
> que a mí y a Marsilla
> prescrito nos fuera,
> nos luce la aurora
> de la recompensa?
> Sí, desde ese trono
> Donde tu grandeza
> Sobre serafines
> Las plantas asienta,
> Benévolo miras
> Las lágrimas nuestras,
> Y al ángel de muerte
> Que rompa le ordenas
> El arca de barro
> Que al alma encarcela.[38]

> Is it not true, My God, | that, after so many sufferings, | your justice is accomplished? | That the time of trial | allotted to me and to Marsilla | is now ended, | and that we see the light | of dawn of our reward? | Truly, from that throne | where in your majesty | you rest your feet | upon the Seraphim, | you look benevolently | upon our tears,/of the angel of death | you demand he break | the vessels of clay | that imprison our souls.

These lines comprise, in effect, a roll-call of the salient components of Stoicism as applied to the Christian faith: suffering in life as a trial, a period of tribulation that may be overcome

[38] Hartzenbusch, *Los amantes de Teruel*, ed. García Castañeda, 142–3.

by faith so that the soul attains its divine reward.[39] In the case of Hartzenbusch's play, it is hardly surprising that a thirteenth-century woman of gentle birth should reveal an intimate reliance on religious faith at such a critical moment in her life. On a historical plane, meanwhile, it was the conscious application of just such a philosophy which, according to the Enlightenment-entailed emphases of nineteenth-century Spanish liberalism, had enabled the Catholic Church to perpetuate the moral enslavement of the people.

Hartzenbusch, however, nuances that tradition in an ending that is clearly meant to provide some kind of solution. In the face of Marsilla's demands in Act 5, Scene 3, Isabel tells him, redirecting the concept of virtue and viewing their love as sacred, 'Marsilla, virtuosos hemos sido | hasta aquí; la pasión que nos inflama | es una virtud más: ¿por qué pretendes | en la última prueba profanarla?' ('Marsilla, we have been virtuous | until now; the passion that inflames us | is one virtue more: | why strive | at this last test to profane it?').[40] This strives to configure love for Marsilla and marital obligation as coexistent rather than mutually exclusive, and the ending of the play, which contains death without violence (the first time in one of the canonical Spanish Romantic plays that either of the chief protagonists had avoided violent death), functions as an explicit attempt at reconciliation: the human embrace and the suppliant attitude of prayer are conjoined in the final stage direction, which reads '(*Arrójase sobre el cuerpo de don Diego, y expira quedando de rodillas abrazada con él.*)' ('She throws herself upon the body of Don Diego, and dies on her knees in his embrace').

There are manifest theological problems here, quite aside of the challenge to verisimilitude: if audiences were minded to accept that both hero and heroine could die almost instantaneously in a sentimental form of internal combustion, then they still confronted the exorcizing of tradition by a recourse to a God whose beneficence would extend to sanctioning and rewarding in the afterlife a love that had become adulterous. It is hardly surprising that Hartzenbusch should crucially amend the explicit suggestion of that final stage direction in his reworked version of 1849 to read '(*Dirígese adonde está el cadaver de Marsilla; pero antes de llegar, cae sin aliento con los brazos tendidos hacia su amante.*)' ('She steps towards Marsilla's corpse; but before she can reach it she falls and expires, her arms thrown out towards her lover)').[41] Less surprising, perhaps, that Larra, in his final theatre review before committing suicide, should have defended the complicated and in many ways unconvincing reconciliation of Hartzenbusch's ending via an appeal to the same sentimental logic in professing 'Las teorías, las doctrinas, los sistemas se esplican; los sentimientos se sienten' ('Theories, doctrines, systems can be explained; feelings are felt').[42]

Hartzenbusch, then, nuances literary tradition while unquestionably writing under its shadow. José Zorrilla, in his *Don Juan Tenorio* of 1844, in order to create an ultimate

[39] See my article 'The Romantic Theology of *Los amantes de Teruel*', *Crítica Hispánica*, 18 (1996), 25–34.

[40] Hartzenbusch, *Los amantes de Teruel*, ed. García Castañeda, 149.

[41] Hartzenbusch, *Los amantes de Teruel* (1849), ed. Carmen Iranzo (Madrid: Cátedra, 1989), 166.

[42] Reproduced in Hartzenbusch, *Los amantes de Teruel*, ed. García Castañeda, 166–73 (173).

reconciliation, effectively overthrows one of Spain's most enduring cultural traditions; Hartzenbusch timidly tinkers, at the end of the day, while Zorrilla much more boldly revises with conscious intentionality. The latter had, of course, acquired a reputation as 'el poeta nacional', as the contemporary writer whose work was most firmly embedded in tradition; it is therefore ironic that he is the playwright who most startlingly turns that tradition upon its head. Perhaps what has received undue attention in this categorically canonical play is the extent to which it might be read textually as a spiritual response to pervasive rationalism, as a Catholic Romanticism overturning Enlightenment prescription.

Zorrilla's famed facility for versification is resiliently displayed in *Don Juan Tenorio*, but so also is the presence, within the play's quite formulaic symbolism and linguistic texture, of an integration, a coherence, an attention to detail, that makes the playwright's consciously diffident claim to have written his drama within a week as one which barely withstands even the most cursory scrutiny. The location of the first part of the play within Carnival, and for many reasons one is tempted more precisely to say the last day of Carnival, *martes de carnestolendas*, is especially calculated to enable its reading as the swansong of the legendary Don Juan's careless hedonism and his approximation to the realm of the spiritual, his apprehension of the metaphysical.

Key here, it seems to me, is the role of Don Luis, the shadow of the eponymous hero, a man whose every word and gesture, whose every immoral feat, functions as a foil to Don Juan in Act 1 of Zorrilla's play. It is Don Luis who is given the first meaningful soliloquy, in Act 2, Scene 3, where he voices anxiety as to the latter's vow to seduce his betrothed on the eve of their marriage. His words here, 'no sé que vago | presentimiento, qué estrago | teme mi alma acongojada' ('I know not what vague | premonition, what harm | my soul in turmoil fears'),[43] appear incongruous from a character whose immorality and licentiousness rival that of Don Juan himself. Less surprising, however, when we come to realize that a linguistic pattern is being established here, in which the world of the tangible and material, the assiduously related sphere of the carnal which they both inhabit, is a rational world whose prescriptions are systematically to be undermined: hence 'vago presentimiento', hence 'alma acongojada', hence the timorousness confessed by the man who has previously feared nothing. Just as telling is the admission, within the intimacy of the monologue, of '¡Por Dios que nunca pensé | que a doña Ana amara así | ni por ninguna sentí | lo que por ella … !' ('By God I never thought | I could love Doña Ana in this way | and never felt for any woman | what I feel for her … !')[44] Is genuine love to intrude into the life of the shamelessly amoral, and if into that of Don Luis, why not into that of Don Juan?

This soliloquy prefigures, I would contend, the intimation of love that is contained in Don Juan's seemingly unpromising meeting with Brígida in Act 2, Scene 9.[45] Don Juan's

[43] José Zorrilla, *Don Juan Tenorio*, ed. Aniano Peña (Madrid: Cáredra, 1988), 120.

[44] Zorrilla, *Don Juan Tenorio*, ed. Peña, 120.

[45] See Judith Arias, 'The Devil at Heaven's Door: Metaphysical Desire in *Don Juan Tenorio*', *Hispanic Review*, 61 (1993), 15–34.

own monologue in the previous scene has apparently done no more than confirm his heartlessness, but Brígida's description of the innocent virtue of Doña Inés as well as her physical beauty means that much more comes to be at stake. The old woman's mercenary portrayal of Inés has an unsuspected effect upon Don Juan, who in an increasingly self-absorbed speech comes to repeat the same pattern earlier enunciated by Don Luis: 'Tan incentive pintura | los sentidos me enajena, | y el alma ardiente me llena | de su insensata pasión' ('Such a suggestive depiction | estranges my senses, | and fill my flaming soul | with senseless passion'),[46] he professes, as reason, logic, and the sensual seem once more to be textually discarded as the anti-hero reveals himself to be susceptible to feelings of a higher order. Thus by the end of the speech Don Juan can reverse the application of the satanic imagery that has typified his own persona and envision himself as Satan's heroic adversary. Brígida appears to speak for the audience when she confesses her own bewilderment at such words. If we initially remain as uncomprehending as she is, however, the miraculous transformation of the anti-hero within a play that is not casually designated 'drama religioso-fantástico' has begun.

Inés's reaction to Don Juan's letter, in Act 3, Scene 3, is also relevant here. The preparation for her later metaphysical role is perhaps foreshadowed in lines that recall textually the earlier ones of both Don Luis and Don Juan. His letter she regards first as a 'filtro envenenado' ('poisoned philter'), a love potion concocted with maleficent purpose; as Don Juan wrote it at the start of the play as the curtain rises, it is. As her speech proceeds, however, Zorrilla effects the recurrence of his chosen pattern of words:

¿Qué sentimientos dormidos
son los que revela en mí?
¿Qué impulsos jamás sentidos?
¿Qué luz, que hasta hoy nunca vi?
¿Qué es lo que engendra en mi alma
Tan nuevo y profundo afán?[47]

What dormant feelings | are these it reveals in me? | What impulses never before felt? | What this light I never saw before today? | What is being born within my soul, | what new and fathomless yearning?

Zorrilla's play, we could say, is as dramatically new as the heroine's incipient emotional experience; it forces audience and reader to grasp the possibilities of a fresh departure, something unprecedented and earth-shattering, whether this be the love between Juan and Inés or the playwright's own rewriting of a tradition seemingly immovably embedded in the national psyche, whose parameters and outcome are so predictable that it is outside of our rational compass to countenance their being overturned.

46 Zorrilla, *Don Juan Tenorio*, ed. Peña, 130–1.
47 Zorrilla, *Don Juan Tenorio*, ed. Peña, 146–7.

Whether we read ulterior meanings into Inés's reaction to Juan's letter or not, there is undoubtedly a recurrent linguistic pattern here, one which militates against the rational and sensual, against the carnal, and which at least allows for foresight of the move to the spiritual and transcendent that we are asked to accept in Act 4, Scene 3, known familiarly in Spanish culture as 'la escena del sofá' (the sofa scene). Zorrilla's language is again exceptionally crafted as that love scene proceeds, as for instance in the timing of Inés's switch from polite to informal mode of speech. I would argue that the examples I have adduced here constitute a coherent foretaste of the words spoken by Don Juan when Inés is apparently emotionally defenceless before his seductive charms, '¡Alma mía! Esa palabra | cambia de modo mi ser' ('O soul of mine! That word changes entirely my being'),[48] and justifying his conclusion that this new-found love has been inspired by God.

Don Juan Tenorio, of course, is not so straightforward. Don Juan's personal demons, his obsessive concern with living up to the persona he has created for himself, are not so easily discarded. His acquisition of personal authenticity will involve, necessarily, the need to overcome the entirety of that persona, and when put to the test by Gonzalo's incredulity and Luis's gleeful mockery he is found wanting. Perhaps a more enduring signal of Don Juan's potential ability to change is effected by Zorrilla between the end of Part I of the play and Act 1 of Part II. The famous lines 'Llamé al cielo y no me oyó, | y pues sus puertas me cierra, | de mis pasos en la tierra | responda el cielo, y no yo' ('I cried out to heaven and it heard me not, | and, since it closes its gates against me, | of my future footsteps here on earth | let heaven bear the weight, not me'),[49] making rhetorically explicit Juan's unwillingness to accept personal responsibility (this is perhaps where the shadow of Rivas's play looms largest), have their pointed counterweight in Don Juan's soliloquy in the cemetery, his contrition before Inés's tomb expressed in the pivotal verses

> Sí, después de tantos años
> cuyos recuerdos me espantan,
> siento que en mí se levantan
> pensamientos en mí extraños.
> ¡Oh! Acaso me los inspira
> desde el cielo, en donde mora,
> esa sombra protectora
> que por mi mal no respira.[50]

> Yes, after so many years | whose memory terrifies me | I feel within me called to life | thoughts which are new and strange. | Oh! Perhaps inspired in me | from heaven, where dwells | that protecting spirit | who, through my evil deeds, breathes no more.

[48] Zorrilla, *Don Juan Tenorio*, ed. Peña, 166.
[49] Zorrilla, *Don Juan Tenorio*, ed. Peña. 179.
[50] Zorrilla, *Don Juan Tenorio*, ed. Peña, 191.

In Zorrilla's play 'pensamientos extraños' or analogous forms of words are always an intimation of a different, more elevated sphere of existence and our capacity to inhabit it. The conjunction with his acceptance of his own moral culpability is an especially telling one; such is the nature of Zorrilla's planning, at every level, that these are the lines which usher in a sequence of *décimas* only previously seen in Act 4, Scene 3, of Part I.

In the Don Juan tradition, the *convidado de piedra*, the statue of Don Gonzalo, had always been the direct means of Don Juan's descent to hell, the vengeful infernal emissary functioning as a guarantor of his damnation. In Zorrilla's play, that spectre of tradition is dismantled since the overturning of literary tradition that made Juan's salvation possible required divine intervention through a different 'sombra protectora', the role that Inés supernaturally brings to bear from entirely outside of rational prescription.

Why, ultimately, should Zorrilla write a version so iconoclastic of the Don Juan legend? Any number of reasons might be adduced, not least the dramatic showboating which the play contains, especially in the ending. Yet if Zorrilla was manifestly writing for Catholic, devoutly religious audiences, then there is something singularly appropriate about a play which casts all forms of rationalism aside, which thrives on the miraculous.[51] The play indisputably possesses an explicit moral in its ending: its final verses are 'es el Dios de la clemencia | el Dios de *don Juan Tenorio*' ('The God of *Don Juan Tenorio* | is a clement God').[52]

Seen in its entirety, Spanish Romantic drama might be said to contain a specifiable trajectory, from the creation of a paradigm in the productions of 1834 through the instances of rebellion against orthodoxy to an attempted reconciliation of the genre with traditional teaching. This would mirror other trends within Spanish Romanticism as a whole, particularly literary criticism. If *Don Juan Tenorio* represents the culmination of Spanish Romantic theatre in Spain, it is at least partly because Zorrilla, with *Don Juan Tenorio*, had left it nowhere else to go; he appeared definitively to have concluded the paradigmatic sequence and to have brought about an impossible reconciliation in the exorcism of personal demons and in the triumphant victory over the various spectres that had haunted its historical evolution.[53] By 1844, in addition, many of the leading figures had departed the scene or moved away from the central concerns of the previous decade. Larra was dead, Rivas wrote no more for the theatre, García Gutiérrez had proved unable to repeat the success of his first play, Hartzenbusch would retract the challenging ending of *Los amantes de Teruel*. It was hard to see what else Zorrilla himself could do in working with the tension, sometimes confrontation, between traditional religious faith and Romantic love.

[51] See Derek Flitter, 'Zorrilla, the Critics, and the Direction of Spanish Romanticism', in Richard A. Cardwell and Ricardo Landeira (eds), *José Zorrilla, 1893–1993: Centennial Readings* (Nottingham: Nottingham University Press, 1993), 1–15.

[52] Zorrilla, *Don Juan Tenorio*, ed. Peña, 226.

[53] For a contrasting point of view, see David T. Gies, 'José Zorrilla and the Betrayal of Spanish Romanticism', *Romanistiches Jahrbuch*, 31 (1980), 339–46.

One further point could be made here. Zorrilla's play stands meaningful comparison with a work of 1843 that would in many ways break the mould in a different artistic form. Wagner's *Flying Dutchman* depicts love as dangerous and demanding, against norms and conventions but ultimately transcendent and redemptive. The endings of Zorrilla's play and of Wagner's opera are almost identical: the souls of Juan and Inés rise into heaven as a legend is at an end, just as the finale of Wagner's 'total art-work' sees the exorcizing of the Dutchman's curse, his body clasped to that of Senta in transfiguration over the sea.

Further Reading

Arias, Judith, 'The Devil at Heaven's Door: Metaphysical Desire in Don Juan tenorio', *Hispanic Review*, 61 (1993), 15–34.

Cardwell, Richard, 'Don Alvaro or the Force of Cosmic Injustice', *Studies in Romanticism*, 12 (1973), 559–79.

Flitter, Derek, *Spanish Romantic Literary Theory and Criticism* (Cambridge: Cambridge University Press, 1992).

Flitter, Derek, 'The Romantic Theology of Los amantes de Teruel', *Crítica Hispánica*, 18 (1996), 25–34.

Flitter, Derek, 'Spanish Romanticism', in Michael Ferber (ed.), *A Companion to European Romanticism* (Oxford: Blackwell, 2005), 272–92.

Gies, David T., *The Theatre in Nineteenth-Century Spain* (Cambridge: Cambridge University Press, 1994).

Gies, David T. (ed.), *The Cambridge History of Spanish Literature* (Cambridge: Cambridge University Press, 2004).

Silver, Philip, 'The Politics of Spanish Romanticism', *Crítica Hispánica*, 18 (1996), 75–80.

Russian

CHAPTER 26

RUSSIAN LITERATURE BETWEEN CLASSICISM AND ROMANTICISM

Poetry, Feeling, Subjectivity

ANDREW KAHN

THE joint discovery of sensibility and subjectivity is the hallmark of early Romanticism in Russia. From the high Enlightenment of Catherine the Great to the end of the Napoleonic Wars, a fresh conceptual model of the self, and new codes of feeling, drive literature. The age of sensibility grew out of an institutional transition away from a court-based patronage system to the private practice of literature that fostered an appreciation of writing as a vehicle for self-expression and cultural statement. Before the appearance in the 1820s of a broader reading public, even then on a smaller scale than that of France and England, homo-social coteries dominated literature as producers and consumers. From the 1760s, the rapid development of a classical idea of literature, a Russian redaction of French neoclassicism informed by a new attention to the ancients, took decades to absorb yet did not block openness to multiple influences from abroad. Even as writers assimilated new trends in European literature a conservative attitude to form, language, and theme persisted. The writers of what Luba Golburt has called the 'first epoch' bequeathed to their younger contemporaries a vernacular verse language that was much fitter for purpose than prose would be until the 1790s. In the 1780s and 1790s, younger writers—mostly amateur men of letters and the occasional noble woman—extended older debates about the elements of style and correct verse form. Writers were able to move between classical models and more experimental forms of subjectivity, especially in the elegy, because a consensus on style survived into the post-Napoleonic period. Debate about the purpose of literature and its national cultural orientation and obligations intensified in the 1820s. At the end of the period covered in this chapter we see the breakdown of support for literature conceived as playful and gentlemanly. The advent of a full-blown Romantic movement, supported by the growth of the reading public, proliferation of literary journals, and the establishment of literary criticism as an institution, caused more writers to take entrenched positions and break with the past.

Discovery of Feeling

From the 1770s, church censorship weakened, liberal press laws were promulgated, academic institutions more actively nurtured pure research, and individuals travelled widely across Europe. These liberating circumstances fostered awareness that the practice of literature was fundamental to the creation of a modern individual sensibility, an inner self fully the complement of the model of a sociable self to which the enlightened gentry aspired. Standard accounts of Russian sentimentalism tend to concentrate descriptions of the cult of feeling on stylized lyric expression. A more ambitious account would map the representation of feeling across genres like autobiography and the diary onto a new awareness of sensibility as a complex interrelation of mind and body. This description of the discovery of feeling accommodates a much broader spectrum of psychological depiction and relations, including *Sturm und Drang*.

Much Western literary depiction of feeling, from Richardson to Fielding, and Laclos to Diderot, derives from Cartesianism and Lockean empiricism whose fictional codes are synchronized with theories about the mechanical body and immaterial soul. Russia discovered feeling and the representation of the passions in the 1770s. Before the second half of the eighteenth century, few Russians had ever used writing to express any sense of inwardness, even in religious spheres where compliance with confessional rites was mainly notional and formal. In the early Enlightenment period Russia never passed through a Cartesian stage of reflection on the workings of the mind and the character of knowledge. 'I feel therefore I am' might be a fair slogan for the discovery of self through feeling that takes place in the second half of the century. Yet from the 1770s, the practice of sensibility proceeds without much of a theory of the body and sensation, confirming a general intellectual trend towards practical experimentation in the arts and literature over academic discovery. In fact, changes in the function of literature, moderate advances in scientific learning, and evolving attitudes to social identity, mainly class-based, stimulate new ideas in Russia about the human subject in the last third of the eighteenth century. The greater availability of a more progressive education, and a newly supple language were also important cultural determinants that unleashed fresh conceptualization and representation of the individual self.

Russia had no philosophical school or established university curriculum. Yet some ideas about sensibility reached St Petersburg, inspiring new and often radical thinking about the mind and feeling in quasi-literary works. The work of imaginative writers often substituted for scientific and philosophical enquiry. Nikolai Karamzin's mind was well-stocked with Enlightenment writings on aesthetics and different aspects of psychology, interests that determined the itinerary of his alter ego, the traveller, who pursues a cosmopolitan tour from one great thinker to the next. His *Letters of a Russian Traveller* (*Pis'ma russkogo puteshestvennika*, 1792) is, among other things, a philosophical Grand Tour of Europe; the itinerary includes meetings with some of the greatest minds of the period from Kant in Königsberg to the medical theorist Bonnet in Geneva. His narrator, a typical example of Karamzinian sensibility—affectionate, tender, highly responsive (and therefore much warmer than the famously reserved Karamzin was in his own actual correspondence)—provides in parallel to his demonstration of feeling an education on contemporary theory about the mind–body duality.

Alexander Radishchev is best remembered now for the radical politics of his *Journey from St Petersburg to Moscow* (*Puteshestvie iz Peterburga v Moskvu*), a prose narrative that channels its critique of the Russian political structure and a serf-based economy through a sophisticated melange of different genres such as the ode, allegorical tale, dream, sentimental tale. Like Karamzin, Radishchev was a prolific and versatile author, a pioneer of literary biography in Russia—*Zhitie Fedoro Ushakova*, The Life of Fedor Ushakov, 1784), a portrait of a materialist intellectual—and of psychological subjectivity—*Dnevnik odnoi nedeli*, The Diary of a One Week, n.d.)—who explored the interrelation of the body and psychological identity. His last great work was the treatise *O Cheloveke, o ego bessmertii i besmertnosti* (On Man, Mortality, and Immortality, 1792), written during his journey into Siberian exile. Like his other masterpieces, this treatise is a hybrid creation, casting philosophical arguments in literary form. It compresses a remarkable amount of state-of-the-art learning on scientific and philosophical theories of human identity and the functioning of organic matter; it remained little known and while it therefore had no impact on literary works of the period it distils a whole chapter in Russian writing and thought in which the concept of sensibility became central to the representation of literary character and human identity.

In Russia, the novel was for the most part a regressive genre, drawing on imitations of folkloric plots or archaic stories. Short fiction rather than the novel proved to be the form most open to exploring questions about feeling as well as representing it. In the 1770s, Russian heroes and heroines, especially as the stock characters of love elegy, did their fair share of weeping to establish their bona fides as true creatures of sensibility. But the emphasis on exterior depiction of feeling gradually begins to support a greater attention to the psychology of feeling, breaking with neoclassical conventions of expressivity in representing subjectivity, and testing social, linguistic, and literary boundaries. Fictions that treat the symptomology of love often contain a meta-fictional counter-narrative in which characters in the process of living out their emotions on the page step back and consider their origins and meaning. In another sign of change, reading itself becomes a stimulus to thinking about the meaning of feeling. Literary heroes and diarists alike increasingly correlated their examination of their emotional histories with fictional lives. Two novellas follow the example of tragic love and suicide established by Goethe's *Werther*. Mikhail Sushkov (1775–92), a poet inspired by Goethe's seminal fiction (and seemingly to suicide as well as literary emulation) employed an epistolary form for his *Rossiiskii Verter* (Russian Werther, 1792) in which the unnamed hero charts his emotional disintegration between 6 July and 28 December, pondering how in a mere five months he could entirely forfeit his emotional self-control. An equally anonymous narrator frames the story with an introduction and concluding paragraph describing how the hero, languishing for a woman trapped in a loveless marriage, hangs himself. These passages interject a note of a sympathy rather than didacticism, but also convey the author's conviction that a true (and somewhat sensational) account deserves to be published because it conforms to an established pattern in fiction (the example cited is the *Russian Pamela*)—and surpasses it. The *Russian Werther* marks a shift in ambitions for fiction by making narrative a vehicle for self-analysis. The eighth letter gives the flavour of a short work that is brief but intense on the subject of a love that transgresses social convention:

You laugh at my letters—well may you laugh, my friend as I often mock myself. I am bored, something is missing and I can hardly comprehend what it is. Writing to you, and receiving your letters, which I reread a hundred times, constitutes part of my routine. In those minutes I feel that I have a friend, that my heart is not entirely empty, and I take pleasure in this. My soul pours forth onto the page and when we are unable to be together then I enjoy conversing with you by letter.

Excesses of sensibility were of a concern for Nikolai Karamzin, who is often regarded as the founding father of the sentimental movement in Russia, a strand in the pre-Romantic period from the 1770s to the early nineteenth century. Karamzin's short fiction contains several notable examples of plots motivated by erotic and sexual interests. 'Bednaia Liza' ('Poor Liza', 1792) tells the story of a young peasant girl who falls in love with Erast (note the 'speaking name'), a member of the landed gentry; he seduces and leaves Liza who drowns herself. The performance of the narrator is a lesson in Rousseauian natural feeling, demonstrating to Karamzin's reader at virtually every turn how to follow the narrator's empathy and achieve close identification with the emotional lives of the characters. Scholarship on Karamzin has helpfully framed his contribution to the fictionalization of sensibility in terms of reader-response. While the story 'Poor Liza' is most famous for a plot about a tryst between a nobleman and an ill-fated peasant girl that is conducted across class boundaries, its opening panorama of the Moscow landscape, church bells in the distance, is a celebrated example of sentimentalist prose because it reads virtually like a master-class, teaching authors how to infuse a landscape with sentiment, and readers how to experience vicariously through the stories of others.

Yet the gentle melancholy of Karamzin's idylls has deflected attention from the darker side of his fiction, partly inspired by Gothic themes, partly reflecting his own apprehension of psychological contradiction. His fiction dramatizes a number of conceptual positions, showing awareness of current important Enlightenment controversies about mind–body duality, and while there are unsolved questions about his philosophical sources (how much of David Hume's thought was known to Karamzin, for instance), the physiological nature of feeling becomes prevalent in Karamzin's work from the 1790s and looks like more than a borrowing from Sterne's fiction. A political conservative and apologist for monarchy, Karamzin set limits on how far feeling might be allowed to run.

Nonetheless, Karamzin pushes his subject matter to boundaries that look emotionally extreme and yet politically cautious. In the early 1790s, he defended Jean-Jacques Rousseau whose *Confessions* and *La Nouvelle Heloïse* he clearly knew, while repudiating his theory of civilization and his putative connection to revolutionary politics in France. In his story 'Ostrov Borngolm' ('The Isle of Bornholm', 1793), Karamzin tackled the question of the limits of natural feeling by using an incest plot. The story follows a textbook definition of the Gothic: it is set on a remote Danish island, features a sinister boatman, a troubled lover, and an incarcerated maiden, privileges the lurid such as a gloomy castle with moat and bolted doors, a rampart, and the melancholy landscape such as moonlight nightscapes, has its share of horrors hidden away in a dungeon, and narrates a tale of emotional repression and excess. The imprisoned maiden tells her story in tones of defiance and remorse, sending through the traveller a message to her father about her plight and her 'heart which has dried up from sorrow, about tears that can never assuage her suffering'. While this hoary elder professes to be a lover of virtue who respects its 'sacred laws', he is responsible for her terrible fate. At this point, Karamzin's narrator interjects, and refuses to impart the elder's terrible secret from whose knowledge he protects the readers and 'friends' to whom he ostensibly tells this story. This failure in disclosure hardly obscures an incest plot. While the story has been read by Yuri Lotman as an allegory for the end of the Age of Reason in the violent passions of the French Revolution, it is even more directly a consideration through fiction of the relationship between social norms and uncontrollable bodily desire, a theme that will later run through much Russian literature, perhaps starting with Alexander Pushkin's *Tsygany* (The Gypsies, 1827) and taken up from a different philosophical premise by Leo Tolstoy in his mature writing.

Perhaps the most intense of Russian excursions into sexual awakening that tests conventional attitudes is Karamzin's 'Rytsar' nashego vremeni' ('A Knight of our Times', 1803), one of the last works of fiction he was to write. Introduced as the history of a single sensibility, the story breaks off with the early adolescence of the hero at a tender moment. Orphaned at a young age, Leon conceives an affection for the wife of the neighbouring landowner who bears a resemblance to the mother of whom he has nearly infantile memories. This young beauty, Emilia, responds maternally to the neglected stripling. But the narrator begins to identify an element of sexual attraction in their affection. Emily can 'only love innocence' and feels unthreatened by adolescent affection, although the boy himself is increasingly troubled by feelings he does not quite understand, indulging in erotic reverie that takes Karamzin, among the most reserved of authors in his personal writings, to the brink of an explicitness about sexual arousal that he resists in 'Poor Liza'. The story breaks off with Leon, a new Actaeon, having contrived to observe his Diana bathing. The narrator had warned that the 'reader might consider that ... we are preparing him for some contravention of innocence. No! The time is ahead! Our hero has only just turned eleven.' But the story breaks off without leaving much doubt about the sexual charge between the young boy and woman. By mapping sexual identity onto conventional ideas of childhood and youth he puts an ideal of innocence under pressure; and by exposing the hidden desire quietly awakened in the young woman he confronts the double transgression of infidelity and with an adolescent.

The *Letters of a Russian Traveller* demonstrated Karamzin's talent for packaging for a domestic readership new, foreign literary models and styles of thought. But beyond its level of generic ambition, and in contrast to the many descriptions of polite society across European capitals, the *Letters of a Russian Traveller* consistently gravitates to tales of extreme emotion whether through erotic catastrophe, radical politics (in the letters concerning the French Revolution), social upheaval (there are several tales about brigands and criminals). A number of the letters look at domestic life in England as a model for familial affection and the gendered roles of parents in the household. Alexander Radishchev and the diarist Andrei Turgenev also treated the question of how to control sexual passion in fiction and diary-writing. In all of these writers ideas about the innate benevolence of man and a belief in moral sentiments were challenged by the awareness of bodily and irrational drives. One signal of the transition from the classical to the Romantic can be found in a change in terminology. 'Strasti', originally used to denote the result of actions done to the senses, increasingly comes to signify 'passion' as an all-consuming desire.

At the end of her reign Catherine turned against some of the writers, including Novikov and Radishchev, whom she had previously supported. She was determined to turn the clock back to the stability and reason of her prime at a moment when trends at court favoured self-expression and intellectual autonomy. This meant not only suppressing republican themes in the theatre, but also putting a lid on religious and emotional representation. In 1795 one of the last sets of books she purchased for her library was a sumptuous set of Plutarch's *Lives*, a sure sign of her commitment to the style of exemplary hero-worship that formed a neoclassical strand in historiography and academic painting of the period. She was determined to turn her back on Rousseau's cult of sensibility and on any cultural movement that authorized a tumultuous, revolutionary individual self. Radishchev may well have assumed that Catherine, who at an earlier point in her realm had clearly wished to reform serfdom, remained true to her Enlightenment principles and would have supported him. He paid a severe price for using the 'man of feeling' he created for his *Journey from St Petersburg to Moscow* as the vehicle for political critique.

Subjectivity and Frontiers of Consciousness

Traditional accounts identify Vassily Zhukovsky's masterful verse translation of Gray's 'Elegy Written in a Country Churchyard' ('Sel'skoe kladbishche', 1802) as the stimulus to a new type of subjective poetry in Russia. (In fact, it is arguable that the most revolutionary aspect of the translation is the emphasis it places on the economics of the countryside, with its reference to landowners as 'slaves of vanity' and patent sympathy for serfs.)

I shall argue that the development of first-person lyric of a nuanced and emotionally viable type originated considerably earlier in Russia. While poets at court continued to celebrate the monarch in strictly neoclassical terms, beyond this public space we find writers searching for an inner word suitable to private feeling. Works for the theatre written and staged in the 1780s repeatedly link moral sensibility and virtue. While the inculcation of virtue (*dobrodetel'*) is part of Catherine's moral vision of the state, behind this view of the rational state is an assumption that individuals will be naturally benevolent and rational. These sentiments eventually find their most powerful outlet in poetry and prose in political attacks on serfdom. But a new emotionality about the private individual also shapes literature. Poets were the most alert to the relation between sensibility and feeling and the reality of death; and it is this awareness of mortality that expands their repertoire of landscapes, their attempts to devise a more probing psychological style and to capture in lyric poems acts of consciousness filled with moral reckoning and awareness of the limits of consciousness as determined by the relation of body and mind.

Poetry on the theme of mortality written in the 1760s treated extinction as an existential fact; while a source of grief, it is not seen as a matter for excessive speculation. More moralists than metaphysicians, poets typically treat sorrow according to Horatian precepts or adopt the manner of Ecclesiastes and encourage readers to contemplate the passage of time and individual mortality. In this earlier part of the period, poems were statements of *memento mori*, expressing perplexity about the disappearance of the dead. Increasingly from the 1770s, self-awareness, awareness of mortal limitations, sensitivity to bodily decay, and the attenuation and tragic rupture of familial bonds stalk the pages of secular Russian writing. Withdrawn and solitary figures inhabit the lyric landscape. Above all, an awareness of death haunts lyric poetry, stimulating new forms of sympathy to one another. This section will characterize the use of graveyard lyrics, representation of subjectivity and elegiac vocabulary in a period that negotiates away from neoclassical convention to a more exploratory style of expression that can be associated with early Romanticism.

The theme of death is pervasive but inspires some original treatments, especially by three of the classic writers of the age, Alexander Radishchev, Gavrila Derzhavin, and Nikolai Karamzin. Derzhavin's reliance on the trope of amplification and abundance reached its culmination in his elegy on the death of Prince Potemkin, a political colossus of the age. One of the most imposing lyrics in all of Russian poetry, a torrent of metaphor and sustained allegory, 'Vodopad' ('The Waterfall', 1794) adheres to classical topoi in arguing the case for the immortality of great men. But it is a great act of both drawing limits and imagining. For on this occasion Derzhavin does not interrogate nature as to the meaning of death. Immortality resides in the cultural institutions that preserve the memories of the great through narrative and through monuments, and the poem itself, while all its resources are dedicated to describing the fluidity of time, through repetition and accretion seems to halt time so that we see through the single vignettes of each stanza how the mighty repeatedly have failed to conquer death. Yet paradoxically the poem also achieves the sublime feat of being both terrible and beautiful because it seems to insert the speaker within the waterfall itself. While the waterfall as emblem represents time it also stands for language that speaks through the poet, a bard in the manner of

Ossian, who serves as the voice of time, a voice of antiquity, the present, and the future. If we wish to see in 'The Waterfall' a movement towards Romanticism, the validity of that claim relates not to the representation of nature, but in the double apotheosis of the subject, Prince Potemkin as the embodiment of nearly supernatural energy, a representation that looks ahead to treatments of Napoleon, and, perhaps above all, in the power and energy ascribed to the poet whose voices merges with time, nature, and ranges over the landscape with the omniscience of a deity. Such visionary grandeur, and such confidence in sublime imaginings, will not be repeated in Russian poetry until the 1830s with the mature lyrics of Evgenii Baratynskii.

But doubt remains whether art can serve as a bulwark against death or assuage a worrying mystery. Among the first works to make out of elegiac themes a drama that is both highly personal and yet universal is 'Na smert' kniazia Mescherskogo' ('Elegy on the Death of Prince Meshchersky', 1779). Derzhavin's poem famously interrogates the funerary bier with a series of terse questions, but the expression of aporia (normally phrased 'Where have you gone?') is a widespread refrain that persists over decades in the poetry of typical figures like Vassili Maikov, Mikhail Murav'ev, Golenishchev-Kutuzov, and Mikhail Kheraskov. The vanity of human wishes and acceptance of the ephemeral nature of life go together, recognizing the limits of human knowledge and restraining the imagination, as Kheraskov (1733–1807) opined in 'Nichtozhnost'' ('Nothingness', 1806): 'No matter the mind's imaginative construction | Every thing I think suffers destruction.' Epistemological anxieties do not hide beneath the surface of these poems. We can only speculate on the degree to which the absence of an elementary philosophical tradition delayed the growth of a more speculative type of lyric until the appearance of a poet like Iakov Kniazhnin (1740–91). Unless motivated by mystical ideas such as entertained in Masonic circles, poets gave frank articulation to a truth much repeated by Russian moralists in the period:

> O death! Your limit is inescapable!
> Changing all into dust,
> You summon us before judgement inevitable,
> To give a reckoning as we must.
> ('Stansy na smert'', 1790?)

Despite the prevalence of these commonplaces, there is also a trajectory within the history of the elegy towards creating subjects capable of representing to themselves (and for the reader) an experiential and meditative drama from death. Writers such as Derzhavin, Nikolai Karamzin, Andrei Turgenev, and then later Konstantin Batiushkov and Zhukovsky undertake the move from a rule-based aesthetic to an aesthetic defined more in terms of emotions and common feelings. Among the first works to make out of elegiac themes a drama that is both highly personal and yet universal is 'Na smert' kniazia Meshcherskogo' ('Elegy on the Death of Prince Meshchersky', 1779). Derzhavin perfects this posture of incomprehension, drawing on classical and biblical wisdom to communicate the message that mankind must surrender to the inevitability of death, and its impenetrability. The poem is remarkable as a specimen of rhetoric, and commentators have rightly drawn attention to its opulent use of figures of speech (sometimes of the relationship it establishes between language and the psychology of the speaker). For the more he protests our ignorance of what lies beyond the 'limit of this world', the greater the profusion of language to fill that absence. Language serves to buttress the speaker's grip on the empirical world by vividly counterpointing the stuff of life with the emptiness of 'non-existence' (*nebytie*). But the poem is open to interpretation as a statement of therapeutic disbelief in the reality of death as nothingness, since the existence of a vacuum cannot be demonstrated or even described. Insofar as the poet intimates that the barrier between existence and non-existence lies in his linguistic incapacity to describe the unknown, the poem subverts the message of resignation and leaves in reserve the possibility of the recuperation of life once language becomes commensurate with the imagination.

Epitaph poetry enjoys a vogue throughout the period, manifesting similar attentiveness to death as a cause for resigned acceptance rather than contemplation: 'Under this stone lies Pl … v. | Above this stone he was such and such | Below it now he's not all that much', wrote Iakov Kniazhnin in an epitaph poem of 1790. The Masonic poet Ivan Khemnitser found his voice in this subgenre. The tombstone inscriptions are written in the manner of the Greek Anthology; they use the *sta viator* motif to command attention and deliver a message about the value of life; or alternatively they aim a satirical arrow at the anonymous subject, using wit to puncture the bubble of ambition, vanity, and illusions of immortality. But the persistence of levity and satire, reflexes of coterie poetry and albums, increasingly makes space for a more overtly serious and melancholy trend that takes death as a pretext to treat the meaning of consciousness and to explore its limitations. From the 1780s, poetry gives evidence of a transition to a more Romantic style as marked by an impulse to engage the unknown, to test the limits of terminology, and, above all, to create within the poem a bond of empathy and co-imagining between the speaker and the implied readers. Elegists repeatedly invoke the notion of indeterminacy—the words 'limit' and 'boundary' recur as points for striving beyond—as a way to fix a tension between resignation and imagining of death as a dramatic struggle.

Prompted to look beyond Orthodoxy by a subculture of Masonic and Pietist ideas, religious thinkers gave consideration to the forms of afterlife and recuperation of the soul, while more subversive natural philosophers such as Alexander Radishchev, representing a small but well educated minority among the urban elite, considered the separation of the spirit from the body at death as strictly material and final. In the treatise *On Man, on his Immortality and Mortality*, Radishchev painted the sundering of the mind and spirit from the body as a passage of excruciating agony, casting the psychological torment in the lurid language of Gothic worthy of Edward Young. Karamzin, on the other hand, avoids any challenges to the official church. Yet much of Karamzin's poetry and prose after 1789 newly considers death less as a matter of religion than as a fact of human society that generates cultural practices of commemoration and mourning. He makes the graveyard visit an important topos well before the translation of Gray. In 'Kladbishche' ('The Graveyard', 1792), Karamzin creates a conversation poem between two of the dead, disembodied and mere voices. There is an element of Gothic horror to the interventions of Voice One whose 'bones quake' and fears that his 'brains nest toads', while the damp earth consumes his rotting corpse under 'a leafless tree'. Point by point Voice Two sets up a binary opposition, saluting the deep sleep of death as 'sweet and simple', welcoming the birdsong and the scent of violets. The two positions on death are brought home to the speaker in the final set of responses in which each imagines the feelings of the wanderer as he passes by the tombs. For Voice One the site must be one of unmitigated horror; for Voice Two the wanderer will see in the spot the 'home of eternal life' and, dropping his staff, remain with them. This dialogue of the dead enacts and articulates a dialectic of rejection and acceptance that other elegiac speakers take up and extend. Inspired by Edward Young, the Freemason Gavril Kamenev (1772–1803) imagined how death would ultimately destroy a graveyard and its monuments. His 'Kladbishche' ('The Cemetery', 1796) pushes the moral of *vanitas vanitatis* to an extreme of decay. No physical monument will suffice to preserve name, rank, and title according to the admonitions of this poem. Social conscience, sympathy, and empathy, the erosion of time on social bonds and individual sensibility, these are the themes that come together in Radishchev's intense elegiac monologue 'Pochto, moi drug, pochto sleza iz glaz katitsia' ('Why, my friend, why does a tear fall from my eye', *c.*1791).

Although Catherine the Great abhorred his political philosophy, Rousseau as a theorist of sensibility and natural religion cast a long shadow in Russia. In the short lyric 'Druzhba' ('Friendship', 1770), Mikhail Murav'ev' rejects the fripperies of neoclassical pastoral in preference for 'heartfelt feeling' (*chuvsvie serdechno*). 'Born to feel', he requires not words but sensations that will enliven his sensibility and speak directly to his heart, the organ that, in the best manner of Jean-Jacques, is a source of intuition and a moral touchstone. For elegists, Rousseau's influence, sporadic but recoverable, provided new techniques of introspection on the relation between feeling, nature, and the mind. In his majestic 'Elegy' (1806), Andrei Turgenev creates an occasion for the consideration of all the major elegiac themes—life as a dream, death as sleep, the vanity of wishes, the regret for youth, the wish for posthumous recognition, the meaning of death as eternal rest or pure disintegration—within a landscape containing all the micro-regions of elegiac style: autumn, pine trees, a graveyard, shade and gloom, and the picturesque.

But Turgenev's poem is particularly important because, following the example of other Rousseauians such as Karamzin in his important 'Poeziia' ('Poetry', *c.*1789), he is one of the first of his generation to see Nature as a force immanent with feeling and determination, a foil to Fate which in this poem seems to stand for History. Ultimately the Nature envisaged here seems akin to that of Shaftesbury—good because beautiful, harmonious because rational—and close to the late Rousseau of the *Rêveries* (from which the epigraph comes) because the speaker also shuns the world, seeking permanent asylum in the forest. Karamzin's mature poems regularly address the texture of sensation and create feeling about feeling, proof of the sensitivity of the soul and its vulnerability to the emotional power of nature. 'Melankholiia' ('Melancholy'), bearing the subtitle 'An imitation of Delille', is a particularly important poem for several reasons. Although an imitation, Karamzin's poem seamlessly bridges the affective lexicons and styles of French and Russian, demonstrating that translation is no barrier to the persuasive expression of sensibility. Behind that effect of technique is also a conceptual point about the universality of feeling, a point that derives from elements of Lockean psychology shared by Russian writers with their Western European counterparts, but also refers to Karamzin's belief that Russian Europeanized elites behave just as the French, English, and Germans do. The poem celebrates a natural propensity that is 'sweeter than all the artificial pleasures and whimsical amusements', a psychological property he extolls as both the cause of sadness and the cure of sadness—in other words, a creator of the bittersweet antinomies from which the poet extracts maximal emotion and proof of his live sensibility. Words like 'grief' (*skorb*) and 'yearning' (*toska*), while already familiar as the vocabulary of neoclassical love elegy, migrate from the description of feeling generated by the engagement of the mind with a moving landscape. A new concentration on the process of poetic activity, combined with an awareness of the interconnection of sensation and consciousness, marks the turn to a Romantic voice. The sound of the nightingale, the celebrated emblem of aesthetic perfection and song for its own sake, captivates Karamzin. 'K solov'iu' ('To the Nightingale', 1794) celebrates again the sweet melancholy engendered by harmonious song, admitting a gap between the listener's reactions and the bird which represents pure song without intention, formally perfect and yet detached from any purpose. Should the poet emulate this model and also aspire to a Kantian aesthetic ideal? This is the didactic message of 'K bednomu poetu' ('To the Poor Poet', 1797) which enjoins the poet to embrace his difficulties as 'good for the heart'; for while nature can seem pitiless in fact it rewards the poet amply by endowing him with a 'fiery heart', a 'mind', 'the art of song', a 'miraculous' and even 'priceless' gift' able to 'enchant hearts with harmony', a set of qualifications extended directly in descriptions of the art of poetry well into the Pushkin period, and verging on the Romantic definition of poetic genius as unique and unrepeatable.

Authorial Genius

In the 1760s and early 1770s Russian poets divided informally as followers of Lomonosov or Sumarokov according to stylistic practice. By the 1780s, sensibility mattered more than diction. Poetic circles or coteries were metropolitan, male in membership, and while mostly drawn from the gentry their ranks were augmented by the sons of clergy such as S. S. Bobrov (1765–1810). Amateur lovers of poetry included government officials like Derzhavin, educators like M. N. Murav'ev (1757–1807), the first rector of Moscow University, artisans like the architect N. A. L'vov (1751–1804), and landowners like the accomplished Horatian poet Vassili Kapnist (1758–1823). They were content to circulate their lyrics and collections in manuscript anthologies, to publish occasionally in literary journals that enjoyed a tiny circulation, and to come together for debate and discussion in literary societies (which by the mid-1810s were factionalized by literary politics). Many poems, and some handbooks, make the correct style of verse a subject of criticism and consideration, and many poets, including the young Pushkin, revel in virtuoso displays of wit and stylistic polish.

Works in celebration of poetic genius go together with epitaphs commemorating figures singled out for posterity's interest. By the mid-1780s, the idea of genius as a special intellectual faculty that elevated elect individuals above most of mankind becomes widespread in Russian writing, usually to denote figures in whom unique aesthetic powers and benevolence are fused. In his *Letters of a Russian Traveller* Karamzin associates genius with a type of ability rather different from the gifts of virtue and bravery that the idea of Great Men extended from Plutarch's exemplary lives. Exceptional intellect unifies figures such as Leibniz, Franklin, Bonnet, and Mendelssohn. Each in their individual spheres devoted their genius to the benefit of mankind. Genius, greater than mere powers of reason, conceptualizes on a different scale. It is mainly in connection with poets that the term genius comes into usage. Homer is one of the first poets referred to as a genius, and the first attested adjectival use is by the poet N. P. Nikolev (1758–1815) in the line 'The ear bent to harken to the mellifluous eloquence and thunderous singing of a new Genius'. Most citations given in the *Dictionary of the Russian Language of the Eighteenth Century* attest the use of the term to denote 'uncommon creative strength' which is linked to an element of craft and 'persistence to an uncommon degree'. The isolation of genius as the defining attribute is all the more powerful because writers do not face the challenge from an anonymous public readership typical of full-blown Romanticism.

While essays on the nature of the imagination do appear, discussions of the nature of inspiration are sporadic rather than systematic. Russia lacked a theorist like Coleridge to bring together a mentalist description of poetic function. Instead the meta-discourse of poetic creativity—whether a mechanical process, a divine type of epiphany, or cultural condition of the role of the *vates*—finds an outlet in lyrics rather than in theoretical exposition. Writers began to extend this principal to poets seen, as Murav'ev states in his poem 'The Power of Genius' (1785, 1792), to possess powers of perception that penetrate the workings of nature and reveal 'in everything its plenitude full delight of existence'. But the cult of sensibility also raised the profile of poets whose individual genius was recognized as exception. Foremost was Derzhavin, who ascribes to the poet of an ideal type near-divine powers of reason. His essay 'Razsuzhdenie o liricheskoi poezii ili ob ode' ('Reflection on Lyric Poetry or the Ode', 1811) describes the imagination of the poet as a sublime gift. From the late 1780s to the end of this period, the role of the poet as a vessel of feeling and heightened consciousness now emerges as a prominent motif. From allegorical waterfalls (as in Derzhavin's imposing elegy on the death of Prince Potemkin) to country graveyards or battlefields (Konstantin Batiushkov's, 'On the Ruins of a Castle in Sweden', 1814) stimulate new powers of vision, introspection, and imagination.

While the word imagination (*voobrazhenie*) appears rarely, poets display an alertness to dreams, a plastic capacity for reverie and fantasy and uncommon eloquence, a facility with association, if not quite a special cognitive faculty, all of which constitute an emerging idea of subjectivity. This combination of greater imagination and greater depth of vision—of the past, of their own age, and sometimes a sense of the future—gradually leads writers to differentiate degrees of poetic talent. Murav'ev discriminated between genius as an aptitude, sometimes an aptitude to satisfy the demands of good taste, and a different capacity to penetrate beneath the 'magical veil' of life. It is the poet whom he identifies as the 'child of a moral Grace', stopping short of Karamzin's encomium of Shakespeare whose glory stems from 'greatness and truth' of his characters and 'penetration into the human heart'. Between the 1790s and 1810s, elegies and eulogies to writers such as Derzhavin and Karamzin himself establish a newfound discourse of genius that celebrates the mortal person for civic or private virtue and vouchsafes an immortal reputation because of perceived genius. Ekphrastic descriptions of sculptural tombs are prominent in Karamzin's travel work; they function within his text as equivalents of *lieux de mémoire* for national figures or domestic grief. Members of the Free Society of Lovers of Literature, Sciences and Arts, an umbrella for informal subgroups aligned by political and intellectual affinity, saw memorial poems as the key to posterity. The early death of the learned and gifted Ivan Pnin elicited a number of such tributes that cast the social ideals of the deceased and his friends as an unbreakable, and holy, monument.

Clearly the search was on in Russia to find a figure who satisfied this idea of genius based on the assumption, articulated by Karamzin, that 'Men of genius are born in every country.' In 1792 the Muscovite antiquarian collector Count Musin-Pushkin discovered a manuscript of a putative lost medieval epic called *The Lay of Igor's Campaign*. While its appearance inspired scepticism about authenticity, it also aroused great enthusiasm because this highly poetic account of a twelfth-century battle represented a boost to the idea of an authentic Russian culture: the bardic narrator, capable of great metaphorical leaps and stirring national history, struck many as a home-grown Ossian (read as authentic) and validation of a tradition of native poetic genius that seemed once again on the rise. Different candidates emerge, including Peter the Great and the scientist-cum-poet Lomonosov whom the writer and philosopher Alexander Radishchev elevates to the status of a mythic, Promethean figure in the final section of his *Journey from St Petersburg to Moscow*, already anticipated twenty years earlier by Nikolai Novikov in his *Attempt at a Historical Dictionary of Russian Writers*. In one of his few essays on the poetic imagination, Derzhavin defined the true poet in terms of the achievement of sublime heights. The polymath, poet, architect, and estate manager N. A. L'vov compared Derzhavin to the ancient bards while paying tribute to the 'elect son of Russia' who combines Horatian wisdom with a Pindaric capacity to generate new images and soar to the sky. This great elegist of others was himself elegized long before his death—but arguably after he had visibly passed his poetic prime and became a relic of a prior age—thanks to his abundant eloquence, his uncommon images, and his larger than life personality. In the 1830s Pushkin lightly mocked his uncouth diction and haphazard learning, but Derzhavin's admirers acclaimed him for a matchless expressivity of language and feeling, proofs of a unique sensibility. When Derzhavin was widowed, Ivan Dmitriev wrote a consolatory elegy ending in aporia and paradox because he argued that only a poet with the powers of Derzhavin could produce the eloquence and wisdom required to console him. On Derzhavin's death, M. V. Milonov, a prominent poet of civic values, produced an elegy spoken by no less a figure than Shakespeare who assures the mourners that Derzhavin's fame is imperishable. Shakespeare's Russian mouthpiece asserts that time itself yields to the poet of genius, a Promethean figure because he defines the terms of true greatness. The minor poet N. M. Shatrov in his 'To the Ashes of Derzhavin', also captivated by the comparison with Pindar, visualizes Derzhavin as he joins a parade of bards, and turns his own text into a monument of a kind by listing the titles of the poems that capture the learning of his pen, the divineness of his language, and the grandeur of his genius. In his poem 'Slavoliubie' ('The Love of Fame', 1822), Vassily Kapnist, a distinguished veteran poet of the previous generation, juxtaposes images of a temple of battle and a temple of poetry. Into the first warriors processed but their fame was not guaranteed because bloodshed had no claim to true renown. By contrast, poets in their own temple were ultimately qualified to erect lasting monuments requiring no more than pen and ink.

Among poets who come of age in the post-Napoleonic period, years that will prove formative for Alexander Pushkin, the idea of genius as a visionary talent becomes a prominent one. Numerous poems about memory as a type of poetic genius—of which Konstantin Batiushkov's 'Moi genii' ('My Genius', 1815) would be a typical example—celebrate the power of association, often when induced by sleep or brought on by a reverie, to unlock experience. In ('Stikhi na son' ('Verses on Sleep', 1905) Ivan Pnin made his ideals of Enlightenment political theory and radical materialism the content of poetic inspiration that Sleep visited on the unconscious, social progress the stuff of his 'visions' and the 'spark of the imagination'. In this vein, the first decades of the century saw a proliferation of Muse-induced epiphanies or yearnings after the naïve powers of the nightingale. Among the most interesting is Vassily Zhukovsky's 'Ia muzu iunuiu byvalo' ('I met my youthful Muse', 1824), which equates poetic power with impressionability and involuntary power of fancy. Minor poets, now better remembered for their progressive views, celebrated the pure art of the songbird whose poignant cries loosened in the mind and heart 'the joy of pure sympathy' and the pure charm of song (A. G. Volkov, 'To the Nightingale', 1799). Instances of pathetic fallacy abound throughout lyric poems. Attitudes to Nature will fall short of the full-blown Schellingian theories of nature and poetic subjectivity that inform the early poetry of Fedor Tiutchev in the late 1820s. Nonetheless, early forerunners of a metaphysical and, to a degree, mystical apprehension of nature, emerge even in the late eighteenth century. In 'Garmoniia mira' ('The Harmony of the World', 1809) and 'Simfoniia natury v chas utra' ('The Symphony of Nature at One a.m.', 1809), the Siberian poet V. V. Dmitriev (1777–1820) picked up where the scientist-poet M. V. Lomonosov left off in his celebrated poem on the Northern lights. This later meditation on the night sky celebrates an 'eternal love' that animates the universe, attributing something like Shaftesbury's principles of order, reason, and beauty to nature.

Literature and Questions of Nation

Secular literature in Russia from the second half of the eighteenth century sees a welter of cross-currents and discontinuous trends that move ahead in a stop-start fashion.

The period features many worthwhile and talented amateur men of letters who use literature as a tool of sociability in forging links with other manifestly enlightened members of the gentry. Anthologies of eighteenth-century lyric give a picture of a dynamic literary culture growing in depth and numbers very rapidly up to the period of Alexander Pushkin's youth. Most writers produced single works or cycles rather than poetic books, works often full of insight into defining questions about social, spiritual, and moral values. Even within the larger trends indicated by terms of periodization such as classicism and pre-Romanticism, many writers went their own way in finding a personal voice that may lead them away from the neoclassical prescriptions about diction and prosody established (and argued over) from the 1750s and 1760s by an earlier generation of theorists.

Discussions about correct style and the linguistic quality of the vernacular, whether based on French salon language or rooted in in neo-Slavonic and thus more authentically Russian, prompted debate. Literary factions and societies who met well into the 1820s were split on prescriptions for poetic style. But it has to be recognized that the literary politics and the theory of literature of the 1810s constituted a retrospective response to a substantial and innovative body of poetry that had assimilated with technical proficiency and artistic finesse European influences. These influences were usually diffuse rather than systematic, and Russian writers imitated promiscuously English, French, and German sources in crafting their own messages. Heterogeneity of style rather than uniformity is the result because for most the message and the lyric voice, rather than the form or genre definition, is paramount. Russia never experienced a Quarrel of the Ancients and Moderns or a Battle of Books. The traditions, and contemporary trends, of European literature ancient and modern were bunched together as Russians read in translation and in the original. When translators domesticated works successfully the distinction between native and foreign, translation and original, collapsed in the minds of readers. Much of the poetry written in the period was classical in form and overtly classical in content. But the degree to which such works were perceived as either European or Russian was a question of reception and attitude.

The existence of literary groups, rather than informal schools inspired by single poets, attests a commitment to literature as at least a pastime and, in some instances, an awareness that literature (much more than music or painting) had acquired stature—and that its purposes required some debating. Questions of taste predominated for the members of Arzamas, who in the 1810s found in literature a game and clever sport, the practice of gifted amateurs whose lightness of touch and tone belied a serious commitment to a polished, transparent style that had the grace of French style and syntax and was entirely compatible with European writing. Younger and older members confirmed their adherence to the canons of style—a conversational tone, regular syntax, standardized expression of emotion through fixed noun-epithet combinations—in which Nikolai Karamzin had written a distinguished body of poetry and prose from the 1780s till his retirement from literature in 1803. For writers of this orientation a polished style did not signify un-Russianness or create a barrier to treating national themes. Cosmopolitan in outlook and reading, these writers absorbed a wide range of European traditions, sometimes through translation and imitation, sometimes through transposition into a specifically native context. The Italian imitations of Konstantin Batyushkov, the translations by Vassily Zhukovsky of German poets, and, above all, his famous version of Gray were judged as works of Russian literature. The translations of Aleksei Merzlyakov, professor of classics at Moscow University, offer an example of how literature crossed the boundaries of the Classical and Romantic, and European and native, at the same time. His strict translations of Virgil's *Eclogues* set a new standard for pastoral verse in Russian. While he preserved the names of Virgil's shepherds, the contemporary idiom and easy style persuaded readers that the ancient was the contemporary, that the European was the Russian, that the universal of the neoclassical also had the national specificity associated with Romanticism.

Directly in this line stands Nikolai Gnedich (1784–1833), eventually renowned for his verse translation of Homer's *Iliad* (1830), who combined the glamour of the classical idyll with a nativizing rustic adaptation in his cycle *Rybaki (Fishermen*, 1822). Poems like these were admired for their combination of the European tradition and its Russian variation. But writers steeped in the European legacy such as Zhukovsky also made notable contributions to the packaging of native material, including folklore and fairy-tales, by translating German and Swiss poetry from Gessner's idylls to Goethe's lyrics of the Weimar period. Initially the ballade proved the most popular genre, overlaying onto the world of the native peasantry the emotional sensibilities of sentimental writers. A direct line stretches from Karamzin's sentimental ballad 'Raisa' (1791), possibly based on a model by Gottfried Bürger, to the verse narratives of Zhukovsky and Kamenev (especially his 'Gromval', 1804). None of these writers depict rural poverty in anything like a naturalistic light. Their unflappable devotion to good taste screened the reader from the actual details of peasant life, as much as in collections of folklore and song anthologies compiled in the period by antiquarians and pioneers such as Mikhail Chulkov. His *Collection of Different Songs* (1774), which went through several reprintings, drew on written versions rather than original fieldwork to present a wide range of popular songs on historic subjects, as well as urban folklore and anonymous literary songs.

Nationalist arguments would eventually factionalize literature in the 1820s when writers clashed over the ballade, its style, and substance. The position of the literary groups that split over issues of genre such as the acceptability of the ballade, the preference for the ode over the elegy, and the use of Slavonicisms in preference to Karamzin's elegant salon style, has often been treated under the larger opposition between Archaists and Innovators. Groupings tend to exaggerate differences; disharmony was the result of multiple factors such as generational rivalry and a tension between nationalist and internationalist views of literature. Membership of groups was a function of age and generation as well as outlook on style. Questions about form, language, and prosody continued to shape discussion, indicating that cross-currents between the classical and the early Romantic marked the practice and theory of literature well into the 1820s. The question of literature as an expression of the quintessence of a nation did colour debates. But difference over genre and language mattered more than any notional opposition between the ancient and modern, Classical or Romantic. Even where groups differed on their linguistic policy they shared attitudes to the interrelation of high genres and popular literature, and the continuation of forms.

Differences of opinion on issues of style that had previously been managed and contained in private correspondence spilled onto the pages of journals. By the 1820s literary criticism had started to gain a hold as a stable medium through which writers could influence readers and probably enhance or damage critical reputations and enhance sales. The transition from friendly societies to public evaluation prompted the acquisition of a polemical critical style that offered value judgements. Style was invested with more ideology as critics floundered in attempts to define the truly popular. In the 1810s some authors who draw most heavily on the classical, and look conservative in literary terms, are most radical in their politics and Romantic when defined from a social point of view. The search for true national identity, in the spirit that Herder had described, led to unexpected positions. Others such as the elderly Derzhavin made common cause with political nationalists and religious conservatives by pinning the definition of Russianness on the use of an outdated linguistic idiom based on the ecclesiastical language rather than the educated vernacular, repudiating at the same time the Karamzinian reforms as extrinsic and inorganic.

Debates deserve to be mentioned at the end of this chapter. They indicate that a consequence of the growth of literature beyond small coteries was the breakdown of consensus on matters of substance and style. The growth of societies, and the development of a literary journalism at the service of different factions, can be taken as signs of the emergence of a full-fledged Romanticism, marked by intergenerational discord and intragenerational misalignments that cannot be disentangled here. In the 1820s Zhukovsky and other practitioners like Petr Pletnev were attacked by both progressive and conservatives for championing the ballade, which was insufficiently Russian, on the one hand, and for betraying the legacy of eighteenth-century classical taste. The definition of authentic Russianness became contested. The poet Pavel Katenin, who called his works 'ballades of the simple folk', rejected charges of faux-Russian style, while Zhukovsky, the darling of an older generation and mentor to the young, had to defend his debt to German literature against detractors who conveniently forgot that he had produced the first modern adaptation of *The Lay of Igor's Campaign* in celebration of a native poetic genius. The Moscow professor and translator of Virgil, Aleksei Merzlyakov saw the style of the ballade as little more than a Russian patina overlaid on a foreign substratum. By contrast he argued that the poetry of the late eighteenth century was truly Russian. In his adaptation of Spartan military songs to Russian metres, Merzlyakov provided his own example of how the Classical could be the Romantic, the ancient now Russian, because he felt they represented popular opposition to the Napoleonic invaders. That line of attack provides a good example of how values could be flipped over.

Further Reading

Primary Sources

For databases containing texts by major and minor figures of the period the most useful websites are: <http://www.rvb.ru/18vek>; <http://www.pushkinskijdom.ru/Default.aspx?tabid=5095> (for lyric poetry of the period). Also useful are these anthologies: *Russkaya sentimental'naia povest'*, ed. P. A. Orlov (Moscow: MGU, 1979); *Russkaia proza XVIII-ogo veka*, ed. G. P. Makogonen'ko (Moscow: Khudozhestvennaia literature, 1971);

Secondary Sources

Brown, W. E., *A History of Russian Literature of the Romantic Period* (Ann Arbor: Ardis, 1986).

Confino, Michael, *Domaines et seigneurs en Russie vers la fin du XVIIIe siècle: Étude de structures agraires et de mentalités économiques* (Paris: Institut d'études slaves de l'université de Paris, 1963).

Ehrard, Marcelle, *V. A. Joukovski et la préromantisme russe* (Paris: University of Paris, 1939).

Eichstädt, Hildegard, *Žukovskij als Übersetzer: drei Studien zu Übersetzungen V. A. Žukovskijs aus dem Deutschen und Französischen* (Munich: W. Fink, 1970).

Golburt, Luba, *The First Epoch: The Eighteenth Century and the Russian Cultural Imagination* (Madison, Wis.: Wisconsin University Press, 2013).

Greenleaf, Monika. *Pushkin and Romantic Fashion* (Palo Alto, Calif.: Stanford University Press, 1994).

Kahn, Andrew, 'Self and Sensibility in Radishchev's Journey from St Petersburg to Moscow: Dialogism, Relativism, and the Moral Spectator', in Laura Engelstein and Stephanie Sandler (eds), *Self and Story in Russian History* (Ithaca, NY: Cornell University Press, 2000), 280–305.

Karamzin, Nikolai, *Letters of a Russian Traveller*, tra. with an introduction and commentary by Andrew Kahn (Oxford: Voltaire Foundation, 2003).

Katz, Michael, *The Literary Ballad in Early Nineteenth-Century Russian Literature* (Oxford: Oxford University Press, 1976).

Kochetkova, N. D., and Panchenko, A. M., eds, *Slovar' russkikh pisatelei XVIII-ogo veka* (Leningard: Nauka, 1988–2010).

Maiofis, M.L., *Vozzvanie k Evrope: Literaturnoe obshchestvo 'Arzamas' i rossiiskii modernizatsionnyi proekt 1815–1818 godov* (Moscow: NLO, 2008).

Maiofis, M. L., and Kurilkin, A. R., eds, *Kritika pervoi chetverti XIX-ogo veka* (Moscow: Izd-vo AST, 2002).

Proskurin, Oleg, *Literaturnye skandaly pushkinskoi epokhi* (Moscow: OGI, 2000).

Ram, Harsha, *The Imperial Sublime: A Russian Poetics of Empire* (Madison, Wis.: Wisconsin University Press, 2003).

Reyfman, Irina, *Vasilii Trediakovsky: The Fool of the 'New' Russian Literature* (Stanford, Calif.: Stanford University Press, 1990).

Schönle, Andreas, 'The Scare of the Self: Sentimentalism, Privacy, and Private Life in Russian Culture, 1780–1820', *Slavic Review*, 57/4 (1998), 723–46.

Todd, William Mills, *The Familiar Letter as a Literary Genre* (Princeton: Princeton University Press, 1976).

Toporov, V.N., *Sel'skoe kladbishche Zhukovskogo: k istokam russkoi poezii* (Amsterdam, 1981).
Vatsuro, V. E., 'Literaturnoe dvizhenie nachala veka. Karamzin. Zhukovsky. Batiushkov', in *Istoriia vsemirnoi literatury*, 8 vols (Moscow: Nauka, 1983–1994), vi. 292–303.
Wirtschafter, Elise Kimerling, *The Play of Ideas in Russian Enlightenment Theater* (DeKalb, Ill.: Norther Illinois University Press, 2003).
Zorin, Andrei, 'Schiller, Gonorrhoea and Original Sin in the Emotional Life of a Russian Nobleman', in Andrew Kahn (ed.), *Representing Private Lives of the Enlightenment* (Oxford: Voltaire Foundation, 2010), 285–303.

CHAPTER 27

ALEXANDER PUSHKIN AS A ROMANTIC

LUBA GOLBURT

To say that Alexander Pushkin (1799–1837) was a Romantic writer is already to advance an argument, one more contentious than stating the same of most other central literary figures of the Romantic period. Generations of critics—starting, shortly after Pushkin's death, with the leading light of nineteenth-century Russian literary canon discussions, Vissarion Belinskii (1811-48)[1]—narrated Pushkin's career as a matter of shedding the trappings of Romantic (primarily Byronic) authorship and gradually yet deliberately progressing towards Realist representation.[2] In the Realist reading, Pushkin is celebrated for attending to the distinctive forms of Russian life and language, making them available—seemingly for the first time—for virtually mirror-like literary representation, one characterized by a lucidity of artistic vision and stylistic transparency. A counter-narrative rejects this post-Hegelian teleology towards Realism, particularly as expressed by Soviet-era ideologues, and sees Pushkin as profoundly rooted in neoclassicist aesthetics, Enlightenment rationalism, and eighteenth-century conceptions of literary circulation and reception oriented towards Western Europe as the cultural centre.[3] Such an epochal designation is more provocatively applied to Pushkin—born ten

[1] See Belinskii's book-length series of articles on Pushkin's oeuvre ('Sochineniia Aleksandra Pushkina'), published in the journal *Notes of the Fatherland* (*Otechestvennye zapiski*) from 1843 to 1846.

[2] Influential Soviet-era studies, informed by a teleological understanding of literary and social history, and foregrounding an advancement from Russian Classicism to Romanticism to Realism as manifested in Pushkin's oeuvre, include Meilakh, *Pushkin i russkii romantizm* (Moscow and Leningrad: Izd. AN SSSR, 1937); and Gukovskii, *Pushkin i russkie romantiki* (Moscow: Khudozhestvennaia lit-ra, 1965) and *Pushkin i problemy realisticheskogo stilia* (Moscow: Gos. Izd. khudozhestvennoi literatury, 1957). On Pushkin's Realism, see also Lidiia Ginzburg, 'K postanovke problemy realizma v pushkinskoi literature', *Pushkin: Vremennik Pushkinskoi komissii*, 2 (1936), 387–401.

[3] On Pushkin's rootedness in 18th-cent. intellectual culture and his 'path to Romanticism', see Viktor Terras, 'Pushkin and Romanticism', in Andrej Kodjak, Krystyna Pomorska, and Kiril Taranovsky (eds), *Alexander Pushkin: Symposium II* (Columbus, Ohio: Slavica, 1980), 49–59. For a study entirely dedicated to Pushkin's engagement with 18th-cent. Russian literature, see Iu. V. Stennik, *Pushkin i russkaia literatura XVIII veka* (St Petersburg: Nauka, 1995). More recently, Andrew Kahn (*Pushkin's Lyric*

years after the French Revolution, and coming of age amid re-examinations and even repudiations of certain of the Russian eighteenth century's artistic and political tenets—than to his older contemporaries (Nikolai Karamzin or Vasilii Zhukovskii). Naturally, this narrative's emphasis on Pushkin's eighteenth-century birthright also complicates his status as Russia's first national poet, a status more comfortably in line with the Romantic conception of the poet as channelling distinctive national genius. If the former account sees Pushkin departing from some loosely defined Romantic practice, or 'overcoming' Romanticism, the latter, in fact, outlines a scenario of his 'becoming' a Romantic.[4]

Inasmuch as both narratives cast Pushkin's Romanticism as a transitional stage always conceived in its dynamic relation to the adjacent periods and aesthetic programmes, they also tend towards a simplified conception of Romanticism, foregrounding those early nineteenth-century conventions absent in the Enlightenment or rejected by Realism: the autonomous lyric subject's orientation towards heightened self-expressivity; the orientalist penchant for the exotic; the fascination with historicity, local colour, and distant pasts; and the privileging of intimate lyrical genres over the public, court-centred poetry of the eighteenth century or the prose of the Realists. Even when Pushkin's Romanticism is not in question, the extent, content, and sources of his Romantic worldview and practice inevitably are, particularly because his own pronouncements on the subject, while numerous, are also far from extensive or conclusive, emphasizing primarily Romanticism's emancipation of literature from neoclassicist formal strictures. The range of Pushkin's reading, moreover, as well as its idiosyncratic trajectories, as he moves from French to English and German literature or from Byron to Shakespeare and Scott, further complicate the task of locating Pushkin in a particular history of Romanticism.

As is often the case with literary figures who find themselves inheriting, rather than first and foremost setting artistic trends, the study of Pushkin's relationship to the pan-European Romantic movement has until recent decades been dominated by inquiry into influence and intertexts. In this context, Pushkin scholarship in the course of the past century has assembled prodigious compendia of the Byronic topoi Pushkin could have gleaned from Amédée Pichot's French prose translations of *Childe Harold's Pilgrimage*, the oriental poems, or *Don Juan*;[5] the transformations of these topoi by

Intelligence, Oxford: Oxford University Press, 2008) has read Pushkin's lyric through the lens of its largely Enlightenment-era philosophical preoccupations.

[4] For a comprehensive critical discussion of scholarship on Pushkin's Romanticism, see Boris Gasparov, 'Pushkin and Romanticism', in David Bethea (ed.), *The Pushkin Handbook* (Madison, Wis.: University of Wisconsin Press, 2005), 537–67. The multiple challenges of chronologizing Pushkin's Romanticism lead Gasparov to conclude (549) that 'the unique poignancy of Pushkin's creative persona consisted precisely in his ability to combine within himself outmoded characteristics with a living sense of the movements and conflicts of his own epoch'.

[5] The most comprehensive account is V. M. Zhirmunskii, *Bairon i Pushkin* (Leningrad: Academia, 1924); see also Tomashevskii, *Pushkin: Kniga pervaia* (Moscow and Leningrad: Izd-vo Akademii nauk, 1956) and Vickery, 'Parallelizm v literaturnom razvitii Bajrona i Puskina', in *American Contributions to the Fifth International Congress of Slavists* (The Hague: Mouton, 1963), ii. 371–401. For an argument against confining Pushkin's engagement with Byron to the earlier period of his career, and against

other versions of conflicted Romantic character, developed, for example, in the fiction of Chateaubriand and Benjamin Constant;[6] and the echoes of Scott's historical novels, manifested in the plots of Pushkin's small but significant historical fiction corpus.[7] If this approach leaves undertheorized the nature of the creative process and authorial self-positioning implicit in this intense reshaping of the other's word, the intertextual study of Pushkin's oeuvre nonetheless provides ample material for such conceptual treatment and paints a rich picture of Romantic-era circulation of texts, motifs, and ideas, a republic of letters whose centres and axes of cultural value are perpetually recharted.

A later, theoretically informed, approach to Pushkin's oeuvre has resisted the desire to see the Romantic republic of letters solely as a network of fully intelligible and documentable textual correspondences; in this view, Pushkin should be included in the epistemological shift towards fragmentary and ironic forms of artistic cognition and selfhood as articulated by the Jena Romantics, and most likely internalized by Pushkin not in reading particular texts, but thanks to his preternatural (and much celebrated) sensitivity to the 'spirit of the age'. Seeing fragmentation in his oeuvre as more than a superficial tribute to European fashion, this approach has highlighted the concomitant fracturing of the subject and the text in Pushkin's corpus, whose many unfinished and fragmented works are indeed replete with gaps that leave a coherent authorial position underarticulated, and might in fact be signposting its dislocation. One crucial breakthrough of this approach has been its recuperation of Pushkin's playfulness and self-aware susceptibility to intellectual fashion as symptoms of a more serious understanding of the Romantic project. In this light, Pushkin's oeuvre is seen to work through numerous creative modalities. Rather than cultivating a cohesive authorial identity, Pushkin partially and ironically inhabits different ones. Surfacing and retreating in response to the particular demands of personal and political circumstance, or of specific literary genres and scenarios of their destabilization and renewal, these identities at the same time ironically engage one another, creating a semblance of biographical continuity for their author. They rearticulate, furthermore, the writer's relationship to his predecessors, contemporaries, and readers, as well as more broadly to both European Romanticism and Russian literary history, each time anew. If Romanticism is to be defined not via its most widespread topoi—not, that is, so as ultimately to demarcate for it a stable and reductive core—but rather as a movement that aspires to undermine various kinds of certainties, be they inherent in generic, biographical, political, or epistemological constraints, then Pushkin, in the very dynamism of his creative positions and ironic self-presentation, is a Romantic par excellence.

limiting the methodological approach to this issue to the intertextual pursuit of echoes and influences, see Monika Greenleaf, 'Pushkin's Byronic Apprenticeship', *Russian Review*, 53 | 3 (1994), 382–98.

[6] Interesting examples of this type of source-criticism are found in the commentaries to *Eugene Onegin* by Vladimir Nabokov and Yuri Lotman.

[7] On Scott and Pushkin, see e.g. Dmitrii Iakubovich, '"Kapitanskaia dochka" i romany Val'ter Skotta', *Pushkin: Vremennik Pushkinskoi komissii*, 4 | 5 (1939), 165–97, and Mark Al'tshuller, *Epokha Val'tera Skotta v Rossii* (St Petersburg: Akademicheskii proekt, 1996).

While 'proteanism'—a descriptive commonplace of both praise and censure accompanying Pushkin's oeuvre since its earliest reception—can thus characterize his versatile and elusive Romanticism, as well as his uncertain and unstable belonging to other periods, movements, and aesthetic persuasions, Pushkin's artistic output is equally, if not more, driven by a syncretic impulse to establish a robust national literary tradition with a legitimate claim to European membership. Pushkin's critical writing and correspondence repeatedly position his works as contributions to this project and urge his fellow writers also to commit to this common goal. Thus, his close friend and lifetime correspondent Petr Viazemskii is pressed to produce analytical prose in order to model for Russia what Pushkin calls 'the metaphysical language',[8] the true Enlightenment's necessary precondition whose absence in Russia Pushkin continually laments; the critic and writer Aleksandr Bestuzhev-Marlinskii is encouraged to treat not Western medieval-chivalric but *Russian* history, and to do so especially in *novels*, to fill his country's void in this genre; Pushkin's own *Boris Godunov* (1825–30), a historical drama set in the Time of Troubles and loosely modelled after Shakespeare's history plays, is pitched to Pushkin's closest interlocutors as an attempt to revolutionize the Russian stage, to put to the test the Russian public's preparedness for new, more organically national forms. Whether in drama or lyric and narrative poetry, critical or novelistic prose, Pushkin's work thus radiates in multiple directions at once. Informing its efforts to assimilate European literary developments is the desire to make the new Russian literary tradition legible to itself and to Europe. The heterogeneity of Pushkin's creative output emerges as a paradoxical product of cultural syncretism, each protean voice differently responding to and synthesizing the multiple traditions Pushkin claims for his own; his originality and his demiurgic status in Russian national literature are built upon a sophisticated and self-conscious derivativeness or, as Fedor Dostoevskii would later define Pushkin's unique gift in a nationalist slavophile vein, his (allegedly Slavic) 'universal responsiveness' (*vsemirnaia otzyvchivost'*[9]).

In this chapter I read Pushkin's engagement with his European cultural context, not as a manifestation of transcendent national character or an entirely innovative approach to literary production, but rather as a radical reworking of the Russian Enlightenment's earlier strategies of cultural Westernization, as well as a commentary on Romantic internationalism and nationalism. If Pushkin's Romanticism is a bid to enter European culture on equal terms, it is hardly the first, and in fact is made by the poet in full awareness of the modernizing culture of imitation and borrowing into which he is born. In the wake of the Petrine reforms, translation and adaptation of foreign texts emerged as one of the most vital strategies of cultural Westernization, enjoying royal support, assuming multiple forms, and ultimately mobilizing and enhancing Russian secular language in a myriad of frameworks. Thus, it was through a free translation (1730) of Paul Tallemant's

[8] Letter to P. A. Viazemskii, cited from Pushkin, *Pushkin on Literature*, tr. Tatiana Wolff (Evanston, Ill.: Northwestern University Press, 1986), 154.

[9] F. M. Dostoevskii, 'Pushkinskaia rech'', in *Polnoe sobranie sochinenii v tridtsati tomakh* (Leningrad: Nauka, 1972–90), xxvi. 145.

narrative allegory *Voyage de l'isle d'amour* (1663) that Vasilii Trediakovskii (1703–68) proposed a new amatory lexicon for Russian, hitherto only minimally endowed with the vocabulary of sentimental interaction; Vladimir Lukin (1737–94) advanced a theory of 'adaptation to Russian mores' (*sklonenie na russkie nravy*) for translating foreign comedies, thereby stressing the need for a native idiom of social critique, and the crucial role of translation in this regard; Catherine the Great's famous voyage along the Volga produced a collective translation by the Empress and members of her retinue of Jean-François Marmontel's *Bélisaire* (1767) and several articles from the *Encyclopédie*, marking translation as a high-brow pastime of state significance. Neoclassicist poetics fit Russian Westernizing ambitions exceptionally well: emulation of the ancients went hand in hand with imitation of Western moderns. Russian poets garnering the proud titles of Russian Pindars or Horaces were, by implication, not only following their Greek and Roman models admirably, but also laying claim to a properly European literary heritage. (The identification of Pushkin as the 'Russian Byron' in the 1820s is undoubtedly a similarly intentioned claim.) Emergent pleas for authorial autonomy at the end of the eighteenth century relate, no doubt, to the pan-European shift towards Romantic individualism and to Russian literature's peculiar institutional history. Its eighteenth-century court- and service-oriented elite, dearth of publication venues, and the virtual impracticability of writing as a profession, that is, are gradually supplanted in the early nineteenth century by a culture featuring a more diverse readership, intelligentsia circles increasingly independent and sometimes critical of the court, a growing number of literary periodicals and publishing houses, and the figure of professional writer embodied first and foremost by Pushkin himself.[10] But these are also, importantly, pleas made in a literature inundated by translations, free translations, imitations, and variations on other authors' themes, where the foreign is often, if not consistently, valued more than the native, and where ownership of discourse is asserted through various degrees of appropriation of foreign sources.

When he makes his literary debut in the 1810s, soon after Russia's triumph over Napoleon, Pushkin enters a polylingual, code-switching, and constantly evolving discursive landscape; and a culture newly rallied around the cause of patriotic self-definition, while at the same time veritably haunted by the spectre of Western Europe. This culture receives different texts in different languages and through intermediaries whose loyalty to the original is questionable, but rarely questioned with any rigour. One wonders, for instance, what it might have meant to read Byron in a French prose translation, all along knowing him to be an English poet (especially if we consider the centrality of the poetry–prose distinction in Pushkin's thinking about his own work and literature generally), or to decipher Shakespeare in English while possessed of only a rudimentary knowledge of the language (as was Pushkin in the late 1820s when working on *Boris Godunov* and *The Little Tragedies*). What kind of discursive flexibility arises when a writer's correspondence with his Russian addressees is conducted in different

[10] For a classic study of Russian literary institutions in this period, see William Mills Todd, *Fiction and Society in the Age of Pushkin* (Cambridge, Mass., and London: Harvard University Press, 1986).

languages: Russian for friends and close acquaintances, and French for women and figures of authority? Most crucially, how might a poet whose avowed ambition is to enliven, and even create, Russian literature and secular literary language work in the context of heated debates over the very existence of such a literature, on the one hand, and a consciousness of robust foreign literary traditions and creative idioms, on the other? Pushkin's Romantic departure from neoclassicism and the eighteenth century lies not in an outright rejection of earlier modes of literary derivation and import, but in their critical overhaul, through which the very act of derivation is reconceived as a performance of originality and critique. This chapter seeks to elucidate Pushkin's strategies of appropriation, revision, and displacement of his European models and interlocutors as developed at different moments of his creative career by examining key selections from his oeuvre, taken from different genres and periods and grouped roughly under two rubrics essential to the history of European Romanticism: Byronism and historicism.

Pushkin's Byronism

Boosted by Romanticism's thriving culture of celebrity, Byron's phenomenal popularity owed most to the idiosyncratic, yet surprisingly far from inimitable, conjunction of fictional and autobiographical identities in his life and work. To imitate Byron meant not only to adopt certain textual practices, but also to align one's biography with them through such Byronic trademarks as the pose of expended youth, aristocratic affectation, exilic and itinerant restlessness, brooding dejection, and a striking blend of political activism and disillusionment in the life of action. All of these elements of the Byronic pose come together for Pushkin in 1820 when he is banished (or, as he insists in his poetry, voluntarily escapes à la Byron) to the south for his political verses and dissipated lifestyle. The early 1820s are doubly (and aptly) marked by Pushkin's formative displacement from the capitals and his growing fascination with Byron. Thus his southern sojourn, which establishes Pushkin as Russia's foremost poet, and as the author primarily of narrative poems reminiscent of Byron's oriental tales, is appropriately bookended by two elegies that consider exile as a Byronic situation: ('Pogaslo dnevnoe svetilo' ('The Orb of Day has Set', 1820) and 'K moriu' ('To the Sea', 1824).[11]

Written on a ship that was to carry the poet further away from his native realm, the former is constructed around a series of refrains—'Clamour, clamour, obedient sail. | Roil beneath me, dismal ocean' (*Shumi, shumi, poslushnoe vetrilo. | Volnuisia podo mnoi ugriumyi okean*[12])—that anchor the lyric subject's agitated reflections as he oscillates,

[11] Reading these elegies (traditionally classified as two of Pushkin's most Romantic texts) in tandem, Andrew Kahn has identified them as the only early lyrics to feature intimate Romantic as opposed to neoclassical conceptions of nature, even as they leave unresolved 'a split in Pushkin between two outlooks [neoclassicist and romantic] on the connection of the poet to the natural world' (*Pushkin's Lyric Intelligence*, 125).

[12] Pushkin, *Sobranie sochinenii v desiati tomakh* (Moscow: Gos. izd-vo khudozh. lit-ry, 1959–62), i. 117.

to the rhythm of the sea's ebb and flow, between disenchanted reminiscences of former passions and half-hearted anticipations of the future, between youth and experience, geographically identified as 'the mournful shores of my foggy homeland' (*bregam pechal'nym tumannoi rodiny moei*) that the poet has abandoned, and the 'magical southern lands' (*zemli poludennoi volshebnye kraia*) he can as yet only imagine. It is the kinetic paradigm, the melancholic bifurcation of the poet's vision between abandoned and imminent realms, that links this elegy with Byron's 'Adieu! Adieu! My Native Shore' from the first canto of *Childe Harold*, a link Pushkin would explicitly signal later by subtitling his poem 'an imitation of Byron' (*podrazhanie Baironu*) in his 1826 verse collection. The poet thus pre-emptively marks whatever Byronic echoes are noticed as fully intended, and at the same time limits his reader's intertextual and biographical probing to a single, most famous, and hence most predictable, direction.[13] In 1820 the poem, for all its participation in common Romantic discourse, offers itself as an imprint of personal experience; in 1826 it becomes an extension of Byron's. If in 1820 the poem, like the emotional state of expectation it describes, has not yet found a ready idiom for its affect and only tends towards the Byronic, in 1826, when Pushkin's identity as the Russian Byron has been repeatedly and all too stiflingly affixed to his creative output, the gesture of marking the text as a Byronic imitation ironically mimics (perhaps at the expense of trivializing the poem) that very predicament: fitting one's poetry and biography into another's mould, that is, becomes a means to possess and overcome one's experience while also making it palatable to the public.

Perhaps the most poignant illustration of this predicament is the 1822 love lyric 'Grechanke' ('To a Greek Girl'), addressed to Calypso Polichroni, a young Greek refugee from Constantinople whom Pushkin met and courted in Kishinev, and who was believed to have previously been Byron's lover. The awareness of Byron as precursor unsettles the poem's presumed initial intention; as a result, what could have developed as an apostrophic description of the poet's beloved gives way to a plea to confirm her *truly* distinguishing feature—her connection to Byron: 'Was it not you who was portrayed | by the poet tormenting and dear ... And [whose] unforgettable image | Lay hidden in the depths of his heart?' (*Uzh ne tebia l' izobrazhal | poet muchitel'nyi i milyi? ... I skrylsia obraz nezabvennyi | v ego serdechnoi glubine?*[14]) Ultimately, the poem configures a love triangle in which the lyric subject's erotic desire is overtly mimetic, borrowed in a strange scenario of apocryphal (or wished) coincidence from a literary precursor. On the one hand, the speaker casts himself as Byron's embarrassed follower and rival, arresting his jealous fantasies at the brink of imagining Byron's and Calypso's physical

[13] The reading of the elegy's Byronic identification in 1826 as a pre-emptive move on Pushkin's part is advanced by Tomashevskii, *Pushkin: Kniga pervaia*, 388–9. Oleg Proskurin has convincingly argued that the elegy's diction situates it not within the Byronic but rather the properly Russian elegiac tradition represented by Konstantin Batiushkov; Pushkin's later identification of the poem as an 'imitation of Byron' in fact masks this literary connection by privileging the demands of autobiographical self-stylization (Proskurin, *Poeziia Pushkina, ili podvizhnyi palimpsest* (Moscow: Novoe literaturnoe obozrenie, 1999), 56–67).

[14] Pushkin, *Sobranie sochinenii v desiati tomakh*, i. 191.

contact ('And you, leaning toward his shoulder ... | No, no, my friend, | I do not wish to feed the fire of jealous dreams': *I ty, sklonias' k ego plechu ... | Net, net, moi drug, mechty revnivoi | Pitat' ia plamia ne khochu*); on the other, in his imagination the girl recedes to the background, and it is 'the depths' of *Byron's* 'heart' that emerge as the poem's true object of yearning. Inasmuch as invoking Byron hinders the fulfilment of the speaker's erotic desire, it also enables a different kind of possession: through the shared object of affection, Pushkin fleetingly inhabits Byron's psyche. The final line, suffused with anxious irresolution, avoids making a choice between the two cynosures, girl and literary idol: 'I fear: all that is dear is false' (*Boius': neverno vse, chto milo*[15]) subsumes both under its totalizing 'all'. While 'dear' as the original's last word resonates with its earlier use to describe Byron ('the poet tormenting and dear'), effectively insinuating some trace of the English bard into the poem's final image, the semantic ambiguity of 'falsehood' (*neverno*) as both betrayal and error references the speaker's jealousy, but also, less obviously, the phantasmal, even misguided nature of the entire scenario of stepping into Byron's shoes. If Pushkin finds it difficult, or impossible, to break away from the literary frameworks that both he and his readers impose on lived experience, the persistent recourse to such frameworks is also shown as an impasse to one's unborrowed creative (in 'To a Greek Girl' rendered as erotic) energies.

Extracting the experience of his own exile from the familiar literary forms of its representation becomes one of the central concerns in Pushkin's lyric of the early 1820s.[16] One of his most remarkable elegiac epistles, 'K Ovidiiu' ('To Ovid', 1821), written in Ovidian elegiac couplets as a gesture of inhabiting Ovid's voice, treats another portentous coincidence, the alleged proximity of Pushkin's place of exile with that of the Roman poet, as an opportunity to overcome the elegiac generic constraints on exilic poetry (as bequeathed from *Tristia* and *Epistulae ex Ponto*). The overcoming of the Ovidian paradigm of lamentation and supplicatory appeals to the Emperor is accomplished first via a brief allusion to a different, Byronic, paradigm of political emancipation and voluntary flight from one's homeland, and then through the assertion of the lyric subject's own vision of his surroundings: 'A stern Slav, I shed no tears, | But I understand them; a wilful exile ... I have repeated your canticles, Ovid | And sought to verify their mournful pictures; | But my gaze has given the lie to deluded dreaming' (*Surovyi slavianin, ia slez ne prolival, | No ponimaiu ikh; izgnannik samovol'nyi, ... Ia povtoril tvoi, Ovidii, pesnopen'ia | I ikh pechal'nye kartiny poverial; | No vzor obmanutym mechtan'iam izmenial*[17]). To be sure, the revised Bessarabian setting Pushkin offers as a corrective to Ovid's still features plenty of melancholy, and the poem's metric form signals its elegiac intent; but Pushkin's

[15] Pushkin, *Sobranie sochinenii v desiati tomakh*, i. 120.

[16] For a study dedicated to the exilic theme in Pushkin's oeuvre, see Stephanie Sandler, *Distant Pleasures: Alexander Pushkin and the Writing of Exile* (Stanford, Calif.: Stanford University Press, 1989).

[17] On Pushkin's conception of the Ovidian and Byronic paradigms as two competing models for stylizing his displacement in the south, see I. V. Nemirovskii, *Tvorchestvo Pushkina i problema publichnogo povedeniia poeta* (St Petersburg: Giperion, 2003), 19–44. Nemirovskii argues that the phrase 'wilful exile' points to his self-stylization as Byron, a rebel and maker of his own fate beyond the reach of political authority.

lyric finds consolation in the luxuriant natural world that for a northerner, a Russian, unlike for a Roman spoilt by lush landscapes, appears to belie the formulas of despondency inherited from Ovid. While 'To Ovid' can be read as one of Pushkin's earliest bids for a voice independent of its own literary origin, 'To a Greek Girl', a far more marginal member of Pushkin's corpus, entertains the possibility of such a voice being stifled by its influential tutors.

'To the Sea', Pushkin's final southern elegy, written in the far-from-southern Mikhailovskoe, the family estate and site of his house arrest upon his readmittance to the Russian heartland, revisits some of the marine imagery first developed in 'The Orb of Day has Set', but unlike in the earlier text, where the poet finds himself wave-borne and his thoughts roiled with the tides, the later elegy is a farewell to the sea, recreated from a physically insurmountable distance that can only be traversed by memory and the spirit. Subsuming in itself reminiscences of the poet's exile and creative quest, together with allusions to the recently departed Napoleon and Byron as heroic embodiments of the elemental forces of nature, this piece's conceptualization of the sea as a mental construct rather than geographical entity produces a totalizing image of personal, literary, and historical experience the poet can export from its original locale wherever he goes: 'Into the forests, into the taciturn wilderness | I, full with you [the sea], shall bear | Your cliffs, your bays, | Your splendor, and shade, and the murmur of your waves' (*V lesa, v pustyni molchalivy | Perenesu, toboiu [morem] poln, | Tvoi skaly, tvoi zalivy, | I blesk, i ten', i govor voln*[18]). Far from a farewell to Romanticism, as the poem has been read by such influential critics as Boris Tomashevskii (with the sea, in this view, representing the Romantic-Byronic-exilic epoch in Pushkin's career[19]), 'To the Sea' stands as the attempt of a maturing writer, removed from the scenery that had lent itself so well to Byronic musings, to recover his earlier Byronic outlook as more than just a youthful pose, to reclaim it as a profound and lasting inner experience.

The lyrics I have considered so far measure the young poet's biographical experience against the poetic language others have provided for its rendering, and in the process distil a new, more precise lyrical idiom befitting the poet's distinctive circumstances and sensibility as well as, by extension, the fledgling Russian literary tradition. The long narrative poems written in the south—*The Prisoner of the Caucasus* (*Kavkazskii plennik*, 1820–1), *The Robber-Brothers* (*Brat'ia-razboiniki*, 1821–2, unfinished), *The Fountain of Bakhchisarai* (*Bakhchisaraiskii fontan*, 1821–3), and *The Gypsies* (*Tsygany*, 1824)—probatively situate various Romantic heroes in a new Russian imperial setting, and offer them to a readership well familiar with these types, but eager to encounter them on native soil and in Russia's own exotic orient. The conflicted heroes of these narratives are subject to various thraldoms, both spiritual and physical; attempting to escape the confining monotony of their habits, they are consumed by passions that ultimately find no satisfying outlet, a recurring predicament lapidarily summarized in the coda to *The Gypsies*: 'And all around, passions fatal, | And no safeguard from the fates' (*I vsiudu strasti*

[18] Pushkin, *Sobranie sochinenii v desiati tomakh*, ii. 38.

[19] Tomashevskii, *Pushkin: Kniga vtoraia* (Moscow and Leningrad: Izd-vo Akademii nauk, 1961), 10.

rokovye, | I ot sudeb zashchity net[20]). Thus, the eponymous Prisoner of the Caucasus flees his Russian past to seek liberty in the wild Caucasian terrain, but spends the entire poem in chains until his final escape with the help of a young Circassian maid who falls in love with him. The two brigands in *The Robber-Brothers* choose their unlawful path, which lands them in prison amid a multi-tribal criminal throng, to break free of their inherited poverty and constraint, but the poem's beginning finds them shackled and, even after their successful escape, the one brother surviving at the end is as tormented by the habits of theft and murder he cannot quit as by the terrible sacrifice of his brother's life he has paid for their crimes. Khan Girei, the protagonist of *The Fountain of Bakhchisarai*, whose anguish we only observe externally, in his often exaggerated gestures and bloodthirsty deeds (a form of overstatement Pushkin later ascribed to his inexperience with the more nuanced rendering of characters' emotional life[21]), desires to experience not the tedious harem pleasure, but true love with his newly acquired Polish noblewoman Maria, inciting the jealousy of his first wife Zarema, which eventually leaves both women dead and Girei pursuing an aimless bloodthirst clearly incapable of quelling his inner turmoil. In *The Gypsies*, the protagonist Aleko, led by his lover Zemfira to join a band of Gypsies roaming the Bessarabian steppes, temporarily escapes the European civilization that had reared him, but this upbringing exercises its fatal grip on his character when, consumed with jealousy, he slays both Zemfira and her new lover, thus proving himself unable to live by the Gypsy codes of complete personal (including amatory) freedom.

The same clash of aspiration and circumstance, innocence and experience, freedom and enslavement (to literary model, imperial decree, or unrequited past passion) that is broached in the southern elegies' accounts of self is in the long narrative poems transposed onto the other, structuring the protagonists' inner conflicts, which are often rendered rather schematically and resolved far more pessimistically than the ultimate striving for personal language and self-understanding afforded by the elegy. Such conflicts, the distinctive scenarios of their resolution in the self and other, the purview and limitations of the elegiac outlook, as well as the pursuit of a Russian poetic language that would exceed inherited clichés and make the perceived world freshly and richly visible—all come together as the governing concerns of Pushkin's most celebrated work, the novel-in-verse *Eugene Onegin* (*Evgenii Onegin*, 1823–31), also begun in southern exile, but completed in the course of seven eventful and prolific years that saw a decided evolution in Pushkin's poetics. Pushkin himself linked his initial conception of the novel (albeit later denying this connection as the work took shape) with Byron's *Don Juan*, a text whose multiple ironies and self-subversive cynicism have been read as deconstructing Byronism itself.[22] If *Eugene Onegin* inherits from Byron's masterpiece its digressive capaciousness and the delicate balance of idealist Romantic enthusiasm and ironic

[20] Pushkin, *Sobranie sochinenii v desiati tomakh*, iii. 180.

[21] Pushkin, *Sobranie sochinenii v desiati tomakh*, x. 67.

[22] See, for instance, Malcolm Kelsall, 'Byronism', in Christopher John Murray (ed.), *Encyclopedia of the Romantic Era, 1760–1850* (New York: Fitzroy Dearborn, 2004), i. 147.

Romantic skepticism,[23] its deployment of Romantic irony is not as corrosive as Byron's, but instead is everywhere checked by sympathy and moments of the narrator's fleeting but indulgent rapprochement with his hero.

The novel's plot is minimal but far from clichéd, its unexpected turns provided mostly in the thorny path by which its heroine Tatiana comes to an understanding of the protagonist Onegin and eventually herself. Eugene has traditionally been construed as an essentially Byronic hero limited to his Byronic pose; developing the argument of Pushkin as interpreter rather than imitator of Byron, I propose instead to read this protagonist as a post-Byronic gloss on the forms of personhood propagated through Byronism, forms so tragically inhabited by the heroes of Pushkin's southern narrative poems, but thoroughly interrogated in *Eugene Onegin*. One of the crucial sources of characterization in the novel is accounts of characters' reading, their interactions being thus interpretable as collisions of competing models available to a late Romantic like Pushkin for the rendering of experience and sentiment in literature. Thus Tatiana is shaped by the sentimental novels of Richardson and Rousseau, and as a result anxiously and dreamily seeks to find in Onegin her soulmate, resorts to the epistolary form, and maintains a uniquely moving relationship with the natural world; Vladimir Lensky, Onegin's friend whom he eventually kills in a foolish duel, is educated in Göttingen, brims with Idealist terminology, and pours out his excessive sentiment in elegiac formulae; most prominent in the title character's reading list, finally, is Byron. Eugene's bookshelf reflects a desire to see his own predicament, for which he himself is all too unforthcoming a spokesman, both moulded and depicted. Onegin reads

> The bard of Juan and the Giaour,
> And some few novels done with power,
> In which our age is well displayed
> And modern man himself portrayed
> With something of his true complexion—
> With his immoral soul disclosed,
> His arid vanity exposed,
> His endless bent for deep reflection,
> His cold, embittered mind that seems
> To waste itself in empty schemes.[24]

This portrait captures Onegin's key traits well enough, but only because Onegin finds in such characters a ready mould for his self-fashioning. By invoking such portrayals in bulk and as part of Onegin's casual reading, Pushkin implicitly claims a different purpose for his work: not to contribute yet another Byronic portrait to a well-populated gallery, but rather to explore the consequences of modelling one's life upon literature.

[23] I borrow this formulation of *Don Juan*'s ironic procedure from Anne K. Mellor, *English Romantic Irony* (Cambridge, Mass.: Harvard University Press, 1980), 42.

[24] Pushkin, *Eugene Onegin*, tr. James E. Falen (Carbondale, Ill.: Southern Illinois University Press, 1990), 166.

If, as Jerome McGann has remarked, Byronic heroes 'face in two directions, "referentially" toward certain socio-historical frameworks, and "reflexively" toward the poetical environments within which they are aesthetically active',[25] then the poetic environment Onegin faces is in fact Byron's, and it comes into conflict with the socio-historical as well as poetic conditions of a world where Byronic personhood is no longer the mark of an autonomous rebel, but rather of a weak individual's susceptibility to fashion.

Starting with its very title, *Eugene Onegin* is a novel that is quite obviously focused on and through its protagonist. The first chapter defines his dandy habitus in high-society Petersburg; the subsequent ones, with the exception of chapter 7, from which the hero is physically absent, stage his confrontations with others: his friendship with Lensky; rejection of Tatiana's affection; ill-advised incitement of Lensky's jealousy at Tatiana's nameday party and murderous duel with his erstwhile friend; his flight from Russia and subsequent return to St Petersburg, where he finds Tatiana in her new, self-aware incarnation of high-society lady and falls in love with her; his letter to Tatiana, symmetrically positioned as an ironic refrain to her naïve epistolary admission in chapter 3; and the final scene in Tatiana's salon where he remains spurned and alone, awaiting the arrival of Tatiana's husband. Despite Onegin's absence, chapter 7 contains the attentive, even revelatory, examination of him by the novel's most sensitive character-observer, Tatiana, who discovers traces of Napoleon and Byron in his study, and fingernail indentations, crosses, and exclamation points in the margins of his books. And yet even at the end of the novel, Onegin's character remains notoriously ill-defined. Is his essential emptiness only poorly masked by fashionable posturing? Does he harbour an unspoken plenitude and depth, persisting despite a modish pretence that threatens to utterly externalize the character, to disperse him into a series of carefully crafted poses? Does the novel allow him a spiritual core that after Lensky's death in chapter 6 becomes a wound? (Not for nothing, after all, does the novel return to the duel as a permanent fixture in Eugene's memory.) In fact, Tatiana's 'discovery' of Onegin in absentia is achieved precisely through such questioning, which assigns to the protagonist partially accurate identities without settling too long on any one:

> What was he then? An imitation?
> An empty phantom or a joke,
> A Muscovite in Harold's cloak,
> Compendium of affectation,
> A lexicon of words in vogue ...
> Mere parody and just a rogue?[26]

In *The Political Unconscious*, Fredric Jameson proposes that we abandon the 'naïve' categories of 'character', 'protagonist', and 'hero' and, harkening to the Lacanian critique of the centred subject, detect in the nineteenth-century novel 'a repudiation of the various

[25] Jerome J. McGann, *Byron and Romanticism* (Cambridge: Cambridge University Press, 2002), 142.
[26] Pushkin, *Eugene Onegin*, 167.

ideals of the unification of the personality or the mythic conquest of personal identity'.[27] Even as he frames and anchors the novel, Eugene in fact ironically embodies just such a pulverization of personality—noteworthy in that, while Byron too may have been sceptical as to the unity of identity, a quite cohesive Byronism was nonetheless embraced by and imposed upon all too many European young men. If Byronism helped disarticulated post-Napoleonic identities to coalesce, but also ossify, then Pushkin's critique of Byronism in *Eugene Onegin* is to represent and chip away at such rigid forms of self-understanding, to reveal the Byronic or any totalizing idiom as in fact precluding the subject's self-expression and self-knowledge.

Pushkin's most powerful pronouncement on the suppression of individual agency and expressivity symptomatic of a self-consciously derivative and belated culture, a culture whose self-determination is inextricably linked with the absorption of other traditions, comes in the very form and language of *Eugene Onegin*. The novel's tour-de-force linguistic performance, its playful cataloguing of the national everyday, which is so perceptively shown to have assimilated and even normalized products of European culture; its rapid-fire conjunctions of different idioms; and above all the spellbinding flexibility, indeed freedom, of its exposition, which appears unmindful of the rigid structure (the so-called 'Onegin stanza' of fourteen lines, iambic tetrameter, and ababccddeffegg rhyme scheme) maintained throughout the novel's eight chapters—all point to a project that foregrounds, indeed celebrates, expressivity and the transcendence of legacies and models while never fully abandoning elegiac musings on their commemoration and overcoming.

When we consider *Eugene Onegin*'s status as Russia's first canonical novel, it is remarkable that what it bequeaths to its immediate followers in the Russian novelistic tradition—Mikhail Lermontov's *A Hero of Our Time* (*Geroi nashego vremeni*, 1840), Nikolai Gogol's *Dead Souls* (*Mertvye dushi*, 1842), Ivan Turgenev's *Rudin* (1855)—is its post-Byronic hero, perturbed by an overabundance of possible scenarios of identity, questing after but also escaping or failing to achieve his own settlement. Yet we might also see the novel within Pushkin's own oeuvre articulating, through the voice of the narrator, the very principles of proteanism that would underwrite the poet's mobile self-presentation throughout his career: his ranging from Ovidian/Byronic outcast to fledgling poet-prophet first encountering the burdens of his civic obligations ('The Upas Tree'/'Anchar', 1828; 'The Prophet'/'Prorok', 1826); to elegist of his passing youth and friends ('Arion', 1827; 'Once more have I visited …'/'Vnov' ia posetil …', 1835); to craftsman seeking to sell his poetic wares for profit ('A Bookseller's Conversation with a Poet'/'Razgovor knigoprodavtsa s poetom', 1824), or by contrast rejecting the pleasure-mongering masses ('The Poet and the Crowd'/'Poet i tolpa', 1828) and asserting the primacy of lofty inspiration ('The Poet'/'Poet', 1827; 'To the Poet'/'Poetu', 1830) and claims to national significance ('Monument'/'Pamiatnik', 1836).

[27] Fredric Jameson, *The Political Unconscious* (Ithaca, NY: Cornell University Press, 1981), 153.

Pushkin's Historicism

Periodizations of Pushkin's career have typically seen him as taking leave of Romanticism and turning to Realism around 1825 upon his return from the south, and particularly after the crushing of the Decembrists, who included many of Pushkin's closest friends, dealt a disastrous blow to presumably 'Romantic' Russian liberalism.[28] We might, however, read the same material rather as a transition (but not outright departure) from preoccupation with Romantic personhood to questions, no less central to Romanticism, of national history and its narrative forms. Here again European models, ranging from Shakespeare's history plays to Balzac's epoch-conscious character typologies to Sir Walter Scott's historical novels, are mobilized to bring Russian history into view through literary forms both familiar and—given the inherent tension of fitting national material to transnational genres—innovative. It was furthermore only in this period that Russian archives were popularized (and many particular ones first excavated) by Pushkin's elder contemporary, the writer and historian Nikolai Karamzin (1766–1826), who in his *History of the Russian State* (1816–29), the magisterial twelve-volume work of Romantic historiography, interpreted native historical material for Russia's Westernized elite. In the preface, Karamzin envisioned for his *History* a dual Russian and European readership, the former enthusing over their national history with sentimental patriotism, the latter finally brought to acknowledge the vast Russian Empire as a historical nation.[29] Describing the fervent reception of the first eight volumes of the *History*, Pushkin, for whom this publication (February 1818) would prove a most formative intellectual event, envisions just such a metamorphosis of Russia's pre-Romanov past from a *tabula rasa* (a myth propagated ever since the launch of Petrine Europeanization in the early 1700s) to a rich patrimony: 'Ancient Russia seems to have been discovered by Karamzin much as America was by Columbus.'[30] Early nineteenth-century cultural discourse in Russia had been marked by unease as to whether a distinctive native language, landscape, history, and national character even existed; but Karamzin's *History* lessened these anxieties, enabling new Russian cultural mythologies and encouraging the search for the new literary forms they might take. Pushkin's was a major voice at this stage of experiment and codification.

Karamzin's history famously stops short of the Romanov dynasty: volumes ix to xi came out in 1821–4 and covered the period immediately following the death of Ivan the Terrible, thus directly inspiring Pushkin's work on *Boris Godunov*; volume xii ends in 1612, i.e. before the 1613 instatement of the Romanovs. When in 1831 Pushkin inherited Karamzin's post as state historiographer, he focused his research, by contrast, on

[28] On the periodization of Pushkin's Romanticism and its putative overcoming in the mid-1820s, see Gasparov, 'Pushkin and Romanticism', 541–2.

[29] N. M. Karamzin, *Istoriia gosudarstva Rossiiskogo* (St Petersburg: Izdanie Evg. Evdokimova, 1892), I, pp. xviii–xix.

[30] Pushkin, *Sobranie sochinenii v desiati tomakh*, vii. 278.

the ruling dynasty, particularly the reigns of Peter I (r. 1696–1725) and Catherine II (r. 1762–96). Unlike his predecessor, he would not so much outright 'discover' Russia's past as offer nuanced illuminations of it, markedly laying emphasis on 'modern' rather than 'ancient' history.[31] Crucially, it is precisely the modern period that is characterized by momentous but also often misguided and authoritarian attempts to bring Russia into the fold of European culture, a project Russian writers—including, as this article has outlined, Pushkin himself—stood both as beneficiaries of and spokesmen for. Writing about modern history, we could thus speculate, was always already a meta-reflective exercise on being a writer in Russia. The famous narrative poem *The Bronze Horseman* (1833) is emblematic in this regard: its first-person poetic voice is complicit in the celebration of state-imposed European modernity ('I love you, Peter's creation'; *Liubliu tebia, Petra tvoren'e*[32]), even as the work as a whole casts this modernity as a problematic, if not outright tragic, inheritance, insisting that the forces shaping St Petersburg, Peter the Great's most visible yet most phantasmal Westernizing legacy, were destructive as well as creative. In a period of increasingly mistrustful censorship, exacerbated in Pushkin's case by Nicholas I's 1826 offer to personally review all his new writing, the author's focus on modernity, in addition to the opportunities it afforded for poetic meta-reflection, precariously opened his historical work to charges of allegorical suggestiveness and subversive political critique.[33] In this connection, the marshalling of scholarly, fictional, and lyrical genres in Pushkin's historical work (a formal agility characteristic of his oeuvre in general) might also be interpreted as testing the capacity of individual genres to convey—or indeed, to smuggle—historical knowledge and analysis with varying degrees of candour and plasticity.

Hardly voluminous, Pushkin's historical corpus nevertheless comprises a surprising range of genres, including a history play (*Boris Godunov*); long narrative poems (*Poltava* and *The Bronze Horseman*) and shorter lyrics (from 'Reminiscences in Tsarskoe Selo' to 'The Feast of Peter I'); historiographical monographs (*The History of Peter the Great*, *The History of Pugachev*); anecdote collections (*Table Talk*); and historical novels (*The Captain's Daughter*, as well as the unfinished *Blackamoor of Peter the Great* and *Dubrovsky*).[34] Seen as a whole, this corpus can be read as a continuous project whose

[31] An important articulation of both the divide and the interconnections between Russian history's 'ancient' and 'modern' periods also belongs to Karamzin, who addresses the question in his brief *Memoir on Ancient and Modern Russia*.

[32] Pushkin, *Sobranie sochinenii v desiati tomakh*, iii. 286.

[33] Wary of the excessive emphasis placed by censors and lay readers alike on decoding present-day political agendas behind the historical settings of fiction (an ideological contraband in which Pushkin no doubt himself participated), Pushkin warns against facilely overlooking the value of literary time travel and reconstruction: 'Thanks to the French, we do not understand how a dramatic author can entirely renounce his own way of thinking so as entirely to relocate to the age that he describes' (*Sobranie sochinenii v desiati tomakh*, vii. 283). In fact, we find Pushkin engaging both the Aesopian and archeological modes of historical writing.

[34] Scholarship on Pushkin's historicism is voluminous; for a recent critical overview and interpretation, see Simon Dixon, 'Pushkin and History', in Andrew Kahn (ed.), *The Cambridge Companion to Pushkin* (Cambridge: Cambridge University Press, 2006), 118–29.

formal diversity masks, yet crucially also enables, a consistent dislodgement of dynastic periodization in favour of a more flexible and analytical understanding of the 'modern', and a thematic convergence upon key moments and rhythms of contestation and consolidation of power, imposture, and legitimacy. In addition, the meta-reflections underlying Pushkin's historical project thematize fundamental epistemological concerns regarding the reliability of historical record and knowledge. On the one hand, Pushkin's experiments with genre highlight the adaptability of documentary evidence to narrative framing and the peculiar aptness of specific literary forms (often imported) to render certain events and periods (mostly native). On the other, they expose the arbitrariness of attempts to narrativize experience, the ideological underpinnings and consequences of imposing genre and interpretation upon material that often resists them.

The publication history of *Boris Godunov* provides a fitting illustration for this cluster of concerns.[35] Evaluating the play, Nicholas I suggested that Pushkin rewrite his fragmented and elusive Shakespearean rendering of the Time of Troubles as a historical novel à la Walter Scott. The Tsar thus appears to ignore the peculiar congruence of the disjointed dramatic form—focused neither on any particular protagonist nor any individual plotline—and the partial, contradictory knowledge of the actual circumstances of regicide, betrayal, and imposture held by participants and later interpreters alike.[36] 'Clothing in dramatic form one of the most dramatic epochs in our modern history',[37] *Boris Godunov* disposed of the classicist unities, the act-bound ordering of dramatic action, and the metrical and stylistic uniformity of language, presenting instead twenty-five loosely linked dramatic scenes written in blank verse and occasionally in prose, thereby puzzling not only those readers who craved the guidance of a novelistic narrator, but also those ambivalent about Pushkin's proposal for the Russian stage—nothing less, he believed, than its much-needed, 'truly Romantic'[38] overhaul. How did the Time of Troubles bear upon Pushkin's contemporary moment? Without the expounding of an authoritative history-teller, the play left this question muddled. Neither a lesson, nor an analogy, nor an unequivocally surpassed earlier moment in the nation's progressive development, the Godunov reign in the play leaves traces notable more for the lacunae they focalize than for any meaning they might definitively ascribe to the epoch. Thus, though the reign and its iniquitous origins form the subject of the final pages of the chronicler-monk Pimen's testimony, the omission of Pimen's account itself only serves to highlight the subversive, indeed denunciatory, power of any chronicler's (or poet's) historical project. Likewise, the culmination of the play in the people's silence at the coronation of Dmitri the Impostor furnishes yet another moment where

[35] For a brief account of this history, see Emerson, 'Pushkin's Drama', in Andrew Kahn (ed.), *The Cambridge Companion to Pushkin* (Cambridge: Cambridge University Press, 2006), 57–74; see also her *Boris Godunov: Transpositions of a Russian Theme* (Bloomington, Ind.: Indiana University Press, 1986).

[36] It is quite possible that Nicholas's acquaintance with *Boris Godunov* came only via a censor-prepared digest; if so, his proposal would be rooted not in any particular objection to the specific form of the play, but rather in a general preference for the historical novel as a genre.

[37] Pushkin, *Sobranie sochinenii v desiati tomakh*, vi. 300.

[38] Pushkin, *Sobranie sochinenii v desiati tomakh*, vi. 282.

the cessation of speech marks an explosive proliferation of interpretive possibilities.[39] The Shakespearean form, with its pluralism and episodic structure, is only in part an organizing brace; more crucially, it yields unsettling silences and ellipses whose interpretive charge is as dangerous as it is elusive. Perhaps, then, Nicholas's preference for the Scottian historical novel, with its ideology of progress and reconciliation, over such interpretive models as eschew closure and foreground epistemic inconsistency, in fact attests to a canny awareness (paradoxically shared by Tsar and writer alike) of literary form as a powerful hermeneutic tool.

Pushkin adopts European historical-narrative templates precisely as hermeneutic tools. The interpretive insight afforded by these borrowed patterns derives as much from their opportune fit with the new material they are brought to shape as from the dissonances born of fitting one to the other. As another case in point, consider *The Captain's Daughter* (*Kapitanskaia dochka*, 1836), a short novel replete with such features of the Scottian narrative as the 'middling' hero stranded between two opposing camps in the midst of a sweeping historical drama; the resolution of the plot's final conflict through the intervention of a female protagonist; the depiction of a central historical personage (Catherine the Great) from the perspective of a character who does not recognize her; and the setting of the novel at a sixty-year remove from the reader's present.[40] These structural resemblances to Scott, along with the construction of domesticity, which Pushkin had earlier praised as central to Scottian narrative,[41] and to which the mundane setting of *The Captain's Daughter* and its protagonist Peter Grinev's unadorned writing pay a definite homage, only partly obscure the suspicion haunting this text that history—particularly Russian history with its underexamined (because then scarcely examinable) forms of tyranny and social unrest—might not lend itself to the optimistic narrative of progress that Scott's plot resolutions of reconciliation and containment appear to privilege.[42] We might in fact construe the radical simplicity for which *The Captain's Daughter* was criticized by some contemporaries, its unabashed resemblance to Scott and apparent lack of poetic invention—in other words, the very mundanity and domesticity that Pushkin seems to lift from the Waverley novels, and further exaggerate

[39] Ironically, the famously fraught final stage direction—'The people are silent'; *Narod bezmolvstvuet*—was introduced to propitiate the censor, who objected to the people's cheering for the impostor in the original.

[40] For a recent overview of the historical novel in Russia, see Dan Ungurianu, *Plotting History* (Madison, Wis.: University of Wisconsin Press, 2007), particularly the section on *The Captain's Daughter* (88–96).

[41] 'The main charm of Walter Scott's novels', Pushkin writes in his two-paragraph sketch on the author, 'is that we are introduced to the past, not with the *enflure* [pomposity] of French tragedy,—not with the primness of the sentimental novel, not with the *dignité* of history, but rather in a contemporary domestic manner' (*Sobranie sochinenii v desiati tomakh*, vii. 535).

[42] For an illuminating treatment of Pushkin's philosophy of history as implicit in *The Captain's Daughter* and as distinct from Western counterparts, see Dolinin, 'Historicism or Providentialism? Pushkin's *History of Pugachev* in the Context of French Romantic Historiography', *Slavic Review*, 58 | 2 (Summer 1999), 291–308, and 'Val'ter-skottovskii istorizm v "Kapitanskoi dochke"', in *Pushkin i Angliia* (Moscow: Novoe literaturnoe obozrenie, 2007), 237–58.

on his own—as expressions of polemical resistance to the falsifications of novelistic closure and evolutionary historical narratives, a defence against the distortive tendencies of imported literary forms in general.[43]

The novel's linear autobiographical narration is repeatedly offset by suggestive repetitions and motivic rhyming; its seeming neutrality, by deep-seated tensions connected to social class and political authority and legitimacy—tensions that strive toward resolution but, unlike the protagonist-centred plotline (with its ending in a happy marriage facilitated by none other than Catherine the Great), never achieve it. Thus, the rift between gentry and peasantry is fleetingly mitigated in scenes of rapprochement between fictional nobleman Grinev and historical peasant Pugachev, but the two protagonists are ultimately revealed to inhabit discrepant ethical and stylistic spaces.[44] Similarly, Pugachev's doomed pretensions to the throne and his ludicrous performance of power are hardly convincing even to his coarsest followers, ruling out any parallel between the classes, let alone some far-reaching scenario of reconciliation. Unlike the masking conceits of Shakespearean drama (the false Dmitrii's imposture, we recall, did succeed both historically and in Pushkin's play), the mundanity of the historical novel, no doubt informed by rationalist Enlightenment epistemology, brings us into intimate proximity with the pretender only to lay bare his illegitimacy all the more glaringly.[45]

Perhaps the novel's most trenchant challenge to Scottian conflict resolution comes from the text's tacit orientation towards its extra-novelistic context. Grinev's eyewitness account is presented as a supplementary document sent to the author Pushkin by the narrator's grandson, who has learned of the former's ongoing historiographical research on Pugachev. Though certainly reminiscent of Scott as well as other fiction of the period, this fabricated provenance markedly directs the reader to inquire beyond the fictitious story of individual adventure, and to bear in mind not only the *History of the Pugachev Uprising* published some two years earlier, but also the existence of material potentially illuminating this episode that never saw the light of print. While focused on the events of 1773–5, Grinev's memoir furthermore repeatedly alludes to that period's resemblance to the no-less-turbulent 1740s, is written by the aged narrator in the early 1800s, and first brought to the public's attention in the 1830s, implying patterns of homologous recurrence in modern Russian history and a persistent lack of resolution for the peasant–gentry conflict. Pushkin's work on the Pugachev uprising indeed coincided with, if not in fact responded to, the peasant unrest of the early 1830s, and his interest in the would-be Peter III could plausibly be seen as grounded in contemporary concerns. Finally, the extratextual knowledge that an informed reading of the novel would activate

[43] For a comprehensive study of Pushkin's prose, which pays particular attention to his engagement with Western models, see Paul Debreczeny, *The Other Pushkin* (Stanford, Calif.: Stanford University Press, 1983).

[44] The influential reading of the novel as negotiating the distance between the two camps, gentry and peasantry, is expounded by Yuri Lotman in 'Ideinaia struktura "Kapitanskoi dochki"', in *Pushkin* (St Petersburg: Iskusstvo-SPb, 1995), 212–27.

[45] Curiously, it is Catherine II's disguise as an ordinary noblewoman in the final scenes of the novel that highlights unpretension as one of the most compelling facets of her legitimacy.

no doubt also includes the recognition of any number of Scott's novels—from *Waverley*, to *Rob Roy*, *The Heart of Midlothian*, or *The Bride of Lammermoor*—as its intertexts. Of all the ways Pushkin creates for his reader a frisson of déjà vu as well as the intellectual experience of reading between the lines, perhaps the most crucial is the novel's recognition of its own status as akin to what readers have already read, that is, as literature, specifically post-Scottian historical fiction. Pushkin's text stages the recognition of the genre to which it proposes to contribute, and the recognition of its very participation in that genre; but in the process it revises this genre's parameters (abbreviates the Scottian long novel to a mere hundred pages; focuses the narrative even more on the mundane aspects of historical experience; problematizes the centrality of developmental, progressive models of national history to the genre) and questions its purchase on Russian history. Repetition and abridgement both instate and erode the comforts of historical adventure and research, and the text that emerges as a result is not another Scottian novel, but that novel's critique.

As I have maintained throughout this chapter, Pushkin's artistic project illuminates a paradoxical convergence of nationalism and internationalism at the core of both European and, perhaps even more exigently, Russian Romanticism; the period's concurrent commitment, on the national as well as individual scale, to creative solipsism *and* to circuits of intellectual exchange opened up by the Enlightenment across Europe (post-Petrine Europeanization in Russia); its introspection and extroversion; its vitalizing yet ambivalent comparatism. Seen in this light, Pushkin's formal and stylistic versatility appears to revel in, but also critically interrogate, the creative possibilities inherent in the predicament of a country striving to fashion its modern national culture by means of appropriation. Thus, the Byronic mask, on the one hand, successfully externalizes the pervasive malaise of the post-Napoleonic individual—perhaps even especially so in a nation that had recently vanquished the Grande Armée, only to find itself bereft of any other outlet for its liberalizing energies—and, on the other, stifles autonomous expression, revealing it as always already borrowed and rigid. The Scottian historical novel imbues local history and landscape—especially of the unspectacular, even dreary, sort that early nineteenth-century Russian intellectuals decried at every turn—with the thrill of adventure and emplotment and the comforting prospect of settlement, but at the same time obscures the precarious rhythms and tensions of the native past. In this treatment, the sway of literary form (no less imposing in the Romantic than in the classicist period, albeit more capacious and flexible) and cultural celebrity (itself, I would argue, experienced as a formalizing constraint) is transcended, or at least destabilized, not via its outright rejection, but rather through its ironic colonization, a self-aware inhabiting of another's voice and culture. This investment in comparative cultural (de)construction, at once playful and serious, persists as a unifying thread throughout Pushkin's otherwise insistently versatile oeuvre, indeed underwrites this very versatility, and could, as I have suggested, be productively singled out as the defining feature of his Romanticism.

Further Reading

Al'tshuller, Mark, *Epokha Val'tera Skotta v Rossii: Istoricheskii roman 1830-kh godov* (St Petersburg. Akademicheskii proekt, 1996).

Belinskii, V. G., 'Sochineniia Aleksandra Pushkina', in V. G. Belinskii, *Polnoe sobranie sochinenii v 13 tomakh* (Moscow: Akademiia nauk SSSR, 1953), vii. 99–579.

Debreczeny, Paul, *The Other Pushkin: A Study of Alexander Pushkin's Prose Fiction* (Stanford, Calif.: Stanford University Press, 1983).

Dixon, Simon, 'Pushkin and History', in Andrew Kahn (ed.), *The Cambridge Companion to Pushkin* (Cambridge: Cambridge University Press, 2006), 118–29.

Dolinin, A. A., 'Historicism or Providentialism? Pushkin's *History of Pugachev* in the Context of French Romantic Historiography', *Slavic Review*, 58 | 2 (Summer 1999), 291–308.

Dolinin, A. A., 'Val'ter-skottovskii istorizm v "Kapitanskoi dochke"', in A. A. Dolinin, *Pushkin i Angliia: Tsikl statei* (Moscow: Novoe literaturnoe obozrenie, 2007), 237–58.

Dostoevskii, F. M., 'Pushkinskaia rech'', in F. M. Dostoevskii, *Polnoe sobranie sochinenii v tridtsati tomakh* (Leningrad: Nauka, 1972–90), xxvi. 129–49.

Emerson, Caryl, *Boris Godunov: Transposition of a Russian Theme* (Bloomington, Ind.: Indiana University Press, 1986).

Emerson, Caryl, 'Pushkin's Drama', in Andrew Kahn (ed.), *The Cambridge Companion to Pushkin* (Cambridge: Cambridge University Press, 2006), 57–74.

Gasparov, Boris, 'Pushkin and Romanticism', in David Bethea (ed.), *The Pushkin Handbook* (Madison, Wis.: University of Wisconsin Press, 2005), 537–67.

Ginzburg, Lidiia, 'K postanovke problemy realizma v pushkinskoi literature', *Pushkin: Vremennik Pushkinskoi komissii*, 2 (1936), 387–401.

Greenleaf, Monika, *Pushkin and Romantic Fashion: Fragment, Elegy, Orient, Irony* (Stanford, Calif.: Stanford University Press, 1997).

Greenleaf, Monika, 'Pushkin's Byronic Apprenticeship: A Problem in Cultural Syncretism', *Russian Review*, 53 | 3 (1994), 382–98.

Gukovskii, G. A., *Pushkin i problemy realisticheskogo stilia* (Moscow: Gos. Izd. khudozhestvennoi literatury, 1957).

Gukovskii, G. A., *Pushkin i russkie romantiki* (Moscow: Khudozhestvennaia lit-ra, 1965).

Iakubovich, Dmitrii, '"Kapitanskaia dochka" i romany Val'ter Skotta', *Pushkin: Vremennik Pushkinskoi komissii*, 4 | 5 (1939), 165–97.

Jameson, Fredric, *The Political Unconscious* (Ithaca, NY: Cornell University Press, 1981).

Kahn, Andrew, *Pushkin's Lyric Intelligence* (Oxford: Oxford University Press, 2008).

Karamzin, N. M., *Istoriia gosudarstva Rossiiskogo* (St Petersburg: Izdanie Evg. Evdokimova, 1892).

Kelsall, Malcolm, 'Byronism', in Christopher John Murray (ed.), *Encyclopedia of the Romantic Era, 1760–1850* (New York: Fitzroy Dearborn, 2004), i. 146–7.

Lotman, Iu. M., 'Ideinaia struktura "Kapitanskoi dochki"', in Iu. M. Lotman, *Pushkin* (St Petersburg: Iskusstvo-SPb, 1995), 212–27.

McGann, Jerome J., *Byron and Romanticism* (Cambridge: Cambridge University Press, 2002).

Meilakh, B. S., *Pushkin i russkii romantizm* (Moscow and Leningrad: Izd. AN SSSR, 1937).

Mellor, Anne K., *English Romantic Irony* (Cambridge, Mass.: Harvard University Press, 1980).

Nemirovskii, I. V., *Tvorchestvo Pushkina i problema publichnogo povedeniia poeta* (St Petersburg: Giperion, 2003).

Proskurin, Oleg, *Poeziia Pushkina, ili podvizhnyi palimpsest* (Moscow: Novoe literaturnoe obozrenie, 1999).

Pushkin, Aleksandr Sergeevich, *Sobranie sochinenii v desiati tomakh* (Moscow: Gos. izd-vo khudozh. lit-ry, 1959–62).

Pushkin, Alexander, *Pushkin on Literature*, tr. Tatiana Wolff (Evanston, Ill.: Northwestern University Press, 1986).

Pushkin, Alexander, *Eugene Onegin*, tr. James E. Falen (Carbondale, Ill.: Southern Illinois University Press, 1990).

Sandler, Stephanie, *Distant Pleasures: Alexander Pushkin and the Writing of Exile* (Stanford, Calif.: Stanford University Press, 1989).

Stennik, Iu. V., *Pushkin i russkaia literatura XVIII veka* (St Petersburg: Nauka, 1995).

Terras, Viktor, 'Pushkin and Romanticism', in Andrej Kodjak, Krystyna Pomorska, and Kiril Taranovsky (eds), *Alexander Pushkin: Symposium II* (Columbus, Ohio: Slavica, 1980), 49–59.

Todd, William Mills, III, *Fiction and Society in the Age of Pushkin: Ideology, Institutions, and Narrative* (Cambridge, Mass., and London: Harvard University Press, 1986).

Tomashevskii, B. V., *Pushkin: Kniga pervaia* (Moscow and Leningrad: Izd-vo Akademii nauk, 1956).

Tomashevskii, B. V., *Pushkin: Kniga vtoraia* (Moscow and Leningrad: Izd-vo Akademii nauk SSSR, 1961).

Ungurianu, Dan, *Plotting History: The Russian Historical Novel in the Imperial Age* (Madison, Wis.: University of Wisconsin Press, 2007).

Vickery, V. N., 'Parallelizm v literaturnom razvitii Bajrona i Puskina', in *American Contributions to the Fifth International Congress of Slavists* (The Hague: Mouton, 1963), ii. 371–401.

Zhirmunskii, V. M., *Bairon i Pushkin: Iz istorii romanticheskoi poemy* (Leningrad: Academia, 1924).

CHAPTER 28

THE GEOGRAPHY OF RUSSIAN ROMANTIC PROSE

Bestuzhev, Lermontov, Gogol, and Early Dostoevsky

KATYA HOKANSON

In the 1820s and 1830s, when Russia's encounter with Romanticism primarily took place, it was a culture caught in a complex debate about its own identity. Russian literature developed late and was dependent at first on that of Ukraine and Poland, and later Western Europe, especially France and England. In its encounter with Romanticism Russian culture had to somehow map broadly European issues and movements on to its own reality. Romantic tropes took on specific cultural meanings; concepts and tropes such as the bold, brooding individual, the focus on interiority, the embrace of the irrational, and the breaking of previous conventions had not only artistic but quite political import in Russia, for example. In a country where the autocratic Tsar, first among a small circle of literate and literary nobility who all knew each other well, read the (carefully censored) works of the best writers as soon as they emerged—and made his opinion about them known—merely to be a writer was an extremely fraught occupation. Many writers, including Pushkin, had personal interviews with the Tsar about their writing. To innovate and to embrace current European trends could lead to approval for furthering the cause of keeping Russian literature up with the times, but also suspicion lest overly independent ideas come with those trends. Most Russian major prose writers of the Romantic period and beyond, such as Pushkin, Lermontov, Bestuzhev, and Dostoevsky, had periods of exile, house arrest, or imprisonment imposed upon them. Prominent writers who participated in the Decembrist Uprising in 1825 were put to death or exiled. As always, to talk about literature in Russia was to talk about something that was far from abstract or academic. Literature, along with historical and later journalistic writing, was the arena in which the issues of the day were debated and opinions expressed.

The Romantic period in Russian literature is indelibly linked with the Caucasus. Pushkin's 1821 narrative poem, 'The Captive of the Caucasus', which drew heavily on

Byronic models but also created a new sensibility, a sense of a new and original Russian hero, was considered a truly Russian piece of literature that was nonetheless set in the Caucasus and not in Russia itself. The narrative poem, which featured a young Russian man being taken captive by Caucasian mountain warriors, was received by critics and fellow literary figures as 'national', a word itself borrowed from the West, at a time when critics were demanding 'national' literature. Pushkin transformed the familiar Byronic figure into a Russian figure fleeing both 'civilization' and political oppression, but also ultimately embracing the Russians' European-like imperial role in the conquest of the Caucasus. Pushkin's captive was succeeded by many other Russian characters whose stories also took place in the Caucasus or Trans-caucasus. The motif was so pervasive that in the 1850s Tolstoy felt he had to 'exile himself' to the Caucasus to become a writer. He followed 'in the steps of the Romantics to systematically destroy their poetics', as Boris Eikhenbaum put it. Tolstoy's character Dmitry Olenin embodied the young man fascinated with the Caucasus:

> His imagination was now turned to the future: to the Caucasus. All his dreams of the future were mingled with pictures of Ammalat-Beks, Circassian women, mountains, precipices, terrible torrents, and perils.[1]

This catalogue was fully sufficient to signify the Romantic Caucasus of Russian literature, literature which in the words of the famous ethnographer Arnold Zisserman had sent scores of young men to seek their fortune in the Caucasus, inspired by their reading of adventurous tales.[2] While for most European literatures Romanticism was a movement that built upon a previous national literary identity, Romanticism appeared in Russian literature at the point when Russians first agreed that they now had a literature they could call their own, one that did not consist merely of translations and borrowings but was fully Russian. The so-called 'southern theme' relating to the Caucasus and to exile was instrumental in this affirmation of a Russian national literature. Along with the 'southern theme', which dealt with the Russian Empire's most prominent theatre of war was the 'Petersburg theme', which similarly interrogated the complexities of Russian national identity, but from the centre rather than the periphery. A long-standing topic of literature, St Petersburg's status as a majestic, orderly 'northern Palmyra' began to come under serious question in the Romantic period, first and foremost as a result of Pushkin's masterpieces 'Queen of Spades' and 'Bronze Horseman', and closely following them, Gogol's and early Dostoevsky's Petersburg texts, which will be considered here.

[1] Tolstoy, *Great Short Works* (New York: Perennial Classics, 2004), 93. Eikhenbaum, *Molodoi Tolstoi* (Berlin, 1922), 108.

[2] A. L. Zisserman, *Dvadtsat' piat' let na Kavkaze* (1842–67; Moscow, 1897), ii. 3: 'Buinak reminded me of the seductive Ammalat-Bek of Marlinsky, that passionate fantasy which once brought to ecstasy inexperienced young souls and enticed me to the Caucasus ...' See also Susan Layton, 'Nineteenth-Century Russian Mythologies of Caucasian Savagery', in Daniel Brower and Edward Lazzerini (eds), *Russia's Orient: Imperial Borderlands and Peoples, 1700–1917* (Bloomington, Ind.: Indiana University Press, 1997), 80–99.

The two most important Russian Romantic prose writers besides Aleksandr Pushkin were Nikolai Vasilievich Gogol and Iurii Mikhailovich Lermontov. Both wrote in multiple genres. Lermontov (1814–41) had a brief but successful career as a writer despite his mere twenty-six years, and set many of his most important works in the Caucasus, including his 1840 novel *A Hero of Our Time*. Nikolai Gogol (1809–52) was of Ukrainian and Polish stock, and was at first in fact perceived as a Ukrainian writer.[3] The Russian Empire was multi-ethnic from its beginnings, and its status as an empire preceded by many decades, if not centuries, its identity as a nation. Contemporaries of Gogol could with ease distinguish between Russian as the language of the empire (and hence a necessary tool to use to make an impact on the St Petersburg-based literary scene), and the non-Russian ethnic identities of individuals. A person who was a citizen of the Russian Empire, who used Russian for many purposes, yet was not ethnically Russian, was a recognizable type, and many military, cultural, and bureaucratic figures came from the ranks of the Empire's non-Russian nobility. For a Ukrainian to write Russian literature was not perceived as contradictory, although with the passage of time Gogol's Ukrainian identity was pushed more and more to the background by nationally minded readers and critics.[4]

Gogol and Lermontov both produced short stories, novels and dramatic work, while Lermontov was also a talented poet, commonly regarded as second only to Pushkin. Besides Gogol and Lermontov there were a number of other important Romantic prose writers. The most popular prose writer of the 1830s was Aleksandr Bestuzhev (1797–1837), who after punishment for playing a role in the 1825 Decembrist Uprising wrote under the pseudonym Marlinsky. From a very prominent family, Bestuzhev was a prolific short-story writer. His novella *Ammalat-bek*, as one might gather from the Tolstoy quotation above, was phenomenally popular, encapsulating the elements that drew Russian writers and readers to the topic of the Russian conflict in the Caucasus—exotic local colour, a dramatic setting, a clash of cultures, bloody plots, and often a simultaneous celebration and critique of imperial conquest. Other important Romantic prose writers of the period included Vladimir Odoevsky (1803–69), Aleksandr Veltman (1800–70), and arguably also the young Fyodor Dostoevsky (1821–81). Though women writers were still few at this point, both Evdokiia Rostopchina (1811–58) and Karolina Pavlova (1807–93) wrote both prose and verse; Pavlova's poetry was later rediscovered and highly valued by the Russian symbolists.

To understand Russian Romanticism, it is essential to be aware that young Russian men in the aftermath of Russia's defeat of the French in 1814 tasted with relish the freedoms of the French capital. When they returned to Russia they found its strict autocratic culture oppressive. They created the secret societies dedicated to the reform of the Russian autocracy that led to the Decembrist Uprising. On 14 December 1825, just as the new Tsar, Nicholas II, was succeeding to the throne, the Decembrists met on

[3] Edyta Bojanowska, *Nikolai Gogol between Ukrainian and Russian Nationalism* (Cambridge, Mass.: Harvard University Press, 2007), 37.

[4] Bojanowska, *Nikolai Gogol*, 78–9.

Senate Square in St Petersburg and called for a constitutional monarchy. The uprising was put down the same day and five of the leaders were later put to death for their actions, with hundreds of others sent into Siberian exile. The flower of the young nobility of Russia, the best and the brightest young men, many from very prominent families well known to the Tsar, was cut off at one fell swoop. The unsuccessful uprising was a watershed moment in Russian history, with the future Decembrists' self-conscious code of behaviour both before and after the uprising constituting a significant component in the formation of Russian culture. For example, *War and Peace*, Tolstoy's epic novel of the Napoleonic War, was originally intended to be a novel about the Decembrists returning from exile in 1856, among them one of his close relatives, Sergei Volkonsky.

Models for Russian Romanticism were not merely literary by any means, but also based on public behaviour by admired individuals, which was in turn was often based on literary models. The Decembrists felt all their actions were part and parcel of themselves and their beliefs. As Iurii Lotman wrote:

> 'We breathe liberty,' declared Ryleev on the square on 14 December. The transferral of liberty from the sphere of ideas and theories into 'breath,' into life, is the essence and the significance of the everyday behavior of the Decembrist.[5]

Pyotr Chaadaev (1794–1856), a military officer during the Napoleonic Wars who was likely sympathetic to the Decembrists' views, although he was not in Russia when the uprising occurred, was someone thought to be exemplary of such public behaviour, famously resigning his commission, possibly as a way to advocate for freedom for the Russian people, and serving as a model for several literary characters, including Aleksandr Griboedov's (1795–1829) famous Chatsky from the witty, satirical play 'Woe from Wit'.[6] Chaadaev also wrote one of the most influential pieces of prose during the Romantic era. His 'Philosophical Letter', written in French in 1829 and widely circulated in manuscript form, took Russia to task for being behind the times and outside of history, unaffected by Western thought, a child among mature nations. Its publication in 1836 led to the closing of the magazine in which it was published and, for a period of time, house arrest for its author, who was declared insane. The genre of the familiar letter, which was the form Chaadaev's letter took, was an extremely important part of Russian literary development of the time and played no small part in the formation of Russian literary vocabulary and style.[7]

[5] Iurii Lotman, 'The Decembrist in Everyday Life', in Iu. M. Lotman and B. A. Uspensky, *The Semiotics of Russian Culture*, ed. Ann Shukman (Ann Arbor: Michigan Slavic Contributions, 1984), 71–123 (119). Kondraty Ryleev (1795–1826) was a poet and co-edited *Polar Star* with Bestuzhev.

[6] See Lotman, 'The Decembrist', 88–92.

[7] See William Mills Todd, *The Familiar Letter as a Literary Genre in the Age of Pushkin* (Princeton: Princeton University Press, 1976).

Aleksandr Bestuzhev-Marlinsky

Aleksandr Bestuzhev, 1797–1837, though now not nearly as well-known as his famous contemporaries, was a writer, poet, critic, translator, editor, and Decembrist leader (he took a leading role in the uprising and was only one of several Bestuzhev brothers to participate). His is a good example of Russian Romanticism's role as a philosophy of life; his political views matched his behaviour and he openly confessed his participation after the uprising. He was sent to Siberia for almost five years, so that his literary activity occurred primarily from 1819 to 1825 and 1829 to 1837. In his early period he translated English and French criticism and then began publishing prose tales in 1821, first Gothic tales based on Livonian (present-day Latvia and Estonia) and Russian history, such as 'Wenden Castle', 'Eisen Castle', 'The Traitor', and then historical adventure tales ('Tournament at Reval', 'Roman and Olga'), as well as society tales ('An Evening at a Bivouac'). For two years, from 1823 to 1825, he edited the highly profitable Decembrist literary almanac *Polar Star* with Kondraty Ryleev, later one of the five main Decembrist leaders, in which he published his own stories and literary criticism. Each issue led with a 'glance' at Russian literature, written by Bestuzhev, who championed national originality, independence from the French language, and neoclassicism; important writers such as Pushkin, Vyazemsky, Zhukovsky, Griboedov, and others published their work in the almanac.[8] From Siberia he was transferred to the Caucasus and reduced to the ranks. He was allowed to publish under the pseudonym Marlinsky. He reached his height of popularity in the 1830s, publishing many stories in Byronic, historical, horror, sea adventure, and Caucasian modes. His most important tales and novellas include 'The Test' (1830), *Ammalat-Bek* (1832), 'Frigate Hope' (1832), and 'Mulla-Nur' (1836).

Ammalat-bek was Bestuzhev's most famous and successful prose work, a fictionalization of the historical story of Ammalat-bek, a real-life Tatar bey (lord) who was captured by the Russians in 1819 and sentenced to death. Verkhovsky, a Russian colonel, asked that Ammalat's life be spared and that he be made Ammalat's sponsor. After a period of apparently harmonious friendship, Ammalat murdered Verkhovsky and later dug up and decapitated his corpse, possibly in a bid to gain permission to marry an Avarian girl, Seltaneta. Instead of marrying, however, Ammalat-bek became an abrek (independent, unattached warrior), and was killed in 1828 in a battle against the Russians. In the novella Bestuzhev gives great attention to daily life in Avaria and Daghestan, and parts of the narrative are journal entries by both Ammalat and Verkhovsky. Ammalat's love for Seltaneta and admiration for Verkhovsky come across quite favourably in the novel, which avoids treating Ammalat as an inscrutable other.

[8] Lauren Leighton, *Alexander Bestuzhev-Marlinsky* (New York: Twain Publishers, 1975), 37–66; see also Lewis Bagby, *Alexander Bestuzhev-Marlinsky and Russian Byronism* (University Park, Pa.: Pennsylvania State University Press, 1995), ch. 3, 'Literary Criticism'.

Ammalat-bek was an immensely popular tale, which probably gave rise to Alexandre Dumas's *Sultanetta* and was translated into English as early as 1843 in *Blackwood's Edinburgh Magazine.*[9] Along with Bestuzhev's other Caucasian tales, it motivated much interest in the Caucasus. Bestuzhev's stories of the 1830s, packed with drama and high-flown rhetoric, gave rise to the term 'Marlinism', denoting a florid and dramatic Romantic style, later criticized for its excesses, although the encounter with Bestuzhev's tales of the Caucasus continued to inspire young readers and Marlinism also provided a foil for writers such as Lermontov, who poked fun at the style while making clever use of readers' knowledge of it. An example of Marlinism is evident early on in the narration of *Ammalat-bek*:

> Nature, in Daghestan, is most lovely in the month of May. Millions of roses poured their blushes over the crags; their odour was streaming in the air; the nightingale was not silent in the green twilight of the wood, almond-trees, all silvered with their flowers, arose like the cupolas of a pagoda, and resembled, with their lofty branches twined with leaves, the minarets of some Mussulman mosque.[10]

Few writers were completely immune to the charms of Marlinsky; Gogol himself was accused of Marlinism at one point when he wrote about Rome.[11] Whatever Bestuzhev's drawbacks, his techniques of writing, especially recasting Byronic tales into prose, and his immense popularity, were noticed by many other writers, especially Pushkin and Lermontov, and he played an important role in Russian literature's turn from poetry to prose in the late 1820s and 1830s.[12] Bestuzhev was ultimately killed in battle in the Caucasus in 1837, living a life that was strikingly in concert with his popular prose.

Iurii Mikhailovich Lermontov

Lermontov is known primarily as a poet, although his prose, primarily his 1841 novel, *A Hero of Our Time*, was quite influential in Russian letters and remains highly esteemed to this day. Because of Lermontov's status as a poet, his poetry will also be briefly treated here. Lermontov, born in Moscow, lived only twenty-six years, dying in a duel in the Caucasus in 1841. His mother died when he was very young and his grandmother had a strong hand in raising him, taking him to the Caucasus at a young age, which strongly influenced him. He tried the University but transferred to the cadet school in St Petersburg, following in his father's military footsteps. He made his name by writing a

[9] *Blackwood's Edinburgh Magazine*, 53/329–32 (Mar., Apr., May, and June 1843).

[10] *Blackwood's Edinburgh Magazine*, 53/329, <http://www.gutenberg.org/cache/epub/12761/pg12761.txt>, accessed May 2013.

[11] William Edward Brown, *A History of Russian Literature of the Romantic Period* (Ann Arbor: Ardis, 1986), iv. 374.

[12] Brown, *History of Russian Literature*, ii. 219.

poem, 'Death of the Poet', upon Pushkin's death in a duel in 1837, implying that the powerful in society played a role in the loss of the great poet. For this poem, which was circulated privately but not published until after his death, he was sent to the Caucasus, a not uncommon punishment, meted out to many members of the military who somehow displeased their higher-ups. The Caucasus, both due to his upbringing and to its political and indeed literary meaning, was amenable to Lermontov, who not only described it in poetry but also painted it in watercolours. Lermontov returned to St Petersburg, but was again sent to the Caucasus for participating in a duel with the French Ambassador's son. He once again participated in Russia's Caucasian war and ultimately died in a duel in Piatigorsk (the setting of much of his novel *A Hero of Our Time*) in 1841.

Lermontov wrote lyric poetry, narrative poems, plays, short fiction, and his novel, *A Hero of Our Time*. Of these, his lyric poetry and novel are counted most highly, along with some of his narrative poems such as 'Demon' (1841) and 'Mtsyri' ('The Novice', 1840). However, Lermontov did not deem many of his works, especially the early ones, publishable, and so his published output during his lifetime was relatively small in comparison with what he had written. Besides being a poet considered second only to Pushkin, and a Romantic writer par excellence, Lermontov is very much distinguished in the Russian literary imagination for his poetry and prose of the Caucasus and his own experience there. Tolstoy envied the personal experience of Pushkin, Bestuzhev, and Lermontov, especially the latter two, who served in and wrote about the Caucasus. Tolstoy served as a cadet in the Caucasus and set his (now realist) tales there; they were clear successors not only to the work of the major three Russian writers of the Caucasus, but also to works by such writers as Denis Davydov (1784–1839), Vasily Grigorev (1803–76), Viktor Tepliakov (1804–42), and Aleksandr Polezhaev (1804–38).

Lermontov aspired both to be like Byron—famous, publicly acknowledged—but also to be unlike Byron, or different from him—to be unique.[13] Russia was in many ways the ideal audience for Byron:

> In effect, only in Russia was Byron read the way he wished, not as a shocking and perhaps puerile immoralist, a self-obsessed Romantic egotist, but as a serious political revolutionary whose words and actions carried real danger to the political status quo. The very fact that Byron's political rhetoric had no published equivalent in Russian literature made it all the more startling when it slipped through the censorial dragnet.[14]

Lermontov's most popular narrative poem 'Demon' is about the love of a supernatural being for a human woman; her joy in life overcomes his unhappy immortality and power, but after he has her betrothed killed, his kiss is fatal to her. The poem was begun

[13] David Powelstock, *Becoming Mikhail Lermontov: The Ironies of Romantic Individualism in Nicholas I's Russia* (Evanston, Ill.: Northwestern University Press, 2005), 88.

[14] Monika Greenleaf, 'Pushkin's Byronic Apprenticeship: A Problem in Cultural Syncretism', *Russian Review*, 53/3 (July 1994), 387.

early in Lermontov's life and written in multiple drafts, at first with an abstract setting, then one in Spain, but once the setting was made Caucasian in the sixth draft, and the human love of the demon specified as Tamara, a Georgian princess, the poem became much more successful. The Caucasian setting is crucial; as William Brown points out, the 'gigantic figure of the Demon is balanced only by the gigantic and magnificent setting of the Caucasus', a technique that Pushkin, too had employed, using the towering peaks of the Caucasus as a foil at times even for the Russian Empire itself.[15]

'Mtsyri', or 'The Novice', was Lermontov's last narrative poem, also set in the Caucasus, but as it featured a character who was a Circassian captured by General Yermolov as a boy and left to be brought up by monks, it was a different kind of interrogation of Romantic freedom. As commentators have noted, the novice's escape into nature is not the panacea it seems it will be; having been cloistered all his life, the young man is not prepared for the wilderness. Nothing makes him intrinsically a part of nature as other literary Circassians are seen to be; he loses his original culture, departs from the monastery, and also is foreign to the natural world, thus encountering a catastrophic loss in his first introduction to independence.

Lermontov's lyric poem 'The Dream', 1841, epitomized the poet at his most masterful. In it a young Russian man lies dying 'in a dale in Dagestan' (the Eastern Caucasus), having been shot by the enemy. The narration is soon revealed to be in the first person; the speaker narrates his own dying moments. In 'deathly sleep', he dreams of a festive party in the capital, where young people are talking about him. One young woman, however, sits apart, grieving because she is dreaming of a 'dale in Dagestan', where she sees a 'familiar corpse' bleeding, with the flowing blood cooling. The dream within a dream, or the prescient crossing of the thoughts of two young people, one dying in the Caucasus, the other thinking of him at a party, thus links the action in the Caucasus, so often seen as distant and foreign to the Russian public, to the centre, where military actions were decided upon. The final stanza closely echoes the first, but is narrated now from the young woman's point of view, as she perceives the dying man (or as he dreams she does). The sounds add a great deal to the whole; the mellifluous blending of d's, l's, and n's convey smoothly the tragic connection between the two being parted. In general Lermontov's prosody is highly regarded.

Lermontov is best known, at least outside of Russia, for his novel, *A Hero of Our Time*. Lermontov's 1840 novel was composed of five individual chapters, approaching the story of the novel from different perspectives and placed chronologically out of order. All four main parts of the narrative, 'Bela', 'Princess Mary', 'Taman', and 'Fatalist', had been written, and several published, prior to the author's grouping them together as a novel with the 'Maksim Maksimych' section created afterwards to hold them together; arguably, one of the pre-existing stories, 'Taman', is not even about the main character, Pechorin.[16] *A Hero of Our Time* in a sense followed in the tradition of Pushkin's *Eugene*

[15] Brown, *History of Russian Literature*, 205.
[16] Brown, *History of Russian Literature*, 243.

Onegin, a novel in verse, by being another kind of unusual novel, one that readers had to actively synthesize both psychologically and chronologically as they read. The main character, Pechorin, is named after a Siberian river—just as Onegin's name was formed from the name of a different (and less turbulent) Siberian river, the Onega. As in *Eugene Onegin*, the main character has a friend and potential rival who is younger and more naïve—Onegin's is Lensky, Pechorin's, Grushnitsky. Unlike Pushkin's novel, where the free-floating narrator is a major character himself, transcending in so many ways the plane of the action, *A Hero of Our Time* has either first or third-person narration, by either Pechorin or other characters.

The entirety of the novel is set in the Caucasus region. The first section of the novel is 'Bela', in which a traveller crossing through the Caucasus encounters a grizzled veteran of the Caucasian wars, Maksim Maksimych, who in turn tells the story of an officer he served with at a military fort, Grigory Aleksandrovich Pechorin. Pechorin, Maksim Maksimych relates, had arranged to steal a Circassian girl, Bela, daughter of a neighbouring chief, and held her captive at the Russian fort, gradually inducing her to accept her captivity and express her love for Pechorin. Meanwhile a young man, Kazbich, whose horse Pechorin had stolen in order to bribe Bela's younger brother to kidnap her, is determined to take his revenge on Pechorin. Ultimately Kazbich stabs Bela, who dies an agonizing death; Maksim Maksimych, the reader understands, mourns her far more than does Pechorin, who had already grown bored of her before the denouement. The end result of 'Bela' is the destruction of Bela's entire family, while Pechorin's military superior but social inferior Maksim Maksimych, though kindly, is powerless against Pechorin's whims.

'Maksim Maksimych' next details how the travelling narrator meets up with him once again; together they become aware that Pechorin has arrived in the town where they are staying, on his way to Persia (possibly as a diplomat, but there is no explanation). The narrator describes Pechorin's physical appearance and notes his coldness toward Maksim Maksimych, who had been overjoyed to see him. In Maksim Maksimych's disgust at Pechorin's aloofness, he gives the travelling narrator Pechorin's papers, which he had been keeping for him.

Part two of the novel begins with an interpolation by the travelling narrator, who apprises the reader that he has discovered that Pechorin has died and so he is at liberty to print his notes, of which he has selected only those that concern the Caucasus, although there are many others. The narrator declares:

> On reading over these notes, I have become convinced of the sincerity of the man who has so unsparingly exposed to view his own weaknesses and vices. The history of a man's soul, even the pettiest soul, is hardly less interesting and useful than the history of a whole people; especially when the former is the result of the observations of a mature mind upon itself, and has been written without any egoistical desire of arousing sympathy or astonishment. Rousseau's *Confessions* has precisely this defect—he read it to his friends.

He continues:

> Possibly some readers would like to know my own opinion of Pechorin's character. My answer is: the title of this book. 'But that is malicious irony!' they will say ... I know not.[17]

Indeed the naming of the novel *A Hero of Our Time* was controversial; Lermontov put in a preface for the second printing, explaining that the portrait was a composite and that (much in the style of Chaadaev's *Letter*, printed a few years earlier), the failings of the hero of our time were a brutally truthful diagnosis of the age, not an endorsement of his character:

> You will say that the cause of morality gains nothing by this book. I beg your pardon. People have been surfeited with sweetmeats and their digestion has been ruined: bitter medicines, sharp truths, are therefore necessary. This must not, however, be taken to mean that the author has ever proudly dreamed of becoming a reformer of human vices. Heaven keep him from such impertinence! He has simply found it entertaining to depict a man, such as he considers to be typical of the present day and such as he has often met in real life—too often, indeed, unfortunately both for the author himself and for you. Suffice it that the disease has been pointed out: how it is to be cured—God alone knows![18]

The story that follows, 'Taman', is named after a town on a peninsula between the Black Sea and the Sea of Azov, in the far Western part of the Caucasus. The first-person narrator, a military man travelling through the area with his Cossack soldier-servant, is presumably Pechorin; perhaps his naiveté and sense of conscience are due to the fact that 'Taman' is chronologically the first story in the book; however, it has even been suggested that the traveller-narrator was at least originally the 'author' of Taman.[19] 'Taman' utilizes some quite conventional Romantic imagery, such as a mysterious blind boy, a beautiful young woman the narrator calls an 'undine' (*rusalka*), and an association of mystery and 'unwholesomeness' with the whole locale of Taman. The narrator, in investigating what he finds to be the strange goings on of the family which provides him with his temporary billet, has his head turned by the mysterious young woman, and agrees to meet her at the beach at night. Despite not knowing how to swim, he agrees to go out with her in a rowboat, whereupon she attempts to drown him. Instead, he throws her into the waves, and returns to the beach to discover her already there; later he finds that his weapons and other valuable goods had been stolen. The girl leaves with her lover (and smuggling partner) Yanko, abandoning the sobbing blind boy on the beach. The narrator regrets that he has ruined the lives of the 'honest smugglers' and departs the scene.

'Princess Mary', which follows, is by far the longest and most complex section in the novel, and ostensibly takes place before the 'Bela' section, although there is no

[17] Lermontov, *A Hero of Our Time*, tr. J. H. Wisdom and Marr Murray (New York: A. A. Knopf, 1916), <http://www.gutenberg.org/cache/epub/913/pg913.txt>, accessed May 2013.

[18] *A Hero of Our Time*.

[19] Brown, *History of Russian Literature*, 245.

mention of its events in 'Bela'. It is in the form of journal entries; Pechorin, a highly placed though possibly disgraced nobleman, is in Piatigorsk, a Caucasian spa frequented by convalescing soldiers and well-off members of the nobility who engage in the fashion of taking the waters. At the spa Pechorin makes the acquaintance of Grushnitsky, a naïve young soldier recovering from a war injury. Pechorin soon determines to best him in his budding flirtation with one of the visiting ladies, the young Princess Mary. Pechorin's erstwhile mistress also arrives, Vera, who is now remarried to a much older man and has come to take the waters for her wasting illness. Vera, Pechorin declares, is the only woman he ever loved and who ever understood him. While seeing Vera behind the scenes, Pechorin gradually steals Mary's attention away from Grushnitsky. Grushnitsky and his circle become enemies of Pechorin, and plan to incite a duel at which they will secretly remove Pechorin's bullet from his pistol. Pechorin uncovers the scheme, and Grushnitsky dies in the duel. Upon returning from the duel Pechorin learns that Vera's husband has discovered her infidelity. She begs him to come and see her one last time; in an attempt to do so he rides his horse to death. Princess Mary's mother has meanwhile expected him to propose, which despite earlier attraction to Mary he cannot do—in part because he also despises and rejects marriage. Pechorin is left to ruminate on his inability to do anything other than spoil the happiness of others.

The final story, 'The Fatalist', also from Pechorin's diary, is said to happen during the time that Pechorin is at the fort. It describes Pechorin's two-week visit to a Cossack village, during which he bets Vulich, a gloomily mysterious Serbian officer, that there is no such thing as predestination. After inviting fellow officers to bet on the fact that no one can die unless he is predestined to do so, Vulich takes down a pistol from the wall and prepares to shoot himself with it. Pechorin, despite his bet, claims a sense of foreboding: 'it seemed to me that I could read the stamp of death upon his pale countenance'.[20] Pechorin warns Vulich that he will die that very day, but he goes through with the shot, which misfires, although the pistol fires properly when next discharged. On his way back to his lodging, Pechorin discovers that Vulich has been hacked to death by a Cossack's sabre. Pechorin concludes that he is right about predestination, but his discussion with the highly practical Maksim Maksimych deflates the claim, since Maksim Maksimych notes that the local pistols are prone to misfiring and that it is foolish to strike up a conversation with a drunken man at night.

There the narrative leaves off, suggesting that there are at least two explanations for Vulich's death, hence allowing the Romantically tinged tale of predestined death to coexist with a practical, relatively realistic interpretation. This ability to view Pechorin both from his own perspective—his cruel disposition, his destructive boredom, his instrumentalization of others for his own ends—and that of Maksim Maksimych and the travelling narrator, allows for a fascinating characterization of Pechorin on his own terms but also a distancing, relativizing view of his character and the many Romantic

[20] *A Hero of Our Time.*

conventions he embodies. Lermontov himself bares the device in other ways, having Pechorin comment on Grushnitsky's knowledge of Romantic conventions of love and heroism.

Despite its rather sutured-together nature, *A Hero of Our Time* is greatly prized for its contribution to the genre of the psychological novel, its beautiful prose, its participation in the construction of the literary Caucasus, and its characterization of a very dark but nonetheless appealing Pechorin, whose manipulating ways ultimately paved the way for other characters, not just the superfluous men whose talents had nothing to occupy them but also, for example, the cruel and polished lasciviousness of *Lolita*'s Humbert Humbert.

Nikolai Vasilievich Gogol

Nikolai Gogol (1809–52), easily the most innovative and unclassifiable Russian writer, was also heavily defined by geography. Although there is little discussion of the Caucasus in his work (a notable exception is the main character of his short story, 'The Nose', who has risen in the ranks due to service in the Caucasus), his depiction of Ukrainian 'local colour' and his audaciously fantastic visions of St Petersburg are crucial to his literary achievement, as well as his unforgettable depictions of the Russian provinces. Gogol's style is daunting to describe, impossible to pigeonhole, but his influence was so huge all of Russian literature was said to have come out from under his 'Overcoat' (the title of his most famous story).[21] Perhaps because of his Ukrainian heritage, his less exalted social class as compared to that of fellow writers such as Pushkin, or his debated sexual orientation, his view of Russia was that of an outsider, although he wrote almost exclusively in Russian. He underlined his stance as an outsider by moving to Italy in 1836, just after the successful debut of his most famous play, 'The Inspector General'. By coming from the margins and later departing the Russian literary scene for distant lands, Gogol fit perfectly a pattern that preceded him—the fact that many of the most prominent Russian writers either came from the provinces or were of mixed parentage, or both, or wrote from a position of exile or distance from Russia. Among them were Mikhail Lomonosov (1711–65), the great eighteenth-century scientist and polymath from the White Sea region, Vasily Zhukovsky (1783–1852), Pushkin's contemporary and an important poet, whose mother was Turkish, the odist Gavrila Derzhavin (1743–1816), from Kazan, with Mongol ancestors, and Pushkin himself, who was one-eighth African. Pushkin's early narrative poems and the beginning of *Eugene Onegin* were written from his southern exile, as were many of Lermontov's works, as well as Aleksandr Griboedov's 'Woe from Wit', written while he was a diplomat in Georgia. The literal or figurative periphery played a vital role in Russian literature, and

[21] The statement, though likely apocryphal, is attributed to Dostoevsky, 'We all came out from under Gogol's "Overcoat."'

the fact that Gogol wrote some of the best Russian literature of all time while abroad in Europe was no exception.

Gogol arrived in St Petersburg in 1828, having grown up in Sorochintsy, in Ukraine, and gone to school in Nizhyn, and immediately published a Romantic poem at his own expense (but under a pseudonym), 'Hanz Küchelgarten'. It was set in Germany and relied heavily on works by Johann Voss and Zhukovsky. It was poorly received. In St Petersburg, the centre of Russian political power and one of the two main centres of publishing, Gogol met other Ukrainian writers such as Orest Somov (1793–1833). Having discovered that all things Ukrainian were in vogue, with the help of family and friends, who sent him material, he wrote his first, very successful stories, set in Ukraine, and called *Evenings on a Farm Near Dikanka*. Gogol adopted a frame narrator, Rudy Panko, a beekeeper, and frequently quoted Ukrainian literature, including the work of his own father, who wrote comedies. Using motifs from Ukrainian puppet theatre and folklore, and utilizing a skaz spoken narrative style, Gogol created a world that included richly imagined, idealized Ukrainian settings, various stock characters such as priests, Russians, Jews, and so on, and supernatural beings such as *rusalki* (mermaids) and apparitions of the devil. His stories in the first collection, published in 1831, included 'Sorochintsy Fair', 'St John's Eve', 'May Night, or the Drowned Maiden', and 'The Lost Letter'.

The first story in the collection, 'Sorochintsy Fair', gives a sense of Gogol's entrancing exoticization of Ukraine, or 'Little Russia'. Although the term originated as a way to designate territorial distance from Constantinople, it grew to have other meanings. Ultimately, the term 'Little Russia' both subordinated Ukraine to Russia and constructed it as a part of Russia itself rather than a separate territory.[22] After a five-line epigraph in Ukrainian, described in Russian as 'from an old legend', the story begins:

> O, the intoxication, the luxuriance of a summer's day in Little Russia! And the unbearable swelter of the midday hours when the very air sparkles with stillness and heat and the infinite ocean of the sky, arched into a voluptuous dome over the earth, appears to have fallen asleep, sated with sweetness, closed in an ethereal embrace with the beauty beneath it … The stout branches of the cherry-trees, plum-trees, apple-trees, and pear-trees sag under the weight of their fruit; above, the sky, gazing into its clear mirror—the river, proudly framed in its embossed green banks … the Little Russian summer is a sheer feast of voluptuous delights![23]

The rapturous description of the countryside soon gives way to far more earthy and less exalted goings-on, as a young man must overcome various forces in order to marry a beautiful young woman he has spied at the fair, while the young woman's mother has a dalliance with a priest's son and apparent demonic appearances frighten the

[22] Andreas Kappeler, '"Great Russians" and "Little Russians"', Adele Marie Barker and Bruce Grant (eds), *The Russia Reader: History, Culture, Politics* (Durham, NC: Duke University Press, 2010), 31–9.

[23] Nikolai Vasilevich Gogol, *Village Evenings Near Dikanka and Mirgorod*, tr. Christopher English (Oxford and New York: Oxford University Press, 1994), 8.

characters. A second volume of *Evenings*, published in 1832, also included four stories, 'Christmas Eve', 'A Terrible Vengeance', 'Ivan Fyodorovich Shponka and his Aunt', and 'A Bewitched Place'. Edyta Bojanowska argues that in his early tales Gogol essentially made Ukraine the centre of the world, with imperial Russia designated as an interloper that is responsible for the inertia and decline of the Ukraine.[24] Another two-volume collection, *Mirgorod* (1835), contained the terrifying supernatural tale 'Viy', whose titular monster has eyelids that drag on the ground and whose gaze can see everything. It also included the humorous 'Old-World Landowners' and 'The Story of How Ivan Ivanovich Quarrelled with Ivan Nikoforovich', which revel in all kinds of absurd situations, grammatical constructions, and vocabulary. In the story about two friends who quarrel, for example, Gogol uses a favourite technique, constructing a sentence that seems as if it will place two similar attributes side by side, but instead creating an absurd 'comparison' of things in completely different categories (not to mention introducing a scatological element to the comparison):

> Ivan Ivanovich is of a somewhat timid disposition. Ivan Nikiforovich, by contrast, has such immensely baggy trousers that if he were to inflate them with air they would accommodate the entire yard, complete with barns and outhouses.[25]

Mirgorod also included the Cossack novella *Taras Bulba*, which was set in a mythical time and took huge liberties with historical Cossacks; Gogol rewrote it in 1842. In 1835 he also published the collection *Arabesques* with some of what were to be called his Petersburg tales, including 'Nevsky Prospekt' and 'The Portrait'. 'Nevsky Prospekt' brilliantly describes St Petersburg's main street during various times of day, with 'synecdochic' descriptions of people, who are reduced to hats, bows, and moustaches, as a backdrop behind a story of dual thwarted love.[26]

> Anyone chancing on Nevsky Prospect will be dazzled by the infinite variety of hats, dresses, and scarves, wispy and brightly hued, which will sometimes retain the affections of their owners for two whole days on end. It is as though an entire sea of butterflies has suddenly taken off into the air, where they hover in a shimmering cloud above the black beetles of the male sex. Here you will encounter waists unlike any you have seen, even in your dreams: slender, narrow waists no thicker than the neck of a bottle ...[27]

An artist, Piskarev, and a military officer, Pirogov, each discover a beauty along Nevsky Prospekt and follow her home. Pirogov's apparation, however, turns out to be a married

[24] Bojanowska, *Nikolai Gogol*, 74–5.

[25] Gogol, *Village Evenings*, 410. See also Brown, *History of Russian Literature*, 289.

[26] Richard Peace, *The Enigma of Gogol: An Examination of the Writings of N. V. Gogol and their Place in the Russian Literary Tradition* (Cambridge: Cambridge University Press, 2009), see esp. 'The St. Petersburg Tales'.

[27] Nikolai Vasilievich Gogol, *Petersburg Tales, Marriage, The Government Inspector*, tr. Christopher English (Oxford and New York: Oxford University Press, 1995).

woman with a vengeful husband, while the artist's ideal woman turns out to be a prostitute, a profession which clashes terribly with the artist's idolization of her. The tale ends badly for both men—Pirogov is soundly beaten by the woman's husband and his friend (a tinsmith and a cobbler with the incongruous names of Schiller and Hoffman), while the artist kills himself after being mocked for proposing marriage to the prostitute. The tale ends with the devil about, lighting the lamps, thus lending the city some of the demonic aspects which hearken back to the Ukrainian tales, and with which the city would come to be identified.

As Edyta Bojanowska points out, Gogol constructed an organic wholeness of the Ukrainian countryside in his early stories, contrasting it with the fragmented city of St Petersburg in Russia. The Romantic interest in national specificity matched his idyllic Ukrainian depictions; Russia was seen quite differently.[28]

Gogol's play 'The Government Inspector' was a satirical portrait of the corrupt officials of a provincial town cast into apprehension, awaiting the arrival of a 'government inspector' whom they then fawn over, realizing only too late that the young man whom they had been wining and dining—and paying bribes to—was an insignificant civil servant, a fact they discover just as the real government inspector arrives. The Tsar himself attended the premier and greatly enjoyed it, cementing Gogol's success as a writer. One of Gogol's most enigmatic stories, 'The Nose', was also published in 1836. The story of an official who wakes up to find that he no longer has a nose (his barber's wife finds it in a loaf of fresh bread, and the barber recognizes it as that of his client, Major Kovalyov), he must cope with his disfigurement and watches in alarm as the nose itself appears in Kazan Cathedral and wears a uniform indicating a higher rank than Kovalyov's himself. The nose attempts to flee the city and is caught, but Kovalyov is unable to reattach it. Kovalyov later awakens to find his nose back where it belonged. There is never an explanation for why this unusual occurrence happened, nor is it explained how the reader should imagine a nose wearing a uniform and riding in a carriage. Interpretations of the story have ranged widely, from Freudian perspectives in which the nose is a phallic object, to a satire of the trappings of rank and bureaucracy, to an interpretation of the nose as a representation of the colonized other.[29] Many critics believe that 'The Nose' was inspirational to Kafka in writing 'The Metamorphosis' and other works, although Kafka does not specifically reference it.[30]

While abroad, Gogol continued to write his novel, which he called a poema or narrative poem, *Dead Souls*, published to great acclaim in 1842. It was received as a brilliant caricature of the backwardness of Russian rural life and bureaucracy. Chichikov, the plump, fatuous, main character (with a silly-sounding name, one of Gogol's specialties), exemplifying untranslatable 'poshlost'' or vulgarity/philistinism, was a nobleman

[28] Bojanowska, *Nikolai Gogol*, 37, 50.

[29] See Ivan Yermakov, 'The Nose', in Robert Maguire (ed.), *Gogol from the Twentieth Century; Eleven Essays* (Princeton: Princeton University Press, 1974), 155–98, and Alexander Etkind, *Internal Colonization, Russia's Imperial Experience* (Cambridge: Polity Press, 2011), 13–15.

[30] See e.g. Neil Cornwell, *The Absurd in Literature* (Manchester: MUP, 2006), 46–8 and 185–6.

who travelled around buying dead souls (or serfs) who remained on the tax rolls, so as to be able to borrow money against their value, though his motivations for buying the souls are not revealed until late in the first part. The townspeople and landowners Chichikov encounters during his travels are fascinating, caricatured figures. Despite the novel's reception, it soon became clear that Gogol saw *Dead Souls* as a kind of *Inferno*, with the *Purgatorio* and *Paradiso* yet to come. Chichikov was to be redeemed in further parts of *Dead Souls*. This was in part because Gogol became increasingly religious in his later years. While experiencing writer's block during writing part two of *Dead Souls* he published the much-maligned *Selected Passages from Correspondence with Friends*, a book of essays that appeared to many to be reactionary and humourless, quite unlike his previous writing. He was able to complete the second part of *Dead Souls*, but was very dissatisfied with it, and in the end burned his manuscript before his death, apparently from starvation, in 1852, although portions of part two have survived in draft form.

'The Overcoat', usually considered Gogol's best story, was published in 1842, and exemplifies the complexity of classifying Gogol's work. It is the story of Akaky Akakievich Bashmachkin, a poor clerk in St Petersburg who lives very modestly by himself and not only enjoys his work as a copyist, he refuses anything more complex than absolute rote copying. Described in vague but pitiful terms, with a 'hemorrhoidal' complexion, he discovers that his overcoat can no longer serve and must be replaced. He accordingly scrimps and saves and finally orders a new overcoat from his tailor. A feminine noun in Russian, the overcoat (*shinel'*) takes on the attributes of a female presence, a 'fair companion', and upon receiving it Akaky's life changes and he is even invited to a party, something unheard of for him, while his new coat is duly admired (perhaps sarcastically) by his previously uncaring co-workers. On the way home, alas, in a square that is so large it looks like a 'fearful desert', his coat is stolen from him by robbers, and the bureaucrat to whom he appeals for its return cruelly rejects his petition. Thereafter he soon dies, apparently of humiliation, and then seems to appear as a ghost, terrifying the official who had not helped him, while coats continue to be stolen in the vicinity.

Interpretations of 'The Overcoat' are if anything are even more numerous than those of 'The Nose', ranging from seeing Akaky as St Acacius, a soul reborn under the influence of love, to reading him as the archetypal 'little man', a realistic depiction of genteel poverty in the city, to a purely aesthetic performance by Gogol, who can be said to have written a story entirely about language. Donald Fanger has noted of Akaky that 'To call him a character is already to assume too much', because his attributes are so flimsy, while the narration itself is shifting and ambiguous, at times apparently sympathetic to Akaky and at other points clearly mocking him.[31] Vissarion Belinsky (1811–48), the influential literary critic, said of Gogol that he was the founder of the 'natural school' in Russian literature, or nascent realism, as William Brown puts it; but simultaneously, his work was fantastic, Romantic, Gothic, grotesque.[32] Fanger considers the late Gogol, like the early

[31] Donald Fanger, *The Creation of Nikolai Gogol* (Cambridge, Mass.: Belknap Press of Harvard University Press, 1979), 156.

[32] Brown, *History of Russian Literature* iv. 347.

Dostoevsky, to be a creator of Romantic realism, a fusing of the two styles. As Fanger writes, 'no other Russian writer combines a verbal magic so undeniable with so intractable an ambiguity of meaning'.[33]

Fyodor Mikhailovich Dostoevsky

Fyodor Dostoevsky, 1821–81, a writer, like Gogol, indelibly linked with the geography of St Petersburg, should also receive mention in a discussion of Russian Romantic prose. Although Dostoevsky is usually considered a realist, in his early period, before his arrest and prison sentence, his short stories have been characterized as expressive of 'Romantic realism', a term promulgated in the Russian context by Donald Fanger and which combines 'the subjectivity of the former and the detached accuracy of the latter'.[34] Fanger finds that Dostoevsky, like the later Gogol, also combines some of the same subjectivity with a growing sense of the realities of the city in his early texts, especially *Poor Folk* (1846), *The Double* (1846), and 'White Nights' (1848). Both writers, along with Pushkin, were instrumental in the construction of St Petersburg as a city of dreams and shadows, with the fantastic and the irrational lurking around every corner. Joseph Frank notes the effect on Dostoevsky of the powerful currents of both German Romanticism (especially German philosophy and writers such as E. T. A. Hoffmann, whose work was also an important model for Pushkin and Gogol) as well as French social Romanticism, whose exemplars such as Victor Hugo emphasized the 'practical application of the Christian values of pity and love; ... The one [type of Romanticism] keeps its eyes devoutly fixed on the eternal; the other responds to the needs of the moment'.[35] Dostoevsky explicitly rewrote Gogol's 'Overcoat' in his epistolary novel *Poor Folk* (the adjective *bednyi* means not just poor but pathetic, pitiable), taking Gogol's character's name Bashmachkin (a last name formed from the word for shoe) and creating for his own character the even more absurd and pathetic name Devushkin, from the word for girl or maiden, yet at the same time bringing what is only suggested or caricatured in Gogol to a more rounded life.[36] Devushkin is also a desperately poor copyist, but he loves (if chastely) a real woman and cultivates an interest in literature. As many commentators have pointed out, Gogol's feminine overcoat becomes in *Poor Folk* an actual young woman, Varvara Dobroselova, who is far younger than Devushkin's 47 years. In the novel Devushkin even reads and criticizes 'The Overcoat', finding it both too close to home and too sad—Dostoevsky

[33] Fanger, 'Nikolai Vasilievich Gogol', in Victor Terras (ed.), *Handbook of Russian Literature* (New Haven: Yale University Press, 1985), 177.

[34] Helen Muchnic, 'Review of *Dostoevsky and Romantic Realism* by Donald Fanger', *Comparative Literature*, 19/1 (Winter 1967), 78–80, 78.

[35] Joseph Frank, *Dostoevsky: The Seeds of Revolt, 1821–1849* (Princeton: Princeton University Press, 1976), 111.

[36] Donald Fanger, *Dostoevsky and Romantic Realism: A Study of Dostoevsky in Relation to Balzac, Dickens and Gogol* (Cambridge, Mass.: Harvard University Press, 1965), 152–3.

takes the irony further and, contrary to Gogol's story, has Devushkin's superior be kind to him and give him money. This, however, does not change the sad ending: in unsentimental style, Varvara marries the rich but coarse man, Bykov. Treated favourably by the famous critic Vissarion Belinsky, who called it a social novel, *Poor Folk* effectively bridged both Romantic and Realist conventions.

Dostoevsky's next novella *The Double*, published only two weeks later, also rewrote a Gogol story, this time 'The Nose'. Once again Dostoevsky 'realized the metaphor', 'appropriating all the fantastic Gogolian coloring and rationalizing it'.[37] Dostoevsky even subtitled it 'A Petersburg Poem' in the style of Gogol's *Dead Souls*. The doubling of Kovalyov due to the escape of his nose becomes an actual doubling in *The Double*, which addresses the Romantic convention of the doppelgänger, as Golyadkin, a poor, already miserable clerk, comes to recognize and be supplanted by his more aggressive double. The story is closely tied to St Petersburg, with its miserable weather and dreamlike fog, which seems to generate the phantom.

A third of these early texts, 'White Nights' (1848), also relies on its St Petersburg setting, during the strange and otherworldly white nights when there is little darkness in a twenty-four-hour period. The main character meets a young girl, Nastenka; they continue to meet and talk in the same place in the city over a succession of white nights. He has been lonely and this contact means a great deal to him. She is kind and caring, no cardboard figure. Despite her telling him that she already has a lover for whom she is waiting, the narrator falls in love with her, but helps her post a letter to her beloved and comforts her as she waits. Finally her beloved returns and, although the narrator's heart is broken, he wishes her well, while he simultaneously fears he will always remain alone. All that he has built up in his imagination will not come to pass, but he is also grateful for what small amount of happiness he has experienced. 'White Nights', too, might be said to be a variation on Gogol; whereas Gogol included both an army officer and an artist in his 'Nevsky Prospekt', Dostoevsky retains only the artist figure, the dreamer.[38] The story was warmly received. Nor would Dostoevsky's appreciation for tender emotion disappear. As Joseph Frank remarks:

> no matter how much Dostoevsky would later belabor the pretensions and the moral vacuity of the Romantic generation of the 'fathers,' he would always prefer the latter to their offspring, who fanatically insisted on reducing 'real life' exclusively to the matter-of-fact, prosaic, and even grossly material.[39]

Although Dostoevsky is best known as a realist, it may well be that the narrator of *Notes from Underground*, written much later, after Dostoevsky's prison sentence, developed from the dreamer of 'White Nights'.

[37] Fanger, *Dostoevsky and Romantic Realism*, 160.

[38] Although most critical texts treat the encounter with Nastenka as real, it has been suggested that she might be merely a figment of his imagination.

[39] Frank, *Dostoevsky*, 347.

The geography of Russian Romantic prose, from the Caucasus to the Russian provinces to the myths and shadows of St Petersburg, played a huge role in the Russian literature to follow. Tolstoy made his name with both his quasi-autobiographical 'Childhood' (set on a provincial Russian estate, written in the Caucasus) and his 'Sevastopol in December', a piece that benefited greatly from his experience writing Caucasian war tales. Dostoevsky's Petersburg, as outlined first and foremost in *Notes from Underground* and *Crime and Punishment*, is legendary, and was elaborated on in Andrei Bely's (1880–1934) great symbolist novel, *Petersburg* (1916 and 1922), and developed further by numerous other writers and poets. Bestuzhev's *Ammalat-bek*, though relegated to adolescent fare, retained a strong influence on generations of readers.[40] There are often elements of Romantic geography in texts that appear at first glance to be quite unrelated; Ivan Turgenev's (1818–1883) 1860 short story, 'First Love', set in Moscow, depends upon the reader's understanding of the Romantic Caucasus, using as motifs several 'southern' texts by Pushkin. A character who is a military officer goes to the Caucasus after despairing of being able to win the hand of the woman he loves—the reader does not have to be told that he is likely to die, either in battle or in a duel.[41] Nikolai Leskov's (1831–95) 1873 novel *The Enchanted Wanderer* spoofs the conventions of both the Caucasus and Gogolian Petersburg. Tolstoy returned to the Caucasus with his magisterial *Hadji-Murat* (1912). Written during the last years of his life, it is unsparing of Russian imperial cruelty. His 1872 short story, 'The Captive of the Caucasus', a realistic revision of Pushkin's narrative poem, has been rewritten again and again, through the end of the twentieth century, and made into a film, only one of many that continue to engage the artistic conventions of the Caucasus.[42]

Indeed, in later texts such as Bely's *Petersburg*, the geographies of Petersburg and the distant imperial periphery, whether explicitly Caucasian or not, ultimately merged and converged. Apollon Apollonovich Ableukhov and his son Nikolai Apollonovich Ableukhov, the two main characters in the novel, contain both Western and Eastern elements, and as their names show, combine Russian and Mongol stock. Apollon Apollonovich believes he loves order and abstraction, and fears the steppe, declaring, 'Russia is an icy plain. It is roamed by wolves!'[43] He does not recognize that he himself embodies the contradictions of Russia, that while admiring the order of his own house and of Petersburg itself he relies on the illusion of an ordered reality. Petersburg itself is on the brink of chaos: 'Beyond Petersburg, there is nothing,' the narrator notes, while the Senator fears the outlying islands with the unfamiliar, vaguely Asiatic swarms of industrial workers.[44] The son, Nikolai Apollonovich, has quarters that are neatly divided

[40] Leighton, *Alexander Bestuzhev-Marlinsky*, 'Conclusion'.

[41] This interpretation was suggested by Edyta Bojanowska.

[42] Sergei Bodrov's film, *Kavkazskii plennik*, was released in 1996. Of 'remakes' of 'The Captive of the Caucasus', see Vladimir Makanin's (b. 1937) short story 'Kavkazskii plennyi', 1995; Andrei Bitov's *Kavkazskii plennik* (2007, written 1969); and numerous others.

[43] Andrei Bely, *Petersburg*, tr., annotated, and introduced by Robert A. Maguire and John E. Malmstad (Bloomington, Ind.: Indiana University Press, 1978), 53.

[44] *Petersburg*, 12.

among East and West, with a bust of Kant appearing alongside oriental elements such as a divan and a hookah. As *Petersburg* and other later texts often indicate, what has been portrayed as distant and 'other' (both people and territory) is ultimately also self. The twentieth-century discourse of Eurasianism advocated embracing the Tatar inside the Russian, as an antidote to the worn-out decadence of the West. Perhaps, it was thought, rather than striving to be part of Europe, Russia should instead embrace all that was Eastern, 'savage' and irrational, as a source of greater power and an affirmation of life and independent identity. This embrace certainly had its roots in the Romantic period. And St Petersburg, already exposed long before as irrational and 'imaginary' to its core, could combine in itself both centre and periphery, reason and savagery, with the revolution, occurring both in the capital and along the far-flung edges of the empire, epitomizing this connection. Ultimately, this foreign territory had long before become recognizable in Russian Romantic prose writing.

Further Reading

Bagby, Lewis, *Alexander Bestuzhev-Marlinsky and Russian Byronism* (University Park, Pa.: Pennsylvania State University Press, 1995).

Barratt, Andrew, and Briggs, A. D. P., *A Wicked Irony: The Rhetoric of Lermontov's* A Hero of Our Time (Bristol: Bristol Classical Press, 1989).

Bojanowska, Edyta, *Nikolai Gogol between Ukrainian and Russian Nationalism* (Cambridge, Mass.: Harvard University Press, 2007).

Brower, Daniel, and Lazzerini, Edward (eds), *Russia's Orient: Imperial Borderlands and Peoples, 1700–1917* (Bloomington, Ind.: Indiana University Press, 1997).

Brown, William Edward, *A History of Russian Literature of the Romantic Period* (Ann Arbor: Ardis, 1986).

Fanger, Donald, *Dostoevsky and Romantic Realism: A Study of Dostoevsky in Relation to Balzac, Dickens and Gogol* (Cambridge, Mass.: Harvard University Press, 1965).

Fanger, Donald, *The Creation of Nikolai Gogol* (Cambridge, Mass.: Belknap Press of Harvard University Press, 1979).

Frank, Joseph, *Dostoevsky: The Seeds of Revolt, 1821–1849* (Princeton: Princeton University Press, 1976).

Frazier, Melissa, *Romantic Encounters: Writers, Readers and the 'Library for Reading'* (Stanford, Calif.: Stanford University Press, 2007).

Greenleaf, Monika, *Pushkin and Romantic Fashiona: Fragment, Elegy, Orient, Irony* (Stanford, Calif.: Stanford University Press, 1994).

Karlinsky, Simon, 'Two Pushkin Studies: I. Pushkin, Chateaubriand, and the Romantic Pose; II. The Amber Beads of Crimea (Pushkin and Mickiewicz)', *California Slavic Studies*, 2 (1963), 96–120.

Layton, Susan, *Russian Literature and Empire: Conquest of the Caucasus from Pushkin to Tolstoy* (Cambridge: Cambridge University Press, 1994).

Leighton, Lauren, *Alexander Bestuzhev-Marlinsky* (New York: Twain Publishers, 1975).

Leighton, Lauren, *Russian Romantic Criticism* (Westport, Conn.: Greenwood Press, 1987).

Peace, Richard, *The Enigma of Gogol: An Examination of the Writings of N. V. Gogol and their Place in the Russian Literary Tradition* (Cambridge: Cambridge University Press, 2009).

Powelstock, David, *Becoming Mikhail Lermontov: The Ironies of Romantic Individualism in Nicholas I's Russia* (Evanston, Ill.: Northwestern University Press, 2005).
Ram, Harsha, *The Imperial Sublime: A Russian Poetics of Empire* (Madison, Wis.: University of Wisconsin Press, 2003).
Scotto, Peter, 'Prisoners of the Caucasus: Ideologies of Imperialism in Lermontov's "Bela"', *PMLA* 107 (1992), 246–60.
Todd, William Mills, *Fiction and Society in the Age of Pushkin* (Cambridge, Mass.: Harvard University Press, 1986).

Polish

CHAPTER 29

POLISH ROMANTICISM

MONIKA COGHEN

Polish Romanticism is not restricted to the literary sphere, but is integral to the understanding of turbulent Polish nineteenth-century history.[1] The bond between Romanticism and history was part of the Polish Romantics' original self-reflection, present in their literary manifestos, where, following Herder and Mme de Staël, they insisted that literature expressed the spirit of the nation at a particular stage of its history. The leading figures of the Romantic movement, Mickiewicz, Słowacki, and Krasiński, not only shared Shelley's conviction that 'Poets are unacknowledged legislators of the world' but also strove to become national spiritual leaders.[2] In the course of the nineteenth century they were recognized as poets-prophets by their reading audience in the country, which was struggling to regain its independence, or at least to preserve its national identity.

The Commonwealth of Poland and Lithuania, which lost its statehood in 1795 after a series of partitions by the neighbouring states of Russia, Austria, and Prussia, had come into being in the late fourteenth century, first as a dynastic union, and then in 1569 as a full political union between the Kingdom of Poland and the Grand Duchy of Lithuania (The Res Publica of two nations). Its territory had included not only the territories of most of present-day Poland and Lithuania, but also considerable parts of Belarus and Ukraine. The Commonwealth had been a multi-ethnic state, with major ethnic groups being Poles, Lithuanians, Ruthenians (Ukrainians), and Belarusians. The leading social group was *szlachta* (the nobility), much more numerous than in the rest of Europe and including members of all the major ethnicities—according to some accounts it accounted for 25 per cent of the population. In terms of nationality most noblemen embraced the overall Polish 'state nationality', though they preserved the sense of their

1 I am very grateful to Peter Cochran and Mirosława Modrzewska for allowing me to quote from their translation of *Beniowski*, and to Patrick Corness and the editors of *The Sarmatian Review* for the permission to use his translation of Norwid's 'Fatum'.

2 Cf. Czesław Miłosz, *The History of Polish Literature*, 2nd edn (Berkeley: University of California Press, 1983), 203.

local homeland.[3] In terms of language, Polish was the language of the nobility, and Lithuanian, Ruthenian, and Belarusian were mainly spoken by the peasantry. Thus, Mickiewicz, who explicitly declared Lithuania to be his native country, did not speak Lithuanian nor Belarusian, and his sense of national identity is expressed in the lines of his 1822 poem 'To Joachim Lelewel': 'from the banks of the Niemen, a Pole, an inhabitant of Europe'.[4]

The sense of overall Polish nationality was so strong that nineteenth-century history offers an account of numerous schemes of regaining independence, thwarted by the partitioning powers, and resulting in increasing oppression, with the Poles constantly looking for political support from the West, particularly to France. At the time of the Napoleonic Wars most Poles linked their hopes and fortunes to Napoleon, who created the Duchy of Warsaw in 1807. After Napoleon's fall, at the Congress of Vienna (1815), the Polish territories were partitioned again among Russia, Austria, and Prussia (and that division persisted without major changes until 1914), but some vestiges of the Polish state were preserved under Russian control in the form of the so-called Congress Kingdom of Poland. Although the Congress Kingdom originally had one of the most liberal constitutions in Europe, it was not respected by the tsarist authorities, who quickly introduced oppressive measures, aimed at thwarting any nationalist movements. The November Uprising (1830–1) broke out as a result of a conspiracy of the cadets of the elitist Warsaw military academy and quickly metamorphosed into a war against the Russian rule. Its failure has traditionally been attributed to lack of consensus among its leaders, which resulted in chaotic military strategy. After some initial successes, the Polish forces were eventually defeated, which led to mass emigration of the people directly involved and to repressive policies at home. For two decades the centre of Polish political and literary life moved to Paris. Yet the works of the Polish Romantics, banned at home, were smuggled to the homeland and, clandestinely distributed, they were well-known and loved.

The November Uprising can be seen as the focal point of Polish Romanticism, with the next military attempt at regaining national independence, the January Insurrection of 1863, as its final benchmark. Both are regarded as ignited by youthful political enthusiasts, largely inspired by Romantic poetry, which provided them with a belief in the power of self-sacrificing fervour. In Poland in the 1820s the *querelle* between the young Romantic writers and the classicist literary establishment, which cultivated neoclassical poetics modelled on French writers such as Jacques Delille, was not only a debate on the shape of national literature but also on the forms of political action. The 'old' proponents of neoclassicism wanted to preserve the status quo; the 'young' Romantics wanted radical change. Lives of many Polish Romantics reveal their radical commitment, for instance: Maurycy Mochnacki (1803–34), a talented pianist, the most vocal critical exponent of new Romantic ideas, strongly influenced by Schelling and the Schlegels,

[3] Piotr S. Wandycz, *The Lands of Partitioned Poland, 1795–1918* (Seattle and London: University of Washington Press, 1974), 5.

[4] In this article, unless otherwise indicated, I am using my own philological translations, mainly in order to show original lexical choices.

was also a clandestine activist, and one of the original members of the cadets' plot. The November Uprising marked the triumph of literary Romanticism, although in political terms it led to a national disaster. The Romantics in their post-1831 writings attempted to confront its consequences, which often took the form of religious mysticism and millenarianism.

The impetus for the renewal of Polish literature came from Lithuania, from a writer whose background reflected the polyethnicity of contemporary Polish society. Adam Mickiewicz (1798–1855) acquired his education at the University of Vilnius, whose academic milieu cultivated the traditions of the Enlightenment and keenly followed intellectual and literary developments in Europe. A considerable part of the activities of the clandestine Society of Philomaths, of which Mickiewicz was one of the leading members, was devoted to the study of French and German publications, which kept the students up to date with the current European trends. Even though the main aim of the society, for which its members were to be persecuted, was the cultivation of Polish culture, they were not satisfied with the existing literary models and looked for inspiration to the West.

In the midst of the debate on how to create a new Polish literature necessary for preserving national identity, Mickiewicz found inspiration in the works of Goethe, Schiller, and Byron, and at the same time drew on local folk traditions. He developed the concept of the common people as a repository of essential moral values, and of 'feeling' as opposed to 'knowledge'. His first volume of *Poezje* (Poetry, 1822), with its cycle of 'Ballads and Romances', traditionally marks the beginning of Polish Romanticism. The ballads drew on the eighteenth-century vogue for the genre, which had, among others, reached Poland in the adaptations from M. G. Lewis's *Tales of Wonder* by Julian Ursyn Niemcewicz.[5] Mickiewicz found his sources in the local folklore, and delighted in the supernatural, coining a new poetic language based on ordinary turns of phrase. The second poem in the cycle, 'Romantyczność' (The Romantic), which is usually seen as his poetic manifesto, challenges a rationalist perception of the world in favour of the truth of feeling and imagination. In a manner following the pattern of well-known ballads, for instance, 'Sweet William's Ghost', we are presented with a dramatic image of a country girl embracing the vision of her dead lover. At the core of the poem lie three responses to the girl's experience: those of the common folk, of a learned old man, and of the speaker. The common folk accept the authenticity of the vision based on the strength of emotion; 'the old man', generally recognized as Jan Śniadecki, the author of a fierce attack on Romantic tendencies in literature, dismisses it as absurd; but the speaker keenly endorses the popular belief. Addressing the rationalist philosopher, he asserts:

> Feeling and faith appeal to me more
> Than the lens and the eye of a sage.
> You know the dead truths, unknown to the common people

[5] Juliusz Kleiner, 'Lewis i jego *Tales of Wonder* jako źródło ballad Niemcewicza', in Juliusz Kleiner, *W kręgu historii i teorii literatury* (Warsaw: Państwowe Wydawnictwo Naukowe, 1981), 144–56.

> You see the world in dust and in each spark of stars
> You don't know the living truths; you won't see a miracle
> Have a heart and look into the heart![6]

The epigraph from *Hamlet*, 'Methinks I see. Where? In my mind's eye', stresses the universal message of the poem, placing it in what was perceived as the 'Romantic' tradition of Shakespeare.

Empirical reason versus faith and feeling became a crucial antinomy in Mickiewicz's thinking. In his second volume of *Poezje* (Poetry, 1823) it found its expression in his poetic drama *Dziady* (*Forefathers' Eve*), parts 2 and 4, the so-called Vilnius-Kaunas text. *Forefathers' Eve*, part 2, continues Mickiewicz's fascination with folk traditions, drawing on the traditional pagan Lithuanian-Belarusian practice of the worship of the dead. What to the enlightened mind and to the church appears as superstition, is granted the status of moral knowledge, as in 'The Romantic'. The dead need the intercession of the living, and the living are to learn from their fate. Yet the communal experience yields space to the drama of an individual by the mysterious appearance of a figure who fails to respond to the exhortations of the group. This marks the dichotomies of Mickiewicz's concerns between the folk community and individualism, between local traditions and his readings in contemporary European literature, preparing for the transition to part 4.

Part 4 focuses on the alienation and revolt of a gifted individual. Its protagonist, Gustaw, seems to be the mysterious figure of dubious ontological status from the end of part 2, presumably that of a Werther-like suicide, who comes to confront his teacher-priest and re-enact his experiences. He is an idealist, completely alienated from society, whose hypocrisy and mendacity he despises. In a breath-taking monologue he recounts his sentimental education based on the reading of what he refers to as 'the robbers' books'—Rousseau, Goethe, Schiller, and, implicitly, Byron—blaming them for forming his sensibility, and sending him on his love quest for a perfect soulmate. His highly idealized beloved, however, in a mundane way, chose a rich, aristocratic husband, which presumably led to Gustaw's suicide, re-enacted by the gesture of stabbing himself with a knife, after which, nonetheless, he continues his passionate outburst of love and despair.

Forefathers' Eve, parts 2 and 4, mark the beginning of Mickiewicz's experimentation with the dramatic form, which found its culmination in *Forefathers' Eve*, part 3, written in Dresden in 1833 (the so-called Dresden text, see below). The fragmentary sequence is generally regarded as a model of Polish Romantic drama. Numerous critics pointed to its dream-like fragmentary structure, and its revolutionary technique, linking together ritual, morality play, lyrical drama, elements of the opera, and political satire. It may seem hard to consider it as whole, with part 1 never completed and part 3 logically and chronologically following part 4. While the pagan ritual may be seen as a prelude to the love tragedy of Gustaw, the two serve as a prequel to a national drama written in

[6] For a literary tr. of the poem, see W. H. Auden, 'The Romantic', *About the House* (London: Faber & Faber, 1966), 76–8.

the aftermath of the November Uprising, and the whole can be seen as indicative of Mickiewicz's development, as Maria Janion put it, from 'a lover of a woman' to 'a lover of his homeland'.[7]

Together with the two parts of *Forefathers' Eve*, volume ii of *Poetry* contained the poetic tale *Grażyna*, a literary form made popular on the continent by Scott and Byron, which was to become characteristic of pre-1830 Polish poetry and to acquire the status of a distinct genre in Polish literary history. *Grażyna* tells the story of an eponymous Lithuanian princess taking to arms against the Teutonic knights, in place of her husband who negotiates with the invaders to advance his selfish interests. Ancient Lithuanian history serves as a cover for present-day political concerns. The poem is often viewed as bearing too many traditional epic features to be classified as a 'poetic tale' proper, since the characteristics of the genre include fragmentariness, intertwining of narrative and lyric features, and a protagonist modelled on the Byronic hero as the focal consciousness.[8]

All these features appear in *Konrad Wallenrod* (1828), another tale from Lithuanian history written during Mickiewicz's forced stay in Russia after his arrest for his involvement in the Philomaths' Society. The very name of the protagonist points to Byron's Corsair and Lara as his literary antecedents, but his real-life model seems to be Konrad Ryleyev, a Russian friend of Mickiewicz's, executed for his role in the Decembrists' plot to prevent the accession of Tsar Nicholas I in 1825. Whereas *Grażyna* deals with a heroic confrontation with the enemy, *Konrad Wallenrod* presents the tragedy of a man who chooses strategies of deceit and treason against the overwhelming power of the oppressor. The protagonist of Byron's romances becomes rewritten by Mickiewicz into a national avenger figure, set against the background of the Teutonic conquest of Lithuania in the fourteenth century. The verse tale recounts the story of the mysterious, guilt-ridden Wallenrod, who, after being elected Grand Master of the Teutonic Order, brings it to destruction in an ineffective military campaign against Lithuania. Konrad turns out to be a Machiavellian figure: he is actually a Lithuanian who was brought up among the German knights but has never forsaken his original identity, which has been fostered by national tales sung to him by the guardian figure of a Lithuanian bard (*wajdelota*) Halban, a figure related to Macpherson's Ossian and to Walter Scott's minstrels. The text examines the moral precariousness and self-destructiveness of his position.

Most critics agree that the poem expresses Mickiewicz's reflections on the possible strategies of Polish struggle for independence at the time when he lived in Russia and witnessed the failure of the Decembrist movement; in particular, the poem is

[7] Maria Janion, 'Literatura romantyczna jako dokument spisków', in Maria Janion, Maria Dernałowicz, and Marian Maciejewski, *Literatura krajowa w okresie romantyzmu 1831–1863* (Cracow: Wydawnictwo Literackie, 1988), 46. Janion sees this transformation as characteristic of Polish Romanticism.

[8] Janina Lasecka-Zielakowa, *Powieść poetycka w Polsce w okresie romantyzmu* (Wrocław: Zakład Narodowy im. Ossolińskich, 1990), 15–27.

seen as his manifesto on the role of national poetry—Halban, the bard who has kindled Konrad's passion for revenge with his tales, is determined to outlive him in order to spread his fame and spur new generations to rebellion. At this point one can observe the transition from the idea of the simple folk to that of the nation, from Romantic primitivism to nationalism. Mickiewicz's Polish contemporaries read the poem as an unequivocal call to arms, completely ignoring the personal tragedy of the protagonist.[9] When in November 1830 the insurgents attacked the Belvedere Palace in Warsaw, the residence of Grand Duke Constantine, who was the commander-in-chief of the military forces in the Congress Kingdom of Poland, a participant of the events commented, 'The word became flesh, and Wallenrod—the Belvedere Palace'.[10]

A different development of the poetic tale appears in Antoni Malczewski's *Maria* (1825), which, under the inspiration of Byron, explores the potential of the fragmentary narrative imbued with deep lyricism. Set against the melancholy landscape of the seventeenth-century Ukraine and based on historical fact, the poem recounts the story of the murder of the beloved wife of a young aristocrat at the order of his proud father, who would not get reconciled to her humbler gentry's descent. Unlike Mickiewicz's tales, which explored current national concerns under the guise of historical events, Malczewski's poem tends towards aestheticism, and exhibits an all-pervading pessimism. It introduces the Ukraine as a favourite Romantic setting: while Lithuania in Mickiewicz's works serves as a synecdoche of the Polish Commonwealth, the Ukraine with its exotic steppe scenery and its turbulent historical relations with Poland can be seen as the poetic counterpart of Scotland in British Romanticism. Seweryn Goszczyński's tale *Zamek Kaniowski* (The Castle of Kaniów, 1828) deploys the poetics of the Gothic and its Cossack protagonist modelled on the Byronic hero to present the 1768 Uprising of the Ukrainian population against the Polish ruling classes (so-called Koliszczyzna), which resulted in massacres on both sides. The Ukrainian setting recurs in many works by Słowacki (see later in this chapter).

Another genre which Mickiewicz developed was the sonnet (*Sonety*, Sonnets, 1826). In the love sonnets, some of them adaptations from Petrarch, he introduced a colloquial poetic idiom to deal with the complexities of sexual relations, and in the Crimean sonnets, under the persona of the Pilgrim, he presented poetic impressions of his travels in the Crimean Peninsula, following the contemporary vogue for orientalism. The sublime of the oriental landscape not only evokes metaphysical experience but also corresponds to the various mental states of the speaker. Although the Pilgrim is a descendant of Childe Harold, his melancholy results from his exile from his homeland, which is constantly present in his memory. For Polish Romantics, this theme of exile was to become a recurring subject.

[9] Dorota Siwicka, '*Konrad Wallenrod*', in Jarosław Marek Rymkiewicz et al. (eds), *Mickiewicz. Encyklopedia* (Warsaw: Horyzont, 2001), 230.

[10] Quoted after Roman Koropeckyj, *Adam Mickiewicz: The Life of a Romantic* (Ithaca, NY, and London: Cornell University Press, 2008), 98.

In the aftermath of the tragedy of the November Uprising Mickiewicz's concerns shifted entirely towards nationalism and religious mysticism. Both of these were combined in messianism, a millenarian conception of history, in which Poland, through the suffering and sacrifice of her children, was to lead other nations towards freedom in a way analogous to Christ, who through his crucifixion won the redemption of man. *Forefathers' Eve*, part 3 (1832), artistically enacts Mickiewicz's metamorphosis from individualism to a belief in the messianic role of Poland. It presents a poetic record of the political trials of young people accused of conspiracy in Lithuania in 1823–4, in which Mickiewicz and his fellow Philomaths were involved. The ordeal of the arrested youths serves as an image of Polish national destiny. The drama sets the suffering of the persecuted against the psychomachia of the protagonist acted out in the fashion of a morality play, with good and evil spirits struggling for his soul. It opens with the transformation of Gustaw, the star-crossed lover from *Forefathers' Eve*, part 4, into Konrad, the poet who casts himself in the role of the Promethean champion of the Polish nation. In the so-called 'Great Improvisation', which presents one of the great flights of Romantic imagination, in an act of sacrilegious self-assertion Konrad as a poet-creator proclaims himself God's equal and demands 'the rule of souls' over his compatriots.[11] Metaphysical rebellion is bound to be self-destructive, but Konrad is saved by a humble Catholic priest, who exorcizes the evil spirit of pride and is granted a vision of Poland as the 'Christ of nations'. The play juxtaposes historical prison scenes and satirical images of the Russian oppressors and Polish elites with elements of medieval plays, and visionary scenes. It is a continuation of Mickiewicz's experiments with hybrid literary forms started in *Forefathers' Eve*, parts 2 and 4. In her 1839 'Essai sur le drame fantastique: Goethe—Byron—Mickiewicz', George Sand ranked it next to Goethe's *Faust* and Byron's *Manfred*, seeing as their common feature the use of the supernatural to tackle philosophical questions, and using Byron's term 'metaphysical drama' to describe them.[12]

If *Forefathers's Eve*, part 3, presents the contemporary tragedy of the Polish nation in the form of experimental Romantic drama, a classical strain in Mickiewicz's work is observable in *Pan Tadeusz* (1834), often viewed as the Polish national epic. The poem presents Polish-Lithuanian society at the eve of Napoleon's invasion of Russia in 1812, with which Poles linked their hopes for national sovereignty. Unlike Mickiewicz's earlier works, it lacks one strongly individualistic protagonist though his traces remain in the character of Jacek Soplica, a swashbuckler with great ambitions who turns into a humble friar in order to atone for his past. In Soplica's deathbed confession, intertextually related to Byron's *The Giaour*, whose translation Mickiewicz was completing at the time, Soplica recounts his story, which seems to be that of the Byronic hero reformed into a Polish Catholic. Not only does Jacek renounce his nobleman's pride and embrace humility, but also he devotes all his efforts to the struggle for Polish independence, which he

[11] Adam Mickiewicz, *Forefathers' Eve*, part 3. Harold B. Segel (ed.), *Polish Romantic Drama* (Ithaca, NY: Cornell University Press, 1977), 105.

[12] George Sand, 'Essai sur le drame fantastique', *Revue des Deux Mondes*, 8 (1839), 489–531.

links to the fortunes of Napoleon, and as a secret emissary he prepares an uprising in Lithuania. The eponymous Tadeusz is his son who is about to enter maturity and in a manner reminiscent of Byron's Don Juan embarks on amatory adventures. The feud between two country families, around which the plot focuses, is a consequence of Jacek's crime and may be seen as an allusion to the anarchy of contemporary Polish politics,[13] as his plans to incite an uprising fall through owing to personal resentments among the local gentry. But the historical timing Mickiewicz has chosen allows him to relive a moment of hope when national unity seems to be possible and the whole community overcomes their prejudices in their support for Napoleon against the Russians in the final canto of the poem. The poem is above all a celebration of memory, which recreates the by-gone way of life of Polish-Lithuanian gentry and the local landscape from the perspective of an émigré living in Paris. The opening words of the poem, known to every Pole, succinctly express Mickiewicz's poetic process:

> Lithuania! my homeland! thou art like good health;
> How much thou should be treasured one can only learn
> Having lost you. Today your beauty in all its glory
> I see and describe as I long for thee.

In the course of the poem Mickiewicz transforms his nostalgia into a series of objective, concrete images, be it of mushroom picking, bear hunting, or love making. The poem interweaves pathos with humour and irony, reveals Mickiewicz's keen eye for detail, and reflects political debates among Polish post-1831 immigrants in Paris.

After *Pan Tadeusz* Mickiewicz renounced writing poetry in favour of political journalism and academic activities. Already in 1832 in Dresden he had written *Books of the Polish Nation and of the Polish Pilgrimage*, which, in biblical-sounding prose, presented his messianic views of the Polish nation and of the special role of the Polish Pilgrims, i.e. Polish political émigrés, in European history. In spite of his nationalism, his ideas of brotherhood among nations and insistence on ethics in political life appealed to a considerable international audience. In Paris he came under the influence of a mystical thinker Andrzej Towiański, and became an active member of his circle. In his lectures on Slavic literatures at the Collège de France (1840–4) he presented not only his ideas on history and literature and what he believed to be the special mission of Slavic nations, but he also used them as a platform for disseminating Towiański's teaching, which led to his dismissal from his university post. Eventually in 1846 he broke free from Towiański's influence; in 1848 he organized a Polish legion to fight in support of Italian liberation from Austria and after the failure of the European revolutions in 1849 he co-edited *La Tribune des Peuples*, a short-lived newspaper with international contributors, which propagated solidarity with oppressed nations and ideologically verged on socialism. Never relenting in his pursuit of the national cause, in 1855 Mickiewicz went to Constantinople to help organize Polish military forces, which were to support Turkey

[13] Andrzej Wajda's film adaptation (1999) emphasizes the topicality of the critique of Polish gentry.

against Russia in the Crimean War. There he died, probably of cholera, a death which brings to mind the death of Byron at Messolonghi.

Mickiewicz's towering presence in the period made other Polish poets define themselves through their stance towards him. Juliusz Słowacki (1809–49) consciously cast himself in the role of Mickiewicz's antagonist and competed with him for the title of the national poet-prophet (*wieszcz*), sharing his belief in poetry as the instrument of forming national consciousness. Unlike Mickiewicz, who addressed in his poetry issues topical to his Polish audience, Słowacki, at least at the beginning of his literary career, believed in the autonomy of art and primacy of the poetic imagination.[14] Born in Krzemieniec in Volhynia (present-day Ukraine), he was a son of a master of poetry and rhetoric at the prestigious local lycée, who later became professor of literature at the University of Vilnius. He lost his father early and was brought up by his literary-minded mother, who ran a salon attended by Vilnius intellectual elites, where young Słowacki had a chance to meet Mickiewicz. Słowacki's relationship with his mother is noteworthy as she not only had a strong impact on the development of his personality, but was to become the addressee of his letters, which are among the greatest achievements of Polish epistolography. Słowacki's poetic sensibility was formed by his omnivorous reading, which made him consciously draw on various literary models. This resulted in a web of intertextual borrowings and allusions in his works, with references ranging from ancient Greece, Shakespeare, Byron, later Calderón, to Polish classics, and finally to his contemporaries.[15] He started his literary career as the author of poetic tales, clearly modelled on Byron and echoing the compositions of his Polish contemporaries, Mickiewicz, Malczewski, and Goszczyński. He was a prolific playwright and his plays are ranked by Polish literary historians next to Victor Hugo's works as highest achievements of Romantic drama. Equally noteworthy are his narrative poems: *Beniowski*, modelled on Byron's *Don Juan*, which in Polish literary criticism is termed a 'poem of digressions', and a mystical poem *Król-Duch* (King-Spirit).

What is already striking in his poetic tales is fascination with the Orient and Polish history, the imagination delighting in the macabre, closer to the Baroque than to the Gothic, and interest in hallucinatory experiences. All these features are salient in *Lambro* (1833), a tale in which he tries to depict the fate of the 1830 generation under the guise of the story of a Greek freedom fighter turned into a corsair, who seeks consolation for his remorse in opium.

Słowacki did not directly take part in the November Uprising, but was sent as an emissary of the Polish insurgent government to Paris and London. This started his life of exile, which he lived in Switzerland and Paris, making also a journey to Italy, Greece, and the Middle East. His first volumes of poetry were poorly received by the Polish émigré literary critics, particularly as his early works made no reference to the

[14] Alina Kowalczykowa, *Słowacki* (Warsaw: Wydawnictwo Naukowe PWN, 1999), 81.

[15] Alina Witkowska, *Romantyzm*, 321, sees 'literariness' as characteristic of Słowacki's early work; Miłosz, *History of Polish Literature*, 233, writes of 'amazing literary cocktails' (borrowing Professor Backvis's term), particularly striking in his dramas.

recent national disaster. Nevertheless, Słowacki aimed at challenging the authority of Mickiewicz, who had already been recognized by his compatriots as the national bard. Whereas Mickiewicz glorified the suffering of the Polish nation and imbued it with messianic meaning, Słowacki examined the reasons for the failure of the uprising and castigated what he considered to be Polish national vices.

His play *Kordian* (1834) offers both a psychological study of the Romantic self and a political examination of the failure of the 1830 Uprising. Its eponymous protagonist is a young aristocrat in quest for the meaning of life. In Act 1 we encounter him as a 15-year-old youth suffering from *Weltschmerz* and attempting suicide; in Act 2 we see him on his Grand Tour, where he becomes disillusioned with both the love of women and human institutions—the British parliamentary system, where all is for sale, and the papacy, which condemns the Poles in their struggle for independence. In a spectacular *Manfred*-like scene on the summit of Mont Blanc, which is a counterpart of the 'Great Improvisation' in Mickiewicz's *Forefathers' Eve*, Kordian realizes his vocation, which is to devote himself to the national cause. This takes the form of his participation in the plot to assassinate Tsar Nicholas I during the ceremony of his coronation as King of Poland in Warsaw in Act 3. The conspiracy, based on historical fact, serves as a metonymy of the 1830 Uprising, showing the rift between Polish national leaders intent on refraining from bloodshed and preserving the legitimacy of power, and the revolutionary drive of the young enthusiasts intent on self-sacrifice, which, they believed, should be sufficient for the restoration of Polish statehood. In spite of being outvoted by his fellow conspirators, Kordian is determined to act on his own. As a cadet keeping guard in the palace of the Tsar, he has the perfect opportunity but is prevented by the devil and personified Imagination and Fear and falls unconscious at the door of the Tsar's bedroom. In a lunatic asylum to which he is confined, the Mephistophelian figure of the Doctor points to him that his patriotic ideas may be delusions, just like the hallucinations of madmen. The drama has an open ending at the point of Kordian's execution; although he has been granted reprieve by the Tsar after performing a stunning horse leap over the raised bayonets at the request of the Grand Duke Constantine, we never know if the pardon arrives in time.

Kordian is a polemical response to Mickiewicz's *Forefathers' Eve*. It abounds in allusions to Mickiewicz's play, with the very name of the protagonist closely echoing the name of Konrad. It seems to juxtapose the idea of active struggle with Mickiewicz's glorification of national suffering, and the concept of Poland as the 'Winkelried of nations' (Winkelried being a medieval Swiss hero who ensured his countrymen's victory over the Habsburg army, making a breach in its ranks by placing the enemy's pikes in his breast), with Father Piotr's vision of Poland as the 'Christ of nations', though both promote the idea of self-sacrifice. Słowacki's drama strikes the reader with its numerous ambiguities, which are encoded in the loose, episodic structure of the play: Kordian's self-fashioning into the national saviour is undermined not only by his eventual inability to act but also by his complete alienation from society and the moral repulsiveness of revenge. The Doctor pronounces ironic metapoetic comments on the Promethean and Tyrtean functions of poetry: 'Why does the nation perish? So that the national bard | Has the content for the poem, and the bard forms the rhyme',[16] which seems to be a reference to Mickiewicz's poetry; on the protest of Kordian the statement becomes reformulated as 'The hymn of the angel flows into the bard; | He sings—the nation perishes because the poet sings',[17] which sounds as an ironic comment on Słowacki's own aspirations. In political terms, the play, particularly through its prologue with the grotesque scene of the creation of the country's governing elites, provides a satire on the leaders of the 1830 Uprising and puts on them the blame for its failure. As Miłosz has noticed, it also criticizes the idea of an individual as a national redeemer, as proposed in Father Piotr's dream, and points to the need for engaging the masses in the national struggle.[18]

In his attempt to develop Polish drama Słowacki found inspiration in Shakespeare and the French contemporary theatre with its love of spectacle, turning to Calderón after his espousal of religious mysticism. He composed numerous dramas on Polish history, both legendary and factual. Among the former the most noteworthy is *Balladyna*, written in 1834 and published in 1839. The play seems almost postmodern with its unique blend of Shakespearean tragedy and comedy fused with Polish folklore and mythical history. Its metadramatic epilogue undermines the veracity of historical records, stressing the power of poetic imagination. The plot draws on a literary ballad about two sisters, who compete for the hand in marriage of a noble knight by picking raspberries, and the elder kills the younger, who has won the competition. The protagonist's name Balladyna stresses the ballad-like quality of the play. We watch her ruthless pursuit of social advancement and power as she rises from an ambitious country girl to the queen. As numerous critics have noticed, she is a compelling character in her psychological complexity, tortured by remorse and yet relentlessly pursuing her goal, acting out deception on others but capable of honesty in her self-judgement. Her succession of crimes concludes in her pronouncing a verdict on herself, which is carried out by a thunderbolt. The *Macbeth*-like plot is interwoven with a subplot of fairies reminiscent of *A Midsummer Night's Dream*.[19] Thus Goplana, a nymph of the Gopło Lake, falls in love with a country oaf Grabiec, Balladyna's original sweetheart. Her efforts to intervene in the human world all go amiss and the results verge on the grotesque. When Grabiec rejects the fairy's advances, she changes him into a willow and as such he witnesses Balladyna's murder of her sister. Then, when Goplana transforms Grabiec into a king to please him, he is murdered by Balladyna, desirous of his crown. Evil seems to prevail in the world where all human efforts at restoring order fail, though the mark of Cain on Balladyna's forehead and the final thunderbolt point to the existence of divine justice.

[16] Juliusz Słowacki, *Kordian*, 3.4. 720–1, *Dzieła wybrane*, iii. *Dramaty* (Wrocław: Zakład Narodowy im. Ossolinskich, 1974), 182.

[17] Słowacki, *Kordian*, 3.4.727, *Dzieła wybrane*, iii. 182.

[18] Miłosz, *History of Polish Literature*, 235.

[19] The echoes from Shakespeare in the play were thoroughly examined by Juliusz Kleiner in his monumental study *Juliusz Słowacki: Dzieje twórczości*. For their succinct account in English, see Peter Cochran et al., Introduction to *Poland's Angry Romantic: Two Poems and a Play by Juliusz Słowacki* (Newcastle upon Tyne: Cambridge Scholars Publishing, 2009), 9–10.

Słowacki's irony found its full expression in his narrative poem *Beniowski* (1841), written in *ottava rima*, in which, like Byron, he displays his poetic virtuosity.[20] As in *Don Juan*, the authorial narrator is the true hero of the poem, being even more neglectful of his protagonist and focusing more on his own self-fashioning than Byron, so that the digressions often overshadow the fragmentary plot. The alleged hero of the poem is a Hungarian-Polish adventurer Maurycy Beniowski, known for his escape from Russian imprisonment in Kamchatka and his daring exploits on several continents, and whose mainly fictitious memoirs achieved wide popularity throughout Europe. Beniowski's escapades started with his participation in the Confederacy of Bar (1768–72), a military union of Polish nobility in defence of their traditional rights and Roman Catholicism, which led to a war against Russia and which in Polish national mythology acquired the status of one of the final struggles to preserve national independence. The poem, of which only the first five cantos were completed, and the fragments published from the manuscript, recounts solely his adventures in the Ukraine. Słowacki's Beniowski has little to do with his historical prototype, being a naïve young man accidently caught in the current of history. He serves as a pretext for the examination of the past and present Polish condition, and for presenting the manifesto of Słowacki's individualism, and his poetic and ideological convictions. The poem contains the poet's response to Mickiewicz's *Pan Tadeusz* with its apparent idealization of Polish-Lithuanian country life, to which Słowacki responds with his condemnation of the Polish gentry for the fall of Poland. He also openly challenges the position of Mickiewicz as the national bard in Polish literature and, fiercely castigating Polish émigré critics, asserts his own poetic superiority. Metapoetic comments interspersed throughout the text reveal his consciousness of his poetic skill, which is well exemplified in the often-quoted stanza:

I mean: the words, now bold, now warm, now faint,
Should follow the quick spirit's every thought:
Sometimes be lightening, swift without constraint,
And sometimes like the steppe's song, sadly wrought,
Sometimes they'll soften, like a nymph's complaint,
And sometimes seem by a starlit angel brought ...
To follow so the mind in all its wit,
The verse should keep the stride, not haul the bit.[21]

In his poem, which is a great assertion of the Romantic poetic self, he moves freely from lyricism to satire, from the pathetic to the grotesque.

In 1841, under the influence of Towiański, Słowacki, like Mickiewicz, turned towards millenarianism, but he quickly shed Towiański's guidance to develop his own philosophical system based on the belief in the immortality of the spirit and its progress

[20] Słowacki's choice of the *ottava rima* must have been inspired by *Don Juan*, but the stanza had a long tradition in Polish literature dating back to the 16th cent.

[21] *Beniowski*, tr. Mirosława Modrzewska and Peter Cochran in *Polish Angry Romantic*, 288.

throughout history, which he revealed in his work of poetic prose *Geneza z Ducha* (Genesis from the Spirit). His late dramas *Ksiądz Marek* (Father Marek, 1843) and *Sen srebrny Salomei* (The Silver Dream of Salomea, 1844), set in the eighteenth-century Ukraine at the time of the Confederacy of Bar and the Cossack revolt, exhibit a blend of the macabre and mysticism, for which Słowacki drew on Calderón, whose *Constant Prince* he translated. In the unfinished narrative poem *Król-Duch* (King-Spirit), of which only one part was published in 1847, he aimed at presenting his mythopoetic vision of Polish history. The dark imagery and evocative moods of his works have earned him the reputation of a precursor of symbolism, and his poetry was highly valued in the later part of the nineteenth century.

In his political thinking he was a democratic radical and believed in the need for revolutionary change, opposing the conservative ideas of his friend Zygmunt Krasiński (see later in this chapter), who in his *Psalmy przyszłości* (Psalms of the Future) postulated the alliance of the nobility with the people and expressed his fears of revolution. Słowacki, in his poetic reply to Krasiński's poem, contended that only radical actions of the '*Spirit*', 'the Eternal *Revolutionary*',[22] can lead to Polish independence, and the poet's role was that of the national spiritual leader. These ideas made Słowacki the poet of the generation growing up in post-1830 Poland, whose idealism was to resonate in the tragic 1863 Insurrection against Russia. Słowacki himself tried to realize his ideas by travelling to Poznań to take part in the abortive 1848 Uprising, but his plans fell through. He died of tuberculosis on his return to Paris in 1849.

Zygmunt Krasiński (1812–59) used to be viewed as the third of the great trio of Polish Romantic poets, but nowadays he is valued mainly for his drama *Nieboska komedia* (*The Un-Divine Tragedy* 1833, published 1835) and his letters. Unlike Mickiewicz and Słowacki, who both descended from the gentry from the east provinces of the former Polish Commonwealth, Krasiński had an aristocratic background. His father, Wincenty, was a domineering presence in his life and he was constantly torn between his loyalty to him, which was also loyalty to his aristocratic social class, and his own national feeling. Wincenty Krasiński had reached the rank of the commander-in-chief of the Polish forces in Napoleon's army. After the Congress of Vienna and the emergence of the Kingdom of Poland, he transferred his allegiance to the Tsar, condemning clandestine nationalist activities. On his refusal to join the November Uprising and subsequent escape to Petersburg, he was regarded as a traitor. The father's actions shaped his son's thinking on the Uprising, which he was persuaded to regard as a revolution aimed at undermining the existing social order, though originally he had considered joining the armed struggle. He managed, however, to resist his father's efforts at setting him on the path of a diplomatic career in the service of the Tsar, owing to his health problems. He lived the life of a cosmopolitan aristocrat in Switzerland, Italy, and France, maintaining close links with the Great Emigration in Paris. In order not to compromise his father and not to cut off the possibility of return to his homeland he published his works

[22] Juliusz Słowacki, 'Odpowiedź na "Psalmy Przyszłości"', ll. 308–9, *Dzieła wybrane*, i. *Liryki i powieści poetyckie*, 143.

anonymously. He started his literary career as an author of Gothic novels based on Polish history, finding his inspiration in the Gothic, Walter Scott, Byron, and the French 'frenetic' school.

It is, however, his correspondence that is regarded as a much more significant literary achievement. Highly valued for its intimate prose, it simultaneously reveals the poet in the act of constant self-fashioning. In his letters to his father, his lover, his English friend journalist Henry Reeve, and numerous Polish men of letters, which later in his career took the place of literary composition, Krasiński assumes different parts towards each of his correspondents, primarily as a Romantic dandy, a patriot, a poet, an invalid, etc.[23]

His prose dramas reveal typically Romantic experimentation with the dramatic form, merging it together with extended narrative and lyrical passages. Like Mickiewicz's *Forefathers' Eve*, part 3, they are metaphysical dramas in which forces of good and evil struggle for man caught in the cataclysms of history, but while Mickiewicz's play is firmly rooted in specific historical events, Krasiński aims at giving his dramas a universal dimension. In *The Un-Divine Comedy*, he created a drama on the Romantic poet and on philosophy of history, which for Miłosz is 'the only European work of the period which dealt with the class struggle in nearly Marxist terms'.[24] The first two parts of the play focus on the critique of Romantic self-fashioning and explore the Romantic concept of the poet as a seer. The protagonist, Count Henryk, is not a 'true' poet as he forsakes love in his quest for poetic beauty. He ruins his domestic happiness in pursuit of the Maiden, who for him embodies poetry, but is actually a decaying corpse brought to life by the power of evil. His obsession with poetry results in the apparent insanity and death of his wife, who strove to become a poet herself to win back his love, and in his young son's being cursed with poetic genius accompanied by blindness. The little Orcio is a seer in contact with the spiritual world; his visionary poetry is juxtaposed against the 'fake' poetry of Count Henryk, whose attempts at the poetic perception of the world are dismissed by a voice accusing him of 'composing a drama'. This bitter deconstruction of the Romantic self comes from the writer who excelled at his own self-fashioning in his own private correspondence and results from what Janion terms Krasiński's 'moralistic conception' of poetry.[25]

The further two parts show Count Henryk entering the realm of public action, by going to the rescue of his fellow aristocrats besieged by the revolutionaries in the Castle of the Holy Trinity. Viewed from the perspective of the morality play, this decision is shown as marking his successive fall—as though political activity was necessarily tainted by an egotistic pursuit of fame. At this point the Count's story becomes part of the dialectics of history. He realizes that his social class, the feudal system, and religion to which they adhere are to be destroyed. He is aware of their responsibility for social oppression, but is determined to defend them as he is bound to them by tradition and honour. His wanderings in disguise around the revolutionary camp reveal the outrages

23 Witkowska, *Romantyzm*, 378–9, 594–6.

24 Miłosz, *History of Polish Literature*, 244.

25 Maria Janion, *Zygmunt Krasiński: Debiut i dojrzałość* (Warsaw: Wiedza Powszechna, 1962), 203.

committed by the revolutionaries in a series of phantasmagoric images, which allude to Dante's journey through hell, with the title of the drama suggesting that it aspires to represent the human realm of history as a counterpart of Dante's *Divine Comedy*. In Count Henryk's confrontation with the revolutionary leader Pankracy, the arguments of both sides are juxtaposed: Pankracy is backed by the suffering of the masses seeking redress and believes in the advent of a new religion of humanity, basing his argument on reason, but he is driven by dictatorial ambitons; Count Henryk firmly defends Christianity and the existing social order, suggesting that the revolutionaries are set on re-enacting the old crimes in their greed and struggle for power. The play's eschatological ending shows the final defeat of aristocracy, with Henryk as the sole remaining defender of its honour stepping to death over the abyss. But the victory of the revolutionaries is undercut by Pankracy's being struck with a vision of the second coming of Christ, and the final words of the dying revolutionary leader are *Galilaee, vicisti*! (Galilean, you have won!), acknowledging the supremacy of divine providence over human, 'undivine' history. The ending is open both to catastrophic and Hegelian interpretations (with Christ marking the 'synthesis' of the new era of Christian regeneration after the 'thesis' of the traditional social order and the 'antithesis' of revolution[26]).

Krasiński's historical thinking was formed by his own fears of social revolt raised not only by the French Revolution, but by the more recent unrest in Britain (which he keenly followed in his correspondence with Henry Reeve), the 1830 Revolution in France, and the 1830 Polish Uprising; thus his play has a universal dimension with unspecified time and place. His Christian conservatism was shaped by his readings in philosophy of history, especially the works of Giambattisto Vico, Jules Michelet, Pierre-Simon Ballanche, Joseph de Maistre, and Hegel. His drama *Irydion* (1836) focuses on the fall of the Roman Empire; the eponymous Irydion is a Greek scheming for the destruction of Rome as a retribution for subjugating Greece, and his revenge is kindled by the satanic spirit of his adviser. In his plot he hopes for the support of the Christians, who, however, refrain from the armed struggle to seek redemption through humility and martyrdom. In the narrative conclusion Irydion is transplanted to 1830s Europe to see the ruins of Rome, for which he has pledged his soul, but he is saved by the intercession of his Christian beloved and sent to serve penance in the enslaved Poland. Traditionally the drama has been seen as a metaphor of the November Uprising, but it aims at presenting a broader vision of mechanisms leading to a decline of civilization and, much more emphatically than the *Un-Divine Comedy*, stresses the redeeming value of Christian sacrifice.

In his further works Krasiński openly moved towards messianism and millenarianism, which is apparent in his poems *Przedświt* (Before Dawn) and *Psalmy przyszłości* (Psalms of the Future), where he presented his providential vision of the progressive evolution of history in which a special, Christ-like part was assigned to the Polish nation, and particularly to its nobility perceived as the preserver of Christian virtues.

[26] Miłosz, *History of Polish Literature*, 246.

At the turn of the nineteenth and twentieth centuries a fourth name was added to the three traditional great Romantic names. Neglected by his contemporaries, Cyprian Norwid (1821–83) was first appreciated by the modernist 'Młoda Polska' (Young Poland) movement and today is recognized as a precursor of Polish modern poetry. It is disputable whether he should be regarded as a Romantic, but chronologically, he belonged to the second generation of the Polish Romantic poets. He was essentially an outsider questioning both the ideology and form of the poetry of Mickiewicz and Słowacki, which he admired but, unlike his contemporaries, rejected as a literary model, in order to pursue his own idiosyncratic conception of poetry.

Norwid grew up in post-1831Warsaw, where he started his training as an artist and made a successful poetic debut. His early poems, still deeply steeped in the Polish Romantic tradition, echoed the pessimism of Malczewski's *Maria*. In 1842 he left Warsaw in order to study sculpture in Florence, never to return to his homeland, because of his conflict with Russian and Prussian authorities. Living in Italy and in Paris, he became acquainted with the leading Polish émigré Romantics including Chopin, whose music embodied for him one of the highest ideals of human creativity through its transformation of Polish folk music into the universal perfection of art, which he expressed in the poem 'Fortepian Szopena' (Chopin's Grand Piano). His poetry met with charges of obscurity in the émigré community, and his attempts to earn a living as an artist proved unsuccessful. In 1852 he decided to try his luck in America and spent a year and a half in New York, working as an illustrator, but his feeling of cultural estrangement, ill health, and financial difficulties made him return to Paris, where he lived the rest of his life in increasing alienation and poverty. From 1877 he stayed in a home for the aged run by Polish nuns, where he died and was buried in a communal grave. Most of his work was published posthumously.

Similarly to the first generation Romantics, his main concern was with history and the individual, but he criticized Polish messianism. He countered the Romantic idea of the nation with a notion of historically evolving human society and asserted the value of the individual in the face of modern industrial civilization. His versatile oeuvre includes dramas, short stories, and essays written in poetic prose. In his philosophical poem *Promethidion* (1851), written in the form of a dialogue, he developed his own concept of the relationship between work and art, reminiscent of the ideas of Ruskin and Morris.[27] He posits the need to bridge the gap between the toil of the common people and artistic creation so that work can become the highest expression of the human spirit on its way to redemption. His most valued achievement is his collection of short lyrics *Vade-mecum*, prepared for publication in 1866, but published only in 1947, where he openly declares a new poetics which, he believed, would set an example for the development of Polish poetry. In their compression and verbal and stylistic experiments, his poems have mostly aptly been compared to those of Emily Dickinson and Gerard Manley Hopkins. A devout Catholic, Norwid

[27] Miłosz, *History of Polish Literature*, 273.

believed in the poet's duty to direct the reader towards the truth, but simultaneously required the reader's intellectual cooperation through the sophisticated use of parable, symbol, and irony. The poem 'Fatum' may serve as a good example of his poetic technique:

I
Such beastly *Anguish*, human-baiting,
With fateful eyes transfixed its prey ...
–Waiting––
Now will he turn away?
II
Instead the stare was fair returned,
As artists size up subjects top to toe;
Aware the human had discerned–
What gain he'd draw
from such a foe,
It shuddered to its very core
––And it's no more![28]

Most Polish literary historians view Norwid as a Romantic primarily owing to his revisionist preoccupation with the problems addressed by his predecessors, though he viewed their poetry as the thing of the past.[29] In the early twentieth century he embodied the figure of the unrecognized solitary genius; later on, his experimentation made him very much a poets' poet. Like Mickiewicz, Słowacki, and Krasiński, he was a Christian idealist. But while they in their effort to confront the burden of nineteenth-century Polish history turned to messianism, he focused on the individual's quest for redemption.

A general overview of Polish Romanticism may lead to misleading oversimplifications and omissions, such as, in the case of this chapter, the development of the historical novel by Józef Ignacy Kraszewski and of the comedy of manners by Aleksander Fredro. The focus of this chapter necessarily falls on the most salient and most characteristic literary developments. The starting point for Polish Romantics was, like for many of their Western counterparts, the focus on the self. But the fate of the individual was seen as irrevocably linked to that of the nation, and personal existence was represented as a worthy sacrifice for the sake of the national cause. In the aftermath of the failure of the 1830 Uprising, pessimism, melancholy, and metaphysical and political rebellion were countered by messianic ideas of the émigré poets. Idealism, which despite their numerous differences the Polish Romantics ultimately shared, led them to religious belief, whether Catholicism or their own less orthodox systems. The confrontation of the individual with history was therefore enacted on the metaphysical plane, and presented mainly in

[28] Tr. Patrick Corness, *Sarmatian Review*, 33/1 (Jan. 2013), 1727 <http://www.ruf.rice.edu/~sarmatia/113/index.html>.

[29] Dorota Siwicka, *Romantyzm 1822–1863* (Warsaw: Wydawnictwo Naukowe PWN, 2002), 226–7.

the dramatic form, which became the dominant genre in the post-1831 period. Through the powerful expansion of the poetic language, and the deep belief in the ethical and social roles of poetry Polish Romantics played a crucial part in preserving the national identity of their readers, truly earning the status of *wieszcz*, the poet-prophet.

Further Reading

Translations

Cochran, Peter, Johnson, Bill, Modrzewska, Mirosława, and O'Neil, Catherine (eds), *Poland's Angry Romantic: Two Poems and a Play by Juliusz Słowacki* (Newcastle upon Tyne: Cambridge Scholars Publishing, 2009). Contains translations of *Balladyna*, *Agamemnon's Tomb* and *Beniowski*.

Krasiński, Zygmunt, *The Undivine Comedy*, tr. Charles Kraszewski (Lehman, Pa.: Libella Veritatis, 1999).

Mickiewicz, Adam, *Pan Tadeusz*, tr. George Rapall Noyes (London and Toronto: J. M. Dent, 1917). Project Gutenberg e-book.

Mickiewicz, Adam, *Pan Tadeusz*, tr. Kenneth R. Mackenzie (New York: Hippocrene Books, 1998).

Mickiewicz, Adam, *Dziady (Forefathers' Eve): Dresden Text*, tr. Charles S. Kraszewski (Lehman, Pa.: LibellaVeritatis, 2000).

Mikoś, Michael J., *Polish Romantic Literature: An Anthology* (Bloomington, Ind.: Slavica, 2002).

Norwid, Cyprian Kamil, *Poems, Letters, Drawings*, ed. and tr. Jerzy Peterkiewicz (poems in collaboration with Christine Brooke-Rose and Burns Singer) (Manchester: Carcanet, 2000).

Norwid, Cyprian Kamil, *Selected Poems*, tr. Adam Czerniawski (London: Anvil Press, 2004).

Norwid, Cyprian Kamil, *Poems*, tr. Danuta Borchardt (New York: Archipelago Books, 2011).

Segel, Harold B. (ed. and tr.), *Polish Romantic Drama* (Ithaca, NY: Cornell University Press, 1977). Contains translations of Mickiewicz's *Forefathers' Eve, Part III*, Krasiński's *The Un-Divine Comedy*, and Słowacki's *Fantazy*.

Secondary Sources

Bachórz, Józef, and Kowalczykowa, Alina (eds), *Słownik literatury polskiej XIX wieku*, 3rd edn (Wrocław: Ossolineum, 2001).

Barańczak, Stanisław, 'Romanticism', *The New Princeton Encyclopedia of Poetry and Poetics*, 3rd edn, ed. Alex Preminger and T. V. F. Brogan (Princeton: Princeton University Press, 1993).

Czerniawski, Adam, 'Polish Poetry', in Peter France (ed.), *The Oxford Guide to Literature in English Translation* (Oxford: Oxford University Press, 2000).

Eile, Stanisław, *Literature and Nationalism in Partitioned Poland, 1795–1918* (Houndmills: Palgrave Macmillan, 2000).

Koropeckyj, Roman, *Adam Mickiewicz: The Life of a Romantic* (Ithaca, NY, and London: Cornell University Press, 2008).

Krzyżanowski, Julian, *Polish Romantic Literature* (London: George Allen & Unwin, 1930).

Miłosz, Czesław, *The History of Polish Literature*, 2nd edn (Berkeley, LA, and London: University of California Press, 1983).

Modrzewska, Mirosława, 'Polish Romanticism', in Stephen Prickett and Simon Haines (eds), *European Romanticism: A Reader* (London: Continuum, 2010).

Ostrowski, Constance J. *Polish Literature in English Translation: A Bibliography of (Guide to) Works in Online, Print, Audio and Video Forms*. Last updated spring 2014. <http://polishlit.org>.

Siwicka, Dorota, *Romantyzm 1822–1863* (Warsaw: Wydawnictwo Naukowe PWN, 2002).

Witkowska, Alina, and Przybylski, Ryszard, *Romantyzm*, 6th edn (Warsaw: Wydawnictwo Naukowe PWN, 2000).

Scandinavian

CHAPTER 30

SCANDINAVIAN ROMANTICISM

KLAUS MÜLLER-WILLE

Origin Myths of Scandinavian Romanticism

According to more traditional accounts in literary history, the exact date in which Romanticism first reaches Scandinavia is precisely determinable. In 1802, the geologist and philosopher of nature, Henrik Steffens, returns to Copenhagen after spending seven years studying and researching in Jena. Back in Denmark, he holds a controversial and widely noted series of lectures that familiarize the Danish audience with the ideas of German Romanticism.[1]

Steffens can be regarded as a model prototype of a border-crosser and cultural mediator between Germany and Scandinavia. In Jena, he was in close contact with the group surrounding the brothers Schlegel, Novalis, and Tieck. The most profound impression, however, was left by his encounter with Schelling, whose first series of lectures on the philosophy of nature (*Naturphilosophie*) were attended by Steffens in 1898. In his own lectures, which he publishes in 1803 under the title *Indledning til philosophiske Forelæsninger* (Introduction to Philosophical Lectures), Steffens consolidates Schelling's new, organic way of thinking with scientific evidence from mineralogy, botany, and physics.[2] The discourse is characterized by audacious analogies between scientific observations and metaphysical reflexions that support Steffens's fundamental thesis of

[1] Fritz Paul, *Henrich Steffens: Naturphilosophie und Universalromantik* (Munich: Fink, 1973); Benedikt Jager and Heming Gujord (eds), *Henrik—Henrich—Heinrich: Interkulturelle perspektiver på Steffens og Wergeland* (Stavanger: Stavanger University Press, 2010).

[2] For more on the close connection between natural sciences and nature philosophy in Danish Romanticism, see Mogens Bencard (ed.), *Krydsfelt: Ånd og natur i guldalderen* (Copenhagen: Gyldendal, 2000).

a nature regulated by spiritual forces. The polemic criticism Steffens voices in the lecture is aimed at the mechanistic reasoning of the Enlightenment, which deconstructs the living unity of nature into its functional elements, thus reducing it to a dead object of an instrumental rationalism

The literary impact ascribed to the lectures is at least equally as relevant as its philosophical content, as the young poet Adam Oehlenschläger was a member of the audience. According to an anecdote in his autobiography, the creation of the first programmatic poem of Scandinavian Romanticism was inspired by a sixteen-hour-long discussion with Steffens. The anecdote of the poem's origin alone shows how Oehlenschläger contributes to the self-referential staging and mythical aggrandizement of the epochal break into Romanticism. The poem in question, which he will publish in 1803 under the title *Guldhornene* (The Golden Horns) in the collection *Digte af Adam Øhlenslæger* (Poems of Adam Oehlenschläger), revolves around epochal events as well.[3] The poet connects the story of the discovery and loss of the famous Golden Horns of Gallehus with the narrative of the vanished Golden Age. In particular, the melting of the Horns, which were stolen from an art chamber in Copenhagen in 1802, is interpreted by Oehlenschläger as a crisis symptomatic of a modern prosaic age. Against the merely economic thinking of his contemporaries he sets the mythical and poetic sentiment that the Golden Horns symbolize.

The Swedish Romantics construct similar strategies of self-mythologization in their establishment of a 'new school' some ten years later in 1810.[4] The centre of these movements is the circle of students from Uppsala around Per Daniel Amadeus Atterbom, Vilhelm Fredrik Palmblad, and Lorenzo Hammarsköld. The members of the so-called Aurora association, in reference to their German role models from Jena, make themselves a name as contributors to collectively published journals, the publication *Phosphoros* (1810–13) being considered the Swedish equivalent to the Schlegel brothers' *Athenaeum* (1798–1800). The Greek god of the Morning Star, Phosphoros, together with his female counterpart, Aurora, is invoked for a literary movement that is first and foremost directed against different representatives of the Swedish Academy. This means that their criticism, in opposition to the corresponding developments in Germany and Denmark, is less directed towards the literary Enlightenment that establishes itself in the context of a bourgeois public sphere, but rather towards an institution of an enlightened court that still adheres to the standards of French classicism.

Taking into account the conditions in Norway, the differences in the development of Scandinavian literatures become even more distinct. Even though Norway gains greater governmental independence in 1814 following the separation from Denmark and the

[3] On the corresponding construction of Danish Romanticism as a 'Golden Age of Danish literature', that is mainly based on the monograph *Guldhornene: Et Bidrag til den danske Romantiks Historie*, published in 1896 by Vilhelm Andersen, see Johan Fjord Jensen, *Efter guldalderkonstruktionens sammenbrud 1–3* (Arhus: Modtryk, 1981); Asbjörn Aarseth, *Romantikken som konstruksjon: Tradisjonskritiske studier i nordisk litteraturhistorie* (Bergen: Universitetsforlaget, 1985).

[4] Louise Vinge, *Morgonrodnadens stridsmän: Epokbildningen som motiv i svensk romantik 1807–1821* (Lund: Gleerup, 1978).

personal union with Sweden, its literary life still remains dependent on Copenhagen for a long time. The strong ties to the cultural scene in Denmark lead to a fairly early reception of Romantic philosophy in Norway, which finds an influential representative in the philosopher Niels Treschow. No literary manifestation of explicit Romanticism, however, is recorded before the works of Henrik Wergeland, who introduces his epic poem *Skabelsen, Mennesket og Messias* (Creation, Man, and Messiah, 1830) with dedicatory poems to Steffens and Treschow. Still it is not possible to talk about a clear formation of a Romantic movement in Norway that could be compared to activities of literary groups in Sweden or in Denmark. The literary debates in Norway are rather characterized by discussions about the possibility and the status of a national literature. The arguments used by the opponents in this public feud can neither be comprehended with the dichotomy between Enlightenment and Romanticism nor with the one between Romanticism and Realism.

Similarly, Finno-Swedish Romanticism, which constitutes itself in the context of the Royal Academy in Åbo, is more concerned with the question of national differentiation than the demand for a clear epochal break. The same is true for Icelandic Romanticism, which still is influenced by the cultural scene in Copenhagen.[5] Steffens's ideas, mediated by Bjarni Thorarensen, had already reached Iceland in the 1810s. However the actual beginning of Icelandic Romanticism is ascribed to the establishment of the Copenhagen journal *Fjölnir* (1835–47). The journal, combining entirely different forms of discourse with articles on politics, economics, science, and poetry, constitutes a new type of decidedly Icelandic public society. It is only through this forum that one of the most important representatives of Icelandic Romanticism, Jónas Hallgrímsson, will be able to raise Icelandic literature to European standards. Apart from writing his own poetry, he publishes translations of current European literature (Heinrich Heine, among others) and establishes an independent Icelandic literary criticism in the journal.

Already this introductory overview of the self-perception of new literary movements in the different countries has revealed the distinct differences in the development of Scandinavian literatures of the early nineteenth century. Although these remarkable disparities make it difficult to speak of a 'Nordic Romanticism', several similarities are still distinguishable.[6] Surely, the most conspicuous link between the national schools is the shared Viking heritage that Romantic authors of all Scandinavian countries refer to in order to form distinctly national literary strategies.[7] Oehlenschläger,

[5] Svein Yngvi Egilsson, *Arfur og umbylting. Rannsókn á íslenskri rómantík* (Reykjavik: Hið Íslenska Bókmenntafélag, 1999).

[6] Comparative studies on Nordic Romanticism can be found in Oskar Bandle et al. (eds), *Nordische Romantik* (Basel: Helbing & Lichtenhahn, 1991); Gunilla Hermansson and Mads Nyggaard Folkmann (eds), *Ett möte: Svensk och dansk litterär romantik i ny dialog* (Göteborg: Makadam, 2008); Annegret Heitmann and Hanne Roswall Laursen (eds), *Romantik im Norden* (Würzburg: Königshausen & Neumann, 2010). Since 2012, studies in Scandinavian Romanticism have been collected under the lead of the Nordic Association for Romantic Studies <http://www.romantikstudier.dk> that publishes the journal *Romantik: Journal for the Study of Romanticism*.

[7] For a representative view, with extensive secondary literature, see Lars Lönnroth, *Skaldemjödet i berget: Essayer om fornisländsk ordkonst och dess återvändning i nutiden* (Stockholm: Atlantis, 1996).

in particular, takes a leading role in reviving medieval Scandinavian literature with his early collections of poems *Nordiske Digte* (Norse Poems, 1807). The poems included in this collection—for instance, the humorous epic poem *Thors Reise til Jotunheim* (Thor's Journey to Jotunheim) as well as the mythological tragedy *Baldur hin Gode* (Baldur the Good)—are subsequently supplemented by a multitude of dramas, stories, and epic poems in which Oehlenschläger reworks material from medieval Old Icelandic literature. His romance cycles, in which he plays with different forms of poetic metre from the Middle Ages and a local folk tradition, have a strong effect on further literary development in Scandinavia. Examples of these romances are the collection of mythological portraits in *Nordens Guder* (The Gods of the North, 1819) as well as the three-part cycle *Helge* (1814), which is later supplemented with *Hroars saga* (1817) and the heroic epic *Hrolf Krake* (1828).

Apart from Oehlenschläger the revival of Old Norse tradition can also be illustrated by the works of Nikolai Severin Grundtvig. In addition to his translations of the *Gesta Danorum* by Saxo Grammaticus and the *Heimskringla* by Snorri Sturluson, he also publishes two noteworthy portrayals of Norse mythology (1808 and 1832), in which he develops a syncretistic reconciliation of the Edda (a collection of Old Norse poems that contains stories of Norse gods and heroes), Christian thoughts, and idealistic philosophy.[8] Grundtvig's syncretistic version of Norse mythology attained great distinction because of his famous activities as a church reformer and founder of the Danish folk high school movement.

In their recollection of Norse mythology, both Oehlenschläger and Grundtvig could refer to Herder's programmatic article *Iduna, oder der Apfel der Verjüngung* (Iduna, or the Apple of Rejuvenation, 1796), in which he explicitly supports an artistic revival of the—in his eyes—'Germanic' mythology. The effect of this article on the constitution of Scandinavian national literatures could likewise be demonstrated with an ample amount of Swedish material pertaining to the subject. The interest in material and motifs from Old Norse literature is especially kindled by a Stockholm association called Götiska förbundet (Gothic League) and its medium of publication, the journal *Iduna* (1811–24). Erik Gustaf Geijer, the publisher of *Iduna*, contributes to its renown with numerous articles and poems. With his famous poems *Odalbonden* (The Yeoman Farmer, 1811) and *Vikingen* (The Viking, 1811) he creates two well-known stereotypes of Nordic masculinity.

Esaias Tegnér follows the lead of Oehlenschläger's *Helge* both formally and content-wise with the Romantic cycle *Frithiof saga* (1825). In contrast to his Danish role model, Tegnér is clearly more concerned about a classicist transformation of the Old

[8] Flemming Lundgreen-Nielsen: 'Grundtvigs Norse Mythological Imagery: An Experiment that Failed', in Andrew Warren (ed.), *Northern Antiquity: The Post-Medieval Reception of Edda and Saga* (Enfield Lock, Middlesex: Hisarlik Press, 1994), 41–68; Sune Auken, *Sagas spejl: Mytologi, historie og kristendom hos N. F. S. Grundtvig* (Copenhagen: Gyldendal, 2004).

Norse material. He even lets the hero travel to Greece and ponder the art of antique temple architecture. Perhaps it is Tegnér's pretentions that lead the *Frithiof saga* to become one of the most internationally successful works of Scandinavian Romanticism, with numerous translations being published all over Europe, especially in England and Germany.

Even though the representation of Old Norse subjects is sometimes connected with a revival of medieval metre, the Mannerist-like stylistic features of Old Norse literature—such as, for instance, the complex metaphorical language of Skaldic poetry—are significantally omitted. However, it is these exact stylistic forms that the most significant representative of Icelandic Romanticism, Jónas Halgrímsson, picks up on.[9] Overall, the formally complex poems by Jónas form a pleasant contrast to other folksy approaches in Scandinavian literature. In his translation of Heine's poems, for example, he deliberately uses Eddic metre, kennings (a special type of Old Icelandic metaphor), and other formal characteristics of the medieval Icelandic literature for literary experiments.

The rediscovery of the Old Norse heritage is, in all countries, accompanied by collections of Scandinavian folksongs, ballads, and fairytales. The interest in folk literature can also be ascribed to the substantial influence of the Brothers Grimm, who regularly corresponded with their Scandinavian colleagues around this time. International attention is especially directed towards Peter Christian Asbjørnsen's and Jørgen Moe's *Norske Folkeeventyr* (Norwegian Folk Tales, 1841–4), which Henrik Ibsen refers to in his *Peer Gynt* (1867).

For many years, in national as well as international literary history, the special nature of Nordic Romanticism was defined by these folkloristic moments, which are naturally closely intertwined with the invention of the modern Nordic nations before and after the Napoleonic Wars.

However, based on a selection of a few chosen genres and authors, it will be argued in the following that Scandinavian Romantics did indeed attempt to enter a critical theoretical dialogue with European Romanticism by the means of aesthetic experiments.[10] Precisely because there is a delay in Scandinavian Romanticism's reactions to European developments, authors tend to vary, modify, or criticize positions or writing techniques of European Romanticism.

[9] Dick Ringler, *Bard of Iceland: Jónas Hallgrímsson, Poet and Scientist* (Madison, Wis.: University of Wisconsin Press, 2002).

[10] On the aesthetic-philosophic potential of Scandinavian Romanticism, see Horace Engdahl, *Den romantiska texten: En essä i nio avsnitt* (Stockholm: Bonniers, 1986); Ulla-Britta Lagerroth and Margareta Ramsay (eds), *Romantiken över gränser* (Lund: Gyllenstiernska Krapperupsstiftelsen, 1993); Karin Sanders, *Konturer: Skulptur- och dødsbilleder fra guldalderlitteraturen* (Copenhagen: Museum Tusculanum, 1997); Lis Møller and Marie Louise Svane (eds), *Romanticism in Theory* (Aarhus: Aarhus Universitetsforlag, 2001); Special issue 'Slöja och spegel—Romantikens former', *Aiolos*, 14–15 (2000).

Philosophical Poetry and Art-as-Religion (Staffeldt, Stagnelius, Wergeland)

The Dane Adolph Wilhelm Schack von Staffeldt, the Swede Erik Johan Stagnelius, and the Norwegian Jonas Wergeland are three Scandinavian authors who react to the religious exaltation of art and the corresponding visionary poetry in European Romanticism. In their poetic visions, nature or the history of mankind is staged as a legible text in order to express the divine as well as the authorial mind hiding behind this inspired semiotic system. However, as repeatedly addressed by the poets themselves, a religious or poetic initiation is necessary in order to perceive and portray nature or history as such an animated sphere of symbols. All three authors thus present the poet as a confident mirror-image of God, who in fact only succeeds in revealing the hidden meaning of nature through his own artistic creations. Coincidentally, all three authors also call attention to the paradoxes and aporias inherent in such a presumptuous claim to a religious poetry.

Staffeldt, who was born on Rügen and died in Schleswig-Gottorp, was far more acquainted with the philosophic and aesthetic discussions of German Idealism than his Danish contemporaries.[11] Most of his poems in the second section of his *Digte* (1804) are devoted to the question of the poetic. In the course of this, Staffeldt consistently places the role of the author on a thin line between narcissistic fantasies of omnipotence and complete despair. On the one hand, the poet is explicitly staged as the founder of a new, pantheistic religion, who achieves a representation of the absolute in his art production. Even the motif of a violently sublime nature that he cultivates in his poems does nothing to contain the omnipotence of this artist, but rather enhances it. The poet at least succeeds in reversing the intimidating experience of the sublime by rendering it aesthetically enjoyable. Conversely, Staffeldt repeatedly shatters this optimistic view of art in his poems. By drawing attention to their own artificiality with an excessive amount of allegory and mythical personifications, they expose the relativity and unreliability of the developed artistic pantheism. Evidently, Staffeldt is very well aware of the fact that the experience of an animated and talking nature ultimately relies on fragile rhetoric figures.

The Swedish poet, Johan Erik Stagnelius, also tries to entangle poetry with religion. As such, his main work *Liljor i Saron* (Lilies in Sharon, 1821), which was published in three booklets and contains poems as well as a drama with the significant title *Martyrerna* (The Martyrs), can be read as proof of an incisive religious conversion. Stagnelius himself elaborates on the theosophical background of his poetry-as-religion

[11] Henrik Blicher, 'Denne Harpe er din Brud', in Ulrik Lehrmann and Lise Præstgaard Andersen (eds), *Læsninger i Dansk Litteratur*, i (Odense: Odense Universitetsforlag, 1998), 279–93.

in an introduction to his collection, which draws on a gnostic tradition reaching from Böhme to Swedenborg and back to a form of Neoplatonism coined by Schelling. In *Liljor i Saron*, Stagnelius interlocks this theosophical tradition with a concept of heavenly love and eroticism, which itself is overshadowed by a death wish. From a psychoanalytic perspective, the poems circle around a libidinously charged death drive—a desire for eternity enhanced into a specific form of knowledge.[12]

A good example for this libidinous concept of religion can be found in the longest piece of the collection, *Kärleken* (Love), which Stagnelius himself calls a 'metaphysical didactic poem'.[13] The piece results in the apotheosis of a heavenly lover with the telling name Amanda. Amanda's function, which is nothing other than an abstract allegory of platonic love, stands in stark contrast to the sensually erotic descriptions of the poetic persona directed towards the beloved's physicality. The signs' ambiguity is a considerable part of the structure of the piece. The antagonism between the pictorial and literal levels of the description leads to unresolvable contradictions and paradoxes within the language.[14] Yet it is this specific form of speech that cannot receive closure, which sustains the infinite desire, in which the speaker really seems to be interested. For a long time, the interpretations of Stagnelius's poetry focused on the religious and philosophical background of his writings. Sometimes these readings obscured from view his keen semiotic interests. Like Novalis's *Lehrlinge zu Sais* (1802, Disciples at Sais), Stagnelius seems to be interested in a language of things. He attributes the legibility of writing and nature to a fundamental poetic ability which he celebrates as the highest of all human intellectual organs. Indeed, he seems to be in favour of letting fantasy roam freely. His poems, for example *Kärleken* (Love), often move across a completely imaginary or metaphoric space that is detached from any kind of reality whatsoever.

Wergeland provides a further example of the formally advanced experiments in Scandinavian poetry of the Romantic Age.[15] His hymn to liberty, set at the centre of his first poetry anthology *Digte, Første Ring* (Poems, First Cycle, 1829), manifests itself on a formal level in a progressive amalgamation of different genres. While the entire collection is marked by a preference for a free form of the ode, he repeatedly breaks the structure through combinations with traditional, rhyming verse forms. The astonishing play with free or incoherent forms should not obscure the fact that Wergeland based his boundary-breaking writing style on many Romantic predecessors and even some late representatives of the sentimental Enlightenment. Content-wise, however, he follows genuine Romantic models. Stagnelius's Amanda finds a Norwegian pendant in Wergeland's Stella. In most of the poems in *Digte, Første Ring* the poet mentions this divine beloved, who appears as a personified form of the world spirit and alternately

[12] Roland Lysell, *Erik Johan Stagnelius: Det absoluta begäret och själens historia* (Stockholm: Symposion, 1993).

[13] Horace Engdahl, *Stagnelius Kärleken* (Nora: Nya Doxa, 1996).

[14] Mads Nyggaard Folkmann, *The Transfigurative Mode of Romantic Discourse: Poetic Models in Novalis, Keats, and Stagnelius* (Aarhus: Dansk Selskab for Romantikstudier, 2007).

[15] Yngve Sandhei Jacobsen (ed.), *Bevegelser i skrift: Bidrag til lesningen av Henrik Wergeland* (Oslo: Cappelen Akademisk Forlag, 2000).

stands for the erotic, aesthetic, religious (pantheistic), or political ideal of the poetic persona. In contrast to Wergeland's early, supposedly progressive work, the potential of his later, tamer work only reveals itself upon a second glance. This is true for the intimate love poetry of the *Poesier* (Poems, 1838) just as much as for *Jan van Huysums Blomsterstykke* (Jan van Huysum's Flower Piece, 1840). The text, which is composed of a series of ekphrases on a painting by Jan van Huysum, deals solely with the poetic process of translating images to text and text to images.[16] It is quite symptomatic of the distanced tendency of the text that it is not the story of a brilliant artist that is being told, but rather one of an delirious father who recognizes the faces of his deceased children in van Huysum's flower arrangement. Lastly, Wergeland achieves the breakthrough to poetic modernism—even before Aloysius Bertrand and Charles Baudelaire—in his collection of four prose poems, which he publishes in 1841 under the ironic title *Sujetter for Versemagere* (Subjects for Rhymesters).[17]

Popular and Academic Metatheatre (Oehlenschläger, Heiberg, Atterbom)

While the lyrical experiments described in the previous section were still committed to the idea of a religious function of literature, this section is mainly concerned with those dramas that use Romantic irony to deal with both art in general and specific aspects of drama and theatre. The fundamental thesis is that the self-referential metatheatre in Shakespeare's and Tieck's work had a particular impact on Scandinavian Romanticism.

Possibly the first literary evidence for the concept of this metadramatic literature in Scandinavia is one of Oehlenschläger's dramas. His *Sanct Hansaften Spil* (A Midsummer Night's Play, 1803) is published in the same collection of poems *Digte* as *Goldhornene*. The particularly loose framework of the series of images is set in an evening at the Copenhagen *Dyrehave* (a predecessor of the Tivoli-fair). The descriptions and comments present, among other things, citizens strolling through the park, performances by travelling artists and puppet masters, a parrot composing poetry, and the series of images from a zograscope. A crucial aspect is the intertextual connection to Shakespeare's *Midsummer Night's Dream*, which is explicitly announced in a second prologue. Shakespeare's double-staging of a play within a play becomes the model for the entire structure of the comedy. By setting a double framework for the play with two contradictory prologues, the audience is prepared for the firework of ideas with which the author will override the three classical unities and the representational

[16] Frode Helland: *Voldens blomster? Henrik Wergelands Blomsterstykke i estetikkhistorisk lys* (Oslo: Universitetsforlaget, 2003); Joachim Schiedermair *(V)erklärte Gesichter: Der Porträtdiskurs in der Literatur des dänisch-norwegischen Idealismus* (Würzburg: Königshausen & Neumann, 2009).

[17] Heinrich Detering, 'Sujetter for Versemagere. Henrik Wergeland og det moderne prosadigt', in Jager and Gujord, *Henrik—Henrich—Heinrich*, 106–24.

function of theatre. Constant breaking of illusion and self-critical comments by the characters—most notably, by a subversive harlequin—exposes the sentimental tradition of Enlightenment and its lachrymosity. Yet the characters also ridicule the Romantic worshipping of pagan Norse monuments as well as the quality and aesthetic of the performed ironic comedy itself. Ludwig Tieck's comedy *Der gestiefelte Kater* (*Puss in Boots*, 1797) was doubtlessly the model for this distinctively self-destructive streak in drama. Remarkably, Oehlenschläger succeeds in combining the self-reflexive approach of the piece with elements of a folk tradition that is simultaneously subverted and supported through the play.

The dramatic poem *Aladdin*, which Oehlenschläger publishes in 1805 in the second volume of the collected works *Poetiske Skrifter*, also deals theoretically with the phenomenon of popular culture and literature. In contrast to *Sanct Hansaften Spil*, the metapoetic significance of *Aladdin* is only revealed at second glance. At first glance, the reader is struck by the almost bizarre simplicity of the character and plot structure of the play. Oehlenschläger never conceals the fact that he is staging a fairytale. The contemplative and ambitious scholar Noureddin and the self-sufficient child of nature Aladdin are two antagonists who are clearly set against each other. They can be described as pure personifications of the two principles of knowledge and fortune. According to this allegorical interpretation the genie in the bottle they fight over can be decoded as an allegory of imagination. Thereby the metapoetic intention of the drama can be unveiled as follows. The grown child Aladdin represents the fanciful genius. It is not knowledge, but natural imagination and fortunate talent that lead to the success of artistic projects. Oranges fall into Aladdin's turban and he is rewarded with a kingdom and a princess despite—or because of—his naïveté and passiveness. It is mainly Hans Christian Andersen who will revert to the corresponding portrayal of the childishly naïve natural genius in his numerous autobiographies, in which he stages himself as the true successor of Aladdin. With his play Oehlenschläger also constitutes a tremendously influential, specifically Danish variety of orientalism, which is more focused on a synthesis of Danish and oriental identities than on a dissociation from the Orient.[18]

Johan Ludvig Heiberg, who will dominate the Copenhagen theatre scene from the 1830s onwards as a dramaturge, theatre critic, and author of numerous dramas, was critically inclined towards Oehlenschläger's cult of naïve artistic production, although he still holds on to Oehlenschläger's fundamental idea of enhancing popular drama.[19] He debuts with a continuation of *Sanct Hansaften Spil*, which he publishes in 1817 under the title *Julespøg og Nytaarsløier* (Christmas Fun and New Year's Jesting). In the piece, he carries the anti-mimetic principle of a Romantic comedy to extremes, amongst other things through reverting to the baroque stylistic device of the allegory. Some of the figures in action apart from the personification of 'Fantasy' are, for example, the 'muse

[18] Elisabeth Oxfeldt, *Nordic Orientalism: Paris and the Cosmopolitan Imagination 1800–1900* (Copenhagen: Museum Tusculanum Press, 2005).

[19] Jon Stewart (ed.), *Johan Ludvig Heiberg: Philosopher, Littérateur, Dramaturge, and Political Thinker* (Copenhagen: Museum Tusculanum, 2008).

Thalia', the 'Purpose', and both 'the Old and the New Year'. Next to these, figures from Holberg's comedies, contemporary Danish dramas, many biblical characters, and several items (a boot, a flute, a book, and so on) appear on stage. The breaking of illusion is perfected in such a way that simply reading the piece causes vertigo. It is not only the theatre scene—presented with actors as well as a feigned audience—that is doubled on stage, but also the technique of breaking illusion itself. A fictional fire on the staged stage causes the entrance of a brigade of firefighters, who in turn get involved in the play within the play and entangled in a dispute with the 'real firefighters' and the 'real audience' about whose auditorium is actually intended and what is truly real.

More important than these early comedies, though, are the entertaining vaudevilles—light operas or musical comedies—that Heiberg publishes from the late 1820s onwards.[20] In these pieces, which are inspired by Eugène Scribe, the self-referential principle of the Romantic comedy is increasingly abandoned in favour of a humorous depiction of bourgeois everyday life. Following a peculiar Hegelian argumentation Heiberg even tries to define the vaudeville as the most valuable genre, in his theoretical treatise *Om Vaudevillen som dramatisk Digtart* (On the Vaudeville as a Theatrical Genre, 1826). Furthermore he tries to appropriate the vaudeville for a national aesthetic. Due to these circumstances, the concept of a national dramatic art in Denmark is, curiously, mainly connected to the Parisian genre 'vaudeville'. Up to the present day, the image of Christian IV is shaped by Heiberg's vaudeville *Elverhøi* (Elves' Hill, 1828), in which the sovereign is staged as a down-to-earth fairytale king.

The Danish tradition of Romantic comedies and musical plays, which is closely connected to a progressive form of popular culture, finds no suitable equivalent in Swedish Romanticism. Here, the concept of metadramatic art is realized in seemingly academic dramas, which circle around highly abstract questions of art theory. This holds especially true for Per Daniel Amadeus Atterbom's extensive play based on fairytales, *Lycksalighetens ö* (The Isle of Bliss, 1824), which can doubtlessly be counted amongst the most important texts of Scandinavian Romanticism.[21] In the play, Atterbom attempts to stage the history or tragedy of poetry. He describes the admittance of King Astolf into the fabled realm of poetry, where he falls for the sensual erotic allure of its ruler, Felicia. The piece ends with an ethical, or rather political, appeal. Facing the decay of his own homeland that has been devastated by a bourgeois debating society of liberal republicans, Astolf sees himself forced to return to the material world and restitute the kingdom in his native land. His attempt to find his way back to Felicia fails. The plot alone emphasizes the allegoric character of this fairytale play. Considering the numerous comments, with which the already allegorically depicted characters allude to their abstract significance, it would even be possible to speak of an emblematic structure of

[20] Jon Stewart (ed.), *Between Vaudeville, Romantic Comedy and National Drama: The Heibergs and the Theater* (Copenhagen: Museum Tusculanum, 2012).

[21] Otto Fischer, *Tecknets tragedi: Symbol och allegori i Atterboms sagospel Lycksalighetens ö* (Uppsala: Acta Universitatis Upsaliensis, 1998); Gunilla Hermansson, *Lyksalighedens øer: Møder mellem poesi, religion og erotik i dansk og svensk romantik* (Göteborg: Makadam, 2010).

the play. This structure is particularly remarkable for its obvious contradiction of the high regard for the animated symbol, which Atterbom advocates in his aesthetic writings of the time. Resorting to allegory and emblem, however, should not be seen as resorting to a baroque set of forms. The allegories themselves are thematized in the play as a historical manifestation of the decline of poetry. They are also problematized by the way they function within the play. This ironic self-reference initiates a complex discussion of different rhetorical figures and tropes. It is not the content of these rhetorical tropes that stands at the centre of the play, but rather the self-conscious use of their specific functional principles. The manner in which a subject from a fairytale is used for the formulation of a philosophic discussion of art is reminiscent of Tieck's analogous endeavour in *Phantasus* (1812–16) or the fairytale of Klingsohr, which Novalis incorporates in *Heinrich von Ofterdingen* (1802).

Similarly complex metadramas are written by Erik Johan Stagnelius and Carl Jonas Almqvist. In their dramas they mainly seek to answer the question of the special conditions and possibilities of a Christian tragedy that emancipates from the classical art of drama.[22]

Universal Poetry, Artist's Novel and Arabesque (Andersen, Almqvist)

Just as it does in other European countries, the epoch of Romanticism leads to a radical new appreciation for the genre of the novel. Friedrich Schlegel's poetological reflections on universal poetry and the arabesque, which he develops, among others, in *Gespräche über die Poesie* (Dialogue on Poetry, 1800), stand as an example for this new esteem of the genre.

On of the first Scandinavian attempts to put the theoretical concept of the arabesque novel into practice is provided by Hans Christian Andersen in his literary debut *Fodreise fra Holmens Canal til Østpynten af Amager i Aarene 1828 og 1829* (A Walk from Holmen's Canal to the East Point of the Island of Amager in the Years 1828 and 1829).[23] The use of *Fodreise* in the title is a first hint at the ironic undertone of the text, which plays with conventions of the travel novel. The subject of the novel, the footpath from Holmen's Canal to the east point of Amager, is by no means a long journey, but rather a short walkway in the centre of Copenhagen that can be covered in fifteen minutes. The text is a loose series of fantastical incidents that happen to the narrator during his walk. He meets all sorts of supernatural creatures, allegories, and personifications: Among others, there

[22] Paula Henrikson, *Dramatikern Stagnelius* (Stockholm: Symposion, 2004); Anders Burman, Roland Lysell, and Jon Viklund (eds), *Dramatikern Almqvist* (Hedemora: Gidlund, 2010).

[23] Jacob Bøggild, *Svævende stasis: Arabesk og allegori i H. C. Andersens eventyr og historier* (Hellerup: Spring, 2012).

are mentions of poetry-writing cats, sleepwalkers, the Eternal Jew, Petrus, a doppelgänger of the narrator, and Death. All these grotesque figures only possess one passion. They are interested in nothing else but literature in general and the *Fodreise* in particular. The book is full of allusions to other books, ranging from vicious satire of contemporary Danish literature to the ambitious citation of classical references. Andersen uses these intertextual references not only to call attention to the violations of the norm and inconsistencies in his own book, but also in order to critically separate himself from his exemplars in German Romanticism—E. T. A. Hoffmann in particular.

This critical distance from German Classicism and Romanticism also characterizes Andersen's first great novel *Improvisatoren* (The Improvisatore, 1835). The hero and narrator of this novel, the sensitive orphan Antonio, finds his way into the highest levels of society due to his clear voice and natural talent for improvised recitation of poetry. In the course of the novel, however, he is constantly revisited by his antisocial past. The novel itself is characterized by strange tensions and fractures, since Andersen follows entirely contradictory traditions of bandits' and artists' novels in choosing his plots. Typical scenes in the first genre, such as those from the lives of Roman beggars and bandits, are set next to pretentious reports of a typical bourgoise esteem of Italian literature and art. Due to the remarkably early thematizations of improvisation techniques, the novel has been invoked as a predecessor of a Scandinavian jazz aesthetic. It seems indeed that the aesthetic excursion with which the first-person narrator distinguishes between the performative qualities of a perpetually changing improvisation and the rigidity of a classical work aesthetic has an impact on the formal dimension of the book as well. By intentionally referencing narrative forms and themes from popular culture, the book goes beyond the formal scope of comparable German artists' novels. The story of the hero's development and romances is merely a vague foil for a loose series of images that simply mirror the bourgeois view of Italy. Even though the author could in fact call upon his own experiences from an extended educational visit to Italy, his depictions show more accurately what had been written about Italy since Goethe than an authentic perception of the country. In playing with bourgeois discourses on Italy, which are blended together with grotesque and erotic elements of the Italy-image in popular culture, the novel offers a fascinatingly collage of citation, in which the author Andersen completely retreats behind the improvising performer Andersen.

It is astonishing that Andersen had already developed an alternative concept with the character of the improvising artist before he questioned the concept of genius in his following novel, *Kun en Spillemand* (Only a Fiddler, 1837). Research long considered *Kun en Spillemand*, like *Improvisatoren* had been before, as an autobiography of Andersen in disguise. It is all the more remarkable that Andersen does not depict a successful story in his novel, but rather the process of artistic failure. None other than Søren Kierkegaard critically dealt with the book in his first publication *Af en endnu Levendes Papirer* (From the Papers of One Still Living, 1838). His negative review shows hat he had a keen intuition for the critical tendencies of the novel. Kierkegaard realizes that Andersen does not attempt to describe a single case. More than that, he realizes that Andersen questions the tame aesthetic doctrine of his time that is geared towards receonciliation and harmony.

A completely different implementation of the Schlegelian novel aesthetic can be found in Sweden. Carl Jonas Love Almqvist's *Fria fantasier hvilka, betraktade såsom ett helt, af Herr Hugo Löwenstjerna stundom kallades Törnrosens bok, stundom En irrande Hind* (Free fantasies, which, seen as a whole, were sometimes called The Book of the Thorn-Rose, sometimes An Errant Hind by Mister Hugo Löwenstjerna, 1832–51) presents a unique European attempt to transpose Schlegel's concept of universal poetry to a single text.[24] Its volume alone is an illustration of this approach. The text, which became known under the title *Törnrosens bok* (Book of the Thorn-Rose) is published in two different editions of either fourteen volumes in the format duodecimo or three massive volumes in an imperial-octave format. Furthermore, a substantial amount of handwritten material which builds on the narrative framework has been passed down. In fiction, all of the texts are described as transcripts from a castle society which originally constitutes itself as an ordinary story-telling circle. The loose narrative framework allows Almqvist to integrate almost his entire production within *Törnrosens bok*. Apart from numerous literary genres from older and newer European as well as oriental literatures, the collection also features essays on religion and art theory, musical notes, and song lyrics. The story-telling circle is later augmented with an academy, which leads to an increase in pseudo-scientific essays in the compilation. The unpublished material of the Thorn-Rose-fiction, from which the manuscript *Svenska Rim* (Swedish Rhymes) stands out due to its size (1400 folio pages), presents only transcripts of academic conversations.

The crucial aspect is that the concept of the collection is presented through the texts included within it. In the framing novels *Jagtslottet* (The Hunting Château, 1832), *Hinden* (The Hind, 1833), and *Baron Julius K** (1835), the members of the story-telling circle not only come up with the idea of a universal artwork but also discuss technical and economic questions concerning the printing and publishing of the *Törnrosens bok*. The notion of a holistic Gesamtkunstwerk is presented as an eccentric idea of a naïve art lover and thereby subverted with Romantic irony. Almqvist thus does not focus on a homogeneous, organic union of different genres, types of art, and discourses, but rather on the tension that arises from merging heterogeneous material.

Almqvist provides two important aesthetic essays on the phenomenon of Romantic irony. *Äfven om Humor, och Stil deri* (Also about Humor, and the Style Therein, 1833) and *Dialog om sättet att sluta sycken* (Dialogue on the Manner of Ending Pieces, 1835) are considered early documents of an open poetology that orientates itself towards the reader. Particularly the novel *Drottningens juvelsmycke* (The Queen's Jewel, 1834) shows Almqvist lives up to his theoretical positions. The innovative character of the text, which is included as the third volume in *Törnrosens bok*, is already made clear in the mixture of different literary and artistic genres and discourses. Dramatic scenes are set next to letters and sections of prose, into which songs, musical notes, as well as historical and juridical documents are incorporated. The plot centres on events from the recent

24 For a representative view, see Klaus Müller-Wille, *Schrift, Schreiben und Wissen: Zu einer Theorie des Archivs in Texten von C. J. L. Almqvist* (Tübingen: Francke, 2005); Gunilla Hermansson, *At fortælle verden: En studie i C. J. L. Almqvists "Törnrosens bok'* (Hellerup: Spring, 2006).

Swedish past, in particular the death of Gustav III, who is murdered in costume at an opera ball. This event representatively stands for the theatricality of an aristocratic culture, in which the difference between theatrical performance and reality, illusion and real life, has been dissolved. The outwardness of the aristocratic court culture is not only criticized in the novel. It s also made productive in the theatrical narration that plays with costumes, illusions, and mistaken identities, which subvert the bourgeois idea of nativeness and subjective identity. This is particularly true for the central character of the novel, who is introduced with an entire series of names—among others, as Azouras, donna Zouras, don Azouras, Lazuli, Tintomara, Tint'om'-Hara, and la Tourneros. Tintomara remains in every way an ambiguous, incomprehensible figure. As a seductive masculine-feminine creature that is equally at home in the artificial world of the stage and in wild nature, she evades the desire of both the female and male protagonists who try to define her into a single identity.

Peculiar Fairytales (Andersen)

The fairytales of Hans Christian Andersen are, without a doubt, the most important contribution of Scandinavian literature to European Romanticism.[25] The texts he publishes in *Eventyr, fortalte for Børn* (Fairytales Told for Children, 1835–42) and his other series—among others *Nye Eventyr* (New Fairytales, 1844–8), *Historier* (Stories, 1852–3), and *Nye Eventyr og Historier* (New Fairytales and Stories, 1858–72)—constitute an entirely new type of fairytale that is neither comparable to traditional folk tales nor the literary fairytales of German Romanticism.

First of all Andersen's fairytales and stories are characterized by a very specific form of language. The discourse, which often follows the rules of an idiosyncratic syntax, is frequently interwoven with moments of direct address and exclamations, and thus conveys the impression of an oral narrative style that almost seems to gain a poetic quality through rhythm, rhyme, and alliterations. This oral style, however, is consciously broken with Mannerist tendencies, such as odd rhetoric or eye-catching punctuation. The dissonant style of the fairytales also has an effect on textual structures at higher levels. Sentimental depictions clash with coarse vernacular, pathos with irony, abstract allegories with sensual descriptions. Furthermore, Andersen uses several entirely different literary traditions in *Eventyr*—folktales, myths, legends, contemporary novels, essays, etc., which are merged in a surprisingly heterogeneous combination.

For a long time, Andersen's experimental style of writing was interpreted as a reference to the wild speech and thinking of the child, whose imagination allegedly also

[25] Fundamental on the literary quality of Andersen's fairytales, see Johan de Mylius, *Forvandlingens pris: H. C. Andersen og hans eventyr* (Copenhagen: Høst & Søn, 2005); Per Krogh Hansen and Marianne Wolff Lundholt (eds), *When We Get to the End ... Towards a Narratology of the Fairy Tales of Hans Christian Andersen* (Odense: University Press of Southern Denmark, 2005).

shapes the subjects of the texts. Due to this interpretation it is not by chance that the fairytales take place in the context of the bourgeois interior. Apart from coffee pots, pins, piggy banks, or tin soldiers, the main protagonists are tame pets, gentle birds, and plants. This fixation on the world of the bourgeois living room may lead to the assumption that the writer was not capable of breaking out of a childish worldview where toys and pets are still animated. Considering the allegory of love in *Sneedronningen* (The Snow Queen, 1845) or the depiction of a storybook career in *Den grimme Ælling* (The Ugly Duckling, 1844), one would tend to agree with this assessment. Following in this vein, the sentimental story of *Den lille Pige med Svovelstikkerne* (The Little Match Girl, 1846) could be interpreted as an allegorical illustration of the art of fairytales. Instead of revolting against social injustice, the narrator takes pleasure from the fairytale-like illusions of the heroine, which even assist her in sweetening her own death.

However, faced with the drastic endings of many of his fairytales, there is no question of Andersen having a conciliatory or harmonizing vision of life. Karen, the little heroine of *De røde Skoe* (The Red Shoes, 1845), as an example, is severely punished for taking pleasure in dancing and pretty shoes. A stern angel condemns her to an eternal dance, and she is only able to escape from it by finding mercy from a headsman, who unceremoniously cuts off her feet. The passion with which Andersen executes such violent scenarios can hardly be harmonized with the image of a gentle friend of children. Many of the *Eventyr* are characterized by a destructive desire by which Andersen first of all attacks the sentimental tendencies of the depoliticized and petit-bourgeois Biedermeier period (roughly 1815–48). The texts are thus not only directed at children, but also address grown-up readers in a type of double coded speech.

The fairytales in no way disguise the existing political circumstances, but rather take a fairly aggressive stance against them—such as in the story of the little soldier in *Fyrtøiet* (The Tinderbox, 1835), which ends with a regicide. Likewise, in what might be the most well-known fairytale of Andersen, *Keiserens nye Klæder* (The Emperor's New Clothes, 1837), recent research has prized highly its abstract theoretical considerations about the complex connection between corporeality, politics, and aesthetics. By addressing sexuality and homosexuality fairly obviously in *Den lille Havfrue* (The Little Mermaid, 1837) or *Dynd-Kongens Datter* (The Marsh King's Daughter, 1858), Andersen exposes further taboo subjects of the Biedermeier.

It is not only these intentional violations of norms that make Andersen a modern author. Several of his fairytales, such as *Det nye Aarhundredes Musa* (The New Century's Goddess, 1861) can be interpreted as poetological conceptions in which the author attempts to transcend a Romantic point of view. He deals very consciously with the far-reaching transformations of modernization and attempts to draw the corresponding aesthetic conclusions.[26] In this sense it is not surprising that Andersen provides the

[26] On the modern potential of Andersen's fairytales, see Elisabeth Oxfeldt (ed.), *H. C. Andersen: Eventyr, kunst og modernitet* (Bergen: Fagbokforlaget, 2006); Klaus Müller-Wille (ed.), *Hans Christian Andersen und die Heterogenität der Moderne* (Tübingen: Francke, 2009); Heinrich Detering, *Hans Christian Andersen* (Berlin: Deutscher Kunstverlag, 2011).

first urban narrative of Scandinavian literature. The fairytale *Dryaden* (The Dryade, 1868) offers a detailed depiction of the world fair, street life, and the system of canals in contemporary Paris. In *Et Stykke Perlesnor* (A String of Pearls, 1859), which is dedicated to the modern theme of travelling by rail, he aesthetically realizes the experience of speed and accelerated perception. Similarly, the short piece *Vanddraaben* (The Drop of Water, 1848) develops a poetic contemplation of microscopic observations. Andersen also discovers new media: the fairytale on doppelgängers, *Skyggen* (1847, The Shadow), has been interpreted as an early response to the spectral medium of photography.

However, some of the fairytales appear to be so absurd that they even push the boundaries of modernity. This holds true, for instance, in *Klods-Hans* (Blockhead Hans, 1855), who wins his princess through the shared consumption of a dead crow and cow faeces. Like other fairytales, this piece revolves around a radical form of sovereignty that holds no respect for the established borders between man and animal.

Literary Philosophy—Philosophic Literature (Søren Kierkegaard)

Søren Kierkegaard's dissertation *Om Begrebet Ironi* (On the Concept of Irony, 1841) provides late evidence of how closely authors followed the poetological debate of European Romanticism in Scandinavia. Even though his criticism of the alleged egocentricity of the Schlegelian concept of irony is based on a misconception, Kierkegaard's ethically motivated criticism of the indecisiveness of a Romantic/ironical stance remains highly relevant.

Kierkegaard's criticism obviously clashes with the usage of irony that characterizes several of his own works.[27] Indeed, the complex play with different narrative frameworks that distinguishes his first great 'novel', *Enten-Eller* (Either/Or, 1843), bears witness to the extent to which the philosopher Kierkegaard adopts the sophisticated literary stragedies of his time. The book is introduced by a fictional publisher, a motif, that Kierkegaard borrowed directly from contemporary German and Danish fiction. The text material is presented as a mysterious manuscript discovered by the fictitious publisher of the book, Victor Eremita. According to this fiction, the texts recorded in the first part of the book, which are designated as A's papers, can neither be chronologically ordered nor attributed to an identifiable author. The loose arrangement of this first text section allows Eremita to unite completely different genres. A's papers thus contain numerous aphorisms und fragments, two aesthetic essays, literary criticism, and

27 On Kierkegaard's intensive examination of literature from German and Danish Romanticism, see the contributions in Jon Stewart (ed.), *Kierkegaard and his Danish Contemporaries*, iii. *Literature, Drama and Aesthetics* (Farnham: Ashgate, 2009); Jon Stewart (ed.), *Kierkegaard and his German Contemporaries*, iii. *Literature and Aesthetics* (Aldershot: Ashgate 2008).

the novel *Førførerens Dagbog* (The Seducer's Diary). The subdued and distant protagonist of this story gives account of a carefully calculated seduction. This character has been called a modern version of Don Juan yet, with his cool manner and his intellectual capacity, he reminds rather of the Vicomte de Valmont, the amoral protagonist of Choderlos de Laclos's *Liaisons dangereuses* (1782).

In contrast to A's papers, B's papers, which are contained in the second part of the book, appear more unified. The ingenious and eccentric style of the first part is replaced by a measured and generally more comprehensible rhetoric and the argument follows a golden thread for the most part. The more disciplined form of the documents is mirrored in the content. Whereas A's loose papers revolve around an aesthetic of the moment and of eroticism, B, who is called Assessor Wilhelm in the fiction, deals with timeless ethical questions. His documents are introduced in the fiction as letters to A, in which he attempts to convince A of the validity of a morally responsible way of life. The cornerstone of his concept is the institution of marriage, which is contrasted with the ironic model of a self-indulgent seduction.

In many respects, *Stadier paa Livets Vei* (Stages on Life's Way, 1845) can be considered as a sequel to *Enten-Eller* (Either/Or).[28] Kierkegaard advances both the dialectical alternative between the standpoints of the aesthetic and the ethical, and the literary technique of *Enten-Eller*. This book is published under a pseudonym as well. This time, a bookbinder functions as publisher, one who simply assembles heterogeneous text material. The principle of the fictitious publisher is further developed in *Stadier*. Altogether, three further publishers assume responsibility for the individual parts of the book. In the first part, *In Vino Veritas*, in which an account of a banquet or symposion is given, publishers and protagonists from Kierkegaard's earlier books appear on the scene. In five speeches, which are devoted to the woman and to love, they develop the theoretical approach of the aesthetic.

At the heart of their speeches lies the principle of a distance-creating reflection, which finds expression in an ascetic-nihilistic contempt for the world or in self-indulgent aestheticism. In the second part, the Assessor Wilhelm features again and counters the five speeches to develop his ethical vision of life. The third part of the text presents a religious, Christian alternative that transcends the viewpoints of aesthetics and ethics—or that unites them on a higher level. In analogy to *Førførerens Dagbog* this part contains a diary of a melancholic young man who gives an account of his dissolved engagement. The faith to which the young man feels bound finds him ethically guilty. Although he is aware of the moral implications of his promise of marriage, he breaks it, in order to do justice not to societal but rather to religious values. His faith, however, offers no new moral security; rather, it causes him to feel the gravity of his ethical breach even more intensely. In this manner, religiousness itself brings about an insoluble ethical conflict. The publisher of this third section, Frater Taciturnus, uses the fictitious document as a

[28] For a representative view, see Robert L. Perkins (ed.), *Stages of Life's Way*, International Kierkegaard Commentary, 11 (Macon, Ga.: Mercer University Press, 2000).

starting point for a theoretical outline in which he emphasizes the profoundly paradoxical form of the religious concept under debate.

The text *Frygt og Baeven* (Fear and Trembling, 1843), which Kierkegaard himself classified as 'dialectical poetry', develops this specific conception of religion with the aid of a biblical example.[29] Abraham, who in his frenzied faith is prepared to defy all natural and societal laws and to sacrifice his son to God, is prevented from carrying out this act by God himself. God thus divests Abraham even of the moral security of having acted correctly in following his faith. Once again, faith leads to a sense of twofold guilt which, paradoxically, serves to strengthen faith.

In his late meta-commentaries *Om min Forfatter-Virksomhed* (In my Work as an Author, 1851) and *Synspunktet for min Forfatter-Virksomhed* (The Point of View for my Work as an Author, 1859) Kierkegaard goes into the reasons why he published his first books anonymously and why he patterned them on literary models. In so doing, he primarily employs rhetorical arguments. The aesthetic mode of production is quite simply intended to awaken the readers' interest. This interest is the necessary prerequisite if the readers are to gradually convert from an aesthetic to a religious understanding of their existence. Kierkegaard's meta-commentaries were long taken literally and his work was reduced to the outlined theory of the three stages of human existence. Yet in and of themselves, the two texts *Om min Forfatter-Virksomhed* und *Synspunktet for min Forfatter-Virksomhed* are subverted by irony and self-contradiction. The superiority of the positions taken by ethics and religion is formulated in an ambiguous argument, that is characterized by aesthetic qualities. Only by means of this ambiguity does philosophy maintain the openness that Kierkegaard demands in opposition to the closed form of a systematic Hegelian thinking. Overall, as a distinctly literary philosopher, Kierkegaard becomes a leading impetus for literary modernism in Europe.[30]

Everyday Realisms (Gyllembourg, Bremer)

While the advent of Scandinavian Romanticism, as previously outlined, has been relatively unanimously associated with the year 1802, there is little accord amongst researchers about the demise of Romanticism and the dawn of poetic Realism.[31] Usually, this ending is associated with the emergence of more realistic forms of representation and a more pronounced political agenda in literature, which in turn is associated with the developments of the late 1830s or even 1840s.

[29] For a representative view, see Robert L. Perkins (ed.), *Fear and Trembling, and Repetition*, International Kierkegaard Commentary, 6 (Macon, Ga.: Mercer University Press, 1993).

[30] Leonardo F. Lisi, *Marginal Modernity: The Aesthetics of Dependency from Kierkegaard to Joyce* (New York: Fordham University Press, 2013).

[31] See Kurt Aspelin, *Poesi og verklighet* (Stockholm: Aklademiforlaget 1967).

In Swedish literary historiography, the end of Romanticism is frequently associated with the publication of the novel *Det går an* (It Can Be Done!, 1839) by Carl Jonas Almqvist. The central scene in this text is a lengthy response by the heroine, in which she argues against marriage and in favour of the concept of a marriage-like partnership based on love. The intense public reactions to the novel are probably due to the fact that the heroine, in her critique of marriage, even seems to be arguing against the model of a marriage based on love. Her comments reveal the paradox that a marriage truly based on love cannot occur with the demand that it last forever. Her arguments against marriage, on the other hand, are of a purely pragmatic nature. As an economically aware business woman, she does not want to subject her business dealings to the imponderabilities of love. The most probable explanation for the massive criticism by the author's contemporaries is precisely this pragmatism being vocalized by a woman. Her factual arguments about matters of the heart hint at a role reversal in the language game of 'love', one which does away with the forms of imagined femininity more than the vague intimations of extramarital intercourse between the protagonists do.

With his prosaic depiction of problems of everyday familial life Almqvist follows a long line of female authors of the 1820s and 1830s.[32] One such writer is Thomasine Gyllemborg-Ehrensvärd, who gained attention in Danish literary history as author of the novel *En Hverdagshistorie* (*An Everyday Story*, 1828). As she did with many of her texts Gyllemborg published this story anonymously in the magazine *Kjøbenhavns flyvende Post*. Owing to its title the story is regarded as the first depiction of an everyday reality that supplants the philosophical speculative literature of early Romanticism. However, what is being told is anything but an everyday story: Similarly to Goethe's *Wahlverwandtschaften* (Elective Affinities, 1809), the plot revolves around a four-way relationship, in the course of which the protagonist and first-person narrator experiences an ethical crisis. At the centre of the narrative lies his relationship with the stepsister of his fiancée, who for her part has been abandoned by her own fiancé. The outrage over this man's irresponsible behaviour does not deter the protagonist from mirroring and repeating the former's betrayal. The reconciliatory conclusion of the novel does little to diminish its abysms: in a double wedding, each of the two betrayed fiancées is matched with the adulterers who betrayed them. Overall, the text seems to follow a precisely calculated experimental concept which, in a type of psychological experiment, thoroughly examines the contingency and temporality of love. Other texts by Gyllemborg are more notable for their theoretically calculated conceptualizations than for their supposed realism. For instance, in the programmatic narrative *To Tidsaldre* (Two Ages, 1845), she literarily depicts the elusive phenomenon of the Zeitgeist. No less a figure than Søren Kierkegaard devotes a comprehensive review to this narrative, which he publishes as a book in its own right, *En litterær Anmeldelse* (A Literary Review, 1846).

At the same time as Gyllembourg, the Swedish author Frederika Bremer established a genre depicting everyday realism with her *Teckningar utur hvardagslifvet* (Sketches

[32] Lise Busk-Jensen, *Romantikkens forfatterinder*, 1–3 (Copenhagen: Gyldendal, 2009).

from Everyday Life, 1828), which she continued to pursue in numerous sequels such as *Familjen H**** (The H— Family, 1830–1), *Grannarne* (The Neighbours, 1837), and *Hemmet* (The Home, 1839). The at times sentimental view of the troubles of family life enjoyed great popularity in Sweden as well as in English- and German-speaking areas and played a decisive role in the establishment of a middle-class aesthetic for novels. It was only in her last novel, *Hertha, eller en själs historia* (Hertha, or the Story of a Soul, 1856) that Bremer formulated explicit criticism of the patriarchal family structure. At this time she was, however, able to look back on a whole series of realistic novels which, by setting their focus on the explicit treatment of socio-politically relevant themes, in part already prefigured fundamental developments in the Scandinavian literature of the Modern Breakthrough (Georg Brandes, Henrik Ibsen, August Strindberg).

Further Reading

Bandle, Oskar, et al. (eds), *Nordische Romantik: Akten der XVII. Studienkonferenz der IASS. 7.–12. August 1988 in Zürich u. Basel* (Basel: Helbing & Lichtenhahn, 1991).

Detering, Heinrich, *Hans Christian Andersen* (Berlin: Deutscher Kunstverlag, 2011).

Egilsson, Svein Yngvi, *Arfur og umbylting: Rannsókn á íslenskri rómantík* (Reykjavík: Hið Íslenska Bókmenntafélag, 1999).

Engdahl, Horace, *Den romantiska texten: En essä i nio avsnitt* (Stockholm: Bonniers, 1986).

Heitmann, Annegret, and Laursen, Hanne Roswall (eds), *Romantik im Norden* (Würzburg: Königshausen & Neumann, 2010).

Hermansson, Gunilla, *Lyksalighedens øer: Møder mellem poesi, religion og erotik i dansk og svensk romantik* (Göteborg: Makadam, 2010).

Hermansson, Gunilla, and Folkmann, Mads Nyggaard (eds), *Ett möte: Svensk och dansk litterär romantik i ny dialog* (Göteborg: Makadam, 2008).

Jager, Benedikt, and Gujord, Hemin (eds), *Henrik—Henrich—Heinrich: Interkulturelle perspektiver på Steffens og Wergeland* (Stavanger: Stavanger Universiy Press, 2010).

Lagerroth, Ulla-Britta, and Ramsay, Margareta (eds), *Romantiken över gränser* (Lund: Gyllenstiernska Krapperupsstiftelsen, 1993).

Lisi, Leonardo F., *Marginal Modernity: The Aesthetics of Dependency from Kierkegaard to Joyce* (New York: Fordham University Press, 2013).

Møller, Lis, and Svane, Marie Louise (eds), *Romanticism in Theory* (Aarhus: Aarhus Universitetsforlag, 2001).

Sanders, Karin, *Konturer: Skulptur- och dødsbilleder fra guldalderlitteraturen* (Copenhagen: Museum Tusculanum, 1997).

Schiedermair, Joachim *(V)erklärte Gesichter: der Porträtdiskurs in der Literatur des dänisch-norwegischen Idealismus* (Würzburg: Königshausen & Neumann, 2009).

Stewart, Jon (ed.), *Kierkegaard and his German Contemporaries*, iii. *Literature and Aesthetics* (Aldershot: Ashgate 2008).

Stewart, Jon (ed.), *Kierkegaard and his Danish Contemporaries*, iii. *Literature, Drama and Aesthetics* (Farnham: Ashgate, 2009).

Greek

CHAPTER 31

THE ROMANTIC CONSTRUCTION OF GREECE

RODERICK BEATON

GREECE, as it exists today, is itself the product of European Romanticism. Out of a decade of bloody, messy warfare was born in 1830 the first newly established nation state in Europe, a blueprint that would become near-universal only after the successful 'unifications' of Germany and Italy, three decades later. So the story of the Romantic movement in Greece is inseparable from the political story of one of the movement's more enduring offshoots, the ideology of nationalism and the nation state.

In Greece, perhaps more than anywhere else, Romanticism appears in its revolutionary guise, a forward-looking thrust to configure the world differently and to forge new institutions and ways of doing things. We are at some distance, here, from the contemplative 'emotion recollected in tranquillity' that generations of students have learned to associate with the English 'Lake poets'. Though many Romantic writers and thinkers were (or became) politically conservative, Romanticism itself is not a conservative movement. The story of Greece shows how a rosy idealism, fashioned in Germany during the second half of the eighteenth century, became yoked to the urgency of survival in the life-or-death struggles of Greeks against their Ottoman overlords. But what makes that story perhaps unique among national struggles is the participation of idealists—Romantics, in the broadest sense—from all over Europe and as far away as the United States of America, in realizing that struggle. For all the chaotic diversity of their backgrounds and aims, and the constant mistrust and misunderstanding between the volunteers and the Greeks they came to help, these revolutionaries risked and often gave their lives in order to make an ideal come true.

Nowhere more than in Greece is it the case that Romanticism was 'the strongest expression and symptom' of a wider, epoch-changing 'revolution'. Or, as a study of the legacy of Romanticism into the twenty-first century has put it, 'The Romantics were thinkers who felt compelled to translate their thoughts into actions. And the actions often took the form of armed conflict.'[1] A constant subtext throughout this chapter will

[1] Isaiah Berlin, *The Roots of Romanticism* (Princeton: Princeton University Press, 1999), pp. xiii,

be the shift from thought to action, or in Lord Byron's words, from 'words' to 'things'. The story of how Greece became a self-governing nation, and its long aftermath, exemplifies this aspect of the Romantic movement to the full. Romanticism *in* Greece, and Romantic thought and action directed *towards* Greece, are almost always as much political as aesthetic.

Greece in the European Imagination (1760–1821)

It started in Germany—or rather, with a German art-collector visiting Rome and Naples. Johann Joachim Winckelmann (1717–68) never got as far as Greece. It was on the basis of his studies of the ancient sculpture available to him in Italian collections, and his knowledge of the literature and history of ancient Greece, that Winckelmann in 1764 produced his *History of the Art of Antiquity*. It was to prove a founding text, at once of German Romanticism and of what has often been termed 'Romantic Hellenism'—that is to say, the elevation of the classical Greek past to the status of an ideal state of mankind.

Winckelmann's joyous astonishment at the artistic and moral superiority that he attributed to the ancient Greeks already allies the aesthetic firmly with the political. 'With regard to the constitution and government of Greece', he writes, 'freedom was the chief reason for their art's superiority. Freedom always had its seat in Greece, even beside the thrones of the kings, who ruled paternally before the enlightenment of reason allowed the people to taste the sweetness of full freedom.'[2] In the same chapter he writes, anachronistically but prophetically, of Greece as a 'nation'. But for Winckelmann, as for most of his German successors until the outbreak of the Greek Revolution in 1821, the condition of aesthetic and political perfection that he ascribes to Greece belongs resolutely to the past—even if a flagrantly unhistorical one. Winckelmann had no thought that political action in his own day might bring back the transcendent glories he ascribed to the Greeks of ancient times.

Among poets, later in the century, Friedrich Hölderlin (1770–1843) seems to have been ambivalent, if not even resistant to the idea. For the Germans, according to Constanze Güthenke, 'modern Greece' was an inherently unrealizable project from the start, because 'Greece' for them stood for an ideal condition of mankind, incompatible with the modern world.[3] It must have mattered, too, that none of the German pioneers of Romanticism in general, or even of Romantic Hellenism in particular, before the 1820s ever set foot in Greece.

1; George Fletcher, *Romantics at War: Glory and Guilt in the Age of Terrorism* (Princeton: Princeton University Press, 2002), 16.

[2] Johann Joachim Winckelmann, *History of the Art of Antiquity*, tr. H. F. Mallgrave (Los Angeles: Getty, 2006), 187.

[3] Constanze Güthenke, *Placing Modern Greece* (Oxford: Oxford University Press, 2008), 71–92.

Of all the poets who addressed the topic of Greece, whether ancient or modern, by far the most influential was Lord Byron. It is not just that unlike the Germans, and unlike his friend and fellow-poet Percy Bysshe Shelley, who comes into this story a little later, Byron actually visited the Greek lands that he wrote about. By the second decade of the nineteenth century, Ottoman-ruled Greece was no longer quite as remote or as exotic as it had been before. A steady stream of European travellers made similar itineraries to Byron; most either published an account of their discoveries or brought them home with them, in the form of looted artworks. (This was the process that brought the Aegina marbles to Munich, the Venus de Milo to the Louvre, and, most controversially, the 'Elgin Marbles' to London.)

Byron's contribution was different. It is not true, as is often said, that he was the first, still less the only, traveller to turn attention to the *modern* inhabitants of the ancient lands and their contemporary plight. Others did so too. But only Byron was able to turn his experiences and opinions into a bestseller. When the first two cantos of *Childe Harold's Pilgrimage* were published on 10 March 1812, the book sold out within hours and had to be reprinted. It was the day when Byron 'awoke to find himself famous'. And the consequence was that Greece, too, became famous overnight. It was the extraordinary literary and commercial success of *Childe Harold*, and of the 'oriental tales' that succeeded it over the following four years, that brought the current condition of Greece and Greeks sharply into the consciousness of readers right across the European continent.

And what had this quintessentially (if also problematically) Romantic poet to say on the subject of Greece? A version of Romantic Hellenism is certainly present in canto II of *Childe Harold*, in which Byron's lightly fictionalized alter ego visits Greece. This is most evident in some of the poem's most often quoted lines:

> and yet how lovely in thine age of woe,
> land of lost gods and godlike men! art thou! ...
> yet are thy skies as blue, thy crags as wild ...
> where'er we tread, 'tis haunted, holy ground ...[4]

But Byron from the start had a political turn of mind (just before *Childe Harold* was published he had made his maiden speech in the House of Lords). He noticed the political predicament of the *modern* Greeks in a way that poets and thinkers who idealized Greece from afar would never have thought of doing. In the poem itself, he imagines the possibility of the Greeks regaining their freedom, but only in guarded terms. In a series of prose 'Notes', jotted down while was living in Athens during the first months of 1811, and published along with the poem, Byron rejected the idea altogether:

> The Greeks will never be independent; they will never be sovereigns as heretofore, and God forbid they ever should! ... To talk, as the Greeks themselves do, of their

[4] *Childe Harold's Pilgrimage*, II. 801–2, 819, 828.

> rising again to their pristine superiority, would be ridiculous; as the rest of the world must resume its barbarism, after re-asserting the sovereignty of Greece.[5]

In the early works of Byron, an idealizing of the ancient past, that has already become conventional, sits uncomfortably with a politically grounded scepticism about the future. The convergence between Romantic Hellenism and the political realities of the 'age of revolutions' had begun.

Byron himself never called unambiguously, in print, on the modern Greeks to rise against their Ottoman masters. One of his most famous poems, the inserted lyric 'The Isles of Greece' in the third canto of his comic epic *Don Juan* (written in 1819), has often been read in this way. But in their context the lines are shot through with ambiguity. Beyond nostalgia for a lost world that was better than the present one, and of which tantalizing traces still survive in the modern climate and landscape, Byron's supposedly patriotic lyric inserted into *Don Juan* gives no clear hint to future action.[6]

It would be left to his friend and fellow-Romantic, the poet Percy Bysshe Shelley, to make good the omission, with his verse drama *Hellas*, written towards the end of 1821 and published in England early the following year. But by that time, the political context would have changed utterly. Against all expectation, by the time Shelley took up his pen to address the subject of *Hellas*, revolution had broken out in Greece. The freedom of Greece was no longer a matter of abstract musing that could be safely consigned to an ahistorical, exemplary past. Romantic Hellenism had come face to face with a political reality in the making.

Before taking this story further, we have first to turn back some decades, to see how Greeks themselves had begun to imagine a political future for themselves. Who *were* those Greeks who talked 'of their rising again to their pristine superiority'? What *were* their aspirations that Byron, in Athens in 1811, found ridiculous?

Greece in the Greek Imagination (1790–1821)

Ordinary Greeks in the late eighteenth and early nineteenth centuries identified themselves not in terms of a yet-to-be-imagined political entity but as adherents of the Orthodox religion which they shared with speakers of other languages. Back in 1453, the capital city of Orthodoxy, Constantinople, had ceased to be also the capital of a Christian empire (known today as 'Byzantine') and become instead the chief city of Islam and the capital of the Ottoman Turks. Among the Christian faithful, millenarian

[5] *Childe Harold's Pilgrimage*, II, 'Notes'.

[6] *Don Juan*, III. 689–784, on which, see Peter Cochran, *Byron's Romantic Politics* (Newcastle upon Tyne: Cambridge Scholars, 2011), 266–72; Beaton, *Byron's War*, 56–9.

prophecies circulated. The reinstatement of the Church of the Holy Wisdom (Hagia Sophia in Greek), the great cathedral of Orthodoxy that had been built under the emperor Justianian in the sixth century, and for the last four hundred years had been turned into a mosque, was an article of faith for them. Songs and legends circulated. Subsequently overinterpreted, what these actually show in their earliest surviving forms is a deep-seated belief in the ultimate vindication of a *religious* identity, that no passing historical or political contingency will ever extinguish.[7] In its way, this millenarian Orthodoxy was as ahistorical as the Romantic Hellenism of the West.

But this was not the whole story. From the middle of the eighteenth century, Greek-speaking educated elites had begun to assimilate, translate, and comment on the ideas emerging from the Enlightenment in the West.[8] It was thanks to the new ideas that these Greek elites first began seriously to think of themselves as the direct heirs to an ancient civilization far older than that of the Orthodox Church to which they belonged. And if Europeans thought that civilization far superior to anything in the world of their own today, then surely its descendants must be marked out in some special way too? In this way, the idea of a revival of ancient Hellas was born.

These elites flourished outside the territory that would later become the heartland of the Greek state: in Constantinople and at the semi-independent courts of Wallachia and Moldavia (where the proxy rule of the Ottoman Empire was exercised through wealthy Greek families from Constantinople); in the Ionian Islands to the west of Greece, where centuries of rule by Venice had established a Western-style aristocracy whose sons were educated in Italy; and further afield in the ports and cities of Europe, where the rise of an enterprising Greek commercial class had led to permanent communities being established (known ever since as the Greek 'diaspora'). These cities included Venice, Pisa, and Livorno in Italy, Vienna and Trieste in the Austrian Empire, Odessa in Russia, and most recently Paris and Amsterdam.

As early as 1791, in Bucharest, the linguistic reformer and educator, Dimitrios Katartzis (*c.*1730–1807), was proposing to his fellow-speakers of modern Greek that they should try to prove themselves the worthy descendants of the ancient Hellenes—and seems at the same time to have been the first systematically to use the Greek term *ethnos* in the sense of a modern nation, following Rousseau's definition of the 'civic' nation in *The Social Contract*. Tellingly, while conceding 'that we are not a nation (*ethnos*) such as to form our own state, but are subject to another more powerful', Katartzis takes comfort from the relative autonomy granted to the Orthodox Christian community by their Ottoman masters: 'Therefore we do represent a nation (*ethnos*) to the extent that we are

[7] Roderick Beaton, *Folk Poetry of Modern Greece* (Cambridge: Cambridge University Press, 1980), 95–100; Michael Herzfeld, *Ours Once More: Folklore, Ideology and the Making of Modern Greece* (New York: Pella, 1986; 1st edn 1982); Marios Hatzopoulos, 'From Resurrection to Insurrection', in Roderick Beaton and David Ricks (eds), *The Making of Modern Greece* (Farnham: Ashgate, 2009), 81–93.

[8] See Paschalis M. Kitromilides, *Enlightenment and Revolution: The Making of Modern Greece* (Cambridge, Mass.: Harvard University Press, 2013); Peter Mackridge, *Language and National Identity in Greece, 1766–1976* (Oxford: Oxford University Press, 2009), 80–101. For a selection of translated texts, see Richard Clogg (ed.), *The Movement for Greek Independence 1770–1821* (London: Macmillan, 1976).

bound by our ecclestiastical authorities with the highest level of administration [taking place] among ourselves ...'[9]

Katartzis was not a Romantic, and his ideas were propagated in manuscript, not in print, so it is hard to tell how much direct influence they had. During the same decade Rigas Velestinlis (1757–98), originally from Thessaly but educated at Constantinople, was also active at the Greek court of Bucharest, translating contemporary French *nouvelles* into Greek and helping to lay the foundations of modern Greek fiction. Rigas is principally remembered today for his revolutionary blueprint of a constitution for a 'Hellenic Republic', freed from Ottoman control and modelled on the French revolutionary constitution of 1793. Rigas published his ideas in Vienna in 1797.[10] Arrested by the Austrian authorities and handed over to the Turks, he was put to death shortly afterwards.

Rigas was no more a Romantic than Katartzis, and no nationalist either. It was in the years following Rigas's death that the idea began to take root of the nation as an organic community, defined by geography, language, and inherited traditions. This way of thinking about the nation originates in the writings in German of J. G. Herder. Exactly how these ideas percolated through to Adamantios Korais (1748–1833) in Paris during the first years of the new century is hard to establish. Korais was a child of the merchant diaspora, but had left commerce behind when he settled permanently in the French capital in 1788, just before the Revolution. There he would remain for the rest of a long life. Like Katartzis, Korais was deeply committed to education as the means to social and political progress, and for him, too, education for the modern Greeks meant principally learning to understand the achievements of their putative ancestors, the ancient Hellenes.[11]

In 1803, Korais addressed a paper in French to the newly formed Society for the Observers of Man, in which he set out the case for the modern Greeks to be recognized as a nation in the modern sense.[12] Korais was frank in recognizing that his countrymen had a mountain to climb. Education was to be the way forward. And he knew, too, that it would take time. By his reckoning, it would not be until 1851 that the Greeks would be ready to assume the burdens of national emancipation—a full thirty years after the initiative would in fact be seized in the Greek Revolution.

Three years after Korais's lecture had been delivered in Paris, an anonymous author writing in Greek, probably in Pisa or Livorno, fleshed out the idea of the self-governing nation. The title *Hellenic Nomarchy* (1806) is a play on words: *nomarchia* transposes two of the letters of *monarchia*. The new coinage means 'rule of law' and the writer, presumably belonging to the same merchant diaspora as Korais, calls for the absolutism of the

[9] Tr. from Dimitrios Katartzis, *Τα ευρισκόμενα*, ed. K. Th. Dimaras (Athens: privately publ., 1970), 44.

[10] Rigas Velestinlis, *New Political Constitution*, extracts in Clogg, *Movement*, 157–63.

[11] See Paschalis M. Kitromilides (ed.), *Adamantios Korais and the European Enlightenment* (Oxford: Voltaire Foundation, 2010).

[12] 'Report on the Present State of Civilization in Greece', tr. in E. Kedourie (ed.), *Nationalism in Asia and Africa* (London: Weidenfeld & Nicolson, 1971), 153–88.

Ottoman Sultan to be swept away and replaced by a consensual form of government, inspired by Rousseau and *The Social Contract* and the republican constitution of the United States, and probably also by some of the ideas of Herder.[13]

With *Hellenic Nomarchy*, with the lecture in French, and anonymous pamphlets and patriotic poems in Greek by Korais, and with the growth and spread of rousing doggerel of the kind that Byron and his friend Hobhouse heard and transcribed on their travels in Greek lands, Romanticism first made its impact among Greeks.

Romantic Poetics, National Revolution (1821–1830)

When the first news of the outbreak of the Greek Revolution reached Livorno and Pisa, on 1 April 1821, Greece in the minds of many of those who greeted it with enthusiasm was still primarily an *idea*. The purpose of the revolution was to realize that idea, to make actual something that until then had existed only in the imagination. The leaders of the local Greek community in Pisa were influential members of the educated cosmopolitan elite who had previously tasted power and exercised patronage in the semi-autonomous province of Wallachia, before being forced into exile by their Ottoman overlords. For the enlightened Orthodox Bishop Ignatios (1765–1828) and for Alexandros Mavrokordatos (1791–1865), the best educated of the future leaders of the revolution in Greece, the project was a hard-headed political one. For the poet Shelley, and his wife Mary, who had become friends with Mavrokordatos in Pisa, the political project was simultaneously cause for wild enthusiasm, and profoundly suspect. Enthusiasm: because here precisely was a vindication of the radical liberalism to which Shelley had been committed ever since his student days. But Shelley had lately been reading Winckelmann. For years, Shelley had been studying the ancient Greek poets and philosophers. He read German fluently and was deeply imbued with the ideas of Romantic Hellenism. For Shelley, scarcely less than for Hölderlin, the actuality of a modern revival of ancient Hellas was a contradiction in terms.

Shelley worked out this dilemma in one of the first poems of substance to be addressed to the subject of the Greek Revolution, and still the most complex. *Hellas* is in form a 'lyrical drama', a reworking of the oldest extant example of Greek tragedy, Aeschylus's *Persians* of 472 BCE, updated and reinterpreted for the present times. The ambiguities of *Hellas* have been much discussed.[14] But in the prose preface that Shelley added before

[13] Translated extracts in Clogg, *Movement*, 106–17. See also Paschalis M. Kitromilides, 'From Republican Patriotism to National Sentiment: A Reading of *Hellenic Nomarchy*', *European Journal of Political Theory*, 5/1 (Jan. 2006), 50–60.

[14] Jennifer Wallace, *Shelley and Greece: Rethinking Romantic Hellenism* (Basingstoke: Palgrave, 1997), 178–207; Roderick Beaton, 'Re-imagining Greek Antiquity in 1821: Shelley's *Hellas* in its Literary and Political Context', in D. Tziovas (ed.), *Re-imagining the Past: Antiquity and Modern Greek Culture* (Oxford: Oxford University Press, 2013), 47–58.

sending the poem for publication in England, at the beginning of November 1821, he is not ambiguous:

> The apathy of the rulers of the civilized world to the astonishing circumstance of *that nation to which they owe their civilization rising* as it were from the ashes of their ruin is something perfectly inexplicable ... We are all Greeks—our laws, our literature, our religion, our arts have their root in Greece.... The modern Greek is the *descendant of those glorious beings whom the imagination almost refuses to figure to itself* as belonging to our Kind ... [emphases added]

In a passage of this preface that his publisher dared not print, Shelley went on to place the current upheaval in Greece at the centre of what he called 'the great drama of the revival of liberty'. For Shelley, the claims of the modern Greeks to be the direct descendants of the ancients, about which Byron had been so sceptical ten years before, are self-evident and unquestioned. That ancient civilization, for Shelley as previously for Winckelmann, had been a 'nation'. Biological kinship therefore creates an imagined debt on the part of modern Europe to that ancestral 'nation', to be repaid in the present and future. Revival of the past is not only possible after all, it is nothing less than a *duty* laid upon all forward-thinking liberal spirits in the early nineteenth century. The liberation of Greece could never, according to this way of thinking, be a purely local affair, of interest only to those about to be liberated. That is the significance of the rousing claim, 'We are all Greeks'. Far more was at stake, in the Greek Revolution, than either the political project for self-government nurtured by enlightened leaders like Ignatios and Mavrokordatos, or the more primitive assertion of power by local leaders, in the name of Orthodox Christianity, that was happening on the ground in Greece.

Educated Greeks recognized the importance of this fact, and were not slow to exploit it. It was for this reason that when hostilities finally wound down, after almost a decade, Greece was able to emerge as a sovereign nation state, recognized by the governments of Europe. In that outcome, another English Romantic poet had played an unexpected part, and one whose full significance has yet to be appreciated.

Lord Byron was a late convert to the Greek cause. It was not until the summer of 1823, when the revolution was two years old, that Byron made up his mind to intervene. He chose his ground for action carefully. He had been ready to take up arms for the Italians, in the cause of a united Italy that was to be freed from Austrian and papal control. But that had fizzled out in February 1821. And Byron had been ambivalent about that particular cause anyway, because as an aristocrat he saw the absurdity of throwing in his lot with a radical *liberal* agenda that logically would have removed or curtailed the privileges of his own class. A *national* revolution was what Byron needed, and in Greece (after weighing up the alternative claims of the South American countries fighting for their independence from European rule), in 1823 he found one. For Byron, the 'Cause', as he came to call it, of Greece became at once the culmination and the negation of his entire career as a Romantic poet. In a number of passages in the poetry of the preceding years, he had speculated wistfully on the relative efficacity and worth of the poet and the man of action, of 'words' and 'things':

> But words are things, and a small drop of ink,
> Falling like dew, upon a thought, produces
> That which makes thousands, perhaps millions think[.][15]

By the early summer of 1823, that was no longer enough. It was time, in Byron's thinking, for words truly to *become* things, for the Romantic poetics of his earlier years to be translated into political action. And the ground for that translation was to be Greece. The political outcome of a revolution was to become the equivalent of an epic poem. The final, lasting achievement of one of the foremost proponents of the Romantic movement in Europe was to be not a work of literature, but a new kind of political organization, that of the nation state as we know it today.

Even before Byron's death, from fever, at Missolonghi on 19 April 1824, poets writing in Greek had already taken up the challenge of adapting the inheritance of European Romantic Hellenism to the realities of revolution. In the earliest works of Andreas Kalvos and Dionysios Solomos to be published in Greek, the 'words' of poetry are already inseparable from the 'things' they celebrate, namely the deeds and aspirations of the revolutionary Greeks.[16]

Both poets belonged to the Ionian Islands, for whose elite a Western education, through the medium of Italian, had been the norm for centuries. Both, before 1821, had written their first poetry in Italian. Kalvos, a peripatetic exile, during the Revolution moved from London to Florence, then to Geneva, where his first book of Greek *Odes* was published in 1824, to Paris where his second appeared two years later, then briefly to liberated Greece in 1826 before making his long-term home first in British-ruled Corfu and ultimately in England. Solomos spent the years of the Revolution in the native island of both poets, Zante (Zakynthos), which at the time, like Corfu, was part of a protectorate administered by Great Britain. Neither poet wrote with any first-hand experience of the Revolution in Greece. But Kalvos devoted all his small Greek-language output to it, and Solomos his most important poems of the 1820s, and indeed many that followed during subsequent decades.

Solomos's *Hymn to Liberty* may have been inspired, in part, by Shelley's 'Ode to Liberty' of 1820, that had been devoted to the liberal revolution in Spain earlier that year.[17] Liberty in Solomos's poem, as in Shelley's, is a semi-divine being who

[15] *Don Juan*, III. 792–4.

[16] For more on these and other Greek literary writers mentioned, and English translations of their work, see Beaton, *Introduction*.

[17] The evidence for this is given by Maria Schoina, '"The prophet of noble struggles": Shelley in Greece', in Susanne Schmid and Michael Rossington (eds), *The Reception of P. B. Shelley in Europe* (London: Continuum, 2008), ch. 17.

had first flourished on earth during the heyday of ancient Greece. Solomos in this poem accomplishes the leap from Romantic Hellenism to a political programme that Shelley had baulked at, and that for Byron would come at the cost of giving up poetry (and as things turned out, also his life). Needless to say, Solomos's youthful outburst of nationalist fervour pays its own price. After the poet's death, its opening stanzas would be adopted as Greece's national anthem; the words are known and sung by everyone who has ever been to a Greek school. But the *Hymn to Liberty* is not among Solomos's finest poems.

In 1824, Solomos and Kalvos both devoted poems to Byron's death. These are not their finest either, but they do play their part in the process whereby the dead English Romantic came to be canonized in Greece, his self-sacrifice for the cause of the Greek nation eclipsing everything else about his life and work, and inaugurating in the country he helped to liberate what has been called a 'century of Byron-mania'.[18]

Two years later, in 1826, Kalvos had fallen silent, perhaps appalled by his brief exposure, in that year, to the reality of the struggle to which he had devoted his best imaginative energies. In the same year, Missolonghi was recaptured by the Turks, after a year-long siege. On the last day of the siege, the old and the sick gathered in the house in which Byron had died. As the Turks entered the town, Byron's former landlord Christos Kapsalis set light to the last supplies of powder and ammunition that had been hoarded in his basement, destroying the house with all those in it, and taking some of the victors with them. Earlier that day, under cover of night, those with enough strength left had made a desperate attempt to break through the lines of the besiegers and reach safety. Most of those, too, died in the attempt, that has been remembered ever since as the 'Exodus of Missolonghi', on 10/22 April 1826.

It was the lowest point of the Greek Revolution. And it was to prove a turning point. Thanks in no small measure to the poets and Philhellenes inspired by the ideas of Romanticism, the liberation of Greece had become a European affair. Four years later, after the decisive victory of the combined navies of Great Britain, France, and Russia in Navarino Bay on 20 October 1827, Greece would be internationally recognized as a sovereign nation.

By that time Solomos, now established in Corfu, the capital of the British Protectorate of the Ionian Islands, was on the way to proving himself the greatest of all Romantic poets writing in Greek, and already at work on the epic commemoration of the siege of Missolonghi that was to occupy him for most of the rest of his life, the never-completed *Free Besieged*.

[18] For texts in translation, see respectively Andreas Kalvos, *Odes*, tr. George Dandoulakis (Nottingham: Shoestring, 2015, first edn 1998); Dionysios Solomos, *The Free Besieged and Other Poems*, tr. Peter Thompson et al., ed. Peter Mackridge (Nottingham: Shoestring, 2000). See also Athina Georganta, *Αιών βυρωνομανής* (Athens: Exantas, 1992).

Consolidating the Nation (1830–1875)

The new state was inaugurated on 6 February 1833. On that date Prince Otto, second son of King Ludwig I of Bavaria, and designated first king of Greece as soon as he should come of age, disembarked at Nafplio in the Peloponnese. The civic and cultural functions of a capital city were already coming together in this well-fortified and once-prosperous town, out of the ruins of almost ten years of war. Writers with literary ambitions had been arriving there over the past few years, the first publishing houses had begun to function. Within a year, however, the decision had been taken to move the nation's capital to Athens, where it has remained ever since.

The aspiring poets and novelists who gravitated first to Nafplio and then to Athens were all of them sons of the pre-revolutionary Greek elites of the Ottoman Empire and the mercantile diaspora. They had of necessity been educated in Europe, since all the earlier centres of Greek learning lay outside the frontiers of the Greek kingdom as these had been drawn (by the Great Powers) in 1832. Panagiotis Soutsos (1806–63) published a verse tragedy and Alexandros Rizos Rangavis (1809–92) a fragmentary narrative poem that follow in the footsteps, respectively, of Byron's *Manfred* and his earlier 'oriental tales', while Soutsos's brother Alexandros may have been indebted to the later Byron's bent for satire—though like Byron himself, Soutsos was also continuing a tradition established in his own language since the previous century. It was in Nafplio, more or less simultaneously with the arrival of the future king, that the modern Greek novel was born—quite programmatically and explicitly, as much part of the furniture for a newly established nation state as the ambitious programme of public building that began in Athens as soon as the capital moved there in 1834 and would continue for almost a century.

The juxtaposition is not facetious. Novel writing and public building were both of them activities predicated, conspicuously and intentionally, on *ancient* Greek precedent. To outward appearance, therefore, the results *look* neoclassical—reviving and repeating aesthetic norms that from the Renaissance to the eighteenth century had been held up for imitation throughout Europe. But their spirit belongs wholly to Romanticism. In the case of fiction, Korais in an influential essay published in 1805 had laid it down that the contemporary European novel had been in origin a *Greek* invention; the fiction destined to be produced by the revived Greek nation must therefore be a continuation of the first novels (also known as 'romances') written in Greek by Heliodorus, Achilles Tatius, and others during the first centuries CE. Duly, for thirty years, beginning with the appearance of *Leander* by Panagiotis Soutsos in Nafplio in 1834, Greek novelists held assiduously to this principle, at the same time as they drew on eighteenth-century precedents such as Lesage, Goethe, Foscolo, and later (from 1850) on the quintessentially Romantic historical tradition established by Walter Scott during the second and third decades of the nineteenth.

In public architecture, the underlying principles were the same, although in this case, throughout the nineteenth century, the creators were mainly Germans and Danes.[19] The

[19] Eleni Bastéa, *The Creation of Modern Athens Creation* (Cambridge: Cambridge University Press, 2000).

buildings of the Athens Academy (designed by Theophil Hansen in 1859 but not completed until 1885) would be derided by Greece's first Nobel laureate, George Seferis, half a century after they were opened, on the grounds that only the empty husk of classical Greek achievement was preserved in their newly fashioned pediments and Doric columns, while the spirit of the exercise was as foreign to Greece as the Danish architect.[20] But even so perceptive a critic as Seferis missed the point: for the brothers Hans Christian (1803–83) and Theophil (1813–91) Hansen, for the Bavarian Friedrich von Gärtner (1791–1847), and the Prussian Karl Friedrich Schinkel (1781–1841), whose grand plan to redesign the Acropolis of Athens was mercifully shelved, as much as for Greeks such as the German-trained Stamatios Kleanthes (1802–62) and the poets and novelists of the time, these 'empty forms' of classical perfection were not just the objects of conventional veneration, to be slavishly repeated: they represented for the modern Greeks what Herder had termed the 'traditions of a people'. For the first generation of Greeks in the new state, and their Philhellenic supporters, it was self-evident that the defining and still-living roots of the revived Greek nation were to be located not in the present or the recent past, but in antiquity. The neoclassical buildings that today still dominate central Athens, just like the less visible productions of the first modern Greek novelists, need to be understood as the local manifestation of the same Romantic ideology as in other parts of Europe at the same time was producing a revival of medieval, 'Gothic' styles.

This rhetoric of revival was the inheritance of Romantic Hellenism, adapted to the new circumstances of a Hellenic nation-state. Its longest-lasting legacy was in the sphere of language. Much has been written on the Greek 'language question', as it has become known, an intellectual controversy that began in the late eighteenth century and peaked in the civil disturbances that rocked Athens at the beginning of the twentieth. Suffice it here to observe that the same logic that led to the revival of the structural forms of the ancient Greek novel and the classical temple also promoted the creation of a hybrid language, that would at once express the organic 'soul' of the people (a principle beloved of Romantic theorists from Herder and Wordsworth onwards) and *revive* the presumed 'glories' of the prestigious language of antiquity.

The 'language question' in Greece has never really been solved. How impossible it was in the middle of the nineteenth century to square this circle can be illustrated by a vignette from 1853. The poet Panagiotis Soutsos was taking an excursion on horseback past the site of the ancient temple and oracle at Delphi, below Parnassus. The archaeological site that now attracts millions of visitors each year was still unexcavated. Like many Western travellers before him, Soutsos lamented that nothing of the wonders of the sanctuary of Apollo could be seen. 'From there', Soutsos' narrative continues, 'I proceeded to the nearest hamlet, following a shepherd who showed me his flock … arriving at the hamlet and enjoying the hospitality of his tiny cottage, little was lacking of the bucolic language of Theocritus, and he almost said to me …'

[20] George Seferis, *On the Greek Style*, tr. Rex Warner and Th. D. Frangopoulos (London: Bodley Head, 1967), 94. Greek original publ. 1938.

There follow three lines, quoted in the original Doric dialect, unintelligible to anyone with a knowledge only of modern Greek. Soutsos's sleight of hand is betrayed by the word 'almost'. As he talks to his shepherd, while listening to the birds singing in the trees and the burbling of the brook nearby, the modern poet convinces himself that this rustic peasant has unconsciously preserved many of the features of the ancient dialects that had in fact completely died out two thousand years before his time. He concludes: 'For an hour I listened to him pronouncing the vowels, the long and the short, always keeping to the ancient melody and more than once deceived myself that I was seeing the Goatherd of Theocritus, it came to me to recite aloud ...' and again he quotes from the ancient text in the original. Once more the circle refuses, obstinately, to be squared: Soutsos has to concede that he 'deceived' himself.[21]

The attempt to reclaim the literary dialects of a two-thousand-year-old civilization as part of the living 'traditions of a people' was bravely made, but ultimately impossible in the terms in which Soutsos tried to make it. By the time when he was writing, in 1853, the paradigm was already changing. The key term, 'revival', was beginning to be replaced by a new one: 'continuity'. This, too, was the legacy of Romantic Hellenism, but now mediated by a new approach to the writing of history that had begun in Germany earlier in the century, and was in turn another manifestation of the Romantic movement. This is the approach known today as historicism. For historicists, history consists above all of *process*. It is in the nature of societies to change over time, in ways determined by context, including inherited culture and geographical environment—the same things that Herder had loosely identified as the traditions that define a people.

This new approach to history came to Greece through the work of the folklorist Spyridon Zambelios (1815–81) and the historian Konstantinos Paparrigopoulos (1815–91). Zambelios was the first to propose that the intermediate stages of Greek history and culture separating the modern 'revival' from its ancient precursor must have constituted a formative process leading to the present condition of the nation. It is therefore the process of change that confirms the desired historical link between the two. In this way the long gap of almost two millennia came to be redefined as the testing-ground on which a modern national identity had been hammered out. This principle was followed through in much greater detail by Paparrigopoulos in his five-volume *History of the Greek Nation*, published between 1860 and 1874. The boldness of the conception is already announced in the title. Paparrigopoulos's achievement was to build on a rhetoric that had already been available since Winckelmann and (in Greek) Katartzis in the eighteenth century: if ancient Greece had been, in some sense, a 'nation', to which the modern revival was heir, then a continuous *national* history could be constructed that would reveal the process of change that had brought the nation from 'there' to 'here'. Described as 'without serious risk of exaggeration ... the most important intellectual achievement of nineteenth-century

[21] Tr. from Panagiotis Soutsos, *New School of the Written Word* (1853), extract from I. M. Panayotopoulos et al. (eds), *Νεοελληνική κριτική*, Series: *Βασική Βιβλιοθήκη*, 42 (Athens: Zaharopoulos, 1956), 48–9. On this work and responses to it, see Mackridge, *Language*, 182–7.

Greece', Paparrigopoulos's *History* could also schematically be proposed as the high-water-mark of Greek Romanticism.[22] Its influence would continue right through the twentieth century and beyond.

Romanticism's Fateful Legacy (1875–1922)

The idea that the Greek national project would not be complete until all the Greek-speaking populations of the Ottoman Empire had been united and the national capital established at Constantinople goes back at least as far as the early years of the Revolution. But its formulation as the 'Great Idea' is conventionally dated to 1844 and a speech addressed to the assembly that had been charged, in that year, with drawing up Greece's first post-independence constitution, which proclaimed a new civilizing mission for the country in the East. Before long, the 'idea' had crystallized around the aspiration to reunite all the Greek-speaking subjects of the Ottoman Empire and recapture Constantinople itself.

During the 1860s the 'Great Idea' gained momentum from the new approaches of Zambelios and Paparrigopoulos to medieval Greek history. This was the time when the millennium-long Christian civilization, known in modern times as 'Byzantine', began to be seriously rehabilitated, among Greek elites, in education and in imaginative literature. The capital of that civilization, from its foundation by the Roman emperor Constantine in 330 until its conquest by the Ottoman sultan Mehmet II on 29 May 1453, had been Constantinople. The newly discovered continuity that by the mid-nineteenth century had come to define Greek national identity gave equal prominence to the legacy of Byzantium as to that of classical Hellas. The last phase of Greek Romanticism, both in literature and in the political life of the country, is defined by the attempt to create an uneasy synthesis between these two very different heritages from the distant past.

Some of the inherent contradictions of the 'Great Idea', at the level of popular consciousness, were highlighted as early as 1872 by the first ambassador of the USA to Greece, Charles Tuckerman. By the time he wrote these words, Tuckerman had left the country under a cloud; he is not a friendly witness. But he does seem to have been an acute observer. Tuckerman's informants had conceded that not all Greeks believed that the conquest of Constantinople was either realizable or desirable as a real political goal. Despite this, he noted, every Greek

22 Paschalis M. Kitromilides, 'On the Intellectual Content of Greek Nationalism: Paparrigopoulos, Byzantium and the Great Idea', in D. Ricks and P. Magdalino (eds), *Byzantium and the Modern Greek Identity* (Aldershot: Ashgate, 1998), 28. On Zambelios, see Ioannis Koubourlis, *La Formation de l'histoire nationale grecque: L'Apport de Spyridon Zambélios (1815–1881)* (Athens: Institut de Recherches Néohelléniques, Fondation Nationale de la Recherche Scientifique, 2005).

> still cherishes it—if not as a practical possibility, as a tenet of his political and religious faith. It is sweet to believe that we are a 'chosen race', destined to carry the symbol of Christianity and the torch of civilization and freedom into the benighted realms of superstition and ignorance, even if circumstances prevent us from attempting the pilgrimage.[23]

No such ambiguities troubled the spirit of Jean Psichari, or Psycharis (as he signed himself, without first name, in Greek) whose intervention in 1888, from his adopted home of Paris, would change the course of the 'language question' for ever. Psycharis was a professional academic linguist who had absorbed the lessons of historicism as they had reached his discipline, through the work of the 'Neogrammarians'. For Neogrammarians, language is of its nature an unstable, therefore changing, system. This branch of linguistics focused on the process of language change, which by the 1880s had been proved to be systematic. Psycharis in 1888 could at last acknowledge the truth that Soutsos, a generation earlier, had tried so hard to elide: that the ancient Greek language had been fundamentally *different* from the language of his own day. It was paradoxically by emphasizing these differences, and proving their systematic nature, that Psycharis and his supporters were able to claim an organic relation between the long-dead language of the ancients and the spoken tongue of the late nineteenth century. It was once again *process* that proved continuity, and process by definition meant change.

Championing the national, 'demotic' or spoken language, over the hybrid that attempted to preserve elements of the ancient, Psycharis in his polemical book *My Journey* equated vindication of the nation's internal linguistic struggles with military victory over its enemies. Outspoken in his support for the 'Great Idea', Psycharis saw the national language and the national army as natural partners in a project that was at once political, military, and poetic:

> The language question is a political question: what the army fights to do to our physical frontiers, our language must do for our intellectual frontiers, both must go much farther, must take in more ground.... Language and fatherland are the same: whether you fight for the language or for the fatherland, you're engaged upon the same task...[24]

The synthesis between the twin heritages of ancient Greece and Christian Byzantium, with their respective 'centres' of Athens and Constantinople, would preoccupy the last major figure in Greek literature to have grown up within the climate of Romanticism. Kostis Palamas (1859–1943) was a prolific poet and critic who also made forays into drama and fiction, and whose legacy in turn would dominate Greek literature throughout the first half of the twentieth century. An early sonnet, published in 1895, encapsulates both the double sense of identity and the ambiguous longing for the 'Great Idea'

[23] Charles Tuckerman, *The Greeks of Today*, 2nd edn (New York: Putnam, 1878), 122, 124.

[24] Tr. from Psycharis, *Το ταξίδι μου* (1888), ed. A. Angelou (Athens: Ermis, 1971), 202.

to be realized. An unnamed Greece, or perhaps better the Greek people, in this poem, is to be represented by a 'double-faced picture'. On one side is depicted the Acropolis of Athens, the 'Sacred Rock' with the sculptures of the Parthenon (the notorious 'Elgin Marbles' taken in the early nineteenth century to be housed in the British Museum in London):

> On this side the Sacred Rock shines bright like topaz
> and the virginal-white chorus of the Maidens Carrying Baskets
> goes forward and shakes the veil of the goddess;
> while on the other sparkle the sapphires of the Bosphorus.
> and through the Golden Gate passes in tumult
> the triumph of victorious Emperors![25]

The 'picture' envisaged here is perhaps hard to imagine as a real object. But evidently for Palamas, as for many of his contemporaries, both sides of the coin—ancient Athens and medieval Constantinople—were equally present, equally valid components of modern Greek identity.

The sequel was to be, from a Greek point of view, tragic. After the defeat of the Ottoman Empire in the First World War, it once again appeared possible that an essentially Romantic 'idea' might be realized in the world of political and military action, as had happened in the Greek Revolution a century earlier. Between 1919 and 1922 Greek troops occupied part of western Anatolia, while Constantinople (today's Istanbul) was occupied by the victorious powers. But this time historical circumstances were to favour the nationalist aspirations not of the Greeks, but of their old adversaries (and *semblables*), the Turks. With the destruction of the cosmopolitan, Greek-dominated city of Smyrna (Izmir) in September 1922 and the enforced expulsion of up to a million Greek Orthodox subjects of the former Ottoman Empire, the sway in Greece of the Romantic movement finally comes to an end.

Further Reading

Bastéa, Eleni, *The Creation of Modern Athens: Planning the Myth* (Cambridge: Cambridge University Press, 2000).

Beaton, Roderick, *An Introduction to Modern Greek Literature*, 2nd edn, revd (Oxford: Oxford University Press, 1999).

Beaton, Roderick, *Byron's War: Romantic Rebellion, Greek Revolution* (Cambridge: Cambridge University Press, 2013).

Beaton, Roderick, and Ricks, David (eds), *The Making of Modern Greece: Nationalism, Romanticism, and the Uses of the Past (1797–1896)* (Farnham: Ashgate, 2009).

Clogg, Richard, *A Concise History of Greece*, 2nd edn (Cambridge: Cambridge University Press, 3rd edn 2013; 1st edn 1992).

[25] Tr. from an untitled sonnet from the collection *Πατρίδες* (*Fatherlands*), first publ. 1895, in Kostis Palamas, *Άπαντα*, iii (Athens: Biris, n.d.), 20.

Güthenke, Constanze, *Placing Modern Greece: The Dynamics of Romantic Hellenism, 1770–1840* (Oxford: Oxford University Press, 2008).

Mackridge, Peter, *Language and National Identity in Greece, 1766–1976* (Oxford: Oxford University Press, 2009).

Pizanias, Petros (ed.), *The Greek Revolution of 1821: A European Event* (Istanbul: Isis Press, 2011; 1st edn 2009, in Greek).

Roessel, David, *In Byron's Shadow: Modern Greece in the English and American Imagination* (Oxford: Oxford University Press, 2002).

St Clair, William, *That Greece Might Still Be Free: The Philhellenes in the War of Independence* (London: Open Book, 2008; 1st edn 1972).

PART II

DISCOURSES

CHAPTER 32

GEOGRAPHIES OF HISTORICAL DISCOURSE

ROBERTO DAINOTTO

un système de *Géographie physique* n'est autre chose qu'un plan méthodique où l'on présente les faits avérés & constans, & où on les rapproche pour tirer de leur combinaison des résultats généraux

a system of Geography is nothing other than a methodical plan where proven and established facts are presented, and where they are brought together in order to draw general results from their combinations.

(Robert de Vaugondy, 'Géographie', *Encyclopédie, ou dictionnaire raisonné des sciences, des arts et des métiers*, 1751–72)

Toute division méthodique, qui n'est fondée que sur des résultats particuliers, est donc fautive, & peut être démentie par de nouvelles combinaisons plus étendues & par des résultats plus généraux ... D'ailleurs, ces divisions méthodiques soulagent la mémoire, & semblent débrouiller le cahos que forment les objets de la nature, lorsqu'on les regarde confusément; mais il ne faut jamais oublier que ces systèmes ne sont fondés que sur les conventions arbitraires des hommes; qu'ils ne sont pas d'accord avec les lois invariables de la nature.

Every methodical division which is only grounded in particulars is consequently faulty and can be contradicted by new, more extensive combinations and by more general results ... Besides, these historical divisions relieve the memory and appear to untangle the chaos of natural objects when they are viewed confusedly; but one must never forget that these systems are nothing but arbitrary human conventions: they are not in agreement with the invariable laws of nature.

(Voltaire, 'Histoire', *Encyclopédie, ou dictionnaire raisonné des sciences, des arts et des métiers*, 1751–72)

The following pages attempt to frame European Romanticism against the background of that 'somewhat enigmatic event' which, between the end of the eighteenth and the beginning of the nineteenth century, has been said to have begun European modernity.[1] Such an 'event,' which in the words of Michel Foucault coincided with the emergence of a new order of things, was nothing less than the discovery of 'the historicity of knowledge.'[2]

It is not, to be sure, that knowledge of the past was unknown in previous epochs—from Thucydides and Herodotus to Strabo and Guicciardini. Yet, as Zachary Schiffman has commented in *The Birth of the Past* regarding early historiography:

> In and of itself, priority in time does not entail difference ... the time prior to the present constitutes an undifferentiated expanse, all of which is equally 'not present.' Even if we were to divide it into years arranged chronologically, it would still remain essentially undifferentiated. An excerpt from the Anglo-Saxon Chronicle epitomizes this homogeneous quality: 803 In this year Hygebald, bishop of Lindisfarne, passed away on 24 June; and Egbert was consecrated in his place on 11 June ... This medieval chronicle, written in at least thirteen different monkish hands, covers the expanse of time from the birth of Christ to 1154, virtually year-by-year. Granted, most of the later entries are more elaborate than these earlier ones, but the annalistic mode—which slots an eclipse of the moon alongside the defeat of a Northumbrian king, and the death of Charlemagne alongside the travels of English bishops and archbishops—renders all entries qualitatively equal. In and of itself priority in time does not entail difference. The distinction between past and present that constitutes 'the founding principle of history' rests on something other than mere priority in time; it reflects an abiding awareness that different historical entities exist in different historical contexts.[3]

Prior to Foucault's 'event,' historiographical thought seemed to lack both a sense of relational causality—how the death of Hygebald was related to the consecration of Egbert and so on—and a sense of qualitative difference between past and present, or even between different past moments. The Renaissance concept of classical imitation is illustrative of precisely this lack of perception of anachronisms—namely, of the fundamental difference between past and present:

> The Renaissance awareness of the differences between past and present had engendered a program of *imitatio* designed to bring the past back to life. For all practical purposes, this living past constituted an undifferentiated collection of entities, all equally relevant to the present.[4]

History was then nothing more than a record of past facts. Moreover, history recorded a chronology that could be known, but that seemed to have no constitutive role in the way

1 Michel Foucault, *The Order of Things*, tr. Alan Sheridan (London: Routledge, 2002), 255.

2 Foucault, *Order of Things*, 81.

3 Zachary S. Schiffman, *The Birth of the Past* (Baltimore: Johns Hopkins University Press, 2011), 229–35.

4 Schiffman, *Birth of the Past*, 204.

in which knowledge itself could operate and function. There could be a knowledge of a historical past, in short, but not knowledge of the fact that knowledge itself *is* historical. History, quite tellingly, never had any place in the classical taxonomy of the branches of knowledge—neatly divided into logics, physics, and ethics—nor in the scholastic encyclopedia codified in Christian Wolff's *Elementa matheseos universae* (1713–15), and still operative, albeit with some modifications, in Immanuel Kant's tripartition of knowledge into pure, practical, and of judgement:

> history has no citizenship rights in ontology, which investigates the essential modes of Being; nor is it the object of psychology, cosmology, or rational theology—because history does not concern the Soul, the physical world, and, even less so, the Supreme Being.[5]

What Foucault had then summarized through his shorthand assertion was an idea that, from Friedrich Meinecke to Reinhart Koselleck, had preoccupied much of (mostly but not uniquely German) historiographical theory. In 1936, Meinecke had opened the discussion by writing on the rise (*Entstehung*) of a new 'historical outlook', which, on the wave of a pre-Romantic *Sturm und Drang*, had found in 'the great German movement'[6] its most coherent expression:

> The whole process depended on the breaking down of the rigid ways of thought attached to the concepts of Natural Law and its belief in the invariability of the highest human ideals and an unchanging human nature that was held to be constant for all ages.[7]

By the middle of the eighteenth century, the monogenetic assumption that humankind was of a single Adamitic origin, created by one God, and universally attending to one divinely ordained natural law, had already fallen into disrepute under the attack of Reason;[8] once Reason too, along with its presumption of one 'unchanging human nature', was being relativized after the European discoveries of different cultures and ancient civilizations—then, a new outlook on life, which Meinecke called *historismus*, 'rose' to change once and for all European culture's very understanding of its world. Knowledge of that world, in Foucault's words, could no longer be held to be absolute and universal. It was now, rather, contingent and 'historical'.[9]

Convinced like Foucault and Meinecke that the years stretching roughly between 1750 and 1850 were some sort of a 'saddle time' (*Sattelzeit*) between the Classical Age and

[5] Pietro Rossi, *Il senso della storia: Dal Settecento al Duemilia* (Bologna: Il Miulino, 2012), 7 (tr. mine).

[6] Friedrich Meinecke, *Historism: The Rise of a New Historical Outlook* (1936), ed. J. E. Anderson and H. D. Schmidt (London: Routledge & Kegan Paul, 1972), 235.

[7] Meinecke, *Historism*, 3.

[8] David N. Livingstone, *Adam's Ancestors: Race, Religion, and the Politics of Human Origins* (Baltimore: Johns Hopkins University Press, 2008), 52–79.

[9] Alphonse Dupront, *Spazio e umanesimo*, ed. Gigliola Fragnito (1946) (Venice: Marsilio, 1993); Paolo Rossi, *Le sterminate antichità: Studi vichiani* (Pisa: Nistri-Lischi, 1969).

the *Sturm und Drang* of modernity, also Reinhart Koselleck believed that a distinctive trait of the latter was to be found precisely in its renewed sense of time and historicity: 'Stating my thesis simply,' he said in his 1965 inaugural lecture as professor of history in Heidelberg, 'in these centuries there occurs a temporalization (*Verzeitlichung*) of history ... which characterizes modernity.'[10]

In that 'saddle time'—after publishers, newspapers, encyclopedists, and *philosophes* had disputed the validity of one idea over another in the widening forum of public opinion (what Kant's second appendix to *Zum ewigen Frieden* famously called *Publizität*, 'publicity')—truth, says Koselleck, could no longer be imagined as one. A new contention, accordingly, had to make its way—namely, 'the claim that it is only possible to discover the truth by adopting a definite position.'[11] This 'position,' which the student of history still recognizes as the 'contextualizing viewpoint' of modern historiography,[12] reorganized the past, from a determinate point of view, as a set of relational causalities: a series of discrete and different facts or events which, as a whole, created as much as recorded a *storia* capable even of explaining the genesis of the present.

Arguably, such a 'contextualizing viewpoint' also posited the first logical problematic proper to this new historical outlook: if the historian can no longer claim to see things absolutely speaking, but rather from her or his point of view, what is then implicitly argued is that *all* truths, rather than being deducible from universally valid first principles, are in fact relative and contextual to the historian's own position. This crisis of absolute values, which Paul Hazard famously called a 'crisis of the European Mind,' was the crisis from which a new sense of history was born.[13]

In this sense, historicization and 'temporalization' of human existence were nothing but the prelude to a Nietzschean 'death of God'—the full relativization and secularization of a 'dis-godded' human life,[14] that is to say, when 'Not one Godhead greets my longing sight.'[15] As Eugenio Donato once commented on this very verse by Schiller, 'the theme of the death of God,' so central to Romantic sensibilities, 'organizes different narrative structures that in turn will produce different "Histories" '.[16] The reason why one privileged *telos* to history had to be replaced now by many different and even 'dissonant' histories, was perhaps best illustrated in a text by Jean Paul—the 'Speech of the Dead Christ from the Universe that There Is No God' (1796)—promptly translated by Mme de

10 Reinhart Koselleck, *Futures Past: On the Semantics of Historical Time*, tr. Keuth Tribe (New York: Columbia University Press, 2004), 11.

11 Koselleck, *Futures Past*, 128.

12 Schiffman, *Birth of the Past*, 217.

13 Paul Hazard, *The European Mind: The Critical Years, 1680–1715*, ed. J. Lewis May (New Haven: Yale University Press, 1953), 3.

14 Owen Barfield, *Saving the Appearances: A Study in Idolatry* (New York: Harcourt, Brace & World, 1965), 130.

15 Johann Christoph Friedrich Schiller, *The Poems of Schiller*, tr. Edgar A. Bowring (London: J. W. Parker, 1880), 74.

16 Eugenio Donato, 'Divine Agonies: Of Representation and Narrative in Romantic Poetics,' *Glyph*, 6 (1979), 93.

Staël into French, and quite influential for the generation of Alfred Vigny and Nerval. In Thomas Carlyle's later Victorian translation into English, we read:

> the dead all cried: 'Christ! is there no God?' He replied: 'There is none.' ... Christ went on: 'I traversed the worlds, I ascended into the suns, and soared with the Milky Ways through the wastes of heaven; but there is no God. I descended to the last reaches of the shadows of Being, and I looked into the chasm and cried: 'Father, where art thou?' But I heard only the eternal storm ruled by none, and the shimmering rainbow of essence stood without sun to create it, trickling above the abyss. And when I raised my eyes to the boundless world for the divine eye, it stared at me from an empty bottomless socket; and Eternity lay on Chaos and gnawed it and ruminated itself.—Shriek on, discords, rend the shadows; for He is not!'[17]

If 'Eternity lay on Chaos'; if the 'eternal storm' of life is 'ruled by none'; and if a sense of life past and present can only be reconstructed from a history generated from a relative 'contextualizing viewpoint'—then a teleological history could hardly be imagined any longer. Histories had to multiply—as many, as particular, and as 'dissonant' or 'chaotic', as there were human events and points of view on earth. It could be no mere coincidence in fact, as Koselleck did notice, that 'parallel expressions like *Verweltlichung* (secularization) and *Verzeitlichung* (temporalization)' remained the discursive essence of modernity.[18] In the classical period, as Foucault would comment with a more openly political bent, knowledge of whatever kind depended on the one Truth maintained by the allegedly universal and absolute power of either pope or emperor. In this sense it was 'perfectly homogeneous'.[19] But with modernity—this was for Foucault the true essence of the *querelle* between ancients and moderns—an old age marked by the absolute power of the monarch and the universal reach of the pope had come to an end, and a new modern time, of which the French Revolution's new calendar was but one symptom, had come into being. 'Temporalization' meant, above all, the recognition that human histories were less a series of teleologically ordained or repeating occurrences, than a series of unique events. As Foucault would reiterate, modernity was nothing else, therefore, than the fragmentation of all classical unities; 'a tendency towards deviation that simultaneously guarantees the existence of history, differences and dispersion'.[20]

Such differences and dispersions, moreover, could only increase exponentially. Because, for instance, as the French Revolution had demolished the absolute Truth of Pope and Emperor, it had in the meantime hypostatized its own truth—the *universal* rights and reason of a universalized 'man'—as just another absolute. As the French troops invaded Germany in 1792 and secured control of Rhineland two years later, it is not surprising that an animosity towards France found exactly in

17 Thomas Carlyle, *Critical and Miscellaneous Essays*, 2 vols (Boston: Brown & Taggart, 1884), ii. 133–4.
18 Koselleck, *Futures Past*, 87.
19 Foucault, *Order of Things*, 343.
20 Foucault, *Order of Things*, 165.

Germany's nascent historicism some tools to fight the battle.[21] Because 'differences,' once discovered, could not be limited merely to the peculiarities of different ages. Differences were to be found in geography, too, as 'geographic space was every bit as constitutive of human experience as historical time'.[22] The age of history and temporalization is then also—for what are strictly interrelated reasons—the age of spatialization and 'classical geography': stretching roughly from the publication of Alexander von Humboldt's *Voyage to the Equinoctial Regions of the New Continent* (1799) to Carl Ritter's monumental *Science of the Earth* (1816–59), a new idea of 'geography according to ... historical development' was being formed in Europe at the same time.[23]

As Koselleck observed, if 'time is not manifest and cannot be intuited' in itself, than only spatial categories could, after all, form the categories of a modern historical thought determined to find differences, relative values, and empirical particularities where the Classical Age had found only unities and absolutes.[24] In Chenxi Tang's iconic image, while Georg Wilhelm Friedrich Hegel was holding his *Lessons on the Philosophy of History* at the University of Berlin, in an office next door Carl Ritter was revolutionizing the discipline of geography by writing the *Science of the Earth*:

> the discovery of historical time around 1800 was accompanied by the discovery of geographic space, and the historicization of society and knowledge went hand in hand with what can be called the geographicization thereof. Indeed, one can speak of the emergence of a distinctively modern concept of geography alongside and in complementarity to the concept of history ... an archaeology of geographic space and geographicization during the age commonly seen as characterized by the rise and absolute dominance of 'historism'.[25]

It is as if, in the last analysis, neither history nor geography per se mattered, but, rather, the will to understand differences in their particularities. Neither modern history, nor modern geography, could attend still to the *résultats généraux*, the generalizable results defining the disciplines for the *Encyclopédie*. A new age had begun, in which ideas of 'cultural difference' and 'enlightened relativism'[26] redefined both history and geography as sciences of the particular. As Alexander von Humboldt put it in 1821, the new task for the historian was 'the study of many particulars, in different places and under different circumstances'. Or, as Michel de Certeau quoted Alphonse Dupront

[21] Zeev Sternhell, *The Anti-Enlightenment Tradition* (New Haven: Yale University Press, 2010), 420.

[22] Chenxi Tang, *The Geographic Imagination of Modernity: Geography, Literature, and Philosophy in German Romanticism* (Stanford, Calif.: Stanford University Press, 2008), 1.

[23] Richard Hartshorne, 'The Nature of Geography: A Critical Survey of Current Thought in the Light of the Past', *Annals of the Association of American Geographers*, 29/3 (1939), 211–77.

[24] Reinhart Koselleck, *The Practice of Conceptual History: Timing History, Spacing Concepts*, tr. Todd Samuel Presner (Stanford, Calif.: Stanford University Press, 2002), 7.

[25] Tang, *Geographic Imagination*, 3.

[26] Sonia Sikka, *Herder on Humanity and Cultural Difference* (New York: Cambridge University Press, 2011), 3.

in the incipit of *The Writing of History*, 'The sole historical quest ... remains indeed a quest for the Other'.[27]

It may not be inopportune then, even at the risk of veering towards some kind of a 'saga in which all the great deeds are done by entities which could not, in principle, *do* anything', to assert a fundamental relation among the abstractions we are accustomed to calling 'Historicism', 'Classical Geography', and 'Romanticism'.[28] What they all 'did' (so to speak!), in a concerted and synergetic effort, was to push 'Europe' (one last abstract entity for our saga) through 'an intellectual crossroads, on the other side of which lies modernity'[29]—a Romantic modernity, that is, predicated on the systematic distinction of *particularities* that could no longer be reconciled within any classical unity of sorts.

Such 'dispersion' of truth into splintered particulars, often expressed in the spurious genres of the aphorism (Kennedy; Malachuk) and the *zibaldone* or miscellany (Leopardi), found one particular form of expression in a Romantic mode *par excellence:*

> the *fragment*. To an even greater extent than the 'genre' of theoretical romanticism, the fragment is considered its incarnation, the most distinctive mark of its originality, or the sign of its radical modernity. This, in fact, is precisely the claim made by Friedrich Schlegel and Novalis, each in their own manner. Indeed, the fragment is the romantic genre *par excellence*.[30]

It is not that the historicist refusal of unities could content itself, in principle, with the mere fragmentariness of events and relativity of knowledge. At the heyday of German historicism, Hegel warned his students 'not to be misled by professed historians'. Opposed to 'the scantiness of the particulars on which [historicist works] are based',[31] he tried one last attempt at a systematic and unitary philosophy of history that could reduce all empirical events to one single, simple and general conception:

> The only Thought which Philosophy brings with it to the contemplation of History, is the simple conception of *Reason*; that Reason is the Sovereign of the World; that the history of the world, therefore, presents us with a rational process. This conviction and intuition is a hypothesis in the domain of history as such. In that of Philosophy

27 Wilhelm Von Humboldt, 'On the Historian's Task (1821)', *History and Theory*, 6/1 (1967), 64; Michel de Certeau, *The Writing of History* (New York: Columbia University Press, 1988), 2.

28 John Dunn, 'The Identity of the History of Ideas', *Philosophy*, 43/164 (1968), 85–104. <http://www.jstor.org/stable/3748838>.

29 Schiffman, *Birth of the Past*, 204.

30 Philippe Lacoue-Labarthe and Jean-Luc Nancy, *The Literary Absolute: The Theory of Literature in German Romanticism* (Albany, NY: State University of New York Press, 1988), 40. See also Clare Kennedy, *An Openness towards the Other: Paradox, Aphorism and Desire in the Writings of Novalis and Derrida* (Edinburgh: University of Edinburgh Press, 2006); Daniel S. Malachuk, 'Coleridge's Republicanism and the Aphorism in "Aids to Reflection"', *Studies in Romanticism*, 39/3 (2000), 397–417; Giacomo Leopardi, *Zibaldone di pensieri*, ed. Sergio Solmi and Raffaella Solmi, 1898 (Turin: Einaudi, 1977).

31 Georg Wilhelm Friedrich Hegel, *The Philosophy of History*, tr. John Sibree (Kitchener, Ont.: Batoche, 2001), 24, 21.

> it is no hypothesis. It is there proved by speculative cognition, that Reason … is *Substance*, as well as *Infinite Power* … On the one hand, Reason is the *substance* of the Universe; viz., that by which and in which all reality has its being and subsistence. On the other hand, it is the *Infinite Energy* of the Universe … It is *the infinite complex of things*, their entire Essence and Truth … That this 'Idea' or 'Reason' is the *True*, the *Eternal*, the absolutely *powerful* essence; that it reveals itself in the World, and that in that World nothing else is revealed but this and its honor and glory—is the thesis which, as we have said, has been proved in Philosophy, and is here regarded as demonstrated.[32]

But also the historicist camp, which against Hegel could not presume a reason transcending history but only many reasons immanent to it, could not confront the danger of fragmentarity too cavalierly. Leopold von Ranke for instance, in 'The Role of the Particular and the General in the Study of Universal History', would speak explicitly of such danger: 'Given the course which historical studies have taken in our times, we are exposed to the danger of losing sight of the general knowledge everyone desires.'[33]

But how could the historicist ever escape such danger and comply with Friedrich Schiller's dictum, 'strive for unity, but do not look for it in uniformity'? What unity could possibly ever be reached if no relative point of view could organize differences once and for all, by hypostatizing itself as absolute, as the ultimate Archimedean point? A 'yearning for harmony', a nostalgia for 'an undivided sensuous unity and … a harmonizing whole',[34] crystallizes into a figure that a recent *Companion to British Romantic Poetry* has called 'romantic science of nostalgia'.[35] It is the Romantic nostalgia for origins, for childhood, and for a past often coinciding with Schiller's image of the south.[36] In 1786, Johann Wolfgang Goethe, tired of the 'environmental mediocrity' of the Weimar's ducal palace, may have inaugurated the trope of the lost classical 'south' with his *Journey to Italy* (published in 1817): 'The idyllic dream of the first men living out of doors and retiring to caves only in an emergency is a reality here.'[37] His example would soon be followed: Samuel Coleridge's search for authentic life in Malta, Naples, and Sicily (1808); Lord Byron's pilgrimage of *Childe Harold* (1812–18); Heinrich Heine's Italian travels (1829); François-Auguste-René de Chateaubriand's *Itinerary from Paris to Jérusalem* (1811); Prosper Merimée's phantasies of Mediterraneity …

32 Hegel, *Philosophy of History*, 22–3.

33 Leopold von Ranke, *The Theory and Practice of History*, ed. Georg G. Iggers and Konrad von Moltke (Abingdon, Oxon: Taylor & Francis, 2011), 77–8.

34 Friedrich Schiller, 'On Naive and Sentimental Poetry' (1795), in *Essays*, ed. Walter Hinderer and Daniel Dahlstrom (New York: Continuum, 1993), 193.

35 Kevis Goodman, 'Romantic Poetry and the Science of Nostalgia', in Maureen N. McLane and James Chandler (eds), *The Cambridge Companion to British Romantic Poetry* (Cambridge: Cambridge University Press, 2008), 195.

36 Roberto Dainotto, *Place in Literature: Regions, Cultures, Communities* (Ithaca, NY: Cornell University Press, 2000), 72–102.

37 Augusto Placanica, *Goethe tra le rovine di Messina* (Palermo: Sellerio, 1987), 23.

Johann Wolfgang von Goethe, *Italian Journey: Et in Arcadia Ego*, ed. W. H. Auden and Elizabeth Mayer (Harmondsworth: Penguin, 1962), 123.

The voyage in search of lost idyllic unities was not the only solution to the fragmentariness of historical existence. A logic of relational causality and a sense of interrelatedness between past and presents—the logic of history as a story with 'a discernible beginning, middle and end'[38]—was just as important as the declaration of differences. Admittedly, however, even this coherence found among disparate events remained of a relative kind—imposed again by a point of view that, without recourse to any absolute, neither reason nor natural law, lacked a final resting point.

Romantic writing then finds itself restlessly torn between fragmentariness and aspiration to wholeness:

> When Friedrich Schlegel notes that 'aphorisms are coherent fragments,' he indicates that one property of the fragment is its lack of unity and completion. But the well-known *Athenaeum* fragment 206 states that the fragment 'has to be ... complete in itself like a hedgehog.' Its existential obligation ..., if not its existence ..., is indeed formed by the integrity and the wholeness of the organic individual.[39]

The central notion of Romantic irony was predicated on the same tension by Friedrich Schlegel in his 'Dialogue on Poetry':

> Every poem should actually be romantic as well as didactic in that broader sense of the word where it describes the general tendency in its deep and infinite sense. We must make this demand everywhere, without using the name ... we demand irony; we demand that events, men, in short the play of life be taken as play and be represented as such ... We are concerned only with the meaning of the whole; and things which individually excite, move, occupy, and delight our sense, our hearts, understanding, and imagination seem to us to be only a sign, a means for viewing the whole at the moment when we rise to such a view.[40]

As Jonathan Arac summarizes well, a resolution of the tension between the desire to escape fragmentariness and the impossibility to revert to any classical unity often required a semantic shift away from the very notion of 'unity':

> Wilhelm's criterion of the 'structure of the whole' is a crucial feature of the new romantic understanding. As Friedrich Schlegel put it, 'there probably is no modern poet more correct than Shakespeare,' when 'correct,' that term so dear to earlier generations, is understood 'in the nobler and more original sense of the word—meaning a conscious main and subordinate development of the inmost and most minute aspects of a work in line with the spirit of the whole.' In the neo-Aristotelian discourse of the eighteenth century, the key term had been *unity*. Coleridge stands as

[38] Hayden V. White, *Metahistory: The Historical Imagination in Nineteenth-Century Europe* (Baltimore: Johns Hopkins University Press, 1973), 5.

[39] Lacoue-Labarthe and Nancy, *Literary Absolute*, 40.

[40] Friedrich Schlegel, *Dialogue on Poetry and Literary Aphorisms*, ed. Ernst Behler and Roman Struc (University Park, Pa.: Pennsylvania State University Press, 1968), 89.

> strongly as Schlegel for a new criterion: 'Instead of unity of action, I should great[ly] prefer the more appropriate, tho' scholastic and uncouth words—Homogeneity, proportionateness, and totality of interest.' This shift in terminology, for Coleridge, brought out the difference between the 'skill of mechanical Talent' and the 'creative Life-power of inspired Genius'.[41]

Through notions of fragmentariness and particularity on the one hand, totality and wholesomeness on the other, a new paradigmatic (yet still problematic) logic, in short, seemed to emerge in Europe—one that could allow for different geographies of Europe to have their own distinctive histories, each productive, in turn, of the specific conditions of knowledge of its different peoples.

If eminent voices from the Enlightenment could still hold that 'mankind are so much the same in all times and places that history informs us of nothing new or strange',[42] Johann Gottfried von Herder, already by 1765, would pit the historical '*diversity* of bodies, of minds (*Gemüter*) etc., of opinions and of tastes, of sensations etc.' against the 'abstractions' and 'metaphysics' of universalizing philosophy.[43] While still under the influence of his teacher Immanuel Kant, the fragments drafted as 'How Philosophy Can Become More Universal' were not only Herder's exordium in the philosophy of relativizing particularities, but also his first step in a direction radically different from the one undertaken by his mentor. For how could Kant's universal and transcendental categories such as reason or morality (the categorical imperative) continue to exist if Herder's philosophy, 'in order to remain philosophy', refused now any transcendence to delve into the immanence of 'my sensations, my strengths, my moral feeling, and my basic drives'?[44]

Far from being a solipsistic call, Herder's early fragment was in fact rooted in the socialized community of 'the people': with an echo of Rousseau's general will, 'I take the word "people" in the general sense of each citizen of the state.' As 'our patriotic friend of humanity Rousseau'[45] had objected to D'Alembert that 'to ask oneself if theater is good or bad in itself is to pose too vague a question',[46] so would Herder observe that nothing is 'in itself unpleasant' or good absolutely speaking.[47] 'There is from one people to another a prodigious diversity of customs, of temperaments and characters', Rousseau had warned. 'Man is one, I admit: but men modified by religions, governments, laws, customs, prejudices and climates becomes so different from one another that we should stop seeking what is good for man in general, and look only for what is good

[41] Jonathan Arac, *Impure Worlds: The Institution of Literature in the Age of the Novel* (New York: Fordham University Press, 2010), 14.

[42] David Hume, *An Enquiry Concerning Human Understanding*, ed. Peter Millican (Oxford: Oxford University Press, 2007), 60.

[43] Johann Gottfried Herder, *Philosophical Writings*, tr. Michael N. Forster (Cambridge: Cambridge University Press, 2002), 27 (Herder's own emphasis).

[44] Herder, *Philosophical Writings*, 15.

[45] Herder, *Philosophical Writings*, 12.

[46] Jean Jacques Rousseau, *Œuvres complètes*, 5 vols (Paris: Gallimard, 1964), v. 17.

[47] Herder, *Philosophical Writings*, 252.

in a particular time in a particular country.'[48] Herder agreed: 'manner of thought and taste change with climate, with regions of the earth, and with countries'.[49] Historicized and given their particular geography, all human things—man, taste, even philosophy, or knowledge—were then neither universal nor purely idiosyncratic: everything became communal, or, *mutatis mutandis*, national. Rousseau signed his letter to D'Alembert as 'J. J. Rousseau, citizen of Geneva', and Herder also stressed his location: 'I am speaking as a German'.[50]

Nor was Herder's historicism a mere continuation of the Enlightened discourse on the differences of people and races that had coalesced around the idea of national 'genius'—the latter notion concocted by the orientalist Amable de Bourzeys for his speech presented at the Académie française on 12 February 1635.[51] Enlightened discourse seemed still determined to resolve those differences in a common progress of humankind understood as a unity. Condorcet's 'Sketch for a Historical Picture of the Progress of the Human Mind' (published posthumously in 1795), for instance, held firm the belief that 'the future condition of the human species can be reduced to ... the destruction of inequality among nations'. Universalizing reason, after all, could be concerned only with such reduction of differences and their resolution into generalizable taxonomic universalities: 'as facts multiply, the human mind learns to classify them and reduce them to more general facts'.[52]

Similarly, Turgot's 'Philosophical Review of the Successive Advances of the Human Mind' (1750) recognized, as much as Hume's empiricism had done, that 'The succession of mankind ... affords from age to age an ever-changing spectacle. Reason, the passions, and liberty ceaselessly give rise to new events.'[53] Yet, exactly like Hume and Condorcet, Turgot too was firm in prophesizing a universal future for a united humankind:

> Self-interest, ambition, and vainglory continually change the world scene and inundate the earth with blood; yet in the midst of their ravages manners are softened, the human mind becomes more enlightened, and separate nations are brought closer to one another. Finally commercial and political ties unite all parts of the globe, and the whole human race, through alternate periods of rest and unrest, of weal and woe, goes on advancing, although at a slow pace, toward greater perfection.[54]

Closer to Herder, even Kant would, in opposition to his pupil's historicist theses, claim a universal and united destiny for humankind—in 'Ideas for a Universal History from

[48] Rousseau, *Œuvres completes*, v. 17 (my tr.).

[49] Herder, *Philosophical Writings*, 247.

[50] Herder, *Philosophical Writings*, 7–8.

[51] Paola Gambarota, *Irresistible Signs: The Genius of Language and Italian National Identity* (Toronto: University of Toronto Press, 2011), 6.

[52] Nicholas de Caritat, Marquis de Condorcet, 'Sketch for a Historical Picture of the Progress of the Human Mind: Tenth Epoch', *Daedalus*, 133/3 (2004), 66, 75. <http://www.jstor.org/stable/20027931>.

[53] Anne Robert Jacques Turgot, *The Turgot Collection: Writings, Speeches, and Letters of Anne Robert Jacques Turgot, Baron de Laune*, ed. David Gordon (Auburn, Ala.: Ludwig von Mises Institute, 2011), 321.

[54] Turgot, *The Turgot Collection*, 322.

a Cosmopolitan Point of View' (1784); 'Conjectures on the Origin of History' (1786); and 'If Humankind is in a Continuous Progress towards Improvement' (1798). However, for Herder's version of cosmopolitanism—because he was a cosmopolitan and even an ardent supporter of the principles of the French Revolution, not the rabid nationalist portrayed in some dubious scholarship[55]—the idea of differences progressively dissolving into unities was an aberration—and an imperial move as well. Each different origin had a different progress, a different development, and a different end. His was the conviction, in Erich Auerbach's words, that:

> every civilization and every period has its own possibilities of aesthetic perfection; that the works of art of the different peoples and periods, as well as their general forms of life, must be understood as products of variable individual conditions, and have to be judged each by its own development, not by absolute rules of beauty and ugliness.[56]

A reading of the early essay on 'The Change of Taste' (1766) offers already the co-ordinates for Herder's new historicist outlook, his nationalism, and his cosmopolitanism, that he will later develop more fully in the ironic *Another Philosophy of the History of the Formation of Humanity* (1774) and in the seminal *Ideas for a Philosophy of the History of Humankind* (1784–91). The essay—which Herder himself saw as 'the precursor of similar observations about the spirit of the changes in various ages'[57]—begins with a simple empirical observation:

> As soon as I find something true or beautiful, as soon as I can convince myself by means of reasons that something is true or beautiful, then nothing is more natural than the expectation that every human being will have the same feeling, the same opinion, with me. Otherwise, of course, there would be no basic rule of truth and no firm basis for taste. As soon as it is shown that what I on the basis of reasons take to be true, beautiful, good, pleasant can likewise on the basis of reasons be regarded by another as false, ugly, bad, unpleasant, then truth, beauty, and moral value is a phantom that appears to each person in another way, in another shape: a true Proteus who by means of a magic mirror ever changes, and never shows himself as the same.[58]

As Auerbach had intuited, it was then an aesthetic preoccupation with 'taste'—the epochal desire to give dignity to national cultural traditions quickly dismissed by the

[55] Karl R. Popper, *The Open Society and its Enemies* (Princeton: Princeton University Press, 1966), 255; Robert Reinhold Ergang, *Herder and the Foundations of German Nationalism* (New York: Octagon Books, 1966), 50.

[56] Erich Auerbach, 'Vico and Aesthetic Historism', *Journal of Aesthetics and Art Criticism*, 8/2 (1949), 110.

[57] Herder, *Philosophical Writings*, 255.

[58] Herder, *Philosophical Writings*, 247.

French Classicism à la Boileau[59]—which opened the way to historicism tout court.[60] What one finds beautiful, another may find ugly—it is, Herder says, just a matter of taste.

The ensuing story is well known. As taste becomes relative, there can no longer be a single literature, but only many different ones, each to be judged according to their own principles. To begin, there is, within Europe itself, a literature 'that comes from the south' and one 'that descend[s] from the north'.[61] As Schiller had already implied in 1795, historical difference (ancient and modern) was, even before becoming aesthetic difference (naïve and sentimental), a geographical one: between the 'serendipitous sky' of the south 'surrounding the ancient Greeks'[62] and the repulsiveness of nature (*Naturwidrigkeit*) of the north, there stood 'two extremely different natures separated by the immeasurable distance between epochs'.[63] Modern northern literature, from this relative point of view, could be neither worse nor better than the classical models, but simply different:

> Nature has given the naive poet the gift of always acting as an undivided unity, of being at each moment a self-sufficient and complete whole, and of dip laying humanity in all its significance ... within the actual world. Nature has endowed the sentimental poet with the power, or rather has imbued him with a vital urge to restore, from out of himself, the unity that abstraction had destroyed within him, in other words, the urge to render humanity perfect in itself, and to pass from a limited condition to an infinite one.[64]

The notion of the two European literatures, popularized in a number of works including Friedrich Bouterwek's *History of Spanish Poetry and Eloquence* (1804), Simonde de Sismondi's *Literature of Southern Europe* (1819), and Edgar Quinet, *Literature and Compared Institutions of Southern Europe* (1843), was being fragmented further into the emerging science of national literature.[65] Herder's 'Fragments on Recent German Literature' (1767–8) and Girolamo Tiraboschi's *History of Italian Literature* (1772–82) are among the first examples of this new trend towards increasing nationalization.[66] On the other hand, no lesser admirer of Herder than 'Goethe formulated the concept of *Weltliteratur* in the 1820s, during the heyday of European nationalism, and it was natural for him then to speak of world literature as based in the interactions of established national literatures'.[67] As Claudio Guillén has noticed, it was precisely the historicist discovery of differences and particularities that engendered both national and 'comparative' literary studies:

[59] Roberto M. Dainotto, *Europe (in Theory)* (Durham, NC: Duke University Press, 2007), 114–19.

[60] Auerbach, 'Vico', 111.

[61] Anne-Louise Germaine Necker, Mme de Staël, *De la littérature considérée dans ses rapports avec les institutiones socialese*, ed. Gérard Gengembre and Jean Goldzink (Paris: Flammarion, 1991), 203.

[62] Schiller, 'Naive and Sentimental', 193.

[63] Schiller, 'Naive and Sentimental', 197.

[64] Schiller, 'Naive and Sentimental', 233.

[65] E. Gillard, 'De l'usage du mot national et, en particulier, de son sens dans l'expression "littérature nationale"', *Cahiers vaudois*, 2 (1914), 5–19.

[66] Giovanni Getto, *Storia delle storie letterarie* (Florence: Sansoni, 1981), 77–102.

[67] David Damrosch, *What is World Literature?* (Princeton: Princeton University Press, 2003), 57.

> Comparative studies properly speaking arose during the span of time from the end of the eighteenth century to the beginning of the nineteenth, when the first works of Romanticism emerged. The idea of national literature and a modern sense of historical differentiation were necessary precursors for the study of comparative literature.[68]

Schiller's 'urge to restore' a lost unity was at work in the nascent concepts of both world and European literature: requests for a new 'European literary science' were voiced loudly, most notably in journals such as *Europa*, founded by Friedrich Schlegel in 1803, in the *Literary Archives of Europe* of 1804, in Giuseppe Mazzini's 'Of European Literature' (1829), and in Henry Hallam's *Introduction to the Literature of Europe in the 15th, 16th and 17th Centuries* (1839).[69] Unlike the cosmopolitan Europe without borders imagined by the previous generation, however, the post-revolutionary, historicist understanding of 'World' and of 'Europe' took into account a new set of differences conceived as national particularities. A relation among such particularities—a new whole—could no longer be resolved into any future unity, but rather restored through that act of translation which characterized both Goethe's world and Mazzini's Europe.[70]

Once the past no longer was to be judged on the basis of Enlightened values taken as absolutes, the Schlegel brothers could also start delving into the riches of literatures and national traditions other than classical ones—the *Niebelungenlied*, the *Edda*, Dante, the Provençal poets, or even the pseudo-Ossian. In the *History of New and Old Literatures*, Friedrich went as far as to call the Middle Ages—so much despised and 'dark' for Enlightenment thinkers—as the 'springtime' of the whole West.[71] As Paolo D'Angelo has further noticed, Herder's historicist opening of the literary field invited also to one more Romantic discovery—that of the Orient (and consequently of Indo-European philology), whose faraway cultural geographies asked to be judged not according to Greek classical norms, as Winckelmann had done, but as autonomous, different expressions whose value had to be measured on the basis of their own specific principles.[72]

Even specific writers long considered 'unreasonable' in light of classical precepts, enlightened reason, and the standards of unities, could now be re-evaluated against

[68] Claudio Guillén, *The Challenge of Comparative Literature* (Cambridge, Mass.: Harvard University Press, 1993), 24.

[69] Adrian Marino, 'Histoire de l'idée de "littérature européenne" et des études européennes', in Béatrice Didier (ed.), *Précis de litérature européenne* (Paris: Presses Universitaires de France, 1998), 14; Yves Chevrel, 'Peut-on écrire une histoire de la littérature européenne?', in Didier, *Précis*, 20.

[70] Mme de Staël, 'De l'esprit des traductions', *Œuvres complétes*, xvii. 1816 (Paris: Treuttel & Wurtz, 1938); Johann Wolfgang von Goethe, 'Some Passages Pertaining the Concept of World Literature', in H. J. Schulz and P. H. Rhein (eds), *Comparative Literature: The Early Years* (Chapel Hill, NC: University of North Carolina Press, 1973), 7; Giuseppe Mazzini, *Life and Writings* (London: Smith, Elder & Co., 1905), 9.

[71] Friedrich von Schlegel, *Geschichte der alten und neuen Literatur: Vorlesungen, gehalten zu Wien im Jahre 1812* (Berlin: Athenaeum, 1841), 200.

[72] Paolo D'Angelo, *L'estetica del romanticism* (Bologna: Mulino, 1997), 56–7.

the judgement of French classicism. Such was the case of Dante[73] and Shakespeare. As Jonathan Arac writes:

> Shakespeare had been criticized in neoclassical criticism for his failure to observe the unities … As Herder put it in the primal text for the German romantic response to Shakespeare, 'whereas in Sophocles's drama the unity of a single action is dominant, Shakespeare aims at the entirety of an event.' The distinction is that Sophocles 'makes a *single tone* predominate,' but in contrast Shakespeare 'uses *all* the characters, estates, walks of life he needs to produce the concerted sound of his drama.'[74]

In short, what historicism had to offer to literature and culture was an expanded geography and a longer history on which to exercise a relative aesthetic judgement. Developing a theme of Winckelmann—the non-repeatability of an artistic epoch in another—Herder's 'Of Taste' claimed the exemplarity of each epoch and place, of each *Volkgeist* with its own right to exist; each with its own values, and each, in fact, with its own 'reasons'—a term that, now historicized as a plural noun, had lost all of a sudden the absolute valence it had had in the historiography of Turgot or Condorcet.

Already in 'Of Taste', however, much more than aesthetic judgement was at stake. All the possibilities and problematics of historicism were already played in it. Because, what does it mean to say that 'what I on the basis of reasons take to be true, beautiful, good, pleasant can likewise on the basis of reasons be regarded by another as false, ugly, bad, unpleasant'? To begin, aesthetics poses already an ethical question here:

> A good, honest man who only knows the world from the market-place, from the coffee-house, and at most out of the *Hamburg Correspondent* is as amazed when he comes upon a story and discovers that manner of thought and taste change with climate, with regions of the earth, and with countries—I say, he is as amazed as Paris can ever be astonished at the arrival of an Indian prince. His astonishment in the end dissolves into laughter: 'But what sort of fanciful stuff' he exclaims 'is there not in books! Who will ever believe this?' Or he takes all these nations to be fools, each in its own way.[75]

Could a man who judges other men from his own relative point of view—from the knowledge acquired from the marketplace, from the coffeehouse, and at most out of the *Hamburg Correspondent*—truly be a good man? And—as the ethical question acquires already geopolitical connotations—can someone judging different nations as 'fools' truly be 'honest' at all? To begin, writes Herder, it is always an 'error when we immediately declare the manner of thought and taste of savages to be fanciful or foolish because it deviates from ours'. But error soon engenders immorality: 'out of ignorance and pride (two dear sisters who never leave each other's side) [they] reject everything

[73] Carlo Dionisotti, *Varia fortuna di Dante: Geografia e storia della letteratura italiana* (Turin: Einaudi, 1967), 255–303.

[74] Arac, *Impure Worlds*, 14.

[75] Herder, *Philosophical Writings*, 247–8.

that contradicts their manner of thought and comprehension. They are so stubborn in support of their opinions and sensations that they are as ready with the names *dumb* and *foolish*'.[76] Pride, the original and most serious of the seven deadly sins and source of all others, makes its way in a mind unable to account for 'the diversity of human beings'.[77] The moral imperative—not a categorical but a relative one—is then predicated on the historicist creed: 'The spirit of changes is the kernel of history'.[78]

In the essay 'Of Taste' there are different cultural geographies that need to be judged in their own right. There are, in other words, nations, whose sovereignty of judgement and cultural self-determination need to be respected. This was undoubtedly the revolution in the *Ius Publicum Europaeum* recorded in 1950 by Carl Schmitt: 'in the 18th and 19th centuries . . . the border between two territorial states of modern European international law did not constitute an exclusion, but rather mutual recognition, above all of the fact that neighboring soil beyond the border was sovereign territory'.[79] What was valid for the law, was also valid for taste and aesthetic judgement. Each nation's taste, writes Herder, is a whole rendered uniform by socialized education—the 'aping of others and a long habituation' to social customs—and by the transmission of national norms from 'ancestors' to 'posterity':[80]

> Every human being in every age thus stands in a middle, so to speak. He can gather about him the extinguished images of his ancestors, he can call forth their shades and, so to speak, make a feast for his eyes when he makes them rustle past before his eyes. But can he also cast a prophetic look into the later times beyond his own grave and, so to speak, see his children and grandchildren walking upon his ashes? History makes the look into the past certain; the prospect into the future is more obscure—but even this shadowy darkness causes pleasure.[81]

The life of the individual, beginning as it were *in medias res*, is then in a historical causal relation with the life of the nation—with its past and tradition; and with its future too, whose history the individual should aspire to make. The individual is then already a 'national allegory',[82] a 'type,' like the character of that new literary genre so indebted to the rise of historicism—the historical novel by Walter Scott:

> For him the historical personality is the representative of an important and significant movement embracing large sections of the people. He is great because his personal passions and personal aims coincide with this great historical movement,

[76] Herder, *Philosophical Writings*, 248.

[77] Herder, *Philosophical Writings*, 249.

[78] Herder, *Philosophical Writings*, 252.

[79] Carl Schmitt, *The Nomos of the Earth in the International Law of the Jus Publicum Europaeum*, tr. G. L. Ulme (New York: Telos Press, 2003), 52.

[80] Herder, *Philosophical Writings*, 252, 253.

[81] Herder, *Philosophical Writings*, 254.

[82] Fredric Jameson, 'Third-World Literature in the Era of Multinational Capitalism', *Social Text*, 15 (1986), 69.

> because he concentrates within himself its positive and negative sides, because he gives to these popular strivings their clearest expression, because he is their standard-bearer in good and in evil.[83]

Also the life of the nation, in turn, is in a historical causal relation with the life of other nations for Herder: nations do not live in isolation, and encounter each other in history. Alas, they often do so presuming with pride their own superiority vis-à-vis the other: they 'believe that everything that they find indispensable because of habituation and education' should be indispensable for the other too[84]—a not too oblique allusion, it seems, to French imperialism's intention to 'transport our revolution' to the whole of Europe.[85]

Once the existence of nations as specific, particular entities with their traditions has been postulated, the only form of cosmopolitanism that Herder's historicism can ever seek is no longer the enlightened progressive reduction and equalization of all differences, but rather the reciprocal acceptance of differences that can only be gained by 'two looks at history [to] dissolve this prejudice'.[86]

However, what is the cost for such dissolution of all prejudices and such embracing of relative values? 'If one were to consider the great diversity that holds sway between opinion and opinion, taste and taste, viewpoint and viewpoint among nations and individual people,' writes Herder, 'then one would almost have to doubt oneself.'[87] The high price that was to be paid, undoubtedly, was clear to Herder himself:

> Could it be that what a nation at one time considers good, fair, useful, pleasant, true it considers at another time bad, ugly, useless, unpleasant, false? And yet this happens! Is not truth, fairness, moral goodness the same at all times? Yes, and yet one observes that propositions for which at certain times each person would have sacrificed his last drop of blood at other times get damned to the fire by precisely the same nation; that fashions which a few years ago each person found fair soon afterwards get hissed off; that ruling customs, that favorite concepts of honor, of merit, of what is useful can blind an age with a magical light, that a taste in these and those sciences can constitute the tone of a century, and yet all this dies with the century. This skepticism should almost put us off trusting our own taste and sensation.[88]

Symptomatically, Herder's writing of the essay on taste breaks off at this point. There is no seeming solution to the impasse but, in theory, to accept its problematic.

The way in which Herder's historicist revolution found its echoes all over Europe can only at this point be summarized rather briefly: once the idea became dominant

83 György Lukács, *The Historical Novel* (Lincoln, Neb.: University of Nebraska Press, 1983), 38.

84 Herder, *Philosophical Writings*, 25.

85 Stuart J. Woolf, 'The Construction of a European World-View in the Revolutionary-Napoleonic Years', *Past and Present*, 137/1 (1992), 78.

86 Herder, *Philosophical Writings*, 255.

87 Herder, *Philosophical Writings*, 249.

88 Herder, *Philosophical Writings*, 256.

that each nation had a specific history, specific values rooted in tradition, and a specific contextual viewpoint from which to give meaning to its past, national histories could proliferate according to these criteria. In each corner of Europe, history became a way to reassess retrospectively a past, or to imagine a future, from a determined national situation.

To give some brief examples, Edmund Burke's *Reflections on the Revolution in France* (1790) would deploy Herder's themes of national traditions pitted against the 'abstractions' of revolutionary France in a relatively conservative key. If Herder's intention had been to theorize a German popular sovereignty *like* that of post-revolutionary France, although not a Germany under French tutelage, for Burke the intention was, quite differently, the preservation of an aristocratic order—but the form of the argument was the same historicist one:

> The people of England will not ape the fashions they have never tried, nor go back to those which they have found mischievous on trial. They look upon the legal hereditary succession of their crown as among their rights, not as among their wrongs; as a benefit, not as a grievance; as a security for their liberty, not as a badge of servitude. They look on the frame of their commonwealth, such as it stands, to be of inestimable value, and they conceive the undisturbed succession of the crown to be a pledge of the stability and perpetuity of all the other members of our constitution.[89]

Exemplary of French historicism in the same reactionary sense are Chateaubriand's *The Genius of Christianity* (1802) and Joseph-Marie de Maistre's *Of Papacy* (1819), both drawing from Herder's—and in general the German Romantics'—exaltation of the Middle Ages in a decidedly anti-revolutionary key. If the Middle Ages had to be re-evaluated against the enlightened indictment, this was so because they offered the best possible model of social organization for Europe: different, autonomous monarchies coordinated by a universal papacy.

Closer to the revolutionary spirit of Herder's historicism was instead, in good part, the Italian case. The very term that Meinecke used in 1936 to label the new historical outlook—*historismus*—was tellingly borrowed from Karl Werner, who had coined it in 1881 to discuss the particular historical method of Giambattista Vico.[90] There has been quite some insistence on the 'miraculous' anticipation of both historicism and Romanticism on the part of Vico.[91] Undoubtedly, there are several commonalities between his *New Science* and Herder's conception of history, starting with their common reaction to enlightened rationalism:

[89] Edmund Burke. *Reflections on the French Revolution; and on the Proceedings in Certain Societies in London Relative to that Event* (London: Dodsley, 1790), 36.

[90] Fulvio Tessitore, *Introduzione a: lo storicismo* (Bari: Laterza, 2009), 4.

[91] Meinecke, *Historism*, 37; Auerbach, 'Vico', 114.

> The poetical irrationalism and the creative imagination of primitive men are concepts common to both; both say that primitive men were poets by their very nature, that their language, their conception of nature and history, their entire life was poetry; both considered enlightened rationalism as unpoetical.[92]

Most likely, however, it was not Vico, but Vincenzo Cuoco's topical reading of the *New Science* in the context of post-revolutionary Italy, which transformed Vico's intuition—that after the Flood the life of the Gentile nations had broken down into different histories, customs, institutions, and forms of knowledge—into a form of 'radical historicism'.[93] Trying to explain the reasons for the failed Neapolitan revolution of 1799, Cuoco wrote a *Historical Essay* (1801) hinging on the notion that the Neapolitan Jacobins had planned a revolution which was 'too French and not Neapolitan enough' to succeed.[94] As for Rousseau and for Herder, what had been good for Paris, was not necessarily good for other histories and geographies such as the Italian one. The same attention to the constitutive forms of the national community, and the same refusal of generalizing abstractions that had characterized Herder's 'How Philosophy Can Become More Universal', were also at work in Cuoco's *Essay*:

> If the constitution, which was guided by abstract ideas of justice, had been based instead on the economic needs and customs of the people; if the revolutionary authorities, instead of speaking a language that the people could not understand, had given them real advantages—maybe, then .... who knows?[95]

But in whatever shape or political colour all new Romantic histories could be conceived, the point is that, as Auerbach once put it, 'historism is a precious (and also a very dangerous) acquisition of the human mind'.[96] If, on the one hand, historicism was 'a revolutionary force which shakes the established order'[97] by demolishing 'prejudices,' discovering otherness, and questioning absolute authority, it was also, on the other hand, a quick descent into the relativistic 'bordello of historicism'.[98] 'Today, we count one hundred opinions,' Cuoco wrote worriedly, 'Tomorrow we will count one hundred and one':

> We oppose ... opinions of a man to another man's opinions; the customs of a people to the customs of another people ... but after so many comparisons and much

92 Auerbach, 'Vico', 115.

93 Fulvio Tessitore, *Nuovi Contributi alla storia e alla teoria dello storicismo* (Rome: Edizione di storia e letteratura, 2002), 91.

94 Vincenzo Cuoco, *Saggio storico sulla rivoluzione di Napoli del 1799* (N.pl.: Tipografia di Francesco Sonzogno, 1806), p. vii; see also his *Platone in Italia*, ed. Antonino De Francesco and Annalisa Andreoni (Bari: Laterza, 2006).

95 Cuoco, *Saggio*, 121–2 (my tr.)

96 Auerbach, 'Vico', 110.

97 Erich Auerbach, *Mimesis: The Representation of Reality in Western Literature*, ed. Willard R Trask, 1946 (Princeton: Princeton University Press, 1974), 270.

98 Walter Benjamin, *Illuminations*, tr. Harry Zohn (London: Pimlico, 1999), 254.

> consideration, confused with so many feelings, so many ideas, so many customs, we can never ever say: 'This is true'.[99]

Twenty years later, Cuoco's friend Alessandro Manzoni, by then well acquainted with the advantages and dangers of historicism (through Dal Busco, Fasano, Mariani, Tellini), put his finger precisely on the implicit peril historicism presented for human social existence. Once judgement can no longer depend on any absolute, not even justice—Don Abbondio is happy to explain in *The Betrothed*—can be 'a question of right or wrong, it's a question of power'.[100] Sure, the narrator's irony does not let the reader fall into complete despair—justice, for Manzoni, is a power above human beings, and in his novel divine providence will make sure that what is right will triumph in the end. Irony—that *Witz* theorized on the pages of the German *Athenaeum* as intimation of a lost absolute—acts as a defence mechanism in front of relativization. It is no surprise, however, that Carl Schmitt could then question exactly such irony, which, refusing to give absolute foundations to right and wrong, let human behaviour vacillate in a perpetual undecidability that only divine intervention could ever solve: 'The origin of Romantic irony lies in the suspension of every decision'.[101]

If the 'saddle time' between two centuries had then been for Schmitt too the 'mutual recognition'[102] of sovereign particularities and the fall of any absolute, then for him the only possibility for decision and action consisted in recognizing that a new law, a new *Nomos of the Earth*, had to be imposed through force alone. The very notion of 'sovereignty', he insisted, is after all a *Grenzbegriff*, a concept bordering potentially with 'the space of the exception'.[103]

Arguably, other solutions than Schmitt's could be found to such Romantic 'irritating contradiction'.[104] Antonio Gramsci for instance, aiming at the formulation of an 'absolute historicism', preferred to consider the latter as a *dialectic* and as an open question, and not, like Schmitt, as a *contradiction* to be solved through the stratagem of the 'state of exception':

99 Cuoco, *Platone*, 284.

100 Alessandro Manzoni, *The Betrothed*, tr. Bruce Penman (Harmondwsorth: Penguin Books, 1972), 53. See Fabio Dal Busco, *La storia e la favola: Il modello manzoniano nel romanzo storico contemporaneo* (Ravenna: Longo, 2007); Pino Fasano, 'L'importazione del romanzo storico in Italia. Scott e Manzoni', *L'imbroglio romanzesco: Una teoria della comunicazione nei Promessi sposi* (Florence: Le Monnier, 2007); Umberto Mariani, 'Evoluzione dello storicismo manzoniano', *Annali d'italianistica*, 3 (1985), 85–96; Gino Tellini, *Manzoni: La storia e il romanzo* (Rome: Salerno, 1979).

101 Carl Schmitt, *Political Romanticism* (New Brunswick, NJ: Transaction Publishers, 2011), 56.

102 Schmitt, *Nomos*, 52.

103 Carl Schmitt, *Political Theology: Four Chapters on the Concept of Sovereignty*, tr. George Schwab (Cambridge, Mass.: MIT Press, 1988), p. xxi.

104 Michael Löwy, *Romanticism Against the Tide of Modernity*, tr. Robert Sayre (Durham, NC: Duke University Press, 2001), 2.

> 'to be above passions and sentiments while living them at the same time' ... this is the kernel of the question of 'historicism' ...: 'how to be critical and men of action at the same time ....'[105]

Recognizing and accepting historicism as a 'question,' however, also required a shift from Romantic irony to a form of passionate and active sarcasm:

> 'Irony' is just for literature, to indicate the detachment of the artist from the sentimental content of his creation. But in the case of historical action, the element of 'irony' would be too literary ... and would indicate a form of detachment connected to a more or less naïve skepticism ... Instead, in this case (in the case of historical action) the characteristic element is 'sarcasm' in a specific form—as a 'passionate' one.[106]

But this is already beyond the temporal limits of Romanticism, and belongs rather to the history of a problematic that the twentieth century simply inherited from the geographies of historical discourse of European Romanticism.

Further Reading

Arac, Jonathan, *Impure Worlds: The Institution of Literature in the Age of the Novel* (New York: Fordham University Press, 2010).

Auerbach, Erich, Mimesis: *The Representation of Reality in Western Literature*, ed. Willard R Trask (Princeton: Princeton University Press, 1974; first publ. 1946).

Auerbach, Erich, 'Vico and Aesthetic Historism', *Journal of Aesthetics and Art Criticism*, 8/2 (1949), 110–18.

Bancheri, Salvatore, *Manzoni and the Historical Novel* (New York: Legas, 2009).

Barfield, Owen, *Saving the Appearances: A Study in Idolatry* (New York: Harcourt, Brace & World, 1965).

Certeau, Michel de, *The Writing of History* (New York: Columbia University Press, 1988).

Chevrel, Yves, 'Peut-on écrire une histoire de la littérature européenne?', in Béatrice Didier (ed.), *Précis de litérature européenne* (Paris: Presses universitaires de France, 1998).

Dainotto, Roberto M., *Place in Literature: Regions, Cultures, Communities* (Ithaca, NY: Cornell University Press, 2000).

Dainotto, Roberto M., *Europe (in Theory)* (Durham, NC: Duke University Press, 2007).

Dal Busco, Fabio, *La storia e la favola: Il modello manzoniano nel romanzo storico contemporaneo* (Ravenna: Longo, 2007).

Damrosch, David, *What is World Literature?* (Princeton: Princeton University Press, 2003).

D'Angelo, Paolo, *L'estetica del romanticismo* (Bologna: Mulino, 1997).

[105] Antonio Gramsci, *Quaderni del carcere*, ed. Valentino Gerratana (Turin: Einaudi, 1975), 1 §28 (my tr.).

[106] Gramsci, *Quaderni del carcere*, 1 §29 (my tr.).

Dionisotti, Carlo, *Varia fortuna di Dante*, Geografia e storia della letteratura italiana (Turin: Einaudi, 1967).

Donato, Eugenio, 'Divine Agonies: Of Representation and Narrative in Romantic Poetics', *Glyph*, 6 (1979), 90–122.

Dunn, John, 'The Identity of the History of Ideas', *Philosophy*, 43/164 (1968), 85–104. <http://www.jstor.org/stable/3748838>.

Dupront, Alphonse, *Spazio e umanesimo*, ed. Gigliola Fragnito (Venice: Marsilio, 1993; orig. publ. 1946).

Ergang, Robert Reinhold, *Herder and the Foundations of German Nationalism* (New York: Octagon Books, 1966).

Fasano, Pino, 'L'importazione del romanzo storico in Italia: Scott e Manzoni', *L'imbroglio romanzesco: Una teoria della comunicazione nei Promessi sposi* (Florence: Le Monnier, 2007).

Foucault, Michel, *The Order of Things* (London: Routledge, 2002; orig. publ. 1972).

Gambarota, Paola, *Irresistible Signs: The Genius of Language and Italian National Identity* (Toronto: University of Toronto Press, 2011).

Getto, Giovanni, *Storia delle storie letterarie* (Florence: Sansoni, 1981).

Gillard, E., 'De l'usage du mot national et, en particulier, de son sens dans l'expression "littérature nationale"', *Cahiers vaudois*, 2 (1914), 5–19.

Goodman, Kevis, 'Romantic Poetry and the Science of Nostalgia', in Maureen N. McLane and James Chandler (eds), *The Cambridge Companion to British Romantic Poetry* (Cambridge: Cambridge University Press, 2008), 195–216.

Gramsci, Antonio, *Quaderni del carcere*, ed. Valentino Gerratana (Turin: Einaudi, 1975).

Guillén, Claudio, *The Challenge of Comparative Literature* (Cambridge, Mass.: Harvard University Press, 1993).

Hartshorne, Richard, 'The Nature of Geography: A Critical Survey of Current Thought in the Light of the Past', *Annals of the Association of American Geographers*, 29/3 (1939), 173–412.

Hazard, Paul, *The European Mind: The Critical Years, 1680–1715*, ed. J. Lewis May (New Haven: Yale University Press, 1953).

Jameson, Fredric, 'Third-World Literature in the Era of Multinational Capitalism', *Social Text*, 15 (1986), 65–88.

Kennedy, Clare, *An Openness towards the Other: Paradox, Aphorism and Desire in the Writings of Novalis and Derrida*, MHRA Texts and Dissertations, 71 (Edinburgh: University of Edinburgh Press, 2006).

Koselleck, Reinhart, *The Practice of Conceptual History: Timing History, Spacing Concepts*, tr. Todd Samuel Presner (Stanford, Calif.: Stanford University Press, 2002).

Koselleck, Reinhart, *Futures Past: On the Semantics of Historical Time*, tr. Keuth Tribe (New York: Columbia University Press, 2004).

Lacoue-Labarthe, Philippe, and Nancy, Jean-Luc, *The Literary Absolute: The Theory of Literature in German Romanticism* (Albany, NY: State University of New York Press, 1988).

Livingstone, David N., *Adam's Ancestors: Race, Religion, and the Politics of Human Origins* (Baltimore: Johns Hopkins University Press, 2008).

Löwy, Michael, *Romanticism Against the Tide of Modernity*, tr. Robert Sayre (Durham, NC: Duke University Press, 2001).

Lukács, György, *The Historical Novel* (Lincoln, Neb.: University of Nebraska Press, 1983).

Malachuk, Daniel S., 'Coleridge's Republicanism and the Aphorism in "Aids to Reflection"', *Studies in Romanticism*, 39/3 (2000), 397–417.

Mariani, Umberto, 'Evoluzione dello storicismo manzoniano', *Annali d'italianistica*, 3 (1985), 85–96.

Marino, Adrian, 'Histoire de l'idée de "littérature européenne" et des études européennes', in Béatrice Didier (ed.), *Précis de litérature européenne* (Paris: Presses Universitaires de France, 1998).

Meinecke, Friedrich, *Historism: The Rise of a New Historical Outlook*, ed. J. E. Anderson and H. D. Schmidt (London: Routledge & Kegan Paul, 1972; orig. publ. 1936).

Placanica, Augusto, *Goethe tra le rovine di Messina* (Palermo: Sellerio, 1987).

Popper, Karl R., *The Open Society and its Enemies* (Princeton: Princeton University Press, 1966).

Rossi, Paolo, *Le sterminate antichità: Studi vichiani* (Pisa: Nistri-Lischi, 1969).

Schmitt, Carl, *Political Theology: Four Chapters on the Concept of Sovereignty*, tr. George Schwab (Cambridge, Mass.: MIT Press, 1988).

Schmitt, Carl, *The Nomos of the Earth in the International Law of the Jus Publicum Europaeum*, tr. G. L. Ulmen (New York: Telos Press, 2003).

Schmitt, Carl, *Political Romanticism* (New Brunswick, NJ: Transaction Publishers, 2011).

Sikka, Sonia, *Herder on Humanity and Cultural Difference: Enlightened Relativism* (New York: Cambridge University Press, 2011).

Sternhell, Zeev, *The Anti-Enlightenment Tradition* (New Haven: Yale University Press, 2010).

Tang, Chenxi, *The Geographic Imagination of Modernity: Geography, Literature, and Philosophy in German Romanticism* (Stanford, Calif.: Stanford University Press, 2008).

Tellini, Gino, *Manzoni: La storia e il romanzo* (Rome: Salerno, 1979).

Tessitore, Fulvio, *Nuovi contributi alla storia e alla teoria dello storicismo* (Rome: Edizione di storia e letteratura, 2002).

Tessitore, Fulvio, *Introduzione a: lo storicismo* (Bari: Laterza, 2009).

White, Hayden V., *Metahistory: The Historical Imagination in Nineteenth-Century Europe* (Baltimore: Johns Hopkins University Press, 1973).

Woolf, Stuart J., 'The Construction of a European World-View in the Revolutionary-Napoleonic Years', *Past and Present*, 137/1 (1992), 72–101.

CHAPTER 33

HISTORIES OF GEOGRAPHY

PAUL STOCK

WHAT does it mean to write about the history of geography? This is not a straightforward question to answer, principally because the word 'geography' can refer both to the physical characteristics of the earth's surface, and to the study and interpretation of those characteristics. When we describe the 'geography' of a space, we are seeking to establish its physical features and arrangement. In empirical terms, therefore, a history of geography might refer to the development of, say, the natural environment in a given period—gradual changes in climate, coastlines, or landforms across geological time. Conversely, it might also refer to the history of a discipline; that is, the academic study of a subject called 'geography' which attempts to analyse the world's properties within codified parameters. Related to this, a history of geography might refer more generally to historical understandings of space: how humans have sought to interpret the world and intervene in it—an enormous topic which might incorporate, among other things, ideas about territory, borders, and attitudes to the environment. Clearly there are a number of complexities here, regarding not only the object of 'geographical' analysis, but also the methods most suitable to acquire geographical knowledge. Indeed, these are issues which still preoccupy the modern discipline with its broad diversity of mathematical and humanistic approaches. What I want to show here is that significant epistemological and methodological questions—questions about knowledge acquisition, and the perception and interpretation of the world—are at the heart of geographical enquiry in the Romantic period. Having outlined the principal trends and tensions in geographical thought, I will then show how two contemporary maps use different methods to justify and represent the limits of 'European' space. Importantly too, I will suggest how an understanding of geographical epistemologies—with their different assumptions about how to comprehend and intervene in the world—can help us interpret the tumultuous political events of the period.

How can we find out what Europeans in the Romantic period thought about geography? Perhaps the best place to look is in geographical texts from the period—specifically, books which attempt to describe the whole earth, and, in doing so, set out methodologies for geographical study. The production of such books increased significantly in the late eighteenth and early nineteenth centuries. Confining ourselves to works in English for a moment, between 1650 and 1770 geographical books for adults (i.e. non-schoolbooks) were published at a rate of roughly four per decade. The 1780s alone, however, saw the publication of thirteen geographical works, followed by another thirteen in the 1790s and fourteen between 1800 and 1810. The pattern is similar in works produced for younger readers or for use in schools. Between 1670 and 1770, there were nineteen such geographies published in Britain, but between 1770 and 1830 there were sixty-two such new titles. These figures do not include multiple editions: for instance, William Guthrie's *New Geographical, Historical and Commercial Grammar*, first published in 1770, went through forty-five editions by 1827.[1] The pattern can perhaps partly be explained by more general increases in book production in the period, and it also seems likely that contemporary events—such as Captain Cook's voyages and prolonged global conflict—stoked interest in reading about different parts of the world.[2] Evidently though, the market for books about 'geography' was sufficiently robust to sustain frequent production of texts with very similar purposes and content.

Working out who might have actually read these books is, of course, a slightly more difficult prospect. Notwithstanding the dangers of discerning readers' identities from the internal evidence of texts, the vast majority of these geographical books make explicit statements about who might benefit from them. They usually present themselves as practical guides for people who need to be well-informed about the world for professional reasons: statesmen, soldiers, merchants, and naturalists. Crucially, though, they also communicate a 'necessary branch of education' for 'people of *every* rank' from 'the lady's library to the tradesman's parlour'.[3] In this respect, geographical books are not straightforwardly elite books, and while there are lavishly expensive editions for limited consumption, there are also a great many cheap titles on poor-quality paper targeting educational and non-elite readerships. It would be naïve to assume that these books straightforwardly express 'popular' mentalities, but on the other hand, their intended reach and evident commercial viability helps us to approximate broad cultural assumptions about geographical ideas in the period. Another key point concerns the internationalism of these texts. Just as the *Encyclopédie* began life as a translation of Chambers's *Cyclopedia*, so too did geographical works freely adapt, borrow, and translate from books in various languages. For example, Anton Friedrich Büsching's *Neue Erdbeschreibung* (1754–68), and Conrad Malte-Brun's *Géographie Universelle* (1810–29) became particularly important source-texts for works in English.[4] Furthermore, some authors employed broad ranges of

[1] Statistics are drawn from O. F. G. Sitwell, *Four Centuries of Special Geography* (Vancouver: UBC Press, 1993), 16–23, 273–84.

[2] William St Clair, *The Reading Nation in the Romantic Period* (Cambridge: Cambridge University Press, 2004), esp. ch. 6.

[3] E. and J. Bruce, *An Introduction to Geography and Astronomy* (Newcastle: Longman, 1805), p. xxiii; Christopher Kelley, *New and Complete System of Universal Geography* (London: Thomas Kelley, 1814–17), i, preface.

[4] Büsching was translated into English twice (in 1762 and in 1778) and was cited by, e.g. the *New and Complete System of Universal Geography* (1796); and John Pinkerton's *Modern Geography* (1802). Rival publishers even alleged that Guthrie's *Geographical Grammar* plagiarized Büsching: see Richard B. Sher,

texts in several languages to compile their works.[5] Indeed, all are drawing on a common stock of classical and Renaissance texts—including Strabo, Pliny, Ptolemy, Münster, and Ortelius—which influenced both the content and procedure of 'geographical' writing. What this means is that, while geographical works in the Romantic period sometimes indulge in patriotic sentiment—proclaiming their country of publication to be superior and so on—they are not uniformly or simplistically 'nationalist' texts, as they often incorporate broader traditions not delimited to particular states or local perspectives.

How, though, do these books write about geography? How do they define their purposes, and how do they structure and present geographical knowledge? Perusal of their contents pages might initially suggest an extraordinary lack of focus: they cover subjects as diverse as astronomy, political constitutions, inhabitants' 'moral character', and other topics which stretch twenty-first-century conceptions of the discipline. In fact, however, as Robert Mayhew has argued, geography books are 'defined very tightly' in this period, operating within established conventions which mandate coverage of specific topics.[6] In this respect, we need to explore the paradigms and expectations which filter and organize spatial knowledge in the period.

A key figure for this investigation is Bernhard Varen (1622–50), the German-born geographer who lived and worked in the Netherlands from 1645. What makes Varen significant is that his two books *Descriptio Regni Japoniae et Siam* (1649) and *Geographia generalis* (1650) together make a rare and explicit statement about the aims and scope of early-modern geographical study.[7] For Varen, geography is 'a science mixed with mathematics, which teaches about the quantitative states of the earth and of the parts of the earth'. As a result, he distinguishes between *general* or *universal* geography, and *special* or *particular* geography. The former 'studies the earth in general, describing ... the phenomena which affect it as a whole': the form and dimensions of the earth; the distribution of lands and water; as well as general questions about latitude, longitude, and climactic zones. By contrast, particular geography focuses on specific places and is subdivided into three broad categories. The first, 'terrestrial', concerns physical dimensions and features: the limits, bounds, and situation of places, and the mountains, rivers, forests, and creatures within them. The 'celestial' category studies a place in relation to the stars: its distance from the equator and poles, its climactic zone, the motion of stars from that position, and so on. Lastly, 'human' particulars focus on inhabitants: their customs,

The Enlightenment and the Book: Scottish Authors and their Publishers in Eighteenth-Century Britain, Ireland and America (Chicago: Chicago University Press, 2006), 156. Malte-Brun (translated 1822–33) is described as 'the most illustrious geographer of modern times' by James Bell's *System of Geography* (Glasgow: Fullarton, 1832), i. 1.

[5] Robert Mayhew, 'Mapping Science's Imagined Community: Geography as a Republic of Letters, 1600–1800', *British Journal for the History of Science*, 38 (2005), 73–92. For a sample source-list, see John Bigland, *A Geographical and Historical View of the World* (London: Longman, 1810), i, pp. ix–xiii.

[6] Robert Mayhew, *Enlightenment Geography: The Political Languages of British Geography, 1650–1850* (Basingstoke: Macmillan, 2000), 32.

[7] See Margret Schuchard (ed.), *Bernhard Varenius (1622–1650)* (Leiden: Brill, 2007).

capacities, government, and histories.[8] These specifications had their roots in ancient sources: Ptolemy's *Geographia* distinguished between the mathematical methods of 'geography', concerned with measuring the whole world, and the descriptive approach of 'chorography', which focused on particular places.[9] However, Varen's expanded designations were, and still are, enormously influential. Though the exact terminology varies, almost all eighteenth- and nineteenth-century geographical works include information on astronomy, the natural world, and human societies: Büsching talks about mathematical, natural, and civil description of the earth; James Playfair divides the subject into mathematical, historical, and 'physical or natural' branches; while Malte-Brun uses the terms *mathématique*, *physique*, and *politique* in his review of different approaches.[10] Even the most recent edition of the *Oxford English Dictionary* (1989) lists the common divisions of the discipline as 'mathematical', 'physical', and 'political' ('geography', definition 1a).

Significantly, these frameworks for geographical enquiry suggest different approaches to the understanding of space. Varen's 'celestial' category—like his 'general' geography—uses universal mathematical laws to interpret the world. Space is understood in terms of abstract calculation premised upon geometric and astronomical principles, and not in terms of materiality, superficial content, or sensation. For example, climate is often defined as 'a certain space upon the surface of the terrestrial globe contained between two parallels, and so far distant from each other that the longest day in one differs half an hour from the longest day in the other parallel'. In other words, it has nothing to do with 'the seasons [or] the quality of the soil': mathematical principles are what distinguish different climactic zones.[11] Sometimes whole continents are understood as geometric shapes. Africa is commonly referred to as a 'pyramid', and some books even describe Asia as a 'cone' and Europe as an 'oblong square'.[12] These phrases define the continents as idealized abstractions, paying relatively little attention to material physicality.

By contrast, Varen's 'terrestrial' category is driven by observation of the physical environment: it defines spaces by the contents of the 'natural world'. Setting the aside the problem of whether it is possible to perceive the world directly, or whether such perception is always filtered and distorted by human senses, the implication here is that the world and its contents are 'out there' in an objective form, separate from, but readily

[8] William Warntz, 'Newton, the Newtonians, and the Geographia Generalis Varenii', *Annals of the Association of American Geographers*, 79/2 (1989), 165–91; J. N. L. Baker, *The History of Geography* (Oxford: Blackwell 1963), 105–18.

[9] Lucia Nuti, 'Mapping Places: Chorography and Vision in the Renaissance', in Denis Cosgrove (ed.), *Mappings* (London: Reaktion, 1999), 90.

[10] Büsching, *A New System of Geography* (London: Millar, 1762), i. 6, 12; James Playfair, *A System of Geography* (Edinburgh: Hill, 1808–14), i, pp. i–ii; Malte-Brun, *Précis de la géographie universelle* (Paris: Buisson, 1810–29), i. 6–7.

[11] *A New Historical and Commercial System of Geography* (Manchester: Sowler & Russell, 1800), p. viii.

[12] Guthrie, *Grammar* (1770), 515; Thomas Bankes et al., *A New Royal Authentic and Complete System of Geography* (London: Cooke [1787/8]), 107; John Smith, *A System of Modern Geography* (London: Sherwood, 1810–11), i. 4.

comprehensible by, humans. In epistemological terms, the emphasis is on empirical experience and observation as the principal means to gather and organize knowledge. Indeed, many works place a high premium on first-hand travel accounts as sources.[13] Particular spaces are therefore defined by their material characteristics: the number of mountains, the length of rivers, the quality of soil, the variety of animals, and so on. Information is observed, collected and delivered, rather than being deduced or calculated by universal mathematical laws.

Lastly, Varen's 'human' particulars—with their focus on customs, government, and history—place human activity and perception at the centre of understandings of space. In other words, spaces are defined by human action and intervention: the construction of towns and borders, for example, or the performance of certain social practices. The epistemological implications of this are significant. In 'terrestrial' geography, spaces and their contents are seen, at least on the surface, as being distinct from their observers. But here, human activities, priorities, and perspectives—including those of the observer—structure how spaces are viewed and understood. In this sense, 'geography' is a human construct, both in the sense that it concerns human intervention in the world, and, more fundamentally, in that it is premised upon interpretative parameters grounded in human perceptions rather than the 'objective' world. In his work on natural history, Oliver Goldsmith says that merely discovering the productions of nature is 'dry, mechanical and incomplete'. But an outline of the 'properties, manners and relations, *which they bear to us*' 'exhibits new pictures to the imagination, and improves our relish for existence by widening the prospect of nature around us'.[14] Goldsmith speaks in terms of 'pictures' and 'prospects', that is to say, constructed perspectives: nature is interpreted and comprehended in terms of its relationship with human observers and their intellectual frameworks. To take another example, Michael Adams says that, in his work, 'the prospect of all the objects will be rendered clear and distinct by the aptness of their arrangement, and the beautiful order of their succession'.[15] In other words, beauty and order lie in the medium and the perspectives offered by it, not directly in the world itself.

Overall, then, Varen's different approaches to geographical study engage with a number of critical issues, including the methods of knowledge gathering, the concept of 'objectivity', and the nature of human perception. It would be misleading to suggest that they present fully articulated positions in an explicit debate; instead, such questions shape a conceptual framework which underpins the way geographical works define and set about their tasks. Nor should we assume that these different approaches are mutually exclusive; indeed, Varen's purpose is to articulate the various methods which can together comprise geographical knowledge. Most geographical books, for example, include a standard section on the two meanings of the word 'horizon'. The 'rational

[13] Some geographical works are effectively edited collections of travel writings. See Cavendish Pelham, *The World, or the Present State of the Universe* (London: Stratford: 1810).

[14] Oliver Goldsmith, *An History of the Earth and Animated Nature* (London: Nourse, 1774), i, p. I; my emphasis.

[15] Michael Adams, *New Royal System of Universal Geography* (London: Hogg, 1794), p. vii.

horizon' refers to the mathematical division of the earth into two equal parts; the 'sensible horizon' to the apparent edge of the earth visible from 'the very place whereon we stand'—that is, the horizon comprehensible by human senses.[16] At such moments, authors acknowledge the different implications of diverse methodologies, but also incorporate both—with their tensions—in the corpus of geographical enquiry. In summary then, geography books engage with some of the key epistemological questions of the Enlightenment and Romanticism: the legitimacy of using universalized laws to interpret reality; the relative merits of pure mathematics and eyewitness observation as means to acquire knowledge; the problem of whether order is intrinsic to the world or an imposition by human systems. We are used to thinking about these questions as the province of elite texts. Here, however, we can see how they both inform and are reflected in popular, high-circulation works intended for utilitarian consumption and educational use.

I now want to amplify these implications by turning to an example especially relevant to a volume on European Romanticism. How do the different approaches I have mentioned affect understandings of European space? How are they related to the political and ideological concerns of the period? Consider these two maps of Europe, both from geography books of the kind just discussed.

One, 'A Map of Europe from the Best Authorities' is from Michael Adams's *New Royal System of Universal Geography* (1794), though the same plate appears to have been previously used in John Seally's *Complete Geographical Dictionary* (1783–4) (Figure 33.1). The other, titled 'An Accurate Map of Europe Compiled from the Best Authorities 1791', is from the ninth edition of Richard Brookes's *The General Gazetteer, or Compendious Geographical Dictionary* (1795). As the title suggests, the plate was in fact first used in the earlier, seventh, edition of 1791 (Figure 33.2).[17] On the surface, these two maps look extremely similar to the point of being nearly identical. They both depict the whole continent of Europe stretching from Iceland to western Russia. They also show surrounding parts of Asia and Africa, though these areas are blank, whereas Europe itself is filled with names (of states and cities) and major topographical features. Both maps overlay the region with a graticule of longitude and latitude, thus placing Europe within the context of an unseen globe comprehensible by mathematical laws. Significantly too, the maps place a strong emphasis on rivers, which are by far the most prominent topographical features on the maps. This, in fact, reflects a theory common to many geography books—that multiple rivers are a defining characteristic of Europe. Rivers apparently facilitate 'intercourse and commerce between different nations', but also 'check the progress of conquest of despotism', thus explaining the prevalence of trade in Europe and the supposed absence of 'oriental' tyrants.[18] In this respect, we can see the influence of

[16] Richard Brookes, *The General Gazetteer* (London: Newbury, 1762), p. vi.

[17] Barbara Backus McCorkle, *A Carto-Bibliography of the Maps in Eighteenth-Century British and American Geography Books* (Lawrence, Kan.: University of Kansas Digital Publishing, 2009), entry nos. 28, 26, 4, and 3: <http://hdl.handle.net/1808/5564>.

[18] See e.g. Guthrie, *Geographical Grammar*, 9th edn (London: Dilly et al., 1785), 59.

FIGURE 33.1 'A Map of Europe from the Best Authorities', from Michael Adams, *New Royal System of Universal Geography* (London, 1794). Courtesy: Library of Congress, G114.A21

FIGURE 33.2 'An Accurate Map of Europe Compiled from the Best Authorities 1791', from Richard Brookes, *The General Gazetteer, or Compendious Geographical Dictionary*, 9th edn (1795). Courtesy: Library of Congress, G102.B87 1795

environmentalist thought: the belief—often particularly associated with Jean Bodin and Montesquieu—that environmental circumstances directly affect the development of cultures and individuals.[19] It is also notable that both maps, and particularly the later one in Brookes, do not show state borders very clearly, if at all. I will return to this apparent lack of interest in state territoriality in due course.

Presently though, I want to focus on the eastern edge of Europe as depicted in both maps; that is, the border between Europe and Asia. The border is not identical in the two maps, but follows a very similar trajectory. Starting in the Black Sea and the Sea of Azov, it follows the River Don for a short distance before traversing to the River Volga. It then continues north, joins the rough location of the Ural mountains, and follows them to the Arctic Circle. By beginning with the Sea of Azov and the Don, these maps tap into an ancient tradition which saw the Don (or Tanais) as marking the limit of Europe. According to some authorities, including Strabo and Ptolemy, the river originated somewhere in the far north near the Northern Ocean and, consequently, formed a barrier of water between Asia and Europe. However, as information about the region grew, the apparent absence of such a definitive demarcation provoked much speculation about alternative sites for the border. In the 1570s, for example, Ortelius proposed a simple straight line linking the Don to the White Sea by Archangel, whereas fifty years later, Philip Clüver suggested the River Ob in Siberia as the probable northern boundary. In the mid-seventeenth century, French cartographer Nicholas Sanson even argued for a boundary-line connecting the White Sea to the River Dnieper in modern Ukraine—thus placing Moscow firmly in Asia. As W. H. Parker explains, controversy about the Europe–Asian boundary continues to the present day: while 'there were at various times prevailing boundaries, each had many variations and rivals ... There was never general agreement about any particular boundary.'[20]

Amidst these uncertainties, the fact that both the Adams map and the Brookes map settle on a similar trajectory is significant. Their chosen line follows very closely the one prescribed by the Swedish military officer Philip Johann von Strahlenberg in his *Das Nord-und Ostliche Theil von Europa und Asia* (1730). Captured in 1709 during the Great Northern War (1700–21), Strahlenberg mapped Russia on behalf of Peter the Great, eventually returning to Sweden to publish his work. Decrying other proposed boundaries as 'fictitious', Strahlenberg settled on the Urals as the most readily comprehensible dividing line. Not only do the mountains separate lands which differ in 'situation and surface', but they also connect with the River Volga's 'high and remarkable shore' and from there to 'a chain of very high mountains' linked to the Don and the Caucasus. In this way, mountains and rivers form 'the visible marks of the bounds between Europe and Asia.'[21] It is surely no coincidence that Strahlenberg's border places a larger section

[19] See Charles Withers, *Placing the Enlightenment: Thinking Geographically about the Age of Reason* (Chicago: Chicago University Press, 2007), 135; David N. Livingstone, *The Geographical Tradition: Episodes in the History of a Contested Enterprise* (Oxford: Blackwell, 1992), 97, 121–4.

[20] W. H. Parker, 'Europe: How Far?, *Geographical Journal*, 126/3 (1960), 278, 281–2.

[21] Strahlenberg, *An Historico-Geographical Description of the North and Eastern Parts of Europe and Asia* (London: Innys & Manby, 1738), 121–2.

of Russia firmly in Europe, and thus serves Peter's wider objective to 'recast the geopolitical self-image of the country' in European terms.[22] The fact that the Adams and Brookes maps reproduce this border suggests the spread and success of this ideological mission: they both show Russia as residing solidly in European space, and thus as a participant in European affairs. Indeed, the Urals boundary would go on to be employed by Immanuel Kant, Malte-Brun, and others deep into the nineteenth century.[23]

Where the two maps differ, however, is in the *way* they depict the European–Asia border. The Adams/Seally map emphasizes the Urals themselves, showing a single uninterrupted line of mountains running from the Arctic to the Volga. Importantly too, they are by far the largest mountains shown: the Alps are tiny in comparison, and the Pyrenees and the Carpathians are the only other ranges on the map. The effect is to grant the Urals both symbolic and material significance: unlike the Alps, they are a physical barrier separating two continents. This implies that the division between Europe and Asia is a natural one, clearly denoted by the obvious physical properties of the earth. In other words, borders are inscribed into the land—they are part of a natural order, perhaps even purposely created according to a divine plan. Of course, there is a sleight-of-hand taking place in that the map depicts the Urals in an exaggerated and stylized manner in order to emphasize their supposed empirical significance. Nonetheless, we can detect here the epistemological implications of Varen's 'terrestrial' geography: specifically, that humans gain knowledge about the world by observing the signs and details intrinsic to the natural order. The task of human learning is therefore to observe the earth and its content closely and discern their inherent purposes and qualities.

This has political implications particularly resonant in the revolutionary period. If borders are engraved in the earth, then this adds credibility to the concept of 'natural frontiers': the idea that certain borders are determined by natural features and that states should fulfil their proper destiny by expanding to fill them. This notion had strong currency in Ancien Régime and revolutionary Europe. Peter Sahlins has shown how 'the idea of natural frontiers was a powerful, recurrent image in the shifting repertoire of French political culture', serving to 'shape the concept of a unified state'. Montesquieu and Rousseau make reference to the 'limites naturelles' of states, and the concept appears to have influenced French expansion and diplomacy in the seventeenth and eighteenth centuries, even featuring in the geographical writings of the royal tutors. In the 1790s, the revolutionaries spoke about 'the ancient and natural limits of France … the Rhine, the Alps and the Pyrenees'.[24] For example, in a debate about whether to incorporate Savoy into the French Republic, the Abbé Grégoire advised the National

[22] Mark Bassin, 'Russia between Europe and Asia: The Ideological Construction of Geographical Space', *Slavic Review*, 50/1 (1991), 5–7. The Ural border was further championed in the 1730s by the Russian historian Vasilii N. Tatishchev.

[23] Parker, 'Europe: How Far?', 286.

[24] Peter Sahlins, 'Natural Frontiers Revisited: France's Boundaries since the Seventeenth Century', *American Historical Review*, 95/5 (1990), 1450, 1430–46; Norman J. G. Pounds, 'France and "Les Limites Naturelles" from the Seventeenth to the Twentieth Centuries', *Annals of the Association of American Geographers*, 44/1 (1954), 51–5.

Convention to 'peruse the archives of nature, to see what the law permits to you, what duty prescribes to you in this regard'.[25] Taken at face value, the implication here is that political practice should follow the guidance of the natural world. Some historians have been tempted to see 'natural frontiers' merely as a rhetorical veneer to the hard calculations of *realpolitik*.[26] Clearly, it would be unwise to discount this in all cases, but nor should we necessarily assume that such ideas are disingenuous. Perhaps a 'territorial' view of geography—in which the earth presents signs to be interpreted—here inspires certain approaches to foreign policy and international relations. In this respect we might see how specific kinds of geographical knowledge can frame and underpin political ideas and activity. Indeed, as Sahlins notes, the interest in natural frontiers marks an important shift in the self-conception of early-modern states—a gradual movement away from feudal kingdoms of accumulated rights and 'overlapping jurisdictions', and towards notions of a shared polity marked by 'bounded, delimited territory'.[27]

In summary then, the Adams/Seally map shows the edge of Europe as a natural border marked by the Ural mountains. The Brookes map is very different. The Europe–Asia border is in roughly the same place, but it does not follow any natural feature: indeed, the Urals are not shown at all. Instead, the border intersects otherwise empty space in what some contemporary texts describe as an 'arbitrary line'.[28] This suggests that any division between Europe and Asia is not founded on objective natural features, but is rather a human imposition. In this respect, borders are contrivances of human culture: they are a creative intervention in the world derived from human politics and history, rather than something intrinsic to the natural order. Evidently, this has quite different epistemological implications to the Adams map. Rather than receiving knowledge by reading the pre-existent signs of nature, humans here impose categories onto the world in order to make sense of it. In other words, we understand the world by inventing terms of reference—and this includes the idea that 'Europe' and 'Asia' are discrete and identifiable spaces. As the *Edinburgh Encyclopaedia* (1830) says rather carefully, 'Europe is the name given to one of the four great divisions into which geographers have divided the earth'.[29] In effect, 'Europe' is something determined by geographers' disciplinary practices, not by observations of the natural environment.

Ultimately, these issues are related to a long-running philosophical debate about whether humans understand the world via perception or conception. This was a topic of great interest to humanist and Enlightenment thinkers, from Francis Bacon's focus on empirical observation to David Hume's scepticism about the reliability of sense experience. Later, of course, it would become a key Romantic theme—we need only think of the famous moment in the *Prelude* when Wordsworth crosses the Alps and reflects

[25] '... *compulser les archives de la nature, voir ce que le droit vous permet, ce que le devoir vous prescrit à cet égard*' (my tr.). Cited in Pounds, 'France and "Les Limites Naturelles"', 54.

[26] See Gaston Zeller 'La monarchie d'ancien régime et les frontières naturelles', *Revue d'histoire moderne*, 8 (1933), 305–33; and 'Histoire d'une idée fausse', *Revue de synthèse*, 11–12 (1936), 115–31.

[27] Sahlin, 'Natural Frontiers', 1424, 1427.

[28] John Pinkerton, *Modern Geography* (London: Cadel & Davies, 1802), i. 2; ii. 465.

[29] David Brewster (ed.), *The Edinburgh Encyclopaedia* (Edinburgh: Blackwood, 1830), ix. 235.

on the relationship between the observed scene and the power of his own imagination. Moreover, this debate also has implications for political practice, especially foreign policy. If borders are not naturally inscribed in the earth, and are instead the products of human imposition as the Brookes map implies, then they can be changed according to political expediency. Every historical period sees new polities and regimes, but the extent of large-scale territorial change in the revolutionary and Napoleonic period is remarkable. An exhaustive summary would require much patience, but in brief France expanded aggressively in the 1790s, absorbing the Austrian Netherlands, the Rhineland, Savoy, and Nice. A number of satellite states were founded under French influence or occupation: the United Provinces became the Batavian Republic and the Swiss Confederacy the Helvetic Republic; in Italy, the Venetian Republic, the Republic of Genoa, the Papal States, and the Kingdom of Naples were abolished and replaced with the Cisalpine, Ligurian, Roman, and Parthenopean Republics respectively. In eastern Europe, Russia, Austrian, and Prussia divided Poland between them, removing it from the map of Europe until its reconstitution in 1918.

Under Napoleon, significant changes continued apace, with more French annexations in the Netherlands, Italy, Spain, and the German states, and new states allied to France, including the Kingdom of Westphalia in northern Germany and the Duchy of Warsaw on former Polish land. Most notably, Napoleon dissolved the Holy Roman Empire, replacing its hundreds of tiny statelets with the Confederation of the Rhine. After Napoleon's defeat the victorious powers reapportioned Europe again at the Congress of Vienna, though in some respects the settlement was characterized as much by new acquisitions and confirmation of Napoleonic changes as by restoration of the Ancien Régime.[30] In short, the continuous wars and treaties of this period meant that borders were open to constant reinterpretation and redesignation: they are the products of human contrivances and endeavours, not fixed by natural laws. Perhaps this is the reason why Adams's *System of Geography* (1794) and Brookes's *General Gazetteer* (1795) both use map plates which make relatively little attempt to outline state territoriality precisely; it is a strategy to cope with unpredictable change. As John Pinkerton says in his *Modern Geography* (1802), describing the present state of European affairs is like 'writing on the sands of a troubled ocean, as the whole may be radically changed in the short space that this sheet is in the press'.[31]

In general terms, the different representations of the Europe–Asia border on these two maps reflect wider uncertainties about how to define and understand borders in the period. This was a question of particular urgency, not merely thanks to the tumult of international conflict, but also due to the intensification of state-building preceding and resulting from those wars. In some respects we can detect rising interest in identifying and enforcing both 'natural' and 'arbitrary' borders. In the late seventeenth and eighteenth centuries, 'maps came to be increasingly used in diplomatic business'

[30] For an excellent summary, see Charles J. Esdaile, *The French Wars: 1792–1815* (London: Routledge, 2001).

[31] Pinkerton, *Modern Geography*, i. 253.

and, as a consequence, 'a firmer grasp of the nature of a linear frontier developed'. This, in turn, contributed to 'a more spatially territorial' conception of statehood; indeed, one might see the definition of 'linear boundaries' as a critical component in wider ideas about 'undivided sovereignty' and the uniformity required by state centralization. For some historians, the French Revolution marks a decisive phase in this process, with its creation of new administrative boundaries, abolition of feudal jurisdictions, and attempts to introduce a universal legal code.[32] As the wars continued, a number of states—especially France and Britain—became concerned to regulate travel and distinguish 'familiar' people from strangers by issuing and passports and travel permits.[33] Underpinning this is an assumption that particular people 'belong' to certain spaces; indeed, that individuals are defined by their containment within specific boundaries. We can also detect increasing interest in economic borders, designed to control the movement of goods and to maximize taxation revenues. The most well-known example is Napoleon's Continental Blockade (1806–13), a large-scale attempt to exclude British goods from French-controlled markets, which stemmed from a longer tradition of maritime and economic warfare. The Blockade required quarantined trading zones and watertight customs barriers, though in the event it was undermined by a lack of sufficient naval and customs resources.[34] In this respect, the reach of centralized power had not caught up with the ambitions of theoretical interest in borders.

All of this might suggest a relentless drive towards tightly defined bordered spaces—a process sometimes proclaimed as central characteristic of modernity.[35] In other respects, however, we can note a strong interest in erasing or breaking down borders—and not simply in the events that saw borders rearranged by military and diplomatic strategy. On the one hand, centralized state-building requires a firmer delineation between countries, but also demands the removal of different taxation and jurisdictional regimes *within* states in order to confirm central control. The French revolutionaries divided France into new *départements* in 1790 precisely in order to abolish the administrative, judicial, and fiscal subdivisions of the Ancien Régime and to both create and control an idea of shared 'national space' governed by the revolutionary centre. Crucially, the *départements* were initially based on a grid scheme and then modified and named according prominent natural features—a technique which tries to evoke mathematical and topographical certainties even as it radically redesigns political and administrative spaces.[36] Napoleon's

[32] Jeremy Black, 'Boundaries and Conflict: International Relations in *ancien régime* Europe', in Carl Grundy-Warr (ed.), *World Boundaries*, iii. *Eurasia* (London: Routledge, 1994), 19–54.

[33] Andreas Fahrmeir, *Citizenship: The Rise and Fall of a Modern Concept* (New Haven: Yale, 2007), 46–50.

[34] Geoffrey Ellis, *The Napoleonic Empire*, 2nd edn (New York: Palgrave Macmillan, 2003), 109–19.

[35] See David Turnbull, 'Cartography and Science in Early Modern Europe: Mapping the Construction of Knowledge Spaces', *Imago Mundi*, 48 (1996), 5–24.

[36] Michael Heffernan, 'The Changing Political Map: Geography, Geopolitics and the Idea of Europe since 1500', in R. A. Butlin and R. A. Dodgshon (eds), *An Historical Geography of Europe* (Oxford: Clarendon Press, 1998), 151–3; Joseph Konvitz, *Cartography in France 1660–1848: Science, Engineering and Statecraft* (Chicago: Chicago University Press, 1987), 43–5.

preference for highly centralized government is well known, but his expansion of common practices across Europe—for example, his introduction of French-based legal codes in the Italian states, Poland, and elsewhere—might be seen as a sustained attempt to break down (inter)national division in favour of centralized uniformity. Some have even interpreted Napoleonic rule as an exercise in European integration, though this perhaps underestimates the degree of French primacy involved.[37] In ideological terms too, we must remember the universalism integral to political debate in the period. The 'Declaration of the Rights of Man and of the Citizen' begins with a reference to 'the French people', but then issues imperatives for 'all men', 'all citizens', and 'any society'.[38] This is a manifesto which recognizes no boundaries and explicitly wants to abolish localized distinctions in favour of universalized principles. Indeed, as Volney remarks in his *Les ruines, ou méditations sur les révolutions des empires* (1791), 'the communication of knowledge will extend from society to society till it comprehends the whole earth. By the law of imitation, the example of one people will be followed by others, who will adopt its spirit and its laws ... and civilisation will be universal.'[39] In 1792, the French revolutionary government even professed universalism to be a cornerstone of its foreign policy, allowing France to assist 'all peoples wishing to regain their liberty'—though there is considerable historiographical dispute about the practical impact of this declaration.[40]

To sum up, the revolutionary and Napoleonic periods saw considerable debate about the role and significance of borders. The international conflict and state centralizations crucial to the period both act to solidify and dissolve (different kinds of) borders, and the different emphases of the Adams and the Brookes maps tap into these contemporary developments. It is significant too that these issues are foregrounded in depictions of the Europe–Asia border. The idea of Europe had long been a problematic issue, but recent scholarship has suggested heightened interest throughout this period in the unity, disunity, and limits of a space called 'Europe'. The late eighteenth and early nineteenth centuries, 'with [their] prolonged military and ideological conflicts, oversaw profound debate about Europe's history and potential future', evident in various media from literary texts to newspapers and diplomatic correspondence.[41] In this respect, the maps participate in wider contemporary concerns, offering different ideas about Europe premised upon 'natural' and 'human' interpretations of space.

Overall, my point is that the maps' different depictions of the Europe–Asia border represent very different ways of understanding the world and gaining knowledge about it. Underpinning this is an epistemological debate about the perception and conception of spaces—an issue which has its roots in continuing methodological discussions about the purposes and scope of geographical study. Nor is this merely an intellectual matter.

[37] Stuart Woolf, *Napoleon's Integration of Europe* (London: Routledge, 1991).

[38] Lynn Hunt, *Inventing Human Rights: A History* (New York: Norton, 2007), 16–17.

[39] Comte de Volney, *The Ruins, or a Survey of the Revolutions of Empires, Translated from the French* (London: Searle, [1795]), 115–16.

[40] T. C. W. Blanning, *The Origins of the French Revolutionary Wars* (London: Longman, 1986), 136–7.

[41] Paul Stock, *The Shelley-Byron Circle and the Idea of Europe* (New York: Palgrave Macmillan, 2010), 10. See also Roberto Dainotto, *Europe (In Theory)* (Durham, NC: Duke University Press, 2007).

I have tried to suggest that these questions have a bearing on contemporary geopolitical activity; that questions about how to interpret and study geographical spaces are integral to contemporary considerations of, say, borders and state-building. This is not to imply that geographical texts and their methodological concerns directly inspire politicians in some teleological sense, although evidently some authors hoped that their books would exert such influence. Rather, it is to situate the contemporary events of international politics—large-scale state formation, interest in 'natural borders', or borderlessness universalism—within a wider set of questions about how humans understand and influence the world.

Importantly, these debates are articulated not simply in elite and specialist texts, but in geographical books for a wider readership, including educational and general reference volumes. This means that geography in the period is alive to some of the crucial philosophical issues of the late Enlightenment and Romanticism. Romantic interest in subjective human experiences, for example, can be seen not in terms of a 'reaction' to the supposed rationalism of the eighteenth century, but within the context of Enlightenment concern with sensibility, human perception, and knowledge gathering. In this sense, some of the great Romantic tropes—a preoccupation with the natural world, say, or (the limits of) sense experience—are firmly located within a set of issues which extend all the way from Kantian metaphysics through to contemporary political undertakings and popular geographical works. The point here is not to see geography—with its methodological breadth and self-defined utilitarian application—as a 'missing link' connecting high philosophy to hard politics in an overly prescriptive or causal way. Instead, it merely is a reminder that a 'history of geography' concerns both the development of disciplined thought and the course of political events 'on the ground'—and both are interrelated at this crucial juncture in European intellectual and political history.

Further Reading

Dainotto, Roberto, *Europe (In Theory)* (Durham, NC: Duke University Press, 2007).

Glacken, Clarence J., *Traces on the Rhodian Shore: Nature and Culture in Western Thought from Ancient Times to the End of the Eighteenth Century* (Berkeley, Calif.: University of California Press, 1967).

Gregory, Derek, *Geographical Imaginations* (Oxford: Blackwell, 1994).

Heffernan, Michael, *The European Geographical Imagination* (Stuttgart: Franz Steiner Verlag, 2007).

Livingstone, David N., *The Geographical Tradition: Episodes in the History of a Contested Enterprise* (Oxford: Blackwell, 1992).

Livingstone, David N., and Withers, Charles W. J. (eds), *Geography and Enlightenment* (Chicago: Chicago University Press, 1999).

Mayhew, Robert, *Enlightenment Geography: The Political Languages of British Geography, 1650–1850* (Basingstoke: Macmillan, 2000).

Stock, Paul, *The Shelley-Byron Circle and the Idea of Europe* (New York: Palgrave Macmillan, 2010).

Wintle, Michael, *The Image of Europe: Visualising Europe in Cartography and Iconography throughout the Ages* (Cambridge: Cambridge University Press, 2009).

Withers, Charles W. J., *Placing the Enlightenment: Thinking Geographically about the Age of Reason* (Chicago: Chicago University Press, 2007).

Withers, Charles W. J., and Ogborn, Miles, *Georgian Geographies: Essays on Space, Place and Landscape in the Eighteenth Century* (Manchester: Manchester University Press, 2004).

CHAPTER 34

ROMANTIC POLITICAL THOUGHT

DOUGLAS MOGGACH

A comprehensive definition of Romanticism has eluded the efforts of generations of scholars.[1] Distinguishing, broadly, immanent and transcendent approaches to nature among authors identified with the European Romantic movement, Arthur Lovejoy recommended using the term only in the plural.[2] In response, René Wellek sought a unity among these writers in their evocations of imagination, nature, and myth.[3] In assessing the political charge of Romanticism, Georg Lukács castigated it for its irrationalism and proto-fascistic tendencies,[4] while Jacques Barzun[5] stressed its anti-totalitarian character, its promotion of individuality and diversity against imposed uniformity and coercion. More recent critics have produced a complex typology of Romantic political critiques of modernity, from restorationist conservative to utopian socialist.[6] For Michael Löwy and Robert Sayre, the common essence of these highly variegated political positions lies in the anti-capitalist character of Romanticism, or its repudiation of capitalist modernity from the perspective of the pre-modern past. This argument in turn has elicited criticisms, perhaps unwarranted, for anachronism, anticipating capitalist development where it is not yet at hand.[7]

[1] On definitions of Romanticism, see Marilyn Butler, *Romantics, Rebels and Reactionaries. English Literature and Its Background 1760–1830* (Oxford: Oxford University Press, 1981), 3–10; in ironic vein, Michael Farber, *Romanticism: A Very Short Introduction* (Oxford: Oxford University Press, 2010), 2–3.

[2] Arthur Lovejoy, 'On the Discrimination of Romanticisms', *Essays in the History of Ideas* (Baltimore: Johns Hopkins University Press, 1948), 228–53.

[3] René Wellek, *A History of Modern Criticism, 1750–1950*, ii. *The Romantic Age* (New Haven: Yale University Press, 1955), 201.

[4] Georg Lukács, *The Destruction of Reason*, tr. Peter Palmer (London: Merlin, 1980), 95–192.

[5] Jacques Barzun, 'To the Rescue of Romanticism', *American Scholar* (June 1940), 147–58; *Romanticism and the Modern Ego* (Boston: Little Brown, 1943).

[6] Michael Löwy and Robert Sayre, *Romanticism Against the Tide of Modernity*, tr. Catherine Porter (Durham, NC: Duke University Press, 2001).

[7] See G. A. Rosso and D. P. Watkins (eds), *Spirits of Fire: English Romantic Writers and Contemporary Historical Methods* (Rutherford, NJ: Fairleigh Dickinson University Press, 1990), part 1, for a debate between Sayre/Löwy and Farber.

Definitional problems of capitalism, and relations between capitalism and modernity, are not within our purview. The following exploration takes its lead from Hegel's diagnosis of modern freedom, and of Romanticism's place in it, locating common elements and variations in Romantic cultural critique. Hegel at times uses the term 'Romantic' broadly, to designate post-classical, Christian ideas of the subject generally;[8] but he is especially concerned to stress, and to differentiate himself from, specific new forms of subjectivity emerging from the Enlightenment. For Hegel, the Enlightenment is a nodal point in human history, the moment of discovery that everything exists for the subject,[9] that all institutions and relations must be assessed in light of their fitness for subjective projects, that norms bind by virtue of the free subjective judgement and endorsement that underlie them.[10] This great progressive movement heralds the emancipation of the subject, but at first these liberated individuals are unable to find themselves at home in the new world of their own construction. If it contains unprecedented possibilities for rational freedom, modernity can also appear as a culture of diremption or fragmentation,[11] an alienated world marked by the shattering of customary relationships; by the loss of wholeness, of the sense of immediacy and connectedness to a community and to nature; by the dissipation of authoritative norms. The unfettering of private interests in emergent civil society also releases their opposition and conflict; the division of labour and its mutual dependencies expand global productive power, but constrict the horizons in which its individual agents live and work.[12] With the collapse of the traditional mediating institutions of the old regime, and with the social transformations operated by the French Revolution, the pressing political question becomes the recursive movement from particularity or isolated individuality to community, universality, or the reaffirmation of common interests: the achievement of a unity compatible with the underlying diversity that is both the glory and the scourge of the modern world. Romanticism is a composite set of responses to this problem.

Romanticism has been described as effecting a cultural transformation, of equivalent significance to the French and Industrial Revolutions, predicated upon absolute inwardness.[13] To speak of absolute inwardness is to evoke Hegel's account of the unhappy consciousness,[14] which Romanticism in many respects resembles. The unhappy consciousness designates for Hegel the initial stance of Christianity as it

[8] G. W. F. Hegel, *Vorlesungen über die Ästhetik, Sämtliche Werke*, ed. H. Glockner, xii–xiv (Stuttgart: frommann, 1964).

[9] G. W. F. Hegel, *Vorlesungen über die Geschichte der Philosophie*, iii, *Werke*, xx (Frankfurt/Main: Suhrkamp, 1971), 332–3.

[10] Charles Taylor, *The Malaise of Modernity* (Concord, Ont.: Anansi, 1991), 81–91.

[11] Hegel, *Ästhetik*, xii. 88, 90–1.

[12] Friedrich Schiller, *On the Aesthetic Education of Man in a Series of Letters*, bilingual edn, ed. and tr. Elizabeth Wilkinson and L. A. Willoughby (Oxford: Clarendon Press, 1967), letter VI.7.

[13] Tim Blanning, *The Romantic Revolution* (London: Weidenfeld & Nicolson, 2010).

[14] G. W. F. Hegel, *Phenomenology of Mind*, tr. J. B. Baillie (New York: Harper & Row, 1967), 251–67; *Philosophy of History*, tr. J. Sibree (New York: Dover, 1956), 343–411.

emerges from its pagan background, further exemplified in the doctrines and institutions of the mediaeval church. This is a subjectivity which knows its essential identity with the divine (because God has become man), but feels itself bereft and abandoned in its earthly, finite existence, from which the divine has withdrawn. The unhappy consciousness yearns for its true destination of unity and harmony, but cannot reach it, and in its desolation creates chains of mediation across the unbearable gulf between itself and the infinite: the gradations of ecclesiastical and political hierarchy respond to this need. While challenging the hierarchical order of the church, the Lutheran Reformation, in repudiating salvation by works, radicalizes further the opposition of person and deed, inner and outer. As Marcuse puts it of Luther, 'Th[e] person is sought in contradistinction to his ("lifeless") works: as the negation and negativity of the works. Doer and deed person and work [sic] are torn asunder: the person as such essentially never enters into the work, can never be fulfilled in the work, eternally precedes any and every work.'[15] Echoes of Luther will reverberate in the Romanticism of Schlegel and Schleiermacher.

But Romanticism is not merely a reprise of older forms of subjectivity. Its specific character emerges in its post-Enlightenment context. From this vantage point, its defining trait is not only inwardness, but modes of relating critically to the world, however fraught with tension that relation might be. Here the Romantics share a similar critical response to modern culture as one of diremption and alienation; the emphasis is on shattered traditional solidarities, the liberation of the subject, and the confrontation of this subject with the rigours of the external world. 'All is grown acrid, divisive, threatening dissolution; and the huge tumultuous Life of Society is galvanic, devil-ridden, too truly possessed by a devil!':[16] the diabolical spirit of Mammon in Thomas Carlyle's account, the fragmentation of experience or the breaking of organic unities, for others. The Romantics elaborate a broadly common theoretical position, focusing on the potentialities and travails of the *modern* subject, and the problems of its insertion into its cultural world. This position on the primacy of the subject is consistent with important normative variations: with different ways of conceiving unity within and between subjects, and widely differing prescriptions for the proper relation which subjects should adopt toward their historical, social, and natural domains. Insofar as Romanticism has a common ground, the unity of unity and multiplicity that it represents is not a polyphonic harmony (as Leibniz would have it). The unity of Romanticism itself appears as a typically Romantic dissonance: a Berlioz symphony much more than a Bach fugue. The stress is on the multiple, with harmony problematic and transient.

The working out of this theoretical agenda entails complex relations with Enlightenment thought. It is no longer current to view Romanticism as a simple repudiation of its precursor, but important continuities between these thought-currents

[15] Herbert Marcuse, *Studies in Critical Philosophy* (Boston: Beacon Press, 1973), 58, referring to Martin Luther, 'Sermon on the Ban' (1520), in *Luther's Works*, xxxix, ed. H. Lehmann (Philadephia: Fortress Press, 1970), 8.

[16] Thomas Carlyle, *Past and Present* [1843] (New York: New York University Press, 1965), 73.

require closer analysis. Some Romantics indeed hold that the Enlightenment itself is one of the sources of the culture of diremption: its abstract ratiocination opposes sense to sensibility, shattering the unity of experience and exacerbating the fragmentation of the self.[17] But an attitude of condemnation is by no means universal among proponents of Romanticism.

Even in its overt criticism of the Enlightenment intellectual context from which it emerges, Romantic thought displays deep affinities with its forebear. These can be seen not only in the centrality of the modern subject, which Romanticism re-emphasizes; but also in the very concepts with which the activities of this subject can be grasped. This is not to equate Romanticism with Enlightenment, but to argue that they share some of the same conceptual apparatus. Three fundamental, interrelated concepts are spontaneity, formativity, and reflection.

Spontaneity refers to the capacity of subjects to be the self-initiating cause of change in themselves and in the external world, and to assess and validate these changes. Action entails not simply a response to external stimuli (and this marks a break with versions of Enlightenment materialism),[18] but is the execution of an inner design. This alternative conception of action as self-causing derives from distinct Enlightenment sources, and is redeployed by the Romantics. Leibniz, who has both idealist and Romantic progeny,[19] had developed this idea in his classical metaphysical system, but it is consciously appropriated for their own purposes by Herder[20] and other Romantics; and analogous ideas appear in various national contexts. The spontaneous subject is the active source of transformation, and not merely a passive reagent, even when, as in Schleiermacher, this restless activity is itself viewed as a source of diremption.

Formativity refers to the capacity of spontaneous subjects to shape objectivity in light of their purposes,[21] or at least to display their subjectivity in transient ways. Everything exists for, and through, the subject: here too Romanticism reformulates an Enlightenment idea. This idea does not presuppose the complete transparency of purposes to the self prior to acting, nor does it necessarily imply successful execution. It is rather the recognition that the world is constructed by subjective effort: it is not simply a given order but a historical result. This is to pose anew the problem of alienation and its overcoming: the stress is on consciousness no longer exclusively in relation to a permanent, transcendent order (as in Stoicism and early Christianity), but in relation to historically contingent and evolving structures, products of human design.

17 For Hegel the recognition of this problem leads him to develop further the Kantian distinction between reason and intellect.

18 G. W. Leibniz, *Philosophical Essays*, tr. and ed. Roger Ariew and Daniel Garber (Indianapolis: Hackett, 1989); *Monadology*, ed. Nicholas Rescher (Pittsburgh, Pa.: University of Pittsburgh Press, 1991), paras 10–13, pp. 66–75.

19 Douglas Moggach, 'Aesthetics and Politics', in Gareth Stedman Jones and Gregory Claeys (eds), *Cambridge History of Nineteenth-Century Political Thought* (Cambridge: Cambridge University Press, 2011), 479–520.

20 Nigel deSouza, 'Language, Reason, and Sociability: Herder's Critique of Rousseau', *Intellectual History Review*, 22/4 (2012), 221–40.

21 Luigi Pareyson, *Estetica: Teoria della formatività* (Turin: Filosofia, 1954).

Such formative shaping does not imply necessarily that subject and object will correspond, or that subjects will succeed in projecting their contents into the outer world. The culture of diremption militates against this result; but, for many Romantics, it does not preclude it. The relation of subject and object raises the question of reflective self-awareness. From his idealistic perspective, Friedrich Schiller defines reflection as the reciprocal relation of self and world, the process by which subjects simultaneously relate to and distinguish themselves from the products of their formative activity.[22] The fundamental ambiguity entailed in the concept of reflection, as a process both of taking up an object as one's own and of separating oneself from it, is of central importance here. In Romantic registers, the problem of reflection, the accord or the non-correspondence between subjects and their deeds, becomes a fundamental issue of modern freedom. This problem is addressed in two distinct ways, whose prehistory bears note.

Among Enlightenment proponents of the doctrine of genius that will play a prominent role in subsequent Romantic thinking,[23] G. E. Lessing (1729–81) argues that, in their formative action, creative artists produce their own rules, instead of deriving them from a divinely sanctioned order,[24] or from mimesis of natural forms. The meaning of artworks is constructed or sanctioned by consensus, not by reliance on transcendent sources.[25] Not given objects, but actions, or subjectivity at work in the world, provide the proper contents of art. Unlike later views of alienation, Lessing stresses the accord of artist and medium, subject and form.[26]

After Lessing, the idea of reflection, the relations of continuity and discontinuity between subjectivity and external forms, is developed (in the Germanic context though with broader European parallels), in two originally complementary senses. J. G. Herder (1744–1803) traces the elaboration of objective form from subjective powers and capacities, seeing externalization as the manifestation of an implicit content. He places sensuousness and rationality in a genetic relationship, showing how the more complex unities of the spiritual realm emerge from simpler, natural antecedents.[27] Schelling and Hölderlin in different ways apply this insight in their quest for the originary unity of thought and being.

[22] Schiller, *Aesthetic Education*, letter XXIV.2.

[23] Darrin McMahon, *Divine Fire: A History of Genius* (New York: Basic Books, 2013).

[24] G. E. Lessing, 'Laocoon', in J. M. Bernstein (ed.), *Classic and Romantic German Aesthetics* (Cambridge: Cambridge University Press, 2003), 25–129; Gérard Raulet, 'Von der Allegorie zur Geschichte: Säkularisierung und Ornament im 18. Jahrhundert', in Gérard Raulet (ed.), *Von der Rhetorik zur Ästhetik. Studien zur Entstehung der modernen Ästhetik im achtzehnten Jahrhundert* (Rennes: Philia, 1992), 146.

[25] Raulet, 'Von der Allegorie', 163.

[26] See Hugh Barr Nisbet, *Lessing: Eine Biographie* (Munich: Beck, 2008).

[27] J. G. Herder, *Sämtliche Werke*, iv (Berlin, 1878), 3–43; viii (1892). Christoph Menke, 'Ästhetische Subjektivität: Zu einem Grundbegriff moderner Ästhetik', in Gerhart von Graevenitz (ed.), *Konzepte der Moderne* (Stuttgart: de Gruyter, 1999), 595, distinguishes Herder's and Mendelssohn's concepts of reflection, but contrasts them with what he calls the metaphysical subject model attributed to Hegel and Heidegger.

For Moses Mendelssohn (1729–86),[28] reflection attends to subjective formative energies as distinct from outward, created forms; it examines the self-aware enjoyment of these powers in their inner richness and potentiality, and in the activity of representation itself.[29] This reflexive separation of subject and form marks the properly aesthetic attitude.[30] The distinction between Mendelssohn and Herder evolves into an alternative that will be decisive for later Romantic thought: reflection as locating a creative force detached from the object, the stance of irony; or reflection as working subjective forces into determinate form, the stance of expressivism. In expressivist versions the separation of self and world is less extreme, and the world is seen as (potentially) the confirmation, not the negation, of the subject. But expressivists too seek ways of confining the dissolving effects of reflection, while acknowledging the spontaneity and formativity of the modern subject.

Expressive and ironic Romanticisms develop contrasting diagnoses of modernity and its pathologies. Diremption may be taken to hold, historically, between subjects and the current, inadequate form of their world: inadequate precisely because it frustrates subjects' authentic expression, but also remediable if new channels of expression can be opened. More radically, diremption may hold, ontologically, between subjects and their deeds, making genuine expression impossible. Sometimes both positions are held. However it is accounted for, the culture of diremption, and the efforts to contain or to liberate the powers of reflection, form the substance of Romantic political thought.

Restoring Unity: History and the People

Jean-Jacques Rousseau (1712–78), widely recognized as one of the progenitors of Romanticism, had criticized Enlightenment rationality as a purveyor of false needs, whose proliferation undermined natural morals and civic virtues.[31] The artificiality and decadence of modern social and political life can be countered by the recovery of an uncorrupted subjective core that lies concealed beneath the accretions of history. Reactivating elements of Stoicism, Rousseau in his discourse *On Inequality* identifies this core with the attitudes of healthy self-love and compassion, *amour de soi* and *pitié*, proper to our native condition.[32] Individuals live freely when they live with

[28] Otto Best (ed.), *Ästhetische Schriften in Auswahl* (Darmstadt: WBG, 1974), 173–97, 207–46; Heinz Paetzold, 'Rhetorik-Kritik und Theorie der Künste in der philosophischen Ästhetik von Baumgarten bis Kant', in Raulet, *Von der Rhetorik*, 10, 21.

[29] Paetzold, 'Rhetorik-Kritik', 13; Menke, 'Ästhetische Subjektivität', 601.

[30] Menke, 'Ästhetische Subjektivität', 603.

[31] Jean-Jacques Rousseau, 'Discourse on the Arts and Sciences' [First Discourse, 1750], *First and Second Discourses*, ed. and tr. Roger D. Masters and Judith R. Masters (New York: St Martin's Press, 1964).

[32] Jean-Jacques Rousseau, 'Discourse on the Origins of Inequality' [Second Discourse, 1755], in *First and Second Discourses*, ed. and tr. Masters and Masters.

authenticity (i.e. when they can view their acts as revelatory of their genuine intents and self-understanding); and with transparency, the mutual expectation of authenticity.[33] Such expectations have been thwarted by history. While these attitudes lie latent deep in the individual heart, the historical process has radically vitiated original *amour de soi* or self-preservation, turning it into competitive *amour propre* or self-affirmation, while *pitié*, or sympathetic reference to other, is distorted into invidious comparison, hypocrisy, deception, and conflict. The loss of original authenticity and transparency as regulators of interactions entails a generalized corruption. Rousseau historicizes the Stoic distinction between *oikeiosis*, recognizing the intrinsic rightness of the world and thus being at home in it, and *allotriosis*, estrangement or alienation from the world, the self, and others.[34] The Stoics consider this a fundamental ethical alternative which the individual will can spontaneously adopt, unconstrained by external causes. Rousseau, however, roots the distinction in history, particularly in the division of labour and the skewed distribution of private property, and traces the perverting effects on the will and on freedom produced by fragmentation, competition, and thraldom to false needs. For Rousseau, the social contract provides a possible cure for the pathologies of the present. The general will is to retrieve the original tendencies of human nature, submerged, but not completely eradicated by history, and to give them a new, political scope. The determination of the general will involves two distinct acts,[35] each exemplifying one fundamental trait of a rejuvenated human nature: in substance, the *volonté générale* expresses the common interest of the citizens, which they consciously ascribe to themselves as their own, thus restoring *pitié* or identification with the other on a new collective basis; and yet formally, the determination of this will requires the assent (Stoic *synkatathesis*) of each independent judgement, reached without extrinsic influence. This is to render *amour de soi* sound again, and to endow transparency and authenticity with new meaning. But such a positive outcome is not universally achievable. It depends on specific conditions of approximate equality of material possessions among a relatively undifferentiated citizenry. Rousseau's republicanism envisages a partial revival of the Greek polis, but does so in a modern spirit, acutely aware of the need to produce harmony by abstracting away from divisive private interests.

In seeking to retrieve putatively natural sentiments,[36] distorted but not destroyed by the historical process, Rousseau shares with Enlightenment contemporaries the idea of a fixed underlying human essence, despite his critique of their ideas of freedom as need satisfaction. In a non-Romantic vein, Adam Smith substitutes a different essential property, the propensity to trade, which had been thwarted by the irrationalities of feudalism, but he likewise affirms the existence of anthropological constants. This idea is

[33] Jean Starobinski, *Jean-Jacques Rousseau: La transparence et l'obstacle* (Paris: Plon, 1957).

[34] Dieter Henrich, *Between Kant and Hegel: Lectures on German Idealism*, ed. David S. Pacini (Cambridge, Mass.: Harvard University Press, 2003), 89–97.

[35] Jean-Jacques Rousseau, *On the Social Contract* [1762], ed. R. D. Masters, tr. J. R. Masters (New York: St Martin's Press, 1978).

[36] Frederick Beiser, *Schiller as Philosopher: A Re-Examination* (Oxford: Oxford University Press, 2005), 11, 158, and n. 66.

challenged by post-Kantians like Fichte, for whom human essence evolves and is practically constituted, and is not a given set of traits.[37] But Rousseau does insist that because of the effects of historical corruption, this retrieval is also a self-transformation, and not simply a loosening of bonds. Some versions of subsequent Romantic expressivism will hold that the essence of the people remains undiluted, and that this essence will emerge immediately once the purely contingent restrictions of feudal, foreign, or ecclesiastical domination have been eliminated; but Rousseau does not advance this view.

For J. G. Herder, the idea of the people or the nation offers a critical vantage point upon the culture of diremption and atomistic individualism.[38] The modern division of labour entails not an increase in social complexity, but a diminution, in reducing workers to identical, interchangeable units; such units are not spontaneously self-directive, but heteronomously determined, obeying external causal forces.[39] Society, once an organism, richly internally differentiated by the variety of skilled work it encourages and the communal bonds it fosters, has been transformed into a lifeless mechanism. Authoritarianism inheres in fragmented modern society as traditional connections and solidarities break, releasing individuals from the integration and protection of intermediate bodies, but subjecting them in their isolation to the oppressive power of the state.[40]

To counter alienation, Herder invokes the redemptive power of the principle of the nation. The culture of diremption is a misshapen world, but underlying it are latent formative energies awaiting release. Unlike the mechanical, imposed unity of the state, the nation is an organic entity, a shared popular life reflecting a dynamic inner principle of cultural creativity, giving voice to a particular understanding of the world and of one's place in it.[41] This idea of the nation recasts Leibniz's monad, whose contents evolve as a purely endogenous process; the active, spontaneous monad has become a collective subject. Herder's expressivist version of Romanticism identifies a continuity in principle between objective cultural forms and the capacities of subjects. In their processes of self-reflection subjects ought to find themselves confirmed in their deeds, authentically rendering in objectivity their own essential content. Such affirmative connections can be blocked by external impositions of state or economic power, but they remain available for activation once these impediments are removed.

Following Leibniz's translation of form into configuration, Herder stresses the aesthetic, formative power of the self. Ethically, an implicit subjectivity must give itself an authentic manifestation in the external world. This authenticity is the hallmark of

[37] J. G. Fichte, 'Destination of the Scholar', *Early Philosophical Writings*, tr. and ed. Daniel Breazeale (Ithaca, NY: Cornell University Press, 1988), 177–84.

[38] On Herder, see Charles Taylor, *Sources of the Self. The Making of the Modern Identity* (Cambridge, Mass.: Harvard University Press, 1989), 368–90.

[39] J. G. Herder, *Auch eine Philosophie der Geschichte zur Bildung der Menschheit, Sämtliche Werke* (Berlin, 1877), v. 534–64.

[40] J. G. Herder, *Ideen zu einer Philosophie der Geschichte der Menschheit*, i (Berlin: Aufbau Verlag, 1965), 27–145.

[41] Martha Helfer, 'Herder, Fichte, and Humboldt's "Thinking and Speaking"', in Kurt Mueller-Vollmer (ed.), *Herder Today* (Berlin and New York: de Gruyter, 1990), 367–81.

freedom, a particular cultural content made manifest, and known and recognized as such. Herder interprets the Leibnizian monad as a national grouping expressing its unique history and consciousness in works of cultural production, language, etc. Each collective subject offers a unique and irreplaceable perspective on the totality of human accomplishments, and realizes a particular aspect of a composite human personality. In following an inner principle of movement, nations generate a spontaneous order, with increasing complexity and differentiation of function. While responding only to inner imperatives, all nations partake in a cosmopolitan task. Each makes a unique contribution to the perfection of the species, which requires the widest possible range: the Leibnizian principle of the unity of unity and multiplicity. The loss of any particular perspective, through suppression or standardization, means the impoverishment of the totality of human capacities, an undesirable reduction in complexity. He thus integrates nationalism into a cosmopolitan perspective, through the Leibnizian presupposition of a pre-established harmony among the capacities and perspectives of these national collective subjects. Herder's contribution to the formation of modern national consciousness has been profound, especially in the revolutions of 1848,[42] though the particularistic aspect of national self-affirmation came increasingly to the fore, with the consequent abandonment of Herder's optimistic framework of cosmopolitan unity in diversity.

Widely heralded, Rousseau's diagnosis of the problems of modern diremption was more enthusiastically received in later Romantic circles in France and Switzerland than were his austere solutions. In distinguishing the ancient military community from modern commercial society, Benjamin Constant (1767–1830) takes issue with Rousseau's attempt to regenerate the polis in modern conditions. Despite the grandeur of his conceptions, which Constant generously acknowledges, Rousseau overlooks the fundamental difference between ancient and modern freedom, and proposes to revive the former as an antidote to present-day alienations. Constant defines the liberty of the ancients as the active, direct sharing in collective power; modern freedom consists instead in the independence of the person and the pursuit of private satisfaction. It depends on the expansion and differentiation of needs effected through trade and expanded economic activity. The preconditions for direct democracy, which Rousseau and his more extreme adherents would revive, are the restricted scale of political and economic interactions, a pre-eminently military cast to the state, and the extensive presence of a slave population. None of these conditions apply to modern political and social life. The predominance of commerce over warfare as means of securing goods demonstrates for Constant the triumph of reason and calculation over passion and impulse. It is a measure of historical progress, not of regression, as Rousseau erroneously deemed history to be. Representative institutions, which Rousseau had repudiated, are the appropriate safeguards of modern freedom. Insofar as citizens exercise oversight over these institutions, the representative system maintains the economic and juridical space in which individual happiness can be sought. It secures independence not in the ancient-inflected,

[42] Juha Manninen, *Feuer am Pol: Zum Aufbau der Vernunft im europäischen Norden* (Frankfurt/Main: Lang, 1996).

Rousseauian sense of proclaiming and participating in the general will, but in the modern acceptance of individual happiness or need-fulfilment. Such happiness can be more efficiently attained by one's own efforts than through paternalistic provision, and hence the representative state is also the limited state. However, Constant declares, the ultimate aim of political association is not mere enjoyment but perfection, the maximal development of the intellectual and cultural capacities of individuals and collectivities.[43] In sketching out the complex relationships between happiness, rights, and moral perfection, Constant's thinking parallels contemporary tendencies in German Idealism, which have been designated post-Kantian perfectionism.[44] Here the boundaries between Romanticism and Idealism are blurred. This body of thought highlights both the value and the problematic nature of modern diversity, and the fragile and contested character of social unity. In contrasting developments from Rousseau, Herder, and other sources, ideas of conflict merge with an ideal of popular unity among other Romantic thinkers, for whom not representative government but the primordial solidarity of the people offers an alternative to the reflexive dissolution of modern life.

A contemporary source identifies the principle of the historiography of Jules Michelet (1798–1874) to be the permanent struggle of *fatalité* and *liberté*.[45] His thought has, in many respects, strong affinities with Herder's.[46] It is based on an expressivist idea of freedom, in which collective subjects, specific facets of a composite human personality, transpose into objectivity their unique perspective on the world. The social ideal of both is 'the greatest diversity … in the most perfect unity'.[47] There are marked differences between the two thinkers, however. Michelet discards Herder's systematic intentions and his organicism.[48] In Michelet's view, history is not a harmonious (Leibnizian) unfolding, interrupted by momentary surface disturbances;[49] it is rather a tumultuous process animated by opposition and conflict. Michelet appeals moreover not to nature, or to given particularities, but to constructions of freedom. The people or the nation is not a naturally determined unity, such as he describes race to be,[50]

[43] Benjamin Constant, 'The Liberty of the Ancients Compared with That of the Moderns', in *Political Writings*, ed. Biancamaria Fontana (Cambridge: Cambridge University Press, 1988), 308–28. On the atavistic character of war in the modern world, and a critique of Napoleonic expansionism, Benjamin Constant [1813], *Cours de Politique Constitutionnelle*, ed. Edouard Laboulaye (Paris: Guillaumin, 1872), ii. 129–82. See also 'The Spirit of Conquest and Usurpation and their Relation to European Civilisation', in Constant, *Political Writings*, 51–84.

[44] Douglas Moggach, 'Post-Kantian Perfectionism', in D. Moggach (ed.), *Politics, Religion, and Art: Hegelian Debates* (Evanston, Ill.: Northwestern University Press, 2011), 179–200.

[45] Louis Le Guillou, 'Michelet et Lamennais (d'après des documents inédits)', *Romantisme*, 5/10 (1975), 129–44 (130); cf. Jules Michelet, *Introduction à l'historie universelle: Tableau de la France. Préface à l'histoire de France* (Paris: Colin, 1962), 35.

[46] On French receptions of Herder, see Stephen A. Kippur, *Jules Michelet, A Study of Mind and Sensibility* (Albany, NY: SUNY Press, 1981), 35–6.

[47] Hayden White, *Metahistory: The Historical Imagination in Nineteenth-Century Europe* (Baltimore: Johns Hopkins University Press, 1973), 152.

[48] White, *Metahistory*, 143.

[49] White, *Metahistory*, 154–5.

[50] Michelet, *Introduction*, 70–1.

but is a work of freedom, forged in struggle. In his histories, especially his histories of France, which is his preferred subject, he traces the breakdown of natural aggregations in favour of constructed unity.[51] He is highly critical of passive and merely internal conceptions of freedom, which he associates largely with the Germanic temperament[52] (hence his explicit rejection of some aspects of Romanticism).[53] For Michelet, freedom is transformative *action*.[54] It is spontaneity and formativity harnessed in a national cause.

In the struggle of fatality and liberty which comprises history, constructed communities emerge. Pre-eminent among these is France, the harbinger of emancipated humanity. Unlike his compatriot and correspondent Félicité de Lamennais (1782–1854), in whose vision of the people functions an express cosmopolitanism,[55] an attempt to transcend national particularities, Michelet thinks that he discovers a particular which bears in itself the universal, the collective interest of humanity. This particular, the French national character, is a composite, a synthesis of unity and diversity, its variegated parts, shaped by the contingencies of locality and climate, spontaneously adhering in a common spirit and in common action. The very construction of this complex unity is a triumph of freedom over necessity, over the fatalities of place, custom, and external causal forces.[56]

A particular formation of the human spirit, France acts nonetheless as a universal guide to progress and emancipation, which other nations will follow as best they can, in light of their own cultural peculiarities. In his survey of world history, Michelet measures the varying prospects for freedom of the European peoples, reversing the assessment of Fichte in *Addresses to the German Nation*. Fichte had held that German culture possessed an inherent superiority rooted in its living language, whose concreteness and vividness offered insight beyond the merely sensuous world into the supersensible as the source of constant renewal and freedom, while French is an offshoot of dead Latin roots, feeble and superficial. Herder too for all his cosmopolitanism evinced a strong preference for the popular German against the overcultivated, highly stylized, and insincere French arts.[57] England Michelet regards as a bastion of narrow egoism. It exemplifies the barren and suffocating aspects of the modern culture of diremption.

In the trajectory of history, Michelet detects alternating moments of analysis and synthesis, breakdown and recomposition, which in their totality attest to a divine

[51] Michelet, *Introduction*, 70.

[52] Michelet, *Introduction*, 53, on Lutheran abnegation and denial of free will.

[53] White, *Metahistory*, 149, notes that Michelet denies that he is a Romantic (insofar as the latter implies passivity and mere inwardness).

[54] Michelet, *Introduction*, 182–3.

[55] Kippur, *Michelet*, 112.

[56] Michelet, *Introduction*, 159–60.

[57] J. G. Fichte, *Addresses to the German Nation*, tr. G. Moore (Cambridge: Cambridge University Press, 2008); J. G. Herder, *Shakespeare*, tr. G. Moore (Princeton: Princeton University Press, 2008).

order made manifest on earth.[58] The providential framework in which he places the essential movement of history is not equated, as it is in Novalis, with a defence of the old ecclesiastical order. Michelet highlights the resiliency of the French, whose long process of formation achieves an invigorating mixture of 'racial' components, notably Gallic and Roman,[59] as also a balanced union of town and country (contrasting with the unilateral urban or rural developments of Italy and Germany, respectively). The unification of the French people was anticipated by the religious and monarchical unity of the Middle Ages,[60] and the kings mobilized the lower orders against the nobility;[61] but the medieval period spawned mere transitional forms, and in no way constitutes an ideal. 'Le droit divin du roi et du prêtre n'existait qu'à condition d'exprimer la pensée divine, c'est à dire l'idée générale du peuple.'[62] Christian doctrines incline towards passivity and otherworldliness,[63] rather than vigorous transformative action, while in its practices Christianity was tyrannical, drowning the world in blood.[64]

The culmination of this lengthy formative process was the French Revolution, which demolished the artificial barriers to sociability that had been erected by the oppressive old regime.[65] 'The Revolution is nothing but the tardy reaction of justice against the government of favour and the religion of grace.'[66] Unification is not complete, however, as long as the social question, the problem of poverty and economic hierarchy, remains unresolved. Michelet praises the moral rectitude and creativity of the poor, the peasantry, and urban workers and artisans,[67] whose social composition and class characteristics he carefully observes. He is vociferous in condemning their oppression. He upholds a national system of education as a means of familiarizing classes with each other, and of healing social divisions.[68] If the *fatalités* of feudalism had been based on geographic and local particularisms, new forms of *fatalité* must now be confronted within the emergent industrial order. The diremptions of the present are neither fatal nor permanent, but can be absorbed in the next historical phase, within a new moment of synthesis and recomposition. The spontaneity and formativity of the people, of the collective subject, are for Michelet the inexhaustible sources of renewal and redemption.

58 Michelet, *Introduction*, 73–4.

59 Michelet, *Introduction*, 61, 70. 'Le croisement des races, le mélange des civilisations opposées, est poutant l'auxiliaire le plus puissant de la liberté', p. 61.

60 Michelet, *Introduction*, 9.

61 Michelet, *Introduction*, 67.

62 Michelet, *Introduction*, 67.

63 Michelet, *Introduction*, 70.

64 Kippur, *Michelet*, 155.

65 Kippur, *Michelet*, 151, 153.

66 Cited in Kippur, *Michelet*, 152.

67 Jules Michelet, *Le Peuple* [1846] (Paris: Flammarion, 1974).

68 Kippur, *Michelet*, 102–4, 111–13.

Restoring Unity: Religion

Other Romanticisms attempt to reconstitute the religious bond as a means of combating the culture of diremption, but without abandoning the ground of the new emancipated subjectivity. In *Le Génie du christianisme* (1802), Francois-René de Chateaubriand (1768–1848) defends Christianity not as a doctrinal system, but as a heightened aesthetic, promoting artistic creativity and reconciling a divided humanity.[69] In his earlier writings Chateaubriand had contested the historical truth of Christianity, whose doctrines he had considered derivative from Platonic and other ancient sources, and he had attacked the oppressive rule of the clergy.[70] He forecast the dissolution of Christianity, which would end either in universal enlightenment or in barbarism.[71] Recanting this position after 1799, when he began composing *Le Génie* in English exile, he now concluded that the merit of Christianity lay not in the literal truth of its dogmatic claims, but in the aesthetic appeal of its doctrine and ceremonies, its vision of worldly order, and its deeper grasp of the relation of finite and infinite than that achieved in classical, pagan art. The ancient Greeks had not yet emancipated themselves from nature, even when their art manifested a dawning spiritual principle, and not mere sensuousness.[72] Christian architecture, arts, and literature express a higher vantage point: the yearning of the finite for a transcendent infinite, towards which it strives and with which it seeks ultimate unity. This is not the mere happy coincidence of self and nature, but the reflective awareness of a loss and reclamation. This attitude endows the arts with unprecedented richness and profundity, from Gothic cathedrals and medieval religious paintings, to the highly reflective writings of Pascal and Fénelon. The Christian mission is to effect an aesthetic education which promotes civilization and reins in the savage passions, offering an antidote to the recent revolutionary upheavals in France. The Revolution reveals a much deeper problem. Though its reflexiveness is ineradicable, modern subjectivity for Chateaubriand has lost its bearings in a fruitless quest for endless satisfactions.[73] The medieval church had succeeded in channelling and disciplining aspirations like these, just as it had earlier salvaged culture from the collapse of the Roman Empire. The church remained a beacon of hope amidst the modern culture of diremption. Chateaubriand attempts to appease the new, post-Enlightenment subjectivity by demonstrating that the traditional religious order, once it is reconceived as an artistic artifice, is in accord with its best aesthetic aspirations, and can restore shattered unities on a higher basis.

[69] Francois-René de Chateaubriand, *Le Génie du christianisme ou Beautés de la religion chrétienne* (Paris, 1802).

[70] Francois-René de Chateaubriand, *Essai historique, politique et moral sur les révolutions anciennes et modernes, considerées dans leurs rapports avec la Révolution française* [1799; repr. 1826] (Paris: Gallimard, 1978), 404–27.

[71] Chateaubriand, *Essai*, 428–31.

[72] Annie Becq, *Genèse de l'esthétique française moderne* (Pisa: Pacini, 1984), ii. 821–2.

[73] John E. Toews, 'Church and State: The Problem of Authority', in Stedman Jones and Claeys, *Nineteenth Century Thought*, 612.

If Chateaubriand evinces a Catholic sensibility in his celebration of ritual and art, the validation of religion offered by Friedrich Schleiermacher (1768–1834) takes as its starting point the Lutheran absolute inwardness of the subject, its solitude and divorce from objective relations, in which it cannot recognize its own formative presence. In the figure of the 'beautiful soul', Schleiermacher gives poignant expression to this interiority of consciousness, reluctant to sully its purity with action, keeping external causality at bay, and distinguishing itself as much as it can from objectivity, which it takes to be mere loss and distraction. In depicting the beautiful soul as the 'unmoved centre of a turning world',[74] which limits its interventions and interactions in order to remain faithful to and reflective upon its own inner impulses,[75] Schleiermacher recasts Leibnizian spontaneity as a goal to be attained, under a kind of ethical imperative to *become a monad*, so that the workings of external causes are minimized. The objective or phenomenal world is devalued before the inner realm of thought and feeling. But such a deracinated self-consciousness is keenly aware of its own limitations; it senses its lack of autonomy and its dependency on higher spiritual powers, on an ineffable absolute, which is present not through rational thought, but in feelings of neediness and subordination. Schleiermacher affirms religious faith as spontaneous submission to this rationally inaccessible power. In such submission lies the basis for a renewed religious community, whose members mutually recognize their common dependency. In this movement of thought, the differences between Romanticism and German Idealism become manifest. From a Kantian perspective, the defect of the Romantic position is that the spontaneity of the subject is not regulated by autonomous self-legislation, but by abjection and heteronomous compliance with an alien (divine) will. From Hegel's perspective, Schleiermacher's Romantic vision fully attests to the culture of diremption even in his efforts to criticize it. This intended endorsement of Christianity is predicated upon a divorce of subject and objective world that threatens to undermine social cohesion.[76] The recognition of this danger provokes Hegel's vigorous anti-subjectivist polemics of the *Philosophy of Right*.[77]

A similar tension recurs in Novalis (Friedrich von Hardenberg, 1772–1801), between the freedom of the individual subject and the overarching providential order to which the religious consciousness gives access. Novalis celebrates the contingent and the accidental for shattering routine and auguring the new: 'All the accidents of our lives are materials from which we can make what we will'.[78] Freedom lies not in the recognition of natural dependency, as in Schleiermacher, nor in rational autonomy, as in Kant; but in

[74] Schleiermacher's *Soliloquy* of 1810, cited in David Simpson, 'Introduction', *German Aesthetic and Literary Criticism* (Cambridge: Cambridge University Press, 1984), 12.

[75] Hegel, *Phenomenology*, 658–66.

[76] Simpson, 'Introduction', 11, 14, 19.

[77] G. W. F. Hegel [1821], *Elements of the Philosophy of Right*, ed. Allen W. Wood, tr. H. B. Nisbet (Cambridge: Cambridge University Press, 1991), 9–23, 180–4; Jeffrey Reid, *L'Anti-romantique: Hegel contre le romantisme ironique* (Quebec: Presses de l'Université Laval, 2007).

[78] Cited in Karl Heinz Bohrer, *Die Grenzen des Ästhetischen* (Munich: Carl Hansen, 1998), p. 12 (my tr.).

indeterminacy, in the capacity to hover between alternatives without fully committing to any: it lies in *Willkür*, or the capacity for unconstrained choice, and not in *Wille*, or submission to universal law. This is another version of the Romantic divorce between individual spontaneity and self-legislation, which marks this current off from German Idealism. Novalis retains nonetheless a teleological perspective on history as an order in which the accidents of individual life are ultimately integrated.[79] He combines a modern view of the reflexive subject with a defence of traditional values and relations, sanctioned by providence. Thus Novalis, in this respect like Herder, views history as redemptive and revelatory of meaning;[80] and like Chateaubriand and the late Wordsworth, he dismisses purely secular solutions to political and social problems as superficial,[81] though preferring the organic solidarities of mediaeval life to the diremptions of the present. Novalis's subject is a modern explorer of creative possibilities; but the world order is fixed and transcendently grounded. It resists the dissolution of modern reflexivity. As such it offers refuge and salvation.

Containing Reflection: Art, Nature, and Tradition

Friedrich Hölderlin (1770–1843) seeks supersensible grounds for the possibility of community among finite spirits, and their claims of freedom.[82] Aesthetic intuition, achieved in art, especially poetry, reveals the primal unity of thought and being, subject and object, preceding the diremptions introduced by the reflective intellect.[83] Though the rending of this initial unity is a necessary stage in the process of human emancipation, the rifts must be healed. Aesthetic access to a pre-conceptual unity brings to rest the infinite regress of subjective reflection, a danger implicit in Fichte's reformulation of Kant, as a process of infinite striving,[84] and operative in modern ideas of deracinated freedom. In evoking a harmony of reflection and objective form, aesthetic insight can prefigure other modes of unity, which complement it: in moral acts which exemplify the activating presence of the universal in the particular, the infinite in the finite; and in history as a movement of continuous realisation of rational ends in the sensuous order, gradually bringing objectivity under the command of reason. This attitude places Hölderlin

[79] Novalis [Friedrich von Hardenberg] [1799], 'Christianity or Europe: A Fragment', in *The Early Political Writings of the German Romantics*, ed. and tr. Frederick Beiser (Cambridge: Cambridge University Press, 1996), 59–80.

[80] White, *Metahistory*, 145

[81] White, *Metahistory*, 146

[82] Bernhard Lypp, *Ästhetischer Absolutismus und politische Vernunft: Zum Widerstreit von Reflexion und Sittlichkeit im deutschen Idealismus* (Frankfurt/Main: Suhrkamp, 1972), 22 n. 24.

[83] H. S. Harris, 'Hegel's Intellectual Development to 1807,' in F. C. Beiser (ed.), *The Cambridge Companion to Hegel* (Cambridge: Cambridge University Press, 1993), 32; Dieter Henrich, *Between Kant and Hegel: Lectures on German Idealism*, ed. David Pacini (Cambridge, Mass.: Harvard University Press, 2003), 279–95.

[84] Terry Pinkard, *German Philosophy 1760–1860* (Cambridge: Cambridge University Press, 2002), 139–44.

in closer proximity to German Idealism than to many of his Romantic contemporaries. An ideal of transparency, as the subordination of contingency to a growing rational control, predominates in his conception of history.[85] Unlike Novalis, it is reason rather than indeterminacy which is the condition of possibility for freedom.

An anonymous, fragmentary text of 1796 or 1797, designated 'The Earliest System Programme of German Idealism',[86] illustrates Hölderlin's influence, though its authorship is in dispute. This short text contrasts the dull and mechanical interaction of parts[87] in the modern world with the idea of free self-determination within a natural order which, following Kant, can be conceived as purposive, a beautiful harmony in accord with subjects' own ends. Kant's philosophy offers a glimpse of this possibility as a regulative ideal, but fails to draw out fully its own implications. Kant's objective is better realized through an aesthetic state of beautiful and harmonized life-conditions, an organic unity of the parts rather than the collisions and frictions of the existing mechanical state. This idea remains rudimentary in the 'System Programme', a mere sketch of the possibility that modern life can be pacified under the beneficent reign of beauty. The aesthetic upholds the ideal of social and political solidarity as an alternative to the culture of diremption.

After Hölderlin the idea of pre-reflexive unity figures in the philosophy of F. W. J. Schelling (1775–1854), who seeks an indifference point where subject and object coalesce, prior to their scission. His *System of Transcendental Idealism* (1800) gives a systematic account of this unity of thought and extension, and of the place of subjectivity and reflection in it. The lack of transparency of consciousness to itself, its partial opacity to its own reflective processes in acts of creation or formativity, means that consciousness is not entirely subject to the laws of causal determination, and thus is able, in this space of freedom, to initiate and innovate. While Hölderlin, like the idealists, seeks to reduce the scope of contingency by submitting it to rational rule, Schelling sees in the contingent the basis of human freedom.[88]

The containment of reflection is an ubiquitous problem among European Romantics. The heterogeneity of British Romanticism is widely acknowledged,[89] William Blake (1757–1827), for example, being associated with an older republican tradition of opposition to the court and to centralized political and economic power in London.[90] In Blake's

[85] Lypp, *Ästhetischer Absolutismus*, 19; G. Raulet, 'Von der Allegorie', 159.

[86] On the disputed authorship of this text, see Martin Gammon, 'Modernity and the Crisis of Aesthetic Representation in Hegel's Early Writings', in William Maker (ed.), *Hegel and Aesthetics* (Albany, NY: SUNY Press, 2000), 145–70. See also Dietrich Mathy, *Von der Metaphysik zur Ästhetik, oder Das Exil der Philosophie: Untersuchungen zum Prozess der ästhetischen Moderne* (Hamburg: von Bockel, 1994), 9–10.

[87] Lypp, *Ästhetischer Absolutismus*, 20.

[88] Andrew Bowie, 'German Idealism and the Arts', in Karl Ameriks (ed.), *The Cambridge Companion to German Idealism* (Cambridge: Cambridge University Press, 2000), 245–6.

[89] Marilyn Butler, *Romantics, Rebels and Reactionaries: English Literature and its Background 1760–1830* (Oxford: Oxford University Press, 1981); G. W. Izenberg, *Impossible Individuality: Romanticism, Revolution, and the Origins of Modern Selfhood* (Princeton: Princeton University Press, 1992).

[90] Marilyn Butler, 'Romanticism in England', in Roy Porter and Mikulas Teich (eds), *Romanticism in National Context* (Cambridge: Cambridge University Press, 1988), 48–9.

aesthetics, the creative process retains its reference to a transcendent order of meaning. His usage of the term 'original' refers not to creation ex nihilo by innovative, creative genius, but to a heightened sense of mimesis or reproduction: the original artist is one who grasps in aesthetic vision the underlying eternal pattern or model, the origin which is to be figured in the work of art.[91]

Many of Blake's contemporaries take a more radical view of modern subjectivity and its innovative potential. Arising from Enlightenment critique, the new thinking about subjectivity and its emancipatory prospects is sharply inflected among its English exponents by the effects of the French Revolution. William Wordsworth (1770–1850) and Samuel Taylor Coleridge (1772–1834) initially welcome the Revolution, but their reflections on its course lead them to politically conservative and quietistic conclusions. The dissolving effects of reflection must be contained by relating subjectivity to an order of transcendent value, whether in nature or in tradition. In a development paralleling the evolution of Richard Wagner half a century later,[92] Wordsworth moves from political optimism and partisanship for the French Revolution, to the devaluation of political solutions for the problems of modern life. This conclusion results from Wordworth's radicalizing the principle of subjectivity itself. His initial support for the overthrow of the old regime arose from his attribution of poverty to the feudal monopoly of property and power, the '*forced* disproportion of … possession'.[93] In this spirit, he collaborated with William Godwin, whose Enlightenment radicalism appealed to the benevolent propensities locked in the individual conscience as the possible basis for political renewal and justice. His reflections on Jacobin politics, however, led him to reject the optimism of Godwin's views. Wordsworth came to equate modern freedom with absolute capriciousness, a purely egoistic spontaneity recalcitrant to law or rational restraint.[94] The problem of subjective self-affirmation is not fundamentally political, and cannot be solved by political means. A partial corrective to the hubris of the modern subject is to be found instead in recognition of the sublimity and infinity of nature,[95] which elevates the consciousness above its shallow egoism and reunites it in a meaningful whole. The nature which Wordsworth invokes is not the immutable order of ancient political thought, but a dynamic and inexhaustible source of potentiality. He transfers the unfettered power of the creative subject, celebrated in other Romanticisms, to the engulfing natural world itself. Like the German Romantic A. W. Schlegel (1767–1845),[96] Wordsworth stresses the dependency of the self on this absolute creative power of

[91] John Barrell, *Political Theory of Painting from Reynolds to Hazlitt: 'The Body of the Public'* (New Haven: Yale University Press, 1986), 225–31, 244–53.

[92] Moggach, 'Aesthetics and Politics', 510–12.

[93] Cited in Izenberg, *Impossible Individuality*, 127.

[94] William Wordsworth [1799–1805], *The Prelude*, ed. J. Wordsworth, M. H. Abrams, and S. Gill (New York: Norton, 1979), 821; Izenberg, *Impossible Individuality*, 122.

[95] William Wordsworth [*c*.1797–1800], *Lyrical Ballads and Other Poems*, ed. James Butler and Karen Green (Ithaca, NY: Cornell University Press, 1992).

[96] A. W. Schlegel, *Über das Verhältnis der bildenden Künste zur Natur* (Landshut, 1808); Becq, *Genèse*, ii. 826.

nature. The individual consciousness emerges from this matrix and creates forms for itself,[97] not in Blake's sense of discovery of the original archetype, but in a reflective self-relation. Reflection is not eradicated, but oriented and restrained in its natural setting. In acknowledging the infinity of nature, subjects are able to limit their hubristic claims of freedom, and to reflect on their own activity within its appropriate frame of meaning.[98] The movement from the diremptions of modern culture to new forms of unity is to be achieved not, as Hegel thought, through rational political institutions, but by a common recognition of natural dependency.

Coleridge, the most cognizant among British authors of contemporary German Romantic and idealist thought, follows a trajectory similar to Wordworth's, from endorsement to critique of the revolutionary heritage. His attempt to confront the unleashed powers of reflection takes a distinct course, looking not to nature but to a complex and highly reflective account of tradition. Within the national body, church and state exist in polarity, complementing each other, at once both an ideal tendency and a concrete configuration, one and many.[99] In working out the dialectic of subject, form, and reflection, Coleridge asks how subjects can view the institutional matrix as their own work, and as confirming rather than vitiating their subjective freedom. How is it possible to reconcile subjective agency with the temporary institutional embodiments in which it reposes; how can we induce a modern *oikeiosis*, in which subjects identify with their deeds? Such identification is neither immediately at hand, as in some expressivist accounts, nor ontologically impossible, as in Romantic irony, but a question of training and education. Coleridge deploys Christian Platonism in attempting to resolve the problem. He identifies the state as the agency of moral perfection, but at the same time distinguishes its ideal and phenomenal forms, the latter being subject to historical contingency, and resistant to imposed reforms. He stresses the formative role of the church, both as universal spiritual community and as variegated national confessions, which promotes the identification of individuals with their social world, and which combats their egoism and self-absorption. While later Romantics like Shelley, inspired by William Godwin, are proponents of the radical Enlightenment,[100] Coleridge is highly critical of Enlightenment materialism for undermining loyalties by liberating individual avidity. The rampant commercial spirit upsets the necessary balance between permanence and progress by subverting the landed classes, the placeholders of the past in the present; but its unlimited scope has dire effects on all classes.[101] The tradition to which Coleridge appeals is not fixed, but mobile, evolving. It responds to the initiatives of subjects but depends also upon their voluntary and

[97] Izenberg, *Impossible Individuality*, 125.

[98] Jonathan Bate, *Romantic Ecology: Wordsworth and the Environmental Tradition* (London: Routledge, 1991).

[99] Samuel Taylor Coleridge [1830], 'On the Constitution of Church and State, According to the Idea of Each', *Collected Works*, x, ed. K. Coburn (Princeton: Princeton University Press, 1976). See Toews, 'Church and State', 617–20; and John Morrow, 'Romanticism and Political Thought in the Early Nineteenth Century', in Stedman Jones and Claeys, *Nineteenth Century Thought*, 49–51.

[100] On Shelley, see Morrow, 'Romanticism', 62–4.

[101] Morrow, 'Romanticism', 49.

conscious adherence, mediated by institutional forms. It is sufficiently ample, he hopes, to contain the reflective tendencies of the present.

Releasing Reflection: Irony and its Aftermath

In Herder's idea of reflection, subjects rediscover themselves and their essential attributes doubled and confirmed in the objective world, whose forms they engender in their activity; but for a distinct current of Romanticism, the movement of reflection can also bring to light deep discontinuities between subject and object. Though he is fleetingly a proponent of revolution and republicanism,[102] Friedrich Schlegel (1772–1829) reverts to Mendelssohn's idea of reflection as the inward turn of the subject away from its outer manifestations. In doing so, he converts into its opposite an idea originally complementary to Herder's. Schlegel's concept of irony implies that external forms cannot be authentic expressions of subjective self-awareness, but are merely transitory moments of creation and destruction,[103] from which the subject stands in conscious isolation. The freedom of the subject consists in its knowledge that no deed, no finite product, can ever embody the plenitude of its own creative power. Schlegel's thought absorbs complex influences from Plato, in that he subjectifies the dialectic of idea and phenomena: he now attributes to the *subject* the infinity of potentialities which can never be adequately manifest in the phenomenal realm, though the latter originates from it and in some measure participates in it.[104] Schlegel's thought contains, too, impulses derived from the initial version of Fichte's *Wissenschaftslehre* of 1794–5,[105] which depicts the incessant struggle of subjectivity against the constraints of the material order, though in Fichte's idealism this process is governed by an ethical imperative to rationalize the world under the command of practical reason. Schlegel typically holds that the gap between subject and object is an ontological one, irremediable by human effort; the correct stance is to acknowledge this diremption, and to revel in it, in ironic detachment.

In its analysis of modern subjectivity, the strand of early Romantic thought deriving from Schlegel confirms Hegel's criticism of its unwitting endorsement of the culture of diremption. In dissociating subjects from their attributes or externalizations, and stressing the contradiction between spontaneity and form, subject and object,[106]

[102] Friedrich Schlegel [1796], 'Essay on the Concept of Republicanism occasioned by the Kantian Tract Perpetual Peace', in *Early Political Writings*, ed. Beiser, 93–112.

[103] Menke, 'Ästhetische Subjektivität', 604, 608.

[104] On the revival of Platonism, see Rüdiger Bubner, *The Innovations of Idealism*, tr. Nicholas Walker (Cambridge: Cambridge University Press, 2003).

[105] Manfred Frank, 'Philosophical Foundations of Early Romanticism', in Karl Ameriks and Dieter Sturma (eds), *The Modern Subject* (Albany: SUNY, 1995), 65–85.

[106] Jörn Rüsen, *Ästhetik und Geschichte* (Stuttgart: Metzler, 1976), 19.

these Romantics attest to an inward-looking, merely subjective morality, which resists the transition to the shared values and practices of ethical life. Here the beautiful soul of Schleiermacher and the ironic subject of Schlegel share the same terrain. Because such subjects fall back on an abstract interiority, and do not derive the standards of judgement and action from the network of social ties and mutual recognition,[107] their ends become contingent and arbitrary, and while they acknowledge this arbitrariness, they are incapable of advancing to reconciliation. Ironic subjectivity exhausts itself in self-absorption, giving voice to the dissonances of modern experience.

The separation of the subject from externality has consequences for the understanding of being and time. Early Romantic thought is characterized by a tension between a Spinozistic or pantheist view of substance as a self-causing continuum,[108] admitting no breaks or gaps, and a view of forms as instantaneous, transient, and discontinuous. While Schlegel still seeks an overarching principle of historical development, in which the chaos of the present might portend undetermined possibilities for new experiences of freedom, late Romanticism opts for a fragmented reality, a 'substanceless punctualisation'[109] of incommensurable possibilities, without recourse to an integrating order.

In Schlegel's developmental account of history,[110] ancient thought and art aim at the mimesis of a natural order. The culture of antiquity depicts the subject as rooted in nature, but at the cost of freedom.[111] Modern forms celebrate liberty as the endless play of subjective creative powers,[112] but also contain[113] a potential for perfectibility and for new and higher syntheses, neither the affirmation of mere subjectivity nor immersion in external nature; but the outlines of this resolution remain vague. In this version, the divorce of subject and object is not grounded in metaphysics, but in the dynamics of successive historical formations; irony or the unconstrained heightening of reflection may mark only a transitional phase, and may not be a permanent ethical bearing on the world.

Subsequent Romanticisms deriving from similar sources, but rejecting the meta-historical framework, break down historical time into a succession of discrete and incommensurable moments, each opening to radically different and unpredictable outcomes.[114] The fantastic, the bizarre, the abnormal, the pathological, and demonic realm of inexplicable effects, predominates in the work of Ludwig Tieck (1773–1853)[115] and in the music of Berlioz (though they have antecedents in such proto-Romantic texts as *The*

[107] Hegel, *Philosophy of Right*, 180–6.

[108] Lypp, *Ästhetischer Absolutismus*, 28.

[109] Bohrer, *Grenzen*, 12–13.

[110] Mathy, *Von der Metaphysik*, 17, 23.

[111] Mathy, *Von der Metaphysik*, 18.

[112] Mathy, *Von der Metaphysik*, 17.

[113] Friedrich Schlegel, 'Vom Studium der griechischen Poesie' (1798). See Walter Jaeschke, 'Ästhetische Revolution: Stichworte zur Einführung', in Walter Jaeschke and Helmut Holzhey (eds), *Früher Idealismus und Frühromantik: Der Streit um die Grundlagen der Ästhetik (1795–1805)* (Hamburg: Meiner Verlag, 1990), 5–6.

[114] Mathy, *Von der Metaphysik*, 16; Bohrer, *Grenzen*, 11, 12.

[115] Bohrer, *Grenzen*, 10–15.

Castle of Otranto).[116] Transcendent powers, whether benign or malignant, increasingly penetrate within consciousness itself, rendering it unstable, impermeable to knowledge, and immune to rational self-determination.

Later German Romanticism, especially in the years preceding the revolutionary outbreaks of 1848, develops in critical polemics with the Hegelian school and with the moral and political thinking of Kant. It involves a defence of personal monarchical sovereignty and the organic connection of king and people, against the artificial and mediated relations of constitutionalism; an invocation of history as the continuous outpouring of a popular spirit, not to be distorted by vapid ratiocination, or forced by reform undertaken in the name of abstract principles (as the French had done, to the detriment of Europe); and an attack on Hegelianism itself for undermining healthy, unreflective social mores through its critical rationalism.[117] On this account, not Romantic frivolity but Hegelian reason is the adversary of ethical life. If the lines of demarcation between Idealism and these modes of Romanticism become increasingly clear in the disputes of the German *Vormärz*, their roots lie much deeper, in the differences between rational autonomy and heteronomy; and in the idealist idea that, if subject and object fail to correspond, they ought to: the ethical task of realizing reason in the world of objectivity is the idealist response to the culture of diremption, which is at the root of Romanticism in its various manifestations.

Formativity and Labour

Like Herder in a different register, Thomas Carlyle (1795–1881) extols the organic solidarity of medieval life, and denounces the reduction of human relations to commodity exchange, the ubiquitous cash nexus.[118] In contrast, the medieval village community had recognized the sanctity of labour, degraded and bestialized under modern conditions.[119] Carlyle protests against the crassness and vulgarity of Benthamite utilitarianism,[120] and proposes heroic and charismatic leadership to mitigate social ills. His diagnosis differs from Herder's, however. Whereas, in his celebration of Shakespeare, Herder had established a close affinity between genius and popular culture, in broadening and deepening a universe of shared meanings,[121] Carlyle views as fraught with tension the relationship

116 Farber, *Romanticism*, 22.

117 On the polemics between Romanticism and Hegelianism: Douglas Moggach, *The Philosophy and Politics of Bruno Bauer* (Cambridge: Cambridge University Press, 2003), 93–5, 99–107; Bernadette Collenberg-Plotnikov, 'The Aesthetics of the Hegelian School', in Douglas Moggach (ed.), *Politics, Religion, and Art: Hegelian Debates* (Evanston, Ill.: Northwestern University Press, 2011), 203–30.

118 Carlyle, *Past and Present*, 187.

119 E. P. Thomson, *William Morris: Romantic to Revolutionary*, 2nd edn (London: Merlin, 1977), 29–32.

120 Richard D. Altick, 'Introduction', in Carlyle, *Past and Present*, pp. x–xi.

121 Cf. Herder's sense of the community of interest rather than conflict between cultural leaders and people: Kristin Gjesdal, 'Shakespeare's Hermeneutic Legacy', <ShakespeareQuarterly.folger.edu>.

between the insight of genius and the inertia of the masses.[122] This struggle of the free will of exceptional individuals against prevailing material limitations serves to elevate life to an awareness of its heroic potentialities, even when the hero is defeated. Despite his reflections on the evanescence of victories over chaos, Carlyle retains a faith in the ultimate justice of the course of the world.[123] He plays the spontaneity of the creative subject against the inertia of the material world, genius against mass mentality.

While he dissociates himself from modern Romantics who lack social engagement, John Ruskin (1819–1900) too defends the ideal of wholeness against fragmentation and diremption; the modern economy does more than merely divide up productive labour, but warps and vitiates the being and identity of the workers themselves.[124] With Herder and Carlyle, he upholds a social ideal of diversity in harmony, which he finds exemplified in aspects of medieval life, and which differs from the alienating divisions imposed under modern market conditions.[125] The medieval period had a keener and truer understanding of freedom than the degraded self-interest and hedonism of the moderns. The Gothic idea of franchise, formulated in the cultural flowering of the twelfth century, revives Greek *eleutheria* and Roman *libertas*, implying the bridling of one's passions and their submission to law, and the steadfast determination to a rightful course of life in the face of blandishments and threats.[126] The Gothic spirit evinces discipline, courage, and justice, while channelling energies and devotions towards worthy objects. Modern Romantics (Ruskin is especially vituperative towards Victor Hugo) have abandoned this correct bearing, in favour of a corrupt sense of self, the sensual, and the grotesque.[127] The decadence can be traced in the works of individual Romantic authors: Ruskin considers the early Wordsworth as approximating the authentic Gothic spirit, at once passionate, creative, and virtuous,[128] whose art bears witness to transcendent truth; but late Wordsworth declines into an ethically empty subjectivism, mundanity, and sensuousness, with critical antisocial implications.

With Ruskin, William Morris (1834–96) shares an abhorrence of the philistinism of modern culture and the degradation and misery of urban life. The coexistence of destitution with obscene abundance and waste demands redress. In Morris's expressivist conception of freedom, form and subjectivity ought mutually to confirm each other, but they fail to accord under modern market conditions. The solution to fragmentation and alienation lies in a new, aesthetically enriched conception of labour, and in the transformation of the conditions of labour itself. As the German idealists and the young Marx also held, the purpose of labour is not only the alleviation of material want, but the

122 White, *Metahistory*, 146.

123 Carlyle, *Past and Present*, 18–19.

124 Cited in Thomson, *William Morris*, 37–8.

125 Kenneth Daley, *The Rescue of Romanticism: Walter Pater and John Ruskin* (Athens, Ohio: Ohio University Press, 2001).

126 John Ruskin, 'Franchise', *Complete Works*, xiii (Philadelphia: Reuwee Wattley & Walsh, 1891), 326–36.

127 Ruskin, 'Franchise', 336.

128 Daley, *Rescue*, 18.

expression of freedom, securing harmony between subject and object, activity and its results. The central image in Morris's work is the unity of unity and multiplicity, a new sense of emancipated community compatible with an expanding range of human powers and satisfactions. The aestheticization of labour is to secure beautiful and affirmative life conditions, intersubjective concord, and harmony with the natural world. Art and ethics coalesce in beauty, a beauty toughened and energized by its alliance with the sublime.[129]

In Morris, beauty represents no mere embellishment, flowers on the chains of the present, but implies throwing off those chains themselves. His thought is not a vapid utopianism, but a critical theory. The undeniable utopian elements in Morris's work function in relation to concrete aims of social transformation. As aesthetic education, they break the unreflective grip of the immediate awareness and interests by positing alternate futures, awakening a critical self-awareness, and opening up new horizons of freedom.[130] They preserve a realm of spirit immunized from corrupt material conditions; but this negative does not *only* abide in the imagination or critical consciousness, but is to be understood on Hegelian lines as identifying a *determinate negation*, the central contradiction that must be resolved if there is to be historical progress. The task is set, as a matter of objective necessity within a specific configuration of social relations, but its resolution is open, an act of creative freedom. Here, in Morris as in Marx (and to some extent in Hegel), the determinate negation is the question of the emancipation of labour, the central problem around which all others revolve, as Morris describes it in *News from Nowhere*.[131] Morris's critical theory is predicated on ideas of spontaneity and self-creation, and is intended to promote the conditions for the practice of freedom. The Leibnizian harmony of interests is reformulated not as a presupposition, but as a (problematic) result to be achieved, through conscious and concerted effort. Morris notes a distinction between self-regarding and community-regarding action,[132] and takes it as a matter of course that such a distinction will be respected in practice, or will be built into the fabric of social interaction in emancipated society; but he offers no institutional means for the enforcement of right, besides reliance on virtue or custom, to guarantee the grounds for the spontaneous actions of the self. His ideal is analogous to the aesthetic state of the Hölderlin-inspired 'System Fragment', where dirempted existence is pacified by beauty, and mechanistic collisions are absorbed in organic unities.

In the *Romantic Revolution*, Tim Blanning describes recurrent cycles of Romantic disaffection and Realist engagement.[133] Among the recent revivals of the Romantic spirit are the counter-culture of 1960s, and postmodern assaults on subjective coherence and rational autonomy. These involve not mere repetitions, but new and unpredictable

129 Thomson, *William Morris*, 83, 791.

130 Michelle Weinroth and Paul Leduc Browne (eds), *'To Build a Shadowy Isle of Bliss': William Morris's Radicalism and the Embodiment of Dreams* (Montreal and Kingston: McGill-Queen's University Press, 2015).

131 William Morris, *News from Nowhere*, ed. James Redmond (New York: Routledge, 1970), 77–83.

132 Morris, *News from Nowhere*, 72–7.

133 Blanning, *Romantic Revolution*, 180–1.

formulations. For all its limitations, the course of Romanticism is not yet run. The culture of diremption imparts to it an inexhaustible impetus.[134]

Further Reading

Ameriks, Karl, and Sturma, Dieter, eds, *The Modern Subject* (Albany, NY: SUNY, 1995).

Barrell, John, *Political Theory of Painting from Reynolds to Hazlitt: 'The Body of the Public'* (New Haven: Yale University Press, 1986).

Barzun, Jacques, *Romanticism and the Modern Ego* (Boston: Little Brown, 1943).

Beiser, Frederick (ed. and tr.), *The Early Political Writings of the German Romantics* (Cambridge: Cambridge University Press, 1996).

Beiser, Frederick, *Schiller as Philosopher: A Re-Examination* (Oxford: Oxford University Press, 2005).

Blanning, Tim, *The Romantic Revolution* (London: Weidenfeld & Nicolson, 2010).

Henrich, Dieter, *Between Kant and Hegel: Lectures on German Idealism*, ed. David S. Pacini (Cambridge, Mass.: Harvard University Press, 2003).

Izenberg, G. W., *Impossible Individuality: Romanticism, Revolution, and the Origins of Modern Selfhood* (Princeton: Princeton University Press, 1992).

Kippur, Stephen A., *Jules Michelet, A Study of Mind and Sensibility* (Albany, NY: SUNY Press, 1981).

Löwy, Michael, and Sayre, Robert, *Romanticism Against the Tide of Modernity*, tr. Catherine Porter (Durham, NC: Duke University Press, 2001).

Lukács, Georg, *The Destruction of Reason*, tr. Peter Palmer (London: Merlin, 1980).

Lypp, Bernhard, *Ästhetischer Absolutismus und politische Vernunft: Zum Widerstreit von Reflexion und Sittlichkeit im deutschen Idealismus* (Frankfurt/Main: Suhrkamp, 1972).

Marcuse, Herbert, *Studies in Critical Philosophy* (Boston: Beacon Press, 1973).

Moggach, Douglas, *The Philosophy and Politics of Bruno Bauer* (Cambridge: Cambridge University Press, 2003).

Moggach, Douglas (ed.), *Politics, Religion, and Art: Hegelian Debates* (Evanston, Ill.: Northwestern University Press, 2011), 179–200.

Mueller-Vollmer, Kurt (ed.), *Herder Today* (Berlin and New York: de Gruyter, 1990).

Stedman Jones, Gareth, and Claeys, Gregory (eds), *Cambridge History of Nineteenth-Century Political Thought* (Cambridge: Cambridge University Press, 2013).

Taylor, Charles, *Sources of the Self: The Making of the Modern Identity* (Cambridge, Mass.: Harvard University Press, 1989).

Taylor, Charles, *The Malaise of Modernity* (Concord, Ont.: Anansi, 1991).

Thomson, E. P., *William Morris: Romantic to Revolutionary*, 2nd edn (London: Merlin, 1977).

White, Hayden, *Metahistory: The Historical Imagination in Nineteenth-Century Europe* (Baltimore: Johns Hopkins University Press, 1973).

[134] The author gratefully acknowledges the support of the Social Sciences and Humanities Research Council of Canada and of the Faculty of Social Science, University of Ottawa.

CHAPTER 35

SCIENCE AND THE SCIENTIFIC DISCIPLINES

BENJAMIN DAWSON

Introduction

EUROPEAN Romanticism coincided with a period of profound reorganization in the sciences, and in particular with the genesis of the modern scientific discipline. In contrast to earlier and other orders of discourse in which disciplines operated largely as archives, that is, as repositories of knowledge, by the early nineteenth century the scientific discipline had begun to play an internal, essential, and active role in epistemic production.[1] Processes of specialization, professionalization, and role differentiation in the sciences were central to this transition, and were supported by the establishment of the earliest research universities (in Göttingen, Leipzig, and elsewhere).[2] Likewise important were changes in the form of scientific communication. Notably, as supplements to the general organs of the scientific institutions established in the seventeenth century, such as the *Philosophical Transactions of the Royal Society* and the proceedings of the Paris Académie, the late eighteenth century saw a proliferation of specialist scientific journals which served both to accelerate the generation of empirical observations and to regulate these communications, governing this great new wealth of fact.[3] Beginning around

[1] On the development of the scientific discipline as the primary unit of internal differentiation and structure formation in the social system of science, see Rudolf Stichweh, *Zur Entstehung des modernen Systems wissenschaftlicher Disziplinen: Physik in Deutschland, 1740–1890* (Frankfurt/Main: Suhrkamp, 1984).

[2] 'Scientific factories (*wissenschaftliche Fabriken*)' was how one commentator described these new institutions. Friedrich Böll, *Das Universitätswesen in Briefen* (1782), cited in Andre Wakefield, *The Disordered Police State: German Cameralism as Science and Practice* (Chicago: University of Chicago Press, 2009), 49. For university reforms prior to the Humboldt era, see Charles E. McClelland, *State, Society, and University in Germany 1700–1914* (Cambridge: Cambridge University Press, 1980), 37–98.

[3] 'The periodical publications of the scientific societies were specialized in the sense that they concerned themselves with the sciences, but they were not limited to any one specialty or discipline.'

1780, journals devoted exclusively to chemistry, physics, mathematics, and philology began in France, Germany, and Britain; and, rather than quickly disappearing again, they became relatively stable sites for the publication of discoveries, the consolidation of specialized vocabularies and criteria of judgement, and hence for the increasing independence of these burgeoning discursive formations.

Beneath this disciplinary redifferentiation of knowledge, changes to the social and moral codes framing intellectual discourse were occurring. In the second half of the eighteenth century, the foundations of the old so-called 'learned class' (*Gelehrtenstand*) were effectively demolished by the ideological and medial forces of the European Enlightenment. The cultural and social interiorization of print played a powerful role in this process, altering the status of the scholarly professions so that, for some observers, the 'Republic of Letters' appeared to have been commandeered by a 'great horde of writers'.[4] 'To attain citizenship of the learned requires only a piece of *writing* (*bedarf es nur einer* Schrift); hence, it is exclusively writers who are named *the learned*.'[5] The old European distinction *literati*/*illiterati*, which had conditioned and sustained the scholarly class within Europe's stratified societies up to and including the natural and 'gentlemen' philosophers of the seventeenth and early eighteenth centuries, was collapsing. And in the academies and universities, late humanist ideals still centred on erudition and eloquence were rendered further obsolete by the intensifying 'research imperative'.[6] Indeed, the emergence at this time of the modern semantics of 'research' (*Forschung*, *recherche*, etc.) ultimately signalled the end of the tradition of European *scientia*, and a redetermination of the totality, and *temporality*, of knowledges of nature: 'In early modern times the transition from the preservation to the enlargement of knowledge could only be perceived as a continual process. In contrast, *research* from about 1800 refers to a fundamental, and at any time realizable, questioning of the entire body of knowledge until then considered as true.'[7]

As the scientific discipline became an internal, generative agent, essential to the production of knowledge in and out of the research university, the form of epistemic

James McClellan III, 'Scientific Institutions and the Organization of Science', in Roy Porter (ed.), *The Cambridge History of Science: Eighteenth-Century Science* (Cambridge: Cambridge University Press, 2003), iv. 87–106 (87). That said, already by the mid-century, articles in the *Transactions* were becoming more determined by professional argument, a tendency supported by the introduction of referees in 1752. See Charles Bazerman, *Shaping Written Knowledge: The Genre and Activity of the Experimental Article in Science* (Madison, Wis.: University of Wisconsin Press, 1988), 136.

4 'Gelehrtenrepublik heißt also der ganze Haufe von Schriftstellern ...' Johann Melchior Gottlieb Beseke, *Vom Patriotismus in der deutschen Gelehrtenrepublik* (Dessau, Leipzig: Buchhandlung der Gelehrten, 1782); quoted in Heinrich Bosse, 'Gelehrte und Gebildete—die Kinder des 1. Standes', *Das achtzehnte Jahrhundert*, 32 (2008), 16.

5 Beseke, quoted in Bosse, 'Gelehrte und Gebildete', 16.

6 See Steven Turner, 'The Prussian Professoriate and the Research Imperative, 1790–1840', in H. N. Jahnke and M. Otte (eds), *Epistemological and Social Problems of the Sciences in the Early Nineteenth Century* (Dordrecht: Springer, 1981), 109–21.

7 Rudolf Stichweh, 'Scientific Disciplines, History of', in Neil J. Smelser and Paul B. Baltes (eds), *International Encyclopedia of the Social and Behavioral Sciences* (Amsterdam: Elsevier, 2001), 13729.

advance became more profoundly discontinuous. An evolutionary progress punctuated by 'epigenetic' breaks displaced or further replaced the contiguous unfolding of natural truth, so that, in science as in politics and art, the period is marked by an increase in power of the present over the past, the new over the established.[8] The transition from continuity to discontinuity seems itself to have been experienced as abrupt rather than gradual—a redoubled or reflexive discontinuity that may lie behind the disorientation discernible in questions such as the 'Where are we?' (*Wo stehn wir*?) of Wilhelm von Humboldt's *The Eighteenth Century* (written already in 1796/7). It also explains, in part, why '1800' could later become the sign of an opaque or 'archaeological' event.[9]

The End of Natural History

Particularly important to the possibility of a Romantic epistemology of science was the fate of the traditional field of 'natural history' as it strove, and failed, to contain the rapidly developing and diversifying discourses of geology, mineralogy, botany, embryology, and zoology, which were each attracting their own communities of authors, observers, and highly motivated experimenters. Mutations of both 'nature' and 'history' were under way.

The category of *historia*—the old name for knowledge from singular cases (*explicatio et notitia rerum singularium*)—was under pressure from modes of investigation which, within the emerging disciplinary economy of research, tended to be both more explicitly *generative* of the phenomena of observation and more methodologically *reflexive*. Already '[b]y the middle of the eighteenth century, "natural history" was no longer seen by the Republic of Letters as a part of history', being rather, as the *Encyclopédie* put it, 'an essential part of physics'.[10] The new distinction, coming at the end of 'natural history', between history (i.e. *temporalized* history) and physics, is important, here, because this distinction became central among those that Romantic science would strive to sublate: 'Not history *of* physics,' Ritter will declare, 'but rather history = physics = history.'[11] The bald and redoubled equation here seems, to say the least, lacking in mediation;

[8] As Wolf Lepenies remarks, 'at the turn of the eighteenth century ... the French Revolution appeared as a model for scientific as well as political upheaval': *Das Ende der Naturgeschichte: Wandel kultureller Selbstverständlichkeiten in den Wissenschaften des 18. und 19. Jahrhunderts* (Munich: C. Hanser, 1976), 107. Foucault discusses the new epistemic and philosophical significance of 'the present' at this time in his many readings of Kant's essay 'What is *Aufklärung*?'. See e.g. Michel Foucault, *The Government of Self and Others*, tr. Graham Burchell (Basingstoke and New York: Palgrave Macmillan, 2010), 11.

[9] Cf. Joseph Vogl, 'Einleitung', in *Poetologien des Wissens um 1800* (Munich: Fink, 1999), 7–10.

[10] Brian W. Ogilvie, 'Natural History, Ethics, and Physico-Theology', in Nancy G. Siraisi and Gianna Pomata (eds), *Historia: Empiricism and Erudition in Early Modern Europe* (Cambridge, Mass.: MIT Press, 2005), 98.

[11] Johann Wilhelm Ritter, *Fragmente aus dem Nachlasse eines jungen Physikers* in *Key Texts of Johann Wilhelm Ritter (1776–1810) on the Science and Art of Nature: Dual Language Edition*, ed. Jocelyn Holland (Leiden: Brill, 2010), 192–3, fragment 140.

yet, as this chapter will try to show, the entirety of Ritter's thought, and a good deal of Romantic science more broadly, is lodged in these = signs. '*Sattelzeit* has two stirrups', writes Rüdiger Campe: 'knowledge of *artes* and even of *theoria*, the exhibition of the universal, underwent historicization. And *historia* ... turns, in the shape of history-in-time (*Geschichte-in-der-Zeit*), into knowledge elevated above knowledge, indeed into a theoretical form of the universal.'[12]

These changes profoundly affected the other term in 'natural history'. For the process of differentiation between scientific discourses entailed a concomitant withdrawal of 'nature' as the direct source and foundation of the divisions between genres of empirical knowledge. In this climate, long-standing, naturally supported divisions between knowledges (such as organic/inorganic, terrestrial/celestial, and so forth) were superseded, as the isolation and resolution of the objects of scientific investigation became increasingly an internal, discursive operation of the disciplines themselves. The European fervour over 'galvanism' (the investigation of 'animal electricity' closely entangled at certain points with Romantic discourse) was partly due to its promise to reintegrate a nature torn apart in the divergence of sciences.[13] In the midst of an 'age of separations' (to borrow Adam Ferguson's phrase), galvanism—a new combined science of physiological, electrical, chemical, and even magnetic phenomena—was to heal the 'wounds of nature' inflicted by ongoing structural transformations in scientific communication.[14] Similarly, the synthetic and reflective discourse of '*biology*— ... the doctrine of the living system in all its states', points to a felt need at this time for a unified science of life.[15] Biology was to combine anatomy, physiology, pathology, embryology, histology, early forms of neurology, etc. into a single (moral as well as medical) discourse. And, in Germany, alongside Treviranus's *Biologie* of 1804 appeared Troxler's *Biosophie* (1807), a document belonging to the idealist programme of a philosophy of nature, another discourse emphatically committed to the unity and systematicity of nature. Here, too, we may locate the scientific programme of Romanticism.

Confronted with an emergent plurality of discourses, Romantic epistemology, alongside the Kantian and post-Kantian philosophy with which it was intricately interwoven, can be seen as attempting to reintegrate knowledge on the basis of the constituent, synthetic unity of the self. Such a perspective no doubt accords with a familiar intellectual history concerning the role of Romantic and idealist agendas

[12] Rüdiger Campe, 'Wahrscheinliche Geschichte—poetologische Kategorie und mathematische Funktion: Zum Beispiel der Statistik in Kants "Idee zu einer allgemeinen Geschichte in Weltbürgerlicher Absicht"', in Joseph Vogl (ed.), *Poetologien des Wissens um 1800* (Munich: Fink, 1999), 209.

[13] See Stuart Strickland, 'Galvanic Disciplines: The Boundaries, Objects, and Identities of Experimental Science in the Era of Romanticism', *History of Science; An Annual Review of Literature, Research and Teaching*, 33 (1995), 449–68.

[14] Ritter, *Key Texts*, 292–3, fragment 337.

[15] Thomas Beddoes, *Contributions to Physical and Medical Knowledge, Principally from the West Country* (Bristol: printed by Biggs & Cottle, 1799), 4. John Brown coins the formulation 'science of life' in his *Elements of Medicine* (1795), *The Works of Dr. John Brown*, ed. William Cullen (London: St Paul's Church Yard, J. Johnson, 1804), ii. 125.

(and, notably, the holistic semantics of *Bildung* and *Wissenschaft*) in the formation of the Berlin University.[16] Closer attention, however, to the actual research practices of Romantic science complicates the traditional story. For, as will become clear, Romantic epistemology was by no means simply synthetic; nor, at least in a banal sense, organicist. 'Practical physics—art of modifying nature—of generating natures as desired', reads a somehow typical fragment of Novalis.[17] A diversifying, multiplying, procreative aspect of Romantic science needs to be acknowledged even (and indeed especially) in its orientation towards the unity and systematicity of the whole as secured, or reflected, by the transcendental subject. The line-drawing of 'Romanticism in science' to be presented in this chapter is intended to show that, and how, dialectical relationships between unity and multiplicity, identity and difference, as also those between self-consciousness and organic nature, history and speculation, which are well known to students of the philosophy of this period, may likewise be observed at the micro-level of research techniques.

The signature of Romanticism in science is, indeed, best looked for at the level of research styles, rather than any particular metaphysics or set of preferred metaphors. Uprooted from real practices of conducting experimental research, the sort of pronouncements often associated with Romantic attitudes in science—concerning, for example, nature as a whole, as an organism, a polarity, a protean, metamorphosing system, or else as an irrational, creative, demiurgic, or daemonic power—must ultimately be reduced to bland abstractions. Bereft of the procedures, processes, and physical experiences in which they arose and to which they gave rise, they appear altogether lacking in concreteness, both in the ordinary sense that they lack empirical reference and the philosophical sense of sounding like unreflective, immediate assertions. Here, however, we also hit upon a major structural problem of Romantic science, namely, its constitutive emphasis on the dialectical negativity of its *process* over the descriptive positivity of its *results*. In places, indeed, what seems to drive this mode of knowledge forward is its own feeling of dissatisfaction and disappointment, the sudden evacuation of interest—or an anxiety about the likelihood of such feelings—when the experiment ends, the object stabilizes, and the ideas that animated and were animated by the experience stare inertly from the page. Nowhere is this tension between the intensity and depth of experimental experience and the propositional limitations of description, between learning and judgment, more pronounced, or more ingeniously and skilfully handled, than in the work of the Silesian chemist and physicist, Johann Wilhelm Ritter. It is towards his work that the chapter moves.

[16] See Elinor S. Shaffer, 'Romantic Philosophy and the Organization of the Disciplines: The Founding of the Humboldt University of Berlin', in Andrew Cunningham and Nicholas Jardine (eds), *Romanticism and the Sciences* (Cambridge: Cambridge University Press, 1990), 38–54; Frederick Gregory, 'Kant, Schelling, and the Administration of Science in the Romantic Era', *Osiris*, 5 (1989), 17–35.

[17] Novalis, *Werke, Briefe, Dokumente*, ed. Ewald Wasmuth (Heidelberg: L. Schneider, 1953), 54. Novalis, *Notes for a Romantic Encyclopaedia: Das Allgemeine Brouillon*, tr. David W. Wood (New York: State University of New York Press, 2011), 8.

Variation and Mediation in Goethe's Epistemology of Science

In a famous exchange on the subject of scientific epistemology, Schiller attempted to correct Goethe's conception of the *Urpflanze* (original plant), by explaining that this was not a possible object of empirical cognition but a rational idea with which no experience could ever be congruent. Goethe's impatient response—'well, so much the better; it means that I have ideas without knowing it, and can even *see them with my eyes*'—has often been taken to encapsulate his strange empiricism.[18] As some recent scholarship suggests, however, Goethe's struggle with the relation between rational ideas and sensible experience led him beyond this well-known outburst towards more complex conceptions and articulations of their 'objective' mediation.[19]

> Dr. Heinroth ... speaks favourably of my nature and activity (*Wesen und Wirken*); in fact, he declares my procedure (*Verfahrungsart*) a unique one. He says, namely, that my mode of thought operates *objectively* (gegenständlich): by which he means that my thinking does not separate itself from objects; the elements of the objects, the intuitions, enter into my thinking and are most intimately penetrated by it; so that my intuiting is itself a thinking and my thinking an intuiting (*die Elemente der Gegenstände, die Anschauungen in dasselbe eingehen und von ihm auf das innigste durchdringen werden, daß mein Anschauen selbst ein Denken, mein Denken ein Anschauen sei*).[20]

The anthropologist, Dr Heinroth, appears to have grasped, with particular acuity, the mimetic and plastic character of Goethe's style of research, his particular way of (to speak with Hegel) surrendering to the life of the object. The choice of the adverb '*objectively*', which Goethe found 'ingenious (*geistreiches*)', marks the connection as well as the distance between Goethe's epistemology and other moral economies of science centred, then and subsequently, upon 'objectivity'. For Kant, we may recall here, objectivity signifies (leaving aside certain differences in his uses of a term he reintroduced into philosophy) a form of the validity and universality of judgements, which derives from the identity of the conditions of the possibility of experience with the conditions of the possibility of the objects of experience. This identity is connected to the impossibility of knowing things in themselves. In contrast to this Kantian notion of objectivity, then,

[18] Quoted from the classic exposition in Erich Heller, *The Disinherited Mind: Essays in Modern German Literature and Thought* (Harmondsworth: Penguin, 1961), 6.

[19] See, in particular, Joseph Vogl's essay 'Bemerkung über Goethes Empirismus', in Sabine Schimma and Joseph Vogl (eds), *Versuchsanordnungen 1800* (Zurich and Berlin: Diaphanes Verlag, 2009), 113–23; and Eckart Förster, *The Twenty-Five Years of Philosophy*, tr. Brady Bowman (Cambridge, Mass.: Harvard University Press, 2012), esp. ch. 11.

[20] Johann Wolfgang von Goethe, *Werke: Hamburger Ausgabe*, ed. Rike Wankmüller and Dorothea Kuhn (Munich: C. H. Beck, 1981), xiii. 37.

Goethe's epistemology maintains both the independence of the form of the object from the knowing subject (the non-intellectual source of its determinateness) and, as a result of this distance, the process of 'mediation' between subject and object—mediation not in reason purely, but at the *empirical* level of experience and experiment.

Goethe's compact discourse on method, 'The Experiment as Mediator of Object and Subject', written in April 1792, proposes a new conception of the role of experiment in natural science. In fact, it is not Kant but Newton who is the implicit, but nonetheless clear, target here. A key text in what has been described as Goethe's 'Protestant Reformation' in science, religious and political concerns are never far from the surface of this treatise on experiment.[21] In the essay, Goethe likens the classical (Newtonian) natural philosopher to a tyrant forcing his subjects (empirical facts) into docile obedience to the dictates of his system.

> We often find that the more limited the data, the more art a gifted thinker will apply. As though to show his sovereignty, he picks out from the slender data available (*vorliegenden Datis*) the few minions which flatter him (*Günstlinge …, die ihm schmeicheln*) and skilfully marshals the rest so they never contradict him directly. Finally he is able to spin (*umspinnen*), entangle, or set aside hostile data and reduce the whole to something more like the court of a despot than a freely constituted republic.[22]

In contrast, Goethe stresses his own pleasure in free collaboration with others and, likewise in perceived opposition to Newton, underlines that the 'value of an experiment consists primarily in the fact that, simple or compound, it can be reproduced at any time given the requisite preparations' (14/13). Such labour of research is 'undertaken for the world and posterity (*Welt und Nachwelt*)' (20/17), and Goethe hopes that, through his own toil, his experiments will have 'become easy to reproduce' rather than 'beyond the scope of so many people'.

It is worth noting, here, an echo of this epistemological republicanism in Schelling's famous letter to Hegel (January 1795): 'Kant has given the results; the premises are still missing. And who can understand results without premises? Doubtless a Kant may, but what is the great many (*der große Haufe*) supposed to do with it? … We must go on with philosophy! Kant has cleared away *everything*,—but how are they to tell?'[23] Schelling's statement and attitude directly reject the view that the *hoi polloi* are to be supplied solely with the positive 'results' of intellectual labour, and spared the process, the negativity, of their production. This is an important political thread running through post-Kantian theoretical philosophy towards Hegel's *Phenomenology*, the preface of

[21] Myles W. Jackson, 'A Spectrum of Belief: Goethe's "Republic" versus Newtonian "Despotism"', *Social Studies of Science*, 24 (1994), 682 and *passim*.

[22] Goethe, *Werke*, xiii. 16. *Scientific Studies*, tr. Douglas Miller, *Collected Works* (Princeton: Princeton University Press, 1994), xii. 15. Subsequent references to, respectively, German and English texts will be given in the text.

[23] F. W. J. Schelling, in *Briefe von und an Hegel* (Hamburg: Meiner, 1969), i. 14.

which unambiguously affirms: 'Only what is completely determined is at once exoteric, comprehensible, and capable of being learned by, and the property of, everyone. The intelligible form of science is the way open and equally accessible to all ...'[24] Goethe's epistemology aims at such complete determination and it, too, may be connected to this Protestant-Enlightenment tradition of popular education. For Goethe, however, there is an important sense in which the process of formation (*Bildung*) is to occur on the side of the *object*, rather than the subject. And this is because, in a gesture that was to prove quite influential, Goethe tends to conceive the determining function of the intellect (constituent subjectivity) as a form of domination (mastery over nature, etc.).

According to Goethe, the Newtonian method conducts and arranges experiments in conformity with its formal arguments. This is problematic not only for the overbearing role it grants to intellectual abstraction; it is also wasteful of sensuous particularity. Once its abstract schema has been filled in with empirical evidence, 'later experiments must be laid aside unused, like bricks brought to a finished building' (20/17). Against Newton, Goethe ventures to say that 'we cannot prove anything by one experiment or even several experiments taken together, that, indeed, nothing is more dangerous than the desire to prove some thesis immediately through experiments' (15/14). In other words, he rejects the idea of the *experimentum crucis*. Experimentation is to be a *mediatory* rather than verificatory process. As such, the essay repeatedly returns to and reinscribes an opposition between immediacy and mediation. As he sees it, the relation between mathematical abstractions and empirical facts characteristic of 'the other method' belies an abstract, insufficiently mediated, and tendentially authoritarian ('despotic') relationship between theory and phenomena, idea and experience.

Importantly, however, Goethe actually believes his own method of experimental science approximates *more* closely to the ideal of mathematical deduction than does the mathematical natural philosophy. For, rather than applying mathematics to phenomena, it strives to emulate the mathematician's 'meticulous care in placing neighbour next to neighbour in series, or rather of inferring one from the other (*das Nächste aus dem Nächsten*)' (18/16).[25] Adhering to the procedure of 'mathematical demonstration, which conducts (*durchführt*) initial elements through their many connections', will, it is hoped, help to restrain the misplaced use of 'imagination and wit' in the practice of empirical science. Goethe does not advocate the use of these artistic faculties in science. His method is, rather, an idiosyncratic synthesis of rationalist and empiricist modes

[24] G. W. F. Hegel, *Phänomenologie des Geistes*, ed. Friedrich Wessels and Heinrich Clairmont (Hamburg: Meiner, 1988), 11.

[25] In the Preface to his *Attempt to Introduce the Concept of Negative Magnitudes into Philosophy* (1763), Kant had stated: 'The use to which mathematics can be put in philosophy consists either in the imitation of its method or in the real application of its propositions to the objects of philosophy. It is not evident that the first has been of a single use, however great the advantage it initially promised ... [Regarding] the second use, by contrast, [... there are] parts of philosophy which, by employing the doctrines of mathematics for their own purposes, have raised themselves to a height to which they otherwise could have made no claim' AA 2: 167; English tr. from *Theoretical Philosophy, 1755–1770*, tr. and ed. David Walford with Ralf Meerbote (Cambridge: Cambridge University Press, 1992).

of demonstration. As Eckart Förster has suggestively argued, it transplants a Spinozan intuitive science (*scientia intuitiva*) from the sphere of mathematical objects and pure concepts onto empirical nature.[26] By the same token (but viewed, so to speak, in the other direction), one could say that it grafts an empiricist (Lockean) form of demonstration qua sensible 'showing' onto a speculative, deductive procedure: 'demonstrations are always more expositions (*Darlegungen*), recapitulations, than arguments' (19/16).

Either way, the first gesture is to posit the unity and systematicity of nature. 'Nothing happens in living nature which does not stand in a connection to the whole' (17/15). As Goethe is fully aware, everything 'hinges on this point'. And yet what is important here is not the metaphysical dimension of the claim, but the methodology Goethe derives from it. As the foundation of the procedure outlined in the treatise, this is neither a metaphysical or empirical proposition nor exactly a regulative idea in Kant's sense. It is, rather, a thesis concerning the whole towards which every limited experience will and must lead, if rigorously pursued. For, if nature is *one*, all that is finally required in studying it is to follow the connections, transitions, or metamorphoses between phenomena; if nature is a whole, then the whole must be present in the transitions between any two phenomenal events, however local or limited they may appear.

> Nothing happens in living nature which does not stand in a connection to the whole.[27] And when experiences seem isolated to us, when experiments are viewed merely as isolated facts (*Fakta*), this is not to say that they are indeed isolated; the question is only: how are we to find the connection of these phenomena, of this occurrence? (17/15)

Thus, whereas in his earlier *Attempt to Explain the Metamorphosis of Plants* (1790) Goethe had sought to detail and describe '[t]he process by which one and the same organ appears in a variety of forms', in 'The Experiment as Mediator', it is not nature directly but, first of all, experimentation which bears and exhibits organic unity and systematic variety.[28] Methodology recapitulates morphology; or rather, it has taken the latter over and into itself. By the time of the essay, it is one and the same *experiment* that recursively 'appears in a variety of forms', for it is diversified and explored in multiple variations. Goethe's 1792 treatise on method is, precisely, an attempt to understand the metamorphosis of experiment. And as such, to recall the insight of Dr Heinroth, Goethe has allowed the elements of the object (plant growth) to enter into and reshape his method, so that his epistemology of experiment resembles, repeats, and refigures the process it formerly ascribed to the intuited object. Empirical claims become

[26] See Förster, *Twenty-Five Years*, 254ff.

[27] 'Living', here, is best interpreted expansively. Schelling remarks that while Jacobi confessed 'not even … being able to *think* matter as living …, Goethe once said he did not know how he should start to think matter as not being living'. F. W. J. von Schelling, *On the History of Modern Philosophy*, tr. Andrew Bowie (Cambridge and New York: Cambridge University Press, 1994), 173.

[28] Goethe, *Werke*, xiii. 64, §4. *The Metamorphosis of Plants*, tr. Gordon L Miller (Cambridge, Mass.: MIT Press, 2009).

methodological rules. And, in the process, the interaction of thought and intuition becomes not simply more explicit but, indeed, external, for the mediation of subject and object now takes place, outside the subject, in and through the geometrical procedure of experimentation.

The culminating claim of 'The Experiment as Mediator' is that, if the 'series of experiments (*Reihe von Versuchen*)' are followed with due care, they will eventually compose themselves into 'a *single* experience' (18/16; emphasis added). Each experiment is to be deduced contiguously from a previous experiment, so that:

> Studied thoroughly and understood as a whole, these experiments could even be thought of as representing a single experiment, just one experience presented in manifold variations (*nur eine Erfahrung unter den mannigfaltigsten Ansichten darstellen*).
>
> Such an experience, composed of many others, is clearly of a higher sort. It sets out the formula, so to speak, by which any number of individual calculations are expressed. I hold it to be the duty of the natural researcher to begin to work toward experiences of this higher sort ... (18/16)

In Goethe's experimental system, the result of any experiment is, ideally, another experiment. Experiments should produce experiments in continual metamorphosis towards ever-higher experiences of nature—experiences which retain and contain those of the *series*, the sequence, and hence the formula, from which they derive. Evidential experience is elevated via a systematic, geometrical, and demonstrative—but also dynamic, exploratory, and improvisatory—process of variation, multiplication, and diversification.[29]

Thus, the twofold innovation of Goethe's scientific methodology, which is essential to an understanding of the epistemology of Romantic science, was to conceive experimentation as *mediation* (of subject and object) and *variation* (of the experimental phenomenon). The 'proper duty of a natural researcher' is the 'diversification (*Vermannigfaltigung*) of each single experiment' (18/16). Rather than verifying predictions, true experimentation systematically varies the contexts in which a particular phenomenon appears. That is, it reproduces the same phenomenon (a specific colour, say) through different means, and hence under a plurality of different conditions. A phenomenon reproduced and experienced in such a diversity of contexts is gradually purified of any single specific context. As such, it is elevated into a universal (what others, but

[29] Emphasizing the procedure of 'diversification' and 'multiplication' in the method of the *Theory of Colours*, Vogl offers a significantly different reading of Goethe to Förster's interpretation. See Joseph Vogl, 'Bemerkung über Goethes Empirismus', in Schimma and Vogl, *Versuchsanordnungen 1800*, 115–16. While Förster indicates the 'Spinozist', speculative-systematic aspect of Goethe's methodology (stressing the analogy with mathematical demonstration and tending to downplay or contain the process of diversification), Vogl points to the 'open-ended', 'improvisatory and exploratory' nature of Goethe's empiricism (115). These apparently contradictory views in fact highlight the peculiar tension of Goethe's ideal work of systematic variation.

not Goethe, would call a concept) not through a process of intellectual abstraction but, on the contrary, through deeper immersion in sensuous being; the phenomenon is liberated from the sensuous immediacy in which it initially appears not through *subtracting* contingent and arbitrary features of that appearance, but rather through *multiplying* the latter so that the idea manifesting itself in the phenomenon gradually stands forth.

In subsequent epistemological reflections titled 'Experience and Science' (1798), Goethe articulated this experimental procedure of purification-through-variation more emphatically: 'it is not causes of phenomena which are the object of inquiry, but rather the *conditions* under which they appear. It is their consequential result, their eternal recurrence in a thousand circumstances, their monotony and their changeability, which are beheld and embraced ...' (25/25). The object of research is now said to pass through three stations: it first appears as an 'empirical phenomenon' (the phenomenon as it is prior to any investigation); subsequently, as the 'scientific phenomenon' (the phenomenon elevated through experiments that 'alter the circumstances and conditions' in which it was initially known); and, finally, as the pure phenomenon (*reine Phänomen*), which 'stands forth as the result of all the experiences and experiments' through which it has passed, and, moreover, which it preserves:

> It can never be isolated, but shows itself in a continuous succession of appearances. In order to present it, the human spirit determines what is empirically unstable (*bestimmt ... das empirische Wankende*), excludes the contingent, separates the impure, unfolds the confused, indeed uncovers the unknown. (25/25)

Such is Goethe's epistemology, a method of experimentation not purposed to test any theory but rather to take a common empirical phenomenon and purify it by varying the material conditions under which it occurs.[30]

Like many of his generation, Goethe associated 'the other method', i.e. Newton's mathematical-mechanical mode of explanation, with the operations of the understanding (i.e. formalistic rationality: *Verstand*) and the discursive, subsumptive, 'juridical' model of cognition anatomized, criticized, and legitimized by Kant. From this angle, the decisive novelty of his method is this: on the classical, discursive view, concepts are, qua genera, necessarily *weaker* in determinate content (i.e. more abstract) than the particulars which fall under them: in order to apply to a multiplicity of individual cases, a concept qua 'law of them all' must be *less* specific or definite than any of those particular cases in isolation. With Goethe, Romantic science, and ultimately Hegel exactly the reverse is true: universals are, as *results* of the series of experiences through which they emerge, necessarily *more* determinate than any particular instance or 'moment' in the course of that development. The universal is not supposed to be staticly external to the particular it subsumes; the particular is a moment internal to the dialectical movement of the universal. The point is that qualitative determinacy, or 'concreteness', is

[30] Cf., on this distinction, Maria Trumpler, 'Verification and Variation: Patterns of Experimentation in Investigations of Galvanism in Germany, 1790–1800', *Philosophy of Science*, 64 (1997), S75–S84.

here a function of mediation, of the *relationships* in which the particular is involved and constituted; from this perspective, nothing is more abstract than the immediate data of isolated sensuous particulars. Ultimately, every individual phenomenon is mediated through every other; and the whole, mediated through every individual, is the most determinate reality: richest in content is the totality which contains (i.e. retains and sustains) each and every particular.[31]

Active Empiricism: The Transition to Romanticism

An extremely bold and speculative fragment from the *Athenäum* reads: 'The scientific ideal of Christianity is a characteristic of the Godhead with infinitely many variations (*Das wissenschaftliche Ideal des Christianismus ist eine Karakteristik der Gottheit mit unendlich vielen Variazionen*).' It is doubtful that Goethe would have directly endorsed Schlegel's peculiar epistemo-christology, but he did conceive the economy of the experiment ('mediator') as a work of elevation through variation. And in this, the Romantics discerned the ideal programme of what Novalis called 'practical physics' or, even more accurately, 'active empiricism': 'he [Goethe] abstracts (*abstrahiert*) with rare exactitude, but never without at the same time constructing (*konstruieren*) the object to which the abstraction corresponds'.[32] For Novalis, it is the *modality* that is crucial—Goethe's 'abstractions' are not possibilities or necessities but actualities. 'With [Goethe] everything is deed—as with others everything is only tendency. He really makes something, while others only make something possible—or necessary. We are all necessary and possible creators—but how few of us are real ones. The scholastic philosopher (*Philosoph der Schule*) would perhaps call this active empiricism.'[33]

Pre-eminent among the 'others' mentioned, here, is Kant. Where transcendental idealism produces only the necessary conditions of possible objects ('a nature in general'), active empiricism produces 'pure phenomena', actual experiences, albeit 'higher' ones. As has often been noted, Goethe treated metaphysical ideas as phenomenal realities. Following the abandoned search for the *Urpflanze* in Italy, however, these ideal realities needed to be constructed, since they were not immediate natural products. And this is what Romanticism seizes upon—the Kantian, critical principle ('reason only has insight

[31] Cassirer indicates a very similar rejection of the traditional theory of the formation of concepts in Lambert's criticism of the logic of the Wolffian school; see Ernst Cassirer, *Substance and Function and Einstein's Theory of Relativity*, tr. W. C. Swabey and M. C. Swabey (New York: Dover Publications, 1953), 19.

[32] Novalis, *Werke*, ed. Gerhard Schulz (Munich: Verlag C. H. Beck, 1969), 410. Novalis, *Philosophical Writings*, tr. Margaret Mahony Stoljar (Albany, NY: SUNY Press, 1997), 112.

[33] Novalis, *Werke*, 409; Novalis, *Philosophical Writings*, 112.

into that which it itself generates (*hervorbringt*) according to its own design'[34]) pushed into an actuality (or effectuality; *Wirklichkeit*) beyond the distinction between appearances and things in themselves: 'We only *know* it, *insofar* we *realize* it.'[35]

Later epistemologists have made comparable assertions.[36] What seems peculiarly Romantic, however, is the idea that this techno-scientific identity of knowing and making, ultimately, or simultaneously, directs the self back towards and into itself. As we shall see, Novalis, Schlegel, Ritter, and others saw the path of nature, studied as a 'whole', leading finally *not* to any pure phenomenon, but back to the human self or *subject*. In this, they were more faithful than Goethe to the spirit of transcendental philosophy.

> *Criticism* … is really the teaching (*Lehre*) which points (*verweist*) us back to ourselves while studying nature, back to inner observation and experimentation (*innre Beobachtung und Versuch*), and while studying our self, to the external world, to external observations and experiments—considered philosophically, the most fertile of all *indications*. It lets us divine nature, or the *external world*, as a human being (*menschliches Wesen*)—it proves that we can and should only understand *everything* as we understand ourselves and our *loved ones* (Geliebten), as we understand us and *you* (*uns und* euch). We catch a glimpse of ourselves in the system, *as component* (als Glied)—consequently, in ascending and descending line, from the infinitely small to the infinitely large—*human beings* of infinite variations.[37]

From the critical, Romantic, and idealist standpoint developing here, the experimental mediation of subject and object in Goethe's methodology has failed to return to 'human beings', to spirit, as the infinite substance and absolute subject of variation. The bipolar experimental system which Goethe described in his epistemological writings of the 1790s, culminates in the externalization of cognition into natural objectivity, with fewer and fewer Romantic 'glimpse[s] of ourselves in the system'. Goethe was, from this angle, in the vanguard of the so-called 'struggle against subjectivism', a campaign which has been seen to span and intellectually define the *Goethezeit*.[38] But, as such, his scientific studies ultimately expose the subject to the *uncriticizability* of its knowledge. Finally, even the rational character of mathematical demonstration, which might have upheld the separation and, hence, potential mediation of the two poles (object and subject, nature and thought), is seen as merely the recapitulation of *nature*: 'its demonstrations

[34] Immanuel Kant, *Kritik der reinen Vernunft*, ed. Jens Timmermann (Hamburg: Felix Meiner, 1998), Bxiii.

[35] Novalis, 'Kant Studies (1797)', tr. David Wood, *The Philosophical Forum*, 32 (2001), 331. Cf. the assertion in the *Hemsterhuis-Studien*: 'We *only know*, insofar *we make*.' Quoted in Frederick C. Beiser, *German Idealism: The Struggle Against Subjectivism, 1781–1801* (Cambridge, Mass.: Harvard University Press, 2008), 431.

[36] Cf. e.g. Bruno Latour's dictum: 'On ne sait rien mais on réalise.' Bruno Latour, *Pasteur: Guerre et paix des microbes. Suivi de Irréductions* (Paris: Editions La Découverte, 2011), 244, proposition 1.1.5.4.

[37] Novalis, *Werke*, 489.

[38] Notably: Beiser, *German Idealism*.

are always more expositions, recapitulations, than arguments'. Mathematical reasoning, with its rigour and perfect contiguity, is ultimately only the mirror of the stringent unity and interrelation of all things in or, rather, *by* nature:

> She has brought me here, she will lead me away. I trust myself to her. She may do with me as she likes (*Sie mag mit mir schalten*). She will not hate her work. I have not spoken of her. No, what is true and what is false, everything has she spoken. Everything is [in] her debt, everything is [to] her credit (*Alles ist ihre Schuld, alles ist ihr Verdienst*).[39]

'In this worldview lies chaos', wrote Walter Benjamin, for whom the fact that, at the limit of Goethe's epistemology, 'even "the word of reason" can be reckoned to the credit of nature' appeared as the summit of a disastrous 'indifference to criticism'.[40] In Romantic natural research, and above all in galvanic self-experimentation, this problem is remedied: the Goethean *Verfahrungsart* of clarification-through-variation receives an axial rotation back toward and into the subject.

Romanticism as a Research Method

For a long time, empirical sciences lay outside the field of scholarship concerned with European Romanticism. In recent years, however, Romanticism's traditional reconstruction in terms of an exclusively literary absolute has been challenged and revised.[41] It is now more frequently acknowledged that even the notion of *romantische Poesie*, which had always appeared to affirm poetry as Romanticism's sovereign form, quickly outgrew any stringently restrictive reference to literature. Initially pointing to an ideal mixture of genres, it came to accommodate more expansive aspirations for the eclectic combination and confusion of multiple discourses and practices within which the experimental sciences played an important role.

[39] Goethe, *Werke*, xiii. 47, xii. 5.

[40] Walter Benjamin, *Selected Writings*, ed. Michael William Jennings and Marcus Paul Bullock, tr. Edmund Jephcott and Rodney Livingstone (Cambridge, Mass.: Belknap Press, 2004), i. 315–16.

[41] The classic argument for the 'literary absolute' is Philippe Lacoue-Labarthe and Jean-Luc Nancy, *The Literary Absolute: The Theory of Literature in German Romanticism* (New York: State University of New York Press, 1988). A particularly concerted effort at revision is Frederick C. Beiser, *The Romantic Imperative: The Concept of Early German Romanticism* (Cambridge, Mass.: Harvard University Press, 2003). With regard to British Romanticism, the challenge has been more vicariously and cumulatively mounted via studies of individual author's interests in particular sciences; e.g. Neil Vickers, *Coleridge and the Doctors, 1795–1806* (Oxford: Oxford University Press, 2004); John Wyatt, *Wordsworth and the Geologists* (Cambridge: Cambridge University Press, 1995); Sharon Ruston, *Shelley and Vitality* (Basingstoke: Palgrave Macmillan, 2005); and the essays collected in Nicholas Roe (ed.), *Samuel Taylor Coleridge and the Sciences of Life* (Oxford: Oxford University Press, 2001).

AMALIA: Is then everything poesy?
LOTHARIO: Every art and every science which operates through discourse (*Rede*), if it wills to be practised for its own sake and if it reaches the highest summit, appears as poesy.
LUDOVIKO: And also each [art and science] which does not force its essence into the words of language (*nicht in den Worten der Sprache ihr Wesen treibt*) has an invisible spirit, and it is poesy.[42]

In these lines from Schlegel's *Gespräch über die Poesie* (1799), the expansion of the semantic field of the term '*Poesie*' beyond the literary—indeed, beyond the linguistic—recapitulates its more general career within the evolution of Romantic discourse. And with regard to Romantic science, the passage is interesting not simply for its explicit inclusion of the sciences as potential species of 'poesy'. Of deeper significance for the question of a Romantic epistemology of science may be the style of reasoning here, the particular way in which the idea (poesy) gets defined and developed.

The participants set out from an abstract and indefinite whole (*is everything poesy?*), introduce a distinction (*all those arts and sciences which* ...), and then, without cancelling this determination, extend it outside its initial sphere of reference (*and also even those that* ...). Crucially, in the transition from Lothario's definition to Ludoviko's, this extension is accomplished via a turn inward, from that which 'appears as poesy' to an 'invisible spirit'. It is this dialectical movement that can be considered characteristically Romantic; it follows, in Schlegel's own terms, 'the path of the whole', along which every idea 'must, in one way or another, go outside itself, in order to be able to return to itself and to remain what it is'.[43]

Romantic science worked through the assumption that the gesture of understanding the physical world must finally coincide with, in Novalis's remarkable formulation, the 'self-penetration of the mind (*Selbstdurchdringung des Geistes*)'. At issue was a method of researching nature, or the ideal of such a method, which would be oriented at once outwards onto the world and inwards into itself. Romanticism developed some exquisitely literal, physical enactments of that intellectual contortion (proceeding outwards through turning inwards) in the practices of self-experimentation that emerged at this time. In these experiments, the body of the researcher oscillated between being the instrument and the object of investigation. To take these practices as the essence of Romanticism in science means, as suggested, looking for the latter less in particular theories about the physical world than in techniques of approaching, observing, and seeking cognitively to interact with it.

Romantic research methods were, indeed, special, concrete implementations of the 'reflecting power of judgment' (to use its Kantian name). In his third *Critique* (1790), Kant had isolated and examined this newly discovered faculty with respect both to aesthetic experience and to the empirical cognition of organic systems (natural purposes). Whereas in cognition of inanimate nature (mechanisms) the mind has a constitutive

[42] Friedrich Schlegel, *Werke in zwei Bänden* (Berlin: Aufbau-Verlag, 1980), ii. 154.
[43] Schlegel, *Werke*, ii. 161–2.

relation to its object, which it determines in accordance with the formal categories of objectivity, in cognition of *living* nature, the organized form of the object is both emphatic and (from a transcendental point of view) exceptional. As such, the ordinary procedure of subsuming intuitions under concepts stalls; if cognition is nonetheless to take place, the mind must pointedly refer to itself in its activity of judgement, drawing on its own rationality, its own systematicity and teleology, and making use of a special power of reflection absent or invisible in ordinary experience and mechanical natural science. The epistemology of Romantic science, especially insofar as it finds its paradigm in self-experimentation, can indeed be read as an explicit setting-to-work of this power of reflection in material techniques and apparatuses.

The continuities between Romantic research practices and Kant's critique of the reflexivity peculiar to judgements of aesthetic and organic form constitute, however, only one side of Romantic epistemology. They must be complemented with reference to that reinvigoration and revision of the Spinozan ideal of *scientia intuitiva* (intuitive science), which we have observed in Goethe, and which was crucial, more generally, to the movement *beyond* Kant in post-Kantian idealism, Romantic theory, and the speculative philosophy of nature. With respect to Romantic practices, it is important to maintain this tension between reflective self-consciousness and active empiricism, between 'Kant' and 'Fichte', on one side, and 'Goethe' and 'Spinoza', on the other.

Here, again, is Schlegel's avowedly Spinozist Ludoviko:

> Physics cannot conduct an experiment without a hypothesis; every hypothesis, even the most limited, if it is thought through rigorously (*mit Konsequenz*), leads to hypotheses concerning the whole, indeed rests on such hypotheses, even if this is without the consciousness of the one using them.[44]

In the epistemology crystallizing here, the *more geometrico* of an intuitive science of essential ideas is to be removed from the sphere of metaphysical and mathematical objects and transposed to physical nature posited, intuited, and progressively understood as a 'whole'.

Whatever else is said of this 'whole', it is crucial to recognize what it is not, namely, a mental abstraction, intellectual generality, or universal category transcending sensible reality: 'deadening generalization (*tötende Verallgemeinerung*) effects exactly the opposite' of the true procedure of science as Ludoviko elaborates it.[45] In this studiously non-classical thought, which bases itself on a certain reading of Spinoza, 'the whole' is not an idea or an empirical concept so much as an intuited or intuitively deduced reality. And what is most remarkable, here, is the attempt to translate a metaphysical doctrine, this 'mystical science of the whole (*mystische Wissenschaft vom Ganzen*)', which Schlegel believes he has discovered in Spinoza, into an applied science—experimentalizing the intuitive ('divine') understanding.

[44] Schlegel, *Werke*, ii. 168.
[45] Schlegel, *Werke*, ii. 135.

This procedure has clear continuities with the methodology of Goethe's experimental science. Peculiarly Romantic, however, is the explicit coincidence, which Schlegel here formulates, of a forward- or outward-moving deductive process and an inward- or backward-moving analytical process: *stringent experimental pursuit of the consequences of an idea or axiom,* Ludoviko claims, *leads to further hypotheses ultimately concerning the totality of the phenomenon, a movement which is, by that very token, and even if beyond the consciousness of the researcher, precisely also the exposition of the origin out of which everything proceeds.* This dialectical movement is a distinctive feature of Romantic natural research. As Dietrich von Engelhardt rightly argues, Romantic science was characterized by a consciousness of history as an ongoing reversion to the origin ('*Geschichte—Rückkehr zum Ursprung*'), of unfolding as rewinding.

> In the course of the history of science, mankind will, according to [J. W.] Ritter, find its way back to a condition of 'concord and connection' ('*Eintracht und Verbindung*') with the world and nature again, the condition it possessed already in its beginning.... Human history is 'memory' ('*Erinnerung*'), is *progressive regress.*[46]

Engelhardt's perspicuous analysis focuses on Romantic conceptions of the history of science, that is, of the development of European sciences as part of an eschatological history of the human race. As we shall see in the next and final section, however, in the case of Ritter, the dialectical path of progressive regress (the way forward as the way back, history as remembering) was also present on the local level of experimental practices.

Romanticism constituted a moment of profound ill-discipline in science, a moment in which metaphysical ideas there was no reason, no right (Kant would have said), to consider as susceptible to empirical experience, observation, and sensible verification were nonetheless pursued through experiments. 'Experience is the test (*die Probe*) of the rational—and the other way round.'[47] As this chiasmus suggests, equally illegitimately—but proceeding in the other direction—sensible phenomena were abducted from the finite realm of appearance and endowed with the status of absolute principles. In so elevating a natural phenomenon directly into a metaphysical principle (electrical fire, chemical fire, galvanic fluid, magnetic polarity, etc.), Romantic scientists were, often quite self-consciously, linking the most up-to-date 'physics' with the most archaic sources of speculative thought. For they were repeating the earliest determinations of the absolute (the indefinite principle or *arkhē* of the Ionian philosophers) in terms of one or other natural phenomenon—as water, air, or, most often, fire. No doubt this repetition formed part of that dialectical-eschatological linking of the origin and goal of history to which Engelhardt points—since the moment of that goal was at hand. The beginning and end of history were coinciding in the present, an intersection that announced a new age. Once again, what is most interesting is the way this

[46] Dietrich von Engelhardt, *Historisches Bewußtsein in der Naturwissenschaft: Von der Aufklärung bis zum Positivismus* (Munich: Karl Alber Freiburg, 1979), 120; emphasis added.

[47] Novalis, *Werke*, 324.

millenarian speculation appeared not only in the philosophy of nature (where attempts to deduce nature from a single principle or element need to be interpreted as highly self-conscious of the history of philosophy and profoundly if complexly embedded in 'Second Reformation' German Pietism[48]) but also in the work-mode of Romantic natural research. For Ritter, this conjunction of origin with eschaton, empirical phenomenon with metaphysical principle, was occurring in the real time of his self-experiments, in a present both physically and spiritually burning with discovery.

Self-Experimentation

In 1795, Alexander von Humboldt began a series of experiments in which, using blistering plasters, he created a pair of open wounds on the backs of his shoulders.

> Nowhere have more appearances of galvanism accumulated than in these experiments. On each shoulder, in order to obtain a fairly large area of stripped skin, I made blisters of the size of a six-franc coin (*Laubthaler*). More precisely, they covered the *Musculus cucullaris* and *deltoides* [trapezius and deltoid muscles].[49]

Humboldt applied different metals to these muscles, using his body as an instrument with which to investigate the electrical, chemical, and physiological phenomena at the centre of the new science of galvanism, or 'vital chemistry', as Humboldt called his research.

> The shoulder and back muscles provide a large, smooth and convenient surface on which to apply the metals securely and (the body being situated horizontally) to sustain the experiment for several hours without interruption.[50]

The more a body-part was 'galvanized' in this manner, the more painful and 'excitable' it became. Humboldt saw, or rather felt, confirmation of his proposition that 'the size of irritation (*Reizung*) x is equal to the product of the stimulus y and the receptivity to irritation (*Reizempfänglichkeit*) of the part z ($x = yz$)'.[51] But his most significant discovery was that '[t]he sensation excited by the metals ... had *not the remotest* resemblance with

[48] See Müller-Sievers's astute (if forbidding) remark that discussion of Schelling's philosophy of nature requires wholesale reconstruction of 'the status of southern German pietism ... at the end of the eighteenth century', Helmut Müller-Sievers, *Self-Generation: Biology, Philosophy, and Literature around 1800* (Stanford, Calif.: Stanford University Press, 1997), 14–15.

[49] Alexander von Humboldt, *Versuche über die gereizte Muskel- und Nervenfaser: Nebst Vermuthungen über den chemischen Process des Lebens in der Thier- und Pflanzenwelt* (Berlin: Rottmann, 1797), i. 324.

[50] Humboldt, *Versuche*, i. 326.

[51] Humboldt, *Versuche*, i. 328–9.

that of electrical current. It is a pain *sui generis* ...'[52] For Humboldt, the particular quality of the pain produced by the metals revealed the biochemical phenomenon at the centre of galvanic researches to be essentially different from ordinary electricity—specifically, the phenomenon was organic.

In subsequent experiments, on top of the discs inserted into his back, he stretched the exposed crural nerve and muscle of a frog.[53] Connecting his own muscular and nervous system to this 'animate matter (*belebte Stoff*)' via the mediation of the heterogeneous metals, he made himself a component of a single unbroken electro-chemico-neuro-physiological chain. Closing the animal-electrical circuit with his own polarized body, he took up a position inside the experimental set-up, physically inhabiting the mediation between technical instruments and research objects, and between theory and phenomena.[54] In these experiments, as in similar auto-experimental procedures that emerged in the course of the galvanic episode in European science, cognition was embodied and extended through the circuit of body-instrument-organism (or mind-technology-object).

The liability of the instrument of investigation actively to interfere with the object of investigation—rather than registering, recording, or measuring it—has, since the beginning of modern experimental science, mostly been understood as a weakness of the experimental set-up. The practitioners of self-experimentation made the material manipulation and practical resolution of the ambiguity, reciprocal interference, and interactive dynamic between instrument and object into the essence of their research procedures. The whole debate over galvanism was animated by the problem of satisfactorily isolating the *source* of the phenomena produced through various conjunctions of exposed nerves, muscles, metals, and electrostatic or electrochemical machines—Leyden jars, Nicholson doublers, Voltaic piles. The invention of the battery (a column of interlaced copper and zinc or silver plates separated by bits of cardboard soaked in brine) occurred in response to the problem facing the Volta-pole of the debate (i.e. those disclaiming the animality of the electrical fluid behind the new phenomenon), which was to find a way of excluding organic material altogether from the production and demonstration of the electrical charge.[55]

[52] Humboldt, *Versuche*, i. 329.

[53] See Humboldt, *Versuche*, i. 331.

[54] Steigerwald discusses the practices in these terms; see Joan Steigerwald, 'Instruments of Judgment: Inscribing Organic Processes in Late Eighteenth-Century Germany', *Studies in History and Philosophy of Science*, C33 (2002), 121ff. For Humboldt's epistemology of experiment, see Michael Dettelbach, 'Alexander von Humboldt between Enlightenment and Romanticism', *Northeastern Naturalist*, 8 (2001), 9–20. For Romantic-period self-experiment, see esp. Simon Schaffer, 'Self Evidence', *Critical Inquiry*, 18 (1992), 327–62; Stuart Strickland, 'The Ideology of Self-Knowledge and the Practice of Self-Experimentation', *Eighteenth-Century Studies*, 31 (1998), 453–71; and Nicolas Pethes, 'Experiment und Leben: Zur Genealogie, Kritik und Epistemologie des Menschenversuchs um 1800', in Vogl and Schimma, *Versuchsanordnungen 1800* 69–84.

[55] For discussion, see Marcello Pera, *The Ambiguous Frog: The Galvani-Volta Controversy on Animal Electricity*, tr. J. Mandelbaum (Princeton: Princeton University Press, 1992), 146–75; Nahum Kipnis, 'Changing a Theory: The Case of Volta's Contact Electricity', in F. Bevilacqua and E. Giannetto (eds),

The addition of the living organism to the field of 'polarities' (magnetic, chemical, electrical) that dominated empirical science in the late eighteenth century was possible on account of fundamental revisions of the basic object of physiological discourse. For, since around 1750, a series of complex, vitalistic concepts of reflex action had increasingly displaced the old mechanical metaphors of the nerves (as tubes, strings, etc.). The new neurophysiological discourse presented the motions and reactions of the body not through the ideas of substance, volition, and mechanism, but rather as relations, interactions, and functions.[56] In this way, the nervous body was, as it were, prepared for its polarization under 'galvanism'. And it was this neurophysiologically reconceived body that, in the galvanic self-experiments of Humboldt, Ritter, and others, would be physically connected to various electrical machines or galvanic agencies (mostly frogs).

The two volumes of Humboldt's *Versuche über die gereizte Muskel- und Nervenfaser* amounted to almost 1000 pages of experimental description and digression. Galvanism was, among other things, a *print* phenomenon. The volume of experimental report, emerging both from inside and outside the universities, was vast. Partly on account of this scale of the output, almost from its inception, the debate and the phenomenon at its centre were subject to narration and historical reconstruction; rarely has a science been so swiftly and immanently interested in its history.[57] In the course of this history extending from the accident of Galvani's initial discovery (which lent itself to narrative rehearsal and embellishment) to the objections from physicists which culminated in Volta's invention of the battery, the basic Galvani-Volta opposition underwent innumerable re-entries, so that the variety of positions multiplied considerably.[58]

The European wave of interest in galvanism served to focus attention, materially and logically, on a variety of scientific problems: notably, on the nature of circuits, and the activity of the 'whole' (i.e. an unbroken chain) on and within the relations of individual component 'parts'; on the difference between open and closed systems; on various physiological powers (especially, sensibility, irritability, excitability, and contractility); on the difference between conducting and non-conducting substances; on accompanying

Volta and the History of Electricity (Milan: Hoepli, 2003), 143–61; and Giuliano Pancaldi, *Volta: Science and Culture in the Age of Enlightenment* (Princeton: Princeton University Press, 2005), 181ff.

[56] For galvanic science's relation to, and role in, the development of the reflex concept, see Edwin Clarke and L. S. Jacyna, *Nineteenth-Century Origins of Neuroscientific Concepts* (Berkeley, Calif.: University of California Press, 1992), 157–211.

[57] See e.g. Humphry Davy, 'Outlines of a View of Galvanism, Chiefly Extracted from a Course of Lectures on the Galvanic Phænomena, Read at the Theatre of the Royal Institution (1801)', in *Collected Works of Sir Humphry Davy*, ed. John Davy (London: Smith, Elder & Co., 1839), ii. 188–209; C. H. Wilkinson, *Elements of Galvanism, in Theory and Practice; with a Comprehensive View of Its History, from the First Experiments of Galvani to the Present Time. Containing Also, Practical Directions for Constructing the Galvanic Apparatus, and Plain Systematic Instructions for Performing All the Various Experiments* (London: J. Murray, 1804); and John Bostock, *An Account of the History and Present State of Galvanism* (London: Baldwin, Cradock, & Joy, 1818).

[58] A table is provided in Helge Kragh, 'Confusion and Controversy: Nineteenth-Century Theories of the Voltaic Pile', in F. Bevilacqua and L. Fregonese (eds), *Nuova Voltiana: Studies on Volta and his Times* (Milan: Università degli studi di Pavia, 2003), 138.

ideas of medium, mediation, and circulation; and, above all, on the identities and differences between life and electricity, organisms and machines. The various, ambiguously physical and physiological, active and passive, stimulating and receptive, objects that emerged from the controversy promised to expose otherwise solely metaphysical distinctions to empirical observation and experiment.

Investigators of different stripes sought, through experimentation, to settle the dispute in their favour. Consciously, they were striving to verify one theoretical explanation or refute another. Observed historically, however, it is possible to recognize, in the course of the controversy, a different and equally vigorous rationality. For, through the hundreds of thousands of pages of report published in the subgenre, 'Experiments and Observations relative to the Phenomenon lately discovered by Galvani, and commonly called Animal Electricity', the phenomenon was multiplied, ramified, and *refined*. Behind their backs, as they argued, the researchers were purifying the essential phenomenon of galvanism. The Voltaic pile, which stands as the objective result of this process, did not so much solve the riddle as objectify it. Those faithful to the electrical physiology of organic bodies could now observe and experiment on its inorganic abstraction in the pile, while viewing the neurophysiological body as an organic battery. Members of the Parisian Galvanic Society claimed to have 'made a voltaic pile with sixty layers of brain, muscle and hat material, and moistened with salt water'.[59] Such galvanists discovered that the presence of metal was not essential so long as there was a difference, asymmetry, or imbalance between the relative conductivity of the two poles (nerve and muscle). And as the voltaists worked to exclude organic parts from the set-up, in order to develop and demonstrate the simple heterogeneity of metals as the essence and source of the charge, the galvanists eventually produced the 'all-animal circuit', that is, nerve-muscle preparations that crystallized what they took to be the identical phenomenon of galvanic action in artificial objects capable of exhibiting contraction despite being composed exclusively of organic materials.[60]

Both these objects, the all-inanimate pile and the all-animal circuit, could appear as physically constructed abstractions of the basic phenomenon of galvanic investigation and reflection, a phenomenon that was fundamentally *relational* or *differential* in form. Electrical fluid was conceptually grasped and experimentally developed in terms of the difference or tension of + and – values, a difference in which neither charge has any qualities outside of its opposition to the other, and in which, as such, both must be grasped as 'poles' which hold their opposite within them. The form of the magnet (closely related to electrical phenomena in Romantic thought) and the chemical polarity of acid/base were considered further specifications of this objectively dialectical form. Across Europe, researchers were finding ways of sensibly exposing what Ritter calls 'the Voltaic law of tension of heterogeneous conductors'; they

[59] C. Sleigh, 'Life, Death and Galvanism', *Studies in History and Philosophy of Science*, C29 (1998), 219 n. 3.

[60] On the 'all-animal circuit' (the possibility of which was confirmed by Humboldt), see Naum Kipnis, 'Luigi Galvani and the Debate on Animal Electricity, 1791–1800', *Annals of Science*, 44 (1987), 127.

were immersing and refining this differential relation in sensible being.[61] Ultimately, through such active empiricism, difference itself, in the form of the concept of *polarity*, was being simultaneously abstracted and realized, comprehended and experienced. Inner or immanent difference (negativity as such) was being given positive, perceivable, corporeally sensible forms.

Rarely has the dialectic been more entangled in empirical positivity than in the scientific research of J. W. Ritter: 'In the nose, the negative pole [of a Voltaic pile] excites an urge to sneeze, finally even [actually excites] this, and sometimes a trace of the smell of ammonia. The positive pole, by contrast, annuls an existing possibility of sneezing and produces a general numbing of the nose, rather like oxygenised muriatic acid (*oxygenierte Salzsäure*).'[62] Use of the ear as a pole in the circuit produces a 'rising sound accompanied by a tone' which, 'when both ears are in the circuit, is distinguishable as *g* of a one-line octave or ḡ.'[63] 'Applied to the tongue, the positive pole of the circuit and battery brings a sour taste', which changes into 'a bitter alkaline' taste once the circuit is broken. Ritter's experimental style resembles the 'accumulator' (storage battery) he invented: accumulating symmetries, strengthening polarity, building tension. Observations pile up on the page.

> First case: Zinc of the battery in the eye.
> Closing [i.e. the circuit]: Occurrence of positive light-state—flash
> Closed: Continuing positive light-state
> Blue colour
> Diminution of external objects
> Less distinct recognition of the same
> Separation [of the circuit]: Withdrawal of positive light-state and
> Transition of the same into the negative—flash
> After the separation: Continuing negative light-state
> Red colour
> Enlargement of external objects
> Distinct recognition of the same
> Gradual return of all these appearances to zero
> Second case: Silver (or copper) of the battery in the eye.
> ...
> Both cases together: absolute subjectivity of all appearances.—[64]

[61] Ritter, *Key Texts*, 282–3.

[62] 'Von den verschiedenen Erregbarkeiten der Sinnesorgane und ihrem Gegensatze' in *Beiträge zur nähern Kenntnis des Galvanismus* (Jena, 1802), i, §86, repr. in Johann Wilhelm Ritter, *Entdeckungen zur Elektrochemie, Bioelektrochemie und Photochemie*, ed. H. Berg and K. Richter (Thun and Frankfurt/Main: Harri Deutsch, 1997), 94.

[63] Ritter, *Entdeckungen*, 94, i, §85. The distinction here seems to be between the note 'g' as heard on a one-line octave scale and a sustained 'g'. (Thank you to Zeynep Bulut for help here.)

[64] Ritter, 'Wirkung des Galvanismus der Voltaischen Batterie auf menschliche Sinneswerkzeuge', *Annalen der Physik*, 7 (1801), repr. in Ritter, *Entdeckungen*, 87.

To which science does this experiment belong? Is this electrical physics, chemistry, optics, neurophysiology, colour theory?

Each aspect here seems equally to function as means and end of the experiment—every *explanandum* is just as much an *explanans*. The light-states and flashes, colours and visible changes indicate the effects of electricity on the eye, the eye helps further to determine the difference between the positively and negatively charged metals, and the metals function in turn as tools for the physiological investigation of colour. This is a science in which the material and cognitive process of research, of experimenting and learning, takes precedence over the confirmation of isolated hypotheses or the production of individual results. The speculative statement with which the experiment ends obviously does not have the simple positivity of a result, but is the acquired perspective of the subject who completes, overarches, and contains the appearances generated by the experimental process as a whole—a series whose shape, structure, and limits are provided by the nervous human body.

For Ritter, sensory organs, here the eye, are human sense-tools (*menschliche Sinneswerkzeuge*). His neurological body is a philosophical instrument—thus, not *his* body, but *a* body. What Ritter reports in passages such as this one are, on one level, not merely his own personal experiences, for the sense-instruments are not his alone, but those of the species. As such, his claims are not merely personal, but intended as scientific findings. Yet, of course, the nature and modes of functioning of these universal human instruments are imperfectly known; they are by no means transparent devices with which to register, record, measure, or transmit effects to the judging mind. Hence, the nerves are as much *objects* of research as its instruments. Furthermore, as a scientific instrument, the Romantic body was understood as a technology that both perceived and *half-created* the natural world. The red and blue colours that occur in this experiment, for example, are not external physical realities which Ritter perceives through his eyes, but exemplary 'physiological colours' in Goethe's sense, i.e. those colours which, neglected and dismissed by traditional optics, 'belong to the subject, because they either completely, or in a great degree, belong to the eye itself'.[65] Romantic self-experiment pioneered the process of exposing the human body to investigation, externalizing its activities and functions. Batteries and dissected organisms were media for turning the nervous body inside out, translating it into an object of study. At the same time, they were media through which external nature (humanity's inorganic body) could be experimentally inhabited, that is, they offered ways of experiencing extra-subjective forces and processes.

When researchers entered the circuit, the philosophical relation between the sentient body and the thinking mind was added to the assemblage of dynamic relations operating within galvanic science. They introduced the human being, human subjectivity in all its Romantic complexity, into the experiment. The mind involved in these experiments was not a discursive understanding, schematizing and subsuming the sensible

[65] *Zur Farbenlehre*, §1; Goethe, *Werke*, xiii. 329.

phenomena transmitted to it by the body. The mind involved in these experiments knew itself, and sought further to know itself, as the seat of active powers, of feeling, of erotic as well as epistemic desires, and of capacities not only for objective judgement (measurement, description, record) but also for self-consciousness, for embodied or aesthetic experience of itself. Indeed, in these experimental performances or rituals, it was above all the self's feeling and experience of itself that was enacted and refined through objects and instruments, organic materials and electrical machines.

> A good physical experiment (*Experiment*) may serve as the model (*Muster*) for an inner experiment, and *is itself* a good *inner* subj[ective] experiment. (see Ritter's experiments).[66]

Novalis's precise gloss on the dialectical style of science radicalized by Ritter begins to indicate what will be its greatest problem. The problem is that the *results* of this research are ultimately irreducible to particular discoveries or explanations. Goethe believed that the result was the 'pure phenomenon'. In Ritter, there is a deeper recognition that the objective result is necessarily also subjective. For, in order for Goethe's pure phenomenon to exist, a memory is required which is capable of grasping, within the singular experience, the *historical succession* of experiments of which it is the archive. With Ritter, Goethe's idea that the result of the research process is higher *experience* is pushed to a kind of logical (and physical) extreme. And, as it is so, the problem with this kind of science appears, namely, that the scientific self, as the bearer of these higher experiences, is as much the product of the process as is anything susceptible to phenomenal description. Or, rather, the phenomenon is bound inextricably to the particular subject who has refined and purified, abstracted and constructed it. Ritter senses this. And he senses, too, the way it is to be solved.

Describing the serial publication of his experiments, the three-volume *Physisch-chemische Abhandlungen in chronologischer Folge* (1806), Ritter insisted: 'It should not merely be a *collection* of my writings; it will be a kind of *literary autobiography* (*literarische Selbstbiographie*), of interest perhaps to anyone who wants or has to educate himself to become a physicist and experimenter.'[67] Beneath the Romantic desire to present *work* and *self* together, a concern can be heard for the value of a science in which positive descriptions and determinate judgements of phenomena have been at least partially subordinated and consumed by the process of experimentation and the evolutionary ascent of experience. Ritter's recognition is that he is *himself* the ultimate product or result of his experiments. And his insight is, thus, that only the *narrative* of his development, his *Bildungsroman*

[66] Novalis, *Das allgemeine Brouillon: Materialien zur Enzyklopädistik 1798/99* (Hamburg: Meiner Verlag, 1993), 386, §647; Novalis, *Romantic Encyclopaedia*, 118.

[67] In a letter to Ørsted, 2 Feb. 1806, cited in Strickland, 'Ideology of Self-Knowledge', 462 n. 46. Cf. Jocelyn Holland, *German Romanticism and Science: The Procreative Poetics of Goethe, Novalis, and Ritter* (New York: Routledge, 2009), 115 and 195 n. 16.

or *biographia litteraria*, can contain that result (the archive of the process, and its *movement*). By doing so, he hopes, after death, to live on as an instrument for the construction of other physicists. It is this ambition which ultimately leads him to the famous Prologue of his last publication *Fragments from the Estate of a Young Physicist* (1809).

The *Fragments* are a miscellany of ideas and notes which Ritter organizes and publishes using the fictional device of an anonymous 'Editor'. In what Ritter called a 'greatly serious jest (*höchst ernsthafte Posse*)', the Editor presents himself as a former friend of the young physicist to whom the fragments have been passed following Ritter's untimely death.[68] As Jocelyn Holland observes, acting as his own literary executor enables Ritter to fuse 'two seemingly distinct bodies of knowledge: a corpus of scientific research into natural phenomena, and a poetic construction of the self as scientist'.[69] By introducing a split between first- and third-person perspectives, his death enables him to *narrate* his science, and thus to subsume the positivity of statements and assertions within the movement of biographical development. As such, the Prologue is both a symptom of, and a brilliant response to, the basic deficiency of 'description' with respect to the *whole* of knowledge, the *history* of experiences, subjectively present in each of the individual fragments.

In his Romantic mode, Ritter registers an epistemological problem which has not disappeared. It is the general problem, namely, of the constitutive 'underdetermination' of knowledge in the modern episteme. As Julian Roberts indicates, underdetermination means 'that we cannot conceptually construct (by "description") the full extent of what we "know" '.[70] If this is an ineluctable effect of the essential temporality that takes hold of reason in the modern thought system, Romantic research in general and Ritter's investigations in particular attempted to acknowledge, endure, and even embrace this time-dependence. By contrast, later scientific discourses have repressed, bracketed, or otherwise black-boxed it, which is undoubtedly necessary for a science that hopes for results. Yet, only results that exhibit the premises and operations of which they are the results afford full comprehension. The attempt to sustain self-consciousness concerning the epistemic processes of object constitution and resolution without foregoing the positivity of description and veridical reference was central to Romantic science, which can, in this sense, be viewed as part of a project to make science more thoroughly exoteric.

[68] As Ritter explained it to Ørsted, 'the prologue contains the biography of the departed, his inner one (*Biographie des Verstorbenen, seine innere*); it is my own, and I wrote it with much honesty and feeling (*Ehrlichkeit und Rührung*). The entire thing is thereby a greatly serious jest (*höchst ernsthafte Posse*)'. Cited in Holland, 'The Workshop as Monument: Fragments from the Estate of a Young Physicist', in Ritter, *Key Texts*, 6.

[69] Holland, 'Workshop as Monument', 115.

[70] Julian Roberts, *The Logic of Reflection: German Philosophy in the Twentieth Century* (New Haven: Yale University Press, 1992), 284.

CONCLUSION

The epistemology of Romantic science was located between two tendencies, active empiricism and critical idealism. Setting out from the physical phenomena of empirical observation, it moved towards an objective refinement of its concept, the universal submerged in sensuous being; alternatively, deploying corporeal nature as the instrument of self-investigation, it tended towards deeper explorations of itself in the interiority of that sensible world. Either way, for Romantic researchers, the movement was to be accomplished not in thought only but using the experiment as mediator. As a result, Romantic research resisted the fully idealizing subordination of empirical positivity (sensible particulars) to the conceptual or dialectical relations which constitute and mediate them, while at the same time it also refused the conceptless positivity and passivity of an empirical science content to narrate and catalogue the data of the world without regard either to the metaphysical presuppositions embedded in its categories, or to the historical, social, and cultural dimensions of its own activity. 'Everything must let itself be squared and not let itself be squared at the same time.'[71] The essential tension of Romantic science is the result of such dual movement: from natural immediacy towards the thought of mediation (the rudest form of which is, perhaps, the self-indexing operation of squaring), and from the ideality of mediation towards an empirical reality that is resistant to being mediated (i.e. intellectually determined) entirely or, so to speak, all at once. As such, it forms a significant detour in the passage between the dualism of form and sensible content in Kant's transcendental idealism and the Hegelian dialectics of abstract and concrete. 'The empirical and the speculative quests are both infinite. To search in both at once—the experimental way, that is the real one.'[72]

FURTHER READING

Beiser, Frederick, *The Romantic Imperative: The Concept of Early German Romanticism* (Cambridge, Mass.: Harvard University Press, 2003).

Brain, Robert M., Cohen, Robert S., and Knudsen, Ole (eds), *Hans Christian Ørsted and the Romantic Legacy in Science* (Dordrecht: Springer, 2007).

Cunningham, Andrew, and Jardine, Nicholas (eds), *Romanticism and the Sciences* (Cambridge: Cambridge University Press, 1990).

Engelhardt, Dietrich von, *Historisches Bewußtsein in der Naturwissenschaft: Von der Aufklärung bis zum Positivismus* (Munich: Karl Alber Freiburg, 1979).

[71] Novalis, *Werke, Briefe, Dokumente*, 100.

[72] Novalis, *Werke*, 475; Novalis, *Romantic Encyclopaedia*, 107. 'Das empirische und d[as] spekulative Suchen ist beides unendlich. In beiden zugl[eich] suchen—der experimentierende Gang, das ist d[er] echte.'

Förster, Eckart, *The Twenty-Five Years of Philosophy*, tr. Brady Bowman (Cambridge, Mass.: Harvard University Press, 2012).

Holland, Jocelyn, *German Romanticism and Science: The Procreative Poetics of Goethe, Novalis, and Ritter* (New York: Routledge, 2009).

Müller-Sievers, Helmut, *Self-Generation: Biology, Philosophy, and Literature around 1800* (Stanford, Calif.: Stanford University Press, 1997).

Schaffer, Simon, 'Self Evidence', *Critical Inquiry*, 18 (1992), 327–62.

Steigerwald, Joan, 'Instruments of Judgment: Inscribing Organic Processes in Late Eighteenth-Century Germany', *Studies in History and Philosophy of Science*, C33 (2002), 79–131.

Strickland, Stuart, 'The Ideology of Self-Knowledge and the Practice of Self-Experimentation', *Eighteenth-Century Studies*, 31 (1998), 453–71.

Vogl, Joseph (ed.), *Poetologien des Wissens um 1800* (Munich: Fink, 1999).

CHAPTER 36

LIFE AND DEATH IN PARIS

Medical and Life Sciences in the Romantic Era

LEON CHAI

In many ways, life in Paris could be said to have become something increasingly fragile and precious after 1789. For the poor, life there had always been difficult: we know, for instance, how rarely clothes were thrown away but rather constantly patched to be worn again, and of how many layers people wore to protect themselves against the cold, as well as how infrequently they removed them.[1] By innumerable ways, all these men and women scratched out their existences, struggled to get through winter, sunned themselves on the quais and embankments along the Seine to keep warm as they waited longingly for spring. Like the crowd in de Sica's *Miracle in Milan*, who follow a solitary ray of sunshine as it moves from place to place ...

No doubt it's also significant that in Revolutionary Paris—as before—people tend to stick together, living in close quarters, keeping a constant eye on each other's movements. So much so that it's not easy to commit suicide anywhere near the centre of Paris without being noticed by somebody. Call it an instinct: like the sense of safety in numbers, the feeling seems to be that if everyone sticks together it's harder for any single person to slip through the net. And if anyone does manage to slip through, there's a whiff of reproach from the *répondants*, the witnesses from the neighbourhood who have to testify to the police, identify the deceased: he or she shouldn't have done that, shouldn't have let the neighbourhood down. Not from sociability, then, but from a far more simple, more primitive instinct: the will to survive.

Nonetheless, despite the tenacious collective will to survive, it's also relatively easy in Revolutionary Paris to die. Today the Place de la Concorde is a wide open square marked mainly by a steady stream of traffic. From 1789 to 1794 it was something quite different: then called the Place de la Revolution, it was the site of the guillotine, where somewhere between 15,000 and 40,000 (mostly *noblesse* and notables) met their end.

[1] Richard Cobb, *Death in Paris* (Oxford: Oxford University Press, 1978), 34–5, 73–4.

Nor did they die alone: here as much as anywhere, the Revolution was spectacle on a massive scale, with a huge crowd as constant witness to almost every death by guillotine. But while the *noblesse* and notables often met their end in spectacular fashion, the same couldn't be said for the poor, many of whom died only a short distance away. From the Place de la Concorde it's a fairly brief walk to the Ile de la Cité, site now as before of the Hôtel-Dieu, then the main hospital of Paris. Today you see a discreet entrance at the north-west corner of the cathedral of Notre Dame, shaded by a row of trees. If you pass through the portal you find yourself in a luminous, spacious foyer: the typical clean, quiet look of the contemporary hospital. But in the early Revolutionary days especially, the Hôtel-Dieu—like any other hospital in Paris—was a nightmare. Only 1,219 beds to accommodate 2,500 patients who could easily become 3,500 or—in the event of an epidemic—as many as 4,500 with four to six patients per bed or as many as eight children, no blankets, no ventilation, beds almost never changed despite the sweat, pus, and secretions that soaked through the mattresses, the dead often not removed for hours or even days, rampant infection, constant screaming from operations without anaesthesia. Here statistics alone suffice to tell the tale: for every fifteen mothers who entered the Hôtel-Dieu to give birth to a child, one would lose her life. Overall, for every four patients admitted to the Hôtel-Dieu, one would die there.[2]

Whether the struggle for life in Revolutionary Paris has anything to do with the study of life there is one of those questions that's obviously difficult if not impossible to answer. In any case, when the National Assembly abolished all the medical and scientific societies of the Old Regime, the one subject it chose to preserve was natural history, in the belief that its study would somehow benefit the people. From the Hôtel-Dieu, significantly, it's only a short walk across the river to the 5th arrondissement where we find the Jardin des Plantes, with its spacious enclosed layout, tall trees, dignified two-storey edifice, and well-kept garden. Inside that edifice were magnificent collections of plants and fossils, and on the grounds a smaller collection of live animals as well. Here, from Revolutionary days onwards, life would be studied.

Naturphilosophie

Typically, when we think of Naturphilosophie we think of German rather than French science. Specifically, Lorenz Oken comes to mind. Walking one day in the Harz Forest in 1806 Oken discovers the blanched skull of a deer which he suddenly sees as an extension of the bones of the spinal column, and out of that Naturphilosophie is born. Earlier, in his *Grundriss der Naturphilosophie* of 1802, he had maintained that the entire animal kingdom could be reduced to five classes, and that these correspond to the different sense

[2] Data on the Hôtel-Dieu from the Jacques Tenon report for the Academy of Science. See Charles Coulston Gillispie, *Science and Polity in France at the End of the Old Regime* (Princeton: Princeton University Press, 1980), 250–6.

organs. In this fashion, the animal kingdom becomes a kind of allegory of the human body. Then in the 1807 inaugural lecture at Jena which secured his fame (with Goethe in attendance), Oken put forward his thesis about the skull as an extension of the spinal column. Nonetheless, he wasn't done there. In *Über das Universum als Fortsetzung des Sinnensystems* from the following year, he would go on to argue that an organism was a combination of all the activities of the universe within a single body. So here we get the macro/micro analogy at the highest level.

Yet for the real origin of Naturphilosophie it might be more useful to look elsewhere: not the Harz Forest in Germany but faraway Egypt in 1802, where a young French naturalist named Étienne Geoffroy Saint-Hilaire had accompanied Napoleon as part of a team of scientific researchers brought to investigate the ancient kingdom. As early as 1795, in his very first paper, Geoffroy had already conceived of the idea of a single plan for all animals. Egypt, however, freed him from professional constraints and allowed him to indulge his speculative fancy. Without the routine of daily work at the Musée d'histoire naturelle, without catalogues or reports to prepare either on his own work or that of others, free to wander the Egyptian countryside, Geoffroy could go wherever he wanted, observe rare species he'd never seen in France, think about connections between species that went far beyond those of the vertebrate group alone, that embraced even the inanimate species. Specifically, Geoffroy concocted a theory of vital fluid (similar to what we find later in Balzac's *Études philosophiques*) in which he attempted to unite physics, chemistry, and physiology.

But the real reason we should look to Geoffroy for the origins of Naturphilosophie rather than Oken has to do with the far greater institutional resources of France. From the outset, the Musée d'histoire naturelle was endowed by the National Assembly with funds for the collections, a library, a journal, and a salaried staff of researchers. So it isn't just a solitary individual carrying on obscure work in a hit-or-miss fashion. Instead, we have science as a major power on the cultural scene, able to intervene on many of the major topical issues. Unlike Oken and other armchair naturalists, the Museum staff carried out many experiments on live animals to add to its knowledge of extinct species. And the Museum collection, helped by generous government support, grew at a spectacular rate to become far and away the finest in Europe. And in part this was due to Geoffroy, who despite fierce British opposition had managed to bring back from Egypt some of the best fossil specimens of extinct species to date. So when Geoffroy, Cuvier, and other Museum staff pontificated on the relation between different species they could do so with the authority that comes from having the best collection of extant and extinct species anywhere.

The Cuvier–Geoffroy Debate

But if Naturphilosophie got off to a great start in France, we have to pursue it further to understand why it didn't remain the dominant science in France, and why Romantic science in France is ultimately more about medicine than about natural history. On this point, it seems to me a lot can be gleaned from the Cuvier–Geoffroy debate. Not only did it expose the weaknesses of Naturphilosophie in France but perhaps—and more importantly—it could also be said to have exposed the weaknesses of natural history as practised at that time. And in that respect, it helps to show why medicine rather than natural history becomes pre-eminent among the Romantic life sciences.

From the standpoint of many eyewitnesses, Cuvier seemed to be the winner of the debate.[3] Initiated by Geoffroy in 1830 on the pretext of a memoir on molluscs sent to the Académie by two young and unknown naturalists (Meyranx and Laurencet), the debate quickly widened out to embrace all the methodological differences between Geoffroy and Cuvier. As historians of science invariably point out, Cuvier had the upper hand because of institutional power: permanent secretary of the Académie des Sciences, he wrote the reports that summarized the year's work in the sciences and so got the last word.

Equally important, he controlled the patronage: who got appointed to which posts at the Museum, the Académie, the Institut. But it wasn't just about institutional power. In fact, when he took the floor at the Académie, Cuvier was frequently able to show that Geoffroy's arguments didn't work, that it wasn't always possible to establish connections across the larger *embranchements* (branches) or groups of species. In his *Philosophie Anatomique*, Geoffroy had argued for the existence of homologous parts between widely different animal species that could change in function as you moved from one species to the next. It was easy for Cuvier to show that these homologies weren't always there, that you couldn't always move so easily via the bridge of homology from one species to the next, especially when these differed widely. It's the same old story: empiricists always win when the argument comes down to detail.

Nonetheless, with some hindsight it's possible to see Geoffroy as the real winner. His idea of trying to track formal homologies across species regardless of the function played by the relevant organs or parts within each species brought a fresh perspective to taxonomy and anatomy, with fruitful research consequences.

Clearly, Cuvier's insistence on how form had to be constantly correlated with function had produced a very static taxonomy: since the functions of organs were always the same for a given species (as far as anyone at that time could tell), and since functions for any given morphological element almost invariably differed between species, everything tended to remain fixed in place (which was exactly the way Cuvier liked it)—no upward or downward mobility, and none sideways across the *embranchements* or larger groups of species. But this makes for boring science, where all you get to do is fill in some blanks from time to time. For many, Geoffroy's approach was much more exciting: because homology could be used to pivot between two species where organs and

[3] For the fullest account, see Toby Appel, *The Cuvier-Geoffroy Debate* (New York: Oxford University Press, 1987), 145–55. Also of interest are her account of Geoffroy in Egypt (pp. 72–81), the genesis of Geoffroy's *Philosophie Anatomique* (97–104), the support for Geoffroy from German Naturphilosophie (pp. 105–9), and Goethe's report on the debate for Germany (pp. 158–61).

functions didn't always square exactly, taxonomy or classification became much more fluid (Geoffroy always thought it was arbitrary anyway), while anatomy gained new life as a way to relate widely different species. More generally, we might say Geoffroy introduced the possibility of flux or mobility in a field endangered by an oppressive status quo. Above all, his notion that homologies could relate species even when the relevant parts functionally differed made taxonomy more imaginative: the possibility of wide leaps across species differences, of new and previously unsuspected relationships, really seemed to open up the field.

Ultimately, though, what the Cuvier–Geoffroy debate revealed was why pre-eminence in the life sciences was about to pass from natural history to medicine. Geoffroy had done everything possible to give natural history a new mobility by showing the possibility of relationships previously unsuspected between larger taxonomic groups. To some extent, that helped to destabilize the boundaries of these larger groups, by showing how elements within them reached out beyond those boundaries. What he couldn't do, however, was to overcome an inherent static quality within the groups themselves. Without evolution (and even Lamarck—a relative outsider—hadn't quite envisioned evolution in the Darwinian sense) there was almost no mobility within each group. Once the traits of a group were fixed, that was it.

In other words, the group itself couldn't change. At most it might be possible to posit relations to other groups. But as long as the groups themselves didn't change, there was no possibility for any more radical movement. Darwin would introduce it later, by an innovative combination of teleology or function and form or morphology: accidental morphological changes within a species become important to its survival because of environmental pressures, hence come to play a key functional role for that species, subsequently become a new morphological trait for that species. So instead of just simple species change through teleology or purposive drive (the progressivism of Lamarck) or a static morphology (Cuvier) we get accidental morphological change ⇒ new functional role as result of changed morphology ⇒ spread of new morphological trait to entire species. In other words, accidental morphology ⇒ new function ⇒ new morphology. But all that was in the future. For the moment, there was only the tyranny of static *embranchements* as defined by Cuvier. Clearly, what everyone wanted was the possibility of movement, development. And if it couldn't come from natural history, that only increased the temptation to look for it elsewhere.

Medical Revolution in France

For any kind of radical reform, a destructive phase seems to be necessary. And so it was for medicine. Here, as elsewhere, the Revolution began by a complete break with the Old Regime: by a single stroke, it abolished the Royal Society of Medicine and the Royal Academy of Surgery. And as of August 1792, all medical instruction throughout France was at an end. The result, predictably, was chaos: no more legal requirements for medical practice, no demands for proof of competence, no quality control. Instead, a flood of untrained practitioners, scores of fake remedies peddled by anyone and everyone, superstition rampant, quackery and charlatanism everywhere. The idea was to do away with privilege. Before the Revolution, medicine had been a genteel armchair profession, practised only by a few, and largely for the wealthy. Under the new regime, medical care was supposed to be for everybody. And that meant a charge of responsibility imposed on the government: public health now gets connected to liberty, equality, and happiness. But organization and competence don't exactly come about by themselves. As a result, from 1789 to 1793–4, the medical situation in France steadily worsened: without private philanthropy (which had helped to provide much of the care under the Old Regime), many medical facilities now went unstaffed. And without the clergy (likewise abolished by the Revolution), virtually no support staff as well.

But if innovation often comes from necessity, necessity often (sadly) comes from war. When the armies of the Republic went out to fight against those of the Coalition, it produced casualties of a kind and scale never seen before. Hence the need for a new kind of medical establishment to address these. Unlike the small, professional forces of the eighteenth century, the citizen-armies of Revolutionary France were engaged in an all-or-nothing effort, committed to the defence of a nation rather than merely of a monarchy. But greater responsibility ⇒ greater risks ⇒ greater cost. So we find inexperienced volunteers charging against artillery firing at point-blank range at places like Aywaille, only to sustain shocking casualties. Likewise, without knowledge of proper sanitary precautions, large republican armies were often decimated by epidemic illnesses. Thus the greater demand placed on the 'health officers' of the republic to care for those who were giving their lives to the national defence. Nonetheless, without some central authority, the sheer magnitude of the problems to which the new republican armies gave rise proved difficult to manage. From 1789 to 1793, French military medical care was clearly on a steep descent into chaos. At this point, forced to recognize a state of total war, the Committee of Public Safety takes over. From now on, negligence and/or incompetence get equated with treason, and treason of course is punished the way you might expect. Faced with this double bind of internal and external pressure, a new group of military doctors rose to prominence: Larrey, Desgenettes, Coste, Percy—all later to become celebrated for their service to the armies of the First Empire. Extreme battle conditions exposed much of eighteenth-century medical theory as pure fluff. Under emergency circumstances, new methods were developed: Larrey demonstrated the effectiveness of wound irrigation by water, bandages that could hold wound edges together, refrigeration to relieve the pain of amputation, catheterization for wounds of the bladder. Briot performed skin grafts on wounds produced by sabres, and Sabatier showed how a severed intestine could be sutured by being wrapped around an ordinary playing card.[4]

[4] David Vees, *Medical Revolution in France 1789–1796* (Gainesville, Fla.: University Presses of Florida, 1975), 185–93.

War also brought about a medical revolution from an organizational or disciplinary standpoint as well. Up to the time of the Revolution, medicine and surgery had gone their separate ways—medicine the genteel armchair discipline, more preoccupied with theory than with making inroads on disease and illness, surgery with the purely instrumental in a fashion not far removed from that of barbers and butchers. War brought about their fusion. Because medicine couldn't solve any of the problems posed by the battlefield, medical theory (of the old style) simply fell out of fashion. In its place, a new kind of practice takes over. Instead of speculative medical theory, we now get an emphasis on the local and on pathology. Rather than just making inferences about the cause or source of illness, health officers resorted to autopsy. What they discovered was tumours, inflammation, and abscesses. To understand how these worked, in turn, they had to combine what they knew about pathology with their knowledge of anatomy. In the process, medicine and surgery gradually came together, to become aspects of a single, more comprehensive medical practice. If anatomy drew at least somewhat from traditional medical knowledge, pathology was a relatively new field, heavily dependent on autopsy and hence on the offices of surgery. Together, they would work their way towards a new medical perspective.

The Emergence of the Hospital

The place where medicine and surgery converged was the hospital. Several reasons helped to bring it about. First, this was where military medicine ultimately had to concentrate its resources. Second, the hospital offered a way to change the demographics of patient care: from now on, medicine would treat everybody, not just the wealthy. Third, the hospital becomes the new medical research centre.

By a kind of logistical necessity, the wars of the First Republic and the First Empire almost forced the creation of the modern hospital. From the outset, the defence of the new republic, with its armies drawn from the population at large, meant that war would now be fought on a new and massive scale. But massive numbers lead easily to massive casualties. How do you deal with that many wounded and dying? Obviously, a new approach was called for. The eighteenth-century style of medicine, with its slow, patient, retail mindset, could no longer suffice: from now on, a quicker, more efficient wholesale outlook becomes necessary. In war, speed is of the essence.

As with the battlefield, so with the military hospital. The key here is to be able to *process* patients as quickly as possible. As chief surgeon, Dominique Larrey set the tone: all amputations within twenty-four hours of the wound's discovery. Likewise, Larrey developed the imperative for quick assessment: from now on, triage according to seriousness of the wound (regardless of rank or nationality), and—when necessary—immediate treatment. But with the huge number of amputations being performed, and the equal or greater number bedridden from illness or disease, casualties couldn't be kept at the front. Hence the need for concentration of resources in central places—which is to say: the hospital.

The hospital also radically changed the demographics of patient care, which was another compelling reason for its emergence as a focal point during the Revolutionary years. Unlike the genteel eighteenth-century medical cabinet practice, the hospital thrived on numbers. We've seen that the Hôtel-Dieu could accommodate as many as 4,500 patients. But the list of Paris hospitals goes on: the Pitié, the Charité, the Necker, the St Antoine, the St Louis, the Bicêtre, the Salpêtrière ... And that meant not just care for the wealthy, but for everyone including the poor. In this respect, the hospital represents a genuine and permanent change ushered in by the Revolution. In fact, the Revolutionary years witnessed not only the revamping and enlargement of existing Paris hospitals but the creation of many more: the St Antoine was new, as were the Enfants Malades (the first children's hospital in the world), the Maternité, the Val de Grâce ... Clearly, the list included many that were meant to serve special groups: women in childbirth, children, the insane. And the fact that many of these were groups not particularly emphasized before the Revolution (mental patients, for instance), showed the new imperative for all-encompassing medical care.

Since the State had shut down the Church, it found itself forced to assume many church prerogatives and duties. The list began with citizen-soldiers of the republican armies, but quickly widened out to take in virtually everyone else. Medicine now took on a distinctly secular quality, nowhere more evident than in the umbrella organization under which all hospitals worked: Assistance publique.[5]

But above all, the Paris hospital became the new medical research centre. And why not? With their vast number of patients, the Paris hospitals could collectively claim an unparalleled pool of subjects for observation and experiment. Better yet, state control of medical care gave French medical practitioners unrivalled access to the patient population. Contrast England, with its private hospitals (St Bartholomew's, Guy's), severely restricted in terms of freedom to conduct autopsies or dissect. During his brief time at the Hôtel-Dieu, Xavier Bichat became legendary for doing 600 cadavers in a year. Compare John Abernethy, the celebrated British surgeon, who in a lifetime had done no more than a handful. Likewise for experiments on the living: wars during the Revolutionary years and later the Empire had brought in massive numbers of wounded, and the danger of death from either wounds or illness eased the way for frequent experiment. Standard practices and centralized control by the state also make it easy to collect data on the condition of patients, what was done to them, and what happened to them. As a result, we find a predilection for statistics and number-crunching in the new Paris medicine. Often, numbers tell the story, and the adroit use of these by medical practitioners there meant they could often rule out by sheer weight of numbers explanations that might gain currency elsewhere.

Finally, concentration of resources in the Paris hospital was bound to yield a huge payoff in terms of education and the transmission of medical knowledge generally.

[5] On the rise of the Paris hospital, see Erwin Ackerknecht, *Medicine at the Paris Hospital 1794–1848* (Baltimore: Johns Hopkins University Press, 1967), esp. 17–28.

Attached to any chief physician or surgeon, there would be, inevitably, a whole team of students, assistants, interns, demonstrators—any or all of whom might well rise in time to become chiefs of surgery or medicine themselves. And that would have the effect of a tenfold multiplication of knowledge. Likewise the existence of hospitals as research centres that would accumulate and keep medical data encouraged researchers to compare results constantly. And that, too, would help to correct, explain, clarify.

The Shift away from Montpellier

Everybody wants to give credit to Montpellier. In the eighteenth century, it was the dominant school, with big stars like Théophile de Bordeu and Paul-Joseph Barthez. Montpellier was all about the link between the physical and the moral, about vitality as a unique phenomenon not reducible to physics, and about a kind of holistic medicine that embraced all aspects of the science of man. On top of that, a number of key people in the formation of Paris medicine were heavily influenced by Montpellier—Cabanis and Pinel come especially to mind. But Montpellier was more humane, more open to concern about environmental influences on health, less into medical intervention and more into belief in the ability of the body to cure itself. From our present standpoint, all this looks pretty good. We don't like too much medical intervention, we like concern about the environment, and in general we want medicine to be more humane. In a recent study, we even find a table of 'winners' versus 'losers', with Paris as the winner and Montpellier as the loser.[6] Here's the table:

Winners	Losers
Paris	Montpellier
Positive method	Philosophical method
Statistics	Prose
Vivisection	Antivivisection
Use of the microscope	Ordinary vision
Reductionism	Holism
Autopsy	Observation of the living
Antivitalism	Vitalism

It's fashionable to suggest Montpellier lost out more from lack of institutional and political clout than from any more purely scientific factors. And that would conform

[6] Elizabeth Williams, *The Physical and the Moral: Anthropology, Physiology, and Philosophical Medicine in France 1750–1850* (Cambridge: Cambridge University Press, 1994), 31. See her discussion and defence of Montpellier, pp. 20–5.

to the kind of history of science favoured by Thomas Kuhn or by Foucault, where winners emerge not because they're more persuasive or better able to square evidence with theory but because their opponents die out or because of some seismic shift that affects people's overall outlook. But before we feel too sorry about Montpellier, perhaps it might be useful to probe the 'winners versus losers' scenario more carefully, to see if there are any other reasons why Paris finally won out, and especially whether its programme was in any way more theoretically constructive, or richer in possibility. From that we might in turn draw inferences about its possible significance for the Romantic period.

We've seen that Paris was into numbers, which Montpellier was not. Years ago I remember going to see a philosophy professor whose specialty was epistemology. On his office door he had posted a baseball box score which gave an inning by inning tally, between 'realists' and 'idealists'. Every innings, the 'realists' would chalk up a lot of runs, while the 'idealists' failed to get any. But the final score was: 'idealists' 1, 'realists' 0. Unfortunately (or fortunately, depending on whose side you're on) it doesn't usually work that way. Instead, numbers have cumulative force. The side that keeps adding up new numbers while its opponent can only reiterate what it has to say in more prose will tend to win out. And not just because we respect numbers more, but because we can see that all the fresh numbers amount to new evidence. In a world where all scientific data have to be qualified to some extent, fresh evidence has the weight of greater probability. Even in current physics, where the numbers are as precise as you're likely to get, everyone knows measurements can still be off. So greater probability from more evidence is all we have to rely on. And the method that can generate fresh evidence gets respect precisely because it has this sort of generative capacity.

A second reason why Paris may have won out over Montpellier has to do with pushing the physical/mechanical further into the realm of the vital. It's not enough just to say Paris was antivitalist as opposed to the vitalism of Montpellier. Everyone in Paris knows perfectly well that vitality isn't exactly the same as the physical/mechanical, that vitality can't be reduced simply or wholly to the laws of physics. To say just this would be to miss the point. The point is, we know something about the laws of physics, whereas we don't necessarily know anything about the laws of vitality. So the further we can push the laws of physics into the realm of the vital, the more of what passes as vitality we can claim to be understandable. From an explanatory standpoint, to talk about vitality as completely different from the physical/mechanical is like throwing up your hands and giving up on it. As long as we can't claim any of it to be physical/mechanical and as long as we don't want to propose any laws of vitality (difficult to do, given the variability of vital phenomena), we lack any kind of explanatory purchase or grip on vitality. And let's face it: we know at least *some* of what passes for vitality has to be reducible to the laws of physics. Take blood circulation, for example. Blood getting pumped out of the heart isn't any different if we're looking at it from the standpoint of blood flow or movement from any other instance of hydraulics. Here as elsewhere, we've got to think about fluid dynamics, about pressure, and so on. And if you ever cut yourself badly and need to try to stop the bleeding, you know you have to keep your hand upright to let gravity do its work. Clearly, then, if we can make *any* explanatory inroads on vitality by showing at least *some* of what it consists of to be explainable in physical/mechanical terms, there's always the possibility we might be able to explain more of it that way. In this fashion, we would gradually gain ground on the inexplicable. Even more important, we'd have some sense of where to go if we wanted to add to the explicability of vital phenomena.

Finally, Paris offered a way to extend the physical/mechanical into the vital: by means of experiment. This is what vivisection and autopsy are all about. From a distance, the Montpellier approach looks nice. You don't violate the vital activity of either person or animal in any way, you allow that person or animal to interact fully with the environment, you don't intervene medically in any fashion that could possibly compromise the health of your subject. The only problem is: you don't learn much either. Unfortunately, observation can only take one so far. Beyond a point (especially if you don't want to use a microscope), there's nothing more to observe. And once you've observed all the naked eye can possibly see, if you still don't understand how a particular vital organ works or what it does, there's nowhere else to go, no other research avenue to pursue. This is where experiment enters the scene. By means of experiment, you alter the conditions under which vitality normally sustains itself and you take note of the result. Typically, altering the conditions of a particular vital activity will alter the nature or mode of that activity. And, by the way it alters it, experiment places you in a good position to figure out what the key factors necessary for any vital activity are, and in some instances even how they bring about that activity. Equally important, experiment can lead very naturally to further experiment: question leads to answer which leads to further question which, when asked by means of new experiment, leads to further answer. Like statistics, then, experiment has a generative capacity, the capacity to produce new knowledge that in turn can generate further inquiry. In that respect, unlike observation, it doesn't have any definite endpoint. Simply put, then, Paris wins out over Montpellier because its programme is more fruitful in research consequences.

Bichat/Magendie/Claude Bernard

What we find in Xavier Bichat and his successors is a perception of life as process. This is what separates Paris medicine from Montpellier, or from the natural history of Cuvier and Geoffroy Saint-Hilaire, as well as German Naturphilosophie. For Bichat, as for Magendie and Claude Bernard later, life is about activity, and activity is about vital processes. Cuvier and Geoffroy Saint-Hilaire, and Naturphilosophie as a whole, had been all about forms. Natural history looks at forms because forms are how we relate past life to present life. Montpellier shifted the focus to the present, and by doing that removed the emphasis from form. But because of its holistic perspective, it couldn't escape a kind of essentialism in talking about the vital principle. Montpellier refused to explore the body internally, and because of that it couldn't get beyond the vital principle to the way it actually worked. So it was only at the Paris hospital, through the autopsy of cadavers and medical operations on the living, that a notion of vital processes gradually emerged.

And because the notion of vital processes could lead to a proliferation of research in ways a holistic perspective couldn't, it gradually comes to define the outlook of its time on the life sciences.

At the very outset of his *Recherches physiologiques sur la vie et la mort* (1800), Bichat defined vitality in terms that would haunt experimental medicine for his time and beyond: 'Life is the ensemble of functions that resist death.'[7] Not a single vital principle, then, but an ensemble of functions: this was where all his dissection of cadavers and experiments on living animals converged. Once you begin to dissect a body (and especially that of a living animal), you immediately realize how many processes are involved in keeping that animal alive. Anyone who's looked at the accounts of different experiments that make up most of the *Recherches* can see this right away: what happens when you cut the windpipe of a dog, what happens if you stop the circulation of blood to the lungs, or to the brain, and so on. From all these experiments Bichat gradually came to realize how vitality continues to sustain itself when some of these processes are stopped, and how it comes to an end when you stop others.[8] And from that he saw that it didn't make sense to talk about vitality as a principle, or a single activity: that it was, in fact, a whole host of different processes that all worked together. Likewise, he discovered the importance of crucial cut-off points: how life could go on if some blood still managed to get to the brain, or if an animal was still able minimally to breathe. So life wasn't just all or nothing: it was also about quantity, numbers.

Vital functions suggests a division of labour, which would ultimately lead Bichat to tissues. Montpellier had talked about the proper or particular life of each organ, but Bichat knew from his frequent dissection of these that such a holistic picture failed to describe things as they really were. Because each time he dissected an organ what he typically found was a number of different tissues. Each tissue, then, had to contribute in some way to the vital function performed by that organ. So if you wanted to talk about vitality you couldn't just stop at the level of organs: if tissues were more basic, you had to move on to tissues. And the fact that you had different tissues helping an organ perform a vital function but not able to exist independently pushed the life sciences very close to chemistry, or to the more purely physical/mechanical.

After all, this was exactly what happened in chemistry: different elements combined to produce a chemical reaction which none of them could have brought about independently. And that meant vitality wasn't so far removed from the physical/mechanical as people had thought. More specifically, it meant you couldn't equate vitality with particular or unique substances. Because tissues, even when dead, still retained all the same chemical/material properties. But if life couldn't be located at the level of tissues, then

[7] Xavier Bichat, *Recherches physiologiques sur la vie et la mort* (Paris: Brosson, 1800), 1.

[8] Hence the emphasis in some of the best Bichat scholarship on experiment over observation: William Albury, 'Experiment and Explanation in the Physiology of Bichat and Magendie', *Studies in History of Biology*, 1 (1977), 47–131; and John Lesch, *Science and Medicine in France: The Emergence of Experimental Physiology, 1790–1855* (Cambridge, Mass.: Harvard University Press, 1984), 61–6, 76–9, 122–4.

it simply couldn't be equated with any particular physical or chemical substances. And that implied the search for the essence of life would have to be taken elsewhere.

For Bichat, what finally defined life was its activity, which consisted of vital processes. If you couldn't identify or equate life with any particular substances, all that was left was the activity of those substances. Here, then, was what life was all about: characteristic, distinctive forms of activity that couldn't be performed by anything else. Take, for instance, nutrition, which comes about via digestion. By this vital process, indisputably, non-vital or inert matter gets assimilated and transformed into something vital, alive. We take in food, which (presumably) at the time we eat it is no longer alive. What happens then? First, a phase of intermixture by which the inanimate gets mixed with the vital, which is to say blood—a phase made possible by the fact that inanimate and vital aren't so far apart. Next, a phase of repulsion: this is where the differences between vital and non-vital come into play, causing these to engage in a 'struggle' of some kind. Life or the vital has to impose itself on the non-vital, on death, or be imposed on. So digestion consumes energy, as life tries to penetrate the non-vital matter. Finally, a third phase: assimilation. Because life can't compete constantly with inanimate matter (whose energies are inexhaustible), it has to find some way to assimilate it, turn it into living matter. Only by doing that can it hope to renew its own vital resources. In the struggle for survival, in other words, you can't just remain as you are: either you expand, or you die. So digestion, by assimilation, is all about expansion, adding to the quantity of living matter so as to find new resources of energy that will allow it to impose on inanimate matter. Obviously, this is an ongoing process. And that's precisely how we recognize it as vital: it doesn't stop until or unless the body dies. Because in the constant struggle between life and death, the inanimate (i.e. dead matter) will always try to impose itself on life. Hence the distinctive quality of vital processes.

With François Magendie, we get less conceptual framework than with Bichat, but—as a result—an even more complete immersion in the mechanics of the vital processes. Unlike Bichat, Magendie had no patience for theory. He didn't care about Bichat's distinction between the vital and non-vital, nor about Bichat's classification of vital properties.[9] To him all the talk in the *Recherches physiologiques* about sensibility and contractility was sheer stuff: only part 2, with its detailed account of Bichat's experiments on living animals and human cadavers, mattered. In the preface to his own *Précis élémentaire de physiologie* (1816–17), he spelled it out pretty plainly:

> Under this form, the facts, the facts alone, serve as a foundation to science; savants will commit to verifying these, to multiplying these as much as possible ... When one engages in experimental research, it's to augment the sum of known facts, or to discover their reciprocal relationships ...[10]

[9] On Magendie and Bichat, see J. M. D. Olmsted, *François Magendie* (New York: Arno Press, 1981; repr. of Schuman's, 1944), 27–34 but see also 161–71.

[10] François Magendie, *Précis élémentaire de physiologie* (Paris: Méquignon-Marvis, 1816–17), Vol. 1, p. ii.

For Magendie, the turning point came when he opted to pursue experimental physiology for its own sake, rather than just as a sideline to medicine. Up to that time, his career had been on a fast track to nowhere, stalled by lack of promotion in either anatomy or surgery within the highly political and competitive Paris medical scene. But backed by support from the Académie des Sciences for his research work, his career took off. And once he'd embarked on a course defined by research rather than clinical practice, he wasn't about to look back.

We get a good idea of how Magendie approached physiology or the study of vital processes from the account of digestion that opens volume ii of the *Précis élémentaire*. In effect, it's like an instant replay in slow motion—120 pages to follow the exact path taken by food through the digestive tract. Magendie begins by looking at the structure of all the organs involved: the mouth, the pharynx, the oesophagus, the stomach, the small intestine, the large intestine. He then takes food (drink gets described separately!) through the entire process. We start with the prehension of food (putting it in your mouth). Then mastication, or chewing it, where we're treated to a long discussion of exactly how the bite works (obviously before dentistry became an independent research field). From there we move on to insalivation (mixing of food with saliva). Here Magendie points out how the temperature of food tends to go up as we chew it. Deglutition, the passage of food from the mouth all the way down to the stomach, is broken down into three separate phases: passage of food from the mouth into the pharynx (throat), crossing over the opening of the glottis and arrival in the oesophagus, passage through the oesophagus into the stomach. Magendie remarks on how many muscles are involved, then goes on to specify which and how they work. The action of the stomach is even more complicated, because now the process becomes chemical for the first time rather than just mechanical. Earlier studies by other researchers, which claimed the chyme or food mass was always the same, are energetically refuted: from having dissected living dogs who were in the process of digesting food, Magendie can say it varies a lot, depending on what they've eaten.

The action of the small intestine leads to the production of gases. Based on his autopsy of condemned convicts who had just been executed, Magendie gives the exact composition (for one who'd eaten bread and Gruyère cheese, and another who'd had beef, lentils, and red wine!). From the small intestine he passes on to the large intestine and beyond—but we won't follow him there.

Compared to Bichat, Magendie is even more purely physical/mechanical in his account of vital processes. Nowhere do we get any sense of the 'lutte' or struggle between vital and non-vital which is the hallmark of Bichat's perspective on physiology. Instead, Magendie sees the interaction between vital and non-vital as no different from any other physical/mechanical interaction. Bichat had already remarked on the analogy between physiological processes and chemistry. Magendie took this to its limit, to a point where we can no longer tell the difference. The upshot is that vital processes become chemical processes. And the effect of that is to emphasize all the more the extent to which they're processes. In 1816–17 chemistry was still a relatively new science on the rise: to use its terminology and its concepts gave Magendie a specificity he couldn't otherwise have claimed in his description of vital processes. At the same time, it was also bound to raise the question of whether there was ultimately *any* difference between chemistry and the life sciences, a question that was bound in turn to require an answer.

If Claude Bernard takes us beyond Romantic medicine, he's nonetheless useful and even necessary as the end to its story. There are a lot of different perspectives on Claude Bernard and his style of medicine and/or experimental physiology: the legalistic tenor of much of his discussion of the relationship between vital and non-vital, the mid-century Victorian industrial sense of science as power, and so on. What I want to stress here, though, is what he does for Romantic medicine as a science of vital processes. If Magendie in his zeal to increase the explanatory power of medicine pushed the physical/mechanical take on vital processes too exclusively, what Claude Bernard does is to rethink the notion of vital process and what it involves. What emerges is a new sense of vital processes. Bernard preserved the functionalist perspective that saw the essence of life in particular vital processes, but he changed the way we think about these by his insistence on specific physical/mechanical or chemical processes as unique to vitality. So where Magendie had been reductive, asserting that all vital processes could be seen either as physical/mechanical or chemical or some combination of these, Bernard retrieves the old sense of vital processes as unique that had been espoused by Bichat. In doing that, he nonetheless took over the physical/mechanical and chemical base established by Magendie.

But where Magendie tries to show how the entire process of digestion can be accounted for by physical/mechanical activity of the muscles of the digestive tract + chemical activity of all the digestive juices, Bernard looks for chemical processes unique to living species, like the production of plant or animal sugar or the role of blood as a vital medium. In his *Recherches physiologiques* Bichat had seen that the medical sciences would have to move towards the investigation of vital processes. Magendie tried to put substance into the claims of medical science by a physical/mechanical or chemical explanation of these. But it would be left to Claude Bernard to try to say what was unique about the vital processes.

Form versus Function

Arguably, the problem with natural history in the Romantic era was its inability to resolve the debate between form and function. We've seen that Cuvier held out for the primacy of function over form: organs or parts of a body became what they were because of what they did, the particular role they had to play. Nor did any part exist within a body without a function—in other words, nothing ever got wasted within the natural economy. And that meant that, as a species changed, all its organs would have to be modified to fit their new functions. So no loose ends, no carryover parts from other species. The upshot, then, was that, with species change, gaps would emerge between different groups, since form always rigidly followed function. To Geoffroy Saint-Hilaire, however, this didn't make sense: given the very palpable resemblances in form between organs or parts of different species, it seemed only natural to try for a more unified perspective, one that would bring the different species together. On top of that, a more unified perspective based on formal resemblances made sense as metascience. Just as contemporary physics has found itself pressed by necessity into the quest for some kind of unified field theory, so early nineteenth-century natural history would likewise have felt a similar pressure. Hence the support for the Geoffroy approach within the Academy of Sciences, and even from Goethe in faraway Germany. But as long as Geoffroy couldn't find a way to reconcile function with form, he couldn't persuade Cuvier. The persistence of a split between form and function meant in turn that the debate would remain a stalemate.

By contrast, the combined use of form and function in the new experimental physiology could perhaps help to explain the ascendancy of medicine among the life sciences in the Romantic era. In the study of vital processes, it all came together: anatomy, chemistry, even the physics of fluid movement or mechanical pressure. Bichat, we recall, had urged medicine to adopt physical and chemical perspectives in thinking about the vital processes: how even organic matter had to be composed of the same basic stuff as all other matter, how the interaction between organs and/or tissues could be understood by analogy with what happened in a chemical reaction.

Likewise, when Magendie explored the digestive process, he took from anatomy the form and structure of the different organs involved, and showed how these worked within the digestive economy. Similarly, chemistry was called upon to explain the interaction between food and the gastric juices, ditto for physics in the passage of food down the digestive tract. With Claude Bernard, the uniqueness of particular vital processes when seen from a chemical standpoint would later lead to the emergence of a new field, organic chemistry. Above all, what the Paris medicine showed was how form and function might come together, not as opposing viewpoints about how to organize the life sciences but rather as different sources of knowledge about what ultimately defined these sciences: the vital processes. By its combination of formal and functional, then, the new physiology might hope to satisfy the Romantic aspiration toward a unified science. Nonetheless, the way it would do that was one that would leave the more traditional conception of Romantic science far behind: it wasn't about holism or a harmony between mankind and nature, nor about some universal archetype for all animal species, nor about a vital principle wholly different from the non-vital. Instead, with its commitment to experimental work rather than any theory about vital forces, the only thing it preserved from all that had come before was a sense of life as ultimately defined by activity, by something ongoing, something always in movement or flux—in other words, by vital processes.

From Romantic Medicine to Nineteenth-Century Science

In many ways the modern sciences can be said to have emerged during the nineteenth century. Nonetheless, the history of each science is different. And if we look at the history of medical science, we can see that it didn't come to a sense of itself as science right away, that only somewhere around the mid-century point did it finally arrive at what we might call a research programme. Precisely for that reason, it seems useful to try to trace briefly the route by which it got there.

In his *Recherches physiologiques* Bichat speaks of two lives (the organic or involuntary, the animal or voluntary), and the same division could well be applied to his work itself. The first half (the discussion of life) is medical theory, classification, distinction. A lot of it harks back to Montpellier, to that eighteenth-century medical style which tried to organize vital phenomena. Yes, Bichat doesn't subscribe to a single vital principle, and he talks about vital functions, which looks forward to the experimental physiology of Magendie and later Claude Bernard. All the same, there's a sense in which all this seems somewhat transitional, like the early Italian campaigns of Napoleon before he had fully worked out the more massive manoeuvres of Jena or Austerlitz. The second half (discussion of death) is almost purely experimental, with a detailed account of ways in which the failure of particular organs will cause people or animals to die. This, then, is where we really see nineteenth-century experimental physiology start to emerge.

Magendie, as we've seen, is all about pure or total immersion in experiment. It's tempting to describe his work as an almost mindless form of experimentation—he hardly seems to know what he's looking for, and hardly seems to care. The preface to his *Précis élémentaire*, with its famous praise of facts alone, offers no research programme of any kind and seems almost clueless about how to formulate one. Nonetheless, it's as if this kind of theoretical mindlessness was almost necessary to the development of experimental physiology as a science. And maybe on some level it was, to free medicine of any earlier theoretical carryovers or influences. What this kind of mindless experimentation did, clearly, was to help develop experimental technique. In volume ii of the *Précis*, Magendie gives a sufficiently detailed account of experiments by himself and others as to allow these to be repeated by other researchers. Like a cookbook, then, the *Précis* seems to have been designed to teach experimental technique. A famous French chef of earlier days, Raymond Oliver, once said: you read Ali Baba for inspiration, you read Escoffier for technique. Likewise we can imagine early nineteenth-century researchers reading the *Précis* with its detailed account of experiments, and from these gaining a sense of how to set up an experiment. Compared to Bichat, certainly, Magendie's experiments have a definite sense of direction, a definite purposiveness. They're all about getting an answer to a question. With Bichat, by contrast, there's a sense of randomness, drift: let's cut the windpipe or a vein, and see what happens ...

All the same, it's no surprise that when we come to Claude Bernard, the student, protégé, and finally collaborator of Magendie, we get a distinct research programme. You might say that where Magendie sets up experiments to get answers to randomly chosen questions, Claude Bernard picks his questions. Where Magendie is wholesale, Bernard is retail. And here, behind the economy of retail, you feel distinct intelligence. It's like the elite Fifth Avenue shop where you see only a few items on display but where each is the best of its kind, and where every one of these has a distinct reason for being there. Unlike Magendie, Bernard realized that despite our best intentions we don't always get there, that we don't always have world enough and time. Hence the need for economy. But he also realized that facts alone weren't sufficient. In his classic *Introduction à l'étude de la médecine expérimentale* he says it's useful to experiment even when we don't have a clear idea of what we're after. But if truth (as he says later) exists only in the form of *rapports* or relations between things, and we never get to know causes or essences, then it's also clear that we won't get there by trial and error alone. Rather, we need what he calls an experimental idea—something that grows out of experiment itself by a kind of personal insight, not just by experimental method. This experimental idea, he says, results from a sort of intuition of the mind which judges that things should occur in a certain way. You notice something because of a lucky conjunction of circumstances or because you're in a receptive state of mind, and suddenly you see in a flash the way things work, how they are, or why they come to be. For Bernard, then, the discovery is finally the idea that attaches to fact, not the fact itself. By itself, in other words, the fact has no significance. It's only the idea that attaches to it which lifts it out of the endless realm of the many, many facts and gives it a special significance. Later he puts this in the form of a more general principle: ultimately, the sole criterion in experiments isn't facts but reason. And the proof of that: the rational (rather than empirical) relation between phenomena and cause.[11] Given that we can only know *rapports* or relations rather than things as they are, we have to construct those relationships. And once we have to construct those relationships, they're not empirical any more. So out of the theory of Bichat and the pure empiricism of Magendie we finally arrive at the reflective science of Claude Bernard—because Bichat focused the study of life on vital processes, and because Magendie tried to explore these experimentally. Nonetheless, it was the generative capacity of these initiatives that made what we call nineteenth century science possible. And that, you might say, was their Romantic legacy.

Further Reading

Ackerknecht, Erwin, *Medicine at the Paris Hospital 1794–1848* (Baltimore: Johns Hopkins University Press, 1967).

Gelfand, Toby, *Professionalizing Modern Medicine* (Westport, Conn.: Greenwood, 1980).

[11] Claude Bernard, *Introduction à l'étude de la médecine expérimentale* (Paris: J. B. Baillière, 1865), 37–8, 51–2, 59–61, 92–3.

Gillispie, Charles Coulston, *Science and Polity in France: The Revolutionary and Napoleonic Years* (Princeton: Princeton University Press, 2004).

Lesch, John, *Science and Medicine in France: The Emergence of Experimental Physiology, 1790–1855* (Cambridge, Mass.: Harvard University Press, 1984).

Temkin, Owsei, 'Basic Science, Medicine, and the Romantic Era', in *The Double Face of Janus and Other Essays in the History of Medicine* (Baltimore: Johns Hopkins University Press, 1977).

CHAPTER 37

RELIGION

THOMAS PFAU

To explore the diverse and unsettled religious landscape of the Romantic era, we might want to begin by offering some working definition, however provisional, of Romanticism. For only so, it would seem, can we avoid sliding into a purely immanent treatment that considers specific religious movements, practices, and controversies strictly on their own terms—a procedure sure to deprive us of a genuinely *critical* standpoint. The matter is rather more complicated, however, since to suppose that the contours and claims of Romantic religious culture ought to be assessed from an extrinsic, 'critical' point of view would itself appear to beg the central question. For it presupposes (but notably fails to argue the point) that Romanticism and, indeed, our own historical moment today must abide by the (Kantian) Enlightenment axiom that the only legitimate form of knowledge is that of 'critique'. In his attempts at delimiting the scope and authority of rationalist models of cognition (from Descartes and Leibniz forward), Kant had evolved a model of *Kritik* characterized by the systematic cultivation of distance and detachment vis-à-vis its specific *sujet*. With its faint Stoic overtones, the overall aura of Kant's critical philosophy is one of principled diffidence vis-à-vis whatever happens to be the *datum* or problem at hand. His philosophy conceives critical knowledge as an aggregate of legitimate propositions about phenomena deemed to be inherently bereft of reason themselves. As the *Critique of Judgment* stipulates, it is only in a strictly hypothetical ('as if') sense that rational purposiveness may ever be imputed to a given natural phenomenon. Like his philosophical and scientific predecessors (Bacon, Gassendi, Locke), Kantian critique pre-emptively estranges us from the objective world, turning it into an epistemological puzzle that can only be solved by articulating the formal conditions under which the experience of a now enigmatic realm of appearances may yet prove possible. Though with important modifications and much circumspection, Kant thus remains true to the Enlightenment's fundamental stance, which treats what is given as an opaque phenomenon that ultimately originates in the inscrutable otherness of the noumenon.

Hence it cannot surprise (and is easily confirmed by even a casual reading of Hume or the French *philosophes*) that when confronting organized religion and subjective belief, the Enlightenment's disengaged or 'buffered self' (C. Taylor) tends to reduce the inner dispositions and outward practices associated with religion to so many instances of superstition, imposture, and illusion. In Descartes, Locke, Voltaire, Hume, and even Kant the prevailing conception of knowledge thus is emphatically hostile to so-called pre-modern views for which human inquiry unfolds as a progressively fuller participation in a world that, far from a shifting inventory of 'appearances', was understood as a timeless rational 'order (*kosmos*)' of 'things' whose teleological constitution furnished human, moral agents with a blueprint for how to inhabit that order. By contrast, an anti-Aristotelian modern sensibility understands religion and individual belief primarily as instances of epistemological illegitimacy whose ostensible lack of a rational (propositional) warrant ought to be critiqued and extirpated. It is just this lacuna within what Alasdair MacIntyre would later term the 'Enlightenment project' to which Hegel objects: '[the] Enlightenment apprehends its object in the first instance and generally ... as pure insight, and, not recognizing itself therein, declares it to be error (*die Aufklärung faßt also ihren Gegenstand zuerst und allgemein so auf, daß sie ihn als reine Einsicht nimmt und ihn so, sich selbst nicht erkennend, für Irrtum erklärt*)'.[1] Paradoxically, then, the Enlightenment places great 'trust' in the substantive identity and coherence of phenomena associated with religious culture, practice, and belief, about which it then proceeds to reach diametrically opposed conclusions. Hegel wryly characterizes the Enlightenment as playing a curious *fort/da* game with religion as 'that wherein [the Enlightenment subject] comes to know itself (*dasjenige ... worin ich mich selbst erkenne*)'. Yet as a result, the critical knowledge so achieved has become 'alienated from its particular individuality, viz. from its natural and contingent existence (*seiner Natürlichkeit und Zufälligkeit entfremdet*)'.[2] Hegel thus alerts his contemporaries (and us) to the implicit kinship that the Enlightenment bears to its own other, thereby undermining its proclaimed emancipation from 'superstition' (*Aberglauben*). In its variously hostile, dismissive, or presumptuous reaction against any stance that fails to accord with its own procedures and objectives of knowing, the Enlightenment has arrived at a 'concept of pure insight' (*Begriff der reinen Einsicht*), to be sure, but it just as notably failed to grasp the true provenance of that concept and thus 'asserts the very opposite of what it maintains regarding faith (*sie unmittelbar das Gegenteil dessen, was sie vom Glauben behauptet*)'. The challenge for Hegel and his Romantic contemporaries thus becomes how to think about 'faith' (*Glauben*) without either naïvely emulating its 'certainty' (*Gewißheit*) or appealing to external evidences and historical proof, in which case the genuine object of religion has already vanished from view, having 'already let itself be corrupted by the Enlightenment (*sich von der Aufklärung verführen lassen*)'.[3]

As Hegel saw so clearly, one of the more troubling consequences of the Enlightenment's engagement with phenomena—religion being an especially prominent case in point—is that in peremptorily ('critically') declaring them to be diametrically

[1] G. W. F. Hegel, *Phenomenology of Spirit*, tr. A. V. Miller (Oxford: Oxford University Press, 1977).

[2] Hegel, *Phenomenology of Spirit*, 334.

[3] Hegel, *Phenomenology of Spirit*, 335, 338.

opposed or 'other' to its own conception of rationality, it tends not so much to comprehend as dissolve them. Religious belief and practice and its underlying emotive or rational foundations are less explained than explained away, in a process whose more advanced phases in Hume, Kant, and Schleiermacher warrant some initial consideration so that we may better understand the conceptual vacuum that the Romantic (Catholic) critique of modernity's liberal-secular view of reason and religion seeks to fill.[4] Hume's *Dialogues concerning natural religion* (published posthumously in 1779) illustrates how the Enlightenment's refusal (or incapacity) to engage the phenomenon of religious belief on its own terms produces a certain 'concept' of religion, to be sure, but fails to grasp the depth and persistence of religious faith understood as a correlate of what J. H. Newman would later term 'real' (as opposed to strictly 'notional') assent. This outcome cannot surprise given that Hume's ahistorical understanding of natural theology appears unaware of its very different function in scholastic theology. We recall how, in the *quinque viae* of Aquinas's *Summa* (*ST* Ia q 2), natural theology or physico-teleological argumentation had been introduced as just *one* of several strategies by which human beings, whose grasp of the divine source and *telos* of their faith remains necessarily imperfect, might achieve a fuller understanding of God's uncreated and transcendent reality and, hence, of the true meaning of their own faith.[5] By contrast, natural theology in Hume's times had been repurposed for the demands of modern epistemology, namely, as an *inferential method* for deducing a transcendent designer or intelligent First Cause from the observable order of natural forms to the idea.

Ingeniously staged as a debate between an orthodox Christian (Demea), a sceptic (Philo), and an adherent of modern natural theology (Cleanthes), Hume's *Dialogues* effectively dismantle the attempt at inferring a divine First Cause from the putative 'evidences' of natural phenomena. Philo's seemingly innocuous suggestion that 'if we distrust human reason, we have now no other principle to lead us into religion' soon bares a more menacing edge as he proceeds to show that there is practically no limit to reason's questioning the so-called 'evidences' of religion. Thus the sceptic, Philo, does not so much *reject* natural theology as simply hobble its progress by intimating that any such 'argument a posteriori' would have to disprove all alternative ways of interpreting the natural evidence it introduces in support of God as First Cause. Leaving aside the underlying Deism of modern natural theology, a weakness primarily explored by the orthodox Demea, our

[4] For a compact survey of Romanticism's varied responses to Enlightenment accounts of religion, see Douglas Hedley, 'Theology and the Revolt Against the Enlightenment', in Sheridan Gilley and Brian Stanley (eds), *The Cambridge History of Christianity* viii (Cambridge: Cambridge University Press, 2006), 30–52.

[5] On the five ways as a form of 'leading' (*manuductio*) towards the intelligibility of God, Rudi te Velde observes that 'the issue for Thomas is not whether God exists as a matter of fact, or even whether we may consider ourselves to be rationally justified in believing that God exists. His focus is in a certain sense not epistemological at all; ... what Thomas is looking for is not so much rational certainty as intelligibility, to wit the intelligibility of the truth expressed and asserted by the proposition "God exists"'. *Aquinas on God* (Aldershot: Ashgate, 2006), 38–9; for a review of competing interpretations of the Five Ways, see Fergus Ker, *After Aquinas* (Oxford: Blackwell, 2002), 52–72.

focus here is solely on Philo's corrosive critique of the mainstream view that proof of God's existence is both necessary and positively attained by a dedicated analysis of the design that imparts specificity and apparent purposiveness to each natural form. Against this hypothesis the modern (Humean) sceptic maintains that the teleological picture suggested by instances of order and structure observable in nature might just as plausibly be the result of chance; that to infer an intelligent, designing First Cause from the uniform order of natural evidence, the Creator from his creation, is to prejudge the whole matter; for 'there is no more difficulty in conceiving, that the several elements, from an internal unknown cause, may fall into the most exquisite arrangement, than to conceive that their ideas, in the great, universal mind, from a like internal, unknown cause, fall into that arrangement.' Whereas Cleanthes is content 'from similar effects [to] infer similar causes', Philo muses on whether such similarity or resemblance can ever be legitimately stipulated, 'unless the cases be exactly similar' (*Dialogues*, 23). Hence, where the aspect of a modern ship might well lead us to form 'an exalted idea ... of the ingenuity of the carpenter', we may ultimately only find 'a stupid mechanic, who imitated others, and copied an art, which, through a long succession of ages, after multiplied trials, mistakes, corrections, deliberations, and controversies, had gradually been improving.' Instead of an overarching, timeless, and perfect design consummated in an instant of divine creation, Philo sees but a long history of blunders, flawed experiments, and adventitious successes: 'Many worlds might have been botched and bungled, throughout an eternity, ere this system was struck out.' Or, as Philo later puts it, there is no reason 'why an orderly system may not be spun from the belly as well as from the brain' (*Dialogues*, 43, 56).

Philo's scepticism essentially recapitulates Hume's critique of causation, which in the present context leads him to reject Cleanthes' inferential account by insisting that there really is no warrant for drawing inferences under any circumstances: 'Nothing seems more delicate with regard to its causes than thought.... Have we not the same reason to trace that ideal world [into which you trace the material] into another ideal world, or new intelligent principle. But if we stop, and go no farther, why go so far? Why not stop at the material world.' In the world we 'have ... experience of particular systems of thought and of matter, which have no order' (*Dialogues*, 39). Moreover, even if elaborate chains of causal inference should prove permissible, this would lead natural theology to become increasingly invested in the study of nature and, concurrently, would render speculation about some putative First Cause increasingly irrelevant. As Philo puts it, 'by this method of reasoning you renounce all claim to infinity in any of the attributes of the deity. For as the cause ought only to be proportioned to the effect, ... the effect, so far as it falls under our cognizance, is not infinite' (*Dialogues*, 42).[6] There is no time here to trace the many brilliant turns in Hume's demolition of what during the previous two centuries had gained widespread acceptance as the most effective strategy for reconciling science

[6] On the genesis of natural (or physico-)theology, see Stephen Gaukroger, *The Emergence of a Scientific Culture: Science and the Shaping of Modernity, 1210–1685* (Oxford: Clarendon, 2006), 129–53; on subsequent mutations of natural theology, see Keith Thomson, *Before Darwin* (New Haven: Yale University Press, 2007), 59–173.

and religion and, seemingly, shoring up the imperiled fortunes of Christian apologetics in the age of Enlightenment. Notably, the demolition of natural theology goes unacknowledged by Cleanthes in Hume's sharply ironic take on the idea of 'Enlightenment', a 'dialogue' whose participants, as far as we can tell, learn nothing from one another.

Yet the relevance of Hume's *Dialogues* for present purposes lies somewhere else. For Hume's book (and specifically Philo's arguments within it) vividly demonstrates two peculiar consequences that arise when the question of religion is framed in strictly epistemological terms and, thus, confined to a protocol of empirical verification and warranted assertibility that Bacon, Gassendi, Hobbes, and Newton had established as the new organon of the modern science of nature. First, the reality of God and the phenomenon of faith are being entertained as legitimate objects of inquiry only on the basis of *counterfactual* reasoning and inquiry. Notably, Philo and Cleanthes are in agreement that the question concerning God is to be framed in terms of modern epistemological method: 'Nothing is demonstrable, unless the contrary implies a contradiction.... There is no being, therefore, whose non-existence implies a contradiction. Consequently, there is no being, whose existence is demonstrable.... The words, therefore, *necessary existence*, have no meaning', quite simply because it is deemed 'absolutely impossible for anything to produce itself, or be the cause of its own existence' (*Dialogues*, 64–5). To know on Cleanthes' account, which Philo's scepticism eventually turns against itself, is to have suspended from the outset the phenomenon of belief. Instead, religion is demoted to a naturalistic and, so it seems, inexplicable occurrence, something that simply happens *in* or, rather, *to* other minds. For religious belief to be recognized as a legitimate object of inquiry, modern inquiry stipulates that religious experience be denuded of its distinctive phenomenology. The *qualia* that would draw the attention of post-Enlightenment thinkers such as Coleridge, Newman, F. Brentano, W. James, von Balthasar, or Marion, as indeed the sheer phenomenological 'givenness' (Marion's *être donné*) of reality is, in Hume's *Dialogues*, peremptorily declared an epistemological *terra incognita*. The incoherence of that self-certifying scepticism is apparent as soon as we consider that in so bracketing reality's qualitative insistence within finite consciousness the Humean sceptic is left with nothing to wax sceptical *about*. Second, and as a result of this pre-trial ruling of Enlightenment scepticism against the *reality* of the phenomena which it purports to adjudicate, the conceptual machinery on which natural theology relies in its attempt to deliver conclusive proof not only dissolves the *factum probandum* of God, faith, and religion but ultimately falls prey to its own, implacable drive for further evidence and further demonstration. Hence, even as the early Enlightenment had mobilized natural theology so as to uphold the theological positions and ecclesiastic authority of a magisterial Protestantism already besieged by various puritanical, millenarian, and Pietist fringe groups, that very framework succumbs to the logical fallacy of *post hoc ergo propter hoc* reasoning—a predicament that Philo exposes with great relish and zeal. Hume's *Dialogues* thus offer a fine instance of what Hegel had in mind when arguing that the Enlightenment was destined to find its own critical and conceptual machinery being unravelled by the same scepticism that had previously led to its development.

A second, arguably more complex figure to be engaged (at least implicitly) by those Romantics attempting a comprehensive revision of liberal and secular modernity is Kant. Written late in his career, Kant's *Religion within the boundaries of mere reason* (1793) undertakes a forceful critique of religion, virtue ethics, and the heteronomous model of agency (dependent on grace) on which they rest. It helps to tarry with this book, since it neatly encapsulates the principal assumptions, claims, and objectives associated with a secular model of reason to which writers like Novalis, Schleiermacher, Schelling, Eichendorff, Görres, de Maistre, Lammenais, and Coleridge among others take themselves to be responding. The fundamental issue here is that the Enlightenment ideal of autonomy seemingly excludes a transcendent authority said to underwrite our initiation into the notion of the good, the just, and the true. Likewise, Kantian autonomy also appears to preclude that the pursuit of such 'hyper-goods' (as Charles Taylor calls them) could ever be anchored in forms of religious belief and practice regulated by an ecclesiastic community and a hierarchical *magisterium*. While Kant retains (however minimally and equivocally) some conceptual space for God and belief, he emphatically severs all connections between the subjective impulse towards religious belief and those normative commitments and institutional practices that such belief had formerly entailed. Furthermore, Kant renders the deity on which belief is focused wholly anthropomorphic and, in characteristic Socinian fashion, treats the notion of a transcendent being as a strictly liminal, inferential case. From the outset, he thus conceives of God in loosely Platonic fashion as 'the idea of a highest good in the world, for whose possibility we must *assume* a higher, moral, most holy, and omnipotent being.... What is most important here, however, is that this idea rises out of morality and is not its foundation.'[7] Inasmuch as Kant's God is 'transcendent' in a strictly notional sense—a 'supersensible' being devoid of observable agency or revealed presence in the world—the *logos* or *ratio* at the heart of Platonic, Augustinian, and scholastic thought is no longer understood as a transcendent *source*. Instead, Kantian *ratio* or *Vernunft* merely delineates an as yet incomplete *project*—one whose progressive realization is to be solely entrusted to the demonstrations of critical philosophy and those finite, secular institutions licensed by it.

Yet in circumscribing God as a 'regulative idea' whose ontology, in good Deist fashion, he declares to be beyond the purview of human reason, Kant jeopardizes his strictly finite notion of moral agency being absorbed into the naturalist and voluntarist tradition that we find in the writings of Hobbes, Locke, Mandeville, and Hume.[8] For Kant, such a model is unacceptable since it supposes that our 'natural inclinations' are merely a function of our 'sensuous nature'—thus compromising the core premise of Kant's critical enterprise, namely, the autonomous nature of human reason. Arguing that 'natural inclinations do not have us for their author' and that 'sensuous nature ... contains too little to provide a ground of moral evil in the human being', Kant insists that the moral law 'imposes itself

[7] Immanuel Kant, *Religion and Rational Theology*, tr. and ed. Allen W. Wood and George di Giovanni (Cambridge: Cambridge University Press, 1996), 58; emphasis mine. Cited as *RLR*.

[8] See Thomas Pfau, *Minding the Modern* (Notre Dame, Ind.: Notre Dame University Press, 2013), chs 9–11.

on [man] irresistibly, because of his moral predisposition (*Anlage*)' (*RLR* 82). Yet what would prevent one from construing such a predisposition as prima facie evidence of a transcendent, providentially ordering God who has fashioned us thus? Does Kant imply an innate (moral) sense after all and, if so, would this not contradict his notion of the human being's rational autonomy and capacity for moral self-legislation? Well aware of what is at stake here and mindful of Adam Smith's objection to moral-sense theories in the 5th edition of his *Theory of Moral Sentiments* (1790), Kant's response appears suffused with variously Stoic and Platonist versions of Christianity as we encounter them in Justus Lipsius, the Cambridge Platonists, and Shaftesbury. Thus he affirms that 'incentives', be they good or evil, never simply operate *in us* but, instead, constitute notions to which we *assent* by 'incorporating them into [our] maxims' (*RLR* 83). Against the naturalist or outright reductionist view that, in his time, had been most forcefully developed in Hume's *Treatise* (1739/1740) and *Natural History of Religion* (1757)—and that has since migrated into neurobiological accounts of the human—Kant stresses that whatever inclination we find within ourselves is *eo ipso* an object of our general *awareness*. Herein he echoes Shaftesbury's earlier conviction that 'we cannot doubt of what passes *within our-selves*. Our Passions and Affections are known to us. *They* are certain, whatever the *Objects* may be, on which they are employ'd'.[9] Likewise, at least in the realm of practical reason, Kant regards self-awareness as a non-negotiable criterion of moral agency. Whatever the sensuous substratum of moral evil, 'it must equally be possible to *overcome* this evil, for it is *found* in the human being as acting freely' (*RLR* 83; last emphasis mine).

Yet if human action is always a function of deliberate choice, rather than being prompted by some unfathomable inclination or compulsion, how can it be stabilized and achieve purposiveness and continuity over time? For moral meanings to achieve communal recognition and significance, their practical instantiation must exhibit both formal coherence and teleological orientation, along the lines of the metonymic progression from inclination to habits to virtues that Aquinas had mapped in his *Summa Theologiae* (I-II, 47ff.). Once again Kant demurs, insisting that 'whatever his previous behavior may have been, whatever the natural causes influencing him, whether they are inside or outside, [man's] action is yet free and not determined through any of these' (*RLR* 86–7). Yet this merely negative response appears to denude Kant's moral agent of any narrative and rational continuity: evidently, there is to be no intrinsic power (habit, virtue), nor any extrinsic, institutional framework (churches, schools) that can be entrusted with authoritatively shaping and normatively guiding the formation of the Kantian subject.[10] As Kant himself realizes, to restrict the operation of the

[9] Shaftesbury, *Characteristicks of Men, Manners, Opinions, Times*, repr. of the 6th edn, 3 vols (Indianapolis: Liberty Fund, 2001), ii. 99.

[10] On this contested issue, see G. Felicitas Munzel, *Kant's Conception of Moral Character* (Chicago: University of Chicago Press, 1999); Barbara Herman, 'Making Room for Character', in S. Engstrom and J. Whiting (eds), *Aristotle, Kant, and the Stoics* (Cambridge: Cambridge University Press, 1996) and 'Training to Autonomy: Kant and the Question of Moral Education', in Amélie O. Rorty (ed.), *Philosophers on Education* (New York: Routledge, 1998); Vivasvan Soni, *Mourning Happiness* (Ithaca, NY: Cornell University Press, 2010), 335–410.

moral law solely to the present instant will not do. For even as that moment of moral self-determination or 'choice' proves crucial and indeed is phenomenologically experienced by a 'corrupt' human being as a dramatic 'change of heart (*Sinnesänderung*)' (*RLR* 92), much depends on the steady implementation of our moral maxims. It is here that Kant appears on the verge of reinstating a (virtue) ethic of small steps such as can only be meaningfully taken if there is an underlying, normative hyper-good *towards* which these steps are teleologically ordered. Thus he acknowledges how the moral agent, taken as an empirical being, can make good on his Augustinian resolutions only by means of 'gradual reform' (*allmähliche Reform*), 'long habituation' (*lange Gewohnheit*), and an 'incessant laboring and becoming (*in kontinuierlichem Wirken und Werden*)' (*RLR* 91–2). Inevitably, this concession transmutes the will's initial act of pure, autonomous self-origination into an enduring moral identity that must be sustained over time, rather than being continually disrupted by new instances of (voluntarist) self-revision and moral self-assertion. That was what Hegel meant when characterizing 'freedom as insight into necessity'.[11]

As it turns out, morality is never merely to do with conspicuous 'resolutions' or 'revolutions' of the modern, Lutheran, hyper-Augustinian (Pietist) variety. For it also involves, crucially, a whole other dimension of empirical practice. However autonomous at the moment of inception, every human act begets objective realities—both within the moral agent (habits, virtues) and external to her (commitments, obligations)—which in time will be experienced as heteronomous forces guiding and circumscribing that same individual's judgements and actions. Were it otherwise, every 'revolution of sense' (*Revolution für die Denkungsart*) would merely turn out as yet another ephemeral, non-cognitive spike or 'passion' of the Humean variety, thus consigning the autonomous subject 'to the sweetness or anxiety of enthusiasm (*Schwärmerey*)' (*RLR* 110).

Among the Romantics, it is above all the young Schleiermacher whose 1799 *Addresses on Religion* would seize upon this implication of a purely emotivist account of religion and the moral life. For his part, trying to ward off precisely that scenario, Kant momentarily comes close to acknowledging that our moral self-formation requires some kind of external presentation, such as an image or exemplar of sorts. Drawing attention to the moral perspicacity of children ('capable of discovering even the slightest taint of admixture of spurious incentives'), he thus concedes that their moral persona is best formed by 'adducing an *example* of good people'. There ultimately remains a role for the outward exemplar (e.g. Christ) and image in the formation of moral character, something that his earlier 'Grounding for the Metaphysics of Morals' (1785) had strenuously opposed. The

[11] Hegel's aphorism as reported by Friedrich Engels, who in 1877 recalls it as follows: 'Hegel was the first who correctly articulated the relation of freedom and necessity. For him, freedom is insight into necessity (*Für ihn ist die Freiheit die Einsicht in die Notwendigkeit*). "Necessity is blind only insofar as it has not been properly grasped [*begriffen*]." It is not in some dreamed-of independence from natural causality that freedom is located, but in our cognition (*Erkenntnis*) of these laws and, thus, in the possibility opening up that we may put them to planned, purposive use (*in der damit gegebnen Möglichkeit, sie planmäßig zu bestimmten Zwecken wirken zu lassen*).' In *Anti-Dühring*, in *Marx-Engels Werke* (Berlin: Dietz, 1979), xx. 106; tr. mine.

image of Christ's descent thus is to serve as a 'prototype' for the rational idea of moral self-improvement. Christ and scripture amount to heuristic fictions aimed at compensating for the fact that the commands and intrinsic objectives of reason cannot be directly intuited but require some mediation: 'We cannot think the ideal of a humanity … except in the idea of a human being willing not only to execute all human duties, … but also, though tempted by the greatest temptation, to take upon himself all sufferings, up to the most ignominious death, for the good of the world and even for his enemies.' Still, Christ's 'prototype is nowhere to be sought but in human reason', and to impute to this 'naturally begotten human being' a transcendent, divine nature will only get 'in the way of the practical adoption of the idea of such a being for our imitation'.

By one line of interpretation, modern Socinian accounts such as Kant's can be traced back as far as Duns Scotus's theory of univocal predication. Though far more carefully circumscribed by Scotus than in the writings of his putative modern descendants, the central ontological tenet appears to be one and the same, namely, that a single substratum of Being is shared by God and man. Such a view paradoxically renders Christ simultaneously more abstract *and* more ordinary, more remote *and* seemingly unintelligible or wholly comprehensible. Ever so tentatively, that is, the vertical (Augustinian/Thomist) axis linking—yet also keeping categorically distinct—the transcendent and uncreated God of Christianity from finite, fallible, and sinful man is being replaced by a horizontal vector. Scotus's contention that '"being is univocal to the created and the uncreated" … aims to conceive of being as a concept quite independently of any revelatory knowledge and independently of th[e] divine–human distinction'. Henceforth, the divine is articulated in quantitative terms on a single ontological plane. God transcends humanity only in 'intensity of being', thereby precluding the kind of analogical reconciliation of God and man that Aquinas had worked out with unprecedented depth. Yet now, 'although there was an ontological continuity between God and humanity (the 'domesticating' move), this also installed an infinite metaphysical gap between them (the 'distancing' move). The 'distancing' move was intended to compensate for the domesticating move, but the combined effect of both was to turn God into an unknowable unfathomable abyss.'[12]

Inadvertently providing a blueprint for modern epistemological approaches to religion, Scotus's univocal concept of Being both moves God closer to creatures *and* moves him further away. For if Christ really is but a 'naturally begotten human being' (*RLR* 104–7), how could he possibly be what, even in Kant's own account, he is meant to exemplify for all human beings? Why speak of a prototype while insisting that it may not differ in anything but degree from ectypal beings? What would render his 'example' compelling if, in fact, it was substantially the same as all other human beings?

[12] Gavin Hyman, *A Short History of Atheism* (London: I. B. Tauris, 2010), 70–1. Hyman's account, which builds on earlier work by Catherine Pickstock, has been vigorously contested. See Richard Cross, '"Where Angels fear to tread": Duns Scotus and Radical Orthodoxy', *Antonianum*, 76 (2001), 7–41; and David Aers, 'Introduction' to *Journal of Medieival and Early Modern Studies*, 46/3 (2016), forthcoming.

As Catholic theologians and Catholic-leaning writers and intellectuals of the next generation, acutely critical of the (Kantian) Enlightenment, would point out, his wholly anthropomorphic conception of God is bound to expire in a radical naturalism that will ultimately undermine the Kantian moral law itself. This paradox would soon be recognized by the Romantics as one of the most bewildering legacies of the Kantian Enlightenment and as a prompt for their own critique of that project. Underlying all the tensions and paradoxes of Kant's late work on religion is his overriding concern with disentangling reason from the notion of transcendence. Though conceding that reason may never be realized in its pure and ultimate form by human beings, and thus remains in strictly logical sense 'transcendent' to us—a point already made in his 'Ideas for a Universal History' (1784)—Kant nonetheless insists that its 'source' must be located in the world of human activity. All notions of transcendence—including ideas of God, Perfection, Immortality, and Freedom—only have auxiliary or 'regulative' function. That is, they serve to focus us on the agenda of reason as something to be incrementally perfected. If Kant's hyper-Augustinian depiction of the human being as inherently sinful and 'saddled with a debt which is impossible for him to wipe out' recalls his Pietist upbringing, he is careful to circumvent the entire Pelagian/anti-Pelagian debate concerning grace as something either solicited through good works or gratuitously conferred. Indeed, Kant attempts nothing less than to dissolve the 2,000-year-old theological distinction between a transcendent/divine and a finite/human plateau of reality into a single, continuous, and anthropomorphic domain. However obliquely, Kantian reason jettisons the idea of grace—transcendently given, unaccountably received, and as such the very foundation of Christian theology—by assimilating it to the portfolio of the modern autonomous individual. While only ever realized in part, Kantian *Vernunft* pivots on an exclusively human-engineered salvation.

Completed in June 1799, and presented at the Michaelis book fair in Leipzig in September of that year, Schleiermacher's *On Religion: Speeches to its Cultured Despisers* adopts a highly rhetorical, at times prophetic idiom that frames religion almost entirely as a matter of subjective, personal experience. In ways that echo Coleridge's lyrics (e.g. 'Religious Musings' or 'Fears in Solitude') and that draw on the sharp critique of rationalism pioneered by J. G. Hamann and F. H. Jacobi's campaign against Lessing's and Fichte's allegedly Spinozist-cum-atheist sympathies, Schleiermacher both diagnoses and reinforces a decisive turn in post-revolutionary thinking about religion. As he sees it, the topic of faith and its consequences for self-expression hangs in the balance, 'especially now, the life of cultivated persons is removed from everything that would in the least way resemble religion' (*On Religion*, 3). Construed as a manifestation of intense religious faith, the rhetorical fervour of Schleiermacher *On Religion* offers a telling instance of what Charles Taylor has defined as the culture of 'expressivism'.[13]

[13] Charles Taylor, *Sources of the Self* (Cambridge, Mass.: Harvard University Press, 1989), 185–98 and 368–92.

From the outset, Schleiermacher portrays himself as 'compelled (*gedrungen*) to speak by an inner and irresistible necessity that divinely rules me' (*On Religion*, 4; translation modified), and he even stipulates that the 'communication of religion cannot be other than rhetorical' (*On Religion*, 22). This expressive imperative to 'set down in pictures or words the impression [that the infinite] made on them ... so as to enjoy it themselves afresh, transformed into another form on a finite scale' is presented in the *Dialogues* as a surrogate type of worship. It unfolds independent of all institutional, liturgical, and dogmatic practice and is deemed valid even (perhaps especially) in the absence of any rational, discursive community: 'they would do it even if no one was there' (*On Religion*, 7). Reminiscent of the strident anti-ecclesiastic and anti-dogmatic stance of seventeenth-century Ranters, Diggers, and Fifth-Monarchy Men or, closer to home, Svabian Pietist communities, Schleiermacher's assertion of the continuing relevance and vitality of religion pivots on the abolition of all frameworks, norms, or practices such as mediate and give objective (and potentially normative) form to religious feeling: 'may it yet happen that this office of mediator (*Mittleramt*) should cease!' For the young Schleiermacher, expression verges on a telepathic transfer of religious feeling that dispenses with lexical specificity and interpretive labour alike: 'the communication of holy thoughts and feelings would consist only in the easy game of now unifying the different beams of this light and then again breaking them up ... The softest word would be understood, whereas now the clearest expressions do not escape misinterpretation' (*On Religion*, 8).

Schleiermacher's attempt at separating subjective, spiritual content from objective forms and practices not only echoes a central intention of Protestantism enshrined in Luther's injunctions of *sola fide* and *sola scriptura*; it also extends tendencies observable in Kant's late writings on religion. Echoing Kant, Schleiermacher rejects the formal claims and deductions of traditional metaphysics (though also those of 'your transcendental philosophy'): 'Religion must not venture too far. It must not have the tendency to posit essences and to determine causes (*Wesen zu sezen und Naturen zu bestimmen*).... It must not use the universe in order to derive duties and is not permitted to contain a code of laws' (*On Religion*, 20). Yet with its repeated insistence that 'religion's essence is neither thinking nor acting, but intuition and feeling' (*On Religion*, 22), Schleiermacher appears to run head-on into the enthusiasm trap that Kant, struggling with his own Pietist upbringing and mindful of similar tendencies in Shaftesbury, had so painstakingly sought to avoid. That, certainly, is the impression left by pronouncements (naturally undemonstrable per se) that 'religion is the sensibility and taste for the infinite (*Sinn und Geschmak fürs Unendliche*)' (*On Religion*, 23) repeatedly interspersed throughout the *Speeches*.

Yet the textual evidence here is more complex and equivocal. Clearly, Schleiermacher wishes to avoid a crude emotionalizing of religious experience, mindful that doing so risks opening the doors for a naturalist and inherently sceptical account of religion *and* emotion as wholly non-cognitive and irrational. Thus he repeatedly stresses the supra-individual dimension of religious feeling: 'I do not wish to arouse particular feelings ... [but] wish to lead you into the innermost depths from which religion first addresses the mind.' The emotion aimed at here is said to raise the believer 'above the common standpoint of humanity (*über den gemeinen Standpunkt der Menschen*)' (*On Religion*, 10–11) and, in a later characterization, acquires a mystical overtones also found in Novalis's *Hymns to the Night* and, eventually, diagnosed by Freud as an 'oceanic feeling' masking the modern subject's profound discontent with a prosaic and inchoate world: 'A manifestation, an event develops quickly and magically into an image of the universe.... my soul flees toward it; I embrace it, not as a shadow, but as the holy essence itself. I lie on the bosom of the infinite world. At this moment I am the holy essence itself, for I feel all its powers and its infinite life as my own' (*On Religion*, 32).

To be sure, *On Religion* cannot be taken as altogether representative of Schleiermacher's broader oeuvre and long-term significance. His extensive writings on ethics, hermeneutics, dialectics, and the philosophy of language over the next three decades show a significant shift and deepening of his intellectual focus. Even so, his contention in the 1822 *Dialectics* that the unity of thinking and willing (what he calls its 'transcendent ground') is to be found in 'feeling' bears obvious affinities to his early arguments about religion, and for his Romantic contemporaries it was above all the highly wrought expressive and subjective rhetoric of *On Religion* that proved influential.[14] Thus, it proves difficult to identify a specific content, let alone ascribe lasting significance to an emotion that resists all articulacy and paraphrase, and that never issues in any distinctive and meaningful type of action or sustained practice.[15] This liability, already observable in Kant's decision to stake the idea of rational self-determination or autonomy on a sudden 'revolution of sense' (*Sinnesänderung*), gradually gives rise to a 'hyper-pluralism' (to borrow Brad Gregory's recent phrase) and to the disaggregation of politics and ethics that deprives Schleiermacher's *Speeches* of any functional and coherent model of community, religious or otherwise.[16] Not only must 'each person ... be conscious that his religion is only part of the whole, [and] that ... there are views just as pious and, nevertheless, completely different from his own', but there is to be no attempt at reconciling these differences. In openly stating that 'religion does not strive to bring those who believe and feel under a single belief and a single feeling' (*On Religion*, 27–8), Schleiermacher's early Romantic account merely continues the redistricting of religion as a province of anti-ecclesiastic and anti-dogmatic, purely subjective and non-negotiable inclinations previously given programmatic expression in Locke's *Letter concerning Toleration* (1689). As a result, objective (ecclesiastic) frameworks, norms, and practices all but disappear from consideration. To suggest that

[14] See *Dialektik*, 265–93. For a compact survey of Schleiermacher's intellectual trajectory, see the article by Christine Helmer in David Fergusson (ed.), *The Blackwell Companion to Nineteenth-Century Theology* (Oxford: Blackwell, 2010), 31–57; and, on Schleiermacher's hermeneutics, Thomas Pfau, 'Immediacy and the Text', *Journal of the History of Ideas*, 51/1 (1990), 51–73.

[15] As one critic, quoted verbatim by Schleiermacher in a letter to Henriette Herz (2 July 1800), had put it, 'the book quite simply cannot be summarized (*eines Auszuges sei die Schrift durchaus nicht fähig*)' (quoted in *On Religion*, 19).

[16] On the 'Subjectivization of Belief', see Brad S. Gregory, *The Unintended Reformation* (Cambridge, Mass.: Harvard University Press, 2011), 180–234.

religious feelings should never 'cause actual actions (*eigentliche Handlungen*)' and to reject as an 'utter misconception' (gänzlicher Mißverstand) the proposition 'that religion is supposed to act' as an 'utter misconception (*gänzlicher Mißverstand*)' (*On Religion*, 29–30; translation modified) denudes religion of all concrete, practical dimensions. It is no longer a communal ritual meant to instantiate concrete theological tenets, and its 'dogmas and propositions' appear denuded of all historical depth and authority; they are 'merely abstract expressions of religious intuitions, and others are free reflections upon original achievements of the religious sense (*freie Reflexionen über die ursprüngliche Verrichtungen des religiösen Sinnes*)'.

Ultimately, revelation (*Offenbarung*) itself is qualified as but the experience of what 'is new to you as an individual (*was für Euch noch neu ist*)' (*On Religion*, 48–9). Soon to be subjected to intense scrutiny by Romantic philosophy (Schelling, Hegel) and by a resurgent Catholic (political) theology, Schleiermacher's stress on the 'immediacy' of religious experience (*Totaleindruck*) not only precludes any process-thinking such as might impart continuity and meaning to the believer's subjective feeling; it also rejects the objective authority of scripture. Though recommended to the individual as a temporary expedient, 'a mediator [or] leader who awakens his sense for religion', scripture for Schleiermacher is paradoxically acceptable only as something to be written rather than be read:

> You are right to despise the paltry imitators who derive their religion wholly from someone else or cling to a dead document by which they swear and from which they draw proof. Every holy writing is merely a mausoleum of religion, a monument that a great spirit was there that no longer exists; for if it still lived and were active, why would [the spirit] attach such great importance to the dead letter that can only be a weak reproduction of it? It is not the person who believes in a holy writing who has religion, but only the one who needs none and probably could make one for himself. (*On Religion*, 50)

Schleiermacher's non-cognitive and anti-institutional account of religion exhibits an inexorable drift, not simply towards a hyper-pluralist conception of moral and political community but towards what might be termed a stance of principled incoherence. The sole criterion capable of authenticating individual belief appears to be its incommensurability with everyone else's: 'for me divinity can be nothing other than a particular type of religious intuition. The rest of religious intuitions are independent of it and of each other (*eine einzelne religiöse Anschauungsart, von der wie von jeder anderen alle übrigen unabhängig sind*)' (*On Religion*, 51).

Even as these words were written, however, the formation of an intellectual opposition (both political and theological) to this line of reasoning and its troubling implications was under way. Thus, while as Schleiermacher's introduction of a radical subjectivism into religious culture and theological argument proved defining of a certain strand of Romanticism, an alternate line of Romantic religious and theological reasoning takes shape after 1800. Unfolding as a sustained, often sharply critical reflection on the legacies of the Enlightenment, this strand of thinking not only questions the excessive self-satisfaction of Enlightenment reason (in the French *philosophes* or *philosophistes*, as de Maistre calls them) but also rejects the non-cognitive sources of selfhood to which Hume's radical naturalism appeals no less than Schleiermacher's sentiment-based theology. Among those deeply critical of a radical subjectivism and implicit non-cognitivism in ethics, theology, and philosophy is Hegel. Arguably, Hegel's practical philosophy as set forth in his *Philosophy of Right* (1820/1821) constitutes the most cogent attempt at reintegrating the individual's moral (*sittliche*) existence with an objective, institutional framework, a project that pivots throughout on Hegel's theory of recognition as first sketched in the *Phenomenology*'s 'lordship-bondage' parable.[17] Yet for present purposes, the more pertinent text is the *Lectures on the Philosophy of Religion* (1827) in the introduction to which Hegel questions attempts (by Jacobi and Schleiermacher) to restrict religious faith to a subjective, immediate, and incommunicable 'feeling of dependency' (*Gefühl der Abhängigkeit*): 'All conviction *that* God is, and regarding *what* God is, rests, so it is surmised, upon this immediate revealedness in the human being, upon this faith. This general representation is now an established preconception.'[18]

As he had observed elsewhere, Hegel here notes that the trouble with appeals to 'immediacy' is not that they are false but that they remain woefully incomplete: 'Not only does philosophy not repudiate this proposition [of the immediate knowledge of God], but it forms a basic determination within philosophy itself (*eine Grundbestimmung in ihr selbst*).' The real difference between Romantic notions of subjective immediacy and Hegel's concept of religious consciousness thus hinges on the seeming absence of any narrative dimension or process-thinking from the former: 'it is noteworthy that the principle [of the immediacy of faith] does not stand still at this simple determinacy, this naïve content. It does not express itself merely affirmatively. Instead the naïve knowledge proceeds polemically against cognition and is especially directed against the cognition or conceptual comprehension of God.' Immediacy, in the way that Schleiermacher and Jacobi (in his work on David Hume) had understood the term, is inherently hostile to conceptual or, more generally, any reasoning activity; it 'is taken as precluding the alternative determination of mediation (*die Unmittelbarkeit des Zusammenhangs wird ausschließend gegen die andere Bestimmung der Vermittlung genommen*), and because it is a mediated knowledge philosophy is disparaged on the grounds that it is only a finite knowledge of the finite (*nur ein endliches Wissen von Endlichem*)'.[19]

Hegel's broader argument in the Introduction to his lectures on religion is directed against what Charles Taylor has recently dubbed the 'subtraction' model of secularization, according to which the incremental advances in scientific knowledge of finite things prove inherently prejudicial to the possibility of religious knowledge.[20] A superb

[17] On Hegel, see Pippin's incisive discussion in *Hegel's Practical Philosophy* (Cambridge: Cambridge University Press, 2008), esp. 3–35 and, on the institutional and recognitive dimensions of sociality, 183–272.

[18] Hegel, *Lectures on the Philosophy of Religion*, tr. R. F. Brown et al. (Berkeley, Calif.: University of California Press, 1988).

[19] Hegel, *Lectures on the Philosophy of Religion*, 86–8.

[20] Charles Taylor, *A Secular Age* (Cambridge, Mass.: Harvard University Press, 2007), esp. 25–89.

diagnostician of the spirit of his age, Hegel is certainly aware that this thesis has met with widespread acceptance (see the chapter epigraph), that Socinianism had effectively come to define Protestantism's christology over the past two centuries, and that the truth claims of earlier theology were now being exclusively treated as contingent historical information:

> One could easily arrive at the view that a widespread, nearly universal indifference toward the doctrines of faith formerly regarded as essential has entered into the general religiousness of the public.... For though Christ as reconciler and savior is still constantly made the focus of faith, ... Christ is dragged down to the level of human affairs, not to the level of the commonplace but still to that of the human.... [Meanwhile] The absolute way in which these doctrines were formed ... is forgotten, and so their necessity and truth is forgotten, too, and the question what one holds as one's own conviction meets with astonishment.[21]

Yet a religious culture whose contents have been pared down to the self-certifying immediacy of a feeling or consciousness of 'dependency' (on God) amounts, its own protestations notwithstanding, to a terminally anthropomorphic and finite conception. For precisely this reason, Hegel contends, it also turns out to be stunted on both philosophical and theological grounds—an enterprise asking not so much to be refuted as simply proving pointless: 'As regards its *contents* this point of view has to be seen as the final step in man's abasement (*Erniedrigung*), even as man himself will conceive of this abasement as the highest and his true destiny.'[22]

Though rightly regarded as the leading philosopher of an emergent Protestant, Prussian nation state, Hegel's analysis significantly overlaps with a political, philosophical, and theological critique of an emotivist conception of religious faith concurrently advanced by a variety of Catholic intellectuals. Like Hegel, and in the case of the Tübingen school of Catholic theology often expressly drawing on his writings, the Catholic critique ultimately regards Schleiermacher's early theology as a (perhaps eccentric) continuation of the Enlightenment's aggressively reductionist and anthropomorphizing outlook on religion.[23] Consistent with Hegel's theorizing of the 'moral life' (*das sittliche Leben*) and religious practice, the Catholic critique now to be briefly considered rejects as fundamentally misguided and incoherent the principal axioms on which the modern, subjective, and emotivist model of religion appears to rest:

(1) an apparent anti-intellectualism and a concomitant failure to take into account the intrinsic fallibility and sinfulness of the so-called 'immediate consciousness' (*unmittelbares Bewusstsein*) of God;

[21] Hegel, *Lectures on the Philosophy of Religion*, 82, 84–5.

[22] Hegel, *Vorlesungen*, i. 44 (not included in the English tr. of Hegel's lectures on religion, which follow the 1827 text).

[23] See Bradford E. Hinze's article on 'Romantic Catholic Theology: Tübingen' in Fergusson, *Blackwell Companion*, 187–213.

(2) a paradoxical commitment to the strict immediacy of faith *and* to a disengaged, historicist protocol that treats (and in time dismisses) all religious tenets, practices, and beliefs as so many fossilized, arcane curiosities;

(3) the loss of supra-individual, dialectically articulated norms and commitments absent which there can be no stable moral and political community;

(4) the failure to adhere to an apophatic (analogical) model of theology that avoids the false choice between univocal predication—such as will in time construe God's transcendence as but an anthropomorphic projection—and equivocal predication according to which 'all words used of God are used in a way completely unrelated to the way in which they are used in ordinary language',[24] and, finally

(5) the failure of Enlightenment naturalism and reductionism to honour the distinction between theoretical and practical rationality, a failure that for Hegel no less than a number of Catholic intellectuals had led modernity to conceive of religious faith strictly as an aggregate of *sentiments, propositions*, or *ascriptions* for which, unsurprisingly, modern epistemological inquiry found itself unable to secure any adequate warrant.[25]

It makes sense to distinguish within the Catholic critique of the Enlightenment project that takes shape during the Romantic era two major strands, with each of them tending to emphasize *some* of these tensions and paradoxes and, as a result, producing a fundamentally different account of the status and function of religion within early nineteenth-century culture and politics. First, there is a strand of 'political theology' whose Catholic (not always fully explicit) orientation fuels a sharp critique of modern, post-revolutionary society and politics, with Edmund Burke, Friedrich Gentz, Adam Müller, Joseph de Maistre, and Felicité de Lamennais as its most prominent representatives. It is this group which offers the most compelling linkage between a Catholic critique of modernity and twentieth-century neo-conservative thought as articulated by Carl Schmitt, Leo Strauss, Michael Oakeshott, and Allan Bloom. In his *Reflections on the Revolution in France* (1790), Burke stresses how the continuity, indeed the perpetuity of the social contract depends on the aesthetic charisma of political institutions and personalities. Any historically contingent political arrangement or 'particular state is but a clause in the great primaeval contract of eternal society, linking the lower with the higher natures, connecting the visible and invisible world' (*RRF* 195). Burke here not only opposes the English 'Jacobins' (Paine, Priestley, Thelwall, et al.) but, obliquely, also Locke's contractual model of a polity in which the legal obligations that connect finite human agents in a 'horizontal comradeship' (Benedict Anderson's phrase) have been

[24] Hyman, *Atheism*, 50.

[25] For critiques of modernity that emphasize its failure to maintain the distinction between practical and theoretical reason, see L. Dupré, *Passage to Modernity* (New Haven: Yale University Press, 1993), 42–64; A. MacIntyre, *Whose Justice? Which Rationality?* (Notre Dame, Ind.: Notre Dame University Press, 1988), 260–280 and 300–25; Pfau, *Minding the Modern*, 283–326.

altogether quarantined from any transcendent norms and obligations. Yet for Burke, the efficacy of modern law depends on a transcendent and richly imag(in)ed divine source. The social covenant is not be 'taken up for a little temporary interest' or adequately grounded as long as it depends on something as fickle as individual assent or 'will'. Rather, Burke insists, any meaningful social compact constitutes *eo ipso* a metaphysical covenant, such that 'the moral and physical disposition of things to which man must be obedient by consent or force' ultimately depends on God, rather than the sovereign, as 'the institutor, and author and protector of civil society' (*RRF* 194–6). For Burke, political community is not to be reduced to some adventitious and expedient 'enterprise association' (to borrow Michael Oakeshott's term). Instead, any meaningful community has metaphysical underpinnings and is invested with prima facie theological significance as a *manifestatio* and image of God. What is left unclear in Burke's reflections—an ambiguity that ultimately results in the bifurcation of Catholic thought during the Romantic era—is whether this appeal to a metaphysical (non-negotiable) model of order is itself but a pragmatic move aimed at staving off the spectre of revolutionary anarchy, or whether Burke is committed to a political-cum-aesthetic theology of the kind that was to flourish in the writings of Novalis, Eichendorff, Chateaubriand, and others.

At first glance, the God of Burke's political theology appears to be a distinctly modern super-agent, the kind of omnipotent deity that had slowly migrated from the voluntarist theology of Ockham's *Quodlibetal Questions* to Hobbes's sovereign will. On this model, reason is only ever imposed by, yet never the source of the sovereign's omnipotence, let alone an (ontological) constraint on how his power is to be responsibly exercised.[26] Inasmuch as God's will constitutes 'the law of laws and the sovereign of sovereigns', rationality and order prove wholly convertible throughout Burke's *Reflections*: 'He who gave our nature to be perfected by our virtue, willed also the necessary means of its perfection—He willed therefore the state—He willed its connexion with the source and original archetype of all perfection' (*RRF* 196). Yet at the same time, beginning with Paine and Wollstonecraft, readers of Burke's *Reflections* have consistently noted how the efficacy and indeed the legitimacy of political power and social order hinge on their aesthetic manifestation. It is Burke's preoccupation with the beauty and splendour of things both made and found that hints at the Catholic undertow of his political theology. An order solely supported by legal, constitutional, and abstract contractual arrangements simply will not do, for it is but an invitation to rampant partisanship fuelled by a 'selfish temper and confined views' (*RRF* 119), yielding but 'a monstrous medley of all conditions, tongues, and nations' and a 'farce of deliberation' (*RRF* 160–1) that ends up paralysing the nation. Hence Burke's vilifies the Jacobins as 'only men of theory ... confined to professional and faculty habits' (*RRF* 128, 133), incapable of grasping that political life is intrinsically practical rather than an implementation of theoretical or speculative tenets. It is this view, of whose Aristotelian and Thomist sources Burke is likely to have been unaware,

[26] On the political and epistemological entailments of Ockham's voluntarism, see Aers, *Salvation and Sin* (Notre Dame, Ind.: Notre Dame University Press, 2008), 25–54; Dupré, *Passage to Modernity*, 174–89; Hyman, *Atheism*, 67–80; and Pfau, *Minding the Modern*, 160–82.

which holds special significance for our present argument. If we take all political meaning and reality to originate in the domain of human praxis, as Burke certainly does, we must also presuppose an underlying teleological framework. Action can never simply be a function of efficient causation, such that 'A' is done merely *in order to* effect 'B'. Indeed, the intention that identifies and aims at '*B*' must itself arise from, and be implicitly sanctioned by, some antecedent, quasi-normative good 'G.' Hence, a particular action aimed bringing about *B* must have been chosen and undertaken *for the sake of* 'G'. Were it otherwise, the act in question would not have been (rationally) *chosen* but, instead, would prove but a transient effect of an inexplicable (quasi-mechanical) compulsion. The objective interest at which a specific action is aimed thus can never be conflated with the underlying good 'G' that renders the pursuit of that objective meaningful and worthwhile.

Yet because human action can only aim at this underlying good through a series of intermediate steps such as comprise the narrative totality of a life, that hyper-good remains *eo ipso* transcendent to the finite agent. Contrary to the interests that fuel epistemological or financial speculation, this Good can never be articulated as an abstract or quantitative proposition. At the same time, a Good that is said to furnish both the supra-individual and trans-generation source *and telos* of human action must yet be rendered intuitable; we must have an image or vision of it.[27] Like Gregory the Great, whose defence of images had stressed that visible beauty should serve 'the unlearned people [who], though *ignorant* of letters, ... might by turning their eyes to the story itself learn what had been done', Burke insists that all political practice and the social order it aims to bring about requires some type of aesthetic mediation.[28] Within the finite realm of the visible, political expediency and social stability can only be secured and legitimated by a theology of divine *manifestatio*.

That this position should bear such seeming resemblance to the 'atrocious and afflicting spectacles' then being staged in revolutionary France in part accounts for Burke's extreme vilification of the Revolution; and indeed, the difference is profound. For whereas French Jacobin spectacle seeks to convey the abstract propositional correctness where 'nothing is left which engages the affections' (*RRF* 172), Burke's aesthetic politics means compensate, indeed atone for the very impossibility of, any truly just and definitive political order in this world. Performed on 'the high altar of universal praise ... all publick solemn acts ... in buildings, in musick, in decoration, in speech, in the dignity of persons' thus serve a dual function of theological and political theodicy. To the finite and refractory subjects of the political realm, institutions ought to present themselves not as embodied theories but as charismatic images. Aside from grounding political authority and ensuring social

[27] On the concept of practical reason and the demise of action in modern thought, see MacIntyre, *Whose Justice?*, 124–45; Hannah Arendt, *The Human Condition* (Chicago: University of Chicago Press, 1998), 175–247; Maurice Blondel, *Action* (1893), tr. Oliva Blanchette (Notre Dame, Ind.: Notre Dame University Press, 2003), esp. 109–44; and Pfau, *Minding the Modern*, 315–18 and 392–402. On the notion of the (hyper-)good as a quasi-Platonic idea, see Iris Murdoch, *The Sovereignty of Good* (London: Routledge, 1971).

[28] Letter of Gregory the Great to Serenus of Marseille (599 CE), in G. E. Thiessen (ed.), *Theological Aesthetics* (Grand Rapids, Mich.: Eerdmans, 2005), 47–8; Gregory continues: 'in [pictures] the illiterate read. Hence, and chiefly to the nations, a picture is instead of reading.'

control, such 'publick ornaments' are also intended to mitigate present discontents and, however discreetly, help cultivate the theological virtue of hope. For Burke, the images and institutions of political order are tokens of 'publick consolation. [They] nourish the public hope. The poorest man finds his own importance and dignity in [them]' (*RRF* 197).

In a melancholic idiom reminiscent of Counter-Reformation writers like Calderón, Gracián, and Cardinal Bellarmine, the *Reflections* unfold a political theology that is both implicitly Catholic and explicitly modern. The latter trait emerges in Burke's deeply pessimistic and proto-existentialist musings on the irremediably flawed nature of all political and social arrangements, in his notorious reference to the 'swinish multitude' and an emblematic depiction of the English body politic as a 'mode of existence decreed to a permanent body composed of transitory parts'—a formal tribute, it would seem, to the frontispiece of Hobbes's *Leviathan*. It is this Hobbesian strain that would soon be taken up by political theorists like Friedrich Gentz (who had translated the *Reflections* into German in 1793), Adam Müller, and Félicité de Lamennais a generation later, and that still resonates in Carl Schmitt's *Roman Catholicism and Political Form* (1923). In the generation succeeding Burke, Joseph de Maistre offers the most extreme version of this voluntarist, naturalist, and deeply pessimistic strand of Catholic political theology. A searing indictment of the revolution, *Considerations on France* (1796) no longer views religious life and ecclesiastic institutions as oriented towards an Augustinian *visio beatifica* or an *unio mystica*, a spiritual tradition integral to Catholicism from Gregory the Great and pseudo-Dionysius to St Gertrude, St Teresa, and St John of the Cross, among many others. Instead, religion's sole purpose now is to contain human rapacity, anarchy, and slaughter. De Maistre's thought thus rests on a dystopic ontology, ample confirmation for which is found in 'the long series of massacres that has soiled every page of history. One sees war raging without interruption' (*Considerations on France*, 24).

The individual counts for nothing except where it is cradled, or confined (like Burke's madman[29]), by a timeless and impersonal order. Unless it is to be but a 'passing phenomenon', de Maistre declares, 'every imaginable institution is founded on a religious concept'. Conversely, 'human power, whenever it isolates itself, can only give its works a false and passing existence'. As to the modern individual's vaunted autonomy and widely supposed ability to create rational order, de Maistre merely scoffs: 'I will never believe in the fecundity of nothingness' (*Considerations on France*, 41–2). Yet to contend that 'the social edifice rests entirely on the cross' (*Considerations on France*, 43n.) and that 'if the religious spirit is not reinforced in this part of the world, the social bond will dissolve' (21) inadvertently exposes the conceptual and spiritual poverty of this strand of Romantic political theology. The result is a kind of reverse Erastianism whereby the institution of the church sanctions an (inherently secular) political order and serves to enforce social control while appearing wholly denuded of all theological and spiritual content. Indeed, de Maistre concedes as much when casually remarking that 'the

[29] 'Am I seriously to felicitate a madman, who has escaped from the protecting restraint and wholesome darkness of his cell on his restoration to the enjoyment of light and iberty?' Edmund Burke, *Reflections on the Revolution in France*, ed. Conor Cruise O'Brien (Harmondsworth: Penguin, 1968), 90.

Catholic Faith has no need ... to return upon itself, to interrogate itself with regard to its belief, and to ask itself why it believes'.[30] Insofar as this reactionary Catholicism has entered into an unholy alliance with the naturalist and existentialist axioms (and political objectives) of Hobbesian thought, its dystopic vision of human existence has effectively abandoned the aesthetic dimension that had still been a prominent and integral feature of Burke's political theology.

Reclaiming an integral spiritual-cum-aesthetic vision, albeit in ways that have shortcomings of their own, is central to another strand within the multi-pronged (Catholic) critique of the Enlightenment. This strand, which we might term the theo-poetics of nostalgia, is principally represented by a number of German Romantics, including Novalis, Eichendorff, Görres, Schelling, Baader, and the later F. Schlegel. Inspired by Edward Young's *Night Thoughts* and Schiller's 'The Gods of Greece', Novalis's *Hymns to Night* (1800) thus conceive of the Enlightenment as an interregnum between the pagan gods of ancient Greece and the return of Christ, with historical mythology of the kind ventured by Winckelmann and Herder yielding to the new idiom of eschatological prophecy: 'Zu Ende neigte die alte Welt sich.... Die Götter verschwanden mit ihrem Gefolge—Einsam und leblos stand die Natur. Mit eiserner Kette band sie die dürre Zahl und das strenge Maaß.'[31] Both in its phantasmagorical imagery and its overt longing for the future reinstatement of a fantasized medieval, organic past, Novalis and his poetic and intellectual heirs (Schlegel, Brentano, and Görres in particular) find in Roman Catholicism above all a rich cultural legacy for giving voice to a pervasive discontent with the two key events bookending their time: the French Revolution and the Napoleonic secularization of Europe. The aesthetic dimensions of Catholicism are expressively cultivated as a virtual reality into which to retreat and from where to articulate dissent from the present: 'Noch reiften sie nicht diese göttlichen Gedanken—Noch sind der Spuren unserer Offenbarung wenig—Einst zeigt deine Uhr das Ende der Zeit, wenn du wirst wie unser einer, und voll Sehnsucht und Inbrunst auslöschest und stirbst.'[32] The *Hymns* mainly continue Novalis's paean to a pre-schismatic world in *Christianity, or Europe* (1799), which among other things had blamed Luther's principle of *sola scriptura* for the infiltration of religion by philology ('nothing is more destructive to the religious sense ... than the naked letter', ii. 737). Here political and social renewal are expressly linked to a nostalgic retrieval of

[30] De Maistre, *Du Pape* (1819), quoted in Richard Schaefer, 'Program for a New Catholic *Wissenschaft*: Devotional Activism and Catholic Modernity in the Nineteenth Century', *Modern Intellectual History*, 4/3 (2007), 438; see also Isaiah Berlin's introduction to *Considerations on France*, esp. pp. xvii–xxxvi.

[31] Novalis, i. 165. 'The old world meets its demise.... Its gods and their descendants have vanished. Nature remains, solitary and inanimate, bound in iron chains by a pale calculus and rigid measure' (tr. mine).

[32] Novalis, i. 159. 'Not yet have the divine reflections yielded fruit. For now, we only detect a few signs of revelation. Once before you unveiled for us the coming end of time, when you will be like us, will be extinguished and die full of fervor and longing' (tr. mine).

magisterial Catholicism: 'Shouldn't Protestantism be ended (*Soll der Protestantismus nicht endlich aufhören*) and cede its place to a new, more permanent church.... Christianity must once again become a living and effective force; and a visible Church that transcends national boundaries must take shape' (ii. 750).

In many ways, such a repurposing of Catholicism as a cultural and intellectual force was only made possible by the post-revolutionary, Napoleonic 'transformation of the Church from an organization based on territorial sovereignty to one based on popular support'. Yet this opportunity was often marred by intellectual carelessness as representatives of a Catholic Romanticism tended to 'idealize a Catholic past that was out of step with the Catholicism of the present'.[33] As early as 1828, Johann Georg Duttlinger sharply criticizes the selective nostalgia and cavalier approach to theology by 'those new-moded, romantic-poetic Catholics and friends of Catholicism ... who simply place certain external poetic and artistic forms in the place of religion and the Church'.[34] Coleridge's insistence that '*Christianity is not a theory* or speculation, but a life; not a philosophy of life, but a living presence' prepares for a shift away from Romanticism's speculative outlook on religion as but an idea and towards the revivalisms (Catholic, Protestant, and Evangelical) of the next generation. By the early 1830s, members of the Oxford (or Tractarian) Movement and similar formations on the continent publicly, and often controversially, insist that religion pivots above all on the individual's acceptance of and commitment to a coherent body of sacramental meanings and devotional practices. Historians have long studied the marked rise in the use of devotions among the Catholic laity, the rise of exclusively Catholic societies (confraternities, sodalities, guilds, or Third Orders), one that often entailed a 'withdrawal of Catholic communities from non-Catholic society'.[35] Newman's eventual claim that religious belief and culture are fundamentally grounded in acts of (simple and complex) *assent* rather than in 'the narrow range of conclusions to which logic, formal or virtual, is tethered' (179) and that 'an image derived from experience or information is stronger than an abstraction, conception, or conclusion' (37)[36] reaffirms the centrality of the image for nineteenth-century religious thought, which concurrently writers such as Eichendorff, Droste-Hülshoff, Stifter, Ruskin, and Hopkins had also maintained. Far more than its reactionary political strand, it is Romanticism's aesthetic-cum-theological rehabilitation of the image which continues to resonate powerfully in works of twentieth-century and contemporary philosophical theology by Pavel Florensky (*Iconostasis*, 1922), Hans-Urs von Balthasar's (*Herrlichkeit*, 1961–9), Marie-José Mondzain (*Image, Icon, Economy*, 2004), Jean-Luc Marion (*In Excess*, 2004), and David Bentley Hart (*Beauty of the Infinite*, 2003) among others.

[33] Schaefer, 'Program', 437.

[34] Quoted in Schaefer, 'Program', 442; reference is to Duttlinger's 1828 *Memorandum* (*Denkschrift*).

[35] Mary Heimann, 'Catholic Revivalism in Worship and Devotion', in Sheridan Gilley and Brian Stanley (eds), *The Cambridge History of Christianity*, viii (Cambridge: Cambridge University Press, 2006), 74.

[36] John Henry Newman, *Essay Written in Aid of a Grammar of Assent* (Harlow: Longmans, 1917), 179 and 37.

Further Reading

Burke, Edmund, *Reflections on the Revolution in France*, ed. Conor Cruise O'Brien (Harmondsworth: Penguin, 1968).

Hegel, G. W. F., *Phenomenology of Spirit*, tr. A. V. Miller (Oxford: Oxford University Press, 1977).

Hegel, G. W. F., *Hegel's Lectures on the Philosophy of Religion*, tr. R. F. Brown et al., 2 vols (Berkeley, Calif.: University of California Press, 1988).

Hume, David, *Dialogues Concerning Natural Religion*, ed. Dorothy Coleman (Cambridge: Cambridge University Press, 2007) [cited as *D*].

Heimann, Mary, 'Catholic Revivalism in Worship and Devotion', in Sheridan Gilley and Brian Stanley (eds), *The Cambridge History of Christianity*, viii (Cambridge: Cambridge University Press, 2006), 70–83.

Hyman, Gavin, *A Short History of Atheism* (London: I. B. Tauris, 2010).

Kant, Immanuel, *Religion and Rational Theology*, tr. and ed. Allen W. Wood and George di Giovanni (Cambridge: Cambridge University Press, 1996) [cited as *RLR*].

Maistre, Joseph de, *Considerations on France*, tr. and ed. Richard A. Lebrun (Cambridge: Cambridge University Press, 1994) [cited as *CF*].

Newman, John Henry, *Essay Written in Aid of a Grammar of Assent* (Harlow: Longmans, 1917).

Novalis [= Friedrich von Hardenberg], *Werke*, ed. Hans-Joachim Mähl, 3 vols (Munich: Carl Hanser, 1978).

Pippin, Robert, *Hegel's Practical Philosophy: Rational Agency as Ethical Life* (Cambridge: Cambridge University Press, 2008).

Schaefer, Richard, 'Program for a New Catholic *Wissenschaft*: Devotional Activism and Catholic Modernity in the Nineteenth Century', *Modern Intellectual History*, 4/3 (2007), 433–62.

Schleiermacher, Friedrich Daniel Ernst, *Dialektik*, ed. Rudolf Odebrecht (Darmstadt: Wissenschaftliche Buchgesellschaft, 1976).

Schleiermacher, Friedrich Daniel Ernst, *On Religion: Speeches to its Cultured Despisers*, tr. and ed. Richard Crouter (Cambridge: Cambridge University Press, 1996).

Taylor, Charles, *A Secular Age* (Cambridge, Mass.: Harvard University Press, 2007).

Thiessen, Gesa Elsbeth (ed.), *Theological Aesthetics: A Reader* (Grand Rapids, Mich.: Eerdmans, 2005).

CHAPTER 38

THEATRE, DRAMA, AND VISION IN THE ROMANTIC AGE

Stages of the New

DIEGO SAGLIA

'Le théâtre est un point d'optique' wrote Victor Hugo in his polemical Preface to *Cromwell* (1827), usually considered as the rallying cry of full-blown French Romanticism. Expanding this definition of theatre as a 'point of view', 'an optical point', or an 'optical vantage point', he remarks further that '[a]ll that exists in the world, in history, in life, in man, everything must and can be reflected in it, although through the magic wand of art'.[1] Through such resolutely visual metaphorics, Hugo announces that theatrical representation encodes, condenses, and filters the cosmos. Simultaneously, he depicts theatre as an optical vantage point, one that grants a specific perspective, and specific purchase, on reality. As a pivotal locus of visuality—i.e. a culture-bound construction of vision—theatre offers access to the deep-seated structures and patterns of the real.

Centred on a staggeringly vast aggregate of world, history, life, and man, Hugo's pronouncement sounds impossibly hyperbolic and its claims bafflingly excessive. In actual fact, Romantic-period statements about theatre (and drama) were just so. Seen as endowed with extraordinary cultural relevance, the stage called forth grandiose declarations. Romantic-era cultures all around Europe invariably proclaimed the crucial relevance of theatre and its metaphorical and transitive aspects, for which, as we shall see, this period coined the term 'theatricality'.

The French Revolution and the myriad forms of spectacle it generated are perhaps the best examples of the pervasiveness of theatre and the theatrical. We need only think of

[1] Victor Hugo, *Cromwell*, introd. Annie Ubersfeld (Paris: Flammarion, 1968), 90 (all trs. are mine, unless otherwise indicated).

the transformation of the Bastille and the Terror into dramatic subjects on the Paris and London stages; revolutionary pageantry and the *fêtes révolutionnaires*; Napoleon's myth, and especially his self-theatricalization through public appearances, portraits, and his carefully stage-managed imperial coronation in 1804; or the Roman-style triumphs parading requisitioned foreign artworks around the centre of Paris. More specifically, in the revolutionary era the French capital saw a drastic reorganization of its playhouses and their activities. Theatre was a crucial tool to promote the education of citizens and shape democratic subjectivities, and in these decades politics became theatre and theatre became a mass ideological institution to instruct and discipline the people. In this respect, the *drame*, the new genre which dominated the late eighteenth-century stage, proved a particularly apt instrument to represent and broadcast the continuity of private and public spheres central to the ideological-political mandates of revolutionary doctrine.

Other countries, too, saw the emergence of comparable theatrical and dramatic manifestations over these turbulent decades. In parts of Italy under the influence of France an often publicly sponsored patriotic (or 'Jacobin') theatre came into being as a means of spreading revolutionary principles. Francesco Mario Pagano became the unofficial dramatist of the Neapolitan Republic of 1799, while, in Milan, Francesco Saverio Salfi translated plays by the *citoyen* Marie-Joseph Chénier and composed texts celebrating the new democratic ideals. In 1800, the renowned economist and political theorist Melchiorre Gioia wrote *Julia, or the Interregnum of the Cisalpine Republic* (*La Giulia, ossia l'interregno della Cisalpina*) for Milan's Teatro Patriottico to provide both topical commentary and ideological instruction for the masses. In the Iberian Peninsula, after the Napoleonic invasion of 1807, General Junot turned Lisbon's theatres into foci of cultural and political propaganda, a function they kept, with all the necessary reorientations, after the British liberated the city in 1808. Spanish cities were also sites of intense theatrical activity during the Peninsular War, with an extraordinarily lively production of pro- and anti-French plays and entertainments. One of Joseph Bonaparte's earliest measures after taking possession of the Spanish throne in 1809 was to regulate the Madrid theatres through legislation echoing Napoleon's imperial edicts of 1806–7 for the Paris stage. Finally, the link between theatre and (counter-)revolutionary ideology was in full view in the momentous assassination of August von Kotzebue, the controversial German dramatist who later in life had become a Russian governmental agent. He was murdered in 1819 by a theology student who aspired to rid humanity of an enemy to liberal ideas. News of his death quickly spread around Europe and conservative commentators did not hesitate to interpret it as just deserts for his earlier immoral and politically subversive dramas. Kotzebue's violent demise incited many reactionary rulers (most notably Austria's Prince Metternich) to pass harsher laws for the control of the press, the banning of public meetings, and the restriction of forms of public representation.

These examples make plain how theatre and spectacle were pivotal and pervasive features in this transitional period. It is not by chance that, as Tracy Davis notes, '[b]y the beginning of the nineteenth century, the idea of the stage's commensurability with theatricality in the social realm was well established, along with the similes likening individuals' behavior to acting, dramatic genres to political spectacle, and spectating to participation in the public sphere'.[2] Aptly, the earliest occurrences of the term 'theatricality' in English featured in Thomas Carlyle's 1837 *History of the French Revolution*.

Around 1800, Europe saw a veritable boom in theatre building and rebuilding. Auditoria got larger, façades became increasingly monumental, and new technologies such as cast and wrought-iron framing were introduced. The new interiors were modelled on those of opera houses, with their Italian-style horseshoe auditoria, proscenium arch stage, pit, and tiers of small boxes. Precious and precious-looking materials were lavished on these interiors, while access areas such as foyers and areas reserved for the wealthier sections of society also became increasingly ornamented. In a socio-economic perspective, these transformations were related to the steady rise of the middle classes as a major constituency that required entertaining in a style reminiscent of aristocratic spaces such as opera houses and court theatres.

Statements about the cultural centrality of drama and theatre were legion in the decades between the eighteenth and nineteenth centuries. In *Corinne, or Italy* (*Corinne, ou l'Italie*, 1807) Mme de Staël wrote that 'Dramatic genius is formed from the public state of mind, history, government, customs, in short from everything which enters into each day's thinking and shapes the moral being'.[3] A major member of her literary salon at Coppet, August Wilhelm Schlegel wrote in the second chapter of his *Lectures on Dramatic Art and Literature* (*Vorlesungen über dramatische Kunst und Literatur*, 1809–11) that a basic prerequisite for the emergence of a national dramatic tradition was the ability of a nation to 'separate and extract the mimetic elements from the separate parts of social life, and to present them to itself again collectively in one mass'.[4] Theatre functions by selecting meaningful elements from a socio-cultural ensemble in order to rearrange them within the texture of the dramatic work and its subsequent staging. In *A Defence of Poetry* (written in 1821), Percy Shelley articulated the paramount effects of this operation: 'The connection of scenic exhibitions with the improvement or corruption of the manners of men, has been universally recognized.'[5] In the same vein, in 1836, the Spanish playwright and critic Mariano José de Larra dubbed literature, and theatre most particularly, as the 'true thermometer of the state of civilization of a people', reworking a commonplace that Gaspar Melchor de Jovellanos had already invoked in his *Report on Shows and Public Entertainments* (*Memoria sobre espectáculos y diversiones públicas*, 1790).[6]

[2] Tracy C. Davis, 'Theatricality and Civil Society', in Tracy C. Davis and Thomas Postlewait (eds), *Theatricality* (Cambridge: Cambridge University Press, 2003), 128.

[3] Mme de Staël, *Corinne, or Italy*, tr. Sylvia Raphael, introd. John Isbell (Oxford and New York: Oxford University Press, 1998), 121.

[4] Augustus William Schlegel, *A Course of Lectures on Dramatic Art and Literature*, tr. John Black, rev. A. J. W. Morrison (London: Henry G. Bohn, 1846), 32.

[5] Percy Bysshe Shelley, *Poems and Prose*, ed. Timothy Webb (London: J. M. Dent, 1995), 259.

[6] 'Literatura', in *La crítica teatral completa de Mariano José de Larra*, ed. Rafael Fuentes Mollá (Madrid: Fundamentos, 2010), 76.

As a defining expression of a national culture, and one to be controlled and policed through strict censorship regulations, theatre was a 'vantage point' to interpret a tumultuous contemporaneity. Reworking Hugo's idea, the Portuguese João Baptista de Almeida Garrett made this clear when, in his May 1843 lecture 'To the Royal Conservatory' ('Ao conservatório real'), he stated that 'the drama is the most genuine literary expression of the state of society', pointedly adding that 'we still ignore what present-day society is: we still ignore what the drama is'; in other words, 'an indefinite society' could be expressed by an equally mutable and open-ended form.[7] One thing, however, was clear to Garrett: 'the writers who illuminate and characterize our period' were playwrights and all French: 'the Victor Hugos, the Dumas, the Scribes'.[8] Hugo himself had no doubts about the primacy of drama and theatre: 'Our age [is] dramatic first and foremost', he wrote in the Preface to *Cromwell*.[9]

Given such radical assertions, it is appropriate that many Romantic manifestos and diatribes were primarily theatrical and dramatic. The stage was one of the main battlegrounds of the new aesthetic doctrines through such major interventions and episodes as Alessandro Manzoni's defence of the tenets of Romanticism and Romantic drama in his polemical 'Letter to M. C[hauvet]' (1820); Stendhal's *Racine and Shakespeare* (1823, 1825), and Hugo's Preface to *Cromwell* (as well as the 1830 'Battle of *Hernani*'); the 1814 *querelle* on Calderón de la Barca between Johann Nikolas Böhl von Faber and José Joaquín de Mora, or Agustín Durán's influential 'Speech on the Influence of Modern Criticism on the Decadence of the Ancient Spanish Theatre' ('Discurso sobre el influjo que ha tenido la crítica moderna en la decadencia del teatro antiguo español', 1828). Calling upon the ancestral glories of a national tradition, yet also frequently setting up Shakespeare as a transcultural model, these texts envisaged new departures for drama and theatre through drastic changes to formal and technical co-ordinates. Such transformations amounted to technological advances, new acting techniques, and a new cultural mythology of the actor and actress, new dramatic forms, themes, and styles. Invested with crucial significance, theatre became a laboratory of aesthetic and technical developments that paralleled and reflected concurrent mutations in society, politics, the economy, the sciences, and technology. These pan-European shifts brought about momentous and long-range changes in the ways of constructing and experiencing theatrical spectacle. In turn, they were symptomatic of some fundamental shifts in eighteenth- and nineteenth-century visual culture through such phenomena as panoramas, historical paintings, and other manifestations of fantastic and realistic illusionism.[10] If Hugo defined drama and theatre as an 'optical vantage-point', Shelley termed them 'a prismatic and many-sided mirror'.[11] Whether viewed as a form of entertainment,

[7] Almeida Garrett, *Frei Luís de Sousa*, introd. J. Tomaz Ferreira (Lisbon: Europa-América, 2003), 123.

[8] Garrett, *Frei Luís de Sousa*, 124.

[9] Hugo, *Cromwell*, 77.

[10] See Gillen D'Arcy Wood, *The Shock of the Real: Romanticism and Visual Culture, 1760–1860* (New York and Basingstoke: Palgrave, 2001); and Sophie Thomas, *Romanticism and Visuality: Fragments, History, Spectacle* (New York and London: Routledge, 2008).

[11] 'A Defence of Poetry', in Shelley, *Poems and Prose*, ed. Webb, 260.

a metaphor, or an interpretative tool, the theatre of Romanticism was a visual point of examination over the complexities of contemporary culture and history, an instrument enabling playwrights, commentators, and audiences to capture a nebulous and indefinite object in the making.

Ways of Seeing

In the February 1828 issue of *Monthly Articles in the History of Dramatic Art and Literature* (*Monatliche Beiträge zur Geschichte dramatischer Kunst und Literatur*), a critic identified as 'H.' observed:

> The splendour of the larger and richer theatres has seduced even the smaller and poorer ones into at least attempting to suggest the same, and [artistic] demands have declined to the point that nothing is wanted but the satisfaction of the coarsest sensuality ... The greater part of the public, including, alas!, educated spectators, grasps at trivia. People want to *see*, actually to see with their own eyes and if possible to be amazed ... What close attention and discussion, altogether distracting from playtext and actors, of the scenery both dead as well as alive. For what are many of the performances other than exhibitions of mobile, colourfully draped pieces of scenery?[12]

These apprehensive words address the question of the public relevance of theatre by implicitly stressing its didactic purpose, one of its most commonly celebrated benefits and a staple of Enlightenment theatrical discourse. They also throw light on the problematic nature of theatre as a mass experience that calls into being an increasingly unmanageable, unthinking public. Indeed, this passage raises the spectre of a theatre in which a predominantly visual surface threatens to efface the word and its semantic depths. It anxiously pinpoints a semiotic inversion that defies inherited ideas about the value of theatre as a *mise en scène* of the word and thus a linchpin of logocentrism.

The Berlin periodical registers the culmination of a series of international developments. The obsession with enhanced visual experience that swept the continent in the Romantic decades had its roots in late eighteenth-century technological developments that sought to provide increasingly exciting forms of optical entertainment. Simultaneously, dissension and critique proliferated everywhere. In his 'Lectures on Shakespeare' of 1812–13, Samuel Taylor Coleridge awarded primacy to the genuine nature of dramatic illusion over the merely optical effects of stage illusion.[13] In 1818, E. T. A. Hoffmann warned that the German stage 'should not resemble a peepshow', and its tricks should only aim at creating 'th[e] higher illusion' of performance.[14] In 1831, Edward Bulwer-Lytton sarcastically defined the

[12] 'The Nineteenth-Century Trend towards Spectacle, 1829', in George W. Brandt (ed.), *German and Dutch Theatre 1600–1848* (Cambridge: Cambridge University Press, 1993), 296–7.

[13] See Frederick Burwick, *Mimesis and its Romantic Reflections* (University Park, Pa.: Pennsylvania State University Press, 2001), 158.

[14] 'Stage Illusionism Criticised, 1818', in Brandt, *German and Dutch Theatre*, 297.

British as the 'Staring Nation' because of their immoderate 'love for shows'.[15] Nevertheless, the appetite for visually charged spectacle was unstoppable. The inexorable progress of technology (as in the shift from oil to gas lighting) and research into optical effects went on undeterred and gradually modified theatrical experience all over Europe.

Specifically, this spectacular craze was a long-term effect of the increasing importance attached to the visual dimension from the mid-eighteenth-century onwards. Focusing on British culture, Peter de Bolla has identified a powerful intersection between a visual 'regime of the picture', dominated by the rules of connoisseurship, and a 'regime of the eye' centred on 'visibility, spectacle, display' and made available through 'the vast array of diversions presented to the eighteenth-century spectator'.[16] The 'regime of the eye', accordingly, stimulated a wide range of techniques and practices aimed at satisfying a seemingly insatiable appetite for visual spectacle. Drawing on traditional forms of illusionism such as magic lanterns (dating back to the seventeenth century), late eighteenth-century experiments with optical techniques produced such phenomena as the *phantasmagoria* and the *eidophusikon*. The latter was the invention of the Swiss émigré Philippe Jacques de Loutherbourg, who, in London's Leicester Square in the early 1780s, popularized a show consisting of a scene displayed on a small stage with appropriate musical accompaniment and lighting operated by oil Argand lamps placed behind the proscenium. The *phantasmagoria* was a projection of supernatural or comical figures accompanied by sound and unexpected lighting effects. Apparently, it was the creation of the magician Paul de Philipstal or 'Philidor', who toured it from Berlin to Vienna and London between 1790 and 1793. Nearer the end of the century, the Belgian Étienne Gaspard Robertson perfected it and made it even more popular by taking it to Paris, Russia, Spain, and America. At about the same time, the vast curved canvasses of the panoramas began to appear in European capitals, attracting large crowds eager for detailed depictions of landscapes or battlefields, and subsequently spawning countless variations such as cosmoramas, myrioramas, and pleoramas.

As evidence of an uncontainable desire to see, these early entertainments reveal a demand for increasingly sophisticated means of producing illusions of reality. Typical of the baroque stage, illusionistic techniques re-emerged as staples (and problems) in late eighteenth- and early nineteenth-century theatre all over Europe—from the 'illegitimate' shows of London to the *teatro de magia* in Madrid or the Parisian *théâtre de boulevard*. The latter originated from the Napoleonic decree of 29 July 1807 which destined entertainments other than comedy and tragedy to four patented playhouses collectively known as *théâtres à spectacle*: the Vaudeville, Variétés, Ambigu-Comique, and Gaîté (the last two also held the monopoly over melodrama). Another decree of 11 March 1809 authorized the reopening of the Porte-Saint-Martin. The success of these venues transformed the Parisian stage into a model of spectacular theatre for the rest of Europe.

[15] Edward Bulwer-Lytton, 'The Siamese Twins' (1831), quoted in Richard D. Altick, *The Shows of London* (Cambridge, Mass., and London: Harvard University Press, 1978), 1.

[16] Peter de Bolla, *The Education of the Eye: Painting, Landscape, and Architecture in Eighteenth-Century Britain* (Stanford, Calif.: Stanford University Press, 2003), 16–17, 69.

Indeed, the French capital may be taken as an emblematic epicentre of the elaboration and diffusion of theatrical innovations in this period. Paris-based professionals such as Louis Daguerre and Pierre Cicéri were exemplary promoters of many decisive optical and visual developments that began on stage before spreading to other fields. The future pioneer of photography Daguerre started as an experimental stage designer at the Ambigu-Comique, where, in the 1810s, he perfected and extended the use of *fermes*—free-standing backdrops winched up from the basement and thus more versatile than retractable wing-flats. Coupled with his realistic depiction of weather phenomena, moonlight, and clouds, this novelty drew large crowds night after night. He also started introducing innovative *spectacles d'optique*, primarily the panorama, into the sets of melodramas. Patented by Robert Barker in 1787 and housed in the purpose-built Leicester Square 'Rotunda' from 1793, the panorama was brought to Paris by the American entrepreneur Robert Fulton. There, it soon became a major attraction at the hands of such artists as Pierre Prévost, Constantin Bourgeois, and Denis Fontaine. In 1804 Daguerre and Prévost opened a space for the exhibition of panoramatic paintings. Simultaneously, panoramas soon began to invade the stage, especially at the dedicated Théâtre Panorama-Dramatique (1821–3) run by Isidore-Justin-Séverin, Baron Taylor, the future manager of the Comédie-Française and a principal promoter of the new Romantic drama at that prestigious (and generally reactionary) venue. In July 1822, moreover, Daguerre and Charles-Marie Bouton, a student of Jacques-Louis David's, opened the 'Diorama' in the rue Samson, a show that became the main rival of the panoramas and exerted a huge influence on nineteenth-century stage decor. This *spectacle d'optique* consisted of a flat or gently curved and slightly transparent canvas illuminated either from the front or the back, so that, for instance, the scene depicted could quickly shift from night to daylight. An interlinked series of innovations, Daguerre's experiments confirm the pervasiveness of optical spectacularity, from the spaces reserved for panorama and diorama exhibitions to more conventional theatres.

That Cicéri was among Daguerre's regular collaborators testifies to the close connection between progress in optical effects and the development of stage painting. This revolutionary designer started his long career in 1806 at the Académie de Musique et Danse and, by the end of it, had painted over 400 decors for all types of playhouses. Known for his picturesque depictions, he particularly excelled at snow-capped mountains, foggy valleys, and ruined castles. In 1828 he created the designs for the opera *The Dumb Girl of Portici* (*La Muette de Portici*, music by Daniel Auber, libretto by Eugène Scribe) where he highlighted local colour by depicting lively Neapolitan settings and surprised audiences with a spectacular explosion of Vesuvius, a scene that had already reaped success at Daguerre's panorama in 1827. For the 1829 premiere of the ballet-pantomime *Sleeping Beauty* (*La Belle au bois dormant*, choreography by Jean-Louis Aumer, libretto by Scribe), Cicéri innovatively adapted the principle of the moving panorama ('cyclorama') by painting a landscape on a canvas that was then unrolled in front of a stationary boat by means of a drum mechanism. In 1830, then, his design for Act 4 of Hugo's *Hernani*, centred on the tomb of Charlemagne, was highly praised for its monumentality, Gothic picturesqueness, and subtly shaded perspectival effects. As he brought scenography in line with painting, Cicéri exemplified a general tendency to invest in strikingly accurate or daringly spectacular backgrounds that might enhance the spectator's visual reaction to, and emotional experience of, the show.

The growing importance of painting also owed much to the fact that the stage was more and more brightly illuminated thanks to gas lighting, a technology that significantly went from the theatre to the city streets and back to the theatre again. In 1803, the German Friedrich Albert Winsor held the earliest gas exhibitions at London's Lyceum Theatre; subsequently, after the creation of the London Gaslight and Coke Company in 1812, gas was increasingly used to light the capital's streets and public buildings; while, in 1817, Drury Lane, Covent Garden, and the Lyceum were entirely lit by gas within days of one another. In Paris the Salle Le Peletier of the Opéra was first lit by gas in 1821; the first theatre to be thus illuminated in Italy was the Fenice opera house in Venice in 1833; whereas Cologne seems to have had the only German gas-lit theatre in the early 1840s. Despite such disadvantages as the great heat, noxious fumes, and increased fire hazard, gas made it possible to darken the auditorium completely and produce subtle shifts from light to darkness and vice versa on stage. Moreover, by making the stage more clearly discernible, designers were under mounting pressure to produce ever more clearly detailed depictions. Almost simultaneously, in 1816, Thomas Drummond invented the limelight, which soon spread as a way of 'spotting' individual performers. In Paris in 1822, Daguerre and Cicéri, who had promoted a variety of experiments with light at the Panorama-Dramatique, collaborated on the fabulously expensive production of *Aladdin, or the Magic Lamp* (*Aladin ou la Lampe merveilleuse*), an *opera-féerie* by Nicolas (or Nicolò) Isouard at the Salle Le Peletier. On this occasion, they fully exploited the possibilities of gas lighting in devising the shining interior of Timorkan's 'Bronze Palace', the dome of which was supported by pillars ornamented by relief elephants, as well as the 'Palace of Light' adorned with a moving sun. This epoch-making production was the first and most spectacular showcasing of the new possibilities of gas lighting on the Parisian stage.

As Cicéri's work on *La Muette* and *Hernani* suggests, advancements in visual effects cut across theatrical and generic hierarchies—from spectacular entertainments to *grands opéras* and Romantic dramas. Productions of serious and, especially, historical texts invested more and more significantly in illusionistic techniques that resulted in fascinating combinations of accuracy and pageantry. A milestone in this respect was the production of Friedrich Schiller's *Maid of Orleans* (*Die Jungfrau von Orleans*) at Berlin's Royal National Theatre in November 1801. On that occasion, the actor and manager August Wilhelm Iffland staged a coronation procession with 200 extras on stage and an astonishing reproduction of the façade of Rheims Cathedral. More on the side of historical reliability, and in line with a pan-European trend for archaeological accuracy, was the first production of Alexandre Dumas's *Henri III and his Court*

(*Henri III et sa cour*) in February 1829, which featured a wealth of carefully researched details including individual stage props. In all of these cases, the appetite for visual entertainment translated into a desire to see the past materialize and experience the illusion of being in the past.

Rather than neat separations between spectacular and 'literary' theatre, the Romantic-period stage offers a continuity of forms of visual spectacle that also contributed to the popularization of new forms of drama. An exemplary text in this respect is the Spanish play *Love Conquers All, or the Goat's Foot* (*Todo lo puede amor, o la pata de cabra*) first performed in Madrid's Teatro del Príncipe on 18 February 1829. This was a translation/adaptation of a French original, César Ribié and A. L. D. Martainville's *Le Pied de mouton* (1806), by Juan Grimaldi, the French director of the Príncipe who almost single-handedly revolutionized drama and theatre in early to mid-century Madrid. Advertised as a play 'de grande espectáculo', *Pata de cabra* introduced new forms of spectacle and ways of staging. It quickly became the most successful play in Spanish theatre of the first half of the nineteenth century. The entire nation was in thrall to this fascinating visual extravaganza and approximately 220,000 people saw the play between 1829 and 1850 in Madrid. Grimaldi developed spectacular moments through complicated stage machinery and tricks including transformations, disappearances, sudden fires, mutated identities, colour changes, and levitations. In addition, although centred on a familiar tale of star-crossed lovers, the play introduced audiences to themes and situations typical of later Romantic drama, such as challenges to authority, the omnipotence of love, and the alternation between comic and serious episodes. *Pata de cabra* is a clear instance of how technological improvements and a demand for visual entertainment set in train changes that radically transformed dramatic writing and theatrical experience alike.

A crucible of international exchanges of techniques and texts, the spectacular component set off major systemic transformations in drama and theatre. These, in turn, triggered repeated denunciations of their increasingly visual nature which seem to testify to a predominant conception of the stage as a repository of essential truths about human nature. If visual spectacle reinforced subjectivity by satisfying a basic human need, it also threatened conventional notions of human nature by privileging mere perception over mental and spiritual processes. Even worse, spectacle promoted the power of technology over an individual's rational and emotional powers, dangerously endorsing spectatorial selves based on crude sensation rather than on stratifications of heritage keyed to the distinctively Romantic idea of 'the power of history to define identity'.[17] The reduction of theatre to visual effects apparently threatened the irreparable loss of substance and depth enshrined in the performed word. In fact, it contributed to some of the most ground-breaking and influential formal developments in drama and performance of the Romantic period.

[17] Erika Fischer-Lichte, *History of European Drama and Theatre*, tr. Jo Riley (London: Routledge, 2002), 230.

Genres and Forms

In July 1822 a cast of English actors (the 'Penley troupe') played at the Parisian Porte-Saint-Martin theatre, usually reserved for melodramas, pantomimes, and one-act comedies in prose mixed with songs. Their debut with *Othello* on 31 July did not bode well, causing an uproar among the audience, whose animosity was also fuelled by strong anti-British feelings. The next performance, Richard Brinsley Sheridan's *The School for Scandal* on 2 August, was again boycotted and stopped after the first scene. If Romantic-period drama and theatre were a network of exchanges, contacts, and transfers, these did not always run smoothly.

Still, this inauspicious tour had some important effects. As a Shakespeare fan, the young Stendhal spent a month in London in 1821 and saw Edmund Kean in *Othello*. After witnessing the debacle of the English performers, he published an indignant article in the October issue of the English-language *Paris Monthly Review*, which then became the first chapter of his polemical Romantic manifesto *Racine and Shakespeare* (*Racine et Shakespeare*, 1823). Another article followed in the January issue, which formed the second chapter, and a second part of *Racine and Shakespeare* eventually appeared in 1825. The emphatic Parisian repulse of Shakespeare moved Stendhal to write these embattled pieces on the state of French theatre, where he advocated reform through the creation of a 'Romantic genre' emerging from, and speaking to, the present.[18] This genre was to be primarily composed of 'tragedies [made] for us', 'national tragedies of a deep and lasting interest'.[19] Also, it should be in prose, recreate 'perfect illusion', and avoid all the 'ridiculous habits' imposed by eighteenth-century treatises, so that ideally 'the new French tragedy should very much resemble that of Shakespeare'.[20]

If there was an insistent demand for the renovation of the French stage, the English playwright came to embody the possibility of jettisoning set patterns and fixing new principles (indeed, of his runaway success *Antony* (1831), Alexandre Dumas *père* said that it was neither a drama nor a tragedy). This refusal of generic labels was part and parcel of a deep-seated need for change, which, as Stendhal's words clarify, comprised formal (prose), thematic (history), and cultural (English theatre) aspects. The latter category, in particular, confirms the coexistence of national and international trends in Romantic-era dramaturgy. Stendhal's treatise takes a European approach to the question, as is patent, for instance, in his coining of the term *romanticisme* from the Italian *romanticismo*. Yet, the most powerful formulation of this call for generic reform was undoubtedly Hugo's Preface to *Cromwell*. There, although he agreed with Stendhal on such points as Shakespeare's primacy, he insisted on verse rather than prose: 'a free, frank and loyal verse, daring to say everything without prudishness, to express

[18] Stendhal, *Racine et Shakespeare*, introd. Bernard Lelliot (Paris: Kimé, 2005), 20.

[19] Stendhal, *Racine et Shakespeare*, 19.

[20] Stendhal, *Racine et Shakespeare*, 29, 42.

everything without affectation.[21] Moreover, by setting up 'nature' and 'truth' as the only proper objects of imitation, Hugo endorsed generic and tonal admixtures, so that formal features would proclaim the new aesthetic and ideological concerns of the *drame*. A mutation of eighteenth-century antecedents, this genre should be neither tragedy nor comedy, disregard imposed doctrines such as the unities, and invest in local colour and, especially, the grotesque as the distinctive code of modern (i.e. post-classical) art. Hugo expanded Stendhal's project for the reform of tragedy into a programme for the wholesale reformulation of the generic system of drama.

Simultaneously, different European cultures manifested this need for new textual forms that might encapsulate new thematic concerns. In Milan, Alessandro Manzoni qualified his first play *The Count of Carmagnola* (*Il Conte di Carmagnola*, 1820) as a reformulation of tragedy, in a preface where, carefully avoiding controversial terms such as 'Romantic' and *drame*, he fixed the co-ordinates of a reformed historical drama. After the traditionalist French critic Victor Chauvet attacked his ideas, in 1823 Manzoni published a lengthy 'Letter to M. C[hauvet] on the Unity of Time and Place in Tragedy'('Lettre à M. C[hauvet] sur l'unité de temps et de lieu dans la tragédie') as an appendix to the French translation of his plays *Carmagnola* and *Adelchis*. There, he vindicated his new departures through some highly sophisticated reflections on historical and poetical forms of truth and by celebrating Shakespeare as a model in some crucial pages on *Richard II* (fittingly so, in an essay published in the same year as Stendhal's *Racine and Shakespeare*). In his 1830 essay 'On Historical Drama' ('Del dramma storico'), Giuseppe Mazzini drew on Manzoni's revolutionary delineation of historical 'tragedy' to promote this genre as the most significant instance of a truly national drama.

In late 1820s Spain, the critic and erudite Agustín Durán similarly championed the emergence of a national drama harking back to the great tradition of the Golden Age. Driven by an overwhelming patriotic impulse, his pioneering 'Speech on the Influence of Modern Criticism on the Decadence of the Ancient Spanish Theatre' ('Discurso sobre el influjo que ha tenido la crítica moderna en la decadencia del teatro antiguo español', 1828) harnessed Romantic principles to a spirited defence of Renaissance and baroque theatre. The best Spanish playwrights of the *Siglo de oro* wrote a type of drama he terms 'national Romantic', which, if better known, might 'resuscitate the enthusiasm of our [literary] youth'.[22] A couple of years later, in his 'Notes on the Historical Drama' ('Apuntes sobre el drama histórico', 1830) Francisco Martínez de la Rosa also proclaimed the quintessential Spanishness of this form as a recurrent component of the national drama. On 19 July 1830, a few days before the Battle of *Hernani*, his play *Aben Humeya* premiered in Paris at the Parisian Porte-Saint-Martin theatre. This historical drama originated from the ideas in the 'Notes', as well as from his familiarity with the tenets expounded in Manzoni's Letter. His subsequent production was another historical play, *The Venetian Conspiracy* (*La Conjuración de Venecia*), first published in Paris in 1830, later staged in Madrid in 1834, and hailed by Larra as an unalloyed expression of a patriotic national

[21] Hugo, *Cromwell*, 95.

[22] See Ricardo Navas Ruiz, *El romanticismo español: Documentos* (Salamanca: Anaya, 1971), 88, 89.

drama and, thus, a demonstration of the fact that 'With all known peoples, [drama] owes its birth to national pride, what we might call a people's self-esteem'.[23]

As is clear, these loud calls for a renovation of serious drama concerned traditional genres and, accordingly, elite cultural discourses. Although radically innovative, they still belonged to aesthetic orthodoxy. By contrast, a largely untheorized form with a far from prestigious cultural pedigree such as melodrama represented a much more deeply transformative, and therefore controversial, generic departure.

An admixture of existing genres characterized by what Peter Brooks has termed 'a mode of excess' in visual, physical, and emotional terms, melodrama dominated the Romantic-period stage all over Europe.[24] Stemming from the social and ideological tensions raised by the French Revolution, it was among the most enduring Romantic legacies to later drama and theatre. The works of one its earliest and most assiduous practitioners, René-Charles Guilbert de Pixerécourt took Paris by storm, first, and then the rest of France and Europe, starting from his enormously successful *Coelina, or the Child of Mystery* (*Cœlina, ou l'enfant du mystère*, 1800). In 1817, the publication of a *Treatise on Melodrama* (*Traité du mélodrame*), a satirical recipe-book for would-be melodramatists, reveals how quickly this genre became a formula. It was the work of three ambitious young writers—Abel Hugo, Armand Malitourne, and Jean-Joseph Ader—whose mockingly hyperbolic remarks throw light on some of the distinctive traits of melodrama. In particular, they stress its absolute modernity, since it 'exclusively belongs to our age' and draws on the *drame* of the previous century, that 'mixed genre' cultivated by Nicolas-Edme Rétif de la Bretonne, Denis Diderot, and Louis-Sébastien Mercier.[25] Melodrama, they say in mock triumphant terms, 'has swept away and invaded everything else' on the strength of its free-wheeling combinations of different genres and modes ('Comedy, ballet, vaudeville, opera, tragedy—melodrama joins everything together. It is a hodge-podge of good things'); and the 'large number of topics it includes' is an incontrovertible sign of its 'superiority over Tragedy'.[26]

Their dismissive intention notwithstanding, these remarks accurately describe melodrama as a mutation of the main serious genre, the popularity of which it soon outstripped. In addition, they clarify its revolutionary nature, lack of classical precedents, and rejection of established notions of decorum. Melodrama effectively transformed serious drama by discarding and rearranging existing norms in order to identify new and relevant sets of moral and aesthetic tenets. Moreover, its innovative import for dramatic and theatrical practice lay in its unabashed exploitation of the Romantic-period vogue for visual entertainment. In Peter Brooks's words, melodrama drew on an aesthetic of the surface and explicitness powered by a 'desire to express all' and, accordingly,

[23] '*La conjuración de Venecia*, de Francisco Martínez de la Rosa', in *La crítica teatral completa de Mariano José de Larra*, 204.

[24] Peter Brooks, *The Melodramatic Imagination: Balzac, Henry James, Melodrama, and the Mode of Excess* (New Haven and London: Yale University Press, 1976), 1–23.

[25] *Traité du mélodrame, par MM. A! A! A!* (Paris: Delaunay, Pélicier, Plancher, 1817), 2, 3.

[26] *Traité du mélodrame*, 7, 13, 66.

to make everything visible.[27] It capitalized on and stimulated further the technologies and techniques of spectacular visuality of this transitional period. By the same token, melodrama provided one of the key spaces for the development and popularization of new ways of acting and new ways of perceiving and appreciating the performers' bodies and the body in performance.

New Bodies

> He hastily threw back his black coat, for he was still in mourning for his father, as if his involuntary contact with it had terrified him. He looked around timidly, as if wanting to see whether the spectre in his breast were actually following him. At last he dared to turn around completely and stood once again with his face to the audience. But he was no longer the same person whom a few moments before we had seen leaving, fall [*sic*] of resolute malice. His features were pallid, his muscles quivered as if trembling with fever, his teeth rattled together, his hollow eyes rolled uncertainly here and there, his hair was standing on end in terror.[28]

With these rapid notations, in 1860 the poet and music critic Heinrich Friedrich Ludwig Rellstab remembered the actor Ludwig Devrient in one of his most acclaimed roles—Franz Moor in Act 4, Scene 2, of Schiller's *The Robbers* (*Die Räuber*). Brimming with physical traits, Rellstab's description records an epoch-making performance consonant with Romantic-era mythifications of actors and their acting style. The same awestruck and emotionally charged language recurred in countless descriptions of Edmund Kean and Sarah Siddons, or Frédérick Lemaître and Mademoiselle George (Marguerite-Joséphine Weimer). In this period, performing bodies invariably took centre stage as perturbing objects, fascinating machines, and the sites of unscripted (hence excitingly unpredictable) manifestations and reactions.

Significantly, Rellstab's words posit the body as an interface of physical and immaterial traits, while also qualifying performance as an intersection of written and embodied feelings. They also highlight the actor's body as the location of a semiotic overload, for, as Rellstab says of Devrient: 'Each step, each twitch of his hand, each turn of his head had meaning.'[29] This meaning, however, is always about to become irrational and non-communicative, for the body in performance has a 'demonic power' that works unexpected effects on the audience.[30]

To be sure, the cult of the actor was not a Romantic prerogative. Yet, in this period, increasing numbers of performers emerged as the targets of widespread enthusiasm

[27] Brooks, *Melodramatic Imagination*, 4.
[28] 'Ludwig Devrient as Franz Moor', in Brandt, *German and Dutch Theatre*, 306.
[29] 'Ludwig Devrient as Franz Moor', 306.
[30] 'Ludwig Devrient's Character as an Artist', in Brandt, *German and Dutch Theatre*, 305.

centring on their physical features and personations. Rapt descriptions abound which depict the actor as a magnetic presence and a body that functions as a collector and relay of intense emotions affecting audiences beyond their control. Perhaps unsurprisingly, one of the most celebrated among these performers was Devrient's predecessor, the *Sturm und Drang* actor Johann Friedrich Ferdinand Fleck. After seeing him as Wallenstein in Berlin in 1799, Ludwig Tieck wrote that 'one felt that the general, so multifariously, so strangely complicated, was caught up in a great horrendous madness', while the audience was 'seized by a mysterious horror'.[31] Later in the period, in spite of his unsuccessful turn in Paris in 1818, Edmund Kean acquired European fame as a revolutionary performer and, only three years after his death, Dumas *père* turned him into an embodiment of Romantic rebelliousness in *Kean; or, Disorder and Genius* (*Kean, ou désordre et génie*, 1836). The title role was aptly played by Lemaître, the personification of *boulevard* theatre and Kean's French counterpart in terms of personal myth and peculiar acting style. Lemaître also starred in Romantic *drames* such as Hugo's *Lucretia Borgia* and *Ruy Blas*, but his technique was especially associated with such melodramatic figures as that of Robert Macaire from *L'Auberge des Adrets* by Antier, Saint-Amand, and Paulyanthe (1823). This character was so successful that Lemaître himself wrote a sequel titled *Robert Macaire* (1834). Of Lemaître, Hugo enthusiastically remarked that 'the lightning flashes of his acting' were not 'a performance, but a transfiguration'.[32]

These outstanding bodies invariably carried connotations of unconventionality and abnormality. Romantic-period popular culture associated some of these mythified figures with irregular lifestyles, physical irregularity (whether of the actor, as in Kean, or of their signature characters), and irregularity in their acting styles through their propensity for emotionally intense interpretations coupled with innovative proxemics. If, in the Romantic era, the body emerged as the 'natural sign of the soul', then drama and theatre showcased a deeply fractured interiority.[33] The most striking productions in this period delineate a theatre of affect wound round an uncontainable physicality that exteriorizes the actor's and character's tortured self. This is evident in reinvented repertoire figures such as the Shakespearean roles that became international favourites, from King Lear and Othello to Richard III and Shylock. New roles were just as affecting, and here the list of male characters might include Schiller's Franz Moor, Maturin's Bertram, Dumas's Antony, Alfred de Vigny's Chatterton, Hugo's Hernani, the Duque de Rivas's Don Alvaro, and Antonio García Gutiérrez's 'Trovador', to select just a few from the more canonical or 'legitimate' output.

As embodiments of irregularity and abnormality, these figures invariably convey marginalized and subversive identities such as outcasts, orphans, rebels, bandits, and lowlifes, an excellent instance being, once again, the melodramatic anti-hero par excellence, Robert Macaire. In Lemaître's magisterial interpretation, this character

[31] 'Fleck's Wallenstein, Berlin, 1799', in Brandt, *German and Dutch Theatre*, 270.

[32] 'Frédérick in *Ruy Blas*, 1838', in Donald Roy (ed.), *Romantic and Revolutionary Theatre 1789–1860* (Cambridge: Cambridge University Press, 2003), 351.

[33] Fischer-Lichte, *History of European Drama*, 165–8.

completely overturned the bourgeois pieties of traditional melodrama, especially in the 1834 sequel, which questioned middle-class hypocrisy even more radically than the original play. Conservative critics damned *Robert Macaire* as an anarchic text and accused it of providing inspiration for Giuseppe Marco Fieschi's attempt on the life of King Louis-Philippe in 1835, and for the criminal career of the notorious Pierre-François Lacenaire, who adroitly turned his 1835 trial into a theatrical spectacle, and whose apologia for crime later inspired Fyodor Dostoevsky for the character of Raskolnikov in *Crime and Punishment*.

As variations on a type of Gothic and Byronic mixture of *désordre* and *génie*, the troubled performers and dark anti-heroes of the Romantic stage personified a society in flux and notions of the self as irregular and unstable. And this was a kind of subjectivity in performance that went beyond the field of acting. Indeed, it possibly found its most impactful embodiment in the figure of Niccolò Paganini, the composer and violinist *virtuoso* whose gaunt and dishevelled body was said to be a physical translation of his tormented art and of the allegedly satanic side of his genius.

It would be incorrect, however, to see this as the only manifestation of Romantic-period acting, for there were equally wildly praised performers who perfected more measured styles, such as John Philip Kemble in London and François-Joseph Talma in Paris. As the most revered tragedian on the late eighteenth-century Parisian stage, the latter popularized an updated version of the classical French tradition of controlled and dignified acting that made him a household name in Europe. Between 1799 and 1801, a young Isidoro Máiquez, the future male star of early nineteenth-century Madrid theatre, obtained a governmental grant, which he supplemented by selling his own costumes and stage ornaments, to travel to Paris and study Talma's technique. Starstruck by his performance in *Hamlet*, Máiquez became a student and subsequently a friend of the French actor, with whom he continued to correspond long after his own return to Spain. That Máiquez had successfully learnt his lessons was confirmed by Martínez de la Rosa, who approvingly noted how the great Spanish performer showed 'the extent to which it may be possible to combine dignity and simplicity; [and] imitate the language of passions through voice, gesture and even silence'.[34] Similarly, Kemble became acquainted with Talma during his trip to Paris in 1802, a meeting that laid the ground for a friendship based on mutual admiration. In 1817 the French star was in London and attended Kemble's farewell performances. Afterwards, Talma's style continued to fascinate actors such as William Charles Macready who saw him in Paris in 1822 and wrote admiringly that his 'genius … rose above all the conventionality of schools', and his 'ease and freedom, whether in familiar colloquy, in lofty declamation, or burst of passion … gave an air of unpremeditation to every sentence'.[35] Talma's natural style, mixed with his hallmark *gravitas*, made him a revered and widely imitated trendsetter.

[34] 'Apéndice sobre la tragedia española' (1827), in *Obras de D. Francisco Martínez de la Rosa*, ed. Carlos Seco Serrano, *Biblioteca de Autores Españoles*, 150 (Madrid: Atlas, 1962), iii.163

[35] 'Macready on Talma', in A. M. Nagler, *A Source Book in Theatrical History* (New York: Dover, 1959), 469.

Of course, actresses were the objects of absolute crazes, too, as their closely scrutinized bodies were praised for their ability to express natural elegance, intense feelings, and strong passions. For instance, of Mademoiselle Mars (Anne-Françoise-Hyppolyte Boutet), Macready noted that 'in person she was most lovely, and in grace and elegance of deportment and action unapproached by any of her contemporaries'.[36] Yet, possibly the clearest testimony of the celebration of the physiques of (female) performers relates to dancers such as the international stars Marie Taglioni (who created the title role in *The Sylph*, 1832) or Carlotta Grisi (who was the first protagonist of *Giselle*, 1841). They were endlessly described by critics and connoisseurs, and reproduced in paintings, prints, and illustrations where their ethereal, almost disembodied, shapes assumed deeply sensual and sexual connotations. On the dramatic stage, rather than embodying rebellion or violence, actresses were most often called upon to embody overwhelming feelings. Embedded in a tradition of sentimentalist discourse that saw the bodies of women as the privileged conductors of intense emotions, the most affecting new roles were women who felt strongly, suffered, and eventually died as victims of fate, intrigue, or love—as in Francesca from Pellico's *Francesca da Rimini*, Adèle in *Antony*, and Leonor in the Duque de Rivas's *Don Alvaro, or the Force of Destiny* (*Don Alvaro o la fuerza del sino*, 1835).

In terms of spectatorial response, then, Romantic-period theatre set off mechanisms of transference whereby the affects shown on stage began to infect audiences and elicit emphatic reactions. As theatrical experience became increasingly emotive, reports abound which detail the effect of performances on spectators who regularly fell prey to what Hugo called the 'lightning flashes' of contemporary acting styles oscillating between hyperbolism and formal restraint. Furthermore, character types and performative styles offered audiences possible models of identity in ways that recall contemporary phenomena such as Wertherism and Byronism. One of the most obvious cases was that of the figures of Antony and Adèle, from Dumas's *Antony*, whose tormented characters (the post-Byronic wanderer and the woman in thrall to an invincible passion) generated forms of emulation among fashionable young men and women.[37]

If, generally, the stage is a crucial location for the display and apprehension of models of identity, Romantic-era drama and theatre specifically constructed the body on stage by prioritizing visible and material aspects through which it could tap into and disclose invisible, often previously unsounded, depths. Performers such as actors, dancers, and musicians displayed their bodies, feelings, and passions through performances of selfhood which touched and induced spectators to adopt and reproduce them. Whether restrained or overflowing with violent passion, the body on stage condensed and made visible notions of identity as alternately a deep or a superficial construct; a condensation of revolutionary and anarchic tendencies or, conversely, reactionary principles; the site of a conflict between norms and abnormality, a grotesque and deformed entity

[36] 'Macready on Talma', 469.

[37] See 'La Reprise d'*Antony*', in Théophile Gautier, *Histoire du Romantisme*, suivi de *Quarante portraits romantiques*, ed. Adrien Goetz (Paris: Gallimard, 2011), 454. On 'Antonisme', see Louis Maigron, *Le Romantisme et les mœurs* (Paris: Champion, 1910), 356–89.

bespeaking the abysses of the soul; or the object of currents of spectatorial repulsion and attraction accompanying as many mechanisms of rejection and self-identification. In this light, the Romantic stage confirms once again its essentially humanist nature by defining an influential lexicon of acting styles and models of selfhood that remained in place until the radical mutations introduced by the twentieth-century avant-gardes.

Romantic Theatre and Nineteenth-Century Visuality

Walter Benjamin's 1935 exposé 'Paris, the Capital of the Nineteenth Century' fashions an evocatively fragmentary account of modernity through an admixture of selected cultural phenomena and relevant transformational forces. Although structurally discontinuous, this portrayal presents several points of cohesion, one of the most conspicuous being an insistence on vision and visuality. Benjamin characterizes nineteenth-century modernity through repeated references to the technological development, proliferation, and consumption of countless forms of seeing and displaying.

Significantly, the arcades emblematizing Benjamin's modernity are made of glass and iron, as well as containing rows of shop-windows. Often ornamented with mirrors, these are places of the new—new building techniques, commodities, and cultural experiences—and spaces of *flânerie*, that eminently spectatorial attitude that offers a detached, and thereby privileged, perspective over reality. Drawing attention to photography, exhibitions, and advertising as distinctive components of modernity in its Parisian epicentre, Benjamin argues for the pervasiveness of practices of display and acts of vision that produced a complex admixture of technology, production and consumption, art and culture. Accordingly, he employs 'phantasmagoria' as a key visual metaphor for the myriad stimulations that surround and invest the subject: world exhibitions are a 'phantasmagoria which a person enters in order to be distracted', while the *flâneur* perceives the 'familiar city … as phantasmagoria'.[38] Not unexpectedly, in view of the preceding discussion, the co-ordinates of this cultural regime are inextricably bound up with the forms of visuality typical of Romantic-period drama and theatre.

Benjamin connects the arcades to the panorama, which he appropriately links to Daguerre and his pioneering pre-photographic experiments. Tellingly, he notes how 'The high point in the diffusion of panoramas coincides with the introduction of arcades'.[39] By invoking this staple of Romantic-era visuality, Benjamin sketches a progressive, century-long development towards a condition of full (or 'panoramatic') visibility in consonance with the pervasive 'desire to express all' which Brooks, as already

[38] Walter Benjamin, *The Arcades Project*, tr. Howard Eiland and Kevin McLaughlin (Cambridge, Mass., and London: Belknap Press of Harvard University Press, 1999), 18.

[39] Benjamin, *Arcades Project*, 5.

mentioned, sees as a central feature of melodrama. Yet, the same condition is linked to the gradual diffusion of gas illumination that soon extended to the arcades ('The arcades are the scene of the first gas lighting').[40] Benjamin places particular emphasis on gas and its dramatic transformation of the experience of urban space. Once again, his composite picture of modernity is not far from the world of the playhouse, since, as already noted, gas went from the stage to the streets and then to the stage again, where it contributed to the development of new illusionistic effects, particularly reinforcing the aspiration of total vision—the illusion of an exhaustive reproduction of reality through panoramatic mimesis.

Although Benjamin does not explicitly mention them, Romantic-period changes in theatre and drama constitute the antecedents of, and therefore fully participate in, his picture. They were part of a time-specific cultural milieu prolonging eighteenth-century regimes of visuality, especially what de Bolla calls the 'regime of the eye', which determined how things were seen and delineated new seeing selves. Stage entertainments offered the possibility of mobile points of view, totalizing vision, reproductions of reality, or visualizations of the imaginary. They also provided spaces where seeing was inextricable from being seen. All of these changes were constitutive of a wider, century-long, scopic regime that grounds Benjamin's notion of modernity. Indeed, the visual greed that worried commentators and inspired writers, actors, and directors was one of the forces impelling the visual reorientations examined in his exposé.

In this perspective, Romantic-period drama and theatre (and visuality more generally) were truly revolutionary and not merely in the sense, suggested at the beginning of this chapter, that the French Revolution had an enormous impact on them. As loci and testimonies of epoch-making cultural developments in Romantic-period Europe, theatre, drama, and related visual practices were sites of transformation of notions and discourses of cultural production and consumption, power and control, socialization, identity-making, and spatial experience. A hyperbolically celebrated 'point of view' and 'optical point' on reality, the stage was a site of multiple and far-reaching mutations anticipating later radical breaks and departures. Rather than mere empty grandiloquence, the Romantics' pronouncements on theatre—from Hugo's and Shelley's to Manzoni's, Larra's, and Garrett's—suggestively and accurately qualify it as a crucial space of cultural reconfiguration and the introduction of the new.

Further Reading

Allévy, Marie-Antoinette, *La Mise en scène en France dans la première moitié du dix-neuvième siècle* (Paris: Droz, 1938).

Bergman, Gösta M., *Lighting in the Theatre* (Stockholm: Almqvist & Wiksell; Totowa, NJ: Rowman & Littlefield, 1977).

[40] Benjamin, *Arcades Project*, 3.

Brooks, Peter, *The Melodramatic Imagination: Balzac, Henry James, Melodrama, and the Mode of Excess* (New Haven and London: Yale University Press, 1976).

Burwick, Frederick, *Illusion and the Drama: Critical Theory of the Enlightenment and Romantic Era* (University Park, Pa.: Pennsylvania State University Press, 1991).

Carlson, Marvin, *Theories of the Theatre: A Historical and Critical Survey, from the Greeks to the Present* (Ithaca, NY, and London: Cornell University Press, 1993).

Cox, Jeffrey N., 'The Death of Tragedy; or, The Birth of the Melodrama', in Peter Holland and Tracy C. Davis (eds), *The Performing Century: Nineteenth-Century Theatre's History* (Basingstoke and New York: Palgrave Macmillan, 2007), 161–81.

Downer, Alan S., 'Nature to Advantage Dress'd: Eighteenth Century Acting', *PMLA* 58 (1943), 1002–37.

Downer, Alan S., 'Players and Painted Stage: Nineteenth Century Acting', *PMLA* 61 (1946), 522–76.

Gies, David T., *The Theatre in Nineteenth-Century Spain* (Cambridge: Cambridge University Press, 1994).

Gillespie, Gerald (ed.), *Romantic Drama* (Amsterdam and Philadelphia: John Benjamins, 1994).

Kindermann, Heinz, *Theatergeschichte Europas*, 10 vols, vi. *Romantik* (Salzburg: Otto Müller Verlag, 1957–74).

Maslan, Susan, *Revolutionary Acts: Theater, Democracy, and the French Revolution* (Baltimore: Johns Hopkins University Press, 2005).

Naugrette, Florence, *Le Théâtre romantique: Histoire, écriture, mise en scène* (Paris: Seuil, 2001).

Thomas, Sophie, *Romanticism and Visuality: Fragments, History, Spectacle* (New York and London: Routledge, 2008).

CHAPTER 39

IDENTITY CRISES

Celebrity, Anonymity, Doubles, and Frauds in European Romanticism

ANGELA ESTERHAMMER

NAPOLEON, Mme de Staël, Goethe, Lord Byron: the Romantic period was dominated by dynamic personalities notable for their travels across the European continent, their media presence as writers and subjects of writing, and their powerful influence on the ideology of the age. The process by which such personalities made an impact on the material world and on a widespread public was perceived by Coleridge when he described 'men of commanding genius' who 'must impress their preconceptions on the world without, in order to present them back to their own view with the satisfying degree of clearness, distinctness, and individuality'.[1] More recent cultural critics have argued that the early nineteenth century saw the emergence of a modern concept of celebrity. Social conditions that included a flood of new periodical publications, the spread of manufactured goods, and the rise of middle-class tourism encouraged the dissemination of mediated and commodified representations of famous people that were easy for the public to collect and to imitate. In contrast to the traditional image of self-sufficient, inward-looking Romantic poets—those whom Coleridge called 'absolute' geniuses who can 'rest content between thought and reality, as it were in an intermundium of which their own living spirit supplies the substance, and their imagination the ever-varying form'[2]—the Romantic celebrity was a product of material culture, the circulation of print, and an ever-expanding reading public.

This chapter addresses the European dimension of nineteenth-century celebrity culture, the extent to which it involved international media networks and figures who, in person and by reputation, crossed borders to engage with multiple publics. Fame on an international scale was facilitated by the reopening of the continent to travel and tourism

[1] Samuel Taylor Coleridge, *Biographia Literaria*, ed. James Engell and Walter Jackson Bate (Princeton: Princeton University Press, 1983), i. 32.

[2] Coleridge, *Biographia Literaria*, i. 32.

after the Battle of Waterloo in 1815—but the post-Napoleonic era also altered the conditions of fame, and as the effects of celebrity culture made themselves felt, so did some ironic countercurrents. In the wake of the personality-driven poetry of Byron or the novels and essays of Mme de Staël, late Romantic literature manifests certain *anti*-celebrity impulses. These trends encompass the anonymous writing that fills literary magazines, collective forms of authorship such as anthologies and annual gift-books, and the use of pseudonyms shared by a coterie of writers. Anonymity and secondariness also seem to be part of a cultural reaction to the death of the great names: Staël in 1817, Napoleon in 1821, Byron in 1824, Goethe in 1832. In response, so many younger writers assumed identities modelled on the personal and textual characteristics of high-Romantic celebrities that the second quarter of the nineteenth century has gone down in German literary history as an age of *Epigonen*—belated, lesser, derivative personalities. The distortions of personality caused by the celebrity condition and the imitative patterns of late Romantic writing contributed to a large-scale preoccupation with identity during an age that foregrounded appearance, performance, and various kinds of reproduction. As they become known across Europe, the identities of Staël, Byron, or Walter Scott crystallized around reproducible features of appearance, behaviour, and style; often they were conflated with fictional (self-)constructions that held special appeal for specific audiences. These processes of abstracting and commodifying identity generated doubts about the uniqueness and cohesiveness of individuals that are reflected in late Romantic literature, both fictional and non-fictional. During the 1820s, in particular, the consequences of a first acquaintance with media-generated celebrity culture intersected with other contemporaneous challenges to personal and authorial identity, including a fascination with doubles and *doppelgänger* as well as elaborate instances of forgery and fraud.

Several critics have argued persuasively that the conditions necessary to create celebrity in the modern sense arose at the turn of the nineteenth century. These include new media and institutions, expanded markets, and a consumer culture that was prepared to collect and consecrate material objects connected to famous individuals. Tom Mole describes celebrity as 'a cultural apparatus consisting of three elements: an individual, an industry and an audience', and contends that 'Modern celebrity culture begins when these three components routinely work together to render an individual personally fascinating'.[3] Technologies and institutions that made possible the emergence of celebrities range from the popularity of portraiture in the late eighteenth century to the invention of photography in the nineteenth century; advances in papermaking, printing, and reproductive engraving; a sharp increase in the number of magazines and newspapers; the introduction of modern techniques of product advertising; and the beginnings of a global distribution network. These multimedia developments made crossover publicity and marketing increasingly prevalent in the early nineteenth century. A popular text could be accompanied not only by reproduction of the author's portrait and visual depictions of favourite scenes, but also by related material products such as jewelry or tableware.

[3] Tom Mole, *Byron's Romantic Celebrity: Industrial Culture and the Hermeneutic of Intimacy* (Basingstoke: Palgrave Macmillan, 2007), 1.

The word 'celebrity' itself, in use since about 1600, became more frequent and changed in meaning during the Romantic period. Mole sums up the semantic change with the observation: 'Celebrity was no longer something you had; it was now something you were'.[4] In contrast to *fame*, which is based on great achievements, develops over time, lasts beyond death, and is often ascribed only after death, celebrity is sudden and ephemeral; it is dependent on the desires and fantasies of an audience as much as on personal accomplishment. One celebrity is vulnerable to replacement by another on the principle that Byron formulates at the beginning of *Don Juan*:

> I want a hero: an uncommon want,
> When every year and month sends forth a new one,
> Till, after cloying the gazettes with cant,
> The age discovers he is not the true one . . .[5]

As Eric Eisner puts it, nineteenth-century literary celebrity subsumes 'various kinds of public notice, including both adulation and notoriety, in which both the writer's personality and the writer's body take on a public significance and a market value of their own'.[6] Insofar as it involves a displacement of identity from internal features inherent in the individual to citable newspaper 'cant' or reproducible material representations, the consecration of celebrities is at odds, however, with the valorization of unique identities and autonomous selves.

Recently, the features and discourses of nineteenth-century celebrity have been explored through a variety of examples from literature, music, theatre, and sport, with special emphasis on female celebrity and on the Victorian period in Britain and America.[7] Although the European dimension has been less systematically studied, celebrity culture manifests itself from the outset as a European phenomenon. A compelling candidate to mark the turn towards a new inflection of identity is Goethe's epoch-making *Sturm und Drang* novel of 1774, *Die Leiden des jungen Werther*. The problematics of identity are in play here on several levels at once, beginning with the epistolary style that places emphasis on the tortuous self-analysis and self-expression of the protagonist Werther, his alienation from conventional social relationships, his self-image as an isolated genius, his suicidal passion for the married Lotte, and his turn

[4] Tom Mole (ed.), *Romanticism and Celebrity Culture, 1750–1850* (Cambridge: Cambridge University Press, 2009), 2.

[5] Lord Byron, *The Complete Poetical Works*, ed. Jerome J. McGann, v. *Don Juan* (Oxford: Clarendon, 1986), 9.

[6] Eric Eisner, *Nineteenth-Century Poetry and Literary Celebrity* (Basingstoke: Palgrave Macmillan, 2009), 2–3.

[7] See Mole, *Romanticism and Celebrity Culture*; Ghislaine McDayter, *Byromania and the Birth of Celebrity Culture* (Albany, NY: State University of New York Press, 2009); Brenda R. Weber, *Women and Literary Celebrity in the Nineteenth Century: The Transatlantic Production of Fame and Gender* (Burlington, Vt.: Ashgate, 2012); and Ann R. Hawkins and Maura Ives (eds), *Women Writers and the Artifacts of Celebrity in the Long Nineteenth Century* (Burlington, Vt.: Ashgate, 2012). One collection with a European focus is Edward Berenson and Eva Giloi (eds), *Constructing Charisma: Celebrity, Fame, and Power in Nineteenth-Century Europe* (New York: Berghahn Books, 2010).

from conventional masculinity towards more stereotypically feminine behaviours such as weeping and outbursts of emotion. On another level, *Werther* generated a distinctive fan response thanks to the identification that Goethe at first cultivated, but later suppressed, between Werther's experiences and his own. Readers' interest in the biographical background led them to make pilgrimages to Weimar in search of more intimate knowledge of Goethe's youthful beloved Charlotte Buff and his suicidal friend Karl Wilhelm Jerusalem.

With regard to both author and protagonist, *Werther* offers an early example of Romantic-era celebrity. The novel sold an unprecedented 9,000 copies within a couple of years of publication and was quickly translated into French (1776) and English (1779), then into seven further languages during Goethe's lifetime. It was adapted to other genres (poetry, opera, ballet, popular theatre) and other media (painting, engraving, porcelain). Werther souvenirs and commodities included jewelry, dinnerware, fans, perfume, and items of dress. As the story lent itself to adaptation, so the character of Werther was subject to imitation, and the wave of *Wertherisme* that spread throughout Europe generated tragic consequences including copycat suicides and (retrospectively) more comic ones such as the imitation of Wertherian attire. Werther's idiosyncratic, recognizable, and easily imitable costume—the blue jacket and yellow vest and trousers he wears the first time he dances with Lotte—is tailor-made for the circulation of a stereotyped celebrity image. Werther himself fetishes these pieces of clothing, having a new set made when the original ones wear out and asking to be buried in these clothes along with the pink ribbon Lotte was wearing on her white dress when he first saw her.[8] This fetishization of fashion leads to the paradox that Werther, whose character is bound up with feelings of uniqueness, embodies his self-image in external appearance and behaviour that lends itself to emulation and replication. Whatever the conjunction of circumstances that led to the immense popularity of *The Sorrows of Young Werther*, therefore, the distinctive way in which that popularity manifested itself was determined, at least in part, by the depiction of Werther's unresolved identity crisis within the novel and by a relationship of (illusory) intimacy among the protagonist, the author, and a geographically widespread readership.

The blurring of the distinction between Goethe's experience and Werther's repeats itself in other paradigmatic examples of Romantic celebrity. A generation later, the eponymous heroine of the novel *Corinne, ou l'Italie* (1807) became indelibly identified with her creator Mme de Staël, the resulting celebrity figure providing a model of the female poet-performer that influenced women authors for the rest of the century. The conditions for Staël's prominence in Romantic Europe were determined by her heritage as the only child of the millionaire Swiss banker Jacques Necker and the Parisian *salonnière* Suzanne Necker, and by her prolific talent for writing in a wide variety of genres, from socio-political essays to aesthetic criticism to fiction. Staël's status as a Romantic-era celebrity, more specifically, is tied up with her unconventional lifestyle that included a household separate from her Swedish-diplomat husband, a series of

[8] Johann Wolfgang Goethe, *Die Leiden des jungen Werther* (Frankfurt/Main: Insel, 1973), 107, 162–4.

affairs and children with different partners, and public media battles with Napoleon that led to her exile from France. It also has to do with her international presence, first as a salon hostess who welcomed the luminaries of Europe at her estate on Lake Geneva and later as a prominent traveller to Italy, the German states, Russia, and England. 'She not only became more famous because of her rootless status', Claire Brock writes, 'but crossed Europe on an effective publicity tour with Britain as her ultimate goal';[9] her arrival in London made 1813 'the year of Madame de Staël'.[10] One nineteenth-century biographer recalled that 'in the immense crowds that collected to see her ... the eagerness of curiosity broke through all restraint; the first ladies in the kingdom stood on chairs and tables, to catch a glimpse of her dark and brilliant physiognomy'.[11] As Staël met members of high society including Byron and the Prince Regent, witnesses commented on her brilliant but incessant conversation, her lack of femininity, her physical unattractiveness, and her craving for attention.

Staël's ability to attract curious crowds across Europe, and the gossip surrounding her physical person as well as her behaviour and relationships, mark her as a modern celebrity. Fascinated by renown—or what she called *la gloire*—on a theoretical level as well, Staël offered a nascent theory of celebrity in her sociological and fictional writings. Her early work *De l'Influence des passions sur le bonheur des individus et des nations* (1796) links intellectual creativity directly to the response of an audience: 'great events occur within you, demanding, in the name of the people, who count on your brilliance, the most lively attention to your own ideas. The cheers of the crowd stir the soul, by inspiring reflections and arousing commotion.'[12] This reciprocal relationship between artist and audience finds its projection and development in the novel *Corinne*, which appeared in English and German translations the same year as the French original. Staël represents Corinne as a multimedia artist, talented at writing, translating, painting, playing the lyre, singing, dancing, and acting; primarily, however, she is an *improvvisatrice*, a public improviser of poetry. By highlighting Corinne's immediate, reciprocal interaction with an audience, this depiction enacts Staël's sense of the close connection between artistic creativity and the response of an adoring crowd.

Corinne first appears in the novel as the star of a public spectacle, a festival held at the Roman Capitol to celebrate her as 'the most famous woman in Italy ... poetess, writer, and improviser, and one of the most beautiful women in Rome'.[13] Together with the protagonist Oswald, who will soon become Corinne's lover, readers of the novel first experience Corinne in performance, as it were from the perspective of her adoring fans. The objectification involved in this perspective reveals itself when Oswald perceives

[9] Claire Brock, *The Feminization of Fame, 1750–1830* (Basingstoke: Palgrave Macmillan, 2006), 159.

[10] Angelica Goodden, *Madame de Staël: The Dangerous Exile* (Oxford: Oxford University Press, 2008), 223.

[11] L. Maria Child, *Memoirs of Madame de Staël, and of Madame Roland*, rev. edn (New York: C. S. Francis & Co., 1854), 87.

[12] Staël, *Œuvres Complètes*, ed. Florence Lotterie (Paris: Honoré Champion, 2008), i/1. 159; tr. from Brock, *Feminization*, 143.

[13] Mme [Germaine] de Staël, *Corinne, or Italy*, tr. Sylvia Raphael (Oxford: Oxford University Press, 1998), 21.

Corinne as if she were a work of art rather than a real woman: her figure is 'in the style of a Greek statue', her dress 'like Domenichino's Sibyl'.[14] Oswald is uncomfortable with the Italian crowd's representation of Corinne—but only because he feels the impulse to paint her differently: 'He felt already that, just by looking at her, he would have produced right away a more true, accurate, and detailed portrait, a portrait which would have fitted no one but Corinne'.[15] Even as he desires to know Corinne as an individual, he imagines taking control of her representation.

As in the case of Werther, Corinne's distinctive attire counterpoints the uniqueness of her talent with the citational quality of her external appearance. Visually referencing Domenichino's early seventeenth-century painting *The Cumaean Sibyl*, her appearance at the opening festival lends itself to further reproduction. At the end of the novel, Oswald is overcome with emotion when he sees the original Domenichino painting in an art gallery in Bologna.[16] Outside of the text, the painting even today helps market *Corinne* by providing the cover image for modern editions such as the Oxford World's Classics. Most significantly, Mme de Staël referenced Corinne's Sibylline dress in one of her most famous self-images: in an 1810 portrait, Staël wears a turban like Domenichino's Sibyl and holds a rose-stem, an accessory she often toyed with in order to draw attention to her elegant hands. An equally famous portrait by Elisabeth Vigée-Lebrun depicts Staël *as* Corinne, holding a lyre and, in reference to one of the most famous scenes of the novel, performing an improvisation in the landscape of Cape Miseno near Naples. The conflation of author and fictional character is also perpetuated by the nickname 'Corinne' or 'Corinna' by which Staël was often known, in person and in print. Thus Byron commemorates the recent death of Staël in a note to canto 4, stanza 54, of *Childe Harold's Pilgrimage* with the declaration, 'CORINNA is no more.'[17]

Byron himself is central to any discussion of celebrity in the nineteenth century. More than any other personality of the age, he has been described as the first modern celebrity due to the suddenness and the geographical extent of his fame, the way his reputation spread through the circulation of image and print, the marketing tactics he and his publishers employed, the wish-fulfilment fantasies he aroused as a good-looking aristocrat, and the role of scandal in shaping his reputation. As with Staël, physical travel and material presence are important components of his impact on readers; the exotic Mediterranean locales of *Childe Harold's Pilgrimage* acquire an aura of authenticity and intimacy thanks to the poet's explicit or implied claim that 'I was there'.[18] Yet modern marketing techniques and the mobility of texts as well as bodies played an equally important role in forging Byron's reputation. Especially in the case of *Childe*

[14] Staël, *Corinne*, 23.

[15] Staël, *Corinne*, 24.

[16] Staël, *Corinne*, 386.

[17] Lord Byron, *The Complete Poetical Works*, ed. Jerome J. McGann, ii. *Childe Harold's Pilgrimage* (Oxford: Clarendon, 1980), 235.

[18] See Stephen Cheeke, *Byron and Place: History, Translation, Nostalgia* (Basingstoke: Palgrave Macmillan, 2003); and Angela Esterhammer, 'Trophies, Triumphs, Tourism, and the Topography of History: Byron's *Childe Harold's Pilgrimage* and its Contexts', *Colloquium Helveticum*, 39 (2008), 25–42.

Harold's Pilgrimage, the sensational success of the first cantos in 1812 was preceded by carefully placed newspaper coverage of Byron's earlier poetry and his political speeches in the House of Lords, and by pre-publication reviews.[19] The construction of Byron's image and that of the fictional Byronic hero take place simultaneously and reciprocally through the composition and reception of *Childe Harold's Pilgrimage* and the oriental verse romances Byron produced between 1812 and 1816. In his preface to canto 4 of *Childe Harold* in 1818, Byron famously (if somewhat disingenuously) admits that the public's conflation of him with Harold is beyond his control: 'It was in vain that I asserted, and imagined, that I had drawn, a distinction between the author and the pilgrim; and the very anxiety to preserve this difference, and disappointment at finding it unavailing, so far crushed my efforts in the composition, that I determined to abandon it altogether—and have done so.'[20]

As with Staël and her alter-ego Corinne, visual images of Byron served to forge his identification with the heroes of his poems while seeming to give access to the physical person of the author, thus creating an illusion of intimacy and making it possible for fans to fashion themselves in his image. Two famous portraits painted by Thomas Phillips in 1813–1814 codified the hallmarks of the Byronic look: three-quarter profile, high forehead, dark curly hair, pensive-disdainful expression, open-shirted neck. These features proved endlessly citable by later Romantic writers, performers, travellers, and dandies. Phillips's three-quarter-length portrait of Byron in Albanian dress puts even stronger emphasis on external attire, which serves as a claim to authenticity since Byron had brought the costume back from his own travels in Albania but also acts as a clichéd marker of exoticism, privilege, and masculinity.

Paralleling the multiplication of Byronic heroes in nineteenth-century literature, a composite image of Byron made up of selected physical attributes together with elements of poetic style, political affiliation, and public behaviour proliferates in the personae assumed by the next generation of writers, artists, and performers across the continent. The Polish 'national poet' Adam Mickiewicz, another restless European traveller, is depicted in an 1828 portrait painted by Walenty Wańkowicz in a distinctly Byronic pose: profiled with chin in hand, pensive, white collar open to expose his neck. In Hungary, the poetry of Sándor Petőfi was likened to Byron's, although the similarity is perhaps more evident in their shared reputation of dying as freedom fighters; in Romania, Mihai Eminescu appeared Byronic due to his unconventional lifestyle and early death. José de Espronceda channelled the influence of Byron into his role as the representative of 'subversive Romanticism' in Spain, and his unfinished mock-epic *El diablo mundo* (1841) is a clear successor to *Don Juan*. Musical and theatrical virtuosi modelled themselves on the Noble Lord, sometimes by imitating a Byronic pose and

[19] See Nicholas Mason, 'Building Brand Byron: Early-Nineteenth-Century Advertising and the Marketing of *Childe Harold's Pilgrimage*', *MLQ: Modern Language Quarterly*, 63/4 (2002), 411–40; Hadley J. Mozer, '"I WANT a Hero": Advertising for an Epic Hero in *Don Juan*', *Studies in Romanticism*, 44/2 (2005), 239–60; Mole, *Byron's Romantic Celebrity*; and McDayter, *Byromania*.

[20] *Complete Poetical Works*, ii. 122.

sometimes by emulating his publicity methods. Franz Liszt, an avowed admirer of Byron, extended the impact of his piano performances through newspaper reports and reproductions of his own visual image, so that 'it was literally the *face*, reproduced ad infinitum in journals, lithograph portraits, and other ephemera, that ... created and sustained Liszt's pan-European celebrity'.[21] The Italian *improvvisatore* Tommaso Sgricci, who became acquainted with Byron and the Shelleys in Italy in the early 1820s, drew on the Byronic profile and in turn influenced the public's perception of Byron as a poet whose poetic genius resembled that of *improvvisatori*. Portraits of Sgricci, such as the one done by François Gérard in 1824, show him in the familiar three-quarter pose with dark curly hair, high forehead, brooding expression, and exposed neck. As with Staël's Corinne, Sgricci's extempore oral performances in the presence of large audiences and in response to their demands epitomize the theatrical and ephemeral qualities of Romantic celebrity.

When celebrities such as Byron, Staël, Sgricci, and Liszt toured Europe, their personal appearances were intensively previewed and reviewed in print media. Stendhal's over-the-top account of Gioachino Rossini's fame at the beginning of his *Life of Rossini* is indicative of the new discourse of celebrity in its emphasis on the geographical range of the composer's renown and the way it consumes public attention:

> Napoleon is dead; but a new conqueror has already shown himself to the world; and from Moscow to Naples, from London to Vienna, from Paris to Calcutta, his name is constantly on every tongue. The fame of this hero knows no bounds save those of civilization itself ...[22]

As celebrities circulate internationally, so do their images—even if the two do not necessarily correspond. An English translation of Stendhal's *Vie de Rossini* appeared in time to create publicity for Rossini's visit to London in 1824 together with his wife, the Spanish soprano Isabella Colbran. Although the tour was a success, Rossini's short, fat presence contrasted with audience expectations that had been built up about his appearance and performance style, his manner while in company, and the speed and facility with which he wrote music; as a result, 'the jolly composite figure of Rossini the composer, made up in equal measure of operas and anecdotes, aural and visual components, [brought] out extreme passions and emotions in public'.[23] Stendhal, a French writer who served as foreign correspondent on Italian culture for English periodicals such as the *London Magazine* and the *New Monthly Magazine*, exemplifies the internationalism of the media networks that disseminated images, reports, and gossip about celebrities.

[21] Dana Gooley, 'From the Top: Liszt's Aristocratic Airs', in Berenson and Giloi, *Constructing Charisma*, 69.

[22] Stendhal, *Life of Rossini*, rev. edn, tr. Richard N. Coe (London: Calder & Boyers, 1970), 3.

[23] Benjamin Walton, 'Rara Avis or Fozy Turnip: Rossini as Celebrity in 1820s London', in Mole, *Romanticism and Celebrity Culture*, 86.

The circulation of visual and verbal images independently of the famous person's physical presence leads to paradoxes inherent in the condition of celebrity; these paradoxes, analysed in recent studies of celebrity culture, already reverberated in the various forms of identity crisis depicted in late Romantic literature. In a phenomenon that Joseph Roach terms 'public intimacy', fandom feeds off the drive to discover and to reveal intimate details of the celebrity's private subjectivity, yet fans have access to him or her only through external representations and reproductions.[24] Celebrity involves a 'branding' of identity that seems to run counter to the unique qualities that should make the individual worthy of renown. Given a geographically widespread mass audience, the celebrity is the object of an anonymous gaze, yet also the object of the individual admirer's desire for a personal relationship and/or self-identification with the celebrity. Even if the fan is never able to *become* the celebrity, the abstracted image offers features for fans to emulate: dress (Werther's blue jacket), accessories (Corinne's turban or Staël's rose-stem), facial expressions (Byron's brooding, averted gaze), habitual phrases or gestures. Imitability, finally, entails the commodification of the celebrity's image: as copies multiply, they lose their connection to an original and become more easily interchangeable with one another.

It is perhaps not surprising, therefore, that the era in which individuals come to be perceived as 'celebrities' (a noun that took hold in its modern sense by the mid-nineteenth century) is also one that raises questions about the autonomy of the self and the authenticity of other people's identities. By the 1820s and 1830s, the effects of celebrity culture intersect with a widespread concern over the durability, cohesiveness, and uniqueness of personal identity that manifests itself in fiction, philosophy, and periodical writing. One aspect of this concern is a new awareness of *anonymity*, a noun and concept that also came into use in the mid-nineteenth century.[25] Its late Romantic expressions include Keats's 'Poetical Character' that 'has no Identity'[26] and E. T. A. Hoffmann's exploration of the effects of print culture on authorial anonymity in late texts such as 'Des Vetters Eckfenster'.[27] Another compelling expression of identity crisis in late Romanticism, the motif of the alter-ego or *doppelgänger*, comes into conjunction with celebrity and anonymity when it is used by writers such as Byron, Scott, and Hoffmann. The protagonist of Byron's late, fragmentary drama *The Deformed Transformed* (1824), for example, is shadowed by his deformed double, and the confusion between two nearly identical

24 See Joseph Roach, 'Public Intimacy: The Prior History of "It"', in Mary Luckhurst and Jane Moody (eds), *Theatre and Celebrity in Britain, 1660–2000* (Basingstoke: Palgrave Macmillan, 2005), 15–30. My discussion is also informed by Chris Rojek, *Celebrity* (London: Reaktion Books, 2001).

25 See Anne Ferry, '*Anonymity*: The Literary History of a Word', *New Literary History*, 33/2 (2002), 193–214, and Jacques Khalip, *Anonymous Life: Romanticism and Dispossession* (Stanford, Calif.: Stanford University Press, 2009), 4. In his introductory chapter (1–24), Khalip explores the theoretical and philosophical ramifications of anonymity as a mode of being that challenges the autonomy and coherence of the Romantic self.

26 *Keats's Poetry and Prose*, ed. Jeffrey N. Cox (New York: Norton, 2009), 294–5.

27 See Carlos Spoerhase, 'Reading the Late-Romantic Lending Library: Authorship and the Anxiety of Anonymity in E. T. A. Hoffmann's Late Work', *Romanticism and Victorianism on the Net*, 57–8 (Feb.–May 2010) <http://www.erudit.org/revue/ravon/2010/v/n57-58/1006511ar.html?vue=integral>.

half-brothers, one virtuous and the other villainous, is a central plot device in Walter Scott's 1824 novel *St Ronan's Well*. Doubles often figure in Hoffmann's experiments with unreliable narrators and unstable selves: his first successful story 'Ritter Gluck' (1809) involves the mysterious double of a famous composer, while 'Der Sandmann' (1816) imagines the inability to distinguish between a living person and a mechanical facsimile. Hoffmann's most disturbing *doppelgänger* novel, *Die Elixiere des Teufels* (1815–16), broaches themes of mental illness, split personality, and demonic possession, leaving its protagonist as well as its readers unable to account for the paranormal relationship between the monk Medardus and his identical half-brother Count Viktorin, among many other uncanny resemblances, repetitions, and mistaken identities that haunt the story. Thanks to the English translation *The Devil's Elixir* that appeared in 1824, Hoffmann's novel likely influenced treatments of the *doppelgänger* theme that appear in English literature of the 1820s and 1830s, including *The Private Memoirs and Confessions of a Justified Sinner* (1824) by James Hogg—a writer who, like Hoffmann, was thoroughly implicated with the pseudonymous personae and falsifications of authorship that filled late Romantic literary magazines.

In his study of the *doppelgänger* theme, Christof Forderer demonstrates that in the early nineteenth century the motif of doubling is no longer used simply to generate comedies of mistaken identity based on external resemblance but, more radically, to question the boundaries of the self. The alternate identities that Hoffmann's protagonist Medardus attempts to take on so that he can engage in licentious and criminal adventures prove to be completely beyond his control; Medardus experiences 'a psychic incapacity for autonomy' as the external mix-up of identities becomes a profound 'internal confusion'.[28] In Hogg's *Private Memoirs*, too, the 'Justified Sinner' Robert Wringhim describes his 'strange distemper' as a condition whereby his self is displaced into two alter-egos that hover 'about three paces off me towards my left side'; 'this occasioned a confusion in all my words and ideas', he reports, 'and I found, that to be obliged to speak and answer in the character of another man, was a most awkward business in the long run'.[29] Hogg's complex novel, like Hoffmann's, speculates on what could happen to the self and society if personal identity can be replicated to the extent that no one, not even the first-person subject, can be sure where the responsibility for speech and action resides.

One may relate (as Forderer does) the psychologizing of the *doppelgänger* theme to the philosophical context of the early nineteenth century, particularly the challenge posed to the autonomous Cartesian 'I' by Kantian epistemology and an increasing scientific awareness of fragmented and unstable psyches. But writers' and readers' fascination with the *doppelgänger* in late Romanticism also coincides with the distortion of personal identity that was brought about by the circulation of mediated images of

[28] Christof Forderer, *Ich-Eklipsen: Doppelgänger in der Literatur seit 1800* (Stuttgart: Metzler, 1999), 54, 57.

[29] James Hogg, *The Private Memoirs and Confessions of a Justified Sinner*, ed. Ian Duncan (Oxford: Oxford University Press, 2010), 116.

celebrities. 'My very identity, my individuality, was cruelly become the game—the mere plaything, of chance', the monk Medardus laments;[30] 'I could not find myself again! … I am that which I seem, and do not seem to be that which I am; to myself an inexplicable riddle, I am at odds with my own self!'[31] The condition of Medardus, like that of Hogg's Justified Sinner, aligns with that of the Romantic celebrity whose private sense of self has become alienated from his public identity, replicated and commodified in appearances, anecdotes, and circulating material objects. 1824, the year in which Hoffmann's *Elixiere des Teufels* appeared in English along with Hogg's *Private Memoirs*, was also the year in which Byron's death sent shock waves across Europe and took the commodification of his identity to another level. In the context of an increasingly media-dependent celebrity culture, the theme of the uncanny and uncontrollable double functions as a critique of the way identity becomes displaced into external appearance and inauthentic performance.

The phenomena of celebrity, anonymity, and illegitimate doubles come together most tellingly and paradoxically in the case of Walter Scott and his European following. Scott provides one of the most unusual examples of Romantic celebrity—one that counters the model of Byron, yet is in its own way a logical consequence of developments in media and the marketplace in the early nineteenth century. While Scott and Byron together dominated European Romanticism for a generation, Scott's fame was never closely correlated with his physical appearance or presence. Instead, the historical novels that brought him international renown, beginning with *Waverley* in 1814 and continuing through the 1820s with triple-deckers that appeared at the rate of more than one a year, were published anonymously with the by-line 'The Author of Waverley'. Even if Walter Scott's authorship was widely guessed, his officially anonymous status, which also earned him the epithet 'The Great Unknown', set the stage for a different kind of authorial identity crisis.

Scott, his publishers, and his readers exemplify a phenomenon that might be termed *anonymous celebrity*. Not only did the public avidly buy, borrow, and read books to which the 'Author of Waverley' brand was attached, but it also participated in a guessing game about their authorship that was actively encouraged by articles in *The London Magazine*, *Blackwood's Edinburgh Magazine*, and other periodicals. 'The perplexity alluded to fans the interest of the novel; and the book itself scarcely excites so much curiosity as the question who is the author', wrote the editor of the *London Magazine*, using this as a reason to chastise the Author of Waverley (whom he guessed to be Scott) for 'raising popular attention at a cheaper rate than by cleverness alone'.[32] Scott himself perpetuates the mystification by making the 'Author of Waverley' into a fictional

[30] E. T. A. Hoffmann, *The Devil's Elixir* [tr. Robert Pierce Gillies] (Edinburgh: Blackwood; London: Cadell, 1824), 137.

[31] E. T. A. Hoffmann, *Die Elixiere des Teufels: Nachgelassene Papiere des Bruders Medardus eines Capuziners*, ed. Hartmut Steinecke and Gerhard Allroggen, in *Sämtliche Werke*, ii/2, ed. Wulf Segebrecht and Hartmut Steinecke (Frankfurt: Deutscher Klassiker Verlag, 1988), 73.

[32] 'Blackwood's Magazine' [by John Scott], *London Magazine*, 2 (Nov. 1820), 517.

character who enters the frame narratives of his novels and converses with their fictional editors and narrators. The 'Prefatory Letter' in *Peveril of the Peak* (1822)—which describes how 'The Author of Waverley entered, a bulky and tall man, in a travelling great-coat, which covered a suit of snuff-brown', to share a beefsteak and ale with the editor, Dr Dryasdust[33]—elides the boundary between the world within the text and the literary marketplace outside the text. Split into a real person and a fictional representation, the Author of Waverley inhabits both planes at once. Similarly, at the beginning of *The Bride of Lammermoor* Peter Pattieson, another of Scott's fictional editors, describes the pleasure he takes in his anonymous celebrity in terms that replicate Scott's own experience as the mystification surrounding the Scotch Novels proliferates through print and conversation:

> Then might I, perchance, hear the productions of the obscure Peter Pattieson praised by the judicious, and admired by the feeling, engrossing the young, and attracting even the old; while the critic traced their style and sentiments up to some name of literary celebrity, and the question when, and by whom, these tales were written, filled up the pause of conversation in a hundred circles and coteries.[34]

With these metafictional ploys, Scott multiplies his own authorial identity and makes the 'Author of Waverley' into a *doppelgänger* of the real-life author.

While Byron's celebrity lent itself to imitation by means of attitude and attire, Scott's anonymous celebrity focused attention on the features of the texts themselves as the identifying characteristics of the Great Unknown. The identity of the Author of Waverley, that is to say, resides in the formulaic patterns of his novels: their three-volume scope, their use of historical setting, local colour, Scottish dialect, adventure themes, recurrent character types and plot motifs. If Scott's official anonymity was in part a marketing ploy designed to keep up a buzz of conversation around his frequent publications, it also created an opportunity for imitators to publish forgeries by copying Scott's formula and appropriating his epithet. The absence of a legal name on Scott's published works, together with a full-fledged 'Author of Waverley' identity that circulated independently of Scott and that could be inhabited by other clever writers, made it impossible for Scott to lodge legal protest against counterfeit Waverley novels. While the fraudulent imitation of celebrated authors is rampant in the Romantic period,[35] Scott forgeries were thus produced with particular enthusiasm in various languages until the mid-nineteenth century.

[33] Walter Scott, *Peveril of the Peak*, ed. Alison Lumsden (Edinburgh: Edinburgh University Press, 2007), 5.

[34] Walter Scott, *The Bride of Lammermoor*, ed. J. H. Alexander (Edinburgh: Edinburgh University Press, 1995), 3.

[35] See Nick Groom, *The Forger's Shadow: How Forgery Changed the Course of Literature* (London: Picador, 2002); and Margaret Russett, *Fictions and Fakes: Forging Romantic Authenticity, 1760–1845* (Cambridge: Cambridge University Press, 2006).

Walladmor, a three-volume German novel that appeared in 1823–4, is an especially compelling example that brings together the various kinds of identity crisis discussed in this chapter: a celebrity author, doubling, mistaken identity, forgery, and international print-culture networks. The title-page, which reads:

Walladmor.
Frei nach dem Englischen
des
Walter Scott.
Von
W .... s.

presents *Walladmor* as a free translation of a Scott novel by an anonymous translator whose first and last initials repeat the initials of Walter Scott. 'W ... s' was outed within the year as 'Willibald Alexis', the pseudonymous alter-ego of Georg Wilhelm Heinrich Häring, a trained lawyer who had already published German translations of Scott's poetry and critical essays on Scott, and who now tried his hand at writing a complete novel—not just in the style of Scott but *as* Walter Scott.

Walladmor is a *doppelgänger* novel, of sorts: the protagonists are identical twins stolen and separated as babies, who are coincidentally brought together again as the only two survivors of a shipwreck off the coast of Wales, where, unbeknownst to any of them, they encounter their father Baron Walladmor. One of the twins is a German-raised writer and artist, Edmund Bertram; the other, James Nichols, is the leader of a band of smugglers. When Bertram is captured by officers in Wales and mistaken for the outlaw Nichols, Nichols comes to his rescue and explains the mistake. Later, though, Nichols is put on trial for his illegal activities, with Baron Walladmor acting as the magistrate who passes a sentence of death on his long-lost son. Thus, *Walladmor* is a novel *about* uncanny resemblance and mistaken identity, and a novel that *enacts* impersonation and fraud by being published as if by Walter Scott. Alexis takes the *mise en abîme* further with the mysterious character Thomas Malburne, who eventually reveals himself to be the 'Author of Waverley' and enters into competition with Bertram when they both claim to be writing *Walladmor*, the very novel in which they both appear. Malburne successfully asserts his claim to be the real author by presenting Bertram with written documents revealing that Bertram is in fact a character in the novel he thinks he's writing. The plot of *Walladmor* thus imitates Scott's trick of bringing the 'Author of Waverley' into his novels as a character, but goes further in the direction of Romantic irony in the style of Hoffmann, a writer whom Alexis knew and admired.[36]

[36] For further interpretation of the effects of Romantic irony in Alexis's *Walladmor*, see Frederick Burwick, 'How to Translate a Waverley Novel: Sir Walter Scott, Willibald Alexis, and Thomas De Quincey', *The Wordsworth Circle*, 25 (1994), 93–100; and Michael Niehaus, *Autoren unter sich: Walter Scott, Willibald Alexis, Wilhelm Hauff und andere in einer literarischen Affäre* (Heidelberg: Synchron, 2002), 14–16.

Becoming something of an international *cause célèbre*, the *Walladmor* forgery led nineteenth-century writers to reflect on authorial identity, especially on why Scott's writing seemed so easy to replicate. In 1835, German journalist Ludolf Wienbarg answered this question by describing Scott-ish writing as purely a matter of technique without connection to an essential self: 'apart from a talent for imitation, he doesn't demand or presuppose anything *of one's own*, no individual view of life, no dominant orientation, no formative spirit—only twitchy fingers and certain plastic techniques.'[37] Willibald Alexis himself wrote that Scott's heroes are 'lovable zeros' and their character 'only an extended negative.'[38] The protagonist of *Walladmor* is, among other things, a self-representation of Willibald-Alexis-imitating-Walter-Scott: as a young would-be writer, Bertram is travelling to Wales to gather local experience with which to write a novel in the style of Scott. Through this self-referential doubling of the action within the novel and reality outside the novel, *Walladmor* simultaneously enacts, explains, and critiques the vulnerability of Scott's fiction to imitation. *Within* the text *Walladmor*, Bertram and Malburne function as doubles of Willibald Alexis and Walter Scott respectively, thus generating Romantic irony. *As* the text *Walladmor*, Alexis's production of a novel under Scott's name, and the publisher Herbig's marketing of it, amount to fraud and forgery. In a further irony, on both these levels the forging of Scott's style reaffirms his celebrity status and the recognizability of his brand. In the absence of any features of Scott's personal or legal identity attached to the novels he produced, their identity comes to reside in a set of thematic features and rhetorical techniques.

German reviewers attributed *Walladmor* to a number of celebrated authors, among them Coleridge and Washington Irving.[39] The most dramatic response, however, came from Thomas De Quincey, who reviewed *Walladmor* anonymously for the *London Magazine* in October 1824.[40] His review exposed the novel as a forgery, but in the process also created demand for it in the English market; publishers Taylor & Hessey accordingly commissioned De Quincey to produce an English translation, which he did at top speed so that it appeared early in 1825. Iterations of the novel continued to multiply when a French translation of De Quincey's English version was commissioned and published within eight weeks.[41]

De Quincey's *Walladmor*—a free adaptation rather than a translation of the German original—removes much of the Hoffmanesque irony of Alexis's novel but retains its reflections on authorial identity and pushes them even further. Alexis had also imitated

[37] Quoted in Jochen Golz, 'Willibald Alexis: Walladmor', *Deutsche Erzählprosa der frühen Restaurationszeit: Studien zu ausgewählten Texten*, ed. Bernd Leistner (Tübingen: Niemeyer, 1995), 235–6.

[38] Golz, 'Willibald Alexis: Walladmor', 242.

[39] Golz, 'Willibald Alexis: Walladmor', 267.

[40] *The Works of Thomas De Quincey*, iv. *Articles and Translations from the* London Magazine; Walladmor *1824–1825*, ed. Frederick Burwick (London: Pickering & Chatto, 2000), 217–61. In an interesting turnabout, Alexis assumed that De Quincey's anonymous review was by Scott himself. Flattered by what he took to be the Great Unknown's attention, he quoted from the review in his preface to the 2nd (1825) edition of *Walladmor*, which he dedicated to the reviewer.

[41] Niehaus, *Autoren unter sich*, 30.

Scott's use of metafictional framing texts: in an ironic 'Dedication to Sir Walter Scott', he complained about the time-pressures under which a translator of Scott was compelled to work, and even asked Scott to confirm his authorship of *Walladmor* lest readers doubt its authenticity. De Quincey translates Alexis's 'German Translator's Dedication' but counters with his own 'Dedication to W***s, the German "Translator" of *Walladmor*', a direct and irreverent challenge to his German counterpart. Preceding these two pseudo-dedications, De Quincey adds an 'Advertisement to the Reader' that more seriously explains the circumstances of the *Walladmor* forgery by locating it within the distinctive circumstances of the German book market. The result is a combination of authentic and fictional paratexts that are filled with comic irony but also probe the relationship among print-culture, imitable celebrity, and personal identity in the late Romantic era.

De Quincey uses a hackneyed anecdote that first circulated among the Scriblerians in the early eighteenth century and that was invoked by philosophers and essayists during the 1820s and 1830s as they resurrected the problem of personal identity. 'Sir John Cutler', De Quincey writes in his mock dedication,

> had a pair of silk stockings: which stockings his housekeeper Dolly continually darned for the term of three years with worsted: at the end of which term the last faint gleam of silk had finally vanished, and Sir John's *silk* stockings were found in their old age absolutely to have degenerated into *worsted* stockings. Now upon this a question arose among the metaphysicians—whether Sir John's stockings retained (or, if not, at what precise period they lost) their 'personal identity.'[42]

While other writers applied the analogy of Cutler's stockings to the identity of persons and bodies, De Quincey applies it to the text of *Walladmor* that he has substantially altered in the process of 'translation'. Is it still the same pair of stockings, he asks rhetorically, or the same novel, once the material has entirely changed? He ends his mock dedication by goading Alexis to translate his new English *Walladmor* back into German, 'and darn me as I have darned you':

> Darn me into two portly volumes: and then I give you my word of honor that I will again translate you into English, and darn you in such grand style that, if Dolly and Professor Kant were both to rise from the dead, Dolly should grow jealous of me—and Kant confess himself more puzzled on the matter of personal identity by the final Walladmor than he had ever been by the Cutlerian stockings.[43]

Challenging Alexis to a potentially infinite back-and-forth series of translations that would, through perpetual change and addition of new material, make forgeries into originals, De Quincey raises valid questions about philosophical, legal, and

[42] Thomas De Quincey, *Walladmor: 'Freely Translated into German from the English of Sir Walter Scott': And Now Freely Translated from the German into English* (London: Taylor & Hessey, 1825), i, pp. xiii–xiv.

[43] De Quincey, *Walladmor*, i, p. xx.

literary definitions of identity. His reference to 'Professor Kant' alludes to his boast that he could, if he applied himself, forge a volume of 'Posthumous Works of Mr. Kant' that would fool German readers up to and including Schelling.[44] But the evocation of Kant by the philosophically astute De Quincey is also an allusion to the way Kantian philosophy itself undermined the concepts of cohesive selfhood and unique identity. Building on the Scottish Enlightenment philosophy of Hume and Smith, who described personal identity as constructed rather than essential, Kant displaced the self's sense of itself into what he called the 'transcendental unity of apperception': 'I am conscious of the self as identical in respect of the manifold of representations that are given to me in an intuition, because I call them one and all *my* representations, and so apprehend them as constituting *one* intuition'.[45] If the Kantian subject is aware of its own unity only as that which bestows unity on manifold intuitions, by De Quincey's time the subject faces additional threats from social and institutional forces that abstract, copy, and forge the identities of texts and persons.

In multiple ways, then, the evolution of celebrity culture and the contemporaneous but contrasting trend towards anonymity put pressure on the private, inward, authentic self that has itself become a Romantic stereotype. The expansion and spread of print media—from newspapers and literary magazines to engravings and political cartoons—has an impact not only on the way personal identity is represented, but also the way it is perceived and conceived. Pan-European internationalism is an equally important context for Romantic celebrity and Romantic anonymity. While the popularity of travel and tourism in the post-Napoleonic era adds the allure of exoticism to the attractions of celebrity, the layers of translation and mediation involved in bringing foreign personalities to a distant public intensify the paradoxical effects of celebrity culture. As audiences expand geographically, they become more anonymous; as periodicals adopt and adapt reports and anecdotes from one another, the information circulating about famous subjects becomes more packaged and clichéd. The speed with which texts and images move among different markets also facilitates the refashioning of identities in different and sometimes fraudulent forms, as can be seen in the widespread imitations of Byron or in the elaborate *Walladmor* forgery. All of this brings the issue of personal identity to the forefront in the literature and culture of the early nineteenth century, a moment when Romanticism's recently awakened concern with unique subjectivity confronts the spectre of externalized, commodified, reproducible selves.

[44] De Quincey, *Walladmor*, i, p. xix.

[45] Immanuel Kant, *Critique of Pure Reason*, tr. Norman Kemp Smith (New York: St Martin's Press, 1965), 155.

Further Reading

Berenson, Edward, and Giloi, Eva (eds), *Constructing Charisma: Celebrity, Fame, and Power in Nineteenth-Century Europe* (New York: Berghahn Books, 2010).
Brock, Claire, *The Feminization of Fame, 1750–1830* (Basingstoke: Palgrave Macmillan, 2006).
Eisner, Eric, *Nineteenth-Century Poetry and Literary Celebrity* (Basingstoke: Palgrave Macmillan, 2009).
Ferry, Anne, '*Anonymity*: The Literary History of a Word', *New Literary History*, 33/2 (2002), 193–214.
Forderer, Christof, *Ich-Eklipsen: Doppelgänger in der Literatur seit 1800* (Stuttgart: Metzler, 1999).
Groom, Nick, *The Forger's Shadow: How Forgery Changed the Course of Literature* (London: Picador, 2002).
Hawkins, Ann R., and Ives, Maura (eds), *Women Writers and the Artifacts of Celebrity in the Long Nineteenth Century* (Burlington, Vt.: Ashgate, 2012).
Khalip, Jacques, *Anonymous Life: Romanticism and Dispossession* (Stanford, Calif.: Stanford University Press, 2009).
Luckhurst, Mary, and Moody, Jane (eds), *Theatre and Celebrity in Britain, 1660–2000* (Basingstoke: Palgrave Macmillan, 2005).
McDayter, Ghislaine, *Byromania and the Birth of Celebrity Culture* (Albany, NY: State University of New York Press, 2009).
Mole, Tom, *Byron's Romantic Celebrity: Industrial Culture and the Hermeneutic of Intimacy* (Basingstoke: Palgrave Macmillan, 2007).
Mole, Tom (ed.), *Romanticism and Celebrity Culture, 1750–1850* (Cambridge: Cambridge University Press, 2009).
Rojek, Chris, *Celebrity* (London: Reaktion Books, 2001).
Russett, Margaret, *Fictions and Fakes: Forging Romantic Authenticity, 1760–1845* (Cambridge: Cambridge University Press, 2006).
Weber, Brenda R., *Women and Literary Celebrity in the Nineteenth Century: The Transatlantic Production of Fame and Gender* (Burlington, Vt.: Ashgate, 2012).

CHAPTER 40

THEORIES OF LANGUAGE

JAN FELLERER

Introduction

THINKING about language is a conspicuously fragmentary branch in the work of many writers typically associated with European Romanticism. Relevant reflections may be harnessed to philosophical ends which are not primarily concerned with language. They may be woven into essays on literary practice, or into the poetic oeuvre itself. However, they rarely amount to an attempt at developing an explicit and comprehensive exposition of the nature and workings of language. This is reflected in the critical literature, either compiling the various ideas of an author, such as Frances Ferguson on Wordsworth, or collating them into a more coherent, but ultimately conjectural system of thought, such as Kristin Pfefferkorn on Novalis. The latter principle has long been extended to particular groups of Romantic writers too, such as Eva Fiesel's synopsis of German Romantic philosophy of language. Her synchronic focus contrasts with diachronic studies in intellectual history which argue for or against lines of continuity, such as Hans Aarsleff's critical reassessments of the role of German Romantics in the history of linguistic thought, in particular that of Friedrich Schlegel. Aarsleff deliberately conjoins traditions in philosophical speculation with developments in data-based linguistic description. Other diachronic surveys place emphasis on either one or the other, such as Anna Morpurgo-Davies's nineteenth-century history of linguistics as a new scientific discipline. Important differences in scope aside, Aarsleff and Morpurgo-Davies move freely between different, predominantly West European traditions, and they both deal with ideas and methods. In contrast, concepts of language among Romantics east of the German and Italian states, and wider social implications beyond ideas and methods, often inhabit altogether separate provinces of scholarship, with exceptions such as Olivia Smith on the politics of theories of language.[1]

[1] Frances Ferguson, *Wordsworth: Language as Counter-Spirit* (New Haven and London: Yale University Press, 1977); Eva Fiesel, *Die Sprachphilosophie der Deutschen Romantik* (Tübingen: Mohr, 1927); Kristin Pfefferkorn, *Novalis: A Romantic's Theory of Language and Poetry* (New Haven: Yale

If nothing else, these few notes on a large research tradition call for some positioning. This survey takes a synchronic approach which identifies key notions about the nature and workings of language and their wider political implications in Europe from around 1789 to the first decades of the nineteenth century. The method will be compilatory, referencing some illustrative texts which give promising access to cross-cultural discourses of language in the Romantic period. There are at least three formations, aesthetic and philosophical, linguistic, and political. Even though treated under separate headings for ease of exposition, they are meant to meet in this introduction in response to more granular surveys. The political dimension in particular tends to be left to historians or to philologists who deal with that part of the continent where it first gained real prominence: East and East Central Europe. Thus, after the first two sections on aspects of philosophy and early linguistics, where the focus is on Germany with France and England, the third section on language and nation moves eastwards to the Slavonic-speaking lands, to finally return back, albeit very briefly, to the West in somewhat unorthodox fashion. The attempted breadth is due to the main purpose of this survey to provide introduction and guidance. It inevitably comes at the cost of depth and nuance.

Philosophy of Language

Three core notions reappear in Romantic writing about the nature of language in its broadest ramifications. Language is the condition of thought, a creative act, and synthesis between subject and object, human and world. The underlying concerns, such as the origin of language and its role in thought, were certainly not new to our period. Romantic responses to them were often not entirely novel either. Relevant discussions in intellectual history abound. Perhaps the most notorious question is whether the eighteenth-century Enlightenment concept of language as a representation or tool of thought is fundamentally different from the Romantic view of language as the organ of thought, or whether this juxtaposition was in fact a nineteenth-century fabrication for specific contemporary purposes as Aarsleff has argued with reference to England.[2] Another notorious debate is about Wilhelm von Humboldt and the extent to which his thought was premised on Kantian philosophy, or even on Condillac and the *Idéologues*, or whether it chiefly emerged 'within the conceptual field of a Romantic understanding of language'.[3] None of this can be pursued further here.

University Press, 1988); Hans Aarsleff, *From Locke to Saussure: Essays on the Study of Language and Intellectual History* (Minneapolis: Minnesota University Press, 1982) and *The Study of Language in England: 1780–1860* (Minneapolis and London: Minnesota University Press and Athlone Press, 1983); Anna Morpurgo-Davies, *Nineteenth-Century Linguistics*, History of Linguistics, 4 (London and New York: Longman, 1998); Olivia Smith, *The Politics of Language 1791–1918* (Oxford: Clarendon Press, 1984).

[2] Aarsleff, *Study of Language in England*, 73–114.

[3] Kurt Müller-Vollmer, 'Von der Poetik zur Linguistik: Wilhelm von Humboldt und der romantische Sprachbegriff', in Klaus Hammacher (ed.), *Universalismus und Wissenschaft im Werk und Wirken der Brüder Humboldt* (Frankfurt/Main: Klostermann, 1976), 225.

I shall, instead, turn to a synchronic outline of the three core notions of the nature of language in Romantic thought.

There was a basic intuition that the relation between humans and their language was even more intimate than had already been established during the eighteenth century. Language came to be viewed as the quintessence of humans and the condition of all thought. In other words, thought 'is essentially dependent on and bounded by language—i.e. one can only think if one has a language, and one can only think what one can express linguistically'. Language is a 'thought organ' in the *Berlin Lectures on Literature and Fine Art* (1801–4) of August Wilhelm Schlegel. Humboldt in particular gave prominence to the conditionality of all thought on language, for example, in his first lecture delivered before the Prussian Academy *On the Comparative Study of Language and its Relation to the Different Periods of Language Development* (1820): 'It is self-evident from the mutual interdependence of thought and word that languages are not so much the means to represent truth once established but rather means to discover truth previously unknown.'[4]

The simultaneity of language with thought raised a host of questions, for example, about the origin of language, which individual writers answered in different ways, in particular the idealist Humboldt as opposed to Romantics proper, such as A. W. Schlegel, F. Schlegel, and Novalis. These differences must play a pivotal role in any account that strives towards an accurate reconstruction of intellectual history. They do not, however, challenge the existence of a more general, distinctly Romantic sensibility to human conditionality on language, shared by such different writers as Humboldt, the Schlegel brothers, and Novalis. By now we have firmly arrived in Germany. Arguably, the prominence which thinking about language acquired here beyond poetics and aesthetics is due to specific historical circumstances, notably the fact that it may be seen as a specific response to Kantian philosophy, and that language was perceived as a special bond among otherwise disunited German states during the Napoleonic Wars. It should therefore be a good place to identify general notions in Romantic discourses on language which travelled easily between European countries.

In this context, the international reception of Mme de Staël's *De l'Allemagne* (1810/1813) is well known. It can be argued that her style too shows signs of a cross-cultural, Franco-German idiom. Müller-Vollmer draws attention to book 8, chapter 18, about German universities. Expounding the didactic advantages of languages over mathematics, de Staël employs French diction reminiscent of Condillac. Take for example the following analogy between grammar and arithmetic: 'La grammaire lie les idées l'une à l'autre, comme le calcul enchaîne les chiffres; la logique grammaticale est aussi precise que celle de l'algèbre.' However, she then continues by transcending these conceptual and

[4] Michael N. Forster, *German Philosophy of Language: From Schlegel to Hegel and Beyond* (Oxford: Oxford University Press, 2011), 25; *August Wilhelm Schlegel: Kritische Ausgabe der Vorlesungen*, ed. Ernst Behler, i (Paderborn: Schöningh, 1989), 399; T. Harden and D. Farrelly, *Wilhelm von Humboldt: Essays on Language* (Frankfurt/Main: Lang, 1997), 18; Wilhelm von Humboldt, *Werke in fünf Bänden*, iii. *Schriften zur Sprachphilosophie* (Stuttgart: Cotta, 1963), 19–20.

analytical qualities of grammar: 'et cependant elle s'applique à tout ce qu'il y a de vivant dans notre esprit ...; ainsi l'on trouve dans la métaphysique de la grammaire l'exactitude du raisonnement et l'indépendance de la pensée réunies ensemble'. Learning languages inspires 'l'activité spontanée de l'esprit, la seule qui développe vraiment la faculté de penser'.[5] Spontaneity, independence, and vivacity of the mind through language are notions congenial to A. W. Schlegel's emphasis on the creative and poetic qualities of language. In the introductory passage to the section on poetry of his Berlin Lectures he says: 'Yet the medium of poetry is exactly the same by which the human mind becomes conscious of itself, and by which it gains control over its thoughts to express and to combine them freely: language.'[6] The partial congeniality of de Staël and Schlegel does not reside in philosophical detail, but in some shared sensibility and notions. What is coming to the fore here is the idea that language is a creative act.[7]

Romantic thinking about language is essentially anchored in reflections on poetry. This does not only apply to A. W. Schlegel. Müller-Vollmer links Humboldt's work on language to his earlier interest in poetics, notably his aesthetic essay on Goethe's *Hermann and Dorothea* and its French version, which appeared, with readers like de Staël in mind, in Millin's *Magasin encyclopédique* (1799).[8] Language as *poïesis* allows mankind to grasp and to form the world. This understanding implies a strong focus on the individual and their creative union with the world whenever they speak. It raises the fundamental problem of accommodating the social nature of language. Even though the solutions offered differed widely, post-Kantian writers typically alluded to a transcendental, ideal essence of language, for example, an a priori linguistic faculty inherent to mankind (Humboldt), or an 'ever changing, ever incomplete poem of all mankind' (A. W. Schlegel). Bestowed upon mankind before all experience, it introduces the possibility of communion with one another because each individual linguistic act is an instantiation of language as such. It is not surprising that the notion was also exploited to locate the beginnings of language beyond the reach of empirical speculation.

A sense of dissatisfaction with Condillac's derivation of linguistic signs from sensations certainly did not start to appear only at the beginning of the nineteenth century. Herder had used it as a peg for his theory of language. More importantly here, in France itself it sparked the emergence of notions which then became prevalent in German Romantic writing on language, for example in the context of a debate of 1795 between Louis-Claude de Saint-Martin and the *Idéologue* Dominique Garat about language and thought. Among the *Idéologues* Condillac's thought retained its influence, which is undoubtedly true of Saint-Martin too. However, he also expressed views which take us into the realm of Romantic theorizing about language: mankind

[5] Mme de Staël, *De l'Allemagne* (Paris: Librairie de Firmin Didot Frères, 1871), 89.

[6] *August Wilhelm Schlegel*, ed. Behler, i. 387.

[7] Kurt Mueller-Vollmer, 'On Germany: Germaine de Staël and the Internationalization of Romanticism', in Richard Block and Peter Fenves (eds), *'The Spirit of Poetry': Essays on Jewish and German Literature and Thought in Honor of Géza von Molnár* (Evanston, Ill.: Northwestern University Press, 2000).

[8] Müller-Vollmer, 'Von der Poetik zur Linguistik', 224–40.

could not invent language, because 'il n'y a rien qui nie vienne pas par une semence et par un germe'; and this must apply in particular to 'le plus beau de nos privilèges, celui de la parole vive et active'. There are similar pronouncements in Saint-Martin's *Poème épico-magique*, most notably 'que nous ayons en nous un germe de désir qui soit comme le mobile radical de l'idée que nous nous proposons d'exprimer'. This is very close to Herder's 'inborn urge' to create language. It thus becomes clear that Saint-Martin argues for a far more intimate and creative relationship between man and language than his adversary could accept. This is very similar to ideas about language from late eighteenth- and early nineteenth-century Germany. Unlike in the case of de Staël, these similarities were not the result of direct contact. It is true that Saint-Martin was known to some in Germany as a theosophist. However, it does not seem that his views on language were noted here. Thus rather than with direct intertextualities, we are dealing with coeval views born out of a critical examination of eighteenth-century philosophy of language.[9]

Related to the two notions that language is the condition of all thought and each instantiation of it a creative act, there was a third concept whose cross-cultural European dimension can be illustrated too. This is the intuition that language in unique fashion unites entities which are otherwise separate. Again, the theme was developed in different ways. For instance, A. W. Schlegel in his Berlin Lectures was particularly interested in primordial language as a union of nature and mind. Through articulation, rhythm, and tone, it is steeped in the sounds of nature. Through signification and meaning it belongs to the creative mind: 'Thus in subjective as well as objective terms primordial language was already a creative representation, both natural and yet characterised by human freedom.'[10] The most immediate example of language mediating between nature and mind is sound symbolism. The debate whether the phonetic shape of linguistic signs is arbitrary, or in some way motivated semantically, was of course by no means new. A. W. Schlegel understood linguistic symbolism very broadly, to include all forms of tropes. It is, therefore, a poetic principle. Primordial language exploited it and must, therefore, be assigned some fundamental poeticity, a special bond with the world it captures in the human mind. It is one of the poet's tasks to re-enact this bond. Similar thinking is present in Coleridge's writing following his studies at Göttingen in 1799. His idea and ideal of 'linguistic harmony' also rests on the iconicity of words and offers a privileged bond between speakers of a language and their world. Thus, language as synthesis between subject and object is a notion which appeared simultaneously in different European contexts of the early nineteenth century. Whether due to direct borrowing or due to congenial thinking, it suggests that there was some common philosophical discourse. It differed considerably from writer to writer, but certain key notions, such as the three proposed here, were mutually intelligible.

[9] *Séances des Ecoles Normales, recueillies par des sténographes, et revues par les professeurs: Débats*, iii (Paris: L'Imprimerie du Cercle-Social, 1801), 12–13; *Le crocodile ou La guerre du bien et du mal: Poème épico-magique en 102 chants* (Paris: Librairie du Cercle-Social, 1799), 287–8.

[10] *August Wilhelm Schlegel*, ed. Behler, i. 400.

Study of Language

The Romantic period of late eighteenth- and early nineteenth-century Europe does not only feature specific sensibilities about the nature of language. It also displays a particular way of talking about the workings of individual languages. Three notions came to the fore over and over again in the work of different writers from different parts of the continent: historicism, organicism, and the diversity of languages. The currency they gained in the Romantic period is embedded in wider historical developments. Prospectively, they related to the rise of data-based comparative-historical linguistics, concisely surveyed by Morpurgo-Davies (see n. 1). Retrospectively, linguistic diversity, albeit from a different angle, played its role in general and rational grammar. Philology, in turn, had long established an interest in older stages of languages. Equally, though often forgotten in the historiography of linguistics, there were strong traditions in didactic, normative, and descriptive grammar of individual languages which continued into our period. As in the previous section, these diachronic topics in intellectual history will not be pursued further here. Instead, the focus will be on a brief synchronic survey of the three key Romantic notions about the workings of individual languages.[11]

An important aspect to the early Romantics' historicism was the intuition that beauty and perfection in languages can only be found in their ancient past. Sanskrit and Sanskrit literature became privileged bearers of hope to this end since Sir William Jones's discourse *On the Hindus* of 1786 and his translation of *Sacontalá, or the Fatal Ring* of 1789 in particular. More likely Jones was driven by the wish to grasp Indian history and law, and by fascination with the Orient, rather than being in search of linguistic and literary ideals in a distant past.[12] However, no other work at the time than his did more to feed early Romantic hopes. The very first sentence of F. Schlegel's *On the Language and the Wisdom of the Indians* (1808) refers to William Jones and the study of the primordial world: 'The anticipations of antiquaries in regard to Indian literature have become very highly raised, particularly since the prolific researches of Wilkins and Sir W. Jones disclosed so many important facts concerning the hitherto obscure history of the primitive world.'[13] Schlegel considered Sanskrit the ancestor language of Greek and Latin and the proto-type of all 'organic', inflectional languages. Superior to 'mechanical', uninflected languages, it is close to the primordial language and, thus, a privileged and most perfect expression of mankind's innate 'sense'. More specifically, Sanskrit allows for proper empirical investigation of linguistic genealogy by way of comparative grammar. It is

[11] See Helmut Gipper and Peter Schmitter, *Sprachwissenschaft und Sprachphilosophie im Zeitalter der Romantik* (Tübingen: Narr, 1985); Sylvain Auroux et al. (eds), *History of the Language Sciences: An International Handbook on the Evolution of the Study of Language from the Beginnings to the Present*, i–ii (Berlin and New York: de Gruyter, 2000–1).

[12] See Michael J. Franklin, *Orientalist Jones: Sir William Jones, Poet, Lawyer, and Linguist, 1746–1794* (Oxford: Oxford University Press, 2011).

[13] *Kritische Friedrich-Schlegel-Ausgabe*, ed. Ernst Behler, viii (Munich: Schöningh, 1995), 107.

true that this idea 'did not spring ready-made from the brain of Friedrich Schlegel'.[14] However, it is more important for our purposes to note that Schlegel idealized historicism and empiricism much more emphatically than other early comparative linguists.[15] To appreciate the difference, suffice it to recall the austere style of Franz Bopp, or that of Rasmus Rask's early and much more astute application of the historical-comparative method in his *Essay on the Origin of the Old Norse or Icelandic Tongue*. Jacob Grimm, to an extent, combined the technical approach with more distinctly Romantic sensibilities, such as a sense of the superiority of earlier stages of languages. Yet his linguistic genealogy was much less an Indo-European than a 'patriotic', Germanic one. It subsequently gained relevance for the Slavs, illustrating once more the quintessentially European character of Romantic thinking about language.[16]

A further key notion which spread fast since the late eighteenth century was the idea that language functions like an organism. Similar to the omnipresent, but many-sided nineteenth-century concept of historicism, organicism took on a number of meanings across disciplines and contexts. A notable distinction included the degree to which it was understood metaphorically. Whereas Franz Bopp appeared to have perceived language as an entirely autonomous organism, this understanding would have been problematic to early Romantic intuition. Even though for F. Schlegel one type of languages was 'organic' with inflecting 'roots' like 'living shoots', and for A. W. Schlegel they formed an 'organic whole', the linguistic organism was still reliant on creative individuals and communities shaping it.[17] Humboldt's writing also abounds in the metaphor, and for him too, the 'organism of language' is not autonomous, but, so he argues in *On the Comparative Study of Language* (1820), it 'originates in the common ability and need of mankind to speak. It is a product of the whole nation. The cultivation of any individual language depends on particular qualities and events and rests to a great extent on specific individuals rising to prominence in the course of time in the nation concerned'.[18] Differences in the early Romantic understanding of language as organism aside, it is interesting to note that organic vocabulary was not restricted to the German lands. Nor was it confined to writers who had direct contact with them, such as Coleridge and de Staël. Applied to language, it also appeared elsewhere, as we have seen with Saint-Martin. According to Aarsleff, even the radically different, sensualist purveyor of speculative etymologies J. Horne Tooke showed 'germs of a very romantic

[14] Aarsleff, *Study of Language in England*, 6.

[15] See Klaus Grotsch, 'Das Sanskrit und die Ursprache: Zur Rolle des Sanskrit in der Konstitutionsphase der historisch-vergleichenden Sprachenwissenschaft', in Joachim Gessinger and Wolfgang von Rahden (eds), *Theorien vom Ursprung der Sprache*, i (Berlin and New York: de Gruyter, 1989), 85–91.

[16] Rasmus Rask, *Investigation of the Origin of the Old Norse or Icelandic Language* [1818], Travaux du Cercle linguistique de Copenhague, 26 (Copenhagen: Linguistic Circle, 1993); Martin Lang, 'Ursprache und Sprachnation: Sprachursprungsmotive in der deutschen Sprachwissenschaft des 19. Jahrhunderts', in Gessinger and von Rahden, *Theorien vom Ursprung der Sprache*, i. 67.

[17] *Kritische Friedrich-Schlegel-Ausgabe*, ed. Behler, viii. 157, and *August Wilhelm Schlegel*, ed. Behler, i. 31.

[18] Harden and Farrelly, *Wilhelm von Humboldt: Essays*, 6; Humboldt, *Werke*, iii. 6–7.

... notion of language', linking language so closely to thought that it almost appeared to acquire 'a soul and a genius'.[19]

A third key interest among Romantics in the study of language built upon the fascination with linguistic diversity. Previous compilations, such as the *Mithridates* (1806–17) and Hervás's *Vocabolario poligloto* and *Saggio pratico* (1787), provided pertinent material. Interest in them continued into our period,[20] but their emphasis on ethnographical classification and their atomistic approach to linguistic data proved unsatisfactory to the empiricists of the early nineteenth century. Humboldt, for example, in his essay *On the Dual Form* of 1827 found himself 'only very rarely ... unable to go beyond general works such as Adelung's "Mithridates" or Balbi's "Atlas" '.[21] In fact, the study of the dual is a prime illustration of Humboldt's call for more thorough and data-based investigations into the anatomy of grammatical categories across the languages of the world.[22] It is interesting to note that the method of comparing the structural properties of languages was in fact akin to Cuvier's comparative anatomy.[23] In the best known passage from his treatise *On the Language and the Wisdom of the Indians* (1808), F. Schlegel explicitly juxtaposed 'comparative grammar' and 'comparative anatomy'.[24] To some extent, however, comparing languages served different purposes for Schlegel and Humboldt. The Romantic Schlegel was in search of genealogical relations, in particular among the Indo-European languages and their sublime 'organic' ancestor. Linguistic diversity beyond Indo-European was instrumental to showing its distinct superiority to 'mechanical' languages, such as Chinese or Amerind languages. Jacob Grimm equally sought linguistic perfection in the distant past, for example, by way of affording ablaut in strong verbs a status of particular beauty in *German Grammar*.[25] Vostokov, in the same vein and explicitly following Grimm, accepted that 'ancient languages, in their correctness and abundance of forms, surpass later languages which are derived from them', including 'ancient Slavonic in comparison with Russian and other [Slavonic, JF] dialects'.[26]

Humboldt did not seek linguistic perfection in ancient or primordial times. He thought of linguistic diversity as forward-looking. It manifests the continued progression of 'the force of the human mind', as he explained in the opening passages of the

[19] Aarsleff, *Study of Language in England*, 54.

[20] See Rask, *Investigation*, 36.

[21] Harden and Farrelly, *Wilhelm von Humboldt: Essays*, 123; Humboldt, *Werke*, iii. 127.

[22] See Frans Plank, 'On Humboldt on the Dual', in R. Corrigan, F. Eckman, and M. Noonan (eds), *Linguistic Categorization* (Amsterdam and Philadelphia: John Benjamins, 1989), 293–333.

[23] See Morpurgo-Davies, *Nineteenth-Century Linguistics*, 94; Ullrich Wyss, *Die wilde Philologie: Jacob Grimm und der Historismus* (Munich: Beck, 1979), 132; Sebastiano Timpanaro, 'Friedrich Schiller and the Beginnings of Indo-European Linguistics in Germany', in E. F. K. Koerner (ed.), *Friedrich Schlegel: Ueber die Sprache und Weisheit der Inder*, Amsterdam Studies in the Theory and History of Linguistic Science, 1 (Amsterdam: John Benjamins, 1977), pp. xxxv–xxxvi.

[24] *Kritische Friedrich-Schlegel-Ausgabe*, ed. Behler, viii. 137.

[25] Jakob Grimm, *Deutsche Grammatik*, i, 2nd edn (Göttingen: Dieterichsche Buchhandlung, 1822), 836; see Wyss, *Die wilde Philologie*, 145.

[26] Alexander Vostokov, 'Rassuždenie o slavjanskom jazykě' [1820], in I. Sreznevskij (ed.), *Filologičeskija nabludenija A. Ch. Vostokova* (St Petersburg: Akademija nauk, 1865), 5.

Kawi Introduction.[27] In distinctly enlightened fashion he sought to study a wide range of different languages in order to reveal general linguistic principles, types, and universals. Yet there was also another side to his pursuit of linguistic diversity which was deeply compatible with the Romantics' emphasis on singularity and historicism. Humboldt believed that each language shaped its speakers' view of the world in a specific way. The idea of linguistic relativity was by no means new. However, more important than the history of the idea is the significance it acquired in due course. In fact, a specific application of it became one of Romanticism's most lasting legacies. This is the view that languages characterize the communities of people who speak them. The idea that there is a close link between language, worldview, and collective, national identity featured frequently in early nineteenth-century European writing. Examples range from Wordsworth's Preface to *Lyrical Ballads* (1800) in the West, via an essay on a suitable European lingua franca by the Bavarian Johann Schmeller (1815), to *Lectures about Russian Literature and Language* by the poet and Decembrist V. K. Kjuchel'beker in the East.[28] In some disciplines, such as rapidly advancing general linguistics and comparative philology, the identification of language and national spirit soon came to be overridden by different scientific agendas. Conversely, in politics its significance grew fast, yielding a privileged link between language and nation that was both progressive and reactionary at the same time.

Language and Nation

Romantic discourses about language were by no means detached from context. There was considerable overlap with other disciplines and periods as the key notions themselves express explicitly. For example, biology and poetics provided vocabulary that is present in metaphors, such as 'language as organism' and 'language as a perpetual human poem'. The one notion that has gained particular and lasting ubiquity across discourses is the assumption of a privileged link between language, worldview, and collective identity. The intricacies of how this link could be modelled, often informed by Herder's treatment of the origin of language, are an important topic in intellectual history. However, once the idea transcended the narrower confines of early nineteenth-century philosophy of language and linguistics and entered the realms of writing and speaking about other subjects, its notional subtleties soon faded into insignificance. What remained was a persuasively straightforward and adaptable stipulation. It goes as follows. Language

27 Humboldt [1836], *Werke*, iii. 368–756, tr. in Michael Losonsky (ed.), *Humboldt: On Language. On the Diversity of Human Language Construction and its Influence on the Mental Development of the Human Species*, Cambridge Texts in the History of Philosophy (Cambridge: Cambridge University Press, 1999).

28 V. K. Kjuchel'beker, 'Lekcija o russkoj literature i o russkom jazyke' [1821], in *Literaturnoe nasledstvo*, 59: *Dekabristy—literatory*, i (Moscow: Akademija nauk, 1954), 366–74. Johann Schmeller, *Soll es eine allgemeine europäische Verhandlungssprache geben?* (Kempten: Dannheimer, 1815).

forges communities to which speakers inalienably belong, typically by birth, and from which they can derive political claims. In many parts of Europe the political dimension soon developed into the more specific demand that linguistically defined communities should have their own state or at least autonomous region, and that this state or region should form a linguistically congruent and homogeneous unit. This is what we have still today. Yet the use of language as a political instrument by European nationalist movements did not spring from Romanticism ready-made. Belonging through language was an assertion regarded as peculiar in our period because it had little to do with then established forms of language planning, notably the prescription of linguistic norms and the imposition of a state language or a lingua franca. Its transfer into other domains produced consistencies, but also contradictions, with the ideological ramifications of these domains, most importantly politics, law, and education.

The discursive leap from language to, eventually, nation posed problems specific to each of Europe's states and provinces. Yet the remarkable ease with which the problems of one place were immediately recognizable to writers of another suggests a shared, pan-European Romantic fashion of politicizing language. One may try and distinguish historically attested types of rendering language instrumental to political ends; for instance, as a means towards unification in Italy and Germany, or to create citizenry in France and Britain, or as a tool of emancipation in South-East and East-Central Europe. Pioneering empirical work in the history of nationalism, such as that of Miroslav Hroch, has in fact shown the usefulness of comparative perspectives. The same author, however, has argued too that simple typological juxtapositions, such as Hans Kohn's popular distinction between German ethno-linguistic nationalism and French civic nationalism (see Meinecke's distinction between *Kulturnation* and *Staatsnation*), are too coarse to adequately capture the complexities of nineteenth-century history.[29] At a more fundamental level, it can be argued that types of nationalism are actually types of theory of nationalism, for example, Ernest Gellner's liberal theory, Eric Hobsbawm's Marxist approach, or Anthony Smith's conservative model. Methodological prudence would therefore suggest that comparison starts from individual cases which were demonstrably interconnected.[30]

Ample illustration can be found in German and Slav Romanticism. There was a close network of textual cross-references from these lands which expounded or implied the principle that people's societal belonging is determined by language and culture. Take for example Jacob Grimm, who linked this principle to the specific agenda of German unification following the Napoleonic Wars. In his foreword to *German Grammar* in

[29] Miroslav Hroch, *Die Vorkämpfer der nationalen Bewegung bei den kleinen Völkern Europas: Eine vergleichende Analyse zur gesellschaftlichen Schichtung der patriotischen Gruppen* (Prague: Univerzita Karlova, 1968); Hans Kohn, *The Idea of Nationalism: A Study of its Origins and Background* (New York: Macmillan, 1944); Friedrich Meinecke, *Weltbürgertum und Nationalstaat: Studien zur Genese des deutschen Nationalstaates* (Munich and Berlin: Oldenbourg, 1908).

[30] Ernest Gellner, *Nations and Nationalism* (Malden, Mass.: Blackwell 2006); E. J. Hobsbawm, *Nations and Nationalism since 1780: Programme, Myth, Reality* (Cambridge: Cambridge University Press, 1992); Anthony D. Smith, *Theories of Nationalism* (London: Duckworth, 1983).

1822, Grimm states that 'we Germans feel the bond of our origin and community only due to the written language ... It seems to me that the development of a people also requires extended external borders for its language, if this language, irrespective of its inner progress, is not to wither away.'[31] In the first edition of 1819 this had been preceded by some scathing remarks about the rise of German as a school subject across all types of education: 'Six hundred years ago every common peasant knew and used the perfection and subtleties of the German language, of which the best language teachers today cannot even dream.'[32] Interestingly, Grimm took back much of this criticism in the foreword to the 2nd edition. There clearly was a tension between promoting standard German as a supra-regional, national standard language on the one hand, and condemning the teaching of norms as spoiling real men's usage on the other. Romantic celebration of the vernacular and of language as a creative act did not combine readily with the equally Romantic yearning for a communal mother tongue which, in its most sublime, typically literary manifestations, would truly express the spirit of the people. The tension between unmitigated authenticity of expression and conscious linguistic planning resurfaced in various discursive formations. Another example comes from conflicting stances on foreign influences. In the aftermath of the formation of the Confederation of the Rhine and Prussia's defeat at Jena and Auerstädt in 1806, Johann G. Fichte wrote his *Addresses to the German Nation* (1808). In the fourth address on the 'principal difference between the Germans and other peoples of Teutonic descent' he warned against the influx of foreign words as they distort authenticity of thought among the people.[33] A. W. Schlegel, on the other hand, in a spirit of early Romantic cosmopolitanism, had dismissed overzealous purism in his *Lectures on Philosophical Art Education* (1798–99).[34] Grimm[35] himself was critical too, but on account of the fact that he considered it an unnecessary interference into the spirit of the vernacular and its natural tendency to sift out undomesticated loanwords. The purist vein should subsequently prevail, but this takes us into the post-Romantic times of by then fully developed linguistic nationalism.[36]

Earlier Romanticism's outlook was decisively cosmopolitan and rooted in thorough study of classical languages and literature. A. W. Schlegel, for instance, considered language a 'poem of all mankind'. Jacob Grimm transcended the local for entirely different reasons. If, as he believed, the native tongue, its history, and textual traditions are a privileged expression of the life and spirit of man, then this will naturally apply to any vernacular language. Grimm, therefore, not only studied the history of Germanic languages and, together with his brother, collected and edited German songs, legends,

[31] Grimm, *Deutsche Grammatik*, 2nd edn (1822), p. xiii.

[32] Grimm, *Deutsche Grammatik* (1819), p. x.

[33] J. G. Fichte, *Addresses to the German Nation*, ed. Gregory Moore, Cambridge Texts in the History of Political Thought (Cambridge: Cambridge University Press, 2008), 47–59; Johann Gottlieb Fichte, *Reden an die deutsche Nation*, Philosophische Bibliothek, 588 (Hamburg: Meiner, 2008), 60–76.

[34] See *August Wilhelm Schlegel*, ed. Behler, i. 32–3.

[35] Grimm, *Deutsche Grammatik* (1819), pp. xiii–xiv.

[36] See August Fuchs, *Zur Geschichte und Beurtheilung der Fremdwörter im Deutschen* (Dessau: Aue, 1842).

and tales. He also translated the 2nd edition of Vuk Karadžić's Serbian grammar in 1824, and he reviewed with enthusiasm Karadžić's collections of (Slavo-)Serbian folk-songs of 1814–1815 and of 1823, including some translations from the original into German.[37] Grimm's interest in folk literature was partly inspired by Herder who himself had included four South Slavonic songs and legends in his anonymously published *Folk Songs* in two volumes of 1778–9. A good decade later Herder renewed the appeal to collect the Slavs' songs and legends in his chapter on 'Slavonic people' in *Ideas for the Philosophy of History of Humanity* (1784–91). The book was widely known and influential among Slav intellectuals of the first half of the nineteenth century. Herder's and Grimm's Romantic interest in the Slavs was informed by the ultimately cosmopolitan tenet that every nation's folk literature and vernacular tongue should be revered as an equally precious compartment of mankind's general wisdom and character. It clashed with one of Romanticism's darker sides where some languages were in fact considered more equal than others, as we saw in the previous section in relation to superior, 'organic' languages. The resolution of this clash in favour of modern popular nationalism and chauvinism takes us well beyond the first decades of the nineteenth century. At that point, the novel idea that native tongue and communal belonging should share some privileged link still had too many other unresolved political, legal, and cultural implications. In Germany, free rein to the genius of the vernacular did not square easily with calls for language planning in the form of purism and supra-regional standardization.

The same Romantic promotion of folk literature and vernacular tongues created contradictions of its own kind in the Slavonic-speaking countries. Returning to Vuk Karadžić, it is characterstic that the Serbian-Orthodox clergy met his publications with hostility. Church representatives rejected his vernacular-based linguistic usage. Instead, they championed Slaveno-Serbian, an artificial, but prestigious written blend of Church Slavonic, Serbian, and Russian elements. The Vuk supporter Jernej B. Kopitar had made Grimm aware of this antagonism in their early correspondence of the 1820s.[38] Grimm took sides uncompromisingly. In his 1824 foreword to the German translation of Vuk's grammar, he defended the 'beautiful Serbian mother tongue' against the clergy's 'patchy style' that resembles an 'unstable, immature stammer'.[39] Meanwhile the metropolis of the Serbian Orthodox Church in the Austrian Empire brought Karadžić to the attention of the Viennese police authorities for his alleged Russian sympathies which could be construed as anti-Austrian. Vuk Karadžić was in fact known to Russian scholars following a visit to St. Petersburg in 1819. However, as with other early Slav Romantics, his linguistic programme did as yet not have any explicit political agenda. We are still firmly in Miroslav Hroch's first phase of national movements where the emphasis is on creating

[37] Jacob Grimm, *Wuk's Stephanowitsch kleine Serbische Grammatik* (Leipzig and Berlin: G. Reimer, 1824); and *Kleinere Schriften*, iv. *Recensionen und vermischte Aufsätze* (Berlin: Dümmler, 1869), 197–205, 427–55.

[38] See Max Vasmer, *B. Kopitars Briefwechsel mit Jakob Grimm*, Slavistische Forschungen, 55 (Cologne and Vienna: Böhlau, 1987), pp. xix–xx.

[39] Jacob Grimm, *Wuk's Stephanowitsch kleine Serbische Grammatik* (Leipzig and Berlin: G. Reimer, 1824), pp. xiv–xvii.

awareness of projected national characteristics, such as the mother tongue. This clearly had political potential though. The Serbian Orthodox clergy and the Viennese police correctly sensed it, and it is also in evidence from an interesting detail of the Vuk reception in Russia.

Here, as elsewhere in the Slavia orthodoxa, including Serbia, the prestigious literary tradition in Church Slavonic weighed heavily on the implemention of a more vernacular-based written standard. However, the ideological connotations were different. Serbia's Orthodox clergy opposed Vuk's Serbian as low in prestige and culturally blasphemous. Russia's supporters of Church Slavonic, on the other hand, contested the new Russian written language, which had been emerging since the 1730s, on partly similar, partly different grounds. For instance, the conservative writer, politican, and admiral A. S. Šiškov (1754–1841) considered Church Slavonic the autochthonous, true written idiom of the Russian people. He thought of it as the prestigious literary variant of the spoken language and, thus, essentially synonymous with Russian. He therefore dismissed the new Russian written language, emerging from the literary practice of a writer such as N. M. Karamzin (1766–1826), as a worthless aberration introduced by unpatriotic cosmopolitans and Gallomaniacs. Even though Karamzinian usage did in fact contain many French calques and borrowings, it was actually much closer to the vernacular than Šiškov's Slavjano-Russian. Ironically, it was thus a more truthful picture of Russia's linguistic and national identity, which Šiškov had made one of his prime concerns. In their controversy with Karamzin and the linguistic reformers, archaizers such as Šiškov targeted borrowings in particular. In a purist vein reminiscent of German Romantics, they rejected direct loans and favoured neologisms based on Church Slavonic and Old Russian which they considered the manifestations of Russia's true linguistic and national identity. The same peculiar contradiction emerges from the writings of the archaizer V. K. Kjuchel'beker. In good Romantic fashion he declared the 'spoken language the people's soul', while his own poems drew heavily on archaic and Church Slavonic elements, not least to distinguish them from the light, elegiac, Gallic verse of his rival V. A. Žukovskij. Another noteworthy aspect of the archaizers' linguistic programme concerns etymology. In a work such as *Essay on Rhetoric* (1811) Šiškov advanced wild etymologies in order to prove the supreme antiquity and superiority of Slavjano-Russian over Western languages. They are somewhat reminiscent of Horne Tooke's pseudo-rational etymological *Diversions of Purley* (1798–1805). This may be linked to the possibility that Šiškov himself had some exposure to elements of rational grammar, which at the time experienced a short period of particular popularity in Russia's secondary schools and universities before more vernacular-based textbook grammar gained ground.[40] In short, Šiškov's application of the idea that there is an exclusive link between language and nation produced remarkable mergers of contradictory ideas: Romantic in outlook, his style of argument appears to be that of a man of the

[40] See Johann Biedermann, *Grammatikographie und grammatische Deskription in Rußland in der 2. Hälfte des 18. und zu Anfang des 19. Jahrhunderts*, Slawische Sprachen und Literaturen, 17 (Frankfurt/Main and Bern: Lang, 1981).

eighteenth century. Also an advocate of the idea that 'language is the soul of the nation', as professed for instance in *Essay on Love of the Fatherland* (1812), he sought the soul in prestigious, yet archaic Russian Church Slavonic. Finally, and even more remarkably, Šiškov, in his capacity as president of the Russian Academy since 1813, became a supporter of Vuk Karadžić and his efforts to promote vernacular Serbian. Vasmer surmises that Šiškov hoped that support for Slavonic vernaculars—other than Russian—would strengthen anti-French, slavophile sentiment among Russia's intellectuals.[41]

The peculiar way in which Šiškov and other archaizers modelled the idea of a privileged link between language and nation was prompted by three political and cultural factors in particular: the Napoleonic Wars, and deep-rooted francophilia among the domestic elite as opposed to Russia's prestigious literary legacies in Church Slavonic. The first two of these factors were important in Germany too, but here they combined with internal political fragmentation which cultural unification sought to overcome. In an empire such as Russia, on the other hand, identifying nation and statehood with one language and culture was more difficult. Ultimately, it proved to be the successful model here too, but this takes us much further into the nineteenth century and beyond. Remaining in the Romantic period proper, let us, after these notes on Serbia, Germany, and Russia, turn to the Czech lands. Here too the idea was the same, that all declared Czech native speakers should form one community to which they inalienably belong, and from which they could derive political claims. And here too, as elsewhere, it met with specific local circumstances which produced consistencies, as well as contradictions, with discourses pertaining to other domains, notably politics, law, and culture. First and foremost, language came to play an even more important role in the Czech lands than in other countries, as the rich research tradition on the Czech national revival has established and assessed from various methodological angles.[42] The transition from writing about linguistic matters to linking them with wider political and legal issues has long been associated with a generational change.[43] At first, learned men of the late Enlightenment turned scholarly attention to the Czech language and its history. Their interests met with new local patriotism among Bohemian noblemen who were discontented with Vienna's centralist strive to curb the historical rights of the provinces' estates. Josef Dobrovský, one of the founding fathers of modern Slavonic philology who recodified written Czech in his *Comprehensive Grammar of the Czech Language* of 1809, was given patronage by the Nostic and Kinský aristocratic families. However, it would have been alien to him to talk more widely about the state and status of the Czech language in its political, legal, and social context. These are the areas into which a subsequent generation of Czech writers and philologists started venturing.

[41] Vasmer, *B. Kopitars Briefwechsel mit Jakob Grimm*, pp. xxiii–xxiv.

[42] See Vladimir Macura's novel semiotic approach in *Znamení zrodu: České obrození jako kulturní typ* (Prague: Československý spisovatel, 1983).

[43] See Robert Auty, 'Language and Nationality in East-Central Europe 1750–1950', *Oxford Slavonic Papers*, NS 12 (1979), 52–83.

One of its most prominent exponents, the lexicographer Josef Jungmann, made a first explicit pronouncement in his *Conversations about the Czech Language* as early as in 1806. In the second *Conversation* the bohemophile Slavomil, essentially Jungmann's voice, refutes the view of his adversary, the cosmopolitan germanophile Protiva, that there is no necessary link between language and nationality: For if one cannot 'imagine a homeland without a nation or a nation without its own language, I would again have to conclude that no one other than he who loves the language of his nation can boast of true love of his country.'[44] Further details of this proposition, such that language is the repository of the experiences, wisdom, and character of the people, show the influence of Herder, whose chapter on the Slavs Jungmann would publish in translation in 1813. Slavomil reserves particular disdain for germanized Czechs who, like Protiva too, do not see any problems in relinquishing Czech in favour of the more widely used German. So far the Romantic proposition of communion with others who share the same mother tongue proved readily interpretable as an alternative model to ever more pronounced German-Czech diglossia. Yet the dispute between Slavomil and Protiva revealed more problematic issues too. Jungmann, and even the third generation of the Czech national revival since the 1830s such as the historian František Palacký and the journalist Karel Havlíček Borovský, were still far from any autonomist, let alone secessionist aspirations.[45] Thus, even though Jungmann's Slavomil rightly understands German dominance in public life as a strong disadvantage to native Czech speakers, he derives from that only very modest claims for improved linguistic rights in some areas of school education and local administration. Disputes about these rights came to be at the centre of Habsburg politics later in the nineteenth century. Were they fundamental civil rights, or were they in fact orthogonal to inherently anational, civil rights? Did they form an individual or collective entitlement? Should they be derived from positive or natural law? These were some of the legal and constitutional issues which the Czech national movement employed in order to call for ever increasing civil, political, and national guarantees, while it shied away from demanding outright independence until the end of the century.

Jungmann himself was in fact a man of the Biedermeier to whom hazardous political activism was a frightful prospect. What is more, his early formative years still fell firmly into the late Enlightenment. This explains in part why, later in life, he considered providing a textbook in Czech rhetoric and poetics a crucial contribution towards general national revival. Dobrovský was of the opposite opinion and labelled Jungmann's *Literature or a Collection of Examples with a Short Treatise on Style* (1820) 'the Bohemian monster'.[46] He generally disliked Jungmann's patriotic 'zeal', as Protiva calls it in the

44 Balázs Trencsényi and Michal Kopeček (eds), *Discourses of Collective Identity in Central and Southeast Europe (1770–1945): Texts and Commentaries*, ii. *National Romanticism: The Formation of National Movements* (Budapest and New York: CEU Press, 2007), 107; Felix Vodička (ed.), *Boj o obrození národa: Výbor z díla Josefa Jungmanna* (Prague: Kosek, 1948), 31–50.

45 See Jiří Štaif, *Obezřetná elita: Česká společnost mezi tradicí a revolucí 1830–1851* (Prague: Dokořán, 2005).

46 Robert Sak, *Josef Jungmann: Život obrozence* (Prague: Vyšehrad, 2007), 109.

second *Conversation*. More specifically, Dobrovský rejected Jungmann's linguistic outlook which gave precedence to contemporary usage. His own ideal was classical written Czech of the Rudolfinian era as enshrined in the Kralice Bible (1579–93). Jungmann, in contrast, used vernacular elements to fill lexical gaps. For example, in *Literature* there were, ultimately unsuccessful, neologisms, such as *přenoška* (now the internationalism *metafora*), *přídoba* (now *parallelismus*), *rovnozvuk* (now *rým*), *přípěv* (now *refrén*).[47] Purism, and the principle that one should write as one speaks, were central to Jungmann's linguistic doctrine. However, he was also still deeply influenced by Dobrovský's generation and their notion of linguistic prestige which could not be derived from the common man's tongue. Slavomil, in his *Conversation* with Protiva, concedes that the status of Czech will be predicated on its literary heritage combined with future lexical development. To that end the Czechs turned to other Slavonic languages.

The initial idea was that there should be cultural exchange and unity among the Slavs. Jungmann did in fact become a moderate supporter of early pan-Slavism. Its beginnings, even though inspired by pan-Germanism, were entirely unpolitical. One of its main attractions for Jungmann must have been the fact that it made accessible a wider range of prestigious literary and linguistic legacies than those of the Czech lands alone. Most notably, it also included Russia where the eighteenth century had seen the emergence of a new literary canon. Thus, pan-Slavism offered the prospect of a solution to an important problem faced by those who wrote in smaller Slavonic languages. To develop and promote their chosen tongue as national language, it was necessary to be able to refer to a literary canon that commanded respect. There was plenty to rely on in Czech literary history from the Middle Ages to the baroque, but the earlier medieval period and the eighteenth century were perceived as gaps. To fill them there were notorious falsifications, such as the alleged medieval *Manuscripts of Dvůr Králové and Zelená Hora*. Pan-Slavism, on the other hand, offered a proper and credible source of additional linguistic and literary heritage. Its actual programme was formulated in the 1820s and 1830s by the poet Ján Kollár and the scholar Pavol Josef Šafárik, both of Slovak origin.[48] It remained expressly unpolitical and cultural in outlook, underpinned by rapid advances in the comparative study of language.

It was a decade later that pan-Slavism started to become, as Ernest Renan put it according to Mousset, 'la philologie comparée transportée sur le terrain de la politique'.[49] In the political arena, pan-Slavism helped to give a more universalist form to types of patriotism, such as Russian slavophilia and Austroslavism. However, its inherent contradictions became ever more evident too. The November Uprising and the Russo-Polish War of 1830–1 had cast unmistakable doubt over Slav unity. Men of the third generation of

[47] Bohuslav Havránek, *Vývoj českého spisovného jazyka* (Prague: Státní pedagogické nakladatelství, 1979), 93.

[48] See Robert Auty, 'Jan Kollár, 1793–1852', *Slavonic and East European Review*, 31 (1952), 74–91; Hans Kohn, 'Romanticism and Realism among Czechs and Slovaks', *Review of Politics*, 14/1 (1952), 25–46; Robert B. Pynsent, *Questions of Identity: Czech and Slovak Ideas of Nationality and Personality* (Budapest: CEU, 1994), 43–99.

[49] Albert Mousset, *Le Monde Slave* (Paris: Société d'éditions françaises et internationales, 1946), 31.

the Czech national revival, such as Karel Havlíček Borovský (1821–56), were aware not only of Austria's reactionary political system, but also of Russian imperialism. What is more, by their time the quest for literary self-esteem was perceived to be proceeding successfully. An example in point is the eventual recognition of Mácha's *May* (1836) as the epic poem of Czech Romanticism. As a result, pan-Slavism became a less pressing proposition. Instead, the Czech liberals of the generation of 1848 like František Palacký and Havlíček Borovský had to face a different problem, as expressed, for example, in *Our Politics*, a series of editorials of April 1848 by Borovský: how should civic rights combine with claims for national and linguistic rights if the former are to be enjoyed by all inhabitants of Bohemia and Moravia, whereas the latter would protect Czech speakers in particular? It was essentially a problem of combining ethno-linguistic particularism with liberal universalism.[50] This, however, takes us well beyond the Romantic period proper.

In Poland on the other hand, where pan-Slavism had limited resonance, the tension between citizenry and ethno-linguistic communion as the *raison d'être* of the state emerged much earlier due to historical circumstances. The traditional constitutional set-up was such that the nobility embodied state and nation, irrespective of language and cultural practices. In fact, the gentry of the Polish-Lithuanian Commonwealth was multilingual, with Ukrainian used alongside Polish in particular. Thus Poland's understanding of its own statehood was essentially agnostic about language. Take for example the *Charta Leopoldina*. This was a constitutional project which a small group of Galician noblemen around Józef Maksymilian Ossoliński presented to the Austrian Emperor in 1790, demanding political autonomy in defiance of Austria's annexation of the province in 1772. The *Charta*, written in French, contained linguistic proposals too. For instance, it included the demand that Poland's traditional language of state administration and jurisdiction should be retained. Crucially, this language was not Polish, but Latin. It is thus not surprising that, at first, there was little concept of equating linguistic with national identity among Poland's Romantic writers of the early nineteenth century, many of whom were of aristocratic or gentry origin themselves. Yet the Partitions and foreign rule soon made the idea attractive that a common native tongue should provide a continued and ingrained bond between the otherwise disenfranchised former citizenry of Poland-Lithuania. As a result, national aspirations were increasingly channelled into culture and language. This could take the more enlightened, civic form of a plan that Polish should become the future lingua franca of the state that was to be won back. The progressive émigré Polish Democratic Society put their hopes in linguistic centralization. However, this could take a more Romantic form too. Maurycy Mochnacki, for instance, Poland's literary critic of the Romantic era attributed a nation-building role to literature and to language in his essay of 1830 *About Polish Literature in the Nineteenth Century*.

Contemporary grammars too, to some extent, manifest the idea that the 'spirit of the language determines the expression of national identity'.[51] Józef Mroziński, in his innovative

[50] Karel Havliček Borovský, *Duch Národnich Novin: Spis obsahujici úvodni články z Národnich Novin roků 1848, 1849, 1850* (Kutná Hora: F. Procházka, 1851), 1–5.

[51] Jadwiga Puzynina, 'Normative Studies in Poland', in Sylvain Auroux et al., *History of the Language Sciences*, ii. 913.

work *First Principles of Polish Grammar* of 1822, expounded the regularities of Polish phonology and morphology without artificially deducing them from categories found in the grammar of classical languages. Nor did he, unlike his Enlightenment predecessor Onufry Kopczyński, derive them from general principles in logical grammar. Mroziński was also a member of the orthographic commission which the Royal Society of the Friends of Science convened in 1814 in an attempt to foster linguistic unity in the face of political disintegration and oppression. After sixteen years' work the commission completed their *Treatise and Proposals on Polish Spelling*, but the partitioning powers banned its dissemination. Jan Nepomucen Deszkiewicz's *Grammar of Polish* (1846) provides a further example. Here, restorative efforts took the form of linguistic archaism, including a proposal to resuscitate the Polish dual. Promotion of archaisms and, in a more progressive vein, support for unified norms based on real linguistic usage were contradictory ideas in early nineteenth-century Polish grammar. Yet they were compatible with wider coeval sensibilities. For instance, we have seen Romantic hankering for the past as well as for future linguistic unification in the German lands. Still, ethno-linguistic nationalism proper remained alien to Poland's ideological landscape even as late as in the 1830s and 1840s. To be sure, nations were central to the worldview of Polish Romantic writers, but they did not attribute the same significance to language as their fellow Slavs from areas with no immediate history of independent statehood. Any explicit argument that the denominator of the nation should be its eponymous language is lacking even from messianist texts, such as Mickiewicz's *Paris Lectures* (1840–4) and Karol Libelt's *Love of the Fatherland* (1844).

Polish Romantic imagination clearly contrasted with that of other Slavs, such as the Czechs and the Serbs, where language played a key role in forging national identity. Similarly, modern standard Ukrainian and Norwegian Nynorsk were emancipatory projects too. Standard German, in turn, is to some extent akin to the Tuscan standard which spread across the Italian peninsula prior to unification. In Greece, the resolution of diglossia in favour of *dimotiki* is partly reminiscent of the situation in the Slavia orthodoxa. These are well established comparisons. At the same time, political, legal, and cultural discourses provided specific local frameworks. The interaction between them and the novel Romantic idea of juxtaposing language with nation offers rich material for further research beyond types and abstract groupings of linguistic nationalism. France and England are no exception. It is true that in the first instance, after 1789, French was to be the language of the state and its citizens. A century later, well into the times of 'turning peasants into Frenchmen', Ernest Renan, in his *Qu'est-ce qu'une nation?* (1882), remains deeply suspicious of building up language into a spiritual link among an allegedly homogeneous primordial nation. However, in France too, as elsewhere, language has assumed Romantic connotations of an innate bond among the members of the nation which expresses and shapes their identity. Brunot suggests that this can in fact be traced back to the Revolution itself. In a civic vein, 'la langue devait être nationale', but, in a less civic vein, it also was 'un des elements essentiels de la nationalité'.[52] The

[52] Ferdinand Brunot, *Histoire de la langue française des origines à 1900*, ix. *La Révolution et l'Empire*, 1. *Le Français, langue nationale* (Paris: Armand Colin, 1927), 420.

latter does not appear to be very well understood and provides further interdisciplinary scope for the study of theories of language in European Romanticism and its aftermath.

Further Reading

Auroux, Sylvain (ed.), *Histoire des idées linguistiques*, ii (Liège: P. Mardaga 2000).

Bär, Jochen A., *Sprachreflexion der deutschen Frühromantik: Konzepte zwischen Universalpoesie und grammatischem Kosmopolitismus*, Studia Linguistica Germanica, 50 (Berlin and New York: de Gruyter, 1999).

Bilenky, Serhiy, *Romantic Nationalism in Eastern Europe: Russian, Polish, and Ukrainian Political Imaginations* (Stanford, Calif.: Stanford University Press, 2012).

Borsche, Tilman, *Sprachansichten: Der Begriff der menschlichen Rede in der Sprachphilosophie Wilhelm von Humboldts* (Stuttgart: Klett Cotta, 1981).

Brown, Roger L., *Wilhelm von Humboldt's Conception of Linguistic Relativity* (The Hague and Paris: Mouton, 1967).

Drews, Peter, *Herder und die Slaven: Materialien zur Wirkungsgeschichte bis zur Mitte des 19. Jahrhunderts* (Munich: Sagner, 1990).

Gardt, Andreas (ed.), *Nation und Sprache: Die Diskussion ihres Verhältnisses in Geschichte und Gegenwart* (Berlin and New York: de Gruyter, 2000).

Hroch, Miroslav, *In the National Interest: Demands and Goals of European National Movements of the Nineteenth Century: A Comparative Perspective* (Prague: Charles University, 2000).

Lotman, Ju. M., and Uspenskij, B. A., *Spory o jazyke v načale XIX veka kak fakt russkoj kul'tury*, Učenye zapiski Tartuskogo universiteta, 358 (Tartu: Tart. gos. Universitet, 1975).

McKusick, James C., *Coleridge's Philosophy of Language* (New Haven: Yale University Press, 1986).

Manchester, Martin L., *The Philosophical Foundations of Humboldt's Linguistic Doctrines*, Amsterdam Studies in the Theory and History of Linguistic Science, III, Studies in the History of the Language Sciences, 32 (Amsterdam and Philadelphia: John Benjamins, 1985).

Nüsse, Heinrich, *Die Sprachtheorie Friedrich Schlegels* (Heidelberg: Winter, 1962).

Schmitter, Peter (ed.), *Geschichte der Sprachtheorie*, iv. *Sprachtheorien der Neuzeit I: Der epistemologische Kontext neuzeitlicher Sprach- und Grammatiktheorien* (Tübingen: Narr, 1999); v. *Sprachtheorien der Neuzeit II: Von der 'Grammaire de Port-Royal' (1660) bis zur Konstitution moderner linguistischer Disziplinen* (Tübingen: Narr, 1996).

Schmitter, Peter, and Roussos, Lefteris (eds), *Geschichte der Sprachtheorie*, vi. *Sprachtheorien der Neuzeit III: Sprachbeschreibung und Sprachunterricht*, 1–2 (Tübingen: Narr, 2005–7).

Trabant, Jürgen, *Apeliotes oder der Sinn der Sprache: Wilhelm von Humboldts Sprachbild* (Berlin: Akademie Verlag, 1986).

Walicki, Andrzej, *Philosophy and Romantic Nationalism: The Case of Poland* (Oxford: Clarendon Press, 1982).

CHAPTER 41

EUROPE'S DISCOURSE OF BRITAIN

PATRICK VINCENT

EUROPE's uncertainty about Britain is nothing new. Long before the creation of the EU, Europeans were strongly divided regarding British exceptionalism and the place of Britain within European civilization. From the late seventeenth century onwards, British influences on Europe were most often progressive, disruptive, and idiosyncratic, whether one refers to the Glorious Revolution in politics, Hobbes and Locke in philosophy, Newton in physics, Shakespeare in literature, Capability Brown in landscape gardening, or Adam Smith in the increasingly hegemonic sphere of commerce. A key member of the European system of states created after the Treaty of Utrecht in 1713 and a participant in the Enlightenment movement to reform manners and forge a modern civil society,[1] Britain was nevertheless imagined as standing alone not just geographically but also culturally—despite John Bull's disparagement of all things European, the island nation appealed to Europeans for its perceived eccentricity. A Romantic-era 'Eurobarometer' of sorts, this chapter will review images of Britain in European discourse and their productive relation to Romanticism between 1750 and 1850.[2] Whether addressing British manners (e.g. common sense, toleration, philistinism, rudeness), ideas (liberalism, capitalism, utilitarianism), or writers (Shakespeare, Byron), these representations of Britain are primarily about individual autonomy and economic prosperity, a view that helped reinforce the Whig narrative of English history as a progressive constitutional development, and which continues to resonate today in official statements on the meaning of Britishness.[3] Although they may appear very distant, even antithetical to Romanticism, with its fondness for irrationality, passion, and excess, they contributed substantially to the development of a liberal, middle-class

[1] J. G. A. Pocock, *Barbarism and Religion*, i. *The Enlightenments of Edward Gibbon* (Cambridge: Cambridge University Press, 1999), 7–9, 110.

[2] For a study of British views on Europe in the same period, see Peter Mortensen, *British Romanticism and Continental Influences: Writing in an Age of Europhobia* (Houndmills, Basingstoke: Palgrave Macmillan, 2004).

[3] Gordon Brown, 'Britishness', British Council Annual Lecture, 8 July 2004.

Romanticism by providing European writers with an aesthetic and ideological middle ground, a *juste milieu* between radicalism and reaction.

The chapter will focus mainly on France, Britain's 'natural' enemy and the nation often viewed as most antipathetic to *les rosbifs*,[4] but will also discuss Germany, a nation with royal ties but also an imagined kinship to England, Switzerland, which acted as an important mediator of British culture on the continent, and Russia, most often associated with France and Germany. While I invoke the term Britain, foreign observers only rarely ventured north or distinguished England from Scotland, Wales, or Ireland, so that their discourse of Britain is most often a discourse on the home counties of England. Keeping in mind Germaine de Staël's insight into the relationship between political institutions, society, and culture, I will propose three moments in Europe's discourse of Britain: the first, running from the mid-eighteenth century up to 1793 when revolutionary France declared war on Britain, coincided with a first wave of anglophilia that was both liberal and cosmopolitan, and which helped foster Romanticism in Germany; the second period, running roughly until 1820, was divided between the radical republicans who viewed Britain as an enemy of democracy, the moderate liberal camp, including members of the Coppet Circle, who appreciated Britain as perfectly balanced between tradition and modernity, and the conservatives who embraced Edmund Burke's chivalric ideal of Britain as a stabilizing force within a reactionary European system; finally, the third period may be identified with what Metternich called Britain's 'great deviation' from post-Vienna Europe and its renewed advocacy of liberty and progress, a shift that triggered a second wave of anglophilia and that contributed to the development of liberal forms of Romanticism in France and across the continent. The chapter ends with the rise of a far more radical European discourse, Marxism, which attacked the myth of English liberty, while at the same time undermining the concept of national character.

Swiss patrician Béat de Muralt published his *Lettres sur les Anglais et les Français* (1725) more than thirty years after his stay in Britain in 1693, and eight years before Voltaire's *Lettres philosophiques* (or *Letters Concerning the English Nation*, 1733), usually cited as the origin of the eighteenth-century phenomenon of anglophilia. His was the first of a series of comparative studies on France and Britain, two nations vying for the military, commercial, but also cultural hegemony of Europe. Among these one may list Louis-Sébastien Mercier's unpublished *Parallèle de Paris et de Londres* (*c*.1780), John Andrews's *A Comparative View of the French and English Nations* (1785), or Mary Berry's *England and France* (1834). Britain was still little known among French speakers at the outset of the eighteenth century. Béat de Muralt and Voltaire helped develop an imprecise, even utopian idea of Britain,[5] representing it as a commercial although not so polite nation, where people were well fed, prosperous, and happy because they could do what they pleased. Muralt writes, 'generally speaking, they have little Education, much Money to spend, and all the possible opportunities to devote themselves to Vice ... Everyone can be who he wants to be, hence the great number of extraordinary Characters ... that one

[4] David Horn, *Great Britain and Europe in the Eighteenth Century* (Oxford: Clarendon Press, 1967), 382.

[5] Francis Acomb, *Anglophobia in France: 1763–1798* (Raleigh, NC: Duke University Press, 1950), 3–4.

sees amongst the English'. Like Voltaire and almost all eighteenth-century commentators on Britain in his wake, the Swiss author attributes this greater freedom and prosperity to the country's constitution and to its parliamentary system, which appeared to successfully guarantee Britons' civil and religious liberties, and enabled the principle of the separation and balance of powers in government.[6] Béat de Muralt was at loggerheads with the authorities in Berne, so that his idealization of British institutions may be seen as a form of oppositional discourse. Taken up in the conditional tense in book 19, chapter 27 of Montesquieu's *De l'esprit des lois* (1748) and by several of the *philosophes*, notably Helvetius, this *liberté anglaise*, as the *Encyclopédie* called it, was essentially a negative form of freedom, the right to property, peace, and happiness. Montesquieu had lived in London between 1729 and 1731, where he was well received and became an inveterate anglophile. His 'Notes sur l'Angleterre', first published in 1818, defends English inhospitality to foreigners as no different from their own rudeness to one another; comments on the new wealth and corruption generated by empire; gives us a sense of the tensions rife between Walpole's ministry and the opposition; yet confidently asserts that, because of its separation of powers, 'England is at present the most free country in the world, no republic excepted'.[7] By the time of the Seven Years War, when Britain's clear military and political superiority led to a first peak in what Fougeret de Montbron negatively labelled as 'anglomania', Great Britain had come to be seen as an *île philosophique*, its ideal of liberty a tradition of thought.[8]

This anglomania predictably sparked an anglophobic reaction, especially during and after the American War of Independence, when more radical advocates of political reform, among them d'Holbach, Diderot, Mably, Sieyès, Robespierre, and Marat, began to question the myth of English liberty. 'Whereas conservatives found English institutions much too republican, some of the liberals thought them not radical enough', Francis Acomb writes. Influenced by classical republicanism and by Rousseau, who famously wrote that Englishmen are free only one day every five years,[9] these populist radicals were more interested in political, or positive, liberty. They criticized Britain's representative government, which they viewed as corrupt, saw political parties as unnecessary in a republic of virtue, and attacked Britain's class inequality and flawed legal system. Clearly not all Englishmen were free nor did they all gorge on beef and beer. Yet in the years of political debate that served as a prologue to the French Revolution, as well as in the debate over the adoption of a parliamentary system at the Estates-General then the National Assembly, English institutions again became an attractive alternative to France's absolutist monarchy. Genevan Jean de Lolme published his *Constitution d'Angleterre* (1771), which glorified Britain's constitutional monarchy.

6 Josephine Grieder, *Anglomania in France: Fact, Fiction, and Political Discourse 1740–1789* (Geneva: Droz, 1985), ch. 2; 'Introduction', Louis-Sébastien Mercier, *Parallèle de Paris et de Londres*, ed. Claude Bruneteau and Bernard Cottret (Paris: Didier, 1982).

7 Montesquieu, *Œuvres complètes*, ed. Daniel Oster (Paris: Seuil, 1964), 331–4.

8 Mercier, *Parallèle*, 23; Grieder, *Anglomania*, 7; Acomb, *Anglophobia*, p. vii; Paul Langford, *Englishness Identified: Manners and Character 1650–1850* (Oxford: Oxford University Press, 2000), 6.

9 Jean-Jacques Rousseau, *Social Contract, The Collected Writings of Rousseau*, iv, ed. Roger Masters and Christopher Kelly (Hanover, NH, and London: University Press of New England), 192.

Texts by the liberal Scottish Enlightenment philosophers were discussed and translated into French, notably Adam Smith's *Richesse des Nations* (1778) publicized in the early 1800s by the liberal anglophile Jean-Baptiste Say. Jacques Necker, Louis XVI's Finance Minister and Germaine de Staël's father, famously admired the British parliament and public finances, in particular its credit system. Other French liberals, including the Girondists Jacques Pierre Brissot and Mme Roland, who both wrote about Great Britain, and engaged with many of the leaders of the Revolution in Roland's salon at the Hôtel Britannique, wished to see the English model adopted.[10] They drew their political ideas from Montesquieu and the *philosophes*, but also from the seventeenth-century English republican tradition, including Milton, Harrington, Sidney, and Nedham, all translated in the revolutionary period.[11] Recollecting his walking tour with Robert Jones across France in the summer of 1790, William Wordsworth could write, 'we bore a name | Honoured in France, the name of Englishmen, | And hospitably did they give us hail, | As their forerunners in a glorious course'.[12] The Jacobins, however, were not ready to satisfy themselves with a mixed government. As an example, Acomb cites French revolutionary Camille Desmoulins in 1789: 'We shall go beyond these English, who are so proud of their constitution and who mocked at our servitude.' After Britain entered the war against revolutionary France in February 1793 and a general decree was declared in October against all British living in France, the community of expatriate radicals that met at White's Tavern in Paris discovered that the name of Englishman had become a liability rather than an honour. The first, cosmopolitan, and liberal phase of anglophilia in France had run its course.

Paul Langford writes that 'Anglomania took its adherents in France, and later in Germany, far beyond an interest in British politics into the realms of manners and culture that raised deeper questions about what constituted Englishness'.[13] Although the distinction between anglophilia and anglomania cannot be precisely drawn, the latter usually refers to an admiration that veers on blind emulation, attaching itself not just to English ideas or institutions, but also to behaviour and even to fashion. Thus the Duc de Chartres and other members of France's aristocratic and bourgeois elite dressed, gardened, bred racing horses, and met in social clubs *à l'anglaise*. Even the court at Versailles adapted what were viewed as Albion's more simple and authentic manners.[14] Although David Hume famously claimed that Britons lacked national character and that this was their distinguishing mark, traits particular to the English very clearly emerged, notably

[10] Jacques-Pierre Brissot, *Testament politique de l'Angleterre* (1780); Jeane Marie Philipon de Roland, 'Voyage en Angleterre', *Œuvres de J. M. Ph. Roland, femme de l'ex ministre de l'intérieur*, ed. L. A. Champagneux (Paris, 1800), iii. 210–86.

[11] Zera Fink, 'Wordsworth and the English Republican Tradition', *Journal of English and German Philology*, 47 (1948), 107–11.

[12] William Wordsworth, *The Prelude 1799, 1805, 1850*, ed. Jonathan Wordsworth, M. H. Abrams, and Stephen Gill (New York: Norton, 1979), 206.

[13] Langford, *Englishness*, 6. For a study of German anglophilia in the 18th cent., see Michael Maurer, *Aufklarung und Anglophilie in Deutschland* (Göttingen: Vanderhoeck & Ruprecht, 1987).

[14] Grieder, *Anglomania*, 14–16.

in the many French sentimental novels written by or about the English.[15] Englishness in the eighteenth century meant more than 'solid breakfasts and gloomy Sundays', as Orwell once put it:[16] Béat de Muralt praises Britons' liberty but also their common sense, privileges their unpolished genius over the polite *esprit* of the French, and justifies their patriotism as the result of their proud independence, economic prosperity, and patent lack of curiosity in all things foreign. This early taxonomy of so-called English manners, which according to David Simpson soon became a commonplace Enlightenment habit, remained remarkably consistent throughout the long eigtheenth century, contributing to the ideology of Englishness.[17] Propagated back home in satirical caricatures of robust, self-satisfied figures such as John Bull and Jack English set in contrast with scrawny, feminized Frenchmen, these images from abroad in turn bolstered Britons' self-esteem.[18] If, as Hume argued, English ideology privileged a culture of individuals rather than types, the English like all other nations were typecast within the increasingly agonistic discursive sphere of Romantic nationalism, where crude stereotypes might be deployed in their favour but also against them.[19] Thus, anglophile liberals in France and elsewhere admired John Bull's pride, patriotism, and roughshod manners as tokens of his commercial spirit and middle-class egalitarianism, whereas royalist conservatives, joined towards the end of the century by left-leaning radicals, criticized the British national character as being too turbulent, selfish, and ill fitted to the French as a nation.[20]

Whereas British rudeness could be seen as progressive in the arenas of politics or of commerce, it had a much harder time making headway in Europe's republic of letters. Many studies have examined the gradual hold on Europe's cultural imagination of the sublime, or 'northern', authors such as Milton, Thomas Gray, Edward Young, and Ossian [James MacPherson], or else the late eighteenth-century fashion for Gothic literature, but it is the history of Shakespeare's reception on the continent which best illustrates the resistance to British national character in the sphere of literature. The modernity of Shakespeare's plays, with their novel emphasis on realism, authenticity, equality, genius, individual subjectivity, and historical and geographical specificity, played a hugely disruptive, even revolutionary role in the various battles waged between the Ancients and the Moderns across Europe, and thus in the development of European Romanticism. In France, which remained the principal arbiter of taste throughout the eighteenth century, François Letourneur published influential translations of Gray, Milton, and

15 David Hume, 'Of National Characters', *Selected Essays*, ed. Stephen Copley and Andrew Edgar (Oxford: Oxford World's Classics, 1993), 119; for a list of 18th-cent. French novels relating to England, see Grieder, *Anglomania*, appendix.

16 George Orwell, 'The Lion and the Unicorn', in *The Penguin Essays of George Orwell* (Harmondsworth: Penguin, 1994), 139.

17 David Simpson, *Romanticism, Nationalism, and the Revolt Against Theory* (Chicago: University of Chicago Press, 1993), 41.

18 See Raphael Samuel (ed.), *Patriotism: The Making and Unmaking of British National Identity* (London and New York: Routledge, 1989); and Linda Colley, *Britons: Forging the Nation 1707–1837* (London: Vintage, 1992), esp. ch. 1.

19 Simpson, *Romanticism*, 42.

20 Acomb, *Anglophobia*, 5–10.

Young in the second half of the century, but Shakespeare made little headway until the 1810s. As Heike Grundman writes, 'For more than fifty years Shakespeare remained a sleeping beauty in a country paralyzed by neo-Classicism.'[21] Shakespeare allowed the Germans, on the other hand, to break away from French neoclassicism much earlier, and helped ignite the *Sturm und Drang* movement with its wildness and woolly emotionalism. The Swiss-German poet and translator Johann Jakob Bodmer, the first of a distinguished line of German-language anglophiles, prepared the way for this revolution in taste starting in the 1730s with translations of Milton, Thomson, and Young, which later inspired the 'wild Swiss' artist Henri Fuseli. He also wrote a 1743 essay that drew on Thomas Blackwell's *Enquiry into the Life and Writings of Homer* to argue for a correspondence between the Homeric period and medieval Germany, enabling modern literature to assert its indepence and launching the Romantic myth of a German nationhood based on medieval Germanic-Christian culture, later developed by Johann Gottfried Herder.[22] Bodmer's friend Christoph Martin Wieland gave added weight to modern literature by producing twenty-two prose translations of Shakespeare in the 1760s, before two members of the avant-garde Jena group, August Wilhelm Schlegel and Ludwig Tieck, came out with their remarkable early Romantic translations of the Bard at the end of the century. At the same time that German travellers, including the intrepid walker Karl Philipp Moritz in 1782, flocked to Britain, generating a 'torrent of travelogues' in the last quarter of the eighteenth century,[23] German readers regularly informed themselves on British art and culture through a number of periodicals. These included the *Neue Teutsche Merkur* (1790–1810), in which Wieland published several essays on Shakespeare, the *Deutsches Museum* (1776–88), and the *Vaterländisches Museum* (1810–11), which contained an early essay on the British Romantics. Much like travellers themselves, these periodicals promoted the circulation of ideas between Britain and Germany, two nations viewed as sharing a common Germanic heritage, contributing in turn to the period's heady combination of cosmopolitanism, nationalism, and literary experimentation, which, alongside the French Revolution, helped give rise to the *Frühromantiker*.[24]

It was largely via August Wilhelm Schlegel and his promoter, Germaine de Staël, that Shakespeare began to be taken seriously in France. For the Germans as for de Staël, Shakespeare stood for 'the democratic and progressive liberal cultural life of England',[25] a cultural life that de Staël famously associates with the Northern imagination but also

[21] Heike Grundman, 'Shakespeare and European Romanticism', in Michael Ferber (ed.), *A Companion to European Romanticism* (Oxford: Blackwell, 2005), 39.

[22] Maike Oergel, 'The Redeeming Teuton: Nineteenth-Century Notions of the "Germanic" in England and Germany', in Geoffrey Cubitt (ed.), *Imagining Nations* (Manchester: Manchester UP, 1998), 77.

[23] Alison E. Martin, *Moving Scenes: The Aesthetics of German Travel Writing on England, 1783–1830* (Oxford: Legenda, 2008), 5–6.

[24] Karen Junod, 'Crabb Robinson, Blake, and Perthe's Vaterländisches Museum (1810–1811)', *European Romantic Review*, 23/4 (2012), 435–51. See also Lawrence Mardsen Price, *The Reception of English Literature in Germany* (Berkeley, Calif.: University of California Press, 1932).

[25] Grundman, 'Shakespeare', 34–40.

with the nascent movement of Romanticism in *De la littérature* (1800). This is the first of her two pioneer comparative treatises, influenced by Montesquieu, that ambitiously demonstrate how history, geography, and political institutions determine culture. De Staël devotes four chapters to Britain, the nation whose genius she associates alongside that of Germany with her liberal ideal of perfectibility, and which she considers as a model to help regenerate the cultures of Southern Europe in a democratic age: 'The poetry of the north', she writes, 'is much better adapted than the poetry of the south to the spirit of a free people.'[26] De Staël published her treatise when even the slightest tie or affinity with Perfidious Albion could be punishable on the grounds of disloyalty to the *Grande nation*. Jacques Mallet Du Pan, her Genevan compatriot who became a virulent anti-Bonapartist pamphleteer and fervent admirer of Burke, had to seek refuge in London to publish his pro-British *Le Mercure britannique* between 1798 and 1800. In the Napoleonic regime's official mouthpiece, *Le Moniteur universel*, the British government was daily depicted as the oppressor of innocent nations and even of its own enchained people, while Englishmen were caricatured as cowardly and treacherous. French anglophiles on the other hand were lampooned as unpatriotic, in works such as Étienne Masse's verse-satire 'Les Anglomanes' (1813).[27] Predictably, reviews of *De la littérature* attacked its thesis on Northern culture on the grounds that it betrayed French national sensibility. Fontanes claimed that it was written in an unfeminine manner that offended national manners and civility, whereas Chateaubriand challenged her argument that Ossianic melancholy was exclusive to Northern countries in order to substitute her liberal theory of perfectibility with his own politically conservative and professionally opportunistic thesis on the genius of Christianity.[28] Reactions to Germaine de Staël's second treatise on nothern culture, *De l'Allemagne*, were even more trenchant: 'Your latest work is not French', wrote Napoleon's Minister of Police, the Duke of Rovigo, in October 1810, before ordering her once again into exile.[29] Despite the Emperor's own taste for Ossian, the book's celebration of Romantic genius, sublime enthusiasm, and Gothic mixture of genres, ideas which de Staël had discovered in Weimar in 1804 thanks in large part to an Englishman, Henry Crabb Robinson, struck the Emperor as being disruptive of republican neoclassicism, but above all as being too foreign.

In the same way that Germaine de Staël's Romantic comparative criticism drew on British and German literature to foster what Fabienne Moore has called 'a European union of arts and letters',[30] her salon conversation and political writings relied on Britain's constitution to imagine a post-revolutionary, liberal Romantic ideal of Europe in opposition to Napoleon's centralizing and homogenizing system of Empire. Praising

[26] Germaine de Staël, *De la littérature*, ed. Gérard Gengembre and Jean Goldzink (Paris: GF Flammarion, 1991), 206 (my tr.).

[27] Quoted in Eric Partridge, *The French Romantics' Knowledge of English Literature, 1820–1848* (Paris: Honoré Champion, 1924), 21.

[28] Jean Pierre Louis de Fontanes, 'De la littérature, par Mme. de Staël-Holstein', *Œuvres de M. de Fontanes* (Paris: Hachette, 1859), ii. 161.

[29] Germaine de Staël, *De l'Allemagne*, ed. Simone Balayé (Paris: GF Flammarion, 1968), i. 30.

[30] Fabienne Moore, 'Early French Romanticism', in Ferber, *Companion to European Romanticism*, 181.

Britain became a shorthand way to claim a Europe made up of distinct, sovereign nations where individual liberties might be respected alongside local differences.[31] French anglophilia was mainly voiced in exile until Napoleon's final defeat in 1815, but even then his critics had to be wary of what they published. In February 1803, for example, the celebrated Whig lawyer James Mackintosh unsuccessfully defended French royalist emigrant Jean-Gabriel Peltier against a libel suit instigated by the French government. The text in question, 'Le 18 Brumaire An VIII', was a satirical ode not only inciting the First Consul's assassination, but also praising England as the only veritably free nation.[32] De Staël, who translated the account of Peltier's trial into French, escaped that same year from Paris and took up residence at her family castle in Coppet, near Geneva, using it as a base from which to visit various parts of Europe over the next ten years, including a winter spent in London in 1813–14. A Protestant city-republic on the cultural divide between Northern and Southern Europe, Geneva had ties to Britain that went back to the Marian persecutions. During the Enlightenment, many young English were sent to Geneva seeking opportunities of improvement as part of their Grand Tour. Geneva's patrician class was likewise fascinated by Britain as a model of civil liberty and as a pioneer of modernity.[33] After flirting with a Rousseauian republicanism inimical to British institutions in her earlier political texts, de Staël became an inveterate anglophile, much like her father Jacques Necker and many of the intellectuals who met in her salon at Coppet, including Benjamin Constant, Jean Charles Léonard de Sismondi, and Charles-Victor de Bonstetten. The Coppet circle, which met off and on during the first fifteen years of the nineteenth century, acted as leading promoters of Britain on the continent during the First French Empire.

De Staël's major political treatise, her posthumously published *Considérations sur la Révolution Française* (1818), is also one of European Romanticism's most important endorsements of British history, society, and culture. The author's stated goal in writing the *Considerations* was to pursue her father's views on Britain by demonstrating that the French Revolution failed when it parted ways with the English Constitution, and by arguing that only the adoption of that time- and experience-tested document might make the French happy.[34] The book's sixth and last part is a 100-page, nuanced analysis of the relationship between England and liberty that responds to European criticism and is largely favourable to Britain, 'the most religious, most moral and most enlightened nation of which Europe can boast'.[35] Information for the book was drawn from de Staël's conversations at Coppet, from her wide reading, but also from her stay in London during the winter of 1813–14, when, hosted by James Mackintosh, she met

[31] Biancamaria Fontana, 'The Napoleonic Empire and the Europe of Nations', in Anthony Pagden (ed.), *The Idea of Europe: From Antiquity to the European Union* (Cambridge: Cambridge University Press, 2002), 125–8.

[32] *The Trial of John Peltier, Esq. for a libel against Napoleon Bonaparte* (London, 1803), 127–8.

[33] See *Genève, lieu d'Angleterre/Geneva, an English Enclave*, ed. Valéry Cossy, Béla Kapossy, and Richard Whatmore (Geneva: Slatkine, 2009).

[34] Germaine de Staël, *Considerations on the Principal Events of the French Revolution*, ed. Aurelian Craiutu (Indianopolis: Liberty Fund, 2008), 'Advertisement of the Author' and ch. 1.

[35] De Staël, *Considerations*, 722.

not just Byron, but many of the nation's leading political, scientific, and cultural figures. Like Béat de Muralt a century earlier, she was struck by the fact that everyone in England, even the animals, looked prosperous owing to liberty. Reviewing the history of British political institutions, she dismisses the myth of Gothic liberty, arguing that the English only became genuinely free after 1688. Her analysis of English liberty balances the progressive views of Godwin and Bentham with a Burkean respect for tradition—the indication, according to Byron, that her politics were 'sadly changed'.[36] As in Constant's *Principes de politique* (1806), she insists on the importance of negative liberty, or government non-intervention in the private sphere, praises the freedom of the press and the jury system, and celebrates what she sees as the nation's greater social equality and aristocracy of talent. Her sanguine review of British institutions does not forbid her from advocating parliamentary reform and the attribution of more rights to Ireland. She also criticizes the nation's manners, in particular English coolness, which she explains as a mixture of timidity and independence. This obviously calls to mind the character of Lord Nevil in her cosmopolitan novel *Corinne, ou l'Italie*, possibly based on Lord John Campbell, a young Scot whom de Staël had courted, apparently with little success.

In accordance with her literary theory, the *Considerations* argues that Britain's perfect institutions have ushered in 'a new age of glory for English poetry; and while everything on the Continent is in a state of degradation, the eternal fountain of beauty still flows from the land of freedom'.[37] Many of the author's views on English literature in fact came from a second important source of information on Britain during Napoleon's reign, the *Bibliothèque britannique* (1796–1815), mainly remembered today for having introduced Byron and Jane Austen to the continent.[38] This was a monthly journal launched by Genevan patricians Marc-Auguste and Charles Pictet, the first an eminent scientist who twice travelled to England, and the second a retired officer who would negotiate Switzerland's neutrality at the Congress of Vienna. Their project's stated aim, to review the latest British works in literature, agriculture, and the arts and sciences, was utilitarian and progressive.[39] It was similar to earlier, typically cosmopolitan and encyclopedic experiments such as Michel de la Roche's *Bibliothèque anglaise* (1716–27) and Desmaizeaux's *Bibliothèque britannique* (1733–47), but deliberately steered clear of political subjects, and in line with Geneva's Protestant heritage, sought to reintroduce religion and morality into public discourse. According to the editors' prefaces at least, the periodical's anglophilia was driven not by love of liberty, but rather by love of progress and the utilitarian faith in a 'free trade of knowledge'.[40] Despite its stated political conservatism, the *Bibliothèque britannique*'s function was subversive in practice,

[36] Byron to Thomas Moore, 22 June 1813, in *Byron's Letters and Journals*, ed. Leslie Marchand (London: John Murray, 1973), iii. 66.

[37] De Staël, *Considerations*, 684.

[38] See David Bickerton, *Marc-Auguste and Charles Pictet: The Bibliothèque britannique (1796–1815) and the Dissemination of British Literature and Science on the Continent* (Geneva: Slatkine Reprints, 1986), 10.

[39] 'Préface', *Bibliothèque britannique*, 1 (Geneva, 1796), 6–8.

[40] *Bibliothèque britannique*, 19 (1802), 5; 22 (1805), 6; 46 (1811), 3.

disrupting the Empire's official anti-British discourse by showcasing the best Britain had to offer, notably in moral philosophy, political economy, education theory, travel, history, and imaginative literature.

Once Napoleon had fallen and the continental blockade no longer made British books a rare commodity, the Pictets renamed their series the *Bibliothèque universelle*. Looking back on twenty years of British literature in its first volume, they wrote: 'As much as a government's jealous and selfish spirit, which even wanted to enslave the mind, allowed it, we spread the knowledge furnished to us by the nation of religion, of liberty, of order and of laws, at a time when all was forgotten, confused, violated on the Continent.'[41] By the time they wrote this, however, the myth of Britain as a moral, liberal, and progressive nation was fast eroding. Prussia, Austria, and Russia, nations that admired Britain not for its liberalism but only for its Burkean conservatism and as a stabilizing force within the Quadruple Alliance, were intent on restoring the status quo and suppressing all reform. From roughly 1816 to 1820, Britain lost the moral high ground it had earned with its fight against Napoleon and with the abolition of the slave trade in 1807. Parliament gagged its citizens' freedom with the Six Acts, at the same time that Castlereagh helped negotiate a concert of Europe at Vienna very different from the liberal, reform-minded ideal of Europe imagined by the Coppet Circle. Like Byron, de Staël criticized Britain's support of the despots on the continent, calling it a 'temporary deviation' from the spirit of 1688.[42] As predicted, the British government's anti-liberal position, at least abroad, became increasingly untenable after 1818. By the time George Canning replaced Castlereagh as Foreign Secretary in 1822, British foreign policy came back 'into harmony with the spirit of the age', as Harold Nicolson writes. Metternich, the Holy Alliance's mastermind and Canning's nemesis, despised Britain's renewed democratic and isolationist foreign diplomacy. For reasons completely opposite to de Staël's, he too lamented what he perceived as Britain's 'grande déviation'.[43]

After the assassinaton of the Duc de Berry in 1820 and the crowning of Charles X in 1824, political reaction intensified in France and the gulf between Britain and the continent further widened. European conservatives became more critical of Britain, whereas liberals across Europe looked again eagerly towards the island nation across the Channel as a beacon of liberty and progress. This led to a second wave of anglophilia and to a new, more left-leaning phase in French Romanticism, branded as 'le libéralisme dans les lettres'. German Romanticism had by then turned to the political right, in effect splitting European Romanticism between liberals and reactionaries. While liberal poet Heinrich Heine's late poem, 'King Richard' (*König Richard*) (1851), may be read as an endorsement of Britain's move away from Austria and the Holy Alliance, Adam Müller's repeated attacks on Adam Smith and on classical political economy starting in 1810 are more characteristic of the *Spätromantiker* worldview, which considered liberalism

[41] 'Coup d'oeil sur la littérature anglaise', *Bibliothèque universelle*, 1 (Geneva, 1816), 15.

[42] De Staël, *Considerations*, 722.

[43] Harold Nicolson, *The Congress of Vienna: A Study in Allied Unity, 1812–1822* (London: Methuen, 1966), 268–74. See also Franklin Ford, *Europe 1780–1830* (London: Longman, 1989).

as 'the English malady'.[44] Twentieth-century German political theorist Carl Schmitt marks the beginning of this conservative turn in 1799, when Friedrich Schlegel first read Burke. Müller's friend Friedrich Gentz translated Burke's *Reflections* into German in 1793, then wrote anglophile articles in his *Historisches Journal* (1799–1801), and was pensioned for his propaganda efforts by the Pitt government. In his earliest work, *Die Lehre vom Gegensatz* (1804), Müller, influenced by his friend and by the anglophile mood at Göttingen, merges Burke with Goethe. By 1810, however, Müller and Gentz had moved on to Vienna, and Burke was largely replaced in German political thought by the monarchist theorists Louis de Bonald, Karl Ludwig von Haller, and Joseph de Maistre.[45] Reacting to Prussia's defeat at Jena in 1806, many German intellectuals and artists including August Wilhelm Schlegel and Johann Gottlieb Fichte defined a more specific German identity based on language to distinguish themselves from Napoleonic France, and to imagine a unified, organic nation. In the 1820s, Hegel developed his theory of the world-historical process driven by individual nations' *Volksgeist* that culminated with the Germans.[46] By 1840, a number of writers associated early on with the Romantic movement, including Ludwig Tieck, Clemens Brentano, and the Schlegels, had taken sides with the new Prussian king, Frederic William IV, against liberalism and in favour of church and state.[47] As Maike Oergel has pointed out, Germans often imagined a shared Teutonic identity with England, and many Tories in Britain returned the favour, especially toward the middle and end of the nineteenth century, the highpoint of English Anglo-Saxonism.[48] British liberal utilitarianism, however, made an awkward bedfellow with German Romantic nationalism, with its visceral distate for materialism and individualism. Nietzsche's aphorism in *Twilight of the Idols* (1889) nicely sums it up: 'Man does not strive for happiness; only the Englishman does.'[49]

The late German Romantics' nationalism, anti-liberalism, and penchant for mysticism was echoed in Russia by the state-sponsored policy of Official Nationality and by the slavophiles, whose skirmishes with the Westernizers, notably the leading Romantic critic Vissarion Belinsky and the political writer Alexander Herzen, dominated the cultural scenes of Moscow and Saint Petersburg during the 1830s and 1840s. Both were familiar with the cosmopolitan Karamzin and Zhukovsky circles, which, starting in the 1800s, had fostered a taste for Western, notably eighteenth-century British authors such

[44] Heinrich Heine, *Selected Verse*, tr. Peter Branscombe (Harmondsworth: Penguin, 1986), 181, and Carl Schmitt, *Political Romanticism*, tr. Guy Oaks (Cambridge, Mass.: MIT Press, 1986), 117. See also Adam Müller, *Die Theorie der Staatshaushaltung und ihre Forschritte in Deutschland und England seit Adam Smith* (Vienna, 1812), *Versuch einer neuen Theorie des Geldes, mit besonderer Rücksicht auf Großbritannien* (Leipzig, 1816), and *Die Fortschritte der nationalökonomischen Wissenschaft in England* (Leipzig, 1817).

[45] Schmitt, *Political Romanticism*, 40–7.

[46] Maike Oergel, 'The Redeeming Teuton', 81. See also Martin Thom, *Republics, Nations, and Tribes* (London: Verso, 1995), part III.

[47] See Harold James, *A German Identity, 1770–1990* (London: Weidenfeld & Nicolson, 1989), 21–5 and ch. 2.

[48] Oergel, 'The Redeeming Teuton', 85–8.

[49] Friedrich Nietzsche, *Twilight of the Idols and the Antichrist* (New York: Dover, 2004), 4.

as Thomas Gray. Although he could be critical of Great Britain, Herzen came to know that nation perhaps better than any other nineteenth-century Russian, living in exile in London between 1852 and 1858. In his autobiography he praises John Stuart Mill's *On Liberty* as well as the civil liberties that he and other political refugees were able to enjoy there: 'In England the policeman at your door or within your doors only adds a feeling of security.'[50] On the other hand, the slavophile ideologues Konstantin Aksakov, Ivan Kireyevsky, and Aleksey Khomyakov not only rejected the values which Great Britain stood for, but all the ideas that came out of Western Europe, from rationalism to individualism, socialism to capitalism. In 'Conversations in the Kremlin' (*Razgavor v Kremle*), a poem written at the height of the Crimean War in 1854, the slavophile salon hostess and German-born Romantic poetess Karolina Pavlova pits an Englishman, a Frenchman, and a Russian against one another, in order to show the superiority of the Russian soul.[51] By the end of the century, the comparison between Westerners and Slavs was commonplace enough for Joseph Conrad to write a parody in *A Secret Agent* (1906) that is among other things a splendid critique of this Romantic extremism. In a conversation at the Russian Embassy, the First Secretary tells Verloc, the novel's terrorist anti-hero that 'England lags. This country is absurd with its sentimental regard for individual liberty.'[52]

Nineteenth-century anglomania could at times come off as extreme as the conservative Romantics' anglophobia. It was most visible in men's dandified poses in imitation of Beau Brummel, in the new women's fashions mimicking the English style, with straw hats, dropped waists, widened skirts, and corsets, but also in the fact that English began to be taught in French schools starting in the 1840s. Even Julien Sorel, the young devotee of Napoleon in Stendhal's *Le Rouge et le Noir* (1830), dresses *à l'anglaise* and plays the dandy in order to negotiate and ultimately reject the Bourbon Restoration's ossified class system. As Mathilde de la Mole remarks at the ball in chapter 39, 'he seemed to have lost that air of cold impassiveness that was so natural to him; he no longer looked English'. The fad for English phlegmatism was of course an offshoot of Byronism, which, alongside the late 'discovery' of Shakespeare, had a dramatic effect on French Romanticism. For many on the continent, Lord Byron was synonymous with England and with the figure of the gentleman, this despite the poet's complicated relation to his homeland, his sharp criticism of its politics, and the fact that his radical cosmoplitanism made him a citizen of the world.[53] According to Richard Cardwell, Byron's complex reception history mirrors the 'preoccupations and obsessions' of the continent.[54] In France, the earlier, royalist Romantics such as Chateaubriand, Nodier, and Lamartine venerated Byron

[50] Alexander Herzen, *My Past and Thoughts*, tr. Constance Garnett (Berkeley, Calif.: University of California Press, 1982), 453.

[51] Patrick Vincent, *The Romantic Poetess: European Culture, Politics and Gender 1820–1840* (Hanover, NH: University Press of New England, 2004), 86–8.

[52] Joseph Conrad, *The Secret Agent*, ed. Roger Tennant (Oxford: Oxford World's Classics, 1983), 29.

[53] See Paul Stock, *The Shelley-Byron Circle and the Idea of Europe* (New York: Palgrave Macmillan, 2010).

[54] Richard Cardwell, 'Introduction', in *The Reception of Lord Byron in Europe*, ed. Richard Cardwell (London and New York: Continuum, 2004), i. 1.

just as fervently as later, democratic-minded authors, including Stendhal, Gautier, and Nerval, helping give some unity to French Romanticism.[55] While all could relate to the brooding sensationalism of his verse, what Sainte-Beuve labelled in 1833 as the *mal du siècle*, it was Byron's politics, shaped by eighteenth-century Whiggism, the French Revolution and Holland House, which made him the hero of Europe's liberal Romantic poets and reformers, from Pushkin, the Decembrists, and Lermontov to Mazzini, the Carbonari, and the Greek revolutionists.

Byron's influence owes everything to the commodification and internationalization of print-culture, abetted by the lack of copyright laws in France and other nations, which helped disseminate British fashions, literature, and ideas, and brought the wind of change to the four corners of Europe. Without Paris's Librairie Galignani, for example, self-proclaimed the 'first English bookshop established on the Continent', Byron would arguably never have become an international celebrity. Opened by a Venetian entrepreneur in 1800, Galignani's became the leading European outpost of British civilization, launching its own newspaper in 1814, *Galignani's Messenger*, available in all the major European cities, and bypassing British copyright laws to produce inexpensive but often high-quality editions of both major and minor British authors. Until Bernhard Tauchnitz launched the even more successful Collection of British and American Authors in Leipzig in 1841, Galignani's and its main competitor, the Librairie Baudry, founded in 1816, had a near-monopoly on English-langage books, supplying circulating libraries and bookshops around Europe with the latest British authors, including Byron, Scott, Moore, Coleridge, Wordsworth, Shelley, Keats, Rogers, White, Campbell, and Montgomery. Thus one could find Galignani editions of Byron and of other male Romantics in the 1830 catalogue of the Librairie Sémen's circulating library in Moscow, alongside titles by a number of female authors from the 1790s, including Charlotte Smith, Helen Maria Williams, and Mary Wollstonecraft.[56] Other specialized periodicals such as *La Revue britannique* (1825–1901) were also created in response to the new demand for British literature. Anglophile statesmen and intellectuals such as François Guizot and Charles de Rémusat helped spread liberal ideas in France by publishing important studies on English history and literature. Finally, essays by literary correspondents in London as well as reviews of new British books appeared regularly in progressive journals such as *Le Globe* and the *Revue des Deux Mondes* in France or *Vestnik Evropy* in Russia, all three of which played an important role in the development of Europe's liberal Romantic movement. Contributors included Philarète Chasles, a translator and mediator of British Romanticism on the continent, Charles-Augustin Sainte-Beuve, France's leading Romantic-period critic and a connoisseur of English literature, and Amédée Pichot, a writer, translator, and publicist of all things British who later became the director of the *Revue britannique*.[57]

[55] Paul Bénichou, *Le Sacre de l'écrivain*, in *Romantismes français* (Paris: Gallimard, 1996), i, 312.
[56] Vincent, *Romantic Poetess*, 80.
[57] Vincent, *Romantic Poetess*, 90–2; Partridge, *French Romantics' Knowledge*, 107.

Pichot's *Voyage historique et littéraire en Angleterre et en Ecosse* (1825) was the most important of several French works on Britain published in this period, among them Louis Simond's *Journal of a Tour and Residence in Great Britain* (1815) and Charles Cottu's *De l'administration de la justice criminelle en Angleterre* (1822). For Pichot, George Canning's nomination as Foreign Secretary put an end to the 'shocking contradiction' between Britain's liberal values and its foreign policy, allowing him to admire that nation once more: 'If M. Canning continues to prudently accept the liberal ideas demanded by the people of Europe after thirty-five years of revolution, can one doubt that the character of the English will be re-established, and that the prosperity of England is the result of its system?'[58] Written in epistolary form as a travel book, the *Voyage* offers a very complete panorama of Romantic-period society and culture, discussing writers but also artists, actors, architects, opera, religion, law, politics, periodicals, agriculture, and the Industrial Revolution in England, Ireland, and Scotland. In the preface, Pichot draws a parallel between his own work and de Staël's *On Germany*: although the author leaves it unstated, British civilization for him clearly demonstrates a genius on par with Germany, and it too can help overhaul France's fossilized classical culture. Claiming like de Staël to be in favour of representative government, without sharing her blind enthusiasm for all things British, he associates classicism with France's corrupt ministry, and aligns the nascent French Romantic movement with Britain's libertarian politics and with its more democratic literature: 'I love liberty, without adopting all its doctrines. I love it the way I love Shakespeare, admiring everything that is grand and beautiful.'[59] One of the *Voyage*'s most original features are the couplings it creates between French and English writers, helping to develop the idea of Romanticism as a European phenomenon and underlining the importance of British literature to the French. Each chapter on an English author is dedicated to a French figure: the chapter on Byron is offered to Chateaubriand, that on Coleridge to Lamartine, the several chapters on Scott to Hugo and others, while Thomas Moore is linked with Nodier, and the Lake Poets with Soulié. Pichot historicizes Byron's reception in France, associating the poet's discovery in 1815 to the shock of the Restoration and to the chaos of the age, yet tempers the impact of Byron and Scott by reminding readers that Chateaubriand and de Staël also played a role in revolutionizing French taste, and by comparing Byron and Chateaubriand, both born according to him for opposition.[60]

Chateaubriand was with Stendhal the European Romantic who could claim to know Britain best. The fact that two authors so at odds politically and personally were able to both admire England and English liberalism nicely exemplifies Britain's role as a bridge between Old Order and Democratic Europe, between tradition and modernity. Chateaubriand was an inveterate anglophile, writing in 1823 that 'I do not share the prejudices of my countrymen against this country; on the contrary I admire this country and its institutions'.[61] His relation to Byron nevertheless contained all the

[58] Amédée Pichot, *Voyage historique et littéraire en Angleterre et en Ecosse* (Paris, 1825), i, pp. x–xi.

[59] Pichot, *Voyage historique*, i, pp. xv, 81.

[60] Pichot, *Voyage historique*, ii. 67–71.

[61] Quoted in Partridge, *French Romantics' Knowledge*, 60.

elements of a psychodrama, the question of who came first being particularly sensitive to Chateaubriand. In his epic, notoriously unreliable autobiography *Mémoires d'outre tombe* (1849), he draws an analogy between his own youth and Byron's, claims Byron copied his *Itinéraire de Paris à Jerusalem* and *René* in *Childe Harold's Pilgrimage*, but still calls him the greatest poet in England since Milton and the leader of the 'new English school' in literature, just as he is the leader of the 'new French school'.[62] Chateaubriand knew English literature better than most of his countrymen, having worked for thirty five years on a translation of Milton's *Paradise Lost*, and helped to publicize British literature in France with a series of articles in *Le Mercure de France* in 1802, republished as his *Essai sur la littérature anglaise* (1836). In books 10 to 12 of the *Mémoires*, written the year his friend Canning became Foreign Secretary, he contrasts the poverty and starvation of his early years as an émigré in London between 1793 and 1800, with the luxury and respect of his 1822 residency as French Ambassador. The tone is a mixture of pride at his success and nostalgia for his lost youth. Citing Burke, he idealizes late eighteenth-century England as the epitome of liberty and order: 'The enlightened aristocracy, placed at the head of this country for the last one hundred and forty years, will have shown to the world one of the most splendid and grandest societies to have honored the human race since the Roman patriciat.'[63]

While Chateaubriand's praise of English politics is Tory-leaning, Stendhal admired Britain for its progressive Whig agenda. He calls his discovery of the *Edinburgh Review* in Milan in 1816, 'a great period in the history of my mind',[64] and became an avid reader of all things English, especially the reviews that he read at Galignani's. Between 1822 and 1826 Stendhal contributed to those reviews; their anti-French views rubbed off on him, giving him the courage to publically reject Racine and Boileau, opening up a new, Romantic literary horizon that was liberal and aligned on Britain rather than on Germany. 'The Romantic system, spoilt by Schlegel's mysticism, triumphs in the form expressed in the twenty-five volumes of the *Edinburgh Review* and as it is practiced by Lord Byron', he wrote in an 1816 letter to his friend Louis Crozet.[65] The controversy surrounding a series of performances of Shakespeare by a British company in 1822 provided the immediate context for *Racine et Shakespeare* (1823–5), Stendhal's famous contribution to the ongoing debate between Ancients and Moderns. Ironically, it was France's liberal press that bashed the actors as a way to express their hatred of the Holy Alliance, famously chanting that Shakespeare was Wellington's aide-de-camp, whereas conservative journalists defended the troupe.[66] Stendhal's essay inverts the political significance of the incident, attacking the classical aesthetic theories of La Harpe's *Lyçée* by passing off the Bard as a Romantic, in other words a modern writer. 'Sur l'Angleterre', a fragment

[62] Chateaubriand, *Mémoires d'outre-tombe* (Paris: La Pléiade, 1951), i. 416.

[63] Chateaubriand, *Mémoires d'outre-tombe*, i. 426.

[64] Pierre Martino, 'Preface', in Stendhal, *Œuvres complètes*, ed. Victor del Litto and Ernest Abravanel (Paris: Honoré Champion, 1970–4), xxxvii, p. xlix. See also Stendhal, *Paris-Londres: Chroniques*, ed. Renée Dénier (Paris: Stock, 1997).

[65] Quoted in Partridge, *French Romantics' Knowledge*, 23.

[66] Martino, 'Preface', pp. xciv–xcvi.

written during Stendhal's stay in England in 1826, reminds us that Stendhal's admiration for British institutions, like that of many of his countrymen, was strong without being wholly uncritical. 'When one is at the Georama', he writes, 'one is struck by the smallness of the English territory, but nevertheless this little island, lacking in everything, has, since Cromwell, shaken up the world'.[67] The author deplores the influence the British aristocracy still exerts on British social and political life, and in true French fashion, complains that the British work too much: 'The English are victims of their work ... Working more than six hours a day diminishes one's happiness'.[68] These images of England, especially of its Whigghish myth of liberty, its commercial wealth, its egalitarianism, and its 'fetishizing of common sense',[69] struck radicals back home in Britain as the disingenuous expression of aristocratic and bourgeois complacency that was wholly ideological. For Wordsworth in 1793, for example, the idea that Britain had already arrived at a state of perfection in government was an insult to reason, whereas Thomas Paine argued that the rhetoric of English national character was pure hypocrisy. Byron preferred to call it cant. For Europeans, however, these images had a different resonance. In absolutist France, they provided the *philosophes* with a working model to challenge, and ultimately uproot, the Old Regime. Beginning in the 1790s, Burke's conservative myth of Englishness lent some counter-revolutionaries a convenient narrative to oppose Jacobinism, but the Coppet Circle's liberal discourse of Britain proved far more influential in helping rid Europe of neoclassicism and of Napoleon. After 1820, writers and revolutionaries from France to Italy to Russia modelled themselves on Britain in order to revolutionize aesthetics and to challenge the Holy Alliance's police state. In other words, Europe's discourse of Britain between 1750 and 1850 was largely subversive, shaking up the world, as Stendhal puts it. It did so, paradoxically, by having a moderating effect on European culture, society, and politics, providing an alternative, liberal form of Romanticism as a counterweight to late German Romanticism and to Metternich. It is in many ways owing to this discourse of Britain, crucially disseminated by the Coppet Circle, that the lasting effect of Romanticism has been 'liberalism, toleration, decency and the appreciation of the imperfections of life'.[70] With the advent of Chartism and what Friedrich Engels titled the *Condition of the Working Class in England* (1843), left-leaning foreign commentators became more critical of Britain and what it stood for, a change registered, for example, in Flora Tristan's *Promenades dans Londres ou l'aristocratie et les prolétaires anglais* (1840). In their Romantic masterpiece, *The Communist Manifesto* (1848), Marx and Engels radicalize the post-Restoration quest for an imaginative politics recently coined by Paul Hamilton as *Realpoetik*, arguing that alienated labour disrupts the full enjoyment of one's humanity, and hence also one's authentic liberty.[71]

[67] 'Sur l'Angleterre', in Stendhal, *Œuvres complètes*, xlv. 295.

[68] 'Sur l'Angleterre', 296.

[69] Simpson, *Romanticism*, 2.

[70] Isaiah Berlin, *The Roots of Romanticism*, ed. Henry Hardy (Princeton: Princeton University Press, 1999), 147.

[71] Paul Hamilton, *Realpoetik: European Romanticism and Literary Politics* (Oxford: Oxford University Press, 2013), 8.

Their pamphlet signals the end of the rhetoric of national character studied in this chapter: 'Modern industrial labour, modern subjection to capital, the same in England as in France, in America as in Germany, has stripped him of every trace of national character.'[72] For Marx and Engels, who wanted to put an end to the bourgeois ideology of liberalism incarnated by Adam Smith's nation of shopkeepers, Britain could be nothing like the images discussed in this chapter. It served them, however, to imagine the end of capitalism just as productively as it did liberals to reimagine the Restoration's 'concert of Europe' as a system of nations based on individual freedom, difference, and toleration.

Further Reading

Cardwell, Richard (ed.), *The Reception of Byron in Europe*, 2 vols (London: Continuum, 2004).

Ferber, Michael, *A Companion to European Romanticism* (Oxford: Blackwell, 2005).

Grieder, Josephine, *Anglomania in France: Fact, Fiction, and Political Discourse 1740–1789* (Geneva: Droz, 1985).

Hamilton, Paul, *Realpoetik: European Romanticism and Literary Politics* (Oxford: Oxford University Press, 2013).

Langford, Paul, *Englishness Identified: Manners and Character 1650–1850* (Oxford: Oxford University Press, 2000).

Martin, Alison E., *Moving Scenes: The Aesthetics of German Travel Writing on England, 1783–1830* (Oxford: Legenda, 2008).

Maurer, Michael, *Aufklarung und Anglophilie in Deustchland* (Göttingen: Vanderhoeck & Ruprecht, 1987).

Pittock, Murray (ed.), *The Reception of Sir Walter Scott in Europe* (London: Continuum, 2007).

Porter, Roy, and Teich, Mikailus, *Romanticism in National Context* (Cambridge: Cambridge University Press, 1988).

Schaffer, Elinor, and Zuccato, Edoardo (eds), *The Reception of S. T. Coleridge in Europe* (London: Continuum, 2007).

Schmid, Susan, and Rossington, Michael (eds), *The Reception of P. B. Shelley in Europe* (London: Continuum, 2008).

Simpson, David, *Romanticism, Nationalism, and the Revolt Against Theory* (Chicago: University of Chicago Press, 1993).

[72] Karl Marx and Friedrich Engels, *The Communist Manifesto*, ed. Harold Laski (New York: Random House, 1967), 144.

Index